Frommer's®

SPAIN

21st Edition

By Peter Barron, Jennifer Ceaser,
Patricia Harris & David Lyon,
Will Shank, Murray Stewart

FrommerMedia LLC

Published by:
Frommer Media LLC

Copyright (c) 2020 by Frommer Media LLC. All rights reserved. No part of this publication may be reproduced, stored in a retrieval system, or transmitted in any form or by any means, electronic, mechanical, photocopying, recording, scanning, or otherwise, except as permitted under Sections 107 or 108 of the 1976 United States Copyright Act, without the prior written permission of the Publisher. Requests to the Publisher for permission should be addressed to Support@FrommerMedia.com.

Frommer's is a registered trademark of Arthur Frommer. Frommer Media LLC is not associated with any product or vendor mentioned in this book.

Frommer's Spain, 21st edition
ISBN 978-1-62887-476-1 (paper), 978-1-62887-477-8 (e-book)

Editorial Director: Pauline Frommer
Editor: Holly Hughes
Production Editor: Heather Wilcox
Cartographer: Elizabeth Puhl
Cover Design: Dave Riedy
Photo Editor: Meghan Lamb
Assistant Photo Editor: Phil Vinke

For information on our other products or services, see www.frommers.com.

Frommer Media LLC also publishes its books in a variety of electronic formats. Some content that appears in print may not be available in electronic formats.

Manufactured in China

5 4 3 2 1

HOW TO CONTACT US

In researching this book, we discovered many wonderful places—hotels, restaurants, shops, and more. We're sure you'll find others. Please tell us about them, so we can share the information with your fellow travelers in upcoming editions. If you were disappointed with a recommendation, we'd love to know that, too. Please write to: Support@FrommerMedia.com.

FROMMER'S STAR RATINGS SYSTEM

Every hotel, restaurant, and attraction listed in this guide has been ranked for quality and value. Here's what the stars mean:

★ Recommended
★★ Highly Recommended
★★★ A must! Don't miss!

AN IMPORTANT NOTE

The world is a dynamic place. Hotels change ownership, restaurants hike their prices, museums alter their opening hours, and buses and trains change their routings. And all of this can occur in the several months after our authors have visited, inspected, and written about these hotels, restaurants, museums, and transportation services. Though we have made valiant efforts to keep all our information fresh and up-to-date, some few changes can inevitably occur in the periods before a revised edition of this guidebook is published. So please bear with us if a tiny number of the details in this book have changed. Please also note that we have no responsibility or liability for any inaccuracy or errors or omissions, or for inconvenience, loss, damage, or expenses suffered by anyone as a result of assertions in this guide.

CONTENTS

LIST OF MAPS

ABOUT THE AUTHORS

After careers at the BBC and Google, **Peter Barron** turned his attention to restoring a barn at his finca on the border between Andalucía and Extremadura. He has been visiting Spain for more than 30 years and loves flamenco guitar, iberico ham, and manzanilla. He divides his time between Spain and London.

Jennifer Ceaser is a freelance writer and editor who has specialized in travel journalism for two decades. A former New Yorker and staff editor at the *New York Post,* Jennifer now splits her time between Berlin and Barcelona. She contributes to a variety of publications, including *Conde Nast Traveler, AFAR, New York Magazine, BBC, Time Out, Coastal Living,* and *Wine Enthusiast.*

Patricia Harris and David Lyon drove almost every twisting mountain road as they researched four previous Frommer's guidebooks about Spain. Founders of HungryTravelers.com, they have a deep appreciation for the perfect codfish croqueta, an honest plate of patatas bravas, or a heap of garlic shrimp. They write about travel, food, wine, spirits, and contemporary art for a range of U.S., Canadian, and British journals. When not on the road, they reside in Cambridge, Massachusetts, where their kitchen is well stocked with saffron from Consuegra, smoked paprika from Extremadura, chorizo from Castilla y León, and a Valencian paella pan to bring them all together.

Trained in Florence, at NYU's Institute of Fine Arts, and at the Harvard University Art Museums in art history and art conservation, **Will Shank** has preserved priceless paintings (Frida Kahlo in Mexico, Salvador Dalí in Madrid) in some of the world's finest museums. In 2000, he decided that working 9-to-5 was not for him, and since leaving his day job at the San Francisco Museum of Modern Art, he has been spotted climbing scaffolding in such places as Pisa, Paris, and Amsterdam, where he has restored aging murals of the American pop artist Keith Haring. Despite his passion for high culture, he is consistently unable to convince his teenage daughter, Stassa, to set foot into an art museum. Will and his husband, artist U. B. Morgan, who emigrated to Spain from the Bay Area in 2006, own a historic home in Barcelona's Gothic Quarter and a terraced vineyard in the cava country of Catalunya, where their rural activities are dictated by the harvests of the grapes, the olives, and a large field of lavender. In the past few decades, Will has shared his deep knowledge of art in such publications as London's *The Art Newspaper* and various travel guides. He has written about LGBT issues for *The Advocate* and *Towleroad* and about preservation topics for *San Francisco Magazine* and *Preservation.* Formerly a film critic for the *Bay Area Reporter* and frequently an art critic for Barcelona's English-language *Metropolitan,* Will finds that he enjoys writing about food and wine as much as he does about culture. He is co-author, with Jim van Buskirk, of *Celluloid San Francisco,* an armchair travel guide to movie locations in the Bay Area.

A proud Scotsman, **Murray Stewart** is an award-winning travel writer who has written, co-authored, and updated several travel guidebooks over the last decade. Prior to 2009, he "enjoyed" a career in corporate restructuring, shutting factories, putting people out of work, and generally spreading mirth and joy across the world of big business. During this time, he received a parliamentary commendation for rescuing a pea-processing factory in the east of England. His traveling has taken him to more than 60 countries, including periods of teaching English in Chile and Mexico as well as corporate consultancy assignments in Spain and Bulgaria. In 2016, his *Basque Country and Navarre* first edition won the British Guild of Travel Writers' Award for "Best Travel Guidebook." A part-time pilgrim, he has walked four routes of the Camino de Santiago pilgrims' route, including the 1,000 miles from Le Puy-en-Velay in France to Santiago de Compostela in Spain, raising thousands of pounds for charity in the process. In his downtime, he keeps fit by swimming and cycling and enjoys the pursuit of lost causes—such as supporting Scotland's national rugby team. He resides in Amersham.

THE BEST OF SPAIN

By Patricia Harris and David Lyon

W e can't verify that Ernest Hemingway once said, "If you visit only one foreign country in your lifetime, make it Spain." But if he didn't say it, he should have. And he could have added that after your first visit, you might never be tempted to go anywhere else.

No other country is quite as flamboyant. Long before Hemingway came to add his macho gloss, 19th-century European writers and painters had mythologized Spain as the quintessential romantic country. It was the land of Moors and Gypsies, of swirling flamenco skirts and narrow-hipped matadors. It was the land of such legendary heroes as El Cid, such wise fools as Don Quijote, and of kings with nicknames such as Pedro the Cruel and Alfonso the Wise.

It's all still true—it's just not the whole truth. Flamenco has enjoyed a renaissance, and many Spaniards are still obsessed with matadors, even as they turn their backs on bullfighting. The current king is likely to be remembered as Felipe the Tall. Yet after being paralyzed by war and dictatorship for much of the 20th century, Spain jumped straight from the 19th century to the 21st. A flamenco beat still drives it, but Spain is now a country of high-speed trains and cutting-edge Internet technology, of a radical avant-garde in food and art, of vibrant modern metropolises like Barcelona, Bilbao, and Madrid that hold their own on the world stage.

The country continues to evolve, and its allures continue to multiply. Ultimately, your own experiences will be the last word on Spain, but we can't resist the urge to share some of our favorite places and activities. As a team of Spain-lovers, here are some of what we think are highlights of the country. Try them and see if you agree.

THE best AUTHENTIC SPANISH EXPERIENCES

- **Being Swept Up in the Passions of Flamenco in Sevilla:** Whether you watch a pure performance at the flamenco dance museum or catch an impromptu shindig at a Gypsy bar in Triana, you'll find you can't get the flamenco rhythms out of your head. See p. 258.
- **Absorbing the genius of Las Meninas in Madrid's Museo del Prado:** Diego Velázquez revolutionized court painting in the 17th century. Join the crowds gazing at his enigmatic portrait of the Infanta Margarita and her retinue, and marvel at the master's brushstrokes. See p. 83.

PREVIOUS PAGE: **Flamenco dancers in Sevilla.**

The Gardens of the Alhambra and Generalife in Granada.

o **Connecting with Moorish Royalty and Commoners in Granada:**
The Alhambra was the crowning artistic glory of Islamic Spain. Once
you've admired its ornate palaces and gardens, wander the medieval
alleyways of the Albaicín. See p. 278.

o **Gaping at the Gaudís in Barcelona:** The Catalan language has the
perfect verb to describe seeing Antoní Gaudí's Modernisme masterpieces: *Badar,* meaning "to walk around with your mouth open in
amazement." See p. 439.

Gaudi's Casa Mila, also known as La Pedrera.

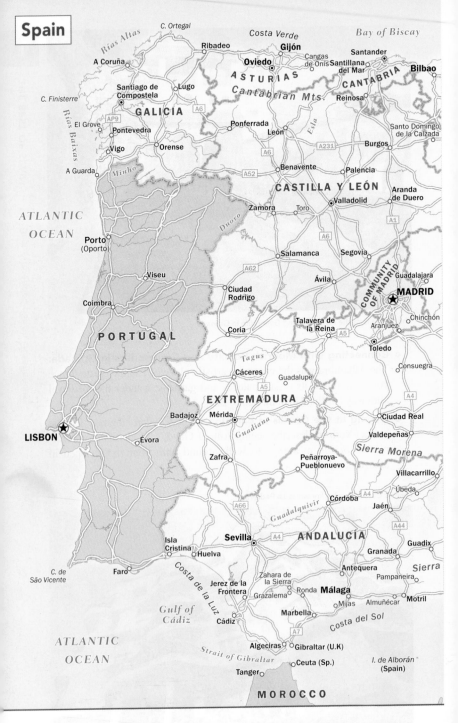

Spain

C. Ortegal · Ribadeo · Costa Verde · Gijón · Bay of Biscay

Rías Altas · A Coruña · Cangas de Onís · Santander

Oviedo · Santillana del Mar · Bilbao

ASTURIAS · CANTABRIA

C. Finisterre · Santiago de Compostela · Lugo · Cantabrian Mts. · Reinosa

A6 · GALICIA · Ponferrada · León · Esla · Santo Domingo de la Calzada

Rías Baixas · El Grove · AP9 · Pontevedra · Orense · A6 · A231 · Burgos

Vigo · Benavente · Palencia · CASTILLA Y LEÓN

A Guarda · Minho · A52 · Aranda de Duero

ATLANTIC OCEAN · Duero · Zamora · Toro · Valladolid · A1

Porto (Oporto) · Salamanca · Segovia · A6

Viseu · A62 · Ávila · Guadalajara

Ciudad Rodrigo · COMMUNITY OF MADRID · MADRID

Coimbra · Chinchón

PORTUGAL · Coria · Talavera de la Reina · A5 · Aranjuez

Tagus · Toledo · Consuegra

Cáceres · Guadalupe · A4

A5 · EXTREMADURA

Badajoz · Mérida · Guadiana · Ciudad Real

LISBON · Valdepeñas

Évora · Zafra · Sierra Morena

Peñarroya-Pueblonuevo · Villacarrillo

Úbeda

A66 · Guadalquivir · Córdoba · A4 · Jaén

Isla Cristina · Sevilla · A4 · ANDALUCÍA · Guadix

Huelva · Granada · Sierra

C. de São Vicente · Faro · Antequera · Pampaneira

Zahara de la Sierra · Ronda · Málaga · Motril

Costa de la Luz · Jerez de la Frontera · Grazalema · Mijas · Almuñécar · Costa del Sol

Gulf of Cádiz · Marbella

Cádiz · A7

ATLANTIC OCEAN · Algeciras · Gibraltar (U.K)

Strait of Gibraltar · Ceuta (Sp.) · I. de Alborán (Spain)

Tanger

MOROCCO

5

- **Trawling for Tapas Around Madrid's Las Letras:** The literary quarter has been a nightlife hub for centuries. Hop from bar to bar, tasting the air-dried ham that hangs over the counter, along with garlic prawns, pickled anchovies, and spicy fried potatoes. See p. 134.

- **Celebrating the Basque Renaissance in Bilbao:** The bold architecture of Frank Gehry's Guggenheim Museum set a new bar for design and sparked a chain of civic improvements. From the new waterfront promenade to various other architectural innovations, Bilbao struts its stuff with pride. See p. 597.

- **Sunning on the Beach at Historic Tossa de Mar:** The ruins of a medieval coastal fortress crouch on one of two headlands bracketing this sandy cove on the often-rocky Costa Brava. See p. 534.

THE best WAYS TO BRING HISTORY ALIVE

- **Driving the White Towns of the Sierra de Grazalema:** Scattered from Ronda to Arcos de la Frontera, these mountainside fortress towns, like flocks of nesting birds. were once the frontier between the Christians and the Moors. See p. 312.

- **Tracing Roman Footsteps in Tarragona:** The oceanside Amfiteatre Romà is a stunning reminder that Rome ruled eastern Iberia from this Costa Daurada port for more than 600 years. See p. 502.

The cathedral of Santiago de Compostela.

Cordoba's La Mezquita.

- **Seeing the Sun Rise in Córdoba's Judería:** Get up early to visit La Mezquita, Europe's greatest surviving medieval mosque, and wander the timeless streets of the Jewish quarter before the crowds arrive. See p. 263.

- **Surveying the Ages in Girona:** From Roman fortifications to Muslim palaces to the largest Jewish Call in Spain, Girona preserves its past. The ramparts above the cathedral show the whole ancient city, raised like dinosaur plates on the spine of a hill. See p. 515.

- **Honoring the Pilgrims' Faith at Santiago de Compostela:** For nearly 10 centuries Christian pilgrims have trekked across northern Spain to the holy shrine of St. James, or Santiago. For the devout, walking into the great cathedral is an earthly taste of the gates of paradise. See p. 655.

- **Walking the Walls of Ávila:** The 11th-century walls around Ávila— some of the most intact medieval walls in Europe—offer stirring views of the countryside, not to mention up-close views of storks nesting on the city's highest buildings. See p. 195.

- **Reliving Roman Entertainment in Mérida:** The ruins of Spain's Roman capital, Emerita Augusta, are the best-preserved outside Italy. Visit in summer to take your seat in the spectacular ancient theater, which hosts a classical drama festival. See p. 713.

THE best HOTELS IN SPAIN

- **Gran Hotel Domine, Bilbao:** It took a lot of architectural chutzpah to erect a contemporary design hotel right next to Frank Gehry's iconic Guggenheim Museum, but this place is up to the challenge. It's a sleek yet comfortable place to stay. See p. 605.

- **Hostal de Los Reyes Católicos, Santiago de Compostela:** Created by royal order to welcome pilgrims coming to Santiago, it's the most history-steeped lodging in town—or maybe in Spain. See p. 660.

- **Hotel María Cristina, San Sebastián:** Opulent in ways that only a Belle Époque hotel can be, this landmark hotel takes its name from a Spanish Queen and delivers royally when it comes to luxury and first-class service. See p. 585.

- **Gran Hotel Inglés, Madrid:** A total refit has transformed this famous old establishment into one of the capital's most stylish boutique hotels, set in a narrow Las Letras street across from Hemingway's favorite sherry bar. See p. 118.

- **Hospedería del Real Monasterio, Guadalupe:** Here's a rare opportunity to lodge inside one of Spain's most beautiful monasteries in this medieval pilgrimage town. Clanking keys, echoing corridors, and pilgrim-friendly prices make this an atmospheric treat. See p. 746.

- **Casa Fuster, Barcelona:** Modernisme's heyday lives again in this deluxe hotel designed as a private home in 1908 by Lluís Domènech i

Frank Gehry's stunning design for the Hotel Marqués in Elciego, in the La Rioja wine country.

Montaner. Private balconies in many rooms open onto leafy Passeig de Gràcia. See p. 466.

o **Hostal de la Gavina, Sant Feliu de Guíxols:** This oasis amid the bustle of the Costa Brava epitomizes gracious living with a hint of Moorish style. See p. 534.

o **Hotel Marqués de Riscal, Elciego:** Rioja wine house Marqués de Riscal hired Frank Gehry to design a "City of Wine" melding production facilities with this striking hotel with a shell of anodized titanium. A kissing cousin to the Guggenheim Bilbao. See p. 610.

o **Las Casas de la Judería, Sevilla:** Comprising 27 traditional houses in the old Jewish quarter, linked by a labyrinth of passages, flower-filled patios and underground tunnels, this eccentric hotel is full of history and character. There's a lovely rooftop pool too. See p. 251.

o **Parador Casa del Corregidor, Arcos de la Frontera:** Once the headquarters of the king's magistrate, this perfectly located *parador* in Andalucía has a modern wing hanging over the cliff edge. Its terraces have exhilarating views of the Río Guadelete plain below. See p. 318.

THE best TAPAS DINING

o **Bergara Bar, San Sebastián:** San Sebastián is well stocked with good tapas bars, but the bright lights of the Bergara shine down on a counter simply groaning with "pintxos creatives." It's considered a national treasure by gastronomes and Spanish chefs. See p. 591.

A classic array of tapas, those iconic Spanish bar snacks.

o **Bodeguita Casablanca, Sevilla:** This busy corner bar near Puerta de Jerez is acclaimed for its deft riffs on traditional dishes. Try the trademark *tortilla al whisky,* cooked carefully to preserve the alcohol and topped with cloves of roast garlic. See p. 256.

o **Casa Bigote, Sanlúcar de Barrameda:** Grab a barrel-top table at this riverside taberna for a plate of rock salt-sprinkled prawns and a cold glass of the town's *manzanilla* sherry. Watch the ferry go back and forth to the Doñana across the Guadalquivir delta. See p. 329.

o **Casa Dani, Madrid:** With a stall inside the beautiful Mercado de la Paz food market, Casa Dani prides itself on making the finest *tortilla española* (Spanish omelet). A huge, gooey slice costs just 2.80€. See p. 135.

o **Casa Juan, Torremolinos:** Mainly a seafood restaurant, Casa Juan serves tapas between meals (i.e., between 5–9pm). It's the perfect spot for a *freidura* of mixed tiny seafood—often called "fried foam"—fried in olive oil. Eat it skin, bones, and all. See p. 362.

o **KGB, Málaga:** Málaga foodies flock here to have fun, and a stream of guest chefs contributes a never-ending variety of novel small plates. The "top secret" tapas are just a joke on the initials for Kuartel Gastronomic Bar. See p. 373.

o **Nou Manolín, Alicante:** Famous chefs from all over Spain (and even France) come on eating holidays to Alicante to treat themselves to Nou Manolín's great fish tapas. See p. 406.

o **Tragatá, Ronda:** At this offshoot of Benito Gómez's exquisite Bardal restaurant, the tapas are little more than a bite, but the Spanish classics and fusion fish dishes are so well-made you might try the whole selection. See p. 311.

o **Tapas 24, Barcelona:** With tapas for breakfast (broken eggs over fried potatoes), lunch (grilled ham and cheese with black truffle), or dinner (hamburger with foie gras), chef Carles Abellean pays homage to the tapas lifestyle. See p. 484.

o **Taberna Bar Cuervo, León:** Michelin-starred chefs throughout Spain have begun to feature the air-dried beef of León on their menus. This taberna has had the best for decades, along with classic León sausages. See p. 229.

o **Taberna Casa Manteca, Cádiz:** Founded by a retired matador in the 1950s, this shrine to the bullfight and flamenco serves *chicharrones* (thinly sliced pork belly) and the local *payoyo* cheese on waxed paper with a glass of sherry. See p. 338.

THE best RESTAURANTS

- **Arzak, San Sebastián:** Co-chefs Juan Marí Arzak and Elena Arzak are passionate about visual presentation and magnificent taste. Yes, the plates are artful, but your palate will be duly rewarded at this restaurant that's been a leader in avant-garde Basque cuisine for more than four decades. See p. 588.

- **José María Restaurante, Segovia:** Segovianos are fanatics about roast suckling pig. Here's where aficionados of *cochinillo* take their families for the crispest crackling skin and the juiciest succulent meat. See p. 195.

- **Lasarte, Barcelona:** Basque chef Martín Berasategui's exquisite fine dining restaurant offers reinterpretations of some of his greatest dishes and innovations by his brilliant chef de cuisine. See p. 483.

- **Dani García Restaurante, Marbella:** At this Costa del Sol fixture, star chef Dani García reproduces some of his classics such as lobster salad with "popcorn" olives (exploded with liquid nitrogen) and suckling pig with pumpkin and orange. See p. 352.

- **El Celler de Can Roca, Girona:** Roca brothers Joan (head chef), Jordi (head pastry chef), and Josep (sommelier) belie the trope about broth and too many cooks. This is Catalan home cooking with surreal twists, as if Salvador Dalí's ghost were in the kitchen. See p. 523.

Suckling pig roasting in a tile oven.

○ **Coque, Madrid:** Representing a new wave of staggeringly sophisticated restaurants, the Sandoval brothers take diners on an avant-garde gastronomic tour, serving scientifically created dishes in several locations within their Chamberí restaurant. See p. 140.

○ **La Pepica, Valencia:** La Pepica's sprawling kitchen is the temple of *paella Valenciana*—and dozens of variations. See p. 398.

○ **Casa Marcial, Arriondas:** Nacho Manzano made his mark in London, but his family restaurant is where he concocts outrageous and delicious dishes such as cucumber soup over green pepper sorbet or roast woodcock with oysters and river eels. See p. 633.

○ **Solla, Pontevedra:** Self-taught Pepe Solla lacks the preconceptions of a classically trained chef—he thinks nothing, for example, of pairing sea bass with braised turnip greens, Galician cabbage, and an orange-lemon sauce. See p. 666.

○ **La Despensa del Etxanobe, Bilbao:** Fernando Canales parades his genius in two adjacent restaurants: **L'Atelier,** the place to celebrate a business deal, and **La Despensa,** which oozes class in its décor, service, and carefully crafted cuisine. His pipeline to foragers and fishermen ensures he has the very best products of the season. See p. 606.

THE best WAYS TO SEE SPAIN LIKE A LOCAL

○ **Shop in the Fresh Food Markets of Barcelona and Valencia:** One look at the culinary riches on display in Barcelona's La Boqueria and Valencia's Mercado Central, and you'll grasp the Spanish obsession with eating. Wait till you taste that orange! See p. 390 and p. 427.

○ **Look for the Good-Luck Frog in Salamanca:** The university city has the wittiest and most phantasmagoric stone carvings in all of Spain. Students look for a frog perched on a skull in the elaborate carvings around the door to the Escuelas Mayores. See p. 207.

○ **Crowd into a Bar to Root for Real Madrid:** Ticket prices for soccer matches at the Santiago Bernabéu stadium have become crazy expensive, but most fans

Flowering patio of Cordoba.

watch the games on television—ideally on a big screen in a bar. See p. 113.

- **People-Watch at El Rastro:** You may not find a bargain at Madrid's venerable Sunday street market at Lavapies, but it's a great place to watch the crowds who come for a wander, a look, and tapas at the bar afterwards. See p. 96.

- **Have a Glass of Catalan Cava:** Sip sparkling wine surrounded by vineyards where those grapes were nourished by the Mediterranean sunshine. In the El Penedés growing region, you can tour Freixenet, Codorníu, Torres, and smaller local wineries. See p. 494.

- **Visit the Private Patios of Córdoba:** During the Córdoba Patio Festival in May, people open their homes so visitors can admire the traditional interior courtyards hung with potted geraniums. See p. 268.

- **Make the Evening Promenade in Marbella:** All over Spain people go out for a leisurely evening walk to show off a beau, visit with neighbors, or just enjoy the cool air. The marble sidewalks of Marbella are an elegant setting for a stroll. See p. 349.

THE best FAMILY OUTINGS

- **Boating on Mallorca's Largest Underground Lake:** The Cuevas del Drach (Caves of the Dragon) hold concerts amid their forests of stalagmites and stalactites. Row around Lago Martel, the largest cavern lake in the world, in illuminated rowboats. See p. 691.

The Cuevas del Drach.

- **Talking to the Animals at the Bioparc Fuengirola:** Moats and landscape features replace bars and cages at this model zoo where you can see more than 140 species of animals. See p. 356.

- **Seeing the Horses Dance in Jerez de la Frontera:** Elegant purebred horses are put through their paces by highly skilled horsemen on Tuesdays and Thursdays at the Andalucían School of Equestrian Art in Jerez. See p. 323.

- **Hiking the Wind-Sculpted Hoodoos of El Torcal:** Andalucía's first natural park is a fantasia of wind-sculpted limestone boulders. Trails lead through the surreal landscape. See p. 375.

- **Kicking Back in Madrid's Parque del Retiro:** Madrid's families flock to the Parque del Retiro to row around the lake, catch impromptu concerts, and let little ones watch old-fashioned puppet shows. See p. 107.

- **Riding the Train to the Beach in Alicante:** Hop the light rail in downtown Alicante and arrive minutes later at the long sands of the barrier beach of Playa San Juan (Platja Sant Joan in Valenciano). See p. 402.

THE best ART MUSEUMS

- **Museo del Prado, Madrid:** Created from the royal collections, this is one of the world's greatest art museums. Its galleries contain Italian,

Bilbao's Guggenheim Museum is as exciting for its architecture as for the art within.

In Sevilla, masterpieces are displayed in the serene setting of a 16th-century former convent.

Dutch and Flemish masters, but it's the Spanish greats who shine, from Diego Velázquez's psychological studies of royalty to Francisco de Goya's journey from early pastorals to late nightmares. See p. 83.

o **Museo Nacional Centro del Arte Reina Sofía:** During the Franco dictatorship, artists fled to countries more hospitable to their modern visions. The Reina Sofía puts them back where they belong. Pablo Picasso's *Guernica,* his *cri de coeur* for the bombing of a defenseless Basque village, is the definitive piece of anti-war art. See p. 87.

o **Museo de Bellas Artes, Sevilla:** The tiled courtyards of this 1594 former convent host Bartholomé Esteban Murillo's florid master-pieces, painted for the convent, and Francisco de Zurbarán's haunt-ingly austere portraits of saints. See p. 242.

o **Fundació Joan Miró, Barcelona:** More than 10,000 works by Joan Miró fill this light-filled museum atop Montjuïc in Barcelona. His sur-real shapes and dreamy spaces have a whimsy of their own, like some-one telling a funny story in another language. See p. 450.

o **Guggenheim Museum, Bilbao:** For some visitors, Frank Gehry's titanium-clad museum building still upstages its own exhibits, whether temporary or permanent. But over time, a penchant for performance pieces and sculpture (some whimsical, some not) on a gargantuan scale ensures that art aficionados will leave fully satisfied. See p. 601.

o **Teatre-Museu Dalí, Figueres:** Salvador Dalí cultivated his image as an eccentric, so it's no surprise that his final monument to himself is a former theater transformed into a non-stop sequence of visual jokes. Here it rains *inside* the car. See p. 526.

- **Museu Picasso, Barcelona:** The artist who redefined art in the 20th century has whole museums dedicated to him in Málaga (his birthplace) and in Paris. The Barcelona museum, housed in five adjoining Gothic structures, lets you observe young Picasso becoming Picasso. See p. 437.

- **Museo de Santa Cruz, Toledo:** Greek mystical painter Domenikos Theotokopoulos adopted Toledo as his home, and the Spanish renamed him El Greco. Some of his finest paintings—elongated religious figures depicted in luminous colors—reside in this beautiful Renaissance building. See p. 162.

- **Museo Carmen Thyssen, Málaga:** The Baroness Carmen Thyssen (of the Thyssen-Bornemisza Museum in Madrid) endowed this institution with a sharply focused collection of Spanish paintings from 1825 to 1925 that document Spain's transition from Romantic cliché to nation with a modern sensibility. See p. 368.

- **Museu Nacional d'Art de Catalunya, Barcelona:** Some of Europe's best Romanesque and early Gothic art was created for Catalan churches. Thanks to heroic rescue efforts in threatened and demolished churches and chapels around Catalunya, much of it is collected here. See p. 452.

THE best OF OUTDOOR SPAIN

- **Hiking the Alpujarra de Granada:** The ancient Moorish mountain villages south from Granada make for great town-to-town hiking on exposed rocky trails. The information center of the Parque Natural de Sierra Nevada in the village of Pampaneira is a good place to start. See p. 303.

- **Cycling to L'Albufera:** The marshlands south of Valencia's port are best explored on two wheels, and there's even a bike path much of the way. See the rice farmers toiling in the marshes, enjoy the almost deserted beaches, and stop for a great paella. See p. 392.

- **Visiting the Illa de Cabrera Natural Reserve:** Although Cabrera was a pirate base in the 13th and 14th centuries, now it is a Natural Reserve off Mallorca where you can see huge colonies of shearwaters and gulls as well as ospreys, falcons, and sea hawks. See p. 678.

- **Surfing the Left-Hand Break in Mundaka:** The long rolling barrel curl in Mundaka on the Basque Coast is famous with surfers around the world. It's also one of the most reliable breaks in Europe. Plan on wearing a wetsuit; the Bay of Biscay can be frigid. See p. 593.

- **Boating the Parque Doñana:** One of Europe's most important refuges for migratory birds, the Donaña marshes spread across the delta of the Río Guadalquivír as it reaches the Bahía de Cádiz. Naturalist-led boat tours leave daily from Sanlúcar de Barrameda. See p. 327.

A surfer tackles the barrel curl in Mundaka.

o **Walking the Fuente Dé Ridge:** You'll have to drive to the téleférico (cable car) station to ride up to a high ridge of Fuente Dé in the Picas de Europe. Walk the ridge, visit the cafe, and marvel at the mountains. See p. 629.

o **Birding in Monfragüe:** This national park of untouched woodland and majestic river gorges is a birdwatcher's nirvana, home to many protected species, including the Spanish imperial eagle, azure-winged magpie, and Europe's biggest population of black vultures. See p. 738.

THE best SMALL TOWNS

o **Trujillo:** It's said that 20 Latin American countries were born in this tough little Extremaduran town, which produced so many conquistadors who colonized the New World in the 16th century. The riches they sent home financed the lavish buildings on its beautiful square. See p. 730.

o **Ronda:** Cleft in two by the dramatic El Tajo gorge, Ronda's old and new towns are connected by a daring stone bridge. Romantic travelers in the 19th century fell in love with its edginess; you will too. See p. 304.

o **Zamora:** When the Christian kings of Castilla took back Zamora from the Moors, they made sure they could hold it by building two dozen fabulous Romanesque churches in the 12th and 13th centuries. The town fortifications have great views along the Río Duero. See p. 211.

o **Elche:** Boasting the largest palm forest in Europe and an archaeological museum devoted to the ancient Iberians, Elche also has the Pikolinos shoe factory outlet at the edge of town. See p. 408.

The hanging houses of Cuenca cling to their clifftop perches.

o **Cuenca:** Spectacularly balanced between earth and sky, Cuenca is famous for its hanging houses, cantilevered onto a precipitous gorge. Abandoned after the Civil War, the upper town was reclaimed by abstract artists, who have regenerated it as striking venue for contemporary art. See p. 171.

o **Deià:** Set on the western end of Mallorca, this high-country village of stone houses draped in bougainvillea was the favored retreat of English poet Robert Graves, who wrote his enduring historical novel *I, Claudius* here. See p. 685.

o **Santo Domingo de la Calzada:** Established in the 12th century as a stopover for pilgrims heading to Santiago de Compostela, this little village in La Rioja eventually grew into a full-fledged pilgrim town where live chickens are kept in the cathedral. See p. 223.

THE best OFF-THE-BEATEN PATH SPAIN

o **Toro:** This dusty little wine town on the Río Duero east of Zamora huddles behind medieval walls. The carvings on the main entry of its 13th-century church are some of Spain's greatest Gothic art. Most Toro shops sell wine—very, very good wine. See p. 216.

o **Cadaqués:** Isolated along the coast over a steep range of mountains, Cadaqués remains the sweet fishing town that has drawn so many artists over the years. The stony beach is better for landing small boats

Spectacular stone carvings adorn a Gothic church in tiny Toro.

than sunbathing. One cove north of the center, Port Lligat was the home and studio of Salvador Dalí, now open to the public. See p. 528.

o **Poblet:** Once the greatest of Catalunya's Carthusian monasteries, Poblet has retreated to near oblivion. Yet the fortified monastery village west of Barcelona has a medieval charm, as if it were plucked directly from Umberto Eco's *Name of the Rose.* The kings of Aragón are buried beneath the church. See p. 506.

o **The Cantabrian Caves:** Whether they were painted 10,000 or 30,000 years ago, the delicate deer and hunched buffalo on the walls of Cantabria's limestone caves remain fresh and vibrant today. See p. 621.

o **Úbeda:** In the 16th century, agricultural wealth financed Úbeda's elegant churches and palaces. When fortunes declined, the building stopped, leaving an open-air museum of Spanish Renaissance architecture. See p. 298.

o **Bardenas Reales:** These "badlands" lie midway between the Pyrenees of northern Navarra and its southern agricultural flatlands. Wind and rain have sculpted spectacular rock formations and if that's not enough, sheep flocks graze here in winter ... while the Spanish air force uses the area for target practice! See p. 568.

o **Teruel:** The Aragonese city of Teruel northwest of Valencia is a treasure trove of Mudéjar architecture—a uniquely Spanish style that came about when Christian patrons engaged Moorish architects and workmen. The synthesis of cultures yielded some of the richest design of the late Middle Ages. See p. 550.

2

SPAIN IN CONTEXT

By Patricia Harris & David Lyon

 One of the few things that the French and English used to agree on was that "Europe ends at the Pyrenees." Those mountains kept Spain in splendid isolation, where it developed along its own path. Consequently, Spain has evolved customs, art, architecture, and even cuisine that owe as much to Islamic North Africa as to its onetime sister provinces of the Roman Empire. The country does not look like, sound like, or even taste like the rest of Europe, and nowhere else is quite as rich or demanding. When you go to Spain, you must surrender to Spain.

You must accept the rhythms of daily life—so unlike the rest of Europe—and think nothing of going to dinner after 10pm and then closing down the flamenco bar after the 3am final set. You must spend the evening in a seafront promenade, walking and talking and nodding at the other walkers and talkers. You must elbow your way to the bar, pointing at the tapas to order, and having your fill. For that matter, you must resolve to eat something new every day that you would otherwise spurn: blood sausage, roasted suckling pig, squid in its own ink. In some places, shops and museums close in the heat of the afternoon, and you must be patient and while away the hours with lunch in a cool, shady courtyard. Do all that, and you will be ready for everything Spain will throw at you.

Rest assured, it will be a lot. The cultural renaissance that followed the 1975 death of dictator Francisco Franco continues to gather steam. Madrid, Barcelona, and San Sebastián have emerged as major European artistic and intellectual centers of cinema, fashion, and gastronomy, while Bilbao has provided a blueprint to the world for using art to transform an industrial backwater into a vibrant cultural capital.

SPAIN TODAY

Spain is a social, cultural, and economic bright spot in Europe. Unemployment is dropping, wages are climbing, yet inflation is low. In practical terms for a visitor to Spain, that means that the country is prosperous yet remains a very good bargain. The bills have been largely paid for the audacious infrastructure investments of the early part of the 21st century, and now Spain enjoys a network of new highways, a high-speed train system that is the envy of Europe, and thoroughly modernized airports.

There has also been a positive sea change in the national mood. When King Juan Carlos I abdicated the throne in 2014, Spaniards welcomed his

FACING PAGE: **Casa Guell in Barcelona.**

El Clásico

Although Spain is a nominally Roman Catholic country, church attendance has fallen off from its historic highs. The true religion of most Spaniards—and particularly of residents of Barcelona and Madrid—is fútbol (soccer). It's a red-letter day on the calendar whenever Real Madrid and FC Barcelona meet. The rivalry is known simply as "El Clásico," and fills the home stadium, while tens of millions of Spaniards tune into the matches on television. Historically, Real Madrid symbolizes the hegemony of the Castilians who have ruled the country since the 15th century, while Barcelona represents the upstart rebelliousness of Catalunya.

son, Felipe VI, perhaps the best educated and most polyglot monarch in centuries. The king and his queen consort, Letizia Ortiz Rocasolano, a former television journalist with CNN, swiftly became symbols of the secularization and liberalization of Spanish cultural life. They were the first Spanish monarchs to enthusiastically welcome an LGBT delegation and Felipe did away with the requirement that office holders swear an oath on a Bible or crucifix.

In June 2018 Spanish voters elected a new government led by prime minister Pedro Sánchez of the Spanish Socialist Party (PSOE). Spain did an about-face on environmental policy, setting new and higher goals for renewable energy. (Nearly 50% of the country's electricity is generated by solar panels and wind turbines—a fact readily evident as you drive past vast wind and solar farms in rural areas.) The new government also took a more active role in European Union affairs. In a reversal of its historic xenophobia, Spain has become an open and immigration-friendly political system and society.

Sentiment in Catalunya for independence from Spain remains high, though the political quarrel has little consequence for visitors—even at the height of the independence protests in October 2017 and September 2018, the main inconvenience for visitors was having to detour around the crowds. The standoff remains, as Catalan nationalists control the regional government by a slim margin and the Sánchez government in Madrid does its best not to poke the bear.

Spain's popular new monarch, Felipe VI, and his queen, Letizia Ortiz Rocasolano, signal the liberalization of the country.

LOOKING BACK AT SPAIN

To understand Spain's accretion of cultures, simply look to any major religious site. The Christian cathedral is often built on the site of a Moorish mosque that was erected on the ruins of a Visigothic church built over the cellars of a Roman temple, which may have used the building blocks and columns from an even earlier Phoenician house of worship.

The peopling of the Iberian Peninsula began around 35,000 B.C., with the arrival of Cro-Magnon refugees from the glaciation of Europe. Traces of the first settlers are scattered and are found mainly in the sophisticated wall paintings in **Altamira** (p. 622) and other caves along the Cantabrian and Basque coasts. The **Basque Archaeological Museum** in Bilbao offers a good overview of what science knows about these first Spaniards.

Two Bronze Age cultures—Iberian and Celtic—had emerged in Spain by the time other Mediterranean cultures made contact. The Iberians are perhaps best known today through a few examples of sophisticated funerary figures, La Dama de Baeza and La Dama d'Elx, both on display in the **National Archaeology Museum** in Madrid (p. 105). Celtic culture flourished around the Atlantic rim of the peninsula; Tartessos, at the mouth of the Río Guadalquivír, became famous throughout the ancient world for its jewelry and for its dance and music. (Tartessans invented castanets.) Examples of exquisite Celtic gold work are in the **National Archaeology Museum** in Madrid (p. 105) and in the **Archaeological and Historical Museum** in A Coruña (p. 649).

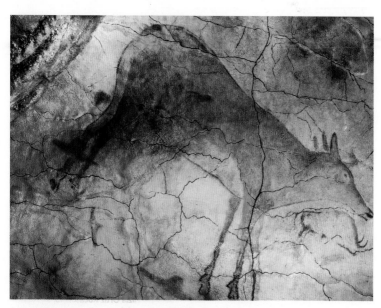

Relics of the earliest Iberians were discovered on cave walls in Altamira.

Phoenician settlement began in Iberia around 1100 B.C., most notably in Málaga and in the peninsular city of Cádiz, where extraordinary Phoenician sarcophagi and some Phoenician jewelry are displayed in the **Museo de Cádiz** (p. 333). Within 200 years, Greek traders began to give the Phoenicians competition, founding the trading post at **Empuriès** (p. 531) on the Costa Brava and pushing into the Balearics and coastal Andalucía.

In 218 B.C., the Romans landed and changed everything. Establishing a beachhead to battle the Carthaginians in the Second Punic War, they proceeded to lay roads across Iberia and either conquer or co-opt everyone they met along the way. The Phoenicians and Greeks had already brought wine grapes and olive trees; the Romans brought wheat, law and order, a hunger for Iberian fish paste, and an insatiable need for soldiers to fight in the Roman legions. By the time of Julius Caesar, Hispania was under Roman law and began a long period of peace and prosperity. **Tarragona** (p. 497), a short trip south from Barcelona, became the administrative center for eastern Hispania while **Mérida** (p. 713) in Extremadura became the western capital. Both retain many Roman structures to this day. The Romans were superb architects and engineers; throughout the country, Roman roads still form the base for many highways. **Segovia** (p. 186), a short trip out of Madrid, boasts one of the greatest of the Roman aqueducts.

Iberia was thoroughly Romanized during this period, although the Basques negotiated a fragile peace with Rome that allowed them to maintain their right of self-governance. Succeeding rulers granted the Basques

Mérida's Roman theater is among Spain's most complete Roman ruins.

Detail of Moorish decoration in the Alhambra in Granada.

the same autonomy until the late 19th century. The Pax Romana prevailed throughout the peninsula, and Latin became the Iberian language.

When the Roman Empire crumbled in the A.D. 5th century, Iberia was first overrun by the Vandals (northern Germans who ultimately kept going south into the mountains of North Africa) and then by the Visigoths from Eastern Europe. Rome had invited them to drive out the Vandals, but local powers decided to keep Iberia for themselves. (The Visigoths' 200-year rule plays out in a few country churches in northern Spain and some of the most sophisticated medieval gold jewelry ever crafted, including the royal jewels and crowns now housed in the **National Archaeological Museum** in Madrid; see p. 105).

Centuries of Holy Wars

In A.D. 711, the game changed again. Led by the great Berber general Tariq ibn Ziyad, Moorish warriors crossed the Straits of Gibraltar from Morocco and set about conquering Iberia. Within 3 years, the Moors controlled all but the far northern fringe of the peninsula, where the Basques and the Asturian Visigoths held out in their mountain lairs.

The Iberian population had collapsed under the chaotic rule of the Visigoths, and the Moors began to repopulate their conquered land, which they called al-Andalus. While northern Europe was foundering in the Dark Ages, the Andalucían capital of **Córdoba** was a model of enlightenment. Religious tolerance was an official policy under the Umayyad Caliphate (A.D. 929–1031). Córdoba's **Great Mosque (La Mezquita;**

p. 268) was erected in this period, and European, North African, Near Eastern, and Jewish scholars flocked to the city. Notable advances were made in agriculture, industry, literature, philosophy, medicine, and mathematics.

By the late 11th century, powerful local kingdoms had arisen in northern Spain with the single-minded goal of restoring Christian rule to Muslim Iberia. When civil war broke out in al-Andalus, the northern Christian warriors pounced. **Alfonso VI** of Castilla seized Toledo, Madrid, and much of central Spain in 1085; the great warlord and national hero **El Cid** won back Valencia and Catalunya (including Barcelona) in 1094. By 1214, only three major powers remained in Iberia: Castilla in the north, west, and center of Spain; Aragón in northeastern Spain; and the Moorish kingdom of Granada, which would flower a century later with the supreme example of Moorish architecture and decorative arts, the **Alhambra** (p. 283).

The Castilian and Aragónese bloodlines would finally meet in Spain's first power couple, **Isabel I of Castilla y León** and **Fernando II of Aragón.** They married in 1469, bringing Toledo (and nearby Madrid) and Barcelona under the same joint rule. Isabel launched the Spanish Inquisition to ferret out heretics, and the Catholic kings (as the Spanish-born pope would dub them) made war on Granada and drove out its last ruler in 1492. Declaring the reconquest complete, Isabel and Fernando decreed that all Muslims and Jews must either convert to Christianity or leave the country.

Later that same year, they dispatched **Christopher Columbus** to find a westward passage to the Spice Islands of Asia, an event memorialized in statuary in the garden of Córdoba's **Alcázar** (p. 237). He sailed from the mouth of the Rio Guadalquivír in Andalucía, and, in October 1492, made landfall instead in the West Indies. His voyages of discovery laid the foundations for a far-flung empire that would bring wealth and power to Spain throughout the 16th and 17th centuries.

A statue in Córdoba depicts Queen Isabel I and King Fernando II sending Christopher Columbus on his voyage to the New World.

Imperial Spain

The grandson of Isabel and Fernando, the Habsburg king **Carlos I,** became the most powerful ruler in Europe when he was crowned Holy Roman

As Holy Roman Emperor, Carlos V ruled over a vast part of western Europe.

Emperor in 1519 and took the title **Carlos V.** He ruled Spain and Naples and the Holy Roman Empire and was lord of Germany, duke of Burgundy and the Netherlands, and ruler of the New World territories. His son, **Felipe II,** inherited the throne in 1556 and 5 years later moved the capital from the closed hilltop medieval city of Toledo to Madrid, where the Habsburg kings had a hunting palace.

Madrid grew quickly from dusty outpost to royal city, setting Spain on its Golden Age of arts and letters, and Madrid on its domination of the national scene. **Miguel de Cervantes** (1547–1616), a career petty bureaucrat, penned the adventures of Don Quijote and set the standard for Spanish prose. The rascal priest **Lope de Vega** (1562–1635) wrote poems and plays incessantly, redefining the Spanish theater in the company of **Calderón de la Barca** (1600–81) and **Tirso de Molina** (1579–1648).

The great painter **El Greco** (1541–1614) came to Toledo from Italy and brought the Italian Renaissance with him, although he could not curry favor at court and remained outside royal circles. **Diego Velázquez** (1599–1660) rose to become court painter to Felipe IV, and the two men were bound like brothers over several decades as Velázquez chronicled the royal family. His paintings, rarely seen in his own day, became public only when the royal art collection was installed in the **Museo del Prado** (p. 83) in the 19th century.

When the crown passed from the Habsburgs to the Bourbon line in 1700, **Felipe V** revoked the autonomy of Catalunya to quash his political foes and turned to re-making Madrid as a proper capital. His first task was to begin construction of the **Palacio Real** (p. 98). His son **Carlos III** transformed the face of Madrid with the aid of Spain's principal neoclassical architect, **Ventura Rodríguez** (1717–85), who laid out the grand boulevard of the Paseo del Prado and worked with **Juan de Villanueva** (1739–1811) on one of Spain's best neoclassical buildings, the Museo del Prado.

Spain in Chaos

Napoleon Bonaparte's 1808 invasion of Spain set off 167 years of instability and political oppression. Noting that Catalunya existed as a buffer

A monument in Madrid celebrates Miguel de Cervantes' great literary creation, Don Quijote, with his squire Sancho Panza.

between the French and the Moors, Napoleon annexed the region (and the riches of Barcelona). The rest of Spain literally took to the hills to fight the French emperor in the War of Independence, finally driving his armies out in 1813. **Francisco de Goya** famously delineated the horrors of French occupation in a series of paintings now in the Prado (p. 83).

The Catalan territory was restored to Spain, along with the Bourbon monarchy, but something in Spanish governance was irreparably broken. **Fernando VII** regained the throne but proved to be no friend of the freedom fighters and spent two decades putting down revolts. His arrogance and inflexibility led to the loss of Spain's most lucrative colonies in the Americas—and subsequent financial hardship for the country.

On the death of Fernando in 1833, civil war broke out between supporters of his daughter (**Isabel II**) and so-called Carlists who favored a more distant—but male—heir to the throne. Two more Carlist wars were fought, mostly in Navarra and the Basque Country, over the next 50 years, and Carlist sympathies festered into the 20th century, fueling both Franco's Falangist movement and Basque separatist sympathies. During this period, Spain was coming apart at the seams, and separatist fervor ran high, especially in Catalunya.

Scholars began to reestablish Catalan as a language of serious letters, and the avant-garde design style known as Art Nouveau in France and Jugendstil in Austria found native expression in Barcelona in the radical architecture of **Modernisme.** Its most extreme practitioner was **Antoni Gaudí** (1852–1926), who seemed as much to grow his buildings as

A stained-glass ceiling dome in Barcelona's Palau de la Música Catalana shows the exuberance of the Modernisme architectural style.

construct them. His masterpiece **La Sagrada Familia** (p. 440) integrates the impossibly soaring arches of High Gothic with a decorative style akin to melted candle wax. Other famous practitioners of Modernisme include **Lluís Domènech i Montaner** (1850–1923), known for the **Palau de la Música Catalana** (p. 438) in Barcelona, and **Josep Puig i Cadafalch** (1867–1956), who designed the **Codorniù bodega** in Sant Sadurní de Anoia (p. 494).

Isabel II ultimately was driven into exile in Paris, but the shaky monarchy was restored in 1874 when her son **Alfonso XII** became king. His sudden death in 1886 left his unborn son as monarch. The child was crowned **Alfonso XIII** at birth; his mother, Queen María Cristina, served as regent until 1902, and her advisors botched both the Spanish economy and Spain's international relations. Although he enjoyed immense personal popularity—he was the first Spanish celebrity king—Alfonso XIII exercised little real power. His chief legacy was to adopt the **Real Madrid** football club and to create the parador hotel system. In 1923, he allowed prime minister **Primo de Rivera** to take over the country as dictator for the next 7 years.

Civil War & the Franco Years

After Primo de Rivera was overthrown, in 1931 Spain declared the Second Republic. Initially progressive and left-wing in its politics, the new government broke into ever-smaller factions. Conservative, fascist-minded parties gained ground in the elections. When a group of right-wing generals declared a coup in 1936, the Civil War began. The world took sides, with Hitler and Mussolini backing **Francisco Franco** and the Nationalist generals. Most of the rest of Europe nominally backed the Republicans, also known as Loyalists or the Popular Front. Germany and Italy sent weapons and military assistance to the right, while the rest of the world sent a few volunteer brigades, including the American contingent called the "Lincoln Brigade." (For those who want insight into the era, Ernest Hemingway's *For Whom the Bell Tolls* is a good read.) It took time to turn untrained militias into an army fit to battle Franco's forces, and time was something the Popular Front did not have.

In the winter of 1936–37, Franco's forces slowly began to establish power, capturing the Basque country and demonstrating his ruthlessness

The Aragonese town of Belchite, reduced to rubble in the Spanish Civil War, has been left in ruins as a sobering reminder of the war's destruction.

by calling in the German Luftwaffe to destroy the Basque town of **Gernika** (Guernica in Castilian Spanish). The horror of the scene, which became the subject of one of Picasso's most famous paintings, *Guernica* (p. 87), repulsed the world.

At the end of the first year of war, Franco held 35 of Spain's provincial capitals, except for Madrid and Barcelona. In 1937, the Republican forces were cut in two, and Madrid was left to fend for itself. The last great offensive of the war began on December 23, 1938, with an attack by Franco's forces on Barcelona, which fell on January 26, 1939, after a campaign of 34 days. Republican forces fled to France. On March 28, some 200,000 of Franco's troops marched into Madrid, meeting no resistance. The war was over the next day, when the rest of Republican Spain surrendered. Lasting 2 years and 254 days, the war claimed 1 million lives. Spain lay in ruins, with Franco atop the smoking pile.

Steering Spain clear of alliances, Franco continued to rule until his death in 1975. He brought order, if not freedom, but he also isolated Spain from the rest of Europe.

Democratic Spain

According to advance provisions made by Franco, **Juan Carlos de Bórbon,** the grandson of Alfonso XIII, became king when the dictator died in 1975. Under the terms of a 1978 constitution, Spain became a constitutional democracy with a monarch whose power is limited to moral suasion. The constitution also devolved much of the government's centralized powers to autonomous regions, addressing long-standing calls for self-government in Catalunya and the Basque Country.

Franco's death was as momentous an event for society as it was for politics. The initial giddiness of Spaniards—dubbed "La Movida"—signified an explosion of freedom that brought to the fore such iconoclasts as filmmaker **Pedro Almodóvar,** who broke into the art-house circuit with his 1988 *Women on the Verge of a Nervous Breakdown,* a wild comedy about Spanish women and their man problems. He promptly became the flag bearer of contemporary Spanish cinema, with a body of work that in many ways defines modern Spanish sensibilities.

Flamenco had been suppressed under Franco but began to rise in popularity in the early 1970s as the dictator's health declined. Young talents, such as guitarist **Paco de Lucía** and singer **Camerón de la Isla** (both now deceased), helped lead a popular revival of the art form. Their emergence as full-fledged international stars in the early 1980s encouraged other artists to come out of the *peñas* (private clubs for flamenco aficionados) where they had labored—some for decades—to play the bars and clubs of Madrid and the cities of Andalucía. Today, Madrid is the epicenter of flamenco, but Sevilla, Jerez, Cádiz, and Málaga remain traditional strongholds.

In a similar vein, Spanish gastronomy underwent a sea change in the mid-1970s when Basque chefs **Pedro Subijana** and **Juan Mari Arzak** applied the principles of French nouvelle cuisine to Spanish food. They in turn inspired a young Catalan cook fresh out of military service named

Hosting the 1992 Olympic Games brought striking redevelopment to Barcelona's waterfront, including Frank Gehry's massive sculpture *El Peix.*

THE SPECTACLE OF death

Whether you love or despise bullfighting, the *corrida* is impossible to ignore. In *Death in the Afternoon*, Ernest Hemingway wrote, "The bullfight is not a sport in the Anglo-Saxon sense of the word; that is, it is not an equal contest or an attempt at an equal contest between a bull and a man. Rather it is a tragedy: the death of the bull, which is played, more or less well, by the bull and the man involved and in which there is danger for the man but certain death for the bull."

We're more conflicted about bull-fights than Papa was. In Spain, lithe (and, yes, sexy) matadors have all the celebrity of rock stars—and we love a good spectacle. But as animal lovers, we've never attended a bullfight in person because we know that no matter how skillful and graceful the matador, we couldn't stomach the baiting, wounding, and eventual killing of the bull. And, yes, we know that the animal is respected in death, and that some of its meat is even distributed to the poor.

Many Spaniards dislike (or simply have no interest in) the sport, and the autonomous region of Catalunya has banned it altogether. But the *corrida* persists as an element of Spanish identity. If you'd like to grapple with your own feelings about this confluence of culture and cruelty, the *corrida* season

lasts from early spring to around mid-October. Fights are held in a *plaza de toros* (bullring), including the oldest ring in remote Ronda and one of the most beautiful in Sevilla. Madrid's Las Ventas is arguably the most important in Spain. The best bullfighters face the best bulls here—and the fans who pack the stands are among the sport's most passionate and knowledgeable.

The bullfighter's greatest honor is to be awarded two *orejas*, or ears. The matador can claim the first by killing the bull with one thrust. The second is awarded by the crowd, with the consent of bullfight officials, for style and show-manship. In Madrid, those so honored are carried through the Grand Portal of Las Ventas by jubilant fans. Win two ears at Las Ventas and doors open at every bullring in the world. A top bullfighter

Ferran Adrià. In his quest for continuous reinvention of food at his restaurant elBulli, Adrià launched a worldwide gastronomic revolution that includes but is hardly limited to the chemistry-set pyrotechnics of molecular gastronomy. Adrià has since closed elBulli, leaving the frontiers of gastronomy to others, but it is nonetheless a great time to eat in Spain. Chefs have never been held in higher regard, finally achieving the fame and status of rock stars and star footballers. (Three-Michelin-star Madrid chef **David Muñoz** was, in fact, a footballer.) Yet not all the great dining in Spain costs 150€ and up (not including wine). The trickle-down of culinary aspiration reaches all the way to Spain's bars, where complex and inventive tapas, or *tapas creativas,* are all the rage.

In a way, Spain's coming-out parties to the world were **Expo '92** in Sevilla and the **1992 Summer Olympics** in Barcelona. The latter spurred the transformation of its host city, completely overhauling the waterfront and heralding Barcelona's reemergence on the world stage. Spain quickly can earn 5 to 6 million euros a year. Spaniards liken it to winning an Oscar in Hollywood—only much more dangerous.

A good alternative to attending a bullfight is to watch one in a neighborhood bar. We were once drinking happily in a small-town bar when the broadcast of a bullfight began on TV. Surrounded by intense fans, we found it impossible not to watch. As it played out on the small screen, the whole event was simultaneously moving and unsettling. Then again, the best travel experiences make you think—and sometimes make you uncomfortable.

placed its cultural treasures on display as well, constructing new major museums across the country, from the Guggenheim (p. 601) in Bilbao and the City of Arts and Sciences (p. 388) in Valencia to Madrid's Museum Nacional Centro de Arte Reina Sofía (p. 87) and Museo Thyssen-Bornemisza (p. 89). Paris's Centre Pompidou even opened its first satellite museum in Málaga (p. 366).

Spain finished its first high speed rail line in time for the Seville Expo in 1992, cutting travel time from Madrid to a mere 2 hours. Recently expanded lines now reach from the central hub of Madrid east to Valencia, north to the edge of the Basque Country, and northwest to A Coruña. Travel times are a fraction of what they once were, and relatively inaccessible parts of Spain are now a short drive or train ride away.

Spain's 2002 decision to join the European Union spurred huge social changes. Pressure to abandon the afternoon siesta finally trimmed the lunch break to 2 hours or less, and many stores, especially in big cities,

TOP 10 souvenirs OF SPAIN

1. **A tin of saffron.** In most countries it is hard to find saffron in anything larger than 1-gram vials. In Spanish markets or specialty shops, you can buy it in containers of 5, 10, 20, and even 50 grams. It's still a splurge, but much less expensive than buying it at home.

2. **An embroidered shawl from Andalucía.** While you're in Sevilla, observe local women to learn how this accessory can become a major fashion statement.

3. **A Basque beret.** More structured than the French beret, a Basque beret is usually made of waterproof wool with a soft leather headband. Ideally, it should be purchased in Basque Country from a man who never takes his off.

4. **A ceramic olive serving bowl.** These bowls have a separate small compartment for placing the pits. Some also have another compartment to hold toothpicks. It will be a great conversation piece at your next dinner party.

5. **A beautiful forged kitchen knife from Toledo.** Toledo steel has been the standard to swear by since knights carried Toledo blades into battle during the Crusades. Blade makers in Toledo now make fabulous kitchen cutlery. Be sure to pack your purchase into a checked bag to fly home.

6. **A bullfight poster.** Any souvenir shop will print your name on a generic poster. Instead, go to the gift shop at a major bullring for exquisite reproductions of posters from recent seasons. A proper bullfight poster is a uniquely Spanish art genre.

7. **A Lladro porcelain figurine.** The firm is a 20th-century invention, but the style harks back to the fine workmanship of 18th-century porcelain.

8. **Canvas espadrilles with rope soles.** This summer classic never goes out of style, and Spaniards make them in both casual and high-fashion editions.

began to stay open without interruption. (Many museums have been reluctant to give up their midday break, however; check hours before visiting. Places that are chronically understaffed tend to close for lunch.) Perhaps the most radical sign that Spain had embraced European social norms came in 2011, when, bowing to E.U. health policies, the country banned smoking in all bars and restaurants throughout the country. Many Spaniards still smoke, but they do it outdoors.

In April 2005, Spain became the third European country to recognize gay marriage. Contemporary Spain is an especially attractive destination for LGBT travelers, and some resort towns, such as Sitges (p. 507) on the coast south of Barcelona, have equal numbers of gay and straight visitors during the height of tourist season. Other popular resort areas for gay travelers are Torremolinos on the Costa del Sol and the island of Ibiza.

Perhaps no change of customs has been more dramatic than the decline in Spaniards' traditional modesty. A generation ago, you could be arrested for going topless on the beach. Now the constitution guarantees

9. **Team jersey from Barcelona FC or Real Madrid.** Football (soccer) is practically a state religion, and these two teams are the most popular in Spain and among the best in the world. State your preference with your jersey.

10. **Paella pan.** It's so flat and thin that it easily slips into a suitcase. Now you can use that saffron.

that you can wear whatever you want—or not—as long as you don't create a stir. As a result, most coastal regions in Spain now have naturist beaches where clothed sunbathers are the odd ones out. It's made Spain a major destination for naturist tourism.

SPANISH ART & ARTISTS

Spain's artistic tradition goes back around 30,000 years if you count the magical cave paintings in the mountains above the Cantabrian coast. (Picasso once quipped, "After Altamira, everything is decadence.") Some of Europe's greatest masters were Spaniards or did their greatest work in Spain. Here are some not to miss—and where to see their art.

BERNAT MARTORELL (d. 1452) This 15th-century painter of retables and manuscript illuminations revolutionized Catalan painting with his complex composition and luminous handling of color and light. One of his greatest surviving works is the *Altarpiece of the Saints John* in the Museu Nacional d'Art de Catalunya (p. 452) in Barcelona.

EL GRECO (1540–1614) The Crete-born artist settled in Toledo in 1577 and spent the next 4 decades filling the city's churches with his singular style. His phantasmagoric color and action-filled application of paint made him an inspiration to 20th-century Expressionists. His work is found extensively throughout Toledo and in the Museo del Prado (p. 83).

FRANCISCO DE ZURBARÁN (1598–1664) The Spanish master of chiaroscuro concentrated on painting ascetic religious meditations for monastery walls, often using the monks as models. Many of his major works are in the Museo del Prado (p. 83) in Madrid, but his greatest masterworks are found in the Museo de Bellas Artes (p. 242) in Sevilla.

DIEGO VELÁZQUEZ (1599–1660) Becoming Felipe IV's court painter at age 25, Velázquez created his greatest works—mostly portraits—while in the royal employ. When the paintings were later deposited in the Museo del Prado (p. 83), where they occupy several galleries, his genius was rediscovered by critics and artists.

> ### Compare & Contrast
>
> When Diego Velázquez painted *Las Meninas* in 1640, he changed the psychology of European painting. This portrait of the royal household of Felipe IV, which focuses on the Infanta Margarita and her maids, includes a reflected image of the artist. It is the star of the Museo del Prado in Madrid and remains a touchstone of Spanish art. Pablo Picasso's obsessive reinterpretations, painted 300 years later, hang in the Museu Picasso in Barcelona.

FRANCISCO DE GOYA (1746–1828) Capable of both giddy pictorialism—as in his bucolic scenes created for the tapestries hung at El Pardo—and harrowing, nightmare images, Goya stands with Velázquez and Picasso in the triumvirate of Spain's greatest artists. His late works painted during the French occupation carry a direct emotional force that was truly new in European art. The best of Goya's work is found in the Museo del Prado (p. 83) and in the Real Academia de Bellas Artes de San Fernando (p. 92), both in Madrid.

JOAQUÍN SOROLLA (1863–1923) Born in Valencia, Sorolla was Spain's premier painter of light and saturated color. Adept at portraiture as well as landscape, his most heartfelt canvases depict his native Valencian shore of churning waves, sun-modeled rocks, and innocently erotic bathers. Although some of his work can be found in the Museo del Prado (p. 83), the best selection fills the Museo Sorolla (p. 106) in Madrid.

PABLO PICASSO (1881–1973) The quintessential 20th-century artist did it all, inventing new styles when he'd exhausted old ones. Many of his early works as well as some seminal 1950s pieces are housed in Barcelona's Museu Picasso (p. 437). The Museo Nacional Centro de Arte Reina Sofía (p. 87) in Madrid displays many Picassos, most notably the iconic *Guernica*. The Museo Picasso Málaga (p. 369) also features a broad selection of his work.

JUAN GRIS (1887–1927) Working with a brighter palette and more mordant wit than either Picasso or Georges Braque, Gris helped pioneer Cubism. He never quit his day job drawing political satire for magazines, allowing him not to take himself too seriously. The Museo Nacional Centro de Arte Reina Sofía (p. 87) in Madrid devotes a gallery to Gris and those who looked to his example.

JOAN MIRÓ (1893–1983) A poet of color and form, Miró is often categorized as a Surrealist. He did sign the Surrealist Manifesto of 1924, but his sense of form derives more from Spain's Neolithic cave paintings than the formal classicism of most Surrealism, and his lyrical celebration of color is unmatched in modern art. His work is best seen in large doses, as at the Fundació Joan Miró (p. 450) in Barcelona and the Fundació Pilar i Joan Miro (p. 677) in Palma de Mallorca. Significant canvases can also be found at Madrid's Reina Sofía (p. 87).

SALVADOR DALÍ (1904–89) The clown prince of Spanish painting, Dalí defines Surrealism in popular culture, employing a hyperrealist style to explore a world of fantasy and nightmare. Dalí lived for a good joke, as the Teatre-Museu Dalí (p. 526) in Figueres shows. Many of his works are in the Museo Nacional Centro de Arte Reina Sofía (p. 87) in Madrid.

EDUARDO CHILLIDA JUANTEGUI (1924–2002) Known mainly for his monumental abstract works in steel and stone, Chillida was born in San Sebastián and returned there from exile in 1959. Major collections of his sculptures are found at Reina Sofía (p. 87) and the Museo de Bellas Artes (p. 602) in Bilbao.

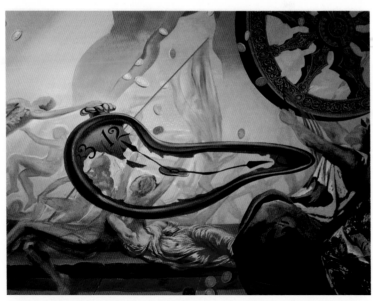

The Teatre-Museu Dalí, designed by the artist himself, is a Surrealist artwork in and of itself.

ANTONI TÀPIES (1923–2012) Nominally an Abstract Expressionist, the mercurial painter experimented with new ideas until his death. Among the first to incorporate marble dust and gravel into his compositions, he moved on to ever-larger objects, including pieces of furniture. Many examples of his work are in the Museo de Arte Abstracto Español (p. 174) and at the Fundación Antonio Pérez (p. 174), both in Cuenca, and in Madrid's Reina Sofía (p. 87). The best collection of his work resides in the Fundació Antoni Tàpies (p. 443) in Barcelona.

FOOD & DRINK IN SPAIN

Eating and drinking are the still points around which the Spanish day revolves. The famous late Spanish dinner is an accommodation for the ferocious heat of summer. In practice, Spaniards eat four meals a day, sometimes supplemented by a sweet afternoon *merienda* (coffee break) with pastry.

The Spanish day starts with **desayuno,** a continental breakfast of assorted rolls, butter, and jam. Most Spaniards drink strong coffee with hot milk: either a *café con leche* (half-coffee, half-milk) or *cortado* (a shot of espresso "cut" with a dash of milk). If you find it too intense, ask for a *café Americano,* which is diluted with boiling water. Be sure to try *churros* (fried doughnut sticks) and very sweet, thick hot chocolate.

Typically the biggest meal of the day, lunch—*almuerzo*—is served from 1 to 4pm, with the busiest time at 2pm. This can be as hearty as a farm-style midday "dinner" in the United States, beginning either with

Churros with chocolate.

soup or hors d'oeuvres called *entremeses*. A main dish might be fish or eggs, or more likely meat with vegetables. Wine is always part of the meal. Dessert is usually pastry or flan, followed by coffee.

After work or an early evening stroll, many Spaniards visit their favorite bars to drink wine or beer and eat ***tapas,*** small plates that can range from trays of olives, a few pickled anchovies, or slices of *jamón serrano* to exquisite small, composed plates that mimic fancy restaurant dishes. The general custom is to have one drink and one tapa (or a larger plate, known as a *ración*) and then move on to the next bar for another drink and a bite, although Barceloneses don't waste time walking between establishments, instead sticking to one place and staking out their patch of bar. Granada has some of the most generous tapas (three drinks with three tapas easily substitutes for dinner). San Sebastián in Basque Country and Alicante south of Valencia have some of the most inventive tapas in Spain.

Depending on the size of your lunch, the ***cena*** (dinner) can also be a big meal with multiple courses. But if you've indulged in a big lunch and lots of tapas, it's quite acceptable to order a lighter meal—perhaps some cold cuts, sausage, a bowl of soup, or even a *tortilla Española* (see below). Many European and American visitors skip dinner altogether in favor of more time at the tapas bars. The chic dining hour is 10 or 10:30pm, but restaurants begin to serve by 9:30pm.

TAPAS FOUND THROUGHOUT SPAIN

Tapas bars all over the country offer many of the same dishes, although *pa amb tomate* (grilled country bread rubbed with tomato, drizzled with olive oil, and dusted with salt) is a Catalan specialty. It sounds simple, but tastes sublime. Bars along northern Spain's Atlantic coast often feature the exquisite tinned seafood of Galicia. Tiny fish fried whole are a specialty on the Andalucían coast. In addition to olives, almonds, and fresh kettle-style potato chips, standard tapas include the following:

Albóndigas Meatballs, usually pork, served in a small casserole dish.

Chorizo Sliced smoked pork sausage seasoned with smoked paprika.

Croquetas Small fritters of béchamel sauce with ham, tuna, or cod.

Gambas a la plancha Shrimp grilled in their shells, called *gambas al ajillo* when grilled with garlic.

Jamón ibérico de bellota Highly prized air-cured mountain ham from Iberian black pigs fed entirely on acorns; the most expensive ham in the world.

Jamón serrano   Thin slices of air-cured mountain ham.

Morcilla   Cooked slices of spicy blood sausage, served with bread.

Patatas bravas   Deep-fried potato chunks with spicy paprika aioli.

Pimientos rellenos   Skinless red peppers stuffed with tuna or cod.

Queso manchego   Slices of La Mancha's nutty sheep's-milk cheese.

Tortilla Española   Thick omelet with potato, usually served by the slice.

SPANISH treats

The breadth of Spain means many regional specialty dishes, and the radical improvements in the Spanish wine industry mean there are more choices than ever to drink with them. Here are some pairings of classic dishes with great Spanish wines.

Cochinillo asado (roasted suckling pig) is served all over Spain but is a specialty of old Castilla, notably Segovia. Drink a **light red from the DO Bierzo region** in northwest Castilla & León, vinted mainly from the Mencia and Garnacha Tintorera grapes.

Paella Valenciana is also served all over Spain, although once you get away from the coast around Valencia, it is rarely the real deal. If you find a great paella Valenciana, eat it accompanied by a **bracing white from the DO Valencia region** or a **Macabeo-Chardonnay white from DO Utiel-Requena.**

Bacalao al pil-pil (codfish served with pil-pil sauce, an emulsion of olive oil, fish juices, garlic, and parsley) is a quintessential Basque dish. The perfect complement is a quintessential Basque wine, the bracing and acidic txakolí from **DO Bizkaiko Txakolina.**

Merluza al horno (roasted hake) is another ubiquitous, reliable dish. We like to drink white wines with it, either a **DO Rueda** (preferably 100% Verdejo grape) or a brisker, more aromatic **DO Rias Baixas** based on the Albariño grape.

Pulpo Galego (octopus with boiled potatoes and paprika) is a specialty of Galicia but is popular around Spain. We find it

pairs very well with a **white DOC Rioja** based on Viura and Sauvignon Blanc.

Suquet is a Catalan fish stew. Some of the best we've ever tasted came from the Empordà district on the Costa Brava. The dish is delicious with a **DO Empordà white** based on the Garnatxa Blanca grape.

Chuleton de buey—a whole beef rib grilled, often over an open wood flame—is a specialty of inland Basque Country and Galicia (a veal version, chuleton de ternera, is a specialty of Ávila). Accompany either with an **aged red DOC Rioja,** based on Cabernet Sauvignon and Tempranillo, or with a **red DOC Priorat.**

Chuletillas de cordero are tiny baby lamb chops, a specialty of Navarra, one of Spain's first great medieval wine regions. It's quickly becoming one of the 21st-century's great districts too. A **red DO Navarra** based on Garnacha Tinta grapes, often blended with Merlot, pairs perfectly with the lamb.

Gambas al ajillo are sweet shrimp grilled in the shells with olive oil and garlic. The perfect accompaniment for this Andalucían specialty is a lightly chilled glass of **sherry from DO Manzanilla de Sanlúcar de Barrameda.**

WHEN TO VISIT

Spring and fall are ideal times to visit nearly all of Spain. The winter months can be very rainy, especially in southern Spain. In summer, it's hot, hot, and hotter still, with the cities in Castilla (Madrid, Toledo, Segovia, Ávila, and Salamanca) and Andalucía (Sevilla, Córdoba, and Granada) heating up the most. Madrid has dry heat; the average temperature can hover around 84°F (29°C) in July and 75°F (24°C) in September. Sevilla has the dubious reputation of being the hottest city in Spain in July and August, often baking under average temperatures of 93°F (34°C), and midsummer temperatures in Mallorca often reach 91°F (33°C). The coasts are somewhat cooler, with summer averages of 81°F (27°C) on the Costa Brava and 77°F (25°C) on the Costa del Sol. The coolest spot in Spain is the Atlantic coast from San Sebastián to A Coruña, with temperatures in the 70s (21°C–26°C) in July and August.

August remains the major vacation month in Europe. Traffic from France, the Netherlands, and Germany to Spain becomes a veritable migration, and it may be difficult to find low-cost rooms in coastal areas. To compound the problem, many restaurants and shops also decide it's time for a vacation, thereby limiting visitors' dining and shopping options.

In winter, the Costa del Sol is the most popular, with temperatures reaching a warm 60°F to 63°F (16°–17°C). Madrid gets cold, as low as 34°F (1°C). Mallorca is warmer, usually in the 50s (low teens Celsius), but it often dips into the 40s (single digits Celsius). Some mountain resorts can experience extreme cold.

Average Daily Temperature & Monthly Rainfall for Selected Cities

BARCELONA

	JAN	FEB	MAR	APR	MAY	JUNE	JULY	AUG	SEPT	OCT	NOV	DEC
TEMP. (°F)	48	49	52	55	61	68	73	73	70	63	55	50
TEMP. (°C)	9	9	11	13	16	20	23	23	21	17	13	10
RAINFALL (IN.)	1.7	1.4	1.9	2.0	2.2	1.5	.9	1.6	3.1	3.7	2.9	2.0

BILBAO

	JAN	FEB	MAR	APR	MAY	JUNE	JULY	AUG	SEPT	OCT	NOV	DEC
TEMP. (°F)	45	48	51	52	55	65	67	67	61	53	52	48
TEMP. (°C)	7	9	11	11	13	18	19	19	16	12	11	9
RAINFALL (IN.)	.9	.8	.9	1.3	1.5	1.2	.6	.7	1.0	1.2	1.4	.8

MADRID

	JAN	FEB	MAR	APR	MAY	JUNE	JULY	AUG	SEPT	OCT	NOV	DEC
TEMP. (°F)	42	45	49	53	60	69	76	75	69	58	48	43
TEMP. (°C)	6	7	9	12	16	21	24	24	21	14	9	6
RAINFALL (IN.)	1.6	1.8	1.2	1.8	1.5	1.0	.3	.4	1.1	1.5	2.3	1.7

SEVILLA

	JAN	FEB	MAR	APR	MAY	JUNE	JULY	AUG	SEPT	OCT	NOV	DEC
TEMP. (°F)	59	63	68	75	81	90	97	97	90	79	68	61
TEMP. (°C)	15	17	20	24	27	32	36	36	32	26	20	16
RAINFALL (IN.)	2.6	2.4	3.6	2.3	1.6	.3	0	.2	.8	2.8	2.7	3.2

Some Spanish public holidays—notably Good Friday, Easter Monday, and Corpus Christi, held 60 days after Easter—depend on the liturgical calendar. Each region of Spain also has some local holidays, usually expressing regional pride.

National holidays include January 1 (New Year's Day), January 6 (Feast of the Epiphany), March 19 (Feast of St. Joseph), Good Friday, Easter Monday, May 1 (May Day), Corpus Christi, August 15 (Feast of the Assumption), October 12 (Spain's National Day), November 1 (All Saints' Day), December 8 (Immaculate Conception), and December 25 (Christmas). If a holiday falls on a Thursday or Tuesday, many Spaniards take off the weekday in between to create an extra-long weekend known as a *puente,* or bridge. Be sure to book hotels well ahead of time. You can always get money from ATMs on holidays, but intercity bus service is sometimes suspended.

Spain Calendar of Events

The dates given below are approximate and will help you start planning. Sometimes the exact days are not announced until 6 weeks before a festival. Check with the Tourist Office of Spain (p. 758) for exact dates.

JANUARY/FEBRUARY

Granada Reconquest Festival, Granada. The whole city celebrates the Christians' victory over the Moors in 1492. Visit www.turgranada.es or call ✆ **95-824-71-46.** January 2.

Día de los Reyes (Three Kings Day), throughout Spain. Parades are held around the country on the eve of the Festival of the Epiphany. Various "kings" dispense candy to all the kids. January 5–6.

Gastrofestival, Madrid. Top international chefs gather for Madrid Fusion, restaurants and tapas bars offer special menus, cooking tours and demos are held, and museums and galleries host food-themed films and programs. Visit esmadrid.com or call ✆ **91-454-44-10.** Last week of January, first week of February.

ARCO (International Contemporary Art Fair), Madrid. One of the biggest draws on Spain's cultural calendar, this exhibit showcases the best in contemporary art from Europe, the Americas, Australia, and Asia. Visit www.ifema.es or call ✆ **91-722-30-00.** Usually mid- to late February.

Festival de Jerez. Annual flamenco festival highlights Jerez's role in the development of the art. Performances range from intimate bars to enthusiasts' clubs to large stage shows. Visit www.turismo jerez.com or call ✆ **95-633-88-74** for tickets. Late February through early March.

Madrid Carnaval. The carnival kicks off with a parade along Paseo de la Castellana and includes a masked ball at the Círculo de Bellas Artes. The festivities end with a tear-jerking "burial of a sardine" at the Fuente de los Pajaritos in the Casa de Campo. Visit www.esmadrid. com or call ✆ **91-454-44-10.** Just before Lent.

Barcelona Carnaval. Compared to other parts of Spain, Carnaval in Barcelona is a low-key affair. In addition to the main parade, stall-owners in local markets compete among themselves for best costume. Just south of the city, in the seaside town of Sitges, the local gay community goes all out for Carnaval. Visit www.barcelonaturisme.com or call ✆ **93-285-38-34.** Just before Lent.

Carnavales de Cádiz. The oldest and best-attended carnival in Spain is a free-wheeling event full of costumes, parades, strolling troubadours, and drum beating. Visit carnavaldecadiz.com or call ✆ **629-332-840.** Just before Lent.

MARCH/APRIL

Fallas de Valencia, Valencia. Dating from the 1400s, this fiesta centers on burning gigantic papier-mâché effigies of winter demons. Bullfights, fireworks, parades, and the mascletà (a series of controlled explosions) add to the merriment. Visit www.fallasfromvalencia.com. Early to mid-March.

Fallas de Valencia.

Semana Santa (Holy Week), throughout Spain. From Palm Sunday until Easter Sunday, a series of processions with hooded penitents carrying icons moves to the piercing wail of the *saeta*. Notable processions are held in Zamora, Cuenca, Jerez de la Frontera, Sevilla, and Madrid; in Barcelona on Palm Sunday, palm leaves are blessed in Gaudí's Sagrada Familia. Spaniards often take holidays on this week, and hotel prices soar to the highest of the year. Unless you are interested in the religious spectacle, it's a good week to avoid. One week before Easter.

La Diada de Sant Jordi, Catalunya. The feast day of St. George (Sant Jordi in Catalan), the patron saint of Catalunya, falls on that same date as the deaths of Miguel de Cervantes and William Shakespeare. On this day, men traditionally give a single red rose to the significant women in their lives, and women give a book in return: Thousands of rose-sellers take to the streets and bookshops set up open-air stalls along major streets. April 23.

Feria de Sevilla (Sevilla Fair). The most celebrated week of revelry in all of Spain includes all-night flamenco dancing, entertainment booths, bullfights, horse-back riding, flower-decked coaches, and dancing in the streets. Book your hotel early for this one. Visit www.turismo sevilla.org or call ✆ **95-448-68-00.** Second week after Easter.

Moros y Cristianos (Moors and Christians), Alcoy, near Alicante. For 3 days, the centuries-old battle between the Moors and the Christians is re-enacted with soldiers in period costumes (*hint:* The Christians always win). Visit www. alcoyturismo.com or call ✆ **96-553-71-55.** Late April.

MAY/JUNE

Festival de los Patios, Córdoba. This is a rare chance to get inside the gates to visit Córdoba's famous patios with their cascading *gitanillas* (little Gypsies), as gardeners call their geraniums. Visit www. patios.cordoba.es for more information. First 2 weeks of May.

Feria de Caballo.

Feria del Caballo, Jerez de la Frontera. This annual livestock fair, held here since the 13th century, focuses on the famous Andalucían breed. It's a week of equestrian events, parades, flamenco, livestock displays, and, of course, sherry drinking. Visit www.turismojerez.com or call ✆ **95-633-88-74.** Mid-May.

Fiesta de San Isidro, Madrid. Madrileños run wild with a 10-day celebration honoring the city's patron saint. Food fairs, folkloric events, street parades, parties, music, dances, bullfights, and other festivities mark the occasion. Make hotel reservations early. Expect crowds and traffic. Visit www.esmadrid.com or call ✆ **91-454-44-10.** Mid-May.

Corpus Christi, all over Spain. This major religious holiday is marked by big processions in Madrid and nearby cathedral cities, such as Toledo. In Catalunya, the streets of Sitges are carpeted in flowers.

May or June, depending on liturgical calendar.

Suma Flamenca, Madrid. This month-long flamenco summit offers performances almost every night in intimate clubs and large concert halls. Visit www.madrid.org/sumaflamenca. June.

Verbena de Sant Joan, Barcelona. For this traditional festival, Barcelona literally lights up, with fireworks, bonfires, and dances until dawn. The highlight of the festival is the fireworks show at Montjuïc. Visit www.barcelonaturisme.com or call ✆ **93-285-38-34.** June 23 (eve of feast of St. John).

Festival Internacional de Musica y Danza de Granada, Granada. Since 1952, Granada's prestigious program of dance and music has attracted international artists who perform at the Alhambra and other venues. Reserve well in advance. For schedule and tickets, visit www.

granadafestival.org. Last week of June to first week of July.

JULY

A Rapa das Bestas (The Capture of the Beasts), San Lorenzo de Sabucedo, Galicia. Spain's greatest horse roundup attracts equestrian lovers from throughout Europe. Horses in the verdant hills are rounded up, branded, and medically checked before being released back into the wild. Visit www.turismo.gal or call ✆ **98-190-06-43.** First weekend in July.

Fiesta de Santiago, Santiago de Compostela. Pomp and ceremony mark this annual pilgrimage to the tomb of St. James the Apostle. Galician folklore shows, concerts, parades, and the swinging of the *botafumeiro* (a mammoth incense burner) mark the event. Visit www.turismo.gal or call ✆ **98-190-06-43.** July 15 to 31.

Fiesta de San Fermín, Pamplona. Vividly described in Ernest Hemingway's novel *The Sun Also Rises*, the running of the bulls through the streets of Pamplona is accompanied by wine tasting, fireworks, and, of course, bullfights. Reserve many months in advance. Visit www.sanfermin.com. July 6 to 14.

Sónar, Barcelona. This international 3-day festival of advanced music and new media art has gained a reputation as one of the world's most innovative. Visit http://sonar.es. Mid-July.

San Sebastián Jazz Festival, San Sebastián. Founded in 1965, this festival brings the jazz greats of the world together in the Kursaal. Other programs take place alfresco at the Plaza de Trinidad in the Old Quarter. For schedule and tickets, visit www.heinekenjazzaldia.com or call ✆ **94-348-19-00.** Late July.

AUGUST

Festival Internacional de Santander. The repertoire includes classical music, ballet, contemporary dance, chamber music, and recitals. Most performances are staged in the Palacio de Festivales, which was custom-built for this event. Visit www.festivalsantander.com or call ✆ **94-221-05-08.** Throughout August.

Fiestas of Lavapiés and La Paloma, Madrid. Festivities begin with the Lavapiés cultural street festival and conclude with the La Paloma celebration on August 15, the Day of the Virgen de la Paloma. Thousands of people race through the narrow streets, and there are children's games, floats, music, flamenco, and *zarzuelas*, along with street fairs. Visit www.esmadrid.com or call ✆ **91-454-44-10.** One week mid-August.

Misteri d'Elx (Mystery of Elche). This sacred drama is reenacted in the 17th-century Basilica of Santa María in Elche (near Alicante). It represents the Assumption and the Crowning of the Virgin. For tickets, visit www.misteridelx.com or call ✆ **90-244-43-00.** August 11 to 15.

Feria de Málaga (Málaga Fair). One of the longest summer fairs in southern Europe, this celebration kicks off with fireworks displays and is highlighted by a parade of Arabian horses pulling brightly decorated carriages. Participants dress in colorful Andalucían garb and wine is dispensed by the gallon. Visit www.malagaturismo.com or call ✆ **95-192-62-20.** Mid-August.

La Tomatina (Battle of the Tomatoes), Buñol (Valencia). This is one of the most photographed festivals in Spain: Truckloads of tomatoes are shipped into Buñol, where they become vegetable missiles between warring towns and villages, followed by music for dancing and singing. Visit www.latomatina.org. Last Wednesday in August.

Semana Grande (Aste Naguisa), Bilbao. Beginning the weekend after the Assumption and continuing 9 days, this festival honors the Virgen de Begoña and celebrates Basque culture. The giant puppet Marijaia is the symbol of the festival; Gargantúa figures parade through the streets "devouring" children, who actually slide through the figures and come out the other end. On the

Semana Grande, Bilbao.

ninth day, Marijaia is burned, only to be reincarnated the next year. Late August.

SEPTEMBER

Diada de Catalunya, Barcelona. The most significant festival in Catalunya celebrates the region's autonomy from the rest of Spain with demonstrations and other flag-waving events. Not your typical tourist fare, but interesting. Visit www.gencat. net. September 11.

San Sebastián International Film Festival, San Sebastián. The premier film festival of Spain takes place in the Basque capital, often at several different theaters. Visit www.sansebastianfestival.com or call ✆ 94-348-12-12. Late September.

Festa de la Mercè, Barcelona. This celebration honors Mare de Deu de la Mercè, the city's patron saint, known for her compassion for animals. A nighttime procession of as many as 50 "animals"

(humans dressed like tigers, lions, and horses) marches through the city with lots of firecrackers and sparklers. Visit www. barcelonaturisme.com or call ✆ 93-285-38-34. Mid-September.

OCTOBER/NOVEMBER

Semana de Santa Teresa, Ávila. *Verbenas* (carnivals), parades, singing, and dancing honor the patron saint of this walled city. Visit www.avilaturismo.com or call ✆ 92-035-00-00. Mid-October.

Fiesta de la Rosa del Azafrán (Saffron Rose Festival), Consuegra. The heart of Spain's saffron-growing region celebrates the harvest with a weekend fair featuring beauty queens, competitions to separate saffron threads from flowers, and a folk festival. Visit www.turismocastillala mancha.es. Late October.

All Saints' Day, throughout Spain. This public holiday is reverently celebrated, as relatives and friends lay flowers on the graves or *nichos* of the deceased. Many bars in Madrid and Barcelona hold Halloween parties the night before—an imported custom that seems to be catching on. November 1.

Christmas Markets, Madrid and Barcelona. More than 100 stalls set up in Plaza Mayor in Madrid to sell handicrafts, Christmas decorations, and Nativity scenes. A similar market sets up in the plaza outside Barcelona's cathedral.

SUGGESTED SPAIN ITINERARIES

By Peter Barron

t would be a delight to get "lost" in Spain, wandering at lei-sure, discovering unspoiled villages off the beaten path. Indeed, we highly recommend this approach. But we also rec-ognize that few will have the time (or money) for an unstruc-tured love affair with the country. A schedule lets you get the most out of your available time, but just because you have an itin-erary doesn't mean that serendipity and surprise can't intervene along the way.

Plan on using various kinds of transportation. Because Spain is big, it's worth covering long distances either by plane or high-speed train. Bear in mind that it may be faster to take a train from Madrid to Barcelona or Sevilla than to go to the airport and wait to get through security; and you'll arrive in the city center. In practice, you may end up using trains, planes, buses, *and* rental cars for maximum convenience and efficiency.

HIGHLIGHTS OF SPAIN IN 2 WEEKS

Spain is so large and so diverse that it's hard to think of hitting all the highlights in just 2 weeks. But this tour strikes most of the notes in the Spanish chord. Most of your travel is by train, making a one-country **Eurail Pass**—which gives you up to 8 flexible travel days for 280€—an economical way to go. See www.eurail.com for details. *Tip:* Make reser-vations as far ahead as possible to visit the Alhambra in Granada (Day 11) and the Alcázar in Sevilla (Day 12).

DAY 1: Madrid ★★★: Pomp & Circumstance

Madrid was a backwater until Felipe II moved his court here in 1561. Start in Habsburg Madrid, with a coffee on **Plaza Mayor** (p. 96), scene of coronations and Inquisition executions. Walk along Calle Mayor, past **Plaza de la Villa** (p. 95) and some of the city's oldest buildings, to the **Palacio Real** (p. 98). The royal palace testifies to the ornate taste of the Bourbon kings; the **Royal Kitchen** and **Armory** tell fascinating stories too. After a snack or lunch on **Plaza de Ori-ente** (p. 97), visit the **Monasterio de las Descalzas Reales** (p. 97) nearby. Royal females once took the veil at this convent and brought their art treasures with them. To stick with the regal theme, visit **Lhardy** (p. 130) for cakes or dinner, or the **Palace Hotel** (p. 116) for a cocktail.

FACING PAGE: **Madrid's elegant Cibeles Fountain, site of post-game celebrations for Real Madrid fans.**

DAY 2: Madrid ★★★: Art & Tapas

Spend the morning at **Museo del Prado** (p. 83), one of the world's great art museums. Concentrate on the Spanish masters: **Velázquez, El Greco,** and **Goya.** After a stroll in **Parque del Retiro** (p. 107) and a quick lunch—maybe a *calamares* sandwich at **El Brillante** (p. 130)—you're ready for the modern masters at the **Museo Nacional Centro de Arte Reina Sofía** (p. 87), where **Picasso**'s *Guernica* is the highlight, alongside works by **Dalí** and **Miró.** Round off a bohemian day with a tapas crawl around **Las Letras** (p. 134) and a flamenco show at **Casa Patas** or **Cardamomo** (p. 146).

DAY 3: Segovia ★★

Swift trains to Segovia start at 6:40am and take less than 30 minutes, so you can pop in for the highlights and keep moving. Admire the 166 arches of the **Roman Aqueduct** (p. 191), then follow the signs through the heart of the city to the fairytale-like **Alcázar** (p. 187). Lunch on the city's signature roast suckling pig at **Restaurante José María** (p. 195) and sleep it off on the afternoon train to Burgos, where you'll spend the night.

DAY 4: Burgos ★★ & Bilbao ★★★

You'll be in the company of pilgrims when you visit the **Catedral de Santa María** (p. 220) in Burgos. Packed with paintings and sculpture, this magnificent Gothic cathedral is the resting place of the swashbuckling Spanish hero **El Cid.** After lunch, take an afternoon train to Bilbao. Explore the narrow streets of the city's old quarter, the **Casco Viejo** (p. 603), and ponder this city's remarkable transformation over a glass of wine and creative *pintxos* in **Plaza Nueva** (p. 604).

DAY 5: Bilbao ★★★

Last night was old Bilbao. This morning is the new city. Get an early start so you can walk the riverfront before spending several hours admiring the **Guggenheim Museum** (p. 601) inside and out. Then head to the **Museo Marítimo Ría de Bilbao** (p. 602) nearby. Built on the site of a shipyard, it tells the extraordinary story of Bilbao's urban reinvention, replacing the scars of centuries of heavy industry with cutting-edge architecture and commerce. Make sure you've reserved seats on the slow afternoon train to Barcelona, which will give you a chance to catch up on sleep. It gets in after 10pm, just in time for a late Catalan dinner.

DAY 6: Barcelona ★★★

Begin exploring this capital of Catalan culture by strolling **Les Rambles** (p. 427), which runs from the waterfront uphill to L'Eixample, going from scruffy to chic along the way. Wander the **Barri Gòtic** (p. 430) and see the **Museu Picasso** (p. 437). After a tapas lunch

Highlights of Spain in 1 and 2 Weeks

nearby, shoot up to Montjuïc to see world-class medieval art at the **Museu Nacional d'Art de Catalunya** (p. 452) and 20th-century whimsy with a panoramic view at the **Fundació Joan Miró** (p. 450).

DAY 7: Barcelona ★★★

Start your day in a state of wonder by visiting Antoni Gaudí's master-piece basilica **La Sagrada Família** (p. 440) and his masterpiece apartment house **La Pedrera** (Casa Milà; p. 445). Spend the after-noon strolling along the harbor, gaping at the yachts in *Port Vell* (p. 418), or working on your tan on the beach at **Barceloneta** (p. 447). Celebrate the evening in the *xampanyerías* (champagne and cava bars) of L'Eixample.

Mosaic sculpture in Barcelona's Parc Güell, designed by Gaudí.

DAY 8: Valencia ★★

Take a morning train to Valencia, and spend the afternoon hitting the Old Town sights, including the **Catedral** (p. 386) and its cool Gothic tower, **El Miguelete.** In the late afternoon, head to **Playa Malvar-rosa** (p. 391), the best of the in-city beaches; that way you'll be ready to eat Valencia's famous paella at one of the beachfront restaurants.

DAY 9: Valencia: City of Arts & Sciences ★★★

Make an early start to visit the **Mercado Central** (p. 390) fresh food market, one of the largest in Europe, a treasure house of locally raised produce. Walk along the Jardí del Túria gardens to reach the **City of Arts & Sciences** (p. 388) and spend the rest of the day inhabiting the future. Unfortunately, rail connections to Granada are still in the past: Your best bet is to take the overnight bus which leaves Valencia at 1 minute to midnight.

DAY 10: Granada ★★★

You'll arrive at 8:30am. After a reviving chocolate and *churros* at **López Mezquita** (p. 296), take a stroll around the central district and visit the **Catedral** and its adjacent royal chapel, the **Capilla Real** (p. 287), where you can see the tombs of Fernando and Isabel, who completed the Reconquest by taking Granada in 1492. From **Plaza Nueva,** take an electric bicycle tour around the hilly *barrios* of Moorish **Albaicín** and **Sacromonte,** with its Gypsy caves (p. 288). Watch the sun go down at the **Mirador de San Nicolás** (p. 297), watching the Alhambra on the opposite hill glow like an object of desire. Then hit Granada's **tapas scene** (p. 297), one of Spain's best.

DAY 11: Granada: The Alhambra ★★★

Months ago, you reserved a ticket with an early entrance time to the **Alhambra** (p. 283). Take lunch with you so you can linger with a picnic in the gardens of the Generalife, and leave time to admire the beautiful Hispano-Muslim art in the Museo de la Alhambra, located in the Palacio de Carlos V. If there's time, walk back into town past the guitar makers and souvenir shops on **Cuesta de Gomérez** (p. 296). You have two options for tonight: Either take the 5pm train to Sevilla to spend a late night tapas hopping (p. 260), or sleep in Granada, then rise early to catch a morning train to Sevilla.

DAY 12: Sevilla ★★★

Whichever time you've chosen to get here, start at the palace fortress of the **Alcázar** (p. 237), having booked online to skip the lines. Marvel at how its palaces represent the synthesis of Moorish design and Christian will. The adjacent **Cathedral** (p. 240) is one of the biggest in Christendom; its bell tower, **La Giralda,** is the city's most emblematic building. Explore the warren of medieval streets in the **Barrio de Santa Cruz** (p. 248) and visit the **Museum of Flamenco Dance** (p. 243), then catch an impromptu late-night performance across the river in **Triana** (p. 248).

DAY 13: Sevilla & Córdoba

Grab a bicycle from any SEVICI rack so you can spend the early morning in the greenery of the **Parque María Luisa,** exploring the museums of **Plaza de América** and the revivalist architecture of **Plaza de España** (p. 245). Then head to Sevilla's most recent landmark, the extraordinary **Setas de Sevilla** (p. 246), for city views and lunch at its covered market stalls. Catch a late afternoon train to Córdoba, where you can take an evening stroll back and forth across the beautifully lit **Puente Romano** (p. 270). Seek out a characterful bar serving Córdoban specialties and brimful glasses of Montilla-Moriles wine (p. 275).

DAY 14: Córdoba ★★

Rise early so you can wander the ancient streets of the **Judería** (p. 265) before the crowds arrive, and at 8:30am visit **La Mezquita** (p. 268) for free, in silence, seeing the holy place at its most mystical. You'll also want to see the **Alcázar** (p. 266), where Fernando and

Isabel based themselves for the conquest of Granada. From there you're well placed to take a tour of Córdoba's famous flower-filled **patios** (p. 268). Depending on the time of your flight the next day, either catch a train back to Madrid or spend another night here and take the early train to Madrid (it's a 2-hr. trip by high-speed train).

HIGHLIGHTS OF SPAIN IN 1 WEEK

It's impossible to do Spain justice in just 7 days, but if that's all the time you have, here's a whistle-stop guide to the main points. Note that some sites will be closed on Mondays, and early trains may not be available at weekends.

DAYS 1 & 2: Madrid ★★★

As described above on p. 49, you'll spend your first day in Madrid exploring the capital's royal connections at **Plaza Mayor** (p. 96), the **Palacio Real** (p. 98), the **Monasterio de las Descalzas Reales** (p. 97). Your second day will be devoted to exploring Madrid's world-class art museums, taking in the Spanish masters at the **Museo del Prado** (p. 83) and modern masters at the **Museo Nacional Centro de Arte Reina Sofía** (p. 87).

DAYS 3 & 4: Barcelona ★★★

An early train takes you to Barcelona, the capital of Catalan culture. On Day 2 you'll stroll around the historic **Les Rambles** (p. 427) and

The Museo del Prado in Madrid.

Barri Gòtic (p. 430), then hit the art highlights at the **Museu Picasso** (p. 437), the **Museu Nacional d'Art de Catalunya** (p. 452), and the **Fundació Joan Miró** (p. 450). Day 4 is all about the stunning architecture of Antoni Gaudí at **La Sagrada Familia** (p. 440) and **La Pedrera** (Casa Milà; p. 445), followed by an afternoon at the beach and harbor.

DAY 5: Granada ★★★

Take an early morning flight from Barcelona to Granada, making sure you've pre-booked an afternoon slot at the Alhambra. Head to the **Cathedral** and **Capilla Real** (p. 287) in the morning before taking a bus or taxi up the hill to the Nasrid palaces of the **Alhambra** (p. 283). Bring a picnic to eat in the gardens of the Generalife. In the evening, book a table at a restaurant with floodlit views of the Alhambra, or start at **Bodegas Castañeda** for a tour of some of Spain's best tapas bars (p. 296).

DAY 6: Sevilla ★★★

The early train will get you to Sevilla by 11am. Follow the plan for Day 12 (p. 53), visiting the **Alcázar** (p. 237), the **Cathedral** (p. 240), the medieval **Barrio de Santa Cruz** (p. 248), and the **Museo del Baile Flamenco** (**Museum of Flamenco Dance; p. 243**).

DAY 7: Córdoba ★★★

Take a morning train to Córdoba (45 min.). Allow plenty of time to visit **La Mezquita** (p. 268), then take a stroll across the **Puente Romano** to the **Torre de la Calahorra** (p. 271), to learn more about the achievements of medieval Córdoba. Seek out a good lunch place for Córdoban cuisine (p. 274) and wander the ancient streets of the **Judería** (p. 265) until it's time to return to Madrid on a high-speed train (around 2 hr.). Spend the night in Madrid before catching your plane home.

THE OTHER SPAIN: EXPLORING THE NORTH

Except for the Guggenheim Museum in Bilbao, the north of Spain doesn't register with most North Americans, who cannot conceive of a Spain without bullfights, flamenco, and parched plains. Walled off from the rest of Iberia by high mountains, the verdant northern rim is a fascinating region, where ancient Celtic and Basque Spain persists.

DAY 1: Santiago de Compostela ★★★

Exhausted yet jubilant pilgrims give Santiago a kind of exuberant joy. To understand the pilgrimage phenomenon over the centuries, visit the **Museo das Peregrinacións** (p. 659). Follow those pilgrims to the **Catedral de Santiago** (p. 658), where you wisely reserved a guided tour spot via the website. Afterwards, have a drink in the bar at the **Hostal de Los Reyes Católicos** (p. 660), founded in 1486 by those famous monarchs Fernando and Isabel.

DAY 2: A Coruña ★

Take a morning train from Santiago, stash your luggage, and make a circuit of the waterfront of this peninsula city. Walk out to the Castillo de San Antón to see the Celtic jewelry at the **Museo Arqueológico e Histórico** (p. 649). Take Bus 1 to the **Acuarium Finisterrae** (p. 647). Don't miss the oldest lighthouse in Europe, the **Torre de Hércules** (p. 650). Spend your evening socializing at **Praza de María Pita** (p. 649).

DAY 3: Oviedo ★★

Rent a car to drive to Oviedo (about 3½ hr.), enjoying some spectacular mountain scenery before you return to the coast. Arrive in time for lunch and then visit the **Catedral de San Salvador** (p. 639). The two stunning pre-Romanesque churches of **Santa María del Naranco** and **San Miguel de Lillo** (p. 641) re-open for tours at 3:30pm, after which you can devote your late afternoon to shopping and your evening to dining and strolling.

DAY 4: Cangas de Onís ★★★

The drive east to this outpost of the Picos de Europa takes just over an hour. You'll have plenty of time to visit Cangas de Onís's **Capilla de Santa Cruz** (p. 629) before heading out to the mountain shrine of **Covadonga** (p. 631). Hike the trails around the ancient battle site and visit the tomb of Pelayo, high on a cliff behind the waterfall. Spend the night in Cangas listening to hikers' tales.

DAY 5: The Edges of the Picos de Europa ★★★

From Cangas, drive east to **Las Arenas de Cabrales** (p. 632) for a lunch of Cabrales cheese and local cider. Continue east on AS-114 about a half hour to N-621, and go south toward Potes, stopping at the **Centro de Visitantes de Sotama** (p. 627) for an orientation to the mountains. Follow signs to **Fuente Dé** (p. 629) for a cable car ride and a ridge hike. In late afternoon, return to Potes and follow N-621 to the coast, then the A-8 east to Santander (1½ hr.), where you can drop off the car.

DAY 6: Santander ★

Enjoy a leisurely day at this elegant beach resort. Spend a few hours on the beach at **El Sardinero** (p. 615) before visiting the **Museo Marítimo del Cantábrico** (p. 617) to learn about the Cantabrian coast's fishing and mercantile history. If you have time, check out the Roman ruins beneath the lower-level chapel at the **Catedral** (p. 617).

The Other Spain: Exploring the North

ATLANTIC OCEAN

Pick up your train tickets so you can catch tomorrow's 8am (week-days) FEVE train to Bilbao.

DAYS 7 & 8: Bilbao ★★★

Visit the **Museo de Bellas Artes** (p. 602), focusing on Basque artists, and then stroll to the nearby **Guggenheim Bilbao Museum** (p. 601). Before entering, walk all around it and across the river to admire its iconic modern architecture. After viewing the Guggenheim's galleries, follow the riverside promenade to the **Casco Viejo** (p. 603), enjoying the *pintxo* bars around Plaza Nueva. On Day 8, take a round-trip bus visit to **Gernika** (**Guernica;** p. 595), the melancholy center of Basque identity captured by Picasso's great canvas. Be sure to visit the thought-provoking **Peace Museum** (p. 596).

DAYS 9 & 10: San Sebastián ★★★

From Bilbao, it's a 75-minute bus ride to this resort city. Start with the **Playa de la Concha** beach (p. 582), where locals stroll morning, noon, and night. Over 2 days you'll have time to catch some rays and still hit the sights: the **San Telmo Museoa** (p. 582) for the region's best rundown on Basque culture and history, then the nearby

The resort town of San Sebastián curves around its lovely bay.

Aquarium (p. 583), with its own intriguing little museum. Get a fabulous overview of the city and bay by riding the century-old funicular to **Monte Igeldo** (p. 584). The essence of a visit to San Sebastián, however, is an evening spent bar-hopping for *pintxos* (p. 590) in the **Parte Vieja** (Old Quarter) or going out for a leisurely dinner. When it's time to go, take a bus direct to the Bilbao airport.

A WEEK IN SPAIN FOR ART LOVERS

This art connoisseur's whirlwind tour ranges from High Gothic to Spanish Surrealism. Book 4 nights' hotel in Madrid, because you'll visit two great art towns as day trips.

DAY 1: Madrid's Museo del Prado ★★★ & More

Hold your horses. Since the Prado is open long hours, start at the museum of the **Real Academia de Bellas Artes de San Fernando** (p. 92), which is only open until mid-afternoon. The great artist Francisco Goya became the academy's director in 1795 and arranged the permanent collection himself, showcasing Spanish, Italian, and Flemish masters. After that, move on to **Museo del Prado** (p. 83), one of the world's greatest museums. Besides *Las Meninas,* almost every court painting by **Velázquez** is here, alongside **Goya**'s

A Week in Spain for Art Lovers

Bay of Biscay

Days 1–2 Madrid
Day 3 Toledo
Day 4 Cuenca
Days 5–6 Barcelona
Day 7 Bilbao

troubling journey from pastoral frolics to the demons of the Black Paintings.

DAY 2: Madrid's Reina Sofía ★★★ & Thyssen-Bornemisza ★★★

The **Museo Nacional Centro de Arte Reina Sofía** (p. 87) picks up chronologically where the Prado leaves off—the early 20th century, with works by Pablo Picasso, Joan Miró, Salvador Dalí, and Juan Gris set in the context of the turbulent times that inspired them. Picasso's *Guernica* is unmissable and haunting. Take a long lunch to clear your head before moving on to Madrid's *third* great art museum, the **Museo Thyssen-Bornemisza** (p. 89). Linger in the Gothic galleries assembled by the Baron Thyssen-Bornemisza or focus on his wife Carmen Cervera's Picassos and American Abstract Expressionists.

DAY 3: El Greco's Toledo ★★★

A half-hour train ride whisks you to Toledo for a day trip to see the city that inspired El Greco. Start with the **Museo del Greco** house museum (p. 161) to set the painter in his 16th-century context, then discover some of his greatest paintings at the **Iglesia de Santo Tomé**

59

(p. 160), the **Catedral** (p. 158), and the **Museo de Santa Cruz** (p. 162), where you can get close enough to see every impasto brushstroke. Jump aboard the motorized tourist train (p. 163) for the same view as in El Greco's famous *View of Toledo.*

DAY 4: Ancient Cuenca's Modern Art ★★

Another high-speed train will take you from Madrid to Cuenca in less than an hour—giving you a long day to explore this rocky citadel that inspired a modern art movement. Begin with the **Museo del Arte Abstracto Español** (p. 174) in one of Cuenca's famous *casa colgadas,* the "hanging houses" cantilevered over the river gorge. The **Fundación Antonio Pérez** (p. 174) gives context to Spanish modern art, along with witty "found objects" from Pérez himself. The **Fundación Antonio Saura** (p. 174) holds temporary exhibitions of contemporary Spanish artists.

DAY 5: Gaudí ★★★ & Picasso ★★ in Barcelona

Catch an early train from Madrid to Barcelona so you have enough time to tour Antoni Gaudí's masterpieces—the basilica **La Sagrada Familia** (p. 440) and his apartment house **La Pedrera** (Casa Milà; p. 445)—before visiting the **Museu Picasso** (p. 437), with its insightful displays of the 20th-century master's works.

DAY 6: Gothic ★★★ to Miró ★★ in Barcelona

Head up to the hilltop of Montjuïc to visit two more wonderful Barcelona museums. Catalan artists were among Europe's finest in the 11th and 12th centuries, and their works from country churches across Catalunya are now displayed at the **Museu Nacional d'Art de Catalunya** (p. 452). Nearby, the **Fundació Joan Miró** (p. 450) concentrates hundreds of paintings and sculptures by that singular Catalan abstract master. (Alternatively, fans of the surreal may want to zip north to Figueres, an hour by train from Barcelona, to delight in the loaf-encrusted **Teatre-Museu Dalí** [p. 526].)

Gaudí's spectacular church La Sagrada Familia in Barcelona.

DAY 7: The Guggenheim in Bilbao ★★★

Take a full day to enjoy the artistic attractions of Bilbao. Start by having a look at Philippe Starck's design for the **Azkuna Zentroa** cultural complex (p. 600) and admire centuries of mostly Basque art at the **Museo de Bellas Artes** (p. 602). Lunch on the riverside plaza, then give yourself the rest of the day to enjoy Frank Gehry's **Guggenheim Museum** (p. 601) inside and out. It's open until 8pm.

CENTURIONS, CASTLES & CONQUISTADORS

This itinerary, through the less-visited regions of Extremadura and Castilla y León, focuses on the enduring Roman, Moorish and Christian monuments that have shaped Spanish history.

DAY 1: Mérida ★★★

Buy a combined ticket for 15€ to visit all the main monuments in Spain's best-preserved Roman town (p. 714). After a tapas lunch at the **bullring** next to the excavation of a Roman villa (p. 721), spend the afternoon at Mérida's world-class **Museo Nacional de Arte Romano** (p. 717). If you visit in summer, try to get tickets for a night-time classical performance at the **Roman theater** (p. 717), and round off the evening with a drink at **Trajan's Arch** (p. 716).

DAY 2: Trujillo ★★

Catch the early-morning bus from Mérida and linger over a cool drink in beautiful **Plaza Mayor** (p. 732), built with riches sent home by 16th-century conquistadors. A huge equestrian **statue of Francisco Pizarro,** who defeated the Incas, looms above. Walk up the hill to visit the **Casa-Museo de Pizarro** house museum (p. 733), where the conquistador is said to have lived, and climb the battlements of the perfect medieval **castle** (p. 733). Dine *al fresco* back in the flood-lit main square (p. 732).

DAY 3: Cáceres ★★★

An early morning bus will drop you in Cáceres in under an hour. Head straight to huge **Plaza Mayor,** gateway to one of Spain's best-preserved medieval cities. Plan to explore the walled hilltop town twice, visiting its churches, palaces, and museums by day, and taking a **flood-lit guided tour** at night (p. 724). Be sure to sample some of this ancient city's cutting-edge **modern cuisine** (p. 729).

DAY 4: Ávila & Segovia ★★★

Bus and train connections are awkward from Cáceres, so your best bet is to rent a car for a day. En route to Segovia, stop off in **Ávila** (p. 195) to walk along the ramparts of Spain's greatest surviving

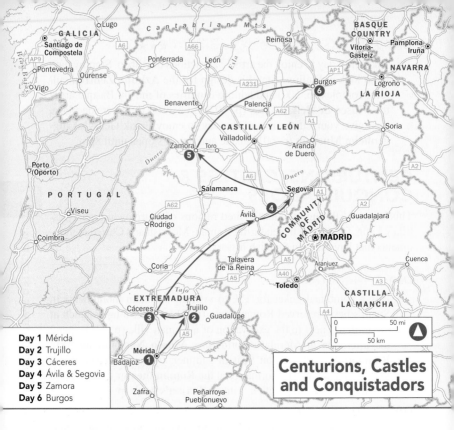

Day 1 Mérida
Day 2 Trujillo
Day 3 Cáceres
Day 4 Ávila & Segovia
Day 5 Zamora
Day 6 Burgos

Centurions, Castles and Conquistadors

medieval fortifications. Continue to Segovia for dinner near the 166 arches of its wonderfully preserved **Roman Aqueduct** (p. 191), lit up at night.

DAY 5: Segovia & Zamora ★★

In the morning, visit Segovia's **Alcázar** (p. 187) for Spain's best example of a storybook castle, extensively reconstructed from the era when Castilian lords poured boiling oil on their enemies from the ramparts. Take a midday train to **Zamora** (p. 211), where the ridge-line bristles with beautiful 12th- and 13th-century churches that staked out the frontier with Moorish al-Andalus. The **Centro de Interpretación de las Ciudades Medievales** (p. 213) gives a vivid picture of life in warring medieval Spain; after that, visit **Santa María-Magdalena** (p. 214) to understand the faith that sustained those warriors.

DAY 6: Burgos ★★★

The morning express bus to **Burgos** (p. 218) will get you into town just in time for lunch. (Burgos originated *estrellitas,* fried potatoes with an egg broken over them as a sauce.) Head to Plaza Mío Cid to

Segovia's dazzling Alcázara looks like a storybook castle.

see the grandiose modern statue of El Cid, the dashing 11th-century warlord who's become a symbol of Spanish patriotism. Pay your respects at his tomb by the main altar of the beautiful Gothic **Cathedral** (p. 220). If you're here from spring to fall, you're bound to notice throngs of pilgrims coming through Burgos, their last urban stop before Santiago de Compostela.

THE SPIRIT OF ANDALUCÍA

The southwest corner of Andalucía provides an intense concentration of Spanishness that's easy to experience in just a few days. Fly into Málaga and out of from Sevilla for a week of flamboyant flamenco, suited matadors, prancing horses, and world-famous wines.

DAY 1: Málaga ★★★

Let Picasso be your guide in this colorful city port. Pick up a map of important sites at his birthplace, the **Fundación Picasso** (p. 367), and spend plenty of time at the unmissable **Museo Picasso** (p. 369). Visit a traditional bodega to taste Málaga's famous wines (p. 371), then dine among the barrels at **El Pimpi.**

DAY 2: Ronda ★★★

Pick up a rental car in the morning and drive the inland route to **Ronda** (p. 304), one of Andalucía's most dramatic towns. Nineteenth-century Romantic travelers fell in love with its spirit and you

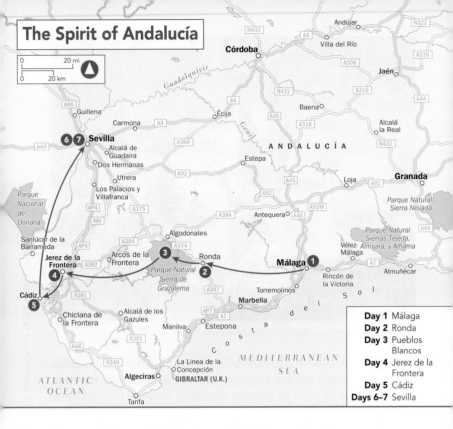

The Spirit of Andalucía

Day 1	Málaga
Day 2	Ronda
Day 3	Pueblos Blancos
Day 4	Jerez de la Frontera
Day 5	Cádiz
Days 6–7	Sevilla

will too. Visit the museum at the **Plaza de Toros** (p. 307), Spain's oldest bullring, and learn about mountain bandits at the **Museo del Bandolero** (p. 306).

DAY 3: Pueblos Blancos

Drive due west across the Sierra de Grazalema through the **Pueblos Blancos** (p. 312)—white towns scattered across the mountains—following signs to **Zahara de la Sierra** (p. 312) for a true mountain-top redoubt, and **Grazalema** (p. 314) for a rustic lunch on the main plaza. Continue west to **Arcos de la Frontera** (p. 316), and, driving carefully, reach the *parador* at top of the town, with spectacular views of the valley. Overnight here.

DAY 4: Jerez de la Frontera ★★

It's a 30-minute drive from Arcos to Jerez, across flat vineyard country. Book a tour at one of the sherry houses—**Bodegas Tradición** (p. 322) has lovely old wines and a fabulous art collection. Visit the **Escuela Andaluza del Arte Ecuestre** (p. 323) to watch a performance of dancing horses and round off the day with a tour of the **tabancos,** and flamenco (p. 324).

DAY 5: Cádiz ★★

It's another 30 minutes by car from Jerez to Cádiz (p. 330), where you can drop your rental car at the railway station. Cádiz's fortified seaside promenades, fried fish restaurants, and characterful bars like **Casa Manteca** (p. 338) are best appreciated on foot.

DAY 6: Sevilla ★★★

There's a fast regular train from Cádiz to Sevilla. After the **Alcázar** (p. 237) and **Cathedral** (p. 240), Sevilla's bullring, the **Real Plaza de Toros** (p. 246) is the city's most visited attraction. It's considered Spain's most important bullring and the area around it

Horses at the Escuela Andaluza del Arte Ecuestre in Jerez de la Frontera.

hums with atmosphere. To stick with the romantic intensity of your trip, visit Murillo's florid masterpieces at the **Museo de Bellas Artes** (p. 242), and nightly flamenco performances at the **Museo del Baile Flamenco** (p. 243). Then tapas crawl until late (p. 260).

DAY 7: Sevilla's Triana ★★

They call it the Independent Republic of Triana, the working-class quarter across the Guadalquivír where so many great bullfighters and flamenco artists were born. If you've fallen in love with Andalucian tiles, visit the **Centro Cerámica Triana** (p. 248) for a history of the local ceramics, and buy a souvenir at one of the workshops nearby. After a riverfront fish dinner, head to **Casa Anselma** (p. 259) for a memorable late-night experience. You can always sleep on your flight home.

SPAIN FOR FAMILIES

This itinerary from Madrid to the Costa del Sol suggests ideas to keep the children occupied and entertained, while allowing parents to enjoy the sights too. Book rooms in Madrid for the first 2 nights, then 1 night in Sevilla, 1 night in Málaga, and 2 nights in Fuengirola.

DAY 1: Madrid ★★★

First of all, take the children to the **Prado** and **Reina Sofía** museums to see *Las Meninas* (p. 83) and *Guernica* (p. 87) respectively.

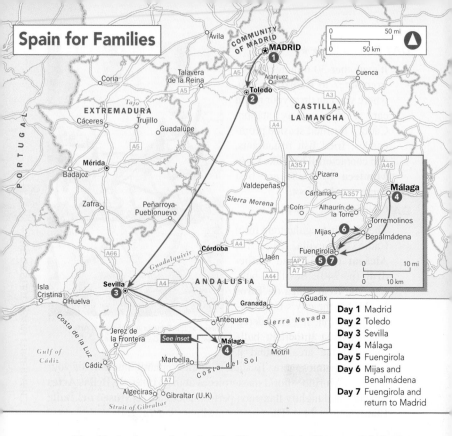

Spain for Families

Ávila · COMMUNITY OF MADRID · ✪ **MADRID** ①

Coria · Talavera de la Reina · Aranjuez · Cuenca

○ **Toledo** ②

EXTREMADURA

Cáceres · Trujillo

Guadalupe

Mérida

Badajoz

Zafra · Peñarroya-Pueblonuevo

Valdepeñas

Sierra Morena

Córdoba

Guadalquivir

Jaén

Isla Cristina · Huelva

Sevilla ③

ANDALUSIA

Granada

Guadix

Costa de la Luz

Jerez de la Frontera · *See inset* · **Málaga** ④

Antequera · Sierra Nevada

Gulf of Cádiz

Cádiz

Marbella

Costa del Sol

Motril

Algeciras · Gibraltar (U.K)

Strait of Gibraltar

CASTILLA-LA MANCHA

Pizarra

Cártama · A357 · **Málaga** ④

Coín · Alhaurín de la Torre · Torremolinos

Mijas ⑥ · Benalmádena

Fuengirola ⑤ ⑦

Day 1 Madrid
Day 2 Toledo
Day 3 Sevilla
Day 4 Málaga
Day 5 Fuengirola
Day 6 Mijas and Benalmádena
Day 7 Fuengirola and return to Madrid

They'll thank you later in life. Then stroll in **Parque del Retiro** (p. 107) for a puppet show and a boat row on the lake. If they have the stamina for the **Palacio Real,** they should enjoy the Royal Armory and Kitchens (p. 99). Relax with an early evening drink in **Plaza Mayor,** while the kids blow huge bubbles on the cobbles (p. 111). Hit **Chocolatería San Ginés** (p. 132) for hot chocolate and churros before bedtime.

DAY 2: Toledo ★★★

Regular trains to Toledo take just half an hour. Once there, the **motorized tourist train** is a fun way for the kids to see Toledo as El Greco saw it (p. 163). Everyone will enjoy the **Museo del Greco** house museum (p. 161), and wince at the museum of **Inquisition Torture Instruments** (p. 165). Then take them to see sword-making and damascene craft (p. 169) and visit the nuns to buy marzipan (p. 167), before catching the return train to Madrid.

DAY 3: Sevilla ★★★

Taking the early AVE train, arrive in Sevilla by 10am. Visit the **Alcázar** (p. 237) and **Cathedral** (p. 240), where the children can play in a garden maze featured in *Game of Thrones,* and climb the 35 ramps of **Giralda** tower (p. 240). Relax in the swooping walkways of the futuristic **Setas de Sevilla** (p. 246), where you can grab lunch in the covered market. In the early evening, treat them to a horse and carriage ride from **Plaza de España** (p. 245), or a riverboat trip from **Torre del Oro** (p. 247).

DAY 4: Málaga ★★★

Take a morning Avant train from Sevilla. Once you're settled, explore the atmospheric fortress ruins of the **Alcazaba** (p. 365). Take water for the hike up the city ridgeline to the **Castillo de Gibralfaro** (p. 366) where, on a clear day, you can glimpse North Africa. If one parent wants to shop the marble-paved Calle Larios, the other can walk the kids along **El Palmeral de las Sopresas** (p. 365) to catch a sightseeing cruise at Muelle Uno. Keep an eye out for dolphins!

DAY 5: Fuengirola ★★

Take the C1 commuter rail from Málaga and check into your hotel. You're finally at the beach. Bring plenty of sunscreen and enjoy a morning swimming and sunning. Lunch at a chiringuito, then spend the afternoon at the **Bioparc Fuengirola** (p. 356), where you'll be

Just above the resort-lined Costa del Sol, the mountain village of Mijas.

immersed in re-created habitats for lowland gorillas, Sumatran tigers, and Madagascan lemurs.

DAY 6: Mijas ★★ & Benalmadena ★★

A half-hour bus ride to Mijas deposits you and the kids in a wholly different world from the beach towns. Hire a donkey taxi to explore this whitewashed mountain village. Hike up to the castle ruins to see the high-rise beach towns spread out below. Return to Fuengirola for some afternoon beach time. After dinner, hop on the C1 to Benalmadena for the amusement park rides at **Tivoli World** (p. 356).

DAY 7: Fuengirola & Return to Madrid

Relax on the beach in the morning, grabbing a breakfast of churros at the kiosks nearby. Allow at least an hour to get back to the Málaga train station, where you'll change from the commuter rail to the high-speed inter-city trains. You'll be back in Madrid in about 3 hours.

MADRID

By Peter Barron

4

You'll never forget your first sight of Plaza Mayor. As you emerge through a shady portico into the vast sun-struck square, you're greeted by a huge equestrian statue of the Habsburg king, Felipe III. Surrounded by crimson, three-storied apartment buildings, Plaza Mayor is the grandest stage set imaginable, where more than 200 balconies become royal boxes on the scene below. It is Madrid in a nutshell: formal, yet casual. This is a regal and a relaxed city, where life is lived on the streets. Friends hop from bar to bar, drinking small beers, ordering tapas and chatting; killing the night, barely sleeping. Antique tavernas with vermouth on tap rub shoulders with restaurants of breath-taking sophistication.

It is urban, but green too. At weekends, families row on the lake in Parque del Retiro, where kings once staged mock naval battles. Its leafy boulevards lead to some of the world's finest art museums, crowned by the Museo del Prado with its masterpieces by El Greco, Velázquez, and Goya. Madrid can get both stifling hot and bitterly cold—its weather has been famously, and a little unfairly, described as "3 months of winter and 9 months of hell." But the *madrileños'* love for their vibrant city is abundantly clear, and countless visitors have fallen for it too. As the saying goes: *de Madrid al cielo:* from Madrid to heaven

If you look at an old map of Spain, you'll see well-established ancient cities like Toledo, Sevilla, and Valladolid, while Madrid appears as little more than a country backwater. In 1561, Felipe II abruptly decided to move the royal court here, for little reason other than it was the geographical center of Spain (and had excellent hunting grounds). So, by Spanish standards, the capital city is relatively new. The vast Royal Palace dates from the 18th century, and Madrid's unloved cathedral next door was not completed until 1993. There is, of course, plenty of history to explore—and some of the world's finest art—but there are no historic sights to equal Granada's Alhambra, Córdoba's Mezquita, or Toledo's cathedral. Instead, Madrid's greatest attraction is the here and now; be sure to make time to appreciate it.

PREVIOUS PAGE: **Parque El Retiro, once for royals only, is now a retreat for all Madrileños.**

ESSENTIALS
Arriving

BY PLANE   Madrid's international airport, **Barajas-Adolfo Suárez** (www.
aena.es; ℒ **91-321-10-00**), lies 15km (9.3 miles) east of the city center.
Most international flights arrive at Terminal 4, the newest and largest terminal. From there, it's quick and inexpensive to get into town. Catch the
yellow **Línea Exprés bus service** at Level 0 Arrivals at Terminals 1, 2, or
4. They run every 15 to 20 minutes during the day, every 35 minutes at
night. Tickets cost 5€; pay the driver (cash only). The trip takes around 40
minutes, stopping at Plaza de Cibeles or Atocha station. There are also
Metro stations on Level 1 at Terminal 4 and Terminal 2 (serving T1, 2,
and 3). To use the Metro, buy a travel card from the machine at the station,
which you can top up whenever you use the subway. From the airport,
take line 8 to Nuevos Ministerios, which connects with the main subway
lines. Tickets to downtown destinations cost 4.50–5€. There are clearly
signed **taxi** ranks at Level 0 Arrivals at all four terminals. Official taxis are
white with a red stripe and have the Madrid city crest on the door; avoid
drivers offering unofficial taxi service. There's a fixed rate of 30€ for the
trip into the city. You'll need cash.

BY TRAIN   Madrid has two major railway stations. **Atocha,** Glorieta
Carlos V is the main station handling commuter trains, regional trains,
and the highspeed AVE linking major cities in the east and south, including Barcelona, Sevilla, and Valencia. **Chamartín** runs AVE trains to

The modern terminal at Baraja airport.

Highways from Madrid

ROUTE	TO	DISTANCE FROM MADRID
A-I	Irún	472km (293 miles)
A-II	Barcelona	626km (389 miles)
A-III	Valencia	354km (219 miles)
A-IV	Cádiz	660km (410 miles)
A-V	Badajoz	408km (254 miles)
A-VI	Galicia	590km (370 miles)

northern and western cities, including Segovia, Valladolid, and León, as well as service to Lisbon and a number of commuter routes. For ticket sales and information, visit www.renfe.com, call ℂ **91-232-03-20,** or go to the ticket office at the railway station.

BY BUS Madrid has several bus terminals, but the main one is **Estación Sur de Autobuses,** Calle Méndez Álvaro 83 (www.estaciondeautobuses. com; ℂ **91-468-42-00**). The two major bus companies ALSA (www.alsa. com) and Avanza (www.avanzabus.com) operate from here.

BY CAR Most of the major highways *(autovías)* within Spain radiate outward from Madrid. Most include toll roads.

Visitor Information

The most convenient and comprehensive **tourist office** in the center of the city is at Casa de la Panadería, Plaza Mayor, 27 (www.esmadrid.com; ℂ **91-578-78-10;** metro: Sol or Opera). It's open daily from 9:30am to 9:30pm. In addition to face-to-face advice, it has self-service terminals where you can download mobile guides and take virtual tours, and lots of flyers and free maps. There's also a ticket office for various attractions, and a souvenir shop. Several smaller, walk-in information points are dotted around the city, including at **Paseo de Recoletos-Colon, Paseo del Prado,** and **Atocha** station. It's worth checking the multi-lingual website before you arrive.

City Layout

Although modern Madrid has long outgrown its original boundaries and sprawls in all directions, it is striking how easy it is to get around. Given that this is Europe's third largest capital—after London and Berlin—its main sights and places of interest are conveniently close together.

MAIN ARTERIES & SQUARES Every newcomer soon stumbles upon **Gran Vía,** which cuts a diagonal swath across the city. It starts next to the Banco de España and climbs to **Plaza de España,** where a long-vacant skyscraper is finally being transformed into luxury accommodation. Gran Vía is lined with international shops and blockbuster cinemas, but—perhaps because it is so wide—feels rather soulless. The narrow streets of Chueca and Malasaña on its north side are much more fun.

South of the Gran Vía lies **Puerta del Sol,** the starting point of Spain's radiating roads; a flagstone marks the spot at **Kilómetro Cero.** It's the bustling crossroads between old Madrid (La Latina, Las Letras, Lavapiés) and the commercial city center. **Calle de Alcalá** begins at Sol and runs a long way northeast, past Retiro Park toward the bullring at Las Ventas. From Puerta del Sol, take the **Carrera de San Jerónimo** east to reach the **Paseo del Prado,** or **Calle Mayor** west to reach Plaza Mayor.

Plaza Mayor is the grand, uniform square at the heart of Old Madrid. It's beautiful, but full of overpriced cafés and caricaturists. Handsome arcades shelter tacky souvenir shops. Exit south through the **Arco de Cuchilleros** to reach the colorful cobbled streets of the *barrios bajos.* Cava Baja is crammed with bars, restaurants, and *madrileños.* Directly west of Plaza Mayor, where Calle Mayor meets Calle Bailén, are the formally laid-out Palacio Royal (Royal Palace) and Almudena cathedral.

Turn right and you're soon back on the Gran Vía. It ends just before **Plaza de Cibeles,** where Real Madrid's fans celebrate their team's victories (they are now banned from draping the fountain with scarves). From there, the broad **Paseo de Recoletos** runs north to Plaza de Colón and on to **Paseo de la Castellana,** flanked by expensive restaurants, foreign embassies, and multinationals.

Head south from Cibeles and you'll soon reach the Museo del Prado, the Museo Thyssen-Bornemisza, and Jardín Botánico (Botanical Garden). To the east lies the **El Retiro,** the magnificent park once reserved for royalty. **Paseo del Prado** continues south to the Atocha railway station. Just off the roundabout is the third of Madrid's great art galleries, the Museo Reina Sofía.

STREET MAPS Make sure you have a suitable map before you set out. You can pick up a free one from the tourist office or download it from the website (www.esmadrid.com/en/madrid-city-map). It's useful for the main landmarks and metro stations but lacks detail in the maze of small streets in old Madrid. Rather than resorting to a large folding map, use the

papa's TOWN

Ernest Hemingway's attachment to Madrid was like an old man's remembrance of the first girl who ever took his breath away. He may have married Paris, but he kept coming back to sleep with Madrid. He was here in the 1920s, looking for a manhood undermined by World War I. He was here in the 1930s, reporting on the fratricidal collapse of a country he loved, and he returned in the 1950s, drawn to the bullring of **Las Ventas,** where he felt that even in a country in the grip of a dictatorship, some elemental truth could be found in the showdown between man and beast. Hemingway's Madrid haunts are well-trodden—from the bullring to the **Matadero** slaughterhouse; from the shabby sherry bar of **La Venencia** to the splendor of the **Palace Hotel;** and, of course, to **Sobrino de Botín,** his favorite restaurant. But it's easy to see why he fell in love.

GPS on your phone, but be careful not to be an obvious target for street thieves.

Madrid's Neighborhoods in Brief

Madrid fans out in three parts. **Old Madrid** lies at the center, crowded around the Plaza Mayor. Also known as the Madrid of the Austrias, after the Habsburgs who established their court here in the 16th century, it contains many of the historic sites and monuments that visitors come to see. **Modern Madrid,** which surrounds it, developed following the demolition of the old city walls in 1860, including Gran Vía and elegant new neighborhoods to the north and east. The huge Nuevos Ministerios government complex was completed just after the Civil War and there was further showy expansion under Franco in the 1950s and 1960s. In recent decades the city has invested heavily in iconic contemporary architecture. **Outer Madrid** stretches out toward the Castilian countryside, taking the greater Madrid population to more than 6 million. Its urbanizations naturally hold less interest for most visitors.

ART DISTRICT & PASEOS The long, broad boulevard of the Paseos forms Madrid's north-south axis, changing its name as it ambles along. The business and diplomatic district of the Paseo de la Castellana gives way to quaint Paseo de Recoletos and its Art Nouveau cafes. As it becomes the Paseo de Prado it grows green with shady parks and gardens and thick with art museums: The Prado, Thyssen-Bornemisza, and Reina Sofía sit here in a triangle just a few hundred yards apart. Some of the city's grandest hotels and restaurants look on. In summer, the Paseos' broad center medians become open-air terraces filled with booksellers and strolling crowds.

PUERTA DEL SOL & LAS LETRAS When medieval walls surrounded Madrid, Puerta del Sol—"Gate of the Sun"—was its east-facing entrance. Today, crescent-shaped Sol is a busy transport hub; once rather seedy, it feels more corporate now after recent renovations. To the south is the *barrio* of Las Letras, bounded by Calles Atocha and Cruz, the Paseo del Prado, and Carrera de San Jerónimo. It was the haunt of writers from Lope de Vega and Cervantes in the Golden Age to Lorca in the 20th century. Plaza de Santa Ana is at its heart, surrounded by crowded tapas bars.

PLAZA MAYOR, LA LATINA & LAVAPIÉS Vast, dignified Plaza Mayor has been at the center of Madrid life since 1617, hosting coronations, bullfights, and, most notoriously, *autos-de-fé*—the public trials and burnings of heretics during the Spanish Inquisition. Mostly, *madrileños* leave Plaza Mayor's cafés to the tourists; locals can be found day and night chatting, drinking, and ordering yet more tapas in the streets below, known as La Latina. From Plaza Mayor, the Arco de Cuchilleros leads through touristy Cava de San Miguel to Cava Baja, where nearly every building contains a bar or tavern. You can stay here too, but it gets noisy. La Latina continues

A welcoming taberna in Chueca.

downhill towards Lavapiés, a long-neglected neighborhood now enjoying a resurgence. Traditionally poor, with a diverse migrant population, it is creative, edgy, and gentrifying.

OPERA & PALACIO REAL   To the west of Plaza Mayor, the cramped old city gives way to elegant open spaces surrounding the Palacio Real, built in 1734 by Felipe V. Across the road, Joseph Bonaparte, Napoleon's brother, built the half-moon-shaped Plaza de Oriente during his brief reign at the beginning of the 19th century. Its crescent of cafés in front of the Teatro Real is a delight. The pedestrianized square around the Opera Metro stop is named after Isabel II, in whose honor the theater was built.

GRAN VÍA, CHUECA & MALASAÑA   Broad, traffic-congested Gran Vía was built at the beginning of the 20th century as Madrid's main street for the automobile era. Spain's first skyscrapers sprang up here, and the boulevard is flanked by department stores, cinemas, and some good hotels. Currently it feels past its prime, something a recent partial pedestrianization may address. Immediately to the north, a huge rainbow across the entrance to Chueca's Metro station announces that this once run-down, still scruffy, district is Madrid's gay capital. By night its streets are thronged with people of all ages—gay and straight, *madrileños* and out-of-towners—surfing its bars and clubs. Neighboring Malasaña, cradle of Spain's post-Franco counterculture (la Movida), is now Madrid's hipster heartland, where traditional tiled bars rub shoulders with gluten-free bakeries and beard-trimming parlors. Both Chueca and Malasaña have plenty of accommodations, from designer hotels to online room rentals.

SALAMANCA, RETIRO & CHAMBERÍ Once Madrid's walls came down in the 1860s, the orderly grid of wide streets to the northeast, Salamanca, became a fashionable address. Calle de Serrano, which runs parallel to the Paseo de la Castellana, is decked out with luxury shopping malls and sleek restaurants; it also hosts the US embassy. Salamanca is where Madrid's rich and beautiful are to be seen—look out for Real Madrid stars and their glamorous partners. The leafy streets near Parque del Retiro are also upscale, but more residential. Chamberí is where you'll find Madrid's young professionals on a night out, chatting in the bars around Plaza de Olavide or tapas-hopping along stylish Calle Ponzano.

GETTING AROUND MADRID
By Public Transit

Madrid has some of Europe's most thorough and least expensive public transit. For an overview, check the website of the **Consorcio Transportes Madrid** (www.crtm.es). Available in Spanish and English, it has a useful tool that recommends ways to get from one place to another using any combination of public transit.

If you expect to travel a lot during a short stay, it may make sense to buy a **Tourist ticket** *(Tarjeta turística)*, which gives you unlimited rides on the Metro and buses. The passes, available at Metro stations and tourist offices, range from 1 day (8.40€) to 7 days (35.40€).

BY METRO (SUBWAY)

The **Metro** system (www.metromadrid.es) is clean, efficient, and easy to use. The first time you travel, buy a **Multi Card** costing 2.50€ at one of the machines at the station. Simply keep it and go to a machine to add more money to your balance as necessary. The standard fare is 1.50€ for the first five stations you go through, 0.10€ for each additional station after that, up to a 2€ maximum in central Madrid. A 10-trip **Metrobus** ticket, good on both the Metro and city buses, costs 12.20€.

Twelve color-coded main lines cover most of the city. The lines aren't labelled by direction, so you'll need to know the final destination of the line you're taking (e.g., on Line 10, Hospital Infanta Sofía trains head north, while Puerta del Sur trains go south). Don't overlook the useful **Circular** line (Line 6), which rotates around the edges of old Madrid, a good way to connect with other lines. The Metro operates from 6am to 2am, and rush hour is best avoided. Ever wonder how *madrileños* manage to stay out so late and still put in a full day's work? Look out for nappers as you ride the Metro.

BY PUBLIC BUS

Public buses, marked **EMT,** are less easy to figure out during a short stay. For the visitor, they are most useful for moving up and down the Paseos, for example from the Bernabéu stadium to the Reina Sofía museum (bus number 27). They run from 6am to 11pm. A single ticket costs 1.50€, which you buy on board, cash only. Or buy a 10-trip Metrobus or Tourist ticket (see above).

BY TOUR BUS

Madrid City Tour (www.madrid.city-tour.com; ⓒ **91-369-27-32**) is the city's hop-on, hop-off sightseeing bus. It's a red double-decker; you can't miss it. Despite a rather boring earphone commentary, it's worth considering, first to get your bearings and then to whisk you to different parts of the city. It costs 19.80€ for 1 day or a better-value 23.50€ for 2 days (children and seniors pay half price, and children under 6 ride free). Buying a ticket entitles you to two different routes: historic Madrid and modern Madrid, the latter of which includes some out-of-the-way places you wouldn't otherwise see. Both tours start at the Plaza de Neptuno next to the Prado museum, but you can jump on anywhere. From March to October, buses operate 9am to 10pm and pass each stop roughly every 10 minutes; from November to February, they run 10am to 6pm, passing each stop every 15 minutes or so. Tickets are widely available, including at the tourist offices and online.

BY COMMUTER RAIL

The **Cercanía** (www.renfe.com/EN/viajeros/cercanias) is Madrid's suburban commuter rail network, denoted by a white "C" on a red circle. It is a cheap and convenient way to visit places in the metropolitan area around Madrid, such as **El Escorial** and **Alcalá de Henares** (p. 149). Fares run from 1.70€ to 8.70€, depending on the zone. Note that *cercanías* are not included on the *Tarjeta turística* or the Metrobus pass.

By Taxi

Madrid's taxis are white with a diagonal red stripe and the city's crest on the front door. At the airport and rail and bus stations, you need to go to a taxi rank, but elsewhere you can hail them on the street. A green light, or the sign "LIBRE," indicates they are available. Fares are pretty reasonable. When you flag down a taxi, the meter should read 2.40€ any time between 6am and 9pm on weekdays (2.90€ from 9pm to 6am and on weekends); for every kilometer after that, the fare increases between 1.05€ and 1.25€. Supplements are charged for certain trips, including to the airport, train stations, bullring, and the football stadiums. It's customary to tip around 10% of the fare. To call a taxi, phone ⓒ **91-547-82-00** or **91-405-12-13.** Travel apps such as **Uber** and **Cabify** operate in Madrid, despite plenty of opposition and occasional strikes by taxi drivers.

By Car

Public transit is so good that inside the city you should leave the driving to the *madrileños*—they're the ones who grew up watching bullfights. Renting a car for excursions is another matter, in which case you should

Madrid Metro

Legend:
- 1 Metro line terminal
- 1 Metro Ligero (light rail) terminal
- Transfer Station
- Transfer to Cercanías (suburban rail)
- ML Transfer to Metro Ligero (light rail)

Paco de Lucía 9
Pitis 7

La Moraleja
La Granja
Ronda de la Comunicación
Palas de Rey
Las Tablas
ML 1
Montecarmelo
Tres Olivos
Fuencarral
Begoña
Chamartín
Duque de Pastrana

Mirasierra
Herrera Oria
Barrio del Pilar
Ventilla

Lacoma
Av. de la Ilustración
Peñagrande
Antonio Machado
Valdezarza
Francos Rodríguez
Guzmán el Bueno
Vicente Aleixandre
Ciudad Universitaria

Valdeacederas
Tetuán
Estrecho
Alvarado

Cuatro Caminos 2
Canal
Ríos Rosas

Plaza de Castilla
Cuzco
Santiago Bernabéu
Nuevos Ministerios 8
República Argentina
Nuevos Ministerios 6
Alonso Cano
Gregorio Marañón

Islas Filipinas
Quevedo
Moncloa 3
Argüelles 4
Ventura Rodríguez
Plaza de España
Príncipe Pío R
Lago
Puerta del Ángel
Alto de Extremadura
Batán
Casa de Campo 5
Colonia Jardín ML
2
3
Campamento
Empalme
Aviación Española
Cuatro Vientos
Aluche
Lucero
Laguna
6
Carpetana
Eugenia de Montijo
Carabanchel
Vista Alegre
Oporto
Urgel

San Bernardo
Noviciado
Santo Domingo
Ópera R
La Latina
Puerta de Toledo
Pirámides
Marqués de Vadillo
Opañel
Plaza Elíptica 11
La Fortuna 11
La Peseta
Carabanchel Alto
San Francisco
Pan Bendito
Abrantes

Iglesia
Bilbao
Rubén Darío
Alonso Martínez
Serrano
Colón
Tribunal
Chueca
Gran Vía
Callao
Sol
Sevilla
Banco de España
Retiro
Tirso de Molina
Antón Martín
Lavapiés
Estación del Arte
Embajadores
Atocha Renfe
Acacias
Palos de la Frontera
Delicias
Usera
Legazpi
Arganzuela–Planetario
Almendrales
Hospital 12 de Octubre
San Fermín–Orcasur
Ciudad de los Ángeles
Villaverde Bajo-Cruce
San Cristóbal
Villaverde Alto 3
Puerta del Sur 10
12

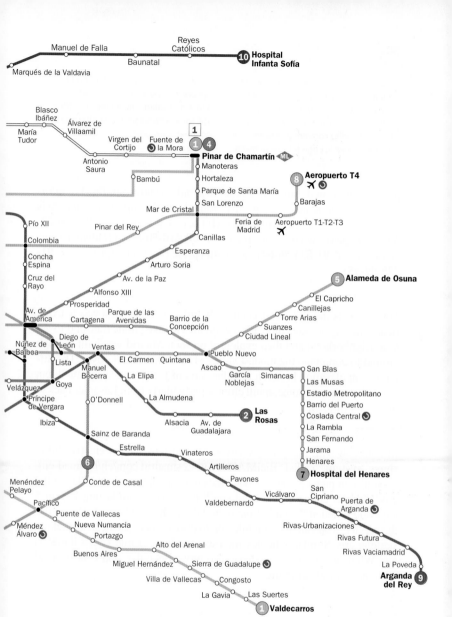

Manuel de Falla Reyes Católicos
Baunatal
10 Hospital Infanta Sofía
Marqués de la Valdavia

Blasco Ibáñez
Álvarez de Villaamil
María Tudor
Virgen del Cortijo Fuente de la Mora
1
Antonio Saura
1 4 Pinar de Chamartín **ML**
Manoteras
Bambú Hortaleza
8 Aeropuerto T4
Parque de Santa María
San Lorenzo Barajas
Mar de Cristal
Pío XII Pinar del Rey
Feria de Madrid Aeropuerto T1-T2-T3
Colombia Canillas
Concha Espina Esperanza
Arturo Soria
Cruz del Rayo Av. de la Paz
5 Alameda de Osuna
Alfonso XIII
Av. de América Prosperidad
El Capricho
Canillejas
Cartagena Parque de las Avenidas
Torre Arias
Barrio de la Concepción
Núñez de Balboa Diego de León
Suanzes
Ciudad Lineal
Lista Ventas El Carmen Quintana Pueblo Nuevo
Velázquez Manuel Becerra La Elipa
Ascao García Noblejas Simancas
San Blas
Goya O'Donnell
La Almudena
Las Musas
Príncipe de Vergara
Estadio Metropolitano
Barrio del Puerto
Ibiza Alsacia Av. de Guadalajara
2 Las Rosas
Coslada Central
La Rambla
Sainz de Baranda
San Fernando
Estrella
Jarama
6
Vinateros Henares
Artilleros
Menéndez Pelayo
Pavones
7 Hospital del Henares
Conde de Casal
Pacífico
Vicálvaro San Cipriano
Puente de Vallecas Valdebernardo
Puerta de Arganda
Méndez Álvaro Nueva Numancia
Rivas-Urbanizaciones
Portazgo
Rivas Futura
Buenos Aires Alto del Arenal
Rivas Vaciamadrid
Miguel Hernández Sierra de Guadalupe
La Poveda
Villa de Vallecas Congosto
Arganda del Rey 9
La Gavia Las Suertes
1 Valdecarros

Walking Tours

We recommend a well-informed wander, but if you feel you need a guide, or have particular interests, the main tourist office offers a range of walking tours (www.esmadrid.com/en/guided-tours-of-madrid). Tours in English focus primarily on Madrid's history and art, but other options include architecture, and food and wine-tasting. Prices vary from 10€–15€ for a history tour to 75€–100€ for a gourmet walkabout.

pick one up from the airport, in order to avoid downtown traffic. For information on car rentals, see p. 751. Rentals at the airport include **Avis** (www.avis.com; ✆ **90-220-01-62**), **Hertz** (www.hertz.es; ✆ **90-230-52-30**), **Europcar** (www.europcar.com; ✆ **90-210-50-55**), **Goldcar** (www.goldcar.es; ✆ **91-834-40-64**), and **Enterprise** (www.enterprise.es; ✆ **91-275-09-95**).

On Foot

You can walk most places in central Madrid, and it's the best way to experience the city. To save time, it's a good idea to take public transport to get to a neighborhood and then explore it on foot. Madrid was built on high ground to command the modest valley of the Manzanares River. The difference in elevation between popular parts of the city is fairly small, but you will encounter some uphill climbs, particularly from Lavapiés back to the center of town.

By Bike & Scooter

In common with many major cities, Madrid now has an **electric bike-share system,** called BiciMAD (www.esmadrid.com/en/bicimad-en). Anyone can pick up one of 2,000 bikes from docking stations all over the city. Register at one of them and you'll be issued a card lasting 1, 3, or 5 days and billed at the end of the period depending on how much you use the service. You can use a mobile app to check where the nearest docking stations are. Similar schemes for **escooter** hire—Lime (www.li.me/es) and Wind (www.wind.co)—have also proved popular, and controversial with the Madrid authorities.

[Fast FACTS] MADRID

Banks & ATMs You'll find ATMs wherever crowds gather in Madrid, especially in shopping districts and around major Metro stations. Most permit cash withdrawals via MasterCard or Visa, and many are linked to networks that will let you access your home bank account. Most offer a choice of language, including English, and charge around 1.95€ per transaction. Major banks include **Banco Santander, BBVA, Caixa and Bankia.** Major overseas banks with a presence in

Madrid include **Deutsche Bank** and **Citibank.** Most Spanish ATMs only accept 4-digit PINs, so if you have a longer PIN and want to use your card in Spain, change it at least a week before departure.

Business Hours   Opening hours can be complicated in Madrid. Expect small shops and banks to open at 10am, close 2 to 5pm for lunch, and open again from 5 to 8:30pm. Shopping centers and some city-center shops stay open continuously from 10am to 9 or 10pm, however.

Doctors & Dentists   For a list of English-speaking doctors and dentists working in Madrid, visit the U.S. Embassy website (see below); look under the tab for "U.S. Citizen Services." For dental services, consult **Unidad Médica Anglo-Americana,** Conde de Arandá 1 (www.unidadmedica.com; ✆ **91-435-18-23**). Office hours are Monday–Friday 9am–8pm (Aug 10am–5pm), and Saturday 10am–1pm.

Embassies & Consulates   See p. 756.

Emergencies   Call ✆ **112** for fire, police, and ambulance services (www.madrid112.org).

Hospitals & Clinics   EU citizens are entitled to free medical care while in Spain; make sure to bring your European Health Insurance Card (EHIC) with you. Citizens of other countries are strongly advised to take out medical insurance before they travel. **Unidad Médica Anglo-Americana,** Conde de Arandá 1 (www.unidadmedica.com; ✆ **91-435-18-23;** metro: Retiro), a private treatment clinic, has staff available by phone 24 hours a day. In a medical emergency, call ✆ **112** for an ambulance. For a list of healthcare centers, visit www.esmadrid.com/en/emergency-services-healthcare.

Internet Access   The city government provides free Wi-Fi (pronounced *wiffy* in Spanish) at hot spots around the city and on public transit, including some Metro lines. For a list of public hotspots visit www.esmadrid.com/en/wi-fi-hotspots. Free Wi-Fi is also often available in cafes and bars. To ask for the password, say: *"la contraseña wifi, por favor."*

Mail & Postage   The post office in the former Palacio de Comunicaciones at Plaza de Cibeles (www.correos.es; ✆ **90-219-71-97**) is open Monday–Friday 8:30am–9:30pm and Saturday 9:30am–2pm. Postage to the U.S. costs around 1.35€; to other European countries 1.25€. You can also buy stamps in tobacconist shops (*estancos*) shops;

look for maroon signs with *Tabacos* in yellow letters.

Pharmacies   To find a pharmacy (*farmacia*), look for an illuminated green cross. Staff often speak English and will gladly give advice on minor ailments. After hours, every pharmacy posts outside a list of nearby pharmacies that are open late. Or check on the pharmacists' website under *Farmacias de Guardia* (www.cofm.es).

Police   The central police station in Madrid is at Calle Leganitos, 19, next to Plaza de España. It is open daily 9am–midnight. The 24-hour number for reporting a crime is ✆ **90-210-21-12.** The National Police have a program called SATE, the **Foreign Tourist Assistance Service** (www.policia.es/wap/oficinas/sate.php), to help tourists file complaints, cancel credit cards or other documents, and contact or locate family members. If you need this service call ✆ **91-548-85-37** or ✆ **91-549-80-08.**

Safety   While Madrid is generally a safe city, purse snatching and pickpocketing are facts of life, especially in areas where there are lots of disoriented tourists paying scant attention to their belongings. Don't let down your guard and you're unlikely to be a victim.

EXPLORING MADRID

Exploring the city is simple if you think of the neighborhoods as clusters. You're likely to spend most of your time in the historic center, but you'd be missing out if you don't get to some of the surrounding areas too. Plan your day and take public transit to the middle of one of the districts and walk from there. An excellent and inexpensive Metro system makes it easy.

Arts District & Paseos

The Paseo del Prado between the Atocha and Banco de España Metro stops is the mother lode for art lovers, with the Museum del Prado, the Museo Thyssen-Bornemisza, and the CaixaForum just a few blocks from each other. Practically just around the corner on the Carlos V traffic circle (*glorieta* in Spanish) stands the Museo Nacional Centro de Art Reina Sofía.

CaixaForum ★ ART MUSEUM It took 5 years to transform this former power station on Paseo del Prado into a dynamo for contemporary art. The Pritzker Prize-winning architectural firm Herzog de Meuron managed to multiply the floor space fivefold while creating a brick structure that seems to levitate above the plaza. One of its many eye-catching features is the 24-meter-high (79-ft.) **Jardin Vertical**—a living wall covered with 250 species of plants. The interior of the building is equally striking. Although La Caixa has permanent collections, it is best known for its constantly changing exhibitions of contemporary art and photography. There are usually three major exhibitions on display at a given time. Many are accompanied by lectures, concerts, and panel discussions.
Paseo del Prado, 36. caixaforum.es/es/madrid. © **91-330-73-00.** Building admission free; exhibition halls 5€, free for kids 15 and under. Daily 10am–8pm. Metro: Atocha. Bus: 10, 14, 27, 34, 37, or 45.

CentroCentro ★ CULTURAL CENTER A Neo-Baroque palace that once housed the central post office and telecommunications service, the Palacio de Cibeles became Madrid's City Hall in 2007. Even the city councilors didn't need something this big, so much of the building has

---

Just the Ticket for Art Lovers

If you plan to visit the big three art museums, it's worth investing in the **Tarjeta Paseo del Arte.** At 29.60€), it saves you 20% on the cost of tickets to the permanent exhibitions at **Museo Nacional del Prado, Museo Nacional Centro de Arte Reina Sofía,** and the **Museo Thyssen-Bornemisza.** Perhaps even more importantly, it lets you skip the queues. You can buy the card at any of the three museums, or online (entradas.museoreinasofia.es). It is good for a year, but note it allows just one entry to each museum—it is worthwhile only if you plan to visit all three. If you only have time to visit one, buy your ticket in advance on-line in order to skip the line. *Tip:* All three museums offer **free admission** during the last couple of hours of each day that they're open, which is great for those on a budget. However, this is no secret, and you may find it hard to get close to the pictures.

been converted into a series of galleries, a concert hall, and other public spaces called CentroCentro. There's a reading area with daily papers and free Internet access, a tourist information office, and a top-notch restaurant (Restaurante Palacio de Cibeles; see p. 129) as well as more casual cafeterias. But the main reason for visiting is the **Mirador Madrid.** An elevator whisks you to the seventh floor, where you can walk around on an open-air balcony for some of the best views of the city.

Plaza de Cibeles, 1. centrocentro.org. ℭ **91-480-00-08.** Building admission free; admission charged to some exhibitions. Mirador de Madrid 3€, seniors and ages 7–14 1.50€, kids 6 and under free. Building Tues–Sun 10am–8pm; Mirador de Madrid Tues–Sun 10:30am–2pm and 4–7:30pm. Metro: Banco de España. Bus: 1, 2, 5, 9, 10, 14, 15, 20, 27, 34, 37, 45, 51, 52, 53, 74, 146, 50, 202, or 203.

A docent gives insight into the Spanish masters at the Museo del Prado.

Museo del Prado ★★★ ART MUSEUM There was a quiet revolution at the Prado in 2013, when the museum rehung the galleries of paintings by **Diego Velázquez** (1599–1660), making his masterpiece, *Las Meninas,* the central focus. They placed it among his royal portraits directly opposite the entrance of the large Sala 12 on the second level of the Villanueva building. You have probably seen reproductions of this extraordinary painting-within-a-painting many times, but the sheer scope and power of the actual canvas will blow you away. The focus of the painting is on the diminutive infanta Margarita, daughter of Felipe IV, and her delicate ladies in waiting *(las meninas).* To the right are two of the court dwarves Velázquez never tired of painting, one of them poking a dog with his foot. An enigmatic Veláquez himself is depicted working on a huge canvas, of which we can only see the back, and on the wall is a shadowy image of the king and queen looking on. What is Veláquez painting—the infanta, or the king and queen? Is their image a painting, or a mirror? *Las Meninas* is easily the most popular painting in the Prado, and you could spend hours looking at it, trying to figure it out. Of course, lots of other people have the same idea, and it is constantly surrounded by tour groups and guides seeking to explain it in multiple languages. If you want to see *Las Meninas* without the crowds, be among the first to enter when the Prado opens at 10am. A Paseo del Arte pass (p. 82), or a print-out of

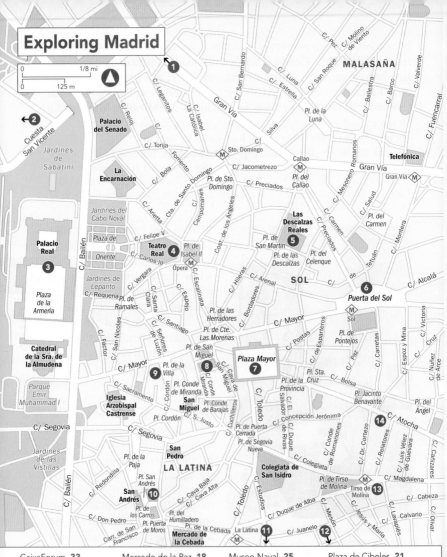

Exploring Madrid

0 ———— 1/8 mi
0 ———— 125 m

MALASAÑA

Telefónica

Palacio del Senado

La Encarnación

Las Descalzas Reales 5

Palacio Real 3

Teatro Real 4

SOL

Puerta del Sol 6

Catedral de la Sra. de la Almudena

Plaza Mayor 7

Iglesia Arzobispal Castrense

San Miguel 8

Plaza de la Villa 9

San Pedro

LA LATINA

Colegiata de San Isidro

San Andrés 10

Mercado de la Cebada

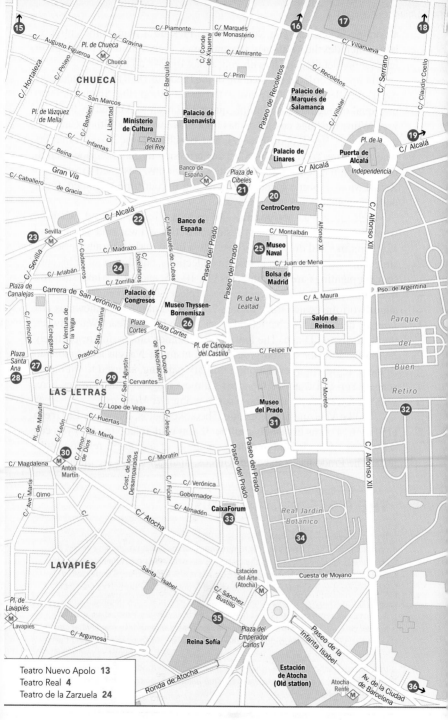

an online ticket, lets you skip the line. Pick up a plan at the entrance, which includes the location of the museum's 45 most famous paintings, or buy a more detailed guide with your ticket for 24€ all in.

Felipe VI ordered the creation of the Prado in 1819 to consolidate the royal art collections and to prove to the rest of Europe that Spanish art was the equal of any other nation (his queen had been impressed by the Louvre). While the huge collection has impressive works by Titian, Caravaggio, Rubens, Rembrandt, Bruegel, and Bosch, it is the Spanish masters who dominate. You could spend all day browsing its galleries, now including a modern extension for temporary exhibitions, designed by architect Rafael Moneo. Some spend a lifetime. But if your time is limited, focus on Velázquez, El Greco, and Goya.

Velázquez was not prolific—he painted what he wanted, when he wanted. Some of his work was destroyed in fire and war, and only around 120 paintings and drawings survive. Most of his early portraits of Sevilla street characters ended up in foreign collections, but almost all of his subsequent paintings are here, in Salas 9A, 10–15, and 15A. Make sure you don't miss his other large-canvas masterpiece, *The Surrender of Breda,* slightly off the beaten track in Sala 9A. The painting, also known as *Las Lanzas,* depicts a vast battlefield scene in the Eighty Years War between the Spanish and Dutch. The looks of defeat and compassion respectively on the faces of the central protagonists, Justin of Nassau and Ambrosio Spinola, represent a revolution in military painting, so used to triumphal scenes. You can examine the artist's almost magical brush strokes here, with far fewer people than those surrounding *Las Meninas.*

Unlike Velázquez, Doménikos Theotokópoulos, known as **El Greco** (1541–1614), was extremely prolific. If you visit Toledo (p. 154) you can see scores of his brightly colored paintings of elongated religious subjects. The Prado has some 40 El Grecos, many of which are displayed in

THE FIRST impressionist

Born in Sevilla in 1599, Diego Velázquez came to Madrid in his early twenties. After completing his first portrait of Felipe IV, he was promised that no one else would ever paint the king. He was to spend the rest of his life working as court painter, and in the process revolutionized Spanish art. His portraits of the king and royal family told a psychological truth rather than some idealized fiction (his later portrait of a sinister-looking Pope Innocent X prompted the reaction: "Too true!"). He painted the hard lives of court servants, jesters, and dwarves. And finally, in *Las Meninas,* he painted himself painting them. Although his masterpieces will be familiar to many, what strikes you when you see them up close are the impressionistic brushstrokes—a slash of white to suggest a collar, a squiggle for a fine silk sleeve, a few fast strokes to capture the movement of a horse's mane. His influence on the French modernist, Eduoard Manet, 200 years later, is clear. Manet called him "the painter of painters" and at the Prado you can see why.

Salas 8B–10B. There are lots of luminous Virgins and saints here too, but the most celebrated is a secular painting, *The Nobleman with his Hand on his Chest*. Painted soon after El Greco arrived in Spain, its solemn pose and the symbolism of his gestures have provoked much debate, not least about who the nobleman was. Some have suggested it is a self-portrait, others that it depicts Cervantes, but the most likely contender is Juan de Silva y Ribera, the military commander of Toledo's Alcázar. His expression, and that of *An Elderly Gentleman* nearby, are so true that you almost feel you know them, or someone just like them.

Francisco de Goya (1746–1828) studied Veláquez's paintings when he began working for the crown in the late 1770s. His early, cheerful side is evident in his paintings of countryside idylls (Salas 85–87), made as cartoons for tapestries to cover the walls of a royal hunting palace. It was his first royal commission. His mature work, especially after Carlos IV made him court painter in 1799, shows an understanding of character on a par with Velázquez. *The Family of Carlos IV* in Sala 32, painted around 1800, reprises the concept of *Las Meninas,* portraying an unhappy royal family in their finery and a king who looks out of his depth. In 1808, Carlos abdicated when the going got tough, and his foolish son invited Napoleon to tidy up Spain. Goya captured the horrors of the French occupation in *Dos de Mayo,* which shows the popular uprising in Puerta del Sol on May 2, 1808, and *El Tres de Mayo,* which depicts the executions of the Spanish partisans by firing squad the following day. These late paintings, which made his modern reputation, are found in Salas 64–65 on the ground level. The disturbing Black Paintings, daubed on the walls of his house in fits of depression and madness in the years after 1819, fill Salas 66–67. These nightmarish images, such as the heart-breaking *The Dog,* didn't reach the Prado until the 19th century, where they became inspiration for German Expressionism and Surrealism. Goya's journey from joyful picnics to *Saturn Devouring His Son* is one of the most astounding and disturbing in the history of art. In between, his portraits of the **La Maja,** with and without clothes (Sala 36), broke daring new ground.

Paseo del Prado s/n. www.museoprado.es. ℭ **90-210-70-77.** Advance tickets at www.entradasprado.com. Admission 15€ adults, 7.50€ seniors, free for students and children under 18. Two visits 22€. Mon–Sat 10am–8pm, Sun 10am–7pm. Free entry Mon–Sat 6–8pm, Sun 5–7pm. Closed Jan 1, May 1, and Dec 25. Metro: Atocha or Banco de España. Bus: 9, 10, 14, 19, 27, 34, 37, or 45.

Museo Nacional Centro de Arte Reina Sofía ★★★ ART MUSEUM

It's a short walk—and a large aesthetic leap—from the Prado to the Reina Sofía, which holds Spain's most significant collection of 20th- and 21st-century works, including Picasso's *Guernica.* Opened in 1990, the main museum consists of an 18th-century former hospital designed by Francisco Sabatini, and the post-modern addition by Jean Nouvel that opened in 2005. They house the museum's collection of more than 22,000 works, as well as an ambitious program of temporary exhibitions, educational

The postmodern architecture of the Reina Sofía's 2005 addition befits the museum's strengths in 20th- and 21st-century art.

events, and talks. The collection is now so large that the museum also uses a couple of palaces in the Retiro park for exhibitions, such as installation art, which require more space (p. 107). The museum's three permanent exhibitions are set out in rough chronological order, with various artistic movements grouped by room. Collection 1, "The Irruption of the 20th Century: Utopias and Conflicts (1900–1945)" fills Level 2 of the Sabatini Building; Collection 2 "Is the War Over? Art in a Divided World (1945–1968)" occupies Level 4. Collection 3, on Level 0 of the Nouvel building, is titled "From Revolt to Postmodernity (1962–1982)" and includes a good collection of American pop art.

Current thinking says that in modern art, context is all. That means paintings by Picasso, Juan Gris, Joan Miró, and Dalí are surrounded by photographs, posters, commercial art, and short films describing the world in which the works were created. This approach is particularly effective in the galleries that deal with art related to the Spanish Civil War and Franco's dictatorship. If you visit nothing else in the museum, it is worth the admission fee to see *Guernica,* in room 206 on the 2nd floor. Painted in June 1937, it was Picasso's response to the unprovoked bombing in April 1937 of the Basque village of Gernika by German and Italian planes at the behest of Franco. Picasso had a commission to produce a large-scale painting for the World's Fair to be held in Paris that summer; *Guernica* became his submission. It is hard to overstate the impact it must have had when first unveiled at the Spanish Pavilion. Seeing its huge, violent, black-and-white images in person is a visceral experience, even today. There are also insightful exhibits about the making of the painting, and regular talks discussing it.

On either side of *Guernica* are two other exhibits that are also well worth your time. Luis Buñuel's surreal documentary *Tierra sin pan* (Land Without Bread) is a portrait of Las Hurdes, in the Extremadura region, where in the 1930s people were so backward and poor that they lived in animal-like squalor. Room 205 houses some of surrealist Salvador Dalí's most famous paintings, including *The Face of the Great Masturbator,* painted in 1929.

Calle Santa Isabel, 52. www.museoreinasofia.es. ℰ **91-774-10-00.** Admission 10€ adults (8€ online), 5€ seniors, students, and ages 17 and under. Wed–Mon 10am–9pm (Sun until 7pm). Closed Jan 1 and 6, May 15, Nov 9, Dec 24, 25, and 31. Metro: Atocha. Bus: 6, 10, 14, 19, 26, 27, 32, 34, 36, 37, 41, 45, 59, 85, 86, 102, 119, C1, C2, or E1.

Museo Naval ★ MUSEUM   Set on the ground level of Spanish Navy headquarters, this museum has a great story to tell. It covers the greatest hits of Spanish naval pre-eminence, including the discovery and exploration of the Americas, the Spanish Armada, and the feared Spanish galleons of the 17th and 18th centuries. Juan de la Cosa's beautiful hand-drawn map from 1500 is said to be the oldest map of Europe that shows the Americas. A scale model of Columbus's flagship, the *Santa Maria,* shows what a fat little tub it was. By contrast, the cutaway model of an 18th-century galleon bristling with cannons can be seen as the birth of the modern warship. Coverage of the Battle of Trafalgar might make you forget that the Spanish lost. At the time of writing the museum was closed for refurbishment, although temporary exhibitions continue. Check the website for updates; when it does reopen, bear in mind you'll need to show your passport to get in. The Navy runs a tight ship. ℰ Paseo del Prado, 5. www.armada.mde.es/museonaval. ℰ **91-523-85-16.** Free admission, voluntary donation of 3€ requested. Tues–Sun 10am–2pm (Aug 10am–3pm). Metro: Banco de España. Bus: 1, 2, 14, 20, 27, 37, 51, 146, 150, and 522.

Museo Thyssen-Bornemisza ★★★ ART MUSEUM   Occupying the Palacio Villahermosa across the road from the Prado, the Thyssen houses one of the greatest private art collections ever assembled. The original collection, spanning 8 centuries of European painting, was compiled by the German-Hungarian industrialists Barons Heinrich and Hans Heinrich Thyssen-Bornemisza, father and son. (The younger Baron's fifth wife, Carmen "Tita" Cervera, a former Miss Spain, was instrumental in convincing him to bring his massive collection to Spain; hundreds of paintings from her own collection, on permanent loan, are exhibited in an extension on the second floor.) Compiled almost in the manner of a stamp collection, the museum, which opened in 1992, contains representatives of practically every major style and artist since the medieval period. Most visitors start on the top floor with the Italian Primitives and work their way down to the pop art of Roy Lichtenstein. But the museum offers some interesting alternatives, suggesting itineraries based on key masterpieces or themes. Whichever way you cut it, you will see familiar images and styles at every turn: the Italian masters Titian, Tintoretto and Caravaggio; Holbein the Younger's instantly recognizable *Portrait of Henry VIII;* Canaletto's unmistakable Venice; the cubism of Picasso, Braque and Gris; Manet's *Woman in a Riding Habit;* Renoir's *Woman with a Parasol;* Degas' *Swaying Dancer;* Jackson Pollack's splashes and Rothko's troubled blocks of color. Many of the Spanish greats are represented, from El Greco, Murillo and Zurbarán to Goya, Dalí and Miró, alongside French impressionists, German expressionists, and Flemish and Dutch heavyweights from Rubens and Rembrandt to Van Gogh. Rubbing shoulders as it does with the Prado and Reina Sofía, you get the sense that the Thyssen has to work harder than it would if it were located elsewhere. It rises impressively to the challenge, with imaginative offers, child-friendly activities, collaborations with other museums, and well-designed apps to help you explore the collection. The cafeteria and museum shop are also excellent.

Palacio de Villahermosa, Paseo del Prado, 8. © www.museothyssen.org. **91-791-13-70.** Admission 12€ adults, 8€ students and seniors, free for ages 17 and under; permanent collection free admission Mon. Mon noon–4pm; Tues–Sun 10am–7pm (extended hours in summer). Metro: Banco de España. Bus: 1, 2, 5, 9, 10, 14, 15, 20, 27, 34, 37, 41, 51, 52, 53, 74, 146, or 150.

Plaza de Cibeles ★ LANDMARK. One of Madrid's most recognizable landmarks, and a dropping-off point for tour buses, this roundabout is dominated by the former Palacio de Comunicaciones (CentroCentro; see p. 82) and by its famous **fountain of Cibeles.** Built in 1782, the fountain depicts the Roman goddess of fertility and agriculture on a sturdy chariot drawn by two lions. Originally it had a practical function, with standpipes providing water for the city and for horses to drink. In recent times it has become notorious as the spot where Real Madrid fans gather to celebrate their team's many triumphs. They used to climb on top and drape the goddess with scarves, but following damage to the marble statue, it's now boarded up on big match days. The **fountain of Neptune,** just along the Paseo del Prado, serves the same function for fans of Real's archrivals, Atlético Madrid.

Metro: Banco de España. Bus: 1, 2, 5, 9, 10, 14, 15, 20, 27, 34, 37, 45, 51, 52, 53, 74, 146, 50, 202, or 203.

Real Fábrica de Tapices ★ FACTORY TOUR   Visiting this working tapestry factory is like stepping back in time. Founded by Felipe V in 1721, it gave Spain its own version of Louis XIV's Gobelins Manufactory in Paris. Almost 3 centuries later, artisans still make rugs and wall tapestries at the original handlooms. Watching their skilled fingers at work will give you a new appreciation for this time-honored craft—a square meter can take up to a year to complete. Francisco de Goya created the designs for Real Fábrica tapestries that still grace the walls of the Palacio Real and El Escorial, and Alfonso XIII insisted the carpets at the Ritz be woven here. When you've finished watching the weavers, you can view Goya's original cartoons as well as beautiful examples of traditional and modern designs. The factory is just to the east of Atocha train station.

Calle Fuenterrabia, 2. www.realfabricadetapices.com. © **91-434-05-50.** Admission 5€ adults; 3.50€ children. Guided tours in English at noon, reservations recommended. Mon–Fri 10am–2pm. Closed Aug. Metro: Menéndez Pelayo. Bus: 10, 14, 24, 26, 32, 37, 54, 57, 102, 141, C1, or C2.

Real Jardín Botánico ★ BOTANICAL GARDENS   The Age of Enlightenment lives on in these formal gardens next to the Museo del Prado at the southwest corner of the Parque del Retiro. Carlos III, the so-called mayor-king, had Juan de Villanueva (architect of the Prado and the Paseos) design the gardens as a collection of temperate zone plants from around the world. The king himself opened the gardens in 1781. Through their history they have had their ups and downs—they fell into years of abandonment after the War of Independence in 1808—but today the meticulously maintained gardens contain more than 6,000 species of plants and trees. Nine self-guided visits are available, including tours focusing on ornamental, medicinal, and edible plants.

Plaza de Murillo, 2. www.rjb.csic.es. © **91-420-30-17.** Admission 4€ adults, 2€ students, 2.50€ seniors, kids under 18 free. Daily 10am–9pm in summer; check website for opening times in other seasons. Closed Dec 25 and Jan 1. Metro: Atocha. Bus: 1, 2, 3, 5, 9, 10, 14, 15, 20, 27, 34, 37, 45, 51, 52, 53, 74, 146, or 150.

Puerta del Sol & Barrio de las Letras

Puerta del Sol is the hub of old Madrid and the principal crossroads of the city's transport systems. It is also the square where *madrileños* have always flocked when trouble is afoot—from the uprising against Napoleon in 1808 to the economic protests of May 2011—and when there is a party to be had (on New Year's Eve, for example).

Just uphill to the southeast are the old streets of the Barrio de las Letras, or literary district, which you'll also hear referred to as Las Huertas. These narrow streets and shady alleys, now embedded with literary quotations, are the same paths walked by playwright Tirso de Molina (1579–1648), novelist Miguel de Cervantes (1547–1616), and the greatest rascal of all, Félix Lope de Vega (1562–1635). Now as then, the neighborhood is home to many of Madrid's liveliest bars and theaters.

Casa de Lope de Vega ★ HISTORIC HOME   Félix Lope de Vega may have been a more complex and fascinating character than any he invented in his many plays. He bought this house in 1610 when he was

In Puerta del Sol, this statue of a bear and a *madroño* tree is a beloved symbol of the city of Madrid.

already an established playwright and lived here for the last 25 years of his life, with his mistress and children by at least three different women. (He fathered 17 in all, although many died in infancy.) This three-story house is an imagined historic restoration from the 1950s, but you can still get a sense of Lope de Vega's extraordinary, hyperactive life. The furnishings reflect the contents listed in his will. He wrote some 500 plays and 3,000 sonnets and became a priest at age 50. He was particularly fond of his tranquil walled garden at the back. "My little house, my peace, my little plot, my study," he wrote to a friend shortly after moving in. All tours are guided, lasting 45 minutes, and it's best to reserve. To guarantee a tour in English, book a couple of days ahead.

Calle Cervantes, 11. casamuseolopedevega.org. ℰ **91-429-92-16.** Free admission. Tues–Sun 10am–6pm (last tour at 5pm). Metro: Antón Martín. Bus: 6, 9, 10, 14, 26, 27, 32, 34, 37, 45, or 57.

Museo de la Real Academia de Bellas Artes de San Fernando ★★ ART MUSEUM The intimate galleries of the Royal Academy are a pleasant change of pace from Madrid's big art museums. Founded in 1752 to teach art students, the museum has amassed a fine collection of paintings and sculptures from the Renaissance period to the present. Spanish artists, naturally, are the best represented, but in some cases, you can compare their work to that of their Italian and Flemish contemporaries. Francisco Goya became director of the academy in 1795, and the collection features 13 of his paintings, including an equestrian portrait of Fernando VII and an absorbing scene of the Inquisition. Most revealing are two Goya self-portraits, one as a dandyish 30-something, the other a world-weary figure in his 60s, before he succumbed to the madness that drove his Dark Paintings. The museum also has his paint-covered final palette. There are paintings by Zurburán, El Greco, and Cano, and the upstairs galleries house 19th- and 20th-century art, including pieces by Picasso (who briefly studied here), Sorolla, and Juan Gris. Salvador Dalí, who was expelled in the 1920s for questioning a professor's competence, doesn't feature.

Calle Alcalá, 13. www.realacademiabellasartessanfernando.com. ℂ **91-524-08-64.** Admission 8€ adults, 4€ students, free for ages 17 and under; free admission Wed. Tues–Sun 10am–3pm. Metro: Sol or Sevilla. Bus: 3, 5, 15, 20, 51, 52, 53, or 150.

Plaza Santa Ana ★★ PLAZA   Sooner or later you're bound to have a drink on Plaza Santa Ana—it's been a center for entertainment and café nightlife since the Corral des Comedias de Príncipe, one of Spain's first theaters, began packing in the crowds in 1583. The open-air theater would stage the plays of Lope de Vega and his more sophisticated successor, Calderón de la Barca, who is honored here with a statue. The 19th-century **Teatro Español** still operates on the east side of the square; a statue paying tribute to the murdered poet and playwright Federico García Lorca faces it, holding a dove of peace. The **Reina Victoria hotel** on the west side was once a favorite of bullfighters; superstitious Manolete always stayed in room 220. On warm evenings, the square is almost entirely filled with the tables and chairs of the bars that surround it, including the Cervecería Alemana, one of Hemingway's favorites.

Metro: Antón Martín. Bus: 6, 26, 32.

Puerta del Sol ★ PLAZA   Many *madrileños* scoff at the idea of spending time on Puerta del Sol, though it is almost always overflowing with people. Think of it like Times Square or Piccadilly Circus, a busy transport hub and tourists' meeting place. Until not so long ago it was a seedy place too, with flop hotels and dodgy vendors, but it has been extensively made over and now has a rather sterile air. It has also been much messed about with. Its famous neon sign advertising Tío Pepe sherry was moved to another rooftop to accommodate an Apple Store; the beloved **statue of a bear and *madroño* tree**—the symbol of the city—was relocated to make way for a Louvre-like Metro entrance. On the plus side, pedestrianization and renovation have made it an attractive place to join the crowds. Embedded in the pavement in front of the old Casa de Correos building is the **Zero Kilometer** marker from which all distances in Spain are calculated. The clock on the former post office displays Spain's

ALL THE NEIGHBORHOOD'S a stage

The earliest record of a theater in Madrid is the Corral de Príncipe, an open-air venue that began staging plays in Plaza Santa Ana in 1583. More than 400 years later, the neighborhood remains a hub of theatrical activity, with five historic theaters in the vicinity. Performances are in Spanish, of course, but musical theater in particular can be enjoyed without a perfect grasp of the language.

Teatro Calderón Madrid's largest theater holds more than 1,000 in its plush red seats and ornate boxes. During its 100 years it has staged everything from flamenco to opera, but following a takeover and refurbishment in 2015, it now focuses on blockbuster international shows like STOMP. Calle Atocha, 18. www. teatrocalderon.es. ✆ **91-429-40-85.** Tickets 30€–70€.

Teatro Español This exquisite 19th-century theater on Plaza Santa Ana presents live Spanish theater and music performances from jazz to classical. Medallions on the façade depict the pantheon of Spanish playwrights, from Calderón de la Barca to Federico García Lorca. Calle Principe, 25. www.teatroespanol.es. ✆ **91-360-14-84.** Most tickets 15€–30€.

Teatro de la Zarzuela If you're curious about Spain's equivalent of Broadway musicals, this theater is the principal venue for the art form known as *zarzuela*. It mixes sketch theater, opera, popular song, and spoken narrative. Hard to follow in detail, but entertaining nonetheless. Restricted view seats can be had for as little as 5€. Calle Jovellanos, 4. teatro delazarzuela.mcu.es. ✆ **91-050-52-82.** Tickets 5€–50€.

Teatro Monumental This former 1920s cinema is home to the Orquesta Sinfónica de Radio Televisión Española. The RTVE orchestra plays a series of broadcast classical concerts from September through June, and the acoustics, as well as the space, are monumental. Calle Atocha, 65. www.rtve.es/orquesta-coro. ✆ **91-429-81-19.** Tickets 10€–25€.

Teatro Nuevo Apolo Formerly the home of the renowned Antología de la Zarzuela company, the Apolo began staging musical variety in the 1930s, but these days focuses on mainstream Spanish and international entertainment shows. Plaza de Tirso de Molina. 1. www. summummusic.com. ✆ **91-369-06-37.** Tickets 25€–60€.

official time. When it strikes midnight on New Year's Eve, Spanish revelers begin eating a dozen grapes—one for each chime. The TV coverage and fireworks come live from Puerta del Sol.

Metro: Sol. Bus: 3, 50, 51, N16, N26, or M1.

Plaza Mayor & La Latina

Madrid was born in La Latina. The neighborhood's boundaries conform closely to the walled medina of the 10th-century citadel known as *al-Majrit*, or "place of water" in Arabic. When Alfonso VI of Castilla y León conquered it in 1085, he turned the mosque into a church and left the walls in place. Four centuries would pass before they were fully torn down to let the village grow, and even today, its narrow streets follow the original Moorish pattern, punctuated almost randomly by little plazas. So, why is it called La Latina? It has nothing to do with the Romans but is named

Cafes crowd around Plaza Mayor, Madrid's roomy main square.

after a hospital founded in 1499 by Beatriz Galindo, a learned woman known as "la Latina." Plaza Mayor was originally the market square outside the city walls, but since the 17th century it has been Madrid's main square.

Mercado de San Miguel ★★ MARKET   Just outside the walls of Plaza Mayor, this long-dormant covered market was renovated and reopened in 2009 as a 21st-century food hall, with more than three dozen stalls housed in its wrought-iron-and-glass shell. The original 1916 market, built to evoke Paris' Les Halles, is an impressive sight, especially at night. Upscale vendors sell a wide range of Spanish favorites—croquettes, *jamón,* seafood, olives, beer, and cava—and it is an enjoyable place to browse at lunchtime or in the evenings. But it does get extremely busy, and you won't find bargains here. For more authentic Madrid markets, see p. 144.

Plaza de San Miguel. www.mercadodesanmiguel.es. ℭ **91-542-49-39.** Sun–Thurs 10am–midnight; Fri–Sat 10am–1am. Metro: Opera, Sol, or Tirso de Molina. Bus: 3 or N16.

Museo de San Isidro ★ MUSEUM   Also known as the Museo de los Orígenes, this interesting museum sits on the site where San Isidro Labrador and his wife, Santa María de la Cabeza, were said to have lived in the 12th century. The humble farm laborer became the patron saint of Madrid, which celebrates him with processions and bullfights during its main fiesta in May. Legend says that their son fell into a deep well and was rescued by their prayers when the waters rose—the first of a number of miracles. The *pozo de los milagros* (well of miracles) is the museum's star exhibit. This free municipal museum also deals with the secular history of Madrid from the arrival of the first humans who hunted along the Río Manzanares some 350,000 years ago through Madrid's apotheosis as Spain's capital. Most exhibits have English translations.

Plaza de San Andrés, 2. www.munimadrid.es/museosanisidro. ℭ **91-366-74-15.** Free admission. Winter Tues–Sun 10am–8pm; summer Tues–Sun 10am–7pm. Metro: La Latina or Tirso de Molina. Bus: 3, 17, 18, 23, 35, 60, 65, or 148.

Plaza de la Villa ★ PLAZA   One of Madrid's most beautiful and historic squares, the tiny Plaza de la Villa holds some of the city's oldest surviving buildings. The plaza has been the site of city government since medieval times, and the **Casa de la Villa,** the old town hall, is located here. The original medieval structure was rebuilt in Renaissance style in 1645 and modified again when Madrid Baroque became the rage. Next door, **Casa Cisneros,** built in 1537 in Plateresque style, was once the home of the nephew of Cardinal Cisneros. Opposite stands the **Casa de los Lujanes,** a 15th-century Mudéjar Gothic manor house, one of Madrid's oldest buildings. It is said that the French king Francis I was held here after his capture at the battle of Pavia in 1525. When he declined to bow to Spain's Carlos V, the door of the tower was lowered, forcing him to bend. Unfortunately, it is currently only possible to admire these buildings from the outside. The Casa de la Villa, which still houses local government offices, used to be open for visits on Mondays at 5pm, but at the time of writing, it was closed for restoration. Check www.esmadrid.com for reopening details, or ask the guards at the door.

Metro: Opera or Sol. Bus: 3, 17, 25, 31, 35, 39, 50, 65, 148, or M1.

Plaza Mayor ★★★ PLAZA   Awash with overpriced cafes, souvenir shops, and caricature artists, this vast square with its red, arcaded apartments is nevertheless noble and beautiful. The site was originally a food market just outside the city walls, and the current square was created by the Habsburgs in 1619 as the city's gathering place. People came to see bullfights, celebrate royal weddings, and witness the *autos-de-fé* of the Spanish Inquisition. With apartments on the square, the royal family had ringside seats. Little remains of those original buildings, as the square suffered three disastrous fires in the 17th and 18th centuries. The zodiac frescoes of Roman gods decorating the **Casa de Panadería** on the north side look old, but they date only from 1992. *Madrileños* tend to leave the square to the tourists, but they come to the plaza for Sunday morning coin and stamp trading and for the annual Christmas market. The square's acoustics are excellent, and musicians often perform in the center near the equestrian statue of Felipe III. The plaza was fully enclosed in 1854, creating the arches that now serve as its gates. The most dramatic is the **Arco de Cuchilleros** (Cutlers' Arch), on the southwest corner. Through it, down the stone steps, are the cave restaurants that have fascinated tourists since the days of Washington Irving.

Metro: Sol, Opera, or Tirso de Molina. Bus: 3, 17, 18, 23, 31, 50, 65, N16, or N26.

El Rastro ★ MARKET   This may sound like heresy, but Madrid's famous flea market is not what it was. Every Sunday, El Rastro sprawls across a roughly triangular district of streets and plazas a few minutes' walk south of Plaza Mayor. Its spine is the **Ribera de Curtidores** (Tanners' Way) and there are still some interesting shops here selling equestrian gear and leather offcuts. But the market itself is full of cheap imported T-shirts, bags, and fake sports team jerseys of the kind you'll find in any city market in Europe. Policemen patrol to check that the stall keepers' permits are in order. The side streets and squares are more interesting—if you want to buy a bird cage, pet supplies, or cobbler's materials, this is the place to come. Good bric-a-brac is harder to find. The optimistically named **Calle Mira el Sol** and **Plaza del Campillo del Mundo Nuevo** are the best places for junk, with vinyl records, vintage soda bottles, and old weights and scales, but there's not much joy in it, and few bargains. It is nevertheless worth a visit to El Rastro to join the wandering crowds, and worth getting there early. Stop for a good-value breakfast at the French bakery **Pan Adoré,** at Plaza de Cascorro, 20, where the staff wear blue and white striped sweaters. For better bric-a-brac, creative and original stalls, and more fun, head to **Mercado de Motores** (p. 108).

Plaza de Cascorro and Ribera de Curtidores. www.elrastro.org. Sun 8am–3pm. Metro: La Latina. Bus: 3 or 17.

Opera & Palacio Real

As you approach Madrid's regal quarter, the narrow streets of the old city open into sun-splashed plazas and the vast formality of the Palacio Real. Comparisons to the Paris Opera and the palace of Versailles are inevitable. Everything you see here was created under Bourbon kings with French taste, or by another Frenchman. During his brief reign, Napoleon's brother Joseph Bonaparte earned the nickname "El Rey Plazuelas," king of the

squares, because of his penchant for demolishing houses to make way for open spaces. The broad expanse between the Teatro Real and palace is Plaza de Oriente, laid out at Bonaparte's behest in the first half of the 19th century. The rearing equestrian statue of Felipe IV employs the same trick as the levitating "living statues" you might see in Plaza Mayor: The horse's hind legs and tail are heavily weighted, while its head and front legs are hollow. It was based on drawings by Velázquez, with scientific advice from Galileo. A crescent of elegant cafés faces it, frequented by ladies who lunch.

The Palacio Real faces onto Plaza de Armeria.

Monasterio de las Descalzas Reales ★★ MUSEUM   In the 16th century, the daughters of nobility had two choices: Be married off to forge alliances with powerful men or opt for a life behind the walls of a convent. Juana de Austria, the charismatic daughter of Carlos V, did both. She married the crown prince of Portugal at age 17, but when he died 2 years later, she requisitioned a royal palace to establish this Franciscan convent. Its name means "Convent of the Barefoot Royals." Each of the noblewomen who took the veil brought a dowry as a bride of Christ, and their treasures still fill the convent. By the 20th century, however, the nuns' circumstances had changed. Also known as the Poor Clares, they were literally starving amid a priceless art collection they were forbidden to sell. The state intervened, and Rome granted special dispensation to open the convent as a museum in 1960, allowing the public to see its riches for the first time. The large hall of the nuns' former dormitory is hung with tapestries woven in Brussels from cartoons by Rubens. Note the floor tiles that delineate each nun's tiny sleeping area. Guided tours are in Spanish, but one glimpse of the magnificent **staircase,** with its 17th-century frescoes of saints, angels, and Spanish rulers, explains the confluence of art, royalty, and faith that defines Spanish history. Other highlights include a plaintive, carved Virgen la Dolorosa by Pedro La Mena, who sits with her hands clasped in one of the choir stalls, and the Plateresque tomb of Doña Juana, who died aged 38 in 1573. This is still a working convent, home to about 20 nuns.

Plaza de las Descalzas Reales s/n. www.patrimonionacional.es. © **91-454-88-00.** Admission 6€; free for children under 5. Tues–Sat 10am–2pm and 4–6:30pm; Sun 10am–3pm. Closed Jan 1, Jan 6, Holy Week, May 1, and Dec 24–25. Free for EU and Latin American citizens Wed and Thurs 4pm–6:30pm. Metro: Opera. Bus: 3, 25, 39, and 148.

Palacio Real ★★★ PALACE   When the old royal palace—a dank, dark *alcázar* captured from the Moors in 1086—burned down in 1734, Felipe V ordered a new palace designed to rival his French cousins' home at Versailles. Having wrested the throne from the Habsburg line in the War of Spanish Succession, it was important for this first Bourbon to eclipse the previous royal dynasty. (He was literally minting coins with the gold and silver flowing from the New World colonies, so money was no object.) The finished product is one of the largest and most lavishly decorated palaces in Europe. Construction began in 1738, and in 1764 Felipe's younger son, Carlos III, finally moved into the 3,000-plus room complex (it was originally intended to be four times larger). Most rooms are reserved for state business, but a significant portion of the palace is open for tours. It remains the official residence of the royal family, although no monarch has lived here since Alfonso XIII fled Spain in 1931. The current king, Felipe VI, lives in the relatively modest Palacio de la Zarzuela outside Madrid.

Free, but Not for All

Unless you're from the European Union or Latin America, you're probably wondering why we're telling you that admission to the **Palacio Real** is free for citizens of those regions for the last 2 hours of the day from Monday to Thursday (Apr–Sept 6pm–8pm; Oct–Mar 4pm–6pm). Free admission at those times can cause real logjams, so plan accordingly. Similar deals apply at the monastery palace at **El Escorial** (p. 147), and on Wednesdays and Thursdays at the **Monasterio de las Descalzas Reales.**

Designed to impress (and even intimidate) visitors, the grand staircase of the Palacio Real still does its job 3 centuries later.

There are often queues to enter the palace on the Plaza de la Armería in front of the cathedral. Skip them by buying your tickets in advance online; you can show your ticket on your phone. The best times to visit are early in the day or at Spanish lunchtime around 2pm, when the lines are shortest. Once inside the ticket office, you have choices. In addition to the main palace visit, which costs 10€, you can visit the Royal Armory (Real Armería), which is included in the cost of the ticket, and take a guided tour of the Royal Kitchen (Real Cocina), with a set start time, for an additional 5€. If you have time, it is worth doing all three. An audio guide costs another 3€.

When you walk into the sunlight of the vast white Plaza de la Armería, most of the people in your line will make a dash for the palace. Ignore them and cross the plaza to start at the **Armory.** You can truly get the measure of Spanish royalty here, as the suits of armor were individually tailored. Felipe I, the handsome Austrian who married Juana la Loca (daughter of Fernando and Isabel) in 1496, stood nearly 6 feet tall—a giant in his day. The armor worn by Carlos V in the equestrian painting by Titian that hangs in the Prado is here, but it is striking how tiny he was in reality. You can also see his parade helmet, with golden hair and beard, and a suit of armor made for his hunting dog. Other points of interest are the 10-foot muskets used in siege warfare, and a sword said to have belonged to El Cid.

Once you enter the palace proper, you're not allowed to backtrack on the rigidly delineated tour through dozens of heavily decorated rooms. An imperial staircase, made from a single piece of marble, leads to the **Hall of the Halbardiers** where you'll see the first of two wonderful ceiling frescos by the Venetian artist Gianbattista Tiepolo, the great Rococo painter of the 18th century. Invited to Spain by Charles III in 1761, he started work on them when he was already well into his 60s (he never returned to Venice). On the ceiling of the magnificent, mirrored **Throne Room** is his master work, *The Apotheosis of the Spanish Monarchy,* an extraordinary piece of political flattery of the king who was paying the bills. It depicts Spain in allegorical form surveying the globe from the clouds, assisted by a panoply of Roman gods. The opulence of the rooms that follow is almost unnerving. You'll see the drawing room where Carlos III had lunch, the over-the-top **Gasparini Room** where he dressed, and the bedroom where he died. Many of the rooms are lined with tapestries made at the Real Fabrica de Tapices, but most of the paintings—including pictures by Goya, Velazquez, and Caravaggio—are copies of originals which hang in the Prado. Other highlights include the **Stradivarius room,** with the world's only string quintet by the great violin maker, and what remains of the royal silver and china collection. (Joseph Bonaparte sold off the best pieces to finance French military adventures.) Finally, you'll reach the vast, chandeliered **State Dining Hall,** first used by Alfonso XII in November 1879 to celebrate his marriage.

Reopened in 2017 after restoration, the **Royal Kitchen** is a treat. These heavy stone cellars, rebuilt in the 1860s and 1870s on the instructions of Isabel II and Alfonso XII, show the downstairs end of the banqueting process. There are hundreds of copper pots and pans, baking trays, fish kettles, and terrine molds—enough to cater state dinners for 140 people. There are roasting spits, warming ovens, and an early telephone, no doubt for conveying culinary commands. The wine cellars have labelled barrels displaying the royal taste from Chateau d'Yquem to Tio Pepe, and menus detailing the wines served on various state occasions. A Real Cocina oven glove from the palace shop at the end of the tour makes a fitting souvenir.

Afterwards, clear your head with a wander in the **Jardines de Sabatini.** Construction of the gardens began in the 1930s on the site of the former royal stables. Formally laid out with a box hedge maze, ponds, and marble sculptures, they were opened to the public by King Juan Carlos I in 1978.

A changing-of-the-guard ceremony takes place every Wednesday and Saturday between 11am and 2pm (in summer 10am–noon) at Puerta del Príncipe. A more elaborate ceremony is held at noon on the first Wednesday of each month (except in summer) in the Plaza de la Armería and is free to the public.

Calle de Bailén, 2. www.patrimonionacional.es. ✆ **91-454-87-00.** Admission 10€ adults, 5€ students and ages 16 and under. Apr–Sept daily 10am–8pm; Oct–Mar daily 10am–6pm. Last tickets sold 1 hr. before closing. Metro: Opera. Bus: 3, 25, 39, or 148.

Teatro Real ★★ THEATER   Begun in 1818, the Royal Opera House finally opened its doors in 1850 in time to celebrate the 20th birthday of Queen Isabel II, and it has seen some dramatic moments since. A partial collapse caused its closure in 1925, and an exploding powder keg during the Civil War meant it sat derelict for some 40 years. After extensive renovation, it finally reopened as an opera house in 1997 with Manuel de Falla's *La Vida Breve* (Life Is Short). Today, it is one of the world's finest settings for opera and ballet, with state-of-the-art technical capacity as impressive as its restored 19th-century grandeur. The best way to appreciate it is to attend a performance, of course, but a variety of guided tours are available, in English by request. They range from a general tour (with guide or audio guide) explaining the history, architecture, and workings of the theater—including a peek into the royal box—to more specialized, and expensive, tours dealing with technical and artistic aspects. During productions, you can even arrange to visit backstage once the final curtain has dropped.

Plaza Isabel II, s/n. www.teatro-real.com. ✆ **91-516-06-60.** Performance ticket prices vary. Audio tour 7€ adults, 6€ for visitors under 26 or over 65; children under 5 free; daily 10:30am–4:30pm. General guided tour 8€ adults, 6€ for visitors under 26 or over 65; children under 7 free; daily 10am–1pm on the half-hour. Other tours 12€–30€, check website for availability. Metro: Opera. Bus: 3, 25, 39, or 148.

Gran Vía, Chueca & Malasaña

The slashing diagonal of Gran Vía was built to represent progress. Alfonso XIII inaugurated the work in 1910 with the announced intention of creating a boulevard to rival any in Paris. Gran Vía was Madrid's first street built for motorcars, and for much of the 20th century, movie theaters, banks, and upscale businesses lined its broad expanse between the Cibeles fountain and Plaza de España. The street, however, began a long, slow slide in the 1970s and has never fully recaptured its former glamour, although the opening of some good hotels and a recent partial pedestrianization have been steps in the right direction. The formerly downbeat neighborhoods of Chueca and Malasaña, immediately to its north, are much further along in their regeneration and have become desirable destinations for shopping, dining, and clubbing. Madrid's street life, rather than monuments, is the main attraction here.

The Carrion Building, an Art Deco landmark on Gran Via.

Circulo de Bellas Artes ★ CULTURAL CENTER   Founded in 1880 by a group of artists and intellectuals, the Circle of Fine Arts became Madrid's first cultural center. It moved into this Art Deco building in 1926 and continues to be one of Madrid's most innovative multidisciplinary spaces, with a couple of stylish cafés. A young Picasso took painting classes here. Today, the non-profit CBA hosts a broad range of art-house exhibitions, films, and workshops, and its rooftop café-restaurant has terrific views over the city. Buy a ticket at the ground-floor reception, take the elevator to the 7th floor, and stare meaningfully into the middle distance.

Calle de Alcalá, 42. www.circulobellasartes.com. ✆ **91-360-54-00.** Exhibitions: Tues–Sun 11am–2pm and 5–9pm; admission 4€. Rooftop café: Mon–Fri 9am–9pm, weekends 11am–9pm; admission 4€. Combined admission 5€. Metro: Banco de España or Sevilla. Bus: 1, 2, 5, 9, 14, 15, 20, 27, 45, 46, 51, 52, 53, 74, 146, 147, or 150.

Museo de Historia de Madrid ★ MUSEUM   Set in a glorious Baroque former hospital, this municipal museum reopened in 2014 after years of refurbishment, and it is a gem. It traces the evolution of Madrid since it became the national capital in 1561. A topographic scale model of the city, meticulously created in wood in 1830, will give you a better sense of the streets of the old town than any paper or digital map. Another exhibit displays models of the mock naval battles that used to take place on the lake of the Retiro park. You can also see Goya's famous *Allegory of Madrid*, which reflects the instability of the 19th century. When it was first painted in 1810 the frame to which the female personification of the city is pointing contained a portrait of the new king, Joseph Bonaparte. In 1812, he was painted out in favor of the word "Constitución," honoring Spain's fledgling democracy. When Bonaparte returned, he had to be painted back in. Eventually, after a hokey pokey of changes, the words "Dos de Mayo" were painted into the frame, in memory of the uprising against the French on that date in 1808. More enduring are the paintings of Plaza Mayor through the ages. The setting barely changes—its inhabitants are simply wearing different costumes.

Calle Fuencarral, 78. www.madrid.es. ✆ **91-701-18-63.** Free admission. Tues–Sun 10am–8pm. Metro: Bilbao or Tribunal. Bus: 3, 21, 37, 40, 147, or 149.

Museo del Romanticismo ★ MUSEUM   This intriguing house museum was originally created in the 1920s by the wealthy collector Marquis de Vega-Inclán, who also founded Toledo's eccentric Museo del Greco (p. 161) and had a hand in creating Spain's parador hotels. It has evolved into a museum focusing on the lifestyle of the upper middle class during the reign of Isabel II (1830–68). Its rooms and furnishings all evoke the romantic charm of the Isabelline style, which has a lot in common with British Victorian.

Calle San Mateo, 13. www.culturaydeporte.gob.es/mromanticismo. ✆ **91-448-10-45.** Admission 3€ adults; 1.50€ seniors and ages 17 and under. May–Oct Tues–Sat 9:30am–8:30pm, Sun 10am–3pm; Nov–Apr Tues–Sat 9:30am–6:30pm, Sun 10am–3pm. Metro: Tribunal or Alonso Martínez. Bus: 3, 37, 40, or 149.

An atmospheric street corner in Malasaña.

Plaza Dos de Mayo ★ PLAZA   Rebellion echoes down the ages in Malasaña. The brick arch at the center of this broad square marks the site of the Monteleón artillery barracks. When the people of Madrid rose up against Napoleon's troops on May 2, 1808, Spanish troops were ordered to remain in barracks. The artillery, under the command of Luis Daoiz de Torres and Pedro Velarde y Santillán, defied the crown and joined the popular uprising. In return, the French reduced the barracks to rubble, killed most of the Spanish soldiers, and martyred their leaders, who are honored in the statues beneath the arch. (The event is chillingly captured in Goya's painting *Dos de Mayo* in the Prado.) At the end of the Franco era, this bohemian neighborhood became a flash point for another rebellion, this time against Spanish authoritarianism: On May 2, 1976, to the delight of onlookers, a couple undressed on top of the arch—an event often cited as the beginning of the countercultural Movida Madrileña. That spirit is alive and well in and around Plaza Dos de Mayo.

Metro: Bilbao or Tribunal. Bus: 3, 21, 40, 147, or 149.

Salamanca, Retiro & Chamberí

After the bustle of Madrid's old city, Salamanca offers a welcome change of pace. The Marqués de Salamanca began constructing this quarter in the 1870s and, by the time it was completed around 1920, it was Madrid's most exclusive address. Situated east of Paseo de la Castellana and north of Parque del Retiro, its broad, tree-lined avenues are laid out in an orderly grid, lined with designer boutiques, high-end shopping malls, and fashionable restaurants. The area around the Retiro park is also leafy and exclusive, while trendy Chamberí to the northwest has become a magnet for Madrid's young professionals.

Estación de Chamberí ★★ MUSEUM   Also known as **Andén 0** (Platform 0), this is an intriguing opportunity to visit the ghost Metro station of Chamberí. Built in 1919 and abandoned since 1966, the old station has been completely restored and you can again walk its ticket halls and platforms and admire the ceramic signage, old advertisements, and vintage fittings. A treat for transport buffs and children, it's also a beautiful exhibition of early 20th-century commercial art.

Plaza Chamberí, s/n. www.esmadrid.com. *©* **91-392-06-93.** Free admission. Thurs 10–1pm, Fri 11am–7pm, Sat–Sun 11am–3pm. Metro: Iglesia. Bus: 3, 5, 16, 40, 61, or 147.

Mercado de la Paz ★★ MARKET   Of Madrid's traditional food markets, Salamanca's is the most beautiful and refined. None can match it for its presentation of just-misted fresh fish and shellfish, perfect fruit and vegetable specimens, carefully aged meats and cheeses, and dozens of varieties of olives. In common with many of Madrid's revived markets (p. 144), there are also plenty of high-tabled spots where you can stop for a snack and a glass of wine, including **Casa Dani** (www.casadani.es),

The abandoned Metro station of Chamberí is now an evocative tourist site.

THE ART OF advertising

In the early 20th century, Madrid shop-keepers began covering their establishments with elaborate tiled scenes to advertise their products and services. Some lovely examples still exist. In Malasaña, **Farmacia Juanse** (Calle San Andres, 5) occupied a large corner site giving ceramic artists plenty of scope to create scenes of men, women, and children taking formulations to cure everything from toothache to constipation. The proprietors of the **Antigua Huevería,** the old egg shop, around the corner (Calle San Vicente Ferrer, 32), embellished their premises with tiled images of hens. It's now a tapas bar—a fitting spot for a slice of *tortilla española.* **La Peluquería Vallejo** in La Latina (Calle Santa Isabel, 22) was founded in 1908 and, a few years later, added its façade of a man and boy at the barbers. Tiled announcements promise unbeatable hygiene and speed. The barbershop is still going strong. As you bar-hop in Santa Ana, you'll see further

Peluquería Vallejo, a vintage barbershop in Las Latinas.

examples. The flamenco venue **Villa Rosa** (Plaza de Santa Ana, 15) is encrusted with tiled scenes of Spanish landmarks. **Bar Viva Madrid** (Calle Manuel Fernández y González, 7), features the Cibeles fountain, alongside exhortations to stop for "Vinos Finos" and "Cervezas, Refrescos y Cafe."

where the *tortilla española* is legendary. Go early, or late, to avoid the rush.

Calle Ayala, 28. www.mercadodelapaz.com. ✆ **91-435-07-43.** Mon–Fri 9am–8pm; Sat 9am–2:30pm. Metro: Velázquez.

Museo Arqueológico Nacional ★ MUSEUM Spain's principal archaeological museum spent more than 6 years redesigning its 19th-century home and its exhibits. The result is magnificently stylish. Spain recognized early on the value of its buried culture and succeeded in keeping most of its treasures inside the country. They range from the intriguing Celto-Iberian statues *La Dama de Elche* and *La Dama de Baeza,* which date from the 4th century B.C., to a wealth of Roman sculpture and mosaics, jeweled Visigothic crowns and crosses, and intricate Islamic art. There is also a reproduction of the cave paintings of Altamira (p. 622).

Calle Serrano, 13. www.man.es. ✆ **91-577-79-12.** Tue–Sat 9:30–8pm, Sun 9:30–3pm. Free admission. Metro: Serrano or Colón. Bus: 1, 9, 19, 51, or 74.

Museo Arte Público ★ MUSEUM   Set in an unpromising spot underneath an overpass on the busy Paseo de Castellana, this open-air sculpture park has 17 pieces by some of Spain's most prominent abstract artists. When the elevated roadway was built in 1970, the artist Eusebio Sempere—who had been commissioned to design its hand railings—had the idea for the park. Bearing in mind that Spain was still in the grip of Franco's arch conservatism, it was a bold idea. The works represent two generations of the Spanish avant-garde including Joan Miró, Eduardo Chillada, and Sempere himself, whose waterfall of alternating wave forms is a highlight. In this location, you might expect it to be dark, dangerous, and graffiti-daubed, but somehow, it's not.

Paseo de la Castellana, 40 (beneath Calle Juan Bravo at Calle Eduardo Dato). www.munimadrid.es/museoairelibre. © **91-467-50-62.** Free admission. Open 24 hr. Metro: Serrano.

Museo Lázaro Galdiano ★★ MUSEUM   The Spanish are enthusiastic collectors, but there are few as enthusiastic as the businessman and patron of the arts, José Lázaro Galdiano (1862–1947). His private collection of more than 13,000 items—bequeathed to the state on his death—fills his Italianate mansion in this refined part of Salamanca. It is astonishing in its breadth, including paintings, sculpture, archaeological artifacts, royal seals, Byzantine jewelry, and medieval armor. The Spanish masters were his main love, and he amassed an extraordinary portfolio including El Greco, Velázquez, Zurbarán, Murillo, and, above all, Goya, who is represented with several paintings, drawings, and prints. He also snapped up pieces by Dutch, Flemish, and English masters, the latter to indulge his wife's taste for Reynolds, Gainsborough, and Constable. But the collection as a whole, its eclecticism and eccentricity, as well as the elegant surroundings of his home, make this museum so fascinating. Each room has a photograph showing how it was decorated and used in Lázaro's day.

Calle de Serrano, 122. www.museolazarogaldiano.es. © **91-561-60-84.** Admission 6€ adults, 3€ students and seniors, free for kids under 12; afternoon guided visits 8€ (reservation required). Tues–Sat 10am–4:30pm, Sun 10am–3pm. Metro: Rubén Darío. Bus: 7, 9, 14, 16, 19, 27, 40, 51, 145, or 150.

Museo Sorolla ★★ HISTORIC HOME   You can see pictures by Joaquín Sorolla (1863–1923) at the Prado and elsewhere in Madrid, but this enchanting museum in his former home has the largest collection by the master of light. Sorolla's paintings, influenced by the French impressionists, enjoyed considerable success among Madrid's new bourgeoisie at the turn of the 19th century, earning enough to build this delightful Andalucían-style family home. The museum offers a window into the comfortable world of the successful painter, balancing his work and domestic life. It's easy to imagine Sorolla at work at one of the unfinished paintings on the easels, surrounded by brushes in pots, or strolling in its restful patios and gardens. The galleries display the range of his work

The garden entrance to the delightful house museum Museo Sorolla.

from portraits and folkloric paintings to his trademark seaside paintings, with parasols, bonnets, and miraculously painted water. Perhaps most blissful is the garlanded mural on the dining room walls portraying his wife, Clotilde García del Costillo, and their daughters. It was Clotilde who decided to turn the property into a museum as a memorial to her husband.

General Martínez Campos 37. museosorolla.mcu.es. ⓒ **91-310-15-84.** Admission 3€ adults, 1.50€ students, free for ages 17 and under; free for all Sat 2–8pm and Sun 10am–3pm. Tues–Sat 9:30am–8pm; Sun 10am–3pm. Metro: Iglesia, Gregorio Marañón, or Rubén Darío. Bus: 5, 7, 14, 16, 27, 40, 45, 61, 147, or 150.

Parque del Retiro ★★ PARK   To see *madrileños* at their most relaxed, spend a Sunday among the families in Parque del Retiro. Originally a playground for the Spanish monarchs, it became a public park at the end of the 19th century. It covers 140 hectares (346 acres) of lawns, lakes, and woodland, but most of the main attractions are close to the central pathway, best accessed next to the triumphal gate, **Puerta de Alcalá.** The park offers gentle recreational activities for everyone—whether they want to watch puppet shows or tango dancers, practice tai chi, play cards or chess, consult a fortune teller, rent rowboats on the lake where Felipe IV used to stage mock naval battles, or just lounge on the grass. From May through September, there are free concerts at the bandstand at the north end of the park on Sundays at noon. Visitors can also enjoy contemporary art: The Reina Sofía museum mounts large-scale exhibitions in two grand pavilions constructed for the 1887 Philippines Exposition, the **Palacio de Cristal** and **Palacio de Velázquez.** At the south end of the park is the **Fuente del Ángel Caído** (Fountain of the Fallen Angel), thought to be Spain's only public monument depicting Satan, and to the west, surrounded by a moat, is the **Forest of Remembrance** for the 191 victims of the 2004 terror attack at nearby Atocha station.

Puerta de Alcala. www.esmadrid.com. Free admission. Apr–Sept 6am–midnight; Oct–Mar 6am–10pm. Palacio de Cristal and Palacio de Velázquez Apr–Sept daily 11am–9pm; Oct–Mar daily 10am–6pm. Metro: Retiro. Bus: 1, 2, 9, 14, 15, 19, 20, 26, 28, 32, 51, 52, 61, 63, 74, 146, 152, 202, C1, or C2.

Outlying Attractions

Ermita de San Antonio de la Florida ★★ CHURCH   Goya's tomb lies in this little hermitage on the banks of the Río Manzanares north of the Palacio Real. But the real draw is the wonderful frescoed ceiling by him, depicting the miracles of St. Anthony with a *trompe l'oeil* balustrade around the cupola. Goya used the labor-intensive technique of applying fresh plaster to the surface, incising his design based on a cartoon drawing, and then applying pigment with a sponge instead of a brush. Many early viewers were shocked that he depicted prostitutes and beggars surrounding the saint, but his patron, Carlos IV, approved. Recently restored to its original glory, it is often called Goya's Sistine Chapel.

Glorieta de San Antonio de la Florida, 5. www.munimadrid.es/ermita. ✆ **91-542-07-22.** Free admission. Tues–Sun 9:30am–8pm. Metro: Príncipe Pío. Bus: 41, 46, or 75.

Matadero Madrid ★ CULTURAL CENTER   This vast contemporary arts complex on the banks of the River Manzanares south of the city center occupies the site of the former Arganzuela slaughterhouse and livestock market. The neo-Mudéjar pavilions of the original site, dating from 1908, have been beautifully restored to create a mini-city devoted to cutting-edge art, culture, and performance. The emphasis is on participation and collaboration across a wide range of disciplines—performing arts, music, design, cinema, architecture—and it is firmly aimed at Madrid's young population rather than visitors, but it is nevertheless an interesting and inspiring place to spend time away from the tourist haunts. You can rent a bike to cruise around the complex and the Madrid Río park nearby, and there are a number of good cafés and bars. Note that most activities take place in the evenings and at weekends.

Plaza de Legazpi, 8. www.mataderomadrid.org. ✆ **91-318-46-70.** Free admission. Complex open daily 9am–10pm; exhibitions and activities Tue–Fri 4pm–9pm, Sat–Sun noon–9pm. Metro: Legazpi. Bus: 6, 8, 18, 19, 45, 78, or 148.

Mercado de Motores ★★ MARKET   On the second weekend of every month, this market for crafts, food, and vintage items takes over the Museo del Ferrocarril railway museum next to Delicias Metro station, south of the city center. Inside, gourmet food stalls and creative jewelry and clothes designers rub up against old steam engines and carriages. Outside, there is plenty of good bric-a-brac—vintage telephones, pop-art lamps, antique beer bottles—accompanied by street food trucks and a

Mercado de Motores street market.

music stage. It is cool, friendly, and great fun—you're more likely to find something interesting and desirable here than you will at El Rastro, be it an antique stock certificate, a Guadarrama goat cheese, or Spanish-made designer shoes. Sponsored by the beer company Mahou, there's a resident DJ and enterprising young people who will babysit your dog, and even your purchases.

Museo del Ferrocarril, Paseo de las Delicias, 61. mercadodemotores.es ✆ **67-231-95-82.** Free admission. Sat 11am–10pm, Sun 11am–9pm. Metro: Delicias. Bus: 8, 19, 45, 47, 59, 85, or 86.

Museo de América ★★ MUSEUM   So much of the history and culture you'll see when you visit Spain relates to the spoils of its imperial adventures in the Americas. This thoughtful museum uses its vast collection of objects from scientific research trips and archaeological digs to record and understand the rich cultures that were forever altered by their interaction with the European explorers and conquistadors. The museum focuses on two key strands: the Knowledge of America, which deals with the story—and myths—of discovery and empire, and the Reality of America, which seeks to explain how Latin America became what it is today. Exhibits re-create the cabinet of curiosities prized by Carlos III in the 18th century—it's intriguing to imagine what it would have been like to see a Mayan carving or golden funerary figure from Colombia for the first time.

Avenida de los Reyes Católicos, 6. museodeamerica.mcu.es. ✆ **91-549-26-41.** Admission 3€ adults, free for students, children, and seniors; free admission Sun. Tues–Sat 9:30am–3pm (Thurs until 7pm), Sun 10am–3pm. Metro: Moncloa. Bus: 1, 2, 16, 44, 46, 61, 82, 113, 132, or 133.

Museo del Traje ★ MUSEUM   You are unlikely to stumble across this fashion museum, located close to the Museo de América in Madrid's university district, but if you are interested in the history of fine clothes, and especially in Spain's famous designers like Balenciaga, it is well worth the trip. Set in a shiny, purpose-built 1970s building, the museum has dimly lit galleries to preserve the delicate fabrics, and fittingly, its displays resemble high-end shop windows. It holds a huge collection, dating from the 16th century through to contemporary designers, and highlights throughout the love of formality and finery you'll still see on the streets of Madrid. The 18th-century *majismo* style, famously captured in the paintings of Goya, was a craze for dressing up in exaggerated versions of traditional Spanish costume. Exhibits focusing on the influential 20th-century designer Cristóbal Balenciaga (1895–1972), are masterclasses in art, science, and gravity.

Avenida Juan de Herrera, 2. museodeltraje.mcu.es. ✆ **91-550-47-00.** Admission 3€ adults, free for seniors and ages 17 and under; free admission Sat 2:30–7pm and all day Sun. Tues–Sat 9:30am–7pm; Sun 10am–3pm. Metro: Moncloa. Bus: 46, 82, 83, 132, or 133.

Plaza de Toros Monumental de Las Ventas ★ BULLRING   The philosopher José Ortega y Gasset said that to truly understand the Spanish you first have to understand the bullfight. Many Spaniards detest the *corrida,* but if you want to get some understanding of it, a tour of this grand, neo-Mudéjar bullring is a good place to start. Huge and rather desolate when there are no crowds around, Las Ventas is Spain's largest ring, with a capacity of 24,000. It opened in 1931 with the intention of offering affordable entertainment to the masses, and tickets for bullfights are still available for as little as 8€, rising to around 200€ for the best seats. There are fights every Sunday at 7pm from March through October, and one every day during the Fiesta de San Isidro in May. Self-guided tours begin at the **Puerta Grande,** through which victorious matadors emerge shoulder-high only if they receive the highest honors from the President. A "point and click" audioguide takes you through the ring, the stands, and the chapel where matadors pray alone before the fight. There's a good

Plaza de Toros Monumental de Las Ventas, one of Spain's most important bullrings.

explanation of the technicalities and traditions surrounding the *corrida,* and a heavy dose of propaganda about the bull's high quality of life prior to the ring. For a few euros more you can pose for a green screen photograph which produces a remarkably convincing picture of you—in a suit of lights, *muleta* in hand—taking on a bull.

Calle Alcalá, 237. lasventastour.com. *©* **68-773-90-32.** Admission 14.90€ adults, 5.90€ children 5–12, free under 5. Tours daily Oct–May 10am–5:30pm; June–Sept 10am–6:30pm; summer night visits Thurs and Sat 8pm–10:30pm. On bullfight days closes 3 hr. before the show. For bullfight tickets, visit www.madridbullfight.com. Metro: Ventas. Bus: 12,21, 38, 53, 106, 110, or 146.

Especially for Kids

Parque del Retiro (p. 107) is the classic family weekend outing, with boats to row on the small lake, puppet shows, street performers, sandy playgrounds, and lots of green grass for running around. The wide, paved paths are one of the few good places in the city for a family bike ride. You can rent bikes at nearby **Rent and Roll,** Calle Felipe IV 10 (www.rent androllmadrid.com; *©* **91-148-49-67;** from 5€). The nearby art museums all have activities for children, and free or reduced admission, but the **Thyssen-Bornemisza** (p. 89) is probably the most child-friendly, with free apps, audio and multimedia guides for kids, and a range of family tours and activities in English. If your children accompany you on a shopping trip to Salamanca, they can run around and touch the artwork at the outdoor **Museo Arte Publico** (p. 106), one of the few places where that is allowed. From there, it's a short walk to the **Carrusel Serrano Madrid,** Calle Serrano, 47 (2€), a vintage merry-go-round in front of Salamanca's branch of El Corte Inglés department store. Madrid's other popular gathering place, **Plaza Mayor,** is also a good spot for families. Kids will find plenty to amuse them watching living statues posing for change, street entertainers blowing huge bubbles, or caricature artists at work. (Expect to pay 15€–20€ if they persuade you to have one done.) Since the traffic-free plaza is enclosed on all sides, you can keep an eye on your children from a café table. For rooftop views of Madrid, take them up to the observatory at **CentroCentro** (p. 82) or to the rooftop café at the **Circulo de Bellas Artes** (p. 102).

Going a little further afield, **Casa de Campo** (daily 11am–7pm; metro: Batán; bus: 33 or 65), the former royal hunting ground across the river from the Palacio Real, is Madrid's largest green space. It contains the **Parque de Atracciones** amusement park (www.parquedeatracciones.es; *©* **90-234-50-01**), with about 40 rides, and the **Zoo Aquarium de Madrid** (www.zoomadrid.com; *©* **90-234-50-14**). Prices to both vary, with significant discounts if you book online, but expect to spend at least 30€ for adults and 20€ for children at each (kids under 100cm/3 ft. 3 in. go free at the amusement park). A good way to reach the Casa de Campo is by the **Teleférico,** Paseo del Pintor Rosales, s/n (https://telefericomadrid.es;

The Teleférico de Madrid.

℗ **90-234-50-02;** adults 6€ round trip, children 5€, under 4 free). Built in 1969 to connect the fairground with the eastern edge of Parque del Oeste—and now operated by Madrid's municipal transport company EMT—the cable car takes passengers on an 11-minute ride high above the city with great views of the parks, the Río Manzanares, and the Palacio Real. Pleasant during the day, the Casa de Campo can be a seedy place at night.

A more modern, and much less expensive, alternative is the **Madrid Río** park, Puente de Toledo s/n (www.madrid.es; ℗ **91-529-82-10;** free admission; daily 24 hr.; metro: Marqués de Vadillo). A huge recreational zone on the banks of the Manzanares near the **Matadero** (p. 108), it has 17 innovative adventure playgrounds for children, with hammocks, bridges and vines in natural, sustainable materials.

There are also plenty of museums and exhibitions tailored for children. The **Museo Nacional de Ciencias Naturales,** Calle de José Gutiérrez Abascal, 2 (www.mncn.csic.es; ℗ **91-411-13-28;** adults 7€, children 3.50€; Tue–Fri 10am–5pm, weekends 10am–8pm; metro: Nuevas Ministerios) has lots of dinosaur skeletons and fossils. For younger children, the **Casita Museo de Ratón Pérez,** Calle del Arenal, 8 (www.casamuseo ratonperez.es; ℗ **63-429-72-94;** 4€, children under 3 free), tells the story of the mouse who is Spain's equivalent of the tooth fairy, and has a collection of the baby teeth of famous people, including Beatrix Potter and Beethoven. Chamberí's ghost Metro station, **Estación de Chamberí** (p. 104), and the **Museo de Ferrocarril,** Paseo de las Delicias, 61 (www.museodelferrocarril.org; ℗ **91-506-83-42;** weekdays adults 6€, ages 4–12 4€, under 4 free; weekends 3€; metro: Delicias), are great for kids who love trains, and soccer fans young and old may insist on touring Real Madrid's **Santiago Bernabéu stadium** (p. 113).

WHERE TO STAY IN MADRID

The good news for summer vacationers is that Madrid hotels don't consider July and August to be peak season and price their rooms accordingly. If you prefer to visit when it is cooler, rates in January and February are also typically low. Prices are highest, and accommodation hard to come by, around Easter and during the fiesta of San Isidro in mid-May. At other times, even in neighborhoods seen as upscale—Salamanca and the area around Opera, for example—you can find good accommodation to suit almost any budget.

If you are staying in Madrid long enough to make an apartment rental worthwhile, **Homes for Travellers** (www.homesfortravellers.com; ✆ **91-444-27-01**) has a good selection, mostly around Chueca and Malasaña, starting at around 50€ a night. Websites such as **AirBnB.com, Home-Away.com,** and **Flipkey.com** are also good sources of affordable rooms and apartments.

Arts District & Paseos

EXPENSIVE

The Ritz ★★★   Madrid's legendary hotel was, at the time of writing, closed for a top-to-bottom refurbishment, but if you are searching for the epitome of Belle Époque indulgence, keep an eye out for its grand reopening in late 2019. When Alfonso XIII married in 1908, he was dismayed that Madrid lacked a hotel befitting his guests. He wanted something to equal the Ritz in Paris or London, so engaged César Ritz to consult on the design and lend his name. No expense was spared. Charles Mewes, architect of the Paris Ritz, was hired, carpets were hand-crafted at the Real Fábrica de Tapices (p. 90), 20,000 pieces of Limoges china were imported from France. Famous guests have included Prince Rainier and Grace Kelly, who honeymooned here; Frank Sinatra serenaded Ava Garner at its piano—she was reputedly wearing nothing but a fur coat; Salvador Dalí unwittingly invented its famous Dalitini cocktail with his own blood. Over its 100-plus years its brocade and velvet have sometimes become a

FIELD OF dreams

Madrid is soccer mad. While it has two passionately supported clubs, **Atlético Madrid** and **Real Madrid,** it is the latter who usually make the headlines, and almost invariably win the trophies. They have won the Spanish league (La Liga) a record 33 times, and the European Cup, or Champions League, an astonishing 13 times. You'll see their crown-topped logo all over the city: on TV screens in bars, on advertising hoardings, in expensive official sports shops, and in counterfeit versions offered by pavement hawkers. Real Madrid's home is the **Santiago de Bernabéu** stadium, north along the Paseo de la Castellana, a huge concrete cauldron which can hold more than 80,000 fans. You can buy tickets for league matches online from around 45€. Tickets for **El Clásico,** any game between Real Madrid and their archrivals Barcelona, are much harder to come by and can cost more than 300 euros. More practical for most visitors is a tour of the stadium, during which you can walk on the pitch where legends from Ferenc Puskás to Cristiano Ronaldo have performed, and marvel at the groaning trophy cabinets. Tickets cost 25€ for adults and 18€ for children; check the website for tour times. Avenida de Concha Espina, 1. www.realmadrid.com. ✆ **91-398-43-00.** Metro: Santiago Bernabéu. Bus: 14, 27, 40, 43, 120, 126, 147, or 150.

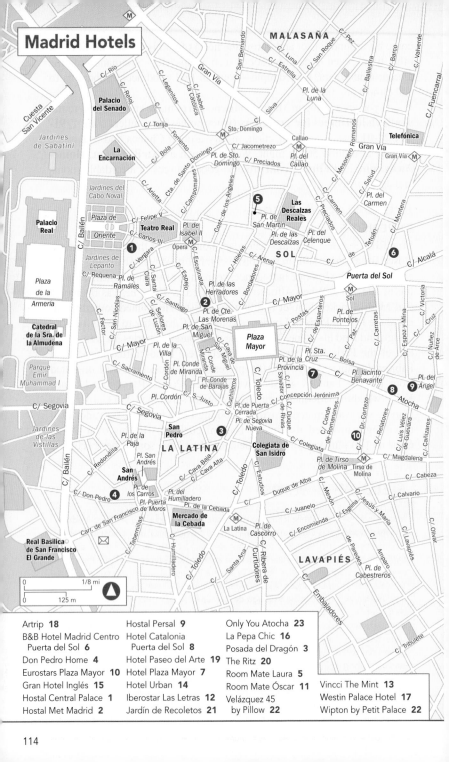

Madrid Hotels

Artrip **18**
B&B Hotel Madrid Centro
  Puerta del Sol **6**
Don Pedro Home **4**
Eurostars Plaza Mayor **10**
Gran Hotel Inglés **15**
Hostal Central Palace **1**
Hostal Met Madrid **2**

Hostal Persal **9**
Hotel Catalonia
  Puerta del Sol **8**
Hotel Paseo del Arte **19**
Hotel Plaza Mayor **7**
Hotel Urban **14**
Iberostar Las Letras **12**
Jardín de Recoletos **21**

Only You Atocha **23**
La Pepa Chic **16**
Posada del Dragón **3**
The Ritz **20**
Room Mate Laura **5**
Room Mate Óscar **11**
Velázquez 45
  by Pillow **22**

Vincci The Mint **13**
Westin Palace Hotel **17**
Wipton by Petit Palace **22**

114

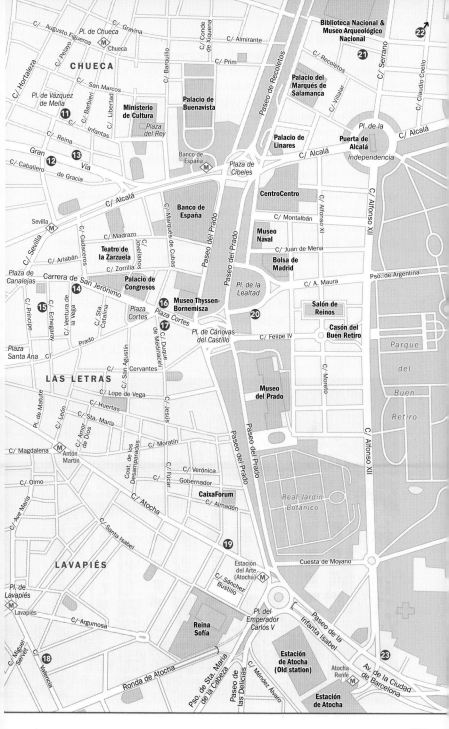

little frayed, and it has changed hands many times, but its latest incarnation promises something special: New owners Mandarin Oriental are spending more than $120 million on the renovation, which will include restoring the original glass dome and creating a 2,000-square-foot royal suite. In truth, few will have the opportunity to stay here, but why not plan to go for afternoon tea? As the Spanish *chanteuse* Lilian de Celis sang: "If I live to be a hundred and six, I'll never forget my afternoons at the Ritz."

Plaza de la Lealtad, 5. www.mandarinoriental.com. ℂ **91-701-67-67.** Rates not yet set at press time. Metro: Banco de España. **Amenities:** Restaurants; bars; concierge; room service; wellness center; terrace; free Wi-Fi.

Westin Palace Hotel ★★ Standing directly opposite the Ritz since it opened in 1912, the Palace has always lived in the shadow of its illustrious neighbor. (You can't help feeling it's enjoyed having the place to itself during the Ritz's refurbishment.) The Palace is, by any yardstick, an extremely grand hotel. It was also commissioned and opened by Alfonso XIII, it was Madrid's building of the year in 1912, and more recently, it got its multi-million-dollar restoration done before the Ritz. Its grandeur is intact, yet a number of 21st-century touches have been added, such as a sushi bar and smooth, taupe-tinted bedrooms. The Palace has also had its fair share of famous guests and scandalous goings-on, all the more so because it never turned away actors and performers, as the Ritz once did.

The Palace Hotel, now operated by Westin, is one of Madrid's grandest luxury hotels.

Hemingway, Orson Welles, and Picasso were all regulars; behind glass, you can see a letter containing a poem by Lorca and a sketch by Dalí in which they seek to borrow money for their impecunious friend, the film director Luis Buñuel. Even if you don't plan to stay here, aim to take a coffee or Sunday brunch (p. 129) in the magnificent stained-glass rotunda.

Plaza de las Cortes, 7. www.marriott.com. ✆ **91-360-80-00.** 470 units. 250€–500€ double; 550€–1,000€ jr. suite. Metro: Banco de España. **Amenities:** Restaurants; bars; concierge; room service; spa and fitness center; terrace; free Wi-Fi.

MODERATE

Only You Atocha ★★   Gloriously eccentric, this hotel could hardly be further away in style from the *grande dames* of the Ritz and the Palace. Set in an unremarkable 19th-century block close to Atocha station, inside it feels like a New York vintage furniture warehouse. The aesthetic is mid-century mishmash: unmatched Danish armchairs, old boxing posters, industrial lighting, a catalogue's worth of different floor tiles. A hatch serving freshly baked pastries is cut from a shipping container. It's the work of the Barcelona-based designer Lázaro Rosa Violán: extremely hip, but great fun at the same time. The guest rooms are cool and calm by comparison, but the urban theme continues: subway-tiled bathrooms with institutional sinks, wooden floors. It's the perfect base for an artsy visit to the Reina Sofía, and there's in-house entertainment, too: cocktails, jazz, and good food, as crazily mixed up as the décor.

Paseo de la Infanta Isabel, 13. www.onlyyouhotels.com. ✆ **91-005-27-46.** 204 units. 130€–250€ double; 195€–300€ jr. suite. Metro: Atocha. **Amenities:** Restaurant; bar; concierge; room service; fitness center; terrace; free Wi-Fi.

Hotel Paseo del Arte ★   This large modern hotel with a business focus is handily located next to Atocha station, across the way from the Reina Sofía museum, 5 minutes from the Prado. Because it hosts many business groups, everything is up for negotiation: Rates rocket when it has a conference and drop through the floor when it doesn't. If you can get them to throw in the excellent buffet breakfast (otherwise a pricey 17.50€ per person), take the deal. Rooms are modestly sized, and functional rather than charming, but you might be able to wangle an upgrade to a more luxurious executive room with private terrace.

Calle Atocha, 123. www.hotelpaseodelartemadrid.com. ✆ **91-298-48-00.** 260 units. 70€–140€ double; 140€–220€ executive room. **Amenities:** Restaurant; bar; concierge; business center; room service; exercise room; spa; free Wi-Fi. Metro: Atocha.

INEXPENSIVE

La Pepa Chic ★   This quirky bed-and-breakfast just around the corner from the Thyssen-Bornemisza museum offers the opportunity to stay right in the heart of the Arts district at knock-down rates. Its rooms are minimalist white with artful splashes of red. Identical pairs of strappy flamenco shoes are mounted like pictures on the wall. Everything is clean, bright, and functional: The beds have crisp cotton sheets, and the white-tiled bathrooms have power showers. Some of the rooms are on the small side, so you might want to ask for a larger one with a view, in the knowledge it will be just as good as the view from the Palace hotel across the street. A simple continental breakfast is included and served in the informal shared space, where free coffee is available all day. Staff are friendly and professional and seem determined to make your stay a good one. If you plan to stay in Madrid for 5 days or more, even greater savings are available.

Plaza de las Cortes, 4. www.lapepa-bnb.com. © **64-847-47-42.** 14 units. 60€–80€ double. Rates include breakfast. Metro: Banco de España. **Amenities:** Free Wi-Fi.

Puerta del Sol & Las Letras
EXPENSIVE

Gran Hotel Inglés ★★★   One of Madrid's oldest hotels, dating back to the 1880s, this classic establishment has just emerged from a total refit which transformed it into one of the city's most stylish boutique hotels. Although the name might make you imagine lawns and fountains, it is set down a narrow Las Letras street, directly opposite the lovely old La Venencia sherry bar (p. 134). But there is nothing dusty and decaying about the Gran Hotel. The sleek Art Deco design is spectacular. The high-ceilinged lobby and chandeliers have the air of a 1920s club—more American than English—with leather stools around an island cocktail bar. Everything is tasteful, solid, understated; service is spot-on. The sound-proofed rooms are a revelation too. Painted all white, they have subtle design flourishes—in some the designer has taken lines of molding and continued them across the ceiling, in others the low attic ceilings resemble the angles of a stealth aircraft. Some rooms have balcony views and free-standing baths, and the beds have Egyptian cotton sheets. The in-house restaurant **Lobo8** continues the sophisticated theme, with an impressively presented tasting menu, good value at 55€, including wine.

Calle de Echegaray, 8. www.granhotelingles.com. © **91-360-00-01.** 48 units. 250€–380€ double, 500€–800€ suite. Metro: Sevilla. **Amenities:** Restaurant; bar; concierge; room service; spa and fitness center; terrace; free Wi-Fi.

Hotel Urban ★★   Situated close to Spain's parliament (Palacio de las Cortes) and convenient for the Prado, the Urban is sophisticated, architectural, and luxurious. It occupies a contemporary building with a soaring central atrium. The style is Art Deco, punctuated by exquisite items of primitive and Oriental sculpture. Large carvings of Papua New Guinean tribespeople loom over reception; there's even a little museum showing the private collection of Jordi Clos, who runs the Derby Hotels group. The spacious rooms have a luxury liner feel, with dark woods, brushed metal, and padded leather upholstery; the suites have a lighter, upper-deck air, and there's a small rooftop pool and terrace. The **Cebo** restaurant, run by head chef Aurelio Morales, is one of Madrid's finest, offering a 17-course tasting menu—a gastronomic tour of every Spanish region.

Carrera de San Jerónimo, 34. www.derbyhotels.com. ✆ **91-787-77-70.** 96 units. 165€–285€ double; 275€–375€ jr. suite. Metro: Sevilla. **Amenities:** Restaurant; bar; concierge; room service; fitness room; outdoor pool, rooftop terrace; free Wi-Fi.

MODERATE

Hotel Catalonia Puerta del Sol ★★   An oasis in the heart of the city, this mid-sized hotel occupies a stately 18th-century building with a cool stone courtyard, a welcome surprise after a hot day's walking. With a high glass roof and air-conditioning, it's so serene that many guests choose to hang out there in the afternoon, encouraged no doubt by the free tapas served between 5 and 7pm. The modestly sized rooms are soundly appointed with new hardwood floors, marble bathrooms, and a soothing autumnal color scheme. Most have large double-glazed windows opening onto the courtyard or Calle Atocha, and outside noise is largely kept at bay. The English-speaking staff are particularly friendly and welcoming, and if you book directly on the hotel's web-site you'll be offered a free glass of cava.

Calle Atocha, 23. www.hoteles-catalonia.com. ✆ **91-369-71-71.** 63 units. 100€–200€ double. Metro: Sol or Tirso de Molina. **Amenities:** Restaurant; bar; cafe; room service; rooftop terrace; outdoor Jacuzzi; free Wi-Fi.

INEXPENSIVE

B&B Hotel Madrid Centro Puerta del Sol ★   Twenty-five years ago an establishment in Puerta de Sol with a name like this would have been a pretty seedy affair. Today, the strung-out name is presumably for the purposes of search engine optimization. This branch of the innovative French B&B chain reflects perfectly what you might call the Apple-ization of Puerta del Sol. Its precision-designed rooms have beds which float on a pool of colored light, bathrooms are a matte glass box, hallway lights sleep to save energy. Free drinks and snacks are available 24 hours a day at what looks just like a tech company microkitchen. The Wi-Fi is, naturally, superfast. The only drawback is that the commotion outside is the same as it ever was, so bring noise-cancelling headphones. And Google the entrance, it's tricky to find.

Calle Montera, 10-12. www.hotel-bb.es. ✆ **91-489-05-91.** 74 units. 75€–150€ double. Metro: Sol. **Amenities:** Vending machine, 24-hr. reception, free Wi-Fi.

Hostal Persal ★   A budget hotel rather than a hostel, this cheap and cheerful place couldn't be better located for the bar-hopping nightlife, but if you are looking for a quiet break this is probably not for you. The Persal occupies a grand, flat-fronted block on a pedestrianized square just off Plaza Santa Ana. You can't miss it—it's painted bright blue. Inside, the mood in the communal areas is student shabby chic: worn leather armchairs and old tomes in the *biblioteca,* and distressed mirrors. The paint is bright and upbeat, and the buffet breakfast at shared kitchen tables is big on fresh fruit. The guest and bathrooms are small and basically furnished, but they're clean, comfortable, and well-serviced, and—let's face it—you probably won't be spending a lot of time there.

Plaza del Angel, 12. www.hostalpersal.com. © **91-369-46-43.** www.hostalpersal.com. 80 units. 50€–100 double. Metro: Sol. **Amenities:** Restaurant; bar; cafe; concierge; free luggage storage; free Wi-Fi.

Hostal Met Madrid ★   There are still plenty of noisy, fleabag *pensiones* in and around Puerta de Sol. Don't go there. This charming guest house shows how you can stay just a few yards from Kilometer Zero for as little as 50€ and get quiet comfort and cleanliness. Set in a little passage just off the Calle Mayor, with a tiny sign on the door, it offers marble-paneled rooms that aren't large, but they are bright, air-conditioned, and spotless. The complimentary water in the fridge always tastes sweeter than the kind you pay for. The staff, too, are the opposite of the tourist trap cliché: welcoming and flexible, happy to offer advice on good places to eat and drink nearby. You are just a hop and a skip away from the San Miguel gourmet market.

Costanilla de Santiago, 2. www.metmadrid.com. © **91-861-69-09.** 9 units. 50€–125€ double. Metro: Opera or Sol. **Amenities:** Free Wi-Fi.

Plaza Mayor, La Latina & Lavapiés
MODERATE

Artrip ★★   There's a framed Spanish newspaper article on the wall at the Artrip headlined: "At last Lavapiés has its boutique hotel." They're right to be proud. This small hotel in Madrid's up-and-coming neighborhood is a joy, and what really stands out is the warmth of the welcome and sense of local pride. The tall, slim townhouse has been smartly renovated to make the most of the limited space. The white-painted rooms have simple, clean lines, good-quality bathroom fittings, and comfortable beds. The exposed beams above your bed on the top floor are perhaps a little low for comfort, but they do add character. There's no restaurant, but the do-it-yourself breakfast is excellent value, and coffee is free all day. As you graze, check out the work by local artists exhibited in the lobby. Because Lavapiés is at the bottom of one of Madrid's few hills, it can feel a little removed from the main sights, but the Metro to whisk you back up the hill is just a few steps away. Or just stay put in the *barrio* everyone is talking about.

Calle de Valencia, 11. www.artriphotel.com/en. © **91-539-32-82.** 17 units. 100€–200€ double. Metro: Lavapiés. **Amenities:** Free Wi-Fi.

Don Pedro Home ★★   In addition to its bars and taverns, La Latina has plenty of historic residential buildings. Why not stay in one? This 18th-century stone-built palace has a studded front door so large you're likely to walk past thinking it belongs to some august institution. Inside, the building has been converted into four designer apartments grouped around a central patio. It's a lovely mix of old and new: exposed stone walls and ancient beams combined with open-plan concrete and girders. The walls are decorated with contemporary art and some well-chosen antique knickknacks. The apartments come in different sizes, sleeping between two and eight people (at a push)—great value for families or groups of friends. Each has a small kitchen and dining space, and a basic breakfast is provided by the host, who will arrange to meet you with the keys. Perhaps best of all is the location, in a sleepy street just 2 minutes' walk from the overflowing bars of Cava Baja.

Calle Don Pedro, 8. www.donpedrohome.com. ✆ **67-362-69-38.** 4 units. Double 100€ to 200€, 3-bedroom apartment 150€-300€. Metro: La Latina. **Amenities:** Free Wi-Fi.

Eurostars Plaza Mayor ★★　Wherever you go in Spain, you're likely to find a Eurostars hotel in a recently renovated building close to the city center. The rates—especially last-minute—are often unbelievably good. Yes, it's a chain, and to international ears the name doesn't exactly ring with romance, but their hotels are invariably high-quality, comfortable, and clean. Everything just works. There are half a dozen Eurostars hotels in Madrid—and close to a hundred across Spain—none more centrally situated than this one, in a renovated 1930s sports arena a short stroll from Plaza Mayor. Its rooms are fitted out with cool, quality materials and big, comfortable beds. A business-style buffet breakfast is served on the seventh floor, which has an outdoor terrace with rooftop views across the city.

Calle Doctor Cortezo, 10. www.eurostarshotels.com. ✆ **91-330-86-60.** 96 units. 60€–175€ double. Metro: Tirso de Molina. **Amenities:** Café; bar; terrace; room service; business center; free Wi-Fi.

Posada del Dragón ★★　Cava Baja is many people's favorite Madrid street, bursting with bar and restaurant life, but you need to be sure you want to stay here. If you are, Posada del Dragón is a great choice. There's been a coaching inn here for 150 years, but today the rooms of this boutique hotel and bar are bright and designer-ish, with a Moorish theme. The accommodation is set around a much more traditional courtyard, and there's a busy restaurant and tapas bar spilling onto the street out front. Make sure you get an upstairs room, either overlooking the street (great views but noisier) or the courtyard (quieter but smaller). Avoid the small ground-floor bedroom right beside the restaurant. Good food choices are everywhere on Cava Baja, but the breakfast and tapas here at the **La Antoñita** restaurant are worth staying in for, offering all the classics—*ibérico* charcuterie, Cadiz-style shrimp fritters, and creamy croquettes).

Cava Baja, 14. www.posadadeldragon.com. ✆ **91-119-14-24.** 27 units. 65€–200€ double. Metro: La Latina. **Amenities:** Restaurant; bar; concierge; bike rentals; free Wi-Fi.

INEXPENSIVE

Hotel Plaza Mayor ★   Great value given its prime location, this curious hotel was carved out of a 200-year-old building adjoining the church of Santa Cruz in 1997. The great mass of stone from that building keeps the interior cool in summer and warm in winter. The downside is that otherwise charming architectural features rather get in the way, with small, irregularly shaped rooms, low ceiling beams, and heavy iron columns in unexpected places. The décor is bright and a little incongruous; the rooms and bathrooms are solid and well-kept. There's one penthouse suite, the Suite de Palomar, which costs considerably more than the standard doubles, but has an outdoor patio with terrific views across the tiled roofs of La Latina.

Calle Atocha, 2. www.h-plazamayor.com. ℰ **91-360-06-06.** 34 units. 55€–85€ double; 100€–125€ suite. Metro: Sol or Tirso de Molina. **Amenities:** Cafeteria; free Wi-Fi.

Opera & Palacio Real

MODERATE

Hostal Central Palace ★★   If you've come to glory in the grandeur of the Palacio Real and its environs, this elegant guesthouse is the place to be. Exclusively located on the Plaza de Oriente directly opposite the palace, it offers a range of stately options, from singles to suites. All are decorated in a style that would make the Bourbons feel at home, but it's not stuffy or faded. The rooms have been recently renovated to a high standard, with white gold *faux* antique furniture, flocked wallpaper, polished floorboards, and more than a hint of irony. Everything is light and airy; the spotless bathrooms are reassuringly 21st-century. The most expensive rooms have privileged views of the royal palace and the mountains beyond, worth the extra outlay if you can get one. Breakfast is served at the Café de Oriente on the crescent below.

Plaza de Oriente, 2. www.centralpalacemadrid.com. ℰ **91-198-32-68.** 21 units 60€–170€ double. Metro: Opera. **Amenities:** 24-hr. reception; free Wi-Fi.

Room Mate Laura ★   The concept at Room Mate hotels is that each is designed around the personality of an imaginary friend who will introduce you to the city (see also Room Mate Óscar; p. 123). Laura is billed as "temperamental, sexy and very creative." Confusingly, the female character portrayed in every room is not Laura, but the rather less sexy Juana of Austria, who founded the nearby Convent of the Barefoot Royals (p. 97) in 1559. Describing your accommodation as temperamental seems to invite trouble, and the vertiginous stairs and open railings in the duplex rooms will not suit everyone, but otherwise Tomás Alía's design is a quirky delight. The small rooms are cleverly and colorfully arranged, with sparse furnishings and glass-box showers stocked with branded toiletries. For an extra fee you can add cooking facilities, in case you want to get creative in the kitchenette. If not, breakfast runs until noon.

Travesia de Trujillos, 3. laura.room-matehotels.com. ℰ **91-217-92-87.** 37 units. 75€–200€ double; 95€–220€ duplex. Metro: Opera or Santo Domingo. **Amenities:** Concierge; cooking facilities; free Wi-Fi.

Gran Vía, Chueca & Malasaña

MODERATE

Iberostar Las Letras ★★   From the moment you step through the revolving door of this grand corner block at the lower end of Gran Vía you know you're in good hands. The English-speaking staff are particularly welcoming and helpful. Behind the 1915 façade, the design is simple, stylish, and literary: bright blocks of color on which quotations from famous Spanish and international writers have been printed. The theme continues in the high-ceilinged, parquet-floored rooms, which are airy and surprisingly quiet given the busy road below. Some have tiny wrought-iron balconies; deluxe rooms have their own terrace and jacuzzi. For the best views, head to the compact rooftop pool and cocktail bar—a great place to watch the sunset before dinner. **Gran Clavel,** the recently retroed restaurant (now with obligatory vermouth bar), serves Madrilenean classics, although you can get more authentic versions in Chueca just across the road. It is worth staying in for the fabulous brunch.

Calle Gran Via, 11. www.hoteldelasletras.com. ℭ **91-523-79-80.** 109 units. 110€–220€ double. Metro: Banco de España. **Amenities:** Restaurant; bar; concierge; room service; fitness center; pool and rooftop terrace; free Wi-Fi.

Room Mate Óscar ★★   Set in the gay district of Chueca, this hotel's imaginary friend is Óscar (see Room Mate Laura; p. 122), who describes himself as "cosmopolitan, night owl, modern, and very friendly." The thumping beats of the colored-glass lobby give way to spotless, spacious

The casual Room Mate Óscar hotel is designed with a personality that fits the Chueca district and its nightlife.

bedrooms, futuristically decked out in lime, orange, and turquoise by designer Tomás Alía. The inside-outside roof terrace is one of Madrid's most sought-out spots for cocktails, but it gets crowded and the service can suffer. Go early to secure a spot. Soundproofing throughout is excellent—a good thing, because Oscar is a party animal, and so are many of his guests. You'll see them coming down for breakfast at 11:45am; luckily, the buffet is set until noon.

Plaza de Pedro Zerolo, 12. oscar.room-matehotels.com. ✆ **91-701-11-73.** 75 units. 80€–200€ double. Metro: Gran Vía or Chueca. **Amenities:** Concierge; roof terrace; free Wi-Fi.

Vincci The Mint ★★   Styled by Barcelona designer Jaime Beriestain, The Mint refers to the color scheme throughout, a range of pale greens and the ever-present teal. The hotel occupies a curlicued former insurance company building in a prime spot at the bottom of Gran Vía, and the understated design incorporates many original features. The atmosphere is quirkier, New York-ier. The first thing that strikes you is that there's no separate reception; you pick up your keys from the bar, along with a welcome drink. The guestrooms are especially clean, the only drawback being that those facing the traffic can get noisy. A gastrobar on the ground floor offers bespoke breakfast options, and in summer a food truck serves fish and chips on the roof terrace. It's painted mint green, of course.

Calle Gran Via, 10. www.vinccithemint.com. ✆ **91-203-06-50.** 88 units 125€–250€ double. Metro: Banco de España. **Amenities:** Gastrobar; room service; roof terrace; free Wi-Fi.

Salamanca, Retiro & Chamberí
EXPENSIVE

Wipton by Petit Palace ★★★   Set in an extensively refurbished building in Madrid's poshest neighborhood, and open only since 2018, the Wipton hums with well-bred luxury and efficiency. The color scheme is straight out of a high-end catalogue—cornflower blue, pastel grays, and moleskin—with hints of vintage aviation. The mid-sized rooms are the last word in comfort: vast beds, dark paneling, and slightly distressed beams. Junior suites have ultra-modern freestanding baths. The service and level of pampering is deluxe: free bike rentals and portable Wi-Fi hotspots, complimentary early evening wine. Children and pets are welcomed. Given the level of comfort and the distinguished address, prices are surprisingly reasonable. Breakfast is excellent, but the menu at the adjoining restaurant, **The Captain,** is less successful: club sandwich–style international fare with a lot of fries. Overall though, the Wipton offers one of Madrid's most comfortable nights—a great place to de-stress on a business trip or for a blow-out family shopping treat.

Calle de Jorge Juan, 17. www.iconwipton.com. ✆ **91-800-49-94.** 61 units. 145€–200€ double. Metro: Velázquez. **Amenities:** Restaurant; bar; bikes; concierge; room service; free Wi-Fi, iPads, and Mi-Fi.

MODERATE

Jardín de Recoletos ★   This contemporary apartment-hotel is set in leafy Recoletos, a short walk from the Parque del Retiro and the boutique shopping of Salamanca. A new build dating from 1999, and recently refurbished, it has a vast marble lobby and paneled ceilings that feel strangely dated, a little bit last-century. But its rooms are spacious and comfortable—and have a kitchenette adequate for preparing a late-night snack. Unless you are in one of the rooms with a private terrace, you shouldn't miss out on the buffet breakfast in the lovely tropical garden.

Calle Gil de Santivañes, 6. www.vphoteles.com. ✆ **91-781-16-40.** 43 units. 135€–180€ double. Parking 23€. Metro: Serrano or Recoletos. **Amenities:** Restaurant; room service; terrace; free Wi-Fi.

INEXPENSIVE

Velázquez 45 by Pillow ★   Set in the most exclusive part of town, between Salamanca's Velázquez and Serrano Metro stations, this 5th-floor guesthouse offers access to the highlife on a budget. Following a recent total refurbishment and rebrand, the decor is tastefully modern with calming colors, hardwood floors, and mid-century furniture. The marble-topped bedside tables have charging points and a master switch for the lights. The Wi-Fi and the bathrooms are solid. The reception area, which has a number of squishy leather sofas, doubles as a breakfast buffet and a lounge for the rest of the day. The rooms are small, but clean and air-conditioned, and most importantly, they are in Salamanca.

Calle de Velázquez, 45. ✆ **91-435-07-60.** 58 units. 80€–160€ double. Metro: Velázquez or Serrano. **Amenities:** 24-hr. reception; free Wi-Fi.

Precioso Estudio en Chamberí ★★   If you plan to go #ponzan-ing—tapas hopping on fashionable Calle Ponzano (p. 135)—this privately rented studio apartment in Chamberí makes an ideal base. Quirkily decorated with exposed brick walls and vintage circus posters, it has plenty of space, with a comfortable living room, an open, split-level double bedroom, and a well-equipped kitchen, including a washing machine. An excellent breakfast is included, and the hospitality of the hosts has sky-high ratings online.

Available on Booking.com, search for title. 1 unit. 75€–100€ split-level apartment. **Amenities:** Free Wi-Fi.

WHERE TO EAT IN MADRID

There are literally thousands of places to dine in Madrid, and when you're first confronted with the choices, it can be overwhelming. Madrid has many long-standing gastronomic traditions, the most developed tapas scene in the world, and access to everything the country has to offer. If you like regional Spanish food, you'll find plenty of examples here. If you like seafood, you're in good company—fresh fish and shellfish are transported from the coast daily. In recent years, young superstar chefs, some

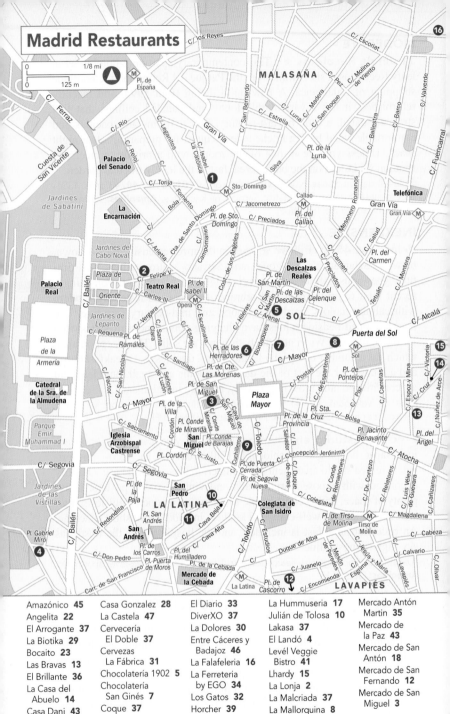

Madrid Restaurants

C/ los Reyes

0   1/8 mi
0   125 m

Pl. de España

MALASAÑA

C/ Ferraz

Cuesta de San Vicente

Jardines de Sabatini

Palacio del Senado

La Encarnación

Palacio Real

Plaza de la Armería

Catedral de la Sra. de la Almudena

Parque Emir Muhammad I

C/ Segovia

Jardines de las Vistillas

Pl. Gabriel Miró

Gran Vía

C/ Torija

Sto. Domingo

Pl. de Sto. Domingo

Jardines del Cabo Noval

Plaza de Oriente

Teatro Real

Ópera

Jardines de Lepanto

Pl. de Ramales

Pl. de las Herraderos

Pl. de Cte. Las Morenas

Pl. de San Miguel

Pl. de la Villa

Pl. Conde de Miranda

San Miguel

Iglesia Arzobispal Castrense

San Pedro

Pl. de la Paja

LA LATINA

Pl. San Andrés

San Andrés

Pl. de los Carros

Pl. del Humilladero

Pl. Puerta de Moros

Mercado de la Cebada

La Latina

Las Descalzas Reales

Pl. de San Martín

Pl. de las Descalzas

Pl. del Celenque

SOL

Puerta del Sol

Sol

Pl. de Pontejos

Pl. Sta. Cruz

Pl. Jacinto Benavente

Telefónica

Gran Vía

Pl. del Carmen

C/ Alcalá

Pl. del Ángel

C/ Atocha

Colegiata de San Isidro

Pl. de Tirso de Molina

Tirso de Molina

LAVAPIÉS

Pl. de Cascorro

Callao

Pl. del Callao

Pl. de la Luna

Amazónico **45**	Casa Gonzalez **28**	El Diario **33**	La Hummuseria **17**	Mercado Antón Martín **35**
Angelita **22**	La Castela **47**	DiverXO **37**	Julián de Tolosa **10**	Mercado de la Paz **43**
El Arrogante **37**	Cervecería El Doble **37**	La Dolores **30**	Lakasa **37**	Mercado de San Antón **18**
La Biotika **29**	Cervezas La Fábrica **31**	Entre Cáceres y Badajoz **46**	El Landó **4**	
Bocaito **23**	Chocolatería 1902 **5**	La Falafeleria **16**	Levél Veggie Bistro **41**	Mercado de San Fernando **12**
Las Bravas **13**	Chocolatería San Ginés **7**	La Ferreteria by EGO **34**	Lhardy **15**	Mercado de San Miguel **3**
El Brillante **36**	Coque **37**	Los Gatos **32**	La Lonja **2**	
La Casa del Abuelo **14**		Horcher **39**	La Malcriada **37**	
Casa Dani **43**			La Mallorquina **8**	

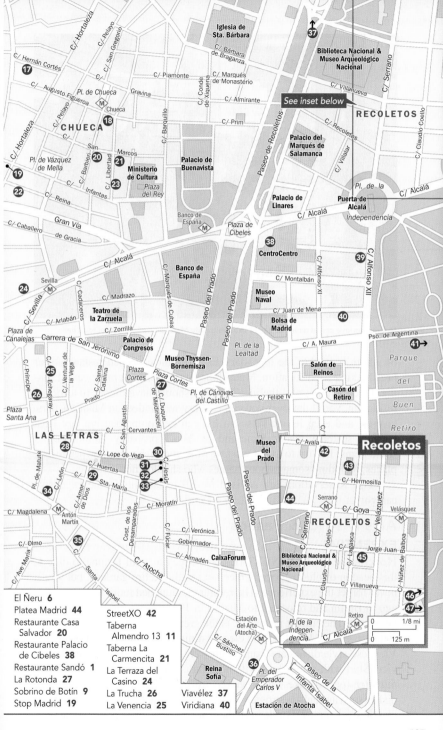

Iglesia de Sta. Bárbara

C/ Hortaleza
C/ Pelayo
C/ San Gregorio
C/ Bárbara de Braganza
Biblioteca Nacional & Museo Arqueológico Nacional

37

C/ Serrano

C/ Hernán Cortés **17**

C/ Augusto Figueroa
Pl. de Chueca
C/ Piamonte
C/ Marqués de Monasterio
C/ Villanueva

Gravina

RECOLETOS

C/ Conde de Xiquena
C/ Almirante

See inset below

C/ Hortaleza

M Chueca

CHUECA

18

C/ Prim

Palacio del Marqués de Salamanca

C/ Recoletos

C/ Claudio Coello

C/ Barquillo

C/ San Marcos

C/ Libertad

Pl. de Vázquez de Mella

20 **21**

23

Ministerio de Cultura

Palacio de Buenavista

Paseo de Recoletos

C/ Villar

C/ Barbieri

22

19

C/ Reina

Plaza del Rey

C/ Infantas

Palacio de Linares

Puerta de Alcalá

Pl. de la

C/ Alcalá

Gran Vía

de Gracia

Banco de España **M**

Plaza de Cibeles

C/ Alcalá

Independencia

C/ Caballero

C/ Alcalá

38

CentroCentro

39

C/ Alfonso XII

Sevilla **M**

24

C/ Sevilla

C/ Cadetos

Banco de España

C/ Marqués de Cubas

C/ Montalbán

C/ Madrazo

Museo Naval

C/ Arlabán

Teatro de la Zarzuela

Paseo del Prado

C/ Juan de Mena

Plaza de Canalejas

Carrera de San Jerónimo

C/ Zorrilla

Palacio de Congresos

Bolsa de Madrid

40

Pso. de Argentina

41→

C/ A. Maura

C/ Príncipe

25

26

Prado

C/ Ventura de la Vega

C/ Santa Catalina

Plaza Cortes

Plaza Cortes

Museo Thyssen-Bornemisza

27

Pl. de Cánovas del Castillo

Pl. de la Lealtad

Salón de Reinos

Parque

del

Buen

C/ Felipe IV

Casón del Retiro

Plaza Santa Ana

C/ San Agustín

C/ Cervantes

Retiro

LAS LETRAS

28

C/ Lope de Vega

C/ Duque de Medinaceli

Museo del Prado

Recoletos

C/ Ayala

42

C/ Huertas

C/ Jesús

30

31

32

33

43

C/ Hermosilla

C/ Matute

C/ León

29

Sta. María

44

Serrano **M**

C/ Goya

Velázquez

M

34

C/ Amor de Dios

C/ Moratín

RECOLETOS

C/ Magdalena

M Antón Martín

Cost. de los Desamparados

C/ Verónica

C/ Serrano

C/ Coello

C/ Lagasca

Jorge Juan

C/ Núñez de Balboa

C/ Olmo

35

C/ Fúcar

Gobernador

C/ Atocha

C/ Almadén

CaixaForum

Biblioteca Nacional & Museo Arqueológico Nacional

45

C/ Ave María

C/ Claudio

C/ Villanueva

Santa Isabel

46→

47→

Retiro **M**

Pl. de la Independencia

C/ Alcalá

0   1/8 mi

0   125 m

Estación del Arte (Atocha) **M**

C/ Sánchez Bustillo

Reina Sofía

36

Pl. del Emperador Carlos V

Estación de Atocha

Paseo de la Infanta Isabel

Madrileños love casual dining at places like the trendy Mercado de San Miguel food hall.

of whom trained at the legendary El Bulli, have opened restaurants of breathtaking sophistication. Madrid, however, excels at more casual dining. Once you get past the idea that you should have dinner in a formal restaurant, you'll discover you can eat very well indeed in Madrid's bars, taverns, and even its markets. No list can be comprehensive, not least because so many places come and go. You'll probably stumble across some gems. But try to avoid wasting time and money on downright bad places, including some famous names who should know better.

Tip: Reservations are advised for all restaurants in the expensive category.

Arts District & Paseos

EXPENSIVE

Horcher ★★ CONTINENTAL   You'll pay a small fortune to dine at this beacon of old-fashioned grace next to the Retiro gardens, but you'll never forget the experience. The restaurant launched more than a century ago in Berlin and relocated to Madrid in 1943 after a run-in with Joseph Goebbels. The current proprietor is the great grandson of the restaurant's founder, Gustav Horcher. The elegant dining room is a period piece; the Viennese-style dishes are from another era, and so is the impeccable service. Start with smoked eel with horseradish or poached egg and *Kartoffelpuffer* (potato cakes) with shaved truffle, before moving on to game dishes such as venison stroganoff and partridge cooked with grapes, or the classic steak tartare. For dessert, there are crepes flamed in brandy at your table, or the extraordinary stacked *Baumkuchen* (cake tree). Men must wear a jacket; women get a cushion to rest their feet.

Calle Alfonso XII, 6. www.restaurantehorcher.com. ✆ **91-522-07-31.** Entrees 35€–59€. Mon–Fri 1:30–4pm and 8:30pm–midnight; Sat 8:30pm–midnight. Metro: Retiro.

Restaurante Palacio de Cibeles ★★ SPANISH   Adolfo Muñoz, the enterprising chef who brought Toledan cooking out of the dark ages, opened this restaurant on the sixth floor of CentroCentro in 2012. Its elegant dining room, with views over the city, serves Muñoz's creative takes on La Manchan classics, such as partridge two ways (stewed in *tempranillo* wine and roasted with sherry sauce) or roast leg of lamb with mountain herbs and *pisto Manchego*—roasted ratatouille vegetables seasoned with sherry vinegar. The regularly changing market fish dishes are also excellent. When the weather's fine, there's a bar menu on the cocktail terrace, with good, but expensive, sharing plates. The croquettes or *pisto Manchego* are the best value. The Colección Cibeles café on the 2nd floor is less special.

Plaza de Cibeles, 1. www.adolfo-palaciodecibeles.com. ✆ **91-523-14-54.** Entrees 25€–33€; terrace sharing plates 12€–36€. Daily 1–4pm; Mon–Sat 10pm–midnight. Metro: Banco de España.

La Rotonda ★★ SPANISH   The lounge under the stained-glass cupola at the Palace Hotel (p. 116) is one of the most spectacular settings in Madrid. You could settle for coffee and cakes here, but if style is a priority and money not an object, the Sunday brunch, accompanied by an operatic performance, is a special experience. The buffet-style brunch, served from 1:30pm each Sunday, is beautifully presented: shellfish, charcuterie, salads, and hot meat and fish dishes, including paella. Attentive waiters circulate to refill your coffee cup or wine glass. If there is a slight sense of being in a high-end international hotel that doesn't feel particularly Spanish, gaze up at the exquisite glass dome, listen to the accomplished performers, and imagine you're back in the Palace Hotel's 1920s heyday. Reservations required.

At Palace Hotel, Plaza de las Cortes, 7. www.larotondapalace.com/en. ✆ **91-360-76-67.** Brunch 85€. Sun 1:30–3:30pm. Metro: Banco de España.

Viridiana ★★ SPANISH   If you like food with wit and panache, you'll love the flamboyant celebrity chef Abraham García. Self-taught, he came to Madrid as a teenager to look for work in its grand restaurants and met the film director Luis Buñuel, after whose 1961 film the restaurant is named. The look is bistro-casual, branded with García's trademark trilby hat; the food is imaginative and delicious. The menu draws on traditional Spanish ingredients (for which García personally prowls the markets), married with international flavors. His curried lentils are served with red shrimp and *sobresada,* a soft chorizo sausage. The grilled pork loin is paired with gnocchi, plums, and smoky chipotle. Green tea panna cotta with papaya rounds things off. A multi-course tasting menu changes according to the market but will almost certainly include García's sublime take on gazpacho. The gregarious chef also makes regular rounds of the tables.

Calle Juan de Mena, 14. www.restauranteviridiana.com. ℗ **91-531-10-39.** Entrees 25€–39€, tasting menu 100€ including wine. Mon–Sat 1:30–4pm and 8:30pm–midnight. Closed Easter week. Metro: Banco de España.

INEXPENSIVE

El Brillante ★ SPANISH   A far cry from the establishments listed above, this Madrid institution with entrances opposite the Reina Sofía and Atocha station is always busy and always scruffy. Its waiters are gruff at best. But it's brilliant. The 4-inch finger-roll *bocadillos* make a good snack, while the 10-inch *bocatas* are lunch. There is a wide range of generous *raciones,* but El Brillante is best known for its *bocadillo de calamares* (fried squid rolls). There's a certain raffish style to standing at the long, stainless-steel bar, letting your napkins float to the floor like everyone else. Or, if you can get an afternoon table outside facing the Reina Sofía, order a sandwich and a beer—served in large, tall glasses—and watch Spanish free runners attempting to scale its steps. Late at night, the output switches to chocolate and churros for revelers on their way home. Given all that, the stainless-steel bathrooms are surprisingly, well, stainless.

Plaza del Emperador Carlos V, 8. www.barelbrillante.es. ℗ **91-528-69-66.** Sandwiches 3€–9€. Daily 7am–midnight or later. Metro: Atocha.

Puerta del Sol & Las Letras

EXPENSIVE

Lhardy ★★ CONTINENTAL   If you enjoyed the Palacio Real, you'll love dining upstairs at this favorite of Isabel II. Madrid's elite has been coming here since Lhardy opened in 1839, bringing *haute cuisine* to Spain for the first time. Once past its slightly shabby exterior close to Puerta de Sol, the restaurant is a rich mix of dark wood and red velvet. The food is old-fashioned and rather heavy—this is a good place to try *cocido,* Madrid's famous stew. Service is, of course, impeccable. Most people passing have no idea that the formal restaurant exists. That's because Lhardy is also the shopfront to a genteel deli on the first floor. It was the first establishment in Madrid to serve single women, and in 1885 introduced self-service consommé so they could have a cup of hot broth while buying provisions. That service still exists, and you can help yourself to a cup of broth from antique urns at the back of the store, and ask for an upmarket snack, which you eat standing up.

Carrera de San Jerónimo, 8. www.lhardy.com. ℗ **91-521-33-85.** Entrees 26€–36€. Cocido menu 67€. Winter hours: Deli Mon–Sat 9am–10pm, Sun 10am–3pm; restaurant Mon–Sat 1–3:30pm and 8:30–10:30pm, Sun 1:30–3:30pm. Summer hours: Deli Mon–Fri 11am–3:30pm and 7:30–10pm, Sat 11am–3pm; restaurant Mon–Sat 1–3:30pm and Mon–Fri 8:30–11pm. Closed Sun. Metro: Sol.

La Terraza del Casino ★★★ SPANISH   Super chef Paco Roncero runs this bastion of contemporary cuisine, having trained with Ferran Adrià, the Spanish master of innovation. The restaurant fills the top floor of the Baroque Casino de Madrid, an elite social club built in 1910. Yet the restaurant is bright and unstuffy, and Roncero's cooking is smart, fresh, and highly experimental. There is an à la carte menu, but it is much better to put yourself in the chef's hands for one of three tasting menus, one of which is available at lunchtime only. The most elaborate and expensive is entitled "Welcome to my world," an extraordinary world of flavor and innovation comprising some 16 tiny courses. The olive oil tasting at the beginning—perfected in Roncero's space-age lab—is an indication of what lies ahead: bending and changing the textures, flavor, and appearance of ingredients at a molecular level. The paired wines are outstanding too. Rather out of character, men must wear a jacket and children under 12 are not welcome to this world.

Calle Alcalá, 15. web.casinodemadrid.es/la-terraza. © **91-532-12-75.** Entrees 45€– 55€, tasting menus 79€–185€. Mon–Fri 1:30–4pm and 9–11:45pm; Sat 9–11:45pm. Closed Aug. Metro: Sevilla or Sol.

MODERATE

La Ferretería by EGO ★ SPANISH   Madrid's oldest surviving iron-monger's shop *(ferretería),* dating from 1888, was converted into this

Chocolatería San Ginés is a classic stop, early or late, for a cup of thick Madrid-style hot chocolate.

FOR dipping

At some point, all Madrid comes into **Chocolatería San Ginés** for a cup of the thick hot chocolate and the fried dough sticks known as *churros*. When the music stops in the small hours of the morning, clubbers from Joy Eslava next door pop in for a cup, and later on, before they head to the office, suited bankers order breakfast. There's sugar spilled on the tables, yet the marble counters are an impeccable tableau of cups lined up with all the handles at the same angle and a tiny spoon on each saucer. During the day it gets horribly busy; if you don't want to queue, **Chocolatería 1902** 2 minutes away is also excellent. **San Ginés:** Pasadizo San Ginés, 5; www.chocolateriasangines.com; ⓒ **91-365-65-46.** Closes briefly early morning for cleaning. **1902:** Calle de San Martín, 2; chocolateria1902.com; ⓒ **91-522-57-37;** 7am–midnight, until 1am Fri–Sat. Metro (for both): Sol or Opera.

bar-restaurant in 2018, leaving many of the antique fittings intact. Screwdrivers and keys grace its cupboards, alongside cocktail tongs. In the window, an industrial contraption has been adapted to display the *jamón* that is its new stock-in-trade. It all works remarkably well, a proud combination of tradition and innovation. And the food is no gimmick. EGO is the initials of Emilio García Ortigosa, a big cheese in the world of ham. Have a glass of wine at the bar and try some of his creations: top-rated (and expensive) acorn-fed ham, carved to perfection; *lagrimas de jamón* (ham "teardrops," with cold *ajo blanco* soup), or delicious Ibérico croquettes. By some extraordinary twist of fate, the new proprietor shares his initials with the original ironmonger, one Esteban G. Ochandatay.

Calle de Atocha, 57. www.ferreteriabyego.com. ⓒ **91-429-71-01.** *Jamón* from 7€–210€. Mon–Thurs 12:30pm–12:30am; Fri–Sat 12:30pm–1:30am. Metro: Antón Martín.

El Ñeru ★ ASTURIAN　You have to push your way through a packed tapas bar to get to the stairs down to El Ñeru's cavernous basement dining rooms. The cuisine at "The Nest" is Asturian, a regional favorite with *madrileños,* and its *fabada Asturiana*—large white beans stewed with ham and sausage—has been named the best in Spain. The menu also has plenty of fish and seafood, including the classic hake braised in cider *(merluza a la sidra),* or you can have your beans with clams. For the more adventurous, there is tripe *(callos),* cooked either in the Asturian or Madrid style. Cider is, of course, the accompaniment of choice—poured at shoulder height—and the bread comes with an interesting spread of butter blended with Cabrales blue cheese. The *menú del dia* is a hearty bargain.

Calle Bordadores, 5. www.restauranteelneru.com. ⓒ **91-548-19-77.** Entrees 13.50€– 25€; set menu 16€. Tues–Sun noon–5pm and 7:30–midnight. Metro: Sol or Opera.

INEXPENSIVE

La Mallorquina ★ PASTRY   This *pastelería* on the edge of Puerta del Sol has been a classic hangout for late morning coffees (the *merienda*) since it opened its doors in 1894. If you can pull yourself away from the exquisitely stocked display cases downstairs, you'll find a little tearoom upstairs where you can order beautifully made sandwiches, glazed pastries, and ice cream concoctions. The prices are remarkably low, service is superb, and although it's right on the Puerta del Sol, it is always full of *madrileños*.

Puerta del Sol, 8. www.pastelerialamallorquina.es. ✆ **91-521-12-01.** Sandwiches 3€–7.50€; pastries 2€–4€. Tearoom 8:30am–9:15pm. Metro: Sol.

Plaza Mayor & La Latina

MODERATE

Sobrino de Botín ★★ SPANISH   Ernest Hemingway really ate here and set a scene in Botín at the end of *The Sun Also Rises.* The establishment has been trading on that publicity ever since, along with the ruling by the Guinness Book of Records that it is the world's oldest restaurant still in business (since 1725). It is of course a tourist trap, but a good

Claiming to be the world's oldest restaurant, Sobrino de Botín excels at an old-school menu featuring such dishes as roast suckling pig.

madrid's **TOP TAPAS**

No one is really sure where the Spanish tradition of eating small plates of food rather than a full meal comes from. The word *tapa* means "lid" and it may be that tavern keepers of old would put a saucer on top of a glass of beer to keep the flies out. Then they started putting a snack onto the saucer to encourage the next drink. Whatever its origins, *madrileños'* capacity to consume tapas seems almost unlimited. You'll see people ordering a saucer of *boquerones* (marinated anchovies) or a slice of *tortilla* (Spanish omelet) at all hours of the day and night. Tapas are ideally eaten standing at the bar and should be a movable feast; enjoy the specialty of the house, then move on to the next stop. It's a good way to try things you're not sure you'll like (like *callos*, or tripe), or delicacies (like top-quality *jamón*) that are expensive for a full plate. In some bars, you'll get a free tapa when you order a drink, so wait to see what appears before ordering more. Many don't take credit cards—cash keeps things moving. The literary neighborhood of Las Letras is a good place to start, but seek out some other gems too.

Las Bravas ★   Fried potatoes smothered in a spicy tomato and paprika sauce are a staple in bars all over Spain. This one claims to have invented the dish—known as *patatas bravas*—and even has a patent on the sauce. You can also get pig's ear, fried baby squid, and even a whole 6-inch *tortilla* covered in it. Calle Espoz y Mina, 13. www.lasbravas. com. ✆ **91-521-35-07.** Tapas 4€–9€. Daily noon–1am. Metro: Sevilla.

La Venencia ★★   It's usually standing room only at this dusty old sherry bar favored by Hemingway. A range of sherries from Jerez and Sanlúcar are served straight from the cask, and go beautifully with olives, salty manchego cheese, or a saucer of pickled anchovies. Your tab will be marked up in chalk on the counter. Taking photographs and leaving tips forbidden. Calle Echegaray. ✆ **91-429-62-61.** Tapas 3€–5€. Daily noon–midnight. Metro: Sevilla.

Calle Jesus ★★   This street in the old newspaper district is a great place for free tapas with your drink. The bars here pour the Mahou *caña* in the old style for maximum creaminess and serve a generous tapa with each. You could drop in to any of a few options—El Diario, La Dolores, Cervezas La Fábrica, Los Gatos—and skip dinner. Metro: Antón Martín.

La Trucha ★   A recent refurb has disappointed some, but this is still the quintessential place for fish tapas. The house specialty is *canapé de trucha*

one—the food, wine, and service are excellent, if pricey. As you enter, peek into the kitchen to see racks of suckling pigs ready to go into the wood-fired oven. If your party is large enough to order a whole one, it is brought to the table with great ceremony and the crisp skin is smashed on top to break it into parts. The daily menu gets you garlic soup with egg as a starter, a large serving of roast suckling pig, a drink, and ice cream. Roast baby lamb is also a house specialty, but if you're on a tight budget, you can eat well on roast chicken for about half the price, and still soak up the 18th-century atmosphere. Reservations recommended. Calle de Cuchilleros, 17. www.botin.es. ✆ **91-366-42-17.** Entrees 15€–32€; set menu 45.90€. Daily 1–4pm and 8pm–midnight. Metro: Opera or Sol.

ahumada, a morsel of smoked trout on a finger of toast. It's so good many go for the *verbena de ahumados*, a selection of smoked fish. Calle Manuel Fernández y González, 3. www.tabernalatrucha.es. ☏ **91-429-58-33.** Tapas 2€–14€. Daily noon–1am. Metro: Antón Martín.

La Casa del Abuelo ★ Choose the original bar on Calle Victoria to savor the patina of age—it opened in 1906 and has been serving shrimp specialties ever since. You can have your *gambas* plainly grilled (*gambas a la plancha*) or with garlic (*gambas al ajillo*), or a tapa of breaded shrimp deep-fried in olive oil. The house wine is great value. Calle Victoria, 12. www.lacasadelabuelo.es. ☏ **91-521-23-19.** Racion of prawns 7€. Daily 1:30pm–1am. Metro: Sevilla.

Casa Dani ★★★ There's much earnest debate in Spain about who serves the best *tortilla española*, with just the right internal gooeyness and properly caramelized onions. You can have an enjoyable time joining the search. **Casa Dani**, which has a stall in Salamanca's Mercado de la Paz, is hard to beat. Calle de Ayala, 28. www.casadani.es. ☏ **91-575-59-25.** Large slice 2.80€. Mon–Fri 7am–4:30pm, Sat 7am–7:30pm. Metro: Serrano.

Casa Gonzalez ★★ A contender for Madrid's most photogenic tapas bar, its antique shopfront advertises *Quesos, Fiambre, Vinos* and that sums it up. Order a cheese plate, a charcuterie plate, and a glass or two of wine. Then soak up the friendly atmosphere, sometimes with live music. Calle del León, 12. casagonzalez.es. ☏ **91-429-56-18.** Half raciones 5€–13€. Mon–Thurs 9:30am–midnight, Fri–Sat 9:30am–1am, Sun 11:30–5pm. Metro: Antón Martín.

Stop Madrid ★ Despite the modern-sounding name, this Chueca pit-stop has been operating since 1929. There are no apparent concessions to modernity in the dusty-bottled bodega, and service can be brusque, but the tapas are terrific. Try *boquerones* with a glass of vermouth. Calle de Hortaleza, 11. stopmadrid.es. ☏ **91-521-88-87.** Tapas 2.50€–4€. Metro: Chueca.

Calle Ponzano ★★★ This street in fashionable Chamberí has so many good tapas bars it has spawned its own verb and hashtag, to go #ponzaning. This is where young *madrileños* go. Hop from classics like Cervecería El Doble (Calle de Ponzano, 58) to youthful hot spots like La Malcriada (Calle de Ponzano, 38) or El Arrogante (Calle de Ponzano, 46), a long way from that old taverner keeping flies off his drinks.

Julián de Tolosa ★★ BASQUE There are lots of good places to eat and graze along busy Cava Baja. This superb Basque *asador* is perhaps the most elegant. Pretty much everything you'll order here will arrive with char-grilled black stripes, and the menu is short and simple. Meat eaters have the choice of *chuletón* (T-bone steak) or *entrecôtte* (ribeye), fish eaters can order *merluza* (hake) or *rape* (monkfish). The starters and side dishes are similarly straightforward: Almost everyone goes for the red *piquillo* peppers, which are smoky and sweet, and, when in season, the fleshy mushrooms *(hongos)*. Many diners prefer the lower dining room with its exposed brick walls and the warmth of the wood grill. The staff do a good job of advising on the size and doneness of your steak (the

GO TO the markets

Most visitors to Madrid quickly come across the **Mercado de San Miguel,** the 19th-century covered market off Plaza Mayor that was converted into a gourmet tapas hall in 2009 (p. 95). But why not seek out some of Madrid's other neighborhood markets for something more authentic? **Mercado Antón Martín,** Calle de Santa Isabel, 5 (www.mercadoantonmartin.com; Mon–Fri 9am–9pm; Sat 9am–3pm; metro: Antón Martín), is still a traditional food market with meat, fish, fruit, and vegetables as well as good tapas bars and pop-ups which carry on after the stalls have closed. In up-and-coming Lavapiés, **Mercado de San Fernando,** Calle de Embajadores, 41 (www.mercadodesanfernando.es; Mon–Thurs 9am–9pm, Fri–Sat 9am–11pm, Sun 11am–5pm; metro: Lavapiés or Embajadores), has a picturesque mix of old-style market characters and hipsters selling artisanal coffee and craft beer. Chueca's **Mercado San Anton,** Calle de Augusto Figueroa, 24 (www.mercadosananton.com; daily 10am–midnight; metro: Chueca), was redeveloped in 2002 as a thriving food court in a huge modern block with a great terrace. For high-end hams, cheese, and wines (and Casa Dani's legendary tortilla), head to the still-traditional **Mercado de la Paz** in upmarket Salamanca (Calle de Ayala, 28; www.mercadodelapaz.com; Mon–Fri 9am–8pm, Sat 9am–2:30pm; metro: Serrano).

chuletón is huge), and on the excellent list of reds from Rioja and Navarre. For dessert, try the typically Basque *Tejas y cigarrillos de Tolosa*—buttery brandy snaps.

Calle Cava Baja, 18. juliandetolosa.com. ✆ **91-365-82-10.** Entrees 22€–30€. Mon–Sat 1:30–4pm and 9pm–midnight, Sun 1:30–4pm. Metro: La Latina.

INEXPENSIVE

Taberna Almendro 13 ★ ANDALUCÍAN   This appealing Andaluz tavern is popular with Spanish families visiting Madrid, so getting a table can be a challenge. But you can enjoy a glass of *manzanilla* from the barrel with a saucer of olives while you wait or opt to eat standing at the bar. Everything looks just as you'd imagine a typical Spanish *taberna:* stone walls, tiled panels, wooden stools, and sherry glasses slotted into racks. The only concession to modernity is the brightly colored laminated menu, supplementing the chalkboard suggestions. *Almendritos* are little rolls, *Roscas* larger rings of bread for sharing, filled with a selection of ham and sausage, black pudding *(morcilla),* and sheep's cheese. For something more substantial, the *tortilla* with caramelized onions is delicious.

Calle Almendro, 13. almendro13.com. ✆ **91-365-42-52.** Entrees 5.50€–12€. Daily 1:30–4:30pm and 8pm–1am. Metro: La Latina.

Opera & Palacio Real

MODERATE

El Landó ★★★ SPANISH   Popular with politicians and celebrities, this famous restaurant is owned by Lucio Blasquéz, who also runs **Casa**

Lucio on Cava Baja. The signature dish at both is the simple, but sensational, *huevos rotos sobre patatas*—effectively egg and fries. As soon as you descend its staircase, covered in photos of famous customers, head waiter Ángel González and his white-jacketed team let you know you are in for a great time. Settle in for a long sharing lunch or dinner in the wood-paneled dining room: perhaps a plate of *jamón ibérico,* wild asparagus and sliced tomatoes in olive oil, then the must-have *huevos rotos,* followed by glorious sliced beef, red in the middle and salty on top, with a bottle of the house Rioja. For dessert, it's hard to resist the *arroz con leche*—rice pudding topped with cinnamon. If you've dined in some of Madrid's more precious restaurants, it may come as a pleasant surprise that simple home cooking and courteous service can be so perfectly enjoyable.

Plaza de Gabriel Miró, 8. No website, search on Facebook. ℰ **91-366-76-81.** Entrees 15€–30€. Mon–Sat 1–4pm and 8:30pm–midnight; Sun 1–4pm. Metro: La Latina. Bus 3 or 148

La Lonja ★ SPANISH You might expect a restaurant on the exclusive Plaza de Oriente crescent right in front of the Royal Palace to be over-priced and under-motivated, but this famous fish restaurant is consistently excellent and remarkably good value. You can eat at the formal restaurant or at the more relaxed *taberna,* and the fare in both sticks to the same classic themes: beautifully cooked fresh fish and seafood rice dishes. Sitting out on the *taberna* terrace with a plate of, say, mixed fried fish and then black rice with baby squid *(chipirones)* to share, a bottle of cold Albariño in the ice bucket, and views towards the Palacio Real, is a fine way to spend an afternoon.

Plaza de Oriente, 6. lalonjadelmar.com. ℰ **91-541-33-33.** Entrees 14.50€–26€. Mon–Thurs noon–midnight, Fri–Sat noon–1:30am. Metro: Opera.

Restaurante Sandó ★★ SPANISH Sandó is the ready-to-wear version of chef Juan Mari Arzak's *haute* restaurant in San Sebastián (p. 588). Of course, off-the-peg won't have quite the hand-stitching and luxuriant fabric of the runway piece, but it has the style and panache. Dishes at Sandó represent some of the creations that Juan Mari and daughter Elena perfected in their laboratory; in classic Arzak style, they marry two seemingly incompatible flavors with great success, like white anchovies and sweet strawberries. You can try a tasting menu here for about a quarter the price of Arzak, and it will still include plates like foie gras ravioli with melon and spinach vinaigrette, or roasted monkfish and chorizo with a vegetable sauce sweetened with honey. Try a couple of inventive tapas plates and a beer for as little as 10€. *Tip:* Arzak also runs the bar at the Hotel Santo Domingo.

At Hotel Santo Domingo, Calle Isabel la Católica, 2–4. restaurantesando.es. ℰ **91-547-99-11.** Entrees 16€–28€. Tues–Thurs 1–4pm and 8–11pm; Fri–Sat 1–4pm and 8pm–midnight. Closed Aug. Metro: Santo Domingo.

4

MADRID | Where to Eat in Madrid

Gran Vía, Chueca & Malasaña

MODERATE

Angelita ★ SPANISH   This family-run wine and cocktail bar in Chueca also does excellent food. The restaurant décor is simple: blonde wood tables and comfortable chairs next to tall glass windows overlooking the street. Attentive service is a key part of this place's appeal, and it is best to allow the staff to talk you through the food and wine options. Whatever else you order, don't miss the plate of chunky chopped tomatoes to start. They come from the family farm, and simply dressed with oil and a little salt, they taste wonderful. After that, there are lots of interesting and flavorful options: oysters; a Korean *sâam* wrap of spicy pig's ear; oxtail cannelloni cooked in Palo Cortado sherry; strong, aged cheeses. You can choose reasonably priced half glasses of wine to accompany each new dish, or just ask your waiter to suggest a good pairing. Word about Angelita has got around, and it fills up very quickly, so it is best to reserve. Calle Reina, 4. madrid-angelita.es. ✆ **91-521-66-78.** Entrees 15€–25€. Tues–Thurs 1:30pm–2am; Fri 2pm–2:30am; Sat 2pm–midnight; closed Sun. Metro: Gran Vía.

Restaurante Casa Salvador ★ SPANISH/ANDALUCÍAN   Too bad Hemingway isn't around to eat at Casa Salvador. The place is a total immersion in Andalucían decor and the cult of the bullfight, with the great matadors staring mournfully from photos and paintings covering the walls. The food is as simple and unaffected as the atmosphere is overwhelming. House specialties include a delicious soupy casserole of white

VEGETARIAN madrid

Vegetarianism is a foreign concept to many Spaniards, whose idea of a vegetable is the fried potato that comes with their pork steak. But times are changing, and you'll sometimes see protests in town squares about Spain's macho attitude towards meat and animal welfare. **La Biotika,** Calle del Amor de Dios, 3 (labiotika.es; ✆ **91-429-07-80**), is the longest-standing vegetarian and macrobiotic restaurant in Madrid, and it looks the part, with veggie burgers, wholegrain bread, and tofu, and a shop selling lentils, beans, and incense. More refined and contemporary is **Levél Veggie Bistro,** Av. de Menéndez Pelayo, 61 (www.levelbistro.es; ✆ **91-127-57-52**), which serves vegetarian sushi and a quinoa timbale with tomato, coriander, and avocado in its airy dining room near Retiro park. Tastiest of all is **La Hummuseria,** Calle Hernán Cortés, 8 (www.lahummuseria.es; ✆ **91-022-62-40**), which bucks the idea that vegetarian food is boring or lacking in flavor. Their freshly made hummus is served with an abundance of fresh vegetables, herbs, and spices, but without additives or preservatives. Share "The Irresistible," with pine nuts, almonds, and warm pita, and a chopped market salad, topped with mint and toasted pumpkin seeds. Then try sister restaurant, **La Falafeleria** (www.falafeleria.es) around the corner at Calle Sta. Bárbara, 4.

beans and ham. If the bullfight pictures don't put you off, opt for oxtail (*rabo de toro*) or a gristly but flavorful sirloin steak.

Calle Barbieri, 12. www.casasalvadormadrid.com. (© **91-521-45-24.** Entrees 12€–30€. Set menu 25€. Mon 1:30–4pm, Tue–Thurs 1:30–4pm and 8:30–11pm, Fri–Sat 1:30–4pm and 8:30–11:30pm; closed Sun. Closed Holy Week. Metro: Chueca.

Taberna La Carmencita ★ SPANISH   The second oldest restaurant in Madrid and one of the most beautiful, La Carmencita's walls are covered with floral-patterned tiles surrounding a lovely wood and zinc bar. Lorca and his literary circle used to hang out here, but the restaurant doesn't rest on the glories of its past. Recently completely renovated, it successfully marries its heritage with contemporary design, and its organically sourced food goes the same way. Fresh farm eggs, slow-cooked lamb, Cantabrian beef, and fish delivered daily from the markets of Santander are the staples of the menu. "Eco" meatballs in a recipe from 1854 sum up the mood. Then there's the *hora del vermú,* just before lunch, when you can wake up your appetite with a glass of bitter vermouth, accompanied by *rabas de Santander,* fried squid rings.

Calle Libertad, 16. tabernalacarmencita.es. (© **91-531-09-11.** Entrees 16€–26€. Mon–Thurs 12:30pm–1am; Sat–Sun 12:30pm–2am. Metro: Chueca.

INEXPENSIVE

Bocaito ★ SPANISH   At this bar-restaurant, separate entrances lead into two rooms served by the same bartenders, who stand in the middle. The menu is cheaper if you stand at the bar. It costs a little more to eat in one of three dining rooms, including the *comedor del jardín,* with potted plants and Andalucían tiles. The food is traditional working-class fare— pork sweetbreads, traditional *cuchara* stews, and *sopa castellana* with bread, garlic, and egg. The name refers to little pieces of toasted bread on which delicious tapas are placed: smoked fish, cockles, or caviar.

Calle Libertad, 4–6. www.bocaito.com. (© **91-532-12-19.** Entrees 11€–24€. Mon–Fri 1–4:30pm and 8:30pm–midnight; Sat 8:30pm–midnight. Metro: Chueca.

Salamanca, Retiro & Chamberí
EXPENSIVE

Amazónico ★★ INTERNATIONAL   Jungle-themed Amazónico, which opened in 2016 just north of the Retiro park, has become the most fashionable table in town, beloved of celebrities and footballers. The interior, the work of the Catalan designer Lázaro Rosa-Violán, is a lush tropical scene, with hanging greenery, a fruit-piled cocktail bar, and a stuffed peacock. The food, by Brazilian chef Sandro Silva, is similarly exotic, a culinary world tour stopping off in Japan, India, and the Mediterranean, as well as Silva's native Latin America. A circular sushi bar serves up a poke of raw red tuna or Peruvian shrimp *ceviche.* Argentinian steaks and skewered sea bass smoke on an open grill. The lighting is nightclub dark, and in the evening, bossa nova sways at the Jungle Jazz club. Cocktails arrive with dragon fruit, sambucus flower, and papaya. This unlikely—and

4

expensive—formula has proved so successful that a branch is due to open in 2019 in London's Mayfair.

Calle Jorge Juan, 20. restauranteamazonico.com. ✆ **91-515-43-32.** Entrees 18€– 52€. Daily 1pm–midnight. Metro: Serrano or Velázquez.

Coque ★★★ SPANISH   The tasting menu at Coque is perhaps the most extraordinary dining experience in Madrid. It is the project of the Sandoval brothers, the third generation of a culinary family who moved their award-winning restaurant from the suburbs to this purpose-designed location in Chamberí in 2017. The building, designed by architect Jean Porsche, is integral to the experience. Over a period of around 3 hours, diners are taken on a tour and served numerous incredible creations in five locations. You start in the cocktail bar with Bloody Mary ice cream and a black sesame taco with guacamole and foie. Then it's on to the spectacular wine cellar for a savory paprika macaroon served with a *fino* sherry. After a pause in the champagne sacristy, you're taken to the kitchen for a beer and hydrolized Spanish omelet. By the time you finally take your seat in the dining room you are about half way through your meal. It is awesomely impressive, great fun, and very expensive, especially if you opt for the dozen or so paired wines.

Calle del Marqués del Riscal, 11. www.restaurantecoque.com. ✆ **91-604-02-02.** Tasting menu 195€, with wine pairing 310€. Tues–Sat 1:30–5pm and 8:30pm–midnight. Metro: Rubén Darío.

DiverXO ★★★ FUSION   Vying with Coque for the title of Madrid's most memorable gastronomic experience is celebrity punk chef David Muñoz's extraordinary restaurant in Chamartín. Influenced by Abraham García, whose Viridiana (p. 129) he visited as a child, Muñoz trained at the London restaurants Nobu and Hakkasan. He describes his pioneering Spanish fusion as avant-garde cuisine in which everything is possible— indeed, his tasting menu is called *Cerdos Voladores* (Flying Pigs). Each course is a work of culinary art, with Jackson Pollock–like splashes and street-art sprays. Expect to use a range of eating utensils: chopsticks, a spatula, your hands. To secure a table you have to buy a non-refundable ticket at 125€, far in advance, which is deducted from your final bill. If that's all too much, you can experience the entertaining and unsettling world of Dabiz (as Muñoz is nicknamed) on a budget at **StreetXO,** on the top floor of El Corte Ingles in the Serrano shopping mall.

At NH Eurobuilding hotel, Calle de Padre Damián, 23. diverxo.com. ✆ **91-570-07-66.** Tasting menu 250€. Wed–Sat 1:30–7pm and 8:30pm–2am. Metro: Cuzco.

MODERATE

Lakasa ★★ SPANISH   Although it's just off fashionable Calle Ponzano (p. 135), Lakasa embodies a similar spirit. It's young, hip and nightclubby, but it doesn't feel exclusive, and the food and service are excellent. You can eat more formally, but there are some ideal sharing dishes and the serving staff are happy to adjust the size to suit your group. Start with the house specialty, *buñuelos de idiazabal,* cubes of sheep's cheese deep fried in batter. Then try a platter of garlicky *chipirones* (baby squid) or a board of *presa ibérica,* acorn-fed pork, pink in the middle. Coupled with good value wine, the price to quality ratio is, as they say around here, *fenomenal.*

Plaza del Descubridor Diego de Ordás, 1. lakasa.es. ✆ **91-533-87-15.** Entrees 15€–30€. Tues–Sat noon–11:30pm. Metro: Ríos Rosas.

Platea Madrid ★★ SPANISH/INTERNATIONAL As you'll have gathered by now, the district of Salamanca is a rather unreal world where the beautiful people go. This huge gastronomic complex in a former cinema is a good place to observe that world without blowing your budget. Set on three levels, this 6,000 square-meter pleasure dome retains the form of the old Carlos III cinema, down to the heavy screen curtains and Wurlitzer lighting. The spaces where the seats used to be are now filled with colorful bars, stalls, and restaurants, serving a range of Spanish and world cuisine, tapas, drinks and cocktails. Center stage, a DJ hunches over her decks, pumping out the soundtrack. You can sit down for a full meal at chic restaurants like Canalla Bistro, but it's more fun to wander around and pick and choose, or just stand and stare.

Calle de Goya, 5-7. plateamadrid.com. ✆ **91-577-00-25.** Sun–Wed noon–12:30am, Thurs–Sat noon–2:30am. Metro: Serrano or Colón.

Viavélez ★★ SPANISH Paco Ron walked away from a Michelin star in an Asturian fishing village to make his assault on the capital. This restaurant, named after the town he left behind, may not have attracted the French star-makers, but it has certainly drawn Madrid gourmets partial to the cold-water fish cuisine of the northern Atlantic coast. Ron splits the establishment between a casual *taberna* and a more formal restaurant. The tavern has a menu of good value canapés (or tapas) and *raciones* of classics like *chipirones* (baby squid) with aioli and *boquerones fritos* (deep-fried anchovies). The restaurant offers some hearty Asturian fish and meat dishes and good value daily and tasting menus.

Avenida General Perón, 10. www.restauranteviavelez.com. ✆ **91-579-95-39.** Entrees 18€–27€; set menu 30€, tasting menu 60€. Tues–Sat 2–4pm and 9pm–midnight, Sun 2–4pm. Closed 3 weeks in Aug. Metro: Santiago Bernabeu.

INEXPENSIVE

La Castela ★★ SPANISH Set on the eastern side of Retiro park, away from the crowds, this unpretentious bar-restaurant serves some of Madrid's best food. You can eat excellent tapas in the bottle-lined bar with a perfectly chilled *caña,* or reserve a table in the slightly dated-looking restaurant at the back. The cooking is classically Spanish, but don't expect *patatas bravas.* The menu leans towards fish and everything is beautifully prepared and presented: clams in *manzanilla* sherry, octopus and squid rice, chickpeas sautéed with langoustines. The wine list is a tour of Spain's D.O. regions. Michelle Obama ate here with her daughters when they visited Madrid, but the *dueño* of the Castela is not the type to shout about it.

Calle del Dr. Castelo, 22. restaurantelacastela.com. ✆ **91-574-00-15.** Tapas from 4€; entrees 15€–20€. Mon–Sat 2pm–5pm and 9pm–12:30am, Sun 2pm–5pm. Metro: Ibiza.

Entre Cáceres y Badajoz ★ SPANISH   A good place to stop for tapas if you are visiting the Las Ventas bullring nearby, this restaurant is named after the rolling expanses of Extremadura which lie between the cities of Cáceres and Badajoz. Yet the food at this busy bullfight-themed place is not particularly *extremeño*. It serves platefuls large and small of mainstream Spanish favorites—*jamón ibérico,* octopus, tomatoes in oil and herbs—and it gets very busy, especially at weekends. The friendly staff are experts at encouraging you to keep ordering plates to share, helped along by free tapas every time you order a frothy beer. When you can't eat any more, there's usually a free piece of cake. Great value and great fun.

Calle de Don Ramón de la Cruz, 109. ✆ **91-401-28-32.** Entrees 10€–20€. Mon–Fri 7am–1am, Sat–Sun 9am–1:30am. Metro: Manuel Becerra.

MADRID SHOPPING

Madrid's main shopping streets contain many of the international brands you'll find in any modern capital, but if you look harder you can find plentiful of characterful Spanish shops. If you don't have time to devote to shopping for its own sake, there are some good options for gifts you can pick up at the museums and monuments you'll visit, while avoiding the tacky souvenir stores. Wherever you go, look out for the word *"rebajas"*

Madrid's enduring department store, El Corte Inglés.

(reductions). Citywide sales generally take place in January and throughout the summer, when you can sometimes find savings of as much as 70%.

Salamanca

For luxury (or window) shopping, head to the Salamanca district, whose avenues are sprinkled with the boutiques of international designers, as well as leading Spanish brands like **Adolfo Dominguez,** Calle Serrano, 5 (www.adolfodominguez.com; ✆ **91-436-26-00;** metro: Retiro); **Balenciaga,** Calle de Lagasca, 75 (www.balenciaga.com; ✆ **91-419-99-00;** metro: Núñez be Balboa); and **Loewe,** Calle Serrano, 34 (www.loewe.com; ✆ **91-577-60-56;** metro: Serrano). Check out Loewe's beautiful—and eye-wateringly expensive—leather bags and jackets, or handle a truly well-made shoe at custom-maker **Gaytan Sucesores,** Calle Jorge Juan, 15 (✆ **91-435-28-24;** metro: Serrano). **Serbal,** Calle de Juan Bravo, 9 (www.serbaldeloscazadores.com; ✆ **91-559-76-46;** metro: Núñez de Balboa), specializes in top-of-the-range hunting gear and can even handle your taxidermy needs. Madrid's smartest shopping mall **ABC Serrano,** Calle Serrano, 61 (www.abcserrano.com; ✆ **91-577-50-31;** metro: Serrano), is nearby. For exquisitely packaged food and wine, visit the Gourmet Experience on the top floors of **El Corte Inglés Serrano,** Calle Serrano, 52 (www.elcorteingles.es; ✆ **90-193-09-30;** metro: Serrano), the food court at **Platea Madrid** (p. 141), or **El Mercado de la Paz** (p. 104).

Chueca & Malasaña

Shoppers with more limited means may prefer these hip neighborhoods. Explore the side streets around **Calle Fuencarral** for up-and-coming designers, graffitied vintage clothes stores, and secondhand books and comics. **Popland,** Calle de Manuela Malasaña, 24 (www.popland.es; ✆ **91-5-91-21-20;** metro: San Bernardo), and **Flamingos Vintage Kilo,** Calle del Espíritu Santo, 1 (www.vintagekilo.com; ✆ **91-504-83-13;** metro: Tribunal), are representative examples, but there are interesting new places popping up all the time. Chueca's main drag, **Calle Augusto Figueroa,** is shoe central, often with bargain prices, and the outlet store of **Salvador Bachiller,** Calle Gravina, 11 (www.salvadorbachiller.com; ✆ **91-523-30-37;** metro: Chueca), is a good place for cheap and cheerfully colored luggage and bags. Nearby **Antigua Casa Crespo,** Calle Divino Pastor, 29 (www.antiguacasacrespo.com; ✆ **91-521-56-54;** metro: San Bernardo), is a lovely old shop selling espadrilles *(alpargatas),* the traditional rope-soled summer shoes.

Around Plaza Mayor & Puerta del Sol

Among some trashy shops in Plaza Mayor, **El Arco Artesanía,** Plaza Mayor, 9 (www.artesaniaelarco.com; ✆ **91-365-26-80;** metro: Sol or Opera), offers appealing contemporary craft items from throughout Spain.

Try **La Favorita,** Plaza Mayor, 25 (www.lafavoritacb.com; *C* 91-366-58-77), or **Casa Yustas,** Plaza Mayor, 30 (www.casayustas.com; *C* 91-366-50-84), for caps *(gorras),* berets *(boinas),* and good-value Panama hats. **Casa de Diego,** Puerta del Sol, 12 (www.casadediego.com; *C* 91-522-66-43; metro: Sol), has been selling beautifully decorated hand-made fans *(abanicos),* shawls *(mantones),* and veils *(mantillas)* for nearly 200 years, and nearby **Capas Seseña,** Calle Cruz, 23 (www.sesena.com; *C* 91-531-68-40), has been making beautiful investment-quality, capes since 1901. For secondhand flamenco and rock CDs and vinyl, **Discos La Gramola,** Calle del Postigo de San Martín, 4 (*C* 63-461-55-84; metro: Sol), is an enjoyable place to rummage around.

Specialty Shops

If you're interested in Spain's great ceramics tradition, don't miss **Antigua Casa Talavera,** Calle Isabel La Catolica (www.antiguacasatalavera. com; *C* 91-547-34-17; metro: Santo Domingo), where the beautiful tile façade alone is worth the trip. Spain's guitar-making craft lives on at **Guitarras Ramirez,** Calle de la Paz, 8 (www.guitarrasramirez.com; *C* 91-531-42-29; metro: Sevilla), which was founded in the 1880s and has made instruments for guitarists from Andrés Segovia to Eric Clapton.

Markets

Sunday morning is the time for the famous flea market **El Rastro** (p. 96), but these days there's too much Made in China and not enough genuine bargains. For the more serious antiques or vintage collector, it's better to return to the neighborhood on a weekday and check out the shops in **Mercado Galerias Piquer,** Calle Ribera de Curtidores, 29 (*C* 60-516-64-47; metro: Puerto de Toledo). If you are visiting Madrid on the second weekend of the month, **Mercado de Motores** (p. 108), is a good bet for bric-a-brac and quirky Spanish designs.

NIGHTLIFE & ENTERTAINMENT

"I have never been to a city where is there less reason to go to bed," wrote Hemingway. The *madrileños'* capacity for night-time revelry is legendary, and the rhythm of life here is simply different. People go out very late, many stay out till dawn, they really do have *chocolate con churros* on the way home, and some simply shower and go straight on to work, napping on the Metro and sleeping at siesta time. If you don't make at least some concession to that rhythm, your stay in Madrid is likely to feel disjointed.

The first part of the evening, from around 8:30pm to 10:30pm, is the time for beer and tapas (see "Madrid's Top Tapas," p. 134). While many visitors gravitate towards the bars around **Plaza Santa Ana,** locals are more likely to head to **Cava Baja** or **Calle Jesus,** or further afield. It's worth seeking out Chamberí's **Plaza de Olavide,** where almost every building surrounding the large, circular plaza has a pavement bar, full of chatting groups of friends. (Try **Bar Méntrida** or **El Cuatro de Copas,** 3 and 4 Plaza de Olavide.) Nearby, **Calle Ponzano** is a great place to hop from one bar to another, as the evening moves towards *copas* (cocktails). The locals call it #ponzaning. The bars of **Malasaña** and **Chueca** have plenty of edgy character, old vermouth fittings, and hipster clientele.

The bars around Plaza Santa Ana make a good first stop on a tapas crawl, but don't stop there.

Where Flamenco Flourishes

Ask a local where to find the best flamenco in town and they are likely to say, without hesitation, **Casa Patas,** Calle Cañizares, 10 (www.casapatas.com; 📞 **91-369-04-96;** 40€; metro: Antón Martín). Authentic and passionately serious, this *tablao* has been instrumental in Madrid's flamenco revival, and the quality is invariably first-rate. The showier, more touristic offerings, are also very good, and may feel more accessible. Good options include **Cardamomo,** Calle Echegaray, 15 (www.cardamomo.es; 📞 **91-369-07-57;** 39€; metro: Sol) and **Villa Rosa,** Plaza Santa Ana, 15 (www.

villa-rosa.es; 📞 **91-521-36-89;** 39€; metro: Antón Martín), behind a tiled façade on Plaza Santa Ana. Usually, the dinner at a flamenco show isn't worth the money. The startling exception is **Corral de la Morería,** Calle Morería, 17 (www.corraldelamoreria.com; 📞 **91-365-84-46;** 39€; metro: Opera), which has a first-class gastronomic menu. The prices above are for the show only, with one drink included. Check websites for show times; most have up to four each evening.

Check out **Taverna Ángel Sierra,** Calle de Gravina, 11, **Casa Camacho,** Calle de San Andrés, 4, or **Casa Baranda,** Calle de Colón, 11.

As the clock moves past midnight, gin and tonic becomes the *madrileños'* drink of choice. **Museo Chicote,** Calle Gran Vía, 12 (https://museochicote.com; 📞 **915-326-737**), founded in 1931, was Madrid's first American-style cocktail bar and a favorite of Hemingway, Sofia Loren, and Luis Buñuel. Or, see if you can get a rooftop spot at the Reina Victoria Hotel, Plaza de Sta. Ana, 14 (www.melia.com; 📞 **91-701-60-00**) or at the uber-stylish Hotel Urban (p. 118). They both stay open until 3am at weekends and you'll need a reservation.

If you prefer jazz or blues, check out **Cafe Central,** Plaza del Angel, 10 (www.cafecentralmadrid.com; 📞 **91-369-41-43;** metro: Antón Martín), or the cavernlike **La Coquette,** Calle de las Hileras, 14 (📞 **91-530-80-95;** metro: Opera). The Malasaña mega-club **Clamores,** Calle Alburquerque, 14 (www.clamores.es; 📞 **91-445-7-38;** metro: Bilbao), often has live jazz in the early evening, before it turns into a late-night disco. In nearby Chueca, Madrid's premier gay bar **Black & White,** Calle Libertad, 34 (www.facebook.com/blackandwhitemadrid; 📞 **91-531-11-41;** metro: Chueca), has a basement disco and a street-level bar with drag shows. For a more mainstream dance club, **Disco-Teatro Joy Eslava,** Calle Arenal 11 (www.joy-eslava.com; 📞 **91-366-37-33;** metro: Sol or Opera), in a 19th-century theater near Puerta del Sol, is open every night of the year. It is conveniently located near **Chocolatería San Ginés** (p. 132) for *chocolate con churros* at dawn.

DAY TRIPS FROM MADRID

By far the most popular short trip from Madrid is to **Toledo** (p. 154), but it's worth spending more than just a day there. If time is tight, the destinations below offer digestible bites of Spanish history, and getting there is easy. The vast monastery palace at **San Lorenzo de El Escorial,** northwest of Madrid, embodies the religious fervor that seized Spanish royalty and drove the Inquisition. By contrast, the small university city of **Alcalá de Henares,** on the plains east of the capital, led a Golden Age flowering of culture. It was the birthplace of Spain's greatest writer, Miguel de Cervantes.

San Lorenzo de El Escorial ★★

Set in the Guadarrama mountains about 50km (31 miles) northwest of Madrid, this little town is dominated by the monastery palace of El Escorial. It's a favorite weekend getaway for people from Madrid, as it is usually several degrees cooler than the capital. Plan to spend around half a day at the royal complex and then have a wander in the town's manicured streets. There are lots of good places for lunch. **Cocheras del Rey,** Calle del Rey, 41 (www.cocherasdelrey.com; ℰ **91-890-70-93**), has a museum and a daily menu at 20€; **El Olivo,** Calle Hernández Briz, 7 (www.facebook.com/restaurantelolivo; ℰ **91-890-35-56**), has a great value menu at 10€. Reservations recommended.

ESSENTIALS

GETTING THERE   Commuter trains *(cercanías)* depart roughly every half hour from Madrid's Atocha, Sol, and Chamartín stations (line C3). The trip takes around an hour and tickets cost 4.05€ each way. For schedule information, visit www.renfe.com/viajeros/cercanias. From the railway station it's a twenty-minute walk through the park to the monastery, or there's a shuttle bus (L1) which will drop you near the entrance. There's also a special tourist train package called the **Felipe II train,** from 20€. Visit www.trendefelipeii.com or call ℰ **91-020-07-82** for more information.

The transport company ALSA operates more than 50 **buses** a day (lines 661 and 664) between Madrid's Moncloa station and El Escorial, reduced to around 20 on Sundays. The trip time is about an hour and a quarter and costs 4.20€ each way. If you're **driving,** take the A-6 from Madrid toward A Coruña. After about a half-hour, fork left onto the M-505 heading toward San Lorenzo de El Escorial. Driving time is about an hour. Parking near the monastery can be difficult; it's best to follow signs to public parking.

VISITOR INFORMATION   The **tourist office,** Calle Grimaldi, 4 (www.sanlorenzoturismo.es; ℰ **91-890-53-13**), is open Tuesday to Saturday 10am to 2pm and 3 to 6pm, and Sunday 10am to 2pm.

EXPLORING SAN LORENZO DE EL ESCORIAL

Real Monasterio de San Lorenzo de El Escorial ★★★ PALACE
Felipe II ordered the construction of this forbidding stone edifice in 1563,

Frescoes adorn the magnificent library at San Lorenzo de El Escorial.

2 years after he moved his capital to Madrid. After the death of the original architect, Juan Bautista de Toledo, it was completed by Juan de Herrera, considered the greatest architect of Renaissance Spain. It took 21 years to build. It must have been a marvel of modernity in its day, and its scale is staggering. Built in granite around a huge quadrangle, it has 2,675 windows and 24km (15 miles) of corridors. The overall effect from the outside is prisonlike; "cold as the grey eye and granite heart of its founder," according to Richard Ford, the great 19th-century writer on Spain.

Once inside, it is worth investing in the audio-guide, but the endless procession of rooms makes a full guided tour feel like hard work. The palace is nonetheless fascinating, and it's worth taking your time. The most intimate and interesting rooms are the **Salones Reales** (Royal Apartments) from where Felipe II ran half the world with scribbled notes of paper. You can see his modest desk and clock, and the tiny bed where he would rest his gouty leg, positioned so he could watch through a window as mass was celebrated in the **basilica,** which sits at the center of the complex. The basilica has 43 altars beneath a dome that emulates St. Peter's in Rome, on which Juan Bautista de Toledo is thought to have cut his architectural teeth. Below it is the **Panteón de los Reyes,** which holds the tombs of a dozen Spanish monarchs. Felipe II built the El Escorial as a burial place for his father, the Holy Roman Emperor, Carlos V, but the gilt and marble bling of the crypt was completed by Felipe IV in the 17th century.

The palace is full of art treasures, although many of the greatest paintings have been moved to the Prado. Highlights in the **Nuevos Museos** galleries include Titian's *Last Supper,* El Greco's *Martyrdom of St. Maurice,* and Velázquez's *La Tunica de José.* The **Hall of Battles** is decorated with meticulous frescoes detailing Spanish military victories, and the vaulted ceiling of the magnificent **Library** is painted with allegorical scenes depicting the liberal arts and sciences. Room after room is bordered in the beautiful blue and white *azulejos* (ceramic tiles) made in Talavera la Reina. Toward the end of the tour you reach the **Palacio de los Borbones,** where the style changes completely. The first Bourbon king, Felipe V, imported Versailles-style furnishings and dressed the cold, stone walls with tapestries designed by Goya. But the Bourbons never spent much time here—austerity wasn't their thing.

Calle Juan de Borbón, s/n. patrimonionacional.es. 🕾 **91-890-59-03.** Admission 10€ adults, 5€ students & children; audio guide 3€; guided tour additional 4€. Apr–Sept Tues–Sun 10am–8pm; Oct–Mar Tues–Sun 10am–6pm. Free for EU and Latin American citizens Apr–Sept Wed–Thurs 5–8pm; Oct–Mar 3–6pm.

Alcalá de Henares ★★

The Spanish Renaissance came to Alcalá de Henares when the powerful Cardinal Cisneros established its university in 1499. While the Inquisition was busy closing minds, Alcalá was opening them. The father of the modern Spanish language, Miguel de Cervantes, was born here in 1547, and the town's elongated square, Plaza de Cervantes, honors him with a fine bronze statue, quill in hand. (Cervantes's family moved away shortly after

---

A Chilling Detour

If you're traveling by car, it is just a 15-minute drive from El Escorial to the **Valle de los Caídos ★** (Valley of the Fallen), a strange and sinister monument to Francoism. Built following the Civil War in the 1940s, it was nominally a neutral memorial to the dead on both sides, thousands of whom are entombed here. But the fact that it was partly built by the forced labor of Republican prisoners, and that the dictators Franco and Primo de Rivera are buried here, has meant it has become a serious bone of contention. It sits on top of a dramatic crag in the Sierra de Guadarrama, surrounded by pine forest and spectacular views toward Madrid. But the bombastic design of its gigantic cross and basilica, built in Neo-Herrerian style into the mountain, is at once ludicrous and chilling. The government has sought to defuse a divisive situation by ordering the removal of Franco's tomb, but at the time of writing the Benedictine prior who runs the mausoleum was not budging. El Valle de los Caídos is a potent symbol of a still-raw history that is worth experiencing, but be sure not to visit on November 20, the anniversary of Franco's death, when things can get heavy. Bizarrely, some young couples choose to get married in its cavernous, gray basilica.

Plaza de Cervantes in Alcaláde Henares.

his birth, but Alcalá is not letting that get in the way of a good story.) After the original university moved to Madrid in the 19th century, Alcalá went into decline, but the arrival of a new university in the 1970s has given this appealing small city another renaissance.

ESSENTIALS

GETTING THERE   Commuter **trains** *(cercanías)* run every 15 minutes or so from Madrid's Atocha station to Alcalá de Henares (lines C2, C7, and C8). A one-way fare costs 3.40€ and the trip takes 40 minutes. The train station in Alcalá is at Paseo Estación (don't get out at the Alcala de Henares–Universidad stop, which is for the campus on the outskirts of town.) For schedule information, visit www.renfe.com/viajeros/cercanias. **Buses** from Madrid, operated by ALSA, depart from Avenida de América 18 (metro: América) every 15 minutes. A one-way fare costs 5€. The Alcalá bus station is on Via Complutense. From Madrid airport, take bus number 824. By **car,** take the A-2 (or R-2 toll road) toward Barcelona and take exit 23 signposted *centro histórico.*

VISITOR INFORMATION   The **tourist office,** Callejón de Santa María, 1 (www.turismoalcala.com; 𝒞 **91-889-26-94**), is open Tuesday through Saturday 10am to 2pm and 5 to 8pm, Sunday 10am to 3pm. Check its excellent website for a variety of guided tours and other suggestions.

EXPLORING ALCALÁ DE HENARES

You can easily explore Alcalá on foot in a day. The stone and red-brick Renaissance buildings of the old town are all close at hand. The city was badly damaged in the Civil War and many art treasures were lost, but extensive renovation means many of the buildings look almost new. Look out for the 90 pairs of storks that nest on nearly every bell tower and rooftop throughout much of the year.

Colegio Mayor de San Ildefonso ★★★ HISTORIC SITE   Adjacent to the Plaza de Cervantes is the university where the playwright Lope de Vega, the Jesuit theologian Ignacio de Loyola, and other Spanish greats studied. Its heavily embellished **façade,** completed in 1553, is one of Spain's finest examples of Plateresque architecture. Stroll through its portal, across the porticoed Patio of Saint Thomas, to reach the Patio of the Three Languages (the university produced the first polyglot bible, in Latin, Greek, and Hebrew in 1517). The atmosphere of ancient learning, mingled with modern student life, is uplifting. The great hall, the **Paraninfo,** has a glorious Mudéjar ceiling of interlaced wood and the names of the university's famous alumni on its walls; every year the King announces the winner of the Cervantes literary prize here (medallions of previous winners, including Mario Vargas Llosa and Octavio Paz, fill the wall outside). The **Capilla de San Ildefonso,** the 16th-century chapel of the original university, has another beautiful coffered ceiling and intricately stuccoed walls. It houses the white Carrara marble tomb of the university's patron, Cardinal Cisneros. Next to the Paraninfo is Alcalá's best restaurant, the historic **Hostería del Estudiante,** run by the *parador* across the street.

Plaza San Diego. www.turismoalcala.com. ✆ **91-885-41-85.** Guided tour 4.50€; audio guides 3€. Tues–Sat noon and 1, 5, 6, and 7pm; Sun noon and 1pm. Capilla Mon–Fri 11am–1pm and 5–7pm; Sat–Sun 11am–2pm and 5–7:30pm.

Museo Arqueológico Regional ★★ MUSEUM   Set in a beautiful red-brick former convent, this is one of Spain's most enjoyable archaeological museums. Clearly laid-out exhibits trace the development of the Madrid region, including natural history as well as human archaeology. Its saber-toothed tiger skull and mastodon jaw are around 10 million years old. An excellent collection of Roman mosaics and artifacts bears witness to the Roman conquest of the area in the 1st century B.C. Complutum, the only Roman city in the Madrid region, had 10,000 inhabitants. There is, notably a wonderfully unsteady-looking statue of Bacchus in the **Jardín de Antigüedades.** When Felipe II moved the royal court to Madrid in 1561 it led to a rapid growth in the manufacture of brightly painted ceramic pots and plates, some of which are evocatively preserved here.

Plaza Bernardas, s/n. www.museoarqueologicoregional.org. ✆ **91-879-66-66.** Free admission. Tues–Sat 11am–7pm; Sun 11am–3pm.

Museo Casa Natal de Cervantes ★ MUSEUM   Bronze sculptures of Don Quixote and Sancho Panza chatting on a stone bench let you know you have arrived at the supposed birthplace of Spain's greatest writer. Their knees are polished by the hands of all the visitors who have posed for photographs with them. Miguel de Cervantes was born in Alcalá in 1547 and lived here only briefly as an infant. In the 1940s, scholarly research suggested that this handsome house may have been his family home, and the city moved quickly to reconstruct it as a museum, done in the same folk-museum style you'll see all over Spain, following the model of the equally tenuous Museo del Greco in Toledo (p. 161). It is nonetheless an interesting and enjoyable look at the life of a comfortably off family in 16th- and 17th-century Spain. Cervantes' father was a barber-surgeon, and you can see a period barber's chair and a brass basin of the kind Don Quijote famously insisted was an enchanted helmet. A small museum upstairs displays Cervantes' great book in various editions and languages. (See "In Search of Don Quijote," p. 170.)

Calle Mayor, 48. www.museo-casa-natal-cervantes.org. ✆ **91-889-96-54.** Free admission. Tues–Sun 10am–6pm.

CASTILLA-LA MANCHA

By Peter Barron

5

n popular imagination, La Mancha is the vast, arid plain where Don Quijote tilted at windmills. As you travel through the region, you'll first see modern wind farms, then—on the occasional hilltop—an array of old-fashioned windmills or the ruins of a medieval castle. Or both. On escarpments high above winding rivers, its cities are reminders of Spain's turbulent past. Every culture from the Romans on made Toledo its citadel; siege was a way of life. Yet the dramatic settings have proved as important to art as to war. El Greco looked out from the walls of imperial Toledo and saw the earth far below and the heavens at eye level— a perspective repeated again and again in his paintings of the Ascension. The eastern city of Cuenca, perched above a deep river gorge, became a haven for abstract artists in the 20th century; its hanging houses (casas colgadas) cling to the rocks like a cubist fantasy.

The name Castilla-La Mancha is a modern administrative fusion of two age-old territories: The first part means land of castles, the second comes from the Arabic *al-mansha,* meaning parched wilderness. The monotonous tableland *(meseta)* supports wheat, olives, sunflowers, herds of sheep and endless, industrial vineyards. The region's celebrated cooking reflects the landscape: roast game and stews, saffron and paprika, hard sheep's cheese, and good red wine.

TOLEDO ★★★

Toledo is one of Spain's most captivating destinations. As the Imperial city, it was the Spanish capital in the era when Spain conquered the New World; it is also a city born of three cultures—Arabic, Jewish, and Christian—who lived here side by side until 1492. Its appearance has changed little since El Greco painted his adopted home at the turn of the 16th century. Even then it was ancient. Wrapped on three sides by a bend in the Río Tajo, Toledo overlooks the plains of La Mancha from a high outcrop, a natural fortress in the center of the Iberian Peninsula. Romans, Visigoths, and Arabs all made it their regional capital, and after the Christian Reconquest, the kings of Castilla made it the capital of Spain. When Philip II moved the royal court to Madrid in 1561, Toledo—then a city of 60,000 people—fell into neglect. Although the church remained the seat of the

Castilla-La Mancha

Madrid
Area of detail

Segovia
Sigüenza
CM110
A1
CM101
A2
N211
Molina de Aragón
AP6
COMMUNITY OF MADRID
Guadalajara
N204
N320
CM210
MADRID
Alcalá de Henares
CASTILLA Y LEÓN
R. Jarama
R. Tajo
Mar de Castilla
Arenas
N403
A5
AP41
A3
N320
Cuenca
Talavera de la Reina
A5
A40
A42
Aranjuez
Tarancón
A40
Saelices
A40
R. Júcar
Toledo
AP36
CASTILLA-LA MANCHA
A3
Embalse de Alarcón
R. Tajo
N502
CM401
CM42
A4
Mora
Tembleque
Quintanar de la Orden
N420
N320
Navahermosa
CM410
CM42
N401
Consuegra
Alcázar de San Juan
El Toboso
A3
Puerto Lápice
Campo de Criptana
N420
AP36
N420
EXTREMADURA
CM403
Villarrobledo
CM42
A43
N320
Malagón
A4
Tomelloso
La Roda
Daimiel
N420
A43
A43
Parque Natural Lagunas de Ruidera
N430
Albacete
Ciudad Real
Manzanares

0 20 mi
0 20 km

primate of Spain (which it still is), time stood still for hundreds of years. When the Romantic travelers visited in the 19th century, they found a city almost unchanged since the 16th century—and were enchanted. Today Toledo is a well-connected hub, capital of the region of Castilla-La Mancha, but it retains more layers of history than almost anywhere else in Spain. Many visitors choose to make the easy day trip from Madrid, but its many riches deserve a longer stay.

Essentials

ARRIVING High-speed **trains** run frequently to Toledo, leaving Madrid's Atocha station between 6:50am and 9:50pm every day. The one-way fare is 13.90€. For train information, visit www.renfe.com or call © **91-232-03-20.** To reach the old city from Toledo's railway station, take bus 5 to Plaza de Zocodover (1.40€); a taxi from the station costs about 8€. There's also regular **bus** service from Madrid, provided by ALSA (www.alsa.es; © **90-242-22-42**). Buses leave daily from Madrid's Estación de Plaza Elíptica (Vía Lusitana), at 15- to 30-minute intervals between 6am and 11pm. Travel time is between an hour and 1½ hours, a one-way ticket costs 5.50€. Once you reach Toledo, you'll be dropped at the Estación de

Cafés ring Plaza de Zocodover, where buses drop off visitors to Toledo's historic center.

Autobuses, which is next to the river about 1.2km (¾ mile) from the historic center. Buses 5 and 6 run from the station uphill to Plaza de Zocodover. Pay the driver directly. By **car,** take the A-42 south from Madrid. The drive takes about an hour. Driving and parking in Toledo's old town isn't fun. It's best to leave your car in a public car park and continue on foot.

VISITOR INFORMATION   There are several tourist offices in town; the one at Plaza Zocodover, 6 (www.toledo-turismo.com; ✆ **92-526-76-66**), is the one you're likely to encounter first, and there's another at the top of the Paseo Recaredo escalator at Plaza de la Merced (✆ 92-525-93-00). They are open daily 10am to 6pm. Pick up a free city map with details of all the main sites and museums, and some suggested walking routes.

Exploring Toledo

Once you've made it up the hill to the old city, Toledo is easy to get around on foot, though you're bound to get lost in its medieval alleyways at some stage. There are so many interesting things to see that, unless you're staying several days, it doesn't make sense to try to do everything. Better to pick a handful of gems and go deeper. At first sight, the *pulsera turística,* a wristband giving access to seven historic sites for 9€ (www.toledo monumental.com) looks attractive, but several key places are not included,

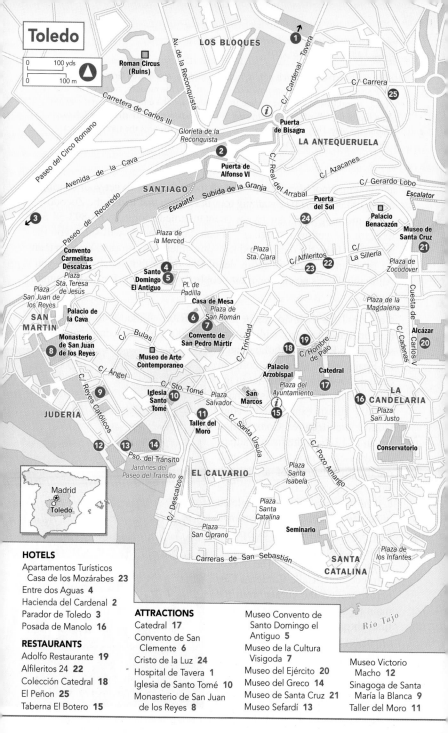

Toledo

0	100 yds
0	100 m

Roman Circus (Ruins)

LOS BLOQUES

Av. de la Reconquista

C/ Cardenal · Tavera

C/ Carrera

Carretera de Carlos III

Paseo del Circo Romano

Glorieta de la Reconquista

Puerta de Bisagra

LA ANTEQUERUELA

Avenida de la Cava

Puerta de Alfonso VI

C/ Real del Arrabal

C/ Azacanes

C/ Gerardo Lobo

Escalator

SANTIAGO

Subida de la Granja

Escalator

Puerta del Sol

Palacio Benacazón

Museo de Santa Cruz **21**

Paseo de Recaredo

Plaza de la Merced

Plaza Sta. Clara

C/ Alfileritos **22**

C/ La Sillería

Plaza de Zocodover

Convento Carmelitas Descalzas

23

Plaza Sta. Teresa de Jesús

Santo Domingo El Antiguo **4** **5**

Pl. de Padilla

Plaza de la Magdalena

Cuesta de Carlos V

Plaza San Juan de los Reyes

Casa de Mesa

Plaza de San Román **7**

Alcázar **20**

SAN MARTÍN

Palacio de la Cava

6

Convento de San Pedro Mártir

C/ Trinidad

18 **19**

C/ Hombre de Palo

Monasterio de San Juan de los Reyes **8**

C/ Bulas

Museo de Arte Contemporaneo

Palacio Arzobispal

Catedral **17**

C/ Ángel

C/ Sto. Tomé

Plaza del Ayuntamiento

C/ Cadenas

LA CANDELARIA **16**

JUDERÍA

9

Iglesia Santo Tomé **10**

Plaza Salvador

San Marcos

15

Plaza San Justo

Conservatorio

12 **13** **14**

Taller del Moro **11**

C/ Santa Úrsula

C/ Pozo Amargo

Pso. del Tránsito

Jardines del Paseo del Tránsito

EL CALVARIO

Plaza Santa Isabela

Seminario

Madrid

Toledo

C/ Descalzos

Plaza Santa Catalina

Plaza San Ciprano

Plaza San Juan

Carreras de San Sebastián

SANTA CATALINA

Plaza de los Infantes

Río Tajo

HOTELS

Apartamentos Turísticos Casa de los Mozárabes **23**
Entre dos Aguas **4**
Hacienda del Cardenal **2**
Parador de Toledo **3**
Posada de Manolo **16**

RESTAURANTS

Adolfo Restaurante **19**
Alfileritos 24 **22**
Colección Catedral **18**
El Peñon **25**
Taberna El Botero **15**

ATTRACTIONS

Catedral **17**
Convento de San Clemente **6**
Cristo de la Luz **24**
Hospital de Tavera **1**
Iglesia de Santo Tomé **10**
Monasterio de San Juan de los Reyes **8**

Museo Convento de Santo Domingo el Antiguo **5**
Museo de la Cultura Visigoda **7**
Museo del Ejército **20**
Museo del Greco **14**
Museo de Santa Cruz **21**
Museo Sefardí **13**

Museo Victorio Macho **12**
Sinagoga de Santa María la Blanca **9**
Taller del Moro **11**

and you may not have time to visit all those that are. To get your bearings, consider taking the free walking tour in English that leaves the Zocodover every morning at 11am (www.cuentametoledo.com; 📞 **60-893-58-56;** look for the yellow umbrella). An entertaining guide will show you the main sites from the outside and tell some interesting stories. You can then go back and explore in more detail the sights that most interest you. Although there's no charge, most people tip around 10€ for the 90-minute tour.

Catedral de Toledo ★★★ CATHEDRAL   Filled with religious art treasures and dripping with history, Toledo's huge cathedral remains the seat of the Roman Catholic church in Spain, long after the political capital moved to Madrid. Set in the center of the old city, it is perhaps Spain's finest example of High Gothic architecture. Construction began in 1226 on the former site of Toledo's chief mosque, itself built on the foundations of a Visigoth cathedral from the 6th century. The cathedral was finally completed under the Catholic Kings Fernando and Isabel in 1493, just as Spain's Muslims and Jews were being persecuted and expelled. The visitor entrance is on Calle Cardenal Cisneros, around the corner from the main façade. To buy your ticket go first through the cathedral shop opposite; the tour with audio guide costs 10€ and you'll need to leave an ID card as a deposit. All that becomes worthwhile once you're inside the cathedral—allow a good 2 to 3 hours to do it justice. The

A ceiling fresco by Luca Giordano adorns the sacristy of the Catedral de Toledo.

detailed, and slightly bossy, audio guide in English will take you step by step through the highlights.

The jaw-dropping Gothic *retablo* (altarpiece) was commissioned in the 1490s by Cardinal Cisneros, the power behind the throne of the Catholic Kings. Its gilded and polychromed wood carvings, telling the story of the life of Christ, took 6 years to complete and enlisted all the great sculptors of the day. Rising the whole way to the ceiling, it is so big that Cisneros demanded the chapel be rebuilt to accommodate it. Perhaps the cathedral's most extraordinary feature, however, is the *El Transparente* altarpiece in the ambulatory. The Baroque sculptor **Narciso Tomé** was unhappy that his mixed media masterpiece depicting Mary and Child and the Last Supper would be shrouded in darkness in the badly lit cathedral. So, he cut a large circular hole high into the ceiling and surrounded it with sculptures of a company of angels and saints. The shafts of light which illuminate the altarpiece and tabernacle in the afternoon are a faithful likeness of heaven. The intricate carvings on the central *coro* (choir) are also worth lingering over. The stalls on the right-hand side were carved in 1539 by **Alonso Berruguete,** those on the left are by **Felipe Vigarny.** They depict Old Testament characters, and is one of Vigarny's more fluid figures showing a Renaissance backside to the rival carvings on the other side? The lower stalls, which date from the 1490s, are carved with scenes from the fall of Granada, still recent news at time. In the *tesoro* (treasure room) the main attraction is the 500-pound (225kg) gilded **monstrance,** which is paraded through the streets of Toledo every Feast of Corpus Christi. It is said to contain the first gold brought back from the New World by Columbus. Look up at the intricately worked *artesonado* **ceiling,** which hangs down like a wasp's nest. When you reach the art gallery of the *sacristía,* don't let the audio guide hurry you along. As you enter, you'll see a 17th-century wooden statue of *St. Francis of Assisi* by Pedro de Mena, deeply moving and remarkably contemporary in appearance. Inside the frescoed gallery there is a wealth of fine paintings by Titian, Caravaggio, Rubens, Zurbarán, Morales, Goya, and, of course, El Greco. The standout masterpiece is the bright red folds of his *Disrobing of Christ* (1579).

For an extra charge, you can have a guided tour of the bell tower, which has great views across Toledo and beyond, but that involves a 138-step climb. There's an easier way to get that view, at Museo del Ejército (p. 161).

Calle Cardenal Cisneros, 1. www.catedralprimada.es. ✆ **92-522-22-41.** Admission 10€; 12.50€ including bell tower. Mon–Sat 10am–6pm; Sun 2–6pm. Special hours during feast days.

Hospital de Tavera ★ ART MUSEUM   Cardinal Juan Pardo de Tavera, the 16th-century Toledo archbishop and close confidant of Emperor Carlos V, was not one to hide his light beneath a bushel. He had this elegant Renaissance palace with twin arcaded courtyards built in a style far more grandiose than necessary to serve as a hospital for the needy—but maybe just grandiose enough to serve as a pantheon recalling the greatness of its patron. (Cardinal Tavera's mausoleum, designed by Alonso Berruguete, is within the adjacent church.) Today this grand building, which represents the finest mature work of Alonso de Covarrubias, is an art museum exhibiting an excellent collection of Spanish paintings from the 15th to the 18th centuries. Among them are five works by El Greco, including a sinister portrait of Tavera himself, and the so-called Virgin of the Good Milk, an early example of public health information through art. The building is clearly visible in unfinished form in El Greco's View and Plan of Toledo in the Museo del Greco (p. 161). A portrait of Carlos V by Titian dominates the banquet hall. It's a bit out of the historic center; to get there, take bus 5 or 6 from Plaza de Zocodover.

Calle Cardenal Tavera, 2. fundacionmedinaceli.org. ✆ **92-522-04-51**. Admission 4€ (6€ includes guided visit to pharmacy). Mon–Sat 10am–1:30pm and 3–6:30pm; Sun 10am–2:30pm. Closed Dec 25 and Jan 1.

Iglesia de Santo Tomé ★ CHURCH   This modest 14th-century chapel, on a narrow street in the old Jewish Quarter, holds two treasures: a de Graaf pipe organ that makes it a choice venue for concerts and recitals, and El Greco's masterpiece *The Burial of the Count of Orgaz* ★★★, painted in 1586. The painting is no longer displayed inside the church; it is mounted in a separate vestibule to accommodate both visitors and the congregants who use the church for worship. To avoid the bus tour groups that often descend to view the painting, go early.

Plaza del Conde, 4. www.santotome.org. ✆ **92-525-60-98**. Admission 2.80€, children under 10 free. Daily 10am–6:45pm (5:45pm in winter). Closed Dec 25 and Jan 1.

Monasterio de San Juan de los Reyes ★ MONASTERY   Fernando and Isabel had this convent built to mark their 1476 victory over the Portuguese and originally intended to be buried here—until the symbolic importance of Granada trumped that plan. It is the epitome of a Franciscan retreat: The cloister's leafy central garden is filled with birdsong, and high-vaulted Renaissance arches flood the arcades with reflected light. Heavily damaged during Napoleon's invasion, it stood vacant until the late 19th century, when restoration began. In 1954, the state returned the property to the Franciscans and it has been a working friary ever since. Located at the western edge of the old city, it's worth seeking out for the serenity of the courtyard and its graceful stone carvings.

Calle Reyes Católicos, 17. www.sanjuandelosreyes.org. ✆ **92-522-38-02**. Admission 2.80€; children under 10 free. Daily 10am–6:45pm (5:45pm in winter). Closed Dec 25 and Jan 1.

Museo Convento de Santo Domingo el Antiguo ★ CHURCH This dusty convent church has the distinction of having lured Doménikos Theotokópoulos, who was to become known as El Greco, to Toledo in

1577 with a commission for nine paintings. His *Assumption,* which still sits over the altar, is not his finest work but it is one of the paintings that made the authorities of Toledo sit up and take notice of his visionary talent. The painter and city proved a good match, and he was to spend the rest of his life here, marrying and raising a family. He is buried in the crypt beneath the church. If you take the museum tour offered by one of the nuns, you can peer through a peephole in the floor and catch a glimpse of his tomb.

Plaza Santo Domingo El Antiguo, 2. www.turismocastillalamancha.es. © **92-522-29-30.** Admission 2.50€. Mon–Sat 11am–1:30pm; daily 4–7pm.

Museo del Ejército (Army Museum) ★★ MUSEUM   Toledo's Alcázar, or fortress, has been destroyed and rebuilt many times through the centuries. It last endured battle in the early months of the Spanish Civil War, when a 3-month siege all but flattened it. Initially General Franco planned to leave the ruins as is, as a paean to Nationalist suffering, but he later changed his mind and had it rebuilt. Given the building's symbolism, it took deft political maneuvering from subsequent governments to reopen the Alcázar in 2010 as Spain's army museum. It is a curious place. There's a large military history collection, including what is claimed to be the sword of El Cid (1043–99), endless suits of armor, and Spanish army uniforms from many eras. But the elephant in the room is the extraordinary story of what happened in this building in 1936. Only one small exhibit deals with the siege, when the ineffectual Colonel José Moscardó somehow held out against Republican bombardment for 70 days before being relieved by Franco's troops; the audio guide devotes just a few seconds to it. It's understandable, given the ongoing sensitivities, but for a chilling sense of what the siege was like, seek out the unadvertised—and completely unrestored—office where Moscardó is said to have sacrificed his kidnapped son in a phone call with his captors. The phone still sits on a table beneath a portrait of the colonel and the shell-shattered ceiling. The office is simply labeled CM on the museum map. The other side of the Alcázar holds a municipal library, and if you take the lift to the top floor there's a little café with the best free views across Toledo and the surrounding plain.

Cuesta de Carlos V, 2. www.museo.ejercito.es. © **92-523-88-00.** Admission 5€; free Sun. Tues–Sun 10am–5pm. Closed Mon. Closed Jan 1, Jan 6, May 1, and Dec 24, 25, and 31.

Museo del Greco ★★ ART MUSEUM   In the early 20th century the Marquis de Vega-Inclán, a wealthy patron of the arts, bought this old house in the Jewish quarter under the misapprehension that it had once belonged to El Greco. The museum he founded, to promote the painter's work and show how life was led in his era, started a trend for a type of art-cum-folk museum you'll see all over Spain: bogus but effective nonetheless. The museum got an extensive makeover ahead of the 400th

Whether or not El Greco ever lived here, the Museo del Greco is a fascinating tribute to the artist.

anniversary of El Greco's death in 2014 and is a delight, with period gardens, Mudéjar cave rooms, and a good collection of El Greco's later works. Among the most notable pieces are a full set of portraits of the apostles (irresistible postcards of which are available in the shop), the *retablo* of San Bernardino, and the celebrated *View and Plan of Toledo*. It's fascinating how the development of the museum, as well as the works it contains, has become part of Toledo's story.

Paseo del Tránsito, s/n. museodelgreco.mcu.es. © **92-522-36-65.** Admission 3€ adults; 1.50€ students; free for seniors and kids under 18; free for all Sun and Sat after 4pm. Tues–Sat 9:30am–7:30pm (until 6pm in winter); Sun 10am–3pm.

Museo de Santa Cruz ★★★ ART MUSEUM   Just a few steps from the Plaza de Zocodover, through the horseshoe arch of the Arco de la Sangre, this is both a magnificent building and a beautifully laid-out museum. A massive former hospital, designed by Toledo's star architect Alonso de Covarrubias, it was commissioned by the powerful Cardinal Mendoza at the end of the 15th century as a refuge for orphaned children. Like the Hospital de Tavera (p. 159), it seems massively over-designed for the job at hand. The front portal is a Plateresque marvel; inside, its cross-shaped galleries have intricate coffered ceilings in Mudéjar and Renaissance

While wandering through the heart of Toledo is a delight, it is just as memorable to view the city from afar. Remarkably, it still looks much as it did when El Greco painted it. For the best perspective, take the Carretera de Circunvalación, the road that runs along the far bank of the Río Tajo. If you don't have a car, the easiest way to get the view is to swallow your pride and hop aboard the motorized tourist train which runs every half hour from the Alcázar, Cuesta de Carlos V (www.toledotrainvision). It makes a circular loop of the river from the Alcántara to the San Martín bridges, and stops at the **Mirador del Valle,** the perfect spot for El Greco–esque photographs. As you return to town, you'll see the *cigarrales,* the recreational country mansions which cling to the hillside (the name refers to the cicadas, or *cigarras,* that congregate on summer evenings). The houses were immortalized by Tirso de Molina, the 17th-century dramatist, in his compendium of tales, *Los Cigarrales de Toledo.*

style; the staircase is laugh-out-loud ornate. The museum is divided into three sections: fine art galleries of painting, sculpture, and furniture; a cloister devoted to archaeological fragments from the Roman, Visigoth, and Muslim periods; and a lovely collection of Spanish and Portuguese ceramic tiles and pottery from the 1238 reconquest of Valencia to the 19th century. The fine art section is particularly informative, as it is laid out chronologically, with information panels in Spanish and English explaining the historical context. The collection of 16th- and 17th-century Toledan art is superb, featuring the finest group of El Greco paintings in town,

Exquisite scrollwork decorates Toledo's 14th-century synagogue, now the Museo Sefardí.

including *The Assumption, The Holy Family,* and the *Veil of Saint Veronica.*

Calle Miguel de Cervantes, 3. cultura. castillalamancha.es. ✆ **92-522-14-02.** Admission 4€, seniors and kids under 16 2€. Mon–Sat 10am–6pm; Sun 9am–3pm. Free for all Wed 4–6pm. Closed Jan 1 and 6; May 1; and Dec 24, 25, 31.

Museo Sefardí (Sephardic Museum) ★★★ MUSEUM/SYNAGOGUE   Five hundred years after the expulsion of the Jews, this museum opened in 1992 to explain the story of the Jewish experience in Toledo and Spain. It is housed in the **Sinagoga del Tránsito,** built in 1355 by Samuel Leví with a dispensation from Pedro I. Leví had significant influence with the king, having served as royal treasurer,

TOLEDO'S spectrum OF CULTURES

While Christian art and architecture dominate Toledo, there are many opportunities to explore the other cultures upon which the city is built. The **Sinagoga de Santa María la Blanca ★**, Calle Reyes Católicos, 4 (toledomonumental.com; ℂ **92-522-72-57;** admission 2.80€; daily 10am–5:45pm, until 6:45pm in summer), dates from 1203 and is believed to be the oldest synagogue in Europe. Its horseshoe arches and intricate moldings echo Córdoba's La Mezquita (p. 268). Like the synagogue, the mosque of **Cristo de la Luz ★**, Calle Cristo de la Luz, 22 (toledomonumental.com; ℂ **92-525-41-91;** admission 2.80€; daily 10am–5:45pm, until 6:45pm in summer), received a Christian name-change after the Reconquest. In a city full of legends, the story goes that a shaft of light guided King Alfonso XII to a crucifix hidden in the walls of the mosque since Visigoth times. Recent analysis shows there was in fact never a Visigoth church on the site. Both sites are part of the *pulsera turística* program, which gives access to seven historic sites for 9€. The **Museo de la Cultura Visigoda ★**, Calle de San Román s/n (cultura.castillalamancha.es; ℂ **92-522-78-72;** admission 2€; Tues–Sat 10am–2pm and 4–6pm, Sun 9am–3pm), underlines the heady cultural mix which makes up Toledo. Its Visigothic artifacts from the 6th to the 8th centuries (with explanation in Spanish only) are housed in the 13th-century church of San Román, an extraordinary mish-mash of Roman, Arab, and Christian design. The small **Taller del Moro ★** museum, Calle Taller del Moro (cultura.castillalamancha.es; ℂ **92-578-82-70;** admission 4€; Tues–Sat 10am–2pm and 4–6pm, Sun 9am–3pm), in a beautifully restored 14th-century palace, focuses on Mudéjar craftsmanship, while the **Museo Sefardí** (p. 163) tells the story of the Jews on the Iberian peninsula. You'll hear plenty of talk about how the three cultures of Christianity, Judaism and Islam lived in harmony in Toledo. Sadly, the historical facts say otherwise.

among other roles. It was the only synagogue in Toledo to escape unscathed in the 1391 pogrom. The building was Christianized after 1492, so only some of the scrollwork on the walls is original—restorations were carried out in the 20th century. Exhibits chronicle Jewish communities on the Iberian Peninsula from the Roman era through 1492. Another gallery looks at the slow changes in 19th-century Spanish law, from the 1802 edict that allowed Jewish religious observances to the formal 1869 retraction of Fernando and Isabel's expulsion order.

Calle Samuel Leví, s/n. museosefardi.mcu.es. ℂ **92-522-36-65.** Admission 3€ adults; 1.50€ students; free for seniors and kids under 18. Tues–Sat 9:30am–7:30pm (until 6pm in winter); Sun 10am–3pm. Free for all after 2pm Sat and all day Sun. Closed Jan 1, May 1, June 7, Dec 24–25, and Dec 31.

Museo Victorio Macho ★ ART MUSEUM   You probably haven't come to Toledo to see modern art (Cuenca is the place for that; see p. 171), but this small museum perched on the edge of the Jewish quarter is worth a visit if you have time. One of Spain's finest modern sculptors, Macho fled at the outbreak of the Civil War and made his name in Latin America. When the Franco regime began courting expatriate artists in the 1950s, he moved back to Toledo to build a home and studio on this dramatic outcrop above the Río Tajo. Following his death in 1966, the site was donated to the city as a museum. Displays include several of Macho's smaller bronzes, some reliefs, and many drawings and sketches. The garden has also fabulous views of the river below the city walls.

Plaza Victorio Macho, 2. realfundaciontoledo.es. ℰ **92-528-42-25.** Admission 3€; children under 12 free. Mon–Fri 10am–2pm and 5–7pm.

Especially for Kids

High religious art and architecture may not exactly rivet kids' attention, but Toledo has plenty of other activities to keep them entertained. A walk through **Bisagra** city gate, around the ancient walls and up one of the escalators to a mirador, will give them a great sense of history and adventure—"I'm the king of the castle" on a grand scale. Of the museums, **Museo del Greco** (p. 161) is probably the most child-friendly, although there's an undeniably morbid appeal to the **Museum of Inquisition Torture Instruments,** Calle de Alfonso XII (exposicion-antiguos-instrumentos-de-tortura.negocio.site; ℰ **92-522-73-27**). Youngsters may be fascinated by Toledo's sword-making traditions and its history of marzipan manufacture. For the truly adventurous, **Fly Toledo,** Puente de San Martín, 2 (fly-toledo.com; ℰ **69-346-48-45; 10€**), a zipline that stretches across the Río Tajo, claims to be the longest of its kind in Europe; it accepts children as young as eight.

Where to Stay in Toledo

Apartamentos Turísticos Casa de los Mozárabes ★ Set in a restored 16th-century townhouse on a narrow, sun-shafted alleyway 2 minutes from the Zocodover, these apartments are a beautiful combination of old and new. The six self-catering units have been expensively renovated leaving many original features intact—exposed stone walls, granite columns, dark beams—while the furnishings and fittings are clean, modern, and functional. A pool table in the basement cave-room illustrates the mood. There's no reception desk, but the host will keep in touch by text message to make sure your arrival is smooth and is a good source of tips about what's hot and what's not in Toledo. The prices, particularly if you share one of the larger apartments with friends, represent terrific value.

Callejón de Menores, 10. www.casadelosmozarabes.com. ℰ **68-976-66-05.** 6 units. 85€–150€ double. Discount parking nearby 13€. **Amenities:** Kitchen; free Wi-Fi.

Entre dos Aguas ★★ This extraordinary boutique hotel was the home of the legendary flamenco guitarist Paco de Lucía, who died in 2014. It's named after his 1970s masterpiece, and his presence and music are all around. The 15th-century house, built around a central patio, is ornately decorated in Andalucían style, while the guest rooms are cool and calm. The setting is harmonious too, close to the convent of Santo Domingo, and the terrace has lovely sunset views across the rooftops. A huge treat for flamenco *aficionados,* who can visit the in-house recording studio where the *maestro* made his final album. *¡Olé!*

Plaza de Santo Domingo, 2. www.casaentredosaguas.es. ✆ **62-761-23-69.** 6 units. 100€–150€ double. **Amenities:** Restaurant; bar; terrace; free Wi-Fi.

Hacienda del Cardenal ★★ You'll be charmed when you make your way through the ancient city walls and find yourself in the tranquil gardens of the former summer residence of one lucky archbishop. The building, dating from the 18th century, has the slightly faded feel of one of the older *paradors,* with worn terracotta tiles and antique lounges, but its rooms are recently renovated and very comfortable. Some have terraces with sun loungers and rates are remarkably low given the privileged setting. Dinner in the spacious dining room (or garden, weather permitting) is at the more expensive end of the scale. The menu is traditional, including *cochinillo* (suckling pig) and Toledo's trademark *perdiz roja estofada* (roast red partridge), which stays long in the mouth and the memory. The hotel is located at the bottom of the hill near the Bisagra Gate, but it is close to the escalator at Paseo de Recaredo.

Paseo de Recaredo, 24. www.haciendadelcardenal.com. ✆ **92-522-49-00.** 27 units. 75€–125€ double. Parking nearby 17€. Bus: 5 or 6 from train station. **Amenities:** Restaurant; bar; outdoor pool; terrace; free Wi-Fi.

Parador de Toledo ★★ The important point to note about Toledo's *parador* is that it sits some 4km (2½ miles) outside the old town, on a ridge across the Río Tajo. The reason, of course, is for the glorious architectural views of the city, but if you stay here, you'll need to take taxis back and forth to visit the sights. The *parador* occupies a handsome stone manor house with heavy wood beams and copies of El Greco's twelve apostles in the reception area, but the guest rooms depart from the usual approach of antique furnishings in favor of clean contemporary lines. Many rooms have balconies, and there's a large outdoor swimming pool and bar terrace, which can get busy when tour groups descend. The restaurant serves all the Castilla-La Mancha standards: roast partridge and lamb, honey ice cream, and *mazapán.* Views of Toledo from your table or poolside recliner are simply magnificent.

Cerro del Emperador. www.parador.es. ✆ **92-522-18-50.** 76 units. 95€–180€ double. Free parking. **Amenities:** Restaurant; bar; room service; outdoor pool; free Wi-Fi.

Posada de Manolo ★ At the budget end of the scale, this family-run guesthouse is perfectly situated less than 100 meters from the cathedral. It's set in a nicely renovated 15th-century building and each of its three floors is themed to the historic cultures which made up medieval Toledo: Arabic, Jewish, and Christian. Rooms are small but comfortable, and there's a reassuring aroma of furniture polish; the keys are the kind you need to leave at reception. The only drawback is the rather noisy plumbing. If you're driving, it's best to leave your car in the San Miguel public car park and make the short walk from there. Optional breakfast costs just 5€.

Calle de Sixto Ramón Parro, 8. www.laposadademanolo.com. © **92-528-22-50.** 13 units. 59€–79€ double. **Amenities:** Terrace; free Wi-Fi.

Where to Eat in Toledo

The first cookbook in Spanish was published in Toledo in 1525, entitled the *Book of Stews, Delicacies and Soups.* Five hundred years on it's not a bad description of Toledo's celebrated cuisine, shaped by the rugged Manchegan landscape and the city's multicultural past. The striking signature dish is *perdiz a la Toledana* (partridge casserole with garlic, herbs, wine, and olive oil), much discussed by visitors to Toledo, not always appreciatively. As James Michener pointed out to a ruddy-faced Englishman in his travel memoir *Iberia:* "I'm afraid there's nothing wrong with your partridge, sir. It's how they serve it in Spain. A delicacy. Well hung." Expect it to be gamy to the point of being high. If that's not to your taste, the roast lamb *(cordero asado)* and suckling pig *(cochinillo)* are superb, as are rustic stews and soups such as *carcamusa,* a rich pork casserole with tomatoes and peas—often served as a bar snack—and *sopa Castellana,* involving garlic, bread, egg, paprika, and lots of the excellent local olive oil. Much of Spain's prized saffron *(azafrán)* is cultivated in the crocus fields of La Mancha, and Toledo's other great delicacy is marzipan *(mazapán),* which you'll see as a finale on many menus. No one is quite sure who first had the idea to mix ground almonds, sugar, and eggs—maybe the Arabs, maybe famine-struck nuns—but the first known recipe for it appears in that same 1525 cookbook. (See "Marzipan from the Nuns," below.)

Adolfo Restaurante ★★ MANCHEGAN   Adolfo Muñoz, the charismatic champion of modern La Manchan cooking, has done more than

MARZIPAN FROM THE nuns

Whether or not they invented it (some say it was originally an Arab treat), the nuns of Toledo began making the confection of ground almonds, sugar, and eggs known as *mazapán* in the 13th century. A flour shortage following the battle of las Navas de Tolosa forced them to improvise to feed a hungry population. The convent of **San Clemente,** Calle San Clemente, 1, claims to be the original source, using the enviable tagline "marzipan and home-made pastries since 1212." If you ring the bell, you'll be buzzed in, and presently a nun will appear behind a grilled hatch. You can buy a range of pre-packaged boxes of marzipan and other sweetmeats from around 20€. In truth, you can get better value—and perhaps better quality too—at the more commercial outlets in town. **Santo Tomé,** competing with nuns since 1856, allows you to assemble your own assortment from the display cases—or just buy one piece for a quick shot of sugar. Look out for extravagant *mazapán* sculptures in their main store at Plaza de Zocodover, 7 (www.mazapan.com; © **92-522-11-68**).

anyone to put Toledo on the culinary map. He has two restaurants in town: the moderately priced gastrobar **Collección Catedral,** Calle Nuncio Viejo, 1 (✆ **92-522-42-44**), and this, the upmarket flagship of the group. Some will tell you that, after 30 years at the top, Adolfo is not as good as it once was, and the dining room and service do feel a little tired, but the tasting menu is nonetheless a memorable performance. Part of what makes Toledan cuisine so distinctive is the Arab-influenced use of both fresh and dried fruit in savory dishes. Muñoz nods to that with beautifully presented dishes like prawn carpaccio with pomegranate, or pig's ear infused with blueberries and passion fruit. The menu changes regularly, but expect roast *ibérico* pork, partridge, and market fish. The 9-course menu can be paired with fine wines from the cellar, served with theatrical high jinks by Adolfo's passionate sommelier Miguel Angel. Reservations recommended.

Calle Hombre de Palo, 7. www.adolforestaurante.com. ✆ **92-522-73-21.** Entrees 25€–45€; tasting menu 76€–100€ with paired wines. Tues–Sat 1–4pm and 8pm–midnight; Sun 1–4pm.

Alfileritos 24 Taberna Restaurante ★★ SPANISH   Old Toledo and new Spain come together in this favorite of young professionals in the heart of the old town. The medieval building, built into the ancient city walls, is split into two sections: a downstairs taberna where you sit under vaulted brickwork, and a sleek upstairs restaurant which surrounds the central patio. The cooking is cosmopolitan, and great value. The *menú del dia,* available only in the taberna, costs just 11.80€ for three simple courses such as *pisto Manchego* (roast vegetables with ham and eggs) or grilled salmon with wok vegetables and *tarta de abuela* (grandma's cake), while the restaurant upstairs offers a full tasting menu for just under 40€. Best of all may be the *pica-pica* sharing dish, which includes creamy partridge and pheasant croquettes, tuna tartare with guacamole, and crunchy duck rolls. Just one gripe: Why is the on-tap beer Heineken? Ask for a bottled Spanish beer instead.

Calle Alfileritos, 24. www.alfileritos24.com. ✆ **92-523-96-25.** Entrees 18€–22€, tasting menu 39.90€. Children's menu. Daily 1–4pm, 7:30–11:30pm (until midnight Fri–Sat).

El Peñon ★★★ MANCHEGAN   This unassuming bar is on a roundabout at the bottom of the hill just outside the old town, so you're unlikely to stumble across it. But it may be the best tapas experience in Toledo, and certainly the best value. At lunchtime it fills up early with locals tasting the wide selection of excellent wines and offers modern *pinchos* at the counter: snacks of *morcilla* (blood sausage) with fried quail's egg and padrón pepper, *boquerones* (anchovies) and goats' cheese, and mini-sliders on black bread. The punchline is that these elaborate and delicious tapas are free with your drinks. After that they start setting up for more formal lunches and dinners of home-cooked specialties at bargain prices.

If you plan to visit the Hospital del Tavera down the hill (p. 159), make sure to time things to include tapas at El Peñon. Then take the nearby escalator back up the hill.

Calle Carrera, 31. www.restauranteelpeñon.es. ⓒ **92-521-33-22.** Entrees 12€–21€. Mon–Thu 8:30am–8pm; Fri 8:30am–midnight; Sat 9:30am–6pm; closed Sun.

Taberna El Botero ★★ SPANISH   Set behind a lovely old red-painted shopfront near the cathedral, El Botero is a lively cocktail bar downstairs with a sophisticated restaurant on top. Everything, from the goldfish bowl *gin tonicas* to the *carbón de bacalao* (blackened cod), is prepared with precision and elegance. Be patient, that cocktail will be worth the wait. The variety of small dishes on offer in the restaurant lean towards fish and are among the most adventurous and attractively presented in town, although they're not cheap. The tasting menu, for one or two persons, may be better value if you're hungry. If not, eat downstairs, where the *degustación de croquetes,* a slate-board selection of six distinct flavors, is first-class finger food.

Calle Ciudad, 5. tabernabotero.com. ⓒ **92-528-09-67.** Entrees 15–20€; tasting menus 40€–70€. Mon noon–5pm; Wed, Thurs, Sun noon–1:30am; Fri–Sat noon–2:30am; closed Tues.

Toledo Shopping

Tourist souvenir shops are just about the only thing that lets Toledo down. From the time of the Crusades, the swordsmiths of Toledo have been renowned for their high-quality weaponry, but the tacky items for sale today are almost all factory-made. Only a handful of traditional sword makers survive. At **Mariano Zamorano**'s workshop, Calle Ciudad, 19 (www.marianozamorano.com; ⓒ **92-522-26-34**), you can—in the winter months—see artisans heating steel bars red-hot on a bed of charcoal, then stretching and shaping the steel into the final blades. If the *Game of Thrones* look is not to your taste, high-quality kitchen knives may be a

POTTERY row

Want to delve deeper into the Spanish ceramic tradition? Consider a trip to **Talavera de la Reina,** 80km (50 miles) west of Toledo, where most of the best pottery is made. Talavera is the province's largest city, so it is hardly a picture-postcard potter's village. Most shops lie along the town's main street, where store after store sells distinctive pieces in the characteristic multi-colored designs. The heavily tiled **Basilica de Nuestra Señora del Prado** ★, Av. Extremadura (www.basilicavirgendelprado.es; ⓒ **92-580-14-45**), is known as the ceramic Sistine Chapel. The stunning, and free, **Museo Ruiz de Luna** ★, Plaza de San Agustin, 13 (turismocastillalamancha.es; ⓒ **925-800-149**), built on the site of a 10th-century convent, traces the design evolution of Talavera's wares from the 16th to the 20th centuries. For a great example of their royal appeal, visit the Palace of the Escorial (p. 147) where blue-and-white *azulejos* (tiles), commissioned from Talavera in the 16th century, line room after room.

IN SEARCH OF don quijote

"In a certain village in La Mancha, which I do not wish to name, there lived not long ago a gentleman…" So Cervantes' masterpiece begins. Miguel de Cervantes was born in 1547 in **Alcalá de Henares** (p. 149), and by the time he got around to writing *Don Quijote* he'd already led an eventful life as a soldier, captive, failed accountant, convict, and struggling author. His two-part epic, regarded as one of the greatest works of fiction ever written, recounts the adventures of the self-styled knight errant and his squire Sancho Panza as they travel the countryside of La Mancha in search of chivalrous deeds. Along the way the deluded Don Quijote mistakes windmills for giants, an inn for a castle, and a garlic-munching farm girl for his fair lady Dulcinea. The story paints a wonderful picture of the life and landscape of golden age Spain, and a day's road trip across La Mancha's empty plains lets you relive it. (Be prepared for an awful lot of so-so metal sculptures of the knight of the sad countenance along the way.)

Consuegra, 45 minutes by car southeast from Toledo, is a good place to start, with 12 picturesque restored windmills and a 10th-century castle above the ugly agricultural town. One windmill is set up as a working museum, where you can see how the wheat was milled; another has been converted into a restaurant and gourmet food store. Ask for details at the first windmill you encounter, which houses the tourist office: **Molino Bolero,** Calle Cerro Caldérico, s/n (www.consuegra.es; © **92-547-57-31**).

Head 20 minutes south to reach the charming village of **Puerto Lápice,** where Cervantes depicted Don Quijote and Sancho staying at its inn. Our hero, mistaking the inn for a castle, persuades its embarrassed landlord to knight him. The inn still stands, though it's now a touristy spot, with a small free museum, obligatory souvenir shop, and restaurant. A better bet for food is to join the locals at **Mesón Cervantes,** Plaza de la Constitución, 6 (www.meson-cervantes.es; © **64-976-03-82**), next to the wooden balustrades of the village square.

better buy: **Artesanía Morales,** Plaza de Conde 3 (www.artesaniamorales.com; © **92-522-35-86**), makes some of the best. Toledo is equally renowned for its *damasquinado,* or damascene work, the Moorish art of inlaying gold and silver threads against a matte black-steel backdrop. Many of the souvenir shops sell inferior machine-made jewelry, but in summer you can still see fine damascene work being done by hand at Mariano Zamoraño's workshop (see above), and at **Damasquinados Suárez,** Circo Romano, 8 (www.espaderias-suarez.com; © **92-528-00-27**).

Toledo Entertainment & Nightlife

Come nightfall, the throngs of day-trippers vanish, and locals seek out nightlife mainly in the modern town, far from the historic attractions. In the old city, **Bar La Abadía,** Plaza San Nicolás, 3 (abadiatoledo.com), is a large stone-built bar and restaurant where Toledans jostle for the house-brand beer. **Bar Ludeña,** Plaza Magdalena, 10, is a friendly local with

Another half hour across the flat, wine-growing country (it produces much of Spain's table wine) will take you to **Campo de Criptana,** which claims to have inspired Don Quijote's most famous episode: the tilting at windmills. In Cervantes' day there were probably as many as 30 windmills standing above the town, easily mistaken for giants. Today 10 remain, 3 of which date to the 16th century. The town is well organized for visitors, with a number of interesting exhibits and an excellent restaurant, **Las Musas,** Calle Barbero, 3 (eltenedor.es/restaurante/las-musas/24687; ✆ **92-658-91-91**). Reserve ahead, as the restaurant gets busy with bus tours. The staff at the tourist office, Calle Barbero, 1 (tierradegigantes.es; ✆ **92-656-22-31**), are rightly proud of what they have here.

Still, the prize for the best exploitation of the Don Quijote story must go to **El Toboso,** home town of the knight's unrequited love, Dulcinea. The **Museo-Casa de Dulcinea del Toboso,** Calle Don Quijote, 1 (turismocastillalamancha.es; ✆ **92-578-82-70**), is of course not where Dulcinea actually lived—being a fictional character, she lived nowhere—but it may have been the house of Ana Martínez Zarco de Morales, upon whom Cervantes based the lady of the knight's imagining. This restored agricultural homestead paints an evocative picture of life in Cervantes' time. Best of all, however, is the **Museo Cervantino** attached to the tourist office on Plaza Juan Carlos I (www.eltoboso.es; ✆ **92-519-74-56**). In the 1920s, the mayor of El Toboso had the bright idea of asking world leaders to send the museum a signed copy of Spain's most famous book in their own language. Today, the museum has around 200 editions signed by leaders ranging from Ronald Reagan to Margaret Thatcher and Nelson Mandela. Two volumes don't contain Don Quijote: Adolf Hitler and Libya's Colonel Gaddafi sent signed books of their own choosing. (Draw your own conclusions.)

If you have more time to spend, there are lots more places of interest along what the authorities have inevitably named the **Ruta Quijote** (www.rutaquijote.es/lugares).

good tapas—try the house speciality *carcamusa* pork stew, which bubbles behind the bar. Next to the Army Museum (p. 161), **Entrecalles Cervecería,** Calle de la Paz (cerveceriaartesana.es), serves more than a hundred types of beer, paired with tapas and classic U.S. rock. **Sala Pícaro,** Calle Cadenas, 6 (www.picarotoledo.com), has regular live events with Spanish indie bands and DJs, while **Taberna El Botero,** Calle Ciudad, 5 (p. 169), is the place for cocktails. Avoid the tourist and burger bars of the Plaza de Zocodover.

CUENCA ★★

Balanced between the earth and sky, this mountain-top city is improbable and beguiling. Islamic soldiers built it in 714 on a high limestone spur surrounded by the gorges of the Júcar and Huécar rivers, which converge here. This strategic fortress repelled many a siege by Christian forces until a 21-year-old Alfonso VIII of Castilla finally took the city in 1177. Of the

Moorish fortifications, only the Arco de Bezudo and sections of crumbling wall remain. Under Christian rule, Cuenca filled with convents and monasteries, and because space on the rock was scarce, buildings went up and up. Cuenca is most famous for its hanging houses *(casas colgadas),* which have played a vital role in the city's recent history. Largely abandoned in the years of poverty following the Civil War, the city was rediscovered in the 1950s by a group of Spanish abstract artists, who admired its surreal angles and high-altitude light, and many relocated here. The abstract art museum which opened in the hanging houses in 1966 began a wave which means that Cuenca now has more contemporary art galleries per head than anywhere else in Spain.

Essentials

ARRIVING   A dozen high-speed trains leave Madrid's Atocha station daily and arrive about an hour later at Estación AVE Fernando Zóbel in Cuenca's new town. The one-way fare costs around 25€. Regional trains cost about 15€ but take more than 3 hours. For information, visit www.renfe.com or call ✆ **91-232-03-20.** Nine intercity **buses** leave from Madrid daily; a one-way ticket costs around 13€ and the trip takes 2½ hours. Buses arrive at Calle Fermín Caballero, 20 (www.avanzabus.com or ✆ **91-272-28-32** for schedule information). A local bus (L1 or L2) will take you up the hill to the old town, costing 2.15€ from the AVE station and 1.20€ from the bus station.

By **car** from Madrid, take the A-3 to Tarancón, and then the A-40, which leads directly into Cuenca. As you climb the hill towards the old town, you'll find public parking at **Aparcamiento Mangana** (Plaza Carmen, 3) with an elevator to take you to the top, or free parking at **Parking Castillo** (Calle Larga) at the top of the town, next to the castle.

VISITOR INFORMATION   The **tourist office** at Calle Alfonso VIII, 2 (turismo.cuenca.es; ✆ **96-924-10-51**), is open daily 10am to 2pm and 5 to 7pm (until 8pm in summer). Pick up a useful map.

Exploring Cuenca

The new city that spreads out at the base of Cuenca is full of life, but it's of limited interest to sightseers. Plan to spend your stay up the hill in the old city and take plenty of time to stand and stare: Cuenca itself is the star. **Plaza Mayor** ★★ is the social center of the old town, flanked by the arch of the *ayuntamiento* (city hall) on one side and the cathedral on the other. A palette of pastel colors on the slim, tall house fronts provides a splendid backdrop to outdoor cafes. Walk (or take bus L2) to the top of the hill past the **Arco de Bezudo** for vistas across the craggy gorge to the ochres and umbers of the buildings that cling to the cliffs opposite. For a different but no less dramatic perspective, the **Mirador de San Miguel** behind the cathedral overlooks the green hillsides of the Júcar valley. Eight old bridges cross the two rivers at the foot of the gorges: Assuming you're not prone to vertigo, walk across the **Puente de San Pablo,** an iron-and-wood footbridge that spans the 60m (197-ft.) drop between the old city and the *parador.* From there you'll get the finest views of Cuenca's hanging houses.

Casas Colgadas ★★★ HISTORIC SITE   These extraordinary structures, built into the sheer rock, date from the 15th century or even earlier. There were once many more of them—as can clearly be seen in a 1565 panorama of the city—but today just a few survive, this group of three being the most celebrated. They were built as private residences by wealthy Cuenca families (you can still see the crest of the canny clergyman who owned them all in the 15th c.) who continued to live in them until the early 20th century, when most others were demolished. They have undergone many changes and renovations over the centuries, accumulating features such as the cantilevered, wooden balconies that jut out over the gorge. In the 1960s the wealthy abstract artist Fernando Zobel, looking for a suitable site to house his collection, leased them from the city of Cuenca, had them restored by local architects, and launched the next chapter in their precarious history. Two now house the **Museo de Art Abstracto Español** ★★★ (see below); the third used to house a fine restaurant, but for now it lies empty.

Calle Canónigos. www.turismocastillalamancha.es.

Catedral de Cuenca ★★ CATHEDRAL   Soon after Alfonso VIII conquered Cuenca in 1177, he commissioned this Anglo-Norman cathedral to please his homesick wife, Eleanor of Aquitaine (daughter of England's Henry II). The masons he brought from Normandy used the same style as the grand Norman cathedral at Chartres, built at the same time. The current façade is not the original—largely rebuilt in neo-Gothic style in 1904 following a disastrous lightning strike, it remains unfinished, but the original soaring alabaster columns are still standing. Highlights inside include a Gothic statue of **Virgen del Sagrario** dating from the cathedral's founding; the **Neoclassical altar** by the great architect of Madrid, Ventura Rodriguez; and a couple of moving El Grecos. The stained-glass windows, which date

One of Cuenca's *casas colgadas*, or hanging houses.

173

from the 1990s, were designed by Cuenca's resident abstract artists. Climb the clerestory *(triforio)* for another stunning view, this time over the Plaza Mayor.

Plaza Mayor. www.catedralcuenca.es. ✆ **96-922-46-26.** Admission, with audio-guide: cathedral only 4.80€; cathedral and triforio 6:30€; cathedral, triforio, and museum 8.00€; family ticket 15€. July–Nov daily 10am–7:30pm. Bus 1 or 2.

Museo de Arte Abstracto Español ★★★ ART MUSEUM   Cuenca's first contemporary art museum, opened in 1966, occupies two of the *casas colgadas* (see above). It's hard to know where to look first—at the details of the Gothic building, out the windows towards the gorge, or at the sometimes-angry art on the walls. In fact, the surreal setting is entirely appropriate. The permanent collection is based around the work of a handful of groups, primarily **Grupo El Paso,** established in the 1950s in response to the stagnating art of Franco's Spain. Once the museum was up and running, a number of artists—among them Antonio Saura, José Guerrero, Gustavo Torner, and Gerardo Rueda—moved into Cuenca's historic upper quarter, whose buildings had been abandoned after the Civil War. In other words, abstract art has been directly responsible for the regeneration of this remarkable city. There are many highlights here—as well as regular temporary exhibitions—but look for Torner's scrap metal landscapes, Guerrero's matchbook blocks of color, and Saura's dark snarls, epitomized by grotesque portraits of **Felipe II** and **Brigitte Bardot.**

Calle Canónigos. march.es/arte/cuenca. ✆ **96-921-29-83.** Free admission. Tues–Fri 11am–2pm, 4–6pm; Sat 11am–2pm, 4–8pm; Sun 11am–2:30pm. Closed Mon.

Fundación Antonio Pérez ★★★ ART MUSEUM   Sigüenza-born Antonio Pérez (b. 1934) chose to base his foundation in this former convent in 1998. He's usually described as a collector, editor, poet, and artist, and it's clear he also has a well-developed sense of humor. His own pieces, categorized as *objetos encontrados* (found objects) and simply labeled A.P., litter the airy galleries. They include roadkill drinks cans, fragments of reinforced concrete, traffic signs in various states of decay, and a set of three bells without their clappers, cheekily entitled *Castrati.* His huge collection of contemporary Spanish art features many of the artists who also appear in the Museo de Arte Abstracto (see above), including Millares and Saura, alongside international stars, such as Andy Warhol, and some lovely pieces of African sculpture. It's all very entertaining, reflecting Spain's post-Franco playfulness. As a bonus, you can buy posters from previous exhibitions for just 2€ apiece, for your own collection of found art.

Ronda de Julian Romero, 20. fundacionantonioperez.com. ✆ **96-923-06-19.** Admission 2€, 1€ seniors and students. Wed–Mon 11am–2pm and 5–8pm (until 9pm in summer).

Fundación Antonio Saura (Casa Zavala) ★ ART MUSEUM   This small city's *third* contemporary art museum opened at the Casa Zavala in

2008, 10 years after the death of the Abstract Expressionist painter Antonio Saura (1930–98). Of all the artists inspired by Cuenca, Saura had the most personal connection. Suffering from tuberculosis as a teenager, he began coming here for his health and grew fascinated by the view from his sickbed window. In a late interview he said he finally realized that without knowing it, he had been painting that view all his life. Oddly, this museum—which has endured financial and family disputes—doesn't primarily feature Saura's work, focusing instead on regular temporary exhibitions of modern Spanish artists.

Plaza de San Nicolas, 1. turismo.cuenca.es. ℂ **96-923-60-54.** Free admission. Summer Mon and Wed–Sat 11am–2pm and 4–8pm, Sun 11am–2pm; winter daily 11am–2pm and 4–7pm.

Museo de Cuenca ★ MUSEUM In stark contrast to all the contemporary art in town, this regional history museum takes the long view, harking back to Neolithic funeral idols. The Cuenca area was once an important mining district for lead and silver, and Iron Age exhibits display a number of Carthaginian, Greek, and Phoenician artifacts that found their way here through trade with the coast. The Romans made peace with local leaders because the mines were so important to the empire; statues and column capitals on display come from nearby Roman settlements at Segóbriga and Valeria. A beautiful 10th-century Islamic capital, found at the archaeological site at Plaza de Mangana in 2001, details the period of Arab dominance. Rooms devoted to the medieval period through the 16th century show how Cuenca emerged as a major center for wine and wool. Kids should appreciate the display of pirate-era gold coins, including the legendary pieces of eight.

Calle Obispo Valero, 12. cultura.castillalamancha.es. ℂ **96-921-30-69.** Admission 3€, 1.50€ seniors and students; free Sat–Sun and Wed afternoon. Tues–Sat 10am–2pm and 4–7pm; Sun 10am–2pm.

Where to Stay in Cuenca

Parador de Cuenca ★★★ It's hard to imagine a hotel with a more dramatic location than the Parador de Cuenca's: on a high outcrop between the deep gorge of the Huécar River and sheer, rocky cliffs. Yet this 14th-century former convent also has an air of solid permanence. It is the top choice in town for secluded luxury, with a strong sense of the monastic life in its church and cloister. The mid-size rooms have clean, simple decor and furnishings; superior rooms have views of the *casas colgadas* across the gorge. The *parador* is connected to the old town by a wooden-sleepered pedestrian bridge high above the river, so it's convenient for sightseeing despite its remove from town. But you'll need a head for heights for the short walk home.

Subida a San Pablo, s/n. www.parador.es. ℂ **96-923-23-20.** 63 units. 95€–250€ double. Parking 18€. **Amenities:** Restaurant; bar; room service; exercise room; outdoor pool; sauna; tennis court; free Wi-Fi.

Posada de San José ★★★ In 1668 the college of San José opened its doors as a home for choirboys of the cathedral just down the hill, in hopes that nearby lodgings would make them more punctual. This historic *posada*, a hotel since 1950, is perfectly located for all the key places in Cuenca and remains resolutely old-fashioned. The front door, with ancient masonry and creeping ivy, is a photo opportunity in its own right. Rooms come in different shapes and sizes and feature plain, wooden furnishings against whitewashed walls. (Mind your head on the low door frames.) If you're willing to forgo a private bathroom, you can get a double room at incredibly low rates; the more expensive rooms have private baths and great views overlooking the Huécar gorge. There's a friendly, family atmosphere here—lots of couples return year after year. *Nonsmokers, be advised:* If your room smells of cigarette smoke, ask to change.

Calle Julián Romero, 4. www.posadasanjose.com. ✆ **96-921-13-00.** 22 units. 40€–55€ double without bath, 65€–100€ double with bath. **Amenities:** Restaurant; bar; terrace; free Wi-Fi.

Leonor de Aquitania ★ This modernly furbished hotel in an 18th-century mansion sits high enough on the hill to offer views of both the old town and the gorge. If you want to get the most out of the setting, splash out on a junior suite with a private terrace and hot tub. The standard rooms are on the small side, but all have cool red-tile floors, tasteful pale walls, and unfussy furnishings. The hotel is attached to a wider food and drink complex occupying the mansion's former stables, which includes the smart Raff restaurant (p. 178).

Calle San Pedro, 60. www.hotelleonordeaquitania.com. ✆ **96-923-10-00.** 46 units. 60€–120€ double; 130€–200€ suite. Free parking. **Amenities:** Restaurant; bar; babysitting; room service; free Wi-Fi, wellness center.

Where to Eat in Cuenca

Cuenca's cuisine owes as much to the mountains east of the city as to the La Mancha plains to the west. Wild game and foraged mushrooms feature prominently, and virtually every bar and restaurant offers the two Cuenca classics: *morteruelo* (a rich terrine of partridge, rabbit, liver, and spices), and *ajoarriero* (a creamy purée of potato, flaked cod, oil, and garlic). Both are usually spread on bread or toast as a starter. This being sheep country, lamb features on most menus. If you're feeling adventurous, try the *zarajos,* grilled lamb's intestines, often available as tapas. Chewy and earthily flavored, they're served coiled like a ball of yarn, wrapped around a vine shoot.

Figón del Huécar ★★ CASTILIAN Set in a lovely old house next door to the Posada de San José (p. 177), this elegant restaurant has fine views of the gorge both inside and out. It's the former home of the hugely successful singer-songwriter José Luis Perales and, like him, it oozes smooth

A row of cafés along Plaza Mayor, near Cuenca's cathedral.

good taste. Although the menu leans towards tradition—*morteruelo, ajoarriero,* and salad with pickled partridge are all available as starters— it brings a modern creativity to Cuencan cuisine with dishes like *bacalao* (salt cod) with honey and mustard, or venison with figs and forest fruits. There's a reasonably priced 3-course *menú del día,* and a tasting menu for an extra 10 euros. Either way, leave room for desserts such as Manchego cheesecake with quince jam. The wine list offers a good opportunity to taste the well-made reds now being produced in the D.O. Cuenca region. Reservations recommended.

Calle Julián Romero, 6. www.figondelhuecar.com. © **96-920-00-62.** Entrees 18€– 25€; set menu 26€; tasting menu 36€. Tues–Sat 12:30–4pm and 7–11pm.

Posada de San José ★★ CASTILIAN You won't be surprised to hear there's a strong traditional flavor to the menu here at Cuenca's posada. For a good introduction to the local cuisine, share a platter of typical starters, including *ajoarriero* and *morteruelo* of course, plus the roast vegetables of *pisto Manchego.* Many local diners start with a knotty plate of *zarajos.* If the tripe and game delicacies are not for you, try the tongue-twisting *solomillo de cerdo a la sidra,* pork loin braised with apples in cider. The most desirable tables are on the terrace surrounded by rose bushes and an olive tree, but the view of the Huécar gorge is just as impressive from the windows of the lovely old dining room, decorated in true Cuenca fashion with abstract modern art. The restaurant is open to the public, and tables fill up fast at weekends, so reserve early.

Calle Julián Romero, 4. www.posadasanjose.com. ✆ **96-921-13-00.** Entrees 12€–17€. Tues–Sun 7:30–10:30pm.

Raff San Pedro ★★ CASTILIAN   Relocated in 2017 to become the house restaurant of the Leonor de Aquitania hotel (p. 176), Raff is beautifully set in the mansion's former stables. Chef José Ignacio Herraiz's cooking is modern fusion, rooted firmly in the fresh flavors of the region. Try the tomato stuffed with scallop *ceviche,* rich game meatballs *(albondigas),* or the intriguing green apple in five textures. The "gastro" menu is a good opportunity to try a contemporary take on the classic dishes of the region; the *trufa de ajoarriero* with apricot packs a lot of flavor into one small ball. Service is friendly and deft: When we visited, an off glass of wine was replaced with smooth grace.

Calle San Pedro, 58. raffsanpedro.es. ✆ **96-969-08-55.** Entrees 16€–24€, set menus 24€ and 35€. Tue–Sat 1–4pm, 8:30–11pm; Sun–Mon 1–4pm.

El Secreto ★★ CASTILIAN   Halfway down the hill towards the new town, this quirky restaurant serves some of Cuenca's best cooking. Decorated to echo the colors of the old city's pastel-painted houses, El Secreto mixes artful presentation with traditional flavors. The 15€ *menú del día* is a delicious and filling bargain, including imaginative combinations such as octopus salad with fruit and coriander, chickpea soup with black pudding, or grilled tuna with guacamole and an abstract slash of *membrillo* (quince jam). Service is both relaxed and attentive. The busy tables and tiny patio, filled with Spanish visitors and lunch-break locals, suggest this place is no longer a secret.

Calle Alfonso VIII, 81. elsecretocuenca.com. ✆ **62-763-74-74.** Entrees 12€–20€, set menu 15€. Daily 1–4:30pm, 8–11pm (no dinner Tues).

Cuenca Entertainment & Nightlife

The bars on Plaza Mayor not only have a spectacular setting, they're good for a drink and tapas, too. **San Juan** (Plaza Mayor, 5) has a serving hatch doing a swift trade in the Cuenca classics, with a free portion of delicious garlic fried potatoes when you order a drink. Around the corner, **Taberna Jovi** (Calle Colmillo, 10) looks like a gentleman's club, with lots of leather, dark wood, and dim lighting. It's a good place for cocktails, with generous free tapas. **La Edad de Oro** (Calle Severo Catalina, 7) has a huge range of gins and plays golden-age music from the 1960s. *Tip:* In summer, the intense heat of the day dissipates suddenly at night, and the streets of Cuenca become so cool that you may want to take a sweater or jacket.

SIGÜENZA ★

This almost perfect medieval town in northeast Castilla-La Mancha has had a turbulent past, from which it is gracefully emerging. Set strategically on the Henares river, its name comes from the Latin Segontia, meaning "dominating the valley," and that prized location means that it has been fought over by everyone since Roman times. The formidable castle at the top of the town was built by the Arabs in the 8th century, finally falling to the Reconquest in the 12th century. The first Christian archbishop built a massive Gothic cathedral here, which looks like a fortress and frequently served as one. Sigüenza played a central role in Spain's medieval civil wars, Napoleonic troops trashed the place during the War of Spanish Independence, and in the 1936 Civil War a 2-month-long battle raged on these streets: Franco's troops occupied the castle, while the Republicans holed up in the cathedral (you can still see the bullet holes in the Plaza Mayor). Today, much of this now-tranquil town has been restored with loads of redevelopment funding, and the castle is one of Spain's most beautiful and evocative *paradors*. Sigüenza's history, architecture, and first-class restaurants make it an appealing place for an overnight stay.

Essentials

ARRIVING   There are 5 **trains** a day from Madrid's Chamartín station, the journey takes between 1½ and 2 hours and costs 12€ to 14€. For information, visit renfe.com or call ℂ **91-232-03-20.** Look for special **medieval train** day trips (esmadrid.com/en/medieval-train-siguenza), which run on certain Saturdays between April and November, featuring troubadours and traditional food. The train, medieval or otherwise, is much easier than the bus: There are around 3 **buses** a day, which may require a change at Guadalajara, costing around 11€ and taking 2½ hours. Check at www.alsa.com or ℂ **90-242-22-42.** From the train or bus station it is a short straight walk to the old town along Calle Alfonso VI. By **car** from Madrid, take the A-2 heading northeast, the trip takes around 1½ hours. The best place to park is right in front of the castle.

VISITOR INFORMATION   The tourist office at Calle Serrano Sanz, 9 (turismo@siguenza.es; ℂ **94-934-70-07**), is open daily 10am to 2pm and Monday through Saturday 4 to 6pm (until 8pm Fri, 7pm Sat). Pick up a free map.

Exploring Sigüenza

It's easy to get around Sigüenza on foot. The new town clusters around the horizontal Alameda park at the bottom of the hill, from which Calle Serrano Sanz leads up to the cathedral and the Plaza Mayor. Calle Mayor takes you the rest of the way to the castle at the apex of the town. There are a few parallel alleyways of medieval buildings—many still undergoing renovation—and that's about it, apart from the surrounding greenery for miles around with some lovely signposted walks.

Despite a turbulent past, Sigüenza has preserved its medieval charm.

Casa del Doncel ★ MUSEUM   Oddly enough, this 13th-century Gothic building with gargoyles and battlements doesn't deal with the story of Martín Vázquez de Arce (El Doncel), although his aristocratic family probably lived here. Instead it houses a curious collection of unconnected things. You can browse a not-very-good exhibition of work by current local artists; a fine collection of antique Spanish guitars and a mocked-up luthier's workshop; and a small working museum of weaving with looms, patterns, and yarn. But what makes the modest entrance fee worthwhile is the wonderful restoration of its Mudéjar rooms, with Islamic inscriptions and carvings. Downstairs you'll find the high-end restaurant Nöla (p. 183).

Plaza de San Vicente, 1. siguenza.es. (C) **94-939-39-06.** Admission 2€. Wed–Sat 11am–2pm and 4–7pm, Sun 11am–2pm.

Castillo de Sigüenza ★★★ CASTLE   The Visigoths first built a fortress on this site in the 5th century and it has undergone numerous reworkings since. Fortified by the Arabs in the 8th century, it was taken by the French-born fighter and archbishop Bernard of Agen in 1123 and converted into an episcopal palace. The castle was home to a succession of bishops for hundreds of years—an 18th-century occupant added windows, balconies and stables—but a disastrous 1830s fire led to it being abandoned. It was further damaged in the Spanish Civil War when Franco's troops used it during the battle for the town—you can see a photograph of the destruction in the reception. It didn't get its final makeover until the 1960s, when it was comprehensively rebuilt to become a *parador* hotel (p. 182). Its near-pristine form means it plays host to many a medieval re-enactment, and film directors Ridley Scott and John Glen both used it as a location for their 1992 films celebrating the 500th anniversary of Columbus' voyage. You can visit the central courtyard even if you're not staying at the *parador.*

Plaza del Castillo, s/n. www.turismocastillalamancha.es. ℭ **94-939-01-00.**

Catedral de Santa María ★★★ CHURCH/MUSEUM   Sigüenza's magnificent 12th-century cathedral and diocesan museum are packed with treasures and fascinating tales. It's worth going first to the museum to buy the combined ticket, which includes a guided tour of the cathedral's chapels. The tour is in Spanish only, but it's the only way to see everything. Star of the show is **El Doncel** (The Boy), whose name and image you'll see all over town. He was Martín Vázquez de Arce, page to Queen Isabel, who died in battle against the Moors in Granada in 1486. His tomb lies in the crypt, topped by a carving of him in languid repose, ankles crossed, reading a book. Spanish philosopher José Ortega y Gasset called it the most beautiful piece of funeral sculpture in the world (you can buy replicas at the cathedral shop). **The Sacristía de las Cabezas** is equally extraordinary. Designed by Alonso de Covarrubias, the master architect of Toledo, its ceiling is carved with hundreds of heads representing all kinds of 16th-century people, from peasants to kings. The entrance to the **Capilla del Espíritu Santo** is a riot of Mudéjar and Plateresque color, and inside—beneath an impressive dome—hangs an *Annunciation* by El Greco. After that, the **diocesan museum,** housed in a pink palace next door, may feel like second-best, but it is beautifully done, including paintings of the Virgin by Zurbarán and Morales—one angelic, the other stern.

Plaza del Obispo Don Bernardo, 6. lacatedraldesiguenza.com ℭ **61-936-27-15.** Admission with guided tour including Diocesan Museum 7€. 3–4 guided tours daily, check times at museum. Daily 9:30am–2pm and 4:30–8pm (museum 11am–2pm and 4:30–7:30pm, closed Tues).

Plaza Mayor ★★ SQUARE   If you were asked to imagine a damsel watching from the gallery as knights of old joust in a tournament below, you'd probably picture a scene something like this Renaissance square. It was commissioned by Cardinal Mendoza, who was bishop of Sigüenza in the 1470s. Along the east side is a row of arcaded 15th- and 16th-century mansions of various heights. To the south is the *ayuntamiento* (town hall), three stories tall, with arcades and galleries from which flags and pennants flutter. It faces the square Tuscan-looking bell tower of the cathedral on the third side. Only the 20th-century bollards break the spell.

Where to Stay in Sigüenza

Alojamientos Victoria ★★ This handsome 15th-century mansion, perfectly situated just off Plaza Mayor, offers 9 loft apartments which are both luxurious and great value. All have memory-foam beds, spotless bathrooms with jetted baths, and small well-equipped kitchens, with a light breakfast included. Some have balcony views of the cathedral, a stone's throw away; others of the surrounding countryside. There's a shared lounge and strong Wi-Fi; guests enthuse about the attentive host.
Calle Mayor, 1. alojamientosvictoria.es. © **94-939-02-53.** 9 units. 65€–88€ double. **Amenities:** Kitchen; terrace; free Wi-Fi.

Hotel El Doncel ★ On the edge of the old town, this stone-built hotel is comfortable, convenient, and good value. It's easy to find, close to the train station on the main road as you come into town, and it's just a short walk up the hill to the cathedral and Plaza Mayor. The guestrooms have stone walls, wooden floors, and quiet air-conditioning, but there is no elevator. Our recommendation for Sigüenza is to stay at the *parador* (see below) but have dinner here at El Doncel's wonderful restaurant (p. 183). If you are inspired by chef Enrique Pérez's exquisite cooking, the restaurant also offers cookery and wine courses.
Paseo de la Alameda, 3. www.eldoncel.com. © **94-939-00-01.** 17 units. 62€–100€ double. **Amenities:** Restaurant; bar; room service; free Wi-Fi.

Parador de Sigüenza ★★★ Given the chance, who wouldn't want to spend the night in a castle? Even by the high standards of Spain's historic state-run hotels, Sigüenza's parador is something special, and remarkably affordable. The central spaces are huge and stately: a cobbled courtyard with box-hedge gardens and fountains; a vast lounge—once the banqueting hall—with thick stone pillars and chandeliers. The spacious guest rooms favor comfort over character; they are simply and cleanly decorated, with tiled floors and modern (rather than medieval) bathrooms. Some have four-poster beds and wooden balconies. The grand stone-arched dining room, with views of the surrounding pine forest, is better for breakfast than dinner, which is traditional and rather heavy. There are better dining options in this burgeoning foodie town (see below).
Plaza del Castillo, s/n. www.parador.es. © **94-939-01-00.** 49 units. 75–200€ double. Free parking. Amenities: Restaurant; bar; garden terrace; free Wi-Fi.

Where to Eat in Sigüenza

Bar Alameda ★★ MANCHEGAN An excellent place for a stand-up lunch, this busy bar has counters piled high with more than 100 kinds of *tapas, pinchos,* and regional delicacies. Over-sized pork scratchings are a local favorite, as are the more challenging *zarajos,* a twisted ball of grilled lamb's intestine. The croquettes, meatballs, and tortilla with ham and cheese are all delicious, as is the fast-flowing regional wine. At around

3pm, the Alameda buzzes with locals and out-of-towners, then suddenly everyone disappears, until the evening session begins.

Paseo Alameda, 2. alamedatapas.es. ℂ **94-939-05-53.** Tapas 2€–8€, entrees 6.50€–10€. Fri–Wed 9:30am–midnight. Closed Thurs.

El Doncel ★★★ MODERN MANCHEGAN   Occupying a low-key space in the El Doncel hotel, this Michelin-starred restaurant is a wonderful surprise. Chef Enrique Pérez combines extraordinary attention to detail and great wit to produce some of the most impressive cooking in the region, indeed in all Spain. His *Pinceladas de Sensaciones* (brushstrokes of flavor) tasting menu changes daily based on market ingredients. It kicks off with 10 tiny snacks, which are hilariously elaborate. Pérez's take on *patatas bravas* is barely thicker than a postage stamp, with miniature blobs of sauce and flower petals, dissolving intensely on your tongue. Eight perfectly served courses follow, headwaiter Eduardo Pérez pairing them with very reasonably priced wines. Flavors abound in dishes such as corvina infused with jasmine tea and *albóndiga de corzo* (game meatball) topped with shavings of truffle. At the end, Enrique appears at your table with a signed copy of the day's menu. A joyful, memorable experience.

Paseo de la Alameda, 3. eldoncel.com. ℂ **94-939-00-01.** Entrees 21–27€, tasting menu 72€, wine not included. Closed all day Sun and Mon evening.

Nöla ★★ MANCHEGAN   Made famous by its appearance on the British gourmet comedy *The Trip,* Nöla serves exquisite cooking at exceptionally good prices. The small dining room is set in the lovely stone basement of the Casa del Doncel museum, though diners can also sit out on a patio in summer. Three tasting menus offer fine regional and fusion flavors for less than 40€ per person. Service and presentation are spot-on. Try the slow-cooked lamb ravioli in a mushroom ragout, or veal sweetbreads with pork scratchings, followed by *torrija,* a block of caramelized French toast served with artisanal ice cream.

Plaza de San Vicente. nolarestaurante.com. ℂ **94-939-32-46.** Entrees 15–19€, tasting menus 27–40€. Thurs–Sat 1:30–3:30pm, 8:30–10:30pm; Sun–Mon 1:30–3:30pm. Closed Tues.

Side Trip to Atienza

If you like a good **castle,** they don't come more emblematic of the region than the one in the small town of Atienza, a 30-minute drive northwest from Sigüenza. It is most striking viewed from a distance—on a clear day you'll see it long before you reach the town. The squat 12th-century tower sits at one end of a huge slab of rock, which lies across the hilltop like a slumbering sea lion. At first, it's hard to tell what is man-made and what is natural. Close up you can see the remains of the walls which once surrounded the rock citadel. There isn't a great deal left to see inside—there's not even an information panel—but climb to the top and the 360-degree views across the plains of Castilla will make you believe you are a medieval lookout, scanning the horizon for the next invading army. The town

The 12th-century castle of Atienza.

itself, at the foot of the hill, is good for a wander, with some attractive medieval features and blazoned mansions.

Restaurante Alfonso VIII, Carretera de Berlanga, 22 (www. restaurantealfonsoviii.es; ✆ **949-306-098**), specializing in wood-fired Castilian roasts, makes an excellent stop for lunch. On the way back to Sigüenza, take a look at the disused salt mines at **Salinas de Imón.** Originally built by the Romans, the tumbledown buildings date from the 18th century. Incredibly, they were active until 1996.

CASTILLA Y LEÓN

By Patricia Harris and David Lyon

o part of Spain speaks so eloquently of the country's warring past as Castilla y León. Its warrior kings carried the battles of the Reconquista to the Moorish conquerors and won back the Iberian Peninsula league by bloody league. The northern pair of cities in this chapter, León and Burgos, held the grand castles from which Christian armies marched and great cathedrals glorified the faith. Just south of them were the fortress cities that staked out the Christian turf in the 7-century struggle between the cross and the crescent. As you approach them, imagine that you are leading an invading army. After a long march, you finally reach the outskirts of Segovia, Ávila, or Zamora. You crane your neck to look up at the walled fortress city high on the hill. Its defenders have been watching your arrival for days, and their swords are ready. . . . It is the tale of central Spain written over and over—only the names of the invaders and defenders changed.

SEGOVIA ★★★

Poor Segovia! Because the city's Roman aqueduct appears on every checklist of Spanish monuments, the city—located at the heart of the castle-rich part of Castilla—often suffers from drive-by tourism. It's easy to park near the aqueduct, take a picture, maybe stop for lunch, and then move on. But Segovia is more than just a pretty Roman face. Outside the perimeter of its old walls lie important religious communities and a mystical shrine of the Knights Templar. In the city proper, Segovia displays a monumental drama from the arches of its Roman aqueduct on one end to the fantasy castle of its Alcázar on the other. Built on a large rocky outcrop, Segovia is a town of narrow, winding streets that have to be covered on foot to visit the Romanesque churches, early Renaissance palaces, and medieval Judería. Isabel herself was proclaimed queen of Castilla at the cathedral here in 1474.

Essentials

ARRIVING More than 2 dozen **trains** leave Madrid every day. Most take less than a half hour from Madrid-Chamartin to Segovia Av and cost 14€ to 25€ each way. The traditional rail station at Segovia is on Paseo Obispo

Quesada, s/n (www.renfe.com; ✆ **90-232-03-20**), a 20-minute walk southeast of the town center. The high-speed train arrives at Segovia-Guiomar; it's served every 15 minutes by bus 11 (2€) to the aqueduct. **Buses** arrive and depart from **Estacionamiento Municipal de Autobuses,** Paseo de Ezequiel González, 10 (✆ **92-142-77-06**). It's about a 7-minute walk to the aqueduct. There are 20 to 35 buses a day to and from Madrid (which depart from Paseo de la Florida, 11; metro Norte; ticket 9€), and about four a day between Ávila and Segovia. If you're **driving,** take the N-VI (on some maps, it's shown as the A-6) in the direction of A Coruña, northwest from Madrid, toward León and Lugo. At the junction with Rte. 110 (signposted segovia), turn northeast (AP-61 or N-603).

VISITOR INFORMATION The **Visitor Reception Center** at Plaza del Azoguejo, 1 (www.turismodesegovia.com; ✆ **92-146-67-20**), open daily 10am to 8pm, offers a free city map and sightseeing advice. The regional tourism office **Tourist Information of Castilla y León,** Plaza Mayor, 10 (www.turismocastillayleon.com; ✆ **92-146-03-34**), is open daily 9am to 3pm and 5 to 7pm. *Tip:* The regional office's city map is easier to use, and they can also give you a good map for Ávila (p. 195).

Exploring Segovia

Segovia is shaped like a wedge of cake plopped on its side. The Roman aqueduct is at the point, while the Alcázar stands atop the thick end above all the frosting. The cathedral and Plaza Mayor are in the middle. You'll find the best shopping in the old city between the aqueduct, the cathedral, and the Alcázar. For local ceramics and souvenirs, cruise **Calle de Juan Bravo, Calle Daoiz,** and **Calle Marqués del Arco.** Thursday is market day.

Alcázar de Segovia ★★ CASTLE   There is a good reason why this fortress looks like a late-19th-century romantic ideal of a medieval castle: Most of it burned in 1862 and was rebuilt to emulate the storybook castles of 16th-century northern Europe rather than the messy fortress-castles of Spain's warrior monarchs of the 1300s. The reconstruction was carried out during shaky political times to burnish the otherwise tarnished image of the monarchy. In effect, it's a museum of the nobler side of the Reconquista.

As you enter (from the city side), the first thing you'll spy are suits of German plate armor for knights and two for their steeds. Spanish monarchs have cultivated this chivalrous image ever since the Habsburgs came to the throne in the 1500s. The castle was a favorite residence of Castilian monarchs throughout the medieval period, and the sumptuous decoration of tapestries, tiles, and Mudéjar woodwork conjures "days of old when knights were bold." In 1474, Isabel took refuge in the original fortress when word came that her brother Enrique IV had died. A mural in the

Galley Chamber tells the rest of that story: Having mustered the support of the royal army, she marched out of the Alcázar to Segovia's Plaza Mayor to be proclaimed queen of Castilla. (She also met Fernando II of Aragón here several years earlier but wisely held onto her rights when they married.) The most dramatic room of the castle is the **Hall of Monarchs,** with its ceiling-level frieze depicting each king or queen in the Castilian line, from Pelayo (Pelagius in Latin) of Asturias, credited with starting the Reconquista in the 720s, to Juana la Loca, Isabel's mad daughter, who is shown seated on a golden Gothic throne. This incredible piece of art and history was commissioned by Juana's grandson, Felipe II, to cement his lineage's claim to the Spanish crown. You can walk the battlements of this once-impregnable castle, from which its occupants hurled boiling oil onto the enemy below, and ascend the 152 twisting stairs of the tower—originally built by Isabel's father as a prison—for a panoramic view of Segovia.

Plaza de la Reina Victoria Eugenia. www.alcazardesegovia.com. © **92-146-07-59.** Admission 5.50€ adults, 3.50€ students, seniors, and ages 5–16; 2.50€ additional for tower. Apr–Oct daily 10am–8pm; Nov–Mar daily 10am–6pm. Bus: 3.

Cabildo Catedral de Segovia ★

CATHEDRAL Segovia's original Gothic cathedral was destroyed in 1520 during the short-lived uprising of the Castilian cities against the Habsburg kings. When the smoke cleared and the lords of Segovia were crushed, Carlos V ordered it rebuilt in the same style, making it Spain's last Gothic cathedral. Just to be on the safe side, he also moved it to Plaza Mayor from its old spot next to the Alcázar. Construction began in 1525, thought it wasn't finally consecrated until 1768. Even on the brightest days, the interior is gloomy, but it's worth visiting to see the swirling, gold-encrusted altar created by José de Churriguera for the Santisimo Sacramento chapel circa 1700, as well as the stained-glass windows, elaborately carved choir stalls, and 16th- and 17th-century paintings.

The soaring vaults of Segovia's late Gothic cathedral.

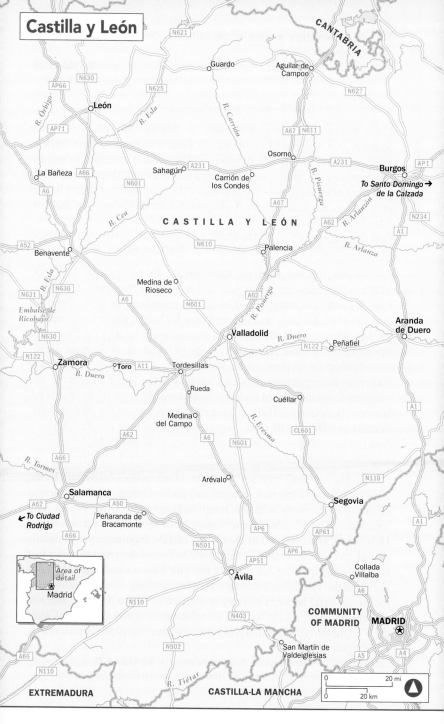

Castilla y León

The serene **cloisters** ★ predate the cathedral. See website for hours of guided tours of the tower.

Plaza Catedral, Marqués del Arco, s/n. www.catedralsegovia.es. ⓒ **92-146-22-05.** Admission to cathedral, cloisters, museum, and chapel room 3€ adults; 2.50€ seniors; free ages 9 and under; cathedral plus tower 7€; free admission to cathedral Sun 9:30am–10:30am. Nov–Mar daily 9:30am–6:30pm, Apr–Oct daily 9am–9:30pm.

Casa-Museo Antonio Machado ★ MUSEUM   When the great Spanish poet Antonio Machado taught French in Segovia from 1919 to 1932, he lived in this boardinghouse. The modest structure is more a remembrance—almost a shrine—than a true museum: Documents, drawings, and other mementos try to conjure the poet, but they aren't half as evocative as the little courtyard overgrown with flowering cacti and hollyhocks gone to seed.

Calle Desamparados, 5. ⓒ **92-146-03-77.** Admission 2.50€, with guided tour 3.50€; free Wed. Daily 11am–3pm, also 3:30–5pm on Mon, Wed, Fri, Sat.

Convento de los Padres Carmelitas Descalzos ★ MONASTERY   The 16th-century mystic and theologian San Juan de la Cruz founded and personally helped build this monastery in 1586. Upon his death in 1591, his body was returned here for burial, where it still rests in the left side chapel of the convent's church. Saint John of the Cross was the confessor of Santa Teresa of Ávila (p. 197) and one of the most significant theologians of the Counter-Reformation. His teachings found new audiences among reform-minded Catholics in the late 20th century, and clergy in Segovia speak of him as if he was merely away for the weekend. His central axiom was that a person must empty his or her soul of "self" in order to be filled with God—a mystical tenet akin to Zen Buddhism.

Paseo de Segundo Rincón, 2. www.ocdcastilla.org. ⓒ **92-143-19-61.** Admission by donation. Church Mon 10am–1:30pm; Tues–Sun 10am–1:30pm and 4–8pm.

Iglesia de la Vera Cruz ★ CHURCH   Built in the 12th century by the Knights Templar more as a shrine than a parish church, this Romanesque edifice still resonates with the rough faith of the warrior monks who founded it. The 12-sided shape (copied from Jerusalem's Church of the Holy Sepulchre), the style of the niches, and the fragmentary wall murals all had special significance in the mystic beliefs of the crusader order that built the church to house a piece of the True Cross. Consecrated in 1246 (1208 on the Gregorian calendar), the church's very existence illustrates the strong bond between military and religious life in Segovia. The site was abandoned when the Knights Templar were disbanded by Pope Clement V in the early 14th century, but the structure was partially restored by the Knights of Malta.

Carretera de Zamarramala. www.ordendemalta.es. ⓒ **92-143-14-75.** Admission 2€. Tues–Sun 10:30am–1:30pm and 3:30–7pm (closes 6pm in winter). Closed Nov.

Museo de Arte Contemporáneo Esteban Vicente ★ ART MUSEUM   Spanish-born Estéban Vicente (1903–2001) found his artistic niche as a member of the pioneering New York school of Abstract Expressionists but chose to donate a significant body of work to his home country. The collection includes oil paintings, collages, a tapestry, and a number of small sculptures. To house and display the collection, the mid-15th-century palace of Enrique IV of Castilla y León (Isabel I's older half-brother) was converted to a white-walled, unadorned, contemporary gallery space. The museum tries to further the spirit of artistic inquiry that characterized the first generation of Abstract Expressionism through temporary exhibitions, which often focus on video.

Plazuela de las Bellas Artes. www.museoestebanvicente.es. ✆ **92-146-20-10.** Admission 3€ adults, 1.50€ students, free for seniors and ages 17 and under; and free for all Thurs. Tues–Fri 11am–2pm and 4–7pm; Sat 11am–8pm, Sun 11am–3pm.

Museo Zuloaga ★★ ART MUSEUM   This fascinating little museum occupies the medieval Iglesia San Juan de los Caballeros, where ceramic artist Daniel Zuloaga (1852–1921) based his family pottery studio starting in 1908. The firm made many of the scenic tiles that decorate the building facades all over Spain, and museum exhibits elucidate the entire artistic process, with an emphasis on the Zuloaga family's masterful painting. Other exhibits highlight the history of the church (parts of it date from the A.D. 6th c., making it one of the oldest Christian sites in Spain). Hours are severely limited, but if Spain's ceramic tradition interests you, this is worth making the effort.

Plaza de Colmenares. ✆ **92-146-33-48.** Admission 1€. Wed 9am–4pm.

Roman Aqueduct (Acueducto Romano) ★★★ ARCHITECTURE Roughly 2,100 years ago, Roman engineers constructed this architectural marvel—a 15km (9⅓-mile) conduit to bring water from the Guadarrama mountains to Segovia. The graceful feat of engineering remains as impressive as it was in the age of the Caesars. While much of the original aqueduct was a ground-level canal, the concluding segments arch high over the city and then continue underground all the way to the Alcázar. The entire structure was built of granite blocks without mortar. Following restorations in the 15th and 16th centuries, it continued to supply the city's water into the late 19th century. The highest of the 166 arches is 28m (92 ft.) and seems even higher when you stand under it and look up. Most visitors focus their attention on the highest arches, but it's fun to follow the structure uphill into residential Segovia neighborhoods.

Plaza del Azoguejo.

Where to Stay in Segovia

Hostería Natura ★★   The owners of this 17th-century guest house, just steps from Plaza Mayor, kept the historic exterior intact but took

Segovia's Roman Aqueduct is a classical marvel of engineering.

colorful, creative liberties with the interior. The cheerful stylishness almost makes you forget that there's no elevator. Bargain-priced rooms 101, 102, and 112 are unusually large quarters furnished with two twin beds, but their airshaft windows don't open. Romantic room 103 has a high, carved-wood four-poster bed, a little private balcony, and walls sponged a deep red. Equally romantic room 114 has a salmon-tinged canopy on the wrought-iron four-poster bed. Room 111 can easily sleep up to five, making it a good bet for families: The parents' private bath-and-bedroom suite, with a queen-size bed and a balcony overlooking a park, connects to a narrow interior room with three twin beds lined up along the wall and a separate bathroom for the kids.

Calle Colón, 5 and 7. www.naturadesegovia.com. ⓒ **92-146-67-10.** 17 units. 35€–105€ double; family room 55€–115€. No parking. **Amenities:** Free Wi-Fi.

Hotel Infanta Isabel ★   If you like being in the thick of things, this hotel is a good option. It sits on Plaza Mayor right across from the cathedral and some rooms have balconies overlooking the square. The Infanta Isabel (1851–1931), the great-great-great aunt of King Felipe VI, used to make a stopover here as she traveled to the summer palace in La Granja.

She would probably still recognize the grand staircase of the otherwise updated property and would likely appreciate the combination of luxurious traditional style and modern amenities. Six triple rooms are good for families.

Plaza Mayor. http://hotelinfantaisabel.com. ℰ **92-146-13-00.** 39 units. 49€–121€ double; 56€–123€ triple. Parking 18€. **Amenities:** Restaurant; bar; babysitting; free Wi-Fi.

Hotel Palacio San Facundo ★★★ This hotel in a 16th-century former noble palace exudes character. Sensitive renovations have maintained its Renaissance-era grace while creating 33 unique rooms that surround the central courtyard. They all have tub-showers, glass-slab sinks on stained-wood bases, and flat-screen TVs. Headboards are either wrought iron or padded dark brown leather, with soft leather trim on the decorative pillows. On the second floor, both 202 and 204 have small balconies with a view of the plaza out front. Many third-floor rooms have even more character, with exposed pine beams on the slanting ceilings and skylights with remote-controlled shades. One especially popular room is 306, with a large bed and decor in deep aubergine tones. Sizes vary a bit, of course. Whatever room you choose, you'll want to spend time in the glassed-over central courtyard with soaring columns and lots of comfortable seating.

Plaza San Facundo, 4. www.hotelpalaciosanfacundo.com. ℰ **92-146-30-61.** 33 units. 79€–160€ double; 160€–190€ jr. suite. Parking 20€. **Amenities:** Bar; room service; free Wi-Fi.

Where to Eat in Segovia

Segovia is justifiably proud—some would say even possessive—of what it considers the city's great contribution to Spanish cuisine: roast suckling pig. There's even a special certification for the dish, *Marca de Garantía "Cochinillo de Segovia,"* indicating a restaurant that only uses milk-fed local pigs, less than 21 days old, that have been processed and cooked in accordance with a strict set of standards. Restaurants without a special oven will fry the piglet, a dish known as *cochifrito.* Segovia is also known for its local lamb, usually offered as *chuletóns de cordero,* or lamb chops, sometimes as *chuletillas de lechal,* or chops from milk-fed lambs. Two common starters on Segovia menus are *sopa castellana*—a soup usually made with a chicken broth base to which chopped ham, bread, sweet paprika, and eggs are added—and *judiones de La Granja,* a dish of white broad beans, chorizo sausage, fresh ham, and onion.

El Bernardino ★ CASTILIAN Just inside the walls of the old city, this traditional *asador* (meat roaster) has been keeping the city fed since 1939. As you look around the dining room (or around at other tables on the terrace), you'll see large wooden platters with roast piglets splayed out

bargains ON SEGOVIAN ROAST SPECIALTIES

Most restaurants offer roast suckling pig as a huge plate with a lot of accompaniments and roast baby lamb only as a dish for two. But two of our favorite casual dining spots serve these Segovian specialties as *raciones*—entrée-size plates with no side dishes. We like **Restaurante la Churrería de San Lorenzo ★** ((*C* 92-104-76-94) because it's in an atmospheric neighborhood outside the old city. Named for its ancient, almost crumbling church, Plaza San Lorenzo is about a 10-minute walk from the aqueduct, and La Churrería is the most popular family restaurant on the plaza. The bar looks as if it was built for a tavern scene in *Man of La Mancha*. Roast piglet or lamb costs 22€, the restaurant's open daily 8am to 4pm and 8pm to midnight.

La Taurina ★ (*C* **92-146-09-02**), located right on Plaza Mayor, organizes each course of the meal as a stage in a bullfight—no great surprise considering the bullfight-themed tiles on the wall and the profusion of matador memorabilia. Unadorned plates of suckling pig or baby lamb are what most people order, though the full menu that adds some sides, bread, dessert, and wine is only 4€ more. On a nice night, sit outside and enjoy a view of the cathedral with your meal. Roast piglet or lamb costs 20€ to 22€; the restaurant is open daily, noon to 5pm and 8pm to midnight.

on top. You'll also notice that the other diners are having a festive time, scraping off big servings of super-tender pork. The restaurant gives the same wood-fired oven treatment to *cordero lechal* (milk-fed baby lamb), lamb quarters from yearlings, and whole chickens. The rest of the menu is a catalog of Castilian mountain food, from the chicken-garlic soup to the *floron* (a kind of Segovian cake) served on a puddle of crème anglaise. Reserve ahead for weekends and holidays.

Calle Cervantes, 2. www.elbernardino.com. *C* **92-146-24-77.** Entrees 13€–20€. Daily 1–4pm and 8–11pm.

La Fogón Sefardí Restaurante ★★ SPANISH/MIDDLE EASTERN The more formal of the dining options at the Casa Mudéjar hotel, "the Sephardic cook" takes the unusual step of incorporating many traditional Spanish Jewish dishes into the otherwise Castilian menu. So while one table might be feasting on the ubiquitous suckling pig, the next will be enjoying a sort of strudel of layers of eggplant with curried lamb and tiny baby vegetables. The kitchen also makes some rather modern dishes, including salmon tacos with a basil-cream sauce. Dessert is the classic *ponche segoviano,* a syrup-drenched, marzipan-encased cake with layers separated by golden custard.

Calle Judería Vieja, 17. www.lacasamudejar.com. *C* **92-146-62-50.** Entrees 16€–20€; set menu 30€. Daily 1:30–4:30pm and 8:30–11:30pm.

Restaurante José María ★★★ CASTILIAN Ask any Segoviano where his family goes for *cochinillo,* and you'll get a big smile and a rambling reverie about the crackling skin and succulent meat served at this culinary landmark. Simply put, in pig-roasting circles, chef-proprietor José María Ruiz is the man. As a result, you'll pay a little more for the privilege of eating in the formal white-tablecloth interior dining room, but if you're going to "pig out," it might as well be on the best. Ruiz also excels at roast suckling lamb *(cordero lechal asado).* To the delight of Spanish diners accustomed to overcooked green beans and canned artichokes, he also invents entire dishes to highlight seasonal vegetables. Reserve ahead for weekends and holidays.

Calle Cronista Lecea, 11. www.restaurantejosemaria.com. ✆ **92-146-11-11.** Entrees 14€–35€. Daily 1–4pm and 7–11pm.

ÁVILA ★★

A UNESCO World Heritage Site, the ancient city of Ávila draws pilgrims for its physical wonders—most notably the well-preserved 11th-century walls and battlements—and for its spiritual history. It was home to Santa Teresa, the dynamic co-founder (with San Juan de la Cruz; see p. 190) of the Carmelitas Descalzos (Barefoot Carmelites). She was born here in

Sunset over the historic walled city of Ávila.

1515, entered the Carmelites at 19, and began her reform of the order at age 45. A prolific writer and a brilliant organizer, Santa Teresa became the practical and political mover of the Spanish Counter-Reformation, while her compatriot San Juan de la Cruz tended to the inner spiritual life of the reform movement. Several sites associated with Santa Teresa remain in Ávila, and the pious visit them as a pilgrimage. If you are coming to Ávila to see the walls, make it a day trip. If you want to delve into the religious history, plan on staying the night.

Essentials

ARRIVING More than two dozen **trains** leave daily from Madrid's Chamartín station for Ávila, about a 1½- to 2-hour trip each way. Tickets cost 9€ to 13€. The Ávila station is at Avenida José Antonio (www.renfe.com; ✆ **90-232-03-20**), 1.6km (1 mile) east of the old city. You'll find taxis lined up in front of Ávila's train station and at the more central Plaza Santa Teresa. For taxi information, call ✆ **92-035-35-45.**

Buses leave Madrid daily from Estación Sur de Autobuses at Calle Méndez Alvaro. One-way tickets are 12€. In Ávila, the bus terminal (www.avanzabus.com; ✆ **90-202-00-52**) is at the corner of avenidas Madrid and Portugal, northeast of the town center.

To drive here from Madrid, head northwest on Highway N-VI (A-6) toward A Coruña, eventually forking southwest to Ávila. Driving time is around 1¼ hours.

VISITOR INFORMATION The **tourist information office,** Av. Madrid, 39 (www.avilaturismo.com; ✆ **92-022-59-69**), is generally open daily 9am to 2pm and 5 to 8pm; from July to September, it stays open 9am to 8pm Monday to Thursday, 9am to 9pm Friday and Saturday.

Exploring Ávila

A Cubist jumble of Gothic convents and palaces slumping down the top of a hill, entirely surrounded by imposing, castellated stone walls, Ávila is the perfect stage set of a Castilian city. It seems a unified whole, making a stronger impression than its individual parts. No visitor can—or should—miss the Murallas, or walls. After that, let your heart and devotion dictate which of the holy spots to visit.

Basílica de San Vicente ★★★ CHURCH One of Spain's finest Romanesque churches, this faded sandstone basilica with a huge nave and three apses stands outside the medieval ramparts—a defiant Christian structure built to claim the high ground in the name of the cross. Its fiercely moralistic carvings, especially on the cornice of the southern portal, play out the struggle between good and evil. The **western portal ★★**, dating from the 13th century, has the best Romanesque bas-reliefs. Inside is the tomb of San Vincente, martyred here in the 4th century. The tomb's medieval carvings, which depict his torture and martyrdom, are fascinating, if disturbing, and reveal medieval Spanish anti-Semitism: The story casts "a rich Jew" as the villain and hastens to note that he was saved by repenting, converting to Christianity, and building this church.

Plaza de San Vicente. www.basiliadesanvicente.es. ℰ **92-025-52-30.** Admission 2.50€ adults, 2.20€ seniors, students, and ages 11 and under. Apr–Oct Mon–Sat 10am–6:30pm, Nov–Mar Mon–Sat 10am–1:30pm and 4–6:30pm.

Carmelitas Descalzas de San José (Barefoot Carmelites of St. Joseph) ★ CONVENT   Also known as the Convento de las Madres (Convent of the Mothers), this is the first convent founded by Santa Teresa in 1562 when she began her reform of the Carmelite order. There are two churches: a primitive one, where the first Carmelite nuns took the habit; and one

Ávila is known for its almost perfect set of medieval walls.

built after the saint's death by Francisco de Mora, architect for Felipe III. The convent's peculiar little museum, consisting of several rooms behind plate glass, holds personal artifacts of Santa Teresa, including her collarbone and the saddle on which she rode around Spain founding convents. One room re-creates her original cell at the convent, including a narrow bed with a log pillow. In the tiny convent church, you might hear the disembodied voices of the cloistered nuns as they sing their prayers.

Calle de las Madres, 4. www.avilaturismo.com. ℰ **92-022-21-27.** Museum admission 1.40€. Daily 10am–1:30pm and 3–6pm.

Catedral del Salvador ★★ CATHEDRAL   Built into the old ramparts of Ávila, this cold, austere cathedral and fortress (begun in 1099 under Alfonso VI) bridges the gap between Romanesque and Gothic, which earns it a certain distinction in Spanish architecture. One local writer compared it to a granite mountain. So heavy is the fortified church that a veritable forest of columns in the local mottled red-and-white stone supports it from within, obscuring many sight lines. Nine hundred years of entombments have filled every nook and cranny of the voluminous cathedral. Dutch artist Cornelius designed the seats of the choir stalls in the Renaissance style. Behind the main chapel is Vasco de Zarza's masterpiece: the beautifully sculpted tomb of Alonso de Madrigal, the powerful bishop of Ávila from 1449 to 1455, who was nicknamed El Tostado ("the toasted one") for his dark complexion. A side altar, naturally enough, honors local celebrity Santa Teresa. Be sure to stop in the Capilla del Cardenal to marvel at its polychrome wooden statues of saints, created by anonymous artists in the 12th and 13th centuries.

Plaza de la Catedral. catedralavila.es. ✆ **92-021-16-41.** Admission 6€ adults, 5.50€ seniors, 4.50€ students and ages 12–18; bell tower additional 2€. Apr–Oct Mon–Fri 10am–8pm, Sat 10am–9pm, Sun noon–7:30pm (until 9pm daily Jul–Aug); Nov–Mar Mon–Fri 10am–6pm, Sat 10am–7pm, Sun noon–5:30pm.

Murallas de Ávila (Walls of Ávila) ★★★ ARCHITECTURE   Ávila's defensive walls are among the best preserved in Europe. They were begun in 1190 on orders of Alfonso VI as part of the re-conquest of Spain. Using the foundations of an earlier Roman fortification, the builders were able to complete the brown-granite construction by 1199, although embellishments continued into the 14th century. Averaging 10m (33 ft.) in height, the walls have nine gateways, 88 semicircular towers, and more than 2,300 battlements. The two most famous gates are the San Vicente and the Alcázar, both on the eastern side. In many respects, the walls are best viewed from the west. You can hire a taxi to drive alongside the walls' entire length of 2km (1¼ miles). Better yet, walk the ramparts, looking eye-to-eye with storks nesting on rooftops and chimneys. Be aware that there are many rough stone steps and some tricky footing, and despite railings, some fully exposed heights. The views are unsurpassed, however, and it's easy to imagine how these fortifications must have awed attacking armies.

Carnicerías, Alcázar, Arco del Carmen, or Puente Adaja gates. muralladeavila.com. ✆ **92-025-50-88.** Admission 5€ adults; 3.50€ seniors and students. Mid-Mar to late Oct Tue–Sun 10am–8pm (Jul–Aug daily 10am–9pm); late Oct to mid-Mar Tue–Sun 10am–6pm.

Museo Teresiano ★★ MUSEUM   Located beneath the Convento de Santa Teresa, which was built on the site of her childhood home, this scholarly museum preserves the garden where Teresa recalled her childhood joy at playing with her siblings. Among the museum's more striking artifacts are painted portraits of Teresa by artists who were her contemporaries, as well as letters between Santa Teresa (strong and forceful penmanship!) and San Juan de la Cruz (a more meticulous but rather florid hand). The museum does a good job of placing Teresa in the context of 16th-century Roman Catholicism, and then tracing the influence of her thought down to the present day.

Calle La Dama, s/n. ✆ **92-021-10-30** or 92-022-07-08. Admission 2€. Tue–Sun 10am–1:30pm and 3:30–5:30pm; closed Jan.

Where to Stay in Ávila

Ávila attracts many religious pilgrims, but hotels are few. Book ahead, especially for July and August, when Spaniards make their pilgrimages and the searing heat means you will certainly want air-conditioning.

Hotel El Rastro ★   The folks who run this hotel seem to have all the lodging (and most of the dining) bases covered in and near Ávila. It's a charming but modern adaptation of an old building that's part of the city walls. Exposed walls of brick and stone and floors covered in large tiles in the public areas create an air of antiquity. Bedrooms, however, have been modernized with plastered walls, wooden floors, and small tiled bathrooms with porcelain fixtures. If the hotel is full, the nearby **Mesón del Rastro** (p. 200) has 10 very modest rooms over the restaurant. And if *that* isn't adequate, they'll offer you a house in the countryside. Personally, we'd stick with the hotel for price, comfort, and convenience.

Calle Cepedes, s/n. www.elrastroavila.com. ✆ **92-021-12-18.** 19 units. 39€–55€ double. Free parking. **Amenities:** Restaurant; bar; free Wi-Fi.

Hotel Palacio de Los Velada ★★★   With a tiled floor and graceful arched colonnades, the central courtyard of this hotel is one of the loveliest in the city. The 16th-century palace-turned-hotel is located near the cathedral, which means you can easily return to lounge on one of the sofas in the courtyard when you feel like taking a break. Guest rooms circle the courtyard and mix comfort with a sense of formality that suits the setting. Many rooms feature unique architectural details such as slanting wooden ceilings or big windows framed by stone arches.

Plaza de la Catedral, 10. www.veladahoteles.com. ✆ **92-025-51-00.** 145 units. 60€–112€ double. Parking 18€. **Amenities:** Restaurant; bar; room service; free Wi-Fi.

Parador de Ávila ★★   Located just inside the city walls 2 blocks northwest of Plaza de la Victoria, this hotel can be hard to find. But once you're settled, it makes a good base for exploring the city. Like most properties in rambling historic buildings, it features wonderful public spaces, including a lovely central courtyard and a formal garden with some archaeological remnants. Some of the nicest rooms look out on the garden. Their traditional furnishings can sometimes seem more dated than evocative of a historic past.

Marqués de Camales de Chozas, 2. www.parador.es. ✆ **92-021-13-40.** 61 units. 108€–175€ double; 230€–350€ suite. Garage 18€; free outdoor parking. **Amenities:** Restaurant; bar; room service; free Wi-Fi.

Where to Eat in Ávila

Ávila is famous throughout Spain for the quality of its veal ribeye steaks, known as *chuletón de Ávila.* The cuisine here is otherwise rather typical Castilian—red meat, dark sauces, wild game, and the potent red wines of the region. Rarely do you need a reservation for dinner, except on Friday and Saturday nights and midday Sunday.

Las Cancelas ★★ CASTILIAN   The best part of this venerable lodging is the terrific, if slightly expensive restaurant that occupies its central courtyard. The heavy wooden tables are set casually with paper covers for the midday meal, but the restaurant turns romantic at night when candles flicker on linen table settings on the patio surrounded by stone columns. Specialties of the house all issue from a wood-fired oven and include crusty loaves of hearth breads as well as leg or shoulder of lamb, the inescapable roast suckling pig, or the classic *chuletón de Ávila* veal chops. It's a popular spot with well-heeled locals, and you'll find the wines of the nearby Castilian countryside to be very good.

Hotel Las Cancelas, Calle Cruz Viejo, 6. www.lascancelas.com. ✆ **92-021-22-49.** Entrees 16€–28€. Daily 1:30–4pm and 8:30–11pm.

Mesón del Rastro ★ CASTILIAN   The inn run by the Hotel El Rastro crew (p. 199) is a more rustic affair than the hotel, and it's very popular with tourists from other parts of Spain who know good if greasy roast meats when they find them. The suckling pig almost goes without mentioning, but the real focus here is on many different roasted preparations of lamb, veal roasts, and—one dish done on top of the stove—pan-fried sweetbreads.

Plaza del Rastro 1. www.elrastroavila.com. ✆ **92-021-12-18.** Entrees 11€–26€; set menu 28€. Daily 1–4pm and 9–11pm.

El Molino de la Losa ★★ CASTILIAN   Outside the walls and across the river, this 15th-century mill converted to a restaurant has a large dining room that retains its rustic origins—a wooden ceiling, wrought-iron chandeliers—as well as a smaller, modern dining room with a nice view of the Río Adaja and its old bridge. While the kitchen does its part to keep up the image of Ávila as carnivore heaven (oven-roasted lamb, baby pig, veal, and duck), the chefs also clearly love vegetables and present them with care and panache. The selection of grilled seasonal vegetables is an excellent option for vegetarians.

Bajada de la Losa, 12. www.elmolinodelalosa.com. ✆ **92-021-11-01.** Entrees 13€–32€, set menu 33€. Tues–Sun 1:30–4pm and 9–11pm.

SALAMANCA ★★★

When the sun is low in the sky, the sandstone cathedrals, convents, and university buildings of Salamanca take on a luminous golden glow. The soft stone lends itself to carving, and virtually every civic structure in the city has been gloriously embellished with flora and fauna, and fables to instruct the illiterate. Only the remnants of a Roman wall suggest historic fortifications—as a university city since 1218, Salamanca has tended to

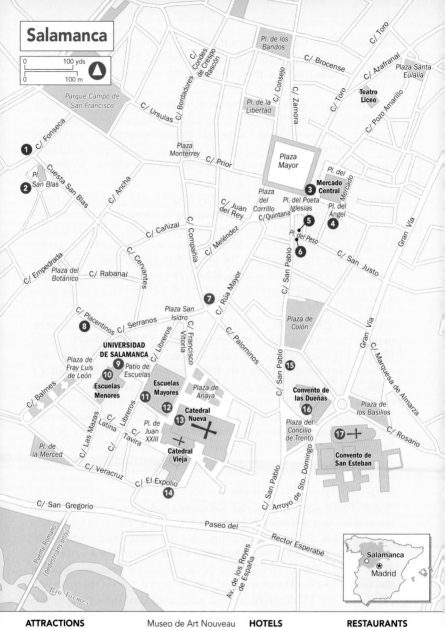

Salamanca

0   100 yds
0   100 m

Parque Campo de San Francisco

C/ Fonseca

Pl. San Blas

Cuesta San Blas

C/ Ancha

C/ Bordadores

C/ Cordes de Crespo Rascón

C/ Ursulas

Pl. de los Bandos

C/ Brocense

C/ Toro

C/ Azafranal

Plaza Santa Eulalia

C/ Pozo Amarillo

Teatro Liceo

Pl. de la Libertad

C/ Consejo

C/ Zamora

C/ Toro

Plaza Monterrey

C/ Prior

Plaza Mayor

Pl. del Mercado

Mercado Central

Gran Vía

Plaza del Corrillo

C/ Juan del Rey

C/ Quintana

Pl. del Poeta Iglesias

Pl. del Ángel

C/ Cañizal

C/ Compañía

C/ Meléndez

Pl. del Peso

C/ San Pablo

C/ San Justo

C/ Empedrada

Plaza del Botánico

C/ Rabanal

C/ Cervantes

C/ Ría Mayor

Plaza de Colón

C/ Placentinos

C/ Serranos

Plaza San Isidro

C/ Libreros

C/ Francisco Vitoria

C/ Palominos

C/ San Pablo

UNIVERSIDAD DE SALAMANCA

Plaza de Fray Luís de León

Patio de Escuelas

Escuelas Menores

Escuelas Mayores

Plaza de Anaya

Convento de las Dueñas

Gran Vía

C/ Marquesa de Almarza

Plaza de los Basilios

C/ Balmes

C/ Las Mazas

C/ Latina

C/ Libreros

Pl. de Juan XXIII

C/ Tavira

Catedral Nueva

Catedral Vieja

Plaza del Concilio de Trento

C/ Rosario

Pl. de la Merced

C/ Veracruz

C/ El Expolio

Convento de San Esteban

C/ San Gregorio

C/ San Pablo

Arroyo de Sto. Domingo

Puente Romano (pedestrians only)

Paseo del

Rector Esperabé

Av. de los Reyes de España

Río Tormes

Salamanca

Madrid

fortify itself with wit and arm itself with wisdom. Instead of archers' battlements or rusted cannons, look for the good-luck frog on the university portal, narrative reliefs of Bible stories on the churches, and sudden surprises of angels or gargoyles overhead.

The University of Salamanca attracts scholars and students from all over the world—including a large contingent of Americans in summer—ensuring a lively nightlife. Although greater Salamanca's population exceeds 180,000, the compact old city retains a charming provincial aura. Most attractions are within walking distance of Plaza Mayor, so the best way to explore Salamanca is on foot.

ARRIVING   A dozen **trains** travel daily from Madrid's Chamartin station to Salamanca (trip time: 1½–3 hr.), arriving northeast of the town center on Plaza de la Estación de Ferrocarril (www.renfe.com; ☏ **90-232-03-20**). The fare is 25€ to 40€. Up to 20 **buses** a day arrive from Madrid, taking 2½ to 3 hours. The fare ranges 20€ to 25€. Salamanca's bus terminal is at Av. Filiberto Villalobos, 71 (☏ **92-322-60-79**), northwest of the town center. If you're driving from Madrid, take the N-VI northwest, forking off to Salamanca on the N-501.

VISITOR INFORMATION   The **Oficina Municipal de Turismo de Salamanca,** Plaza Mayor, 32 (www.salamanca.es; ☏ **92-327-83-42**), is open Monday to Friday 9am to 7pm, Saturday 10am to 7pm, and Sunday 10am to 2pm. The regional **Oficina de Información Turística de Castilla y León,** Rúa Mayor at Casa de las Conchas (www.turismocastillayleon. com; ☏ **92-336-85-71**), is open July to mid-September Monday through Friday 9am to 2pm and 4:30 to 8pm, Saturday 10am to 8pm, Sunday 10am to 2pm; from mid–September to June, hours are Monday through Friday 9am to 2pm and 4 to 6:30pm, Saturday 10am to 6:30pm, Sunday 10am to 2pm.

Exploring Salamanca

You probably won't want to visit Salamanca in August, when the scorching midday heat makes even lizards dash across the plazas in search of a sliver of shade. But at any other time, this is a stroller's city, where new delights catch the eye at every turn. The **Plaza Mayor ★★★** is the heart of the community, an embodiment of the conflicting academic styles of this university city. The regimented, orderly layout reflects the neoclassical style of the 18th century, when it was constructed from plans by one member of the Churriguera family. Other family members then decorated the surfaces in their characteristically full-blown Spanish Baroque style. Salamantinos gather here at all hours of the day and night to connect with each other, to talk, and (most of all) to eat and drink. When the sun sets and the stone plaza begins to cool, cafe tables spill out from beneath the arcades and *tunas* (student singers in old-fashioned academic cloaks) wander from table to table singing for tips.

The Baroque architecture of Plaza Mayor.

About a quarter of the old city is devoted to buildings of the University of Salamanca, still one of Spain's most prestigious centers of scholarship. Courtyards around university buildings are generally open to the public; the **Patio de Escuelas Menores** is a popular gathering point for tour groups as well as Salamantinos. Standing proudly in the center is a statue of 16th-century poet and scholar **Fray Luis de León,** the city's poster boy for intellectual freedom and defiance of tyranny. Imprisoned for 4 years by the Inquisition for translating the Bible's Song of Solomon into Castilian, the scholar began his first lecture after returning to the classroom, *"Decíamos ayer . . . ,"* or "as we were saying yesterday. . . ."

Casa de las Conchas (House of Shells) ★ ARCHITECTURE It's hard to miss this restored 1483 house on the street between the University and Plaza Mayor; the facade consists of 400 simulated scallop shells, the symbol of Santiago (St. James), patron saint of the Reconquista. It was created by a medical professor at the university as a tribute to the pilgrimage city of Santiago de Compostela (p. 655). Today it holds the regional Castilla y León tourist office.

Calle de la Compañía, 2. ✆ **92-326-93-17.** Free admission. Courtyard Mon–Fri 9am–9pm, Sat 9am–2pm and 4–7pm, Sun 10am–2pm and 4–7pm.

Casa-Museo Unamuno ★★ HISTORIC HOME   To understand the intellectual, humanistic side of Salamanca, visit this 18th-century house where early-20th-century poet/philosopher/novelist Miguel de Unamuno lived during his first term as university rector. Never have we seen a home where the life of the mind was so manifest, from his library of world masterpieces to his own photographs showing him with the top intelligentsia of his era. A man of principle, he had to leave the country when dictator Primo de Rivera came to power and demanded that he censor his scholarship. When de Rivera fell, Unamuno returned exultant, but the euphoria was short-lived. Unamuno was the symbol of a humanistic era of lofty values and high ideals, crushed in Spain's descent into chaos. Indeed, he died of an apparent broken heart shortly after the Civil War began. Unamuno loved his adopted city deeply, once writing in a poem, "I keep your very soul in my heart. And you, my golden Salamanca, will keep my memory when I die." And so it has.

> ### A Twisted Family
>
> Spanish Baroque architecture takes the impulse for distortion to an extreme. The Churriguera family carved out a name for themselves with a family style that owes a great deal to the forms assumed by twisted rope. **José Benito Churriguera** (1665–1725) and his brothers **Joaquin** (1674–1724) and **Alberto** (1676–1750) were stone sculptors who became architects. Their work in Salamanca, especially with altarpieces and the stucco work on building facades, spawned many imitators in Spain as well as in Mexico—hence the term *Churrigueresque.*

Calle de Libreros, 25. museo.usal.es. ℰ **92-329-44-00.** Admission 4€ adults; 2€ seniors and students. Mon–Fri 10am–2pm.

Catedral Salamanca ★★★ CATHEDRAL   Salamanca actually has two impressive cathedrals connected to each other, located in the south end of the old town. If you're just entering for worship or to say a prayer, you'll go into the "new" cathedral. If you want to tour the spaces, though, you'll be added to a group and handed a multilingual audioguide which follows a strict itinerary—there's no jumping around to the "good" parts. The **Catedral Vieja (Old Cathedral)** is a squat Romanesque structure begun in 1140, with sight lines to the altar obscured by the sheer bulk of its interior supports. Nonetheless, it has some powerful religious art, most notably the mid-15th-century altarpiece of 53 scenes painted by Nicholas of Florence to delineate the life of Christ and scenes of the Virgin Mary. Two chapels are of particular note: the **Capilla de San Martín** with frescoes painted in 1242, and the **Capilla de Santa Catalina,** replete with gargoyles. The **Catedral Nueva (New Cathedral)** isn't all that new—it was launched in 1513 in an old-fashioned style that made it "the last gasp of Gothic style," as architectural historians put it—but it's still the largest and highest building in the city. The soaring spaces inside welcome pious

Salamanca's Cathedral Vieja.

contemplation. All three Churriguera brothers (p. 204) served as supervising architects during the cathedral's ongoing construction (it wasn't consecrated until 1733), so many of the surface details and twisted-rope columns are truly Churrigueresque. (One bas-relief column, for example, resembles a cluster of palm trees.) The tradition of inspired stone carving continues: When the lower portion of the Puerta Ramos on the west side was rebuilt in 1992, the stonemason and restorers decided to update the carvings with the image of an astronaut floating in space, a monkey eating an ice cream cone, and a stork carrying a branch in its beak. (Panhandlers hanging out near the entrance will point them out for a tip.) After viewing the two churches, the tour continues through the enclosed cloisters.

Plaza Juan XXIII. www.catedralsalamanca.org. © **92-321-74-76.** Free for worship; tours 6€ adults, 5€ seniors and students, 4€ ages 7–16. Apr–Sept daily 10am–8pm; Oct–Mar daily 9am–6pm.

Cielo de Salamanca ★★ MUSEUM Sometimes the best attempts at understanding the universe fail as science but survive simply because they are beautiful. This fresco of the night sky, painted by Francisco Gallego in 1474, covers part of the ceiling of the old university library; it's just off the plaza that separates the university's graduate school from its undergraduate campus. Working without the benefit of Copernicus' and Galileo' scientific breakthroughs, Gallego attempted to merge myth, science, and religion by mashing up astrology and night-sky astronomy. You'll have to wait a few minutes after entering for your eyes to adjust to the low light, but the vision is the very definition of magic.

Patio de Escuelas Menores, s/n. museo.usal.es. No phone. Free admission. Apr–Sept Mon–Sat 10am–2pm and 4–8pm, Sun 10am–2pm; Oct–Mar closes 7pm.

Convento de las Dueñas ★★★ CONVENT

Unlike the brothers at adjacent San Estéban (see below), the Dominican nuns are cloistered, but their cloister and intensely fragrant rose garden are open to visitors. Originally a noble palace, it was donated to the order in 1419 and subsequently altered and enlarged. The 16th-century cloister designed by Rodrigo Gil de Hontañón is a hidden treasure: Capitals on the arcade pillars represent some of the city's most inspired stone carving—any fan of gargoyles or modern graphic novels should make the effort to see them. They're a sample book of contorted human bodies, angels, griffons, devils, flying goat heads, winged horses, and other fantastic creatures. The carvings are so vivid that it's hard to believe the poor nuns can sleep at night.

Plaza del Concilio de Trento, s/n. ✆ **92-321-54-42.** Admission 2€. Mon–Sat 10:30am–12:45pm and 4:30–7:30pm.

Convento de San Estéban ★ MONASTERY

Dominicans from this monastery accompanied Columbus on his voyages. Not only did they proselytize to the natives of the New World, they argued that indigenous people around the world had souls and human rights. While the dignity of all persons seems common sense in the 21st century, it was a radical concept in the 16th, and the Dominicans of Salamanca suffered for it. Nonetheless, they persevered and continue to agitate for social and economic justice, finally convincing Pope Paul III to declare indigenous people as human beings. Their convent is a pleasure to tour, highlighted by the elaborate gilded José Benito Churriguera altar in the church and a stunning Baroque choir with an illustrated hymnal big enough that all 118 monks could read the music from their seats.

Plaza del Concilio de Trento, s/n. www.saintstephenspriory.com. ✆ **92-321-50-00.** Admission 3€ adults; 2€ seniors and students. Daily 10am–2pm and 4–8pm.

Mercatus ★ STORE

The official university store has the usual branded merchandise, but it also sells some terrific souvenirs that won't embarrass you once you get home. Enamored of the student singing groups, or *tunas,* on Plaza Mayor (p. 202)? You can purchase CDs here. Silk scarves reproduce the Cielo de Salamanca (p. 205) in all its mysterious beauty; you can also purchase T-shirts, tote bags, puzzles, and drink coasters emblazoned with the same image. Or go tacky and buy your budding scholar a bright stuffed frog, the good-luck talisman of Salamanca students.

Cardenal Plá y Deniel, s/n. mercatus.usal.es. ✆ **92-329-46-92.** Mon–Sat 10am–8pm; Sun 10am–2pm.

Museo de Art Nouveau-Art Déco ★ MUSEUM   Masterful Art Nouveau glass by Emile Gallé and René Lalique are the artistic highlights, but the 1,500-plus-piece collection of the Manuel Ramos Andrade Foundation also embraces jewelry, paintings, furniture, and marble and bronze figurines. All the works date from the late 1880s through the 1930s, and while some are mainstream Art Nouveau or Art Deco, others are fascinating Spanish outliers of the two styles. Many visitors are surprised to find a world-class collection of more than 400 porcelain dolls, courtesy of collector Manuel Ramos Andrade.

Calle El Expolio, 14. www.museocasalis.org. ℂ **92-312-14-25.** Admission 4€ adults; 2€ students; free for ages 13 and under. Apr–Oct Tues–Sun 11am–8pm; Nov–Mar Tues–Fri 11am–2pm and 4–7pm, Sat–Sun 11am–8pm.

Museo de Salamanca ★ ART MUSEUM   Only steps from the grandly carved main entrance of the University, this attractive little museum is packed with religious art confiscated from convents and monasteries in the mid–19th century. Most of the churches from which the 15th- to 17th-century carvings and paintings were taken no longer exist, and in a few cases, the art is exhibited with the altar or niche from its original church. The contrast between rude architecture and polished artistry is striking—a reminder that for rural people, the church was often the most beautiful thing in their lives. One highlight is a golden Churrigueresque altarpiece crafted between 1697 and 1704. In addition to the permanent collections, the museum has begun a very active program of thematic exhibitions combining pieces from its collection with works borrowed from other municipal and regional museums around the region of Castilla y León.

Patio de las Escuelas, 2. www.museoscastillayleon.jcyl.es/museodesalamanca. ℂ **92-321-22-35.** Admission 1€, free to all Sat–Sun. July–Sept Tues–Sat 10am–2pm and 5–8pm, Sun 10am–2pm; Oct–June Tues–Sat 10am–2pm and 4–7pm, Sun 10am–2pm.

Universidad de Salamanca ★ HISTORIC SITE   Established in 1213 and granted its full charter in 1254, Salamanca was organized on the model of the University of Bologna—that is, it gave precedence to humanistic scholarship over the study of theology favored by the University of Paris. Its intellectual heyday was in the 15th and 16th centuries, but it remains a major force in Spanish intellectual life and the most popular place in the country for foreigners to study the Spanish language. The original college, the **Escuelas Mayores,** boasts one of the **best carved portals** ★★★ in a city of pretty impressive doorways. Carved in 1534, this "doorway to heaven" was intended to emulate the goldsmith's art. The main medallion in the first register depicts the Catholic monarchs Isabel and Fernando. Crowds gather to scrutinize the fine details, but they are not looking for the Catholic monarchs; they are looking for the carved frog perched on a human skull on the right-hand side of the door. Legend holds that students who can spot it will do well on their exams. Although Salamanca is not known for its business school, Salamantino entrepreneurs have capitalized on the legend by making the *rana* (frog) a whimsical if unofficial symbol of Salamanca. Every imaginable trinket can be purchased emblazoned with its likeness.

Given such a great entrance, it's a little disappointing that the only tour inside the university is restricted to a self-guided walk around the Renaissance arcades of the Escuelas Mayores. Let your nose lead the way. The chapel has the lingering odor of sanctity (actually, frankincense), while the wonderful old library on the upper level smells of paper and old leather, even through the closed glass doors. You can also visit the lecture hall of Fray Luis de León (p. 203), fitted with crude wooden benches.

An elegant lecture hall at the ancient University of Salamanca.

Patio de las Escuelas, 1. www.usal.es. ☏ **92-329-44-00.** Admission 10€ adults, 5€ seniors and students; audioguide 2€. Mon–Sat 10am–7pm (until 8pm Apr to mid-Sept), Sun 10am–2pm. Enter from Patio de las Escuelas.

Where to Stay in Salamanca

You'll want to stay within the old city to avoid a long walk from a hotel on the outskirts. Besides the usual ultra-high seasons of Christmas and Easter, Salamanca hotels command a premium from late September through October due to a succession of festivals and annual conferences. Visitors coming for Spanish language courses of a month or more might consider a furnished apartment through **Homes for Travellers** (www. homesfortravellers.com; ☏ **91-444-27-19**).

Abba Fonseca Hotel ★★ Adjoining a classic 17th-century university college, this modern hotel behind a massive golden sandstone facade appear to have been part of the university campus for centuries. The immediate neighborhood consists of graduate colleges, so on-street parking is easy, and the scholarly conference clientele guarantees a truly usable desk, plenty of outlets for plugging in your gear, and Wi-Fi that lives up to its high-speed billing. The beds are some of the best we've encountered in Spain. The hotel is only a short walk to the cathedrals, yet sufficiently removed from the main student areas that it's extremely quiet at night.

Plaza San Blas, 2. www.abbahotels.com. © **92-301-10-10.** 86 units. 69€–150€ double; 105€–210€ suite. **Amenities:** Restaurant; bar; babysitting; fitness center; sauna; room service; free Wi-Fi.

Hotel Soho Boutique Salamanca ★   If you'd like to stay close enough to the Plaza Mayor to stroll in for drinks without having to endure lusty fun-seekers under your windows while you try to sleep, this small hotel a 2-minute walk from the plaza is just your ticket. The rooms are all quite new and surprisingly spacious. The décor is very Spanish—the trim on the furniture is gold, and so is the travertine that lines the bathrooms. It's a comfortable place with a decent bar and café. The location is unbeatable for the price.

Plaza Angel, 5. en.sohohoteles.com. © **92-399-39-00.** 23 units. 95€–110€ double. **Amenities:** Bar-cafeteria; free Wi-Fi.

Microtel Placentinos ★★   Aptly named—with just nine rooms it really is a micro-hotel—Placentinos is a marvel of design and interior decorating. There are three single rooms and six doubles in this tiny 16th-century building amid the looming blocks of the old university. Most rooms have at least one wall of exposed stone. Comfortable but contemporary furniture may strike a muted palette, but the simple rooms are anything but spartan. Bathrooms in the doubles have whirlpool tubs and some even have a sauna shower. The location is spectacular—steps from the cathedrals.

Calle Placentinos, 9. www.microtelplacentinos.com. © **92-328-15-31.** 68€–125€ double. **Amenities:** Jacuzzi on terrace; free Wi-Fi.

Where to Eat in Salamanca

Salamancan cuisine is similar to Segovia and Ávila, but the university city does have a few distinctive specialties: thinly sliced dry mountain ham from Guijuelo; a spicy, crumbly sausage called *farinato* that is more bread crumbs than meat; and *hornazo,* a pastry stuffed with cheese, sausage, and ham. Students traditionally feasted on these meat pies during Easter week to celebrate the return of prostitutes to the city after Lent; the dish is now available year-round and not only for young men with raging hormones.

Tourist restaurants along **Rúa Mayor** offer acceptable if uninspired meals at slightly inflated prices; restaurants lining **Plaza Mayor** attract tourists and locals alike. To join Salamantinos in a more tranquil setting, go to **Paseo Carmelitas** between Calle La Fuente and Puerta de Zamora, where a leafy green park is full of terraces popular for afternoon snacks.

Casa Paca ★★ CASTILIAN   The classic choice among Salamantino restaurants, Casa Paca has been serving its meat-heavy menu since 1928.

Ancient dishes like *alubias* (white beans stewed with pig's tails and ears) and *cocido* (a meat stew of all the trimmings from several kinds of animals) are on the menu, but diners making a night of it tend to ask for meats *a la brasa volcánica,* or cooked on the wood-fired grill. Favorites include suckling pig, thick beef steaks, and racks of baby goat chops. The atmospheric dining room with alternating wood-paneled and ancient stone walls is a real throwback to old Castilla. Honestly, we find it all a little overwhelming and usually opt to eat and drink on the bar side, where some of the most generous tapas in central Spain are provided "free" with drinks. (Beer and wine go up to 3.50€–5€ at meal times.) There's an array of tapas displayed—slices of *tortilla Española, farinato* sausage with scrambled eggs, pig's ears in tomato sauce *(orillas),* pastry squares filled with goat cheese and quince jam, small casseroles of meatballs, cod-stuffed red peppers, potato salad. Just ask (or point) when you order your drink.

Plaza del Peso, 10. www.casapaca.com. ℂ **92-321-89-93.** Entrees 20€–27€. Daily 2–4:30pm and 9–11:30pm. Bar daily 11am–midnight.

La Hoja 21 ★★ CONTEMPORARY SPANISH   One of the things we love about the menu at La Hoja 21 is chef Alberto Lopez's penchant for cooking with fresh vegetables. Maybe that's because the establishment is just steps from the city's farmer's market. The tasting menu changes with seasonal ingredients, but almost always features mushroom risotto with fresh veggies and braised cheeks of the local heritage beef called Morucha. You can also expect crab crepes and little pasta purses filled with cheese, shrimp, and minced vegetables. One of the regional specialties here is roasted leg of mutton with potato cakes.

Calle San Pablo, 21. www.lahoja21.com. ℂ **92-326-40-28.** Entrees 16€–22€; set menu 16€. Tues–Sat 2–4:30pm and 9–11:30pm, Sun 2–4:30pm.

Méson Cervantes ★ CASTILIAN   Combination plates are the mainstay of dining on Plaza Mayor, and this venerable restaurant offers some of the best prices as well as some of the best food. For about 10€, you can get a small steak with two fried eggs and fried potatoes, while lamb chops with lettuce, tomato, and fries might set you back a few euros more. It's one of the few spots serving generous vegetarian plates—our favorite includes white asparagus, green beans, peas, lettuce, tomato, marinated artichokes, and steamed squash. The darkly atmospheric upstairs bar (the restaurant has no plaza-level dining room) is jammed at midday with locals drinking beer and eating such plates as rice-filled blood sausage with red peppers or scrambled eggs and *farinato* drizzled with honey.

Plaza Mayor, 15. www.mesoncervantes.com. ℂ **92-321-72-13.** Entrees 17€–23€. Daily 10am–midnight or later.

Restaurante Arzobispo Fonseca ★★★ SPANISH   Every major college town has a restaurant where faculty and staff take guests for inexpensive meals in a fancy setting. In Salamanca, it's this beauty in the

chilling ON PLAZA MAYOR

On hot summer nights, you'll find as many people eating ice cream as dining on Plaza Mayor. If you want a cone, join the line outside **Café Novelty** (Plaza Mayor, 2; ℭ **92-321-49-56;** daily 8am–midnight). During colder months, an artsy crowd convenes in the Art Nouveau interior. Local specialty cold drinks can be just as refreshing; we like the plaza tables of **Cafetería Las Torres** (Plaza Mayor, 26; ℭ **92-321-44-70;** daily 8am–midnight) for sipping *leche helada* (a smooth concoction with hints of vanilla, cinnamon, and citrus rimmed with whipped cream) or *blanco y negro* (vanilla ice cream melting in a double shot of espresso).

formal 16th-century courtyard of the Colegio Arzobispo. The tables are set in pristine white linens, and you'll be dining with dons and university administrators. The *menu del día* is clearly subsidized, offering a choice of two first plates (typically a salad or a rice dish) and two second plates (sole or chicken, for example), along with wine, bread, and a pastry.
Plaza Fonseca, 4. www.usal.es/restaurante-fonseca. ℭ **608-923-865.** Entrees 12€–26€; set menu 15€. Daily 1:30–4pm and 9–11:30pm.

Río de la Plata ★ CASTILIAN   Rafael and Josefa Andrés Lorenzo opened this basement restaurant in 1958, naming it for Josefa's native Argentina. It became a favorite hangout for the bullfight crowd and those ubiquitous Americans, Ernest Hemingway and Orson Welles. It remains a popular dining room for an artsy university crowd as well as curious tourists. Josefa's daughter Paulina oversees the kitchen now, making homey dishes like garlic soup, grilled sausages, or local trout with ham. If you hanker for Castilian dishes not available at most restaurants, consider the brains fried in batter or stewed kid with almonds.
Plaza del Peso, 1. www.restauranteriodelaplata.es. ℭ **92-321-90-05.** Entrees 11€–28€; set menu 25€. Tues–Sun 1:30–3:30pm and 9pm–12:30am. Closed 2 weeks in July.

ZAMORA ★

Until the recent installation of high-speed rail, few North Americans beyond architecture buffs ever visited Zamora. While it has some modern hotels and terrific restaurants, the city seems little changed since its years of dusty decline in the 17th century, when the majority of its populace emigrated to South America, establishing several Zamoras across that continent. Yet scholars often refer to Zamora as an open-air museum of Romanesque architecture, and the old churches—most of them well-preserved and still functioning as neighborhood parishes—are powerfully moving. The processions, or *pasos,* during Holy Week (the week before Easter) are some of the largest and most spectacular in Spain. Reserve far ahead to visit then but expect hotel sticker shock.

It is surprising that Zamora's monuments have survived so many centuries, as the city has been the site of fierce battles. It was here that León finally captured the city from the Moors in the 11th century; Zamora was also the scene of fierce battles in the 15th-century war between Isabel I and Juana la Beltraneja, Isabel's illegitimate half-niece—a struggle whose memory is preserved in the old Spanish proverb *No se ganó Zamora en una hora,* or "Zamora wasn't won in an hour."

Essentials

ARRIVING   Seven high-speed **trains** travel daily to and from Madrid. They take about 90 minutes and cost 25€ to 53€ each way. The train station is at Calle Alfonso Peña (www.renfe.com; ℭ **90-232-03-20**), about a 15-minute walk from the edge of the old town. From Salamanca, there are close to two dozen **bus** connections a day (www.zamorasalamanca.es); the express (6.50€) takes 50 minutes, while the regular bus (5.40€) takes 1 hour. The town's bus station lies a few paces from the railway station at Calle Alfonso Peña, 3 (ℭ **98-052-12-81**). Call ℭ **90-202-00-52** for bus schedules and price information. If you're driving from Madrid, take the A-6 superhighway northwest toward Valladolid, cutting west on the N-VI and west again at the turnoff onto 122.

VISITOR INFORMATION   The **Oficina Municipal de Turismo,** Plaza de Arias Gonzalo, 6 (turismo-zamora.com; ℭ **98-053-36-94**), is open Monday to Saturday 10am to 2pm and 4 to 7pm, Sunday 10am to 2pm.

Exploring Zamora

Zamora's Romanesque churches are a delight to explore, but you'll have to check the doors for the hours of Mass to get inside most of them. These priceless monuments, 700 to 800 years old, are still active parish churches. A handful open for prayers in the mornings at 10am, close before lunch, and open again in the early evening, 5 to 8pm.

It's also a treat to explore the city walls. The **Portillo de la Traición** (Treason Gate) on the northwest corner of the city commemorates the assassination of Castilian king Sancho II in 1072, when he and El Cid were laying siege to the city in a battle over succession to the crown of León. The upshot of Sancho's death was that his brother Alfonso united the crowns of Castilla and León.

Catedral San Salvador ★★ CATHEDRAL   With its ribbed blue-and-white Byzantine-style dome, there's no mistaking Zamora's cathedral. Built swiftly between 1151 and 1174 (although the transept wasn't finished until 1192), it has a stylistic unity that is unusual in Spain, where cathedrals were generally completed over centuries rather than decades. Set on the high point of Zamora's ridge, the cathedral looks as much like a fortress as a church when viewed from the riverbanks below. Yet it opens

A procession during Holy Week in Zamora.

into the city with a harmonious plaza that gives viewers the distance to appreciate its full grandeur. Some Gothic towers have been added to the Romanesque temple, of course, and the interior decorations stretch out across the centuries. The choir stalls, carved 1512–16 by Juan de Bruselas, are especially notable for their lively scenes of country life in addition to the usual images of saints and famous figures from antiquity. The cathedral's museum, located inside the cloister, contains the city's greatest artistic treasure, the so-called "Black Tapestries," woven in Flanders in the 15th century. They illustrate scenes from the Trojan War as well as Hannibal's campaign in Italy. They are called "black" because several show people about to be decapitated.

Plaza de la Catedral. catedraldezamora.wordpress.com. © **98-053-06-44.** Admission 5€ adults, 3€ seniors and students. Cathedral admission free Sun afternoon. Apr–Oct daily 10am–8pm; Nov–Mar daily 10am–2pm and 4–7pm.

Centro de Interpretación de las Ciudades Medievales ★

MUSEUM   Since so much of Zamora remains medieval, it was a logical spot to open this center for the study of medieval cities. The cutting-edge facility built into the exterior of a city wall has a series of galleries that explore the historical, social, and cultural side of medieval life in central

Spain with dioramas, scale models, and multilingual panels. You'll make your way down to the lowest level of the museum, which is known as the Zen overlook, or "Mirador Zen." It overlooks the Rio Duero from a softly lit room filled with faint music.

Cuesta del Pizarro, s/n. © **98-053-62-40.** Free admission. Tues–Sun 10am–2pm and 5–8pm (closes 6:30 Nov–Mar).

Iglesia de Santa María-Magdalena ★ CHURCH   One of the most beautiful of the many Romanesque churches in Zamora, the Magdalena was begun in 1157 for the Order of San Juan and completed early in the 13th century. The form is a simple parish church of its era—a single narrow rectangular nave with a semicircular apse. What sets this church apart (beyond the extensive restoration carried out in the late 20th c.) is its remarkable stone carvings. Right at the main door, you'll see four pairs of columns, their capitals embellished with dragons that have both human and animal heads. The exquisite carvings continue inside the church—notice the laughing heads on the moldings over the arches. Two tabernacles are embedded in carved stone, and there is a magnificent tomb of a now-anonymous woman watched over by a pair of carved angels.

Rua de los Francos, s/n. © **98-053-18-45.** Free admission. Tue–Sat 10am–1pm and 5:30–8pm (open Mon but closed Tue Jul–Sept), Sun 10am–2pm.

Where to Stay in Zamora

Hotel Sercotel Horus Zamora ★★   A former Banco de España building from the 19th century, this hotel was transformed into a rich merchant's mansion in the early 20th century and later served as a newspaper headquarters. At the opening of the 21st century, it was converted into a boutique hotel that retains the Art Nouveau decoration of the original building but upgrades the interiors in a minimalist modern style. Even the smallest rooms are spacious and airy, and the largest rooms are huge. Just a 2-minute walk from the Plaza Mayor, the location is ideal for sightseeing.

Plaza del Mercado, 20. www.hotelhorus.com. © **98-050-82-82.** 45 rooms. 60€–105€ double; 95€–115€ jr. suite. **Amenities:** Bar; restaurant; room service; spa; free Wi-Fi.

NH Palacio del Duero ★★   Barely outside the old city walls of Zamora, this hotel occupies the 14th- to 15th-century convent of San Juan de Jerusalem as well as the 16th-century Comendadores convent and part of a 20th-century winery. All those properties have been nicely integrated, but the path to some rooms can seem a bit like a maze. The rooms themselves are spacious, modern, and serene, and some have private terraces while others open onto a hidden courtyard where some guests like to sunbathe. The location is perfect for walking to the center (under 5 min.) or making a quick getaway with your car, since it's outside the medieval street maze.

Plaza de la Horta, 1. www.nh-hotels.com. © **98-050-82-62.** 49 units. 61€–93€ double. **Amenities:** Bar; restaurant; free Wi-Fi.

Parador de Zamora ★ Medieval armor, heavy tapestries, hanging lanterns, and reproduction antique furniture give this *parador* a gravitas that other lodgings in Zamora lack. Built in the mid–15th century on the site of an earlier Roman fortress, the building features a beautiful staircase and a dignified wood-and-stone interior courtyard with a well in the center. The two levels of guest rooms are arrayed around the central patio and most have big windows with heavy wooden shutters. The decor mixes richly colored fabrics with dark wood furnishings for a modern interpretation of traditional style. The location is within convenient walking distance of attractions.

Plaza de Viriato, 5. www.parador.es. ✆ **98-051-44-97.** 52 units. 90€–156€ double, 170€–195€ jr. suite. **Amenities:** Restaurant; bar; outdoor pool; room service; free Wi-Fi.

Valbusenda Hotel Bodega & Spa ★★★ On the road to the Castilian wine capital of Toro, this magnificent modern country retreat is geared to wine-lovers. Set in the middle of D.O. Toro vineyards, the hotel was constructed as an integral piece with a small winery. (Guests get a free tour.) Grape products figure in the spa treatments, and the restaurant menus are constructed to put the choice of wine before the choice of main dish. The rooms mimic a modern men's private club: Walls are paneled with light wood, large windows take in vast views of the countryside, and the upholstery, bedding, and drapery are all in neutral tones. The graciously landscaped grounds include a "library" vineyard of grape varietals. The hotel makes an excellent base for touring Toro wineries as well as the historical attractions of Zamora.

Carretera de Toro a Peleagonzalo, s/n. www.valbusenda.com. ✆ **98-069-95-73.** 35 units. 157€–192€ double, 282€–317€ jr. suite. **Amenities:** Restaurant; bar; spa; fitness center; 2 pools (1 indoor); tennis court; free Wi-Fi.

Where to Eat in Zamora

Zamora sits on the north bank of the Río Duero just downstream from the wine districts of Rueda and Toro and just upstream from the Arribes del Douro vineyards. To the north, the landscape rises rapidly into mountain woodlands that supply the foraged mushrooms and wild trout often found on Zamoran menus. Historically, the city was an important stop on the Roman "silver road" to Galicia, and the Galician penchant for octopus continues even in this dusty Castilian city.

Asador Casa Mariano ★★ CASTILIAN Classic dishes of Castilla y León dominate the menu at this homey restaurant devoted to its wood-fired brick oven. Segovia has its roast piglet, but Zamora was historically a wool-raising town and the specialty here is wood-roasted milk-fed lamb. (The owners helped found the Asociatión de Asadores de Lechazo de Castilla y León, the professional association that sets the standards for the dish.) Every Wednesday the chef also prepares a traditional Castilian *cocido,* a stew full of sausages, offal, chickpeas, and a rich broth. In keeping with regional tradition, most of the fish dishes feature salt cod, except for the hake and octopus brought in from A Coruña. The local *morcilla Zamorano* is a particularly rich blood sausage roasted like a cut of meat.

Avda Portugal, 28. www.asadorcasamariano.com. *C* **98-053-44-87.** Entrees 14€– 28€; set menus 14€–39€. Mon–Sat 9am–4pm and 6:30pm–midnight, Sun 9am–4pm.

La Bóveda ★★ CONTEMPORARY SPANISH   Located in the old Banco d'España vault at the Hotel Horus (p. 214), La Bóveda ("The Vault") is a treasure. The chef adapts several classic Spanish dishes from different regions—*bacalao al pil-pil* with piquillo peppers from Basque country, for example, or suckling pig with crispy skin from Castilla—and gives them a modern twist. The wine list features the splendid reds from nearby Toro. Although it's perhaps the dressiest restaurant in Zamora, La Bóveda offers exceptional value for the price.

Plaza del Mercado, 20. www.hotelhorus.com. *C* **98-050-82-82.** Entrees 12€–22€, set menu 16€–22€. Mon–Sat 1:30–3pm and 9pm–midnight, Sun 1:30–3pm.

Libertén ★★ SPANISH   Very chic yet affordable, this restaurant strikes a note of high contrast right away with pale birch furniture and floors as a background for the black tablecloths and staff uniforms. The crispness carries over into the dishes' presentation—great piles of shellfish graced with Dublin prawns, beautiful chop and steaks piled high with golden fried potatoes. Lamb and veal chops come with a sauce of aged Zamoran cheese. The extensive, well-curated wine list draws from all four nearby regions: reds from Ribera del Duero, Toro, and Arribes del Duero, and spectacular whites from Rueda. A rarity among Castilian restaurants, Libertén excels at desserts, offering a rotating list of at least five chocolate treats. If you finished your red wine, the bar also offers a selection of sweet Pedro Ximenez by the glass.

Calle Puerta Nueva, 2. http://restauranteliberten.com. *C* **98-053-66-64.** Entrees 10€–18€; menu de día 10€. Tue–Sat 1–3:30pm and 9–11pm, Sun 1–3:30pm.

A Side Trip into Wine Country ★★

With its location atop the ridgeline over the Río Duero, Zamora is the perfect staging ground for quick visits to three of Spain's major wine districts. Most wineries ask that you arrange visits in advance, but some permit drop-ins.

The closest district, **D.O. Toro,** centered on the medieval city of Toro, a 40-minute drive east of Zamora on the A-11. In addition to warfare and religious conversion, the Castilian kings employed the persuasive properties of wine to take back Iberia from the Moors, then claimed the reconquered turf around Toro by planting vineyards. Building on those first 11th-century plantings, Toro has become the heart of its own D.O. wine

Decorations on a float at the annual wine festival in Toro.

district, source of some powerful red wines. Ever since scientific wine-makers in the 1980s began to tame the powerful *tinto de Toro* grape (an ancient strain of Tempranillo), the biggest names in Spanish viticulture have flocked here to establish vineyards. On the way to Toro (actually, on its western outskirts), **Bodega Valbusenda** (Carretera de Toro a Pelea-gonzalo; www.valbusenda.com) offers tastings and winery tours as part of a wine resort complex (see p. 215 for its hotel). Downtown Toro's single main street is lined with shops offering free tastings and selling the local wines—so many that if you're not careful, you'll be woozy by the time you get to the 13th-century Colegiata church, officially **Santa María la Mayor,** on Plaza Santa María (torosacro.com; *✆* **98-069-03-88;** summer Tues–Sun 10:30am–2pm and 5–7:30pm, winter Tues–Sun 10am–2pm and 4:30–6:30pm). Note that you enter the church from the rear (4€ admission except during Mass), mostly because the main entrance, the **Pórtico de la Majestad (Portal of Majesty) ★★★**, is one of Spain's most magnificent examples of Gothic stone carving; you have to go through the church and back out to view it. The carved figures of the Last Judgment—all still painted in sun-blasted pastels—reveal something of the carver's theology: First to be saved, even before the Virgins and the

Martyrs, are the musicians. If you want to visit area wineries, inquire at the **D.O. Viños de Toro** office at Calle Isaías Carrasco, 4 (dotoro.com; ✆ **98-069-03-05**), for a list with addresses and contact information.

A half hour east of Toro on the A-11 and A-6, the village of Rueda is headquarters for **D.O. Rueda,** home some of the best white wines in Spain. Two grapes are especially important here: verdejo and sauvignon blanc. Some cellars in town date from the 12th century, but in the late 1970s, rediscovery of the verdejo grape and the introduction of controlled cold fermentation rocketed Rueda's whites to world-class status. Sauvignon blanc was reintroduced to the area by Rioja growers late in the 20th century—ironic, considering that genetic sleuthing suggests the grape may have originated here before it was taken to France. Several bodegas have shops along the main street of Rueda, but to get a more complete picture of the town's historic winemaking, reserve ahead to visit **Bodegas Antaño Mocén,** Calle Arribas, 7–9 (www.bodegasantano.com; ✆ **983-86-85-33**). Its 400- to 500-year-old cellars stretch 2.5 miles (4km) underground; the winery, however, is a model of stainless-steel tanks and computerized controls. The on-site shop does a tasting (15€ Mon–Sat) of wines ranging from fresh young whites to elegant verdejos aged in French and American oak.

About an hour further east along the Río Duero (take the scenic CL-610, CL-600, and N-122), **Peñafiel** is the de facto capital of the **D.O. Ribera del Duero.** Since the turn of the 21st century, the region has rivaled—some say surpassed—D.O. Rioja as the source of Spain's best red wines. Small outlets for major producers abound; the tourist office at Plaza San Miguel de Reoyo, 2 (www.turismopenafiel.com, ✆ **98-388-17-15**), sells a "wine pass" for 5€ that opens the doors for winery visits at more than a dozen bodegas in the area. The remarkable Peñafiel castle—which looks like a great ark marooned on a hilltop—is home to the **Museo Provincial del Vino** (✆ **98-388-11-99;** admission with wine tasting 10€), which recounts wine history, winemaking techniques, and the finer points of appreciating local wines. Signage is in Spanish, but a headset CD player provides English commentary.

BURGOS ★★

Spain's greatest conqueror, El Cid Campeador—the Spanish hero immortalized in the epic *El Cantar de Mío Cid*—was born near Burgos, and his remains have a kinglike prominence in the grand cathedral. On a less heroic note, during the Spanish Civil War, General Francisco Franco made the conservative city his Nationalist army headquarters, doing his clumsy best to represent himself as a modern El Cid. His attachment to the city means that Burgos remains more intact than most medieval Spanish cities. It definitely lives up to its roots as the "cradle of Castilla." Employing a distinctive lisp (their hero is "El Theed"), Burgos residents speak textbook Castellano—of course, they wrote the textbooks. Burgos is a provincial capital on the desert *meseta.* Ferociously hot in summer, it comes alive at night as students flock to the cafes and dance clubs.

Essentials

ARRIVING   Burgos is well connected by **train** from Madrid (trip time: 2–4½ hr.) and Bilbao (trip time: 2½–3 hr.). Fares from Madrid range from 31€ to 40€; from Bilbao, 16€ to 20€. The Burgos-Rosa de Lima train station is about 7km (4.3 miles) northeast of the old city on Avenida Príncipes de Asturias, s/n. Visit www.renfe.es or call ✆ **90-232-03-20.** Some 18 **buses** a day make the 2¾-hour trip from Madrid. A one-way fare costs 19€ to 27€. The Burgos bus depot is at Calle Miranda, 4 (www.alsa.es; ✆ **94-726-20-17**), which intersects the large Plaza de Vega, due south of (and across the river from) the cathedral. Burgos is well connected to its neighbors by a network of highways. It's a 3-hour drive from Madrid (follow the N-1 north) and only a 90-minute drive from Bilbao.

VISITOR INFORMATION   The CITUR **tourist office,** Calle Nuño Rasura, 7 (www.turismocastillayleon.com; ✆ **94-728-88-74**), is open July to September daily 9am to 8pm. From October to June it's open daily 10am to 2pm and 4 to 7:30pm.

Exploring Burgos

The south side of the medieval part of Burgos is lined with beautiful parks along the Río Arlanzón. The most dramatic entrance into the old city is through the ancient **Arco de Santa María,** decorated with early-16th-century sculptures of famous Burgos burghers. The plaza before you is one of the busiest pedestrian crossroads of Spain: Two different pilgrimage routes to Santiago converge in Burgos, and every pilgrim pays respects at the marvelously hulking **Catedral de Santa María,** built into the remnants of the city's defensive walls. East of the cathedral, you'll find a warren of shops and tapas bars en route to the Plaza Mayor. Slightly farther east, a modern equestrian statue of E Cid strikes an iconic heroic pose. Cross back across the river to visit the **Museo de la Evolución Humana** (p. 221), a thoroughly modern museum about the first humans living in Europe.

Casa de Cordón ★ HISTORIC SITE   History records that on April 23, 1497, Christopher Columbus met with Isabel and Fernando in this 15th-century palace (now a bank and cultural center), after his second voyage to the New World. Also in this building, in 1506, Felipe el Hermoso (the Handsome) suffered a heart attack after a game of jai alai; his grieving wife, Juana, dragged his body through the streets of Burgos, earning her the sobriquet Juana la Loca (the Mad).

Plaza de la Libertad s/n. ✆ **94-725-81-00.** Mon–Sat noon–2pm and 7–9pm. Free.

Cartuja de Miraflores ★ CHURCH   Located 4km (2½ miles) east of the center of Burgos, this florid Gothic charterhouse was founded in 1441.

King Juan II (father of Isabel I) selected it as the royal tomb for himself and his wife Isabel of Portugal. By 1494, the **church** ★ was finished, its sober facade belying the treasure-trove of decoration inside. The stunning attraction of the interior is the **sculptured unit** ★★★ in the apse (said to have been built with the first gold brought back from the New World) by Gil de Siloé, who also designed the polychrome wood altarpiece. The remains of the king and queen lie in a white marble mausoleum designed like an eight-pointed star, decorated with exuberant Gothic cherubs, pinnacles, canopies, and scrolls.

Carretera de Burgos a Cardeña Km 3. www.cartuja.org. © **94-725-25-86.** Free admission. Mon–Sat 10:15am–3pm and 4–6pm; Sun 11am–3pm and 4–6pm (Nov–Mar closed Wed).

Catedral de Santa María ★★★ CATHEDRAL   Begun in 1221, this celebrated cathedral is one of the best examples of French Gothic on the Iberian Peninsula. Ornamented 15th-century bell towers flank the three main doorways by Juan de Colonia. The 16th-century **Chapel of Condestable,** behind the main altar, embodies Flamboyant Gothic architecture; it's richly decorated with heraldic emblems, balconies, a sculptured filigree doorway, figures of apostles and saints, and a stained-glass window

Burgos claims the Spanish hero El Cid as a native son.

The Museo de la Evolución Humana.

of an eight-sided star. Equally elegant are the two-story 14th-century **cloisters,** filled with haunting Spanish Gothic sculptures. The cathedral's **tapestries,** including a well-known Gobelin, are rich in detail. In one of the chapels you'll see an old chest linked to the legend of El Cid; the warrior had it filled with gravel to be used as collateral to trick moneylenders. The remains of El Cid himself, together with those of his wife, Doña Ximena, are buried beneath marble slabs in front of the altar and beneath the cathedral's lanternlike dome. At midday, bright colored lights from the stained glass play down on them.

Plaza de Santa María s/n. www.catedraldeburgos.es. © **94-720-47-12.** Admission 7€ adults, 6€ seniors, 4.50€ students, 2€ ages 7–14, free for children 6 and under. Mid-Mar to Oct daily 9:30am–7:30pm; Nov to mid-Mar daily 10am–7pm.

Museo de la Evolución Humana ★★★ MUSEUM   Since the early 20th century, archaeologists have been excited about finds in caves in the nearby Sierra Atapuerca, but only recently did science prove conclusively that some of these human fossil remains date back 800,000 years. That makes Atapuerca Europe's earliest site of human inhabitation by a long shot—literally hundreds of thousands of years before the emergence of *Homo sapiens* or even *Homo neanderthalis.* What's all the more remarkable is that these limestone caves have been in more or less continuous use ever since. This extraordinary museum, opened in 2010, chronicles the successive waves of hominids in Spain, even explaining what appears to be human's earliest use of fire. Subterranean galleries deal with the Atapuerca excavations, while the Evolution gallery dominates the ground floor. The next level up deals with cultural evolution, and the top floor is a platform for admiring the museum's dramatic and quite beautiful architecture by Juan Navarro Baldeweg.

Paseo Sierra de Atapuerca s/n. www.museoevolucionhumana.com. ℭ **94-742-10-00.** Admission 6€ adults, 4€ seniors and students, free under age 8; free to all Wed evening. Jul–Sept Tues–Sun 10am–8pm; Oct–June Tue–Fri 10am–2pm and 4:30–8pm, Sat–Sun 10am–8pm.

Where to Stay in Burgos

Hotel NH Collection Palacio de Burgos ★★★   Right on the Río Arlanzón across a small bridge from the cathedral, this nearly 500-year-old palace makes a luxurious setting for a visit to Burgos. The graceful rhythms of the 16th-century cloisters alone are worth the stay. But the rooms are hardly monastic—they are large by Spanish standards and furnished with dark wood furniture, wooden floors, and earth-toned bedding and drapery. The slight remove from the heart of the city helps guarantee a good night's sleep. The hotel makes a good touring base; book a superior or premium room for only a small step up in price.

Calle de la Merced, 13. www.nh-collection.com. ℭ **94-747-99-00.** 110 units. 78€–154€ double, 140€–173€ jr. suite. Parking 19€. **Amenities:** Restaurant; bar; gym; sauna; solarium; roof terrace; free Wi-Fi.

Hotel Rice Reyes Católicos ★★   It's a bit of a surprise to find a hotel that features classic British-style decor in the heart of Castilian Spain, but this boutique hotel is a good bet for its attention to comfort (luxury mattresses, excellent marble bathrooms) and convenient location about 0.8km (½ mile) north of the city center. Family rooms can accommodate two adults and two children. The Rice also has some pet-friendly rooms for a 20€ supplement.

Av. Reyes Católicos 30. www.hotelrice.com. ℭ **94-722-23-00.** 50 rooms. 50€–95€ double; 70€–135€ family room. Parking 14€. **Amenities:** Restaurant; bar; free Wi-Fi.

Mesón del Cid ★★ CASTILIAN   With its striking views of the adjacent cathedral, it's hard to beat the location of Mesón del Cid. While the decor is rather stodgy, everything about the hotel is welcoming and comfortable, and the old-style Castilian furnishings are actually newly manufactured. Once the city's most elegant address, the hotel has been superseded by several newer chain properties: That competition means that prices are as old-fashioned as the metal bedframes. The hotel's restaurant is just the place to take your aging aunt for traditional cuisine.

Plaza de Santa María 8. www.mesondelcid.es. ℭ **94-720-87-15.** 56 rooms. 60€–75€ double; 124€–140€ suite. **Amenities:** Restaurant; bar; free Wi-Fi.

Where to Eat in Burgos

Burgos is often cited (especially by Castilians) as the gastronomic capital of Spain, in no small part for its superb and spicy blood sausages, the prevalence of roasted meat dishes, and a lively tapas scene. The vast majority of tapas bars are almost unbelievably good bargains—short-term visitors rarely look much farther.

Casa Ojeda ★ CASTILIAN   Established in 1912, Casa Ojeda is the Burgos standard-bearer for traditional Castilian cuisine. With its modestly priced bar-cafe and downright inexpensive deli in the same building, Casa Ojeda's spacious dining room features service as classical as the menu, along with a wood-burning stove to warm the room in chilly weather. Spit-roasted meats are excellent (if pricey), but the kitchen prides itself on more modest plates like tongue with pickled wild mushrooms, blood sausage roasted in the oven with stuffed red peppers, and crab salad with noodles and grated black truffle. Reserve at least 3 days ahead.

Calle Vitoria 5. www.restauranteojeda.com. ✆ **94-720-90-52.** Entrees 16€–36€. Mon–Sat 1:30–4pm and 9–11:30pm, Sun 1–3:30pm.

La Quinta del Monje ★★ SPANISH   It's hard to decide between the main dishes and the incredible tapas at this inventive spot, a favorite of local foodies, with dishes ready-made for Instagram. Blood sausage here is not the usual small roasted slices—it's a tempura-fried lollipop with piquillo pepper sauce. Soft-boiled egg is served with flecks of foie gras and mushroom jam. Perhaps the most umami-packed dish is a small crunchy pork-jowl burger with chimichurri sauce. If you have a bigger appetite, consider the seared tuna belly with pistachio ragout or the roast chicken with sautéed potatoes. Ask about the desserts of the day. The chef always has some gorgeous trick up his sleeve.

Calle San Lorenzo, 19-21. laquintadelmonje.com. ✆ **94-720-87-68.** Tapas 2€–5€, entrees 9€–17€. Mon–Fri 9am–12:30am, Sat 10:30am–1am, Sun 10:30am–12:30am.

La Favorita Taberna Urbana ★★ CASTILIAN   Widely acclaimed for the charcoal-grilled beef, pork, and wild game dishes that dominate its dining room menu, La Favorita also has an atmospheric tapas bar where exposed brick-and-stone walls lend a rustic flavor to its urban location. The proprietors are justifiably proud of their regional specialties, many of them available at the bar as inexpensive tapas. On a chilly day, warm up with *estrellitas* (half-cooked eggs over fried potatoes) or a mini-tower of *habitas con foie* (baby broad beans with ham and duck liver).

Calle Avellanos 8 E. www.lafavoritaburgos.com. ✆ **94-720-59-59.** Tapas 2€–3€, *raciones* 6€–14€, entrees 11€–19€. Daily 11am–11pm.

Side Trip to Santo Domingo de la Calzada ★

Pilgrims have streamed across northern Spain for nearly 1,000 years to reach Santiago de Compostela (p. 655). To see the pilgrimage route up close, make a day trip to **Santo Domingo de la Calzada,** 68km (42 miles) east of Burgos. Established in the 12th century by Saint Dominic as a stopover for pilgrims, its core has changed little over the centuries. The town's landmark 12th-century Gothic **cathedral** ★ (www.english. catedralsantodomingo.es; ✆ **94-134-00-33**) contains the crypt of its founder. A centuries-old legend is attached to the cathedral: Supposedly a cooked rooster stood up from the dinner table and crowed to protest the innocence of a pilgrim who'd been accused of theft and sentenced to hang. To this day, a live cock and hen are kept in a cage on a church wall; you can often hear the rooster crowing at Mass. The cathedral is open Monday to Friday 9am to 8pm, Saturday 9am to 7pm, Sunday 9am to 12:20pm and 2 to 8pm. Admission is 5€ adults, 3€ ages 8 to 18, and free for everyone on Sunday for Mass. Motorists can reach Santo Domingo de la Calzada by following either of the traffic arteries paralleling the river, heading west from the Burgos cathedral until signs indicate N-120. If you want to stay the night, you can't do better than the **Parador de Santo Domingo** ★★★, Plaza del Santo, 3 (www.parador.es; ✆ **94-134-03-00;** 95€–130€ double). Built next to the cathedral in the 12th century as a hostelry for pilgrims, its modern rich linens, lofty beds, and spacious rooms make it anything but ascetic.

LEÓN ★★

Once the leading city of Christian Spain, León has one of the most inspiring Gothic cathedrals in Europe. Long the capital of a broad feudal kingdom, León went into eclipse after uniting with Castilla. Today it serves as a gateway between Castilla and Galicia's pilgrimage routes to Santiago de Compostela. The modern city sprawls, but the most important monuments, restaurants, and hotels are concentrated in the center. Like Burgos, the region is renowned for its soft-spoken, pristine Castellano Spanish. León is an excellent place to experience the tranquility of the Spanish heartland; it's also obligatory for students of medieval architecture.

Essentials

ARRIVING León has 10 **trains** daily from Madrid (trip time: 2¼–4½ hr.). The station, Estación del Norte, Av. de Astorga, 2 (www.renfe.es; ✆ **90-232-03-20**), is on the western bank of the Bernesga River. Cross the bridge near Plaza de Guzmán el Bueno. A one-way ticket from Madrid ranges from 30€ to 55€. Most of León's **buses** arrive and depart from the Estación de Autobuses, Paseo Ingeniero Sáenz de Miera (✆ **98-721-10-00**). Three to five buses per day link León with Zamora and Salamanca, and there are 11 per day from Madrid (trip time: 4¼ hr.). A one-way ticket on a direct regular bus from Madrid costs 24€ to 40€ for the *supra* (comfortable) service. For more information on prices, visit www.alsa.es or call ✆ **90-242-22-42.** León lies at the junction of five major highways

León's claim to Gaudí fame: the 1893 Casa Botines.

coming from five different regions of Spain. From Madrid, head northwest on the N-VI superhighway toward A Coruña; at Benavente, bear right onto the N-630.

VISITOR INFORMATION   The **tourist office,** Plaza de San Marcelo, 1 (www.turismoleon.org; ✆ **98-787-83-27**), is open daily 9am to 8pm.

Exploring León

Casa Botines ★★ MUSEUM   If you're not planning to visit Barcelona to see the mind-boggling architecture of Antoni Gaudí, here's your chance in León. When León's cloth merchants wanted to build a new headquarters, one of their Barcelona counterparts, Carles Güell, recommended Gaudí, the architect Güell had commissioned to design his own home (p. 429). The resulting structure, dedicated in 1893, expresses the medieval revival side of Modernisme, right down to the façade's high-relief sculpture of St. George sticking it to the dragon. Inside, the architectural details reveal Gaudí's flair. Some rooms exhibit a collection of 19th- and 20th-century Spanish paintings. You can also climb the tower but only on guided tours, which are offered in English and Spanish.

Plaza San Marcelo, 5. www.casabotines.es. ✆ **98-735-32-47.** Admission 5€ adults, 3€ students and seniors; 8€/5€ with a guide. Tues 11am–2pm and 5–9pm, Wed 5–9pm, Thurs–Sat 11am–2pm and 5–9pm, Sun 5–9pm.

The Catedral de León.

Catedral de León (Santa María de Regla) ★★★ CATHEDRAL

This is why almost everyone visits León—to see the sun shine through the most dramatic stained-glass windows in Spain. There are 125 in all (plus 57 oculi), dating from the 13th century. They are so heavy that the roof of the cathedral is held up not by the walls, but by flying buttresses. In the church-building frenzy of the Middle Ages, every Gothic cathedral vied to distinguish itself with some superlative trait. Milan Cathedral was the biggest, Chartres had the most inspiring stained-glass windows, Palma de Mallorca had the largest rose window, and so on. Structurally, though, the boldest cathedral was at León. This edifice set a record for the greatest proportion of window space, with stained-glass windows soaring 34m (112 ft.) to the vaulted ceiling, framed by the slenderest of columns. The windows occupy 1,672 sq. m (nearly 18,000 sq. ft.), or almost all the space where you'd expect the walls to be. Inside, the profusion of light and the illusion of weightlessness astonish even medievalists. The 13th-century architects (Juan Pérez and Maestro Enrique) who designed the cathedral were, in effect, precursors of architect Mies van der Rohe, 7 centuries before the age of steel girders and plate-glass curtain walls. The experience of being surrounded by color and light makes this cathedral so special.

Plaza de Regla. www.catedraldeleon.org. © **98-787-57-70.** Admission free for worship; cultural visits 6€ adults, 5€ seniors and students, 2€ children. May–Sept Mon–Fri 9:30am–1:30pm and 4–8pm, Sat 9:30am–noon and 2–6pm, Sun 9:30am–11am and 2–8pm (closed Sun afternoons in May); Oct–Apr Mon–Sat 9:30am–1:30pm and 4–7pm, Sun 9:30am–2pm;

MUSAC (Museo de Arte Contemporáneo de Castilla y León) ★

ART MUSEUM   We seriously doubt that the city of León will ever rival, say, Berlin for international hipness, but even León deserves a taste of the avant-garde, which this museum supplies in spades. From the exterior, its stained-glass panels evoke a box of Crayola crayons or a rack of paint chips in the "bold" collection. Even on a dreary winter day MUSAC looks cheery and inviting. Collections focus mostly on artists under the age of 40, and the programming has won a number of European awards for innovation, for presenting conceptual pieces like a re-created car accident. Marcel Duchamp is no doubt chuckling in his grave.

Av. de los Reyes Leoneses 24. musac.es. © **98-709-00-00.** Admission 3€ adults, 2€ students, 1€ ages 8–18. Tues–Fri 11am–2pm and 5–8pm; Sat–Sun 11am–3pm and 5–9pm. Bus: 7, 11, or 12.

Real Colegiata de San Isidoro ★★★ CHURCH   The Leónese boast that "León had 24 kings before Castilla even had laws." Eleven of them (along with 14 queens and many other nobles) are entombed here in this 12th-century burial vault, a marvelously spooky Romanesque room with fanciful ceiling frescoes of biblical scenes and court life. It's a magical space, which the Leónese understandably call the "Sistine Chapel of Spain." The church is no slouch either: Its treasury has some rare finds—10th-century Scandinavian ivory, an 11th-century chalice, an important collection of 10th- to 12th-century Asian fabrics—and the library museum contains many ancient manuscripts and rare books, including a Book of Job from A.D. 951, a Visigothic Bible, and a Bible from 1162, plus dozens of miniatures.

Plaza San Isidoro 4. www.museosanisidorodeleon.com. © **98-787-61-61.** Admission 5€. Mon–Sat 10am–2pm and 4–7pm, Sun 10am–2pm. Bus: 4 or 9.

Where to Stay in León

Hotel Alfonso V ★★   We usually expect hotels named after Spanish monarchs to be steeped in history, but this mid-20th-century property in León's commercial center features modern décor, its soaring seven-story lobby ringed with interior balconies and filled with sculpture. The mid-sized guest rooms are a bit less dramatic, decorated in bright contemporary Spanish style with lots of color pops, simple Scandinavian furniture, and bathrooms awash in marble and nickel-stainless fixtures. Soundproofing is excellent. The top-floor bar is a dramatic place to get a drink at night, with sweeping city views.

Calle Padre Isla 1. www.hotelalfonsov.com. ☎ **98-722-09-00.** 62 units. 63€–90€ double; 120€–140€ suite. Parking 19€. **Amenities:** Restaurant; bar; free Wi-Fi.

Hotel Posada Regia ★ The two buildings renovated to make this hotel neatly bracket León's period of greatest importance: One dates from the 14th century and the other from the 19th. Furnishings evoke the latter, with their Isabelline lines (comparable to Victorian) and extensive use of silk broadcloth upholstery. The family that runs the Regia and its tavern took advantage of the buildings' different architecture to expose beams in some rooms and to strip plaster from brick or stone walls in others. The color palette tends to favor bold, saturated, warm tones. Many of the spacious bathrooms have corner tubs. Top-floor rooms, tucked under the eaves, are the most romantic. The central location makes the Posada Regia very convenient for seeing the sights.

Calle Regidores, 11. www.regialeon.com. ☎ **98-721-31-73.** 36 rooms. 59€–130€ double; discounts for pilgrims with pilgrim card. **Amenities:** Restaurant; bar; free Wi-Fi.

Hotel Real Colegiata de San Isidoro ★★★ The church, museum, and pantheon of the kings of León (p. 227) constitute one of León's great sights. But if this Romanesque Augustinian monastery really captures your imagination, spend the night. After walking past a lovely fountain in the majestic courtyard, you'll find yourself surrounded by antique furnishings and glittering chandeliers in the sumptuous common areas. The rooms are less over the top—in fact, some are downright tight, rented at accordingly low prices as "monastic" rooms. Standard and "superior" doubles are quite spacious, though, and each room has a window to the central courtyard cut through the deep stone walls. Think of it as a "night at the museum."

Plaza de San Marcos, 7. www.hotelrealcolegiata.com. ☎ **98-7787-50-88.** 46 rooms. 89€–96€ double. Free parking. **Amenities:** Restaurant; bar; chapel; free Wi-Fi.

Where to Eat in León

Pablo ★★★ LEONESE If you have trouble imagining how classical Leonese dishes can be prepared in an upscale, minimalist way, then sign up for the tasting menu at Pablo. The humblest of dishes, blood sausage, is somehow transformed when it's roasted on oak twigs, and the city's famous dried beef assumes a rich lustiness when it's paired with wild mushrooms in a salad. It's a bold step for a restaurant to serve only a tasting menu, usually eight courses; diners have to trust the chef implicitly. But it works at Pablo. Reservations have been suggested since the restaurant opened in 2005; after it won a Michelin star in 2019, they became essential.

Avda Los Cubos, 8. www.restaurantepablo.es. ☏ **98-721-65-62.** Tasting menu 45€. Tues–Sat 1:30–3:30pm and 9–11:30pm, Sun 1:30–3:30pm.

Taberna Bar Cuervo ★ TAPAS   The streets and squares just south of the cathedral—Barrio Húmedo—are filled with small restaurants and bars that take advantage of León's cured meats, famous throughout Spain. Charcuterie here is often just called *embutidos,* or sausages, but the term goes way beyond ground meats stuffed into casings. Many Spanish gourmets consider the local dried beef, *cecina de León,* equal to the best air-dried hams of Andalucía. This tavern has an unusually good selection of charcuterie as well as plates of the local cheeses.

Calle de la Sal 6. ☏ **98-725-40-03.** Raciones 7.50€–15€. Daily 11am–midnight.

León Entertainment & Nightlife

Few other cities in Spain evoke the mystery of the Middle Ages like León. To best appreciate the city's old-fashioned eloquence, wander after dark around the Plaza Mayor, the edges of which are peppered with simple cafes and bars. None is particularly distinct from its neighbor, but overall the effect is rich, evocative, and wonderfully conducive to conversation and romance. One of the best places for drinks is **León Antiguo,** Plaza del Cid, 16 (☏ **98-722-66-95**), which is open Monday to Wednesday 7pm to midnight and Thursday to Saturday 7pm to 4am. Drinks cost 3€ to 6€.

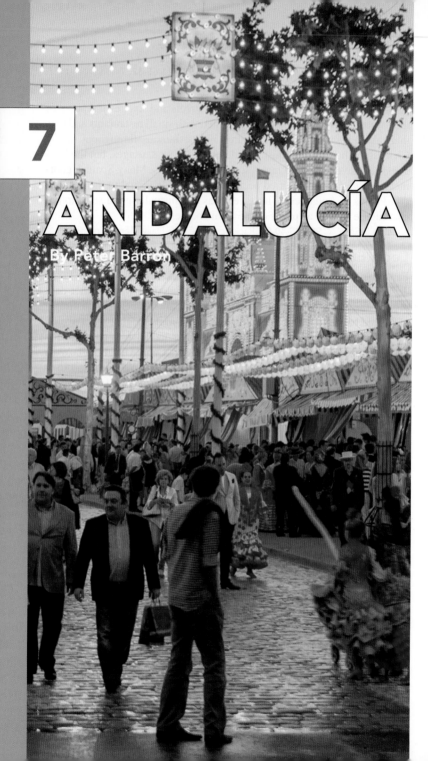

7

ANDALUCÍA

By Peter Barron

Much of what the world imagines as Spain is, in fact, Andalucía. It's the sun-drenched land of sombreros and sherry, where bulls are bred and matadors are more famous than rock stars. It is the passionate cradle of flamenco, with its flouncing dresses and percussive guitar. Of course, some Andalucíans reject these stereotypes, but many more embrace and celebrate them. Nothing here is done by half. Flowers are brighter, fiestas more intense, and the music is both more joyful and more melancholy.

Andalucía was the last redoubt of the Moors, who held al-Andalus for nearly 8 centuries until 1492, and it still shines with the glories of medieval Islam: the world-famous Alhambra of Granada and Mezquita of Córboda, Sevilla's Alcázar and the hybrid minaret of La Giralda. Many of Andalucía's smaller towns are hauntingly beautiful: whitewashed mountain villages, the Renaissance grace of Úbeda and Baeza, the romance of gorge-split Ronda. The dramatic landscapes that surround them are protected in natural and national parks, where rare birds and wildlife flourish. Add the aristocratic languor of Jerez de la Frontera and the glittering personality of Cádiz, and whether you spend a week or a month here, you will only have skimmed the surface.

This sunny, mountainous region also includes the Costa del Sol—led by Malaga, Marbella, and Torremolinos—the beachside playground of southern Spain, which is covered in Chapter 8. Go to the Costa del Sol for beach resorts and nightclubs; visit Andalucía for its rich history and architectural wonders, its traditional tapas, music, and sheer beauty.

SEVILLA ★★★

Sevilla is Andalucía's largest, most self-assured, and most sophisticated city. Style matters here: Almost every *sevillana* owns at least one flamenco dress to wear during the famous April *feria*. A *sevillano* would never sport a tie with a horseman's wide-brimmed sombrero: *¡No es correcto!* It may also be the most elaborately decorated city in Spain: No country does Baroque like the Spanish, and no city does Spanish baroque like Sevilla, where the style represents the hybrid offspring of Moorish decoration and the patronage of the Catholic church.

Sevilla has been Andalucía's center of power since Fernando III of Castilla threw out the Almohad rulers in 1248. Although he rebuilt their

Alcázar fortress, he wisely left the Giralda and the Barrio Santa Cruz intact, and the tangled streets of the Judería still make the medieval era palpable. As the first major city in Andalucía to return to Castilian hands, Sevilla has a markedly Christian countenance, jeweled with churches and former convents. Its Holy Week *(Semana Santa)* processions are the most passionate in Spain.

Essentials

ARRIVING Sevilla's **Aeropuerto San Pablo** (www.aena.es; ✆ **91-321-10-00**) is served by nearly two dozen airlines, including Iberia, Vueling, Air Europa, British Airways, Lufthansa, EasyJet, and Ryanair. The airport lies 10km (6¼ miles) from the city center along the A-4 highway. Linea EA buses (www.tussam.es; ✆ 95-501-00-10) leave Arrivals for the city center every 20 minutes (fare 4€). It terminates at the bus station at Plaza de Armas, but for most visitors it will be more convenient to get off in the city center at Torre del Oro. Official **taxis** (white with a yellow stripe) charge a flat fare to the city center: 22.20€ during the day, 24.75€ after 9pm.

The **train** station, **Estación Santa Justa,** is on Avenida Kansas City (www.renfe.com; ✆ **91-232-03-20**). More than 20 high-speed AVE trains per day run from Madrid to Sevilla (trip time: 2½ hr., cost: 45€–80€ if you avoid the morning commuter rush). Regular trains from Córdoba to Sevilla leave roughly every 20 minutes (trip time: 45–75 min., cost: 14€–30€). There are around a dozen trains daily from Málaga (trip time: 2–3½ hr., cost: 24€–44€) and four from Granada (trip time: 3¾ hr., cost: 30€).

The bus station at **Plaza de Armas** (✆ **95-490-80-40**) handles long-distance connections, while regional Andalucía buses use the **Prado de San Sebastián** (✆ **95-441-71-11**), near Plaza de España. Several companies operate from these stations: ALSA covers most of the main routes (www.alsa.es; ✆ **90-242-22-42**).

By **car,** Sevilla is 530km (329 miles) southwest of Madrid, 145km (90 miles) west of Córdoba, and 205km (127 miles) northwest of Málaga. Several major highways converge on Sevilla; it is easy to drive to, but very difficult to drive around in. Parking can be nightmarish. If you arrive by car, ask your hotel about parking arrangements and leave your car there for the rest of your stay. Parking costs around 20€ a day.

GETTING AROUND Fortunately, Sevilla is easily walkable—there are no hills to speak of and most key sights cluster in a small area on either side of the river. If you need to get from one end to another in a hurry, hop on a bus (1.40€ per trip) instead of paying around 10€ for a taxi. The municipal bicycle rental program, **SEVICI** (www.sevici.es; ✆ **90-090-07-22**), provides access to red bikes parked on racks at 260 stations across the city, each with a kiosk where you can subscribe by credit card. A 1-week membership is 13€; it's free for the first half hour, 1€ for the next hour, 2€ an hour after that. The city **tram** and **Metro** system are good for

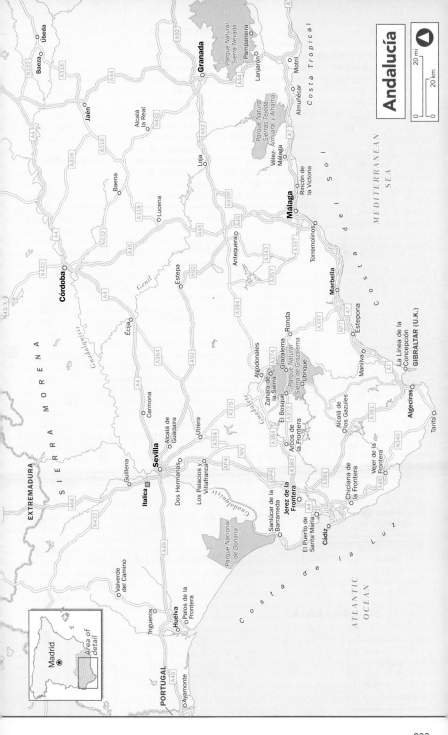

Andalucía

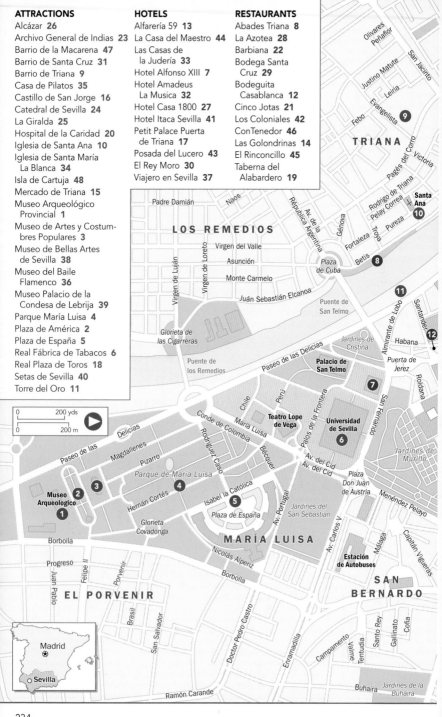

ATTRACTIONS

Alcázar **26**
Archivo General de Indias **23**
Barrio de la Macarena **47**
Barrio de Santa Cruz **31**
Barrio de Triana **9**
Casa de Pilatos **35**
Castillo de San Jorge **16**
Catedral de Sevilla **24**
La Giralda **25**
Hospital de la Caridad **20**
Iglesia de Santa Ana **10**
Iglesia de Santa María
  La Blanca **34**
Isla de Cartuja **48**
Mercado de Triana **15**
Museo Arqueológico
  Provincial **1**
Museo de Artes y Costum-
  bres Populares **3**
Museo de Bellas Artes
  de Sevilla **38**
Museo del Baile
  Flamenco **36**
Museo Palacio de la
  Condesa de Lebrija **39**
Parque María Luisa **4**
Plaza de América **2**
Plaza de España **5**
Real Fábrica de Tabacos **6**
Real Plaza de Toros **18**
Setas de Sevilla **40**
Torre del Oro **11**

HOTELS

Alfarería 59 **13**
La Casa del Maestro **44**
Las Casas de
  la Judería **33**
Hotel Alfonso XIII **7**
Hotel Amadeus
  La Musica **32**
Hotel Casa 1800 **27**
Hotel Itaca Sevilla **41**
Petit Palace Puerta
  de Triana **17**
Posada del Lucero **43**
El Rey Moro **30**
Viajero en Sevilla **37**

RESTAURANTS

Abades Triana **8**
La Azotea **28**
Barbiana **22**
Bodega Santa
  Cruz **29**
Bodeguita
  Casablanca **12**
Cinco Jotas **21**
Los Coloniales **42**
ConTenedor **46**
Las Golondrinas **14**
El Rinconcillo **45**
Taberna del
  Alabardero **19**

Sevilla

commuters but of little value to visitors. **Taxis** are easy to find on the street and at cab ranks; a green light on the roof and a sign (libre) in the windshield indicates if they are free. To order a **cab,** call **Tele Taxi** (© 95-462-22-22) or **Radio Taxi** (© 95-458-00-00). Apps like Uber and Mytaxi also now operate in Sevilla.

VISITOR INFORMATION   There are several tourist offices around the city; the main ones are next to the cathedral at **Plaza del Triunfo, 1;** beside the town hall at **Plaza de San Francisco, 15;** and by the Torre del Oro on **Paseo Alcalde Marqués del Contadero.** They're open Monday to Friday 9am to 7:30pm, weekends 10am to 2pm. For information before you travel, visit **visitasevilla.es**, or call © **95-547-12-32.**

EVENTS   By far the most popular times to visit Sevilla are during the **April Fair**—the most famous *feria* in Spain—and during **Holy Week** *(Semana Santa),* when the streets are filled with religious processions and robed penitents (p. 242). Book lodging well in advance for both.

Exploring Sevilla

A city of 700,000 people, Sevilla sprawls in every direction from its historic heart. But the old city, where you are likely to spend most of your time, is quite compact. The Cathedral, Giralda, and the Alcázar sit next to each other around the **Plaza del Triunfo.** The ancient, narrow streets of the **Barrio de Santa Cruz** spread north from there, with the green spaces of the **Parque María Luisa** to the south. Along the eastern bank of the river is the **Arenal,** the former ship-building district now dominated by the bullring. Across the bridges to the west lies **Triana,** the old fisherman's and Gypsy quarter, famous for its bullfighters, flamenco artists, and painted ceramics. The commercial center spreads northward from **Plaza Nueva** along the pedestrianized streets of Calles Sierpes and Cuna towards the **Plaza de la Encarnación** and Sevilla's newest landmark, Las Setas. The neighborhood north of Encarnación is called **Macarena** after the basilica which is at the heart of Sevilla's Holy Week. It stretches past

---

Tour Guides for Sevilla

In Sevilla, sightseeing buses face one issue: Many of the city's medieval streets can't accommodate large vehicles. To compensate, **City Sightseeing** (city-sightseeing.com) offers hybrid bus and walking tours, but the pre-recorded commentary on the bus section is rather dull. Hop-on, hop-off tickets cost 21€ (10€ children) for unlimited use in a 24-hour period. More lively and informative are the free tours offered by **Heart**

of Sevilla (www.heartofsevilla.com; © **64-404-52-42**). Former history students lead a variety of 90-minute walks daily—taking in the monuments, Triana, and Macarena—with plenty of entertaining stories. Tours are free, though most people give 10–15€ at the end of the tour. Several companies offer guided Segway and bike tours from around 30€; **Jetwalk** (segwaysevilla.com; © **61-815-71-95**) is one of the most highly rated.

BEAT THE queues

The last thing you want to do during your stay in Sevilla is to stand in line for an hour or more in the hot sun. The lines for the **Alcázar** (see below) often stretch far across the Plaza del Triunfo. Skip them by booking online in advance for an extra 1€, and aim for an early slot. At 9:30am you can often walk straight in, ahead of the tour groups. To buy your ticket for the **cathedral** (p. 240), don't go to the cathedral: Head instead to the **Iglesia de San Salvador** in Plaza San Salvador, where you'll quickly be able to buy a 9€ combined ticket that gives you access to that church, the cathedral, and the cathedral's bell tower, the **Giralda.** Once inside the cathedral, you'll see another queue to climb the Giralda; it's often a long queue, and at the top you'll need to wait your turn to see the view. For views without queues, go to the **Setas de Sevilla** (p. 246), where there is an elevator and a panorama that includes the Cathedral and the Giralda.

the once seedy, now fashionable, **Alameda de Hercules** to the Moorish walls at the northern limit of the old city. Across the river, north of Triana, the rather desolate **Isla de Cartuja** was the site of Expo '92 and now holds a contemporary art museum, concert hall, and amusement park.

Alcázar ★★★ FORTRESS   Technically the oldest European royal residence still in use—the king and queen stay here when in Sevilla— this complex of palaces and fortifications dates from the rule of the Abbadid dynasty in the 11th century. Destroyed and almost entirely rebuilt after the 1248 reconquest of Sevilla, it has been much tinkered with by successive kings and queens. Entry is via the **Puerta del León,** with its striking red crenellated wall and ceramic panel depicting a lion, which leads to a series of courtyards and royal residences. The older, more austere building is the **Palacio Gótico,** built by Alfonso X in the 13th century. Carlos V modified its halls to celebrate his wedding in 1526 to his Habsburg cousin, Isabel of Portugal. Huge tapestries celebrate his conquest of Tunisia. The much larger and far more beautiful **Palacio Mudéjar ★★★,** built in the 14th century by Pedro I, is perhaps Spain's finest example of Mudéjar architecture, the style of decoration created by Muslim artisans working under Christian rule. The term means "those who stayed on"; the palace employed some of the same craftsmen who had worked on the Alhambra in Granada. It's a tour de force of carved plaster and stone, delicate calligraphic friezes, tooled wooden ceilings, and decorative tiles. The **Patio de las Doncellas** (Court of the Maidens) most clearly resembles the Alhambra; some inscriptions here refer to Pedro as "the sultan" and others proclaim "there is no conqueror but Allah." The patio's upper columned arches, added by Carlos V, bear his motto "Plus Ultra" (Still Further). The **Patio de las Muñecas** (Court of the Dolls), which served as a children's play area (look for two tiny children's faces peering out from one of its arches) is a good example of architectural recycling: The columns come

A dome at the Alcázar's Salón de Embajadroes.

from the Roman settlement of Itálica just outside Sevilla (p. 263), the capitals from Medina Azahara near Córdoba (p. 263). The exquisitely decorated **Salón de Embajadores** (Hall of Ambassadors) was Pedro I's throne room. Its cupola of carved and gilded wood, representing the heavens, is the palace's most spectacular sight (it is also known as the *media naranja,* or half orange). Subsequent monarchs added wrought-iron balconies and a frieze of 16th-century royal portraits.

The Catholic Kings, Isabel and Fernando, also spent time at the Alcázar; they received Columbus here on his return from America. The **Casa de la Contratación** (House of Trade) was founded by Isabel in 1503 as the crown agency to oversee Sevilla's monopoly on commerce with the New World; inside you'll find the *Virgin of the Navigators* by Alejo Fernández, the first European painting to depict native Americans, sheltering under the Virgin's mantle. For an additional 4.50€ you can visit (with audioguide) the **Cuarto Real Alto,** the upper quarters still used by the royal family when in Sevilla. Round off your visit by wandering in the extensive gardens, a rambling collection of terraces, fountains, mazes, and pavilions featuring centuries of alterations. Fans of the TV show *Game of Thrones* may know them better as the Water Gardens of Dorne.

Plaza del Triunfo s/n. www.alcazarsevilla.org. ⓒ **95-450-23-24.** Admission 11.50€ adults, 3€ seniors and students, free kids under age 17. Apr–Sept daily 9:30am–8pm; Oct–Mar daily 9:30am–6pm (last admission 1 hr. before closing). Bus: T1.

Archivo General de Indias ★ HISTORIC SITE Administering its overseas empire from Sevilla, the Spanish government generated a huge amount of paperwork, which was eventually filed away here. This austere 16th-century building was designed by the architect of El Escorial, Juan de Herrera, as the Stock Exchange *(Lonja)*. Bollards and chains surround it and the cathedral next door, demarcating the jurisdictions of Mammon and God. As the city's trading fortunes began to wane, the building became Sevilla's Academy of Art, with Murillo among its founders. Then in 1785, during the reign of Carlos III, it was turned over for use as the records office for the Indies and amassed some 80 million pages on miles of shelving. Today the bulk of the documents are safely stored in air-conditioned vaults nearby (the boxes you'll see lining the shelves are empty). Exhibits include letters between Columbus and his patron Isabel and from Cervantes to the king, unsuccessfully seeking a posting abroad before he discovered his true calling. Free and queue-free, the Archivo's marble halls are a relaxing place to pause after the Cathedral and Alcázar.

Av. de la Constitución. www.andalucia.org. ✆ **95-450-05-28.** Free admission. Mon–Sat 9:30am–5pm; Sun 10am–2pm. Bus: T1.

Casa de Pilatos ★ HISTORIC SITE This 16th-century seat of the dukes of Medinaceli is one of Sevilla's finest palaces, combining Gothic,

Courtyard at Casa de Pilatos.

Mudéjar, and Renaissance styles in its courtyards, fountains, and salons. It owes its grandeur to the first Marquis of Tarifa, who went on a pilgrimage to Jerusalem via Italy in 1518 and returned to Sevilla buzzing with architectural ideas. It is said to be a reproduction of Pontius Pilate's house in Jerusalem, but its strong Italian and Mudéjar influences suggest otherwise. You can visit the ground floor and the first floor with a guide; the rest of the palace is still used by the Medinaceli family. Throughout, the house features magnificently decorated *azulejos* (tiles) and wooden *artesonado* ceilings; the staircase is a marvel. The art collection on the upper floor includes paintings by Sebastiano del Piombo, Pacheco, and Goya. The lush gardens are a further treat—the palm trees, box hedges, and cascading bougainvillea are a striking symbol of wealth and opulence in Sevilla's hot, dry climate.

Plaza Pilatos 1. www.fundacionmedinaceli.org. ℂ **95-422-52-98.** Entire house 12€; ground floor, patio, and gardens 10€. Daily 9am–6pm (7pm in summer).

Catedral de Sevilla & La Giralda ★★★ CATHEDRAL   The largest Gothic building in the world, the Catedral de Sevilla was designed with the stated goal that "those who come after us will take us for madmen." Construction began in the early 15th century on the huge rectangular base of the Almohad mosque and took a hundred years to complete. From the outside, its vast, low, profile is rather ungainly; the British writer Laurie Lee described it as "hugging the ground like an encrusted turtle." Inside, its scale is staggering. There are 20 chapels arranged around its naves, closed off by elaborate wrought-iron grilles *(rejas),* Iberia's unique contribution to cathedral art. The domed **Capilla Real** (royal chapel) houses the remains of Fernando III, who retook Sevilla in 1248, alongside the tombs of Alfonso X and Pedro I. The Capilla de San Antonio contains one of Murillo's finest paintings, the *Vision of St Anthony.* It is said that

---

PAINT THE TOWN red

As you walk around Sevilla, you'll notice that many of the grandest buildings, including the entrance to the Real Alcázar, are painted red or pink. The color became highly fashionable following the colonization of the New World, and it comes from an unlikely source. For thousands of years Mexicans had harvested and dried the parasitic cochineal beetle which lives on the prickly pear cactus. Once crushed, the beetles produce carmine, a natural red pigment used in paint, fabric dyes, and food coloring. The first cochineal arrived in Sevilla in the 1520s, and Carlos V quickly recognized its value, instructing Hernán Cortés to get hold of more of it. It looked brighter and held faster than existing European red dyes. At the height of the trade, ships brought some 300,000 pounds (136,000kg) of cochineal to Sevilla every year, alongside the more conventional spoils of silver and gold. Latin America still exports large quantities of it, used to color products from lipstick to Red Velvet cakes. If you see Natural Red 4 or E120 on a food label, it has colored by the crushed beetles of the New World.

A detail from the altar at Catedral de Sevilla.

young women pray before the huge painting, asking Anthony, patron saint of the lovelorn, to send them a husband. In a portal on the south side of the cathedral, the **tomb of Columbus**—not created until 1892—is held aloft by four carved pall-bearers, representing the four kingdoms of Spain. Whether his bones are here is another matter: His remains have been removed, reinterred, mixed up, and lost on a number of occasions since his death in 1506, and the Dominican Republic, known in Columbus' time as Hispaniola, claims them too. In the central nave, the bulky carved choir *(coro)* leads to the cathedral's gilded highlight: the huge, **Gothic altarpiece** *(retablo)* depicting the life of Christ in 45 panels. It is the life's work of the Flemish sculptor, Pieter Dancart, and took more than 40 years to complete. On feast days three times a year, six choirboys *(Los Seises)* perform a ceremonial dance on the altar dressed in Renaissance plumed hats, wielding castanets. In the sacristies, seek out remarkable paintings by Zurbarán, Campaña, and Goya, the last of which depicts Sevilla's martyr saints Justa and Rufina, with the Giralda tower in the background. Legend says that they were early Christian potters from Triana, who were tortured and killed by the Romans after refusing to make pots for a pagan celebration. They are revered in Sevilla, especially in Triana, and are said to protect the Giralda. The oval-domed Chapter House has more paintings by Murillo, of which the *Immaculate Conception* takes center stage. After touring the cathedral's somber interior, you emerge into the sunlight of the **Patio de los Naranjos** (Court of the Orange Trees), originally the mosque's main courtyard, where worshippers performed their ablutions before prayer. The central fountain dates from Visigothic times, and above the doorway hangs a stuffed crocodile, said to have been a gift from the Sultan of Egypt to Alfonso X. Leave via the **Puerta de Perdón,** the entrance to the old mosque, which retains its exquisitely carved horseshoe arch.

    La Giralda, the bell tower of the cathedral, is the city's most emblematic and most beautiful monument. Erected as the minaret of the mosque between 1171 and 1198, it was built on Roman and Visigothic

APRIL IS THE craziest month

Every April, Sevilla hosts not one but two full-on popular festivals. Its **Semana Santa** (Holy Week) processions are the biggest and most passionate in Spain. Huge floats called *pasos* bearing statues of the Virgin and Christ are shouldered through the streets for hours on end. Around 70 church brotherhoods (*confradias*) take part, leading the procession in the sinister-looking robes and pointed hoods of the *penitentes*. The high point is Holy Thursday, when the processions to the Cathedral carry on through the night. You can find details of where and when to see them on the newspaper ABC's website: sevilla.abc.es/pasionensevilla. Two weeks later, everyone is at it again, for the **Feria de Abril**. This week-long non-religious festival, originally a horse-trading gathering, takes place at the fairgrounds (*Recinto Ferial*) to the west of the river. Shuttle buses leave regularly from Plaza de San Sebastián, but it's usually quicker to walk. Almost everyone dresses in flamenco or traditional equestrian gear and stylish couples ride into town on horseback or in carriages, a glass of *manzanilla* in hand. There are also daily bullfights at the Maestranza. Some complain that the *feria* is an exclusive, unwelcoming event—*sevillanos* themselves jockey for years to get access to one of the *casetas*, the tents where non-stop eating, drinking, and dancing goes on until the small hours. In recent years public *casetas* have opened, but they are so busy that you can stand in line for an eternity for a glass of *rebujito* (*manzanilla* mixed with lemonade) and a plate of prawns. It's best just to go with the flow, wander the sandy avenues, and enjoy the spectacle. For more information, visit www.visitasevilla.es

foundations—you can see Latin inscriptions on some of the blocks at its base. Its brick latticework, different on each of its four sides, creates beautiful shadow effects as the sun crosses the sky. Initially, the minaret was shorter and topped with bronze spheres, which were replaced with Christian symbols in the 14th century. In 1568 the Renaissance balconies, bell chamber, and pinnacle were added. The weather vane on top—the *giraldillo*, which gives the tower its name—takes its height to 104m (341 ft.). Inside, 35 gently climbing ramps lead to the top, constructed so that the *muezzin* could ride up on a horse or donkey; today it is accessible by wheelchair. Entry is through the cathedral; admission is included in the combined ticket, but frankly the Giralda is better appreciated from the outside, from vantage points across Sevilla.

Av. de la Constitución s/n. www.catedraldesevilla.es. ⓒ **95-421-49-71.** Cathedral and tower 8€ adults, 3€ students 25 and under, free for kids 14 and under. July–Aug Mon 9:30am–3:30pm, Tues–Sat 9:30am–4:30pm, Sun 2:30–6:30pm; Sept–June Mon 11am–3:30pm, Tues–Sat 11am–5pm, Sun 2:30–6pm. Bus: T1.

Museo de Bellas Artes de Sevilla ★★ MUSEUM The former convent that houses this extensive collection of Spanish art almost upstages the paintings inside. Built in 1594 for the order of the Merced Calzada de la Asunción, it benefited greatly from Sevilla's golden age of painting and ceramics; its tiled cloisters are enthralling. Inside, the galleries hold the finest collection of Spanish masters outside of the Prado.

Although Madrid got the majority of the great Velázquez paintings, the rest of the artists of the Sevillian school are well represented, including the greatest works by Murillo, notably a gigantic *Immaculate Conception* originally painted for the Convento de San Francisco. A room is devoted to canvases painted for this convent by Pacheco, tutor and father-in-law to Velázquez, and Zurbarán is represented by three large canvases painted for Sevilla's Carthusian monastery (Cartuja), depicting the austere lives of the monks.

Plaza del Museo 9. www.museosdeandalucia.es. ✆ **95-554-29-42.** Admission 1.50€, free to E.U. residents and students. Tues–Sat 9am–9pm; Sun 9am–3pm; closed Mon. Bus: 03.

Museo del Baile Flamenco ★★ MUSEUM   It is said there are no schools to create flamenco performers, just as there are none to create poets. Cristina Hoyos, the founder of this museum, drew instead on her depth of feeling to become one of the most celebrated flamenco dancers of the late 20th century. This darkly lit museum with curtained doorways is relatively short on artifacts and signage, and long on video clips that immerse the viewer in the art of the dance. One of the most engrossing exhibits features short videos that demonstrate the seven styles *(palos)* of flamenco. In an opening video, Hoyos advises you follow your emotions. It's not necessary to understand flamenco, she says, it must be felt. See for yourself at a nightly show (p. 259).

Calle Manuel Rojas Marcos, 3. www.museodelbaileflamenco.com/en. ✆ **95-434-03-11.** Admission 10€ adults, 8€ students and seniors, 6€ children. Daily 10am–7pm.

Museo Palacio de la Condesa de Lebrija ★ HISTORIC HOUSE Officially a museum of architecture and interior decoration, this historic house is also a portrait of the Countess of Lebrija, who owned the 16th-century palace from 1901 until 1914. An avid archaeologist and collector,

SEVILLA'S OTHER great painter

Sevilla's most famous artist is undoubtedly **Diego de Velázquez,** born here in 1599. In his early twenties, he left for Madrid with his portraits of street sellers and was promptly snapped up by Felipe IV as his court artist. He, and most of his paintings, never returned to Sevilla. Today, the Prado (p. 83), in Madrid, is the place to see Velázquez; Sevilla is the place to admire the prolific output of **Bartolomé Esteban Murillo.** Born in 1618, he also went to Madrid as a young man, but returned in 1645 and dedicated most of his life to decorating Sevilla's churches, convents, and monasteries with his huge Baroque paintings of religious subjects. His style, seen by some as overly sentimental, fell out of favor for many years, but in 2018 the Sevilla authorities clasped Murillo to their bosom with a year-long celebration to mark the 400th anniversary of his birth. Many canvases have been cleaned and restored to their original glory. You can see numerous examples of Murillo's florid style in the Museo de Bellas Artes, the Cathedral, and the church of Santa María la Blanca, among others.

CARMEN & don juan

Two of Sevilla's most famous inhabitants are fictional characters, but they are linked to real people and places. The picaresque novella **Carmen,** the basis of Bizet's famous opera, was written by French novelist Prosper Mérimée in 1845 after a visit to Sevilla; he claimed it was a true story. Carmen was a beautiful, sensuous, gypsy woman (*gitana*) who worked in Sevilla's cigar factory; she was killed by her soldier lover Don José after betraying him for another. The cigar factory, the **Real Fabrica de Tabacos** on Calle San Fernando, is now Sevilla's University; you can walk through its courtyard to evoke the drama. In the 19th century all the workers here were women, whose fingers were considered nimbler for rolling cigars. At the peak of production, the factory employed some 6,000 workers, and conditions were anything but the beauty and romance of Mérimée's imagination. It continued to produce cigars, cigarettes, and snuff until 1965.

Don Juan was originally the creation of the dramatist Tirso de Molina, whose parable has inspired many versions, including Mozart's opera *Don Giovanni*. Many claim that the model for Don Juan was local nobleman **Miguel de Mañara** (you can visit his birthplace on Calle Levíes, 27; www.andalucia.org; ✆ **95-503-69-00;** Tues and Thurs 11am; free admission, booking required). In fact, the play was published when de Mañara was still a baby. What is more likely is that the story of a notorious womanizer and libertine provided the model for de Mañara's lifestyle: He is said to have watched a performance of the play as a teenager and left the theater saying: "I will be Don Juan." Whatever his sins, he eventually repented, using his great wealth to build the **Hospital de Caridad** (Hospital of Charity) and its lavish church. On the threshold is an inscription by de Mañara, saying he isn't fit to be buried in the church. His grateful beneficiaries disagreed, and "Don Juan" lies in the crypt. Calle Temprado, 3. www.santa-caridad.es. ✆ 95-422-32-32. Daily 10am–7:30pm (closed for Mass Sun 12:30–2pm). Admission 8€ with audioguide; 5€ seniors, 2.50€ children under 18. Free to all Mon 3:30–7:30pm.

she installed several ancient mosaics (including Roman treasures lifted from Itálica; see p. 263) and filled the house with a surprisingly harmonious collection of Roman, Greek, and Persian statues, fabulous tiles salvaged from a convent, and Louis XVI furniture. You can roam around the ground floor at will and take a guided tour of the living quarters upstairs, including an impressive library.
Calle Cuna, 8. www.palaciodelebrija.com. ✆ **95-422-78-02.** Admission 6€ ground floor, 10€ both floors. July–Aug Mon–Fri 10am–3pm, Sat 10am–2pm, closed Sun; Sept–June Mon–Fri 10:30am–7:30pm; Sat 10am–2pm and 4–6pm, Sun 10am–2pm.

Parque María Luisa ★ PARK   Once owned by Isabel II's sister, these green, open spaces to the south of the city were originally the gardens of the **Palacio de San Telmo.** The 17th-century palace, with a foaming Churrigueresque facade, was built as a school for navigators. When the Infanta María Luisa died in 1897, she left the gardens to the city, and in 1929 Sevilla hosted the **Exposición Iberoamericana** here. The world's fair was intended to improve relations with the United States and Latin America following the loss of empire, to modernize a decaying city, and to reinvent Spanish architecture. It was largely successful, despite terrible timing, opening 6 months before the Wall Street crash. Pavilions showcasing Spain, Portugal, and a dozen participating countries were erected in and around the park, and many still stand, serving as foreign consulates, museums, and university buildings. The park is a remarkably open and tranquil place, given its proximity to the city center, and attracts both *sevillanos* and visitors to its boating ponds and shady, flower-bordered paths. If you're going to succumb anywhere in Spain to the temptation to take a horse and carriage tour, this is the place to do it; expect to pay 45€ for an hour-long tour of the gardens and the city.

Plaza de América ★ PLAZA   This oblong plaza at the south of the park houses some of the grandest pavilions left over from the 1929 Expo. Two have been converted into museums that are worth a look. The **Museo Arqueológico Provincial** ★ (www.museosdeandalucia.es; ℂ **95-512-06-32**) is perhaps the most comprehensive archaeology museum in Andalucía, with artifacts from prehistoric times through the Roman and Visigothic to the end of the Moorish period. The highlight is the **Carambolo Treasure,** discovered in 1958 by workmen in a Sevilla suburb: a dazzling hoard of gold jewelry from the 9th to 6th centuries B.C. Its exquisite pendants, bracelets, and plaques offer a tantalizing glimpse of the semi-mythical city of Tartessus, whose exact location has never been established. In the neo-Mudéjar pavilion opposite is Sevilla's folklore museum, the **Museo de Artes y Costumbres Populares** ★ (www.museos deandalucia.es; ℂ **95-471-23-91**). The ground floor displays artifacts of traditional occupations, including a forge, a baker's oven, a wine press, and a tanner's shop. The ceramics collection on this floor is first-rate. Upstairs is devoted to fashion and costumes, including court dress of the 19th century and embroideries from the factories of Sevilla.

Museo Arqueológico: Admission 1.50€ adults, free for students and E.U. residents. Sept–June Tues–Sat 9am–9pm, Sun 9am–3pm; July–Aug Tues–Sun 9am–3pm. **Museo de Artes y Costumbres Populares:** Admission 1.50€ adults, free for students and E.U. residents. Sept–June Tues–Sat 9am–8pm, Sun 9am–3pm; July–Aug Tues–Sun 9am–3pm.

Plaza de España ★★ PLAZA   The centerpiece of the Exposición Iberoamericana, this huge crescent was designed and its building supervised by the great Sevillian architect Aníbal González, whose statue stands facing it. The style is known as Regionalism, intended to reinvent Sevilla's architecture by paying homage to its past. (You'll see examples of Gonzalez's work all over town, including the tiny **Capilla del Carmen** on Triana bridge.) The grandiose structure here is full of symbolism. The broad arc represents Spain's openness to the New World, its canal the Atlantic Ocean, and its Venetian-style bridges the links to the old kingdoms of Spain. You can rent a pleasure boat to row on the canal's flat waters or wander around its porticos. Set into the vast, curving wall are tiled murals advertising the charms of Spain's 50 provinces, from Álava to Zaragoza.

Real Plaza de Toros ★ LANDMARK   Dating from 1761, the Real Maestranza de Caballería de Sevilla is neither Spain's oldest bullring (that's in Ronda; see p. 307) nor the largest (that's in Madrid; see p. 110), but it is considered the most important. During the bullfight season around the April *feria,* couples dress up in flamenco gear and sombreros, light cigars, and pour chilled *manzanilla* to revel in the *corrida;* tickets change hands for large sums. After the Alcázar and the Cathedral, the Plaza de Toros is Sevilla's most visited attraction. Although you are not allowed to step onto the hallowed *albero* sand of the ring, you can tour the *tendidos* (stands) and survey the gates where the matadors and bulls enter, the gate where the slaughtered bulls are dragged out by three mules, and the gate where matadors exit in triumph if they receive the highest honor from the officials. A museum displays paintings, prints, and sculptures that trace the history of the spectacle from an aristocratic demonstration of bravery to a populist sport in which bullfighters from lowly backgrounds (like Triana, across the river) can achieve the status of nobility. The shop sells posters advertising the bullfight season going back to the 1990s, each year's poster designed by well-known Spanish artists.

Paseo Colón, 12. www.realmaestranza.com. ✆ **95-421-03-15.** Admission 8€ adults, 5€ seniors and students. Apr–Oct daily 9:30am–9pm, Nov–Mar daily 9:30am–7pm (during *feria* 9:30am–3pm). Closed Dec 25. Bus: 03, 40, 41, or C5.

Setas de Sevilla ★★★ LANDMARK   Finally completed in 2011, this controversial wood-and-steel structure—resembling a hobbyist's model on an enormous scale—dominates the Plaza de la Encarnación. Officially known as the **Metropol Parasol,** it was quickly nicknamed Las Setas (The Mushrooms). Many in this city, where new architecture has tended to draw on the past, still haven't come to terms with it. The plaza had previously been the site of a century-old public market; when excavations began to build this new market, important Roman and Moorish ruins were discovered, delaying the process for years. Underground, you can visit those relics in the **Antiquarium** (setasdesevilla.com/antiquarium; ✆ **95-547-15-80**), an excellent archaeological museum. Above, avant garde canopies designed by German architect Jürgen Mayer-Hermann are draped over an upscale market with tapas bars and food stalls. It's hard to imagine its elliptical wooden pieces will still be here in 500 years' time—expensive maintenance is another bone of contention among *sevillanos*—but it is great fun to promenade around its upper decks, which have a bar, a restaurant, and some of Sevilla's best views.

Plaza de la Encarnación, s/n. www.setasdesevilla.com. ✆ **60-663-52-14.** Viewing level 3€; Antiquarium 2.10€. Market Mon–Sat 8am–3pm. Antiquarium Tues–Sat 10am–8pm, Sun 10am–2pm. Viewing level Sun–Thurs 10:30am–11:45pm, Fri–Sat 10:30am–12:45am.

Torre del Oro ★ LANDMARK The Almohad rulers of Sevilla erected this tower and another just like it across the river in 1220 as a defense mechanism—a stout chain linking the two prevented ships from moving in and out of the port without authorization. The system worked until the 1248 siege, when a Castillian admiral broke the chain. The matching tower vanished centuries ago, but the Torre del Oro has survived, serving at various times as a warehouse, prison, and administrative offices. You'll hear different accounts of how it got its name, the Tower of Gold: Some say it's because it was once covered in the yellow tiles you can see on its roof, others say it's because the gold brought back from the Americas was stored here. The most likely explanation for the name is that the tower served as a checkpoint at which a hefty tax was levied—in gold—for entry into the port. These days the tower serves as the **Museo Maritimo,** which recounts the history of Sevilla's port from its Almohad era to its shipping heyday of the 16th and 17th centuries.

Paseo de Cristóbal Colón, s/n. www.visita sevilla.es. ✆ **95-422-24-19.** Admission 3€ adults, 1.50€ seniors and students; free to all Mon. Mon–Fri 9:30am–6:45pm; Sat–Sun 10:30am–6:45pm.

Once a defensive tower, Torre del Oro now houses Sevilla's Museo Maritimo.

Sevilla's Barrios

Barrio de La Macarena ★ NEIGHBORHOOD The district around the **Basilica de La Macarena,** north of the center, was once the poorest slum in Spain. These days it's an appealing blend of gritty working-class tradition and hipster creativity that doesn't yet feel over-gentrified. Its cobbled streets house vintage clothing shops, quirky cafés, and artists' collectives alongside traditional bars and a lot of churches. The district takes its name from the 17th-century statue of the **Virgen de la Macarena,** one of the most venerated during the Holy Week processions. You'll see her tear-dropped face all over town. The five emerald brooches she wears were given to her by the legendary bullfighter Joselito—after he died in the ring in 1920, La Macarena was dressed all in black for the next Semana Santa. You can visit the basilica and museum at Calle Bécquer, 1 (herman daddelamacarena.es; ✆ **95-490-18-00**), daily 9am to 2pm and 5 to 9pm

(6–9:30pm in summer). Admission, with audioguide, is 5€. Sevilla's oldest flea market, **El Mercadillo de Jueves,** takes place on nearby Calle Feria every Thursday from 7am to 3pm. The street also has an excellent food market, with a mix of traditional fruit and vegetable stalls, artisanal cakes and coffee, and great tapas. It's open Monday to Saturday, 8:30am to 8pm. A couple of blocks towards the river lies the 16th-century **Alameda de Hércules,** a huge public promenade. By the late 20th century it had become a notorious center for drugs and prostitution, but it has now been successfully regenerated. Surrounded by bars and restaurants, it's Sevilla's main gay district.

Barrio de Santa Cruz ★★ NEIGHBORHOOD   The narrow, whitewashed streets of the old Jewish quarter are Sevilla's main tourist zone. There are plenty of souvenir shops and jaded restaurants here, but despite the crowds, the district has kept more of its character than the overrun Judería in Córdoba (p. 265). Almost every visitor to Sevilla will spend a few hours wandering its medieval alleyways, with names like **Vida** (Life) and **Muerte** (Death, renamed Calle Susona). You can shade from the sun in twisting streets built for just that purpose; discover secret squares, peer into flower-filled patios, and pause for a drink in its antique bars. After the Reconquest of Sevilla in 1248, Fernando III confined the city's Jewish population to this area; several of its churches, like **Santa María La Blanca** (Calle de los Reyes Católicos, 4), were originally synagogues, converted after the expulsion of the Jews in 1492. To learn more about the area's Jewish history, including the sad story of Susona and the skull which marks her house, visit the **Centro de Interpretación Judería de Sevilla,** Calle Ximénez de Enciso, 22 (www.juderiadesevilla.es; ✆ **63-571-97-96**). It's open daily 11am to 7pm and costs 6.50€. Afterwards, pause for a glass of *manzanilla* down the street at the charming bars of **Casa Plácido** or **Las Teresas.**

Barrio de Triana ★★ NEIGHBORHOOD   Just across the Guadalquivir from the city center, Triana is fiercely independent. You'll see ceramic plaques on houses saying "nació en Triana" (born in Triana) and souvenir shops which never mention the name Sevilla. This working-class neighborhood is the traditional quarter of fishermen and Gypsies *(gitanos)* and the birthplace of many famous bullfighters. It is also the neighborhood of the *alfarerías,* makers of the traditional decorative tiles *(azulejos)* and pots for which Sevilla is famous. Ceramics have been made here for millennia—legend says that Triana's patrons, the 3rd-century martyrs Santa Justa and Santa Rufina, were potters. Many of the large ceramics factories whose kilns once polluted the Triana air have now closed, but there are still several workshops and salesrooms concentrated around Calle San Jorge, and the excellent museum **Centro Cerámica Triana,** at Calle Callao, 16 (www.visitasevilla.es; ✆ **95-434-15-82**), is well worth a visit. It's open Tuesday to Saturday 11am to 5:30pm, Sunday 10am to 2:30pm, and costs 2.10€. The **Iglesia de Santa Ana,** on Calle Vázquez, is Sevilla's oldest church, dating from 1280. It is nicknamed the cathedral of Triana, and a ceramic plaque gives a clue to the origin of the neighborhood's name: It depicts the Virgin Mary's mother, Santa Ana, with the Virgin and Christ: the trinity of Ana. The riverfront along Calle Betis is filled with *tabernas* and *marisquerías* (shellfish restaurants) that set up outdoor tables during the warm weather; it's a good place for early evening tapas and impromptu late-night flamenco. At the end of Puente Isabel II (always called the Puente de Triana here), the historic market, the **Mercado de Triana,** was redeveloped as a gourmet market in 2013 and has become a popular destination, with a number of excellent tapas bars that carry on long after the food stalls have closed. Next to the market, the remains of the large Moorish fortress, **Castillo de San Jorge,** has archaeological displays showing its Almohad origins and a serious exhibition about the Spanish Inquisition, which was based here from 1481 to 1785. It's open Tuesday to Saturday 11am to 5:30pm, Sunday 10am to 2:30pm; admission is free.

Especially for Kids

Unlike some of Spain's historic cities, Sevilla has plenty of things to keep children interested and entertained, with free admission to many key sites. The maze in the *Game of Thrones* gardens at the **Alcázar** (p. 237), the swooping walkways of **Las Setas** (p. 246), and the A to Z murals of **Plaza de España** (p. 245) are all obvious destinations. If they need to run off some energy, try the 35 ramps of the **Giralda** (p. 240), but note that children must be accompanied to the top.

Pabellón de la Navegación ★ MUSEUM   North of Triana, Isla de Cartuja, the often-overlooked site of Expo '92, has several features that appeal to children. Interactive displays (in Spanish and English) at this pavilion tell the story of the great Spanish explorers, along with detailed models of historic ships. There are also child-centered temporary exhibitions and the 60m-high (196 ft.) **Torre Schindler,** which has an observation tower with terrific views of the city.

Camino de los Descubrimientos. www.pabellondelanavegacion.com. ✆ **95-404-31-11.** Nov–Apr Tues–Sat 10am–7:30pm, Sun 10am–3pm; May–June and Sept–Oct Tues–Sat 11am–8:30pm, Sun 11am–3pm; July–Aug Tues–Sun 10am–3pm.

Rotonda Isla Mágica ★ AMUSEMENT PARK   Also on the site of Expo '92, this amusement park offers fairground rides, entertainment, and a waterpark. Various discounts are available, including much cheaper tickets on Friday afternoons.

Rotonda Isla Mágica. www.islamagica.es. ✆ **90-216-17-16.** Admission 32€ adults, 26€ children. Jul–Aug daily 11am–11pm (until midnight Sat), more limited hours rest of year; check website.

Where to Stay in Sevilla

Sevilla has plenty of good value accommodation across the range, but during Semana Santa and the Feria de Abril rates skyrocket. The second figure quoted in the listings below is an indication of likely high season prices, but they can go even higher. If you're planning to be in Sevilla at these times, book far in advance and arrive with an ironclad reservation and an agreed price before checking in.

EXPENSIVE

Hotel Alfonso XIII ★★★ A landmark in its own right, this neo-Mudéjar fantasy was built for the 1929 Exposición Iberoamericana. It is the work of architect José Espiau, who won a competition to design what was intended to be Europe's most luxurious hotel. It took 12 years to build. For generations it has been the most exclusive address in Sevilla, attracting international royalty and movie stars; after a complete refit in 2012, its inlaid arches, marble floors, and ceramic friezes again shimmer like a mythical Andalus palace. The guest rooms are extraordinarily sumptuous, with buttery leather upholstery, Nasrid-style plasterwork and coffered ceilings. Staying here is an expensive luxury, but even if you're

The elegant courtyard of the Hotel Alfonso XIII, built in 1929.

not a guest, you can wander through its lobby and courtyards, peruse its historical exhibits, and order an exquisitely served coffee or cocktail.

Calle San Fernando, 2. www.hotel-alfonsoxiii-seville.com ℭ **800/535-4028** in U.S. and Canada, or 95-491-70-00. 147 units. 275€–675€ double. Parking 22€. **Amenities:** Restaurants; bars; concierge; room service; fitness center; outdoor pool; terrace; tennis court; free Wi-Fi.

MODERATE

Las Casas de la Judería ★★★   One of the most characterful places you are ever likely to stay, this hotel is comprised of 27 traditional houses in the old Jewish quarter, linked by a labyrinth of passages, flower-filled patios, and underground tunnels. Lodging here feels like stepping into your own private version of the past. The hotel has 134 historic rooms in all manner of shapes and sizes, decorated in traditional style with rough-hewn painted beams, antique furniture, and wood floors. In places it feels a little rickety. The bathrooms make more of a concession to modernity, with marble surfaces and solid fittings. Above it all, linking several buildings, a spacious rooftop terrace and pool offer fabulous views and a bar in summer. The hotel is located on the eastern edge of the old town, close to the church of Santa Maria la Blanca, a former synagogue. It's a 10-minute stroll to the cathedral.

Calle Santa María la Blanca, 5. www.lascasasdelajuderiasevilla.com. ℭ **95-441-51-50.** 134 units. 100€–250€ double. Parking 24€. **Amenities:** Bar; terrace; outdoor pool; spa; free Wi-Fi.

Hotel Amadeus La Musica ★   In addition to flamenco, Sevilla is a great place for traditional and classical music—you'll see wandering bands of black-cloaked minstrels *(las tunas)* playing mandolins and hear high-quality classical buskers. Set on a narrow alleyway in the heart of the Barrio Santa Cruz, this family-run hotel embraces those traditions. Inside it is surprisingly spacious, occupying two restored houses. The rooms are simply but elegantly decorated, with white walls, classical-era furniture, and wood or antique-tiled floors. There is a good-sized roof terrace with a plunge pool where you can have your breakfast and admire the nearby Giralda. The Moorish-tiled patio contains a variety of musical instruments which you are invited to play (in a sound-proofed room) and the hotel also hosts regular concerts of chamber music.

Calle Farnesio, 6. www.hotelamadeussevilla.com. ℭ **95-450-14-43.** 13 units. 90€–250€ double. **Amenities:** Bar; terrace; pool; music; free Wi-Fi.

Hotel Casa 1800 ★★   The red carpet that covers the pavement outside this charming hotel a few steps from the cathedral signals the ambience within. Painstaking renovation has given this 19th-century mansion, built for the mayor of Sevilla, an air of solid refinement. The pale-toned rooms have hardwood parquet floors and original exposed brick and beams; the furniture is stately yet understated. Guest rooms are arranged around a central patio with a marble floor and a huge glass chandelier, where breakfast and complimentary afternoon tea are served. A decked rooftop terrace offers a small pool and close-up views of the Alcázar and cathedral. There's no restaurant, but plenty of eating options, including Bodega Santa Cruz (p. 256), lie just beyond that red carpet.

Calle Rodrigo Caro, 6. www.hotelcasa1800.com. ✆ **95-456-18-00.** 33 units. 130€–230€ double. **Amenities:** Bar; concierge; terrace; pool; free Wi-Fi.

Petit Palace Puerta de Triana ★★ Completely renovated in 2018, the Puerta de Triana has been beautifully decorated with simple blocks of contemporary color and the occasional floral flourish. Its public areas are modern, spacious, and light-filled; its guestrooms are on the small side, but they're elegant and uncluttered. Beds are large and comfortable, and the bathrooms have high-quality fittings and well-stocked toiletries. The buffet breakfast is particularly good, with plenty of fresh fruit and vegetarian options, and guests have access to free iPads, mobile Wi-Fi and bikes. This stylish hotel, set on the broad avenue leading to Isabel II bridge, is well located for Triana, the riverside bars, and the bullring, and it's only a 10-minute walk from the cathedral.

Calle Reyes Católicos, 5. www.petitpalacepuertadetriana.com. ✆ **95-421-62-59.** 19 units. 70€–170€ double. **Amenities:** Bar; terrace; jacuzzi; bikes; free Wi-Fi.

Posada de Lucero ★ A refurbished 16th-century hostelry, the "Morning Star Inn" is a lovely blend of historic and modern. This nationally listed building has been in constant use as an inn for more than 400 years; all kinds of rogues and rascals have stayed here. These days, following a top-to-bottom refit, it's a classy and comfortable lodging that marries Roman columns and exposed brickwork with sleek contemporary design. A couple of minutes' walk from Las Setas, and close to some excellent restaurants and tapas bars, the Posada is quiet, clean, and much appreciated for its helpful and friendly service.

Calle Almirante Apodaca, 7. www.hotelposadadellucero.es. ✆ **95-450-24-80.** 42 units. 80€–160€ double. **Amenities:** Bar; concierge; terrace; outdoor pool; free Wi-Fi.

El Rey Moro Hotel ★ Created in 2009 from a handsome 16th-century manor house, the family-run El Rey Moro spans the centuries with colorful contemporary rooms inspired by historic motifs. Walls are painted in vivid colors, and the furnishings are quirky, one-of-a-kind pieces. The rooms are arranged on two levels around a central courtyard with beautiful wooden galleries and an old Moorish fountain; many retain the exposed beams of the original house. There is a small rooftop terrace and Jacuzzi, and some rooms have spa baths. Everything is spotless. This corner of Barrio Santa Cruz is a 5-minute walk from the cathedral, and guests have free use of house bicycles. Note, however, that the hotel doesn't accommodate children.

Calle Lope de Rueda, 14. www.elreymoro.com. ✆ **95-456-34-68.** 19 units. 80€–180€ double. **Amenities:** Bar; terrace; jacuzzi; free Wi-Fi.

INEXPENSIVE

Alfarería 59 ★★   Possibly the friendliest guesthouse in Sevilla, this bed-and-breakfast in the heart of Triana's pottery district offers a lovely experience. Hosts Rosa and Carlos have converted an old house into a spacious open-plan lodging where you are welcomed like one of the family. The rooms are modern, well-appointed, and functional, with electric shutters, air conditioning, and a spa bath with bathrobes. Don't miss breakfast, served at a long shared kitchen table, laden with sticky Arab pastries, whiskey-cured ham, and regional cheeses. If you like anonymous hotels, this is probably not for you—but if, like Rosa and Carlos, you love to meet people, chat, and even hug, this is a wonderful introduction to Triana.

Calle Alfarería, 59. casaalfareria59.com. ✆ **95-434-13-17.** 5 units. 50€–160€. **Amenities:** Kitchen; laundry; free Wi-Fi.

La Casa del Maestro ★   Named after the famous flamenco guitarist Niño Ricardo (1904–72), who lived here, this charming little hotel near Plaza de Encarnación is decorated in bold, intense colors. The building has the classic format of three floors around a central courtyard, plus a small rooftop terrace with views of the Giralda. A large street-level lounge provides a place to get coffee and hang out. Rooms are snug but attractively decorated; each is themed around one of Niño Ricardo's compositions.

Calle Niño Ricardo, 5. www.lacasadelmaestro.com. ✆ **95-450-00-06.** 11 units. 60€–180€ double. **Amenities:** Free Wi-Fi.

Hotel Itaca Sevilla ★   Set in a former mansion on a narrow street just off the Plaza de la Encarnación, this handsome hotel delivers a lot of style for the price. The guestrooms surround a pretty courtyard painted in yellow and red, just like the bullring; all have exterior views through soundproofed windows. Simple, dark wood furniture, marble flooring, and crisp white linens give the rooms a clean, contemporary air. They are small, but well designed to make maximum use of the space, and there's also a compact rooftop pool and terrace.

Calle Santillana, 5. www.itacasevilla. ✆ **95-422-81-56.** 23 units. 55€–250€ double. **Amenities:** Free Wi-Fi.

Viajero en Sevilla ★   This cheap (except in Apr) and cheerful bed-and-breakfast sits right in the center of town, ideally placed for everything. The friendly host will give you a map, and mark lots of suggestions of good places to go. Rooms are small, but clean and comfortable, with free Wi-Fi and very hot water in the showers. A cooked breakfast in the small reception area is included in the rate, which is a bargain. The only drawback is the noise: Double-glazed windows reduce the hubbub of late-night revelers on the street outside, but the sounds of the building's old plumbing, and early leavers dropping their keys in the letter box, reverberate through the building. Bring earplugs.

Calle Fernán Caballero, 4. ✆ **63-723-38-73.** 6 units. 25€–200€. **Amenities:** Bike rental; free Wi-Fi.

Where to Eat in Sevilla

The North African influence on Sevilla's cuisine is obvious from the abundant use of almonds, saffron, and lemons, and in the honey-sweetened pastries and desserts. Gazpacho was made here with ground almonds and garlic long before tomatoes arrived from the New World, and unleavened bread is still baked in ancient ovens. Fish and seafood from the mouth of the Guadalquivir river feature on most menus, and look out for pork-based oddities like *solomillo al whisky* and *montadito de pringá*. There are thousands of places to eat in Sevilla, many very good, some cynical and disappointing. Be sure to venture beyond the tourist traps that line Calle Mateos Gago near the cathedral. These recommendations lean towards tapas, because that's what most *sevillanos* do.

EXPENSIVE

Abades Triana ★★ ANDALUCÍAN/INTERNATIONAL   The strip of restaurants overlooking the river from the Triana side, opposite the Torre del Oro, undoubtedly has the finest dining views in town. But be careful, it can be an expensive and disappointing experience. Abades is easily the most stylish and expensive of the bunch and is often booked solid for weddings and business events. If you avoid summer Saturday evenings, however, its outdoor terrace with a lightbox floor is a memorable place for a special dinner. The style is contemporary, with smallish, artful plates of roast fish and meat. The à la carte menu, including romantic treats like caviar paired with champagne, can get very expensive, but a range of set menus is available, starting at 38€—not unreasonable given the setting.

Calle Betis, 69. abadestriana.com/en. ✆ **95-428-64-59.** Entrees 22€–60€, fixed-price menus 38€–180€. Daily 1:30–4pm and 8pm–midnight. Bus C3, 5, 40, or 41.

MODERATE

La Azotea ★★★ FUSION   Now with four locations in Sevilla, La Azotea serves great-value modern tapas. The setting is contemporary and informal with stool seating, the young serving staff is attentive and fun, and the short menu and daily specials are superb. Beautifully presented dishes are strongly rooted in Andalucían tapas tradition but include all sorts of creative twists and nods to other cuisines. The traditional *ajo blanco* cold almond soup is served with mango, dried tuna, and basil oil; the combination of zucchini carpaccio, anchovies, and shaved goat's cheese is wonderful. Tapas and half or full *raciones* are available. This branch, on touristy Calle Mateos Gago, bucks the culinary trend on that street.

Calle Mateos Gago, 8. laazoteasevilla.com/en. ℰ **95-421-58-78.** Tapas 4€–7€; entrees 12€–19€. Daily 9am–midnight.

Barbiana ★★ ANDALUCÍAN/SEAFOOD   If you've tasted Barbiana *manzanilla* sherry from Sanlúcar de Barrameda, you know what kind of food to expect at this related restaurant next to Plaza Nueva. Bone-dry, fresh and tangy, it's a perfect complement to fish from the Huelva coast and crustaceans from Sanlúcar, and that's exactly what Barbiana serves. There's a glorious selection of traditionally served seafood, from heavy stews and rice dishes to deep fried *puntillitas* (baby squid) and crunchy *tortillitas de camarones,* a fritter of tiny whole shrimp. If there's room after that, don't miss the raisin ice cream with sweet Pedro Ximénez sherry.

Calle Albareda, 11. www.restaurantebarbiana.com. ℰ **95-422-44-02.** Entrees 9€–27€. Mon–Sat noon–5pm and 8pm–midnight.

Cinco Jotas ★★ ANDALUCÍAN   You can get good *jamón ibérico* in almost every bar and restaurant in Sevilla—and it will be expensive wherever you go—but it doesn't come much better than this. Spain's finest ham comes from the village of Jabugo, 100km (62 miles) north of Sevilla, where free-range *pata negra* pigs feed on the acorns of the *dehesa* meadows. The five Js of the title represent the best of the best. The modern, informal bar and sit-down restaurant inside get very busy—particularly if there's a bullfight at the Maestranza nearby—so reservations are a good idea. The expertly carved and intensely flavored ham, married with wines and sherries from the Osborne group who own the brand, is one of Andalucía's great pleasures. The *parrillada de carnes,* a selection of grilled *ibérico* pork cuts, is pretty irresistible too.

Calle Castelar, 1. cincojotas.es/restaurante-5-jotas. ℰ **95-421-07-63.** Entrees 14€–23€; *jamón* half *ración* 17€, *ración* 29€. Reservations recommended. Mon–Thurs 8am–midnight; Fri–Sun noon–1am.

ConTenedor ★ FUSION   Hip and adventurous, this slow-food restaurant in the Macarena district serves carefully prepared Andalucían and fusion dishes. The philosophy here goes against the traditional standing-at-the-bar tapas approach—the menu, which changes regularly, is chalked up on a blackboard and fresh ingredients from the market are in full view. The English-speaking servers take pride in explaining the cooking. The seafood and duck rice dishes are particularly impressive, and there's an interesting, well-priced beer and wine list. The restaurant also serves as a cultural space, with regular flamenco and jazz performances.

Calle San Luis, 50. restaurantecontenedor.com. ℰ **95-491-63-33.** Entrees 13€–21€. Reservations advised. Mon–Sat 1:30–4pm and 8–11:30pm; Fri–Sat 1:30–4:30pm and 8:30–midnight, Sun 1:30–4:30pm and 8:30–11:30pm. Bus 3 or C4.

Taberna del Alabardero ★★ ANDALUCÍAN   The upstairs dining rooms of this elegant town house near the Plaza de Toros have earned a reputation as one of the finest restaurants in Sevilla. But it's probably more fun to eat off the bistro menu in the tile-encrusted dining room downstairs: Its dishes are less precious, and everything is prepared and served by students of the hotel and hospitality school, which is headquartered here. The regularly changing set menu includes hearty soups, fish, and meat courses; it's an excellent value at 14.50€ on weekdays. The restored mansion also serves as an inn, with spacious and elegant guest rooms.

Calle Zaragoza, 20. www.tabernadelalabardero.es. ✆ **95-450-27-21.** Entrees 19€– 32€; set menu 14.50€ weekdays, 18€ weekends. Daily 1:30–4:30pm and 8:30pm– midnight. Closed Aug.

INEXPENSIVE

Bodega Santa Cruz ★ ANDALUCÍAN   Although the signs say Bodega Santa Cruz, no one ever calls it that: This popular bar, close to the tourist center but always full of locals, is known as **Las Columnas** because of the stone pillars out front. Seafood, and a small stewed pork sandwich called a *pringá montadito,* are the house specialties. Fight your way to the bar, order, say, a plate of *calamares* (battered squid), *gambas* (prawns), or *ensalada rusa* (seafood potato salad), with a cold *caña* of beer. And a *pringá* for good measure. The bartender will tot up your account in chalk on the counter. Then take it outside, stand beneath the columns as the world goes by, and enjoy. It is also a good spot for coffee and *tostada* at breakfast time.

Calle Rodrigo Caro, 1. www.facebook.com/BodegaSantaCruzSevilla. ✆ **95-421- 8618.** Tapas 2.20€–3€; entrees 11€–12.50€. Daily 8am–midnight or later.

Bodeguita Casablanca ★★ ANDALUCÍAN   The pavement outside this corner bar near the Puerta de Jerez starts to fill up as soon as it opens for the evening at 8pm. Run by Tomás and Antonio Casablanca, this bull-fight-themed restaurant is justly acclaimed for its deft riffs on traditional dishes. The Casablancas convert the ubiquitous *tortilla española* into their trademark *tortilla al whisky,* cooked carefully to preserve the alcohol and topped with cloves of roasted garlic. Elsewhere on the lengthy menu, sea-food comes to the fore: garlic clams, salt cod croquettes, cuttlefish balls in squid ink sauce. Most diners graze on tapas outside while expert servers do the rounds, but inside you can sit down and order full plates, including a huge roast leg of lamb.

Calle Adolfo Rodríguez Jurado, 12. www.bodeguitacasablanca.com. ✆ **95-422-41- 14.** Tapas 2.50€; entrees 12€–20€. Mon–Fri 7am–5pm and 8pm–midnight, Sat 12:30– 5:30pm. Closed Sun and Aug. Bus: T1.

Los Coloniales ★★ ANDALUCÍAN   One of the most enjoyable places for evening tapas, this traditional taberna near Las Setas has an outdoor hatch, a busy bar, and a backroom *comedor.* Servers at the bar engage in non-stop good-natured banter with each other and with the clientele. Every minute or so, generous and delicious-looking plates emerge from the kitchen. Order a drink and watch the performance for a while, then make your choice from a menu that favors meat dishes. The *solomillo al whisky* (pork loin stewed in whiskey) and *chorizo* sausage topped with quail's eggs seem to be the locals' dishes of choice; the tender *solomillo,* served with fried potatoes and glassy pieces of stewed whole garlic, is simply superb. There's a larger sister branch near the bullring.

Plaza Cristo de Burgos, 19 and Calle Fernández y González 38. tabernacoloniales.es. ✆ **954-50-11-37.** Tapas 2.10€–4€; entrees 10€–22.50€.

Las Golondrinas ★ ANDALUCÍAN   At lunchtime, Triana's Las Golondrinas is a spectacle of crowded tapas consumption and frantic service that is both impressive and a little daunting. You may or may not get a table upstairs, but you can order food at the bar or even a couple of rows back. There is a menu, but it's best to keep it simple and order what everybody else seems to be having, namely *chipirones* (baby squid) and *champiñones* (stuffed garlic mushrooms). The cheese platter and *montadito de lomo* (pork loin sandwich) are also excellent. Given the task at hand, service can be rather abrupt, but once you've got your order in, the dishes should be sashayed to you in an instant. After an exhausting hour or so the crowds suddenly disappear and all is calm again, until the evening. Confusingly, Las Golondrinas has two establishments just around the corner from each other. If one is too full, go to the other (Golondrinas 2 is at Calle Pagés del Corro, 76).

Calle Antillano Campos, 26. www.barlasgolondrinas.com. ✆ **95-433-16-26.** Tapas 2.40€–3.50€; entrees 12€–18€. Daily noon–4pm and 8pm–midnight. Bus: C3 or 5.

El Rinconcillo ★ ANDALUCÍAN   El Rinconcillo was established in 1670 on the corner of this small street near Plaza de la Encarnación and claims to be the oldest bar in Sevilla. It has no doubt been updated at some point in the last 350 years, but not recently. The lights are dim; hams dangle from ceiling hooks; dusty bottles furnish the bar walls and the stone floor looks as if it has been here since 1670. It is popular with locals and visitors, but this no tourist trap. You can reserve one of the marble-topped tables in the *azulejo*-tiled dining room, or stand at the counter where the bartender chalks up your tab. The food is simple but tasty—try the house *croquetas* and the traditional chickpea and spinach stew *(garbanzos con espinacas).* And while you're in the neighborhood, visit also the friendly **Los Claveles** bar across the street, for good *montadito* sandwiches and lots of religious imagery.

Calle Gerona, 40. www.elrinconcillo.es. ✆ **95-422-31-83.** Tapas 2.50€–3.50€; *raciones* 9.50€–18€; set menus 28€–55€. Daily 1pm–1:30am.

Sevilla Shopping

The pedestrianized streets around Calles Sierpes and Cuna are Sevilla's main shopping zone. There are some tacky souvenir stores around here, but also interesting old emporia selling classic *sevillano* goods. **Sombrería Maquedano,** Calle Sierpes, 40 (facebook.com/sombrerosmaquedano; ✆ **95-456-47-71**), has a beautiful window display of hats, including the wide-brimmed *sombrero cordobés.* **Juan Foronda,** Calle Sierpes, 33 (juanforonda.com; ✆ **95-422-76-61**), sells investment-quality embroidered silk shawls *(mantones)* and veils *(mantillas),* as well as more modestly priced fans *(abanicos).* The staff are always helpful, whether you're spending 500€ or 15€. Near Plaza de la Alfafa, **Sombreros Antonio García,** Calle Alcaicería de la Loza, 25 (www.sombrerosgarcia.com; ✆ **95-422-23-20**), has everything the *caballero* needs: rabbit-fur sombreros and wonderfully stylish *traje corto* riding suits for men, women and children. **Lina,** Calle Lineros, 17 (www.lina1960.com; ✆ **95-421-24-23**), is the place for flamenco dresses, beautifully blending traditional and contemporary designs.

For ceramics, head across the bridge to Triana. The tile-encrusted facades of **Cerámica Santa Ana,** Calle San Jorge, 31 (www.ceramicatriana.com; ✆ **95-433-39-90**), and **Cerámica Ruiz,** Calle San Jorge, 27 (www.ceramicaruiz.es; ✆ **95-518-69-41**), are photogenic, but the items for sale are rather touristy. Wander around the surrounding streets to find more authentic pieces, such as those at **Cerámica Rocio-Triana,** Calle Antillano Campos, 8 (www.facebook.com/ceramica.rociotriana; ✆ **95-434-06-50**). **La Cartuja de Sevilla** (lacartujadesevilla.com), founded by the Englishman Charles Pickman in 1841, still makes china dinner services of the kind owned by many a *sevillano* family. The factory and shop are on the outskirts of Sevilla, but you can buy the dishes, and individual items, at **El Corte Inglés** department store, Plaza del Duque de la Victoria, 8 (elcorteingles.es; ✆ **95-459-70-00**). Back in the Barrio Santa Cruz, **Populart,** Pasaje de Vila, 4 (www.populartsevilla.com; ✆ **95-422-94-44**), has antique ceramic tiles and pottery at uptown prices.

Confitería La Campana, Calle Sierpes, 1–3 (confiterialacampana.com; ✆ **95-422-35-70**), sells traditional pastries in lovely old-fashioned tins. See also the beautifully packaged confectionery at **Despensa del Palacio** on Calle Villegas (ladespensadepalacio.com; ✆ **95-591-45-25**). For top-of-the-range regional hams, cheeses, and wine to take home, head to **Flores Gourmet,** Calle San Pablo, 24 (floresgourmet.es; ✆ **80-757-59-77**).

Sevilla Nightlife & Entertainment

FLAMENCO

Flamenco is in Sevilla's blood. Along with Jerez and Cádiz it is the cradle of the art form, and many of Spain's most famous performers grew up in the Gypsy quarter of Triana. Apart from Madrid, the city has the busiest performance schedule in the country. There are several different formats to choose from.

Two cultural centers offer very pure flamenco in a style intended to be as educational as it is entertaining. The **Museo del Baile Flamenco,** Calle Manuel Rojas Marcos, 13 (www.museodelbaileflamenco.com; ✆ **95-434-03-11**), offers daily dance-oriented performances in its courtyard, at 5pm, 7pm, and 8:45pm. Admission is 22€ adults, 15€ seniors and students, and 12€ children. The **Casa de la Memoria,** Calle Cuna, 6 (www.casade lamemoria.es; ✆ **95-456-06-70**), has two shows a night in a small courtyard, usually featuring a small troupe focusing on early 20th-century styles. Shows are at 7:30pm and 9pm. Admission is 18€ adults, 15€ students, and 10€ ages 6 to 11.

The flamenco nightclub spectacle, or *tablao,* of choreographed flamenco performances can be expensive, and *aficionados* grumble about the quality. Most give you a drink with the admission price and offer dinner for an extra 20€ to 40€. The dinner is rarely worth it, but you may get better seats. **El Patio Sevillano,** Paseo de Cristóbal Colón, 11 (www.elpatio sevillano.com; ✆ **95-421-41-20**), has 90-minute shows twice nightly at 7pm and 9:30pm. Admission is 38€. **El Arenal,** Calle Rodó, 7 (www. tablaoelarenal.com; ✆ **95-421-64-92**), has two nightly shows at 7:30pm and 9:30pm. Admission is 39€. At **Los Gallos,** Plaza de Santa Cruz, 11 (www.tablaolosgallos.com; ✆ **95-421-69-81**), the 90-minute shows begin at 8:30pm and 10:30pm. Admission is 35€ adults, 20€ children 6-10 years. For a flamenco performance on a budget, head to **La Carbonería,** Calle Céspedes, 21 (lacarbonerialevies.blogspot.com; ✆ **95-422-99-45**), a big no-frills place with a student bar feel. Admission is free, charcuterie and cheese on wax paper costs 10€, and the beer comes in English-style pint mugs. A series of short sets starts around 10pm.

Sevilla is famous for its spontaneous flamenco bar scene, where you may or may not encounter someone playing and/or dancing, and you don't have to sit politely on folding chairs. Three of the best are on the Triana riverfront: **El Rejoneo,** Calle Betis, 31B; the dance club **Lo Nuestro** next door at Calle Betis, 31A, on Tuesdays and Thursdays; and **T de Triana,** Calle Betis, 20. They all open between 11pm and midnight and stay open until dawn.

Finally, there is Triana's legendary **Casa Anselma,** Calle Pagés del Coro, 49 (www.facebook.com/CasaAnselma; ✆ **95-421-28-89**). Not, strictly speaking, a flamenco venue, it is an old, square bar with a central performance area where locals and Spanish tourists crowd for an evening of popular song, dance, and audience participation. Queues form around 11pm and eventually Anselma appears to manage the door, picking and choosing guests at will. If you can get in, admission is free, but she makes it very clear you must buy a drink. Eventually Anselma herself gets up to sing some standards, her elderly voice aided by wannabes in the audience.

She'll pause mid-song to make sure the audience are still drinking. It's a good, old-fashioned get-together that goes on late into the night.

BULLFIGHTS

The bullfighting season at the **Real Maestranza** (p. 246) runs from April through October. The most important *corridas* take place during the Feria de Abril, when ticket prices are highest. Most start at 6:30pm, with some later shows at 9pm (famously, the bullfight is one of the few things in Andalucía that always starts on time). While you can buy tickets at the box office *(taquilla)*, it is advisable to book online ahead of your trip—seats are snapped up quickly. Several websites offer tickets; the official site (plazadetorosdelamaestranza.com; ✆ **95-430-13-82**) lets you avoid additional charges and inflated prices. Prices range from 15€ to 300€ for the best seats.

DRINKS & TAPAS

For most *sevillanos* there is little or no distinction between going out to eat and going out for a drink. You simply do both, and the places listed in the inexpensive section of "Where to Eat" (p. 256) are also recommended for a drink. At a certain point as the evening wears on, beer and tapas give

A matador faces down a bull at Sevilla's iconic bullring Real Meastranza.

Encore, Encore

In addition to *Carmen* and *Don Giovanni,* around 150 librettos have been inspired by Sevilla, yet the city didn't get its own opera house until the 1990s. The **Teatro de la Maestranza,** Paseo de Colón, 22 (www.teatromaestranza.com; ✆ **95-422-33-44**), quickly became one of the world's premier operatic venues. Its season focuses on works inspired by the city; flamenco, jazz, and Spanish *zarzuelas* (operettas) are also performed here. Tickets can be purchased daily from 10am to 2pm and 5:30 to 8:30pm at the box office in front of the theater. The opera house may be visited only during performances.

way to *copas,* very often enormous goblets of gin and tonic. To bar-hop like a local, kick off at the standing tables outside the two crowded bars on Plaza de San Salvador, **La Antigua Bodeguita** and **Los Soportales,** and take it from there. **Taberna Álvaro Peregil** is an atmospheric hole in the wall on touristy Calle Mateos Gago for a glass of *vino de naranja* (orange wine) and *chicharrones*—salty, thinly sliced pork belly from Cádiz. From there it is a hop to the locals' favorite, **Las Columnas** (p. 256). **Bar Garlochí,** Calle Boteros, 26, has the lavish decoration of a Baroque chapel, and the terrace at **Hotel Inglaterra** on Plaza Nueva is the height of sophistication for a *gin tonica.* As evening turns to night, head to the **Alameda de Hercules** for its cocktail bars and dance clubs, which don't get going until after 11pm. Most are at least gay-friendly, and those that are overtly gay welcome a straight crowd. **Bar 1987,** Alameda de Hercules, 93, feels exactly like 1987, and the well-named **Bar El Barón Rampante,** Calle Arias Montano, 3, has flamenco performances on Sundays from 6:30pm on.

Side Trip to Carmona ★

An easy trip by bus or car 35km (21 miles) east of Sevilla, Carmona is an ancient and beautiful walled town with plenty of fine buildings and fascinating Roman remains. One of the oldest settlements in Europe, it was fortified in turn by the Carthaginians, Romans, and Moors. Julius Caesar called it the best defended town in Andalucía, and you can still see why. The **Puerta de Sevilla,** one of four defensive gates, is a good place to start. Enter its **alcázar** (fortress) via the **tourist office** at Alcázar de la Puerta de Sevilla (turismo.carmona.org; ✆ **95-419-09-55;** 2€ adults, 1€ students and seniors) and climb to the top to admire the town's whitewashed houses and church towers gleaming in the sun. After that, it's an easy walk around the main sights of the town. There are little arrows embedded in the pavement suggesting a route, but they're rather confusing, and besides, you want to be looking up rather than down. Be sure not to miss the **ayuntamiento** (town hall) with its near-perfect Roman mosaic depicting Medusa, and the **church of Santa María,** which was built atop an old mosque and retains its tranquil orange-tree patio. The nearby **Museo de la Ciudad** (museo ciudad.carmona.org; ℭ **95-423-24-01;** 2.50€ adults, free for seniors and children) has an interesting collection of archaeological finds from the various cultures who settled here, including the mysterious Tartessians from the 4th century B.C. (it also has a good restaurant and tapas bar). The restaurants on **Plaza San Fernando** make a good stop for lunch, with set menus for as little as 10€. The only part of town that's a bit of a walk away is the area named after Jorge Bonsor, the French/English archaeologist who discovered the Roman amphitheater and necropolis here in the 19th century. The well-maintained **necropolis,** Avenida de Jorge Bonsor, 9 (turismo.carmona.org; ℭ **60-014-36-32;** 1.50 €, free to EU citizens),

The Parador de Carmona, built inside a medieval fortress, is worth visiting even if you're not staying overnight.

contains the house-sized family tombs of Romans who lived in and around Carmona between 200 B.C. and 400 A.D. The Elephant tomb is named after the now trunkless statue found there, which may denote a temple to Mithraism, a cult which once rivalled Christianity. If you plan to stay overnight, try the elegant and atmospheric **Casa de Carmona ★★,** Plaza de Lasso, 1 (www.casadecarmona.com; ℭ **95-419-10-00**). And whether or not you plan to stay, it's worth the trek up the hill to the modern **Parador de Carmona ★★,** Alcázar, s/n (www.parador.es; ℭ **95-414-10-10**), built inside the ruins of another fortress, once home to the 14th-century king Pedro "the Cruel." The view from its terrace, down to a huge swimming pool and the parched countryside beyond, is spectacular. From Sevilla, buses to Carmona leave three times a day from the Plaza de Armas and cost 3€; for information, contact ALSA (www.alsa.es; ℭ **90-242-22-42**). By car, take the A-4 toward the airport and stay on the road towards Córdoba; the turning for Carmona is clearly signposted. As it's convenient for the airport, Carmona may make a good stop for the last night of your tour.

Side Trip to Itálica ★

Lovers of Roman history shouldn't miss **Itálica,** the extensive ruins of an ancient city at **Santiponce** on the northwest outskirts of Sevilla. After his victory in the second war against the Carthaginians in 206 B.C., the Roman general Scipio Africanus founded Itálica for his veteran fighters (the name means "Little Italy") to remind them of home. The city quickly grew in importance as an exporter of wheat and olive oil, and two of the most famous Roman emperors, Trajan and Hadrian, were born here. The enthusiastic builder Hadrian commissioned much of its development, including the **amphitheater,** which, with a capacity of 25,000, was among the largest in the Roman Empire. (It featured as a location in an episode of the TV epic *Game of Thrones* in 2017.) For centuries after the fall of the Roman Empire, the people of Sevilla treated Itálica as a ready source of building materials for dams, roads, and grand buildings, scavenging its elegant Roman columns, mosaics, and masonry. Today, it is properly protected as a leading site for ongoing archaeological research. Wandering around the grid of ancient streets, you can look in on the wealthy homes with elaborate mosaic floors depicting gods, birds, and the days of the week. The **Traianeum** was a huge temple built by Hadrian to honor his uncle and adoptive father, Trajan. In the small visitor center, you can see a reconstruction of what it once looked like and understand why Itálica became a go-to place for marble columns. On a separate site in the village of Santiponce is the well-preserved **Roman theater.** There are some good options for lunch nearby—try **La Caseta de Antonio,** Avenida Rocio Vega, 10 (lacasetadeantonio.es; ✆ **95-599-63-06**), for excellent paella and stews.

To visit the ruins, head to the **Conjunto Arqueológico de Itálica,** Avenida Extremadura, 2 (www.museosdeandalucia.es; ✆ **60-014-17-67**). Admission is 1.50€, free to E.U. residents. From April through June, it's open Tuesday to Saturday 9am to 9pm, Sunday 9am to 3pm; July to September, hours are Tuesday to Sunday 9am to 3pm; and from September to March, it's open Tuesday to Saturday 9am to 6pm, Sunday 9am to 3pm. (It's closed on Jan 1 and 6, May 1, and Dec 24 and 25.) By car from Sevilla, head for the northwest periphery and follow signs for the E-803, direction Zafra. Bus numbers M-170A and B leave Sevilla's Plaza de Armas every half hour or so for the 30-minute trip.

CÓRDOBA ★★★

To visit Córdoba is to glimpse what might have been. A millennium ago, Muslims, Christians, and Jews lived and worked together to create western Europe's greatest city—a cosmopolitan center of poetry, art, philosophy, and cutting-edge science and medicine. Until the 11th century, Córdoba was the capital of western Islam, described by one contemporary writer as "the ornament of the world." The Mezquita, the largest medieval mosque in Europe, remains its star attraction, and the narrow streets and whitewashed buildings of Andalucía's most intact Moorish city endure, albeit with a thick coating of 21st-century tourism.

Built on the north bank of the river Guadalquivir, the city was founded by the Romans as Corduba, and became the capital of Baetica, famous for its olive oil and poetry. The Moors quickly made it their capital too, but after the Reconquest in 1236 Córdoba fell into a long decline, becoming at one point a plague-driven backwater. By the 18th century its population had dwindled to just 20,000 inhabitants. A century later, the Romantic travelers, so enamored of Sevilla, Granada, and Ronda, were unimpressed by Córdoba. (The English writer George Borrow called it a "mean, dark, gloomy place.") Today, it remains a smallish city, with around 300,000 people, but the industries of jewelry, olive oil, and especially tourism have brought prosperity and color. The city's strong sense of identity—in its Arab-influenced cuisine and flower-decked patios, its under-appreciated wine and art—make it a rewarding place to spend a few days, all the more so if you can break away from the tourist epicenter and experience something of the real Córdoba. In summer, the city gets extremely hot—registering Spain's highest temperatures—so spring and fall are the best times to visit.

Essentials

ARRIVING   Located in the center of Andalucía, Córdoba is a junction for high-speed rail links between Madrid and Sevilla, Madrid and Málaga, and Málaga and Sevilla, as well as for *media distancia* (MD) trains between Jaén and Sevilla. About 30 **high-speed trains** a day arrive from Madrid, taking around 1 hour 45 minutes, costing 63€ each way. AV City trains take around 2 hours and cost 40€ to 50€. To visit from the Costa del Sol, take one of 19 trains a day from Málaga, all take about an hour and cost 42€ for AVE, 28€ for AVANT. The main train station is north of the old city at Glorieta de las Tres Culturas, off Avenida de América. Bus 3 runs between the station and the historic center; a taxi will cost around 6€. Otherwise, it's a 30-minute walk south, along Avenida de Cervantes and Paseo de la Victoria. For train information, visit www.renfe.com, or call ✆ **91-232-03-20.**

ALSA (www.alsa.es; ✆ **90-242-22-42**) provides **bus** service to Córdoba from several cities, dropping passengers at the station on Glorieta de las Tres Culturas. There are seven buses a day between Sevilla and Córdoba, taking 2 hours and costing 12:30€ one-way. Between Granada and Córdoba eight buses a day make the 3-hour run, costing 15€ for a one-way ticket.

Driving in Córdoba can be a scarring experience. Traffic in the old town is strictly limited—you can be fined unless you ask your hotel to let the police know you're authorized—and the parking signs linked to hotels are merely places where you can stop briefly to drop off bags. It is much

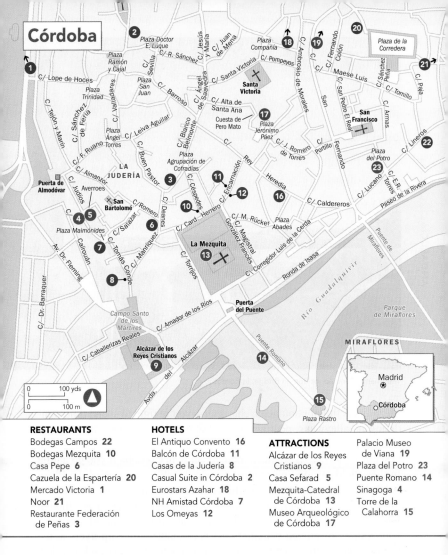

Córdoba

less frustrating to avoid driving in the old town altogether, and find a parking lot on the edge, say, at **Parking Mezquita,** Calle Cairuan, 1 (parkinglamezquita.com), which will cost around 15€.

VISITOR INFORMATION Córdoba's new visitor center is a large brick building on Plaza del Triunfo (www.andalucia.org; ℂ **95-735-51-79**), between the Mezquita and the river. It is open Monday to Friday 9am to 7:30pm, Saturday and Sunday 9:30am to 3pm.

Exploring Córdoba

It's all too easy for the visitor to Córdoba to slip into the **Judería** and scarcely leave. Of course, this warren of narrow streets behind the

The Puente Romano, or Roman Bridge, in Córdoba.

Mezquita is full of photogenic character—you're right to spend time wandering its alleyways, peering into its patios—but it is also depressingly full of tacky gift shops, overpriced restaurants, and flamenco shows. And, yes, tourists. There is so much more to enjoy in Córdoba if you go a little further afield. A good place to start is on the sloping apron of the **Plaza del Triunfo,** in front of the **Puente Romano** (Roman Bridge). From here, there are easy and interesting walks to all points of the compass, though you'll keep gravitating back to the area that surrounds the Mezquita. A wide variety of guided walking tours is available—pick up flyers at the visitor center on the square—but they can get both expensive and crowded. The hop-on, hop-off city bus tour, which also starts from here, is a quick way to get a sense of the wider city. Owing to the narrow streets of the old town, it uses a combination of small and large red buses and a walking tour of areas that are inaccessible by transport. Tickets, valid over 2 days, cost 18.50€.

Alcázar de los Reyes Cristianos ★★ CASTLE   A short walk along the river southwest from the Plaza del Triunfo stands the Fortress of the Christian Kings. Commissioned in 1328 by Alfonso XI, it became the base from which Isabel and Fernando governed as they prepared to re-conquer Granada, the last Moorish stronghold in Spain. While not nearly

Early-Bird Incentives

The best time to explore the Judería is first thing in the morning, before the crowds arrive, and while the tourist shops are still shuttered. Then, you can hear the echo of every footstep on its timeless streets and see the sunrise turn the tower of the cathedral golden.

There's another great incentive to get up early: Between 8:30 and 9:20am each morning (except Sun), entry to the Mezquita is free, and group visits are not allowed. You can appreciate its meditative power in silence, with just a few other souls.

as inspiring as the Mezquita, the Alcázar is interesting because of the important historical events it witnessed. Christopher Columbus came here in 1486 to lobby the monarchs about his plans to find a western sea passage to the East Indies; in the gardens, a group statue commemorates this apparently awkward encounter and the rulers' eventual agreement to underwrite his discovery of America in 1492. Also, the regional branch of the Spanish Inquisition was based here from 1490 until 1821; the circular **Torre de la Inquisición** once housed its grim paperwork. After that the castle served as the city's prison right up until the Franco era. Today it's a tranquil place. Some of its rooms display Roman mosaics unearthed in

A garden at the Alcázar de los Reyes Cristianos.

Córdoba, while the formal 19th-century gardens have long lines of sculpted cypresses, fragrant orange trees, fish ponds, and fountains. Climbing the battlements gives you views across the city and the river, and at night, the fortress hosts a light, sound, and water spectacle called **Noches Mágicas en el Alcázar** ("Magical Nights at the Castle").

Calle Caballerizas Reales. s/n. www.reservasturismodecordoba.org. ✆ **95-742-01-51**. Admission 4.50€ adults, 2.25€ students and seniors. Daily Apr–Sept 9:30am–7pm, Oct–Mar 9:30am–5pm. Noches Mágicas 6.50€ adults, 3.25€ students and seniors; shows in summer Tues–Fri 10pm and 11pm, Sat midnight, rest of year Tues–Fri 9pm. Bus: 2, 6 or 9.

Mezquita-Catedral de Córdoba ★★★ HISTORIC SITE   No visitor to Córdoba should miss its mosque, one of the world's great architectural achievements. It was begun in 784 by the Emir Abd al-Rahman I, and extended several times by succeeding rulers. Its mesmerizing forest of identical arches, striped red and white, seems to go on forever. Until, that is, it is rudely interrupted by the **Roman Catholic cathedral,** plonked in the middle of the mosque in the 16th century, an enduring symbol of Christian hubris. Carlos V, who also committed acts of architectural vandalism at the Alhambra in Granada, gave the go-ahead for the cathedral in 1523, ignoring pleas from the town council. At least he later admitted his mistake, telling the church: "You have built what you or others might have built anywhere, but you have destroyed something that was unique in the world." It is certainly unique, but far from being destroyed. What was once the religious focus of the mosque, the glittering *Mihrab* ★★★, was part of the huge extension carried out in the 10th century by al-Hakam II.

INSIDE THE blooming PATIOS

If you're lucky enough to visit in the first fortnight of May, it is the season for meeting Córdobans inside their homes. They are so proud of the flowers they grow in their patios that many of them open up to visitors for the **Concurso de los Patios de Córdoba,** the Córdoba Patio Festival (www.amigosdelospatioscordobeses.es). Pick up a map of participants from the tourist office. When you enter people's homes, you'll see their ancient patios arranged around a well or fountain with whitewashed walls hung with pots of blazing geraniums, or *gitanillas* ("little gypsies"). You might be offered a glass of *fino*. Admission is free, but it's customary to leave a few coins in a tip tray to help with upkeep. If you miss the festival, there are other ways to get an idea of the patios so central to Córdoban life. Several privately run tours are available; you'll find flyers at the tourist office. **Rutas de Patios en San Basilio** (www.depatios.com; ✆ **95-794-18-81**) is one of the most highly rated, costing 5€. Or visit the **Palacio Museo de Viana ★**, Plaza de Don Gome, 2 (www.palaciodeviana.com; ✆ **95-749-67-41**), which has 12 patios representing various eras and architectural styles. It's open September to June, Tuesday to Saturday 10am to 7pm, Sunday 10am to 3pm; July and August Tuesday to Sunday 9am to 3pm. Tickets cost 5€ for patios only, 8€ including the palace.

The Mezquita's Patio de los Naranjos.

He asked the Byzantine emperor Nicephorus to send him a craftsman capable of equaling the decoration of the great mosque in Damascus. The Christian emperor not only agreed but threw in a load of gold *tesserae* (mosaic pieces) for good measure. The horseshoe-arched prayer niche they decorate served two purposes: to indicate the direction of Mecca and amplify the voice of the imam throughout the mosque. Its wonderful mosaics and inscriptions survived because it was bricked up at the time of the Reconquest and not rediscovered until the 19th century. After contemplating the mosque, linger in the **Patio de los Naranjos** (Courtyard of the Orange Trees), which has beautiful fountains where worshippers once performed their ablutions before prayer.

A range of options to visit the Mezquita is available, from the early morning free entry to expensive tours with official guides (25€), audioguides at an additional 4€, and nighttime tours at 18€. Given the excessive tourism which surrounds it, it still feels refreshingly uncommercial. You might want to visit more than once during your stay.

Calle Cardenal Herrero, 1. mezquita-catedraldecordoba.es. © **95-747-05-12.** Admission 10€ adults, 5€ ages 10–14, under 10 free. Free entry Mon–Sat 8:30–9:20am; paid entry 10am–6pm (7pm in summer), Sun 8:30–11:30am and 3–6pm (7pm in summer). Bus: 3 or 7.

Museo Arqueológico de Córdoba ★★ MUSEUM   The new building for this excellent collection of artifacts opened in 2011 next door to the Renaissance palace that previously held the museum. The site was originally a Roman amphitheater—you can tour intact portions of it in the basement of the new structure. The museum chronicles life in and around Córdoba since the earliest settlers, with an emphasis on everyday tools, household items, and funeral objects. Well set-out displays begin with the Copper and Bronze Age, followed by Phoenician and Greek artifacts, Iberian statuary, and extensive Roman remains, including an exceptional glass funerary urn. Moorish artifacts, of course, are abundant. Among the most interesting are the hoards of coins hidden away during uneasy times as the caliphate staggered to an end in the 11th century. A magnifying glass allows you to examine their inscriptions in detail. Information panels are in Spanish and English.

Plaza Jerónimo Páez, 7. www.museosdeandalucia.es. ⓒ **95-735-55-17.** Admission 1.50€, free for EU nationals. Tues 2:30–8:30pm; Wed–Sat 9am–8:30pm; Sun 9am–2:30pm. Bus: 3 or 7.

Plaza del Potro ★★ PLAZA   This small, elongated square east of the Mezquita was originally a horse market; the fountain at its center is topped with a rampant colt (*potro* in Spanish). Some excellent museums are set around this historic square. The **Posada del Potro** gets a wry mention as a den of vice in Cervantes' *Don Quijote;* when you enter its 15th-century courtyard you are transported back to the age of stables and innkeepers. It now houses the **Centro Flamenco Fosforito** ★★ (centroflamenco fosforito.cordoba.es; ⓒ **957-476-829;** admission free), a museum tracing the roots, styles, and stars of flamenco. The modern audiovisual displays sit a little uneasily with the historic surroundings, but the explanations—in Spanish and English—are excellent. Have a go at trying to keep the rhythm of the various flamenco forms and ask about free flamenco performances. Most of the year it's open Tuesday to Friday 8:30am to 8:15pm, Saturday 8:30am to 4pm, and Sunday 8:30am and 2pm; in summer it's open daily 8:30am to 3pm. Across the square, the **Museo Julio Romero de Torres** ★★ (museojulioromero.cordoba.es; ⓒ **95-747-03-56;** admission 4.50€, same hours as Centro Flamenco Fosforito) is dedicated to Córdoba's beloved painter, who died in 1930. You'll see prints of his symbolist masterpieces all over town; most of the originals are in this beautifully laid-out gallery. Look out in particular for his melodramatic tribute to flamenco, *Cante Jondo* (Deep Song), and *La Chiquita Piconera* (The Little Coal Girl), which portrays a beautiful, yet deeply disenchanted, young woman tending a tray of embers. Symbolism indeed.

Puente Romano ★★ BRIDGE   Córdoba's Roman bridge, stretching across the Guadalquivir river just south of the Mezquita, is a popular place for an afternoon stroll to the sound of flamenco guitar buskers. Built in the 1st century B.C., it has been restored so many times that none of its 16 arches is original. It was used for road traffic right up until this century, when the new **Puente de Miraflores** (known locally as the *puente oxi-dado,* or rusty bridge) relieved it of that duty. Halfway across you'll see the **shrine to San Rafael,** the city's guardian angel, often surrounded by worshipers lighting candles and leaving flowers. San Rafael was credited with ending the plague that decimated the city in the 17th century, and the people of Córdoba haven't forgotten. At the far end of the bridge stands the **Torre de la Calahorra** ★, a sturdy gate built in the 12th century by the Almohad caliphate to defend the bridge against Christian attack. It too has been heavily restored. It houses the **Museo Vivo de al-Andalus** (www.torrecalahorra.com; ✆ **95-729-39-29;** admission 4.50€), a rather cheesy audiovisual presentation which nonetheless gives a good sense of the Muslim, Jewish, and Christian characters behind medieval Córdoba's great achievements.

Sinagoga ★ SYNAGOGUE   This is one of only three remaining pre-Inquisition synagogues in Spain. It was built in 1315, a couple of blocks west of the northern wall of the Mezquita, and is small because of the restrictions placed on Jewish building at the time. The synagogue is noted for its elaborate stuccowork, including Mudéjar patterns on the entrance and Hebrew inscriptions from the Psalms inside. The east wall has a large niche where the Torah Ark and scrolls were placed, and you can still see the balcony where women worshipped. After Spain expelled the Jews in 1492, the synagogue was converted into a hospital, and later a Catholic chapel. Nearby **Casa Sefarad** ★, Calle Judios (www.casadesefarad.com; ✆ **95-742-14-04**), is a small museum chronicling Jewish life in the 11th and 12th centuries, when Córdoba was the de facto capital of Sephardic Jewry. Exhibits highlight Sephardic musical and literary traditions and the traditional craft of making gold thread; it also celebrates the Jewish, Muslim, and Christian women of Córdoba's heyday who were leading poets, philosophers, and scholars.

Calle de los Judíos 20. www.turismodecordoba.org. ✆ **95-720-29-28.** Free admission. Tues–Sun 9am–2:30pm.

Especially for Kids

In addition to the **Alcázar** (p. 266) and the **Museo Vivo de al-Andalus** (see above), both of which children should enjoy, Córdoba has a good **zoo,** just along the river to the southwest on Avenida Linneo, s/n (zoo. cordoba.es; ✆ **95-720-08-07;** adults 5.50€, children 3€; Tues–Sun 9:30am–6pm). The surrounding gardens include the recently remodeled adventure playground **La Ciudad de los Niños,** Avenida Menéndez Pidal (ciudaddelosninos.cordoba.es; ✆ **95-720-00-18;** admission 1€, kids under 5 free; Tues–Sun 11am–6pm).

Where to Stay in Córdoba

At peak times, especially in May, Córdoba has too few hotels to meet demand, and prices spike accordingly. Reserve as far in advance as possible.

EXPENSIVE

Balcón de Córdoba ★★★   Set in a beautifully renovated old house just a few yards from the Mezquita, this boutique hotel nevertheless feels apart from the clamor of the Judería—its narrow street is surprisingly quiet and free of tourist shops and bars. Once inside you are immediately in a cool patio with orange trees and Roman archaeological remains. The smallish guestrooms are tastefully appointed in pale colors; top-quality fittings share the space with some well-chosen antiques. The hotel's restaurant, **Pairi Daeza,** serves well-presented Middle Eastern-influenced cooking, and if you book early you can dine on the rooftop balcony with views across the night-lit mosque and cathedral. Service throughout is impeccable and friendly.

Calle Encarnación, 8. www.balcondecordoba.com. ℰ **95-749-84-78.** 10 units. 160€–425€ double. Parking 25€. **Amenities:** Restaurant; bar; room service; terrace; solarium; live music; free Wi-Fi.

Casas de la Judería ★★   Full of charm and character, this romantic hotel sits on the edge of the Judería, between the Mezquita and the Alcázar. Once you step through its studded front door you'll feel as if you're in another world. Created by combining a number of 17th- and 18th-century city palaces, it features wood-beamed guest rooms in all shapes and sizes. The beds have traditional tooled leather headboards and sumptuous bedding. But the public areas, reached by labyrinthine corridors, are the real joy of the hotel—taste the noble Córdoban way of life as you lounge in its patios and shaded arcades.

Calle Tomás Conde, 10. www.lascasasde lajuderiadecordoba.com ℰ **95-720-20-95.** 64 units. 105€–375€ double. Parking 19€. **Amenities:** Restaurant; bar; room service; pool; terrace; solarium; valet parking; free Wi-Fi.

The charming hotel Casas de la Judería was created by combining several old townhouses.

MODERATE

Eurostars Azahar ★★   This modern hotel in a handsome red-painted building is close to Plaza de las Tendillas, the busy old town square where Córdobans meet for a night out. It's a great base from which to see the city beyond the Judería. Opened in late 2018, it has the advantage that everything has been designed to meet modern needs—right by your bed there's a master light switch and a socket where you can charge your phone. The rooms are clean, bright, and comfortable—the large beds especially so—and there are lots of appealing touches: complimentary water, apples, and sweets in the lobby; dental and shaving kits in the bathrooms in case you forgot to pack yours; a travel book on your bedside table. Rates, as usual at Eurostars hotels, are extremely reasonable at off-peak times.

Calle García Lovera, 1. www.eurostarshotels.com. ⓒ **95-721-12-96.** 45 units. 49€–195€. No parking. **Amenities:** Bar/café; fitness center; sauna; free Wi-Fi.

NH Amistad Córdoba ★★   Set right into the old city walls close to the 14th-century synagogue, the Amistad was created by cleverly combining two 18th-century mansions into a large and gracious hotel, mixing modern design and original features; another building across the Plaza de Maimónides was later added for suites. A historic Mudéjar-style patio lies at the heart of the property, but the spacious rooms are decorated in a clean-lined modern style, with wood paneling and pale colors. A highlight is the geometrically shaped swimming pool.

Plaza de Maimónides, 3. www.nh-hoteles.com. ⓒ **95-742-03-35.** 108 units. 100€–215€ double. Parking 20€. **Amenities:** Restaurant; bar; room service; pool; solarium; free Wi-Fi.

INEXPENSIVE

El Antiguo Convento ★   Old meets new in this renovated former convent a 5-minute walk west of the Mezquita. Arranged around a leafy traditional patio, the white-painted rooms are simply yet quirkily decorated with bright, modern designs, while maintaining their original patterned-tiled floors. There's an upbeat attitude among the staff and a backpacker hostel atmosphere among the guests. Breakfast in the patio is generous at 4.75€, including fruit juice, yogurt, and home-made cakes; free coffee is available all day. Rates are among the lowest you'll find in Córdoba, and you'll save even more if you stay longer.

Calle Rey Heredia, 26. www.antiguoconvento.com. ⓒ **95-747-41-82.** 35€–80€. 14 units. No parking. **Amenities:** Cafeteria; terrace; bike rentals; free Wi-Fi.

Casual Suite in Córdoba ★★   These little apartments on a quiet square north of the Judería are beautifully thought-out and a great value. The decor is bright, modern, and designer-ish, yet everything has been geared for stripped-down efficiency; the limited room space is maximized with open clothes rails and tiny kitchenettes. There is no key—an easy-to-remember code gives you access to the front door and your room. Drinks are self-service—leave money in the tray. And there is no reception—the host will text you to arrange to meet. If that all sounds a little impersonal, he's very friendly and will give you tips and flyers for recommended restaurants and activities.

Calle San Felipe, 11. casualsuite.es. ⓒ **62-607-63-63.** 5 units. 45€–120€. **Amenities:** Kitchen; free Wi-Fi.

Los Omeyas ★ This budget hotel sits on a quiet street just yards from the Mezquita. At these prices, in this location, you might expect a fleapit: It's not. The modest front door doesn't prepare you for the sight of the airy arcaded patio at the heart of the building. The guest rooms are a little dated, but they are clean and functional. If you can get one, those on the top floor have city views. A simple toast and coffee breakfast in the patio costs 4.50€.

Calle Encarnación, 17, www.hotel-losomeyas.com. ✆ **95-749-22-67.** 39 units. 35€–90€ double. Parking 15€. **Amenities:** Bar; terrace; free Wi-Fi.

Where to Eat in Córdoba

Córdoba is much celebrated for its cuisine, which draws extensively on Arabic cooking, liberally mixing sweet and savory flavors—you'll taste spices such as cumin, turmeric, and cinnamon. Córdobans are proud of a number of classic dishes that are served in almost every restaurant and tavern; you shouldn't leave without trying at least some of them. They include the cold, tomatoey *salmorejo* soup topped with ham and egg, *berenjenas con miel* (eggplant with honey), gooey *rabo de toro* (oxtail), and *flamenquines,* rolled ham and pork loin deep-fried in breadcrumbs. The Judería is full of restaurants good and bad, including some famous names which are not what they were, but to truly eat like a Córdoban, seek out distinctive eateries away from the tourist center.

EXPENSIVE

Noor ★★★ ANDALUCÍAN Paco Morales' lauded restaurant is in a tree-lined suburb that's a 10-minute taxi ride from the Mezquita. It's well worth the journey. Inside, the restaurant is a kind of modernist Moorish fantasy, and so is the dining experience. Three tasting menus with paired wines are available, each a festival of the senses. The Beréber menu is a perfectly choreographed succession of surprising combinations, served on elaborate arabesque tableware. Its nine courses are interpretations of Andalucía's 1,000-year-old culinary heritage: saffron bread with cured ox, cod with orange and olive juice, sheep's milk ice-cream with *ras-al-hanout* spices. Morales—who trained under the legendary Ferran Adrià—is ever present, performing in the open kitchen and visiting tables. One of Spain's finest restaurants, this is a dream date. Reservations are essential, as far in advance as possible.

Calle Pablo Ruiz Picasso, 8. noorrestaurant.es. ✆ **95-710-13-19.** Tasting menus 85€–150€, with wine pairing 40€–80€ more. Reservations essential. Wed–Sat 1:30–3:30pm and 8:30–10:30pm. Bus: 1, 3 or 7.

MODERATE

Bodegas Campos ★★ ANDALUCÍAN This prestigious wining-and-dining complex near Plaza del Potro is where Córdobans go for a celebration dinner. Founded in 1908 as an aging cellar for the wines of Montilla-Moriles, its richly dark halls are lined with barrels and vintage festival posters. Several dining rooms are arranged across a number of houses and courtyards: You can sit down for a formal dinner, served by white-aproned waiters alongside well-dressed family groups, or have a more casual meal at the bar. Rich roast meats and fried fish dominate; half portions *(media ración)* of some dishes are available. The *salmorejo* here is legendary and the wines are, of course, superb. Incidentally, Bodegas Campos has the best car park in town, decorated with antique tiled wine advertisements.

Calle Lineros, 32. www.bodegascampos.com. © **95-749-75-00.** Entrees 10€–18€. Sun–Thurs 12:30–4pm and 7:30–11pm, Fri–Sat 12:30–4pm and 7:30–11:30pm.

Casa Pepe ★★ ANDALUCÍAN   The best of the famous names of the Judería, Casa Pepe is a tourist restaurant, but a good one. Established in 1930 and reinvented in the 1990s, it oozes class. It's not cheap, but the food and service are excellent. All the classics are here—*salmorejo*, oxtail, eggplant and honey—as well as such interesting signature dishes as lamb sweetbreads with mushrooms and pine nuts, and slow-cooked *bacalao* (salt cod) with chickpeas. Presentation is stylish. The setting, in a handsome white-washed building, celebrates the restaurant's roots, and includes some good paintings by Córdoban artists. In summer the roof terrace has lovely night views of the cathedral.

Calle Romero, 1. restaurantecasapepedelajuderia.com. © **95-720-07-44.** Tapas 3.50–4€; entrees 11€–20€. Sun–Thurs 12:30–4pm and 7:30–11pm, Fri–Sat 12:30–4pm and 7:30–11:30pm.

A Glassful of Montilla-Moriles

While free *tapas* is less of a tradition in Córdoba than in, say, Granada (p. 297), the drinks measures here are very generous. In bars and taverns you'll see people drinking *fino* from flute glasses filled to the brim. The wine is from the Montilla-Moriles wine region in the south of Córdoba province. While made and categorized in a similar way to the better-known sherries of Jerez, they are not fortified with additional alcohol, and have perhaps an even more subtle flavor. The dark, sweet *Pedro Ximénez* is usually served in a glass two-thirds full. Just don't ask for a glass of sherry.

Cazuela de la Esparteria ★★ ANDALUCÍAN   A marketplace during the day, the grand Plaza de la Corredera is filled with drinkers and diners at night. Its large dimensions and low lighting make it a little uninviting after dark, but luckily this restaurant, just off the square, has an abundance of atmosphere. By 9pm it's crammed with people standing at tables outside, perching in the bar, or bagging a table in the large restaurant inside. Somehow the friendly staff manage to get everyone fed. You can opt for tapas or half or full *raciones* of all the classics, but it's particularly good for fish. Try eggplant with salmon, batter-fried cuttlefish *(chocos)*, or *tomate con ventresca* (tuna belly), accompanied by a brimful glass of Montilla-Moriles *fino*.

Calle Rodríguez Marín, 16. lacazueladelaesparteria.es. © **95-748-89-52.** Tapas 2€; entrees 9€–18€. Mon–Thurs 12:30–4:15pm and 8pm–midnight, Fri–Sat 12:30–4:15pm and 8pm–12:30am, Sun 1–4pm.

INEXPENSIVE

Bodegas Mezquita ★★ ANDALUCÍAN   Originally a deli and wine store, Bodegas Mezquita has expanded its successful formula into a string of bar restaurants around town. Most of the North African-influenced dishes are offered in a choice of sizes, making it easy to order several to share. The lunchtime two-person tapas menu is great value at 14.90€, including the sublime *berejenas califales* (eggplant fritters in a sweet PX wine reduction) and meatballs *(albondigas)* flavored with almond and saffron. An excellent wine list emphasizes the Montilla-Moriles region but includes good bottles from all over Spain.

Calle Céspedes, 12. www.bodegasmezquita.com. ℂ **95-749-00-04.** Tapas 2.65€–4.50€; entrees 6.50€–15€; tapas menu 14.90€; set menu 14.85€. Daily noon–midnight.

Restaurante Federación de Peñas ★★ ANDALUCÍAN   Looking for a good dinner and a flamenco show on a budget? Look no further. You'll spot this Judería institution by the set menus on blackboards outside. They really do offer a 12€ evening dinner that includes a free flamenco show. The 150-seat restaurant is set in a typical Córdoban patio with red-and-white arches that mimic those of the Mezquita; Julio Romero de Torres nudes grace the walls. Drop in during the afternoon to reserve a table—they'll let you take your pick—or book online. The show starts at 8:30pm, so aim to get there shortly after eight. Dinner is simple, but good: say, *gazpacho,* a large mixed salad, *albondigas* (meatballs), followed by apple and cinnamon tart, with a large glass of wine and coffee. The flamenco show is honest, passionate, and sweaty, the audience reassuringly local. It may be the best 12€ you spend in Córdoba.

Calle Conde y Luque, 8. federaciondepeñas.es. ℂ **95-747-54-27.** Set menu 12€–15€, tapas menu 12€. Daily noon–4pm and 7pm–midnight.

Córdoba Shopping

In some streets of the Judería, almost every building contains a shop selling mass-produced souvenirs—Moorish-inspired prints, inlaid boxes,

---

CÓRDOBA'S THRIVING gastromarket

A short distance northwest of the Judería, this 19th-century fair pavilion was transformed in 2013 into Andalucía's first gastronomic market. **Mercado Victoria,** Paseo de la Victoria, s/n (www.mercadovictoria.com; ℂ **95-729-0707**), has around 30 stalls offering small platefuls of Córdoban and Spanish favorites, plus a sprinkling of world cuisine. Stroll around and take your pick of *jamón,* oysters, cold *salmorejo* soup, Argentinian *empanadas,* Japanese *tempura,* and much more, including good vegetarian options. You'll also find colorful outside terraces, a workshop kitchen for classes and demonstrations, and a kids' playground. By early evening, the complex is jammed with people eating and drinking, making it one of the liveliest tapas scenes in town. It's open every day from noon to midnight, on Fridays and Saturdays until 2am. The worn ceramic floor tiles tell the story of its success.

A CALIPH'S pleasure palace

Conjunto Arqueológico Madinat al-Zahra ★★, a kind of Moorish Versailles just outside Córdoba, was built in the 10th century by the first Umayyad caliph of al-Andalus, Abd ar-Rahman III. He's said to have built it out of love for the favorite of his harem, Al-Zahra (the Brilliant), but more probably it was to demonstrate his power to other regional bosses. Ten thousand workers slaved to build this mammoth palace, which once contained 300 baths and 400 houses. It took 25 years to complete but lasted only 65 years after that—the Berbers sacked the palace in 1013, and by 1031 the Umayyad dynasty's brief rule of al-Andalus was over. Through the centuries, the site has been repeatedly plundered for building materials (many stones were used to build the Alcázar; see p. 266). The **Royal House,** where ministers were received, has been meticulously restored, but in other parts you will need to use your imagination. The award-winning modern museum and research center next to the archaeological site uses a variety of innovative methods to bring this huge and complex palace to life.

Madinat al-Zahra is at Carretera Palma de Río, Km 8 (www.museosde andalucia.es; ✆ **95-735-28-74**). Admission is 1.50€ (free to EU residents). From mid-September to March, it's open Tuesday to Saturday 9am to 6:30pm, Sunday 10am to 5pm; from April to May, the hours are Tuesday to Saturday 9am to 8pm, Sunday 10am to 5pm. From June to mid-September, it's open Tuesday to Saturday 10am to 3:30pm, and Sunday 10am to 5pm.

Two to three buses a day leave from Córdoba's Paseo de la Victoria; the roundtrip costs 9€ (ages 5–12 5€). A shuttle bus at the site is included in the cost of the ticket, which can be purchased at the tourist office or online (reservasturismodecordoba.org). If you are driving, take the A-431. It's well sign-posted from the center of town.

glass tea cups. They are pretty terrible, but there are also shops selling good quality foods to take home: vacuum-packed *jamón,* olive oil, and the under-marketed wines of Montilla-Moriles. **Delicias del Califato** (Calle Tomás Conde, 1) has an appealing selection of loose teas and spices. For better quality arts and crafts, try **Zoco** (Calle de Judios, 24), where a range of local artisans show their original jewelry and ceramics; **Meryan** (Calleja de las Flores, 2) for traditional tooled leather known as *Córdobanes;* or the shop at the **Casa de las Cabezas** museum (Calle Cabezas, 18; www.casadelascabezas.com). If you're in Córdoba over a weekend, the Sunday morning flea market **Mercadillo del Arenal** (Calle del Enfierno) offers plenty of colorful junk, but also some good pottery, leatherware, and bric-a-brac. The rather thin bullfighting museum, **Museo Taurino** (Plaza Maimónides, 3) has a little shop outside where the most interesting items are facsimile bullfight posters of local heroes El Cordobés and Manolete (including the bullfight in which Manolete was gored to death in 1947).

Oddly, the **Julio Romero de Torres** museum (Plaza del Potro, 1) doesn't sell prints or postcards of the images in the museum, but you can buy a well-produced guide to his work, including postcards of his best-known paintings, from a machine outside for 3€, or prints from the souvenir shop on the square.

Córdoba Nightlife

There are plenty of places to go for a drink in the Judería, but it's worth seeking out where the locals go. Many gather at the tiny **Bar Correo,** Calle Jesús María, 2 (www.facebook.com/BarCorreoCordoba), just off the Plaza de las Tendillas. Inside, it's little more than a counter, but crowds stand at its outside tables every evening for beer at 1.20€ a glass. **Casa El Pisto,** Plaza de San Miguel, 1 (www.casaelpisto.com), is a grand old bar filled with bullfighting memorabilia (including a charming painting of Manolete in a business suit), where ham carving is an art form and a fat *tortilla espanola* sits on the counter. There's a brisk trade in *fino* wine and huge gin and tonics. Nearby **Taberna Góngora** has a rustic vibe, great tapas, and low prices. Try their famous *boquerones al limon* (marinated anchovies) with a beer.

There are many options for flamenco shows, with or without dinner. **Tablao El Cardenal,** Calle Buen Pastor, 2 (www.tablaocardenal.es; ✆ 69-121-79-22), set in a beautiful patio 5 minutes north of the Mezquita, is one of the best. For music other than flamenco, try **Long Rock,** Calle Teniente Braulio Laportilla, 6 (www.longrock.es/cordoba), **Urban,** c/ Alfonso XIII, 3 (urban-bar.negocio.site), or the **Jazz Café,** Calle Rodríguez Marín, 1 (www.facebook.com/jazzcafecordoba). You can probably tell by the names which one is for you.

GRANADA ★★★

When Boabdil, the last Nasrid ruler of Granada, went into exile in 1492, he took the bones of his ancestors with him. But he left behind their magnificent fortress-palace, the Alhambra, and a legacy of nearly 8 centuries of Islamic culture. Legend has it that as he turned to look back at Granada, he wept, at a mountain pass now known as Suspiro del Moro ("The Moor's Sigh"). The Catholic kings Isabel and Fernando had completed the reconquest of al-Andalus, but in Granada they lost the history. Few come to this beautiful city to see the tombs of Los Reyes Católicos in the Capilla Real (although you should)—they come for the exuberant ornamentation of the Alhambra, the unmistakably Arabic face of the Albaícin, and the haunting *zambras,* the gypsy flamenco songs that echo from the hills of Sacromonte. The Spanish composer Isaac Albéniz, who paid musical homage to the city, wrote: "I want the Arabic Granada, that which is art, which is all that seems to me beauty and emotion."

Essentials

ARRIVING Iberia (www.iberia.com; ✆ **800/772-4642** in the U.S., 90-111-15-00 in Spain) flies to Granada from Madrid five times daily.

Vueling (www.vueling.com; ☏ **80-720-01-00**) has four direct flights a day from Barcelona. Several international airlines, including British Airways, Lufthansa, and Easyjet, fly directly to Granada. **Federico García Lorca Airport** is 17km (10½ miles) west of the center of town on Carretera Málaga; check www.aena.es or call ☏ **91-321-10-00** for information. A bus links the airport with the center of Granada, daily 6am to 11:30pm; the one-way fare is 3€, trip time is 45 minutes. A taxi will cost around 25€.

Granada is well linked by **train** with the most important Spanish cities, especially others in Andalucía. The train station, **Estación de RENFE de Granada,** is at Avenida de Andaluces, s/n (www.renfe.es; ☏ **91-232-03-20**). Four trains daily arrive from Sevilla (trip time: 3–4 hr.; cost: from 30€ one-way); from Madrid, there are five trains daily (trip time: around 4 hr.; cost: from 30€).

Granada is served by more **buses** than trains. The main bus terminal, **Estación de Autobuses de Granada,** Carretera de Jaén s/n, has links to virtually all major towns and cities in Andalucía, and to Madrid. There are 10 buses a day from Sevilla to Granada (trip time: 3 hr.; cost: one-way ticket 23€–31€), 9 from Córdoba (trip time: 3 hr.; cost: 16€ one-way). If you're on the Costa del Sol, around 20 buses a day make the 2-hour trip from Malaga, costing around 14€ for a one-way ticket. For bus information, contact **ALSA** (www.alsa.es; ☏ **90-242-22-42**).

By **car,** Granada is around 4 hours due south of Madrid via the A-4 and A-44. From Sevilla, on the A-92 heading east, the journey takes around 2 hours and 45 minutes; from Córdoba, the trip via the A-45 and A-92 takes around 2 hours

Houses in Granada's old quarter, the Albaicín.

and 15 minutes. Driving and parking in the center of Granada can be tricky, but there is a large car park next to the Alhambra, costing 19€ per day.

GETTING AROUND Granada's small-scale red buses, which race through its narrow streets, will take you pretty much anywhere you need to go. The #30 and #32 buses (fare 1.50€) run continuously from Plaza Isabel la Católica to the ticket office of the Alhambra, while #31 and #34 buses leave Plaza Nueva for the Albaicín and Sacromonte. The standard fare is 1.40€, but it's even lower if you buy a multi-trip travel card **(tarjeta Credi-Bus),** available at tobacconists and newspaper kiosks. Taxis are relatively inexpensive, costing about 7€ to go from Plaza Nueva to the Alhambra.

VISITOR INFORMATION   The **Patronato Provincial de Turismo de Granada,** Calle Cárcel Baja, 3 (www.turgranada.es; ℂ **95-824-71-28**), is open Monday to Friday 9am to 8pm, Saturday 10am to 7pm, Sunday 10am to 3pm. For information on both the city and surrounding area, the tourist information office of **Junta de Andalucía,** Calle de Santa Ana, 4 (www.andalucia.org; ℂ **95-857-52-02**), is open Monday to Friday 9am to 7:30pm, Saturday and Sunday 9:30am to 3pm.

Exploring Granada

One school of thought says that after seeing the Alhambra you can die happy and not bestir yourself to see anything else in Granada. Many visitors get straight onto the tour bus and leave. But Granada is one of Spain's most interesting and vibrant cities, and it would be a pity to overlook it. After visiting the Alhambra, aim to spend at least a full day and evening exploring the city. As you'll see, some visitors have decided to spend a lifetime here.

Despite its name, the oldest extant square in Granada is **Plaza Nueva,** which under the Muslims was the site of the woodcutters' bridge. Today the river Darro runs under the square. On the plaza's east side is the 16th-century **Iglesia de Santa Ana,** built by Diego Siloé. Many start their visit here—the tourist office is on the corner, and English-speaking guides on Segways wheel about the square offering tours.

If you don't have time for a tour, walk a couple of minutes northeast along the banks of the Darro to the **Paseo de los Tristes** for your first proper view of the Alhambra. (The name, meaning Promenade of the Sad Ones, was coined because it was the route to the 19th-c. cemetery built in after an outbreak of yellow fever.)

As with any place where tourism is the mainstay, parts of Granada are overrun with tourist shops and restaurants, but this city of 230,000 also has a strong, authentic identity. Downtown, away from the Alhambra and the hillside *barrios,* it is an easy and pleasant place to stroll around, particularly if you are hopping from tapas bar to tapas bar.

Albaicín ★★ NEIGHBORHOOD   Also known by its Arabic name **Albayzín,** this ancient quarter on one of Granada's two main hills stands

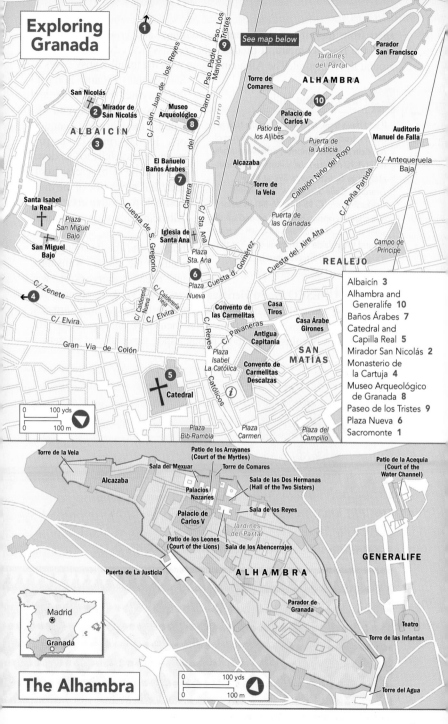

Exploring Granada

San Nicolás

2 Mirador de San Nicolás

Museo Arqueológico 8

ALBAICÍN

3

El Bañuelo Baños Árabes 7

Santa Isabel la Real

Plaza San Miguel Bajo

San Miguel Bajo

C/ Zenete

4

C/ Elvira

Gran Via de Colón

Cuesta de S. Gregorio

Carrera del Darro

Iglesia de Santa Ana 6

Plaza Sta. Ana

Plaza Nueva

C/ Caldereria Nueva

C/ Caldereria Vieja

C/ Elvira

Convento de las Carmelitas

Casa Tiros

C/ Pavaneras

Antigua Capitania

Casa Árabe Girones

Plaza Isabel La Católica

Convento de Carmelitas Descalzas

SAN MATÍAS

C/ Reyes Católicos

5

Catedral

Plaza Bib-Rambla

Plaza Carmen

Plaza del Campillo

Pso. Los Tristes

Pso. Padre Manjón

9

Torre de Comares

ALHAMBRA

Jardines del Partal

Parador San Francisco

10

Palacio de Carlos V

Patio de los Aljibes

Puerta de la Justicia

Auditorio Manuel de Falla

C/ Antequeruela Baja

Alcazaba

Callejón Niño del Royo

C/ Peña Partida

Torre de la Vela

Puerta de las Granadas

Campo de Principe

Cuesta del Aire Alta

REALEJO

See map below

Darro

C/ San Juan de los Reyes

C/ Sta. Ana

Carrera del Darro

Cuesta d. Gomerez

0 100 yds
0 100 m

The Alhambra

Torre de la Vela

Patio de los Arrayanes (Court of the Myrtles)

Sala del Mexuar

Torre de Comares

Patio de la Acequia (Court of the Water Channel)

Alcazaba

Sala de las Dos Hermanas (Hall of the Two Sisters)

Palacios Nazaríes

Palacio de Carlos V

Sala de los Reyes

Jardines del Partal

Patio de los Leones (Court of the Lions)

Sala de los Abencerrajes

Puerta de La Justicia

GENERALIFE

ALHAMBRA

Parador de Granada

Teatro

Torre de las Infantas

Madrid

Granada

Torre del Agua

0 100 yds
0 100 m

apart from the city of 19th-century buildings and boulevards. A relic from the Nasrid empire, it predates the Renaissance city that sprang up around the cathedral. The Albaicín (along with the uphill Gypsy caves of Sacromonte) became home to the marginalized Muslims and Gypsies declared beyond the pale by the Christian conquerors. Its labyrinth of narrow streets was too hilly to tear down in the name of progress; ironically, it is now some of the most desirable real estate in Granada. Albaicín's alleyways, cisterns, fountains, plazas, whitewashed houses, and the decaying remnants of the old city walls have all been preserved—it was declared a UNESCO World Heritage site in 1994. Walking around, you can glimpse the walled gardens of the private houses called Carmens, with their fruit trees and fountains. And then there are the views. The **Mirador San Nicolás** is the most popular spot, especially at sunset—it

---

Head for the Hills

If you have time, an electric bicycle tour is a good introduction to the historic *barrios* of **Albaicín** and **Sacromonte,** otherwise a hilly walk. A 90-minute tour, suitable for moderately able cyclists, costs 39€ at **Play Granada,** Calle Santa Ana, 2 (sixthrills1.trekksoft.com; ✆ **95-816-36-84**). A lazier and cheaper option is to hop on and off the small local buses (#31 and #34), which rotate around the hillside districts all day. For that, it's worth buying a travel card (p. 280).

Detailed mosaic work in the Alhambra.

reserving **FOR THE ALHAMBRA**

The Alhambra is so popular—it has 3 million visitors a year—that the government has limited the number of people who can enter each day. You can buy tickets at the ticket office, but each day's quota sells out quickly, so it's strongly advisable to buy them online or by telephone, well in advance. Take care when booking online—there are lots of sites offering expensive tours and tickets, but the only official one is **tickets. alhambra-patronato.es** (✆ **85-895-36-16**). Be careful, too, when choosing which ticket to buy; there are several different options and not all of them give access to the Nasrid Palace, which you don't want to miss. The **Alhambra General** website ticket at 14€ allows you to visit all public areas within the complex: the Alcazaba, the Nasrid Palace, and the Generalife. You can choose when to visit the Nasrid Palaces, but note that you must show up at the time specified on the ticket. Once you've bought your ticket online either print it out or collect it at a vending machine at the entrance, using your reservation number. (You can show your ticket or your phone, but don't let it run out of charge as you approach the head of the queue!) Allow at least 3 hours to visit the palaces and the gardens.

gets very busy, colonized by buskers, hawkers, and jugglers, but the view is achingly beautiful. If you're willing to keep walking you can find more secluded miradors, with views to the snowy peaks of the Sierra Nevada, but it's best to avoid these winding streets after dark. To get there, take bus 31 or 32.

Alhambra and Generalife ★★★ HISTORIC SITE   Spain's most popular visitor attraction, the **Qalat Al-hamra** (Red Castle) is perhaps the most remarkable fortress ever built. Islamic architecture in Spain reached its apogee in this palace once occupied by Nasrid princes, their families, and functionaries. Although the Alhambra was converted into a lavish palace in the 13th and 14th centuries, it was originally constructed for defensive purposes on a rocky hilltop above the Darro River. The modern city of Granada was built nearby across the river.

When you first see the Alhambra up close, its unadorned exterior may surprise you. The astonishing ornamentation lies within. Enter the complex at the modern concrete pavilion on Paseo de la Sabica (bear in mind it's a 10-min. walk from there to the Nasrid Palaces). Most visitors won't need an expensive guide, or even an audioguide: It's best simply to immerse yourself in the Alhambra and its gardens and try—as Washington Irving suggested—to shut your eyes to everyday life.

CARLOS V'S PALACE   As you wait for your slot at the Palace of the Nasrids (Palacio Nazaríes), take a look at the **Palacio de Carlos V** ★★. The Holy Roman Emperor—who also allowed the cathedral to be built in the middle of the great mosque at Córdoba (p. 268)—didn't think that Granada's Nasrid palace was grand enough, so in 1526 he ordered Pedro

Machuca, a student of Michelangelo, to design him a fitting royal residence. To add insult to injury, Carlos financed his Renaissance pile by levying a tax on the Muslims. Stunningly innovative in its day, the square exterior opens to reveal a huge circular courtyard with two arcaded stories high and open to the sky. But the emperor never lived here: The palace remained unfinished and roofless until the 20th century. Inside, the **Museo de la Alhambra** ★★ (www.alhambra.org; © **95-802-79-00**) displays artifacts retrieved from the Alhambra, including fragments of sculpture, ceramics, and even perfume burners used in the harem. The most outstanding objects are the richly decorated Nasrid amphorae and the *Pila de Almanzor*, a 10th-century ablution basin adorned with lions, stags, and ibex.

MEXUAR As your time slot arrives, from the Mexuar you'll be ushered on a strictly controlled tour of the **Palacio Nazaríes.** The first, modestly decorated, hall was a reception area where the sultan and his ministers heard appeals from members of the public. It was converted into a Catholic chapel in the 1600s; note the Christian motto *Plus Ultra,* topped by a crown, on the tiled walls. At the back of the hall the **oratory** and **mihrab,** with views of the Albaicín below, were heavily restored in the 20th century following a gunpowder mishap in 1590. Pass through the **Cuarto Dorado** (Gilded Room), so-called because of its embellished ceiling added by the Christian kings, and you'll find yourself in the **Patio del Mexuar.** The facade here is perhaps the most elaborate of all, as it is the doorway to the **Serallo,** or inner court. The public wouldn't have been allowed past this point.

Emperor Carlos V's Palace at the Alhambra.

The stucco inscriptions repeat the Arabic phrase "there is no conqueror but Allah."

SERALLO The Serallo, built during the reign of Yusuf I in the 14th century, is arranged around the **Patio de los Arrayanes** (Court of the Myrtles), which contains a narrow reflecting pool hedged by myrtle bushes.

Note the decorative tiles, among the finest in the Alhambra. At the northern end is the antechamber known as the **Sala de la Barca.** Its magnificent wooden ceiling suggests the hull of a boat, or *barca,* but in fact the name comes from the Arabic *baraka,* or blessing, a word repeated again and again in the plasterwork. Beyond, in the **Comares tower,** is the **Salón de Embajadores** (Hall of the Ambassadors), the palace's largest and grandest room, where the Nasrids carried out their diplomatic business. Perfectly square, it contained the sultan's throne. Its cedar dome evokes the seven heavens of the Muslim cosmos. It was in this room that the ill-starred Boabdil signed the terms of his surrender to the Catholic Kings.

HAREM   An opening off the Court of the Myrtles leads to the greatest architectural achievement of the Alhambra, the **Patio de los Leones** (Court of the Lions), constructed by Muhammad V. This was the heart of the palace, the private section where the sultan and his family retreated. The court is an architectural representation of paradise, and shows Christian influences in its cloister, lined with arcades supported by 124 slender marble columns. At its center is Andalucía's most famous fountain, resting on 12 marble lions. The lions represent the hours of the day, the months of the year, and maybe even the tribes of Israel. To one side is the **Sala de los Abencerrajes.** It is said that during a banquet here, Boabdil's father, Muley Hacén, slaughtered 16 members of the Abencerraj family because their chief was sleeping with his favorite wife. Two other remarkable salons open onto the Court of Lions: The Hall of the Two Sisters, **Sala de las Dos Hermanas** (so named for the two identical marble slabs in the pavement) with its stunning honeycomb dome of carved plaster; and the **Sala de los Reyes** (Hall of Kings), the Alhambra's great banquet hall, with its 14th-century ceiling paintings on leather.

From here a gallery leads to the **Patio de la Reja** (Court of the Window Grille). This is where Washington Irving lived in the Emperor's chambers in 1829, and where he began to write his famous book *Tales of the Alhambra.* As you leave the Nasrid palace and walk through the gardens towards the Generalife, with the fortress walls on your left, you'll reach the **Torre de las Infantas** (Tower of the Princesses), scene of one of Irving's most famous stories. Three beautiful princesses, Zayda, Zorayda, and Zorahayda, fell in love with three captive Christian soldiers. To cut a long story short, two sisters got their man, but the third, Zorahayda, couldn't betray her father and died broken-hearted, locked in the tower. The story goes that she is buried in these gardens, where a single rosebush grows.

GENERALIFE   Keep left across the bridge at **Torre del Agua** and you'll soon reach the gardens and the main building of the **Generalife.** Set in 30 lush hectares (74 acres), it was built in the 13th century as a sultan's escape from the scorching summer heat and palace intrigues. Its name, pronounced *hen-ah-rah-lee-fey,* means "garden of the architect." Don't expect an Alhambra in miniature—its open windows, arcades, and white painted walls were designed for comfort rather than splendor. The gardens, on the other hand, are magnificent, although they have been much altered over the centuries. Highlights include the **Patio de Polo,** where visitors on horseback would dismount; the **Escalera del Agua,** a gently flowing water staircase; and the **Patio de la Acequía,** an enclosed Oriental garden with rows of water jets making graceful arches above it. The **Patio de la Sultana** is said to have been the secret rendezvous point for Zoraya, wife of Sultan Muley Hacén, and her lover, chief of the unlucky Abencerrajes. So much for escaping palace intrigue. The gardens of the Generalife are the unsurpassable setting for Granada's International Festival of Music and Dance, which takes place over 2 weeks in early summer (www.granadafestival.org).

ALCAZABA   At the beginning or end of your visit, try to see the **Alcazaba,** the rugged 9th-century fortress that is the oldest part of the complex. For spectacular views, climb the **Torre de la Vela** watchtower. From here you can get a great sense of the Alhambra and Generalife, and the whole city and province of Granada are laid out before you, stretching towards the snowcapped mountains of the Sierra Nevada. It was on this parapet in January 1492 that the cross was again raised over Granada, after nearly 800 years of Moorish rule.

Calle Real de la Alhambra s/n. tickets.alhambra-patronato.es. ℂ **95-802-79-71.** General ticket, including Alhambra, Nasrid Palace, and Generalife, 14€; garden visit 7€; night visit 8€. Mid-Oct to Mar daily 8:30am–6pm; Apr to mid-Oct daily 8:30am–8pm; night visit days and times vary, check website. Museo del Alhambra, admission free; Wed–Sat 8:30am–6pm (summer until 8pm), Sun and Tues 8:30–2:30pm.

Baños Arabes ★ HISTORIC SITE   It's remarkable that these 11th-century "baths of the walnut tree," as they were known by the Moors, escaped destruction during the reign of the Reyes Católicos, who considered public bathing decadent. Among the oldest buildings still standing in Granada, and among the best-preserved Arab baths in Spain, they predate the Alhambra. Many of the stones used in their construction show signs of Visigothic and Roman carving, especially the capitals. The 5€ admission ticket also gives you access to two other historic Arab buildings in the

---

Walking to the Alhambra

Most visitors opt to take a taxi or the bus from the town to the Alhambra, but some hardy souls enjoy the uphill climb from Plaza Nueva. Start on the Cuesta Gomérez and follow the signs indicating the zigzagging road that leads to the top. The walk takes about 30 minutes. For those staying at the *parador* or other hotels near the Alhambra, walking into town and catching a bus or taxi back up the hill is a happy compromise.

Granada's Baños Arabes.

Albaicín. (For a modern Arab bath experience, there are several options in town. **Hammam Andalus,** Calle Santa Ana, 16 [granada.hammamandalus. com; ℂ **95-822-99-78;** from 30€] is one of the most popular.)
Carrera del Darro 31. www.granadatur.com. ℂ **95-802-79-00.** Admission 5€. Daily 10am–5pm.

Catedral and Capilla Real ★★ CATHEDRAL   Granada's Renais-

sance cathedral feels too big for its setting, boxed in and partially hidden by later buildings. It was begun in 1523 on top of the city's main mosque and not completed until 1704. It was largely designed by Diego de Siloé and later by Granada's Alonso Cano, known as the Spanish Michelangelo, who was responsible for its towering Baroque facade. Inside, it's a wedding cake of white and gold, with an impressive starry cupola, stained-glass windows, and canvases and sculptures by the multi-talented Cano. Behind the cathedral (and requiring a separate admission fee) is the Isa-belline Gothic **Capilla Real** (Royal Chapel). Built between 1505 and 1517, this is where the remains of the Catholic Kings Isabel and Fernando lie. It was their wish to be buried in recaptured Granada, not in their home kingdoms of Castilla or Aragón. Their Carrara marble tombs lie side by side with those of their daughter, Juana la Loca (Joan the Mad), and her husband, Felipe el Hermoso (Philip the Handsome). The gilded grille here is one of the finest in Spain. In the crypt below, you can see their lead coffins, alongside the tiny casket of Miguel, Prince of Portugal, who died as a child. The Sacristy museum contains items belonging to the Catholic Kings: a crown and scepter, sword, and Isabel's mirror, as well as her personal **art collection,** including Botticelli's *Oration in the Garden of Olives.* An excitable audioguide tells a good story, but everything in the Capilla Real is so tangible, it's better to press pause and take it all in first hand.

Gran Via de Colón, 5. catedraldegranada.com. Catedral: ℰ **95-822-29-59;** 5€ with audioguide; Mon–Sat 10am–6:30pm, free admission Sun 3–5:45pm. Capilla Real: ℰ **95-822-78-48;** 5€ with audioguide; Mon–Sat 10:15am–6:30pm, free admission Wed 2:30–6:30pm. The cathedral shop on Calle Alcaicería sells a range of combination tickets.

Monasterio de la Cartuja ★★ MONASTERY

In the outskirts of Granada, a couple of kilometers north of the center, this 16th-century Carthusian monastery is well worth the trip. It is sometimes called the Christian answer to the Alhambra, and you can't help thinking its architects and craftsmen must have taken the Nasrid palace as a challenge. It starts austerely with a peaceful cloister planted with orange trees. Portraits of martyred monks and a *tromp l'oeil* wooden cross are the only decorations in the refectory. But when you get to the church it bursts into full-blown Baroque fantasy. The ornamentation here is perhaps the pinnacle of Spain's Churrigueresque style; plasterwork froths like ocean waves crashing onto a rock, and the sanctuary's frescoed cupola is way up there with the Transparente in Toledo's Cathedral (p. 159). In the midst of it all is a small, baleful statue of St Bruno, founder of the silent Carthusian order, by José de Mora.

Paseo de Cartuja s/n. www.archidiocesisgranada.es. ℰ **95-816-19-32.** Admission 5€. Sun–Fri 10am–6pm, until 8pm summer; Sat 10am–1pm and 3–8pm. Bus: 8.

Museo Arqueológico de Granada ★ MUSEUM

One of Spain's oldest archaeological museums, this well-presented museum on the banks of the Darro inhabits the 16th-century Castril palace, which has a fine Renaissance facade and patio. Its collection of artifacts ranges from the Iberians through to the Nasrids, a period spanning 1.5 million years. Its most remarkable exhibit is the **Astrolabe of Ibn Zawal** from 1481, a circular bronze instrument used to calculate the beginning of Ramadan and the times and direction of prayer, based on the position of the stars. It is the only known example made for the latitude of Granada. Explanations are in Spanish and English.

Carrera de Darro, 2. www.museosdeandalucia.es. ℰ **60-014-31-41.** Admission 1.50€, EU citizens free. Sept–Jun Tues–Sat 9am–9pm; Jul–Aug Tues–Sat 9am–3pm.

Sacromonte ★★ NEIGHBORHOOD

Pushed out of town by the Christian rulers, hundreds of Gypsies *(gitanos)* once lived in caves on the

Inside a Gypsy cave in Sacromonte.

"Holy Mountain" on the outskirts of Granada above the Albaicín. Nearly all the Gypsies who remain are in one way or another involved with tourism; these days many of them commute from homes in the city. You can walk uphill, but to save time take a bus or taxi (and definitely use transport after dark). A bike tour (p. 282) is a good way to get off the beaten path. To see inside the caves and learn something of Gypsy culture, visit the **Museo Cuevas del Sacromonte** ★, Barranco de los Negros (www. sacromontegranada.com; ☎ 95-821-51-20), which displays several cave homes, as well as others set up as studios for traditional weaving, pottery, and metalwork. The museum is open mid-October to mid-March daily 10am to 6pm, until 8pm in summer. Admission is 5€; take bus 34 to get here. In the evenings, many caves become performance venues for the Granada Gypsy flamenco style known as *zambra*. If you're feeling adventurous, you can even lodge in a cave house: **Las Cuevas de Abanico,** Calle Verea de Enmedio, 89 (www.cuevaselabanico.es; ☎ 95-822-61-99), offers one- and two-bedroom units with whitewashed walls, tiny bathrooms, and a corner equipped for minimal cooking. Most are rented by the week. At the time of writing they were closed for restoration, so check the website. Various cave houses are offered for rent on Airbnb.com.

Where to Stay in Granada

EXPENSIVE

AC Palacio de Santa Paula ★★★   An austere exterior hides what only the *parador* rivals as Granada's most luxurious stay. This sanctuary on the Gran Vía combines two historic buildings: the 16th-century Convento de Santa Paula and a 12th-century palace. It's an impressive blend of ancient and modern architecture in which the beautiful brick cloister and smaller Moorish patio are connected with glass and steel. The ample guestrooms are simply and elegantly decorated in warm earth colors, with large beds and well-stocked mosaic-tiled bathrooms, including bathrobe and slippers for the in-house *hammam*. The restaurant, **El Claustro,** is one of Granada's finest, set in the grand former refectory. A 50€ tasting menu offers creative takes on Andalucían cuisine with good value wine pairing.

Gran Vía de Colón, 31. www.marriott.com. *©* **95-880-57-40.** 76 units. 150€–250€ double. Parking 18€ per day. **Amenities:** Restaurant; bar; exercise room; hammam; free Wi-Fi.

MODERATE

Casa Morisca ★★   Lovingly restored by a renowned Granada architect, this 16th-century mansion in the Albaicín retains a central patio and Moorish *alberca* (pond), Nasrid columns, and coffered ceilings. The Granadino style, influenced by the decoration of the Alhambra, is showcased throughout. The Mirador suite, which costs considerably more than the standard rooms, has a window view of the Alhambra's Comares Tower. There's no restaurant, but a good buffet breakfast (12€) is served in the brick-vaulted cave room.

Cuesta de la Victoria, 9. www.hotelcasamorisca.com. *©* **95-822-11-00.** 14 units. 60€–200€ double; 120€–300€ suite. Free parking (arrange in advance). **Amenities:** Bar; free Wi-Fi.

Casa del Capitel Nazarí ★   This centrally located hotel by the river Darro takes its name from the original Nasrid column capital that helps keep it standing. A renovated 16th-century palace, it is arranged around a central courtyard with a pebble-mosaic patio where breakfast and complimentary afternoon drinks are served. The rooms have Renaissance wooden ceilings, tiled floors, and most have showers rather than baths to maximize space. Historic building regulations precluded an elevator, but ground-floor rooms are available. Skip the extra charge for a room with a view of the Alhambra—the view's seriously obstructed—and enjoy this great value hotel in its own right.

Cuesta Aceituneros, 6. www.hotelcasacapitel.com. *©* **95-821-52-60.** 18 units. 55€–185€ double. **Amenities:** Free Wi-Fi.

Casa Palacete 1822 ★★   Six beautifully designed rooms make up this elegant boutique hotel, opened in 2015 close to the Puerta Real in the city center. Each room in the renovated 1822 mansion is named after a

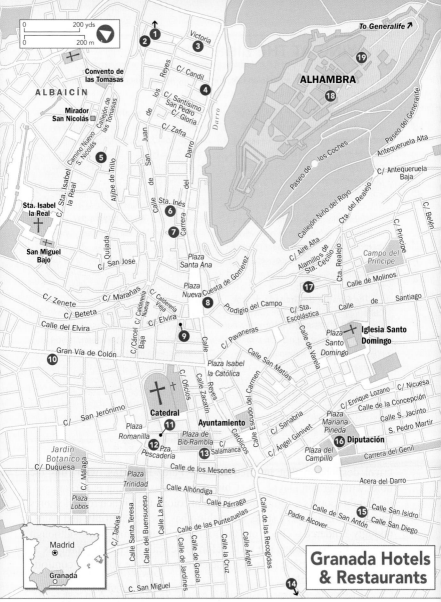

HOTELS

AC Palacio de Santa Paula **10**

Casa de la Catedral **11**

Casa del Capitel Nazarí **7**

Casa Morisca **3**

Casa Palacete 1822 **15**

Cuevas de Abanico **1**

Hotel América **18**

Hotel Los Tilos **13**

Hotel Palacio de Santa Inés **6**

Parador de Granada **19**

RESTAURANTS

Arriaga **14**

Bar Los Diamantes **8**

Bodegas Castañeda **9**

Chikito **16**

Cunini Restaurante & Marisquería **12**

Damasqueros **17**

El Huerto de Juan Ranas **5**

Mirador de Morayma **2**

Ruta de Azafran **4**

STAYING AT THE alhambra

"I lived in the midst of an Arabian tale, and shut my eyes, as much as possible, to every thing that called me back to everyday life."

The American writer Washington Irving was lucky enough to lodge in rooms within the Alhambra for several months in 1829. That privilege is sadly no longer available, but there are two places where you can stay within the walls of the palace complex—one luxurious, the other more modest. If you'd like to wander the grounds after the tourist crowds have gone, plan to reserve a room far in advance, but bear in mind that both lodgings are inconvenient for visiting the rest of Granada. You'll need a bus or taxi to bring you back up the hill.

The **Parador de Granada ★★★**, **Calle** Real de Alhambra, s/n (www.parador.es; ✆ **95-822-14-40**), is Spain's most exclusive parador. Set in a sand-colored 15th-century monastery overlooking the gardens of the Generalife, it is beautiful, peaceful, magical. The public areas are all shady courtyards, fountains, ancient tiles, and stucco work. The guestrooms and fine restaurant are

contemporary, subtly echoing the decorative style of the Alhambra. Doubles range from 225€ to 500€ a night, suites from 500€ to 800€. The level of service matches the surroundings. Free parking is available.

Hotel América ★, Calle Real de Alhambra, 53 (www.hotelamerica granada.com; ✆ **95-822-74-71**), is a 19th-century house converted in the 1930s into a 17-room hotel. The small rooms and home cooking are fairly rudimentary, but the atmosphere is friendly, and the location for the Alhambra unbeatable—less than a minute's walk from the Nasrid palace. At night it is strikingly quiet, until the street cleaners start their work bright and early. If you plan to spend most of your time in and around the palace grounds this is a good and economical option. Doubles range from 110€ to 220€, depending on the season. Valet parking is available.

travel destination that inspired Patricia Pérez-Higueras, who runs the hotel with her son David. The Chinese room has hanging paper lanterns, the Hindu room is a commotion of bright colors, the French room features sumptuous Louis XVI style. Everything has been beautifully and painstakingly rendered—check out the tooled ceilings throughout—although some of the bathrooms put style before practicality. The hospitality is as warm as the decor; the team seem determined to make your stay comfortable and memorable.

Call San Isidro, 16. www.casapalacete1822.com. ✆ **95-825-87-43.** 6 units. 80€–200€ double. Paid parking nearby. **Amenities:** Concierge; coffee shop; shared lounge; free Wi-Fi.

Hotel Palacio de Santa Inés ★★   A pioneer in transforming Albaicín's Mudéjar mansions into lodgings for tourists, the Palacio de Santa Inés opened in this prime location in the mid-1990s. Set across two 16th-century houses, it has a central patio featuring fragments of original Renaissance frescoes on its walls. Ornate wooden galleries rise towards coffered ceilings. Spacious family rooms have an additional bed on a

The Parador de Granada is actually within the Alhambra, in the former convent of San Francisco.

mezzanine level and some rooms have views of the Alhambra. Helpful staff, sparkling bathrooms, and an excellent breakfast (included in the rate) make this hotel much in demand. Book well in advance.

Cuesta de Santa Inés, 9. www.palaciosantaines.com. © **95-822-23-62.** 35 units. 60€–200€ double. Parking 19€. **Amenities:** Room service; afternoon tea; spa treatments; free Wi-Fi.

INEXPENSIVE

Casa de la Catedral ★★   These nicely designed rooms above a café on the cathedral square offer amazing value in a great location. Double, triple, and quadruple rooms are available, each with a kitchenette including a microwave and fridge—ideal for young families. Decor is fresh and simple, with pastel-painted wooden headboards and furniture. The friendly café Rollo below is a good place for breakfast, with close-up views of the cathedral; hotel guests get a 10% discount there for lunch or dinner.

Plaza de las Pasiegas, s/n. catedral-es.book.direct. © **95-825-35-95.** 10 units. 40€– 190€ double. **Amenities:** Café/restaurant, packed lunches, free Wi-Fi.

Hotel Los Tilos ★   Set on the Plaza Bib-Rambla, surrounded by covered cafes and restaurants, Los Tilos is a bargain for budget travelers. The bright rooms are spacious, clean, and surprisingly quiet given the downtown location; most have views over the plaza. There's a tiny elevator and a rooftop terrace where guests often gather to share a bottle of wine. The substantial buffet breakfast, including bacon, eggs, and *tortilla,* will set you up for a long day's sightseeing.

Plaza Bib-Rambla, 4. www.hotellostilos.com. ✆ **95-826-67-12.** 30 units. 40€–70€ double. **Amenities:** Free Wi-Fi in public areas.

Where to Eat in Granada

The gastronomy of Granada draws heavily on the city's Arab past—lots of spices, almonds, and dried fruit are used—and you'll also see many a Moroccan restaurant serving couscous and *harira.* As well as the Spanish standards there are some unusual regional delicacies: fava beans and ham, plates of snails, and Sacromonte omelet (which sometimes includes lamb's brains and testicles). Seafood and fried fish are also a favorite, trucked inland from Motril. But the big news is that Granada is Spain's capital of free tapas. Every time you buy a drink at a bar, you'll be given a plate of something interesting. The portions in some places are so generous that you may not need dinner.

EXPENSIVE

Damasqueros ★★★ ANDALUCÍAN   Having trained with some of Spain's top chefs, Lola Marín opened Damasqueros in the Realejo district in 2009. Marín cooks from her Andalucían roots, referencing traditional dishes, but she presents them in a carefully edited fashion that would grace the cover of any food magazine. There is just a tasting menu, available with or without paired wines, which changes regularly. Tiny pieces of octopus in a pepper soup are matched with a Galician Albariño. A mushroom ravioli with a yolk on top mimics ham and eggs. Fried fish and *migas* (breadcrumbs) echo the tapas served in downtown bars, served with barrel-fermented Chardonnay. The surroundings are simple and soothing, cream leather chairs and pendant lighting; the young waitstaff is knowledgeable and committed. A joy.

Calle Damasqueros, 3. www.damasqueros.com. ✆ **95-821-05-50.** Tasting menu 39.50€, with wine pairing 59€. Tues–Sat 1–3:30pm and 8:30–10:30pm, Sun 1–3:30pm.

MODERATE

Chikito ★ ANDALUCÍAN   Back in the 1920s, this was the location of the Alameda, where Federico García Lorca and his artistic circle known as El Rinconcillo used to meet. A statue at a corner table marks the spot. The food and atmosphere seem unchanged from those days, and although you'll find tourists, you'll also find old gents propping up the bar and young families dropping in after a shopping trip. The restaurant offers plenty of Andalucían classics: salt cod salad with shredded oranges, "Nasrid" steak with sultanas and almonds, sweet *pionono* pastries (named after Pope Pius IV: Pio Nono). Free tapas at the bar come on generous

TABLES WITH a view

What could be more relaxing than dinner on a balmy terrace with spectacular views of the Alhambra, where the food and wine is delicious, the service friendly, and the bill reasonable? Unfortunately, it doesn't always work out like that. If you've watched the sunset at the Mirador de San Nicolas it's tempting to consider **El Huerto de Juan Ranas,** Calle de Atarazana, 8 (www.elhuertodejuanranas.com; ✆ **95-828-69-25**), for dinner. The views are second to none, but the food is expensive, and the service gets grumpy reviews. A pre-dinner drink on the terrace may be a better bet. Don't expect free tapas. For dinner, take a short walk to **Mirador de Morayma,** Calle Pianista García Carillo, 2 (miradordemorayma.com; ✆ **95-822-82-90**), and try the traditional *remojón* salad of salt cod, orange, and olives.

The restaurants that line the Paseo de Los Tristes, with views looking up at the Alhambra, can also be frustrating. **Ruta de Azafran,** Paseo del Padre Manjón, 1 (rutadelazafran.com; ✆ **95-822-68-82**), feels less jaded than most, with a selection of light and bright North African–influenced dishes, and some bargains on its wine list. For completely different, but equally spectacular views, book a table at **Arriaga,** Avenida de las Ciencias, 2 (www.restaurantearriaga.com; ✆ **95-813-26-19**). Set at the top of a skyscraper near the science park (a taxi ride from the center), its picture windows offer incredible nighttime vistas of the city. The tasting menus are superb and the service impeccable, although it's not cheap. Tasting menus 50€ and 65€, wine pairing adds 12€ or 20€.

rectangular plates; the walls are covered in photos of famous guests, from the Spanish king to Maradona.

Plaza del Campillo 9. www.restaurantechikito.com. ✆ **95-822-33-64.** Entrees 12€–30€. Thurs–Tues 12:30–4:30pm and 8–11:30pm, closed Wed.

Cunini Restaurante & Marisquería ★★ SEAFOOD   In a city that is extraordinarily generous with free tapas, Cunini is more generous than most. You can sample much of the seafood menu here by standing at the undulating marble bar and ordering drink after drink. The tapas seem to get better with each, and that's not the beer talking. If you want the full seafood blowout, take a seat in the restaurant or on the covered plaza outside for a procession of fresh shrimp *(quisquillas),* barnacles *(percebes),* baby squid *(chipirones),* and turbot *(rodaballo),* to mention just a few.

Plaza de Pescadería, 14. www.marisqueriacunini.es. ✆ **95-825-07-77.** Entrees 13€–33€. Mon–Sat noon–2am.

INEXPENSIVE

Bar Los Diamantes ★★ SEAFOOD   Frying fish for Granadinos since 1942, Los Diamantes has a number of bars across town. The original on Calle Navas is fabulous but hectic, or try the newer, larger branch on Plaza Nueva. If you want a full meal, ask at the counter for a seat at one of the bench tables. If you prefer tapas to share, grab a stool or stand at the bar. Order, say, a plate of mixed fried fish *(surtido de pescado)* and a couple of beers, and you're likely to get a free starter of a plate of clams; once you've polished off the hot battered fish, you might get a free finisher of garlicky mushrooms. Servings are large, so half portions *(media racion)* may suffice. It may also be the only restaurant in Granada whose menu offers brains *(sesos),* sweetbreads *(mollejas),* and chicken nuggets. Service is friendly and fast.

Calle Navas, 28 or Plaza Nueva, 13. www.barlosdiamantes.com. © **95-822-70-70** or **95-807-53-13.** Entrees 15€–21€, half portions 10€–13€. Daily 12:30pm–midnight (Calle Navas branch closes 4:30–8:30pm).

Bodegas Castañeda ★★★ ANDALUCÍAN Just off the Calle Elvira, this is a must-visit bar for a drink, tapas, or even a sit-down meal. It's a classic old wine dispensary with barrels behind the bar and hams over it. It could be three-deep at the counter and the friendly bar staff might suggest throwing you your drink and free tapa. There are a few tables around the edge of the bar; if you can get one, order either the hot or cold platter *(tabla caliente/fria)* from a roving waiter. It will arrive lightning fast, passed over the heads of drinkers at the bar, and is plenty for two. The food isn't going to win any gourmet prizes, but it's interesting and tasty stuff, and anyway, the main reason to come here is to see this nightly food and drink machine in action. Try their signature drink, *calicasas,* a potent blend of different wines. (One should be enough.) Note that there are two establishments with the same name on this block, the result of a family dispute. The address below is the one you want.

Calle Almireceros, 1. m.facebook.com/BodegasCastaNeda. © **95-821-54-64.** Tapas 2.50€–6€; medium platter 15.50€. Mon–Fri noon–1am, Sat–Sun noon–2am.

Granada Shopping

Next to the cathedral in the lower city, the narrow alleys of the rebuilt **Alcaicería,** once the Moorish silk market, are filled with souvenir and craft shops. It's fun to wander, but it's all pretty touristy stuff. It's a similar story on **Calderería Vieja** and **Cuesta de Gomérez,** which have the feel of Moroccan souks. There are lots of wall hangings, marquetry boxes, and Arabic tile fridge magnets for sale, but it's worth seeking out something more original. Across from the entrance to the Capilla Real, look for the **Madraza** cultural center run by the University of Granada, Calle Oficios, 14 (tienda.ugr.es), which sells modern Moorish-inspired designs on fabrics and tiles. **Rocio,** Calle Capuchinos, 8 (www.elrocio.es; © **95-826-58-23**), is where Granadinos buy their flamenco gear for festivals. There are a number of Spanish guitar-making workshops *(guitarerrías)* where you can watch the craftsmen in action: Try **Guitarrería German Perez,** Cuesta de Gomérez (www.guitarerria.com; © **95-822-70-33**), or **Guitarras Bellido,** Paseo de las Palmas (www.guitarreriabellido.com; © **95-822-84-03**). **López Mezquita,** on Calle Reyes Católicos (© **95-822-12-05**), is

WHERE TO SEE flamenco

In both Sacromonte and in town, the standard and authenticity of flamenco performances can be variable, and you can be easily parted with your money, so choose carefully. If you want to see a *zambra* performed in a genuine cave, **Venta El Gallo,** Barranco Los Negros, 5 (www.ventaelgallo.com; ✆ **95-822-84-76**), is a good option. It's expensive at 26€, but there's a free drink and no pressure to spend more. The biggest drawback can be the tour groups, who seem determined to record the whole performance (despite the "no video" sign) and talk throughout. The show starts at 9:30pm. For a more intimate, high-quality show, try the nightly concerts at **Palacio de los Olvidades,** Cuesta de Santa Inés, 6 (www.flamencolosolvidados.com; ✆ **95-819-71-22**), which weave together flamenco and the works of Federico García Lorca in a wonderful way. Shows are at 8:15pm and 9:30pm and cost 15€. For flamenco with dinner, **Los Jardines de Zoraya** in the Albaicín, Calle Panaderos, 32 (www.jardines dezoraya.com; ✆ **95-820-62-66**), has a lovely patio, good food, and an intense performance. Shows are at 8pm and 10:30pm; there's also a 3pm show on Saturday and Sunday afternoons. They cost 49€ with dinner, 20€ without. If you yearn for a spontaneous performance away from the *tablaos,* try **El Encuentro Asador,** Calle Escudo del Carmen, 10 (✆ **95-821-60-31**), where song and dance breaks out on Thursday and Friday evenings around 9pm, and at Sunday lunchtime.

a grand old *pasteleria* selling beautifully packaged cakes and sweets. You can buy loose teas and spices from stalls near the cathedral, or have your name written in Arabic—on a card or on your arm—at the **Mirador de San Nicolás.**

Granada Nightlife

If you enjoy bar-hopping, Granada is for you. Wander loosely from Calle Elvira towards Calle Navas and you'll pass scores of atmospheric bars and restaurants, almost all of them offering generous free tapas. Here are a few you shouldn't miss: **Bodegas Castañeda,** Calle Almireceros, 1 (p. 296); **Bodegas la Mancha,** Calle Joaquín Costa, 10; **Casa Julio,** Calle Hermosa, 5; **Enoteca Pacurri,** Calle Gracia, 21; **Los Diamantes,** Calle Navas, 28, or Plaza Nueva, 13 (p. 295). If you prefer a guided visit to some out-of-the-way eateries, contact **Granada Tapas Tours** (www. granadatapastours.com; ✆ **61-944-49-84**).

In recent years, a number of Moroccan-style teashops *(teterías)* have popped up around the Albaicín, especially on Calle Calderería Nueva. For atmosphere, Arab pastries, and hookah pipe-smoking *(cachimba),* try **Tetería Nazarí,** Calle Calderería Nueva, 14, or **Tetería del Bañuelo,** Calle Bañuelo, 5, which has a pleasant patio with views of the Alhambra.

For music other than flamenco, head to **Booga Club,** Calle Sta. Bárbara, 3, or **Six Colors,** Tendillas de Santa Paula, 6, Granada's liveliest gay bar.

Side Trip to Úbeda & Baeza ★★

Less than 2 hours from Granada by car and a little longer by bus, through a landscape of endless olive trees, the provincial town of **Úbeda** is completely different in atmosphere. Granada is the ultimate Moorish city, but Úbeda's old town is filled with Spain's finest Renaissance architecture—it is sometimes called the "Florence of Andalucía." The most striking buildings are the work of Andrés de Vandelvira, who in the 16th century created his own interpretation of the new style from Italy. The best way to appreciate this unspoiled World Heritage Site is to wander around its wide-open plazas and admire its honey-colored Renaissance palaces and blazoned mansions. Allow time too to visit Úbeda's shops, which specialize in beautifully decorated ceramic bowls, esparto grass basketry, and artisanal olive oil. After the crowds and trashy souvenirs of Granada, its streets feel refreshingly tranquil and authentic.

And if finding one Renaissance pearl in the middle of the Spanish countryside is a surprise, what's even more pleasing is that there is another just 10km (6 miles) down the road. **Baeza,** with a population of 16,000, is about half the size of Úbeda and has almost as many Renaissance buildings.

ARRIVING   The easiest way to visit Úbeda is to take one of the 10 **buses** per day from Granada (www.alsa.es; ⓒ **90-242-22-42**). They take 2 to 3 hours and cost 13€ each way. The bus station is on Calle San José in the new part of the city; signs point downhill to the zona monumental. To drive, take the E-902/A-44 north from Granada; at Jaen, follow the A-316 spur northeast. There's parking in Plaza de Andalucía.

VISITOR INFORMATION   Pick up a walking map at Úbeda's **tourist office** next to the clock tower, Plaza de Andalucía, 5 (www.andalucia.org; ⓒ **95-377-92-04**). It is open Monday to Friday 9am to 7:30pm, Saturday 9am to 3pm and 5 to 7:30pm, Sunday 9:30am to 3pm. Baeza's **tourist office** (www.andalucia.org; ⓒ **95-377-99-82**) occupies a 16th-century building on the Plaza del Pópulo. It's open Monday to Friday 9am to 7:30pm, weekends 9:30am to 3pm.

EXPLORING ÚBEDA

Andrés de Vandelvira's patrons were local nobility who had become fabulously wealthy through royal connections and monopolies on the olive oil and textile trades. You'll see the names of the two most powerful families, Cobos and Molina, all over town.

With the exception of the Hospital de Santiago on its own to the west, Úbeda's monumental zone comprises a series of spacious squares at the bottom of Calle Real where almost every building is a 16th-century gem, palaces built in *piedra dorada* (golden stone). In the 17th century the town fell into sharp decline, which explains the absence of later architectural styles. Úbeda suffered damage during the Civil War and years of neglect, but it's recently been beautifully restored, making the area feel like a Renaissance architectural park.

Barrio Alfarero ★ NEIGHBORHOOD   Calle de Valencia is the heart of the *barrio alfarero* (potters' district), where a handful of pottery workshops line one short strip, plus a ceramics museum. You'll see the Tito name everywhere: Several generations of the same family are engaged in producing intricately decorated ceramic bowls—usually green—fired in traditional kilns. You can pick up a beautiful medium-sized bowl for around 15€. You'll see Paco Tito's award-winning ceramics shop in the Plaza Ayuntamiento in the monumental quarter, but the prices there are much higher than they are here.

Museo de Alfarería Paco Tito, Calle de Valencia, 22. pablotito.es/museo. ℂ **95-375-14-96.** Free admission. Mon–Sat 8am–2pm and 4–8pm; Sun 10am–2pm.

Casa Museo Andalusí ★ MUSEUM   Don't miss this extraordinary private museum in a 15th-century Jewish *converso* mansion. It is the life's work of Francisco Castro, a history enthusiast who has amassed a huge collection of traditional Andalucían art and craft from across the region. Ring the bell and his daughter will proudly show you round. Church doors, fragments of *artesonado* ceiling, Moorish masonry, popular ceramics, cheese presses, spinning wheels, a magnificent inlaid writing chest with secret drawers, and a magical cellar are just some of its treasures.

Calle Narváez, 11. vandelviraturismo.com. ℂ **61-907-61-32.** Admission 5€. To arrange visit, contact Vandelvira Turismo, Calle Real, 61 ℂ **65-950-87-66.**

Hospital de Santiago ★★ HISTORIC SITE   This huge, austere building was Vandelvira's last masterpiece, completed in 1575, the year of his death. It was commissioned by Diego de Los Cobos y Molina, the Bishop of Jaén, and continued to be used as a hospital until the 1970s. The sandstone exterior is remarkably free of embellishment, earning it the nickname "Andalucía's Escorial." Over the main entrance is Vandelvira's trademark, a carving of Santiago Matamoros on horseback—St. James in full Moor-slaying mode. Today, the building is in constant use as a cultural complex, hosting exhibitions and conferences in its double-tier arcaded courtyard and concerts in the exquisitely decorated chapel. Note the monumental staircase leading upstairs from the patio.

Calle Obispo Cobos, 28. turismodeubeda.com. ℂ **95-375-08-42.** Free admission. Mon–Fri 7:30am–2:30pm and 3:30–10pm; Sat–Sun 7:30am–2:30pm and 5–10pm. Closed weekends Aug.

Iglesia de San Pablo ★ CHURCH   This church in the center of old town is almost as fascinating as the El Salvador (see below). One of Úbeda's oldest buildings, parts of it date back to Visigothic times. It's like a primer on architectural styles: The front entrance, called the carpenters' door, is Romanesque; the south portal, added in 1511, is in Isabelline Gothic style; the tower is Plateresque. Vandelvira himself designed one of the chapels, which are all enclosed with fine wrought-iron grilles. As you leave, stroll past the old town hall (**Antiguo Ayuntamiento**) in the corner of the square. It's now a musical conservatory, from which lovely sounds waft.

Plaza 1 de Mayo. turismodeubeda.com. ✆ **95-375-06-37.** Free admission, 1€ donation appreciated. Tues–Sat 11am–1pm and 6–8pm; Sun 11am–1pm.

Sacra Capilla Funeraria de El Salvador ★★ CHURCH   One of the finest examples of Spanish Renaissance architecture, inside and out, this church was designed by Diego de Siloé and the work was carried out by Vandelvira—his first major architectural project. It was built as a family chapel and mausoleum for Francisco de los Cobos, who was secretary to Emperor Carlos V (it's still privately owned by his descendants). The richly embellished portal is mere window dressing for the wealth of decoration inside. The **altarpiece** by Alonso Berruguete is a dazzling display of gilded wood representing the transfiguration of Christ. It is mostly a restoration, having been badly damaged in the Civil War. The **sacristy,** designed by Vandelvira himself, is even more impressive, crammed with allegories of vice and virtue. The door, representing the gates of Eden, is extremely unusual, occupying the corner of the chapel. The ceiling is a

The richly decorated Sacra Capilla Funeraria de El Salvador in Úbeda.

mind-boggling piece of decoration by the French sculptor Esteban Jamete, who also carved the facade.

Plaza Vásquez de Molina, s/n. www.fundacionmedinaceli.org. © **60-927-99-05.** Admission 5€, with audioguide. Mon–Sat 9:30am–2:30pm and 4:30–7:30pm (6pm in winter); Sun 11:30am–3pm and 4:30–7:30pm (7pm in winter).

EXPLORING BAEZA

Start in **Plaza de la Constitutión,** a beautiful cobbled square containing a fountain adorned by lions and the arches of the **Puerta de Jaén,** through which Carlos V passed in 1526 on his way to marry Isabel of Portugal. Take the left-hand arch and climb the Cuesta de San Gil towards the cathedral. The **Catedral de Santa María** was started shortly after the Reconquest, on top of the town's former mosque (look for remnants of the mosque in the Gothic cloister), but in the mid–16th century, it was reconstructed by the region's master architect, Andrés Vandelvira. Admission is 4€, with audioguide. You can climb the bell tower for views over the town and the olive groves beyond (another great viewpoint is the **mirador** a short distance behind the cathedral, when you reach the city walls to the south of the town). Next to the cathedral stands the stout **Casa Consistoriales Altas,** the old town hall, which bears the coat of arms of queen Juana "the Mad" and her husband, Felipe "the Handsome." As you start to descend the hill along Cuesta de San Felipe, you'll see the 15th-century **Palacio de Jabalquinto,** one of Baeza's finest palaces, with an intricate Isabelline facade reminiscent of Salamanca's House of Shells (p. 203), and the **Antigua Univeridad,** whose walls are covered with antique graffiti. It was traditional for graduating students to write their name and dates on the wall in bull's blood. The buildings are still used for University language courses. Wander back towards the large, elongated town square, **Plaza de la Constitución,** via the ancient **Arco del Barbudo.**

WHERE TO STAY & EAT IN ÚBEDA & BAEZA

Baeza's Plaza de la Constitución has a pleasant arcade of restaurants with tables on the sidewalk in summer. **Los Arcos,** Portales Alhóndiga, 11 (© **66-976-93-36**), offers a hearty set menu at 15€.

Asador de Santiago ★ ANDALUCÍAN   This big restaurant next to Úbeda's Hospital de Santiago often caters for groups attending concerts and conferences there. You can perch at the bar out front and eat good tapas or main dishes or have a full sit-down dinner in the formal dining room. Wood-fire roast meats are the specialty. The slow-cooked lamb and *presa ibérica* (pork shoulder) are excellent, if expensive; service is spot-on. It may however take the prize for the worst painting ever on a restaurant wall—an inexplicable recent rendering of Jonah being swallowed by a whale.

Avenida Cristo Rey, 4. asadordesantiago.com. © **95-375-04-63.** Entrees 18€–26€. Mon–Sat 1:30–4pm and 8:30pm–midnight, Sun 1:30–4pm.

Palacete Sol de Mayo ★★   There can't be too many places on earth where you can rent a holiday home built in the 13th century. This ancient restored Úbeda mansion has Gothic arches, a stone-pillared central courtyard, its own olive press with huge 500-year-old amphorae in the cellar—and four double bedrooms. It is often booked up for grand dinner-party weekends, but during the week you can rent the whole place for a song. Apart from the rather strange modern art on the walls, it is like spending the night in a museum.

Callejón Ventaja, 8 www.apartamentossoldemayo.com. © **60-882-55-23.** 1 unit. 100€–300€.

Parador de Úbeda ★★ ANDALUCÍAN   The huge paved square on which the *parador* stands is one of the most beautiful in all Spain. The hotel stretches along one flank of the Plaza Vázquez de Molina. On one side is the church of El Salvador; on the other, a little box-hedge garden leads to further Renaissance treasures. Even if you don't plan to stay overnight, you should take a look inside this 16th-century palace. The classically plain facade opens up to a double galleried interior courtyard where you can linger for a drink. A grand staircase leads to spacious and exquisitely tiled guestrooms. The whole place exudes a calm nobility. The restaurant feels more rustic, featuring classic regional dishes such *andrajos*

The Parador de Úbeda sits next to the El Salvador church on Úbeda's main square.

de Úbeda (a traditional soupy stew), shoulder of kid, and almond desserts (entrees 16€–24€, set menu 34€). Note that you are not allowed to park in the pedestrianized square, beyond dropping off your luggage, and can quickly get a fine.

Plaza Vázquez de Molina, s/n. www.parador.es. © **95-375-03-45.** 36 units. 100€–200€ double. **Amenities:** Restaurant; bar; free Wi-Fi.

Side Trip to the Alpujarra de Granada ★★

Nowhere in Andalucía retains its Moorish mien like the rustic mountain villages of Granada province on the south flank of the Sierra Nevada. Isolated until the 1950s by poor roads, the architecture echoes Berber houses in northern Morocco. These green valleys and rugged hills terraced with olives and vines are spectacular. The twisting mountain roads are best explored by car, as public transit is spotty.

LANJARÓN ★

The first town of the Western Alpujarra reached along the A-348 is perhaps the least typical. Lanjarón is famous all over Spain for the water bottled from its springs; it's been a spa town since Roman times. Six mineral-rich springs bubble up from its rocks, each with different alleged healing properties. The town revolves around the spa hotel, the **Balneario de Lanjarón,** Avenida de Madrid, 2 (balneariodelanjaron.com; © **95-877-04-54**), built in 1928. Twice a day, residents and visitors line up in the lobby to fill bottles with water from its springs. The spa makes a relaxing retreat, with an eco-friendly restaurant and services from thermal baths to ozone therapy. Double rooms range from 100€ to 150€ depending on the season, treatments from 64€ to 124€.

PAMPANEIRA ★★

The lowest spot in town is 1,000m (3,281 ft.) above sea level, and every street leads steeply up from there. This tiny village of 350 inhabitants is the tourism center for the High Alpujarra; its small shops sell excellent local ham, artisanal chocolate, and colorful, shaggy cotton rugs *(jarapes de Alpujarra)* and other crafts. But the main reason to come here is to hike. Do not set out on a trail without first inquiring about trail conditions at the **Punto de Información Parque Natural de Sierra Nevada,** Plaza de la Libertad, s/n (www.nevadensis.com; © **95-876-31-27;** in summer daily 10am–3pm, in winter Wed–Sun 10am–2pm). The center arranges group hikes and rock-climbing excursions. Hikers are encouraged to follow well-marked trails from Pampaneira to the nearby ridgeline villages of Bubión and Capileira. The distance is about 6km (3¾ miles), with an elevation rise to 1,455m (4,773 ft.), and should take a couple of hours. If you plan to stay overnight, book well ahead for the **Hostal Pampaneira,** Avenida de la Alpujarra, 1 (www.hostalpampaneira.com; © **95-876-30-02**). All 15 simple and cozy rooms have televisions and heating—air-conditioning is never needed. Double rooms start at just 42€ per night.

south from **GRANADA**

"It was a poor village, standing high above the sea, with an immense view in front of it. With its grey box-shaped houses of a battered Corbusier style, all running down the hill and fusing into one another, and its flat clay roofs and smoking chimneys, it suggested something that had been made out of the earth by insects."

A member of Britain's Bloomsbury literary set, **Gerald Brenan** decided after fighting in the First World War that he didn't want to return to a stifling life of privilege in Britain, so he settled in Spain. He chose as his home the remote village of **Yegen** in the Eastern Alpujarra, where life had remained almost unchanged since the Middle Ages. His memoir, *South from Granada*, paints an extraordinary picture of a Spanish mountain village in the 1920s and 1930s, where windows had no glass, witches were still active, and dating rituals involved the *reja*, or window grille. (Brenan memorably wooed a beautiful girl at her window, only to discover when they met that she was a midget and had been standing on a box.) You can visit his house, known locally as **Casa del Inglés** and marked with a ceramic plaque, in the still tiny village.

RONDA ★★★

"Ronda is, indeed, one of those places that stands alone," wrote the English travel writer Lady Tenison in 1850. "I know of nothing to which it can be compared." It is a truly incredible sight. The city is cleft in two by the 120m-deep (390-ft.) Río Guadalevin gorge, known as **El Tajo.** Its houses and hotels hang off each side of the sheer drop, and a daringly tall stone bridge, the **Puente Nuevo,** spans the divide. Located at the eastern edge of the mountain ridges that separate the Costa del Sol from the Cádiz plain, Ronda is the gateway to the Serranía de Ronda—the jagged ridges that harbored bandits and rebels from the Roman era until the 1930s. The Romantic travelers fell in love with Ronda's edginess in the 19th century, and in the 20th, Ernest Hemingway and Orson Welles fell for the drama of its bullring, the oldest in Spain. The city is divided into the old part across the bridge—first Moorish, later aristocratic—and the newer town on the north side of the gorge, begun after the Reconquest in 1485. The old quarter is the obvious draw, with its narrow, rough streets and buildings with a marked Arab influence. But don't ignore the new side, whose gardens offer cliff-edge views that will make you gasp.

Essentials

ARRIVING   Ronda's main **train** station is at Avenida Andalucía (www. renfe.com; ✆ **91-232-03-20**). There are three trains a day from Granada. The trip takes 2½ to 3 hours and costs 20€ one-way. There is one direct train per day from Málaga, taking 2½ hours and costing 15€. Two trains daily connect Madrid and Ronda. The trip takes around 4 hours and costs 76€ one-way.

The main **bus** station is at Plaza Concepción García Redondo, s/n (© **61-690-94-83**). There are five buses a day from Sevilla, taking around 2½ hours and costing 20€ one-way. From Málaga, three buses a day take 2½ hours, costing 17€ one-way. From Marbella, there are seven buses a day, taking 1 hour and costing 9€ one-way.

By **car** from Sevilla, take the A-375 and then the A-374. From Granada, take the A-92 heading west. From Málaga, take the A-357 and then A-367; from Marbella head northwest on the A-397. The drive to Ronda is not difficult in any direction, but it is best to avoid driving in town. Taking the exit to Ronda North will bring you to the newer part of town where plenty of public parking is available.

VISITOR INFORMATION   The **tourist office** on Paseo de Blas Infante, s/n (www.turismoderonda.es; © **95-218-71-19**), is open Monday to Friday 10am to 6pm (7pm in summer), Saturday 10am to 5pm, and Sunday 10am to 2:30pm.

Exploring Ronda

There is plenty to see and do in Ronda, but by far the most impressive sight is the town's extraordinary setting. Make sure to leave plenty of time just to wander and take it all in. There are many miradors, cliff paths, and places to pause for a drink or lunch to marvel at the view. You're likely to start on the **Plaza de España,** next to the *parador,* and cross the **Puente Nuevo** on foot into the old town. Climb the main **Calle Armiñán** and explore the palace-strewn streets which cluster around it on both sides. After that, cross back into the newer **Mercadillo** quarter for the **Plaza de Toros,** the charming **Plaza de Socorro,** and more stunning views from the **Mirador de Ronda.**

Baños Arabes ★★ HISTORIC SITE   Off to the left as you climb Calle Armiñán, close to the town's two old bridges (Puente Viejo and Puente de San Miguel), Ronda's 13th-century Arab baths are among the best preserved in Spain, although recent restoration has given their distinctive humps some incongruous glass covers. Inside, the structure is wonderfully intact, with barrel vaults, octagonal brick columns, and star-shaped skylights, which the glass protects from the elements. In the style of Roman baths, they include cold, warm, and hot rooms, through which bathers would rotate several times. A 5-minute animated film gives an excellent explanation of the mechanism used to deliver and heat the water. Calle Molino de Alarcón, 11. www.rondatoday.com/rondas-arab-baths. © **65-695-09-37.** Admission 3€. Mon–Fri 10am–6pm (7pm in summer); weekends 10am–3pm. Free on Sun.

Centro de Interpretación del Puente Nuevo ★ MUSEUM   Ronda's greatest architectural achievement is its skyscraper-high bridge spanning the terrifying El Tajo gorge. The town's citizens petitioned the crown for a new bridge in 1542, but 2 centuries passed before technology

not just **FOR THE KIDS**

As you walk through the old town of Ronda, you'll see signs advertising a couple of private museums which at first sight look a little trashy. Both, however, are worth a second look.

Museo Lara ★★, Calle Armiñán, 29 (www.museolara.org; © **95-287-12-63**), displays the extraordinary collection of Juan Antonio Lara Jurado, who has spent a lifetime amassing a vast cabinet of curiosities including guns, clocks, cameras, opera glasses, and scientific instruments. There are archaeological artifacts, suits of lights, old wine barrels, and gruesome exhibits dealing with the Inquisition and Witches (the latter includes a "consolation device" that will take some explaining to the children). The museum is open daily 11am to 7pm and costs 4€, free for children under 10. Just up the street, the **Museo del Bandolero ★**,

Calle Armiñán, 65 (www.museo bandolero.com; © **95-287-77-85**), recounts the history and myths of the bandits who used to hide out in the mountains surrounding Ronda. These Robin Hood characters, with names like El Tragabuches and El Tempranillo, fired the imaginations of the 19th-century Romantic travelers. The last bandit, known as Pasos Largos (Long Legs), was finally shot dead by the Guardia Civil in them thar hills in 1934. The museum is open 11am to 6:30pm Sunday to Friday, Saturday 11am to 7pm. Admission is 3.75€ for adults, free for children under 8.

had advanced enough to attempt it. The first bridge on this spot opened in 1739—and collapsed 2 years later, killing 50 people. The current 98m (320-ft.) structure was started in 1759 and took 34 years to build, requiring the intervention of master architect José Martin de Aldehuela to complete the job. The visitor center is inside the structure of the bridge itself and is worth a visit as much for its setting and views of the turbid waters as for the exhibits. The interactive screens don't offer a great deal of information but show some interesting old pictures of Ronda and its extraordinary bridge.

Plaza España s/n (entry next to the parador). www.rondatoday.com/history-of-the-puente-nuevo. © **64-996-53-38.** Admission 2€, 1€ seniors, kids under 14 free. Mon–Fri 10am–6pm; Sat–Sun 10am–3pm.

Palacio de Mondragón ★ MUSEUM Once the private home of the last Moorish king, Abomelic, this charming palace was renovated after the Reconquest to receive Isabel and Fernando. Later changes, and the facade, date from the 18th century. Inside there is a trio of courtyards in different architectural styles—Mudéjar and Castilian—featuring Moorish mosaics and wonderful views of El Tajo and the Serranía de Ronda. The Noble Hall has a beautiful, highly decorated wooden ceiling. The museum upstairs doesn't have many artifacts, but it does have a remarkably detailed explanation—in Spanish and English—of the history of settlers in the region, with life-size models of cave dwellings and dolmens. Rather oddly, it finishes just as Moorish rule begins.

Plaza Mondragón, s/n www.museoderonda.es. ℗ **95-287-08-18.** Admission 3.50€. Mon–Fri 10am–6pm (7pm in summer), Sat–Sun 10am–3pm. Free entry Tues from 3pm for EU citizens.

Plaza de Toros ★★ BULLRING/MUSEUM   Ronda's majestic bull-ring, built in 1785, is the oldest in Spain. It is the setting for the annual **Feria Goyesca,** which takes place in early September in honor of Ronda's own Pedro Romero (1754–1839), the legendary matador and inspiration for Goya's famous bullfight etchings and paintings. During the festival, *toreros* dress in the 18th-century costumes depicted by Goya. If you visit only one bullfighting museum while in Spain, make it the **Museo de la Tauromaquia,** set within the curved halls of the ring. Exhibits and a good audioguide document the history of Ronda's two great bullfighting dynasties, the Romero and Ordóñez families. Francisco Romero, born in 1700, invented the *muleta,* the red cape used in the last phase of the bullfight. His grandson Pedro killed more than 5,000 bulls during a 30-year career without serious injury, a feat never surpassed. In the modern era, Cayetano Ordóñez and his son Antonio were immortalized by Ernest Hemingway in *The Sun Also Rises* and *The Dangerous Summer,* respectively.

Ronda's Plaza de Toros.

The museum shop sells back-number posters for the Corrida Goyesca, designed by famous Spanish artists, including Picasso.

Calle Virgen de la Paz, 15. www.rmcr.org. ✆ **95-287-41-32.** Admission 7€, 8.50€ with audioguide. Daily 10am–6pm (8pm in summer), except during bullfight festival.

Where to Stay in Ronda

Ronda has a wide range of good lodgings, many with spectacular views. Rates are generally reasonable, but spike at Easter and during the bullfight festival.

EXPENSIVE

Parador de Ronda ★★★   As is so often the case, the *parador* has the best location in town: perched right on the edge of El Tajo gorge next to Puente Nuevo. It occupies the former town hall, a stern arcaded building with a clock at the center of its facade. The interior style is modern, with an airy atrium and simple, elegant guest rooms with wood floors and subdued colors. Nothing distracts from the extraordinary views, which are the point of staying here. Rooms look across the thrilling ravine to the old city or toward the bullring on the other side. Many have tiled private

Ronda's handsome parador sits right on the edge of El Tajo gorge, with spectacular views.

balconies, and all guests can enjoy the bar terrace, gardens, and swimming pool at the edge of El Tajo.

Plaza de España s/n. www.parador.es. (℗ **95-287-75-00.** 79 units. 100€–250€ double. Parking 18€. **Amenities:** Restaurant; bar; room service; terrace; outdoor pool; free Wi-Fi.

MODERATE

Hotel Catalonia Reina Victoria ★★

This elegant spa hotel, built in 1906 by an Englishman, is the last word in genteel comfort. Set in the newer north side of the town, a walk away from the historic quarter, it feels like a place of retreat. The Bohemian poet Rainer Maria Rilke stayed here (in room 208) for several months in 1912, in search of inspiration; a small museum here displays his writing desk, and there's a statue of him in the gardens. A hundred years later, a thorough renovation has given the airy guest rooms a clean-lined contemporary feel, fitting its new role as a spa and wellness center. The scenery from its clifftop setting is superb, but bear in mind that it isn't the classic view of the El Tajo ravine.

Calle Jerez, 25. www.hoteles-catalonia.com. (℗ **95-287-12-40.** 95 units. 100€–200€ double. Parking 15€. **Amenities:** Restaurant; bar; room service; outdoor pool; terrace; spa; gym; free Wi-Fi.

Hotel Catalonia ★★

Ronda's second Catalonia hotel has spectacular views of a different kind. Recently renovated and beautifully furnished, this grand corner building sits opposite the bullring, and many of its rooms, its restaurant, and its rooftop pool have panoramic views over the huge arena and the countryside beyond. If you plan to stay here during the Goyesca bullfight season in early September, you'll need to book many months in advance and expect to pay dearly for that privileged vantage point. Food and service are excellent.

Calle Virgen de la Paz, 16. www.hoteles-catalonia.com. (℗ **95-287-75-00.** 80 units. 90€–200€ double. Parking 22€. **Amenities:** Restaurant; bar; room service; outdoor pool; terrace; free Wi-Fi.

INEXPENSIVE

Enfrente Arte ★★

Located close to the Baños Arabes in the old part of town, Enfrente Arte looks like just another small hotel on the outside. Inside, this Belgian-run place is one of the most memorable lodgings in Andalucía. The style is predominantly '70s pop-art, with a scattering of Moroccan hippy trail. It's all bright orange and Mediterranean blue, mod plastic furniture, mosaics, fishponds, and stepping stones. The individually decorated rooms might feature a huge orange hand as a chair, or a wrought-iron four-poster, and there's a higgledy-piggledy pool terrace with countryside views. Help yourself to drinks at the honesty bar and don't miss the delicious cooked breakfast, where you pick up plates and utensils from the trunk of a sawn-in-half Seat 500.

Calle Real, 40. www.enfrentearte.com. (℗ **95-287-90-88.** 14 units. 80€–150€ double. No parking. **Amenities:** Bar; café; outdoor pool; terrace; live music; free Wi-Fi.

Apartamentos Ronda-Centro ★ Perfectly located just on the new town side of the Puente Nueva, these self-catering apartments offer exceptional value. The compact, air-conditioned rooms are simply and cleanly decorated; each has a kitchenette, washing machine, microwave, and toaster. Some have views over Plaza España and the bridge, others have private terraces with mountain views. Prices start from as little as 70€ in the low season. They also have the distinct advantage of being next door to Ronda's finest restaurant, **Bardal** (see below).

Calle José Aparicio, 1A. www.apartamentosrondacentro.com. ⓒ **60-819-09-99.** 8 units. 70€–120€ double. Parking 12€. **Amenities:** Kitchen; washing machine; terrace; free Wi-Fi.

Where to Eat in Ronda

EXPENSIVE

Bardal ★★★ ANDALUCÍAN Occupying the same space as the now defunct star restaurant Tragabuches, chef Benito Gómez's restaurant is one of Andalucía's finest—the standard of cooking, presentation, and service is simply astounding. Just two lengthy tasting menus are available, with wine pairing on top. It's a succession of miniature masterpieces that draw on Andalucían roots, but surprise again and again with their inventive flavor combinations, such as almond milk with eggplant, sardine, and herring roe. The decor and design, behind an unassuming exterior, is as exquisite as the food and wine. A deposit is required when making a booking, but you'd be crazy not to show up.

Calle José Aparicio, 1. restaurantebardal.com. ⓒ **95-219-02-91.** Tasting menus 85€ and 100€, wine pairings add 45€ or 50€. Tues–Sat 1:30–3:30pm and 8:30–10:30pm.

MODERATE

Casa María ★★ ANDALUCÍAN When you walk into this tiny family-run bar right at the top of the old town, host Elias Vega will tell you this is a different kind of restaurant. There is no menu, just a set price of 30€ for whatever he and Isabel Alba prepare that day from the market—you can choose between fish or meat. The bar counter is stocked with fresh ingredients and spices. A huge slice of bread with tomatoes and olive oil will get you started. The cooking is simple, fresh, and excellent, particularly the perfectly grilled beef and pork, which might come with a spicy Romesco sauce. After a sticky pudding, peruse the fine selection of whiskies and brandies. There are just four tables, so a reservation is strongly advised. And arrive hungry.

Plaza Ruedo Alameda, 27. ⓒ **95-108-36-63.** Set menu 30€. Daily noon–4pm and 7–10:30pm.

Restaurante Pedro Romero ★★ ANDALUCÍAN This famous restaurant across from the bullring is at the traditional end of the scale, but the cuisine is more complex than the matador photos and stuffed bull's head might suggest. Well-presented dishes include mountain recipes like wild partridge stew, confit rabbit, and Ronda *migas* (fried breadcrumbs with sausage and garlic). There is also a surprisingly good selection of fish. Less surprising is Pedro Romero's signature dish, *rabo de toro* (oxtail). Make a reservation if you expect to eat here on the day of a bullfight, when it will be packed.

Virgen de la Paz 18. www.rpedroromero.com. ✆ **95-287-11-10.** Entrees 18€–25€; set menus 18€ and 27€. Mon–Sat noon–3:30pm and 7–10:30pm, Sun noon–3:30pm. Closed Mon June–Aug.

Tragatá ★★ SPANISH   To sample the Benito Gómez magic on a budget, head to his brightly lit tapas bar on Calle Nueva. Each dish is little more than a bite, but they're all so good you may find yourself trying the whole day's selection. The classics are here—cold *salmorejo* soup, homemade croquettes, *bocadillo de calamar* (spicy squid sandwich)—but everything is prepared and presented in fine dining style. Main courses have an Asian fusion twist—try Thai sea bass or duck tataki—and there are some interesting, if expensive, cured fish tapas, such as *mojama de atún roja* (red tuna carpaccio), served with apple and roast almonds.

Calle Nueva, 4. tragata.com. ✆ **95-287-72-09.** Tapas 2.75€–4€; entrees 10€–22€. Tues–Sat 1:15pm–3:45pm and 8–11pm; Sun 1:15–3:45pm.

INEXPENSIVE

Entrevinos ★★ ANDALUCÍAN   A great place for lunch or evening tapas, this busy wine bar has a selection of more than 100 local wines, enticingly displayed behind the counter. Take a seat at the bar and order a selection of delicious and imaginative tapas—garlic mushrooms, squid in a nest of black pasta, caramelized red peppers—and ask the barman to

prehistoric CAVE PAINTINGS

The prehistoric paintings at **Cueva de la Pileta ★★** (www.cuevadelapileta.org; ✆ **68-713-33-38**), 25km (16 miles) southwest of Ronda, compare with those at the better-known caves of Altamira in northern Spain (p. 622). In the wilds of the Serranía de Ronda, José Bullón Lobato, grandfather of the present owners, discovered the cave in 1905. More than a mile long and filled with oddly shaped stalagmites and stalactites, it also contains fossilized human and animal skeletons. The paintings depict animals and mysterious symbols in red, black, and ocher. A highlight is the **chamber of the fish,** which contains a wall painting of a black seal-like creature about 1m (3¼ ft.) long. This chamber, the innermost part of the cave, ends in a precipice that drops vertically nearly 75m (246 ft.). Guided visits are limited to 25 people and must be reserved in advance. There are around five scheduled tours a day, more at weekends and fewer in winter. They last an hour and cost 10€ for adults and 5€ for ages 5 to 10. The caves sit in a valley parallel to Ronda's, separated by a steep range of hills. It's easiest to get here by car, or you can take the train or bus to Benaoján and walk from there, about 4km (2½ miles).

recommend a glass or two of the reasonably priced wine. Don't miss the hot chocolate pudding for dessert.

Calle Pozo, 2. ✆ **65-858-29-76.** Tapas 1.50€–2.50€; entrees 6€–10€. Mon 8pm–midnight, Tues–Sat 12:30–4pm and 8pm–midnight. Closed Sun.

La Duquesa de Parcent ★ ANDALUCÍAN   This perfectly situated restaurant, overlooking the gorge back towards the parador, gets bad reviews for being a tourist trap. It is, but you can beat the trap. First, dart in and see if one of the seven tables on the balcony is free. If not, skip it. If you can get a table, ignore the overpriced à la carte menu and the terrible pizzas and ask about the *platos combinados,* which are advertised outside but don't appear on the menu. There are four choices: *lomo* (pork loin), *pollo* (chicken), *rosada* (pink fish), or *albondigas* (meatballs), all served with a fried egg, freshly made French fries, and a few fresh vegetables. Throw in a glass of wine, bread, oil, and a coffee, and you can have a good simple lunch with one of the most exhilarating views in town for less than 20 euros. Take cash—the card machine never works. If all goes well, you may even get a free *chupito* digestif.

Calle Tenorio, 12. ✆ **95-287-1965.** Set menu 12.50€. Daily 11am–10:30pm.

A DRIVING TOUR OF THE PUEBLOS BLANCOS

Scattered across the provinces of Cádiz and Málaga, the villages and towns of inland southwest Andalucía are called the **Pueblos Blancos** (white towns) because their houses settle on the mountainsides like snow. If you have a car you can visit a handful in the course of a day and take in some of Spain's most dramatic scenery along the way. Several towns in this area are tagged *de la Frontera* because this was once the frontier between the Christians and Muslims. Although the Reconquest eventually prevailed, it is the Moorish influence that makes these towns so appealing, with their labyrinths of narrow cobbled streets, fortress walls, and whitewashed houses with wrought-iron grilles *(rejas).* The drive is not difficult, but the roads do twist and turn, and climb steeply in places. Lodging and eating options are limited, but we have included a few recommendations for those who want stay longer for hiking, outdoor activities, and even trout-fishing. The best times to visit are in spring, when the wildflowers are in bloom, and in the fall.

Zahara de la Sierra ★

From Ronda, take the A-374 northwest, following the signs toward Algodonales, a village best known for **Fly Spain,** Calle Sierra, 41 (www.flyspain.co.uk; ✆ **65-173-67-18**), a first-rate paragliding center. Once past Montecorto, take a left signposted to Zahara de la Sierra, the most perfect of the province's fortified hilltop pueblos. The drive from Ronda is about 40 minutes.

The white houses of Zahara de la Sierra.

Zahara lies at the edge of the 50,000-hectare (125,000-acre) **Parque Natural Sierra de Grazalema.** Shaded with pine trees and oak forests, it is an important habitat for griffon vultures. Before hiking in the park, visit the **Information Office** at Plaza del Rey, 1 (www.zaharadelasierra.es; © **95-612-31-14**), open Tuesday to Sunday from 10am to 2pm in summer, and from 4 to 6pm in spring and fall There are five major routes; for most you'll need to ask permission at the office, which also organizes horseback riding, canoeing, and bike trips.

The village itself exudes civic pride. Its neatly arranged streets of whitewashed houses rise to a heavily restored Muslim fortress on the outcrop above. You can climb to the castle via the zigzagging path or wooden staircase near the Arco de la Villa hotel. Allow a good 20 minutes to reach the top, more than 500m (1,640 ft.) above sea level. It's worth the effort. Once on the battlements, you can see a number of white villages arrayed across the landscape. When you get back to the cobbled center of the village, you'll have earned coffee and a snack. Join the locals at **Rincon de la Ermita,** Calle San Juan, 14 (© **66-543-68-02**), for a brown-bread *tostada* with tomato and the cloudy local olive oil. When you leave town, heading south on the Carretera de Grazalema, drop in at **El Vínculo** (www.molinoelvinculo.com; © **95-612-30-02**), a mill that has been producing olive oil since 1755.

WHERE TO STAY & EAT IN ZAHARA DE LA SIERRA

Arco de la Villa ★   Tugasa, the rural tourism arm of the province of Cádiz, built and maintains this little stone inn on the west side of the village. Rooms are basic but spacious; the beds are comfortable, and the tiled bathrooms have abundant hot water. There is a restaurant with a good set menu at 15€. If you plan to hike in the area, Arco de la Villa makes a good base.

Camino Nazarí, s/n. www.tugasa.com. © **95-612-32-30.** 17 units. 69€ double. Free parking. **Amenities:** Restaurant; bar; free Wi-Fi in public areas.

Grazalema ★★

The drive from Zahara to Grazalema is one of the most spectacular in all Spain, but the roads are steep and narrow. From Zahara, follow the CA-9104 heading south. You will cross the high point of the mountains at the dramatic **Puerto de las Palomas** (Pass of the Doves), with an elevation of 1,356m (4,450 ft.). When you reach the junction with the main A-372, follow the signs east into Grazalema. The 17km (10-mile) drive takes about half an hour—longer if you stop for photos.

Grazalema comes as a surprise when you round a turn and first spot it nestling in the valley of the Río Guadalete. It was founded in the 8th century by Berbers from Saddina, a peaceable lot who chose a green valley over an arid peak and never fortified the town. As a result, Christian and Muslim armies passed them by. It is the wettest town in Spain, receiving 2,160mm (85 in.) of rain a year. The **tourist office,** Plaza de España, 11 (turismograzalema.com; © **95-613-20-52**), is open Monday to Friday 10am to 2pm and 4 to 8pm, Saturday and Sunday 10am to 2pm. It hands out hiking trail maps and serves as a clearing house for guide services.

Towering limestone crags overlook the town. For the best views, climb to a belvedere near the 18th-century chapel of San José. Grazalema takes pride in its idiosyncratic bull-running festival, **Toro de Cuerda,** dated from Celtic times, in which the animal is tethered on a rope. A sculpture on the main street celebrates the festival, which takes place every July. The village is also known for its local crafts, especially handwoven wool blankets and rugs. It's a 5-minute walk from Plaza de España to **Artesanía Textil de Grazalema,** Carretera de Ronda (mantasde grazalema.com; © **95-613-20-08**). At the small factory, open to the public, you can buy blankets and ponchos made from local wool using handoperated looms and antique machinery. It's open weekdays from 8am to 6:30pm (until 2pm on Fri; closed in Aug).

WHERE TO STAY & EAT IN GRAZALEMA

Hotel Villa de Grazalema ★★   Built by the provincial tourism agency to encourage family vacations in Grazalema, this little complex has simple rooms and apartments with a garden swimming pool and views of the village. It feels like a junior *parador,* and the subsidized prices are terrific value. The restaurant has a 15€ menu whose specialty is locally caught trout stuffed with mountain ham. The complex is an easy 10-minute walk to the center of Grazalema village.

Carretera Olivar, s/n. www.villa-turistica-grazalema.com. ✆ **95-613-22-13.** 24 units, 38 apartments. 45€–75€ doubles; 75€–140€ apartments. Free parking. **Amenities:** Restaurant; bar; outdoor pool; self-service laundry; free Wi-Fi.

Cádiz El Chico ★★ ANDALUCÍAN   This grand old building on the main square was Grazalema's first proper restaurant and remains the best in town. It made its name among Spanish gastronomes by reviving the region's traditional lamb and kid stews and persuading local shepherds to sell it their best produce rather than shipping to big-city markets. Try the *sopa de Grazalema* to start: bread, garlic, diced ham, sausage, and egg, a meal in itself. After that, perhaps the *paletilla de cordero lechal* (slow-cooked shoulder of lamb), venison in red wine, or wild boar with raspberries—mountain cooking at its best.

Plaza de España, 8. ✆ **95-613-20-67.** Entrees 10€–20€. Set menu 16€. Daily 1–4pm and 8pm–midnight.

El Bosque ★

After the mountain drive from Zahara to Grazalema, the relatively flat westward drive to El Bosque feels easy. It is 20km (12 miles) through deep forest on the A-372. The town here is of less interest, but it makes an ideal base for hiking the beautiful woods and streams. The **information center** (Calle Federico García Lorca, 1) handles access to the Sierra de Grazalema natural park from the western side; you will need permission before you set off. It's open mid-June to mid-September Tuesday to Saturday 8am to 2pm; in spring and fall hours are 4 to 6pm. Next to the tourist office is **Quesos El Bosqueño,** Calle Antonio Machado (www.quesoselbosque.com; ✆ **95-671-61-56**), an excellent cheese shop with a small museum, whose *payoyo* cheeses have won prizes among the world's best. If you plan to stay over for hiking, **Las Truchas,** Avenida Diputación, s/n (www.tugasa.com; ✆ **95-671-60-61**), is another *parador*-style hotel and restaurant run by the provincial authorities, with clean, simply furnished rooms from 60€. Even if you decide not to hike in the area, follow the stream across the road from Las Truchas for a 5- to 10-minute stroll. This icy waterway is the **Río Majaceite,** the southernmost trout stream in Europe.

Ubrique ★

At this point you may want to press on to Arcos de la Frontera, but if you have a weakness for leather handbags, a diversion to Ubrique—15 minutes south on the A-373—is a must. The largest of the white towns, it is picturesque as you arrive, and a hive of industry in the center. Finding a parking space can be a challenge. A center of the leather trade since Moorish times, in recent years Ubrique has fashioned a role for itself as a producer of handbags to high-end designers. Some of the biggest and most expensive international brands, including Louis Vuitton, Gucci, and Chanel, have leather goods made here (although the factories themselves are sworn to secrecy). Almost every shop is a leather goods outlet with high-quality items and real bargains. Check the website (www.ubrique turismo.es/zona-de-interes-artesanal) or pick up a list at the **Tourist Office,** Calle Moreno de Mora, 19 (© **95-646-49-00**), open weekdays 10am to 2pm and 4 to 7pm, Saturday 11am to 2pm and 4 to 7pm, Sunday 11am to 2pm.

Arcos de la Frontera ★

If you can, arrange to reach Arcos de la Frontera from the south east, taking the C-334. The views as you approach the town along the twisting Guadalete river are fantastic: a plunging sandstone cliff, church towers perched at the edge, whitewashed houses tumbling down its sides. This old Moorish stronghold is a highlight of the Pueblos Blancos and its *parador,* which you'll see hanging out over the cliff, is a dramatic spot for an overnight stay.

Known to the Romans as Arco Briga, the town became an independent Moorish *taifa,* or kingdom, in the 11th century. As with all the towns

Small whitewashed houses line the streets of the hilltop town of Arcos de la Frontera.

bearing the name Frontera, it was on the frontline between Arab and Christian forces; it fell to Alfonso X in 1264. You'll spend most of your time on the narrow medieval streets of the **Medina**—unless you're staying at the *parador* it's best to park on the Plaza de España and walk up the hill. The **tourist office** at Calle Cuesta de Belén, 5 (turismoarcos.com; ✆ **95-670-22-64**), occupies a lovely old palace on the way. It's open Monday to Saturday 9:30am to 2pm and 3 to 7:30pm, Sunday 10am to 2pm.

The old town's main square, **Plaza de Cabildo,** sits at the top. From the **Balcón de Arcos** you can see the other end of the view you had as you arrived: mile after mile across the fertile plain of the river Guadalete. Behind you is **Santa María de la Asunción,** a 15th-century church built—as was so often the case—on top of the old mosque. Its Plateresque western facade is magnificent, but the bell tower—rebuilt after a 1755 earthquake—is something of an under-achievement. It was originally intended to rival Sevilla's Giralda, but a lack of funds meant the church had to settle for an unfinished 37m-high (120-ft.) tower. Inside, there's a mixture of styles: Gothic vaulting, a Renaissance altarpiece, and a Baroque choir. The church is open Monday to Friday from 10am to 12:45pm and 4 to 6:45pm, Saturday 10am to 1:30pm. Admission is 2€, or 3€ for a combined ticket which also gives access to the **Iglesia de San Pedro.** The Moorish-era castle on the main square is privately owned and closed to the public.

The **Iglesia de San Pedro** sits right at the edge of the cliff beyond the parador. As well as lavish 15th-century gilding, it contains a couple of interesting paintings by Francisco Pacheco, tutor and father-in-law of Velázquez, and some rather spooky relics. You can climb its bell tower for more amazing views, although that's not for the faint-hearted. It's open Monday to Friday 10:30am to 2pm and 3:30 to 6:30pm, Saturday 10:30am to 2pm. On your way back, drop into the **Convento de las Mercederías** (Plazuela de Botica, 2), where the cloistered nuns sell almond cookies at a *retorno,* a revolving window in the wall.

WHERE TO EAT & STAY IN ARCOS DE LA FRONTERA

Bar Alcaraván ★ ANDALUCÍAN   The most atmospheric bar in town lies through a flowerpot-festooned entrance in cellars below the Plaza del Cabildo. It's a friendly place for good value tapas. Along with plenty of hearty meat and sausage plates, it does a good line in seafood. Despite being far from the coast Arcos has a strong tradition of eating fish, which is rushed up the hill from the port of El Puerto de Santa María. Try roast peppers with mackerel *(melva)* or *albondigas de chocos y gambas,* cuttlefish balls with prawns. In summer you can eat on the steps outside.

Calle Nueva 1. ✆ **95-690-72-93.** Tapas and *raciones* 4€–12€. Daily 1–5pm and 8pm–midnight.

A welcoming lounge in the Parador Casa del Corregidor.

Parador Casa del Corregidor ★★ The *parador* has the best location in town, holding down one side of the Plaza del Cabildo. Once the headquarters of the king's magistrate, this 18th-century building has a modern wing that hangs over the cliff edge; its guest rooms have terraces with exhilarating views of the plain far below. The restaurant has great views too, and a good-value sharing menu at 21€ per person, plus interesting stew-based specialties of Arcos. Even if you aren't staying at the *parador* you can still order a drink on the terrace.

Plaza del Cabildo, s/n. www.parador.es. *Ⓒ* **95-670-05-00.** 24 units. 90€–145€ double. Limited free parking on plaza. **Amenities:** Restaurant; bar; free Wi-Fi.

JEREZ DE LA FRONTERA ★★★

Jerez is not the region's most beautiful nor architecturally rich city, but you'd be hard pressed to find anywhere that better embodies the spirit of Andalucía. This busy, commercial hub is defined by three quintessentially Spanish things: sherry, horses, and flamenco. You can experience them all to the highest standard during even a short stay.

The pedestrianized plazas and cobbled streets around the old town are dotted with stylish restaurants, tiny sherry depots *(tabancos),* and gypsy-infused flamenco bars. Upon this stage, smartly dressed *jerezanos* stroll with an aristocratic ease. They know they've got the good things in life sorted out, even if the city's wealthiest days are behind it. The soundtrack is the quick-paced *bulería,* the cheeky form of flamenco which originated in the *barrios* of San Miguel and Santiago. Jerez is the perfect base from which to explore the countryside and towns which make up the celebrated Sherry Triangle.

Essentials

ARRIVING Several airlines offer direct **flights** to Jerez, from Madrid, Barcelona, Palma, London, Frankfurt, Düsseldorf, and Munich. For details, visit www.aena.es, or call ✆ **91-321-10-00.** The airport on Carretera Jerez-Sevilla is about 11km (6¾ miles) northeast of the city center (follow the signs to Sevilla). A *cercanía* train runs from the airport to downtown Jerez.

There are 15 **trains** a day from Sevilla, which take an hour and cost 11.50€ to 20€ one-way. A dozen trains from Madrid arrive daily; tickets cost 50€ to 80€, and the trip takes 3½ to 4 hours. The beautifully tiled Mudéjar revival railway station, on Plaza de la Estación (www.renfe.com; ✆ **91-232-03-20**), is a landmark in its own right. **Bus** connections are also frequent; the bus terminal is adjacent to the train station on Calle Cartuja, a short walk east of Plaza del Arenal.

Jerez is easy to get to by **car;** it lies on the toll highway (AP-4/E-5) connecting Sevilla with Cádiz. Take exit 78. There's plenty of underground parking in town, including a huge lot under Plaza del Arenal.

VISITOR INFORMATION The main **tourist office** is on Plaza del Arenal, s/n (www.turismojerez.com; ✆ **95-633-88-74**). It's open in winter Monday to Friday 8:30am to 3pm and 4 to 6:30pm, weekends 9am to 3pm. Summer hours are Monday to Friday 9am to 3pm and 5 to 7pm, weekends 9am to 2:30pm (Aug weekends 8am–4pm). Helpfully, it posts a weekly digest of what's on in the window, including details of free walking tours, and you can pick up flyers for most of the things you'd like to see, do, eat, and drink.

EVENTS Jerez hosts many festivals and fairs relating to its key attractions. The **Feria de Caballo** (horse fair), usually held in the second week of May, began as a horse-trading gathering in the Middle Ages and has evolved into a week of general revelry which vies with Sevilla's Feria. Hotel prices spike accordingly. Around the beginning of September, the **Fiesta de la Vendimia** (Harvest Festival) celebrates the end of the grape harvest with a ceremonial trampling on the steps of the cathedral; the **Fiesta de la Bulería** flamenco festival kicks off around the same time. Since 1987, the Spanish motorcycle grand prix has been held at the **Circuito de Jerez** in early May. On that weekend, tens of thousands of leather-clad bikers from all over the world roar into town.

Exploring Jerez de la Frontera

TOURING THE BODEGAS ★★

The **Plaza de Arenal** isn't a particularly interesting square in itself, but it is the heart of the town, where all the winding, cobbled streets eventually lead. Good-natured beggars recline on the benches and of an evening there might be a children's flamenco performance, watched by proud parents. The plaza's cafes are okay for a cooling drink, but you can do much better nearby. People tend to meet at the equestrian statue of the 1920s dictator and son of Jerez, **Miguel Primo de Rivera** (1870–1930), for whom some locals still have a sneaking regard.

If you've come this far, chances are you'll want to get straight to the sherry houses. There are scores of bodegas all over town and almost all of them offer tours and tastings. Some people are a little sniffy about **Gonzalez Byass** (see below), makers of the ubiquitous **Tío Pepe** ("you can drink that anywhere," a guide at one of the smaller houses told us), but a visit to Jerez without calling on Tío Pepe would be a bit like going to Venice and ignoring the canals. It's a short walk, signposted from the Plaza del Arenal.

Besides the bodegas reviewed below, there are plenty of others to visit, tracing the histories of the predominantly British families who

Celebrity-signed barrels of Tío Pepe sherry.

THE STORY OF sherry

They've been making wine in and around Jerez since the Phoenicians first brought vines here 3,000 years ago. The city's Moorish name was Sherish, from which the names of both Jerez and sherry derive. A fortified wine, it is made from two white grape varieties—Palomino Fino and, for the sweeter wines, Pedro Ximénez—and to be called sherry it must be produced within the wine region which stretches between the towns of **Jerez, Sanlúcar de Barrameda,** and **Puerto de Santa Maria.** It's this area's dry, chalky soil, known as *albariza,* and the way the wine is made, that makes sherry so distinctive.

The *solera* system ensures a consistent quality by aging the wine in three rows of barrels. The top row contains the youngest wine, which is then blended with that in the lower rows to produce the finished article from the bottom barrels. Sherry has no vintage—each bottle contains wine from several different years.

A bodega tasting tour will help you appreciate the many different styles. *Fino* is pale and fresh, produced when a yeasty froth called *flor* forms on top of the wine in the barrel. **Manzanilla** is a *fino* produced in the town of Sanlúcar, where aging in the sea air gives it a salty tang. **Amontillado** is a *fino* that has been exposed to oxygen, giving it a toffee color and nutty character. **Oloroso** is a darker and richer style on which flor doesn't develop because more alcohol has been added. All of these are naturally very dry; sweeter styles are created by adding sweet wine or must. **Cream** is the blend traditionally favored by the British, while **Pedro Ximénez** is the sweetest of all, a black, raisiny syrup.

Sherry's international appeal owes much to Sir Francis Drake. When he destroyed the Spanish fleet at Cádiz in 1587, he made off with 2,900 barrels of sherry, sparking a British love affair with the drink which has endured ever since. Take care when tasting: All sherry is significantly stronger than table wine, ranging from 15% to 22% alcohol.

founded famous cellars here. Some also offer equestrian and flamenco shows and paired menus. They include **Harveys** (www.grupoemperador spain.com), **Sandeman** (www.sandeman.com), **Alvaro Domecq** (www.alvarodomecq.com), **Lustau** (www.lustau.es), and **Williams and Humbert** (www.williams-humbert.com). You can pick up their flyers at the tourist office.

Bodegas Gonzalez Byass ★★ WINE TOUR   The world's best-known sherry maker's bodega is so large (it covers 92 hectares/227 acres) that part of the tour is made aboard one of those motorized tourist trains. Before you set out, however, there's a 20-minute video—narrated by an actor playing **Tío Pepe** himself—to give you a primer on this robust wine and brandy dynasty. The tour is rich in history and anecdote, including the **Apostoles** *solera* built for the visit of Queen Isabel in 1862; the vine-shaded **Calle de Ciegos,** billed as Jerez's loveliest street; numerous barrels signed by Spanish and international celebrities; the famous sherry-drinking mice (now just a photograph, a glass, and a little ladder); and the world's largest weather vane. After that, you can taste a selection of mainstream sherries, paired with tapas for an extra charge, and then *salida por tienda* (exit via the gift shop), for an impressive demonstration of marketing featuring Tío Pepe's sombrero-wearing, guitar-wielding logo.

Calle Manuel María González, 12. www.bodegastiopepe.com. ✆ **95-635-70-00.** Admission 15.50€, 7.75€ ages 5–17. No reservation required. Tours in English Mon–Sat noon, 1, 2, and 5:15pm; Sun noon, 1, and 2pm.

Bodegas Tradición ★★★ WINE TOUR   Much more refined than the Tío Pepe operation, this boutique house specializes in sherries classified as V.O.S. (aged 20 years or more) and V.O.R.S. (aged more than 30 years). The Rivero family who owns the bodega has amassed an extraordinary private collection of Spanish art from the 15th to the 20th centuries, including works by Velázquez, Zurbarán, and Goya, as well as the *Surrender of Granada* by Pradilla Ortiz and the wonderfully roguish *Bandolero Torero* (Bullfight Bandit) by Jiménez Aranda. Once you've finished the wine tour and tasting you can take a glass of sublime old Pedro Ximénez into the gallery and peruse the collection at your leisure, a rare glimpse into the privilege of the world of sherry.

Plaza Cordobeses, 3. www.bodegastradicion.com. ✆ **95-616-86-28.** Reservation required, tour and tasting 20€.

TOURING THE HISTORIC SITES ★

Alcázar ★★ CASTLE   Standing opposite the mammoth Gonzalez Byass bodega, flanked by lemon trees, is the Moorish Alcázar. The *frontera* in Jerez's full name was the frontline between the Christians and the Almohads, and this fortress was built in the 11th century as a bulwark against Christian encroachment. The bent entrance of the horseshoe-arched *Puerto de la Ciudad* demonstrates the emphasis on security. After many years of decay, the huge site has been largely restored, showcasing an austerely beautiful mosque, authentically recreated gardens, and one of the best-preserved Moorish bathhouses in Andalucía. Its star-shaped skylights create a magical effect. Although the mosque was converted into a church when the Christians prevailed in 1264, its *mihrab,* or prayer niche, has been preserved. In the 18th century the Alcázar housed a new-fangled olive oil mill, now beautifully restored to working order (if you had a donkey to turn its huge stone presses). The fortress also contains the **Palacio Villavicienco,** home to the wealthy family who ran the olive oil operation. It has a tower with a *camera obscura* which projects images of the city in a darkened room. The well-managed tour starts with a short introductory video. In summer, look for atmospheric nighttime visits, including theatrical costumes.

Alameda Vieja, s/n. www.turismojerez.com. ✆ **95-614-99-55.** Alcázar only 5€ adults, 1.80€ students and seniors; with camera obscura 7€ adults, 4.20€ students and seniors. July–Sept Mon–Fri 9:30am–5:30pm, Sat–Sun 9:30am–2:30pm; Oct–Jun daily 9:30am–2:30pm. Closed Dec 25, Jan 1, and Jan 6.

ay, CABALLERO!

The Spaniards' love for their horses is as strong today as when Neolithic artists painted equine images in the caves near Ronda 20,000 years ago. The museum at the **Fundación Real Escuela Andaluza del Arte Ecuestre ★★★**, Avenida Duque de Abrantes, s/n (www.realescuela.org; ✆ **95-631-96-35**), traces the evolving bond between man and steed, emphasizing the skills of horsemanship and the breeding of the Pura Raza Española, or Spanish purebred horse—what English-speakers call the Andalusian. The breed's top blood lines were first established at Carthusian monasteries in the 15th century and the horse's compact, elegant form has changed little since. The Real Escuela, founded in 1973, schools riders in the art of taming and training horses to perform exquisite balletic dance routines. Performances of "How the Andalusian Horses Dance" usually take place on Tuesdays and Thursdays, with variations depending on the season (check the website). Before and after the show (Mon–Fri 10am–2pm, Sat 10am–3pm), you can tour the grounds and visit the museums of equestrian art and carriages. You can also visit on non-performance days and watch training sessions, which perhaps give even more insight into the extraordinarily close relationship between horse and rider (magnificent in dove-gray sombrero and the *traje corto*, short-jacketed suit). Beware of imitations—some hotels carry flyers for similar-looking horse spectacles that are not the *Real* thing.

Cathedral ★ CHURCH Built over a period of 80 years from 1695 on, the cathedral of San Salvador has a one-piece-at-a-time feel, incorporating several architects and styles: Gothic, Baroque, and Neoclassical. Its concatenation of flying buttresses, ornate facades and sculpted pinnacles is formidable rather than beautiful, and it has attracted its fair share of criticism. The first great travel writer on Spain, Richard Ford, called it vile, adding that the "architect did not by accident stumble upon one sound rule." Its detached **bell tower** is also a hybrid, 15th-century Gothic-Mudéjar on the bottom and 17th-century Baroque on top. Inside, the main points of interest are the intricately carved vaulting of the central nave, a lovely painting of the Virgin as a girl by Zurbarán, and a **secret staircase** which, by dint of the many architects on the job, leads nowhere. Although intended at the outset as a church worthy of becoming a cathedral, that wish was not granted until 1980, and a statue of Pope John Paul II stands in gratitude outside.

Plaza Encarnación, s/n. www.catedraldejerez.es. ☏ **95-616-90-59.** Admission 6€, 7€ including bell tower; children under 12 free. Mon–Sat 10am–6:30pm (Apr–Sept until 8pm, except Mon).

Plaza de la Asunción ★★ PLAZA   This is the most beautiful square in Jerez and a lovely place to relax in the evening light surrounded by architecture spanning 6 centuries. The oldest building is the **Iglesia de San Dionisio,** a plain-fronted Gothic-Mudéjar church from the 15th century with a single round window and pointed arch entrance. On the south side is the **Antiguo Ayuntamiento,** the old town hall, built in the 16th century in Italian Renaissance style, with a porticoed gallery on the left and Corinthian columns, pedimented windows, and decorative friezes on the right. Stately mansions from the 19th century and a 20th-century central sculpture representing the Assumption complete the picture. Although the whole square has been recently and beautifully refurbished, it still feels refreshingly underexploited, with just one, very lucky, bar.

Centro Andaluz de Flamenco ★ CULTURAL INSTITUTION Before you venture out to a performance, drop in to this beautiful old palace **(Palacio Pemartin)** in the Santiago district, which, alongside the barrio de San Miguel, is the cradle of Jerez flamenco. An academic center—the atmosphere is rarefied and reverent—it holds the world's largest public archive of books, scores, and performance videos of flamenco. Engravings and paintings capturing the *duende* (spirit) of performance grace the walls and the melodies of *bulerías* and *soleares* drift into an idyllic courtyard. In the foyer you'll find pinned-up details of upcoming performances,

---

TOURING the tabancos

A great way to combine the joys of sherry and flamenco is to go on the tabanco trail. Tabancos originated in Jerez as kiosks with sherry barrels where workers could pick up supplies on their way home. (The name is probably a fusing of *estanco*, or government-run shop, and *tabaco*, or tobacco.) Over time they developed into tiny meeting places with simple food and impromptu music. A few years ago, they were in danger of extinction, but today they're back in fashion and dozens have popped up around the old town. There's even an official **Ruta de los Tabancos** (facebook.com/rutadelostabancosdejerez). Which is best? For all-round atmosphere, passionate flamenco, excellent tapas (try the *chicharrones*, thinly sliced pork belly served on waxed paper), and sherry from the barrel at a euro a glass, it's hard to beat **Tabanco El Pasaje** (c. Santa Maria, 8). Try also the bullfight-themed **Tabanco Las Banderillas** (c. Caballeros, 12), **Tabanco San Pablo** (c. San Pablo, 12), run by the same family since 1936, and for raucous and hilarious flamenco, **Tabanco a la Feria** (Calle Armas, 5).

festivals, and classes. Ask the staff for advice, they will be delighted you're interested in Andalucía's great art form.

Plaza de San Juan, 1. www.centroandaluzdeflamenco.es. © **95-690-21-34.** Admission free. Mon–Fri 9am–2pm, closed weekends

Where to Stay in Jerez de la Frontera

If you're on a tight budget, hotel rooms are available in Jerez for as little as 35€, but for the same money you'll be much better off with one of the many rooms and apartments offered on **Airbnb.com** and other online sites.

Hotel Casa Grande ★★   Ideally located a short walk from the Plaza del Arenal, this cool, clean hotel in a former grand townhouse is exceptionally good value. Its air-conditioned rooms have white marble floors, high ceilings, and simple furnishings in Andalucían style. There's a spacious central courtyard, a small bar where the courteous staff will offer you a complimentary drink, and a shared rooftop terrace with views across town. It's a soothing place to repair to after a hot day's walking.

Plaza de las Angustias, 3. www.hotelcasagrandejerez.com. © **95-634-50-70.** 15 units. 60€–120€ double. Limited free parking. **Amenities:** Bar; terrace; free Wi-Fi.

Palacio Garvey ★★   Set in a substantial sherry family palace in the old town, Palacio Garvey has an efficient, business-traveler feel. Its decor mixes traditional and modern, striking contemporary art and glass doors blending with 19th-century grandeur. The spacious air-conditioned rooms are well equipped with flat-screen TVs, strong Wi-Fi, and mini-bars; the mosaic-tiled bathrooms have quality fittings. The hotel's restaurant, **La Condesa,** has attracted favorable attention in its own right, serving regional dishes with a modern twist, and there's a leafy patio where breakfast is included.

Calle Tornería, 24. www.hotelpalaciogarvey.es. © **95-632-67-00.** 16 units. 65€–120€ double. Parking 12€. **Amenities:** Restaurant; bar; room service; patio; free Wi-Fi.

Hotel Villa Jerez ★★   Staying at this five-star hotel north of the old town offers a taste of sherry aristocracy. Rooms in the mansion are spacious and full of light, and they look out onto terraces, palm-treed gardens, and a large swimming pool. The decor is elegantly traditional, with pale walls, classic wood furniture, and wrought-iron balconies. Budget rooms are in a separate, smaller building. The hotel is plugged into the sherry trade, offering tastings in the restaurant and arranging private tours of the bodegas for guest. The only drawback is the 25-minute walk to Plaza del Arenal, although horse-lovers will be glad to know that the Real Escuela is just around the corner.

Av. de la Cruz Roja, 7. www.villajerez.com. © **95-615-31-00.** 18 units. 80€–130€ double. Free parking. **Amenities:** Restaurant; bar; free Wi-Fi.

Where to Eat in Jerez de la Frontera

For traditional fried fish, head to the immaculately run **Freiduria Gallega El Nuevo Jerezano,** Calle Arcos, 5 (© **95-634-6347**). It's more a take-away than a restaurant—you can stand at the counter and attack mounds of vinegary, battered fish and squid sold by weight and served on a sheet of greaseproof paper. For a simple breakfast of coffee, orange juice, and toast with olive oil and tomato, **La Moderna,** Calle Larga, 67 (www.facebook.com/lamoderna.jerez; © **95-632-13-79**), is a lovely old intellectual café with antique sherry ads, newspapers on poles, and a wooden fridge. It must have been modern once. There are plenty of ice cream parlors in town, none more architecturally interesting than **Rosa d'Oro,** Calle Consistorio, 5–7 (www.larosadeoro.net; © **95-633-84-08**), where the counter is built into the old city walls which run, like raspberry ripple, through the shop.

Bar Juanito ★★ ANDALUCÍAN Locals will tell you they never visit this Jerez classic just off the Plaza de Arenal because it's too expensive or too touristy, but every time we've visited, lots of people were speaking Andalucían Spanish at the colorful patio tables, bar, and dining room. You might pay a small premium for the famous name, and the food is traditional and tasty rather than artful, but it's worth it for the atmosphere, honed over 75 years. Try the fresh tuna salad in sherry vinegar, meatballs in *oloroso* sauce, or *mollejas salteadas,* sautéed sweetbreads.

Calle Pescadería Viejo, 8–10. www.bar-juanito.com. © **95-633-48-38.** Tapas and *raciones* 4.50€–8€. Mon–Sat 1–4:30pm and 9–11:30pm, Sun 1–4:30pm.

La Carboná Restaurante ★★★ ANDALUCÍAN If you only have time for one big dinner in Jerez, make it La Carboná. It's set inauspiciously on a dark back street, but once inside this former sherry warehouse you are in great hands. The setting is delightful: a large, white, wood-beamed bodega with generously spaced tables and soft, hanging lighting. Chef Javier Muñoz has created an experience based around high-quality meat and fresh fish roasted on a charcoal brazier, in which sherry—often thought of only as an aperitif—takes you the whole way through. Go straight for one of two five-course sherry tasting menus *(menu maridaje),* good value at 45€ and 70€ given the quality of the food and fine wines offered. The menu changes regularly, but one staple is roast loin of Cantabrian beef, served with a reduction of sweet Pedro Ximénez, coupled with a dry *oloroso.* The risotto of wild mushrooms and squid with parmesan, accompanied by a glass of *amontillado,* is simply glorious. The youthful waitstaff clearly care a lot about what they're doing and seem delighted that their efforts are appreciated.

Calle San Francisco de Paula, 2. www.lacarbona.com. © **95-634-74-75.** Entrees 20€–25€; sherry-pairing menu 45€ and 60€. Wed–Mon 12:30–4:30pm and 8pm–12:30am.

La Cruz Blanca ★★ ANDALUCÍAN A lovely place for a people-watching lunch close to the Plaza de la Asunción, La Cruz Blanca rather immodestly advertises its many accolades on a huge sign outside. They are deserved: The stylishly presented dishes, leaning towards fish and seafood, both look and taste great. You can go for a range of Japanese-influenced tapas or a more formal menu, at reasonable prices given the quality and prime location. Fashionable young locals come here to tuck into Galician octopus salad and diced tuna cooked in *palo cortado* sherry. Nearby **Albores,** Calle Consistorio, 12 (www.restaurantealbores.com; ✆ **95-632-02-66**), is also excellent.

Calle Consistorio, 16. www.restaurantelacruzblanca.com. ✆ **95-632-45-35.** Tapas 1.60€–4.50€; entrees 12€–23€. Daily noon–midnight.

Jerez Shopping

The best shopping in Jerez involves the city's three big preoccupations. Designer shops along Calle Larga draw their inspiration from tailored equestrian outfits and flouncy flamenco dresses. Visit **Amparo Macia,** Calle Larga, 55 (www.facebook.com/amparomaciajerez; ✆ **68-545-53-29**), for exquisite modern designs. **Hipisur,** Calle Circo, 1 (www.hipisur.com; ✆ **95-632-42-09**), has everything the horseman or woman needs, including stylish leather boots at excellent prices. **Antonio García,** Calle Larga, 33 (sombrerosantoniogarcia.com; ✆ **95-633-91-96**), is the place for wide-brimmed sombreros, leather belts, and purses. **Abrines,** Calle Lancería, 10 (abrinesmusica.com; ✆ **95-634-29-99**), has been supplying the city's flamenco artists with guitars and strings since 1948. They sell instruments for beginners as young as 2 years old. Try **Mala Música,** Calle Medina, 10 (✆ **95-632-55-40**), for second-hand CDs and vinyl.

And then, of course, there is sherry. There are wine shops all over town, but few as charming as **Casa de Jerez,** Calle Divina Pastora, 1 (lacasadeljerez.com; ✆ **95-633-51-84**). Most of the bodegas can ship wines to your home, and if you're worried about taking liquids in your hand luggage, the marketing folks at **Gonzalez Byass** (p. 321) have thought of that: how about a box of six tasting miniatures, and a couple of glasses, branded with Tio Pepe's bottle, sombrero, and guitar?

Day Trip to Sanlúcar de Barrameda ★★

Sanlúcar de Barrameda's harbor at the mouth of the Guadalquivir was once so deep that Columbus launched his third voyage to America here. But centuries of silting have made the river shallow, creating lovely in-town beaches and protecting the wetlands of the **Parque Doñana** on the opposite shore. Sanlucár's sandbars and strands make it a playground of the South, and the estuary ecosystem is a fisherman's dream. Well-heeled Spaniards flock here around Easter to bask in the sun, ride horses on the beach, and eat mounds of fresh seafood in the restaurants along the Bajo de Guia riverfront.

The simplest way to get to Sanlúcar from Jerez is to drive the 25km (15 miles) on the A-480. Regular bus service takes 40 minutes, costing 2€. From the bus station on Avenida Guzmán el Bueño, it's a short walk to the **tourist office** at Avenida Calzada Duquesa Isabel, s/n (www.sanlucar turismo.com; ℰ **95-636-61-10**), which is open Tuesday to Saturday 10am to 2pm and 5 to 7pm, Sunday and Monday 10am to 2pm.

Sanlúcar is the home of *manzanilla* sherry, a pale, delicate style with a salty tang obtained by aging in the sea air. When Magellan set sail from here in 1519 to circumnavigate the globe, he reportedly spent more on *manzanilla* than he did on armaments. To understand why, visit one of the many bodegas in town. **Bodegas Barbadillo ★★**, Calle Sevilla, 1 (www. barbadillo.com; ℰ **95-638-55-00**), is by far the biggest producer and also makes Spain's top-selling white table wine. Its **cathedral bodega,** a symmetrical, high arched monument to *manzanilla,* is an awe-inspiring sight. The bodega offers guided tours in English Tuesday to Sunday at 11am (10€ per person; reservations recommended). Other well-known makers offering tours include **Bodegas Hidalgo,** producers of the La Gitana brand (www.lagitana.es; English tours Mon–Sat at 11:30am; 12€); **Bodegas Delgado Zuleta** (www.delgadozuleta.com; English tours Mon–Sat at 11am; 6€); and **Bodegas La Cigarrera** (www.bodegaslacigarrera.com; English tours Mon–Fri at 11am; 5.50€). You'll see the appealing antique artwork of their logos on bar awnings all over town. Check websites for special tours and tastings, such as food pairings and nighttime visits.

Parque Nacional Coto Doñana ★★★ NATURE RESERVE   Sanlúcar is the departure point for boat trips to the marshlands *(marismas)* at the mouth of the Guadalquivír River. Much more than merely scenic, they sustain the Bay of Cádiz fisheries, provide sanctuary for hundreds of thousands of migrating birds, and were finally recognized in the late 20th century as one of the most important wetland systems in Europe. The Coto Doñana was once the hunting ground for the Dukes of Medina Sidonia; it was named after the 7th duke's wife, Doña Ana, in the 16th century. The vast area became a national park in 1969 after a long campaign by Spanish and international conservationists who eventually persuaded the dictator Franco not to destroy it for economic development. The wetlands host an extraordinary array of birds and wildlife, including migrating flamingos, the Spanish Imperial eagle, red and fallow deer, the exceptionally rare Iberian lynx, and even dromedary camels (who may or may not have been introduced during the Moorish conquest). The park is heavily protected and constantly under threat from neighboring development. Large parts are inaccessible to the public and private cars can only skirt its borders, but there are good options to visit. For a quick trip to walk along the deserted dunes and admire the skyline of stone pines, simply hop onto one of the small open ferries which go back and forth across the river from the Bajo de Guia all day (5€ round-trip; make sure to check when the last boat back leaves). For a more detailed excursion, and additional information about Doñana, go to the visitor center at the beautifully tiled old ice factory **Fábrica de Hielo,** where you can book a riverboat trip, or a combined boat and four-wheel-drive trip, to explore the ecosystems of the park. Both visits last about 2½ hours and have limited capacity, so it's best to book in advance.

Centro de Visitantes de Fábrica de Hielo, Av. Bajo de Guia s/n. www.visitasdonana. com. ✆ **95-636-38-13.** Visitor center free, daily 9am–8pm. Boat trip only: 15€ adults, 11€ seniors; 7.50€ children; boat and 4×4 trip 35€. Children under 5 free on both.

WHERE TO EAT IN SANLÚCAR DE BARRAMEDA

Casa Balbino ★★ ANDALUCÍAN   A Sanlúcar institution, this always busy eatery on the main square, Plaza del Cabildo, is well worth a visit. There is no table service—you give your order to the staff behind the glass counter who juggle multiple food and drink requests and somehow it all works. The house specialty is the crunchy yet chewy *tortillita de camarones* (shrimp fritter); the *jamón* hanging over the counter is also first-rate. The walls are covered with historic scenes of Sanlúcar life, including a hair-raising photograph of the day a bull escaped from the ring and made its way through the crowded stand. All in all, the place is great fun, with cheerfully low prices.

Plaza del Cabildo, 14. www.casabalbino.es. ✆ **95-636-05-13.** Tapas 2€–3€, entrees 10€ –15€. Daily noon–5pm and 7pm–midnight.

Casa Bigote ★★★ ANDALUCÍAN   All the restaurants along the Bajo de Guia riverfront serve excellent seafood, but this is the most famous and clearly the locals' favorite. At lunchtime, it's not unusual to see several restaurants on the strip empty and Casa Bigote already doing a roaring trade. There's a formal restaurant with river views upstairs and an intensely busy *taberna* downstairs where the tables are upturned barrels. A plate of langoustines here, accompanied by a glass of cold *manzanilla* straight from the barrel, is an experience to savor. Reservations are recommended for the restaurant; no reservations at the bar.

Calle Pórtico de Bajo de Guia, 10. www.restaurantecasabigote.com. ✆ **95-636-26-96.** Tapas 3€–5€, entrees 10€–20€. Mon–Sat 1–4pm and 8:30–11:30pm, closed Sun and Nov.

Horse Racing on the Beach

Each year in August, the beaches of Sanlúcar thrum with the sound of hooves as horse-racing takes over the town. The world-famous and colorful **Carreras de Sanlúcar** are held in two bursts over the second and fourth weekends of the month, when hotel and restaurant prices are at a premium (www.carrerassanlucar.es).

Restaurante Mirador de Doñana ★★ ANDALUCÍAN   As the name suggests, the view across the river to Doñana is the thing, and if you can get a table upstairs the setting is superb. The extensive menu, mainly seafood, is also excellent, with a number of interesting rice dishes and stews in addition to a mind-boggling—and rather expensive—selection of *gambas, langostinos,* and *cigalas* (prawns of various sizes). Reservations are recommended for the best views.

Av. Bajo de Guia, 0. www.miradordonana.com. ⓒ **95-636-42-05.** Entrees 10€–30€. Daily noon–5pm and 8pm–1am, closed Jan–Feb.

CÁDIZ ★★

Surrounded by the Atlantic Ocean on three sides and connected to the mainland by a narrow strip of land, Cádiz has a lot going for it. Its perfect natural harbor has attracted settlers, traders—and brigands—throughout history. It claims to be Western Europe's oldest continuously inhabited city—the Phoenicians founded a trading post called Gadir here in 1100 B.C. and the inhabitants of Cádiz still call themselves *gaditanos.* The city grew rich in the 16th century as a haven for the galleons of New World trade, but it had its fair share of setbacks, first from devastating English raids and then in 1755 when much of the town was destroyed by the earthquake that also leveled Lisbon. With its rebuilt grid-system streets surrounded by lively *barrios,* it is reminiscent of that city, but so far has remained largely untouched by international tourism. That may be changing. In recent years the city has invested heavily in renovating its grand but crumbling buildings, and its vibrant local culture, picturesque beaches, and wonderful seafood make it one of Andalucía's most appealing cities.

So Many Places . . .

Unlike most cities, it's a little difficult to say where the center of Cádiz lies. The old town is made up of several distinct *barrios* (districts) and most have their own leafy squares and centers of activity. **Plaza de San Juan de Dios,** given a makeover in 2012 for the 200th anniversary of the Spanish constitution, is probably what most would consider the center, but then there are the **Plaza de la Catedral,** the refined **Plaza de Mina,** and the wide-open **Plaza de San Antonio,** where the composer Manuel de Falla lived. Not to mention the marketplace of **Plaza de la Libertad,** and adjoining **Plaza de Topete** (also called Plaza de las Flores). And those are just the big ones. Seek out the lovely **Plaza de la Candelaria, Plaza de San Francisco,** and **Plaza del Mentidero** for a relaxing break among exotic trees, fountains and statues of famous gaditanos.

Essentials

ARRIVING   Fifteen **trains** arrive daily from Sevilla (trip time: 2 hr.; cost: 16€–24€ one-way), most of them stop at Jerez de la Frontera and El Puerto de Santa María along the way. The train station is on Plaza de Sevilla (www.renfe.com; ℂ **91-232-03-20**), on the southeast side of the main port. Four **buses** run daily from Madrid to Cádiz. Trip time is 8¼ hours and a one-way ticket costs 28€–38€. The service is operated by **Socibus** (www.socibus.es; ℂ **90-222-92-92**). The terminal is on the north side of town, a few blocks west of the main port. By **car** from Sevilla, the A-4/E-5 toll road will bring you into Cádiz across the magnificent new **Puente de la Constitución de 1812** suspension bridge.

VISITOR INFORMATION   The **tourist office,** Paseo de Canalejas, s/n (ℂ www.turismo.cadiz.es; ℂ **95-624-10-01**), is open in summer Monday to Friday 9am to 7pm, Saturday to Sunday 9am to 5pm; in winter Monday to Friday 8:30am to 6:30pm, Saturday to Sunday 9am to 5pm. The office hands out a useful map with color-coded walking routes.

Exploring Cádiz

On the map, Cádiz looks uncannily like an outstretched arm and hand giving a thumbs-up sign. Most visitors will spend their time on the hand, which is less than 2km (1¼ miles) from knuckles to wrist. A good way to start is to promenade around the seawall, the Castles and Bastions route on your tourist office map. It's an easy walk, but there are also lots of places in town where you can hire bikes, scooters, or Segways. The broad oceanfront walkways pass the silent remains of the city's fortifications. They were built out of grim necessity: In 1587, Sir Francis Drake attacked the harbor and waylaid the Spanish Armada, the so-called "singeing of the King of Spain's beard." Then, in 1596, English and Dutch troops torched Cádiz, taking several of its prominent citizens hostage. Philip II—beard well and truly on fire—responded by commissioning a series of fortifications around the fist of the city, which would repel raids for the next 200 years.

At the north end of the Playa de La Caleta bay stands the **Castillo de Santa Catalina,** Calle Antonio Burgos (www.turismo.cadiz.es; ℂ **95-622-63-33;** admission free; daily 11am–7:30pm, until 8:30pm Jul–Aug). Built in 1598, it has a star-shaped floor plan and a moat on the land side, making it extremely secure. Once used as a military prison, it now houses art exhibitions and cultural events. The **Castillo de San Sebastián** on the south end sits on an island across a long causeway. It is named after a chapel built in the 15th century by the crew of a Venetian plague ship who were allowed to stay on the island to recuperate. Between the castles lies **La Caleta** strand, one of the city's two European blue-flag beaches. In the

Calle de la Virgen in Cádiz.

evening it's a beautiful place to watch the sun go down, with small boats bobbing in the glittering bay and the whiff of frying fish in the air. Heading north, past the modern *parador,* the *paseo* takes you through one of the city's many public gardens, the mannered **Parque Genovés,** with exotic trees and plants from around the world. Past yet another fortress, the **Baluarte de la Candelaria,** you'll reach the less formal gardens at **Alameda Marqués de Comillas,** with its ancient, twisted tree trunks and fishermen casting from the ramparts. Along the way, plain-fronted seaside apartments echo the no-nonsense design of the earlier fortifications.

Catedral de Cádiz ★★ CATHEDRAL   The last great Spanish cathedral financed by the riches from the New World, this hulking church was begun in Baroque style in 1722 and finally finished with the help of volunteer labor in 1838. The later parts—including the yellow-tiled dome and hexagonal bell towers—are Neoclassical. It's impressive rather than beautiful, but the 7€ admission, including access to the clock tower and cathedral museum, is worth spending. The tour is slick, with a detailed audioguide in several languages, museum-style exhibits, and a gift shop.

Highlights are an elaborately carved **cedar choir** from 1702 and the huge 390kg (860 lb.) **silver monstrance** that is shouldered through the streets during the feast of Corpus Christi every June. The circular crypt contains the tomb of the Cádiz-born composer **Manuel de Falla.** After the tour, you can climb the eastern clock tower **(Torre de Reloj),** whose entrance is to your right as you exit the cathedral. The views—particularly of the port and the city's magnificent new bridge—are spectacular, but take care not to get lost in photography: The bells just above your head sound every 15 minutes and are painfully loud. The **cathedral museum,** next to the much simpler old cathedral **(Iglesia de Santa Cruz),** is in a beautifully restored Mudéjar building where the most significant object is the decree to abolish the Spanish Inquisition.

Plaza Catedral. www.catedraldecadiz.com. ✆ **95-628-61-54.** Cathedral admission 5€, 3€ seniors and students; Torre de Reloj 5€. Mon–Sat 10am–6pm, Sun 1–6:30pm. Bus: L2.

Museo de Cádiz ★★ MUSEUM   There's something touching about the two 5th-century B.C. Phoenician sarcophagi in the archaeological collection of this dignified museum. The man's carved coffin was unearthed in 1887, and when the matching woman's sarcophagus was excavated in 1980, the pair, buried together for eternity, were reunited. Many of the most evocative objects in the archaeological collections are Phoenician and Carthaginian. The ancient gold jewelry discovered at the Cádiz necropolis is as advanced in design and construction as any modern work—it's astonishing to note it was created some 2,500 years ago. The Roman room includes a giant statue of Emperor Trajan excavated at nearby Bolonia in 1980—look at the difference in quality between his head, carved in Rome, and his togaed torso, probably knocked out locally. The fine arts collection on the arched upper floors includes a lovely set of pictures of the saints by Zurbarán, painted in the 1630s from monks he met at the Carthusian monastery at Cartuja, and the last painting by Murillo *(The Marriage of Saint Catherine),* on which he was working when he died in 1682. His student completed the job.

Plaza de Mina s/n. www.museosdeandalucia.es. ✆ **95-620-33-68.** Admission 1.50€. Mid-Sept to mid-June Tues–Sat 10am–8:30pm, Sun 10am–5pm; mid-June to mid-Sept Tues–Sat 9am–5pm, Sun 10am–5pm.

Roman Theater ★★ ARCHAEOLOGICAL SITE   If you approach the crumbling theater from the sea front it looks like a sad affair: Heavy railings forbid access; a contractor's sign announces emergency repairs. But follow the signs around the block and you'll reach the recently completed visitor center, which is both beautifully designed and offers surprisingly good access to the theater. Built in the first century B.C., it was one of the largest in the Roman empire, capable of holding 20,000

7

ANDALUCÍA

Cádiz

spectators. Known as *Gades* by the Romans, Cádiz became a valued port and naval base; Julius Caesar granted its inhabitants citizenship of Rome in 49 B.C. The theater was discovered by chance in 1980 when a warehouse on the site burned down, which explains its cramped setting among much later buildings, making further excavation tricky. The exhibition and explanations, in Spanish and English, are coolly and clearly presented.

Calle Mesón, 11. www.turismo.cadiz.es. **67-798-29-45.** Free admission. Apr–Oct Mon–Sat 11am–5pm, Sun 10am–4pm; Oct–Apr Mon–Sat 10am–4:30pm, Sun 10am–4pm. Closed 1st Mon of month.

Torre Tavira ★ LANDMARK   In the late 18th century, when Cádiz handled three-quarters of Spain's commerce with the Americas, the city was dotted with 160 watchtowers to monitor the comings and goings of ships in the harbor. The tallest still standing is Torre Tavira, a square Baroque tower erected on the highest point of the old city in 1778. Exhibitions on two levels tell tales of the trading heyday of Cádiz, but the undoubted highlight is the rooftop view of the city, its harbor, and the sea beyond. When you reach the top, you enter a **camera obscura** that casts live 360-degree images of the city onto a concave screen.

Calle Marqués Real Tesoro, 10. www.torretavira.com. **95-621-29-10.** Admission 6€; seniors and students 5€. Oct–Apr daily 10am–6pm; May–Sept daily 10am–8pm.

Where to Stay in Cádiz

There are good options at the rock-bottom end of the scale. **Pension Cadiz,** Calle Feduchy, 20 (pensioncadiz.es; **95-628-58-01**), has simple, clean rooms and shared bathrooms in an old townhouse, a deal at around 35€ a night; **Casa Caracol,** Calle Suárez de Salazar (casacaracolcadiz.com; **95-626-11-66**), is a backpacker classic with colorful dorms, group activities, and prices as low as 15€ a night. **Airbnb** offers a good range of well-located rooms and flats at great rates.

Apartamentos Turísticos Plaza de la Luz ★★   These new apartments close to the restaurants and bars of the Barrio La Viña are our bargain pick, with prices as low as 45€ a night. The spotless, coolly tiled studios are simply but elegantly furnished. Each has a kitchenette with a cooktop, microwave, and fridge, and a small lounge with TV and Wi-Fi. Everything is efficiently handled by staff at the separate reception down the street. The location, a couple of minutes from La Caleta beach and a 10-minute walk to the center of town, is ideal, not least because it's on the same street as the lovely Casa Manteca bar (p. 338).

Corralón de Los Carros, 62. www.plazadelaluz.com. **85-617-00-84.** 25 units. 45€–80€. Parking 20€. **Amenities:** Kitchenette; laundry; terrace; free Wi-Fi.

Hotel Boutique Convento Cadiz ★★   If you're looking for something with more of the character of old Cádiz, this former convent has all

Unlike many state-run paradors, the one in Cádiz is sleek and modern.

the charm of an historic *parador* coupled with the amenities of a boutique hotel. The building dates from the 17th century and is still owned by the Dominican order—you'll see white-robed monks wandering around its ornate chapels. The central cloister, with its checkerboard floor tiles and arched colonnades, is a lovely place for breakfast. The bedrooms have clean, modern lines, blond wood furniture, a capsule coffee machine, and minibar. Well-located for the port and train station and the restaurants on Calles Plocia and Sopranis, the Convento is great value too.

Calle Santo Domingo, 2. www.hotelconventocadiz.com. ✆ **95-620-07-38.** 26 units. 55€–175€. Paid parking nearby. **Amenities:** Breakfast room; fitness center; library; free Wi-Fi.

Parador de Cádiz ★★★ A government-run *parador* has occupied this beautiful spot between Parque Genovés and La Caleta beach since the system launched in the 1920s. This latest incarnation, opened in 2012, is a striking ultra-modern block. Every light-filled room has a terrace overlooking the ocean and huge beds from which you can gaze out through floor-to-ceiling glass. The in-house spa runs the gamut of beauty and wellness treatments across wood-decked rooftop pools. The beach at La

Caleta is just a minute or two away. The only caution is that, with its own shops and restaurant, it feels a little remote from the street life of Cádiz, more luxury retreat than city break.

Avenida Duque de Nájera, 9. www.parador.es. © **95-622-69-05.** 124 units. 95€–220€ double. Parking 16€ per day. **Amenities:** Restaurant; bar; shops; concierge; room service; indoor and outdoor pools; spa; free Wi-Fi.

Where to Eat in Cádiz

There's plenty of good modern cooking in town. Besides the more formal restaurants listed below, gastrobars **La Candela,** Calle Feduchy, 3 (www.facebook.com/LaCandelaTapasBar; © **95-622-18-22**), and **Sonambulo,** Plaza de La Candelaria, 12 (www.facebook.com/sonambulocadiz; © **66-208-68-75**), are getting great reviews for their imaginative takes on Cádiz cuisine. At lunchtime the **Mercado de Abastos** (Plaza de la Libertad) has a lively courtyard food market; and for breakfast, where better for *churros con chocolate* with atmosphere than the market traders' favorite, **La Marina** (Plaza Topete, 1; © **95-622-23-97**)?

La Bodeguita de Plocia ★★ SEAFOOD/ANDALUCÍAN   There are lots of good restaurants on Calles Plocia and Sopranis in the Santa Maria *barrio,* but the constant turnover of diners here bodes well, locals happily waiting for a table even on a Monday night. Great-value fresh fish and swift service are the order of the day. Grab a stool at the bar, peruse the poetic list of names on the blackboard, and see if you can work out what the *gaditanos* are ordering. The *zamburiñas* (scallops) are particularly popular. Or leave it to chance and ask for *pescado frito mixto* (mixed fried fish). Then make way as cheerful waitstaff sway past carrying a couple of high-piled plates in one hand and three *cañas* of beer in the other.

Calle Plocia, 11. © **95-625-13-64.** Tapas 1.70€–4.50€; entrees 7€–15€. Mon–Fri 8am–midnight; Sat–Sun 1pm–midnight.

El Faro ★★★ SEAFOOD/ANDALUCÍAN   El Faro is acknowledged by most as the grandest restaurant in Cádiz. Its big rooms have an old-school feel with dark woodwork, painted ceramic plates, and photographs of celebrity diners (from former king Juan Carlos to Pierce Brosnan and Halle Berry, who shot the James Bond movie *Die Another Day* in Cádiz). Specialties include whole sea bass *(lubina)* or gilthead bream *(dorada)* baked in a casing of salt, and the black rice squid dish *arroz negro con chocos guisados.* Most of the fish dishes are priced by weight. If you don't fancy the full-blown formality and expense, the adjoining wooden-topped tapas bar is also superb, where a couple of flavorsome small plates and a glass of good local wine or *manzanilla* will set you back less than 10€. Service in both is immaculate. Reservations recommended.

Calle San Félix, 15. www.elfarodecadiz.com. © **95-621-21-88.** Entrees 17€–25€. Daily 1–4pm and 8:30pm–midnight.

constitution & **CARNAVAL!**

It was Cádiz that gave the world the political label "liberal." During the Napoleonic occupation, the Cortes de Cádiz became the country's first national assembly and in 1812 los Liberales drew up a constitution remarkable for its progressiveness. The **Constitution of Cádiz,** also known as La Pepa, sought to abolish feudalism, establish a constitutional monarchy, and allow for freedom of the press. "The object of the government is the happiness of the nation," it declared. The optimism was short-lived: In 1814, King Ferdinand VII returned from exile, tore up the constitution, and re-established absolute monarchy. Yet the liberal spirit of the *gaditanos* has never dimmed. During the Franco era, the general tried to ban decadent celebrations like the annual carnival, but the stubbornly independent citizens of Cádiz carried on regardless.

Today, the **Carnaval de Cádiz,** which spans two weekends at the end of February, is of course a riot of dressing up, drinking, and dancing. But it is also deeply political, revelers using anarchic humor to satirize the issues of the day, thumbing their painted noses at the powers that be. If you plan to visit during carnival, be sure to book accommodation well in advance.

Restaurante Café Royalty ★★ INTERNATIONAL   This magnificently decorated grand café on the corner of Plaza de Candelaria has a remarkable history. Opened in 1912 to celebrate the centenary of Spain's constitution, it became the meeting place for intellectuals, musicians, and artists. The Cádiz-born composer Manuel de Falla gave concerts here. Then on the eve of Civil War in the 1930s, its doors closed, and it fell into disrepair for the next seven decades. In 2008, a wealthy *gaditano* couple bought it and painstakingly restored it to its original glory, just in time for the bicentenary of the constitution in 2012. You'll come mainly for the high society ambience and gorgeous decor, but the food and service are top notch too, especially Sunday brunch.

Plaza de Candelaria, s/n. www.caferoyalty.com. © **95-607-80-65.** Entrees 24€–30€; set menu 40€; brunch 20€. Mon–Fri 11am–11pm, Sat 9:30am–midnight, Sun 9:30am–11pm.

Cadíz Shopping

The pedestrianized shopping streets around Calle San Francisco are dominated by mobile phone stores and lingerie chains, but if you persevere you can still find interesting independent stores and genuine bargains. **Confiteria Maype,** Calle Corneta Soto Guerrero, 3 (© **95-621-46-52**), is a glorious pastry and sweet shop selling gift-wrapped confections. In the kiosks by the central market, **El Melli,** Calle Libertad, s/n (elmelli.com; © **95-621-39-33**), sells an extensive and well-priced selection of flamenco CDs and carnival memorabilia. **Deportes Bernal,** Calle Pelota, 2 (www.deportesbernal.es; © **95-626-57-10**), sells last season's yellow-and-blue shirts of Cadiz FC, the heavily supported but long-suffering local soccer club, for as little as 9€. And look for **Casa Serafin,** Calle Compañía, 3 (*©* **95-622-24-01**), a lovely old knife and scissorsmiths next to the equally traditional **Bar Brim** coffee shop, Calle Compañía, 2 (*©* **95-622-19-63**).

Cádiz Nightlife

Given the *gaditanos'* love of witty conversation and good food, it's no surprise that much of the nightlife here revolves around eating and drinking. For character, it's hard to beat **Taberna Casa Manteca,** Corralón de los Carros, 66 (www.facebook.com/tabernamanteca; *©* **95-621-36-03**), founded by a retired matador in 1953 and still run by his family. Bullfight and flamenco memorabilia cover its walls like religious paintings, and the sherry and tapas are as good as the atmosphere. Try *chicharrones* (thinly sliced pork belly) and the celebrated *payoyo* cheese served on wax paper, or first-class *boquerones en vinagre* (marinated anchovies). **Taberna La Manzanilla,** Calle Feduchy, 19 (www.lamanzanilladecadiz.com; *©* **95-628-54-01**), is an authentic old bodega where you can taste bone-dry *manzanillas, olorosos,* and *amontillados* straight from the barrel, accompanied by a saucer of fat, green olives. It's run by Pepe, who chalks up your account on the wooden counter and will happily tell you the history of the bar, in his family for three generations. You can also buy a bottle to take home. **Cafe de Levante,** Calle de Rosario, 35 (www.cafedelevantecadiz. com; *©* **95-622-02-27**), attracts a younger *gaditano* crowd for its well-priced coffee, cakes, and *cañas,* while the seafront seating at **La Colonial,** Alameda Apodaca, 15 (www.facebook.com/lacolonialalameda; *©* **85-617-15-27**), is a great place for a sundown cocktail.

For flamenco, head during the day (except Sun) to the **Centro de Interpretación del Flamenco,** Calle Santiago, 12 (www.facebook.com/ FlamencoCadiz; *©* **95-607-36-77**), in Barrio de la Merced. They can give you a print-out of upcoming flamenco shows at the handful of venues in town, including **La Cava,** Calle Antonio López, 16 (www.flamenco lacava.com; *©* **95-621-18-66**), **La Perla,** Calle Concepción Arenal, 0 (www.perladecadiz.com; *©* **95-625-91-01**), and **Pelicano Musicafé,** Av. Fernández Ladreda, 1 (www.facebook.com/ElPelicanoMusiCafe; *©* **95-628-84-26**). Pelicano is a beautiful venue built into an ocean-facing bastion, where sea air blows through an open window to cool the performers. Most shows start around 9:30pm and lean more toward song and guitar than dance.

At the top end of the cultural spectrum, the Cádiz city government runs the **Gran Téatro Falla,** Calle Virgili, 9 (www.teatrofalla.com; *©* **95-622-08-34**). This turn-of-the-19th century theater, honoring the Cádiz-born composer Manuel de Falla, presents everything from contemporary and classical plays to flamenco superstars, modern dance, and opera. In May

The Gran Téatro Falla, named after Cádiz-born composer Manuel de Falla.

each year it hosts an international classical music festival, including works by Falla himself.

Day Trip to El Puerto de Santa María ★

The third point of the Sherry Triangle, and the least well-known, is **El Puerto de Santa María.** Next to Jerez and Sanlúcar it feels a little neglected, but it nevertheless makes an enjoyable day trip from Cádiz. The simplest way to get there is to take the catamaran ferry from the harbor in front of Plaza de San Juan (www.catamaranbahiacadiz.es; © **90-245-05-50**). The frequent, 20-minute crossing costs 2.75€ each way. From Jerez, it's a 25-minute drive on the A-4.

This deep-water port has a long and storied history. Columbus' flagship, the *Santa María,* hailed from here, and a plaque on the 13th-century **Castillo de San Marcos** honors local mariners who took part in the 1492 voyage. El Puerto, as it's known locally, grew wealthy as a merchant town trading with the New World and earned the nickname *ciudad de los cien palacios* (city of a hundred palaces), some of which you can still see scattered around the town, embellished with family coats of arms. The **tourist**

office, Plaza Alfonso X El Sabio (www.turismoelpuerto.com; ✆ **95-648-37-15;** Mon–Sat 10am–2pm and 4–6:30pm, Sun 10am–2pm), is in one such palace; its staff can suggest interesting walking routes. Today, Santa María is a low-key port filled with shrimpers and deep-water tuna boats, a tourist destination for Spanish families with some pleasant beaches and sailboats in the harbor, and headquarters to a number of prestigious sherry houses. Improbably, it also has the third most important **bullring** in Spain after Madrid and Sevilla.

Osborne, Calle los Moros, 7 (www.bodegas-osborne.es; ✆ **95-686-91-00**), has the best-known bodega in town. Famous for its black bull logo (see "Osborne's Brandy Bulls," below), it is also Spain's biggest producer of brandy. Guided tours of this handsome winery take place in English every day at 10am, ranging from 8€ to 55€ with tastings; pre-booking is required. After that, you have many choices for lunch in this traditionally food-loving town, though the economic downturn of the last decade means a number of them lie abandoned.

If you're interested in top quality *jamón ibérico,* paired with some rare old sherries, then **Toro,** Calle los Moros, 7 (torotapaselpuerto.com; ✆ **95-690-50-20**), the stylish modern tapas restaurant attached to the Osborne bodega, is a great choice. It's open Monday to Friday 8:30am to 5pm and 8 to 11:45pm, Saturday 10am to midnight, Sunday 10am to 5pm and 8 to 11:45pm. If you prefer fish, head to **Romerijo,** Calle José Antonio Romero Zarazaga, 1 (www.romerijo.com; ✆ **956-54-12-54**), which is open daily 12:15pm to 12:15am. A seafood complex which dominates El Puerto's riverfront *marisquerías,* it's a restaurant of many parts: a *freiduría* for fried fish, *cocedero* for cooked shellfish, and a *cervecería* for beer with both. There's also a takeaway counter serving fish-filled paper

OSBORNE'S brandy bulls

As you drive through Spain, every now and then you'll see the 14m-high (45-ft.) silhouette of a black bull that has become synonymous with the country. The image appears on bumper stickers, T-shirts, and flags, and many assume it's part of an official Spanish marketing campaign. Its history is much more interesting, however. The signs were first erected in the 1950s as brandy advertisements painted black, white, and red, with the lettering "osborne veterano." When the Spanish government outlawed roadside alcohol advertising in the 1980s, the signs were painted solid black in order to comply. Then in 1994 the government declared they should be removed altogether, under a law banning billboards on national highways. By then they'd become a much-loved part of the landscape and Spanish identity, and outcry followed. A court eventually ruled that the Osborne bull has "cultural and aesthetic significance" and the signs were reprieved. Some 90 of them still loom over highways across Spain.

cones, and an online shop. Long tablefuls of middle-aged Spanish couples spend lunchtime devouring plate after plate of shellfish, turning their empty white wine bottles upside down in the ice-bucket, chatting non-stop. Try also the subtle seafood *gazpacho* and delicious *tortillitas de camarones* (shrimp fritters), accompanied perhaps by a glass of Osborne's Bailén *oloroso*. Then, all too soon, it's time to catch the catamaran back to Cádiz.

THE COSTA DEL SOL

By Patricia Harris and David Lyon

S ome of Spain's nicest beaches—and worst traffic congestion—coexist along the Mediterranean shoreline of the Costa del Sol, the sandy strip along the southern coast of Andalucía. From the quiet sands of Estepona, it stretches east to the jet-set resort of Marbella and the port city of Málaga, then continues east as the Costa Tropical to Almuñécar. Strands are lined with sandy coves, whitewashed houses, olive trees, lots of new townhouse apartments, high-rise megahotels, fishing boats, golf courses, souvenir stands, fast-food outlets, theme parks, and surprisingly varied flora and fauna. Millions of travelers are willing to ignore the high-rise concrete architecture and brave the traffic jams for one good reason: With an average of 325 days of sunshine a year, the Costa del Sol lives up to its name.

It's best to know yourself before you go. Do you want to simply bake on the beach? Do you crave nightlife? Do you long to hobnob with the beautiful people? Or do you hanker for a relatively undeveloped fishing village? Whichever you choose, there's one overall strategy to enjoying the Costa del Sol: When you leave the highway and enter a thicket of unattractive concrete buildings, keep heading toward the water and look for the old city center, where narrow, twisty streets have defied development.

Golfers have lots of choices as well. If you prefer grassy greens to sandy strands, a couple of the best resorts are **Los Monteros** (www.monteros.com; ℭ **95-277-17-00**) in Marbella, which has the leading course; and **Hotel Guadalmina Spa & Golf Resort,** also in Marbella (www.hotelguadalmina.com; ℭ **95-288-22-11**). With more than 60 courses, the "Costa del Golf" could keep you busy all summer, even if you played a different course each day. Ask your hotel reception desk to arrange tee times at least a day in advance.

Thanks to highway investments, it's easier to get around the region than it used to be. The infamous N-340 highway from Málaga to Estepona has become a fast, safe, six-lane road. For those traveling long distances along the coast, the **Autopista del Sol,** a toll expressway with four lanes, has greatly relieved traffic congestion.

From June to October, the coast is mobbed, so reserve far in advance. At other times, innkeepers are likely to roll out the red carpet. Northern European retirees come in droves during the bargain winter season, but

FACING PAGE: **Playa de Nueva beach in Punta Banús.**

beaches: THE GOOD, THE BAD & THE UGLY

It was the allure of beaches that originally in the 1950s put the "sol" in the Costa del Sol. But in truth, not all of the Costa del Sol is a paradise for swimmers.

The roughest beaches—mainly pebbles and slates—are on the east end at **Málaga, Nerja,** and **Almuñécar.** Moving westward, you encounter the gritty, grayish sands of **Torremolinos.** The best beaches here are at **El Bajondillo** and **La Carihuela,** which borders an old fishing village. Another good stretch of beach is along the meandering strip between **Carvajal, Los Boliches,** and **Fuengirola.** In addition, two good beaches—**El Fuerte** and **La Fontanilla**—lie on either side of Marbella. However, all these beaches tend to be overcrowded,

especially in July and August. Crowding is worst on Sundays, May through October, when family picnickers join sunbathers on the strands.

All public beaches in Spain are free. Don't expect to find changing facilities—there might be cold showers on the major beaches, but that's it.

Although it's not sanctioned by the government, many women go topless. To bare it all, head for the **Costa Natura,** about 3km (1¾ miles) west of Estepona. It's the oldest established naturist resort (with day passes) along the Costa del Sol.

many hotels, restaurants, and attractions close or keep limited hours between New Year's Day and Easter, when the weather can be overcast and rainy.

If you're planning an extended family holiday on the Costa del Sol, consider renting self-catering accommodations—anything from a studio apartment with kitchenette to a multi-bedroom villa. The "rentals" tab on the web site **Andalucia.com** gives you a huge range of options—including cave houses and camping. Just be aware that all the bookings go through the Booking.com portal, an Expedia company.

ESTEPONA ★

A town of Roman origin, Estepona is a budding beach resort, less developed than Marbella or Torremolinos and, for that reason, more likable. Estepona contains an interesting 15th-century parish church, with the ruins of an old aqueduct nearby (at Salduba). Its recreational port is an attraction, as are its beaches: **Costa Natura,** N-340 Km 257, the first legal naturist beach along the Costa del Sol; **La Rada,** 3km (1¾ miles) long; and **El Cristo,** only 550m (1,804 ft.) long.

Essentials

ARRIVING The nearest rail links are in Fuengirola. However, Estepona is on the **bus** route from Algeciras to Málaga. If you're driving, head east from Algeciras along the E-5/N-340.

The Costa del Sol

VISITOR INFORMATION   The **tourist office,** Av. San Lorenzo, 1 (www. estepona.es; ✆ **95-280-20-02**), is open Monday to Friday 9am to 8pm, Saturday 10am to 1:30pm.

Exploring Estepona

Estepona's old city remains remarkably untouched by the easy money and glitz of the resorts on its fringes. It's fun to poke around its narrow streets, eat and drink at local bars, and shop the morning **street markets** that take place on Wednesday at Children's Park and Sunday at the Port. The Sunday morning market at the ABC Plaza specializes in crafts. One new attraction has substantially brightened the old center: The **Orquidarium** ★★, Calle Terrace, 86 (www.orchidariumestepona.com; ✆ **95-151-70-74**), features more than 1,300 species of orchids beneath a parabolic dome roof. It's open Tuesday through Saturday 9am to 2pm and 3 to 6pm, Sunday 10am to 2pm. Admission is 3€ adults, 1€ ages 4–11.

Where to Stay in Estepona

Moderately priced hotels are in the town center, while some of the coast's most expensive and luxurious resorts are out of town along the coast.

Hotel Buenavista ★   We've long loved this working-class hotel *residencia* in the middle of town, just across the road from Estepona's main beach. Rooms on the front have little balconies, and on a clear day you can see the green hills of Africa across the straits. The new window-mounted air-conditioning is needed less for cooling than to cut the noise from traffic on the road and boisterous vacationers on the promenade. Even in the highest season, Buenavista is a bargain for an old-fashioned beach vacation. If you're planning to go in July or August, book far ahead to get a jump on the Spanish families who flock here.

Av. de España, 180. www.buenavistaestepona.com. ✆ **95-280-01-37.** 38 units. 57€–100€ double. **Amenities:** Restaurant (separate building); free Wi-Fi.

Hotel TRH Paraíso ★   Panoramic views, dramatic architecture, and all the amenities of a good resort make the TRH Paraíso the leader in the moderate price category along this stretch of the Costa del Sol. It's across the highway from Playa Costalita some 12km (7½ miles) from the center of Estepona. Built in the 1980s, the resort is a little longer in the tooth than some of its competition, which shows in the somewhat smaller bedroom size. But every room has a balcony looking out on the ocean. Guests enjoy discounts at 25 area golf courses, and a special playground and pool are reserved for children.

Carretera de Cádiz, Km 167. en.hoteltrhparaiso.com. ✆ **95-288-30-00.** 171 units. 57€–167€ double, 86€–291€ suite. Free parking. **Amenities:** 2 restaurants; 4 bars; children's center; Jacuzzi; 2 pools (1 indoor); sauna; free Wi-Fi.

Kempinski Hotel Bahía ★★★   This sprawling estate hotel between Estepona and Puerto Banús has such broad landscaped lawns that it looks like it should have a golf course. But, no—that landscape is part of the charm of an oasis hotel, though the golf desk can arrange tee times at any of nine nearby courses. All rooms and suites have private balconies or terraces, with garden or sea views. Fresh from a contemporary but Art Deco-inspired makeover, the rooms are spacious, the beds are soft, and the large bathrooms are paved in marble. Families favor the Bahia for its excellent children's center and its connections to English-speaking babysitters. Meals are literally a moveable feast, from an indoor breakfast buffet to lunch by the sea to romantic dining in the gardens.

Carretera de Cádiz, Km 159, Playa el Padrón. www.kempinski.com. ✆ **95-280-95-00.** 145 units. 190€–430€ double, 334€–593€ jr. suite. Garage parking 20€; outside parking free. **Amenities:** 4 restaurants; 3 bars; children's center; 4 pools (1 heated indoor); spa; outdoor tennis court; free Wi-Fi.

Where to Eat in Estepona

In summer, the cheapest places to eat in Estepona are the *chiringuitos,* little dining areas set up by local fishermen on the beach. They feature seafood, including sole and sardine kebabs grilled over an open fire. Tapas bars are often called *freidurías* (fried-fish bars), and you'll find most of them at the corner of Calle de los Reyes and La Terraza. Tables spill onto the sidewalks in summer. *Gambas a la plancha* (shrimp) are the favorite (but not cheapest) dish to order.

La Alcaría de Ramos ★ SPANISH   There's a definite international cast to the nominally Spanish cuisine here, betrayed in part by extensive use of French on the menu. That said, grilled sole with vegetables and potatoes is almost always a pleasant light dish in any language, and grilled sea bass in a Basque red pepper sauce is a dependable treat. The owners, the Ramos brothers, reserve much of their inventiveness for salads and soups, offering treats like a baby squid salad with Emmentaler cheese and lemon vinaigrette, or raspberry gazpacho with yogurt and mint sorbet. Opt for dining in the terrace garden if the weather permits.

Carretera de Cádiz, Km 167. www.laalcariaderamos.es. ⓒ **95-288-61-78.** Entrees 15€–26€. Reservations recommended. Mon–Sat 7:30pm–midnight.

PUERTO BANÚS ★

A favorite resort for international celebrities, the coastal village of Puerto Banús was created almost overnight and made to look as if it had been there forever. It's exactly what a set designer would think a Costa del Sol fishing village should look like—except that the harbor is filled with yachts rather than scruffy fishing boats, and the amplified bells of the King Abdul Aziz Mosque call the faithful to prayer. Expensive bars and restaurants line the waterfront. To reach the town, take one of 15 buses that run daily from Marbella, or drive west from Marbella along E-15.

Where to Stay in Puerto Banús

H10 Andalucía Plaza ★   Despite being attached to the Marbella Casino (p. 355), this Costa del Sol pioneer hotel has rebranded itself as family-friendly. During the summer, it operates the Daisy Club entertainment program for children, and the bouncers at the casino doors make sure no one under 18 enters. Recent renovations have restored some of the hotel's luster, with silver and gold trim shining from the walls and movie star portraits prominent in the public areas. Rooms vary from tight doubles to larger doubles and suites, but most have balconies or terraces. Casino admission is free for guests. The beach is a 10-minute walk away, through a highway underpass.

Urbanización Nueva Andalucía, s/n. www.hotelh10esteponapalace.com. ⓒ **95-281-20-00.** 400 units. 92€–255€ double; 150€–274€ jr. suite. Free parking. **Amenities:** 2 restaurants; 2 bars; bikes; 3 pools (1 indoor); spa; free Wi-Fi.

Park Plaza Suites Hotel ★   Located right next to the yacht harbor, this small hotel often houses yachtsmen in need of a break from the boat.

The chic harbor at Puerto Banús.

Despite the name, most rooms are doubles (just six real suites) but they are spacious and comfortable in a very contemporary style, and there are nearby apartments that range up to three bedrooms. Floors are wood laminate and bedspreads and draperies are designer Mediterranean chic. Every room has a large balcony or terrace as well as cooking facilities and a washer/dryer. You can walk out the door to restaurants and nightclubs—or enjoy a private stretch of beach. Minimum stays are required in July and August.

Paseo Marítimo de Benabola, s/n. www.parkplazasuiteshotel.com. ✆ **95-290-90-00.** 51 units. 78€–258€ double; 108€–465€ suite and apartments. Parking 26€. **Amenities:** Restaurant; bar; exercise room; Jacuzzi; free Wi-Fi.

Where to Eat in Puerto Banús

Lounge La Habana ★ SEAFOOD/SPANISH   It may not be Valencia, but the rice dishes here are as authentic and balanced as you'll find on the Costa del Sol—even if they are all labeled "paella." The black rice tinted with squid ink (a Catalan dish) is especially good, and the rice with red king prawns *(carabineros)* is satisfyingly salty and sweet. Fish dishes are the real stars of the menu, though, especially the octopus with creamy potatoes.

The wine list—especially the sparkling wines—is unusually extensive for the Costa del Sol. Many dockside eating establishments around here have gone ultra-casual, but La Habana retains an old-fashioned sense of decorum.

Muelle de Levante, 7. www.lahabanalounge.es. © **657-671-432.** Entrees 15€–28€. Tues–Sun 1pm–midnight.

Los Bandidos ★★ INTERNATIONAL   Despite the name, you won't get robbed at Los Bandidos. This savvy restaurant has negotiated the changing trends of international cuisine since the late 1980s, and its current incarnation combines classical French service, a dining room plastered with photos of bygone celebrities, and an adept menu with just enough Nordic touches to suggest a passing acquaintance with the cooking of Rene Redzepi. That said, the strength of the kitchen lies with the classics: Chateaubriand, grilled turbot, veal fillet with foie gras, or sole in white wine sauce.

Muelle Ribera, 35. losbandidos.es. © **95-281-59-15.** Entrees 16€–40€. Daily 1–4pm and 7pm–midnight.

Shopping in Punta Banús

The **Nueva Andalucía Artisan Market,** Avenida Manolete, next to the bullring in Puerto Banús, is one of the largest and most colorful flea markets on the Costa del Sol. More than 120 vendors offer their merchandise on Saturdays from 9am to 2pm.

MARBELLA ★★

Although it's nearly as packed with tourists as Torremolinos, Marbella is the nicest resort town along the Costa del Sol. The big difference is money: Some of the region's finest upscale resorts coexist here with budget hotels. A long-ago visitor to the coast, Queen Isabel II, is said to have exclaimed, *"¡Qué mar tan bello!"* ("What a beautiful sea!"), and the name stuck.

Essentials

ARRIVING   The main **bus** link is between Málaga and Marbella, with **Avanzabus** (www.avanzabus.com; © **91-272-28-32**) running more than 30 buses a day. The trip takes 45 minutes to 1¾ hours and costs 6.35€ to 8.70€ one-way. Madrid and Barcelona each have three daily buses to Marbella. The bus station is located on the outskirts of Marbella on Avenida Trapiche, a 5-minute ride from the center of town. If you're driving, Marbella is on the N-340/E-15.

VISITOR INFORMATION   The **tourist office,** Glorieta de la Fontanilla, s/n (turismo.marbella.es; © **95-276-87-60**), is open Monday to Friday

Kite-surfing in Marbella.

9:30am to 9pm, Saturday 10am to 2pm. Another tourist office with the same hours is on the Plaza de los Naranjos (© **95-277-46-93**).

Exploring Marbella

Even if you don't stay here, you might want to spend a day exploring. Marbella retains traces of its origins as a pleasant seaside town at the foot of the Sierra Blanca. That past persists in the palatial town hall, medieval ruins, and ancient Moorish walls.

Marbella's most charming area is the **Old Quarter** of narrow cobblestone streets centered on **Plaza de los Naranjos.** From the wide promenade along the beach, you simply climb a set of marble stairs past several Salvador Dalí bronze statues and cross the **Alameda,** a leafy park with tiled benches. Suddenly you're in a tangle of medieval streets and whitewashed houses hung with pots of geraniums.

The biggest attractions in Marbella, however, are **El Fuerte** and **La Fontanilla,** the two main beaches, which are lined with often very good and reasonably priced fish restaurants. There are other, more secluded beaches, but you need your own transportation to get there.

Where to Stay in Marbella

EXPENSIVE

Don Carlos Leisure Resort & Spa ★★   This long-time Marbella favorite reinvented itself (yet again) with the addition of the adults-only "Oasis by Don Carlos" section of the resort. This wing is devoted to fitness and wellness, with an emphasis on slimming and toning already bronzed and pampered bodies. The rest of the resort remains as it has been for years: an oasis of gardens spilling downhill from the stand of pines behind the main hotel to the edge of one of the best beaches on this section of the coast. Small business conferences sometimes take over the hotel during the off-season, but Don Carlos is oriented to a leisure clientele.

Carretera de Cádiz Km 192. doncarlosresort.com/en/. © **95-276-88-00.** 256 units. 165€–439€ double, 460€–527€ villa. Free parking. **Amenities:** 3 restaurants; 2 bars; babysitting; exercise room; 2 outdoor pools, 1 indoor pool; sauna; spa; 12 outdoor tennis courts (lit); free Wi-Fi.

Marbella Club ★★★   When the Marbella Club opened in 1954, there was almost nothing else around it. Exclusive and expensive from the outset, it swiftly established Marbella as an alternative to the French and Italian Rivieras for aristocrats, tycoons, and yachtsmen who prefer their weather sunny and their beaches sandy. Three generations later, all those lovely gardens and trees have matured, and the clusters of bungalows and garden pavilions have evolved a homey yet clubby ambience. Rooms vary a lot, but they are without exception spacious and decorated like a magazine photo spread. All of them have either private balconies or terraces. Service is discreet and superb.

Bulevar Príncipe Alfonso von Hohenlohe, s/n. www.marbellaclub.com. © **95-282-22-11.** 121 units. 425€–865€ double; 490€–3,945€ suite. Free parking. **Amenities:** 2 restaurants; bar; bikes; concierge; golf course; 3 pools (1 indoor); spa; free Wi-Fi.

Puente Romano ★★★   Neighbor to the Marbella Club and, for some guests' money, every bit its equal, Puente Romano began as a cluster of vacation apartments but came into its own as a luxurious and beautifully landscaped colony of high-end lodging in the 1970s. The intervening decades have only seen it mellow further to become an Andulucían seaside village for the well-to-do. Guest rooms are spacious and have private or semi-private balconies or terraces. The grounds are a veritable maze of paths leading past fountains and little waterfalls, beneath arbors enshrouded in vines or flowers, and patches of blooming gardens. Complimentary greens fee and shuttle service to the 18-hole golf course is included with the room.

Bulevar Príncipe Alfonso von Hohenlohe, s/n (Carretera de Cádiz Km 177). www.puenteromano.com. © **95-282-09-00.** 285 units. 224€–410€ double, 314€–2,380€ suite. Limited free parking. **Amenities:** 3 restaurants; 2 bars; babysitting; children's center; concierge; health club; 3 outdoor pools; sauna; 10 outdoor tennis courts (lit); free Wi-Fi.

8

THE COSTA DEL SOL

Marbella

MODERATE

The Town House ★★   Looking like an interior designer's portfolio of old-school luxury, this boutique hotel was created from an old house in the center of Marbella's venerable Casco Antiguo, or old quarter. The walls were re-stuccoed and whitewashed and the tile floors re-laid, and it now gleams like a brand-new hotel. The architecture helps make the experience, and you'll find yourself spending as much time as possible on the roof terrace at the start and end of the day (it's too hot at midday). Views from the terrace stretch over a jumble of Old Town rooftops down to the boardwalk on the beach, a 10-minute walk away.

Plaza Tetuán, Calle Alderete, 7. www.townhousemarbella.com. ℭ **95-290-17-91.** 9 rooms. 125€–185€ double. **Amenities:** Bar; room service; free Wi-Fi.

INEXPENSIVE

Hostal Enriqueta ★★   The most charming of the modest hotels in the old quarter of Marbella, the Enriqueta is a classic example of Andalucían architecture, its rooms arranged around a flower-filled central courtyard. Rooms 208 and 202 have balconies overlooking that courtyard. All rooms have air-conditioning, but guests rarely turn it on because the thick-walled old building tends to stay quite cool. Rooms are very plain and very small, but the family that runs the *hostal* is warm and friendly. Stairs are steep and narrow, and there is no elevator. If climbing is a problem, request one of the four rooms on the ground level.

Calle de los Balleros, 18. www.hostalenriqueta.com. ℭ **95-282-75-52.** 20 rooms. 35€–100€ double. **Amenities:** Free Wi-Fi.

Where to Eat in Marbella

EXPENSIVE

Dani García Restaurante ★★★ CONTEMPORARY SPANISH This eponymous restaurant at the Puente Romano resort (p. 351) showcases the talents of Marbella's most innovative and star-bedecked chef. García launched this elegant venture with just 50 seats in the main dining room and 20 more in a private dining room. While the venue features some of García's iconic dishes, like "popcorn" olives (exploded with liquid nitrogen) with lobster salad, or suckling pig with pumpkin and orange, it also serves as a showcase for his newest experiments. Make reservations as far ahead as possible.

Bulevar Príncipe Alfonso von Hohenlohe, s/n (Carretera de Cádiz Km 177). www.grupodanigarcia.com. ℭ **95-282-09-00.** Fixed-price menus 145€–220€. Tues–Sat 1:30–3:30pm and 8:30–10:30pm.

Marbella Club Grill ★★ INTERNATIONAL   The Marbella Club (p. 351) has reorganized its dining into several discrete venues, all under the talented direction of executive chef Juan Gálvez. Most guests take lunch at the bountiful buffet at the **Beach Club,** which is open to non-guests as well. Diners seeking out avant-garde contemporary Spanish cuisine gravitate to the **MC Café.** The old standby, however, remains the **Marbella Club Grill,** with seating both indoors and outside on a terrace. You dine amid blooming flowers, flickering candles, and strains of live music—perhaps a Spanish classical guitarist, a small chamber orchestra playing 19th-century classics, or a Latin American vocalist. The contemporary pan-European menu changes seasonally. You might begin with a lobster cocktail with diced mango and honey truffle dressing, or perhaps a spicy coconut soup with lemongrass. Specialties include beef entrecôte with mushroom pepper sauce, and seared tuna with ginger dressing.

Bulevar Príncipe Alfonso von Hohenlohe s/n. www.marbellaclub.com. ✆ **95-282-22-11.** Entrees 27€–45€. Summer daily 9pm–12:30am; winter daily 8–11:30pm.

MODERATE

Casa de la Era ★ ANDALUCÍAN   This erstwhile country house retains its rustic charm inside, although the "country" around it has evolved into an industrial park. The restaurant emphasizes coastal Andalucían cuisine. House specialties include *fideos* (noodles cooked like rice in a paella) with monkfish and clams; fried eggplant drizzled with honey; and oxtail braised in the Córdoba style. One unusual choice is a succession of grilled seasonal vegetables brought to the table on skewers until you say "enough!"

Carretera de Ojén Km 0.5. www.casadelaera.com. ✆ **95-277-06-25.** Entrees 12€–21€. July–Aug daily 8–11pm; Sept–June Sat–Sun 1–4pm.

Shopping in Marbella

You will find many international brands in this upscale town. If you'd like to purchase some of Andalucía's regional ceramics, a good bet is **Cerámica San Nicolás,** Plaza de la Iglesia, 1 (✆ **95-277-05-46**). For a serious piece of art, **Galleria d'Arte Van Gestel,** Plaza de los Naranjos, 11 (✆ **95-277-48-19**), in the Old Town is one of the most established galleries in Marbella. It's worth stopping in just to see how harmoniously contemporary art fills the spaces of a historic home. **Vinacoteca La Cartuja,** Plaza Joaquín Gómez Agüera, 5 (lacartuja.wine/; ✆ **95-277-52-03**), is dedicated to carrying as many Spanish wines as possible.

Marbella Nightlife

You will need to pack more than a bathing suit and flip-flops if you want to join the nightlife scene. There's more international wealth hanging out in the watering holes of Marbella, and a wider choice of glam (or pseudo-glam) discos than virtually anywhere else in Spain. Foremost among them is **Discoteca Olivia Valere** on Carretera Istan, N-340 Km 0.8 (www.oliviavalere.com; ✆ **95-282-88-61**), which can hold up to 1,000 people. It's open from 9pm to 7am and charges a cover of 30€. Fashionable club wear is essential.

A MARBELLA tasca CRAWL

Marbella boasts more small tapas bars than virtually any other resort town in southern Spain. Even if you set out with a specific place in mind, you'll likely be distracted en route by a newer, older, bigger, smaller, brighter, or just more interesting joint you want to try—which is half the fun.

Prices and hours are remarkably consistent: The coffeehouse that opens at 7am will switch to wine and tapas when the first patron asks for it (sometimes shortly after breakfast), and then continue through the day dispensing wine, sherry, and, more recently, bottles of beer. On average, tapas cost 3€ to 10€, but some foreign visitors configure them into *platos combinados*.

Tapas served along the Costa del Sol are principally Andalucían in origin, with an emphasis on seafood. The most famous plate, *fritura malagueña*, consists of fried fish based on the catch of the day. Sometimes *ajo blanco*, a garlicky local version of gazpacho made with almonds, is served, especially in summer. Fried squid or octopus is another favorite, as are little Spanish-style herb-flavored meatballs. Other well-known tapas include tuna, grilled shrimp, *piquillos*

rellenos (red peppers stuffed with fish), *bacalao* (salt cod), and mushrooms sautéed in olive oil and garlic.

Tapas bars line many of the narrow streets of Marbella's historic core, with rich pickings around **Calle del Perral** and, to a somewhat lesser extent, **Calle Miguel Cana.** In August especially, when you want to escape wall-to-wall people and the heat and noise of the Old Town, head for one of the shoreline restaurants and tapas bars called *chiringuitos*. All serve local specialties, and you can order a full meal, a snack, tapas, or a drink. **Restaurante Los Sardinales,** Playa de los Alicates (www.lossardinales.com; ✆ 95-283-70-12), serves some of the best sangria in the area. Another good bet is **Chiringuito La Pesquera,** Playa Marbellamar (www.lapesquera.com; ✆ 95-277-03-38), where you can order a plate of fresh grilled sardines.

You can enjoy a more low-key night in the heart of historic Marbella in its *bodegas* and taverns. **La Venencia Los Olivos,** Avda Miguel Cano, 15 (bodegaslavenencia.com; ℂ **95-285-79-13**), is conveniently located adjacent to one of the town's widest thoroughfares. Its wide choice of sherries, wines, and tapas draws lots of chattering patrons.

Although hardly authentic, **Flamenco Los Chatos Ana María,** Plaza Santa Cristo, 4 (hardoklaamann.wixsite.com/flamencomarbella; ℂ **634-366-578**), is a good start for foreign visitors who speak limited Spanish. The long, often-crowded bar area sells tapas, wine, sherry, and a selection of more international libations. This is late-night entertainment—the doors don't open until 9pm, and the crowd really gets going between midnight and 3am. Cover and one drink cost 25€.

Seven kilometers (4⅓ miles) west of Marbella, near Puerto Banús, **Casino Marbella,** Hotel H10 Andalucía Plaza, Urbanización Nueva Andalucía (www.casinomarbella.com; ℂ **95-281-40-00**), is a favorite with visitors from northern Europe. Jackets are not required for men, but T-shirts are frowned upon, and shorts and athletic shoes are not allowed. Casino hours are daily from noon to 4am for the slot parlor, daily 8pm to 4am for the main floor. A passport is required for admission.

FUENGIROLA & LOS BOLICHES ★

The former fishing towns of Fuengirola and Los Boliches lie halfway between the more famous resorts of Marbella and Torremolinos. Less-developed Los Boliches is just 0.8km (½ mile) from Fuengirola. These towns don't have the panache of Marbella or the range of facilities of Torremolinos, but except for two major luxury hotels, Fuengirola and Los Boliches are cheaper and attract large numbers of budget-conscious northern European tourists. The best beaches—**Santa Amalja, Carvajal,** and **Las Gaviotas**—are broad, clean, and sandy.

Essentials

ARRIVING   Fuengirola is on the C1 commuter rail *(cercanía)* route from Málaga, with trains every half-hour all day. The station is at Avda. Jesús Santos Rein, s/n, 3 blocks from the leisure port and the beach, or a 15-minute stroll down the street from the zoo. The trip takes 45 minutes and costs 3€. To drive from Marbella, take the N-340/E-15 east.

VISITOR INFORMATION   The **tourist office,** Paseo Jesús Santos Rein, 6 (www.fuengirola.org; ℂ **95-246-76-25**), is open Monday to Friday 9am to 6pm, Saturday and Sunday 10am to 2pm.

Exploring Fuengirola & Los Boliches

Everybody goes to the big **flea market** at Fuengirola on Tuesday. Many British retirees who live in the holiday apartments nearby attend this

family-friendly COSTA DEL SOL

The Costa del Sol may have one of the hottest nightlife scenes in Spain, but it is also a great destination for families. When you and the kids need a break from the beach, there are plenty of attractions to keep everyone happy.

In 2010, President Obama and his family visited **Selwo Aventura** (www.selwo.es; ✆ **95-257-77-73**), highway A7, km 162.5 in Estepona. The wildlife park focuses on mega-fauna—Asian elephants, cheetahs, lions, giraffes, white rhinoceroses, and hippopotamuses. Daily feeding times for many of the animals are posted. A trampoline area, zipwire, and hanging bridges are great for active kids. The wildlife park is closed January and early February; in July and August it's open daily 10am to 8pm, with shorter hours the rest of the year. Adults cost 26€, seniors and children 18€; online advance purchases get significant discounts.

Benalmádena draws families with a cluster of three attractions. **Sea Life Benalmádena** (www.visitsealife.com; ✆ **95-256-01-50**) at Malapesquera Beach features a tunnel-like aquarium, a rock pool, and habitats for sharks, giant turtles, and rays. It's open daily 10am to 6pm. Discounted admission, purchased online, is 12€; treat the kids to a round of minigolf for only 3.50€ more. **Selwo Marina,** Parque de la Paloma, s/n (www.selwomarina.es; ✆ **95-257-77-73**), features dolphin and sea lion encounters and an exotic bird exhibition. Its Penguinarium has one of the most notable collections of penguins in Europe. The marina is open mid-February through October daily from 10am to at least 6pm with later hours in summer. It is open weekends only in November. Admission is 21€ adults, 15.50€ seniors and children; there are significant discounts for online advance purchases. For good old-fashioned fun, **Tivoli World,** Arroyo de la Miel (www.tivoli.es; ✆ **95-257-70-16**), has about 40 different amusement rides and a full schedule of entertainment. It's open July and August daily 5:30pm to 1:30am, with more limited days and hours March to June and September to October. Park entrance for adults is 8€, for seniors 5€; an unlimited-rides pass is 15€.

Also see **Bioparc Fuengirola,** p. 356, in the town of Fuengirola, and **Museo Alborania,** p. 368, in Málaga.

sprawling market, later stopping in at one of the Irish or British pubs for a pint, just like they used to do back home.

Bioparc Fuengirola ★★ ZOO   Now one of Europe's model zoo facilities, this sensitive presentation of animals in four different ecosystems is easily the top attraction on the Costa del Sol. There are no cages, but design keeps animals and humans apart with moats and landscape features. The zoo replicates the tropical rainforests of Madagascar, Equatorial Africa, Southeast Asia, and the Indo-Pacific islands with 1,300 animals representing 140 species. There is a children's play area as well as a couple of restaurants and cafes.

Calle Camilo José Cela, 8–10. www.bioparcfuengirola.es. ✆ **95-266-63-01.** Admission 21€ adults; 17€ seniors; 16€ ages 3–9. Daily July–Aug 10am–11pm, more limited hours rest of year.

Castillo Sohail ★ CASTLE Fuengirola may have been built up as a discount beach resort town, but it retains one remnant of its Moorish past. The Almohad dynasty built this castle in the 12th century on the hill overlooking the beach where both Romans and Carthaginians had earlier settled. The castle was modified many times after it fell into Christian hands (the armies of Isabel and Fernando) in 1485. Restored by Fuengirola trade school students, it is surrounded by beautiful green lawns. To find it, walk east along Paseo Marítimo toward the elegant cable-stay bridge over the Río Fuengirola.

Paseo Marítimo, s/n. ⓒ **95-246-74-57.** Free admission. Tues–Sun 10am–2pm, also 3:30–6:30pm May–Sept.

Where to Stay in Fuengirola & Los Boliches

Hotel Villa de Laredo ★ We always think of the skyline in Fuengirola as "the city by the sea," since so many high-rise hotels shoot straight up into the sky at the edge of the sand. This rather modest hotel with a rooftop swimming pool has a great view of the sandy scene below. It is located smack-dab in the middle of everything, which means that you can easily leave the hotel to dine and shop elsewhere. Some rooms have small terraces opening onto the beachside promenade, but the quarters, even in these, are rather tight. (A mirrored closet door makes the room look a little bigger.) All in all, if you plan mostly to be out soaking up sun and hitting the bars, a room here offers a pleasant spot to sleep.

Paseo Marítimo Rey de España, 42. www.hotelvilladelaredo.es. ⓒ **95-247-76-89.** 74 units. 63€–128€ double. **Amenities:** Restaurant; bar; outdoor pool; free Wi-Fi.

Occidental Fuengirola ★ Formerly known as Las Piramides before a 2019 top-to-bottom renovation, this pair of 10-story towers joined by a large marble lobby is one of the best of Fuengirola's large properties. The rooms are surprisingly spacious, with pale walls and wood floors. Bathrooms are decked in marble, from the walk-in showers to the floor and walls. Best of all, each room has a sea-view balcony with a sliding door and chairs for sitting outside and listening to the surf.

Calle Miguel Márquez 43. www.barcelo.com. ⓒ **95-247-06-00.** 316 rooms. 116€–188€ double. Parking 20€. **Amenities:** Restaurant; 2 bars; 2 pools (1 indoor); free Wi-Fi.

Where to Eat Around Fuengirola & Los Boliches

Charolais Bodega Restaurante ★★ SPANISH The Charolais began as a wine bar, and its cellar holds more than 400 choices. You can enjoy a glass of wine with a wide variety of creative tapas in a contemporary bar, or in the more sedate restaurant (note that they have separate entrances). The owner is a big fan of Spanish red wines, so the menu tends to emphasize dishes best consumed with *tintos*. The house specialties are baby lamb chops and duck breast with mushrooms and port wine sauce.

Calle Larga, 14. www.bodegacharolais.com. ✆ **95-247-54-41.** Tapas 4€–11€, entrees 14€–30€, set menus 30€–40€. Reservations essential on summer weekends. Mon–Sat 1–4pm and 7–11:30pm. Closed Dec–Feb.

Sollo ★★★ INTERNATIONAL   Locals have dubbed Sollo's Diego Gallegos "the caviar chef" because of his nibbling menu featuring Granada-farmed caviar. The restaurant, in fact, is named for the Andalucían sturgeon, which he serves with great gusto. But that's just the beginning: Gallegos serves all sorts of freshwater fish, which is unusual on the Mediterranean coast. Some are locally farmed (tilapia, catfish), and some, like eel, are wild-caught species. The restaurant offers only tasting menus—one short, one longer—both studded with dishes you've never tried before.

In the Doubletree by Hilton, Avda del Higuerón, 48. www.sollo.es. ✆ **95-138-56-22.** Tasting menus 75€–100€. Mon–Sat 7:30pm–midnight.

MIJAS ★

It's hard to believe that this mountain "White Town" (so called for the whitewashed buildings tucked into the hillside) could even exist just 8km (5 miles) north of the frenzied coastal road N-340/E-15 and the beachside resorts. Mijas sits at the foot of a mountain range near the turnoff to Fuengirola, and from its lofty height—450m (1,476 ft.) above sea level—you get a panoramic view of the Mediterranean.

There's frequent bus service to Mijas from the terminal at Fuengirola, 30 minutes away. To drive from Fuengirola, take the Mijas road north.

Exploring Mijas

Celts, Phoenicians, and Moors preceded today's tourist throngs to Mijas. Today the charming town itself is the attraction, more than any specific sight. The easiest way to get around its cobblestone streets is to walk, though many tourists opt instead to rent a so-called "donkey taxi"—either riding astride the donkey or in a donkey-pulled cart.

If you consider Mijas overrun with souvenir shops, head for the park at the top of Cuesta de la Villa, where you'll see the ruins of a **Moorish fortress** dating from A.D. 833.

Every Saturday from May into October, busloads of bullfight fans descend on Mijas for the heavily advertised weekly *corridas*.

Where to Stay & Eat in Mijas

Restaurant-Café Meguiñez ★ INTERNATIONAL   So few people live full-time in Mijas that it has no authentic local cuisine, but this cheerful little restaurant and wine bar serves a good range of generic Spanish dishes ranging from oxtail stew to fried pork chops with egg. Most folks

A vacation ritual: riding the "donkey taxis" in Mijas.

like to order a variety of tapas and a bottle of wine and chill out under the grape arbor patio out back—a pleasant respite from the village's tourist bustle.

Calle San Sebastian, 4. restaurantemeguinez.wordpress.com. ✆ **95-248-54-79.** Tapas 4€–7€, entrees 9€–16€, set menu 12€. Daily 10am–1am.

Hotel TRH Mijas Beach & Cultural ★   This was one of the pioneer hotels of the Mijas hillside, built in the 1970s before the Mijas-Costa developments got underway. Despite the name, it's not on the beach, but it has great ocean views from most public areas and guest rooms. Consider this hotel for its pleasant grounds where you can sit sipping drinks in the brilliant sun (or beneath an umbrella), leaving it to others to sweat it out on the beach. If you're driving, it's a good base for touring the region.

Urbanización Tamisa, 2. www.trhmijas.com. ✆ **95-248-58-00.** 204 units. 97€–147€ double. Parking 15€. **Amenities:** Restaurant; bar; bikes; outdoor pool; sauna; tennis court; free Wi-Fi.

La Cala Resort ★★   Cabell B. Robinson called the terrain here the most challenging of his career when he designed the first two 18-hole courses at this contemporary golf resort (there's now a third). The property is 7km (4⅓ miles) from the beach, so your focus here is likely greens and fairways, and the only sand you'll find is in the bunkers. Rooms are reasonably spacious and furnished in a low-key contemporary style.

La Cala de Mijas. www.lacala.com. ℂ **95-266-90-16.** 107 units. 99€–144€ double. **Amenities:** 2 restaurants; bar; exercise room; 3 18-hole golf courses; 2 pools (1 indoor); room service; spa; 2 outdoor tennis courts (lit); free Wi-Fi.

TORREMOLINOS ★

This Mediterranean beach resort stands for everything good and bad about the Costa del Sol. Europeans and Americans flock here for the bargain rooms, the sweaty social scene, and the preponderance of English-speaking bars and coffee shops. Many relax here after a whirlwind tour of Europe— the living is easy, the people are fun, and there are no historical monuments to visit. A sleepy fishing village until the 1950s, Torremolinos has been swamped by cookie-cutter cement resort hotels. But overdevelopment has its upside: Hotels must slash room prices to win over customers, making Torrie one of the best bargains on the Costa del Sol.

Essentials

ARRIVING   Nearby Málaga airport (p. 364) serves Torremolinos. Frequent **trains** to Torremolinos run from both the airport and the Málaga

Resort hotels line the beach in Torremolinos.

train station. For train information, visit renfe.com or call © **90-232-03-20. Buses** also run frequently between Málaga and Torremolinos; call © **90-214-31-44** for schedules. Drivers should take the N-340/E-15 west from Málaga or the N-340/E-15 east from Marbella.

VISITOR INFORMATION The **tourist information office** at Plaza Comunidades Autónomas (turismotorremolinos.es/en; © **95-237-19-09**) is open daily 8am to 3pm (in winter Mon–Fri 9:30am–2:30pm).

Where to Stay in Torremolinos

MODERATE

Hotel Tropicana & Beach Club ★★ At the east end of La Carihuela beach, the Tropicana has an edge on most Torrie hotels, being a little removed from the crush of lodgings closer to the city center. It even has its own beach club—i.e., the legal right to claim a piece of the long strand. A tropical theme dominates, with lots of large palms and pastel colors. The somewhat forced conviviality doesn't quite disguise the fact that the Tropicana is yet another salmon-tinted stucco hotel, bristling with private balconies, overlooking the beach. But the prime location puts it close to the many restaurants of La Carihuela.

Calle Trópico, 6. www.hotelmstropicana.com. © **95-238-66-00.** 84 units. 55€–216€ double. Free parking. **Amenities:** Restaurant; bar; outdoor pool; free Wi-Fi.

Meliã Costa del Sol ★ There's no denying the behemoth size of this grand hotel, located right on Playa de Bajondillo. The Meliã group has revamped this veteran—one of the first generation of Costa del Sol resorts—to make public areas more majestic and elegant and has brought guest rooms more in line with contemporary expectations. Floors 5–9, a.k.a. "the Level," enjoy such perks as a lounge with snacks. What really distinguishes this hotel, though, is the size of the rooms. The smallest are 32 sq. m (344 sq. ft.), and suites are nearly twice that size.

Paseo Marítimo, 11. www.meliacostadelsol.solmelia.com. © **95-238-66-77.** 538 units. 60€–234€ double; 135€–300€ jr. suite; 310€–365€ suite. Free parking. **Amenities:** 2 restaurants; 2 bars; bikes; concierge; health club and spa; 2 outdoor pools; free Wi-Fi.

Roc Lago Rojo ★★ The 1970s architecture, inspired by the Habitat apartments built for the 1964 Montreal Olympics, looks like it was sprung from Woody Allen's *Sleeper,* but complete renovations have kept these studio-style rooms in touch with contemporary decor. Each has a terrace with sea view. The hotel's "adults only recommended" policy focuses on romantic retreats for couples. Small pets (up to 22 lb./10kg) are permitted only in the junior suites.

Calle Miami, 5. www.roc-hotels.com. © **95-238-76-66.** 188 units. 108€–186€ double; 125€–195€ jr. suite. Parking 17€. **Amenities:** Restaurant; bar; babysitting; outdoor pool; free Wi-Fi (must reserve through website).

INEXPENSIVE

Hotel Los Jazmínes ★   We happen to think that Playamar, the stretch of beach in front of Los Jazmines, is one of the best strands in Torremolinos: Located east of the town center, it gets fewer day-trippers. This nearby hotel faces a plaza at the foot of the shady Avenida del Lido. Smallish rooms furnished with queen or double beds overlook either the hotel garden or the beach. Apartments have two bedrooms, a kitchen, living room, bath, and outdoor terraces.

Av. de Lido, 6. hotellosjazmines.com. 𝒞 **95-238-50-33.** 100 units. 47€–135€ double, 75€–160€ apartment. **Amenities:** Restaurant; bar; outdoor pool; free Wi-Fi.

Hotel Residencia Miami ★   Built in 1950 as the summer home of Granada Gypsy queen and flamenco dancer Lola Medina, this white stucco palace became a hotel in 1957, and has matured as a grand complex with an air of mystery. Gardens surround the property and the walls drip with bougainvillea and fuchsia. The rooms are not large, but they feel more compact than small. There's a massive fireplace in the rustic lounge.

Calle Aladino. 14. www.residencia-miami.com. 𝒞 **95-238-52-55.** 26 units. 52€–76€ double. **Amenities:** Bar; outdoor pool; free Wi-Fi.

Where to Eat in Torremolinos

A good spot to try is the food court at **La Nogalera,** the major gathering place between the coast road and the beach. Head down Calle del Cauce to this compound of modern whitewashed Andalucían buildings. Open to pedestrian traffic only, it's a maze of passageways, courtyards, and patios for eating and drinking. You can find everything from sandwiches and pizza to Belgian waffles and scrambled eggs.

IN TORREMOLINOS

Casa Juan ★ SEAFOOD   We seriously doubt if La Carihuela's shrunken fishing fleet could keep this semiformal, 170-seat restaurant in seafood for more than an hour. It is part of a small empire of seafood restaurants in the immediate neighborhood, but we're suckers for the splendid display of crustaceans and shellfish at Casa Juan's entrance. If you don't order the mixed-shellfish platter *(mariscada de mariscos),* try the cod with saffron sauce or the *zarzuela* (seafood stew) of shellfish.

Calle San Gines, 18–20. www.losmellizos.net/casajuan. 𝒞 **95-237-35-12.** Entrees 12€–45€. Daily 12:30–4:30pm and 7:30–11:30pm. Closed Dec.

El Figón de Montemar ★ ASTURIAN/ANDALUCÍAN   The menu here is a rather unusual combination, matching the bacon and beans (and hard cider) of Asturias with the fried foam of the Andalucían coast. Yet somehow the combination of chilly Cantabrian coast with the sunny Mediterranean works, and the cozy decor with walls covered in wine racks is welcoming. Small-time fishermen stream in all day with the whiting, red mullet, and other small fish that they bring up in nets. If one brings a nice fat octopus, then there's suddenly a special on the menu.

Av. Espada 101. www.elfigondemontemar.com. ℰ **95-237-26-88.** Entrees 14€–26€. Daily 1–4pm and 8pm–midnight. Closed mid-Jan to mid-Feb.

IN BENALMÁDENA-COSTA

Where Torremolinos ends and Benalmádena-Costa to the west begins is hard to say. The two resorts seem to merge (although driving east, there *is* an ancient sign welcoming visitors to Torrie). Benalmádena offers some of the better restaurants in the area.

Ventorrillo de la Perra ★ ANDALUCÍAN/SPANISH   When this 1785 inn turned smugglers' warehouse was rescued from ruin in 1972 to become a restaurant, the owners took great care to restore the original architecture and decorate in an 18th-century style. The menu is equally old-fashioned and, for the most part, Castilian, featuring oven-roasted wild game, large portions of meat, and whole fish. One of the house specialties is *gazpachuelo malagueño,* a traditional coastal fish stew thickened with new potatoes and spiked with a little sherry and vinegar. It's worth the 15-minute walk from the beach to see one of the rare remnants of pre-development coastal life.

Av. Constitución, 85 (Km 13, Arroyo de la Miel). ℰ **95-244-19-66.** Entrees 17€–32€. Tues–Sun 1–4pm and 8pm–midnight.

Torremolinos Nightlife

Torremolinos has more nightlife than any other spot along the Costa del Sol. The earliest action is always at the bars, which stay lively most of the night, serving drinks and tapas until at least 3am. Note that some bars are open during the day as well.

Bar La Bodega, San Miguel, 40 (ℰ **95-238-73-37**), relies on its colorful clientele and the quality of its tapas to draw customers, who rank this place above dozens of other *tascas* in this popular tourist zone. Many guests come here for lunch or dinner, making a satisfying meal from the plentiful bar food. You'll be lucky if you find space at one of the small tables, but once you begin to order—platters of fried squid, pungent tuna, grilled shrimp, tiny brochettes of sole—you might not be able to stop. Tapas and beer start at 3€. La Bodega is open daily noon to midnight.

Ready to dance off all those tapas? **Octan,** Palma de Mallorca, 36 (octan.es), a well-designed nightclub in the town center, is one of the most convivial in Torremolinos. Strobes, spotlights, fog machines, and a state-of-the-art sound system set the scene. Expect to pay 6€ or more for a drink; the cover charge is from 25€, including one drink. The club is open from 11pm to 6am in summer months only.

For unabashed tourist flamenco, try **Taberna Flamenca Pepe López,** Plaza de la Gamba Alegre (www.tabernaflamencapepelopez.com; ℰ **95-238-12-84**), in the center of Torremolinos. Many of the artists come from the bars of Sevilla and Granada, and from May to October they perform

Wednesday through Saturday at 10pm (shows are much less frequent the rest of the year). Check website or call to confirm first. A 30€ cover includes your first drink and the show.

Gay men and women from throughout northern Europe are almost always in residence in Torremolinos. **Plaza de la Nogalera** and **Plaza de los Tientos** are centers of gay nightlife.

One of the Costa del Sol's major casinos, **Casino Torrequebrada,** Avenida del Sol, Benalmádena-Costa (www.casinotorrequebrada.com; ✆ **95-257-73-00**), is on the lobby level of the Hotel Torrequebrada. In addition to slot machines, it has tables devoted to blackjack, baccarat, poker, and two kinds of roulette. The gaming hall is open daily 8pm to 5am, the restaurant from 9pm to 2am. There is live music on weekends. Casino admission is 3€. Bring your passport to be admitted; you must be over age 18 to enter.

MÁLAGA ★★

Málaga seems to prove the adage that flamenco styles reflect their birthplace, for Andalucía's second-largest city is as deeply nuanced and improvisational as the *malagueña*. Yet travelers often give it short shrift as they rush from the airport or train station to the Costa del Sol resorts, not realizing that Málaga has superb beaches of its own, historic sites and museums, and a strong identity with native son Pablo Picasso. To have it all, base yourself in Málaga, use the train to spend a few hours a day on a Costa del Sol beach, and return to the vibes of a real Spanish city by nightfall. The city of weekday commerce changes into a grand tapas-hopping scene in the evenings and a beach community on the weekends. The redeveloped port district has a striking yacht marina, a romantic walkway by the water, and a new district of shopping, restaurants, and nightlife stretching from the Parque de Málaga to the harbor lighthouse.

Essentials

ARRIVING   More than 40 airlines from around the globe fly into **Aeropuerto Málaga-Costa del Sol** (www.aena.es; ✆ **91-321-10-00**). Travelers from North America can transfer for Málaga in London, Paris, Amsterdam, or Madrid. Within Europe, Air Europa, Vueling, Ryanair, and Iberia offer connections from several cities. There's an 8-minute train connection (3.60€) from Terminal 3 to the main rail station, Estación María Zambrano, on the western edge of the city; change trains there for a "Centro Ciudad-Alameda" train to get to the town center.

Twelve AVE **trains** per day arrive in Málaga from Madrid (trip time: 2½ hr.). Ten trains a day connect Sevilla and Málaga, usually via Córdoba (trip time: 2–2½ hr.). For ticket prices and rail information in Málaga, contact RENFE (www.renfe.com; ✆ **90-232-03-20**).

Buses from all over Spain arrive at the terminal on the Paseo de los Tilos, behind the RENFE offices. Buses include 8 per day from Madrid (trip time: 7 hr.), 5 per day from Córdoba (trip time: 3 hr.), and 10 per day from Sevilla (trip time: 3 hr.). Call ✆ **90-242-22-42** for bus information.

From coastal resorts, you can drive to Málaga along the N-340/E-15.

VISITOR INFORMATION The tourist office, at Plaza de la Marina, 11 (www.malagaturismo.com; ✆ **95-192-62-20**), is open daily 9am to 8pm. The website features several themed audiotours in English, and a free downloadable app with extensive detail on 85 sites around the city. Several firms offer walking tours; inquire at the tourist office.

SPECIAL EVENTS During the second week in August, the city celebrates its Reconquest by Fernando and Isabel in 1487 with parades and bullfights.

Exploring Málaga

Although the train and bus stations are west of the river, almost everything you will want to see in Málaga is located to the east. The skyline makes it easy to navigate: The spire of the one-armed **cathedral** rises in the center of the old city, while restored Moorish walls stitch their way up the Gibralfaro hillside from the old **Alcazaba,** or fortress, a short distance from the waterfront. In the main part of town, elegant **Calle Larios**— paved with marble and lined with top boutiques—links the main **Plaza de la Constitución** to the water-front parks. Tree-lined **Alameda Principal** leads west from the port.

> ### Málaga on Two Wheels
>
> For an old, congested city, Málaga has con-venient and well-marked bicycle paths. For a two-wheel overview of the city, connect with **Bike Tours Málaga,** Calle Vendeja, 6 (www.biketoursmalaga.com; ✆ **650-677-063**). Of the company's several tours, the general "City Bike Tour" takes 3 hours and costs 24€ adults, 19€ students, and 16€ children.

The **Parque de Málaga,** full of subtropical plants, sepa-rates the urban city from the waterfront. The dock areas south of the Parque de Málaga have become the playground of the city, with the former Muelle Dos redeveloped as the delightful walkways of **El Palmeral de las Sopresas,** and **Muelle Uno** as a shopping, nightlife, and dining destination.

Alcazaba ★ PALACE This combination palace and fortress tells the story of the warrior potentates of the Taifa period in Andalucía, when the central Moorish empire had disintegrated into small squabbling king-doms. It does not occupy the highest ground but does command an irregu-lar rocky spur that towers over most of the city. Begun shortly after the Arab conquest of 711, the largest sections were built between the 11th and 14th centuries. Just as Catholic churches often reused stones from Moor-ish buildings, the Alcazaba is filled with fluted Greek-style columns dat-ing from 200 to 300 B.C., and occasional blocks of Roman stones with Latin inscriptions still visible. The most evocative part of the complex is the well-preserved interior palace, with its palpable air of domesticity.

Málaga's Alcazaba, a palace and fortress all in one.

Tip: The main entrance to the Alcazaba lies up a long series of steps on Plaza de la Aduana, but there's an elevator behind the Ayuntamiento (city hall) at Calle Guillén Sotelo and Calle Francisco Bejarrano Robles.

Plaza de la Aduana, Alcazabilla. ℂ **95-222-72-30.** Admission 3.50€ adults; free Sun 2pm–closing. Combined admission with Castillo de Gibralfaro 5.50€. Apr–Oct daily 9am–8pm; Nov–Mar Mon–Sat 9am–6pm, Sun 9am–2pm. Bus: 4, A, 11, 16.

Castillo de Gibralfaro ★ CASTLE The ruins of this Moorish castle-fortress crown a hill overlooking Málaga and the Mediterranean. The walls are crumbling in spots and the keep is overgrown, but views are spectacular. Walking to the castle from town is fairly strenuous, and muggings have been reported over the years. Still, the walk can be atmospheric if it's not too hot. Otherwise, take the bus from the cathedral.

Castillo del Gibralfaro. Admission 3.50€ adults; free Sun 2pm–closing. Combined admission with Alcazaba 5.50€. Daylight hours. Microbus: 35, hourly from cathedral.

Centro Pompidou Málaga ★★ MUSEUM Nicknamed "El Cubo," this multi-colored glass cube is a highlight of the renovated dock area. Its collection comes from the Paris museum, but tends to highlight modern and contemporary artists with ties to Spain and the Mediterranean. Changing temporary exhibitions mean that there's always something new—and usually provocative—to see.

Muelle Uno, s/n. centrepompidou-malaga.eu. ℂ **95-192-62-00.** Admission to permanent collection and temporary shows 9€ adults, 5.50€ seniors; free under age 18. Wed–Mon 9am–8pm. Bus: 1, 3, 4, 11, 14, 19, 25, 32-37, 40, C1, C2.

Fundación Picasso ★ MUSEUM Picasso was born in Málaga in 1881 in a rented apartment at Plaza de la Merced, 15, and moved two doors down in 1883. He lived there until the family moved to A Coruña in 1891. Arguably the greatest painter of the 20th century, Picasso never really worked in Málaga, but the city was a profound influence. The Fundación Picasso preserves his birth home as a small museum, showing artifacts that range from baby Pablo's umbilical band and christening dress to some paintings by his father, painter José Ruiz Blasco. Other exhibits flesh out the family and city influences, and explore Picasso's insistence on his Spanish identity, especially as regards his love of bullfighting and flamenco. When you leave the Casa Natal, look for blue and white tile plaques around the Plaza de la Merced that indicate the second family home, the place where his father used to hang out with other artists, and the Iglesia Santiago where Pablo was baptized.

Plaza de la Merced, 15. fundacionpicasso.malaga.eu. ✆ **95-192-60-60.** Admission with audioguide 3€, 2 € seniors and students, free ages 17 and under; free to all on Sun after 4pm. Daily 9:30am–8pm. Bus: 36, 1, 37.

Málaga Cathedral ★ CATHEDRAL Nicknamed *La Manquita,* or the "one-armed lady" because of its unfinished second bell tower, this church collapses a lot of history into one hulking mass of stone. It sits at the foot of the Alcazaba where the Moorish mosque used to be, a symbolic obliteration that was not lost on the Spanish royalty, who took back Málaga from the Moors in 1487. Construction of the cathedral didn't begin until 1528, and the builders finally gave up in 1782. The striking 17th-century choir stalls carved of mahogany and cedar are a visual highlight: The 40 images of saints are largely the work of Pedro de Mena, one of Spain's most celebrated wood sculptors. Both daytime and nighttime visits to the roof can be arranged at fixed times, although roof access is free 9am to 10am Monday through Thursday.

Plaza Obispo. malagacatedral.com. ✆ **95-221-59-17.** Admission 6€ adults, 5.50€ seniors, 4€ ages 18–25, 3€ youth 14–17, kids 12 and under free. Jun–Sept Mon–Fri 10am–9pm, Sat 10am–6:30pm, Sun 2–6:30pm; shorter hours rest of year. Bus: 14, 18, 19, or 24.

Mercado Central ★ MARKET Also known as the Mercado Atarazanas because it sits on the site of the old Moorish shipyard, this 14th-century building has a front door with a perfectly preserved horseshoe arch from the Nasrid period. The building was substantially changed in the 19th century, when it became the city's food market. Visit for a vivid display of local fish and subtropical fruits and vegetables grown along the coast.

Calle Atarazanas, s/n. No phone. Mon–Sat 8am–3pm.

Muelle Uno ★★ LANDMARK Recent development of the stretch of waterfront from Plaza de General Torrijos to the 1817 Malagueta lighthouse has created Málaga's newest dining, shopping, and nightlife district. Broad walkways line the waterfront, and glass cubes containing boutiques, bars, and restaurants stretch the entire distance. Walking along the waterfront at night provides a romantic view of the lighted Moorish walls that zigzag up the hill from the city below. Right where the waterfront turns onto Muelle Uno, you'll find a number of **cruise boats.** Their 90-minute cruises tour the bay between the two main beaches, one east and one west of the city. Keep your eyes peeled for dolphins.

La Pinta Cruceros, Muelle Uno. www.malagaenbarco.com. ⓒ **64-581-59-15.** Boat tours 12€ adults, 8€ children. Bus: 1, 3, 4, 11, 14, 19, 25, 32-37, 40, C1, C2.

Museo Alborania ★ MUSEUM   If you follow the seashells, starfish, and other marine life forms embedded in the sidewalks around El Palmeral de las Sopresas, you'll end up at this waterfront museum that calls itself a "classroom of the sea." Geared to small children more than to adults, this collection of aquariums shows marine life in reasonable facsimiles of their native habitats, exhibits intended to inculcate a sense of stewardship of the marine world.

El Palmeral de las Sopresas (Muelle 2), s/n. www.museoalborania.es. ⓒ **95-160-01-08.** Admission 7€ adults, 5€ seniors and students; family passes available. July to mid-Sept daily 11am–2pm and 5–8pm; mid-Sept to June Thurs–Sun 10:30am–2pm and 4:30–6:30pm. Bus: 1, 3, 4, 11, 14, 19, 25, 32-37, 40, C1, C2.

Museo Carmen Thyssen Málaga ★★ MUSEUM   Located just off the Plaza de la Constitución in the Renaissance-era Palacio de Villalón, this museum displays the Spanish paintings circa 1825 to 1925 collected by Carmen Thyssen of the Museo Thyssen-Bornemisza in Madrid (p. 89). By concentrating on this narrow slice of European art, the baroness was able to acquire the very best work of the era. Moreover, because the museum limits its scope, the interpretation is sharp and succinct. Ground-floor galleries feature the romantic paintings of the early and mid–19th century that would make Spain one of the most popular artistic clichés of the day—colorful landscapes with even more colorful inhabitants: Gypsies, flamenco dancers, bullfighters, and ladies clad in mantillas demurely fluttering their fans. One floor up, galleries showcase a more naturalistic, moody style, as well as the parallel "précieux" style in which every flower petal and costume ruffle is articulated in exquisite detail that rivals damascene metalwork. Look for Alfred Derhondenq's 1851 vision of a Lenten procession in the streets of Sevilla, which shows the transition from the merely picturesque to a more considered realism. By 1867, Marià Fortuny i Marsal is rendering a bullfight with dramatic intensity and thick palette-knife clusters of paint that show his debt to Cezanne. As the exhibition progresses in time and style, it arrives at possibly one of the greatest paintings in the museum, the 1905 *Salida de un baile de mascaros* ("Exit from the Masked Ball") by José García y Ramos. The central figures in this parody of high society are a coachman and a doorman, standing in front of a theater smoking as a man in top hat and tails and his lady in full ball gown race down the steps. On the right, the red-nosed musicians are taking their leave. On the left, scantily clad and masked ladies are moving in on the society men.

The second-floor gallery is devoted to the "old masters," a mix of Italian and Spanish sculpture and painting from 13th-century Gothic through the museum's sole Velázquez portrait. The third floor hosts temporary exhibitions.

Plaza Carmen Thyssen, Calle Compañía, 10. www.carmenthyssenmalaga.org. ℗ **90-230-31-31.** Admission 10€ adults, 6€ seniors and students, ages 17 and under free. Tues–Sun 10am–8pm. Bus: 11, 20.

Museo Picasso Málaga ★★★ MUSEUM   Picasso last visited Málaga at the age of 19, but toward the end of his life expressed the wish that his work be displayed in the city of his birth. That wish became a reality in 2003. Continued gifts by Picasso's daughter-in-law and grandson have brought the collection to 285 works, most of which are unfamiliar since they were kept in the artist's private collection. Because Picasso's greatest hits are elsewhere, this museum focuses on teasing out the artist's multi-faceted genius and showing his different styles of working at different times. During the period that he was making abstract Cubist portraits, for example, he also drew delicate portraits of his son so realistic that they could be photographs. Through early 2020, the museum's permanent collection galleries are augmented by works held in a foundation overseen by Picasso's grandson Bernard and his wife.

Calle San Agustín, 8. www.museopicassomalaga.org. ℗ **95-212-76-00.** Permanent collection 8€ (6€ seniors and students), temporary exhibitions 6.50€ (4€ seniors and students); ages 16 and under free. Free to all last 2 hr. daily. July–Aug daily 10am–8pm; Mar–June and Sept–Oct 10am–7pm; Nov–Feb 10am–6pm. Bus: A, 4, 11, 16.

Málaga honors its native son Pablo Picasso with not one but two museums.

Where to Stay in Málaga

EXPENSIVE

AC Málaga Palacio ★★   One of the largest downtown hotels geared to both leisure and business travelers, the Palacio sits across the street from the Parque de Málaga a short distance from the cathedral and at the foot of the pedestrian shopping artery Calle Larios. You'll pay an extra 20% for a balcony room with a view of the port and the plaza below. But a basic room here is very pleasant, with a good desk. The free Wi-Fi is adequate for email, but if you need broadband, you'll have to spring for a wired network connection.

Cortina del Muelle, 1. www.marriott.com. ℂ **95-221-51-85.** 214 units. 129€–203€ double; 270€–319€ suite. Parking 25€ nearby. Bus: 4, 18, 19, or 24. **Amenities:** Restaurant; bar; concierge; exercise room; outdoor pool; free Wi-Fi.

MODERATE

Hotel MS Maestranza ★   There's a lot to like at the Maestranza, which is named for the adjacent Plaza de Toros. In fact, the bullring is so close that guests in rooms on the Calle Maestranza side can see bullfights from the balconies on floors 9 to 12. The other views are not exactly shabby, either, taking in the beautifully reconstructed yachting port and the lighted Moorish walls rising from the seaside city to the Gibralfaro. Regular rooms are a little tight but well-designed, and the location is perfect for enjoying the nightlife and restaurants of Muelle Uno across the street.

Av. Canóvas del Castillo, 1. www.mshoteles.com. ℂ **95-221-36-10.** 90 units. 81€–196€ double. Bus: 11, 14, 25. **Amenities:** Bar; spa; Jacuzzi; sauna; free Wi-Fi.

Hotel Petit Palace Plaza Málaga ★   Tucked into a small street just a few paces off Plaza de la Constitución, this high-tech hotel offers a laptop in every room. Moreover, guests also get 30MB of city Wi-Fi to use in the streets of Málaga. Furnishings are smoothly contemporary, and the bathrooms have new porcelain fixtures and high-tech hydromassage showers. Big beds make the small double rooms tight, but they work well once you figure out how to store your luggage. Triple and quad rooms are also available.

Calle Nicasio, 3. www.hthoteles.com. ℂ **95-222-21-32.** 66 units. 77€–128€ double; 92€–165€ triple, 135€–172€ quad. Bus: 4, 18, 19, or 24. **Amenities:** Restaurant; bar; concierge; exercise room; free Wi-Fi.

Room Mate Larios ★★   A striking Art Deco–era building near the head of Calle Larios, this Room Mate is set up with several self-sufficient apartments ranging from studios with a cooking corner to units with a separate bedroom and upstairs loft sleeping area. Expanses of contrasting marble and high-sheen black paint make the public areas look as if they had traveled in time from Paris circa 1930. The rooms continue the deco look with smoothly streamlined furniture and lots of black, gold, and taupe. Standard rooms are tight but well-designed; apartments are spacious. The Picasso Museum is about a 5-minute walk away, and the city's best shopping is just outside the front door. If Larios is full, Room Mate may suggest its other hotel, Lola, which is a fine hotel in a less convenient neighborhood.

Calle Marqués de Larios, 2. www.room-matehotels.com. © **95-222-22-00.** 41 units. 119€–210€ double; 166€–250€ jr. suite; 145€–225€ studio apt. Bus: 4, 18, 19, or 24. **Amenities:** Restaurant; bar; free Wi-Fi.

INEXPENSIVE

Sercotel Los Naranjos ★   Set on the section of Playa Malagueta known as Baños Carmen, about a mile (1.6km) east of central Málaga, Los Naranjos is an ideal setting for spending more time at the beach than sightseeing in the city. Rooms are reasonably spacious, and the strand and its accompanying beach bars are literally across the street. It can seem a little desolate in the off-season, but rates are very low then. Several rooms have balconies with a sea view. Triple rooms have three twin beds.

Paseo de Sancha, 35. www.hotel-losnaranjos.com. © **95-222-43-16.** 41 units. 55€–135€ double, 80€-130€ triple. Parking 13€. Bus: 11. **Amenities:** Restaurant; bar; free Wi-Fi.

Where to Eat in Málaga

EXPENSIVE

José Carlos García Restaurante ★★ SPANISH   Málaga's star chef José Carlos García pioneered fine dining when he opened this waterfront restaurant, which attracts gastronomes all up and down the Costa del Sol. There are two menus and two dining rooms, with the glass box of a kitchen in between. The a la carte menu features some of the chef's greatest hits (like a sumptuous hand-cut steak tartare) as well as newer inventions like white prawns served with frozen white almond-garlic gazpacho. There's also a daily menu of five half portions. The tasting menu is a

---

WHAT & HOW TO drink IN MÁLAGA

Malagueños pride themselves on having a slang term for everything, and the place to decipher the language of coffee is **Café Central,** Plaza de la Constitucíon, 11 (www.cafecentralmalaga.com; © **95-222-49-72**), where the tiled lexicon on the wall explains everything from a *solo* (full glass of black coffee) to a *mitad* (half-coffee, half-milk) and a *nube,* or *cloud* (a splash of coffee topped by almost a full glass of milk). Although many people order *churros* with their coffee at Central, the classic spot for thick hot chocolate and *churros* is **Casa Aranda,** Calle Herrería del Rey (no phone). If it's too warm for hot drinks, **Casa Mira,** Calle Larios, 5 (© **95-221-24-22**), makes excellent crushed-ice drinks called *granizados.* The two traditional flavors are coffee and lemon. But the most traditional drink in the city is the sherrylike Málaga wine, and the most traditional place to drink it is **Antigua Casa de Guardia,** Alameda Principal, 18 (antiguacasade guardia.com; © **95-221-46-80**), founded in 1840. Wines are served from giant oak barrels, and the barman chalks up your tab on the sticky wooden counter.

10- to 14-course extravaganza of incredible bites like sea urchin roe with tapioca pearls or roast suckling pig in pineapple sauce. Wait for your table with a drink on the outside terrace. Reserve as far ahead as possible.

Muelle Uno, Plaza de la Capilla. en.restaurantejcg.com. ⓒ **95-200-35-88.** Entrees 25€–35€, set menu 66€, tasting menu 140€. Tues–Sat 1:30–3:30pm and 8:30–11pm. Closed July 1–15. Bus: 251.

MODERATE

El Chinitas ★ SPANISH   Heir to the legendary 19th-century cafe-theater by the same name, El Chinitas cultivates a timeless look of straight-backed wooden chairs, wood-paneled walls, and white linen tablecloths. The menu hails from the same era, representing the best of coastal seafood and the meat traditions of central Spain. Fish is mostly fried; meats are braised or grilled. In keeping with tradition, other than the obligatory green salad, green beans, artichokes, and asparagus, vegetables are an afterthought. It is a great spot to enjoy *rabo de toro* (braised oxtail), steamed prawns, or scrambled egg dishes. The tapas set menu is a bargain of seven varied tapas and dessert.

Calle Moreno Monroy, 4. https://el-chinitas.business.site. ⓒ **95-221-09-72.** Entrees 12€–21€, set menu 40€, tapas menu 17€. Daily noon–midnight.

Godoy Marisquería ★★ SEAFOOD   Like José Carlos García, Godoy was a pioneer on Muelle Uno. This glittering glass jewel box of a restaurant offers a menu primarily of shellfish, augmented by some fin fish, a couple of steaks, and a few ham-based appetizers. The house specialty is a Málagan version of *zarzuela* consisting primarily of large pieces of monkfish with clams and cockles in a tomato-fish broth. For more casual munching, order a good white wine and an assortment of fried anchovies, red mullet, tiny squid, and pieces of flounder.

Muelle Uno, 34–35. www.marisqueriagodoy.com. ⓒ **95-229-03-12.** Entrees 12€–31€; shellfish tasting menu 63€. Tues–Sat 1:30–3:30pm and 8:30–11pm. Bus: 251.

INEXPENSIVE

Restaurante Gorki Central ★★ SPANISH   Located just off Calle Larios, this handsome dining room with an equally attractive group of tables in the street can serve you everything from a single oyster with a sip of manzanilla to a full-blown multi-course meal accompanied by a bevy of wines. There are burgers, finger sandwiches of smoked salmon or curried chicken, and big plates of melted goat cheese over fresh tomatoes. For a more substantial meal, order a seared tuna steak or black rice with sautéed cuttlefish and saffron aioli.

Calle Strachan, 6. www.grupogorki.com. ⓒ **95-222-14-66.** Tapas 2.50€–7€; entrees 11€–18€. Daily noon–midnight.

Restaurante Bar La Bouganvilla ★ SPANISH   Tucked into one corner of Plaza del Siglo, this unprepossessing little eatery resembles an American quiche bar of the 1980s—except that the food is a lot better. The menu consists of about a dozen tapas, ranging from a *pincho de* *tortilla* to ceviche to a half-dozen shrimp grilled with garlic. Add a few variations on green salad, a range of fresh and aged cheeses, and a couple of variations on small pieces of grilled meat, and you have the full picture. Prices are excellent, service is quick, and the food is some of the best of its kind, making La Bouganvilla a great spot to grab a bite if you're shopping your way across Málaga.

Calle Granada, 22. labouganvilla.com. © **95-100-61-03.** Tapas 3€–7€, entrees 12€–18€. Daily 10am–11pm.

La Cosmopolita ★ SPANISH   Set a few paces off Plaza del Siglo, this breezy little spot is a midday favorite for Malagueños in the know. Many show up just for the big sandwiches made on baguettes from Las Garrochas bakery. The signature sandwich is the Don José, aka Pepito, with sliced veal, roasted peppers, and grilled octopus. Other highlights include a creamy baby squid risotto, veal steak in mustard sauce, and fried eggs with baby fava beans. On weekdays, La Cosmopolita also serves breakfast.

Calle José Denis Belgrano, 3. www.lacosmopolita.es. © **95-221-58-27.** Tapas 2.50€–3.50€, entrees 12€–19€. Mon–Sat 8:30am–midnight.

KGB Málaga ★★ TAPAS   Practically next door to Gorki, KGB Málaga trades on its name to offer "top secret" tapas—though the initials actually stand for Kuartel Gastronomic Bar. The brains behind this creative reimagining of a tapas bar is José Alberto Callejo, novelist and university professor. The tapas change frequently, and guest chefs are always adding new ideas. One standard is a holdover from the days when Dani García had this space: The *rabo de toro* sliders taste exactly like braised oxtail. This is where foodies come to have fun.

Calle Fresca, 12. © **95-222-68-51.** Tapas around 5€, *raçiones* around 9€. Daily 1–4:30pm and 8pm–midnight.

Málaga Shopping

Calle Larios has most of the city's top boutiques, though many are familiar international brands. For unusual eyewear, stop at the head of the street at **Óptica Fernández Baca,** Plaza de la Constitucíon, 12 (© **95-221-11-54**),

---

A PERFECT MÁLAGA beach EVENING

It takes about an hour to stroll along Playa de la Malagueta from the port to Playa Pedregalejo. You'll pass surfcasters, colonies of feral cats living in the rocks, and on a Saturday afternoon, barefoot brides having their pictures taken on the beach. Fish-house restaurants line the beach at Pedregalejo. One of the value spots is **El Caleno** ★, Paseo Maritimo El Pedregal, 49 (© **95-229-91-48**), open Tuesday to Sunday 2 to 6pm and 8pm to midnight. Main dishes cost 12€ to 20€. Specialties include grilled sardines and a *fritura Malagueña* of mixed fried fish. Linger as long as you want and then walk 2 blocks up from the beach to Avenida Juan Sebastian Elcano to catch the 11, 33, or 34 bus back to Alameda Principal.

Shopping along Calle Larios in Málaga.

which carries frames from European designers rarely seen in the U.S. **Calle Nueva,** which runs parallel to Calle Larios, is lined with good, less expensive shops. For hip Spanish fashion, **Piel de Toro,** Calle Nueva, 27 (www.pieldetoro.com; © **95-221-12-20**), carries preppy-style clothing for men and women with a playful embroidered bull logo. A rather sweet Málaga tradition is to create porcelain flowers as a way to enjoy their blooming season year-round. **Rincón de la Biznaga,** Calle Granada, 53 (© **95-222-68-18**), is run by folks who continue this craft.

If you're searching for a fan or beautiful embroidered shawl, check the offerings at charmingly old-fashioned **Celyan,** Calle Marqués, 3 (© **95-125-74-68**).

The new **Muelle Uno** is also lined with shops, including **Reuníon de Creadores,** Local 1.B (© **629-609-404**), which features the work of contemporary craftspeople. Their jewelry and bags are particularly striking. A number of craftspeople set up outdoor booths along the Muelle several Sundays per month.

Málaga Nightlife

As in most big Spanish cities, in Málaga Spaniards gather at bars and restaurants to drink, snack, and talk. You'll find tapas scenes on the side streets from Calle Larios, along Calle Granada, and along Muelle Uno. For live music and dancing, try **ZZ Pub,** Calle Tejón y Rodríguez, 6 (www.zzpub.es; © **95-244-15-95**), which is big with university students. Performances start around 10:30pm and end 4 to 5am.

The best-established of the flamenco *tablaos*—essentially nightclub performances by a troupe—is Tablao Flamenco Los Amayas, Calle Vélex Málaga, 6 (www.flamencomalagacentro.com; ✆ **95-151-23-90**). Performances are Monday through Saturday at 7pm and 9pm. In addition to the resident troupe, Los Amayas often hosts touring artists. Show tickets start at 25€, with tapas dinner 45€.

Two beautifully restored theaters—**Teatro Echegaray,** Calle Echegaray, 6 (www.teatroechegaray.es; ✆ **95-222-41-09**), and **Teatro Cervantes de Málaga,** Ramos Marin, s/n (www.teatrocervantes.es; ✆ **95-222-41-09**), present musical concerts, flamenco, dance, and theater. The Cervantes is also home to the Málaga Philharmonic Orchestra.

Side Trip to El Torcal de Antequera ★★

In less than an hour, you can drive north from Málaga to the desert hills of **El Torcal de Antequera,** designated in 1929 as Andalucía's first natural park. A paved road swishes back and forth through the bone-dry landscape, providing constantly changing perspectives on the wind-sculpted limestone hoodoos. Three well-marked trails depart from the visitor center (www.torcaldeantequera.com; ✆ **95-224-33-24;** daily Nov–Mar 10am–5pm, Apr–Oct 10am–7pm; admission free). If you stick to the trails, you run a good chance of spotting several of the 30 species of wild orchids that flourish in this harsh landscape, or even seeing an eagle swoop down on a lizard. Guided tours (10€–16€) explore more remote areas of the park. The landscape is so spooky that El Torcal has the dubious distinction of having more UFO sightings than any other place in Spain. An on-site restaurant has great views from its terrace. Just over 50km (31 miles) north of Málaga, El Torcal is reached by driving A-45 north to Antequera, A343 south from Antequera, then local road MA-3310 to El Torcal.

NERJA ★

Nerja puts its best face forward. The village is picturesque and charming, and the flowering plants that do so well in its protected climate trim the whitewashed buildings in ebullient color. Everything in town focuses on the main square overlooking the ocean, the **Balcón de Europa ★★**, a palm-shaded promenade that juts defiantly out into the Mediterranean. It is the most gracious spot on the coast east of more upscale Marbella.

Balcón de Europa in Nerja.

Nerja is known for its good (if pebbly) beaches and small coves, its seclusion, its narrow streets and courtyards, and the peculiar flat-roofed architecture of its houses. Nearby is one of Andalucía's top geological attractions, **La Cueva de Nerja** (see below). To reach the best beaches, head west from the Balcón and follow the shoreline.

Essentials

ARRIVING   At least 19 buses per day make the 1-hour trip from Málaga to Nerja, costing 4.60€ one-way. Service is provided by Alsa (www.alsa. es). If you're driving, head along the N-340/E-15 east from Málaga or take the N-340/E-15 west from the Motril junction with A-14 coming south from Granada.

VISITOR INFORMATION   The tourist office, at Calle Carmen, 1 (www. nerja.es; ✆ 95-252-15-31), is open Monday to Friday 10am to 2pm and 3 to 6:30pm, Saturday and Sunday 10am to 2pm.

Exploring La Cueva de Nerja

The most popular outing from Málaga and Nerja is to the **Cueva de Nerja (Cave of Nerja)** ★★, Carretera de Maro, s/n (www.cuevadenerja.es; ✆ 95-252-95-20). Scientists believe this prehistoric stalactite and stalagmite cave was inhabited from 25,000 to 2000 B.C. It was rediscovered in 1959, when a small group of boys found it by chance. Once fully opened, it revealed a wealth of treasures left from the days of the cave dwellers, including Paleolithic paintings depicting horses, deer, and other prey.

The Cueva de Nerja.

Only a small fraction of the paintings lies in the galleries open to the public, but the striking geology compensates: You can walk through stupendous caverns where ceilings soar to a height of 60m (197 ft.).

The cave is in the hills near Nerja, where you can enjoy panoramic views of the countryside and sea. It's open daily 9am to 3pm (open until 5:30pm Jul–Aug). Admission is 13€ adults, 11€ children 6 to 12, and free for children 5 and under. (A discount is available for online ticket purchases.) Buses (www.alsa.es) to the cave leave hourly from Paseo de los Tilos, s/n, in Málaga, from 7am to 8:15pm (trip time: 1 hr.; cost: round-trip 10€). Hourly municipal buses from Avenida de Pescia, s/n, in Nerja run from 8:30am to 9:40pm (cost: round-trip 2.4€). Return buses run hourly until 9:45pm.

Where to Stay in Nerja

EXPENSIVE

Parador de Nerja ★★   The Spanish *parador* system does not let the lack of a suitable historic building stop it from offering a hotel in some of the country's most scenic and popular areas. In Nerja, this modern hotel sitting on a cliff above the ocean compensates for its lack of historic atmosphere with striking views and a lovely garden. Most of the fairly spacious rooms have balconies facing the sea, and understated furnishings don't distract from the views. For all the sense of privacy, it's only about a 5-minute walk to town center.

Calle Almuñécar, 8. www.parador.es ✆ **95-252-00-50.** 98 units. 133€–339€ double. Free parking. **Amenities:** Restaurant; bar; outdoor pool; outdoor tennis court (lit); free Wi-Fi.

MODERATE

Carabeo ★★   It's hard to find a place with more character than the Carabeo, which occupies a former schoolhouse in Nerja's atmospheric old fisherman's quarters. Owners have done an admirable job of mixing antiques and art to make a comfortable retreat. But however charming the quarters, Nerja is really about the sea, and Carabeo delivers on that front also. The property sits on a cliff overlooking the water and is only about a 5-minute walk to a swimming beach. The owners made all seven rooms unique. What they have in common are spacious dimensions, rich fabrics, and solid wood furniture. Several have a private terrace or balcony.

Hernando de Carabeo, 34. www.hotelcarabeo.com. ✆ **95-252-54-44.** 7 units. 90€–115€ double, 190€–210€ jr. suite, 206€–225€ suite. Free parking nearby. Closed late Oct–Apr. **Amenities:** Restaurant; bar; exercise room; outdoor pool; sauna; free Wi-Fi.

Hotel Balcón de Europa ★   If you like to be in the heart of the action, this nine-story modern hotel built in the 1970s sits on the right bank of the Balcón de Europa. Most of the rooms have a terrace to enjoy the sea view, and all have been renovated to seem fresh and bright. Fabrics in rich colors and patterns set a tone of elegance. Views from the pool are stunning, and a small private beach allows guests to escape the crowds.

Paseo Balcón de Europa, 1. www.hotelbalconeuropa.com. © **95-252-08-00.** 110 units. 108€–280€ double; 168€–436€ suite. Parking 12€. **Amenities:** 2 restaurants; bar; outdoor pool; sauna; free Wi-Fi.

INEXPENSIVE

Hostal Ana ★   To save money in this fairly expensive city, book one of the rooms here that has a small kitchen. With a plain white facade and wrought-iron accents, the relatively new building—constructed in 1998—seems right at home in the historic center of the city, yet within easy walking distance of the Balcón de Europa. Liberal use of colorful Andalucían-style tiles adds character. Some of the rooms are small, but all have simple, comfortable furnishings. The innkeepers are friendly and helpful. There's a 4-night minimum during July and August.

Calle La Cruz, 60. hostalana.es. © **95-252-30-43.** 17 units. 28€–90€ double. **Amenities:** Hot tub; free Wi-Fi.

Hotel Plaza Cavana ★   Small wrought-iron balconies add an air of grace to this two-story hotel near the Balcón de Europa. Though they're not large enough for lounging, the balconies do offer a great vantage point to take in the scene and let fresh sea air into the rooms. The fairly spacious rooms were designed by someone with a good eye for pairing bright colors with neutrals for a harmonious and tranquil effect. Guests share a garden patio. Innkeepers often offer amenities such as a free buffet breakfast or late checkout for online booking; be sure to ask.

Plaza Cavana, 10. www.hotelplazacavana.com. © **95-252-40-00.** 39 units. 70€–139€ double. Parking 15€. **Amenities:** Restaurant; bar; bikes; exercise room; Jacuzzi; 2 pools (1 indoor); sauna; free Wi-Fi.

Where to Eat in Nerja

Oliva Restaurante ★★ MEDITERRANEAN   Choose between a bustling modern dining room or a tranquil courtyard patio for a relaxed meal with excellent service. Some definite international influences play out on the menu here, notably sautéed duck foie gras and the use of Jerusalem artichokes as a foil for fresh scallops. The fish side of the menu is where the kitchen really shines—seared bluefin with crunchy veggies, smoked wild sea bass, or John Dory in black tempura with sherry spinach.

Calle Pintada, 7. www.restauranteoliva.com. © **95-252-29-88.** Entrees 16.50€–25€. Mon–Sat 12:30–3pm and 7–11pm.

Restaurante Rey Alfonso ★ SPANISH/FRENCH   It's easy to miss this restaurant, which is located in a glass case below the Balcón de Europa and reached by small staircases on either side of the promontory. Even if you don't want a meal, stop in for a drink—you can't really get much closer to the ocean without getting wet, and the views, especially at sunset, are quite remarkable. The meals are rather conventional *platos* *combinados* of meat, starch, and vegetable. Make a reservation ahead for weekends.

Paseo Balcón de Europa s/n. ✆ **95-252-09-58.** Entrees 11€–20€. Mon–Sat noon–3pm and 7–11pm; Sun noon–3pm. Closed 4 weeks in Jan–Feb.

ALMUÑÉCAR ★

Almuñécar is an excellent choice for travelers who like their beach time with a generous side of history. The most important coastal resort of Granada province, the town has a long stony beach dotted with *chur-rerías,* which open early for breakfast. The Phoenicians founded Almuñé-car in the 8th century B.C., naming it Sexi and establishing the first *garum* (fermented fish paste) works near the main beach. The Romans took over in 218 B.C. and kept the *garum* business going, as Sexi's fish paste was traded as far away as Greece and Turkey. The town became a more traditional fishing port under the Moors, who also introduced sugar cane farming. Its subtropical climate also makes the Rio Verde valley a hothouse for fruits and vegetables.

Essentials

ARRIVING   Eight buses per day make the 75-minute trip from Granada to Almuñécar, costing 2.85€ one-way. From Málaga to Almuñécar, there are 10 buses a day, costing 7.50€ each way. Service is provided by Alsa (www.alsa.es; ✆ **90-242-22-42**). If you're driving, head along the N-340/E-15 east from Málaga or take the A-14 south from Granada. Driving time is about 1¼ hours from both cities.

The beach in Almuñécar.

The **Almuñécar tourist office,** Paseo de Altillo, s/n (www.turismoalmunecar.es; *C* **95-863-11-25**), is open Tuesday through Sunday 9:30am to 1:30pm from April through October; from November through March, it's open Thursday to Sunday.

Exploring Almuñécar

A complex of parks and ruins in **Barrio San Miguel** near the beach explains Almuñécar's rich history. The **Parque Botánico El Majuelo** in the central city next to the ruins of the Roman fish paste factory is filled with tropical and subtropical species that flourish in the warm microclimate.

Castillo San Miguel ★ CASTLE Archaeologists have found ceramics here that date these fortifications back to a Carthaginian compound in the 3rd century B.C., and there's ample evidence that the Romans also fortified the spot. (That *garum* trade was worth protecting, apparently.) The castle that survived, though, was built in the 13th century by the same Nasrid dynasty that constructed the Alhambra (p. 283). The structure was famous for its prison and the dungeon where political prisoners were kept. Spanish monarchs modified the structure but kept its prison operative until 1808, when the castle was severely damaged by English bombardment.

Barrio San Miguel. www.turismoalmunecar.es. *C* **650-027-584.** Combined admission with Museo Arqueológico 2.35€ adults, 1.60€ seniors and children. Tue–Sat 10:30am–1:30pm and 4–6:30pm, Sun 10:30am–1pm.

Parque Ornitológico Loro-Sexi ★ ZOO More than 1,500 birds representing more than 100 species fly in large caged areas in this modern aviary. Scarlet macaws, toucans, and peacocks provide colorful splendor.

Calle Bikini, s/n, Plaza Rahman. www.turismoalmunecar.es. *C* **95-863-56-17.** Admission 4€ adults, 2€ seniors and children. Tues–Sun 10:30am–2pm and 4–6pm.

Museo Arqueológico ★ MUSEUM The structure itself is perhaps the greatest artifact in this local history museum: It occupies a portion of the Roman ruins (La Cueva de Siete Palacios) set into the city hills. The rather elegant vaulted space contains artifacts from the various cultures that once called Almuñécar home, including the Romans, Moors, and Phoenicians. The most unusual artifact suggests the cosmopolitan nature of this historic city. It's an Egyptian glass, carved from solid quartz, with hieroglyphics that date from the 17th century B.C. The antique curiosity most likely reached Almuñécar aboard a trading vessel.

Calle Cueva de los Siete Palacios, s/n. www.turismoalmunecar.es. *C* **607-865-466.** Combined admission with Castillo San Miguel 2.35€ adults, 1.60€ seniors and children. Tues–Sat 10:30am–1:30pm and 4–6:30pm; Sun 10:30am–1pm.

Where to Eat & Stay in Almuñécar

Digame Pepe ★ SEAFOOD This casual restaurant does a bang-up business with English-style breakfasts in the morning, along with *churros* for those who want to sit down, rather than stand at a beachside *churrería,* to eat the crisp hot treats. Digame Pepe is right on the beach, so folks return in the evening to watch the sun set while they eat fried or grilled fish or fish stew.

Paseo de los Flores, s/n. © **95-834-93-15.** Entrees 8€–20€. Daily 8am–10pm.

Hotel Helios Costa Tropical ★★   Opened in 1989, this large white hotel helped usher in tourism in Almuñécar. It remains our favorite lodging in town. Located right across the street from the Playa San Cristobal, it takes advantage of the setting with sea-view terraces on most of the fairly spacious guest rooms. The Helios has a number of resort features including a pool, game rooms for kids, meeting rooms, and even a hairdresser. But friendly and helpful staff provide the kind of personal attention we usually expect in smaller properties. Two especially nice features are the 10th-floor solarium and the heated pool, open November through March for winter getaways.

Paseo San Cristóbal, 12. www.helios-hotels.com. © **95-863-44-59.** 227 units. 50€–186€ double. Parking 12€. **Amenities:** Restaurant; bar; exercise room; pool; free Wi-Fi.

VALENCIA & THE COSTA BLANCA

By Patricia Harris and David Lyon

V alencia is a lyrical metropolis with world-class architecture and (according to at least two popes) the Holy Grail. Go for the white sand beaches, the blue water, and the green riverbed of parkland that encircles the old city. And bring your appetite—it was the Valencians who first combined Moorish rice with vegetables and legumes, shellfish, and rabbits and snails from their gardens to give the world paella. Eat the dish here and you'll never settle for the imitations served in the rest of the country.

VALENCIA ★★★

Geography is destiny in Valencia. As the easternmost sheltered harbor on the central Iberian coast, during the Moorish occupation it became a stepping-stone from North Africa to central Spain and back. El Cid prevailed against the Moors here—and they recaptured the strategic port by driving his successors back into the hills. A millennium ago, the city changed hands with staggering frequency. Today, container ships and petroleum tankers ensure that the city's lifeblood is still the port. Yet industry is so sequestered and clean that visitors only see it (and then at a distance) if they bicycle along the coast to L'Albufera (p. 392).

Floods engulfed Valencia in 1957; to prevent another disaster, the Rio Túria, which had encircled the city, was moved underground. This feat of earthworks engineering set Valencia on a path to reimagining itself. The dry riverbed was transformed into a 10km (6¼-mile) linear park, where the City of Arts and Sciences was ultimately erected on the southeastern corner. Its futuristic architecture by native son Santiago Calatrava and Spanish-Mexican architect Félix Candela rivals Frank Gehry's Guggenheim Bilbao. Emblematic of the new city, these soaring modern masterpieces have sparked a renaissance of Valencia.

Essentials

ARRIVING More than 40 airlines serve **Manises Airport** from more than 70 European and North African destinations. **Iberia Express** (www.iberiaexpress.com; ✆ **901-200-424**) flies to Valencia from most major Spanish cities, while **Ryanair** (www.ryanair.com; ✆ **902-585-230**) and **Vueling** (www.vueling.com; ✆ **902-808-022**) have the most European connections. The airport is 8km (5 miles) southwest of the city center. To reach downtown, take Metro line 3 or 5 (1.50€–3.90€) or bus 150 (1.50€). For more information, call ✆ **900-461-046.** A taxi (✆ **963-703-333**) from the airport to the town center costs 15€.

FACING PAGE: **For centuries, Valencia has been defined by its splendid seafront.**

Trains run to Valencia from all parts of Spain. The landmark Modernista building of **Estación del Norte,** Calle Játiva 2, sits just south of the heart of the city. Its information office on Calle Renfe (www.renfe.com; ⓒ **90-232-03-20**) is open Monday to Friday 8am to 9pm. From Barcelona, 16 trains arrive daily, including several 3½-hour TALGO trains. At least 20 trains daily connect Madrid with Valencia; Alvia high-speed trains take about 2 hours and the AVE only 100 minutes. From Málaga, on the Costa del Sol, the trip takes 4 to 7 hours, depending on connections.

Buses arrive at Valencia's Estació Terminal d'Autobuses, Av. de Menéndez Pidal, 13 (ⓒ **96-346-62-66**), about a 30-minute walk northwest of the city's center. Take bus 8 to reach the Plaza del Ayuntamiento. Thirteen buses a day run from Madrid (trip time: 4 hr.), 10 from Barcelona (trip time: 5 hr.), and 5 from Málaga (trip time: 8 hr.).

Ferries connecting Valencia with the Balearic Islands (p. 670) run year-round to Palma (Mallorca) and Ibiza (note that there's only one weekly ferry to Ibiza in winter). Travel agents in Valencia sell tickets, or you can buy them from the **Trasmediterránea** office at the port, Estació Marítim (www.trasmediterranea.es; ⓒ **90-245-46-45**). To reach the port, take bus 4 or 19 from the Plaza del Ayuntamiento.

From Barcelona, the easiest **driving** route is the express highway (AP-7) south (toll: 41€). From Madrid, use national highway E-901. From Alicante, take the E-15 express highway. From Málaga, drive north to Granada and cut across southeastern Spain on the 342, which links with the 340 into Murcia; from there, take the road to Alicante and then the E-15 highway.

VISITOR INFORMATION   The main **tourist information office** at Calle Paz, 48 (www.visitvalencia.com; ⓒ **96-398-64-22**), is open Monday to Saturday 9am to 6:50pm and Sunday 10am to 1:50pm.

Getting Around Valencia

Valencia has completely modernized its **public transit** system under the EMT (Empresa Municipal de Transportes). A digital chip pass card called **MÓBILIS** (2€ at tobacconists, kiosks, and EMT office) can be loaded for multiple rides, although paper tickets (1.50€) are still sold on local buses. The MÓBILIS card usually comes loaded with a 10-trip Bonobus pass (8.50€), which is valid for both bus and Metro. The **Metro** system (www.metrovalencia.es; ⓒ **90-046-10-46**) is more efficient than the bus, covering the Old Town well and branching out to the outskirts, including the beaches. Most **local buses** leave from Plaza del Ayuntamiento 22; bus 8 runs from

> ### The Local Lingo
>
> Don't be surprised if you see signs around Valencia in a language that's neither Spanish nor Catalan. It is **Valenciano,** closely related to Catalan. Often you'll be handed a "bilingual" menu in Castilian Spanish and in Valenciano. English is also widely spoken. Most street names appear in Valenciano.

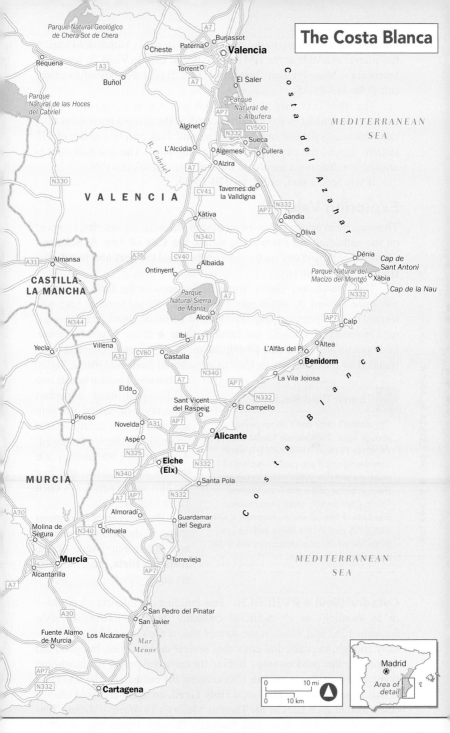

The Costa Blanca

Plaza del Ayuntamiento to the bus station at Avenida Menéndez Pidal. A bus map is available at the EMT office (Calle Correo Viejo, 5; www.emt valencia.es; Mon–Fri 9am–2pm and 4:30–7:30pm). For bus information, call *C* **96-315-85-15.**

The MÓBILIS card also gives you access to the city's bike rental program, **Valenbisi** (www.valenbisi.com), at the cheap annual subscriber rate. Valencia is flat and easy to pedal around. Pick up a bike at any of 275 stations around the city and drop off at any other. The first half hour is always free. You must register at the web site and select a PIN.

If you need a **taxi,** call *C* **96-370-33-33.**

Exploring Valencia

There are three primary areas of interest in Valencia: the **old city,** centered on the cathedral and Plaza de la Reina; the **City of Arts & Sciences,** southeast of the old city on the dry riverbed, and the **port and beach district,** east of the old city.

The 14th-century Gothic Torres de Serranos on the north side of the city once formed the main gate to Valencia; the old western gate was formed by the Torres de Quart. Just west of Torres de Quart, near the original University of Valencia, the **Jardí Botànic ★** (Calle Quart, 80; www. jardibotanic.org; *C* **96-315-68-00;** metro: Túria or Angel Guimerà) was founded by the university in 1567 as a garden of medicinal plants. Today the botanical garden boasts one of Europe's most important collections of varied tree life and palms, with nearly 45,000 international species displayed. Admission is 2.50€ adults, 1.50€ seniors and students, and free for kids under age 7. It's open 10am to dusk.

The city's other large green space is the former riverbed, now the green swath of the **Jardí del Túria,** great for walkers and cyclists.

> ### Tourist Card Roulette
>
> City discount cards don't always deliver enough value. The **Valencia Tourist Card** for 24, 48, or 72 hours (15€/20€/25€) is worth considering only if you plan to visit lots of museums and ride public transit between them. A better deal is the 7-day Valencia Tourist Card for 12€, which gives museum discounts or free admission. Augment it with a MÓBILIS card for the Metro and bus systems. See valenciatouristcard.com and order online for a 10% discount.

Catedral (Seu) ★★ CHURCH Few buildings in Valencia are as old—or as looming—as its medieval cathedral, built in fortresslike style between 1252 and 1482 on the former site of the Grand Mosque. Naturally enough, the cathedral embodies several design styles, but good old Spanish Gothic predominates. Behind the cathedral proper is a handsome domed basilica. Since the late 15th century, the cathedral's claim to fame is that it possesses the purported **Holy Grail,** an agate-and-gold chalice celebrated in such tales as Sir Thomas Malory's *Le Morte d'Arthur,* Tennyson's *Idylls of the King,* and Wagner's *Parsifal.* Depending on which

Valencia

Puente
San José

Puente de
las Artes

C/ Guillem de Castro

C/ Na Jordana

1
IVAM

**Centro Cultural
la Beneficencia**

C/ Corona

C/ Dr. Beltrán Bigorra

EL CARMEN

C/ Salvador Giner

**Casa Museo
Benlliure**

**Iglesia del
Carmen**

Plaza
Carmen

C/ Alta

C/ Baja

C/ Portal
d. Valldigna

C/ Caballeros

JARDINES
DEL TURIA

C/ Blanquerias

**Torres de
Serranos**

Plaza
Fueros

Plaza
Cisneros

C/ Serranos

PONT DE
FUSTA Ⓜ

C/ Cronista Rivelles

Puente de
Serranos

C/ Conde de Trénor

**Real Monasterio
de la Trinidad**

**Museo de
Bellas Artes**
6

C/ San Pío V

Puente
Trinidad

7

8

LA SEU

C/ Pintor López

**Torres
de Quart**

C/ Quart

C/ Murillo

C/ Pinto Domingo

C/ Guillem de Castro

C/ Carniceros

C/ Balmes

C/ Camarón

C/ Bany

**Iglesia
del Pilar**

←**17**

C/ Hospital

MUVIM

C/ Guillén de Castro

Plaza
Tossal

**San
Nicolás**

C/ Bolsería

Plaza Don
Juan de
Vilarrasa

**Santos
Juanes**

**Mercado
Central**
3

**EL
PILAR**

C/ Tomo d. Hospital

Avenida Barón de Cárcer

**La
Lonja**
2

Av. María Cristina

C/ Músico Peydro

Ayuntamiento

San
Agustín

C/

Av. Marqués de Sotelo

**Basílica de Nuestra
Señora de los
Desamparados**

Plaza
la Virgen

Catedral
12

11

**Santa
Catalina**

Plaza de
la Reina ⓘ

C/ San Vicente Martir

18

Plaza
Ayuntamiento

C/ Barcas
19

C/ Correos
20

✉

C/ Ribera

C/ Alicante

XÁTIVA Ⓜ

ⓘ
**Estación
del Norte**

Xátiva

**Plaza de
Toros**

Almudín

C/ Trinitarios
5

**Museo de
la Ciudad**
10

C/ del Mar

C/ de la Paz

4

13
**Museo de
Cerámica**

Plaza R.
Botet
16

C/ Moratín

El Patriarca ⓘ

**Universidad
de Valencia**

C/ Pintor Sorella

C/ Don Juan Austria

C/ Pascualy Genís

C/ Sagasta

C/ Roger de Llúria

Paseo Ruzafa

21

Plaza
del Temple

9

**LA
XEREA**

Plaza
Tetuán

**Santos Tomás y
San Felipe Neri**

Jardines
de la
Glorieta

Plaza Alfonso
El Magnánimo
14

15

C/ Poeta Quintana

Ⓜ C/ Sorni
COLÓN

**EL PLA
DEL
REMEI**

C/ de Colón

C/ Hernán Cortés

22

23

C/ Cirilo Amorós

C/ Félix Pizcueta

C/ Pizarro

Gran Vía del
Marqués del
Turia

Madrid
⊛
Valencia

0 ___ 150 yds
0 ___ 150 m

Valencia's Catedral.

legend you prefer, the vessel was either used by Jesus at the Last Supper or by Joseph of Arimathea to collect Jesus's blood as it dripped from the cross. It is the focal point of its own chapel within the cathedral. An audioguide lets you tour the cathedral at your own pace; afterward, you can climb the stairs inside the unfinished 47m-high (154-ft.) Gothic tower known as **Miguelete** ★ ("Micalet" in Valenciano). It affords a panoramic view of the city and the fertile orchards and truck gardens beyond.

Plaza de la Reina. www.catedraldevalencia.es. ⓒ **96-391-81-27.** Admission free for prayer; cultural visit with audioguide 7€ adults, 5.50 € seniors and kids under 12. Mon–Sat 10am–6:30pm, Sun 2–6:30pm (Nov to mid-Mar until 5:30pm, closed Sun). Miguelete 2€ adults, 1.50€ kids under 14; daily 10am–1pm and 4:30–7pm. Bus: 94, 4, 5, 9, 19, 80, or 81.

Ciutat de les Arts i les Ciències (City of Arts and Sciences) ★★★

MUSEUM   Since the Palau de les Arts Reina Sofía opened in 2005 as the final jewel in its cultural crown, the City of Arts and Sciences has become as emblematic of Valencia as Frank O. Gehry's Guggenheim Museum is of Bilbao. Valencianos' chests swell a little bigger as they inform you that Valencia didn't have to go overseas for a great architect—it already had native son Santiago Calatrava, the engineer-architect previously known for visionary bridge designs. His construction innovations helped to create soaring vistas and seemingly weightless structures in this 36-hectare (89-acre) site south of the city, set on the dry riverbed created by channeling the Río Túria underground. Félix Candela, a Spanish architect who'd spent most of his career in exile, contributed one of the structures, and his technical expertise with thin-shell concrete was critical to Calatrava's designs for the other three major buildings in the complex.

The first building to open (1998) was Calatrava's **L'Hemisfèric** ★★, a structure resembling a giant eye and eyelid; inside is a massive IMAX theater, a planetarium, and a laser show. The science museum, **El Museu de les Ciències Príncipe Felipe** ★, has a similarly playful construction, recalling the skeleton of a whale. Its interactive exhibits are designed mainly to get children excited about science, so they rely heavily on "gee-whiz" elements such as lightning in a bottle or the science of sports. If your time is limited or you don't have kids in tow, this building is best admired from outside.

Candela's chief design contribution, **L'Oceanogràfic** ★★, is the largest oceanographic aquarium in Europe. He designed it in the shape of a water lily, using an exaggerated parabola to maximize the concrete structure's ability to support itself without buttresses. Viewed from a distance, it's both graceful and otherworldly, yet inside the enveloping structure, the individual displays of marine habitats seem intimate and immediate. The areas are connected by underwater glass walkways.

Panoramic elevators and stairways connect the multiple levels at the airy **Palau de les Arts Reina Sofía** ★★, a 14-story glass-and-metal opera house and performing arts center (p. 388). The "palace" has four massive rooms for performances, surrounded by walkway plazas and a landscape that contains as much open water as solid ground.

The entire complex is a favorite of skateboarders, who find its angles, ramps, parallel walks, and other features terrifically challenging. It's also

Airy modern architecture at the Ciutat de les Arts i les Ciències.

popular with fashion photographers, who find the abstraction and grand scale of the architecture a particularly dramatic setting. It's a great place for family outings, too. The "city" also hosts the annual **Festival Eclèctic** in July, which features four to five free outdoor concerts and several days of free performances by acrobats, martial artists, and street performers. *Tip:* If you plan to visit more than one site, check for discounts on combined admissions

Av. Autopista del Saler. www.cac.es. ℭ **90-210-00-31.** L'Hemisfèric: admission 8€ adults, 6.20€ seniors and kids 12 and under; open daily 10am–9pm. Museu de les Ciències Príncipe Felipe: admission 8€ adults, 6.20€ seniors and kids 12 and under; daily 10am–7pm (closes 9pm July–Sept, 6pm Jan–Mar). L'Oceanogràfic: admission 32.20€ adults, 24.20€ seniors and kids 12 and under; daily 10am–7pm (closes 9pm July–Sept, 6pm Jan–Mar). Metro: 3 and 5, Alameda.

Institut Valencia d'Art Modern (IVAM) ★ ART MUSEUM   IVAM opened on the western edge of the old city in 1989 as Spain's first contemporary art museum. Don't come expecting the latest 21st-century work—IVAM focuses on the development of Modernism and the avant-garde before World War II. It's in an ultramodern building, though, anchored by the signature welded-iron sculptures of abstract/Cubist artist **Julio González** (1876–1942), who bequeathed 394 works ranging from drawings and paintings to jewelry and sculpture. The museum also possesses an extensive collection of works by Valencian painter **Ignacio Pinazo** (1849–1916), whose stylistic experiments were notably abstract and avant-garde in their day. Other strengths of the collection include 20th-century photography and photo-collage, pop art, and new media.

Calle Guillém Castro, 118. www.ivam.es. ℭ **96-317-66-00.** Admission 6€ adults, 3€ students, free for seniors and children under 10. Tues–Sun 10am–7pm (until 9pm Fri). Bus: 5, 8, 28, 29, 79, 80, 81, 95. Metro: Túria.

Lonja de la Seda ★ LANDMARK   Master mason Pere Compte constructed this fortified hall between 1482 and 1533 as Valencia's silk exchange. Listed as a UNESCO World Heritage Site, it is considered a top example of Gothic civic architecture. A forest of twisted-wheat columns supports the main trading hall, and the tranquil central courtyard features orange trees and a fountain. School children on field trips are usually extremely amused by the gargoyles, which represent bodily functions usually performed outside of public view.

Plaza Mercado, s/n. ℭ **96-208-41-53.** Admission 2€ adults, 1€ seniors and students, free Sun. Mon–Sat 9:30am–7pm, Sun 9:30am–3pm. Bus: 4, 7, 27, 28, 60, 81. Metro: Xàtiva or Colón.

Mercado Central ★★★ MARKET   This Modernista cathedral of food is one of the grandest food markets in Spain, rivaling La Boqueria in Barcelona (p. 427). It's a great place to pick up Valencia oranges (in season) and to see the exquisite produce grown in the little truck farms *(huertas)* that surround the city. Near the front of the market you'll find several stalls where smoked paprika is piled in high cones and tins of saffron can be purchased for a comparative bargain. Even if you're not buying, visit to see which produce is in season and what fish are truly fresh, to guide you in picking the best dishes at a restaurant.

Plaza Mercado, s/n. www.mercadocentralvalencia.es. © **96-382-91-00.** Mon–Sat 7am–3pm. Bus: 4, 7, 27, 28, 60, 81. Metro: Xàtiva or Colón.

Museo de Bellas Artes ★★ ART MUSEUM   This charming museum's prize exhibition hall is the **Sala Sorolla,** hung with major works by the gifted Valencian painter Joaquin Sorolla (1863–1923). It's the most extensive collection of his paintings outside the Museo Sorolla in Madrid (p. 106) and chronicles his career from art student years in Rome to some of his final compositions. The museum is also strong in Flemish art and includes a smattering of most of the major Spanish painters from Ribera and Murillo through Goya. Unique is the collection of so-called Valencian "primitives," who continued to work in a Gothic style well into the 14th and 15th centuries.

Calle San Pío V, 9. www.museobellasartesvalencia.gva.es. © **96-387-03-00.** Free admission. Tues–Sun 10am–8pm. Bus: 94, 6, 11, 16, 26, 28, 79, or 95. Metro: Pont de Fusta or Alameda.

Museo Nacional de Cerámica ★ MUSEUM   This late Gothic palace was remade in the 18th century with a rococo exterior dominated by Ignacio Vergara's figures of "Dos Aguas" (Two Waters), now the palace's namesake. The building was a landmark long before the private ceramic collections of Manuel González Martí and his wife Amelia Cuñat were installed here in 1947 to create the Museo Nacional de Cerámica. With its long history of fine ceramic art, Valencia was a fitting location. The museum is of most interest to collectors, who will find the nuances of regional styles fascinating.

Calle Poeta Querol, 2. mnceramica.mcu.es. © **96-351-35-12.** Admission 3€ adults, 1.50€ students and seniors. Tues–Sat 10am–2pm and 4–8pm, Sun 10am–2pm. Bus: 31, 70, 6, 8, 9, 10, 11, 27, 70, 71. Metro: Colón.

Outdoor Activities

BEACHES

Valencia boasts more than 20 km (12½ miles) of European blue-flag beaches, including **Playa Arenas** ★ and **Playa Malvarrosa** ★, just minutes from the city center. Adjoining these beaches is the seafront promenade, **Paseo Marítimo** ★. If you head south toward **El Saler,** you'll find more natural, dune-backed beaches and less competition for a spot on the shore.

BOATING

Real Club Náutico de Valencia, Camí del Canal, 91 (www.rcnv.es; © **96-367-90-11**), has a sailing school that rents boats for scuba diving and snorkeling. It maintains a full yacht-service facility.

THE fires THAT CLEANSE

Valencia goes insane every year from March 15 to 19. It's the only way to explain the whirlwind of parades, music, fireworks, controlled explosions outside city hall, and general madcap revelry that continues around the clock. The festival is called **Las Fallas,** and it's not for the faint of heart—or the easily startled.

The origins of Las Fallas are vague but seem to lie in the 18th century, when Valencian carpenters would celebrate spring by burning their winter lampposts. A century later, the lampposts had morphed into satirical figures that were burned in a main plaza on St. Joseph's Day (Mar 19). Modern materials like foam core and polyester film have allowed *fallero* artists to grow ever more outrageous. The figures, erected in 300 or more city squares, may be as high as eight stories and can cost up to $1 million each. Representing a wide array of political and pop cultural subjects, the satire can be both biting and bawdy.

Yet solemn piety is also a part of Las Fallas. During the day, parades of characters who seem to have stepped out of a Goya painting bring bouquets of pink, white, and red carnations to the Plaza de la Virgen. The men look like 18th-century dandies, the women like ladies of the court in full-skirted silk brocade dresses, hair combs, and mantillas. After they hand over their flowers, which are affixed to the skirts of a five-story-high Madonna, they weep and take pictures.

The strangest spectacle of all is the *mascletà,* a pyrotechnic extravaganza whose main purpose must be to sell hearing aids. Thousands of people crowd the streets around City Hall Plaza waiting for the fuses to be lit on approximately 1 million firecrackers and other concussive devices. They begin exploding with an innocuous pop-pop-pop and build to bone-shaking booms.

The grand finale occurs between midnight and 1am, when all but two "pardoned" figures are torched in a blazing inferno that feels like a cross between Mardi Gras and the bombing of Baghdad. For Valencianos, it's a way to get rid of the old and welcome in the new. To the uninitiated, it is both unnerving and exhilarating.

The **Museu Faller** (Plaza de Montolivet, 4; www.fallas.com; ☎ **96-208-46-25**) preserves some historic figures from past festivals along with photos, paintings, and posters of the exuberant excess. Admission is 2€, 1€ seniors, it's open Monday to Saturday 10am to 7pm, Sunday 10am to 2pm.

Outlying Attractions

PARQUE NATURAL DE L'ALBUFERA ★★

Only about 13km (8 miles) south of the city center on N-332, this stunning region is also easily visited by bicycle, as much of the roadway is paralleled by a bicycle path. (See p. 386 for bike-sharing details.) Nowhere is the contrast of built and natural environments as striking as at the beach in the nearby village of **El Saler:** Its eastern view zeroes in on cargo ships and tankers in Valencia's industrial port, yet shore birds practically cover the beach of smooth flat stones.

Rice farmers have labored since the A.D. 700s in the flooded fields around **L'Albufera,** an inlet that has been closed off from the sea for so long

The seafront promenade Paseo Maritimo runs along Malvarrosa beach.

that the water has become fresh. The ecosystem of freshwater lake, lagoons, and barrier beach and dunes was declared a natural reserve in 1986. Rice fields still cover about two-thirds of the area, and produce the bulk of the tall, hard-to-cultivate Bomba strain that makes the best paella. You may see fishermen in small, flat-bottomed boats on the lake, mostly catching mullet or collecting American red crayfish, so prized for paella. The wetlands between the lake and sea rank among Iberia's most important breeding grounds for more than 5,000 pairs of herons and four varieties of terns. For details on birding in the park, guided tours, and excursions in traditional boats, stop at the **Racó de l'Olla Centre d'Interpretación** (parques naturales.gva.es; 𝄐 **96-386-80-50**), located at the El Palmar turnoff from CV-500. The center is open daily 9am to 2pm. Take Bus 25 to get here.

Shopping

You haven't seen Valencia until you've visited the 1920s **Mercado Central** ★★★ (p. 390) to marvel at the beautifully displayed meats, fish, and produce, and to purchase *bomba* rice, smoked paprika, and a paella pan to bring home.

If you're in town on a Sunday morning, head to the open-air market at **Plaza Redonda,** near the cathedral. Vendors offer traditional Valencian handicrafts, including ceramics, ironwork, silver items, and inlaid

Shop for fresh food at Mercado Central.

marquetry. You'll also find colorful items from other parts of Spain and even Morocco. If you're more interested in seeing what Valencianos have been storing in their attics, head to the Sunday flea market on Avenida de Suecia.

Spain's ubiquitous **El Corte Inglés** department store has several locations in Valencia, including Calle Pintor Sorolla, 26, and Calle Pintor Maella, 37 (www.elcorteingles.com; ✆ **96-315-95-00**). We like the fact that these stores usually stock local handicrafts and other goods along with more general merchandise. They are often a good bet for one-stop shopping. Serious shoppers will enjoy browsing around the **Plaza del Ayuntamiento** and along the streets of **Don Juan de Austria, Colón, Sorní,** and **Cirilo Amorós.** The **Mercado de Colon** (Calle Jorge Juan, 19; ✆ **96-337-11-01**), a Gaudi-inspired fantasy dating from 1916, is a good stop for a café break. Also in the old city center, **Mercado de Tapinería** (Calle de la Tapinería, 15; www.tapineria.com; ✆ **69-222-79-67**) has several bars and restaurants, as well as pop-up stores that change weekly.

Valencia is known for its embroidered shawls, and **Nela** (Calle San Vicente Mártir, 2; ✆ **96-392-30-23**) has an excellent selection, along with fans, leather goods, and other items. Spain's famous Lladró porcelain figurines are made in a factory just outside the city; for a full range displayed in an elegant setting, seek out **Lladró** (Calle Poeta Querol, 9; www.lladro. com; ☎ **96-351-16-25**). If you wish to visit the **Lladró Museum** in the suburb of Tavernas Blanques, ask the shop staff to assist with reservations.

Where to Stay in Valencia

In July and August, when Valencia can be uncomfortably hot and humid, some hoteliers lower prices significantly. It never hurts to ask. In mid-March during Las Fallas (p. 392), expect rates quoted below to double.

EXPENSIVE

Hotel Neptuno Valencia ★★★   A well-established beach hotel right on Playa Malvarrosa, the Neptuno has clean modern lines, and if the standard rooms are a little on the small side, who cares? You're not staying at the beach to stay in your room. Sea-view rooms command a premium, and the spacious suites are even pricier. The rooftop solarium has great views along the shore and a tiny pool for cooling off between tanning sessions; it's a very popular point for watching yacht races in the harbor. The beachfront terrace has a bar, so you can lie back on a chaise lounge and nurse a cool drink.

Paseo Neptuno, 2. www.hotelneptunovalencia.com. ☎ **96-356-77-77.** 50 units. 148€–170€ double; 324€–398€ suite. Parking 20€. Metro: Marina Reial Joan Carles I or Neptú. **Amenities:** Restaurant; bar; gym; spa; free broadband ADSL and Wi-Fi.

Palacio Marqués de Caro ★★★   Located on a quiet, narrow street east of the cathedral, this venerable palace has been remade as a sleekly contemporary boutique hotel with 26 utterly different rooms, each of which looks like a stage set. Such decorative details as Moorish vases, a neoclassical frieze, even a room with a preserved medieval wall, all echo the city's Roman and Moorish pasts. The Jardi Túria is literally steps away, and it's an easy walk to more central attractions. Some rooms are on the small side, so ask to see yours when checking in.

Carrer de l'Almirall, 14. www.carohotel.com ☎ **96-305-90-00.** 26 units. 143€–225€ double; 322€–391€ jr. suite. Parking 25€. Metro: Alameda. **Amenities:** Restaurant; bar; pool; free Wi-Fi.

MODERATE

Hotel Ad Hoc Monumental ★★   Exposed brick walls and wood beams lend a sense of warmth to this small hotel in an 1880s building. Well-maintained guest rooms are comfortably, if somewhat sparely, furnished; several have outdoor terraces, and all are well soundproofed. The hotel's location is a real plus, northeast of (but near) the cathedral and on the banks of the Jardí del Túria green pathway. It's convenient for exploring the central city—and for walking or bicycling to the City of Arts and Sciences. Bicycle rental is available.

Calle Boix, 4. www.adhochoteles.com. ☎ **96-391-91-40.** 28 units. 87€–120€ double. Parking 17€. Bus: 9, 35, 70, 71. Metro: Alameda. **Amenities:** Restaurant; bikes; free Wi-Fi.

Hotel Mediterráneo ★ Bright and functional rooms in a modern minimalist style combine with a heart-of-the-city location, near many attractions, to make this modest property an excellent choice for leisure travelers. It's close to the city hall plaza, so the surrounding streets can be busy at night, but excellent double-paned windows and air conditioning make sleeping easy even during the summer. Families with children should inquire about triples, usually priced just a few euros more.

Avenida del Oestre, 45. www.hotelmediterraneovalencia.com. ✆ **96-351-01-42.** 34 units. 108€–120€ double. Bus: 13, 62, or 70. Metro: Xàtiva. **Amenities:** Bikes; free Wi-Fi.

Hotel One Shot Palacio Reina Victoria 04 ★★ One Shot Hotels take their name from the concept of a photograph capturing a moment in time: The neoclassical Palacio Reina Victoria captures the spirit of 1913, when a new king was trying to make Spain relevant to Europe again. The guest list has included everyone from King Alfonso XIII and bullfighter Manolete to Federico García Lorca and Pablo Picasso. When One Shot took over in 2016, they renovated with wood, iron, and tile to update the original interiors by a full century. Changing photo exhibitions in public spaces add to the ambience. Rooms remain small to mid-size but now have luxurious American mattresses. The central location—roughly equidistant to the Plaza de Toros and the cathedral—is definitely handy for sightseeing on foot.

Calle Barcas, 4. www.husareinavictoria.com. ✆ **96-352-04-87.** 96 units. 64€–225€ double, 89€–260€ jr. suite. Parking 20€. Bus: 4, 6, 7, 8, 14, or 27. Metro: Colón, Xàtiva. **Amenities:** Restaurant; bar; free Wi-Fi.

SH Inglés Boutique Hotel ★★ For a treat, try to book a room with a view of the Museo Nacional de Cerámica so that you can wake up to a vision of its stunning baroque facade. Occupying the 18th-century former palace of the Duke of Cardona, this hotel maintains a sense of quiet decorum, from the graceful main stairway to the tasteful traditional furnishings in the guest rooms. As you might expect of an older building, rooms tend to vary in size, shape, and amenities. Some have private balconies

---

DRINK LIKE A local

To emulate the Valencianos, head to Barrio del Carmen to visit **Sant Jaume,** a cafe at Calle de Cavalleros, 51 (cafesantjaumevalencia.com; ✆ **96-391-24-01**), for an *agua de Valencia,* a mixture of orange juice, Cointreau, and cava. The drink is said "to cure all that ails you," so it's appropriate that the building itself used to be an apothecary. Foodies flock to **Vuelve Carolina,** Calle Correos, 8 (vuelvecarolina.com; ✆ **96–321–86–86**), for cocktails and upscale tapas on the ground level of the same building as El Poblet (p. 399). The city's most famous drink, *horchata,* made with ground tiger nuts, is best at **Horchatería Santa Catalina,** Plaza Santa Catalina, 6 (www.horchateriasanta catalina.com; ✆ **96-391-23-79**).

and others are fairly small; inquire carefully when booking. A central location on an architecturally distinguished street is a plus.

Calle Marqués de Dos Aguas, 6. www.inglesboutique.com. ☎ **96-351-64-26.** 63 units. 100€–132€ double. Parking 30€. Bus: 6, 9, 31, or 32. Metro: Colón. **Amenities:** Restaurant; bar; bikes; free Wi-Fi.

Vincci Lys ★★   In many ways, Vincci Lys has the best of two worlds, being close to the train station but also centrally located for sightseeing. Sitting on a pedestrian street lined with cafes and restaurants, the hotel has a welcoming, neighborhood feel. Light wood floors, pale walls, and clean-lined furnishings emphasize the generous proportions of many of the rooms, while dark fabrics add a bit of romance. If you are not bothered by street noise, request one of the rooms with a private balcony.

Calle Martínez Cubells, 5. en.vinccilys.com. ☎ **96-350-95-50.** 101 units. 89€–186€ double; 178€–312€ jr. suite. Parking 30€. Bus: 4, 6, 8, 16, 35, or 36. **Amenities:** Restaurant; bar; concierge; free Wi-Fi.

INEXPENSIVE

Catalonia Excelsior ★★   This hotel in a 1950s building near the Plaza del Ayuntamiento is a good bet for travelers on a budget. You can opt for a simple, basic double with modest furnishings or upgrade to a larger room, a room with a terrace, or a room with a hydromassage tub to work out the kinks after a day of sightseeing. All guests, however, enjoy the convenient location, good attention to housekeeping, common terrace, and exterior windows.

Calle Barcelonina, 5. www.hoteles-catalonia.es. ☎ **96-351-46-12.** 81 units. 91€–120€ double. Bus: 19, 35, 70, or 71. Metro: Colón. **Amenities:** Bar; free Wi-Fi.

Hostal Venecia ★★   Budget travelers are usually pleasantly surprised when they arrive at the Venecia and behold this beautiful building right in the heart of town, across the plaza from the city hall *(ayuntamiento)*. Because the Venecia shares a staircase with private apartments in the same building, it is considered a *hostal* rather than a hotel, which by law limits the rates it can charge. Travelers reap the benefit, as the Hostal Venecia operates with all the efficiency of a small hotel, and staff tend to be friendly and knowledgeable. Wood paneling and decorative wallpapers lend a touch of style to the clean, simply furnished (and often small) rooms.

Plaza del Ayuntamiento, 3. www.hotelvenecia.com. ☎ **96-352-42-67.** 54 units. 63€–90€ double. Bus: 19, 35, 70, or 71. Metro: Colón, Xàtiva. **Amenities:** Bikes; free Wi-Fi.

Where to Eat in Valencia

EXPENSIVE

Eladio ★★ GALICIAN   One glance at the menu signals that chef-owner Eladio Rodríguez has not forgotten his Galician roots, even if he's transplanted them to a warmer and sunnier coast. The tank of live shellfish is just one signal that he's obsessed with freshness, and the menu itself basically advertises the fish of the Galician coast—hake, monkfish, fresh cod, salt cod, and turbot—prepared "Galician style." In general, this means simply roasted in an extremely hot oven with minimal garnish. He does serve cod with the Basque green sauce *(pil pil)* and offers some Valencian treats like red mullet with almond sauce. Meat eaters are in luck at Eladio as well, since Galicia prides itself on extraordinary beef. The kitchen already has a wood charcoal fire going for the fish, so it's no trouble to throw a T-bone on the coals or tuck a chateaubriand (for two) into the grill.

Calle Chiva, 40. www.restauranteeladio.es. ℰ **96-384-22-44.** Entrees 22€–32€; tapas 12€–17€; tapas menu 30€. Mon 1–4pm; Tues–Sat 1–4pm and 9–11:30pm. Closed Aug. Bus: 3, 70, or 72. Metro: Av. del Cid (line 3 or 5).

La Pepica ★★★ SEAFOOD/VALENCIAN   The Picassos of paella are the cooks in La Pepica's sprawling kitchens. The restaurant faces onto Playa Malvarrosa, but if you approach from the town side, you can walk through those kitchens to the dining room. Founded in 1898, La Pepica has wowed royalty, movie stars, and yes, even Ernest Hemingway with its spectacular seafood and multiple versions of paella. Don't hesitate to take pictures when the waiter in striped vest and bowtie brings the paella pan to your table for presentation, before taking it to a station for plating. The place is huge, seating more than 400 diners, yet every table gets impeccable service. La Pepica's paella is the benchmark for the dish everywhere else in the world.

Paseo Neptuno 6–8, Playa Malvarrosa. www.lapepica.com. ℰ **96-371-03-66.** Entrees 20€–35€; tasting menu 31€. Mon–Sat 1–4pm and 8:30–11pm, Sun 1–4pm. Closed last 2 weeks Nov. Bus: 32. Tram: Marina Reial Joan Carles I.

La Sucursal ★★ CONTEMPORARY SPANISH   In a country where cutting-edge food is considered one of the liveliest indigenous art forms, it's only fitting that this delightfully inventive restaurant sits on the roof of the landmark Americas Cup building (known locally as Veles e Vents, or "sails and winds"). Bright and airy, it's easily one of the most glamorous eateries in the city. While La Sucursal earned its initial reputation for

---

TALK ABOUT market CUISINE

The marvelous Art Nouveau **Mercado Colón** ★★ (Jorge Juan, 19; mercadocolon.es; ℰ **96-337-11-01**) still has a few gourmet butchers, fishmongers, and produce vendors in the basement, but the main action these days is at street level. The space is filed with three restaurants, seven bars and coffee shops, and even a pair of *horchaterías.* Propane heaters on the outdoor terrace at **La Mie Dorée** (ℰ **96-351-38-86**) make the bar a favorite for hanging out in the evening and sipping from the extensive gin menu. From breakfast through late night, Mercado Colón offers you someplace or other to get a bite and a sip.

reinterpreting the Spanish culinary canon, it has evolved into one of the region's most avant-garde kitchens, offering new takes on seafood with cultural references all around the Mediterranean. Expect to be surprised by such combinations as razor clams in tiger milk; sea cucumber with egg yolk, thistle, and an eel sauce; or Wagyu beef with smoked pumpkin.

Muelle du la Aduana s/n. restaurantelasucursal.com. ℂ **96-374-66-65,** reservations ℂ **645-201-679.** Fixed-price menus 45€–90€. Dinner reservations essential 1 week ahead for dinner. Mon–Fri 1–3:30pm and 8:30–11:30pm; Sat 8:30–11:30pm. Closed 1 week in Aug. Bus: 92. Metro: Marina Reial Joan Carles I.

MODERATE

El Poblet ★★★ VALENCIAN/MEDITERRANEAN Chef-owner Quique Dacosta hails from the coastal village of Dénia (famous for its shellfish) and rose to fame as one of Spain's most provocative young chefs. His philosophical writings deconstruct the traditions of seafood cuisine in eastern Iberia and then reconstruct them to match a contemporary avant-garde aesthetic. That all sounds very high-falutin' and has certainly made him the darling of critics, but he can also walk the walk; his radical cuisine looks beautiful, tastes delicious, and is reasonably priced. His comfortable contemporary dining room in the heart of the city features an a la carte menu grounded in coastal traditions—dishes like cold red prawns served as a centerpiece of a dinner salad, or Senia rice with blue duck meatballs and artichokes.

Calle Correos, 8, 2nd fl. www.elpobletrestaurante.com. ℂ **96-111-11-06.** Entrees 24€–35€; tasting menus 88€–123€. Mon and Wed–Sat 1:30–3:15pm and 8:30–10:15pm; closed Sun and Tues, also closed Mon in Aug. Bus: 10, 13, 81, N1, N8. Metro: Colón.

La Lola ★ MEDITERRANEAN/INTERNATIONAL This snazzy little restaurant in Barrio del Carmen has definite attitude, with a contemporary decor harking back to Op Art and a kitchen inspired by elBulli on a budget—right down to Adrià's rediscovery of simplicity. It's possible to start with something as straightforward as a single perfect anchovy with toast smeared with tomato, or as complex as braised octopus with creamy potatoes and roasted red peppers. Lola also serves a full range of *caldosas,* rice dishes a little soupier than paellas. Regulars favor the version with duck, wild mushrooms, and crisp bits of ham.

Calle Subida del Toledano, 8. lalolarestaurante.com. ℂ **96-391-80-45.** Entrees 19€–27€; set lunch menu 15€ (Mon–Fri) or 22€ (Sat–Sun), set dinner menu 25€. Daily 1:30–3:30pm and 8:30–11:30pm. Bus: 2, 4, 6, or 7.

Palace Fesol ★ VALENCIAN More than a century old, the "bean palace" earned its name with recherché fava bean dishes, but the restaurant has evolved into a rather elegant dining room specializing in all manner of traditional Valencian cuisine. If you want to know how a local dish is cooked in the classic manner, order it here. There are many variants of

VALENCIA & THE COSTA BLANCA

Valencia

paella and *caldosa* on the menu, and even a few fava bean dishes. Chances are, though, the waiter will advise that you try the catch of the day. He'll be right, and you can always get favas as a side dish.

Calle Hernán Cortés, 7. www.restaurantepalacefesol.com. ✆ **96-352-93-23.** Entrees 17€–30€. Reservations advised. Tues–Sun 1–4pm and 9–11pm. Closed Sat–Sun July–Aug. Bus: 5. Metro: Colón.

INEXPENSIVE

Casa Montaña ★ TAPAS   Hungry Valencianos have bellied up to the bar at this bodega since 1836. The once-rough neighborhood used to be inhabited by fishermen and dock workers, but Casa Montaña led the area's revival (some would say gentrification). Dock workers still come in, but they're as likely to be crew off the racing yachts as stevedores. Class truly doesn't matter here, as everyone is welcome. The room is jammed with large wine barrels (most of them full), and the kitchen serves an almost encyclopedic range of tapas, with an emphasis on fish. Don't miss the ancient Saracen *titaina* casserole made with tuna belly, chopped tomatoes and peppers, and toasted pine nuts. The wine cellar is extensive; if you admire the list, owner Emiliano Garcia might invite you to tour the cellars.

Calle José Benlliure, 69. www.emilianobodega.com. ✆ **96-367-23-14.** Tapas 5€–20€. Mon–Sat noon–3:30pm and 8–11:30pm; Sun 12:30–3:30pm. Metro: Mediterrani. Tram: Grau–Canyamelar.

Valencia Entertainment & Nightlife

Valencia is famous for its *marcha* (nightlife) and for its bohemian bars, but where you go at night in Valencia depends on when you visit.

The best area in the cooler months is historic **Barrio Carmen,** in the city center. **Calle Alta** is a good street on which to start your bar-crawl, as is the historic core around **Plaza del Ayuntamiento.** A longtime local favorite is **Cafeteria Barcas 7,** at the same address as the name (✆ **96-352-12-33**), among banks and office buildings directly north of Estación del Norte. It serves drinks and tapas (including small servings of paella) at the stand-up bar, and often has live music in the evening. You could stop here for your first cup of coffee at 7am and for your final nightcap at 1am. Drink prices start at 1.50€, and tapas cost 4€. **Disco City,** Calle Pintor Zariñena, 16 (✆ **96-391-41-51**), a dance club with black-on-black decor and a wall of mirrors lining the

---

Rainbow Pride in Valencia

Valencia is Spain's third-largest city and, after Madrid and Barcelona, the country's biggest gay center. Most of the action is in the historic center's **Barrio Carmen,** particularly along Calle Quart. Valencia is a progressive, liberal city, and visitors need have no fear about being "out" on the street. A good publication for what's happening, and when, is Madrid-based *Shangay,* distributed free in gay establishments and available online at **www.shangay.com.**

Valencia's Plaza de Toros.

dance floor, attracts the under-30 crowd, who come here to dance to funk, soul, and R&B. It's definitely for late-nighters: The scene doesn't get rolling until 3am. Cover is usually 15€.

In summer, the emphasis switches to the beach, **Playa Malvarrosa.** Everyone from teens to 40-somethings congregates around open-air bars, which play music, often have dance floors, and are open from late May to September. Drinks usually cost 4€ to 6€. There are also discos in this part of town, one of which is the salsa room at **Akuarela Playa,** Calle Eugenia Viñes, 152 (www.akuarelaplaya.es; ⓒ 96-337-47-20). Cover is 12€ to 17€, and drinks are several euros more than in the open-air bars.

PERFORMING ARTS

The **Palau de la Música ★★**, Paseo de la Alameda, 30 (www.palau valencia.com; ⓒ 96-357-50-20; metro: Alameda), presents an impressive array of 200-plus programs a year. The most prestigious orchestras in the world, as well as directors and soloists, appear here; it's also home to the Valencia Orchestra throughout its season. The hall seats 1,793 and has wonderful acoustics (Plácido Domingo once declared "Palau is a Stradivarius"). Ticket prices vary but are generally in the 10€-to-90€ range.

Valencia's grand opera house, **Palau de les Arts Reina Sofía ★★**, Autopista del Saler, 1 (www.lesarts.com; ⓒ 96-197-58-00), is housed in a futuristic, helmet-shaped building, part of the City of Arts and Sciences (p. 388). Some of the world's most prestigious opera companies perform here. Hourlong guided tours of this Calavera masterpiece building are 10.90€ adults, 8.50€ seniors and students. Performance tickets range from 15€ to 200€ and can be purchased online or at the box office.

SPECTATOR SPORTS

Neighboring Catalunya may have outlawed bullfights, but *corridas* still figure prominently in Valencian life. The first fight season of the year is during Las Fallas in March; fights resume from Easter through May and start up again in early October. Valencia's **Plaza de Toros,** one of the largest rings in Spain, is adjacent to the rail station at Calle de Xàtiva, 28. If you don't want to attend a corrida but are curious about the culture of bullfighting, you can visit the **Museo Taurino,** Pasatje Doctor Serra, 10 (*©* **96–388–37–38**), and then enter the ring itself. The museum is open all year, Sunday and Monday 10am–2pm, Tuesday through Saturday 10am–6pm; admission is 2€ adults, 1€ seniors and students.

ALICANTE ★★

Alicante, capital of the Costa Blanca, is popular in both summer and winter, especially with Brits and northern Europeans who have been coming here in droves since the mid–20th century. The compact city combines an atmospheric old quarter, a dramatic and historic bluff-top fortress, a sparkling yacht harbor, and excellent beaches. The waterfront promenade is a delight of swirl-patterned pavements. The substantial number of African immigrants, many of whom wear the dress of sub-Saharan Africa, gives the city a cosmopolitan air.

Playa San Juan ★, the largest beach in Alicante, is 5km (3 miles)

Alicante's Explanada d'Espanya.

east of the old city and can be quickly reached by tram. It is lined with villas, hotels, and restaurants. The bay of Alicante has two capes, and on the bay is **Playa Postiguet ★**, at the foot of the bluff topped by a castle.

Essentials

ARRIVING   Alicante's **Internacional El Altet Airport** (www.aena.es; *©* **96-691-90-00**) is 19km (12 miles) from the city. Dozens of carriers fly here from all over Europe and North Africa, with **Ryanair** (www.ryanair. com; ✆ **902-585-230**) dominating the schedule. The C6 bus runs from the airport to the city every 20 minutes (fare: 3.85€).

Ten **trains** a day connect with Valencia (trip time: 1½–2 hr.; fares: 22€–32€). Eight trains a day come from Barcelona (trip time: 5–5½ hr.), and 13 a day from Madrid (trip time: 2¼–3½ hr.). The RENFE office is at **Estación Alicante,** Avenida Salamanca (www.renfe.es; ✆ **90-232-03-20**).

Bus lines from various parts of the coast converge at the terminus, Calle Portugal, 17 (✆ **96-513-07-00**). There is almost hourly service from Valencia (trip time: 4 hr.). Buses also run from Madrid, a 5- to 6-hour trip.

To drive here, take the E-15 expressway south along the coast from Valencia. The expressway and N-340 run northeast from Murcia.

VISITOR INFORMATION   The **tourist information office** at Rambla de Mendez Núñez, 41 (www.alicanteturismo.com; ✆ **96-520-00-00**), is open Monday to Friday 10am to 6pm, Saturday and Sunday 10am to 2pm.

Exploring Alicante

With its wide, palm-lined avenues, this town was made for sauntering. The magnificent **Explanada d'Espanya** ★ wraps around part of the yacht harbor under a parade of palm trees. Its mosaic sidewalks have wave patterns so realistic that they've been known to give inebriated visitors a touch of motion sickness. Off the esplanade are lovely marble-paved squares such as **Plaza Gabriel Miró** and **Portal de Elche** of the entire harbor.

Many people come to Alicante for its sparkling beaches, including El Postiguet in the city center. The beach spreads out from the foot of the high hill topped by stately if decrepit **Castell de Santa Bárbera,** which towers over the bay and capital city. On the slopes of Castillo de Santa Bárbara behind the cathedral is the **Barrio de Santa Cruz** ★. Forming part of the **Villa Vieja (Old Quarter),** it's a colorful section with wrought-iron window grilles, flowers, and a view of the entire harbor.

Castell de Santa Bárbera ★★ FORTRESS   The Greeks called this fort Akra Leuka (White Peak). Its original defenses, erected by the Carthaginians in 400 B.C., were later used by the Romans and the Arabs. The fortress has all the medieval castle accoutrements, including a moat and drawbridge, huge cisterns, powder stores, dungeons and high breastworks. The ramparts offer panoramic views over land and sea. Five rooms are devoted to the free **Museo de la Ciudad de Alicante** ★ (daily 10am–2:30pm and 4–8pm). The castle is accessible via elevator from the Explanada d'Espanya; otherwise you can drive or walk to the top—a paved road off Avenida Vásquez de Mella leads directly to a parking lot beside the castle.

✆ **96-592-77-15.** Admission via elevator 2.70€, free if you drive or walk. Summer open daily 10am–10pm; winter daily 10am–8pm.

Castell de Santa Bárbera.

Museu de Arte Contemporáneo Alicante ★ ART MUSEUM
Alicante isn't all ancient. Facing Iglesia Santa María, housed in the
baroque Casa de la Asegurada (originally constructed in 1685 as a gra-
nary), this contemporary art museum features works by Miró, Calder,
Cocteau, Dalí, Giacometti, Gris, Picasso, Tàpies, Chagall, Kandinsky, and
Braque. You'll also see a musical score by Manuel de Falla. The museum
was formed in 1977 with the donation of a private collection by the painter
and sculptor Eusebio Sempere, whose works are on display.
Plaza de Santa María, 3. www.maca-alicante.es. © **96-521-31-56.** Free admission.
Tues–Sat 10am–2pm and 4–8pm, Sun 10am–2pm.

Museo Volvo Ocean Race ★ MUSEUM   At the port, this new
museum details with interactive exhibits the thrilling history and complex
technology behind the ocean race formerly known as the Whitbread
Round the World Race—the so-called "Everest of sailing." Alicante has
been the race's start point since 2008.
Muelle de Levante, 10. museovolvooceanrace.esatur.com. © **96-513-80-80.** Admission free. July–Aug Mon–Sat 11am–9pm, Sun 11am–3pm; Sept Tues–Sat 11am–
9pm, Sun 11am–3pm; Oct–June Tues–Thurs 10am–2pm, Fri–Sat 10am–6pm, Sun
10am–4pm.

Where to Stay in Alicante

EXPENSIVE

Meliã Alicante ★   All 544 rooms at this ocean-liner-sized beach hotel face outward to look at Playa Postiguet on one side or the spiffy Alicante marina on the other, and each has a small balcony to step onto to enjoy the sea air. The hotel was built in 1973, and all rooms are identically sized at 26 sq. m (280 sq. ft.), while the junior suites are all 54 sq. m (580 sq. ft.). The current decor plays up the vast expanses of travertine marble with pops of saturated primary colors in the draperies and bedspreads. For a more luxe experience, upgrade to "The Level" for rooms with somewhat finer finishes, access to a private lounge with open bar, and an elevation that provides even better views. It's perfect if you left the kids at home, as it's limited to adults only.

Plaza del Puerto, 3. www.melia.com. ℂ **800-336-3542** in the U.S., or 96-520-50-00. 544 units. 102€–203€ double; 167€–295€ suite. Parking 23€. **Amenities:** Bar, 2 restaurants; exercise room; spa; outdoor pool; free Wi-Fi.

Sercotel Spa Porta Maris & Suites del Mar ★★★   Dominating the pier on the cruise port jetty, this pair of sister hotels is our hands-down choice for a luxurious stay in Alicante. We especially enjoy turning off the air-conditioning and sliding open the door to the terrace to go to sleep to the sound of the waves. The Porta Maris section was built first, and its rooms, while spacious by Spanish standards, are smaller than those in the posher Suites del Mar. They share an entrance, a reception area (different desks), the spa, and a casual restaurant. The Suites del Mar' suites are larger and more comfortable; its guests also have exclusive use of a pool, sauna, exercise area, and lounge, as well as a separate café for breakfast and daytime snacks.

Plaza Puerta del Mar, 3. www.hotelspaportamaris.com. ℂ **96-514-70-21.** 141 units in Porta Maris; 39 units in Suites del Mar. 118€–181€ double; Porta Maris suites 172€–235€ with breakfast; Suites del Mar 154€–180€. **Amenities:** 2 restaurants; 2 bars; exercise room; health club; spa; free Wi-Fi.

MODERATE

Eurostars Lucentum ★★   Admittedly, it's 10 blocks uphill from the port, but you get a lot of value by stepping back from the waterfront. Set in the middle of the main shopping district, the Lucentum is as close to the castle as to the beach. However, there's a tram stop across the street at the market, which will whisk you to the beach in minutes. The hotel has a polished elegance and lots of green plants around. The modest price jump to a superior room is worth it for the king-sized bed and even more space to stretch out.

Avenida Alfonso X El Sabio, 11. en.eurostars.com. ℂ **96-659-07-00.** 169 rooms. 63€–85€ double; 104€–145€ suite. Late Apr–mid-Sept rates include breakfast. Parking 15€. **Amenities:** Bar, sauna, laundry, gym; free Wi-Fi.

INEXPENSIVE

Bed & Breakfast La Milagrosa ★★   Who says you can't do a beach town on the cheap? Located three blocks from the beach, this family-run guesthouse is adding private baths to all its double rooms but expects to have some shared baths for the next few years. Superior rooms have small balconies overlooking the basilica. Some apartments with cooking facilities will sleep up to six. Even guests in the most modest rooms are free to use the kitchen and to eat on the terrace—making the whole experience feel very much like home away from home.

Calle Villavieja, 8. lamilagrosa.eu. ✆ **96-592-92-44.** 20 units. 38€–51€ double with shared bath; 65€–135€ en suite apartments. Free parking. **Amenities:** Bar, laundry; free Wi-Fi.

Hostal Les Monges Palace ★★   A rather charming hodgepodge of conjoined buildings with exposed brick and stone and extensive tilework, Les Monges has served as a lodging since 1989. The location near the city government offices places you smack in the middle of town; the room decor, while modest, is hardly as monkish as the name would suggest. The hotel's one suite is decorated with Japanese-style furnishings, including a bed so low that you almost have to kneel first to lie down. There's a whimsical charm about it all, and the family that operates the "palace" has a real sense of hospitality. They are genuinely excited to share their beloved Alicante with guests. The shared rooftop patio has charming views of the roofs and chimneys of old Alicante.

Calle San Agustín, 4. www.lesmonges.es. ✆ **96-521-50-46.** 18 rooms. 51€–70€ double; 100€–110€ suite. Parking 12€. **Amenities:** Bar; free Wi-Fi.

Where to Eat in Alicante

Alicanteros eat rice in almost every imaginable way. The most typical sauce is aioli, a kind of mayonnaise made from oil, egg yolks, and garlic. Dessert selections are the most varied on the Costa Blanca; *turrón de Alicante* (Spanish nougat) is the most popular.

Nou Manolín ★★ TAPAS/VALENCIAN   The fish tapas of Alicante are famous all over Spain—top Michelin-starred chefs often come to town on tapas-eating holidays. One of the places they come is Nou Manolín, where everyone from deckhands to stevedores to upscale tourists mingles at the bar, drinking local wines and making a meal of little plates of batter-fried anchovies, garlicky grilled shrimp, sizzling casseroles of sausages—more than 50 choices in all. The elegant upstairs dining room emphasizes local fish and the beautiful vegetables of the Alicante coast. In 2018, the founder was honored with the Premio Nacional de Gastronomía for his lifetime body of work. The menu features many rice dishes, but you can't go wrong with the catch of the day baked in a salt crust.

Calle Villegas 3. www.noumanolin.com. ✆ **96-520-03-68.** Entrees 21€–34€. Daily 1–4pm and 8:15pm–midnight. Bus: 22.

Restaurante Dársena ★ VALENCIAN   If you're looking for paella in Alicante, look no further. Dársena offers more than 100 versions of the baked rice dish, including a number using various organ meats. Located on a pier in the harbor, this glamorous dining room is often the first choice of the yachtsmen who put in at Alicante. Generally speaking, all rice dishes are prepared for a minimum of two diners. The menu also offers a half-dozen meat options and another half-dozen fish plates. The fish are usually the best bet; be sure to ask about the catch of the day. To eat farmed salmon (which is on the menu here) would be a shame, given that the Mediterranean laps at the pilings beneath the restaurant.

Marina Deportiva, Muelle de Levante, 6. www.darsena.com. ℂ **96-520-75-89.** Entrees 15€–32€; fixed-price menus 25€–65€. Lunch reservations essential. Mon–Sat 1:30–4:30pm and 8:30–11:30pm, Sun 1:30–4:30pm. Bus: 22.

Restaurante Monastrell ★★★ VALENCIAN   Since relocating to the main promenade, Monstrell now has breathtaking design and sweeping port views to complement its imaginative cuisine. María José San Román is the city's only Michelin-starred chef, and she earned it the hard way, having trained with top Basque chefs Martín Berasategui and Juan Marí Arzak and worked at the Girona's El Celler de Can Roca (p. 523). Yet San Román has forged a sophisticated style all her own, grounded in local Levantine gastronomy. The restaurant is named for the area's indigenous black grape, and San Román probably uses more Alicante saffron in her cooking than any other chef in Spain—she's celebrated for her innovative ways of using saffron to enhance flavors without imparting the characteristic aroma. Main dishes draw on hearty cooking of the interior (roast lamb with crisp red peppers and bread crumbs) as well as the coast (tuna neck confit with potato sauce and sea vegetables). For something lighter than the fixed-price menus, an outdoor passageway offers an innovative tapas menu.

Avenida Julian Guillén Tato, 1. www.monastrell.com. ℂ **96-520-03-63.** Tasting menus 66€–96€, bar tapas 8€–17€. Vegetarian options available. Dining room reservations essential. Mon–Sat 1:30–3:30pm and 8–11pm, Sun 1:30–3:30pm; closed Mon in winter. Bus: C6, 6, 9, 21, 22, 4.

La Taberna del Gourmet ★★ TAPAS/VALENCIAN   This snazzy contemporary tapas restaurant is Alicante's other destination for visiting gourmet chefs. Essentially a gastrobar of what its owners call "auteur cuisine," it is run by Geni Perramón, daughter of María José San Román of Monastrell (above). Far more than a bar, La Taberna del Gourmet is a deli, a dining room, and a virtual museum of contemporary tapas. The full menu offers more than 100 dishes, ranging from a few bites of goat cheese with herbs and honey to a bowl of black rice with cuttlefish, prawns, artichokes, and red peppers. Special tapas tasting menus are available for a minimum of two people.

Calle San Fernando, 10. www.latabernadelgourmet.com. ℂ **96-520-42-33.** Tapas 4€–16€, *raciones* 12€–32€, tasting menus 29€–59€. Daily 11am–12:30am. Bus: 1, 2, 10, 21, 22, C6. Tram: Mercado.

9

VALENCIA & THE COSTA BLANCA

Alicante

Alicante Entertainment & Nightlife

Alicante is a great city for socializing. One of the town's densest concentrations of watering holes lies adjacent to the port. Night owls wander from one bar to the next along the length of **Muelle del Puerto** (aka the Explanada d'Espanya). There are at least 20 spots that rock through the night. Alternatively, barhop on the narrow streets of Alicante's **Villa Vieja.** Some of the most sociable streets are **Calle Laboradores, Calle Cien Fuegos,** and **Plaza Santísima Faz.**

ELCHE

South of Alicante on the road heading toward Murcia, Elche (Elx in Valenciano) is one of the oldest continuously inhabited cities in Spain, and a cradle of Iberian civilization. It is known for its lush groves of date palms, shoe and sandal making, and the **Misteri d'Elx (Mystery of Elche),** reputedly the oldest dramatic liturgy in Europe. Every August 14 and 15 for the last six centuries, this pageant has celebrated the Assumption of the Virgin, with songs performed in an ancient form of Catalan. The play takes place at the 17th-century Basilica de Santa María. For tickets, visit www.misteridelx.com or call © **90-244-43-00.**

Elche's Palm Grove.

Essentials

ARRIVING Local **train** service arrives at Estación Parque, Avenida del Ferrocarril, with 5 trains a day from Murcia. As AVE service is built out, Elche expects to rejoin the national rail network; for updates, see www.renfe.com. The **bus** station (© **96-661-50-50**) at Avenida de la Libertat has hourly service to and from Alicante. If driving, take the N-340 highway from Alicante and proceed southwest.

VISITOR INFORMATION The **tourist information office** at Plaza Parque (www.visitelche.com; © **96-665-81-96**) is open Monday to Friday 9am to 7pm, Saturday 10am to 7pm, Sunday 10am to 2pm (winter hours shorter).

An industrial park on the edge of Elche is home to factory outlet stores of two dozen Spanish makers of clothing and—most notably—shoes. Marked-down, discontinued styles or sample sizes can save you up to half off retail. The best shop is **Pikolinos Tienda Museo ★**, Calle Marie Curie, 33 (www.visitpikolinos.com; ☏ **96-568-12-34**). Ask at the tourist information office for directions and a list of factory outlets.

Exploring Elche

Apart from the mystery play, Elche's **Palm Grove ★★** is the town's biggest draw, a 200,000-tree palm forest that is unrivaled in Europe. There's a 2.5km (1½-mile) walking tour through the grove; ask at the tourist office for a map. It's said that Phoenician (or perhaps Greek) seafarers originally planted the trees, while medieval Moors created the irrigation system that still maintains the palms. Even if you don't tour the entire grove, stroll through the **Huerto del Cura (Priest's Grove) ★★**, open daily 10am to dusk, to see the palm garden and collection of tropical flowers and cactuses. Look for the Palmera del Cura (Priest's Palm) from the 1840s, with seven branches sprouting from its trunk. Admission is 5€, 3€ students and seniors.

A replica of the ancient limestone bust La Dama de Elche (the original is at Madrid's archaeology museum; see p. 105) presides over the **Museo Arqueológico y de Historia de Elche (MAHE) ★★**, Calle Diagonal del Palau, 7 (www.elche.es/museos/mahe; ☏ **96-665-82-03**), installed in the old Altamira Palace. These archaeological exhibits, many of them in underground galleries, illuminate Elche's significance as a center of Iberian Celtic culture from the late Neolithic era on, even before the Phoenician traders arrived. It's open Monday to Saturday 10am to 6pm, Sunday 10am to 3pm. Admission is 3€ adults, 1€ students, and 1.50€ seniors and large families (free admission on Sun).

Where to Stay & Eat in Elche

Hotel Huerto del Cura ★★★   If the palm oasis has drawn you to Elche, then you would be nuts to stay anywhere else but this colony of duplex and triplex bungalows in the middle of the Huerta del Cura (Priest's Grove), the most beautiful part of the palm forest. Amid the palms, tropical fruit trees, and flowers, a winding red-slate path connects various buildings with patios where you can sit and enjoy the beauty and tranquility. If that's not enough, the new Oasis Zen Garden has a sauna and rooms for body treatments and massages. The on-site restaurant, **Els Capellans,** features contemporary Mediterranean cuisine (entrees 14€–28€; tasting menus 35€–50€).

Porta de La Morera, 14. www.hotelhuertodelcura.com. ☏ **96-661-00-11.** 81 units. 81€–90€ double; 117€–127€ jr. suite. Parking 12€. **Amenities:** Restaurant; bar; outdoor pool; free Wi-Fi.

Restaurante La Finca ★★★ MEDITERRANEAN   A landscaped terrace surrounds this handsome country house that's home to Elche's only Michelin-starred restaurant. Susi Díaz's contemporary cooking is creative and solidly based in local products, including Riofrio farmed caviar. The chef encourages diners to assemble their own tasting menus of two snacks, two seasonal appetizers, two starter plates, one main dish, dessert, and coffee. First courses include such surprises as red tuna carpaccio, sea cucumbers and peas, and roasted pigeon with apples. For a main course, consider the grilled pigeon with apples and Calvadós, or lobster with pistachios and baby vegetables.

Partida de Perleta, 1–7. www.lafinca.es. (𝒞 **96-545-60-07.** Entrees 25€–29€; tasting menu 79€. Tues–Sat 1:30–3:30pm and 8:30pm–10:30am (Oct–May closed for dinner Tues–Wed). Closed 2 weeks Jan, 1 week at Easter, 1 week Oct.

10

BARCELONA

By Will Shank

T he Catalan language has a verb that must have been invented for Barcelona. "Badar" means (more or less) to walk around with your mouth wide open in astonishment. You'll be doing a lot of that in Barcelona. The city's artists have always had a fantastical vision—from the gargoyles along the roofline of the cathedral, to Antoni Gaudí's armored warrior chimneys on La Pedrera, to the surreal amoeboid sculptures of Joan Miró (they're on a roof, too).

Barcelona really is an original, with its own unique history, language, gastronomy, and overall sense of style. When Madrid was still a dusty fortress village on the Río Manzanares, Barcelona was already a force to be reckoned with on the Mediterranean. It has been at the intersection of cultures—Iberian, Roman, Visigothic, Moorish, French, and Aragonese—for 2,000 years. Today it is the capital of the autonomous region of Catalunya, forever chafing to leave the federal fold of Spain but enjoying near-country status within the European Union.

Having won back its identity from Spain, Barcelona is profoundly Catalan, yet generous about conducting business and pleasure alike in Catalan and Castilian—as well as in English. Whatever tongue its visitors speak, Barcelona knows how to impress. Whether you are floating above the city on a cable car, rambling the medieval streets of the Barri Gòtic, devouring peel-and-eat shrimp at a beachside cafe, or sipping fresh strawberry-melon juice at La Boqueria, remember to keep your eyes wide open: You never know what will amaze you next.

ESSENTIALS

Arriving

BY PLANE Barcelona's international airport (BCN) is **El Prat** (www. aena.es; ✆ **90-240-47-04**), located 12km (7½ miles) southwest of the city center. (Beware of being flown into the "other" Barcelona airport, which in fact is near Girona, a 90-minute drive from Barcelona.) BCN has two passenger terminals connected by shuttle buses. The newer terminal, T1, serves the majority of international carriers, as well as the local low-cost airline **Vueling.** A handful of international carriers—most notably discount airlines **Ryanair, EasyJet,** and **Norwegian**—operate from the old airport, now called T2 (which includes terminals A, B, and C).

Many U.S. travelers to Barcelona fly to Madrid and change planes there, although there are some nonstop flights to Barcelona on various carriers from New York, Washington-Dulles, Philadelphia, and Atlanta, and now also the upstarts **Norwegian** (which offers nonstop flights between Barcelona and Newark, Oakland, and Los Angeles), and **Level** (which does West Coast routes and Boston). Bargain hunters willing to do the research and put up with some inconvenience can often find the cheapest overall airfare by flying transatlantic to Ireland or the United Kingdom, then taking EasyJet, Ryanair, or Vueling to Barcelona. **Iberia** (www.iberia.com; ✆ **800-772-4642**) offers daily shuttle flights between Barcelona and Madrid every half-hour at weekday peak hours; Vueling shares many Iberia routes. Often cheaper than Iberia, **Air Europa** (www.air-europa.com; ✆ **90-240-15-01**) also shuttles between Madrid and Barcelona.

GETTING FROM THE AIRPORT TO DOWNTOWN   A **RENFE train** runs between the airport's Terminal 2 and Barcelona's Estació de Sants every 15 to 30 minutes daily from 5:13am to 11:14pm (from Sants) or 5:42am to 11:38pm (to Sants). The 20-minute trip costs 4.60€. Be warned, however, that reaching the starting point of the train from the primary Terminal T1 can add some time to your arrival, and if you're jet-lagged, you may not welcome this hassle. Poorly adapted city buses shuttle between the two terminals, and there's almost no room for your luggage. If you do decide to take the train into the center, you can then catch the Metro from Sants to almost anywhere in Barcelona. The new **metro Line 9S** (S is for South) started serving both airport terminals in 2018. Unfortunately, it doesn't arrive at any central metro stations, although it could be a convenient option if you're headed for the big Fira Gran Via convention center. A one-way ticket between the airport and any stop on the 9S line costs 4.60€. If your hotel is near Plaça d'Espanya or Plaça de Catalunya, you should probably take the cost-efficient **Aerobús** (www.aerobusbcn.com; ✆ **93-415-60-20**). This system was recently simplified so that you can choose either bus T1 that runs to/from Terminal 1 or bus T2 that does the same route to and from the smaller terminal. They run every 10 minutes starting at 5am and ending at 12:30am from the airport, and you can catch a bus from a stop in front of the Corte Ingles Department store in Plaça Catalunya until 1:05am; all buses make a stop at Plaça d'Espanya. Midday service runs every 5 minutes; the fare is 5.90€ for a single trip, 10.20€ round-trip. A **taxi** to the center from the airport costs between 25€ and 30€, with an added airport surcharge as well as one for putting bags in the trunk. The good news is that taxi drivers absolutely do not expect a tip.

BY TRAIN   Barcelona has two major railway stations. Most national and international trains arrive at **Estació Central de Barcelona-Sants** (Metro: Sants-Estació), including high-speed AVE trains from Madrid and the high-speed Trenhotel from Paris. Some slower trains arrive at the under-used and beautiful **Estació de França** (Metro: Barceloneta, L3). For general RENFE (Spanish Railways) information, visit www.renfe.com or call ✆ **91-232-03-20.** There are two train options between Barcelona and Madrid: the "express trains" (trip time: 4½–9¾ hr.; cost: 68€–93€) and the high-speed AVE (Alta Velocidad Española) trains (trip time: 2½–3¼ hr.; cost: 108€–181€). You will want to purchase tickets, especially on high-speed trains, in advance. The RENFE website is notoriously difficult to negotiate, even though there is an English translation, so be patient. The wide range of pricing options can be confusing, too. It can be much less frustrating to plan your train trip by talking in person to a station ticket agent.

BY BUS Bus travel to Barcelona is possible, but it's pretty slow and less comfortable than the train. Barcelona's Estació del Nord, Carrer d'Alí Bei, 80 (Metro: Arc de Triomf) serves **Alsa** (www.alsa.es; ✆ **90-242-22-42**) buses to and from southern France and Italy. Alsa also operates 27 buses per day to and from Madrid (trip time: 7½–8½ hr.). A one-way ticket from Madrid costs 26€ to 44€. **Eurolines Viagens,** Carrer Viriato (www.eurolines.es; ✆ **93-490-40-00**), operates seven buses a week from Frankfurt and another five per week from Marseille.

BY CAR From **France** (the usual European road approach to Barcelona), the major access route is at the eastern end of the Pyrenees. You can choose the express highway (E-15) or the more scenic coastal road. If you take the coastal road in July and August, you will often face bumper-to-bumper traffic. You can also approach Barcelona via **Toulouse.** Cross the border at Puigcerdà, near the Principality of Andorra. From there, take the N-152 to Barcelona. From **Madrid** the drive takes at least 6 hours via the AP-2 and A-2 highways.

BY FERRY **Trasmediterránea,** Muelle de Sant Bertran, s/n (www.trasmediterranea.es; ✆ **90-245-46-45**), operates daily trips to and from the Balearic Islands of Mallorca (8 hr.) and Menorca (8 hr.). **Balearia** (www.balearia.com) also connects with the Balearic Islands, and **Grimaldi Lines** (www.grimaldi-lines.com) go back and forth from Barcelona and the west coast of Italy (Savona/Civitavecchia). In summer especially, it's important to have a reservation as far in advance as possible.

Visitor Information

Barcelona has two types of tourist offices. The **Catalunya regional office** deals with Spain in general and Catalunya in particular, with basic information about Barcelona. It has two locations at the El Prat airport (Terminal 1: ✆ **93-478-47-04;** Terminal 2: ✆ **93-478-05-65**), both in the Arrivals hall after you pass Customs. Hours are daily 8:30am to 10pm. These offices are co-managed with **Turisme de Barcelona** (see below). Another large office in the center of Barcelona at the **Palau de Robert,** Passeig de Gràcia, 107 (www.gencat.net; ✆ **93-238-80-91**), is open Monday to Saturday 9am to 8pm, Sunday and holidays 9am to 2:30pm.

The **Oficina de Informació de Turisme de Barcelona,** Plaça de Catalunya, 17-S (www.barcelonaturisme.com; ✆ **93-285-38-34**), also offers deals exclusively with the city of Barcelona. The main office is underground on the southeast corner of the plaza. In addition to getting detailed information about the city, you can purchase the **Barcelona Card** (p. 426) or tickets for the **Barcelona Bus Turístic** here. In the same space you'll also find the **FC Barcelona** shop, which sells football match tickets along with all the souvenirs imaginable, and an information desk for the **Ruta de Modernisme** (p. 426). The office is open daily 9am to 10pm, Sunday until 2pm.

City Layout

Barcelona is a port city surrounded by two small mountains (**Montjuïc** on the southwest, **Tibidabo** on the north) that form a natural bowl around the port. Although the city sprawls on its east side, the main sections of interest to travelers are the **waterfront, Ciutat Vell** (old city), **L'Eixample** and **Gràcia** (19th-c. extensions inland from the old city), and **Montjuïc.**

The central artery of the Ciutat Vell is **Les Rambles,** a broad avenue with a pedestrian center strip. It begins at the waterfront at Plaça Portal de la Pau, with its 50m-high (174-ft.) monument to Columbus, and stretches north to Plaça de Catalunya, changing names several times along the way.

The promenade of Les Rambles lies at the heart of the old city.

Along this wide promenade you'll find bookshops and newsstands, stalls selling birds and flowers, and benches or cafe tables where you can sit and watch the passing parade. West of Les Rambles is **El Raval,** a sector of the old city that has rebounded in recent years, evolving a good restaurant and bar scene. Just off Les Rambles to the east is **Plaça Reial,** the most harmoniously proportioned square in Barcelona. The neighborhood immediately east of Les Rambles is the **Barri Gòtic** (or Gothic Quarter), and east of the **Barri Gòtic** are the neighborhoods of **El Born** (where the waterfront transitions into the medieval city) and **La Ribera.**

Plaça de Catalunya is intersected by **Gran Via Corts Catalanes,** which is the approximate divider between the old and new cities. Ringed with hotels and restaurants, the plaza is a crossroads of bus and Metro routes. North of Gran Via, the streets of L'Eixample assume an orderly grid. **Passeig de Gràcia** is the most elegant of the north-south boulevards. The exception to the grid is the slash across "new" Barcelona, the **Avinguda Diagonal,** which separates the grid of L'Eixample from the grid of Gràcia.

FINDING AN ADDRESS/MAPS   Barcelona abounds with long boulevards and a complicated maze of narrow, twisting streets. Knowing the street number, if there is one, is essential. The designation s/n *(sin número)* means that the building has no number. It's crucial to learn the cross street if you're seeking a specific address. The rule about street numbers is that there is no rule. Most streets are numbered with odd numbers on one side, even numbers on the other. But because each building counts as a single number and some buildings are much wider than others, consecutive numbers (like 41 and 42, for example) may be a block or more apart.

Arm yourself with a good map before setting out. The free maps given out at the tourist office will do, but they often leave off the names of many of the small streets. The Barcelona Streetwise map from **Michelin** (formerly Falk) is good as well as durable. It is available at most newsstands and kiosks. However, finding your way with a massive folding map is usually impractical and, frankly, makes you more vulnerable to pickpockets. **Google Maps** (http://maps.google.com) are very detailed for Barcelona and largely accurate. If your phone or tablet has local service, you can use them while walking around. Otherwise, download an app that allows you to save the maps for offline reference.

Barcelona's Neighborhoods in Brief

LES RAMBLES & EL RAVAL   Originally the drainage canal that ran down the western edge of the 13th-century city walls, **Les Rambles** is now a broad, 1.5km-long (1-mile) avenue running between the waterfront and Plaça de Catalunya. The large pedestrian strip down the middle hosts a stream of street entertainers, flower vendors, news dealers, cafe patrons, and strollers. In the 15th century, convents and monasteries were built on the southwest side of Les Rambles; the last of them was razed in the 19th century. When they left, brothels moved in, and **El Raval,** west of Les Rambles, became Barcelona's red-light district. Nonetheless, a few important Modernisme landmarks were constructed in Raval, and today it is a resurgent neighborhood, with the university campus and contemporary arts scene on the north end. The newly developed **Rambla del Raval** is a charming neighborhood park, complete with Fernando Botero's giant bronze cat, "El Gato del Raval," and a loud flock of wild monk parrots nesting in the trees.

BARRI GÒTIC   East of Les Rambles is Barcelona's main medieval quarter, the atmospheric **Barri Gòtic,** where thoroughly modern shops stand cheek by jowl with museums and historic churches. King Jaume I encircled it with a wall in the 13th century, of which little remains. Built atop the old Roman city of Barcino, it is a tangle of narrow streets that radiate from and connect to plazas around the cathedral and other Gothic churches. Buried deep within the Barri Gòtic are the remnants of the **Call,** the medieval Jewish neighborhood.

LA RIBERA & EL BORN   **La Ribera**—literally, the shore—was constructed in medieval times where the sea encroached east of the city walls. Part of it was destroyed to build a fortress, now the Parc de la Ciutadella. **El Born** was the name given to the area of small, ancient streets west of the fortress. The north-south **Via Laietana** forms its western boundary, and **Passeig de Sant Joan** and Parc de la Ciutadella its eastern boundary. Somewhat more open than the Barri Gòtic, this area is home to the **Museu Picasso.**

Lamp posts in elegant L'Eixample were designed by Antoni Gaudí.

L'EIXAMPLE & GRÀCIA   North of Plaça de Catalunya and Gran Via de les Corts Catalanes, **L'Eixample** is the elegant planned "expansion" built in the late 19th and early 20th centuries. Catalan Modernisme, a local version of Art Nouveau architecture, reached its apex here. Famous landmarks include Antoni Gaudí's **Basilica de la Sagrada Familia** and Casa Milà, aka **La Pedrera.** The main north-south axis is **Passeig de Gràcia.** At its northern end, it is transected by the broad swath of **Avinguda Diagonal.** North of the Diagonal, the working-class neighborhood of **Gràcia** consists of several formerly rural villages annexed by Barcelona over the years.

417

LA BARCELONETA & THE WATERFRONT   Back when Barcelona was a sailor's town, the waterfront was colorful but a little iffy after dark. The 1992 Olympics changed all that, bringing a complete redevelopment of the Port Vell—now a yacht harbor—and installing **L'Aquarium Barcelona** and the **Maremagnum** shopping center on a newly created island, the Moll d'Espanya. Another quay was transformed into the **Moll de la Fusta,** a popular walking and cycling path. At the east end of Moll de la Fusta, **Passeig de Joan de Borbó** goes to the tip of **La Barceloneta,** once the neighborhood of fishermen and now a hip bohemian address noted for its seafood restaurants and sandy beaches.

POBLENOU   A neighborhood in transition, the "new town" of **Poblenou** is a former industrial zone occupied primarily by textile factories. One by one these spaces have been redefined, and the intrepid traveler who has had enough Gaudí can discover, with a short metro ride from the historic center, the hipster cafes and galleries of Barcelona's "Williamsburg." Locals will tell you that the beaches of this eastern stretch of the city are better—and invariably less crowded—than those of Barceloneta.

MONTJUÏC   Rather disconnected from the rest of the city, **Montjuïc** is a small mountain that's not so small when you're walking up it in August. It begins at **Plaça d'Espanya,** where the city's convention center is located, and goes up to the old Palacio Nacional, now the **Museu Nacional d'Art de Catalunya.** The mountain was developed for the 1929 Barcelona International Exposition, when the **Mies van der Rohe Pavilion** and the **Poble Espanyol** area of "typical" Spanish architecture were built. It is also the home of the **Fundació Joan Miró.**

GETTING AROUND
On Foot

You can walk most places in Barcelona's old city, or through the main points of interest in L'Eixample. But it's a good idea to use public transport to a starting point and then set off on foot to explore.

By Public Transit

Barcelona's public transit system includes extensive and interlinked networks of buses, subway trains, trams, and "rodalies" (local commuter rail). For a full overview, check the website of **Transports Metropolitans de Barcelona** (www.tmb.cat). This site, available in Catalan, Spanish, and English, recommends ways to get from one place to another using any combination of public transit and walking. Individual tickets on subway and buses within the central city cost 2.20€; 10-ride tickets, available in machines in any metro station, cut the per-ride cost in half.

You'll save a bundle by visiting an automatic machine in any metro station on your first day and buying a 10-trip card for Zone 1 (essentially anywhere in the center); that will lower the per-ride price to just over a euro. It's good for transfers for 90 minutes, from the time you first

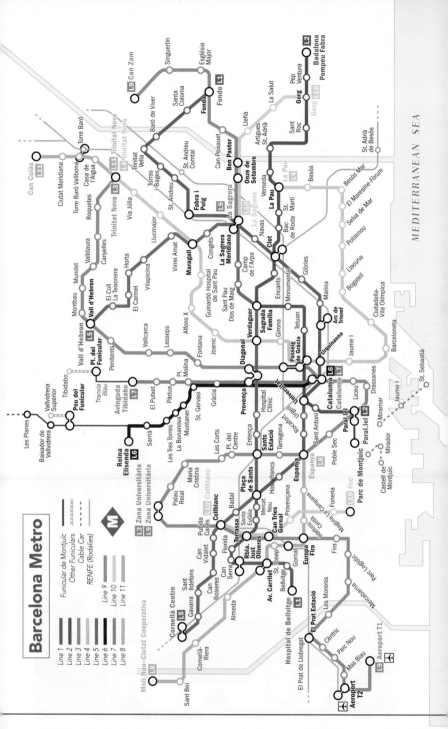

419

validate it on a bus or in a metro station turnstile. Most—but not all—metro stations have disabled access via elevators to/from the street level, and many buses "kneel" to allow a wheelchair to roll through a middle door.

BY SUBWAY

The six lines of Barcelona's Metro system crisscross the city more frequently and with greater speed than the bus network. Service operates Sunday to Thursday from 5am to midnight, Friday 5am to 2am, and a full 24 hours on Saturday. Each Metro station entrance is marked with an "M" in a red diamond. The major station for all lines is **Plaça de Catalunya.**

BY BUS

About 190 bus lines traverse the city and, not surprisingly, you don't want to ride them at rush hour. Most buses run daily 6am to 10pm; some night buses go along the principal arteries from 10pm to 6am. You can buy your

The hop-on-hop-off Barcelona Bus Turistic is one good way to get a quick overview of the city.

ticket when boarding or buy a multiple ticket in a machine in any metro stop. **Red buses** cut through the city center during the day; **yellow** ones operate at night. A recent streamlining of the bus system has tried to make routes clearer by re-naming east-west routes with an H (for "horizontal"), north-south routes V ("vertical"), and D for diagonal. Tickets, good for 90 minutes, are interchangeable between the metro and the bus system.

By Barcelona Bus Turistic

The most established of the sightseeing buses, the double-decker **Barcelona Bus Turistic** travels three routes that can deliver you to almost every major tourist attraction in the city. The bus includes running commentary (through headsets) in 10 languages, and a choice of outdoor seating with great views or indoor seating with heat or air-conditioning. It also claims free on-board Wi-Fi (it never worked on any buses where we tried it). Circuits on the red route (old city, Montjuïc, and the waterfront) and the blue route (L'Eixample and Gràcia) each take about 2 hours. The green route, which shuttles along the neighborhoods and beaches east of Port Olimpic, takes 40 minutes. You can get on and off all day, but be forewarned: You can wait as much as a half-hour to get onto a crowded bus in high season. These buses are useful if you don't want to use regular public transportation, but they're much less efficient. *Our advice:* Take these buses for a good overview on your first day in the city (one day on the bus will also snag you a booklet of discounts good on many attractions, including La Pedrera and La Sagrada Familia). Buy tickets online in advance to save time. The cost is 30€ for 1 day (25€ seniors, 16€ ages 4–12), 40€ for 2 days (35€ seniors, 21€ ages 4–12), ages under 4 free.

By Taxi

Each yellow-and-black taxi bears the letters sp *(Servicio Público)* on its front and rear. A lit green light on the roof and a libre sign in the window indicate the taxi is free to pick up passengers, and you can flag them down on the street, or find one at a taxi stand. The basic fare begins at 2.15€, with each additional kilometer costing 1.13€. Supplements might apply— 1€ for a large suitcase placed in the trunk, for instance. Rides to the airport carry a supplement of 3.10€, and rates are higher between 8pm and 8am and on some holidays. For a taxi, contact **Ràdio Taxi** (www.radiotaxi033. com; ✆ **93-303-30-33**). The phone app service **MyTaxi** (https://es.mytaxi. com) also works in Barcelona, as does **Uber,** although its antagonistic relationship with the local taxistas has been tense, resulting in the occasional taxi strike.

By Funicular & Rail Links

It takes some planning to visit the mountains of Tibidabo or Montjuïc. To visit Tibidabo (p. 456) by public transport, take the **Funicular de Tibidabo.** The fare is 7.70€, or 4.10€ if you're also purchasing admission to the Tibidabo amusement park. The funicular operates every 15 to 20 minutes. From mid-April to September service is daily 10am to 8pm; the rest of the year it usually operates only Saturday and Sunday 10am to 6pm. To get to the funicular, take Metro Line 7 to Avinguda Tibidabo, exit onto Plaça Kennedy, and take Bus 196 (the usual 2.20€ fare) to the funicular. The 1901 **Tramvía Blau** (Blue Streetcar; 4€) is currently shut down for repairs, but once it's back, that's another way to reach the funicular from Plaça Kennedy.

Getting to **Montjuïc** by funicular is a simple ride from the Paral.lel Metro station; it's considered part of the Metro network, so the ride up the hill comes at no extra cost. Once you're on the mountain, you can ride **Telefèric de Montjuïc** to the castle on top (adults 12.70€ round-trip, 9.20€ for ages 4–12).

By Car

No matter how attached you are to your car back home, **don't** drive around congested Barcelona. Parking is expensive (especially in hotels), public transit is more efficient, and generally it's not worth the hassle. Save car rentals for excursions. Both Avis and Hertz have offices at the airport; **Avis** is also at Carrer Corçega 293–295 (www.avis.es; ℰ **90-211-02-75**) and **Hertz** at Carrer de Viriat, 45 (www.hertz.es; ℰ **93-419-61-56**), adjacent to the Estació Barcelona-Sants rail station. Both are open Monday to Friday 8am to 9pm, Saturday 8am to 8pm, and Sunday 8am to 1pm. *Tip:* It is usually cheaper and easier to arrange your car rental before leaving home. Prices vary little among companies, so stick with whichever one dovetails with your frequent-flyer program.

[FastFACTS] BARCELONA

Banks & ATMs You can usually find a bank—or at least an ATM—wherever crowds gather in Barcelona, especially around major Metro stations. Most permit cash withdrawals via MasterCard or Visa. The most prominent ATM networks in Barcelona are **La Caixa** and **Banco Santander,** but they may charge a high commission; shop around for smaller banks that do not. Note that most Spanish ATMs accept only 4-digit PINs, so if you have a longer PIN, change it at least a

week before departure. Many banks now have "dynamic currency conversion," allowing the bank to charge your withdrawal in dollars rather than euros. The exchange rate is even worse than the one your bank at home will give you, so always answer "NO" and ask to be charged in euros.

Consulates National embassies are all located in Madrid, but there are some consular offices in Barcelona. The **U.S. Consulate,** Carrer Reina Elisenda, 23 (https://es.usembassy.gov/

embassy-consulates/ barcelona; ℰ **93-280-22-27**), is open Monday to Friday 9am to 1pm; you need to make an appointment unless you have an emergency like a lost/stolen passport. Before going, check https://es.usembassy. gov/embassy. The **Canadian Consulate,** Plaça de Catalunya, 9 (www.canada international.gc.ca/spain-espagne/offices-bureaux/ consul_barcelona; ℰ **93-412-72-36**), is open Monday to Friday 9am to 12:30pm. The **U.K. Consulate,** Avinguda

Diagonal, 477 (www.gov.uk/ world/organisations/british-consulate-general-barcelona/ office/british-consulate-general-barcelona; ☏ **93-366-62-00**), is open Monday to Friday 8:30am to 1:30pm.

Doctors & Dentists

Barcelona has many hospitals and clinics, including **Clínic Barcelona** (www. hospitalclinic.org; ☏ **93-227-54-00**) and **Hospital de la Santa Creu i Sant Pau,** at the intersection of Carrer Cartagena and Carrer Sant Antoni María Claret (www.santpau.cat; ☏ **93-291-90-00**). For dental needs, contact **Clínica Dental Barcelona,** Passeig de Gràcia, 97 (www.clinica dentalbarcelona.com/en; ☏ **93-487-83-29**), open daily 9am to midnight.

Emergencies Call

☏ **112** for general emergencies. To report a fire, call ☏ **080;** to call an ambulance, ☏ **061;** to call the police, ☏ **088.**

Internet Access Most

lodgings offer free Wi-Fi, at least in public areas. Typically, bandwidth on free

hotel Wi-Fi is good enough to surf the web and check e-mail, but not for streaming videos or music. The city government provides free Wi-Fi at over 2,000 spots around the city. You will have to sign up for a free account to use it (ajuntament.barcelona.cat/barcelonawifi/en/#connectar). Buses and some Metro lines also have free Wi-Fi.

Language Catalunya

has two official languages: Catalan and Castilian Spanish. Catalan (Catalá in its own language) takes precedence for signage, television, radio, and most publications. A romance language resembling both Spanish and French, Catalan is much preferred among locals, especially so during these times of separatist zeal. English is often a better bet, and it is widely spoken—if not well—in the tourism sector.

Mail & Postage The

main post office is a beautiful beaux-arts building at the foot of Via Laietana, on Plaça d'Antoni López (www. correos.es; ☏ **93-486-80-50**). It's open Monday to

Friday 8:30am to 9:30pm and Saturday 8:30am to 2pm.

Newspapers & Magazines Barcelona's

leading daily newspapers, which often list cultural events, are *El Periódico* and *La Vanguardia. Time Out Barcelona* is useful for arts listings.

Pharmacies The cen-

trally located **Farmacia Montserrat,** Les Rambles, 118 (☏ **93-302-43-45**), is open daily 9am to 8pm. Pharmacies take turns staying open late at night; those that aren't open post the names and addresses of nearby pharmacies that are.

Safety Barcelona is a big

city with many disoriented tourists paying scant attention to their belongings. Pickpockets and purse-snatchers treat the unwary like the weak antelopes straggling at the back of the herd. Don't be one of them. Be careful with cameras, purses, and wallets wherever there are crowds, especially on Les Rambles, on buses, or while standing in line at a tourist attraction.

EXPLORING BARCELONA

Most of Barcelona (with the notable exception of the Gothic Quarter and Raval, near the sea) is laid out on a grid. Locals refer to the sea (mar) or mountain (montaña) side of streets to give directions, but for the sake of explanation here, we'll place the Mediterranean to the south (which it isn't exactly) and to the north the mountains that you can see from almost anywhere in the city. There are essentially four parts of Barcelona that will interest you most: the **Old City** of the Romans and the Middle Ages; the 19th-century planned city, called **Eixample;** the **waterfront;** and the mountain called **Montjüic.**

In the oldest part of town, **les Rambles** (pronounced "las ramblas") is a central north-south artery from Plaça de Catalunya down to the sea.

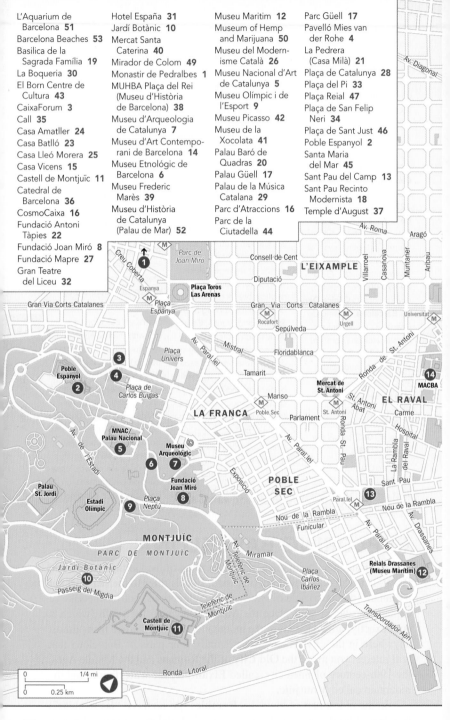

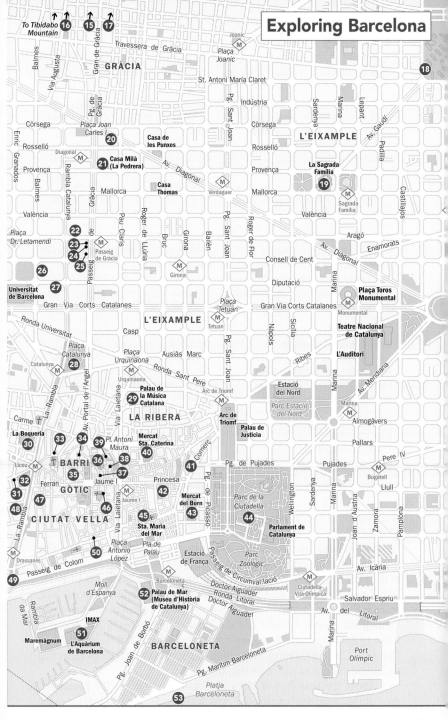

To Tibidabo Mountain

16 15 17

18

Joanic

Travessera de Gràcia

Plaça Joanic

GRÀCIA

St. Antoni María Claret

Indústria

Còrsega

Plaça Joan Carles I

20

L'EIXAMPLE

Rosselló

Casa de les Punxes

Còrsega

Rosselló

La Sagrada Família

19

Diagonal

Casa Milà (La Pedrera)

21

Provença

Provença

Av. Diagonal

Casa Thomas

Sagrada Família

Mallorca

Mallorca

Verdaguer

València

València

Plaça Dr. Letamendi

22

Aragó

Enamorats

23

24

Passeig de Gràcia

Consell de Cent

Av. Diagonal

25

26

Girona

Diputació

27

Plaça Toros Monumental

Universitat de Barcelona

Gran Via Corts Catalanes

Plaça Tetuan

Gran Via Corts Catalanes

Monumental

Teatre Nacional de Catalunya

Ronda Universitat

L'EIXAMPLE

Casp

Tetuan

L'Auditori

Plaça Catalunya

Plaça Urquinaona

Ausiàs Marc

Ronda Sant Pere

Catalunya

28

Urquinaona

Estació del Nord

Palau de la Música Catalana

29

Arc de Triomf

Parc Estació del Nord

Carme

LA RIBERA

Arc de Triomf

La Boqueria

30

33 34

Pl. Antoni Maura

39

Mercat Sta. Caterina

Palau de Justícia

Almogàvers

Marina

Liceu

32

BARRI

36

38

40

Pallars

31

35

GÒTIC

Ferran

Jaume I

37

41

Princesa

42

Pg. de Pujades

Pujades

Pere IV

Bogatell

Llull

47

48

46

Jaume I

Mercat del Born

43

Parc de la Ciutadella

CIUTAT VELLA

45

44

Parlament de Catalunya

Sta. Maria del Mar

Pla de Palau

Plaça Antonio López

50

Estació de França

Parc Zoològic

M

Drassanes

Passeig de Colom

Barceloneta

Ciutadella-Vila Olímpica

49

Moll d'Espanya

52

Palau de Mar (Museu d'Història de Catalunya)

Doctor Aiguader

Ronda Litoral

Doctor Aiguader

Salvador Espriu

Av. del Litoral

IMAX

Maremàgnum

51

L'Aquàrium de Barcelona

BARCELONETA

Pg. Marítim Barceloneta

Port Olímpic

Platja Barceloneta

53

425

SAVINGS ON exploring

There are four discount programs that may or may not work for you, depending on what you want to see and how you're planning to get around.

A ticket on the **Barcelona Bus Turistic** (p. 421) gets you a coupon book good for the calendar year. Most discounts are modest, and the Museu Picasso is not included, but if you decide to ride the bus, be sure to use the coupons.

The **Barcelona Card** features several free museum admissions and allows you to skip the lines. It also provides discounts on other admissions and tours, including 15–20% on admissions to major Modernista buildings. Unlimited use of Metro, buses, and commuter rail can be a plus. Available at all Barcelona Turisme offices and El Corte Inglés department stores, it costs 45€ for 72 hours, 55€ for 96 hours, 60€ for 120 hours. The corresponding prices for children ages 4 to 12 are 21€, 27€, 32€. A 2-day option, the **Barcelona Card Express,** costs only 20€, but gives you discounts rather than free museum admissions; it also gives you free public transit for 48 hours, including to/from the airport.

The **Articket BCN** is geared to the major art museums, providing priority entry to six museums for 30€: Museu Picasso, Museu Nacional d'Art de Catalunya, Fundació Joan Miró, Fundació Antoni Tàpies, the Centre de Cultura Contemporània de Barcelona (CCCB), and the Museu d'Art Contemporani de Barcelona (MACBA). Tickets to the first three alone will cost more than the pass. The pass also allows you to skip the line—a huge timesaver at the Museu Picasso.

Purchasing the **Ruta de Modernisme guide** (12€) at any bookstore or tourist office supplies you with a coupon book with up to 50% off entrance fees to the Modernista buildings. The guide itself and its accompanying map make invaluable, if highly detailed, references to 116 Modernista sites around the city.

When weighing the options, keep in mind that on the first Sunday of each month, **admission is free** anyway at the Museu Picasso, the Museu Nacional d'Art de Catalunya (MNAC), and the Museu d'Història de Catalunya. Museu Picasso is also free every Sunday after 3pm, while MNAC is free every Saturday after 3pm.

It's actually a succession of streets, whose names—Rambla de Santa Mònica, Rambla dels Caputxins, Rambla de Sant Josep, Rambla dels Estudis, Rambla de Canaletes—recall the various religious orders that were once located here. To the west of it lies the **Raval** neighborhood, and to the east, the oldest part of Barcelona: the **Barrio Gotico** and **El Born.** The Picasso Museum, the Cathedral, the church of Santa Maria del Mar, and the Palace of Catalan Music are found in the warren of narrow streets holding the Gothic Quarter and the Born neighborhoods. The Raval is home to the Museum of Contemporary Art and the CCCB (Contemporary Center of Catalan Culture), along with lively eateries and shops reflecting the ethnic culture of recent immigrants.

Above the busy hub of Plaça de Catalunya stretches the **Eixample,** the Catalan word for "expansion," which is exactly what took place in the second half of the 19th century after Barcelona's medieval walls were demolished in 1860. Urban planner Ildefons Cerdá freed up the city from the narrow twisting alleys of the Gothic Quarter, shooting his wide thoroughfares and identically spaced blocks of buildings northward, which connected old Barcelona with the village of Gracia; the Rambles were extended beyond Plaça de Catalunya as the Passeig de Gracia (or "the passage to Gracia"), now a chic shopping boulevard.

Les Rambles & El Raval

If you're not jazzed walking up and down **Les Rambles** ★★★ (Las Ramblas in Spanish), check to make sure you still have a pulse. You can spend a day here just exploring the street life, cafes, and shops. But you'll want to take some of that time to turn into El Raval on streets named Nou de la Rambla, Sant Pau, Hospital, Carme, and Elisabets. You'll find both the wonderfully *récherché* world of old Raval, and the modern, hip neighborhood of the arts. Get to Les Rambles by one of three Metro stops: Drassanes at the waterfront, Liceu halfway up, and Plaça de Catalunya at the top.

La Boqueria ★★★ MARKET   Foodies visiting Spain consider the Mercat de Sant Josep de la Boqueria (its official name) a temple deserving reverential pilgrimage. The spot has been a marketplace since medieval days when Raval farmers sold their produce to the inhabitants of the walled city. The current market is the largest of Barcelona's 35 public markets. It has a sidewalk mosaic in front created by Joan Miró in the

La Boqueria, the grand food market on Les Rambles.

1970s, and the metal-roofed structure is an amalgam of building styles erected between 1840 and 1914. From the outside, it resembles a train station. Inside, it is jammed with stalls selling every imaginable type of fresh produce, fish (segregated to one side), and meat (toward the back). There are bakeries and sandwich stalls and juice bars and cafes all tucked into the mix. Even if you're not someone normally intoxicated by food, it's an important spot to visit. Pay attention to what the stalls are selling, and you'll quickly learn what's fresh and in season, and can order accordingly at restaurants.

Les Rambles, 91. www.boqueria.barcelona. No phone. Mon–Sat 8am–8:30pm. Metro: Liceu.

Gran Teatre del Liceu ★★ THEATER   Despite its plain exterior, this 2,700-seat Belle Epoque opera house is opulent inside. One of the world's grand theaters, it was designed in 1861 to replace an earlier one destroyed by fire. Flames gutted the opera house again in 1994, but it was restored to its 19th-century glory. It's also a great place to take in opera, dance, or a concert. The Liceu also offers **guided tours** of the public areas, and a limited number of guided tours of the stage and service areas.

Les Rambles, 51–59. www.liceubarcelona.cat. ⓒ **93-485-99-00.** 30-min. tour Mon–Sat 1pm, 6€ adults, 5€ students and seniors; 45-min. tour Mon–Fri hourly 2–5pm, Sat from 11am, 9€ adults, 7.50€ students and seniors; 50-min. tour Mon–Fri 11am and noon, 16€ adults, 12€ students and seniors; 80-min. tour (includes backstage areas) at 9:15am, 24€ adults, 18€ students and seniors (select dates to be pre-booked). Metro: Liceu.

Museu d'Art Contemporani de Barcelona ★ MUSEUM   This white elephant displaced several historic blocks of the Raval neighborhood when it was built in the 1990s, and it's still trying to define its role in the art world. Conceived as a showcase for contemporary art from the mid-20th century on, MACBA tends to install exhibitions of the most esoteric—and incomprehensible—nature, scaring away potential visitors. (It doesn't also help that the museum promotes its exhibitions in the square outside only in Catalan.) What it HAS done for the neighborhood is to bring youth and vibrancy to the formerly seedy district—in the form of hundreds of skateboarders, who are drawn to the ramps in front of the building. Save your money and, if you're a Richard Meier fan, admire the building's architecture from the outside. Two of MACBA's most striking artworks can be viewed in the square near the entrance without paying admission: a forceful black-and-white ceramic mural by Basque sculptor Eduardo Chillida, and a reconstruction of Keith Haring's cautionary 1986 AIDS mural that was originally painted in a nearby square. A gothic chapel near the museum, the Convent dels Angels, which is part of MACBA, frequently installs the work of individual artists, and the lovely 16th-century stone space can work well as a contemporary exhibition gallery.

Plaça dels Angels 1. www.macba.cat. ⓒ **93-481-22-68.** Admission 10€ adults, 5€ students, free seniors and ages 14 and under. Mon and Wed–Fri 11am–7:30pm; Sat 10am–8pm, Sun 10am–3pm. Metro: Plaça de Catalunya.

Exploring Barcelona

BARCELONA

Museu Marítim ★★ MUSEUM

A dazzling replica of a 16th-century warship at the Museu Marítim.

Recently re-opened, this museum chronicles Barcelona's maritime history from the time when Rome established the trading port of Barcino up to the 21st century. The museum is housed inside medieval royal shipyards, the Drassanes Reiales. (Yes, the waters of the Mediterranean used to reach the front door of this building; the sea has gradually moved a block away.) Built between 1255 and 1378, these shipyards were so vast that thirty galleys could be built at a time; as a result, the crown of Aragón became one of the most powerful naval forces in the Mediterranean. It's a marvelous example of adaptive re-use of an enormous building, creating a successful and intelligently mounted museum that brings its history alive. Admission includes entrance to the historic three-masted schooner *Santa Eulália,* moored across the street. The high-ceilinged, elegant **Norai** restaurant offers a delicious fixed-price menu and outdoor seating in good weather. Make sure that you and your kids peek through the porthole of the wooden submarine in the courtyard.

Avinguda de les Drassanes, s/n. www.mmb.cat. ℂ **93-342-99-20.** Daily 10am–8pm, Sun free after 3pm. Admission 10€, or 5€ students and seniors. Metro: Drassanes.

Palau Güell ★★★ HISTORIC SITE   Constructed between 1886 and 1890 for aristocrat and industrialist Eusebi Güell, this was Antoni Gaudí's second commission—and yet the architect's budding originality was such that it already looks almost as if it were grown rather than built. The family quarters are conventional—"a normal Venetian palace," a guide once sniffed on one of our tours—but the architect's imagination ran wild above and below. The underground forest of brick columns and vaults in 10 musty cellars creates a honeycomb of stables and servants' quarters, and functions as much as a root system as a foundation. The rooftop is even more startling, for Gaudí wrapped the chimneys with swirling abstract sculptures. Not only are they embedded with mosaics of broken pottery, they also employ artistic symbols from ancient Catalan tradition. After the restraint of the main residence, the rooftop is an exultation of the spirit.

Carrer Nou de la Rambla, 3–5. www.palauguell.cat. ℂ **93-472-57-75.** Admission 12€ adults, 9€ students, 5€ ages 10–17 and seniors. Apr–Oct Tues–Sun 10am–8pm, Nov–Mar Tues–Sun 10am–5:30pm. Metro: Liceu.

Plaça de Catalunya ★ PLAZA Considered the heart of the city, this large circular plaza is where the old city and the 19th-century extension meet. Since its last renovation in 1929, it has also been the crossroads of the Metro system. Shoppers flock to a large branch of the Spanish department store El Corte Inglés, and a recent addition grabbed a prime location on the busy square: the Apple Store. Plaça de Catalunya is also known for its fountains. Legend says that anyone who drinks from the Font de Canaletes will inevitably return to Barcelona.
Metro: Catalunya.

Sant Pau del Camp ★★ CHURCH The antithesis of Gaudí's La Sagrada Familia, the modest ancient church and monastery of Sant Pau del Camp (St. Paul of the Fields) is one of the most serene and most moving religious spaces in Barcelona. According to his gravestone, which was unearthed in 1596, the monastery was founded between 897 and 911 by Guifré Borrell, then count of Barcelona (and son of Wilfred the Hairy). The church was sacked by Al-Mansur's Moorish troops in 985, but the whole complex was rebuilt during the 13th century—the period of the charming cloister and its stone capitals carved with Biblical tales. Centuries of erosion have not dimmed Eve's sudden embarrassment about her nakedness or the ferocity of the reptilian devil being skewered by archangel Michael. The intimate piety of the church and its small altar are striking. A side chapel holds a beautiful polychrome Gothic statue of María del Deu, as well as the founder's gravestone. The posted opening hours schedule should not be taken literally.
Carrer Sant Pau, 101. ✆ **93-441-00-01.** Admission 5€ adults, 4€ students and seniors. Mon–Sat 10am–6pm. Masses Sat 8pm, Sun noon. Metro: Paral.lel.

Barri Gòtic

Barcelona came into its own as a Mediterranean power in the 12th century when the Aragonese King Jaume I erected a defensive wall around the city. This area—roughly from Les Rambles east to Via Laietana and from the waterfront north to Plaça de Catalunya—is the **Barri Gòtic (Gothic Quarter)** ★★★, which retains much of its medieval street pattern. It's a fascinating neighborhood of narrow streets and pocket squares, most fronting on Gothic churches. Plan on spending at least a half-day exploring, knowing that you will get a little lost, no

The Barri Gòtic.

matter how good your map. The area assumes a special magic on Sunday mornings, when you can emerge from a warren of small streets onto a square where a musician may be playing for change. Metro stops for the Barri Gòtic are Liceu and Jaume I.

Call ★ HISTORIC NEIGHBORHOOD   Barcelona had one of the most robust Jewish communities in Iberia from the 12th century until 1391, when the community in the heart of the Barri Gòtic came under siege. Six centuries of absence have wiped away most evidence of Jewish presence, but since the 1990s, a concerted effort by scholars and community activists has helped establish the old limits of the Call and has begun to restore the remains of the principal synagogue. The main street of the Call (a Jewish word meaning "small street") was Carrer de Sant Domènc, where the great synagogue, the kosher butcher's shop, and the homes of the leading Jewish citizens were located. An information center and display of artifacts recovered through excavations is operated by the Associació Call de Barcelona in a shop above the remains of the **Sinagoga Mayor.**

Carrer Marlet, 5. www.sinagogamayor.com. ℂ **93-317-07-90.** Admission 2€ adult, 1.50€ seniors and ages 29 and under. Mon–Fri 10:30am–6:30pm, Sun 10:30am–3pm. Metro: Jaume I.

The Catedral de Barcelona, a showpiece of Catalan Gothic architecture.

Catedral de Barcelona ★★
CHURCH   A celebrated example of Catalan Gothic architecture, Barcelona's cathedral was begun at the end of the 13th century and more or less completed by the mid–15th century. One notable exception, the western facade, dates from the 19th century when churchgoers felt that the unadorned Gothic surface was somehow inadequate. If you really want to get a feel for the cathedral, skip the "tourist visit" completely and go to Mass, or at least sit silently and reflect. The high naves, which have been cleaned and lit in recent years, are filled with terrific Gothic architectural details, including elongated and tapered columns that blossom into arches in their upper reaches.

The separate **cloister** has vaulted galleries that surround a garden of magnolias, medlars, and palm trees, along with the so-called "well of the geese" (13 geese live in the cloister as a symbol of Barcelona co-patron Santa Eulalia, the teenage Roman martyr who is buried in the crypt). The cloister also contains the cathedral's museum, of which the most notable piece is a 15th-century *pieta* by Bartolomé Bermejo. For an extra 3 euros, you can also take an elevator to the roof, which has a number of fanciful gargoyles and terrific views of the rest of the Barri Gòtic.

Plaça de la Seu, s/n. www.catedralbcn.org. © **93-315-15-54.** Admission 7€. Mon–Fri 12:30–7:15pm, Sat 12:30–4:45pm; Sun 2–4:45pm. Metro: Jaume I.

Museum of Hemp and Marijuana ★★ MUSEUM   What do Betsy Ross, Henry Ford, Popeye, and John Wayne have in common? They all championed the cause of different uses of the *cannabis sativa* plant, one of the oldest agricultural crops on earth. This is not at all the "stoner" museum that you might be expecting, but rather a thoughtful presentation of the various ways in which hemp and marijuana have been used historically in industry, in medicine, and in pop culture. Additionally, the Dutch instigator of the museum (he also opened one in Amsterdam) placed it in one of the most beautiful Modernista flats in the Gothic Quarter, and building's history is highlighted along with a focus on the objects on view. The experience is complemented by whimsical moments like a selfie machine that will place you and your friends or family in a virtual marijuana field or dressed as scientists in a pot greenhouse, and the shop is full of irresistible souvenirs.

Carrer Ample, 35. www.hashmuseum.com. © **93-319-75-39.** Admission 9€ adults, free for ages 12 and under if with adults. Daily 10am–10pm. Metro: Drassanes.

MUHBA Plaça del Rei ★★★ MUSEUM/ARCHAEOLOGICAL SITE The Museum of the History of Barcelona has several sites around town, this being the central one. Here you can get a fascinating look at ancient Roman times through a tour of underground walkways over the excavations of Barcino, the city founded in the 1st century B.C. (the Moors leveled it in the A.D. 8th c.). It's set in part of the 11th-century Palau Reial Major, palace of the kings of Aragón and Catalunya (also in this palace complex: the **Museu Frederic Marès;** see below). Although they are partially visible from Plaça del Rei, the last remaining Roman walls and defensive towers of Barcino—a section from the A.D. 4th-century second enclosure—are easier to make out from the museum's other side, on Plaça Ramon Berenguer on Via Laietana. Embedded within the wall are the royal chapel of Santa Ágata and a 14th-century segment of the Palau Reial.

Plaça del Rei, s/n. www.museuhistoria.bcn.es. © **93-256-21-00.** Admission 7€ adults, 5€ students and seniors, free under age 16. Tues–Sat 10am–7pm, Sun 10am–8pm. Metro: Jaume I.

Museu Frederic Marès ★★ MUSEUM   Just because you already own 500 medieval polychrome sculptures of the Madonna and Child, is that any reason not to buy a few hundred more? That must have been the sort of quandary that faced sculptor Frederic Marès (1893–1991) during the many decades he spent assembling this extraordinary group of objects, now the permanent collection of the museum that bears his name. The museum has an enviably central location in the Gothic Quarter (literally in the shadow of the Cathedral), and it presents one of Spain's most thorough—one is tempted to say obsessive—collections of sculpture and decorative arts. It's important to pace yourself, as at a certain point you may want to hold up your hand and say, "Enough!" (Will I focus on the daguerreotypes, the unicycles, or the hat pin collection?) The great joy of seeing so many related objects installed side-by-side is that it reveals the subtle differences in the hand of each anonymous sculptor of the crucifixes or the Gardens of Eden, for instance. The museum, acknowledging the vastness of its collections, allows you to use your admission ticket for a return visit. Handicapped access is somewhat limited, although an elevator goes to most levels of the rambling historic building. There's a delightfully shady courtyard under the entrance arches, and a pleasant café (**Café d'Estiu**) where, between April and September, you can enjoy a light lunch before or after your visit to the galleries.

Plaça de San lu, 5. www.museumares.bcn.cat. ℂ **93-256-35-00.** Admission 4.20€ adults, 2.40€ seniors and students. Free Sun 3–8pm. Mon and Wed–Sat 10am–7pm, Sun 11am–8pm. Metro: Jaume I.

Plaça de Sant Just ★★ PLAZA   Most people find this tranquil little plaza because they want to dine at **Cafè de L'Acadèmia** (p. 476), but in Roman times, Jews and Christians came here to trade. The 13th-century church on the plaza, the **Basilica dels Sants Just i Pastor,** honors two Roman boy martyrs. The Gothic church stands on the site of the original 4th-century Christian basilica in Barcin; glass openings in the floor allow you to glimpse remains of a previous Romanesque church that stood here, which was the seat of the archbishop until the city's cathedral was constructed. Only one tower of two planned towers was built on the asymmetrical building; you can go to the top for awesome views of the Gothic Quarter. The interior is full of mysterious surprises, including several images of the damned burning in hell. The fountain in the plaza, said to be the city's oldest water source, was carved of Montjuïc stone in 1367. Above its three pipes you'll see an image of one-handed Sant Just, another of the royal shield, and a third of a shield showing a hawk catching a partridge.

Plaça Sant Just. http://basilicasantjust.cat. ℂ **93-301-74-33.** Free admission. Church open Mon–Sat 11am–2pm and 5–9pm, Sun 10am–1pm. Metro: Jaume I.

Plaça del Pi ★ CHURCH   Three pretty contiguous plazas surround the Gothic church of **Santa María del Pi** ★, acclaimed for its rose window, one of the world's largest. The 15th-century original was destroyed when the church, like many others, was set on fire by anti-clerical troops at the beginning of the Civil War in 1936. The modest admission fee is worth paying for access to a well-drawn history of the various churches that have existed on the site, along with the context of the neighborhood as Barcelona grew from a Roman walled town to an early Christian city. Recent archaeological finds have opened a window onto the Romanesque structure that preceded the current Santa Maria del Pí. Views from the historic bell tower make you feel you're right at the center of the Gothic

The immense rose window of Santa María del Pi overlooks lovely Plaça del Pi.

Quarter. Frequent evening concerts, often featuring flamenco guitar, give you a chance to savor the historic interior. The main square out front is the officially called Plaça del Pi; the adjoining **Plaça de Sant Josep Oriol** leads behind the church to tiny **Placeta del Pi.** Some of the buildings on the lovely squares feature the unusual *sgraffito* decorative technique, an 18th-century style imported from Italy. These welcoming spaces are also popular for a weekend artisans' market and open-air cafe-bars.

Santa María del Pi, Carrer del Cardenal Casañas, 16. http://basilicadelpi.cat. *©* **93-318-47-43.** Church admission 4€ adults, 3€ students, seniors, and ages 7–14. Guided tour to bell tower 8.50€. Daily 10am–6pm, tower tours at noon and 1pm. Metro: Jaume I, Liceu.

Plaça Reial ★ PLAZA   Barcelona's first big urban renewal project in the 19th century, this large and harmonious square occupies the former site of the Santa Madrona Capuchin monastery, which was demolished at mid-century. Inspired by the renewal projects of Paris, architect Francesc Daniel Molina conceived the Plaça Reial as a residential square formed by buildings with two stories and a partial upper floor. These days it's surrounded largely by cafes, and although it attracts many more tourists than locals, it is still a great place to sit beneath an arcade, drink beer, and observe the scene. The fountain of the three graces in the center is flanked by handsome Art Nouveau lampposts that were Antoni Gaudí's first commission (1878). He decorated them with a caduceus (a messenger's wand with two snakes entwined around it) and winged helmets—attributes of Hermes, patron of shopkeepers.

Metro: Liceu.

Plaça de Sant Felip Neri ★ HISTORIC SITE This quiet little plaza is one of the few spots in the city to bear witness to Barcelona's suffering during the Civil War. Pockmarks on the facade of the Sant Felip Neri church recall the Nationalist bombs that fell here on January 30, 1938. Twenty children and 22 adults who were taking refuge in the church cellars were killed. The fall of Barcelona took place 10 weeks later, when Franco and his forces dropped 44 tons of bombs on the civilian population. Franco saw himself as uniting the country. Many Catalans still see it as genocide.

Metro: Liceu.

Temple d'August ★★ ARCHAEOLOGICAL SITE One of the four columns of this A.D. 1st-century temple is incorporated into a display of the Roman wall on Plaça Ramon Berenguer. The other three remain where they were originally erected, now awkwardly enclosed within a 19th-century building. The temple once formed part of the Roman Forum dedicated to Emperor Caesar Augustus. The ruins are part of the citywide collection of the Museu d'Història de la Ciutat (MUHBA) and can be visited free of charge.

Carrer Paradis, 10. www.museuhistoria.bcn.es. ℂ **93-256-21-22.** Free admission. Mon 10am–2pm, Tues–Sat 10am–7pm, Sun 10am–8pm. Metro: Jaume 1.

La Rivera & El Born

With streets a little wider, buildings a little newer, and street patterns that at least approach a grid, **La Ribera and El Born ★★** push the Barri Gòtic eastward, still obviously part of the old city, though both districts have become gentrified since the 1990s (there's little or no laundry hanging from the balconies in Born these days, replaced in most cases by flower planters). Both neighborhoods have sprouted gelaterias and tapas bars every few steps. Metro stops include Jaume I, Arc de Triomf, and Urquinaona.

El Born Centre de Cultura ★

ARTS CENTER When the old wholesale Born market, a glorious 19th-century cast-iron structure built in imitation of similar buildings in Paris, underwent demolition in the 1990s, the plan was to turn it into a high-end retail destination, or perhaps a public library. But then ruins of streets and building foundations were discovered during the excavation, and the plan was put on hold while urban archaeologists did their

The neo-Mudéjar Arc de Triomf, built for Barcelona's 1888 world's fair.

work. Plans for the building shifted radically as city governments came and went, and when the smoke cleared and the Cultural Center opened in 2013, a glass floor at street level revealed basements similar to the buildings that still surround the market house. Why? In a transparently political move, the archaeological site was deemed significant because the ruins represent the siege of 1714, when the Spanish took over Catalunya. Is it worth visiting? Some of the center's temporary exhibitions, like those highlighting the history of the building's use as a market and the sociology surrounding that era, are edifying. Admission to the core of the center is free; you get what you pay for.

Carrer del Comerç 12. www.elbornculturalmemoria.barcelona.cat. © **93-256-68-51.** Free admission. Tues–Sat 10am–7pm, Sun and holidays 10am–8pm. Metro: Jaume I, Barceloneta.

Mercat Santa Caterina ★ MARKET   That amazing undulating roof is the masterpiece of Catalan architect Enric Miralles, who topped Barcelona's oldest (1848) enclosed market house with a spectacular sombrero in 2001. Glazed tiles in 67 hues form the rainbow covering of la Boqueria's rival in La Ribera, which is still a lively retail market full of fresh produce. Enclosed in glass on one side of the food market, an archaeological site run by the Museu d'Història de la Ciutat (MUHBA) includes excavations tracing Barcelona culture from the Bronze Age to present. Chief among the ruins are the Dominican monastery of Santa Caterina, established here in 1219 and torn down in the anti-clerical fervor in 1835. The interpretive site is open Monday, Wednesday, and Saturday 7:30am to 3:30pm and Tuesday, Thursday, and Friday 7:30am to 8:30pm. Admission is free.

Avinguda de Francesc Cambó, 16. www.mercatsantacaterina.com. © **93-319-57-40.** Mon 7:30am–2pm; Tues–Wed, Sat 7:30am–3:30pm; Thurs–Fri 7:30am–8:30pm. Metro: Jaume I.

Museu de la Xocolata ★ MUSEUM   The space is really too small to tell the chocolate story effectively, and the museum has decided to fill most of the galleries with wacky chocolate sculptures (of Messi, of Don Quixote, of the Virgin of Montserrat) instead of focusing on teaching kids and their parents about the relationship between Barcelona and chocolate, or the story of how it's made. The city claims to have been the entry port of chocolate into Europe, based on the arrival of a 1520 shipment of cacao from Mexico. A Cistercian monk in the New World sent it to the Monasterio de Piedra in Aragón, complete with a recipe for a chocolate drink. This little museum is really designed to make you crave chocolate; even your ticket is a chocolate bar.

Carrer Comerç, 36. www.museuxocolata.cat. © **93-368-78-78.** Admission 6€ adults, 5.10€ students and seniors, free under age 7. Mon–Sat 10am–7pm, Sun 10am–3pm.

Museu Picasso ★★ MUSEUM The primary charm of this museum lies in the environment that has been created by stringing together five gothic buildings and filling them seamlessly with a series of white cube galleries. It is not the encyclopedic collection of the "other" Picasso Museum (the one in Paris), since the artist left Barcelona as a teenager, so most of what stayed behind is art school work. Pace yourself going through the first galleries of these paintings and drawings and reserve your energy for the real treasures toward the end. These include a collection of whimsical painted ceramics donated by Picasso's widow Jacqueline Roche in the 1980s, and the artist's version of *Las Meninas.* The museum did a disservice to its visitors by removing a helpful installation explaining the source of Picasso's inspiration for *Las Meninas,* Velazquez's 17th-century masterpiece in the Prado, but if you do some homework before coming here, there's great joy in viewing Picasso's abstracted renditions of these princesses, dwarves and dogs, all painted during the summer of 1957. The museum hosts a series of lively temporary exhibitions

The courtyard of Museu Picasso.

related to various aspects of the life and work of the Spaniard who was arguably the greatest artist of the 20th century.

Carrer Montcada, 15–19. www.museupicasso.bcn.cat. ✆ **93-256-30-00.** Admission 12€ adults (14€ with temporary exhibition), 7€ seniors, students, and ages 18–25; free 17 and under; free Thurs 6–9:30pm and all day 1st Sun of month. Mon 10am–5pm, Tues–Sun 9am–7pm (Thurs until 9:30pm). Metro: Jaume I.

Palau de la Música Catalana ★★★ LANDMARK   One of the most extreme and exciting of the Modernista buildings, this structure may be Lluís Domènech i Montaner's masterpiece. Commissioned by the Orfeó Català choral music society, the architect laid the first stone in 1905 on St. George's Day (May 5, the feast of Catalunya's patron saint). It finally opened in 1908—a marvel of stained glass, ceramics, statuary, ornate wrought iron, and carved stone. In the architect's signature style, the facade features exposed brick combined with colorful ceramic mosaics. The sculptures are symbolic and, frankly, nationalistic. The stone prow, a work by Miquel Blay, is an allegory of popular music with two boys and two old men embracing a nymph while St. George protects them with the Catalan flag. Inside, the vaults of the foyer are lined with Valencian tiles. The concert hall itself is topped with an enormous stained-glass skylight representing a circle of female angels surrounding the sun as a choir—quite appropriate for a choral society. If you want a detailed explanation of all the imagery, plan to take a guided tour. We find that the best way to enjoy the hall is to attend a concert. Arrive early and you can study the rich details from your seat.

Carrer Palau de la Música 4-6. www.palaumusica.org. ✆ **93-295-72-00.** Guided tours 20€ or self-guided tours 15€. Daily 10am–3:30pm, with longer hours in summer. Box office daily 9:30am–3:30pm. Metro: Urquinaona.

Parc de la Ciutadella ★ PARK   When Barcelona picked the losing side in the War of the Spanish Succession (1701–14), the victorious Felipe V repaid the city by leveling a neighborhood to erect a citadel. The fortification proved of little use against Napoleon, and the fort was torn down in the mid–19th century. Lakes, gardens, and promenades fill most of the park that took its place, and admission to the park itself is free. The large green patch is also the site of the **Zoo de Barcelona ★** (www. zoobarcelona.cat; ✆ **90-245-75-45**), which covers 13 hectares (32 acres) and is home to more than 300 species. Animals run the gamut from lumbering hippos to jumpy Saharan gazelles, from western lowland gorillas to Komodo dragons. Zoo admission is 11.40€ adults, 12.95€ ages 3–12, with 50% discounts available on-line. The zoo is open daily 10am to 7pm in summer, 10am to 5:30pm the rest of the year.

Parc de la Ciutadella. Metro: Ciutadella.

Santa Maria del Mar ★★ CHURCH   Built by the trade guilds rather than the nobility, this church is the city's most harmonious example of the Catalan Gothic style. Construction began in 1329 and was more or less finished in 1383 (the bell towers were added in 1496 and 1902). Three

Ornate fountains flow in Parc de la Ciutadella.

soaring naves are supported by wide-spaced columns that bloom like thick stalks as they reach the ceiling. Stained-glass windows throughout fill the church with light during the day. Guided views of the roof and towers are available daily, weather permitting.

Plaça de Santa María. www.santamariadelmarbarcelona.org. ℭ **93-215-74-11.** Admission 5€ adults, 4€ students and seniors. Mon–Sat 9am–1pm and 5–8:30pm; Sun 10am–2pm and 5–8pm. Tower tours 8.50€ adults, 7€ students and seniors. Metro: Jaume I.

L'Eixample & Gràcia

Where Les Rambles meets Plaça de Catalunya, the tangled web of streets of the old city are released into the orderly grid of **L'Eixample ★★★**. Strolling its wide boulevards can seem like a breath of fresh air, which was precisely the effect Ildefons Cerdá envisioned when he designed and built it between 1890 and 1910. The Eixample will enthrall you with its major sites of 19th-century architecture, but don't overlook the small details like the Modernista light posts designed by Gaudí, and the hexagonal paving tiles with floral patterns (also Gaudí-designed) which you can still spot on some of the sidewalks of Passeig de Gràcia and nearby cross streets. Take a break on one of the gracefully styled tile benches on the street corners. Modernisme was one of the first movements to emphasize "design for living," and those designs still bring delight more than a century later.

You can escape the tourist throngs by venturing a bit north (via an easy metro ride to Fontana) into a "real neighborhood," the former village of Gràcia, now a charming low-rise neighborhood full of lovely plazas, cafes, and shops run by designers and local entrepreneurs.

Basilica de la Sagrada Familia ★★★ CHURCH   Architect Antoni Gaudí (1852–1926) was a profoundly religious man, and from 1912 forward he made the design of this soaring basilica his life's work. If it is not the grandest church in all of Spain, it is certainly the grandest constructed within living memory. This "Church of the Holy Family" is a strange and wonderful structure, part retro-Gothic cathedral and part Modernista fantasy, with some bowls of fruit tossed in for color at the tops of the towers. The soaring interior really seems like a place of worship now, after decades as a construction site that stood open to the elements; the roof finally went on a few years ago, and the target date for completion—still almost a decade away—now seems within reach. The massive project was held up by some dramatic roadblocks: The original plans were burnt during the Spanish Civil war, and a grassroots attempt rose to halt the digging of a train tunnel within a few blocks of the basilica, deemed a threat despite seismic studies to the contrary. (The tunnel was dug, and the structure remained upright.) Because Gaudí left the structure unfinished

Gaudí's famous Basilica de la Sagrada Familia.

at the time of his death, and his plans went missing, what you see today is a hodge-podge of guesswork by subsequent teams of architects. The west portal (the Façade of the Passion) is especially inharmonious, with clunky white protrusions that look like overgrown Lego blocks. The east façade (of the Nativity), where you will enter, is more in the spirit of Gaudí's pious Christian view of the New Testament stories, although they appear to have been carved out of volcanic stone, cobwebs, and bat droppings. Dragons and gargoyles hang off corners, and an entire Noah's ark of preposterous animals (rhinos! elephants!) are carved in stone. And that's just the outside.

The central nave resembles a gleaming white sci-fi spaceship, although Gaudí's original intent was to create the illusion of a forest of impossibly tall palm trees, which allow a maximum of light to stream through their fronds from very tall stained-glass windows. And in fact, it is that play of magical light on the walls and floors of the interior that give the Sagrada Familia a true sense of spirituality and earns Gaudí the moniker "God's architect." The cost of the elevator ride up the towers, where the true magnificence of Gaudí's creation is most visible, is absolutely worth the extra euros. Construction of the church came to a near halt at the outbreak of the Civil War and languished until the late 1980s. Yet new construction techniques (and more tourist admissions) have sped up the process. Since the church was consecrated in 2010, the builders have been racing toward a much-publicized projected completion date of the 2026 centenary of Gaudí's death. (He is buried in the Chapel of Carmel, one level down from the main church.) Buying tickets online in advance has become essential, at least in the busiest seasons, in order to avoid the wait of an hour or more.

Entrance from Carrer de Sardenya or Carrer de la Marina. www.sagradafamilia.cat. © **93-208-04-14.** Admission 15€ adults, 13€ students and anyone under 30, 11€ seniors, ages 10 and under free; admission to towers costs 14€ more. Apr–Sept daily 9am–8pm, Mar and Oct daily 9am–7pm, Nov–Feb daily 9am–6pm. Closed Dec 25–26, Jan 1, and Jan 6. Metro: Sagrada Família.

Casa Amatller ★★★ HISTORIC HOME   Three of the greatest residential Modernista buildings in Barcelona stand along the block of Passeig de Gràcia between Carrer del Consell de Cent and Carrer d' Aragó. Labeled by tourism promoters as the Quadrat D'Or, or Golden Quarter, it's also referred to with a wink as the Mançana de la Discòrdia (Block of Discord), a name alluding to the mythical Judgment of Paris, in which an apple was the prize in a contentious beauty contest among three goddesses (in Catalan, "apple" is the same word as "city block"). Casa Amatller is a 1900 masterpiece by Josep Puig i Cadalfach, a key architect from the generation before Gaudí. After many decades as an office building, a massive facelift restored its original look as the home of chocolatier Antoní Amatller; it re-opened to the public in 2015. This Modernista wonder reflects the architect's—and the era's—fascination with northern European Gothic style as the apex of nostalgic Catalan history. It stands in striking contrast to its next-door neighbor, Gaudí's **Casa Batlló** (see below). Puig i Cadafalch made extensive use of ceramics, wrought iron, and fanciful sculptures to achieve this gingerbread creation. The guided tour includes, appropriately, a chocolate tasting, and if you're still hungry, the pleasant Café Faborit out back makes a nice stop after the tour.

Passeig de Gràcia, 41. www.amatller.org. © **93-461-74-60.** Admission 19€ adults, 17.10€ seniors and students, 9.50€ ages 7–12, kids 6 and under free. Daily 10am–6pm. Metro: Passeig de Gràcia.

Casa Batlló ★★★ HISTORIC HOME   Next door to Casa Amatller, Casa Batlló was designed by Gaudí in 1905. The facade's sinuous curves give the structure a lush organic appeal, and the balconies, like those at La Pedrera (p. 445), seem to be sculpted ocean waves. Floral references in the ornamentation turn more faunalike as the building rises, with the roof evoking the scaly skin of a dragon. Touring means climbing the spiral staircase around the central light shaft and starting with the Batlló family

Swirling ceilings surround a skylight in Casa Batlló.

quarters, where Gaudí's architectural flourishes and his furniture designs vie for your attention. Señor Batlló's office has a little nook with two benches and a stove for warmth—perfect for a courting couple to sit on one side and their chaperone on the other. Even this smallest of the rooms has a skylight to let in natural light. All the decor, including waterlike eddies in the swirling ceiling, allude to the marine world; in the sewing room, which overlooks an interior courtyard, an ingenious ventilation system of sliding slats seems inspired by fish gills. The roof terrace has chimneys designed to evoke the backbone of the dragon slain by Sant Jordi (St. George), patron saint of Catalunya. It's not the cheapest admission in town, but a cool new interactive program makes the high price almost worth it: As you walk through the house with a smart phone, an app deletes the other tourists from your view and reinstates original furnishings, even "lighting" a fire in the fireplace. Fun! Gawkers crowd the sidewalk in front of the eccentric building, and lines for admission can get quite long; it's smart to get your ticket online ahead of time, which will save you 4€; for an extra 5€ you can zip to the front of the line. The outdoor terrace has live music with cocktails from mid-May through October.

Passeig de Gràcia, 43. www.casabatllo.cat. ℰ **93-216-03-06.** Admission 24.50€ adults; 21.50€ seniors and ages 18 and under; kids 6 and under free. Open daily 9am–8pm. Music and cocktails (mid-May to Oct) 8pm, 39€. Metro: Passeig de Gràcia.

Casa Lleó Morera ★ ARCHITECTURAL SITE   The third member of the Golden Quarter, Casa Lleó Morera was designed by the third architect of the Modernista triumvirate, Lluís Domènech i Montaner. The 1905 home was revolutionary in its day for its extensive use of different forms of artisanry on the interior (alas, closed to the public) to realize the architect's distinctly floral design. Because it occupies a corner, the house has two beautiful facades that mirror each other with a tower of sorts dividing them. Domènech i Montaner's signature floral capitals appear in several variants, and he created a gallery of columns on the top floor that evokes the rhythm of a convent cloister. The one part of the ground level that can be visited—the shop of Loewe, purveyor of fine leather goods—does not retain the architect's designs.

Passeig de Gràcia, 35. No phone. Metro: Passeig de Gràcia.

Casa Vicens ★★★ MUSEUM The earliest residence designed by Gaudí, an 1883 summer home for Barcelona stockbroker Manel Vicens and his family, became available for sale to the highest bidder a few years ago. Luckily it was purchased by a bank, which implemented an exquisite renovation of the building and its interiors and then opened it to the public in 2017 as a museum. The exterior's mishmash of textures and colors, completed by another architect in a 1920s expansion of the house, strikes the approaching visitor as, well, gaudy. But beautiful interior finishes and handcrafted details will delight, and you can gain insight here into the early work of the great Catalan architect. Go up to the photogenic rooftop for a selfie and you will see evidence of the young Gaudí experimenting with elements that distinguish his later work, like his whimsically colorful chimneys. Signboards in almost every room are a wealth of information, but it's worth the extra 3€ to pay for an in-depth hour-long guided tour. A small café in the garden offers tasty dishes and drinks from the high-end Hofmann restaurant and bakery, known locally for its desserts.

Carrer de les Carolines, 24. https://casavicens.org. © **93-547-59-80**. Admission 16€ adults, 14€ seniors and ages 17 and under, kids 5 and under free. Apr–Sept daily 10am–8pm; Oct–Mar Mon 10am–3pm, Tues–Sun 10am–7pm. Metro: Fontana.

Fundació Antoni Tàpies ★★ ART MUSEUM Dedicated to Antoni Tàpies (1923–2012), Catalunya's leading late 20th-century artist, this museum tends to emphasize late works and large-scale pieces (the collection is largely based on gifts from the artist and his wife). Changing exhibitions show Tàpies's evolving viewpoints and underscore his role in bringing unconventional materials (gravel, broken sticks, chunks of cement) into high art. Seeing so many works by Tàpies in one place illuminates how, like many Spanish artists, he returned repeatedly to the motif of the cross for works both secular and (in his own abstract way) sacred. Since it's in L'Eixample, it's no surprise that the museum occupies a Modernista landmark: the former home of publishing company Editorial Montaner i Simon, built by Lluís Domènech i Montaner from 1880 to 1882 (the company belonged to his mother's family). The pioneering structure has a jaunty Moorish cast to it. *Tip:* Make sure to check the schedule online, because the whole museum closes between exhibitions.

Carrer Aragó, 255. www.fundaciotapies.org. © **93-487-03-15**. Admission 7€ adults, 5.60€ students and seniors. Tues–Sat 10am–7pm (Fri until 9pm), Sun 10am–3pm. Metro: Passeig de Gràcia.

Museu del Modernisme Català ★ MUSEUM You may think you've come to the wrong address when you arrive at what appears to be a storefront in Eixample. This modest museum's small collection of decorative arts includes several pieces of furniture designed by Gaudí in collaboration with Josep Maria Jujol. The building itself, an adapted Modernista warehouse, was designed by Enric Sagnier and built between 1902 to 1904, but not much of that remains visible. A few treasures here include marbles by Eusebi Arnau, who did some major sculptures for the over-the-top proscenium of the **Palau de la Música Catalana** (p. 438). Mostly the museum feels like a less-than-professional showcase for a spotty private collection.

Carrer Balmes, 48. www.mmcat.cat. ℂ **93-273-28-96.** Admission 10€ adults, 7€ seniors and students, 5€ ages 6–16. Mon–Fri 10:30am–2pm and 4–7pm. Metro: Passeig de Gràcia or Universitat.

Parc Güell ★★★ PARK Gaudí began this splendid park in Gràcia as a real-estate venture for his patron, Catalan industrialist Eusebi Güell. Although it never came to fruition, Gaudí did complete several public areas, which some consider his crowning professional achievement, even more than the Sagrada Familia. Where does the land end and the architecture begin? On the upper terraces, the landscaping melts into the architecture, and the outdoor sculptures look like earthworks. Of the originally planned model community of 60 dwellings, Gaudí did construct a grand central plaza with a market below it, and lined the plaza with its famous serpentine bench, studded

Colorful mosaics adorn the terraces of Parc Güell.

with his trademark trenchadí (bits of broken ceramics). The Doric columns of the market space below are hollow, part of Gaudí's drainage system. Only two houses were ever completed, however. One of them (designed by Ramón Berenguer, not Gaudí) was the architect's home from 1906 to 1925; it's now the **Casa-Museu Gaudí ★** (www.casamuseumgaudi.org; ℂ **93-219-38-11;** admission 5.50€ adults, 4.50€ students and seniors; May–Aug daily 9am–8pm, Oct–Mar 10am–6pm), a museum containing Gaudí models, furniture, drawings, and other memorabilia. The central mosaic "dragon" fountain, a symbol of Barcelona, has become a major photo op . . . if you can get close to it.

Parc Güell was formerly just that, a park, but a few years ago its popularity necessitated charging a fee to enter the "Monumental Core" of the park. Buy tickets online in advance if you can; all tickets have set entry times. The Casa-Museu Gaudí is located in the free part of the park, but it has its own admission fee.

Calle de Olot for park entrance, Carrer del Carmel, 23 for Casa-Museu Gaudí. Parkguell.barcelona. ⓒ **93-219-38-11.** Park admission: (timed tickets): 17€ adults, 14€ seniors and ages 7–12, kids 6 and under free. Daily May–Aug 8am–9:30pm, Apr and Sept–Oct 8am–8:30pm, Nov–Mar 8am–6:15pm. Metro: Lesseps for main entrance, Bus 64 for free upper entrance and Casa-Museu Gaudí entrance.

La Pedrera (Casa Milà) ★★★ HISTORIC HOME   It took the neighbors a long time to warm up to Modernisme. When Gaudí's last secular commission, Casa Milà, was finished in 1912, they took one look at the undulating lines of seemingly wind-eroded rock and dubbed the building La Pedrera ("the stone quarry"). The shock of its novelty has faded, but the nickname has stuck as a term of endearment. With a sinuous, rippling facade, it is one of the most beloved of Gaudí's works (and another spot where purchasing an advance ticket online will save you precious time as well as several euros). The tour includes the patios and the Espai Gaudí, a handsome maze under the roof rafters with engineering and architectural didactics that help you to get into Gaudí's mind. (He calculated, for instance, the loads an arch could bear by hanging weights on knotted cord to get the shapes he wanted, then extrapolating to life size.) The Pedrera Apartment evokes an era when the elegant apartment house was new, complete with Gaudí furniture. Substitute a modern music system for the Edison phonograph, and most visitors would be ready to sign a lease on the spot. Gaudí saved his grandest gestures for the rooftop, transforming

Gaudí's La Pedrera.

functional chimneys into a sculpture garden of swirling mosaic forms and ominous hooded warriors. Gaudí intended the roof as an open-air terrace, and during the summer, jazz musicians hold forth several evenings each week. Amid the chimneys Gaudí built a lovely parabolic arch to frame the towering steeples of his masterpiece, La Sagrada Familia; if you are patient long enough for the crowds to part, it's the classic Barcelona selfie. For a more intimate (and more expensive) nighttime visit, choose the "Origins" tour, which includes a glass of cava on the rooftop.

Carrer Provença, 261–265. www.lapedrera.com. © **90-220-21-38.** Admission 25€ adults, 19.50€ seniors and students, 14€ ages 7–12, free ages 6 and under. "Origins" tour 34€ adults, 17€ ages 7–12, free ages 6 and younger. Mar–Nov daily 9am–8:30pm (night tour 9–11pm) Nov–Feb 9am–6:30pm (night tour 7–9pm). Metro: Diagonal.

Sant Pau Recinto Modernista ★★★ ARCHITECTURAL SITE
Why visit a former hospital? Because this was a medical facility unlike any other. After almost a decade of refurbishing, this extraordinary UNESCO World Heritage complex recently opened to the public as a convincing argument that doctors a century ago had some intriguing ideas about what constituted good care—and that Gaudí did not come out of nowhere. Designed in 1901 by Lluis Domènech i Montaner, it was

---

beyond GAUDÍ

If you'd like to explore the city's hidden treasures of Modernisme, those that aren't open specifically as historic museums, consider putting these beauts on your itinerary:

Caixa Forum Near Plaça d'Espanya, this former factory built by the major Modernista architect Puig I Cadalfach re-opened in 2002 as a handsome venue for La Caixa bank's traveling art exhibitions. If you don't want to pay for the art shows, you can still roam around the brick pavilions and go up on the undulating rooftop, which you will probably have pretty much to yourself. Av. De Francesc Ferrer i Guárdia, 6-8, www.caixaforum.es.

Fundació Mapre The elegant Casa Garriga Nogués, an extraordinary Modernista mansion by Enric Sagnier in l'Eixample, is now (since 2015) also a space of traveling art exhibitions, which rarely cost more than 3 € to enter. Carrer de Diputació 250. Complete information at www.fundacionmapfre.org/fundacion/en/exhibitions/casa-garriga-nogues.

Hotel España This still-operating hotel in Raval (p. 462) was renovated by

Doménech I Muntaner in 1903-04 and given another facelift in 2010. Guided tours offered by the hotel (Tues 12:15pm and Fri 4:30pm) highlight Modernista features like the outrageous alabaster fireplace by sculptor Eusebi Arnau, which still dominates one of the dining rooms. Carrer de Sant Pau 9-11, www.hotelespanya.com.

Palau Baró de Quadras Open by appointment only, the former residence at Av. Diagonal 373 has been chopped up over the years, but many stunning original elements are still intact. To make an appointment, contact Cases Singulars at www.casessingulars.com.

Want to see more in the company of a local expert? Try the architectural tours at **Insight Barcelona** (www.insight-barcelona.com); their tours access a number of sites that aren't usually open to the public.

conceived as a hospital village to look after all the needs of its patients, providing a freestanding library, parks and gardens for the healing powers of pleasant reflection, and personal services such as a barber shop. Domènech i Muntaner's use of graceful sculpture, stained glass, and exquisite mosaic tiles defines the best of the era that was the generation before Gaudí. It covers the equivalent of 9 city blocks, although the architect set it at a 45-degree angle to the L'Eixample grid to make it an architectural island in the city. Now that the beautiful landscaping is back in place, visitors can experience the sense of peace and tranquility that must have comforted hospital patients (and the medical staff). Reconstructed interiors of some pavilions—communal patients' rooms, sunrooms, even a sunlight-flooded circular surgery center—help visitors picture the former use of the spaces. The complex is about a 10-minute stroll up Avinguda Gaudí from La Sagrada Familia—stop halfway and you can gaze up and down the street for a view of each masterpiece. We recommend attending an evening musical event in the administrative building; audiences get time to savor the over-the-top ornamentation and listen to visiting artists play the piano that belonged to famed Barcelona soprano Victoria de los Angeles, who gave her name to the concert series: www.lifevictoria.com.

Carrer Sant Antoni Maria Claret, 167. visitsantpau.com. ℰ **93-553-78-01.** Self-guided tour 14€ adults, 9.80€ seniors and ages 29 and under, kids 11 and under free. Apr–Oct Mon–Sat 9:30am–6:30pm, Sun 9:30am–2:30pm; Nov–Mar Mon–Sat 9:30am–4pm, Sun 9:30am–2:30pm. Metro: Hospital de Sant Pau/Dos de Maig.

La Barceloneta & the Waterfront

Barcelona has always lived by the water, and fishing boats, trade vessels, and ferries continue to come and go in its harbor. But there's new vitality along the **waterfront ★★**, from the Mirador de Colom east to Port Olimpic along the Passeig de Colom and the pedestrian **Moll de la Fusta ★**. Starting in the late 1980s, Barcelona built new quays and waterfront paths and even constructed new islands to house a world-class aquarium and a shopping and entertainment complex. At the same time, it preserved the barrier-beach sand-spit of **La Barceloneta ★★**, the former fishermen's village that also boasts the city's finest recreational beaches.

Spend some time exploring the back streets of La Barceloneta, where the residents still hang their laundry on the balconies. As you tromp the length of Moll de la Fusta, you'll find two playful pieces of public art: the giant fiberglass lobster that Xavier Mariscal created for the restaurant Gambrinus, and pop artist Roy Lichtenstein's *Barcelona Head* at the foot of Via Laietana (not his best work, but still a splash of color on the waterfront). Continue east up the beach to Port Olimpic, and you'll encounter Frank O. Gehry's abstract sculpture *Peix* (Fish), which has become the de facto symbol of Barcelona's rejuvenated waterfront. This district is the place to enjoy a casual seafood lunch and catch some rays at the beach. Plan on spending a full day, with time to take a boat tour and to see some

Sharks swim in their huge tank at Barcelona's aquarium, set amid modern development on the waterfront.

of the sights. Three Metro stops provide access to the sites below: from west to east, Drassanes, Barceloneta, and Ciutadella/Vila Olimpica.

Barcelona Beaches ★★ BEACH   You don't have to leave the city to hit the beach. European blue flags (indicators of the highest water quality) fly on all 10 of Barcelona's beaches. Four of the best lie along the strand from the tip of La Barceloneta east to Port Olimpic. Each has showers, bathrooms, snack bars, umbrella and hammock rentals, and lifeguards. They are all free. **Platja de Barceloneta** and adjacent **Platja del Somorrostro** (near Port Olimpic) also have changing rooms and lockers. (Carmen Amaya, perhaps the most famous flamenco dancer of all time, was born in the shanty town that once stood on Platja del Somorrostro.) These two beaches and the more westerly **Platja de Sant Sebastià** and **Platja de Sant Miquel** can be reached from Metro stops Barceloneta or Ciutadella/La Vila Olimpica. A little farther east at Metro stop Poblenou, you'll find the most popular beach with college-age Barcelonans and visitors alike, **Platja de Mar Bella.** It, too, has all the facilities, including lockers, and is the only beach in Barcelona with a section set off for nude sunbathing and swimming. Food options on the water become slimmer between November and April when the beach *chiringuitos* close for the season, but don't worry, there are plenty of waterfront restaurants where you can still order that paella.

Metro: Barceloneta, Ciutadella/Vila Olímpica, or Poblenou. Bus: N6, N8.

Mirador de Colom ★★ MONUMENT   Les Rambles meets the waterfront at this monument to Christopher Columbus that was erected for the Universal Exposition of 1888. Bas-reliefs on the plinth recount the feats of the great navigator, and various symbolic sculptures in florid Victorian style surround the base. At the top of a 50m (174-ft.) Corinthian column stands a bronze sculpture of Columbus pointing to the New World, although the precision of his compass might be questioned. Inside the iron column, a small elevator ascends to the lookout from the "crown" just below Columbus's feet (*warning:* It sways on windy days). It provides a unique panoramic view of Barcelona and the harbor and a chance to play "name that spire," as every church in the city pokes up just above its surrounding buildings. A surprising element of the gift shop on the below-grade level is a good stock of hard-to-find local wines, with wine tastings available.

Portal de la Pau. www.barcelonaturisme.com. ⓒ **93-285-38-32.** Admission 6€ adults, 4€ seniors and ages 4–12, free for kids 3 and under. Daily 8:30am–8:30pm, closed Dec 25 and Jan 1. Metro: Drassanes.

Museu d'Història de Catalunya ★★ MUSEUM   This museum uses "the memory of a country" as its tagline, and it's one of the best cultural history museums we've seen anywhere. The coverage begins in the Lower Paleolithic era and works its way up to the present—quickly. Historic exhibits linger at some high points of the Catalan experience, such as the reigns of Jaume I and Jaume II when Catalunya was a major Mediterranean power, and the 19th-century industrial revolution that made Catalunya in general and Barcelona in particular rich and powerful. The 20th-century coverage is almost giddy as it depicts a vibrant Barcelona in the first few decades—and almost numbing as it accounts the horrors of the Civil War and the four decades the region then spent as Franco's whipping boy. (The era since Franco's death seems less well digested, but history museums usually have the advantage of hindsight.) It's worth visiting just to appreciate the building, the Palau de Mar, the last surviving 19th-century Barcelona warehouses. The 4th-floor restaurant, **1881,** has a spectacular terrace with great views of the port and waterfront. It's not necessary to book a meal—most people come just for a drink and the view.

Plaça de Pau Vila, 3. www.mhcat.cat. ⓒ **93-225-47-00.** Admission 4.50€ adults, 3.50€ students and seniors. Tues and Thurs–Sat 10am–7pm, Wed 10am–8pm, Sun 10am–2:30pm. Metro: Barceloneta.

Montjuïc

Residents of Barcelona used to quarry stone, harvest firewood, and graze livestock on this flat-topped hill southwest of the old city. **Montjuïc** ★ began to assume its current shape in the early 20th century, when parks were planted and the 1929 International Exposition was held here. Many of the park's structures, including the **Palau Nacional** (now the National Art Museum of Catalunya), and the popular and kitschy **Magic Fountain** (*Font Màgica*) date from this period. The 1992 Olympics brought even more structures to Montjuïc, including world-class pools that are still used for international swimming meets. The biggest attractions on the mountain are two stunning art museums, **Fundació Joan Miró** (p. 450) and MNAC, the **National Art Museum of Catalunya** (p. 452). (It takes some effort to reach MNAC, but it's worth it.) The most useful bus lines are Route 55 from Plaça d'Espanya and the small buses that route around the Montjuïc roads. The funicular (mostly underground) from the Paral.lel Metro station delivers you to the Telefèric de Montjuic station, a stone's throw from the Miró Foundation; the funicular train is included in your metro fare. The **Bus Turistic** (p. 421) also visits Montjuïc, making stops at all the attractions. If you're up for a moderately steep climb, you can also walk from Plaça d'Espanya through the Magic Fountain and up the ceremonial staircase of the Museu Nacional d'Art de Catalunya. There are also outdoor escalators that make the climb less daunting.

Castell de Montjuïc ★ HISTORIC SITE In sharp contrast to its often grim history, this mass of military stone is now surrounded by serene gardens where Barcelonans often come for Sunday picnics. The fort last saw action in the Civil War when it kept changing hands and was used by both sides for political and military executions. In 1940, the Franco government prevailed on Germany to hand over the refugee president of Catalunya and summarily executed him here. The fort then served as a prison for political prisoners until Franco's death. The city assumed control of the property in 2007 and launched a development program to create a memorial to Catalan political martyrs, though the 2008 economic crisis halted those plans. Today the fortress is just a place to enjoy the views and the gardens. The best way to get here is on the 8-passenger cable cars of the **Telefèric de Montjuïc,** or by public bus 150.

Ctra. de Montjuïc 66, www.ajuntament.barcelona.cat/castelldemontjuic. © **93-256-44-40.** Castle admission 5€ adults, 4€ seniors and students, free 1st Sun of month and every Sun after 3pm. Daily Mar–Oct 10am–8pm, Nov–Feb 10am–6pm, closed Dec 25 and Jan 1. Telefèric: Avinguda Miramar (opposite Montjuïc Municipal Swimming Pool) 12.70€ round-trip adults, 9.20€ ages 4–12; June–Sept 10am–9pm, Mar–May and Oct 10am–7pm, Nov–Feb 10am–6pm; closed late Jan to mid-Feb. Montjuïc funicular; Bus 55 or 150.

Fundació Joan Miró ★★★ MUSEUM This comes close to being the perfect art museum. Even if you don't care about the work of Catalan artist Joan Miró (1893–1983), the hilltop location of the Foundation has an inspiring panoramic view, with whimsical painted metal sculptures on its easily accessible roof, and the gleaming white building (by architect Josep Lluís Sert) is a marvel in itself. The Barcelona native (there is a small plaque on his birthplace in the Passatge de Crédit in the Gothic Quarter) achieved fame as part of the surrealist movement in Paris in the early 20th century, but his boldly abstracted graphic style and vibrant palette are rigorously Spanish/Catalan. The rich permanent collection of paintings and drawings from all periods of Miró's life can be embraced in an hour or so, a satisfying visit that doesn't exhaust the visitor. And then

Barcelona native son Joan Miró is celebrated in this hilltop art museum.

there's still time to take in one of the always-enticing traveling exhibitions in the temporary galleries. There are few dining options up on Montjuïc, but the museum itself offers a pleasant indoor-outdoor café, as well as a well-stocked gift shop of Miró-related merchandise.

Plaça de Neptú, Parc de Montjuïc. http://fundaciomiro-bcn.org. ✆ **93-443-94-70.** Admission 12€ adults, 7€ seniors and students, kids under 15 free. July–Sept Tues–Sat 10am–8pm (Thurs until 9pm), Sun 10am–3pm; Oct–June Tues–Sat 10am–6pm (Thurs until 9pm, Sat until 8pm), Sun 10am–3pm. Bus: 50 (at Plaça d'Espanya) or 150, or via Funicular from Metro Parallel.

Jardi Botànic ★ GARDEN   The Botanic Gardens of Barcelona, originally established in 1930, were completely overhauled in the 1990s. They are now a beautifully landscaped green space that showcases Mediterranean-climate plants from all over the globe, including Africa, Australia, California, the Canary Islands, and Chile. The collection continues to evolve—new species are grown in greenhouses every year and planted in the gardens. The 71 planting zones are connected by walking paths, many of them crossing small bridges and walkways over ponds. If you're also planning to visit the **Museu de Ciénces Naturals (Museu Blau,** across town in Parc del Forum), you'll save some money by buying a combined admission. You can stroll through the stunning cactus garden on the other side (facing the port) of Montjuïc for free.

Carrer Dr. Font i Quer, 2, Parc de Montjuïc. www.jardibotanic.bcn.es. ✆ **93-256-41-60.** Admission 3.50€ adults, 1.70€ seniors, free ages 15 and under; free 1st Sun of month and every Sun after 3pm. June–Aug daily 10am–8pm, Apr–May and Sept–Oct 10am–7pm, Nov–Mar 10am–6pm. Metro: Espanya (then a 35-min. walk) or Funicular Montjuïc and bus 55.

Museu d'Arqueologia de Catalunya ★ MUSEUM Busloads of local school kids love to come to the MAC, at the foot of Montjuïc, to learn about their ancestors' history. But there are rewards for foreign visitors as well, even if the three-language wall texts are a little inconsistent. Housed, a bit awkwardly, in a pentagonal building built for the 1929 International Exposition, this museum deals with pre-history somewhat plodingly, but the artifacts left behind by Phoenicians and Greeks show clearly how Catalunya related to the rest of the Mediterranean basin ("The Great Blue Bridge"). There is an amazing mosaic floor unearthed from a patrician home in ancient Roman Barcino and a beautiful collection of fragile objects of ancient glass. The museum recently dusted off its medieval section, and the new installation is an eye-opener: How often to you get a chance to see belt buckles and household objects of the Visigoths? Passeig Santa Madrona, 39–41. www.mac.cat. ℂ **93-423-21-48.** Admission 5.50€ adults, 4.50€ seniors and students, free under age 8. Tues–Sat 9:30am–7pm, Sun 10am–2:30pm.

Museu Etnológic de Barcelona ★ MUSEUM A bit off the beaten track compared to its big brothers on the Parc de Montjuïc, this museum gets fewer visitors. But that's a shame, as it's not the dusty old place one might expect of its name: The museum has made a successful effort to remain contemporary and to reflect the sociology of the life of the vibrant city that rages around its quiet hillside location. Go downstairs and visit the clean, well-lighted, see-through storage cases for an extensive collection of objects not on display. Passeig Santa Madrona, 16–22. www.mac.cat. ℂ **93-256-34-84.** Admission 5€ adults, 3.50€ seniors and students, free ages 15 and under. Tues–Sat 10am–7pm, Sun/holidays 10am–8pm. Metro: Espanya. Bus: 55.

Museu Nacional d'Art de Catalunya ★★★ MUSEUM It is an open secret among residents of Barcelona that one of the greatest art treasures in the city is housed at the National Museum of Art of Catalunya. While many of the collections of paintings and sculptures are mediocre, the magical, mystical installation of medieval frescoes is unparalleled. Most of these treasures were discovered at the beginning of the 20th century in crumbling ancient churches in the Pyrenees. When one such church was sold to Boston's Museum of Fine Arts, it set off a storm of outrage over losing Catalunya's cultural patrimony, leading to church after church being purchased by public institutions. Skilled conservation teams then detached fragile and fading mural paintings from the walls and ultimately moved them to this museum. MNAC displays more than a hundred pieces from the churches, accompanied by contemporaneous panel paintings and polychrome wood carvings, most of them dating from the 11th to 13th centuries, a fundamental period in Catalan art. Elsewhere in the vast museum building (originally built for the 1929 Barcelona International Exposition), lower level galleries are devoted to a wide range of popular traveling exhibitions; a Modernista section displays treasures like

Museu Nacional d'Art de Catalunya.

a 1907 fireplace by Domènech i Montaner and paintings by second-generation Modernista artist Joaquim Mir, as well as works by Catalunya's only noted Impressionist painter, Marià Pidelaserra. The museum interior was given a facelift for the 1992 Olympics, based on plans by architects Gae Aulenti and Enric Steegmann. Take a break from the galleries and go up to the roof for a spectacular view.

Palau Nacional, Parc de Montjuïc. www.mnac.es. ℗ **93-622-03-76.** Admission 12€ adults, 8€ seniors and ages 15 and under; free to all Sat after 3pm, 1st Sun of month. May–Sept Tues–Sat 10am–8pm, Sun/holidays 10am–3pm; Oct–Apr Tues–Sat 10am–6pm, Sun/holidays 10am–3pm. Metro: Espanya.

Museu Olimpic I de l'Esport ★ MUSEUM   It's sort of like arriving after the game has ended, but it's still a thrill to see the leftovers of the games that changed Barcelona in such a big way: the 1992 Olympics. To the accompaniment of a piped-in soundtrack that blares out a subliminal message of The Thrill of Victory, the visitor gets a chance to revisit the history of the games all the way back to the ancient Greeks, with many stops along the way, to consider additions (the first taekwondo competition, Sydney 2000) and adaptations (female athletes! Paris 1900). Interactive stations in the Hall of Fame let you dial up your own favorite Olympic moments while comfortably seated in front of a personal screen, and a display of whimsical figures of performers at the opening and closing Barcelona ceremonies (the self-proclaimed "best Games in history") closes out the fun.

Avinguda de l'Estadi 60. www.museuolimpicbcn.cat. ℗ **93-292-53-79.** Admission 5.80€ adults, 3.60€ students and seniors, ages 6 and under free. Apr–Sept Tues–Sat 10am–8pm, Sun/holidays 10am–2:30pm; Oct–Mar Tues–Sat 10am–6pm, Sun/holidays 10am–2:30pm. Metro: Espanya.

Pavelló Mies van der Rohe ★★ ARCHITECTURAL SITE   Architecture devotees flock to this mecca of modern architecture, originally built for the 1929 exhibition. Gaudí had been dead only 3 years when German architect Mies van der Rohe placed his sleek steel-and-glass pavilion in the Plaça d'Espanya, and the Catalan master might quite possibly still be spinning in his grave: What could be further removed from the swirls and curlicues of Gaudí and company than this elegant minimalist design from the architect whose motto was "Less Is More"? The Barcelona chair, that icon of modern furniture design, was designed for this space, and the original served as a 20th-century throne for the visiting king of Spain during the pavilion's inauguration. The building was reconstructed in the 1980s by Mies fans who acknowledged the significance of this monument of modern architecture, creating the movement to re-create it in a preservation project above reproach.

Avinguda Francesc Ferrer i Guárdia, 7. http://miesbcn.com. 🕐 **93-215-10-11.** Admission 5€ adults, 2.60€ students, free for seniors and kids under 16. Mar–Oct daily 10am–8pm, Nov–Feb 10am–6pm. Metro: Espanya.

Poble Espanyol ★ HISTORIC SITE   This faux Spanish village was designed in 1929 by Josep Puig i Cadalfach for the International Exposition. Each plaza or street in the village simulates the architecture of some corner of Spain from Galicia to Valencia. Buildings are full-scale, and after more than 8 decades of patina, some portions are authentic enough to make you do a double-take. Romantic couples have been noted kissing under flower-laden balconies in "Seville," having been carried away by

The open-air Poble Espanyol is an intriguing mash-up of architectural replicas from all over Spain.

the romance of finding themselves *almost* in the real thing. Hats off to Barcelona for figuring out how to give new life to this quaint relic of the past (consider the fate of similar international fabrications like the structures built for the New York World's Fair of 1964–65.) The main plaza is ringed with restaurants and cafes, and there are many shops selling quality crafts and souvenirs. To make the site less hokey, management has invited real contemporary craft artists to use the workshops. A dynamic new (2018) addition is the continuous showing of the multi-screen FIESTA, an 8-minute wordless tour of Spain via some intense you-were-there footage of festivals like Pamplona's running of the bulls and the Catalan towers of people called Els Castallers (entrance included with admission ticket). The village also houses the **Fundació Fran Daurel** contemporary Spanish art collection, which presents some irreverent artworks like an all-male version of the famous cubist *Desmoiselles d'Avinyon,* as well as some actual works by Pablo Picasso. If you decide to take a mini-trip to the musical world of Andalucia by buying tickets for the **Tablao de Carmen flamenco show** (p. 491), you get free admission to Poble Espanyol any time after 4pm, giving you plenty of time to look around and have dinner before the show.

Avinguda Marqués de Comillas, 13, Parc de Montjuïc. www.poble-espanyol.com. ✆ **93-508-63-00.** Admission 12.60€ adults, 10.50€ students, 9€ seniors and ages 4–12, free for kids 3 and under; family tickets available. Mon 9am–8pm, Tues–Sun 9am–midnight (until 3am Fri, 4am Sat). Metro: Espanya. Bus: 13, 23 or 150.

Farther Afield

Monastir de Pedralbes ★★ MUSEUM Not the most centrally located cultural site in the city (monasteries by their nature tend to be remotely placed, to ensure tranquility), this extraordinary former convent is worth the effort to reach it. Occupied for almost 7 centuries by an order called the Poor Clares, the convent has the largest Gothic cloister in Europe. The peaceful site also holds a superb collection of artworks and artifacts, many of them donated by wealthy 14th-century families who wanted their daughters to become novices in the same convent where Queen Elisenda was also in residence. Make a point of visiting the small Chapel of Sant Miquel, which has frescos from the 1340s that were recently restored to their exquisite original colors; the intimate room is one of Barcelona's least known, and most beautiful, treasures.

Baixada del Monestir, 9. www.monestirpedralbes.bcn.cat. ✆ **93-256-34-34.** Admission 5€ adults, 3.50€ seniors and students under 30, free for kids 15 and under; free to all Sun after 3pm. Tues–Fri 10am–1:30pm; Sat–Sun 10am–4:30pm. Metro: Reina Elisenda.

Barcelona for Families

Family-friendly attractions include the **Zoo de Barcelona** (p. 438), the **beaches** (p. 448), and **L'Aquarium Barcelona** at the Moll d'Espanya (www.aquariumbcn.com), with its giant ocean tank that wraps around an

80m (262-ft.) corridor with a moving walkway on one side. It opens daily at 10am and closes between 7:30 and 9pm, depending on the season, with admission prices 20€ adults, 15€ kids 5 to 10, and 7€ kids 3 to 4 (family tickets are available as well).

The fantastical details of Gaudí's architectural works generally intrigue youngsters. Parents who want to see **La Sagrada Familia** (p. 440) can reward the youngsters with the tower tour, while at **La Pedrera** (p. 445), Gaudí's mosaic-covered rooftop chimneys may remind kids of the hooded Darth Vader of *Star Wars*. The smartphone tour of **Casa Batlló** (p. 441) will astound everyone, but for a price.

If the kids accompany you to the Fundació Miró and the Museu d'Art Nacional de Catalunya on Montjuïc, treat them to the **Telefèric de Montjuïc** cable car ride to the **Castell** (p. 450). Other thrilling journeys are the **gondola** between Montjuïc and the Barceloneta beach (p. 447) and the tiny elevator inside the **Columbus Monument** (p. 449) for a 360-degree view. Sports fans of all ages will appreciate the **Olympic Museum** (p. 453). The innovative science museum **Cosmo Caixa** (Carrer d'Isaac Newton, 26; www.cosmocaixa.es), a favorite with school groups, is filled with lots of cool interactive installations, like a walk through a rain forest, a chance to leave your handprint in a block of ice, or a scan of your body that shows where all of the bacteria live. It's open daily 10am to 8pm, and general admission is 2.50€.

The most popular family excursion is the trip up **Tibidabo Mountain** to a century-old amusement park (see below). The ride on the

Ride the funicular up Tibidabo to enjoy panoramic views of the city, as well as a fun amusement park.

Funicular de Tibidabo (7.70€, or 4.10€ with amusement park entries) costs more than the public bus, but it's more fun. To reach the funicular, take Metro Line 7 to Avinguda Tibidabo, exit onto Plaça Kennedy, and take **Bus 196** (2.20€) to the funicular. The historic 1901 **Tramvía Blau** (Blue Streetcar) was shut down for repairs as of this writing, but it's usually a colorful alternative to the bus.

Parc d'Atraccions ★ AMUSEMENT PARK   Tibidabo provides nostalgic appeal for several generations of locals and visitors because of its downright charming retro rides—a carousel, an "airplane" that spins around a pole, whirling teacups—along with modern attractions like a roller coaster, a pirate ship, and a haunted castle. A family visit can be fairly expensive, but you may be able to limit costs by focusing on the Panoramic Area of the park and the adjacent 255m (837-ft.) communications tower, **Torre de Collserola,** a 1992 Olympics structure by Norman Foster, with its observation deck.

Plaça Tibidabo 3–4, Cumbre del Tibidabo. www.tibidabo.cat. © **93-211-79-42.** Ticket for all rides: 28.5€ adults, 9€ seniors, 10.30€ children up to 1.2m (4 ft.) in height, free for children under 90cm (3 ft.). Apr–July Wed–Sun 11am–9pm (daily in Aug), Mar and Sept–Dec weekends and holidays only, daily Jan 1–5, closed Jan 6 to end of Feb. Panoramic Area: 12.70€ adults, 7.80€ under 1.2m tall, 6.70€ seniors, daily except Christmas–Feb 1; Torre de Collserola 5.60€ adults, 3.30€ seniors and ages 4–12, free ages 3 and under. Discounts for online purchases.

Organized Tours

Barcelona is best appreciated on foot, and the Barcelona tourist office has developed a number of **Barcelona Walking Tours** that are offered in English. Tours cover the Barri Gòtic, Picasso's Barcelona (including the Museu Picasso), and Modernisme masterpieces in L'Eixample. A gourmet tour based in the old city includes visits to noteworthy shops and food outlets, with a few tastings. For full listing of tours, visit bcnshop.barcelonaturisme.cat, call © **93-285-38-32,** or inquire at the tourist office on Plaça Catalunya. Adult tickets start at 16€; some tours are free for children, others 7€ for kids. There's an easy walking tour of the Gothic Quarter for those with mobility problems (13.50€) called **Barcelona Walking Tours Easy Gótic.** Discounts for online purchases.

Free tours of the Barri Gòtic and Gaudí's greatest hits are offered daily by **Runner Bean Tours** (www.runnerbeantours.com). Seasonal ghost tours and a special family itinerary are also available. Guides expect a tip, and most participants give generously. The website gives meeting places and times.

Discover Walks (www.discoverwalks.com; © **93-181-68-10**) are led by Barcelonans eager to share their enthusiasm for their city. These personal and often quirky walks are held daily from spring through fall (Fri–Mon in winter) and advance booking is recommended. There's a free Old Town tour that leaves at 11am daily from the Cathedral (tips are expected). The Gaudí tour (22€) departs from the front of the tour of Casa Batlló.

The Rambles and Barri Gòtic walk (19€) departs from in front of the Teatre del Liceu (p. 428) at 3pm Tuesdays, Thursdays, and Saturdays. A good way to see a real neighborhood, Gràcia, is to pay 55€ (39€ for kids under 18) for Discover Walks' 2-hour Barcelona's #1 Food and Beer Tour, which meets at the Fontana metro stop Thursdays and Saturdays at 11:30am.

Barcelona Eat Local (https://barcelonaeatlocal.com) offers rich 3-hour culinary tours of other neighborhoods, like the Gothic Quarter and colorful Le Raval, which emphasize wine pairings. They cost 75€, 55€ youth, 35€ kids.

If you are comfortable riding a bicycle in big-city traffic, several firms offer guided bike tours. **Barcelona Ciclo Tour** (www.barcelona ciclotour.com; ✆ **93-317-19-70**) has a 3-hour tour for 22€, departing from the Plaça de Catalunya daily at 11am and also at 4:30pm from mid-April through October. A night tour for the same price is also offered Thursday through Sunday from June through September, and Friday and Saturday in October, at 7:30pm. A free (tips expected) bike tour run by **Free Bike Tour Barceloneta** (www.freebiketourbarcelona.com) leaves the Barceloneta metro station daily at 2pm and lasts 3 hours.

If you'd rather enjoy the city lights and cooler evening air in a more leisurely fashion, the **Barcelona Bus Turistic** (p. 421) offers 2-hour tours from 9am to 7pm in the winter and 9am to 8pm in summer. It costs 30€ adults, 16€ children, 25€ seniors, and departs from Plaça de Catalunya. It's a good way to get oriented on your first day, and you save a bit per day by getting a ticket for 2 consecutive days (40€ adults).

For a tour that picks you up in your hotel lobby, consider the 4-hour city tour (59€) in 12-passenger vans from **Barcelona Day Tours** (www. barcelonadaytours.com; ✆ **93-181-52-87**). The same company offers a half-day tour to Montserrat (p. 491) for 69€ or full-day options that combine Montserrat with a city tour (99€) or with a visit to the sparkling wine region (89€).

WHERE TO STAY IN BARCELONA

Hotels in Barcelona are among the most expensive in Spain, but that doesn't mean you can't find good values. Many visitors gravitate to hotels on or near **Les Rambles** for convenience, but better bargains can be found in **El Raval** as well as in the **Barri Gòtic.** Although not quite as convenient to public transit, lodgings in **La Ribera** and **El Born** tend to offer the best combination of price and value. Hotels along the **waterfront** tend to be new and flashy, and priced accordingly. **L'Eixample** hotels, while typically more expensive than in the old city, are also usually more spacious. Expect many mid-to-upper level hotels to have rooftop "pools," but the vast majority of them are tiny and could hardly qualify as swimming pools, as they are mostly for show. If you choose to drive in Barcelona, you will usually pay a high price for hotel parking, but pay it if you must: Street parking is at a premium.

Les Rambles & El Raval

EXPENSIVE

Casa Camper ★★   The Camper shoe company took its offbeat shoe design aesthetic and used it to convert a 19th-century Raval tenement building near the contemporary art museum into a designer hotel. Rooms have a breezy and playful decor, and each one features a rope hammock as well as a bed. They're designed to appeal to well-heeled hipsters—just spare enough to be modern, not so empty as to look barren, and each is a mini-suite with separate sleeping and sitting areas. There's also one real suite on each floor where the living and sleeping areas are linked through a pocket sliding door. Should you feel overwhelmed by the city, you can catch a nap in a hammock on the roof terrace. The lobby has a snack buffet available around the clock.

Carrer Elisabets, 11. www.casacamper.com. ℂ **93-342-62-80.** 25 units. 158€–178€ double; 227€–396€ suite. Metro: Plaça de Catalunya. **Amenities:** Bar; babysitting; bikes; restaurant; room service; free Wi-Fi.

Hotel Bagués ★★★   This is our choice for a romantic getaway in the old city, for both its looks and its high level of hospitality. The staff provides friendly and helpful service without putting on airs. The hotel's Modernista design is a holdover from the building's heyday as a jewelry store; the modern comforts don't detract one iota from the stunning visuals of the original designs. Walls and wardrobes in the rooms are enhanced with gold-leaf accents and panels of Madagascar ebony. The hotel even has a Masriera Museum, showcasing the jewelry of the Art Nouveau master, and it sports Fortuny lampshades in its dining room. Most rooms are called "standard," but are larger than most hotel suites.

Les Rambles, 105. www.derbyhotels.com. 31 units. ℂ **93-343-50-00.** 181€–271€ double; deluxe rooms from 295€. Dogs allowed on request. Metro: Plaça de Catalunya. **Amenities:** Bar; restaurant; room service; business center; outdoor pool; solarium; spa; gym; limousine service; free Wi-Fi.

MODERATE

Citadines Aparthotel ★★   At the upper end of Les Rambles near the Plaça de Catalunya, these self-sufficient apartments, constructed in 1994, were renovated and completely refurnished in late 2013. With gray wood floors, muted earth-toned bedspreads and draperies, dark wood furniture, large showers in the bathrooms, and fully equipped if compact kitchens, even the smallest of these units is twice the size of most hotel rooms. The kitchen makes it easy (and cheaper) to prepare breakfast and gives you an excuse to shop at La Boqueria. The location, just steps from the Plaça del Pi in the Barri Gòtic, is prime. The Aparthotel has two buildings that share a gym and coin-op laundry. There's no minimum stay, but prices per night decline with longer bookings.

Les Rambles, 122. www.citadines.com. ℂ **93-270-11-11.** 131 units. 110€–245€ studio apt, 200€–490€ 1-bedroom apt. Metro: Plaça de Catalunya. **Amenities:** Gym; free Wi-Fi.

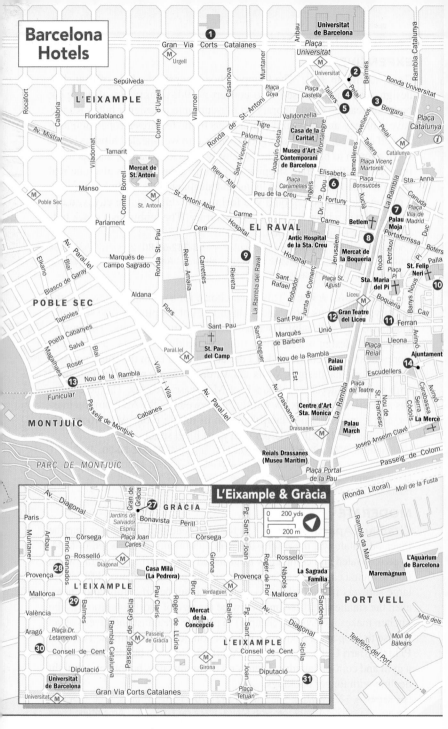

Barcelona Hotels

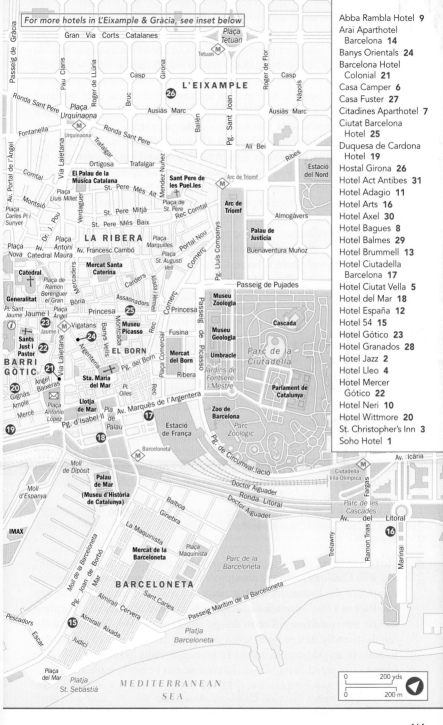

For more hotels in L'Eixample & Gràcia, see inset below

Gran Via Corts Catalanes

Plaça Tetuan

L'EIXAMPLE

LA RIBERA

EL BORN

BARRI GÒTIC

BARCELONETA

MEDITERRANEAN SEA

Abba Rambla Hotel **9**
Arai Aparthotel Barcelona **14**
Banys Orientals **24**
Barcelona Hotel Colonial **21**
Casa Camper **6**
Casa Fuster **27**
Citadines Aparthotel **7**
Ciutat Barcelona Hotel **25**
Duquesa de Cardona Hotel **19**
Hostal Girona **26**
Hotel Act Antibes **31**
Hotel Adagio **11**
Hotel Arts **16**
Hotel Axel **30**
Hotel Bagues **8**
Hotel Balmes **29**
Hotel Brummell **13**
Hotel Ciutadella Barcelona **17**
Hotel Ciutat Vella **5**
Hotel del Mar **18**
Hotel España **12**
Hotel 54 **15**
Hotel Gótico **23**
Hotel Granados **28**
Hotel Jazz **2**
Hotel Lleo **4**
Hotel Mercer Gótico **22**
Hotel Neri **10**
Hotel Wittmore **20**
St. Christopher's Inn **3**
Soho Hotel **1**

| 0 | 200 yds |
| 0 | 200 m |

461

Hotel Brummell ★★★ Slightly off the beaten track, this hipster heaven up the hill from the shabby streets of Raval clings to the hillside under Montjuïc. The nearest Metro station—a 10-minute walk—will take you to the center of things (and the foot of Les Rambles) in one stop. Impeccable designer taste is evident in every space of this cozy boutique hotel. The beds are extremely comfortable and outfitted with high-quality cotton sheets and towels. Guests can use the yoga studio next door free of charge with a little advance planning. The hillside location under Montjuïc Park puts you in the middle of a tranquil residential neighborhood, but you are surrounded by several of Poble Sec's other up-and-coming establishments, which the helpful reception staff will be glad to direct you to. In fact, a welcome packet of personal favorites from the management will open a world of little-known Barcelona destinations to you. Two decks out back provide ample breathing space and not only sun beds and a small pool but a vegetable patch! Breakfast features yummy home-baked pastries, and although there is no restaurant, room service is delivered from the awesome eatery Flax and Kale.

Nou de la Rambla, 174. www.hotelbrummell.com. ✆ **93-125-86-22.** 20 units. 120€– 250€ double. Metro: Paral.lel. **Amenities:** honesty bar, vending machine, free tea time, outdoor pool, terrace, sauna, free yoga and high-intensity training, free Wi-Fi.

Hotel España ★★ Erected as a rooming house in 1859, this handsome structure just steps from Les Rambles was transformed into a Modernista hotel in 1903 by Lluís Domènech i Montaner. (Guests get a discount on the "Beyond Gaudí" architectural tour; see p. 446.) The hotel was renovated in 2010 to restore its historic flair while also installing contemporary technology and plumbing. The styling is serene and simple, with dark wood tones and taupes that coordinate nicely with the Modernista design. The smallest rooms are a little tight (roughly 12×12 ft.), but most are larger. The main floor and the **La Fonda** restaurant shine with Modernista splendor, and the lounge's over-the-top alabaster fireplace by sculptor Eusebi Arnau is to die for.

Carrer Sant Pau, 9–11. www.hotelespanya.com. ✆ **93-550-00-00.** 82 units. 102€– 232€ double. Metro: Liceu. **Amenities:** Bar; restaurant; business area; terrace; pool; free Wi-Fi.

Hotel Jazz ★ The Jazz aims to be both clubby and chic. Located off Plaça de Catalunya near the contemporary art museum and the downtown campus of the University of Barcelona, it's true to its name, evoking the Rat Pack era (for some reason, a Spanish fascination) without replicating it. The new renditions of retro design are timeless. This is an unusually family-friendly design hotel, even providing complimentary cradles for infants. In an odd nod to an old-fashioned amenity from the 1950s, the rooms offer piped-in music—a feature that can be easily turned off.

Carrer Pelai, 3. www.hoteljazz.com. ✆ **93-532-96-96.** 108 rooms. 106€–166€ double. Parking 27€. Metro: Plaça de Catalunya. **Amenities:** Bar-cafe; business center; outdoor pool; rooftop terrace; room service; free Wi-Fi.

INEXPENSIVE

Abba Rambla Hotel ★   Built in 2005, this sleekly modern and friendly hotel was a pioneer of fine lodging in El Raval, an area once known for budget pensions. It fronts the park of La Rambla del Raval, an up-and-coming cafe district. Rooms are compact but well-designed with adequate space and contemporary bathrooms, most with tub-showers. Set just far enough off Les Rambles to avoid the crowds, it's still convenient to walk to the contemporary art museum as well as most attractions in the Barri Gòtic.

Carrer La Rambla del Raval, 4C. www.abbahotels.com. ✆ **93-505-54-00.** 49 units. 63€–135€ double. Parking 22€. Metro: Liceu. **Amenities:** Bar; cafeteria; business center; solarium; free Wi-Fi.

Hotel Ciutat Vella ★★   A red-white-and-black color scheme gives this place a lot of visual pop. Rooms have an uncluttered but functional design that has the ease of use of a good website. The clientele tends to skew young, but that could be because the art school and university are also nearby. It might be the brightest and airiest lodging in El Raval, and the low-season prices make it one of the best bargains. A rooftop terrace with a Jacuzzi tub and solarium is a nice extra touch.

Carrer Tallers, 66. www.hotelciutatvella.com. ✆ **93-481-37-99.** 40 units. 62€–91€ double. Metro: Plaça de Catalunya or Universitat. **Amenities:** Free lobby snacks and drinks 24 hr./day; rooftop terrace, Jacuzzi, solarium; free Wi-Fi.

Hotel Lleó ★   Surrounded by designer boutique hotels where all the furnishings are dark wood, all the floors are Pergo, and all the soft goods are shades of brown and taupe, the Lleó is a Spanish throwback of blond wood furniture, tan walls, and hardwood floors. It's like finding a caramel in a box of chocolates—different but just as good in its own way. The hotel is penalized a star in the official ratings for no restaurant, so it's a bargain for the quality. Rooms are adequately sized with decent desks, comfortable beds, and small but well-designed bathrooms. In summer, the rooftop terrace and pool are welcome surprises in this price range.

Carrer Pelai, 22 y 24. www.hotel-lleo.com. ✆ **93-318-12-12.** 92 rooms. 64€–153€ double. **Amenities:** Rooftop terrace and pool; business center; Jacuzzi; billiards room; free Wi-Fi.

St. Christopher's Inn ★   One of the newest (2012) in this European chain of deluxe backpacker hostels, the Barcelona version touts the city's late-night revelry, the nude beach (there is one, but it's not close), and the youthful vibe of the city. The four private rooms can be as expensive as nearby hotels, but the dorm rooms are a pretty good deal. Male, female, and mixed dormitories are available, and they're clean and bright. All ages are welcome, but most guests are younger than 25.

Carrer Bergara, 3. www.book.st-christophers.co.uk ✆ **93-667-45-88.** 11 rooms. 13.80€–33€ dorm bed; 51€ private double. Metro: Plaça de Catalunya. **Amenities:** Kitchen facilities; bar-restaurant; towel rental; free Wi-Fi.

Barri Gòtic, La Ribera & El Born

EXPENSIVE

Arai Aparthotel Barcelona ★★ You will think you've stepped onto a movie set when you enter the lobby of the Arai, with its extravagant balustrades and graceful stone staircase. This luxury boutique hotel in the heart of the Gothic Quarter is a good choice for families, as several of their very plush rooms are designed to accommodate more than a couple. All of them have nicely designed kitchens (which is what makes it an "aparthotel") in exquisitely furnished rooms within a framework of 18th-century stone walls. The suite sleeps four in two private rooms separated from each other, which provides privacy for two couples, and it features two terraces, each with a Jacuzzi. The whole eclectic mishmash of design elements, from oriental to baroque, in woods, metal, leather, and glass, somehow works together to create a beautiful overall hotel environment. Rooms have balconies with a view either toward the mountains or the lovely Plaça la Verónica below. And as if that's all not enough, the Arai also welcomes your dog.

Carrer d'Avinyó, 30. www.hotelneri.com. 31 units. ℂ **93-320-39-50.** 154€–369€ double; 341€–422€ suite. Metro: Jaume I. **Amenities:** 2 restaurants; pool; hot tub; gym; sauna; free Wi-Fi.

Hotel Neri ★★★ Most of this delightful boutique hotel at the edge of the Call in the Barri Gòtic lies within a rebuilt medieval noble home, with a modern restaurant wing harmonizing nicely with the ancient stone. Reception sits on the Call, while the restaurant terrace opens onto Plaça Sant Felip Neri, one of Barcelona's most storied old squares. The building skillfully combines 9 centuries of architecture while keeping the rooms open, airy, and timeless. Abstract Expressionist art hangs throughout the hotel, evoking a modern sensibility in a structure rooted in the very non-abstract materials of stone and exposed wood. The rooftop terrace (complete with hammocks as well as tables and chairs) functions as an auxiliary bar, weather permitting. The Neri's location makes it a popular choice for travelers on Jewish heritage holidays.

Carrer Sant Severe, 5. www.hotelarai.com. 22 units. ℂ **93-304-06-55.** 260€–286€ double; 341€–463€ suite. Metro: Liceu or Jaume I. **Amenities:** Restaurant; bar-cafe; babysitting; free Wi-Fi.

Hotel Mercer Gotico ★★★ Occupying a privileged location in the heart of the stone corridors of the Gothic Quarter, this is a collection of buildings of great architectural significance, with souvenirs of the past cropping up everywhere. The rooms are exceptionally spacious, with attention to design details and soothing low-key colors. Suites all have a separate sitting room. The hotel is built around a courtyard, so it is surprisingly filled with light, and many rooms have interior courtyard views. The rooftop lounge with its small pool and sunbeds is a great place to hang out after a day of sightseeing. The staff is supremely professional and helpful.

Walk out the door and you're 5 minutes from the Picasso Museum or the Jaume I metro stop; the lovely Plaza Sant Just is less than a minute away.

Carrer del Lledó, 7. www.mercerbarcelona.com. © **93-310-74-80.** 28 units. 288€–437€ double; 502€–1,156€ suite. Metro: Jaume I. **Amenities:** Restaurant; bar-cafe; pool; free Wi-Fi.

Hotel Wittmore ★★   Located on a tiny alley hidden away in the Gothic Quarter, the Wittmore is one of the most recent of several boutique establishments in the old city. A living wall in the small atrium can be seen from almost all the rooms, which face inward. In fact, the lack of noise is the single most outstanding feature of the Wittmore; it feels absolutely silent despite its central location. Although the rooms are called "Tiny," "Small," and "Extra Small," the names shouldn't be taken too seriously—the "Small," for instance, has a massive shower. Downstairs is a beautiful library, and decor throughout features lots of dark wood with splashes of intense red. Breakfast, lunch, and dinner are served in the handsome salon bar, and there's a rooftop with lovely city views. The staff is as professional and accommodating as you would expect in a place of this quality. There is a no-children and a no-photography policy. To ensure the privacy of celebrities?

Carrer de Riudanarenes, 7. www.thewittmore.com. © **93-550-08-85.** 22 units. 215€–364€ double; 409€–499€ suite. Metro: Jaume I. **Amenities:** Restaurant; bar-cafe; babysitting; free Wi-Fi.

INEXPENSIVE

Banys Orientals ★★   Located in historic El Born at the doorway to the Barri Gòtic, this boutique hotel sits on a beautiful pedestrian street. It offers quality and comfort at an affordable price in a 19th-century private mansion turned modern hotel. Bathrooms gleam with marble, floors are stained a dark walnut, and the crisp white linens stand out in high contrast. In addition to doubles, there are several suites, some with private patios. If you like the location, consider the upgrade to a suite, as doubles are beautiful but too tight to have more than one suitcase open at a time. Try the hotel's traditional Catalan restaurant **Parellada,** a destination for locals and tourists alike.

Carrer Argentería, 37. www.hotelbanysorientals.com. © **93-268-84-60.** 43 units. 77€–143€ double. Metro: Jaume I. **Amenities:** Restaurant; room service; free Wi-Fi.

Barcelona Hotel Colonial ★★   Set in a handsome 19th-century building that once housed the Banco Hispano, this hotel is convenient for exploring Barcelona's waterfront as well as the old city. Right behind the historic post office building, it's less than a 5-minute walk from the Moll de la Fusta and just a few hundred yards from the Museu Picasso. Perhaps because it's a former bank building, this lodging has a grander lobby than many old city hotels, especially those in Born. Rooms are rather less spacious than the lobby, though just as tastefully appointed. Triple rooms with a sleeper couch are available.

Vía Laietana, 3. www.hotelcolonialbarcelona.com. © **93-315-22-52.** 81 rooms. 77€–153€ double. Metro: Jaume I or Barceloneta. **Amenities:** Cafeteria; free Wi-Fi.

Ciutat Barcelona Hotel ★★   A bargain-priced design hotel for grown-ups, the Ciutat Barcelona has a soothing contemporary look to its rooms, including chairs and light fixtures that could have come straight from the showroom at Design Within Reach. Spaces are compact but well-designed, and the rooftop terrace is like having a private oasis in the middle of the city. There is a side entrance for wheelchair users, and some of the rooms are accessible. The small pool is big enough to make kids happy.

Carrer Princesa, 35. www.ciutatbarcelona.com. ℂ **93-269-74-75.** 78 rooms. 70€– 135€ double. Metro: Jaume I. **Amenities:** Internet corner; rooftop pool; free Wi-Fi.

Hotel Adagio ★   Barcelona hotels with an official two-star rating can be pretty grim, but Adagio is a delightful exception following substantial renovations in early 2013. Located about halfway between Plaça Reial and Plaça de Catalunya, Adagio fronts onto Carrer Ferran, one of the broader east-west streets of the Barri Gòtic. The reception area is tiny, as it was moved back to make room for the excellent tapas restaurant **Adagiotapas** (p. 480) in the front. Rooms are small but very clean. Location on the lively shopping street is superb, but it's best to keep windows closed and use the air conditioning as the narrow stone streets can be noisy at night. Exceedingly friendly and eager-to-please staff helps compensate for the lack of luxury.

Carrer Ferran, 21. www.adagiohotel.com. ℂ **93-318-90-61.** 38 units. 55€–155€ double. Metro: Liceu or Jaume I. **Amenities:** Free Wi-Fi.

Hotel Gótico ★★   This hotel at the crossroads of Jaume I/Princesa and Via Laietana is our favorite among the cluster of Gargallo family hotels on the same block. The historic building from 1823 was transformed into a hotel in 1999 and completely renovated in 2012. Acres of marble cover the entry foyer (as well as the bathrooms) and golden accents glimmer against wood inlay and exposed brick. Guest rooms are a little snug but are simply decorated with furniture that reinterprets the Modernista aesthetic through the lens of Danish Modern. The location is terrific for walking swiftly to the cathedral in one direction, the Museu Picasso in the other. Friendly and solicitous staff make the experience of staying here all the more pleasant.

Carrer Jaume I, 14. www.hotelgotico.com. ℂ **93-315-21-13.** 81 units. 76€–171€ double. Parking 25€. Dogs permitted. Metro: Jaume I. **Amenities:** Bar-cafe; room service; terrace; free Wi-Fi.

L'Eixample

EXPENSIVE

Casa Fuster ★★★   This stunning Modernista building, designed by Lluís Domènech i Montaner for the Fuster family in 1908, was reported at the time to be the most expensive home constructed in the city. Modernisme's heyday lives again in this deluxe hotel decked out in a palette of magenta, mauve, and taupe. Private balconies in many rooms open onto

Built in 1908, the Modernista mansion Casa Fuster is now a luxury hotel.

leafy Passeig de Gràcia. The hotel's Viennese cafe is one of Barcelona's best jazz clubs, but soundproofing is so good that you won't hear a single saxophone honk in your room. The location isn't all that convenient for exploring the city, but if you have your heart set on sleeping in a full-blown Modernista landmark, Casa Fuster is your place.

Passeig de Gràcia, 132. www.hotelcasafuster.com. 96 units. ✆ **93-255-30-00.** 196€–280€ double; suites 504€–2100€. Parking 37€. Metro: Diagonal. **Amenities:** Restaurant; bar; babysitting; concierge; exercise room; Jacuzzi; outdoor pool; room service; sauna; free Wi-Fi.

MODERATE

Hotel Axel ★★ Several LGBT travel publications give Axel their imprimatur, and it's easy to see why. A huge mural of two men embracing adorns the lobby, there's gay erotic art in most guest rooms, the on-site boutique sells skimpy men's bathing trunks, and there's a strong flirting scene at the rooftop pool, sun deck, and cocktail bar. Still, the hotel advertises itself as being hetero-friendly, and with its rich linens, larger-than-usual rooms (with true king beds instead of two twins pushed together), and a full menu of pillow choices, Axel should appeal to travelers of all orientations, but adults only.

Carrer Aribau, 33. www.axelhotels.com. ✆ **93-323-93-93.** 105 units. 119€–188€ double; 129€–299€ suites. Parking 24€. Metro: Universitat. **Amenities:** Restaurant; 2 bars; health club and spa; outdoor pool; room service; free Wi-Fi.

Hotel Balmes ★★ Smartly priced Hotel Balmes shares the serene modern style of the Derby Group chain, which we'd call a cross between a small art museum and a well-appointed gentleman's club. (The Derby Group's owner is an indefatigable art collector.) In this case the art consists of an extensive collection of sub-Saharan African masks and small wooden sculptures in both public areas and individual guest rooms. Even standard rooms are spacious, and several superior rooms feature small outdoor terraces. If you're interested in a larger space with a kitchenette, the hotel also has a few flats available in a building behind the courtyard, **Balmes Residences.** You'll wake up under a gilded Modernista ceiling.

Carrer de Mallorca, 216. www.derbyhotels.com. ✆ **93-451-19-14.** 105 units. 79€–171€ double, apartments 215€–242€. Metro: Diagonal. **Amenities:** Bar; restaurant; sauna; free Wi-Fi.

Hotel Granados ★★   The stone-and-glass facade of this converted 19th-century hospital is accented with oxidized iron trim in an effort to give it what the designer thought was a "New York" Soho look. In truth, it couldn't be anywhere but Barcelona, and the hotel itself is quietly and confidently posh without being the least bit snooty. Like the Balmes (see above), it is a Derby Hotel, and maintains the company style of dark wood, polished glass, and artwork everywhere. In this case, the art is from South and Southeast Asia. There are also a few Egyptian artifacts, and guests are given a free pass to the Museu Egipci of Barcelona. (The hotel's owner is on the board.)

Carrer Enric Granados, 83. www.derbyhotels.com. 77 units. ✆ **93-492-96-70.** 97€–264€ double. Metro: Diagonal. **Amenities:** Restaurant; bar; exercise room; outdoor pool; room service; free Wi-Fi.

INEXPENSIVE

Hostal Girona ★   Early Modernista architect Ildefons Cerada designed this building in the 1860s, and it retains some significant traces of its design heyday. The hostel is located on an upper floor, and only some rooms show their history. Almost all units have private bathrooms, but you can save a bit if you're willing to share. Four units have balconies; for the full Modernista effect, ask for one of the two large rooms with terraces.

Carrer Girona, 24 (piso 1, puerta 1). www.hostalgirona.com. ✆ **93-265-02-59.** 19 units. 39€–71€ double. Metro: Girona or Urquinaona. **Amenities:** Free Wi-Fi.

Hotel Acta Antibes ★★   Modern and rather pretty with its spare black-and-white decor with pops of red, this pleasant and functional hotel, just a 7-minute walk from La Sagrada Familia, is a breath of fresh air in a neighborhood where most lodgings have grander pretensions. Rooms are compact, so don't plan on spreading out, but they're tidy and bright, and the staff is cheerful. Lacking a restaurant or even a cafeteria (there is a breakfast room), the hotel only gets two stars from the official rating agency. That's okay—it guarantees a lower price for a quality lodging. You can rent a bike for 16€ per day.

Carrer de la Diputació, 394. www.hotel-antibesbarcelona.com. ✆ **93-232-62-11.** 71 units. 51€–100€ double. Parking 19€, or 9:50€ on the website. Metro: Tetuan. **Amenities:** Internet corner; free Wi-Fi.

The Hotels Arts, built in 1992 as a centerpiece of the Barcelona waterfront's pre-Olympic makeover.

Soho Hotel ★★ Barcelona-born designer Alfredo Arribas collaborated with Verner Panton's design company to create the organic minimalist look for this well-priced designer hotel. Certain contemporary clichés creep in, like the clear glass cube showers and beds so low that you're nearly on the floor. But those beds are super-comfortable, and those showers have great shower heads. Lower-level rooms can be noisy with Gran Via traffic, so ask for a courtyard room. Expensive seventh-floor suites feature wood-decked terraces with terrific city views.

Gran Via de les Corts Catalanes, 543. www.hotelsohobarcelona.com. ℭ **93-552-96-10.** 51 units. 63€–140€ double; 84€–176€ double superior with terrace. Parking 28€. Metro: Plaça de Catalunya. **Amenities:** Bar; outdoor pool; free Wi-Fi.

Waterfront

EXPENSIVE

Hotel Arts ★★★ A landmark from the 1992 Olympics waterfront makeover, the Ritz-Carlton–managed Hotel Arts occupies the lower 33 floors of a 44-story skyscraper known for its contemporary art collection. It's about 2.5km (1½ miles) southwest of the old city, next to Port Olimpic. Spacious well-equipped guest rooms have built-in headboards, bedside tables, generously sized desks, and sumptuous beds. Pink marble dominates the bathrooms, and views from the windows take in the skyline and the Mediterranean. The hotel also has the city's only beachfront pool.

Carrer de la Marina 19–21. www.ritzcarlton.com. ℭ **800/241-3333** in the U.S., or 93-221-10-00. 483 units. 467€–517€ double; 533€–1200€ suite. Parking 55€. Metro: Ciutadella or Vila Olimpica. **Amenities:** 5 restaurants; 2 bars; children's programs; concierge; exercise room; outdoor pool; room service; spa; Wi-Fi 30€ per day.

MODERATE

Duquesa de Cardona Hotel ★★   This 16th-century former noble home was transformed into a boutique hotel in 2003. The developers' gentrification optimism about the strip between the Barri Gòtic and the harbor may have been a little premature (a low-rent backpacker hostel still operates two doors away). But it's hard to fault the fabulous views across the Moll de la Fusta to Port Vell, or the upper-level views back to the Columbus Monument and up the coast to Port Olimpic. Rooms on the front (an extra charge for waterfront views) are larger and more romantic than some of the tighter quarters on the back that face into El Born.

Passeig Colom, 12. www.hduquesadecardona.com. © **93-268-90-90.** 40 units. 128€–291€ double; 252€–385€ jr. suite. Parking 30€. Metro: Barceloneta or Drassanes. **Amenities:** Restaurant; babysitting; concierge; room service; free Wi-Fi.

INEXPENSIVE

Hotel 54 ★   If you can't score a room with a view at this pleasant hostelry in the former fishermen's association building, then console yourself by hanging out on the fifth-floor terrace to enjoy a 270-degree view of the harbor and city skyline. The location is terrific: You can cut through residential Barceloneta to walk to Platja San Sebastiá, and Les Rambles is a 15-minute walk up the Moll de la Fusta. A major renovation installed nice decorative touches like colored LED mood lights over the beds and cast-glass sinks in the bathrooms. The website calls the rooms "modern and functional," and so they are.

Passeig Joan de Borbó, 54. www.hotel54barceloneta.com. © **93-225-00-54.** 28 units. 61€–148€ double. Metro: Barceloneta. **Amenities:** Bar-cafe; room service; rooftop terrace; free Wi-Fi.

Hotel Ciutadella Barcelona ★★   Set between the Parc de Ciutadella and Barceloneta, this hotel opened in fall 2012 with bargain-priced contemporary design rooms. The location is great for exploring the dining and nightlife of El Born—or spending the day at the beach. Most rooms are compact, but they're so well-designed that they seem more spacious. Views along the avenue are unremarkable, but ample double-glazed windows ensure that the light gets in and the noise does not. Terrifically friendly and helpful staff make the Ciutadella a very pleasant choice.

Avinguda Marquès de L'Argentera, 4. www.hotelciutadellabarcelona.com. © **93-268-90-70.** 59 units. 71€–168€ double. Metro: Barceloneta. **Amenities:** Free Wi-Fi.

Hotel del Mar ★   Handy to both the beaches and the old town, the Hotel del Mar has been doing what it does for decades, and if the rooms are a bit plain, everything is clean, and the staff is very enthusiastic. Each room has a terrace with a view of the port—even if a bit distant—and a couple have a view of the sea, hence the name. Ample attractive public spaces on the level above reception give guests a place to stretch out. Continental breakfast is included.

Pla del Palau, 19. www.hoteldelmarbarcelona.com © **93-319-33-02.** 72 units. 84€–137€. Rates include breakfast. Metro: Barceloneta. **Amenities:** Free Barcelona tour, no Wi-Fi.

WHERE TO EAT IN BARCELONA

One reason why Barcelona has evolved into one of the world's top gastronomic destinations is La Boqueria. The great market displays *everything* that is available in the city, from the catch of the day to still-warm-from-the-sun berries. With no mystery about ingredients, the chefs and cooks have to work their magic to make a dish that is somehow even better than the pristine ingredients you saw in the market. Sometimes that's as simple as *pá amb tomate*—toasted or grilled bread rubbed with fresh tomato, drizzled with olive oil, and sprinkled with sea salt. In tomato season, it is served instead of a breadbasket.

You can eat fabulously at some of the most old-fashioned and casual spots in the city—places like Cal Pep (p. 477), or the ultimate comfort food restaurant, Los Caracoles (p. 478). But Barcelona is one of the world's great eating cities, so it's worth splurging here if you can. It need not break the bank; some of the top chefs have opened tapas restaurants and other bargain venues to showcase their culinary creativity using less expensive materials. Barcelona dining hours are closer to the European standard than in Madrid. Lunch is usually served from about 1:30 to 3pm

Street cafes in the historic center.

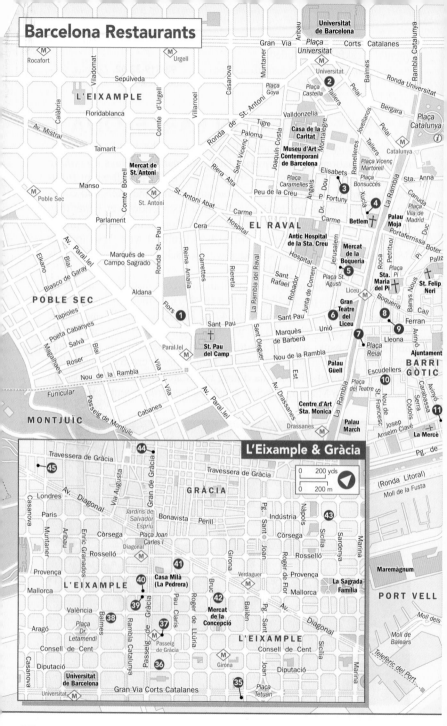

Barcelona Restaurants

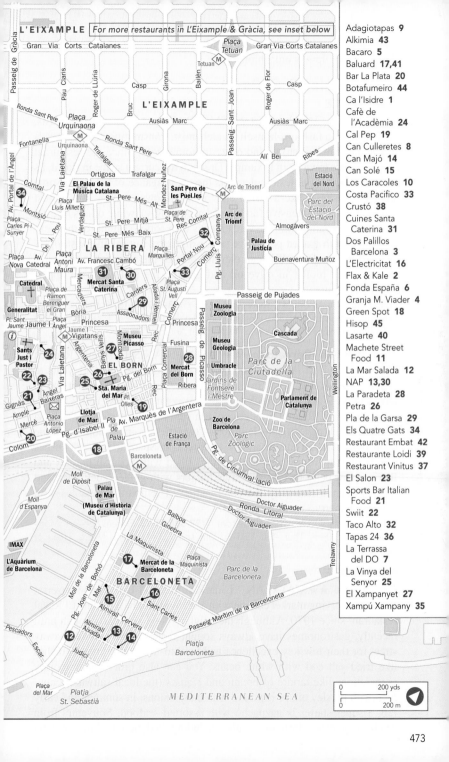

(and can represent a great bargain), and dinner starts around 8pm, although dining before 9pm is unfashionable.

Les Rambles & El Raval

EXPENSIVE

Alkimia ★★ CATALAN CONTEMPORARY   As the name suggests, chef Jordi Vila fashions himself an alchemist, transmuting base materials of Catalan cuisine into a kind of gastronomic gold. Since the restaurant moved across town from Eixample Dreita to the current space in Raval, its lush environment now complements the extravagance of his food. Some signature dishes—like a "fried egg" of cauliflower cream—are almost impossibly labor-intensive (and priced accordingly), while others like the roast chicken cannelloni, the veal kidneys with coffee crumbs, or the pickled oyster with glazed pork have surprising tastes but relatively straightforward preparations. Vila can elevate some of the simplest ingredients, poaching red mullet in olive oil and gracing the plate with an apple-cucumber chutney.

Ronda de Sant Antoni, 41. www.alkimia.cat. ✆ **93-207-61-15.** Entrees 24€–70€; fixed-price menus 98€–158€. Reservations required. Mon–Fri 1:30–3:30pm and 8–10:30pm. Closed 3 weeks in Aug. Metro: Sant Antoni or Urgell.

Dos Pallillos Barcelona ★★ ASIAN/SPANISH   Albert Raurich heads this oddball tapas restaurant, and given that he spent 11 years at elBulli (the last 6 as head chef under Ferran Adrià), the restaurant had to have a twist. When he and Adrià ate their way through New York's Chinatown on a visit, Raurich thought up dim sum tapas. Located in the Casa Camper hotel (p. 459), Dos Pallillos—"two sticks"—pays homage to the chopsticks of Asian cuisine and the toothpicks of Spanish bar food. Dishes run the gamut from Chinese dumplings filled with Spanish prawns and Iberico pork belly to Japanese-style burgers with ginger, cucumber, and miso. Regulars swear by the combination of tempura vegetables with glasses of sherry.

Carrer Elisabets, 11. www.dospalillos.com. ✆ **93-304-05-13.** Entrees 85€–95€. Mon–Tues 7:30–11:30pm, Thurs–Sat 1:30–3:30pm and 7:30–11:30pm. Metro: Liceu or Catalunya.

MODERATE

Ca L'Isidre ★★ CATALAN   Isidre Gironés and his wife Montserrat have been serving market cuisine with a seafood emphasis at this El Raval restaurant since 1970. Although the neighborhood was fairly rough until recently, gastronomes have always sought them out on a hidden-away street for their low-key excellence and hard-to-find old-fashioned dishes like fried salt cod with white beans. You can also order contemporary preparations like tartare of bream and *cigalas* (the local saltwater crawfish) with parsley oil, or roast kid with baby onions. In summer and early fall, a super starter is gazpacho with assorted seafood. Souvenirs from celebrity guests adorn the walls, including Federico Fellini, Giulietta

Masina, Salvador Dalí and Woody Allen (and the rumor of a former monarch). The owner is known to have actually turned down a Michelin star rating, for reasons known only to him.

Carrer Les Flors, 12. www.calisidre.com. ✆ **93-441-11-39.** Entrees 20€–60€; weekday lunch menu 35€. Reservations required. Mon–Sat 1:30–4pm and 8:30–11pm. Metro: Paral.lel.

Fonda España ★★ BASQUE

The value for price ratio is very high at this superb restaurant in the Hotel España (p. 462) in El Raval. The menu is created by star chef Martín Berasategui (see p. 483 for his high-end Lasarte), who's based in Basque country but visits often. Because he focuses on traditional fare rather than the more inventive dishes served at his other restaurants, he's charging less (and using fewer organ meats, a blessing for squeamish diners). Look for grilled kid chops (like lamb chops), baked monkfish, or fried mullet. The most Basque of the desserts is a glass of slightly sparkling txacolí wine with strawberries and a scoop of lemon peel ice cream. Management recently restored the main dining room to Lluís Domènech i Montaner's designs; the Art Nouveau mosaics positively gleam. For guided hotel tours, see p. 446.

Carrer Sant Pau, 9. www.hotelespanya.com. ✆ **93-550-00-10.** Entrees 18€–26€; weekday lunch menu 28€; dinner menus 40€–114€. Reservations suggested. Mon–Sat 1–4pm and 8–11pm, Sunday 1–4pm. Metro: Liceu.

Flax and Kale ★★ FISH/VEGETARIAN

Non-meat eaters were thrilled when Teresa Carles opened this innovative "flexitarian" eatery a few years ago, and it was an immediate hit. It's not exclusively vegetarian,

In a classic Art Nouveau interior, Fonda España features the cooking of star chef Martín Berasategui.

Raw vegan lasagna is among the creative yet healthful dishes at Flax and Kale.

but its original and healthful dishes with clever names (one is called "Don't Call Us Tacos/No Digas Tacos") are a relief from the *jamon*-heavy cuisine of most traditional restaurants. The soaring dining spaces are handsome—be sure to check out the upper level terrace. Go for the gluten-free pizzas and yummy curries, but skip the desserts, which try too hard and often fall flat.

Carrer dels Tallers, 74b. www.teresacarles.com. ✆ **93-317-56-64.** Entrees 13€–18€. Reservations recommended. Mon–Fri noon–5pm and 7–11:30pm, Sat–Sun 7–11:30pm. Metro: Catalunya or Universitat.

INEXPENSIVE

Granja M. Viader ★ CATALAN One of Barcelona's original "milk bars," M. Viader invented the drink you see next to the sodas in every cooler: Cacaolat. It's exactly what you might think from the name—chocolate milk—and Catalans of a certain age gush with nostalgia over it. The founder was instrumental in getting pasteurized milk products out to the public, and this wonderfully old-fashioned cafe, founded in 1870, still serves coffee, pastries, sandwiches, exceedingly thick hot chocolate (a "suiza" is topped with whipped cream), and, of course, chocolate milk. In the morning, you can also get hot *churros* to go with the hot chocolate.

Carrer Xucla, 4–6. www.granjaviader.cat. ✆ **93-318-34-86.** Sandwiches 3–5€; pastries 1.80€–4€. Mon–Sat 9am–1:15pm and 5–9:15pm. Metro: Liceu or Catalunya.

Barri Gòtic, La Ribera & Born
MODERATE

Cafè de L'Acadèmia ★★★ CATALAN Whether you reserve a table in the charming little plaza Sant Just in warm weather, or sit under the

15th-century stone arches inside during the winter, you are in for a treat at this inventive restaurant, which serves variations on traditional Catalan cuisine at a reasonable price. Chef-owner Jordí Castellvi, who also has a vineyard at the foot of Montserrat, prepares market cuisine, offering up yummy dishes like a cold carrot soup with a dollop of pesto in warm weather. The offerings change daily but original dishes, like a roasted salt cod gratinée with artichoke mousse, almost all exceed expectations. Castellvi has maintained a loyal and friendly wait staff for many years, perhaps in part because they get every weekend off—this is a weekdays-only foodie destination. The fixed-price menu at lunch is a good deal, but you may have to ask for it, as it's usually printed only in Spanish/Catalan.

Carrer Lledó, 1. ⓒ **93-319-82-53.** Entrees 10€–14€; midday set menu 16€, lower prices at counter. Reservations required. Mon–Fri 1:30–4pm and 8:30pm–1am. Closed last 2 weeks in Aug. Metro: Jaume I.

Cal Pep ★★★ CATALAN   The only bad thing about Cal Pep is that it closes after dinner on Saturday and doesn't reopen until Monday dinner. Swarms of happy people dine on Pep's small dishes, *media raciones* (that is, bigger than a tapa and smaller than a *racion*). There are some Catalan classics among the 70 or so dishes available on a given day, but most are the restaurant's own inventions—the "atomic" omelet with crumbled sausage, chewy beans, and potent garlic sauce, for example, or baked artichokes stuffed with onions and black olives. Gravel-voiced Pep himself still sometimes plays host, making sure everyone is having a good time and recommending what they should try next. There's a small dining

Fresh seafood and other Catalan favorites are lovingly prepared by chef Cal Pep and his crew.

room in the back, but the real show happens at the counter seats up front, where the friendly waiters will be glad to make recommendations.

Plaça des les Olles, 8. www.calpep.com. ☎ **93-310-79-61.** Reservations for groups of 4–20 only. Entrees 6.50€–25€. Mon 7:30–11:30pm, Tues–Sat 1–3:45pm and 7:30–11:30pm. Closed last 3 weeks in Aug. Metro: Barceloneta or Jaume I.

Can Culleretes ★ CATALAN   Tucked onto a tiny side street near the Plaça Reial, Culleretes has been serving traditional Catalan fare since 1786—dishes like spinach cannoli with salt cod brandade, stewed wild boar, or partridge casserole. The priciest meal (32€ for two) is the assorted fish and shellfish, a three-course spread that starts with garlic shrimp and steamed shellfish, moves on to assorted fried fish (usually monkfish and squid), and concludes with grilled prawns, scampi, and baby calamari.

Carrer Quintana, 5. www.culleretes.com. ☎ **93-317-30-22.** Entrees 8.50€–20€, set menus 24€–32€. Reservations recommended. Tues–Sat 1:30–4pm and 8–10:45pm, Sun 1:30–4pm. Closed late July–mid-Aug.

Los Caracoles ★ SPANISH   It is a rite of passage for tourists to dine at "The Snails," where the Bofarull family has been welcoming hungry travelers since 1835. As you arrive, you can't miss the picturesque sight of whole chickens roasting over a spit in an open window. The snails, for which the restaurant was renamed in the mid–20th century, are good and garlicky, but most diners come for the comfort food: chicken and ham croquettes, roast chicken, roast suckling pig, and the pricey lobster paella. The menu has basically remained unchanged since Los Caracoles was featured in the inaugural edition of Frommer's *Spain on $5 a Day*. Honest food without subtext never goes out of style.

Carrer Escudellers, 14. www.loscaracoles.es. ☎ **93-301-20-41.** Entrees 11€–45€. Daily 1:15–3:30pm and 6–11:30pm. Reservations recommended. Metro: Liceu or Drassanes.

Cuines Santa Caterina ★★ ASIAN/MEDITERRANEAN   This soaring adjunct to the Mercat Santa Caterina (p. 436) is one of the classiest eating halls in Barcelona. A simple tapas bar stands at the entrance, but the main action is in the dining room, where chunky wooden tables are surrounded on two sides by open kitchens. That's right, "kitchens" in the plural. Order paella and it comes from the Spanish kitchen; order fried rice and it comes from the Asian kitchen. The restaurant prides itself on total integration with the market, and many dishes are suitable for vegetarians, if not always for vegans. Light vegetable tempuras are offered, as are vegetable sushi rolls and excellent sashimi cut to order. Spanish and Catalan market food—roast duck, monkfish, and clams with romesco sauce—is just as plentiful and just as good. You can eat at the bar all day starting at 9am. You can't make reservations, so show up early or be ready to wait.

Mercat de Santa Caterina, Avinguda Francesc Cambó, 17. www.grupotragaluz.com/restaurante/cuines-santa-caterina. ☎ **93-268-99-18.** Entrees 9€–37€. Sun–Thurs 1–4pm; Fri–Sat 1–4pm and 7:30–11:30pm. Metro: Jaume I.

La Paradeta ★★ SEAFOOD This is one of seven in a local family-run chain, and the one with the coolest location, right across from the former Borne Market. When you walk through the door, you pick out the best-looking fresh fish or shellfish for the chef to cook for your lunch or dinner. Everything is market price, so they weigh your fish and you say, "More," or "less please," and then…"grilled" or "steamed." Add a salad and some wine for a good price, and take a seat while the fish cooks. The atmosphere is fun and very casual. A mural on the wall shows the family at work.

Carrer Commercial, 7. www.laparadeta.com. *€* **93-268-19-39.** Entrees 5€–20€. Tues–Thurs 1–4pm and 8–11:30pm, Fri–Sun 1–4pm and 8–midnight. Metro: Jaume I or Barceloneta.

Els Quatre Gats ★ CATALAN Nobody goes to Els Quatre Gats for its fine cuisine, as most of the offerings are rather bland versions of traditional Catalan fare. But the restaurant is full of the ghosts of a bygone era, and the management has taken advantage of the building's rich history to attract a curious crowd of visitors, who come for a look and stay for a meal or a few shared plates of tapas. The restaurant has recently made more of an effort at presentation, serving some dishes on tiles based on Modernista designs, dressing the wait staff in snappy traditional black-and-white, and generally re-creating the heyday of the restaurant, which lasted only 5 years at the turn of the last century. Teenage Picasso hit the mark in 1900 when he had his first exhibition on the walls of Els Quatre Gats, which was a hangout for Modernista art stars of the previous generation (Santiago Rusiñol, Miquel Utrillo, Ramón Casas). He also designed the menu cover, which is still used, signing it with his given name, "P. Ruiz Picasso" (he later dropped the more pedestrian surname of his father). The exterior of the building is an 1897 marvel of Neo-Gothic and Catalan art nouveau elements designed by Puig i Caldalfach.

Carrer Montsió, 3. www.4gats.com. *€* **93-302-41-40.** Entrees 17€–125€, tapas 3€–18€. Reservations required Sat–Sun. Daily 9am–2am. Metro: Plaça de Catalunya.

La Terrassa del DO ★ CATALAN The casual dining space of the grandly named DO Plaça Reial Boutique Hotel Gastronomic is only marginally more expensive than its less accomplished neighbors on the Plaça Reial. The forte here is drinks with tapas, but even the tapas are a welcome respite from most bar food. Imagine a glass of cava with a salad of escarole, mango, and grilled fresh Atlantic bonito, or a glass of Priorat red with griddled calamari and garlic. The DO kitchen also prepares solid comfort food like charcoal-grilled octopus with mashed potatoes, roasted catch of the day with vegetables of the season, or a burger made with Galician veal (the closest thing to American beef you'll find in Spain). There are many tables inside and (weather permitting) more outdoors, so reservations aren't an issue.

Plaça Reial, 1. www.hoteldoreial.com. *€* **93-481-36-66.** Tapas 2.30€–27€, entrees 18€–60€. Daily Apr–Oct 11am–1am, Nov–Mar 12:30pm–midnight. Metro: Liceu.

INEXPENSIVE

Adagiotapas ★★ CATALAN   Chef/owner Jordi Herrera—a revered former culinary professor at Barcelona's hotel school—is a master of tradition and innovation alike. His capacity for giving old dishes new legs won him a Michelin star at his fine-dining restaurant, but in mid-2013 he also opened this creative tapas operation in a modest Barri Gòtic hotel. Some dishes are straightforward, like the briny oyster with ginger mignonette, while others are clever re-inventions of classics, such as a *tortilla* with caramelized onion that's finished in the oven as a small tart in a cupcake paper. Instead of conventional ham croquettes, he serves delicious rabbit croquettes encrusted with shredded phyllo and accompanied by dabs of ratatouille. The wine list is short and inexpensive.

Carrer Ferran, 21. www.adagiotapas.com. ✆ **93-318-90-61.** Tapas 4€–10€. Set menus 12€–16€. Mon 7–11pm, Tues–Sun 1–4pm and 7–11pm. Metro: Liceu or Jaume I.

Bar La Plata ★★ TAPAS   Do a few things, and do them well. There is no simpler food emporium in Barcelona than Bar La Plata, named for the short Gothic Quarter alley where it is located. There is no menu. There are six, usually crowded, tables, but most patrons stand. Since 1945, customers have ordered four simple tapas plates over the marble counter, and it has proven to be a winning formula. Your choices are crispy fried sardines *(pescaditos)*, buttifarra sausage, a salad of tomato wedges and raw onions, or anchovies and olives. Longtime fixture Pepe Gómez will serve it all to you, along with a glass of wine (or if you're brave enough to try it, a stream of vino blanco from a glass porrón), and there you have it: tapas perfection for a few euros.

Carrer Mercé, 28. barlaplata.com. ✆ **93-315-10-09.** Tapas 2.50€–5€. Mon–Sat 10am–3:15pm and 6:15–11pm. Metro: Drassanes.

Petra ★★ CATALAN   Even if the interior is a hippy-era retro version of a Modernista original, the ambience of this little restaurant, which is literally in the shadow of the church of Santa Maria del Mar (p. 438), feels authentic and warm. We like the gimmick of printing the menu on wine labels. Owners Sam and Joan make diners feel welcome, and the comfort-food dishes fill the soul and the belly. A specialty is the egg dish *huevo de calaf,* served over potatoes and accompanied by cod, liver, or the local sausage called *butifarra.* A modest wine list features local wines at a good price; try the Montsant red.

Carrer dels Sombrerers, 13. www.restaurantpetra.com. ✆ **93-319-99-99.** Entrees 7€–12€. No reservations. Mon–Thurs 1:30–4pm and 8:30–11pm, Fri–Sat 1:15–4pm and 8:30pm–midnight, in winter also Sun 1:30–4pm. Metro: Liceu.

Pla de la Garsa ★★ CATALAN   Although a new generation is in charge, this venerable family restaurant retains its terrific collection of Modernista graphic art, its 18th-century tiles and wrought iron, and its commitment to the dark and savory side of traditional Catalan cookery. The kitchen makes its own pâtés and terrines—the anchovy-black olive

WHEN something spanish JUST WON'T DO

Spaniards and Catalans do many things well in the kitchen. But among the weak links in the local cuisine are bread (usually bland and lacking in texture), pasta, and ice cream. So once you've had your fill of tapas, remember that neither France nor Italy are far away.

Superb **breads** and buttery croissants (unlike the local "normal" version which is made of lard or olive oil), for instance, can be found in Barcelona in a few places, like the delectable **Crustó** in Eixample at Carrer Valencia, 236 (www.crusto.es), or the two **Baluard** bakeries, one in Eixample at Carrer Provença, 279, and the original at Carrer Baluard, 38, in Barceloneta (www.baluardbarcelona.com).

Authentic Italian **gelato** is proudly mixed daily by a couple who are half-American (wife Tracy) and half-Italian (husband Giovanni) in **Swiit,** a friendly gelateria with a lovely Gothic Quarter location at Baixada de Viladecols, 2c (www.swiitbarcelona.com).

Real Neapolitan **pizza** is dished out by real Neapolitans at several locations, including the homey but delicious **Sports Bar Italian Food,** Carrer Ample, 51, and at **NAP (Neapolitan Authentic Pizza)** in two locations, one in the Born and one in Barceloneta (www.facebook.com/nap. pizzeria).

Can't wait for that next trip to Italy for the perfect dish of **pasta?** Visit the cozy and friendly trattoria **Bacaro,** behind the Boqueria on a narrow alley called Jerusalem #6 (www.bacarobarcelona.com).

Mexican food is finally finding an audience here (Iberians don't like it *picante*), and a host of taquerias offer variations on the Mexican theme, where you can order it hot, or not. Our favorites are **Costa Pacifico** on the lovely Plaça Sant Augurtí Vell (www.costapacifico.es), dirt-cheap **Taco Alto,** Carrer del Portal Nou, 62, near Arco de Trionfo (www. tacoalto.es), and the hip **Machete Street Food** in the Gothic Quarter on Carrer Ample, 20 (no website).

10

BARCELONA | Where to Eat in Barcelona

terrine *(garum)* is especially good—and offers a wide array of traditional sausages and cured meats, including the air-dried beef usually only found in mountainous western Catalunya. When it's available, ask for the sturgeon carpaccio starter with cava vinaigrette. (Sturgeon cooked in cider is also usually on the menu as a main dish.) Duck is a staple here; one of the restaurant's most popular dishes is duck three ways (gizzards, liver, and thighs). The short and powerful wine list is strong on Priorat, and for dessert you can't go wrong with any of the Catalan cheeses.

Carrer Assaonadors, 13. www.pladelagarsa.com. © **93-315-24-13.** Entrees 9€–16€, 2-person set menu 24.50€ each. Reservations recommended Fri–Sat. Daily 7pm– 1am (closes at midnight Sun). Metro: Jaume I.

El Salon ★★ CATALAN   Americans will be glad to find a place where they can dine at something close to the supper hour they're used to in this atmospheric restaurant on a small street in the Gothic Quarter. The high-ceilinged stone room creates just the right environment for a romantic dinner, with service that's friendly but unobtrusive. Dishes are beautifully presented, most of them twists on traditional Catalan themes, like a tender sea bass in a tomato sauce and *calamares a la plancha* beautifully rolled into cylinders and served on a bed of white beans. Save room for dessert; there's an interesting twist on the classic *tarte tatin*.

Carrer de l'Hostal d'en Sol, 6. ② **93-315-21-59.** Entrees 12€–20€. Sun and Tues–Fri 5pm–midnight, Sat 5pm–2am, closed Mon. Metro: Jaume I.

La Vinya del Senyor ★★ VINOTECA/TAPAS   It doesn't get much better than spending an afternoon on the terrace of La Vinya del Senyor taking in the glorious Gothic facade of the church of Santa María del Mar (p. 438)—especially if there's a wedding taking place. The vinoteca serves glasses of wine with a modest tapas menu. It's not uncommon to find several Priorats, several more Riojas, and a selection of Ruedas and Albariños by the glass. If you're drinking a bottle, you can choose from more than 300 still wines and cavas, sherries, and Moscatels. Tapas include many usual suspects—Manchego cheese, *jamón serrano*—and some Catalan surprises like walnut rolls drizzled with Catalan olive oil. La Vinya also serves the sweet, crisp version of *coca,* a Catalan flatbread scented with anisette and rolled in sugar and pine nuts. Because it absorbs the tannins in your mouth, it's a great complement to a powerful red wine.

Plaça Santa María, 5. www.lavinyadelsenyor.com. ② **93-310-33-79.** Wines by the glass 2€–25€, tapas 2€–20€. Sun–Thurs noon–1am, Fri–Sat noon–2am. Metro: Jaume I or Barceloneta.

El Xampanyet ★ TAPAS   One of the city's best-loved "champagne bars" since 1929, El Xampanyet knows that no bar ever went broke by selling inexpensive drinks. By day it keeps a low profile just across from the Museu Picasso; the corrugated steel door does not roll up until the museum closes. In minutes, Xampanyet is jammed, as drinkers assemble next to wine barrels, marble-topped tables, or the long zinc bar as if someone were about to start shooting a party commercial. Tapas are simple and salty (olives, ham, croquettes), and the house cava (white or pink) is a great deal.

Carrer Montcada, 22. ② **93-319-70-03.** Tapas 2€–8€. Mon–Sat noon–3:30pm and 7–11pm, Sun noon–3:30pm. Closed Aug. Metro: Jaume I.

L'Eixample

EXPENSIVE

Botafumeiro ★★ SEAFOOD   Owner Moncho Neira hails from Galicia and holds the opinion (shared by much of Spain) that Galicians know more about fish than anyone. Neira sources his fish from auctions on the Catalan and Galician coasts and presents them in an old-world fine-dining setting, where waiters wear white jackets and diners are expected to dress accordingly. Begin with a selection of clams and oysters from the raw bar, or take Neira's advice and start with his spider crab pie. Because he has access to the Galician catch, he always has live lobsters, "Norway lobster" (scampi), and two or three species of crab, clams, mussels, and percebes (goose barnacles) in enormous tanks at the restaurant entrance. Diners who prefer meat can choose from a few steaks, some veal dishes, and traditional Galician stewed pork with turnips. The wine list is as Galician as many of the fish, with several bracing *albariño* whites from the Rias Baixas along with a nice selection of Catalan cavas.

Carrer Gran de Gràcia, 81. www.botafumeiro.es. ✆ **93-218-42-30**. Entrees 29€–45€. Reservations recommended. Daily noon–1am. Metro: Fontana.

Hisop ★ CATALAN   Oriol Ivern Bondia and Guillem Pla wowed their fellow chefs when they opened Hisop in 2001 to serve radically reinvented Catalan cuisine. Pla has moved on, but Ivern keeps Hisop percolating in a more streamlined style, constantly reimagining the flavors of the region in pure, unmuddled form. This results in some marvelously stripped-down dishes—whole grilled red mullet with a zucchini flower, or a John Dory with cockles steamed in a vanilla broth. Suckling pig is made all the more unctuous by an accompaniment of roasted plums. The menu changes four times a year, with weekly adjustments. (What chef can resist the tomato harvest or a seasonal fish spawn?) Hisop's desserts are equally brilliant combinations of flavors—peach with ginger and coffee, chocolate with basil and almonds, pistachio with kaffir lime.

Pasatje Marimon, 9. www.hisop.com. ✆ **93-241-32-33**. Entrees 21€–28€; 10-course tasting menu 65€, with wine pairing 95€. Reservations required. Mon–Fri 1:30–3:30pm, 8:30–11pm; Sat 8:30–11pm. Closed 1st week Jan. Metro: Hospital Clínic.

Lasarte ★★★ BASQUE   If you consider yourself a foodie and have plans for one big splurge in Barcelona, Lasarte might be your best bet. It's the elegant Barcelona outpost of much-decorated Basque chef Martín Berasategui, and since 2009 has held two Michelin stars of its own. Berasategui is known for his innovations, but also for mentoring young chefs, so chef de cuisine Paolo Casagrande interprets the classics of the master and adds dishes of his own. This is world-class dining, and it doesn't come cheap. Many dishes are no more than four bites, which translates to more than 10€ per bite. But they are dishes that will form part of your sensory memory bank, the plates against which you will measure all others. Red prawns, for example, come into the restaurant live from the boat. The kitchen prepares them in a sea urchin flan topped with a sheep's milk "caviar" (thanks to the miracles of spherification) and sends them to the dining room on a wet black slate to evoke the dark ocean where they swam only hours before. Tuna belly might be flash-grilled over charcoal and served with mango and capers in soy sauce and a tiny bowl of raw celery minestrone for an orgy of sweet, salt, and umami. If this is all just too breathtaking (especially the price), consider the more casual **Loidi** (see below) or **Fonda España** (p. 475).

Carrer Mallorca, 259 (in Hotel Condes de Barcelona). www.restaurantlasarte.com. ✆ **93-445-00-00**. 7-course menu 205€, 10-course menu 235€. Smart dress and reservations required. Tues–Sat 1:30–3:30pm and 8:30–10pm. Metro: Provença.

Restaurante Loidi ★★ BASQUE   Also part of the Hotel Condes de Barcelona, Loidi is Berasategui's gastro bistro. Loidi is much more casual, though many diners dress smartly for dinner anyway. Dishes are less elaborate than at Lasarte (see above), but are available only as set menus, of which the whole table must order the same number of courses. The six-course Martín Selection gives you most of the menu for about the cost of a main dish at Lasarte (a three-course version is also available). Dishes might include large veal ravioli candied in carrot juice and served with meat broth, or fish with cauliflower purée and beet couscous.

Carrer Mallorca, 248–250. www.loidi.com. ☎ **93-492-92-92.** Tasting menus 31€–51€. Sun 1–3:30pm, Mon–Sat 1–3:30pm and 8–11pm. Metro: Provença.

MODERATE

Restaurant Embat ★★ CATALAN   Another stalwart of Barcelona's bargain-priced "bistronomic" restaurants, Embat has just 10 tables in a modest space designed in white minimalist style. It bustles at lunch, when the menu usually has three main dishes, none more than 12€, and often requires reservations at night, when prices rise and choices expand dramatically. The dishes are not radical—just re-thought. Gazpacho comes with a few shrimp and a small ball of burrata (cream-filled mozzarella) with a flurry of basil. The classic monkfish with spinach and creamy potato is complemented by a thin sheet of crackly almond praline. Desserts are a specialty; one favorite is the hot chocolate pudding with walnut ice cream.

Carrer Mallorca, 304. www.embatrestaurant.com. ☎ **93-458-08-55.** Entrees 10€–22€, tasting menu 42€. Mon–Wed 1–3:45pm, Thurs–Sat 1–3:45pm and 8:30–11pm. Metro: Girona or Diagonal.

Tapas 24 ★★ TAPAS   Prices have increased, but success has not spoiled food star Carles Abellan, whose basement restaurant in L'Eixample is his personal homage to the tapas lifestyle. Come for breakfast, and you can order *estrellitas*—fried potatoes with a broken fried egg stirred in on top, with or without extra sausage, ham, or foie gras. (Catalan chefs love foie gras, which is local and inexpensive.) You cannot reserve a table, but take your chances at an off-hour, as service is nonstop from morning through evening. The menu keeps changing as the day progresses, but count on being able to order a bowl of lentils stewed with chorizo, or the "McFoie" burger (a hamburger

Barcelona's tapas scene inevitably includes seafood.

topped with foie gras). Abellan is famous for his "bikini" grilled ham and cheese sandwich with black truffle. There are now a couple other Tapas 24 restaurants in town, but the original remains a treat, with its colorful graphics and helpful wait staff.

Carrer de la Diputació, 269. www.carlesabellan.es. ℰ **93-488-09-77.** Tapas 5€–24€. Daily 9am–midnight. Metro: Passeig de Gràcia.

INEXPENSIVE

Restaurant Vinitus Madrid-Barcelona ★ CATALAN   Locals mourned the closing of the classic Madrid-Barcelona restaurant that occupied this location for decades, named for a former train stop on Carrer Aragó where the inter-city railroad arrived for a century until 1960. The new owners kept the famous sign when it reopened as Vinitus in 2018, and if it lacks the former establishment's patina of age, it has the same cozy ambiance, thanks to the graceful mezzanine level that overhangs the bar. Mommy meals abound, and the kitchen excels at seafood. Try the *huevos estrellados,* a specialty, and the crunchy camembert. The yummy desserts, at 2.80€ each, may be the best deal in town.

Carrer Aragó, 282. clubcomerbien.com/restaurante-vinitus-barcelona. ℰ **93-853-30-85.** Entrees 5.75€–12.15€. Sun–Thurs 11:30am–am; Fri–Sat 11:30am–1:30am. Metro: Passeig de Grácia.

Xampú Xampany ★ CATALAN   One of the last of the city's old-fashioned *xampanyerías,* this no-frills spot on the corner of Carrer Bailèn at Plaça de Tetuan functions as a wine store that specializes in cavas, the Catalan sparkling wines that used to be called "champagne" before E.U. rules kicked in. It is also a bar that usually has at least a half-dozen cavas in the ice bucket. On top of that, it is also a casual restaurant that serves breakfast food, sandwiches, and small plates of sausages and grilled fish. The omelet sandwich (French omelet—just eggs) makes a good breakfast for a few euros. This being Spain, many breakfast customers also have a glass of cava. Like most things involving inexpensive sparkling wine, it looks a lot more romantic after dark.

Gran Vía de les Corts Catalanes, 702. xampuxampany.com. ℰ **93-265-04-83.** Mon–Sat 8am–1:30am. Metro: Girona or Tetuan.

Waterfront & La Barceloneta

EXPENSIVE

La Mar Salada ★ CATALAN/SEAFOOD   One of the more prominent members of Barceloneta Cuina, a restaurant organization that aims to promote the seafood gastronomic traditions of the fishermen's neighborhood, La Mar Salada serves old-fashioned dishes like *bombas* (potato balls with a bit of blood sausage in the middle) or heavily breaded and deep-fried squid. Both dishes are usually bathed in the garlicky Catalan eggless mayonnaise called "allioli." But this inventive restaurant is also known for its lobster fritters and a dynamite version of rape *suquet,* a seafood soup made with monkfish, clams, onions, tomato, saffron, and sweet paprika. Desserts are out of the ordinary and presented with flair.

Passeig Juan de Borbo, 58–59. www.lamarsalada.cat. ✆ **93-221-10-15.** Entrees 9.50€–28.50€, set menu 19.50€. Reservations recommended. Mon and Wed–Fri 1–4pm and 8–11pm, Sat–Sun 1–11pm. Metro: Barceloneta.

MODERATE

Can Majó ★ CATALAN/SEAFOOD   Literally steps from the beach, this family restaurant dates from 1968 and is now run by two generations of the Majó family. The dining room resembles a country tavern, but as long as the weather is good, everyone wants to eat outdoors at the white-linen-clad tables beneath umbrellas. Not all the seafood is local—they fly in amazing oysters from Galicia and France for the raw bar. Many of the shellfish are cooked over a wood-fired grill, which gives them a smoky tang. The restaurant is known, however, for fish soups—both the simple fish and shellfish in a fish broth, and the more elaborate *zarzuela,* a Catalan dish where the mixed fish are more important than the broth. On request, the kitchen will prepare a very similar French bouillabaisse.

Almirall Aixada 23, Barceloneta. www.canmajo.es. ✆ **93-221-54-55.** Entrees 14€–44€. Reservations recommended. Tues–Sat 1–4pm and 8–11:30pm, Sun 1–4pm. Metro: Barceloneta.

Can Solé ★★ CATALAN/SEAFOOD   Proprietor Josep Maria Garcia adheres to the traditional plates of La Barceloneta. That could mean starting with a briny bowl of tiny sweet clams or cabbage hearts stuffed with tuna. Some vanishing dishes make their last stand here, like the fried cod and onions with sweet currants that hint at its North African roots. And then there's the *zarzuela,* the most expensive dish on the menu because it is an encyclopedia of the Barceloneta catch, jammed with everything including whiting, shrimp, cigalas, bream, mackerel, clams, mussels, and even lobster.

Carrer Sant Carles, 4. www.restaurantcansole.com. ✆ **93-221-50-12.** Entrees 12€–28€. Reservations suggested. Tues–Thurs 1–4pm and 8–11pm; Fri–Sat 1–4pm and 8:30–11pm, Sun 1–4pm. Metro: Barceloneta.

Green Spot ★★ VEGETARIAN   This is the kind of place that gives vegetarian cuisine a good name. Green Spot is one of the creations of Tomás Tarruella, and the brand Grupo Tragaluz whose unique restaurants have helped to revolutionize eating in Barcelona. The space itself is an elegant wooden environment by Brazilian designer Isay Weinfeld, which makes you feel at ease from the moment you stroll down the long oak-lined entry corridor. Imaginative food combines international flavors from Asia and the Mediterranean, with such healthful offerings as quesadillas of avocado and kimchi, or to-die-for combinations like sweet potato tagliatelle in a sauce of walnuts, macadamias, and black truffles. Pizzas fill out the menu for those who prefer something traditional (hold the salami please), and the food is complemented by a serious wine menu.

Live music on Thursdays completes the sophisticated effect. "Veggies for veggies. Veggies for non-veggies," says their website. Indeed.

Carrer de la Reina Cristina, 12. www.encompaniadelobos.com. ℰ **93-802-55-65.** Entrees 9.75€–16.50€. Sun–Thurs 1pm–midnight, Fri–Sat 1pm–2am (reduced menu 4–8pm). Metro: Barceloneta.

INEXPENSIVE

L'Electricitat ★★ TAPAS   Possibly the favorite neighborhood bar of all of Barceloneta, this restaurant's midday atmosphere matches the name—it's positively electric. It's a great place to have steamed mussels or clams, maybe a bite of fried fish, some anchovies, a finger sandwich with smoked trout, and then perhaps a small crab salad. There's beer on tap and a lot of inexpensive Catalan wines. In cold weather, they also tap the big barrels of house vermouth that are more or less ornamental the rest of the year.

Carrer Sant Carles, 15. ℰ **93-221-50-17.** Tapas and *raciones* 1.50€–12€. Mon–Sat 8am–3pm and 7–10:30pm, Sun 8–3:45pm. Metro: Barceloneta.

SHOPPING IN BARCELONA

If you don't want to spend a lot of time shopping, museum shops are your best bet for offerings not available elsewhere. Our favorites are the **Museu Picasso** (p. 437) and the **Fundació Joan Miró** (p. 450). They have broad selections of jewelry, scarves and other accessories, books, posters, and interesting home accessories at reasonable prices. If by some chance you are in the market for an original piece of graphic art by a Spanish master, check out the shop at the **Fundació Antoni Tàpies** (p. 443). The shops at **La Pedrera** (p. 445) and **Casa Batlló** (p. 441) have merchandise inspired by the Modernisme movement. At Casa Batllo, you can even find nail polish in Gaudí-inspired colors.

Elegant Passeig de Gracia is Barcelona's luxe shopping destination.

Sports fans should check out the merchandise at **FC Botiga,** the official shops of Barcelona's wildly popular football club. (The most convenient locations are Carrer Jaume 1, 18, ✆ **93-269-15-32;** and Ronda Universitat, 37, at the corner of Plaça de Catalunya, no phone). For last-minute shopping, there are FC Botiga outlets at terminals T1 and T2 at the airport and at the Sants train station.

The football club also has a shop in the **Arenas de Barcelona** (Gran Via, 373–385; www.arenasdebarcelona.com; ✆ **93-289-02-44;** metro: Plaça d'Espanya), originally Barcelona's bullring, built 1889 to 1900. Six floors of shops and a movie theater are augmented by an excellent food court. But if you're expecting to see any remains of the bullring other than a few exterior bricks, you'll be disappointed; thank British architect Richard Rogers for what's known as "façadism," which means that the original character of the building has completely disappeared.

Shoppers and window shoppers alike will probably find neighborhood streets more interesting. To see how the other half lives, check out the boutiques along **Passeig de Gracia,** Barcelona's most prestigious shopping promenade. For our (more limited) money, the streets of the Barri Gòtic and adjacent Born and La Ribera are more interesting to explore and the shops more fun and unpredictable. For an overview of regional handcrafts, check out **Artesania Catalunya** (Carrer dels Banys Nous, 11; ✆ **93-467-46-60;** metro: Liceu or Jaume I). Craft and fashion merge in the humble espadrille, made since the 1940s at **La Manual Alpargatera** (Carrer Avinyo, 7; www.lamanual.net; ✆ **93-301-01-72;** metro: Jaume I or Barceloneta); the shop claims that Salvador Dalí was an aficionado of its iconic shoes. Dalí Gaudí, and Picasso inspired jewelry designers at **BCN Art Design** (Carrer Argenteria, 76, metro: Jaume I; and Carrer Princesa, 24, metro: Jaume I; www.bcnartdesign.es; ✆ **93-268-13-08**). **Krappa** (Carrer Freneria, 1; www.krappa-bcn.com; ✆ **93-442-51-00;** metro: Jaume I) makes engravings based on historic woodcuts. Many maps, cards, bookplates, and larger prints here are colored by hand. You can buy from local designers ("del autor") in modestly priced shops along the Carrer d'Astúries in the Gràcia neighborhood; try **Jose Rivero** at number 43 (✆ **93-237-33-88**) for one-of-a-kind men's and women's clothing made of felt and other feel-good materials.

And if you can't find it anywhere else, try the sprawling department store **El Corte Ingles** on the Plaça de Catalunya. It also has the largest supermarket in the city center.

Street Markets

Hagglers will enjoy Barcelona's street markets. **El Encants** antiques market is held 9am to 8pm (some dealers leave earlier) on Monday, Wednesday, Friday, and Saturday in Plaça de les Glòries Catalanes (www.encantsbcn.com; metro: Glòries). A market has operated here since the 14th century, but in 2013 El Encants moved into a soaring new pavilion with a distinctive mirrored ceiling, and it's a prime destination for local bargain hunters. The flea market at the recently re-opened **Mercat Sant Antoni,** in a sprawling octagonal 1880s market house, is open Monday and Wednesday through Saturday from 10am to 8:30pm. The farmers' market inside is open Monday to Saturday from 8am to 8pm (www. mercatdesantantoni.com; metro: Sant Antoni).

One of the best weekly flea markets is held Sundays from 10am to 7pm in Raval on **Plaça Salvador Seguí,** where the real bargains can be found just before closing (metro: Paral.lel). Try also the Thursday (9am–8pm) market, more antiques than second-hand items, in **Plaça Nova** at the base of the Cathedral of Barcelona (metro: Jaume 1). There's a smaller flea market 10am to 7pm Saturday and Sunday near the **Mirador de Colom** (metro: Drassanes). **Plaça Reial** (metro: Liceu) is the site of a stamp and coin market 10am to 8pm on Sunday. **Plaça del Pi** (metro: Liceu) hosts an art fair (www.pintorspibarcelona.com) with dozens of artists on Saturday 11am to 8pm and Sunday 11am to 2pm, while contemporary artisans line **Carrer Argentería,** from Santa María del Pi to Via Laietana, on weekends 10am to 5pm. A useful website to track down the location of the roving flea markets is https://fleamarketbcn.com.

Food Shopping

La Boqueria (p. 427) and **Mercat Santa Caterina** (p. 436) are the best fresh food markets. These food extravaganzas are perfect for buying spices and other packaged goods to bring home, although every Barcelona neighborhood has its own market house. For great chocolate, visit **Cacao Sampaka** (Carrer Consell de Cent, 292; www.cacao sampaka.com; ✆ **92-272-08-33;** metro: Passeig de Gràcia), which was co-founded by Albert Adrià, brother of famed chef Ferran. If your taste runs more to nuts or the traditional *torron* (nougat made with honey and almonds), check out the ancient (since 1851) nut roaster **E & A Gispert** (Carrer dels Sombrerers, 23; www.casagispert. com; ✆ **93-319-75-75;** metro: Jaume I). For gourmet olive oils from around Spain, specialty dried beans, and canned fish and shellfish from Galicia, check the floor-to-ceiling shelves of upscale caterer **Colmado Quilez** (La Rambla de Catalunya, 63; www.lafuente.es; ✆ **93-215-23-56;** metro: Passeig de Gràcia).

Shopping for fresh produce in Mercat Santa Caterina.

The ornate interior of the Palau de la Música Catalana.

ENTERTAINMENT & NIGHTLIFE

Barcelona is as vibrant by night as it is by day. To get into the rhythm of the city, enjoy an early evening promenade along Les Rambles (watch your wallet), and a stop in a tapas bar or two, followed by a late dinner. If you don't want to dine in a nearly deserted restaurant—or among other tourists only—plan to arrive in your chosen restaurant sometime after 9pm. Most nights, that will probably be all the entertainment you need.

But Barcelona also has a rich cultural scene, and the landmark venues of **Palau de la Música Catalana** (p. 438) and **Gran Teatre del Liceu** (p. 428) come alive when performers take the stage. As the name suggests, the Palau de la Musica specializes in musical performances, which present no language barriers. Although the Liceu is known for its opera and theatrical productions, it also schedules an interesting mix of dance and music.

There are also several notable theater venues on Montjuïc, including **Teatre Grec** (Passeig de Santa Madrona, 36; www.bcn.cat/grec; ☎ 93-316-10-00; metro: Espanya), an atmospheric open-air amphitheater on the site of a former quarry; and **Mercat de Les Flors** (Carrer Lleida, 59; www.mercatflors; ☎ 93-426-18-75; metro: Espanya or Poble Sec), set in a building from the 1929 International Exposition, and known for championing innovative drama, dance, and music. These two venues, along with **Teatre Lliure** (Passeig Santa Madrona, 40–46; www.teatrelliure.com; ☎ 93-289-27-70; metro: Espanya), host Barcelona's acclaimed Grec Festival in July—an extravaganza of dance, theater, music, and even circus arts.

During the summer, one of the best places to enjoy jazz is on the rooftop of **La Pedrera** (p. 445). Otherwise, check out the schedule of jazz, blues, and world music at **Sala Jamboree** in the Barri Gòtic (Plaça Reial, 17; www.masimas.com/jamboree; ☎ 93-319-17-89; metro: Liceu), which features both up-and-coming and established artists. **Santa María del Pi** (p. 433) also has a summer concert series in the church's "Secret Garden."

A cluster of bars along Calle Ample in the Gothic Quarter is popular with the college crowd. The somewhat old-fashioned **Poble Espanyol**

(p. 454) has a surprising number of popular spots, including the open-air disco **La Terrazza** (www.laterrazza.com; ✆ **93-272-49-80**), with its great city views, and **The One** (www.poble-espanyol.com/en/night), a trendy club. **Razzmatazz,** the most happening club in Poblenou, attracts an international crowd of late-night revelers (www.salarazzmatazz.com).

Big-name pop performers book the massive sports stadium atop Montjuïc, **Palau Sant Jordi,** and a bit of advance planning might turn up a couple of available seats there (www.palausantjordi.cat). There's also a summer concert series in the pleasant garden venue of the **Palacio Real de Pedralbes** where everybody from Sting to Tom Jones has been known to show up recently (www.festivalpedralbes.com).

Barcelona is not in the forefront of the flamenco revival, but several venues present colorful and enjoyable performances with dancers, singers, and musicians. **Flamenco Tablao Cordobes** (Les Rambles, 35; www.tablaocordobes.com; ✆ **93-317-57-11;** 42€; metro: Liceu) occupies a lovely Moorish-style performance space with tilework and arched ceilings. **Flamenco Tablao Patio Andaluz** (Carrer Aribau, 242; www.jesuscortes.net; ✆ **93-209-35-24;** 33€; metro: Gràcia) features dancer Jesús Cortés, a member of an accomplished family of flamenco artists. At Poble Espanyol, **El Tablao de Carmen** (www.tablaodecarmen.com; ✆ **93-325-68-95;** 39€) is named for the Barcelona-born dance legend Carmen Amaya. Note that prices quoted here are for the performance and one drink. Most clubs offer dinner as well, but you are better off eating elsewhere.

You can get a deep dose of Gothic atmosphere during the Flamenco show (and sometimes jazz) on Carrer Montcada, at Palau Dalmases across the street from the Picasso Museum, where you will be enveloped in medieval charm and candlelight while enjoying the performance (www.palaudalmases.com; ✆ **93-310-06-73**).

Wherever you begin, end your evening with a glass of cava, as Catalunya's sparkling wine is called, at one of the city's classic *xampanyerias* like **El Xampanyet** (p. 482) or **Xampú Xampany** (p. 485).

DAY TRIPS FROM BARCELONA

You don't need to pack a suitcase for these day trips into the countryside around Barcelona. And the two destinations could not be more different. The monastery at **Montserrat** is one of the most important religious pilgrimage sites in Spain. **Sant Sadurní d'Anoia** is for oenophiles; more than 40 winemakers in the village open their cellars for tastings of cava, the Catalan sparkling wine.

Montserrat ★★

Thousands flock to this mountainside monastery each year to see and touch the medieval statue of **La Moreneta** (the Black Virgin). Many newly married Catalan couples come here for her blessing on their honeymoon, and many name their daughters "Montserrat" ("Montse" for short).

If you want to meet Catalans, visit on Sunday, especially when the weather is nice; for smaller crowds, visit on a weekday. The winds blow cold on the mountain, even during summer, so bring a sweater or jacket.

ESSENTIALS

GETTING THERE The best way to get to Montserrat is via the Catalunyan railway, **Ferrocarrils de la Generalitat de Catalunya** (FGC; R5-Manresa; www.fgc.es; ✆ **93-237-71-56**), with 12 trains a day leaving from the Plaça d'Espanya in Barcelona. The R5 line connects with an aerial cableway **(Aeri de Montserrat),** which is included in the fare of 35.30€ round-trip. An excellent alternative to the Aeri (especially when windy weather grounds the cable car) is the **Cremallera de Montserrat,** a 15-minute funicular ride from the village below the mountain. You get off the train one stop sooner at Olesa de Montserrat, and transfer to the funicular. The fare is also 35.30€ round-trip. Either combination ticket can be purchased at any FGC train station. Alternatively, a Tot Montserrat package, which includes the train and choice of cable car or funicular, admission to the museum and the new interactive audiovisual gallery, and a self-service lunch is sold online (http://barcelonaturisme.cat) and in the brick-and-mortar stores of **Turisme de Barcelona** (p. 415) for 53.85€.

VISITOR INFORMATION The **tourist office,** Plaça de la Creu (www.montserratvisita.com; ✆ **93-877-77-77**), is open daily from 10am to 5:45pm.

EXPLORING MONTSERRAT

You can see Montserrat's jagged peaks from all over eastern Catalunya; the almost otherworldly serrated ridgeline is a symbol of Catalan identity. As a buffer state between Christian France and often Islamic Spain, medieval Catalunya espoused a fierce and intense Christian faith that reached its apogee in the cult of the **Virgin of Montserrat,** one of the legendary "dark" virgins of Iberian Catholicism. A polychrome carving of the Virgin and Child (in Catalan, Maria del Deu) was discovered in a grotto on the mountainside in the 12th century, and many miracles have been ascribed to the figure.

The **Basilica de Montserrat** and a Benedictine monastery have grown up on the site. Most believers are less interested in the glories of the basilica than in getting close to the statue. To view **La Moreneta,** enter the church through a side door to the right. The meter-high carving is mounted in a silver altar in a chapel high above the main altar. You will be in a long line of people who parade past the statue, which is mostly encased in bulletproof acrylic to protect it from vandalism. The casing has a cutout that lets the faithful kiss her extended hand. If you are around at 1pm daily, you can hear the **Escolanía,** a renowned boys' choir established in the 13th century, singing "Salve Regina" and the "Virolai" (hymn of Montserrat). The basilica is open daily from 8 to 10:30am and noon to 6:30pm. Admission is free.

The sculpture "Eight Stairs to Heaven" in Montserrat alludes to this holy site's spectacular mountaintop setting.

At Plaça de Santa María, you can also visit the **Museu de Montserrat** (www.museudemontserrat.com; © **93-877-77-77**), a repository of art donated by the faithful over the years. Many of the works are religious subjects, some by major artists like Caravaggio and El Greco, but others are purely secular pieces, including an early Picasso ("El Viejo Pescador" from 1895) and some lovely Impressionist works by Monet, Sisley, and Degas. The museum is open daily 10am to 5:45pm, or 10am to 6:45 weekends, feast days, and in summer; admission costs 7€ adults, 6€ seniors and students, 4€ ages 8 to 16.

You can also make an excursion to **Santa Cova (Holy Grotto),** the purported site of the discovery of La Moreneta. The natural grotto was reworked in the 17th century, and a small church in the shape of a cross was built here. You go halfway by funicular but must complete the trip on foot. In 2013, the monastery and the Catalunya government transformed the church into a gallery with a permanent exhibition of religious art. The grotto is open daily 10am to 1pm and 4 to 7pm. Round-trip fare is 4€.

If waiting in line to see holy relics isn't your thing, you might just enjoy a day of hiking in the spectacular scenery that surrounds this special site while your family shops the Disney-like souvenir shops of Montserrat.

Sant Sadurní d'Anoia ★

Plenty of terrific wine is made in the countryside around Barcelona, but only Sant Sadurní d'Anoia is easily visited on public transportation—a must if you're planning to taste a number of the sparkling wines (cava) for which the village is famous.

ESSENTIALS

GETTING THERE   The easiest way to get to Sant Sadurní is to take an R4 train from Plaça de Catalunya or Barcelona-Sants station in the direction of Sant Vicenç de Calders. Trains run about every half-hour from 5:30am until 11:15pm, and the journey takes 45 to 50 minutes. The fare is 4.20€ each way.

VISITOR INFORMATION   The tourist office at Carrer del Hosital, 26 (www.turismesantsadurni.cat; ✆ **93-891-31-88**), is open Tuesday through Sunday 10am to 2pm.

EXPLORING SANT SADURNÍ D'ANOIA

Thick-walled 19th-century cava cellars fill the town, but you should make your first stop the new **Centre d'Interpretació del Cava** ★ (Carrer de l'Hospital, 23; www.turismesantsadurni.cat; ✆ **93-891-31-88**). Located inside an old distillery, it mixes old-fashioned and high-tech exhibits to introduce visitors to the history of cava, the grapes used to make it, and the entire production process. You can even hold a (dead) phylloxera louse, just to drive home the history of cava. (When phylloxera struck the vineyards of champagne, the makers there desperately sought new territory, thus giving birth to the Catalan cava industry.) The center charges 6€.

Staff at the tourist office inside the center (admission free) can help you plan your excursion in Sant Sadurní, including making calls to cava operations that require reservations. Cellars that are open for visits and tastes (usually for a token fee or no charge) are listed on the interpretation center's website. Sometimes a paper printout is available, but don't count on it. Some small cellars make a few hundred cases of cava; some are bigger—much bigger. Note that many cellars close on Friday and Saturday afternoons and all day Sunday. Just walking around the village and stopping at some of the tiny operations with open doors by their loading docks can be a lot of fun. Two of the larger producers that put the town on the map offer excellent overviews of the traditional champagne process.

At the edge of town, the massive **Freixenet** ★★ (Carrer Joan Sala, 2; www.freixenet.es; ✆ **93-891-70-96**) pioneered U.S. distribution of cava as a less expensive alternative to champagne. Since the winery gets large groups, much of the tour is via video and includes a heavy dose of marketing, complemented by a quick trip into the deep cellars to see aging bottles and—finally—a tasting. The entire tour takes about 90 minutes and should be reserved in advance. The basic tour costs 15€ for adults, 10€ for ages 9 to 17, and is free for ages 8 and younger. Tours are offered Monday through Saturday 9:30am to 4pm and Sunday 10am to 1pm. Reserve tours by phone, or on their website.

The other giant of Sant Sadurní cava production, **Codorníu** ★★ (Avinguda Jaume Codorníu, s/n; www.codorniu.es; ✆ **93-891-33-42**) is worth visiting to see the so-called "Cathedral of Cava," the winemaking and storage facility built 1895 to 1915 and designed by Modernista architect Josep Puig i Cadalfach. If you know Codorníu from its entry-level cava, the tasting will open your eyes (and palate) to some extraordinary high-end selections. Several options are offered, from a standard tour and tasting to extended tastings or even a tapas lunch. The basic tour starts at 16€; times vary; book ahead. A variety of other tours, including one focusing on architecture, are available. Reserve by phone or e-mail at reserves@codorniu.es.

Vilafranca del Penedés, which is the center of *cava* country, also has a wine center in its old town, **Vinseum** on Plaça Jaume I, 5 (www.vinseum.cat; ℭ **93-890-05-82**). Summer hours are daily 10am to 7pm; the rest of the year it's open 10am to 2pm and 4 to 7pm (closed Mon). Admission is 7€ adults, seniors and students 4€; it includes a wine tasting.

For a more personal experience, if you have a car and an extra day to explore wine country, there are other charming wineries to visit that excel in organic wines. In Sant Pau d'Ordal the lovely winery **Albet i Noya** (www.albetinoya.cat; ℭ **93–899-48-12**) is open Monday to Friday 9am to 1:30pm and 3 to 6pm, weekends and holidays 10am to 2:30pm. Book a tour of their cellars and grounds for 13€.

Or try or the organic ("bio-dynamic") vineyard of **Parés Balta** in Pacs del Penedés (www.paresbalta.com; ℭ **93-890-13-99**) for their variety of cavas and still wine. You can book a delicious wine pairing here. It's open daily, except for some bank holidays, from 9:30am to 6:30pm. A basic tour costs 15€ and includes four wine tastings. For a special wine country experience, consider their special 4×4 tour that goes through their *terroir* and lasts 4 hours, including a sommelier tasting for 66€ or a gourmet tasting for 77€.

A larger and more established winery that is more about still wines (also they do produce cava) is the **Familia Torres** just outside Vilafranca, where you can book a winery tour, or enjoy delicious pairings of wine and food. Reserve on line at www.torres.es or call ℭ **93-817-74-00.** Tours cost 12€ and include a tasting of two wines.

If you're making a long day of it, put one of these two special restaurants on your itinerary. It's not pretty, but the local food is first-rate at **Cal Xim** in Sant Pau d'Ordal (Plaça Subirats, 4; ℭ **93-899-30-92**). You will have a view of the vineyards at the elegant dining room of **Cava and Hotel Mastinell** restaurant (www.hotelmastinell.com; ℭ **93-115-6-1-32**), located near the town of Vilafranca del Penedés inside a bizarre structure built to resemble a wine rack. Its 22€ prix-fixe lunch Tuesday to Friday is a good deal; from Tuesday through Thursday, dinners are the same price, which includes all the wine you can drink. Bon profit!

COSTA DAURADA

By Jennifer Ceaser

efore there was Barcelona, there was Tarragona, which was the Roman capital of the east end of the Iberian Peninsula for more than 700 years. It still boasts some of Spain's most extensive Roman ruins. They have been respectfully assimilated into the modern city, creating a sense of timelessness that, in its own provincial way, rivals eternal Rome. Closer to Barcelona, the beach resort of Sitges has grown up into a genuine city that offers art and culture to round out your stay when you've had enough sea, sand, and sun. If you seek more of the shore experience, head south of Tarragona to the long crescents of golden sand—each with a small village—that punctuate the Golden Coast (Costa Daurada) en route to the great fan delta of the Ríu Ebre.

TARRAGONA ★★★

For sheer historic sites, the Roman port city of **Tarragona** is one of the grandest, yet most overlooked cities in Spain. A natural fortress, the city perches on a rocky bluff 82m (269 ft.) above its deep and sheltered harbor. Although the Romans landed farther north at Empúries in 218 B.C. to savage the Carthaginians during the Second Punic War, they made their military and administrative headquarters at Tarraco, now Tarragona. At its Roman apogee, Tarraco boasted a population of nearly 1 million people and launched the legions on the conquest of the peninsula, bringing the western reaches of Europe under Roman control.

The most famous of the Roman roads in Iberia, the Via Augusta, connected Rome to Tarraco, and pieces of it remain in the plazas of the city. Tarragona's extensive Roman ruins were declared a UNESCO World Heritage Site in 2000, although not all the architectural elements remain where the Romans placed them. Just as the Catalans absorbed Roman culture, they also appropriated the Roman architecture, mining the monuments for building blocks that appear in the medieval city that clusters around the cathedral.

Essentials

ARRIVING There are trains from Barcelona-Sants station to Tarragona about every 15 minutes. Tarragona has two train stations. The one called Tarragona, conveniently located in the city center, is mainly serviced by slower regional trains. Camp de Tarragona, a modern station about 10km outside the city, has high-speed Avant, AVE, and Alvia services. Trains take from 31 minutes to 1¼ hours and cost 6.35€ to 54.20€. AVANT trains have the best combination of speed and value; 35 minutes for 17.30€. In Tarragona, you'll find RENFE offices in the train stations, in the city center at Plaza Pedrera, s/n (www.renfe.com; ☏ **90-232-03-20**), and at Camp de Tarragona (Mas L'Hereuet, s/n). There are also about 10 **buses** per day from Barcelona to Tarragona (trip time: 1½ hr.), but the bus is slower, less convenient, and often more expensive than the train. Call ☏ **90-242-22-42** for more information. To drive, take the A-2 south-

Ruins of the ancient Roman highway, the Via Augusta, in Tarragona.

west from Barcelona to the A-7, and then take the N-340. It is a fast and costly toll road, with one-way tolls of 7.35€.

VISITOR INFORMATION The main **tourist office** is at Calle Major, 39 (www.tarragonaturisme.cat; ☏ **97-725-07-95**). From July through September, it's open Monday through Saturday 10am to 8pm, Sunday 10am to 2pm; the rest of the year it's open Monday to Friday 10am to 2pm and 3 to 6pm, Saturday 10am to 2pm and 3 to 7pm, and Sunday 10am to 2pm.

Exploring Tarragona

Central Tarragona consists of a new city organized around the broad avenues of Les Rambles on fairly flat terrain, and a partially walled old city that huddles around the cathedral on high rocky ground. Traces of Roman Tarroco are found in both the old and new cities, as are a few gems of Modernisme architecture and design. In the new city, the **Balcó del Mediterráni (Balcony of the Mediterranean)** seaside belvedere connects the old and new Rambles. Be sure to stroll the main artery, **Rambla Nova,** a fashionable, wide, tree-lined boulevard. Running parallel with Rambla Nova to the east, the **Rambla Vella** marks the beginning of the old town; it was once part of the Roman Via Augusta. Just off Rambla Vella, the **Plaça de La Font** functions as the go-between from old to new cities. It has a lively cafe scene as well as the offices of city government.

Catedral ★ CHURCH Begun in the mid–12th century and finally consecrated in 1331, the cathedral spans the transition from Romanesque to

Gothic architecture. Standing at the highest point of the city, it has a fortresslike quality. The immense rose window of the main facade is balanced by the Gothic upper tier of the octagonal bell tower, where windows flood the interior with light. The most striking work of art in the church is the altarpiece dedicated to Santa Tecla, patron of Tarragona, carved by Père Joan in 1430. Two flamboyant Gothic doors open into the east end of the church, where you'll find the **Museu Diocesà,** with a collection of Catalan religious art.

Plaça de la Seu. ✆ **97-722-69-35.** Cathedral and museum 5€. Mid-June to mid-Sept Mon–Sat 10am–8pm, Sun 3–8pm; mid-Mar to mid-June and mid-Sept to Oct Mon–Sat 10am–7pm; Nov to mid-Mar Mon–Fri 10am–5pm, Sat 10am–7pm. Bus: 1.

Tarragona's cathedral features an immense rose

Museu d'Art Modern de Tarragona ★ MUSEUM

"Modern" at this museum is more a statement of era than style, as the paintings ignore all the avant-garde movements of the 20th century. It was founded by the donation of several sculptures by Julio Antonio that had been in his family's possession. Additional bequests have expanded the collection, which includes many more Catalan artists, especially the painter Josep Sancho i Piqué and sculptors Santiago Costa i Vaqué and Salvador Martorell i Ollé. Along the way, curators also acquired an extensive collection of late-20th-century Catalan photography.

Carrer Santa Anna, 8. www.dipta.cat/mamt. ⓒ **97-723-50-32.** Free admission. Tues–Fri 10am–8pm; Sat 10am–3pm and 5–8pm; Sun 11am–2pm.

Museu Nacional Arqueològic de Tarragona ★★ MUSEUM

Catalunya's oldest archaeology museum was established in the first half of the 19th century and continued to add to its collection as urban expansion and building projects unearthed more evidence of the city's early history. Currently the museum is under renovation, but highlights of the collection have been moved to a temporary building, a former passenger terminal on the port. Head here to get an overview of Tarragona's Roman era before you explore the ancient sites that still dot the city. The museum's displays of household objects such as jewelry, cups and plates, cooking utensils, and children's toys bring a human touch to history. They are balanced by works of great artistry, such as a carved head of Medusa, and intricate mosaic murals of peacocks and marine life.

Tinglado 4, Moll de Costa. www.mnat.cat. © **97-723-62-09.** Admission 4.50€. June–Sept Tues–Sat 9:30am–8:30pm, Sun 10am–2pm; Oct–May Tues–Sat 9:30am–6pm, Sun 10am–2pm. Bus: 22.

EXPLORING ROMAN TARRAGONA

Since the Roman ruins are distributed throughout the city, we have drawn them together here for travelers who want to immerse themselves in the remains of Tarraco. Apart from the sections of the Roman aqueduct still standing on the northern fringe of the city proper, most of the Roman ruins are grouped together under the umbrella of the **Museu d'Història de Tarragona** (**Tarragona History Museum;** Calle Cavallers, 14; www.tarragona.cat/patrimoni/museu-historia; © **97-724-22-20**). The museum itself is distributed among a few historic houses owned by the city (included in the combined admission pass), but visitors will find the Roman sites themselves of greater interest. To see the best Roman artifacts, visit the Museu Nacional Arqueològic de Tarragona (above).

Single site admissions to the Roman monuments are 3.30€ adults, 1.70€ seniors and students, free ages 16 and younger. Combined admission to all the museum's sites costs 11€ adults, 5.50€ seniors and students; you can buy this pass at any of the sites. From April to September, they're open Tuesday to Saturday 9am to 9pm, Sunday and holidays 9am to 3pm (June–Aug also open Mon 9am–3pm). From October to March, the hours are Tuesday to Friday 9am to 7:30pm, Saturday 9am to 7pm, Sunday and holidays 9am to 3pm. Closed December 25 and 26, January 1, and January 6. All sites can be reached by city bus 2 (1.50€).

modernisme AMID THE ROMANS

Just as Tarraco was a provincial reflection of the glories of Rome, modern Tarragona can boast some glimmers of the Modernista masterpieces of Barcelona. When you're making your promenade on Rambla Nova in the new city, stop in to see the Modernista interior of the **Teatre Metropol** (Rambla Nova, 46; © **97-724-47-95**), built in 1908 and still used for live theater, dance, and concerts. At the edge of the old city, **L'Església de Sant Francesc** (Rambla Vella, 28) has a striking Modernista chapel well worth the time to visit (Mon–Sat 11am–1pm and 5–8pm; free admission). If you're continuing uphill to the old city through Plaça de la Font, pop into the **Ayuntament** (City Hall) to see the Modernista ship-shaped tomb of Jaume I of Aragón (1208–76), the conqueror who brought together the political fates of Aragón and Catalunya and stands today as a rallying symbol for Catalan autonomy, if not outright independence from Spain. The Ayuntament is open Monday through Friday 9am to 9pm, Saturday and Sunday 10am to 2pm; admission is free.

The ancient Amfiteatre Romà has a commanding site overlooking the Mediterranean.

Amfiteatre Romà ★★★ ANCIENT SITE   This A.D. 2nd-century theater was carved from the cliff that rises above the crashing ocean. Contrasted against the vast spread of seaside sky and the abrupt and rugged cliff, the amphitheater must have been one of the most dramatic in the ancient world. Even in ruins, it's a sight you won't soon forget. In its day, up to 14,000 spectators would gather here for bloody gladiator battles, other games, and executions. The tiered seats that they sat upon are the same ones you'll see today. Beautiful as the site is, a monument reminds us that "Many innocent lives were taken in this amphitheater."
Parc del Milagro. ⓒ **97-724-25-79.**

Passeig Arqueològic ★★ ANCIENT SITE   When the Romans decided to enclose their city of Tarraco in the A.D. 2nd century, they built their walls on top of huge boulders. About a third of the original 3,500m construction still stands, and you can follow a gardenlike path for about 0.8km (½ mile) of that length. Historic markers show the way; there are also opportunities to climb up onto the ramparts for views of the sea and country. History is layered here: You'll also find cannon placed in battlements by the Spanish in the early 18th century.
Av. Catalunya, s/n. ⓒ **97-724-57-96.**

Pretorì i Circ Romà ★★ ANCIENT SITE   In the A.D. 1st century, the Romans selected a hillside location to build this three-level complex, with each floor dedicated to a different activity: worship (the top level), government (the middle level), and the circus (the lower level). The well-preserved circus, with a capacity of 30,000 spectators, is the most visited and evocative part of the site. It was used for horse and chariot races, and it's still possible to imagine the winners exiting through the grand, arched Porta Triumphalis.

Plaça del Rei, s/n. ✆ **97-722-17-36.**

Where to Stay in Tarragona

AC Hotel by Marriott ★★   Squarely aimed at business travelers, this contemporary hotel is a bit of a walk from major sites but close to the strollable Rambla Nova and the bus station. Rooms are pleasant and clean, if somewhat corporate in feel, with parquet floors, comfortable beds, and a desk. Triple rooms offer a small seating area. The back of the hotel overlooks a park; the front is along a busy street, though soundproofed windows block out most of the traffic noise. There's a nicely equipped top-floor gym and a sprawling solarium.

Av. de Roma, 8. www.marriott.com. ✆ **97-724-71-05.** 115 units. 71€–90€. Parking 13€. **Amenities:** Restaurant; room service; gym; free Wi-Fi.

Hotel Lauria ★   Guests here enjoy a large outdoor pool and close proximity to the Balcony of the Mediterranean promenade. In fact, the hotel is well-situated for sightseeing in general. The rooms range from small to medium and have comfortable, but spare, modern furnishings brightened with bold pops of color. For an ocean view, ask for a room at the back.

Rambla Nova, 20. www.hotel-lauria.com. ✆ **97-723-67-12.** 72 units. 50€–80€ double. Public parking nearby 12.50–13.50€. **Amenities:** Bar; outdoor pool; room service; gym; pet-friendly; free Wi-Fi.

Hotel Plaça de la Font ★   Photo murals behind the beds bring images of Tarragona's stately architecture and rocky coast into the small guest rooms. But if you like to turn in early, take note that the hotel sits on a lively old city plaza and you may find you can't escape the cafe noise at night. Many consider it a minor inconvenience for the charming and convenient location and the good price for simple, modern rooms.

Plaça de la Font, 26. www.hotelpdelafont.com. ✆ **97-724-61-34.** 20 units. 58€–78€. **Amenities:** Bar; restaurant; free Wi-Fi.

Hotel SB Ciutat de Tarragona ★★★   Set right on the main city park (a good spot for joggers), this sleekly modern hostelry offers downtown Tarragona's fanciest digs. It's convenient for sightseeing; everything (except the beaches) is within close walking distance. The rooftop deck around the pool is especially popular for families, as are the special family rooms with extra beds and a layout designed to give both parents and kids a little privacy. Triple and quad rooms are also available for adults traveling together. Free parking is provided if booked through the hotel website.

Plaça Imperial Tarraco, 5. www.hotelciutatdetarragona.com. ✆ **97-725-09-99.** 58 units. 65€–141€ double; from 92€ junior suite. **Amenities:** Restaurant; bar; café; gym; outdoor pool (seasonal); room service; sauna; pet-friendly; free Wi-Fi.

Where to Eat in Tarragona

Cooking in Tarragona is rather Janus-like, looking out to the sea for all the bounty of the Mediterranean and glancing over its shoulder to the mountainous country that begins a short distance from the coast. As a result, its menus are always brimming with both coastal fish like sea bream and bass, and deep-water predators like yellowfin tuna. At the same time, the local lamb and kid are as good as any in Spain, from herds that feed on the rosemary scrub of nearby hillsides.

Barquet ★★ CATALAN/SEAFOOD   One of Tarragona's most established seafood restaurants (since 1950), Barquet's nautically themed dining rooms may look a bit old-fashioned, but the food is fresh, and the kitchen really knows how to cook and present both fish and shellfish. Look for the local specialty of fried fish with toasted noodles called *fideos rossejat*. Local oysters are available on the half-shell as well as roasted, and the garlicky steamed mussels are the equal of any on the coast. One of the best bets is often the grilled catch of the day (usually sea bream or bass); diners who don't care for fish have a few grilled options of veal and chicken. The house selections of D.O. Terra Alta wines are good, economical complements to most dishes. Once one of Tarragona's more expensive options, Barquet has introduced several less expensive set menus.

Carrer Gasometro, 16. www.restaurantbarquet.com. ✆ **97-724-00-23.** Reservations recommended. Entrees 20€–30€; set menus from 25€, tasting menus 27€–43€. Mon–Fri 12:30–3:30pm; Sat 1–3:30pm; Tues–Sat 8:30–10:30pm. Closed Jan 1–7 and Aug 15–Sept 15.

El Llagut Taverna Marinera ★★ CATALAN/SEAFOOD   El Llagut considers itself a Slow Food restaurant, and does indeed use local meat, fish, fruits, and vegetables. But it is blessedly free of foodie pretensions. The rough stone walls and checked tablecloths give diners the message that they can relax and enjoy their meal, and staff take the time to fully explain unfamiliar dishes. Rice dishes with seafood are the sure winners here. Some are a veritable encyclopedia of the local catch, while the *arròs negre* focuses on just one species, gaining its flavor and color from the squid and squid ink.

Carrer Natzaret, 10. elllagut.com. ✆ **97-722-89-38.** Entrees 11€–20€, Slow Food menu 21€–24€.; Tues–Sat 1–4pm and 8:30pm–midnight; Sun–Mon 1–4pm. Closed mid-Dec to Jan 31.

The main segment of the Costa Daurada consists of the sandy beach towns southwest of Tarragona, stretching from Salou, just outside Tarragona, roughly 60km (37 miles) to the old Roman port of L'Ampolla.

Salou is the largest beach town of the Costa Daurada, but the community has managed to hold onto the elegance of its main beach. Local legend has it that the Passeig de les Palmeres, a broad promenade lined with towering palms, was modeled on the promenade in Nice. An impressive sculpture celebrates the departure of Jaume I from Salou in 1229 to recapture Mallorca. Modernista villas lining the promenade attest to Salou's long-standing wealth and good taste. The counterpoint to that graciousness is the **Port Aventura** theme park (www. portaventuraworld.com/en; ☏ **08-082-343-399;** admission 48€, ages 4–10 and seniors 40€), located outside of town. Polynesia, Aztec Mexico, China, and Wild West areas have their own thrill rides and dance spectacles, and its Costa Caribe Aquatic Park offers dozens of water adventures. It's open mid–March through January 6.

Just south of Salou is the salty village of **Cambrils,** where beachgoers and commercial fishermen share the strand, and tourists gather to watch the boats unload their catch around 4pm.

The easiest (and least expensive way) to get on the water here is to take the **catamaran shuttle service** between Salou and Cambrils (12€ round-trip). It is operated by **Creuers Costa Daurada** (Avinguda Diputació, 15;

www.creuerscostadaurada.com; ☏ **97-736-30-90**); other cruises costs 30€–59€).

To get up into the hills above Cambrils, hike up the easy **Miró in Montroig del Camp trail** from Pixerota beach for 8km (5 miles) to the hilltop chapel of La Mare de Déu de la Roca. As a young man, Joan Miró spent summers in these hills above Cambrils, and there are 10 benches along the trail marking spots where he painted various pictures.

At L'Ampolla, the coast changes character from golden sands to the broad, flat, and stunningly beautiful delta of the Riú Ebre (known elsewhere in Spain as the Río Ebro). Land and water are so interspersed here that it is hard to tell where one ends and the other begins. The delta is a major rice-growing region and an important habitat for water birds. So many thousands of flamingos breed here that they cease to seem like a novelty. Much of the delta lies within the **Parque Natural del Delta de l'Ebre.** Its **Ecomuseu del Parque Natural** (Carrer Doctor Martí Buera, 22; parcsnaturals. gencat.cat/en; ☏ **97-748-96-79;** admission by donation; Tues–Sat 10am–1pm and 3–5pm, Sun 10am–1pm) has exhibits explaining the park's human and natural features. The information desk can also advise on boat trips, bicycle rentals, and birding guides.

Braseria Taula Rodona ★★ CATALAN   This casual restaurant offers good value and a warm tavern ambience dominated by the towering chimney. Tarragona may be a city on the sea, but this establishment showcases excellent steak, veal, pork, lamb, and kid from the nearby mountains. Everything is grilled over an open wood fire, and the place is inevitably packed with local students, courting couples, and even entire large families.

Carrer La Nau, 4. braseriataularodona.eatbu.com. ☏ **97-789-65-06.** Entrees 12€–20€. Tues–Sun noon–4pm and 8–11pm.

Les Coques ★★ CATALAN   If you are looking for a meal with a sense of occasion, Les Coques is a good choice. The restaurant is set within thick stone walls and features arched entrances and wood-beamed ceilings. As befits the setting, some dishes, such as the veal with foie gras, can be on the pricier side. But you can enjoy the setting and fine service just as well if you stick with the less expensive and more homey dishes such as baked sea bass or duck confit in port-wine sauce.

Carrer San Llorenç, 15. www.les-coques.com. ✆ **97-722-83-00.** Entrees 12€–24€. Set lunch menu 18€. Mon–Sat 1–3pm and 9–11pm.

Les Voltes ★★ CATALAN   Thick plate glass and stainless surfaces harmonize surprisingly well with the ancient stone to create a very upscale look for this modern restaurant in the vaults of the Roman circus. It's a bit of a circus itself, as it seats 250 people and is popular with tour groups as well as individual travelers. Despite an almost all-tourist clientele, Les Voltes has very good prices for expertly grilled and roasted meats, including lamb shoulder and a spicy casserole of pork trotters. It also offers an excellent black rice with squid (12€, minimum of two people per order) and a number of Tarragona fish dishes, including baked sea bass with potatoes.

Carrer Trinquet Vell, 12. www.restaurantlesvoltes.cat. ✆ **97-723-06-51.** Entrees 10€–20€. Tues–Sat 1–3:30pm and 8:30–11:30pm; Sun 1–3:30pm (July–Aug closed Sun). Closed last 2 weeks July.

Side Trip to Poblet

If you rent a car, you can make a 30- to 45-minute drive through picturesque mountain passes to one of Catalunya's most evocative and atmospheric monasteries. As a side benefit, it's smack-dab in the middle of an up-and-coming wine-growing district. **Monestir de Poblet** ★★ (Plaça Corona d'Aragó 11, Poblet; www.poblet.cat; ✆ **97-787-00-89**) is a UNESCO World Heritage Site. Its most striking feature is the pantheon of the old kings of Aragón—a catacomb of royal tombs. Constructed in the 12th and 13th centuries and still in use, Poblet's immense basilica reflects both Romanesque and Gothic architectural styles. Re-established in 1940 as a Cistercian monastery after remaining vacant since 1835, Poblet is one of the largest Cistercian communities in Europe. The monks pass their days writing, studying, working a printing press, farming, and helping restore the building, which suffered heavy damage during the 1835 revolution.

The monastery is also surrounded by vast stretches of Pinot Noir grapes, originally introduced by Cistercian monks from Burgundy. The monastery's winery has been rebuilt by the Cordoniú group and is open for free tours and sales. It belongs within the D.O. Conca de Barberà wine region but is one of the few properties making reds from Pinot Noir rather than Garnatxa (Grenache) or Ull de Llebre (a local clone of Tempranillo).

The graceful cloister of Poblet's Cistercian monastery, a UNESCO World Heritage site.

Admission to the monastery costs 8.50€ adults, 5.50€ seniors and students. It's open Monday to Saturday 10am to 12:30pm and 3 to 5:55pm (closes 5:25pm in winter), Sundays 10am to 12:25pm and 3 to 5:25pm. Guided tours are mostly in Spanish with occasional English translations.

SITGES ★★

Sitges is one of the most popular vacation resorts in southern Europe. Long a beach escape for Barcelonans, it became a resort town in the late 19th century as artists, authors, and industrialists transformed fishermen's houses into summer villas. The Modernisme movement took hold in Sitges by the late 1870s, and the town remained the scene of artistic foment long after the movement waned, attracting such giants as Salvador Dalí and poet Federico García Lorca. The bohemian exuberance and intellectual and artistic ferment came to an abrupt halt with the Spanish Civil War. Although other artists and writers arrived in the decades after World War II, none had the fame or the impact of those who had gone before.

The beach is as dramatic ever, making Sitges the brightest light on Catalunya's Costa Daurada. It becomes especially crowded in the summer with affluent and young northern Europeans, many of them gay, and there's a lively art and gallery scene, mostly featuring bright, loosely representational but expressive painting. Sitges is also famous for its raucous celebration of Carnestoltes, or Carnival, in the days leading up to Lent.

Essentials

ARRIVING There are commuter rail *(cercanías)* **trains** to Sitges every 15 to 30 minutes between 6am and midnight from Barcelona-Sants station. Travel time is about 30 minutes, and the fare is 4.10€. In Barcelona, call ✆ **90-232-03-20** or visit www.renfe.com for details on schedules. Sitges is a 45-minute drive from Barcelona along the C-246, a coastal road. The express highway A-7 is less scenic but faster on weekends when the free coastal road is clogged with traffic.

The 17th-century Església de Sant Bartomeu i Santa Tecla overlooks Sitges harbor.

VISITOR INFORMATION The **tourist office** is at Plaza Eduard Maristany, 2 (www.sitgestur.cat; ✆ **93-894-42-51**). Summer hours (mid-June to mid-Oct) are Monday to Saturday 10am to 2pm and 4 to 8pm. Sunday 10am to 2pm. The rest of the year, it's open Monday to Friday 10am to 2pm and 4 to 6:30pm, Saturday 10am to 2pm and 4 to 7pm, and Sunday 10am to 2pm.

Exploring Sitges

Sitges was once a fortified medieval town on the hillside above the beach, and bits and pieces of that fortress persist. The modest former castle, for example, is now the seat of the town government. The oceanfront **Passeig de la Ribera** is much more emblematic of modern Sitges. A favorite spot to promenade in the early evening, it is defined by two landmarks of different eras and sensibilities. A sign on **Chiringuito ★** (Paseo de la Ribera, 31; ✆ **98-894-75-96**), a beachside restaurant/bar founded in 1913, identifies it as the probable source of the name now used by all similar casual spots along the Spanish coast. At the east end of the promenade, booming surf soaks the stone steps leading to Plaça del Baluart, where the 17th-century baroque **Església de Sant Bartomeu i Santa Tecla ★** overlooks the harbor. So does a single cannon, the last of six that drove off English warships in 1797. Behind the landmark church are the Museu Cau Ferrat and the Museu Maricel (p. 510).

Most people come here to hit the beach, which comes equipped with showers, bathing cabins, and stalls; kiosks rent motorboats and water-sports equipment. Beaches on the eastern end and inside the town center, such as **Aiguadoiç** and **Els Balomins,** are the most peaceful. **Playa San Sebastián, Fragata Beach,** and the **"Beach of the Boats"** (below the church and next to the yacht club) are the area's family beaches. A some-what hipper, more youthful crowd congregates at **Playa de la Ribera** to the west.

All along the coast, women can and certainly do go topless. Farther west at the most solitary beaches, the attire grows even skimpier, especially along the **Playas del Muerto,** where two tiny nude beaches lie between Sitges and Vilanova i la Geltrú. The first beach draws nudists of all sexual orientations, while the second is principally if not exclusively gay.

Fundació Stämpfli-Art Contemporani ★ MUSEUM   This organi-zation brings the artistic reputation of Sitges up to date—the oldest works are from the 1960s—and injects an international perspective to the sea-side art colony. Small but growing, the permanent collection includes around 90 works by 60 artists from 22 different countries. A recent expan-sion allows the gallery to better accommodate its current collection and have more space for temporary exhibitions and events. Rotating exhibi-tions explore aspects of contemporary art, from pop art of the 20th cen-tury to video art of the 21st.

Plaça de l'Ajuntament, 13. www.fundacio-stampfli.org/fundacio. ℂ **93-894-03-64.** Admission 5€ adults, 3.50€ seniors and students; combination ticket with Museu Cau Ferrat and Museu Maricel 13€, 9€ seniors and students. July–Sept Fri 5–8pm, Sat–Sun 11am–2pm and 4–8pm; March–June and Oct Fri 5–7pm, Sat–Sun 11am–2pm and 4–7pm; Nov–Feb Fri 4–6pm, Sat–Sun 11am–2pm and 4–6pm.

Museu Cau Ferrat ★★ MUSEUM   After a several-year restoration project, this museum even more brilliantly captures the life, lifestyle, and art of the early years of Sitges as an art colony. In the late 19th century, modern artist Santiago Rusiñol (1861–1931) created his combined studio, home, and art gallery by joining two 16th-century fishermen's cottages. His unique property soon attracted Catalan bohemians whose presence helped spur the transformation of the town into a popular seaside resort. Upon his death in 1931, Rusiñol willed the house and his collection to the city, and visitors can see examples of his work as well as work by his con-temporaries. The collection includes a few notable pieces by Picasso and El Greco. But the appeal of the museum lies less in any individual work of art than in the way that it captures the excitement, allure, and tensions of an avant-garde artistic salon in the years before the Spanish Civil War.

Carrer Fonollar. www.museusdesitges.com. ℂ **93-894-03-64.** Admission 10€ adults, 7€ seniors and students (includes a visit to Museu Maricel). Tues–Sun 10am–8pm (Mar–June and Oct closes 7pm; Nov–Feb closes 5pm).

Museu Maricel ★ MUSEUM
One of the people attracted to the Sitges art scene was American industrialist Charles Deering (heir to the company that would become International Harvester), who had this charming palace built right after World War I. Today it displays the collection of Dr. Jésus Pérez Rosales, which ranges from Gothic and Renaissance altarpieces to Catalan ceramics. The town's own art collection is of more local interest as it features work created by Sitges artists in the 19th and 20th centuries, including the members of the Sitges "Luminist School," a movement that preceded Catalan Modernisme. The enclosed Mirador offers magnificent views over the sea, with grand arches punctuated by impressive *noucentista* sculptures.

Carrer Fonallar. www.museusdesitges. com. ✆ **93-894-03-64.** Admission 10€ adults, 7€ seniors and students (includes a visit to Museu Cau Ferrat). Tues–Sun 10am–8pm (Mar–June and Oct closes 7pm; Nov–Feb closes 5pm).

Museu Maricel displays the works of artists drawn to Sitges's creative scene from the 19th century on.

Where to Stay in Sitges

Book far ahead if you're planning a visit in July or August, as every room in Sitges will be full. Between mid-October and Easter, you might find most lodgings closed.

Galeón Hotel ★ Part of a three-hotel group all located a 2-minute walk from the beach near the Plaça d'Espanya, the Galeón offers a great balance between price and comfort. Nicely maintained, it's been updated to place streamlined furniture in the wood-paneled rooms and to provide a pillow menu for the firm, comfortable beds. Public areas are small, but if you're not in your room at Sitges, you're likely at the beach. The hotel provides guests with beach towels and umbrellas—a nice touch.

Carrer Sant Francesc 44. www.hotelsitges.com. ✆ **93-894-13-79.** 74 units. 84€–122€ double. Parking 18€. **Amenities:** Restaurant; bar; outdoor pool; free Wi-Fi in public areas.

Hotel El Xalet ★★ in the city center a good 10-minute walk from the beach, the hotel occupies a Modernisme landmark building constructed by architects Gaietà Buigas i Monravà in 1901. The ornate stonework, carved trim, fanciful spires, and stained glass in floral motifs reflect the neo-medieval side of Modernisme design. The lobby and reception areas are filled with period tile mosaics and marble, while the guest rooms feature original details complemented by antique furniture. Some rooms have terraces. Nicely maintained gardens surround a small pool, and breakfast is served (weather permitting) on a roof terrace. There is also a summer-only restaurant.

Carrer Illa de Cuba, 35. www.elxalet.com. © **93-811-00-70.** 17 units. 63€–110€. **Amenities:** Restaurant; outdoor pool; free Wi-Fi.

Hotel Medium Romàntic ★   Created by combining two 19th-century townhouse villas, the Romantic has a kind of casual sprawl that's part of its charm. The hotel makes the most of the art-colony history of Sitges, practically plastering the walls with bright, often whimsical canvases that make up in enthusiasm what they might lack in execution. The paintings continue into the guest rooms; they certainly beat the generic posters of other hotels striving for an arty, romantic atmosphere. Both gay and straight travelers from all over Europe congregate here and get the day off to a grand start with breakfast in the lovely garden. A companion property,

The number-one reason most visitors come to Sitges: its glorious beach.

Hotel de la Renaixenca, is used for overflow guests, who have full use of the grounds. The beach and train station are nearby. Note that there is no elevator.

Carrer de Sant Isidre, 33. www.hotelromantic.com. © **93-894-83-75.** 36 units. 70€–110€. Rates include breakfast. **Amenities:** Bar; free Wi-Fi.

ME Sitges Terramar ★★★   The trendy ME by Meliá brand has overhauled what was formerly the hulking 1960s-era beachfront Terramar Hotel, breathing some much-needed contemporary design into Sitges' rather tired hotel landscape. It feels like a bit of Miami in the midst of the Mediterranean, with playful yet elegant décor and a youthful (albeit well-heeled) vibe. The rooftop bar with panoramic sea and Sitges views is one of the hottest nightlife scenes in town, which means you might want to avoid upper-level rooms if you crave sleep. The outdoor pool is pleasant with ocean breezes, while a protected cove just across the street is ideal for swimming, sunning, and drinking at the on-site beach club. Nearly all the sleekly decorated, minimalist rooms have sea views, but opt for one with a balcony if you can afford it. Also splurge for the breakfast, with a buffet that sprawls across three rooms. The hotel is a 20-minute stroll along the promenade to the center of town.

Passeig Marítim, 80. www.mebymelia.com. © **93-894-00-50.** 213 units. 175€–300€. Parking 13€. **Amenities:** Multiple bars; restaurant; outdoor pool; gym; spa; free Wi-Fi. Closed Dec–Jan.

Where to Eat in Sitges

Seafood always seems best at the beach, and Sitges restaurants serve a wide variety of Catalan rice plates or stews with fish and shellfish. But hilly pastoral country is literally just a few miles inland on the other side of the coastal mountains, and meat dishes are also popular.

El Pou ★★ CATALAN   Chef Oscar Massó's contemporary interpretation of traditional tapas makes the diminutive El Pou a very popular spot among locals and tourists alike. Many starters have a distinctly Asian flair, like lightly fried baby squid punched up with kimchi mayo, sardines marinated in soy sauce and tomato, or garlicky skewers of yakitori chicken. Standout main courses include a tender Iberian pork jowl flavored with

SITGES after dark

In true Spanish fashion, nightclubs and bars with live entertainment rarely open before 11pm, and in Sitges, most cater to a gay clientele. The greatest concentration is on **Carrer Sant Bonaventura** in the center of town, a short walk from the beach (near the Museu Romàntic). A map detailing gay bars and their style—from leather to black rubber to disco-ball dancing—is available at the bars themselves and online at www.gaysitgesguide.com

Thai spices and served on a hearty roll. Purists can find more typically Catalan tapas such as sliced Iberian ham, a plate of local cheeses, and of course anchovies. Don't miss the chef's twist on patatas bravas: fried potatoes stuffed with aioli and artfully presented like a sushi roll. Weekend reservations are a must in high season.

Carrer de Sant Bonaventura, 21. www.elpoudesitges.com. ℂ **93-013-47-98.** Entrees 9€–15€. Mon, Wed, Thurs 8–11pm; Fri–Sun 1:30–3:30pm and 8:30–11:30pm.

Fragata ★★   Located on the beach at the edge of Plaça Baluarte, Fragata is a contemporary jewel box of a restaurant: all glass, with taupe and nutmeg upholstery and table linens. Even the impressive wine cellar is a frosted glass cube. There's a bit of an international air to parts of the menu—veal with Stilton and mustard sauce, for example—but beautifully presented Catalan seafood carries the day, whether as an *all cremat* soup, with chunks of fish and caramelized garlic, a ceviche of wild sea bass, or a paella with shrimp, cuttlefish, mussels, and monkfish. The mixed grill of fresh fish is always a good bet—except on Sunday, when the fishermen stay ashore.

Passeig de la Ribera, 1. www.restaurantefragata.com. ℂ **93-894-10-86.** Reservations recommended. Entrees 18€–25€. Daily 1:30–4:30pm and 8pm–midnight.

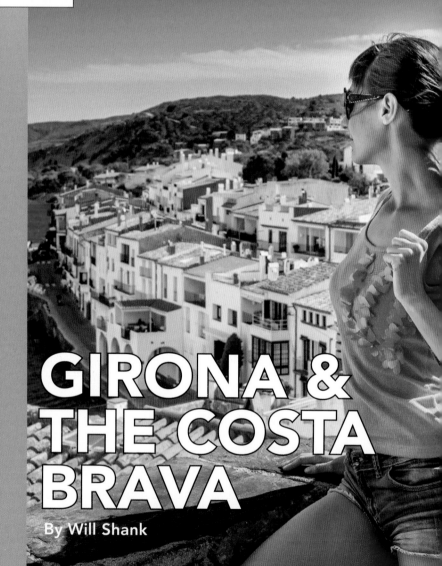

GIRONA &
THE COSTA
BRAVA

By Will Shank

S pain's northeast corner was almost ruined in the 1960s when real estate speculators somehow decided that its medieval fishing coves could be turned into sun-and-sea resorts to rival the already overgrown Costa del Sol in Andalucía. Fortunately, geography conspired against the Costa Brava, or "Wild Coast" (as the region was dubbed), from going too far down the road of overdevelopment. Yes, there are some blights on the landscape, and some of the communities closest to Barcelona sold their character to the holiday package industry. But other communities resisted and have preserved their identities along with their historical buildings, wild natural scenery, and sweeping crescent beaches.

GIRONA ★★★

Girona is Barcelona's country cousin—slower-paced and more compact, yet strikingly sophisticated and cosmopolitan. It is the perfect escape valve when the pressure of the Barcelona crowds begins to get to you. Girona is simply a charming, disarming Catalan city with lots to look at and some delicious things to eat. It was founded by the Romans on a hill crouching above the Ríu Onyar, and the shape of the city remains as Roman as it was 2,000 years ago. As those Romans realized, the river crossing here was so strategically important that Girona has been besieged 25 times over the centuries, beginning with Charlemagne in 785. The most devastating siege was by Napoleon in 1809, when he starved the city into submission.

Fortunately, Napoleon did not destroy Girona, and the elegant and graceful city retains traces of the Roman era along with medieval buildings on the Roman street structure. Gorgeous 19th-century pastel houses line the riverfront. As a citadel city, Girona is blessedly compact and, while steep, walkable. A stroll along the perimeter of the medieval walls gives you amazing views, and it's absolutely worth the climb to reach them. Working up an appetite is a good idea because, like Barcelona, Girona is a city with a passionate local food culture.

Essentials

ARRIVING More than 25 **trains** per day run between Barcelona and Girona. Trip time ranges from 37 minutes on AVANT and AVE trains to 1½ hours on the slow regional. Tickets range from 10€ to 32€ one-way, with the best combination of time and price being the AVANT trains at 38 minutes and 16.20€ to 31.30€. The cheapest way to cover this distance by train is to buy a ticket from a red machine in Sants Station for an unreserved coach on Renfe's Media Distancia system, but you can't reserve on line. The journey will be 70 to 90 minutes long, for only 11.25€ one-way. Yes, it's confusing; ask a station manager for help if you can't sort it out. All of these trains arrive in Girona at the Plaça Espanya (www.renfe.com; ☏ **90-232-03-20**).

The low cost and convenience of trains on this route has practically put inter-city **buses** out of business. But if you want to take a bus, **Sagalés** (www.sagales.com; ☏ **90-213-00-14**) is the company that does the route up and down the Costa Brava, and it does an airport route, Line 604, stopping at Barcelona and Girona for 16€. **Alsa** (www.alsa.es) operates a few buses between Barcelona's Estació del Nord and Girona (with a stop at Girona airport). Fare is 14.50€ and the journey takes about 1 hour, 50 minutes.

VISITOR INFORMATION The tourist office, at Rambla de la Llibertat, 1 (www.girona.cat/turisme; ☏ **97-201-00-01**), is open Monday through Friday 9am to 7pm, Saturday and Sunday 9am to 2pm. The **Welcome Point,** Carrer Berenguer Carnicer, 3 (☏ **97-221-16-78**), is open July through mid-September, Monday through Friday 9am to 7pm, Saturday 9am to 5pm, and Sunday 9am to 2pm. The rest of the year it's open Monday through Friday 9am to 3pm and weekends 9am to 2pm. In addition to providing information on lodging, dining, attractions, and transport, the Welcome Center offers guided tours.

Exploring Girona

Crossing the **Ríu Onyar** is much easier than it was in Roman times. From the vast city parking lot and train station, simply walk east over the pedestrian footbridge to the 14th-century Romanesque hulk of **Església de Sant Feliu** (p. 520), one of the oldest churches outside the Roman walls. The **Plaça de Sant Feliu** is a central meeting point for Gironans and visitors alike. Take note of the statue of a

The narrow medieval passages of the Call, or Jewish Quarter, of Girona.

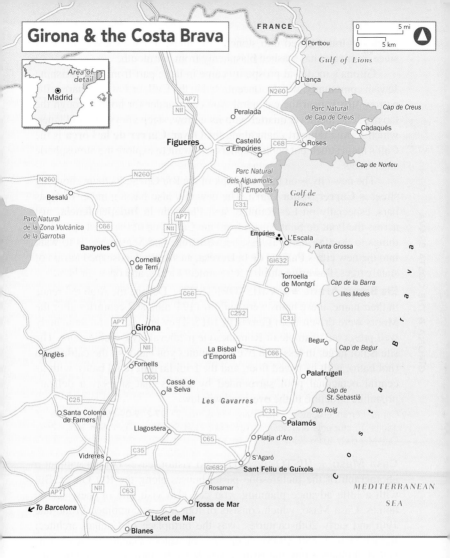

Girona & the Costa Brava

FRANCE

Portbou

Gulf of Lions

Llança

Peralada

Parc Natural
de Cap de Creus

Cap de Creus

Cadaqués

Figueres

Castelló
d'Empúries

Roses

Cap de Norfeu

Besalú

Parc Natural
de la Zona Volcànica
de la Garrotxa

Parc Natural
dels Aiguamolls
de l'Empordà

Golf de
Roses

Banyoles

Cornellà
de Terri

Empúries

L'Escala

Punta Grossa

Torroella
de Montgrí

Cap de la Barra

Illes Medes

Girona

La Bisbal
d'Empordà

Begur

Cap de Begur

Anglès

Fornells

Cassà de
la Selva

Palafrugell

Cap de
St. Sebastià

Santa Coloma
de Farners

Les Gavarres

Cap Roig

Palamós

Llagostera

Platja d'Aro

Vidreres

S'Agaró

Sant Feliu de Guíxols

Rosamar

MEDITERRANEAN

To Barcelona

Tossa de Mar

SEA

Lloret de Mar

Blanes

*Area of
detail*

Madrid

lioness mounted on a stone column. Tradition holds that a Gironan returning from a journey must kiss the statue's hindquarters to prove his good
citizenship (tourists do it, too).

If you walk around behind the church and uphill, staying outside the
walls, you will find the **medieval baths** (p. 518) and the handsome Benedictine monastery of Sant Pere de Gallignants (St. Peter of the Cock
Crows), which houses the **Museu d'Arqueologia** (p. 520).

Alternatively, you can pass through the walls at the towering Roman
gate on Plaça de Sant Feliu to the plaza in front of the **Catedral de Girona**
(p. 518), centerpiece of the medieval old city. According to another Gironan legend, the witch gargoyle on the cathedral was once a human witch,

magically transformed into stone in the midst of curses and rants. Ever since, rainwater has washed blasphemy from her mouth.

Girona's medieval prosperity came in large part from its flourishing Jewish community, which concentrated in the **Call,** or Jewish Quarter, the narrow streets near the cathedral. You can wander for hours through the labyrinthine medieval quarter with its narrow, steep alleyways and lanes, which form a rampart chain along the Onyar. **Carrer de la Força** is the Call's main street, but photographers will want to explore the atmospheric side streets.

The new city is on the west bank of the Ríu Onyar. Its main shopping street is **Carrer Santa Clara.** The new city also has a number of tapas bars, especially on Les Rambles and **Plaça de la Independència,** just across the Pont de Sant Agustí from the Call. One of the most appealing things to do after dark, at least between June and September, is to walk into the new city's **Parque de la Devesa,** an artfully landscaped terrain of stately trees, flowering shrubs, refreshment kiosks, and open-air bars.

Els Banys Àrabs ★★★ HISTORIC SITE Despite the Arab reference in their name, these baths were built in 1194, almost 2 centuries after the Moors were driven from Girona in 1015. They are a rare and amazingly well preserved example of Romanesque medieval civic architecture. The site is not large; in less than twenty minutes you can visit the **caldarium** (hot bath), with its paved floor, and the **frigidarium** (cold bath), with its central octagonal pool surrounded by pillars that support a delicate prismlike structure in the overhead window.

Carrer Ferran el Católic. www.banysarabs.org. ✆ **97-219-09-69.** Admission 2€ adults, 1€ students and seniors. Apr–Sept Mon–Sat 10am–7pm, Sun 10am–2pm; Oct–Mar daily 10am–2pm.

Casa Masó ★ HISTORIC SITE No visitor leaves Girona without a photograph of the picturesque pastel houses along the Riú Onyar. But with a little advance planning, you can also visit one of these iconic homes. Casa Masó, which consists of four houses combined in the late 19th and early 20th centuries, was the birthplace of Catalan architect Rafael Masó (1880–1935). A disciple of Antoni Gaudí, his work was heavily influenced by the British Arts & Crafts movement, and the furnishings and decorations in the home show an interesting blend of Catalan Modernisme, British Arts & Crafts, and French Art Nouveau. Admission is by guided tour only and requires an advance reservation.

Carrer Ballesteries, 29. www.rafaelmaso.org. ✆ **97-241-39-89.** Admission 6€ adults, 5€ students, 3€ seniors, free under age 16. Tues–Sat 10am–6pm.

Catedral de Girona ★★★ CHURCH The magnificent cathedral is Girona's leading attraction, but visiting is not for the weak of limb. To enter, you must climb a 17th-century baroque staircase of 89 steep steps. (Fitness enthusiasts race up and down the steps in the early morning.) The

Visiting Girona's baroque cathedral requires climbing a flight of 89 stairs.

cathedral dates from the 14th century, so the basic structure bridges Romanesque and Gothic. What is most evident, though, is the surface decoration that is pure Catalan baroque. As you climb the stairs, you'll be staring at a facade added in the late 17th and early 18th centuries. The bell tower, which rises from a cornice, is crowned by a dome capped with a bronze angel weather vane. Go through the cathedral's main door and enter the nave, which at 23m (75 ft.) is the broadest Gothic nave in the world.

Most of the cathedral's extensive art collection is displayed in its treasury. Girona's greatest single treasure is the **Tapestry of the Creation ★★★**, an exquisite piece of 11th- or 12th-century Romanesque embroidery that depicts humans and animals in the Garden of Eden along with portraits of Girona citizens, including members of the city's prominent Jewish population. The other major work is a 10th-century manuscript, the **Códex del Beatus,** which contains an illustrated commentary on the Book of the Apocalypse. From the cathedral's **Chapel of Hope,** a door leads to a **Romanesque cloister** from the 12th and 13th centuries, with an unusual trapezoidal layout. The cloister gallery, with a double colonnade, has a series of friezes that narrate scenes from the New Testament. Guides tout them as the prize jewel of Catalan Romanesque art, but even more fantastic are the carved capitals of the cloister, which vividly narrate moral tales in intricate twists of stone. From the cloister you can view the 12th-century **Torre de Carlemany (Charlemagne's Tower),** the only surviving section of the 12th-century church that the cathedral displaced.

Plaça de la Catedral. www.catedraldegirona.cat. ✆ **97-221-58-14.** Cathedral admission free; cloister and museum with audioguide 7€ adults, 5€ students and seniors; 1.2€ under age 17; free under age 7. Nave, treasury, and cloister are free Sun (audioguide 1€). Cloister and museum daily, Apr–June 10am–6:30pm; July–Aug 10am–7:30pm, Oct–Mar 10am–5:30pm. Cathedral daily 9am until museum closing time.

Església de Sant Feliu ★ CHURCH   Eight Roman and early Christian sepulchers are the main attractions of this Romanesque church with Gothic flourishes. (The two oldest date back to the A.D. 2nd c., and one shows Pluto carrying Persephone to the underworld.) The church itself was built slowly over the 14th to 17th centuries on the spot held by tradition to be the tomb of the 4th-century martyr Feliu of Africa. The structure is significant in Catalan architectural history because its pillars and arches are Romanesque while the nave is Gothic. Besides the sepulchers, other exceptional works within the church include a 16th-century altarpiece and a 14th-century alabaster statue of a Reclining Christ. One chapel contains the remains of city patron Sant Narcís—according to legend, flies escaping from his tomb drove away the French armies during the 1285 siege of Girona.

Pujada de San Feliu. www.catedraldegirona.cat. ✆ **97-220-14-07.** Free admission. Mon–Sat 10am–5:30pm, Sun and holidays 1–5:30pm.

Museu d'Arqueologia ★ MUSEUM   Everyone from Celtic Iberians, Greeks, and Carthaginians to Romans, Moors, and Visigoths passed through Girona and the surrounding countryside at one point, and the very thorough collections of this regional branch of the **Museu d'Arqueologia de Catalunya** (p. 520) chronicle them all. The museum occupies the Catalan Romanesque building that once housed the Benedictine monastery of Sant Pere de Gallignants (St. Peter of the Cock Crows). Most of the artifacts represent the Roman period and the quality overall is very high.

Plaça Santa Llúcia, s/n. www.macgirona.cat. ✆ **97-220-26-32.** Admission 4.50€ adults, 3.50€ seniors and under 25, free under age 8. Tues–Sat 10am–7pm (closes 6pm Oct–Apr), Sun and holidays 10am–2pm.

Museu d'Art ★★ ART MUSEUM   As you have probably already gathered, the people of Girona love a good legend. So it is only fitting that the 10th- to 11th-century altar stone of Sant Pere de Roda is one of the most prized objects in the museum. Made of wood and stone, it depicts both religious stories and Catalan legends. It's just one piece in a collection that brings together Catalan art from the 12th to the 20th centuries. Your kids—and you—will enjoy the rooms that colorfully explain precisely how both medieval panel paintings and stained glass are made, start to finish. After your visit, don't miss the shaded gardens behind the museum, the Jardins de la Francesa. A staircase in the gardens lets you ascend to the ancient city walls, where you can walk for a considerable distance to gain a unique panoramic perspective on the medieval city.

Pujada de la Catedral, 12. www.museuart.com. ✆ **97-220-38-34.** Admission 4.50€ adults; 3.50€ students and seniors, free under age 16. Tues–Sat 10am–7pm (closes 6pm Oct–Apr), Sun 10am–2pm.

Museu del Cinema ★ MUSEUM Film buff and historian Tomàs Mallol assembled more than 25,000 artifacts relating to the art of cinema: early crude camera obscura devices, Chinese shadow puppets, the earliest attempts to animate photography when that technology was still in its infancy. The collection dates from early history (including the original camera of the Lumière brothers) up to about 1970. Cinema aficionados from around the globe come here to study the origins of their art form.

Carrer Sèquia, 1. www.museudelcinema.cat ✆ **97-241-27-77.** Admission 6€ adults, 3€ students and seniors, free for ages 13 and under; free admission 1st Sunday of month. July–Aug Mon–Sat 10am–7pm and Sun 10am–2pm; Sept–June Tues–Sat 10am–6pm.

Museu d'Història dels Jueus ★★ MUSEUM The Jewish population of Girona flourished in the 12th century, when scholars, including the great rabbi Nahmanides, made it one of Europe's most important philosophical centers of Kabbalistic mysticism. In keeping with European tradition, the Jewish Quarter, or "Call," grew up in the protective shadow of the cathedral—until Isabel and Fernando expelled all the Jews from Spain in 1492. As part of the 1992 nationwide reassessment of Spain's gains and losses from the events of 1492, the Girona government set up a nonprofit organization to recover the Jewish history and culture of the city. One part of that effort was to establish this museum. In the decades since it opened, it has grown to an extensive warren of 11 galleries that examine community life, festivals and traditions, synagogues and forms of worship, and even the diaspora and the tricky matter of conversions during the Spanish Inquisition. Some of the most striking exhibitions deal with Jewish artistic and cultural traditions specific to Catalunya, while some of the most poignant include carved sepulchers unearthed during excavations at the old Jewish cemetery on Montjuïc.

Carrer Força Vella 8. www.girona.cat/call/eng/index.php. ✆ **97-221-67-61.** Admission 4€ adults, 2€ seniors and students, under age 14 free. July–Aug Mon–Sat 10am–8pm, Sun 10am–2pm; Sept–June Tues–Sat 10am–6pm, Sun–Mon 10am–2pm.

Museu d'Història de Girona ★ MUSEUM This collection covers the sweep of local history and prehistory from the flint and iron tools of the first Neolithic peoples through the glories of medieval Girona to the dark days of the Spanish Civil War, when the city built an underground shelter to protect its children from relentless bombardment by Franco's forces. One of the more interesting themed exhibits deals with the traditional sardana circle dance and the cobla band that accompanies the dancers. Although the 18th-century Capuchin Convent de Sant Antoni has been transformed into a modern museum, one room does retain a macabre feature from the old convent: 18 niches where dead friars were propped up in a seated position until their bodies became naturally mummified.

Carrer de la Força 27. www.girona.cat/museuhistoria/eng/index.php. © **97-222-22-29.** Admission 4€ adults, 2€ students, free under age 16. May–Sept Tues–Sat 10:30am–6:30pm, Sun and holidays 10:30am–1:30pm; Oct–Apr Tues–Sat 10:30am–5:30, Sun and holidays 10:30am–1:30pm.

Where to Stay in Girona

Bellmirall ★★ At least one rough stone wall in each room reminds visitors that this building in the center of the old Call dates from the 14th century. If you want to immerse yourself in the atmospheric old city, this lodging is a good choice at a good price. The rooms are small to midsize and feature simple furnishings, but you can also take advantage of the small courtyard. You'll find a TV in the common living space, but the bedrooms are TV- and phone-free (as well as smoke-free). There is a garage for bicycles and motorcycles.

Carrer Bellmirall, 3. www.bellmirall.eu. © **97-220-40-09.** 7 units. 44€ single to 88€ double. **Amenities:** Free Wi-Fi.

Ciutat de Girona ★★ This contemporary hotel is centrally located at the corner of two pedestrian streets, on the west side of the river between the San Feliu footbridge and Parque de la Devesa, a popular evening gathering spot in the summer. The generously sized bedrooms feature contemporary furnishings and up-to-date technology. Families will be pleased that there's an indoor swimming pool. When you're ready to see the sites, the cathedral is only about a 10-minute walk away.

Carrer Nord, 2. www.hotelciutatdegirona.com. 44 units. © **97-248-30-38.** 107€–135€ double; 4-person apartment 160€, triple 142€, family room 244€. Parking 21€. **Amenities:** Restaurant; bar; room service; pool; free Wi-Fi in public areas.

Hotel Històric ★★★ Architecture buffs should not miss this lodging, which in its own way encompasses Girona's history: The 9th-century building, now a hotel, includes a portion of a Roman wall and a 3rd-century aqueduct. Lodging options include both guest rooms and apartments that can accommodate three or four people. Most guest rooms have beautiful stone walls, balconies, and stylish modern furniture. The apartments have more rustic, but comfortable, decor and are a good choice for families. If it's full, the Històric also manages an equally charming place made of ancient stones a few blocks away, and the management will open the doors to you at Casa Cundaro.

Carrer Bellmirall, 4A. www.hotelhistoric.com. © **97-222-35-83.** 15 units. 113€–150€ double; 198€ junior suite. Apartments 89€ for up to 3 people, 118€ up to 4. **Amenities:** Restaurant; room service; free Wi-Fi.

Hotel Museu Llegendes de Girona ★★   Is Girona for lovers? This hotel thinks so. Three "Eros" rooms have two levels and feature romantic decor. The Suite Margarita Bonita goes farther with rather explicit artwork, a bed mounted on a stage, liberal use of mirrors, and a sofa designed for tantric exercise. For those not on honeymoons, the 9th- to 10th-century building adjacent to Sant Feliu also has lovely, unthemed rooms that are comfortable, stylish, and a convenient base for exploring the old city.

Portal de la Barca, 4. www.llegendeshotel.com. ℂ **97-222-09-05.** 15 rooms. 110€ double, 156€ junior duplex suite. **Amenities:** Restaurant; room service; free Wi-Fi.

Where to Eat in Girona

The residents of Girona take Catalan gastronomy very seriously, making it one of the best cities its size for contemporary fine dining. The gourmet emphasis trickles down to more casual and less pricey venues as well, and it's easy to make a meal of tapas. One good area for tapas-hopping is the Plaça de la Independència, just across the Pont Sant Augusti from the Call.

Boira Restaurant ★ CATALAN   Boira has some seating outdoors on Plaça de la Independència, but we prefer a romantic table overlooking the river in the tranquil upstairs dining room. In contrast to the more traditional menus of surrounding restaurants, Boira emphasizes seasonal, local food. Creamy goat cheeses from the Catalan countryside could show up in a small tart; in springtime, local asparagus often graces fish plates; and in the fall, mushrooms abound. Part of Boira's appeal is the daily menu of starter, main dish, dessert, and wine for less than the cost of a main dish in many restaurants. Accordingly, portions are modest. Some of the most fit people in Girona—professional cyclists who train here—eat regularly at Boira.

Plaça de la Independència, 17. www.elboira.com. ℂ **97-221-96-05.** Entrees 12€– 14€, Set menu 14€–20€. Mon–Fri 7am–midnight, Sat–Sun 7am–1am.

Casa Marieta ★★ CATALAN   While in Girona, fans of quirky local foods should try the *trinxat*, a casserole of rice, ham, cabbage, and potatoes. This regional dish is available, appropriately enough, in this, the oldest restaurant in town. Casa Marieta is also a reliable place to enjoy *suquet*, the seafood stew served throughout Catalunya. Art Nouveau–style stained glass and banquette seating enhance the dining experience.

Plaça de la Independència, 5-6. www.casamarieta.com. ℂ **97-220-10-16.** Entrees 8€–27€. Reservations recommended. Sun–Thurs 1–3:30pm and 8–10:30pm, Fri–Sat 1–4pm and 8–11pm. Closed Feb.

El Celler de Can Roca ★★★ CATALAN/INTERNATIONAL   Named the best restaurant in the world in 2013 by the readers of *Restaurant* magazine, El Celler de Can Roca picked up the avant-garde baton when Ferran Adriá closed the famous elBulli. With Roca brothers Joan (head chef),

Jordi (head pastry chef), and Josep (sommelier) in charge, the restaurant belies the old trope about too many chefs and spoiled broth. The cuisine is firmly rooted in classic Catalan home cooking but with sometimes surreal twists, as if the ghost of Salvador Dalí were in the kitchen. For example, the simple appetizer of local olives is served as caramelized olives—on a bonsai tree. (Be careful with the branches, as they need the tree for the next customer.) The meal begins with small bites from the El Mundo section of the kitchen (a spicy ball of frozen fish broth coated in cocoa butter, for example), followed by inventive main dishes of the moment. Rarely are they repeated, although the veal tartare with mustard ice cream, spicy ketchup, and fruit compotes is one stalwart. Jordi is famous for inventing desserts that re-create the aromas of classic perfumes. For a once-in-a-lifetime experience, it's worth the splurge and the cost of a cab ride, as the restaurant sits about 2km (1¼ miles) from the center of town. Online reservations open at midnight on the first day of the month; phone reservations can be made farther ahead.

Carrer Can Sunyer, 48. www.cellercanroca.com. © **97-222-21-57.** Reservations essential. Fixed-price menus 95€–215€. Tues 9–11pm, Wed–Sat 1–4pm and 9–11pm.

Divinum ★★★ CATALAN If you don't have months to wait for a reservation at Can Roca (see above), head straight for the exceptional dining experience offered at Divinum. This is the type of elegant establishment where the waiters march through the dining room in matching uniforms with epaulettes, placing linen napkins on your table using a serving fork and spoon instead of their fingers; as soon as you're seated a complimentary glass of cava arrives. You can order a la carte, but the Petit Menú Gastrónomic is a memorable experience. One after another, 13 beautifully styled courses are presented, and each one is more mouth-watering than the one before. A little red globe that looks like a cherry but bursts on the tongue into a spicy Bloody Mary; bib lettuce served still growing in a little flowerpot; a flight of four different kinds of Spanish olive oil and three kinds of coarse salt; delicate fillets of red mullet served in a brine and grape sauce. When the second dessert arrived, it was almost—but not quite—too much. With or without wine pairings (an extra 30€) or the optional cheese cart (really? yes!), the evening adds up to a memorable food event, with impeccably correct service from the super-attentive wait staff. (The larger Menú Gastrónomic features 17 dishes, if I counted correctly, and charges 40€ additional for wine pairings.) If you're up for a splurge, the price of a meal here is half of what such a special experience would cost in Barcelona.

Carrer de l'Albereda, 7. www.dvnum.cat. © **87-208-02-18.** Entrees 18€–30€; fixed-price menus 58€–70€. Reservations recommended. Mon–Sat 1:30–3:30pm and 8:30–10:30pm.

Massana ★★ CATALAN We love the advice that Pere Massana gives to diners who hesitate to try the sea cucumbers that he offers as a starter.

After the description on the menu he adds, "Do not ask. Taste them." That's good advice overall, and diners would be wise to simply trust Massana's sure hand at combining flavors and textures into winning dishes. Even though he is now the proprietor of one of Catalunya's best restaurants and the recipient of a Michelin star, he has not forgotten the great Catalan culinary traditions. One section of the menu is devoted to "The Pure Product, barely touched" and includes such plates as Palamós prawns from the Costa Brava roasted in coarse sea salt.

Bonastruch de Porta 10. www.restaurantmassana.com. ℂ **97-221-38-20.** Entrees 25€–49€; tasting menu 110€. Reservations recommended. Wed–Mon 1:15–3:30pm and 8:15–10:30pm; Tues 1:15–3:30pm.

Mimolet Restaurant ★ CATALAN   Some of the tastiest dishes here are found among the starters, including tempura-fried small fish, salmon tartare with basil oil, mussel salad with creamy wasabi dressing, and Iberian ham croquettes with red wine reduction. For a set price, you can choose a starter and a main dish, and the chef will surprise you with dessert (usually some combination of genoise, fresh fruit, cream, and chocolate). Vegetarians are always provided with options here, too.

Carrer Pou Rodó, 12. www.mimolet.net. ℂ **97-229-79-73.** Entrees 15–25€, set menu 38€, tasting menu 38€. Tues–Fri 1–3:30pm and 8–10:30pm, Sat–Sun 1–4pm and 8–11pm.

Side Trip from Girona

CASTELL GALA DALÍ DE PÚBOL ★★

Salvador Dalí created a persona that was bigger than life and, in some ways, better known than his actual work. His greatest composite work of art is the Teatre-Museu in Figueres (below), and it's packed with some of his best works. The **Castell Gala Dalí de Púbol** (Carrer Gala-Salvador Dalí s/n, Púbol; www.salvador-dali.org; ℂ **97-248-86-55**) is less about his art and more about his neuroses and his strangely submissive relationship with his wife, Gala. In 1969, the couple stumbled onto this 11th-century castle, which lay in ruins (no roofs, cracked walls). Dalí promptly bought it for Gala and redecorated the interiors to create a series of comfortable (if often bizarre) rooms without making the exterior look as if the property had ever been repaired. It was Gala's refuge, and he agreed not to visit unless she invited him—something she rarely did. Dalí used the castle as a studio for 2 years after her death, moving out in 1984 when his bedroom caught fire one night. The artistry here is conceptual—it's all in how Dalí treated the architecture and furnished the rooms. Of the three sites run by the Gala-Salvador Dalí Foundation (the third is his seaside studio near Cadaques), this one is the most "normal." Admission is 8€ adults, 6€ students, and free for children 8 and under. It's open from daily 10am to 6pm, with extended hours until 8pm mid-June through mid-Sept (it closes at 5pm Nov–Dec). Púbol is 21km (13 miles) east of Girona on highway C-66.

FIGUERES ★★

The most famous native son of Figueres is Salvador Dalí, the Surrealist painter who put this otherwise-undistinguished small city in northern Catalunya on the international art map. Seeking to capitalize on the artist's fame, the mayor of Figueres invited him to create a museum there in 1961. Dalí chose the ruins of the old municipal theater in the town center because his first childhood art show had been hung there. With no disrespect to the community, the chief reason to visit Figueres is to tour the strange and wonderful world of the Teatre-Museu Dalí, one of the most-visited tourist destinations in Spain.

Essentials

ARRIVING   RENFE (www.renfe.com; ☏ **90-232-03-20**) has hourly train service between Barcelona-Sants and Figueres. The trip takes around 2 hours, and costs 12€ to 16€, one-way, depending on type of train. Be sure to book for the Figueres station, not Figueres Vilafant, which is the high-speed rail station in a neighboring town. Trains from Girona take 30 to 40 minutes and cost 4€ to 7€. Figueres can also be reached by car on the AP-7 from Girona.

VISITOR INFORMATION   The Figueres **tourist office** is at the Plaça de l'Escorxador, 2 (www.ca.visitfigueras.cat; ☏ **97-250-31-55**). The office is open July through September Monday through Saturday 9am to 8pm and Sunday 10am to 3pm; hours the rest of the year are Monday through Friday 9:30am to 2pm and 4 to 6pm. It's closed around the Christmas/New Year holidays.

Exploring Figueres

Teatre-Museu Dalí ★★★ MUSEUM   There is something for everyone to like, or at least to be astounded by, inside this bewildering museum, which is essentially a monument to the mad genius of Salvador Felipe Jacinto Dalí i Domènech. Many of the surrealist's most famous works—like the melting clocks in "Persistence of Memory"—hang elsewhere, but his early paintings here are a reminder of what a gifted craftsman Dali was and why he became famous in the first place. Upon entering, visitors

The whimsical Teatre-Museu Dalí.

are first faced with the artist's Cadillac in the courtyard, where it rains *inside* the car! Far from a traditional series of white cubes, the contents of this grouping of buildings are more like snapshots of corners of his psyche, all collaged together inside a carnival funhouse. Dalí began his career in the 1920s as one of Spain's three *enfants terribles* (the others were writer Federico García Lorca and filmmaker Luis Buñuel). For most of his life, he was engaged in an obsessive and dependent relationship with the Russian-born Elena Ivanova Diakonova, known as Gala. He remained tenaciously loyal to her until her death in 1982 (although the same can't be said of Gala toward Dalí).

Many of the works in the Teatre-Museu relate to this relationship and Dalí's complicated feelings about sexual intimacy. It took the artist a long time to assemble the museum, since he made all the initial placements of objects. It finally opened in 1974. When the artist died in 1989, thousands of artifacts and artworks from throughout his life passed to the Gala-Salvador Dalí Fundació, which maintains the museum, and the exhibits have been moved around—but not so much to jeopardize Dali's claim that it is the largest surreal object in the world. Dalí spent his final 4 years living adjacent to the museum in the Torre Galatea, named for Gala. He was buried beneath the theater's great dome, which he had painted as the eye of a fly as seen through a microscope. Our favorite single artwork is the ceiling mural portraits of Dalí and Gala as seen from below the ground. (You're looking at them dirty-feet-first.) And even if your kids don't know who Mae West was, the visual trick of recreating a woman's face out of furniture will amaze everyone. Be sure to visit the installation next door that features Dali's amazing jewelry, some of which moves, as it's included in your ticket to the museum. *Tip:* In August there's a special "Theater-Museum by Night" for 15€ from 10pm to 1am.

Plaça de Gala-Dalí 5. www.salvador-dali.org. ✆ **97-267-75-00.** Admission 14€ adults, 10€ students and seniors, free ages 8 and under. Closed Mon except in the summer. Apr–Sept 9am–8pm, Oct 9:30am–6pm, Nov–Feb 10:30am–6pm, Mar 9:30am–6pm.

Where to Stay & Eat in Figueres

Duran Hotel & Restaurant ★ CATALAN We don't know what Salvador Dalí ordered when he ate at this restaurant that occupies an old inn dating from 1855. But you can't go wrong with the sole in orange sauce with shrimp ravioli, or a *fideù* (paella with noodles instead of rice) of monkfish and prawns. The Duran also offers a number of game dishes, such as saddle of hare with chestnut puree and raspberry jam. The hotel occupies a newer part of the property and features 65 rooms with crisp, neutral-toned furnishings punctuated by playful headboards of undulating wooden slats. Some rooms can accommodate three or four people, and some have been adapted to be wheelchair accessible.

Carrer Lasauca, 5. www.hotelduran.com. ✆ **97-250-12-50.** 65 rooms. 54€–63€ double. Restaurant entrees 14€–29€; set lunch menu 22€. **Amenities:** Restaurant; bar; free Wi-Fi.

El Motel ★★ CATALAN   You wouldn't guess it from its name, but El Motel is the most elegant place to eat in Figueres, offering the type of fine dining that the locals reserve for a long family luncheon on a Sunday. As it's a bit out of the center, it isn't the most convenient place for Dalí fans to dine, but if you're arriving in this part of the world in a car, a meal here can be a special experience. We like the fact that the chef/owner Jaume Subirós has menu offerings for different appetites. On the Market Menu, diners can opt for starter and dessert only, or main course and dessert only. His Tasting Menu is a multi-course extravaganza with appetizer, four main dishes, cheeses, and dessert. Both menus rely on fresh ingredients from the market, so you never know what to expect, but rest assured that Subirós is equally inventive with fish and meat. The family-run restaurant has been an institution since its founding in 1961, and the Hotel Empordá upstairs is a good place to stay if you don't want the parking hassles and noise of the old town, which is about 1km away.

Av. Salvador Dalí, 170. www.elmotelrestaurant.com. © **97-250-05-62.** Entrees 18€–64€; set menus 20€–60€. Wed–Sat 12:45–3:30pm and 8:30–10:30pm, Sun–Mon 12:45–3:30pm; closed Tues.

CADAQUÉS ★★

The last resort on the Costa Brava before the French border, Cadaqués feels truly off the beaten path. The remote seaside town was the summer home of Salvador Dalí's family, and it gained a reputation as an artist hang-out in the 1920s, attracting luminaries like director Luis Buñuel, writer Federico Garcia Lorca, and painter André Breton. Despite the publicity it received when Dalí later lived in the adjacent village of Portlligat, it still feels unspoiled and remote, although unsightly developments have begun to creep up the surrounding hills. Still, the center of the lovely white village wraps around half a dozen small coves, with a narrow street running along the water's edge. Scenically, Cadaqués is a visual feast of blue water, colorful fishing boats, old whitewashed houses, narrow twisting streets, and a 16th-century parish church on a hill.

Essentials

ARRIVING   Three to four **buses** per day run from Figueres to Cadaqués. Trip time is 1¼ hours. The service is operated by **SARFA** (www.sarfa.com; © **90-230-20-25**). Driving from Barcelona, follow the A-7 northeast until you come to the town of Figueres, where you'll see signs leading east to Cadaqués, which is the other side of a winding mountain road.

VISITOR INFORMATION   The **tourist office,** Cotxe, 2 (www.visit cadaques.org; © **97-225-83-15**), is open Monday to Saturday 9am to 9pm, closed on Sunday.

Exploring Cadaqués

Seeing the "sights" in Cadaqués basically means strolling around the narrow streets and enjoying the stony beach. The one landmark is the **Església de Santa María,** Calle Eliseu Meifren, a 16th-century Gothic church with a baroque altar; it dominates the narrow, hilly streets in the old section of town. It's usually open for visits from 9am to 5pm—assuming someone comes to unlock it.

Hop in a taxi (or take a good stroll through the town—less than half an hour from the center) to the former fishing community of Portlligat and the **Casa-Museo Salvador Dalí** in Portlligat (www.salvador-dali.org; ✆ **97-225-10-15**). From the secluded cove of Port Lligat you can spot the Dali house by its distinctive egg-shaped towers. (He loved eggs.) This museum is another part of the "Dalí triangle," which includes the Teatre-Museu Dalí at Figueres (p. 526) and the castle at Púbol (p. 525).

Originally a series of fishermen's huts, the structure was converted by Dalí into his summer home starting in 1930. Over the years he kept adding on and decorating the rooms with collected objects ranging from dried flowers to stuffed animals. He and Gala lived here for many years, and their private quarters are the most interesting rooms, which gives you intimate insights into how this couple lived and entertained; their whole life was an art piece. Inside the house, which is chockablock with memorabilia, you'll be greeted by a giant polar bear and discover such oddities as the couple's bed and a pop-art miniature of Granada's Alhambra. Out back is a lip-shaped sofa and a penis-shaped swimming pool as well as an ahead-of-its-time sculpture made of Pirelli tires and sangria bottles. You can also see the studio where Dali painted, with his easel, brushes, and paints still in place.

Very important: Advanced reservations are *mandatory.* Adult admission is 12€ for the house and olive garden, 8€ for students under 16 and

The richly decorated baroque altar of Eglésia de Santa Maria in Cadaqués.

seniors, free for kids ages 8 and under. The olive garden only is 6€, or 5€ for students and seniors. Opening hours change by the season: mid-September through January 10:30am to 6pm; February through mid-June 10am to 6pm, mid-June to mid-September 9:30am to 9pm. It's open daily except November through mid-March, when it's closed on Mondays.

Where to Stay & Eat in Cadaqués

Hostal S'Aguarda ★   A good choice if you're planning to visit Dali's house, this pleasantly old-fashioned casual *hostal* has an elevated view of the village on the high road to Portlligat. Rooms have all the modern conveniences, but none of the slickness of a resort hotel. Bathrooms are unusually large, and many rooms have either a private balcony or access to a shared terrace—both with great panoramic views.

Carretera de Portlligat 30. www.hotelsaguarda.com. © **97-225-80-82.** 28 units. 88€–170€ double; 102€–170€ suite. Free parking. Closed Nov. **Amenities:** Bar; outdoor pool; room service; free Wi-Fi.

Hotel Rocamar ★★   This traditional hotel that hangs dramatically above the beach is elegant enough for a couple's getaway, yet has enough activities (indoor and outdoor pools, sauna, mini-golf, and tennis court) to keep a whole family happily entertained. For that romantic getaway, consider one of the rooms with a balcony or terrace and sea views. Many of the other rooms have mountain views, but no balconies. It's closed for the winter by late October, like many hotels in this part of the world. As of this writing, the Rocamar is closed for renovations but check their website for updates.

Dr. Bartomeus, s/n. www.rocamarcadaques.com. © **97-225-81-50.**

GOLF DE ROSES

This small bay enclosed on the north by the Cap de Norfu and on the south by Punta Gross is lined by a swampy shoreland that forms the **Parc Natural dels Aiguamolls de l'Empordà,** one of the largest wetlands in Catalunya. The marshes are home to more than 300 species of birds, making the park one of the prime birding destinations in Spain. The pink creatures found on the beach, especially in July and August, are the package tourists from northern Europe who flock here to sun on the sands of Roses, the town just north of the natural park. South of the wetlands stand some of the most evocative classical ruins in northeast Spain, **Empúries,** the erstwhile site of Greek Emporion and the landing site of the Romans when they first invaded the Iberian Peninsula to oust the Carthaginians. Both sets of ancient ruins have been excavated and are explained by a fascinating museum on site.

Essentials

ARRIVING   Roses can be accessed by bus from Figueres or Cadaqués— **SARFA** (www.sarfa.com; © **90-230-20-25**)—but it's easiest to reach driving east from Figueres on C-68. From Roses, the coastal road south leads through the park to the village of L'Escala, where the ruins of Empúries are located.

VISITOR INFORMATION The **Oficina de Turisme de Roses** (www. en.visit.roses.cat; © **97-225-73-31**) is located at Avinguda Rhode, 77–79. From mid-June to mid-September it's open daily 9am to 9pm except holidays; the rest of the year the hours are Monday to Saturday 10am to 2pm and 3 to 6pm, Sunday 10am to 1pm.

Exploring the Golf de Roses

Roses is a pretty little town out of season, but resort development has completely obscured the ancient Greek settlement here.

A short distance south of Roses, the wetlands of the **Parc Natural dels Aiguamolls de l'Empordà ★** begin. The ecological preserve lies at the mouth of Ríu Fluvià and provides an important haven for migratory birds, including pink flamingos. Some birders prefer to explore the waterside paths by bicycle, but there are also well-signed lookout points along the shore road.

The main attraction along the Gulf is **Empúries ★**, where Greek commerce and Roman might are both writ large. The archaeological site,

The Empúries ruins.

Canals lace through the Golf de Roses resort town of Empuriabrava.

which is just north of the village of L'Escala, has been under excavation since 1908. Greeks founded the city in 600 B.C. as a trade port, then built a second city slightly inland in 550 B.C., naming it Emporion, or "trading place." The first settlement lies buried under a fishing village, but the extensive city of Emporion and its cemetery make up the greater part of the ruins. Farther inland, Scipio Africanus founded a military camp in 219 B.C. to stage his first invasion to oust the Carthaginians from the Iberian Peninsula. An amphitheater and villas with mosaics still attest to the flourishing Roman presence. At the site, the **Museu d'Arqueologia de Catalunya** interprets the three towns and chronicles the archaeological excavations. The famous sculpture of Asclepios (god of medicine) was returned to the site from Barcelona in 2008. The museum is on Carrer Puig i Cadafalch, s/n (www.macempuries.cat; ✆ **97-277-02-08**). Admission is 5.50€ adults, 4.50€ students and seniors, free children under 8. It is open June to September daily 10am to 8pm, the rest of the year 10am to 6pm (closes at 5pm mid-Nov to mid-Feb).

You can also walk along the seaside path from the ruins to the flourishing village of **L'Escala.** Salted anchovies from the town are famous all over Spain, and exhibits at the **Museu de l'Anxova i de la Sal** explain the local fishing industry from the 16th century to present. The little museum is at Av. Francesc Macià, 1 (www.museudelanxovaidelasal.blogspot.com; ✆ **97-277-68-15**). Admission is 2.15€, 1.10€ students and seniors, free under age 12. Summer hours (July–Aug) are Monday to Saturday 10am to 1pm and 5 to 8pm, Sunday 10am to 1pm; winter hours (Sept–June) are Tuesday through Sunday 10am to 1pm.

SOMETHING fishy FOR SURE

Founded in 1279 by the king of Aragón, **Palamós** remains the only major fishing port still active on the Costa Brava. Its fleet is legendary for going far to sea for large fin fish such as yellowfin tuna and for harvesting vast quantities of sweet shrimp from coastal waters. Tourism development has been contained south of the village, leaving the medieval architecture and the working docks intact. To understand both the fish and the fishing industry, try the **Museu de la Pesca** (Moll Pesquer, s/n; www.museudelapesca.org; ✆ **97-260-04-24;** admission 5€ adults, 2.50€) students and seniors, kids under 6 free). It's open Tuesday to Saturday 10am to 1:30pm and 3 to 7pm, Sunday 10am to 2pm and 4 to 7pm, with extended hours in summer. It's not the most professional museum you've ever visited, but you'll glean some pearls of wisdom about the local industry so key to the Costa Brava. In October, **Palamós Gastronòmic** celebrates the town's foodie heritage with special menus, food demonstrations, cooking classes, and a shrimp-eating contest on the docks. If your schedule brings you to this part of the coast for an overnight stay, try the **Hostal La Fosca** (www.hostallafosca.com), where you can have a quiet respite right on a lovely cove outside town, and also enjoy a meal and a shop that features the management's own line of local wines and olive oils, Brugarol (you can also arrange to tour their farm and vineyards).

SANT FELIU DE GUÍXOIS ★★

Sant Feliu de Guíxols is a beautiful harbor and former fishing port framed on one side by a rocky headland holding the luxury residential area of S'Agaro and on the other by a 10th-century Benedictine monastery.

Essentials

ARRIVING Direct **bus** service from Girona takes about 45 minutes and costs 8.30€ via **SARFA** (www.sarfa.com; ℰ **90-230-20-25**). If you choose to drive, it takes about 40 minutes on C-45 and C-55.

VISITOR INFORMATION The **Oficina Municipal de Turisme Sant Feliu de Guíxols** (www.guixols.cat; ℰ **97-282-00-51**) is located on the main beach at Passeig del Mar 8–12. It is open Monday to Saturday 10am to 1pm and 4 to 7pm, and Sunday 10am to 2pm.

Exploring Sant Feliu de Guíxols

The chief attraction of Sant Feliu is its natural setting. The Platja Sant Pol is one of the least crowded beaches on the Costa Brava and is well furnished with adjacent bars and restaurants for cold drinks and inexpensive

Sant Feliu's Platja Sant Pol is one of the Costa Brava's loveliest beaches.

meals. The hills around Sant Feliu are crisscrossed with well-marked hiking paths that offer splendid views of the sea and coast. Ask for a trail map at the tourist office.

The most striking buildings in Sant Feliu belong to the complex of the medieval Benedictine monastery. The monastery is no longer active, and the buildings are undergoing a slow restoration process (made even slower by Spain's economic doldrums). But the beautiful Romanesque **Mare de Déu dels Angels** remains an active parish church filled with a millennium of religious art, some of it quite powerful. It's located on the Plaça del Monestir and is open daily 9am to 12:30pm and 7 to 8:30pm; admission is free.

Also a part of the monastery complex, the **Museu d'Història** (www.museu.guixols.cat; ℰ **97-282-15-75**) explains the local cork industry that made Sant Feliu wealthy in the late 19th century. Cork barons built the marvelous Modernisme houses you'll see along Platja Sant Pol and in S'Agaro. The museum is on the Plaça del Monestir adjacent to the church, and admission is 2€ adults, 1€ students and seniors, free for kids under 8. It is open Monday to Friday 10am to 2:30pm, Saturday 10am to 6pm, and Sunday 10am to 2pm.

Where to Stay & Eat in Sant Feliu de Guíxols

Hostal de la Gavina ★★★   This elegant property is a surprisingly secluded retreat on the often crowded—and not always elegant—Costa Brava. It sits on a small peninsula that juts out into the ocean, with beaches on two quiet bays. The core of the property is a gleaming-white 1932 former private villa with a hint of Moorish style. Expanded over the years, it holds most of the guest rooms, which are confidently luxe in style with rich fabrics, carved and sometimes gilded furniture, and lovely architectural details. Superior double rooms have private balconies. You could easily pass many happy days exploring the manicured grounds and hanging out at the outdoor saltwater pool. There's even a hammam for women in the spa. The Candlelight Restaurant and the adjoining El Patio de Candlelight (in warm weather) epitomize romantic gourmet dining.

Plaça de la Rosaleda, S'Agaro. www.lagavina.com. ⓒ **97-232-11-00.** 74 units. 320€–450€ double; 500€-650€ suites. Free parking outside; garage 20€. Closed Nov–Apr. **Amenities:** 2 restaurants; 2 bars; bikes; health club; 2 pools (1 indoor, 1 outdoor); room service; spa; 2 outdoor tennis courts; free Wi-Fi.

Hotel Sant Pol ★★   A dozen of this beachside hotel's 22 rooms have direct sea views, and five have hydromassage baths—making the Sant Pol a personalized small-lodging option to nearby oversized resort hotels. Styling is simple, contemporary, and bright with extensive tile, marble, and nickel-chrome fixtures in the spacious bathrooms. Ideally situated for sunbathing and swimming at the Sant Pol beach (on the north end of the village), the hotel offers free parking if you book online. Note that rates from mid-July through August include half board. The Restaurant Sant Pol is an unpretentious dining room with excellent preparations of local fish and a three-course menu at lunch (17€) and dinner (22€).

Platja de Sant Pol 125. www.hotelsantpol.com. ⓒ **97-232-10-70.** 22 units. 88€–208€ double. Parking 10€–13€. Closed Nov. **Amenities:** 2 restaurants; bar; room service; free Wi-Fi.

TOSSA DE MAR ★★

The gleaming white town of Tossa de Mar, with its 12th-century walls, labyrinthine old quarter, fishing boats, and good sand beaches, is perhaps the most attractive base for a Costa Brava vacation. Not only does the town have more *joie de vivre* than its competitors, it is shielded from overdevelopment by the towering cliffs that surround its main cove. In the 18th and 19th centuries, Tossa was a significant port for the cork industry. But when the cork business declined in the 20th century, many of its citizens emigrated to America. In the 1950s, thanks in part to the Ava Gardner movie *Pandora and the Flying Dutchman,* tourists began to discover the charms of Tossa, and a new industry was born.

Essentials

ARRIVING Direct **bus** service is offered from Blanes and Lloret de Mar. Tossa de Mar is also on the main Barcelona-Palafruggel route. Service from Barcelona is daily from 8am to 8:30pm and takes 1½ hours. For information, call © **90-230-20-25.** To drive, head north from Barcelona along the A-19.

VISITOR INFORMATION The **tourist office** is at Av. El Pelegrí, 25 (© **97-234-01-08;** www.infotossa.com). In April, May, and October, it's open Monday to Saturday 10am to 2pm and 4 to 8pm; November to March, Monday to Saturday 10am to 1pm and 4 to 7pm; and June to September, Monday to Saturday 9am to 9pm, and Sunday 10am to 2pm and 5 to 8pm.

The view from the walls of Vila Vella, Tossa de Mar's medieval core.

Exploring Tossa de Mar

Tossa was once a getaway for artists and writers—Marc Chagall called it a "blue paradise." To experience the charms of Tossa, walk through the 12th-century walled town, known as **Vila Vella,** built on the site of a Roman villa from the A.D. 1st century. Enter through the Torre de les Hores. Then, descending from the Old Town, follow signs to Plaça del Pintor J. Villalonga, where you'll find steps that let you walk along the medieval ramparts.

In 1914, archaeologists uncovered in Tossa the ruins of one of the grandest Roman villas on the Costa Brava, **Els Ametllers Roman Villa.** Inhabited from the 1st century B.C. to the A.D. 6th century, it was the headquarters of a vast tract of vineyards producing wine for export to Rome. During the summer, beautiful mosaic floors of the rooms are uncovered for viewing.

Tossa itself has two main beaches, **Mar Gran** and **La Bauma.** The coast near Tossa, north and south, offers even more possibilities.

Where to Stay in Tossa de Mar

EXPENSIVE

Gran Hotel Reymar ★   Built in the 1960s on a rocky outcrop above Mar Menuda beach, this gleaming white hotel has almost become a landmark in its own right. The architectural design allowed for several terraces for sunbathing away from the beach crowds. For more privacy, some rooms have their own balconies with sea and garden views. Modern wood-grained furniture and light walls give a breezy, relaxed feel. The hotel is about a 10-minute walk southeast of the town's historic walls.

Playa Mar Menuda, s/n. www.tossagranhotelreymar.com. ℃ **97-234-03-12.** 166 units. 127€–274€ double; 184€–387€ suite. Parking 16€. Closed Nov–Apr 17. **Amenities:** Restaurant; 3 bars; bikes; children's center; exercise room; Jacuzzi; outdoor pool; room service; sauna; outdoor tennis court; free Wi-Fi.

MODERATE

Best Western Mar Menuda ★★   This may not be the fanciest lodging in town, but it has the best terrace with a panoramic view of the sea and the town. Many of the midsize to spacious guest rooms also have sea views, and all are comfortably decorated with clean-lined furniture and bright white linens and feature good-size bathrooms. If you're interested in watersports (scuba diving, windsurfing, or sailing), staff can offer advice. If you just want to lie by the pool, that's okay, too. Breakfast is included.

Playa Mar Menuda, s/n. www.bestwesternhotelmarmenuda.com. ℃ **800/528-1234** in the U.S., or 97-234-10-00. 50 units. 86€–177€ double; 92€–215€ suite. Rates include breakfast. Free parking. Closed Nov–Dec. **Amenities:** Restaurant; bar; babysitting; children's playground; outdoor pool; room service; free Wi-Fi.

Hotel Diana ★★   Our favorite is this historic boutique hotel in a villa designed by a disciple of Gaudi, who employed decorative paving stones, brightly patterned tiles, and elegant painted ceilings to great effect. Though set back from the esplanade, the hotel has great ocean views, and many rooms have private balconies. Rooms are spacious with traditional furnishings and modern bathrooms, but most guests spend their time on the covered terrace overlooking the beach or on the charming inner patio—a true oasis with vine-covered walls, cafe tables, huge palm trees, and fountains.

Plaça de Espanya, 6. www.diana-hotel.com, ✆ **97-234-18-86.** 21 units. 70€–170€ double; 120€–250€ triple. Parking nearby 10€. Closed Nov–Apr 5. **Amenities:** Restaurant; bar; room service; free Wi-Fi.

INEXPENSIVE

Hotel Cap d'Or ★★   This small hotel has a lot going for it. It's family-run, with good, personal service, and enjoys an enviable location snuggled up to the stone walls of the old castle on the south end of town. And it's right on the beach. Small is the operative word, however, and the 11 very tidy and simply decorated rooms tend to be compact. Some have lovely ocean views, but all guests can enjoy the vistas from the outdoor terrace, where breakfast and other light fare, prepared by the women in the family, is served. Reserve early.

Passeig de Vila Vella, 1. www.hotelcapdor.com. ✆ **97-234-00-81.** 69€–110€ double; 139€–169€ family room (2 adults and 2 children). Parking nearby 23€. Closed Nov–Mar. **Amenities:** Restaurant; bar; free Wi-Fi.

Hotel Tonet ★   We like the fact that Tossa de Mar is a real little town rather than simply a beach resort. This modest, family-run hotel sits on one of the town plazas and is a good place to hear church bells call people to Mass and to observe daily life from the upper-level terrace/solarium. Yet it is only about a 5-minute walk to the beach. Many of the simply furnished rooms are on the small side and a bit dated, and there is no air-conditioning.

Plaça de l'Església, 1. www.hoteltonet.com. ✆ **97-234-02-37.** 36 units. 51€–65€ double. Parking nearby 10€. **Amenities:** Bar; free lobby Wi-Fi.

Where to Eat in Tossa de Mar

La Cuina de Can Simón ★★ CONTEMPORARY CATALAN   This rustic-seeming dining room of rough stone walls dates back to the mid-18th century, when Tossa was a fishing village and fortress town rather than a seaside preserve for the well-to-do. The food here, however, is anything but rustic, representing instead the finesse of contemporary Catalan cooking. Dishes are available a la carte, but most diners opt for the tasting menu, which begins with small bites before moving on to raw oysters (in season), a soup, a fish plate (say, scallops with sea urchin roe), a fish *fideù* (like paella with noodles), a whole baked fish, and then either a small grilled steak or a mound of steak tartare. The dessert platter always features fresh fruit and some form of pudding or ice cream.

Carrer Portal, 24. www.restaurantcansimon.com. ✆ **97-234-12-69.** Entrees 28€–48€; set menus 68€ and 98€. Reservations required. Wed–Sat 1–3:30pm and 8–10:30pm, Sun 1-3:30.

Restaurant Sa Muralla ★ CATALAN   You needn't get dressed up to eat at "The Wall," a grill restaurant offering simple, straightforward food. Born as a fishermen's bar, it's evolved into one of the best casual restaurants in Tossa, and it recently expanded to a less atmospheric, but more airy, upper floor. Pescaphobes have a choice of grilled chicken, veal, pork, and lamb, though the grilled catch of the day is what most people order—unless they're enjoying the Tossa classic, *cim-i-tomba,* which consists of layers of fish and potato in a casserole, served with a whole head of roasted garlic and ALSO some very garlicky aioli.

Carrer Portal, 16. www.samuralla.com. ✆ **97-234-11-28.** Entrees 9€–27€, set menus start at 29€. Daily noon–4pm and 7–11pm.

ARAGÓN

By Jennifer Ceaser

L andlocked Aragón, along with adjacent Navarra, forms the northeastern quadrant of Spain. Most travelers find this ancient land *terra incognita,* which is unfortunate because Aragón is one of the most history-steeped regions of the country, associated especially with two former residents: Fernando of Aragón, whose marriage to Isabel, queen of Castilla y León, in the 15th century led to the unification of Spain; and his daughter Catalina de Aragón (better known in English as Catherine of Aragón), the unfortunate first wife of Henry VIII of England.

Aragón prides itself on its exceptional Mudéjar architecture, a synthesis of the architectural forms of Christian Europe with the decorative motifs and construction techniques of the Muslim world.

ZARAGOZA ★★

According to legend, the Virgin Mary appeared to Santiago (St. James the Apostle), patron saint of Spain, on the banks of the Rio Ebro and ordered him to build a church there. Today Zaragoza, which sits at the center of a rich alluvial plain, is a bustling, prosperous, commercial city of wide boulevards and arcades. Its handsome cathedral is a Mudéjar landmark, and its ornate basilica is an important pilgrimage center.

Founded by Carthaginians, Zaragoza first flourished as the Roman colony of Caesaraugusta. As an independent Muslim principality in the 11th century, it played a pivotal role in Christian-Muslim political relations; after being conquered by Christian forces, Zaragoza became the seat of the medieval kingdom of Aragón.

Today, Zaragoza is a city of nearly 700,000 people—nearly three-quarters of the entire population of Aragón live here in the province's capital. With more than 33,000 students, the Universidad de Zaragoza has livened up this once-staid city. Cafes, theaters, restaurants, music bars, and taverns have boomed in recent years.

Essentials

ARRIVING Zaragoza's airport (ZAZ) has limited service via Ryanair from London, and by Air Europa from Paris (seasonal), Brussels, and Milan. The city is so well-connected by train that it no longer has commercial domestic flights. Approximately 30 **trains** arrive daily from

Aragón

Barcelona (trip time: 1½–5¼ hr.) and 19 from Madrid (trip time: 1¼–3½ hr.). Trains pull into Estación Zaragoza-Delicias, Calle Rioja, 33 (www. renfe.com; © **90-232-03-20**). All but a few trains per day are high-speed rail. There are also 8 direct **buses** a day between Zaragoza and Barcelona (trip time: 3½ hr.) and 18 direct buses from Madrid (trip time: 3½ hr.). By car, Zaragoza is easily reached on the E-90 (A-2) east from Madrid or west from Barcelona.

VISITOR INFORMATION The **tourist office,** Plaza del Pilar, s/n (www. zaragozaturismo.es; © **97-620-12-00**), is open daily 10am to 8pm. It's closed December 25 and January 1.

SPECIAL EVENTS   One of the city's big festivities is the **Fiesta de la Virgen del Pilar,** held the week of October 12, with top-name bullfighters, religious processions, and general merriment.

Exploring Zaragoza

Basílica de Nuestra Señora del Pilar ★★ CATHEDRAL   Considered a co-cathedral with La Seo del Salvador (below), this grandiose 16th- and 17th-century basilica on the bank of the Río Ebro has an almost Byzantine aspect with its domes and towers. Thousands of the faithful travel here annually to pay homage to the tiny statue of the *Virgen del Pilar* in the Holy Chapel. The basilica's name, **El Pilar,** comes from the pillar upon which the Virgin is supposed to have stood when she asked Santiago (St. James) to build the church. (Like "Montserrat," "Pilar" is a common Spanish woman's name, often conferred by devout parents.) During the second week of October, the church is a backdrop for an important festival devoted to Nuestra Señora del Pilar (Our Lady of the Pilar), with parades, bullfights, fireworks, flower offerings, and street dancing. For art lovers, the basilica's main attraction is its frescoes painted by Goya, who was born nearby. The baroque cupolas in the Temple of

The multi-towered Basilica de Nuestra Señora del Pilar rise over the banks of the River Ebro in Zaragoza.

Pilar were decorated by Goya and Francisco Bayeu, another Zaragoza artist and Goya's brother-in-law. The attached **Museo Pilarista** houses the jewelry collection used to adorn the Pilar statue, as well as sketches by Goya and other local artists.

Plaza de la Nuestra Señora del Pilar. ℂ **97-639-74-97.** Free admission to cathedral; museum 2€. Cathedral Mon–Fri 6:45am–8:30pm (until 9:30pm in summer), Sat and Sun 6:45am–9:30pm. Museum Mon–Fri 10am–2pm and 4–8pm; Sat 10am–2pm. Bus: 22 or 36.

La Seo del Salvador ★ CATHEDRAL This Gothic-Mudéjar church, built between 1316 and 1319 and enlarged and renovated into the 18th century, is in many ways even more impressive than El Pilar. The rich white facade is a fine example of the Aragonese Mudéjar style and the structure is an exemplar of Aragonese Gothic architecture. Among its more important features are the main altar and a fine collection of French and Flemish tapestries from the 15th to the 17th centuries, which are housed in the adjacent museum.

Plaza de la Seo. ℂ **97-629-12-311.** Admission 4€ (includes Tapestry Museum). Mid-June to mid-Oct daily 10am–9pm; mid-Oct to mid-June Mon–Fri 10am–2pm and 4–6:30pm, Sat 10am–12:30pm and 4–6:30pm, Sun 10am–noon and 4–6:30pm. Bus: 21, 22, 29, 32, 35, 36, 43, 44, or 45.

Museo de Zaragoza ★ MUSEUM There's a marvelously old-fashioned feel about this museum of local antiquities, beginning with its flamboyant Beaux-Arts building, which was constructed for the Hispano-French Exposition of 1908 (commemorating the centenary of Napoleon's siege of the city). The building survived fierce bombardment during the Spanish Civil War, and the heroic statues that surround it speak of a pre-war era that romanticized antiquity: Three main sculptures represent Painting, Architecture, and Sculpture itself, and a pair of Art Nouveau sculptures allude to Archaeology. Most of the ground-floor exhibits are the results of local digs, and represent prehistoric, Carthaginian, Roman, and Muslim eras in Zaragoza. Most notable is a fine bust of Caesar Augustus, for whom the original Roman city was named.

Plaza de los Sitios 6. www.museodezaragoza.es. ℂ **97-622-21-81.** Free admission. Tues–Sat 10am–2pm and 5–8pm; Sun 10am–2pm. Bus: 30, 35, or 40.

Museo Goya-Colección Ibercaja ★★ ART MUSEUM Set in a marvelous Renaissance home in the middle of the city, this small museum recently was renamed to focus on the region's most famous native son, Francisco de Goya. The first floor features mostly Spanish religious paintings from the 15th to 18th centuries, while a few Goya paintings, including a self-portrait, are highlights of the Sala Goya on the mezzanine. The real attraction is the low-lit second floor, which displays five Goya etching series, including *Los Caprichos* and the wrenching *Los Desastres de la*

Guerra. The third floor is devoted to little-known (and fairly unexceptional) Spanish artists from the 19th and 20th centuries.

Calle Espoz y Mina, 23. museogoya.ibercaja.es. ☏ **97-639-73-87.** Admission 4€. Mid-Mar to Oct Mon–Sat 10am–8pm; Sun 10am–2pm; Nov to mid-Mar Mon–Sat 10am–2pm and 4–8pm; Sun 10am–2pm. Bus: 30, 35, or 40.

Museo Pablo Gargallo ★ ART MUSEUM   Pablo Gargallo (1881–1934) was Aragón's contribution to the artistic avant-garde of the early 20th century. A great friend of Picasso and Juan Gris, he was born in Maella, Aragón, but spent his most productive years in Paris. He introduced Cubism's jarring dimensional changes into sculpture by creating three-dimensional figures from flat metal plates. He was also among the first of the avant-garde to appropriate celebrities as images, creating sculptures modeled on Greta Garbo. The museum holds 100 of his works.

Plaza de San Felipe 3. www.zaragoza.es. ☏ **97-639-25-24.** Admission 4€. Tues–Sat 10am–2pm and 5–9pm; Sun 10am–2:30pm. Bus: 35 or 36.

Where to Stay in Zaragoza

Hotel Alfonso Zaragoza ★★   On the border of the historic city center and the bustling shopping area around Plaza España, this 12-story modern hotel has one of the city's best locations. The nice-sized rooms feature bright, contemporary furnishings, parquet floors, and automated window treatments. Spring for one of the 16 upper-floor junior suites with separate seating areas, kitchenettes, and free-standing bathtubs in the open bathrooms; some come with spacious terraces with great city views. The rooftop pool is a rare find in the city, though the larger indoor pool on the basement level is more suitable for swimming.

Calle Coso, 15-17-19. www.palafoxhoteles.com. ☏ **87-654-11-18.** 120 units. 80€–161€ double. Public parking nearby 16€. **Amenities:** Cafeteria; room service; indoor and outdoor pools (both seasonal); free Wi-Fi.

Hotel Reino de Aragón ★   This up-to-date business hotel is less than a 5-minute walk from the medieval historic center and steps away from the tapas-hopping district on the ladder streets between calles Coso and San Miguel. Service is polite and helpful, and the rooms are comfortable despite the spare, modern decor. This is one high-rise where we opt for an upper floor, as the hotel has enough elevators to avoid long waits. For a slight splurge (about 10€ more), choose one of the superior rooms on the sixth floor to enjoy an outdoor terrace.

Calle Coso, 8. www.hoteles-silken.com. ☏ **97-646-82-00.** 117 units. 75€–160€ double. Parking 16€. **Amenities:** Restaurant; bar; gym; free Wi-Fi.

NH Gran Hotel ★★★   NH Hoteles seems to specialize in finding neglected gems and bringing them back to life. Created in 1929 as one of a national string of fine hotels, the Gran enjoys wonderful bone structure—that is, a fine Art Deco exterior and well-laid-out public rooms. NH basically gutted the guest floors to create contemporary rooms in soothing shades of gray with contrasting dark wood floors, while maintaining the original high ceilings, tall windows, and crown molding. The hotel is a top venue for weddings and other life-landmark celebrations, while the meeting rooms make it a popular choice with businesses. For sightseers, it's a 10-minute walk to the basilica, plus the pretty, leafy streets surrounding the hotel are brimming with upscale boutiques and pleasant cafes.

Calle Joaquín Costa, 5. www.nh-hoteles.com. ✆ **97-622-19-01.** 133 units. 80€–154€ double; from 117€ junior suite. Parking 16€. **Amenities:** Restaurant; bar; gym; sauna; room service; free Wi-Fi.

Zenit Don Yo ★ There are budget hotels and then there are bargain-priced hotels. We consider this Zenit affiliate one of the bargains, as the hotel is fresh and contemporary, and while the rooms are modestly furnished, they're pretty large by Spanish standards and their beds are top-notch. The location is best for business but fine for sightseeing—right next to the Plaza de Aragón and Plaza de la Independencia.

Calle Juan Bruil, 4–6. www.zenithoteles.com. ✆ **97-622-67-41.** 147 units. 55€–79 € double; from 86€ junior suite. Parking 12€. **Amenities:** Restaurant; bar; room service; gym; free Wi-Fi; pets allowed.

Where to Eat in Zaragoza

Bodegón Azoque ★★ SPANISH   Fish from Galicia, chorizo from Navarra, shrimp from Huelva: This cozy, rustic, two-story restaurant excels at sourcing the best regional products from all over Spain. It's an extensive menu, with symbols detailing the ingredients in each dish—helpful if you're a picky eater but otherwise a bit overwhelming. Easiest is to check the chalkboard for whatever's in season, order a few dishes, and let the quality of ingredients shine in the preparation. Don't miss the

---

ON THE menu IN ARAGÓN

Aragón has a cuisine built on meat, from the famous Teruel ham to mountain lamb. The plains of the Río Ebro produce much of Spain's native wheat and barley. Specialties of the Aragonese table include:

- Lamb or kid roasted on a spit
- Fried slices of Teruel ham with tomato sauce
- Wild trout from mountain streams
- *Cecina* (air-dried beef)
- Wild mushrooms and black truffles
- Artichokes stewed with local ham and almonds

signature Ensalada Azoque, a mix of spinach, mushrooms, bacon, and fried goat cheese chopped and served tableside. If you're eating at the usual Spanish time for dinner (9pm or later), be sure to make a reservation and ask for a table on the buzzier main level.

Calle Marqués Casa Jiménez, 6. www.bodegonazoque.com. *℃* **97-622-03-20.** Reservations suggested. Entrees 12€–25€. Set menu 22€. Tasting menu 45€. Mon–Sat 11:30–4pm and 7pm–midnight, Sun 11:30–4pm. Bus: 21, 38; tram Plaza Aragon.

La Rinconada de Lorenzo ★ ARAGONESE An old-fashioned favorite, "Larry's Little Corner" has acquitted itself of stodginess by introducing a line of creative tapas that have swept the local awards for the last few years. It's in the university area, which means that the bar is always hopping even when the dining room is quiet. The fare is traditional for Aragón, favoring roasted meats, especially the D.O. Ternasco de Aragón, a special variety of lamb. The lamb even shows up stewed, as in the dark and unctuous bowl of trotters. The wine list is short on whites but has multiple reasonably priced red options from the Aragonese delimited wine districts of Calatayud, Somontano, and Cariñena.

Calle La Salle 3. www.larinconadadelorenzo.com. *℃* **97-655-51-08.** Reservations required. Entrees 10€–22€. Mon–Sat noon–4pm and 8–11:30pm, Sun noon–4pm (June–Aug closed on Mon). Bus: 20, 24, 33; tram to San Francisco.

mudéjar **ARCHITECTURE**

BRICKS: Most Mudéjar buildings in Aragón are constructed of brick, which lends itself well to sophisticated geometric decoration. Walls of Romanesque and Gothic churches tended to be very thick, allowing the craftsmen to configure the surface bricks with protruding corners that create complex decorative patterns.

WOOD: Sophisticated combinations of carved panels and geometrically arrayed beams and boards characterize Mudéjar wooden ceilings. They are usually found in rooms where the ceiling span does not exceed 20 feet, such as private chambers in palaces, small rooms in convents and monasteries, and anterooms in churches. A major exception is the coffered ceiling of the main nave of the Teruel cathedral.

PLASTER: Plaster carving figured prominently in many Islamic architectural styles in Andalucía, and adaptations of those techniques decorate doorways, windows, and even entire walls in Mudéjar buildings constructed in the Christian-dominated north.

TILES: Muslim craftsmen introduced tile artistry to Sevilla in the 8th century, and their abstract geometric tiles still persist as a popular decorative element in Spanish buildings. Mudéjar buildings often feature tiled floors, half-tiled walls, and tile decorations on their exteriors. The tower of San Salvador in Teruel is often cited as one of the most harmonious combinations of Mudéjar tile- and brickwork.

Restaurante Riskomar ★★ BASQUE With its self-consciously *vanguardista* design and unabashedly Basque menu, Riskomar offers a full-immersion dining experience of strong flavors, contrasting textures, and a little bit of culinary theater. Many dishes are prepared over an open flame in emulation of Basque master chef Victor Arguinzoniz of Asador Etxebarri. Several of the best plates use *cocochas,* the cheeks of big hake or cod, which are both the chewiest and most flavorful parts of the fish. Shellfish are impeccable here; try the pink and white shrimp, Galician clams, and langoustines.

Calle Francisco de Vitoria, 16–18. www.restauranteriskomar.com. ✆ **97-622-50-53.** Reservations required. Entrees 20€–32€. Tasting menus 28€–45€. Mon–Sat 1:30–4pm and 9–11:30pm, Sun 1:30–4pm. Closed 2 weeks at Easter. Bus: 33.

Entertainment & Nightlife

Zaragoza is a university town, so things perk up around 11pm. A good place to begin an evening's bar- and pub-crawl is Plaza Santa Cruz.

A popular tapas bar worth a visit is **Casa Luis,** Calle Policarpo Romea, 8 (✆ **97-629-11-67**). Shellfish tapas include oysters, shrimp, and razor clams in little bundles. The house *cojonudos* (toast topped with quail's eggs, ham, and roasted red pepper) is the best version in town. Casa Luis is open most of the year (closed in June and last 3 weeks of Nov) Tuesday to Sunday 1 to 4pm and 7 to 11pm. House wine starts at 1.50€, and tapas range from 2€ to 8€.

TARAZONA ★

The kings of Aragón once lived here, and before them, it was a Roman center. But this handsome city on the border with La Rioja and Navarra is really noted for its Mudéjar architectural landmarks. The Mudéjar style reached its apogee in medieval Aragón, where Christians and Muslims collaborated in the design, decoration, and construction of major buildings.

Essentials

ARRIVING Six **buses** arrive daily from Zaragoza. Trip time is 1 hour, and a one-way fare costs 9.50€. For bus information and schedules, contact Therpasa (www.therpasa.es; ✆ **97-622-57-23**). If you're driving, head west from Zaragoza along the A-68, connecting with the N-122 to Tarazona.

VISITOR INFORMATION The **tourist office,** at Plaza San Francisco 1 (www.tarazona.es; ✆ **97-664-00-74**), is open daily until 6:30 or 7pm, with a mid-day closure from 2:30 to 4pm.

Exploring Tarazona

Tarazona is laid out in tiers above the quays of the Rio Queiles. The city's major attraction is its Gothic **cathedral** ★ begun in 1152 but essentially reconstructed in the 15th and 16th centuries. It's a superb example of the Aragonese Mudéjar architectural style of that era, especially in the elaborate lantern tower and belfry. It's worth going inside (admission is 4€ adults, 3€ seniors and students, free under age 12) to see some fine plasterwork and a striking cloister. The church is generally open Tuesday to Sunday 11am to 2pm and 4 to 7pm (closes Sun 6pm). From mid-October until late March, it's closed on Tuesdays as well, and closes weekdays at 6pm.

Tarazona's cathedral is another striking example of the Mudéjar architectural style.

The handsome 16th-century **Ayuntamiento (Town Hall)** has reliefs across its facade depicting Carlos V entering Bologna in 1529 to be crowned Holy Roman Emperor. The emperor is upstaged, however, by even grander murals depicting heroic deeds of Hercules, which tradition says were performed on a mountain southeast of town. Follow the Ruta Turística, a scenic walk, from city hall up to the church of **Santa María Magdalena,** which has a Mudéjar tower that forms the chief landmark of the town's skyline; its *mirador* opens onto a panoramic view.

Where to Stay & Eat in Tarazona

Hotel Brujas de Irués ★   The setting for this recently remodeled modern hotel couldn't be nicer. Just outside of town on the Zaragoza road, the hotel looks out on the spires of the medieval city on the front, and on a sweeping mountain range in the back. There is a business center, and the hotel even has meeting rooms, but the clientele seems to be an equal mix of businesspeople and tourists. Rooms are modest and simply decorated and some bathrooms have tubs. The street level has a perfectly pleasant restaurant that serves an international menu and features an affordably priced, three-course *menú del día.*

Teresa Cajal, 30. www.hotelbrujas.com. ℭ **97-664-04-00.** 56 units. 52€–60€ double. Free parking. **Amenities:** Restaurant; cafeteria; free Wi-Fi.

Condes de Visconti ★★   You definitely feel surrounded by history at this delightful small hotel in a 16th-century in-town palace. Even the Renaissance arcade of the courtyard is lined with Tuscan columns. Because it's right in the heart of the old city, it makes an ideal perch for exploring the medieval streets. While the bones of the hotel are classic, the decor is a harmonious blend of antiques with contemporary furniture and art. The romantic bedrooms, many with canopy beds, all feature tubs in the bathrooms—whirlpool tubs in most instances.

Calle Visconti, 15. www.condesdevisconti.com. ℂ **97-664-49-08.** 15 units. 62€–85€ double. **Amenities:** Bar; restaurant; free Wi-Fi.

NUÉVALOS/PIEDRA ★

The town of Nuévalos, with its one paved road, isn't much of a lure, but thousands of visitors flock to the **Monasterio de Piedra.**

Essentials

From Madrid, **train** connections reach Calatayud; take a taxi from there to the monastery. Driving from Zaragoza, take the A-2 motorway in the direction of Madrid-Barcelona and exit at Nuévalos. If you're driving from Madrid, take the A-2 motorway in the direction of Madrid-Barcelona and exit at Alhama de Aragón.

Exploring the Monastery

Nuévalos's major attraction, the **Monasterio de Piedra ★★★** (www. monasteriopiedra.com; ℂ **97-687-07-00**) is a virtual Garden of Eden—it even has a 60m (197-ft.) waterfall. It was here in 1194 that Cistercian monks built a charterhouse on the banks of the Rio Piedra. It is said the original monks moved to this site because they wanted a "foretaste of paradise"; actually, they were escaping the political intrigues at the powerful Monestir de Poblet (p. 506) in Catalunya. The monks left in 1835, but their former quarters are now a hotel (below).

Two pathways, marked in blue or red, meander through the grounds, and views are offered from several levels. Tunnels and stairways dating from the 19th century are the work of Juan Federico Mutadas, who created the park. Slippery steps lead down to an iris grotto, just one of many quiet, secluded retreats. You can wander through the grounds from 9am to 7pm (Oct–Mar until 6pm). The monastery is open daily 10am to 6pm. Admission to the park and monastery is 16€.

Where to Stay & Eat

Monasterio de Piedra ★★★   You'll feel more like a bishop on retreat than a monk when you stay at this luxurious hotel on the grounds of the monastery. Rooms have views either of the surrounding parklands or the 12th-century cloister, and the spa is nothing short of sumptuous.

The hotel grounds meld into the landscaped grounds, and guests enjoy free entry to both the monastery and the park. The dining room, which is also open to non-guests, serves traditional Aragonese cuisine.

Calle Afueras, s/n. www.monasteriopiedra.com. ✆ **97-687-07-00.** 62 units. 98€–282€ double. Rates include buffet breakfast. Restaurant entrees 14€–25€. Free parking. **Amenities:** 3 restaurants; 3 bars; outdoor pool; free Wi-Fi.

TERUEL ★★

Virtually an open-air museum of Mudéjar architecture (see the sidebar on p. 546), Teruel is visually stunning. In 1986, UNESCO designated its cathedral and three other churches in town as the Mudéjar Architecture World Heritage Site. The sheer beauty of the town makes it worth a trip if you're anywhere in the vicinity.

That being said, Teruel was once even more architecturally distinguished than you'll find it today. It was the site of the bloodiest battle of the Spanish Civil War, with the city changing hands several times between December 1937 and February 1938 in the worst winter cold recorded in Spain up to that time. More than 140,000 soldiers died and many of the city's medieval structures were destroyed in the bombardment.

Essentials

ARRIVING   Four **trains** per day arrive from Zaragoza in the north and Valencia in the south. Travel time is about 2½ hours from either direction, and fares range from 15€ to 20€. Trains pull into Estación Teruel, Camino de la Estación (www.renfe.com; ✆ **90-232-03-20**).

VISITOR INFORMATION   The **tourist office,** at Plaza de los Amantes (www.turismo.teruel.es; ✆ **97-862-41-05**), is open daily 10am to 2pm and 4 to 8pm (10am–8pm in Aug).

Exploring Teruel

Most visitors approach the old city from the north, walking up the 1920s neo-Mudéjar **L'Escalinata** stairs to enter town through the arch of the elaborate 14th-century **Torre El Salvador.** The narrow street opens into the city's main square, **Plaza del Torico,** built around a fountain flowing from the mouth of a bull. The bull has been a civic symbol since Alfonso II captured the city in 1171. Among the buildings on the plaza, the striking **Casa El Torico,** a lilac-blue confection with white floral designs, is an example of 19th-century Modernisme architecture, which was greatly inspired by Teruel's Mudéjar style.

Architecture experts consider the **Catedral de Santa María de Mediavilla ★★★** to be the most beautiful surviving example of Mudéjar architecture. Its towers, dome, and roof are all designated as part of

A fountain in Teruel's Plaza del Torico features a bull, the city's symbol.

UNESCO's World Heritage, but the coffered ceiling of the central nave is also a masterwork. It is located on the Plaza de la Catedral (✆ **97-861-80-16**). Admission is 3€ adults, 2€ seniors and students. It is open daily until 8pm in summer; the rest of the year it is open Monday to Saturday 11am to 2pm and 4 to 7pm and Sunday 4 to 7pm.

The 14th-century Mudéjar masterpiece **Iglesia San Pedro** ★★ (www.amantesdeteruel.es; ✆ **97-861-83-98**) contains a chapel dedicated to Los Amantes, ill-fated medieval lovers whose legend looms larger than the church's towers. Entrance to the mausoleum, which has high-tech displays about the Romeo-and-Juliet tale, costs 4€, while San Pedro alone is only 2€. We recommend the 8€ package ticket that includes the church, the Mudéjar tower attached to it, and the walkway in between, but if you have the time and actually like tales of doomed lovers in antiquity, go for the whole 9€ package of mausoleum, church, tower, and walkway. The complex is open daily 10am to 2pm and 4 to 8pm (10am–8pm in Aug).

Where to Stay & Eat in Teruel

Hotel Reina Cristina ★★ Beautifully renovated in 2013 by the Gargallo group, one of northeast Spain's leading hoteliers, the Reina Cristina sits just outside the old city walls at the Torre El Salvador. It's an easy, if slightly uphill, walk to see the major sights of town. While the rooms are not especially large, they are carefully thought-out to avoid wasting space. Views are either of the city or of the dramatic countryside. Parking is always a problem in Teruel, but the Reina Cristina has its own dedicated lot. The hotel restaurant, which serves traditional Aragonese cuisine, serves an excellent large breakfast buffet (inquire when booking).

Paseo del Óvalo, 1. www.hotelreinacristinateruel.com. ✆ **97-860-68-60.** 101 units. 68€–80€ double. Parking 13€. **Amenities:** Restaurant; bar; free Wi-Fi.

Parador de Teruel ★★   When you drive up to this *parador* on the outskirts of Teruel (about 2km/1⅓ miles from the city center), you might do a double take. The building is a substantial country house built in a modern version of the Mudéjar style, right down to the carved plaster, tile decorations, and the use of repeating ogival arches. The garden landscaping even gives the property a quasi-Moorish feel. Rooms are large and modern, and the bathrooms are filled with marble. The restaurant serves Aragonese cuisine with a special emphasis on roasted, grilled, and stewed lamb.

Carretera Sagunto-Burgos, N-234 km122.5. www.parador.es. © **97-860-18-00.** 60 units. 80€–104€ double; 180€–203€ suite. Free parking. **Amenities:** Restaurant; bar; outdoor pool; free Wi-Fi.

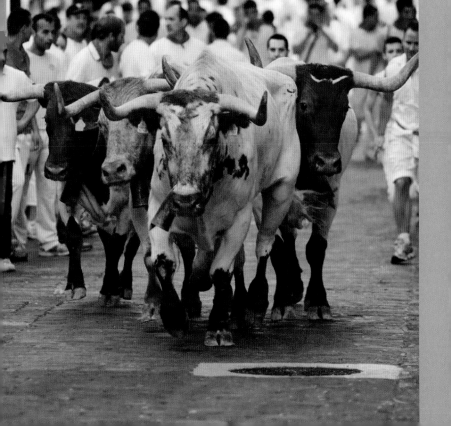

NAVARRA &
LA·RIOJA

By Murray Stewart

14

The ancient kingdom of Navarra (Nafarroa in Basque) shares a 130km (82-mile) frontier with France, with its many Pyrenean crossing points making it an important link between Iberia and the rest of the European continent. As a border region, Navarra has seen its share of conflict, and to this day the remains of isolated castles and fortified walled towns bear witness to historic struggles. But this proud land, one of the most ancient on the peninsula, has preserved its own government and—at least north of the capital, Pamplona–some strong Basque traditions. While Castilian Spanish is the official language throughout the autonomous region, Euskera is an official language in northern Navarra, where it is spoken. Economically, this is also one of Spain's richest communities.

Romans, Christians, French, Muslims, and Jews have all left their stamp on Navarra, and its architecture is as diverse as its landscape. Rich in folklore, here pagan rites were blended with Christian traditions to form an engrained mythology that lives on today in Navarra's myriad festivals.

Navarra is well-endowed with natural attractions, from the mighty northern Pyrenean peaks, through dramatic gorges in the east and high sierras in the west, down to its central vineyards and even arid semi-desert landscapes in the south. Most foreign visitors miss these when they come in July to see the **Fiesta de San Fermín** and its chaotic bull-running through the streets of Pamplona. If you do visit for the festival, try to explore the surrounding region as well.

Adjoining Navarra is **La Rioja,** by population and terrain the smallest autonomous region of mainland Spain. By virtue of its world-famous wine, this province punches well above its weight. The provincial capital is lively Logroño, a city of some 200,000 that sits both on the Ebro, one of Spain's most significant rivers, and on the Camino de Santiago, its most important pilgrimage route.

PAMPLONA/IRUÑA ★

Ernest Hemingway's descriptions of the running of the bulls in his 1926 novel, *The Sun Also Rises,* made **Pamplona** universally famous. Those romantics who read the book, then rush off to Pamplona to see the

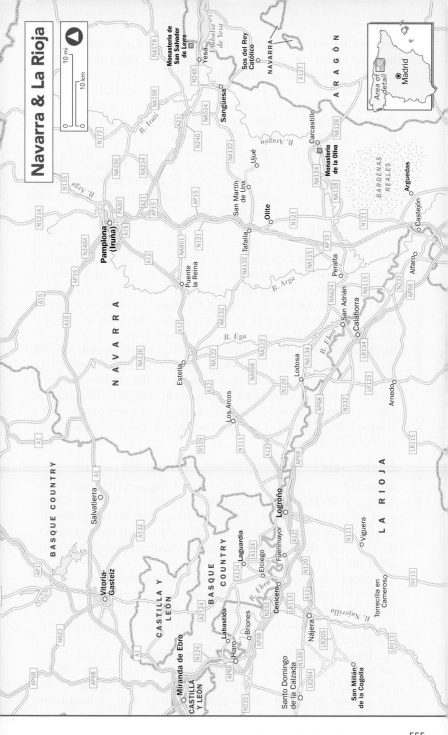

encierro (running of the bulls) during the Fiesta de San Fermín, generally miss the author's ironic depiction of manliness. This raucous festival remains a superstar attraction, the focal point of the city's calendar. Beginning on July 6 and lasting 9 days, the revelry is accompanied by fireworks, Basque flute concerts, and many other lively sideshows. Finding a bed in Pamplona during fiesta time means reserving a year in advance or planning to stay elsewhere in the region and "commuting" by bus.

But Pamplona is far more than just a city with a popular annual festival. Long the most significant community in Spain's Pyrenean region, it was also a major stopover for those traveling either of two frontier roads: the Roncesvalles Pass or the Velate Pass. Once a fortified city, it became the capital of the ancient Basque kingdom of Navarra in 824.

In its historic core—best explored on foot—the Pamplona of legend lives on, but the city has been engulfed by modern real-estate development. Nevertheless, there are many green spaces, including La Taconera, a spacious swath of fountain-filled gardens and parkland west of the old quarter, popular with university students and strutting peacocks.

Pamplona's Golden Age came at the beginning of the 15th century during the reign of Carlos III of Navarra (called "the Noble"), who gave the city its cathedral, where he was later buried. Over the years, the city has been the scene of many battles, with various factions struggling for control. Those who lived in the old quarter, the Navarrería, wanted to be allied with Castilla y León, whereas those on the outskirts favored a French connection. Castilla y León eventually won out, although some citizens today would prefer Pamplona to be part of a new country with a Basque identity. South of the city, that identity and Basque nationalist sentiment diminishes.

Essentials

ARRIVING   Few people fly to Pamplona's **Aeropuerto de Noaín** (www. aena.es; © **91-321-10-00**), since service consists of only a few flights a week from Madrid on Iberia (www.iberia.com; © **90-111-15-00**). It's located 6.5km (4 miles) from the city, connected hourly by bus Line A to the city center and bus and train stations. A taxi into the center will cost about 16€.

Nine **trains** connect daily to and from Madrid (trip time: 3–6 hr.) and six with Barcelona (trip time: 4 hr.) Pamplona also has four daily connections with San Sebastián to the north (trip time: 1¾ hr.). Zaragoza, Burgos, and Vigo can also be reached directly. Visit www.renfe.com for train details and bookings.

Buses connect Pamplona with several Spanish cities and regional towns: seven per day with Madrid (trip time: 6 hr.), six per day with Barcelona (trip time: 5½ hr.), eight per day with Zaragoza (trip time: 2¼ hr.), and a dozen daily with San Sebastián (trip time: 1 hr). Information is

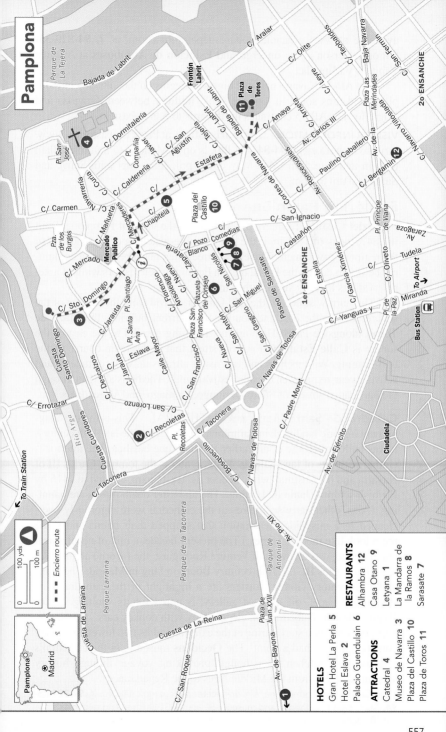

Pamplona

Encierro route .... (dashed line legend)

0 ——— 100 yds
0 ——— 100 m

Parque de La Tejera

Bajada de Labrit

Parque de Larraina

Parque de La Taconera

Parque de Antoniuti

Cuesta de Larraina

Cuesta de La Reina

To Train Station

Río Arga

C/ Errotazar

Pza. de los Burgos

Pl. San José

C/ Dormitalería

C/ Carmen

C/ Navarrería

C/ Curia

Pl. de la Compañía

C/ Javier

C/ San Agustín

C/ Tejería

Frontón Labrit

Bajada de Labrit

Plaza de Toros

C/ Aralar

C/ Olite

C/ Leyre

C/ Amaya

C/ Arrieta

Av. Carlos III

Paulino Caballero

Av. de la Navarro Villoslada

Plaza Las Merindades

Baja Navarra

San Fermín

2º ENSANCHE

C/ Bergamín

C/ Teobaldos

Estafeta

C/ Calderería

C/ Chapitela

C/ Mercaderes

C/ Manueta

Sto. Domingo

C/ Mercado

Mercado Público

Plaza del Castillo

C/ San Ignacio

C/ Pozo Blanco

C/ Comedias

C/ Castañón

C/ Estella

C/ García Ximénez

C/ Oliveto

C/ Tudela

Pl. Príncipe de Viana

Av. de Zaragoza

To Airport

Bus Station

Miranda

Pl. de la Paz

C/ Yanguas y Miranda

1er ENSANCHE

Paseo de Sarasate

C/ San Nicolás

C/ San Miguel

C/ San Gregorio

C/ San Antón

C/ Nueva

Plazuela del Consejo

Plaza San Francisco

C/ San Francisco

Pl. Santa Ana

Eslava

Calle Mayor

C/ Jarauta

C/ Descalzos

C/ San Lorenzo

C/ Recoletas

Pl. Recoletas

C/ Taconera

C/ Bosquecillo

C/ Navas de Tolosa

C/ Pedre Moret

Av. de Ejército

Ciudadela

Av. Pío XII

Plaza de Juan XXIII

Av. de Bayona

C/ San Roque

Cuesta Santo Domingo

C/ Cuesta Curtidores

C/ Florencio Ansoleaga

C/ Nueva

Pl. Santiago

C/ Santiago

HOTELS
Gran Hotel La Perla 5
Hotel Eslava 2
Palacio Guendulain 6

ATTRACTIONS
Catedral 4
Museo de Navarra 3
Plaza del Castillo 10
Plaza de Toros 11

RESTAURANTS
Alhambra 12
Casa Otano 9
Letyana 1
La Mandarra de la Ramos 8
Sarasate 7

Pamplona
Madrid

557

available at www.estacionautobusesdepamplona.com, at ✆ **94-820-35-66,** or in person at the underground **Estación de Autobuses** at Avenida Yanguas y Miranda.

The AP-15 Navarra national highway begins on the outskirts of Pamplona and runs south to join the A-68, midway between Zaragoza and Logroño. The AP-15 continues northwards to San Sebastián.

VISITOR INFORMATION   The **tourist office,** at Plaza Consistorial (www.turismo.navarra.es; ✆ **94-842-07-00**), is open Monday to Saturday 10am to 2pm and 3 to 5pm (Mar–May until 7pm, June–Sept until 8pm), and Sunday 10am to 2pm.

Exploring Pamplona

Plaza del Castillo, formerly the bullring, is the heart of Pamplona. Built in 1847, today this square is the city's people-watching center and seat of the regional government. The elegant tree-lined plaza becomes a communal bedroom during the Fiesta de San Fermín, when visitors without hotel reservations literally sleep in the streets.

The narrow streets of the Old Quarter extend from three sides of the square. Just to the east and south is the current bullring, the **Plaza de Toros,** alongside Paseo Hemingway. Running parallel to the east of the square is **Calle Estafeta,** a narrow street that is the main course of the bull-running. With its bars and taverns, it attracts university students and is lively year-round even outside festival times. The bulls also run through the barricaded streets of Santo Domingo, Santiago, and Mercaderes.

Catedral de Santa María ★★ CATHEDRAL   This is the most significant historic landmark in Pamplona. Dating from the late 14th century, it was built on the site of an earlier Romanesque basilica. The interior is Gothic with lots of fan vaulting. At the center is the tomb of Carlos III of Navarra and his Castilian wife, Leonor de Trastámara, created in 1416 by Flemish sculptor Janin de Lomme. The alabaster death masks are haunting. (Alas, other early sculptures in the cathedral were vigorously over-cleaned in a misguided restoration that stripped their patina and made them look like modern copies.) The present facade, a mix of neoclassical and baroque, was the work of Ventura Rodríguez, the favorite architect of the other Carlos III, the 18th-century Bourbon king in Madrid. The 14th- and 15th-century Gothic cloisters are a highlight of the cathedral. The Barbazán Chapel, off the east gallery, is noted for its vaulting. Victor Hugo called the cathedral "an elegant lady with donkey ears." Cruel, perhaps, but once you start staring at the exterior and its two towers, you may conclude that he had a point! The **Occidens** museum, in the cathedral's refectory and kitchen, is a thought-provoking voyage through history spanning the era from the Middle Ages to the Renaissance.
Calle Curia/Calle Dormitalería, s/n. www.catedraldepamplona.com. ✆ **94-821-25-94.** Admission to cathedral and museum 5€ adults, 3€ children and pilgrims. Mon–Sat 10:30am–6pm (closes 4pm in fall and winter). Bus: 11.

A detail from the Catedral de Santa Maria in Pamplona.

Museo de Navarra ★ MUSEUM "To make the past present" is this museum's motto, written large above the entrance of what was once a hospital. Its earliest piece, a stone carving called the Mapa de Aboutz, dates from roughly 12,000 years ago, when much of Navarra was covered by glaciers. This carving is a landscape map, leading from the cave where it was found to a spot where hunters would find a herd of goats. Marvelous stone carvings from the A.D. 2nd century indicate the assimilation of Roman art in the area. One beautiful example shows Bacchus returning in triumph from India. And don't miss the splendid examples of Muslim carving from Córdoba, dignified Gothic religious paintings, and Goya's excellent portrait of the Marqués de San Adrián painted in 1804. Local Navarrese artists and sculptors also feature.

Calle de Santo Domingo, 47. www.cfnavarra.es/cultura/museo.© **94-842-64-92.** Admission 2€ adults, 1€ students and seniors, free for ages 15 and under; free for all Sat afternoon and all day Sun. Tues–Sat 9:30am–2pm and 5–7pm; Sun 11am–2pm. Bus: 14.

Where to Stay in Pamplona

Prices here are mostly reasonable, but during the Fiesta de San Fermín, you will pay triple or quadruple those listed below. Unless you're visiting for San Fermín, avoid the city at that time.

THE RUNNING OF THE bulls

Beginning at noon on July 6 and continuing to July 14, the Fiesta de San Fermín is one of the most popular events in Europe, a bucket-list favorite drawing thousands of tourists who severely overtax Pamplona's limited facilities and put a strain on their personal capacities to consume alcohol.

The actual bull-runnings start on July 7. Get up early (or don't go to bed at all) because to watch you'll need to be in position behind the barricades along Calle Estafeta no later than 6am (the run starts at 8am). Actually, taking part is dangerous: Several people die each year in such events across Spain. Each bull-running ends at the bullring.

Tickets for a good seat in the ring go on sale the day before each *corrida* (bull-fight). They can be bought at the bull-ring's ticket offices or online (http://feriadeltoro.com). Tickets cost around 6€ and sell out quickly, and therefore tourists often must use scalpers.

The fiesta draws well over half a million visitors, many of whom camp in the city parks. Temporary facilities are set up, but there are never enough beds. Hotel reservations should be made a year in advance and confirmed *at least* 6 months beforehand—the tourist office will not make any recommendations during the festival. If you look respectable, some Pamplónicos may rent you a room, but they may gouge you for the highest price they think you'll pay, and your room might turn out to be a dirty floor shared with others in a slumlike part of the city. Many young visitors sleep on the grounds of the Ciudadela and Plaza Fueros traffic ring, but muggings can occur. Longtime visitors to Pamplona advise that it's better to sleep in a group, on top of your belongings, and during the day. If you can't find a room.

As for bars and restaurants, ignore all the times given in the listings beginning on p. 561. Most establishments operate round-the-clock during the festival.

Gran Hotel La Perla ★★ This dowager lives up to its reputation as Pamplona's grand hotel. It's said that this is where Hemingway installed his wife, while he went elsewhere to frolic with his mistresses. Built in 1881, its classical facade wears its years with dignity. Renovations have freshened everything without making radical changes in the low-key modern furnishings. The right address to be in the thick of things, it sits on the main square and some rooms overlook Calle Estafeta, where the bulls run in the *encierro* of San Fermín.

Plaza del Castillo, 1. www.granhotellaperla.com. ✆ **94-822-30-00.** 44 units. 181€–250€ double; from 425€ suite. Valet parking 30€. Bus: 3, 5, 8, or 11. **Amenities:** Restaurant; gastrobar; free Wi-Fi.

Hotel Eslava ★ If you're on a budget, the Eslava is the best inexpensive lodging in the town center. It is clean, fairly quiet, and decorated in a no-nonsense old-fashioned style that doesn't vie to be trendy. It's located a short distance from the Plaza de Recoletas, and, of course, not far off the Ruta de Santiago pilgrimage route. Pilgrims like the big bathtubs offered by some double rooms, allowing them to soak away the aches of several days of walking. Staff at the family-run Eslava are extremely hospitable and the breakfast is well-priced.

Plaza Virgen de la O, 7 (corner with Calle Recoletas, 20). www.hotel-eslava.com. ✆ **94-822-22-70.** 28 units. 55€–80€ double. Parking nearby 13€. Bus: A, 16, 17, or 21. Closed Dec 24–Jan 6. **Amenities:** Free Wi-Fi.

Palacio Guendulain ★★★ You can pretend you were born to nobility when you stay at this plush boutique hotel carved out of an 18th-century family home built by the viceroy of northern South America, Sebastián de Eslava. His descendants still live on the second floor, but the ground level has become the hotel reception area and restaurant, while the third and fourth floors are given over to sumptuously appointed guest rooms, decorated with antique-style furnishings and a smattering of real antiques. The family's collection of fancy carriages is on display, and the polished dark woodwork and gilt-edged furniture can make the hotel sometimes feel like a museum. Nonetheless, it is easy to get used to living in this style, especially since the "classic" rooms are modestly priced. (There are more expensive deluxe rooms and two suites.)

Calle Zapatería, 53. www.palacioguendulain.com. ✆ **94-822-55-22.** 26 units. 130€–180€ double, 370€–420€ suite. Parking 18€. Bus: 3, 8, or 10. **Amenities:** Restaurant; bar; free Wi-Fi.

Where to Eat in Pamplona

Pamplona looks to the Basque Country for gastronomic inspiration, with many bars offering the mouthwatering, creative, tapas-style small plates called *pintxos.*

EXPENSIVE

Alhambra ★★ NAVARRESE/BASQUE   A touchstone of contemporary Navarrese cuisine, Alhambra has been one of Pamplona's top restaurants since it opened in 1985. Chef Javier Diaz Zalduendo knows all the classic dishes, but he is no slave to tradition. Try his boneless trotters with boletus sauce, given a squeak of zest with slices of Granny Smith apples, or savor his Iberian lamb dish flavored with thyme, chestnuts, and Armagnac. Local Araiz pigeon is always on the menu, sometimes stewed with tomatoes, at other times boned and served with a roasted mushroom risotto.

Calle de Francisco Bergamín, 7. www.restaurantealhambra.es. ⓒ **94-824-50-07.** Entrees 25€–28€; set menus 58€–69€. Reservations recommended. Mon–Sat 1–3:30pm and 9–10:45pm. Bus: 1, 5, 9, 11, or 17.

MODERATE

Casa Otano ★★ NAVARRESE/BASQUE   While the innovative Basque chefs of the Alhambra (above) prepare gorgeous avant-garde food at reasonable prices, there's an equally appealing, far more casual style of Navarrese cooking that pops up in old-fashioned taverns like Casa Otano. Their creative *pintxos* mirror the style of San Sebastián and Bilbao, but for the great spit-roasted meats, grilled octopus, or lamb chops with fried potatoes, you'll have to grab a table upstairs. Casa Otano has been a local favorite since the 1950s.

Calle San Nicolás, 5. www.casaotano.com. ⓒ **94-822-70-36.** Entrees 12€–22€. Reservations recommended. Mon–Sat 1–3:30pm and 8:30–10:45pm, Sun 1–3:30pm. Bus: 3, 8, or 10.

INEXPENSIVE

Letyana ★★ BASQUE   Located in a section of town known for its tapas and drinking bars, Letyana is vying for the title of "king of *pintxos* in Pamplona." One spectacular plate is the medallion of monkfish mounted on a crab shell, stuffed with crabmeat, on top of scampi cooked in butter and a little squid ink. Another favorite is the loin of venison roasted with prunes and raisins and topped with sauce made with ham, almonds, and cava.

Travesía Bayona, 2. ⓒ **94-825-50-45.** *Pintxos* 3€–5€; *raciones* 6€–18€. Mon–Sat 1–4pm and 8–10:30pm, Sun 1–4pm. Bus: 3.

La Mandarra de la Ramos ★★ BASQUE PINTXOS   Slap-bang in the lively cauldron that is Calle San Nicolás—Pamplona's party street—this local favorite merits a stop on everyone's night out. Fifty huge hams hang from the beamed ceiling, giving a clue as to what might feature heavily in the delicacies on the bar counter. Yes, here they mix it with scrambled egg, top it with seasonal mushrooms, or decorate it with red peppers. The *pintxos* here are not only tasty, but much bigger than those elsewhere. Tables at the rear welcome diners looking for a full meal, which will include octopus or steak, cooked simply. Do take time out from grazing to admire the floor, with its impressive bull-running décor. Calle San Nicolás, 9. www.lamandarradelaramos.com. ℰ **94-821-26-54.** Entrees 8€–15€, set menu 16€. Daily 11am–midnight (Fri–Sat until 1am). Bus: 3, 8, or 10.

Sarasate ★ VEGETARIAN This lovely, largely midday restaurant is an anomaly in meat-loving Navarra. Except during the San Fermín festival, when they revert to carnivore ways and serve meat and fish to satisfy the hordes, Sarasate is strictly vegetarian and has been since 1979. The menus are pretty limited, featuring the usual suspects like creamy rice with mushrooms, a strudel of spinach and feta cheese, and red bean burger with quinoa. Most dishes are gluten-free, and several are vegan. All meals are fixed-price, with fruit juices extra. Calle San Nicolás, 19. www.restaurantesarasate.com. ℰ **94-822-57-27.** Set menus 11€–16.50€. Sun–Thurs 10am–5pm; Fri–Sat 10am–5pm and 8–11pm. Bus: 3, 8, or 10.

Shopping

You'll find Navarrese handicrafts everywhere in shops across the old town. For a good-quality memento, visit **Gurgur,** Calle Estafeta, 21 (ℰ **94-820-79-92**) which is packed to the roof with largely Navarrese products such as *txistorra* sausage, Pamplona chorizo, Navarrese chocolate, jams, honey, wine, and much more. Now in its fourth generation, **Las Tres ZZZ,** Calle Comedias, 7 (ℰ **948-22-44-38**) is the place to find a local wineskin from which to quaff your *vino* (an essential accessory at festival time). Founded in 1873, much of the company's product is manufactured from traditional goatskin, but the company also produces wineskins from corduroy and synthetics.

Wooden bowls and spoons are popular Navarrese craft items.

Pamplona Nightlife

It's not hard to find good nightlife in Pamplona. Four streets in particular—**San Nicolás, Estafeta, Naverrería,** and **Jarauta**—are lined with bars and restaurants. San Nicolás is the pick, but elsewhere you'll find the following two bars, which boast significant history.

Dating from 1888, the stunning Art Deco **Café Iruña,** Plaza del Castillo 44 (www.cafeiruna.com; © **94-822-20-64**), contains the Rincon de Hemingway bar, frequented by the Bohemian writer. You'll be dazzled by the café's ornate interior, but in summer you'll want to lounge on its popular outdoor terrace. The winter crowd is likely to congregate around the bar, ordering meals and snacks in addition to drinks. Popular with office workers, the lunchtime *menú del día* (menu of the day) is 15.90€. Entrees cost from 10€ to 12€ and breakfasts and *pintxos* are also available. The café is open Monday to Thursday 8am until midnight, Friday to Sunday 9am to midnight.

Almost as old, but not nearly as fancy as Iruña, **Café Roch,** Calle Comedias, 6 (© **94-822-23-90**), lies just off the main square and pulls in its own eclectic crowd. Customers of all ages and backgrounds fill this compact bar to exchange tidbits of gossip, huddling over their drinks while nibbling on various flavorsome croquettes—the house special—ordered at the bar and diligently prepared upstairs and delivered through a hatch. Roch opens Monday to Friday 9:30am to 3pm and 6:30 to 10:30pm, Saturdays 11:30am to 3pm and 6:30 to 11pm. Sundays it opens noon to 3pm and 6:30 to 10:30pm.

OLITE ★

Dominated by its turreted castle, historic Olite is also an important focus for the wine industry and a center for the region's agriculture, which thrives on a climate characteristic of the distant Mediterranean: short, mild winters and long, hot summers. Local wine merchants hold a festival each year in mid-September, preceded by the town's August Medieval Fair.

Essentials

ARRIVING   Three **trains** per day run from Pamplona to Olite, taking 40 minutes. For rail information, visit www.renfe.com or call © **91-214-05-05.** The **bus** company **Alsa** (www.alsa.es; © **94-822-10-26**) connects Olite to Pamplona with 7 to 15 buses per day. The trip takes 40 to 55 minutes. By **car,** take the A-15 expressway south from Pamplona.

VISITOR INFORMATION   The **tourist office,** at Plaza de los Teobaldos 10 (www.turismo.navarra.es; © **94-874-17-03**), is open May to mid-October Monday to Saturday 10am to 2pm and 4 to 7pm, and Sunday 10am to 2pm. Mid-October to April, hours are Sunday to Thursday 10am to 2pm, Friday and Saturday 10am to 2pm and 3 to 6pm (with the exception of Easter week, which has the same hours as summer).

Exploring Olite

In the 15th century, this Gothic town was a favorite address of the kings of Navarra. Carlos III put Olite on the map, ordering in 1406 the building of

The Gothic church of Santa María la Real de Olite.

the **Palacio Real** (www.guiartenavarra.com; ✆ **94-874-12-73**), Plaza Carlos III el Noble, one of the most luxurious castles of its time. Fully restored in the 1930s, it's a romantic place to visit, with its twirly, turreted towers and lookouts. It's open daily 10am to 7pm (to 8pm in July and August, to 6pm October to March). Tickets can be bought online, advisable in high season and holidays. Admission is 3.50€ adults; 2€ seniors and ages 6 to 16. A guided tour is available for 4.90€ but has to be booked at least a day in advance.

Next to the castle on Plaza de los Teobaldos stands the town's Gothic church, **Santa María la Real de Olite** (www.olite.es), with a splendid 12th-century doorway decorated with flowers—a favorite backdrop for wedding photographs. The church opens for visits generally from 11am until 1pm and 4 until 5:30pm, though times vary according to the season. Entrance costs 1.50 €.

Sharing the tourist office building—and its opening hours—is the informative **Museo de la Viña y el Vino** (www.museodelvinodenavarra. com; ✆ **948-74-12-73**), which chronicles winemaking in Navarra since Roman days, while also explaining recent advances in viticulture and technology. Admission is 3.50€ adults, 2€ seniors and students.

The red Navarra wines are well-rated in Spain, a close third behind Rioja and Ribera del Duero, as ancient vineyards have met modern viticulture and an eager domestic market. The local rules permit "French" grapes like Cabernet Sauvignon and Merlot as well as the traditional indigenous varieties like Tempranillo and Graciano. Wine is nowadays becoming a cornerstone of the region's tourism, and several bodegas can be visited near Olite. **Bodegas Marco Real** (www.familiabelasco.com; (𝄐 **94-871-21-93**) outside town has English-language tours of their two wineries and tastings that will open your eyes—and taste buds—to Navarra wine. The main winery is located at km38 on N-121. A guided tour and tasting costs 7€ to 10€, depending on how many wines you want to sample. Most months, tours run Friday to Sunday and public holidays only (July and August daily), at set times, and must be reserved. Specify that you are an English speaker!

Where to Stay & Eat in Olite

Parador de Olite ★★   There really is no question that the most characterful place to stay is in Olite's former palace. Part of the state-owned *parador* network, the hotel has just 16 guest rooms in one of the wings of the Palacio Viejo, which preceded the Palacio Real (p. 565) located virtually next door. Walls crafted from huge stones, high ceilings, and suits of armor all add to an ambience heavy with history. (The kings of Navarra were always at war with someone, usually the French, the Castilians, or the Aragonese.) The other rooms are located in the modern 1963, brick-built addition, which tries hard to emulate the Gothic style. The parador evokes the days of Carlos III ("el Noble") and his Castilian queen, Leonor de Trastámara, and two of the most romantic rooms (106 and 107), equipped with four-poster beds and huge stone fireplaces, are named for them; to advance book either of these, you pay a significant premium which includes half-board and a visit to the Palacio Real.

Plaza de los Teobaldos, 2. www.parador.es. (𝄐 **94-874-00-00.** 43 units. 90€–160€ double. **Amenities:** Restaurant; bar; cafeteria; free Wi-Fi.

Restaurante Teobaldos (Parador de Olite) ★ NAVARRESE   If you're staying in the parador, no need to stray far for dinner. And if you're not a resident, this is your chance to soak up some age-old ambience while feasting on Navarrese specialties. Food is unpretentious, making the most of southern Navarre's high reputation for good-quality vegetables. Changing seasons might bring in green asparagus to accompany truffled eggs or offer up artichokes to be stuffed with duck. A tasting menu is also available, focusing on more Navarrese rural treasures such as *migas de pastor* (shepherd's breadcrumbs) and cold pear soup from Rincón de Soto in neighboring La Rioja.

Plaza de los Teobaldos, 2. www.parador.es. (𝄐 **94-874-00-00.** Entrees 18€–25€. Reservations required in high season. Daily 1–3:30pm and 8–10pm.

Side Trips from Olite

High up on a mountain a half-hour's drive east of Olite, **Ujué** seems plucked from the Middle Ages. Built as a defensive town, it is a place of cobbled streets and sturdy stone houses clustered around a hilltop church-fortress, **Iglesia-Fortaleza de Santa María do e Ujué ★**, Calle San Isidro, 8 which dates from the 12th to the 14th centuries. The heart of Carlos II ("the Bad") was placed to rest here. The church towers open onto views of the flat countryside, extending to Olite in the west and the Pyrenees to the north. Admission to the church is free and it is open daily 10am to 5:30pm. On the Sunday after St. Mark's Day (April 25), Ujué is an important pilgrimage center for Navarrese people, many of whom, barefoot and wearing tunics, carry large crosses. They come to Ujué to worship Santa María, depicted on a Romanesque statue dating from 1190.

You might also visit the **Monasterio de la Oliva ★** (www.monasterio delaoliva.org; $\mathcal{C}$ **94-872-50-06**), 34km (21 miles) south of Olite, founded by Navarra king García Ramírez in 1164. An excellent example of Cistercian architecture, it is home to a small band of monks from that order. Once hugely influential, it nearly met its demise after the Laws of Confiscation, which swiped Church properties, but a 20th-century restoration saved it. Note the distinguished portal and two rose windows that adorn the late 12th-century church. The monastery was built to solidify the Christian hold on what was, in the 12th century, a borderland between Muslim and Christian rule. Cistercian monks brought from Burgundy not only their signature architecture and stern Christianity, but also grapes and the know-how to cultivate them. Reds and rosés can be bought in the monastery shop, evidence that the surrounding lands still produce good wine 800 years later. The monastery is open Monday to Saturday 9:30am to noon and 3:30 to 6pm, Sunday 9:30 to 11:30am and 4 to 6pm. Admission is 2.50€.

Half an hour's drive south from the monastery, you will encounter a natural curiosity, the semi-desert of **Bardenas Reales ★★**, designated as a biosphere reserve. Start by picking up a park map at the **Centro de Información de Bardenas Reales de Navarra** (www.bardenasreales.es; ✆ **94-883-03-08**), accessed from the NA-8712 near Arguedas. It is open in summer from 9am until 2pm and from 4 to 7pm; in winter, hours are 9am to 2pm and 3 to 5pm. The park itself is open from 8am until 1 hour before sunset. Twenty communities co-own the park with the nearby Monasterio de la Oliva (above). Every winter, shepherds bring sheep from the Pyrenean valleys to graze here, before returning in April or May. Bizarrely, the flocks share the park with the Spanish air force, who drop dummy bombs onto a central firing range—a quite extraordinary sight (and sound!). But the most photographed feature of the park is the Castildetierra, a skewed spike of a hill crafted by centuries of wind and occasional rain to leave a natural wonder that surely belongs in Arizona.

This strange desert and its stunning scenery are popular with film producers; Bardenas Reales has appeared in various movies, including Ridley Scott's *The Counselor.* Birdlife here is abundant, with golden eagles and black kites present as well as the rarer and smaller Dupont's lark.

LOGROÑO ★

La Rioja's capital, Logroño, is an excellent base for touring this compact region's major attractions. Although much of this small city is a typical agricultural business center, its old quarter is encased in medieval walls and worthy of an hour or two's exploration on foot. It's familiar to pilgrims crossing this region on their way to distant Santiago de Compostela (p. 655), still nearly 4 weeks' walk away. The quarter's most typical and beautiful streets are **Muro Francisco de la Mata** and **Breton de los Herreros.** But keep in mind that this is a wine town: The main activity is not sightseeing but rather sipping at a bar, eating a few bites, having a pleasant conversation, and then moving on to another bar to repeat. For that, seek out **Calle Laurel,** home of all the action.

Essentials

ARRIVING   Four or five **trains** (www.renfe.com; ✆ **90-232-03-20**) daily connect to and from Barcelona (trip time: 4–5 hr.) and six per day with Madrid (trip time: 3½–4 hr.). From Bilbao in the north, two trains arrive per day (trip time: 2½ hr.). Six **buses** arrive daily from Pamplona (www.laestellesa.com; ✆ **94-823-65-09,** trip time 1½ hr.) and six from Madrid (www.plmautocares.com; ✆ **90-214-41-74,** trip time 5 hr.). If you're arriving by car, take the N-111 southwest from Pamplona or A-68 northwest from Zaragoza.

The **tourist office,** at Calle Portales, 50 (www. lariojaturismo.com; ✆ **94-129-12-60**), is usually open Monday to Saturday 9am to 2pm and 4 to 7pm, and Sunday 10am to 2pm. From July to September the office is open daily 9am to 2pm and 5 to 8pm (Sun to 7pm).

Exploring Logroño

A 12th-century manuscript called the "Codex Calixtinus," the earliest known guide to the Camino de Santiago pilgrimage route, singles out Logroño as a safe haven for travelers. Pilgrims entered the east end of town on the 11th-century **Puente de Piedra** (stone bridge), which still

crosses the Rio Ebro, though it had to be rebuilt in the 19th century and has lost its three fortified guard towers. At the bridge's southern end, turn right into **Rúavieja,** the pilgrim's path. A road steeped in history, its junction with the Travesia Palacio marks the rear of the 12th-century **Iglesia de Santa María de Palacio** (entrance on Calle Marqués de San Nicolás), once part of a royal palace. The palace part dates from 1130, when Alfonso VII offered his residence to the Order of the Holy Sepulchre. Most of what he left is long gone, of course, but there remains a pyramid-shaped spire from the 13th century.

Return to the **Rúavieja,** which soon becomes the Calle Barriocepo and leads to the ancient **Pilgrim's Fountain.** Here, pilgrims rested and washed (pilgrimage is a smelly business) before going to pray in the 16th-century **Iglesia Santiago El Real** across the street. The

The streets of Logroño's old quarter are full of wine bars and cafes.

church itself is of less interest to non-pilgrims, however, compared to the giant **Concatedral de Santa María de la Redonda,** Plaza Constitución. Its vaults date from the 1400s, but the Baroque facade only from 1742. Inside, you can visit the 1762 Chapel of Our Lady of the Angels, octagonally shaped with rococo adornments. Constructed on top of an earlier Romanesque church, today's cathedral is known for its broad naves and twin towers. Admission is free. It's open Monday to Saturday 8:30am to 1pm and 6 to 8:45pm.

In the very heart of Logroño, explore the gardens of the broad **Paseo del Espolón,** where in the late afternoon, Logroño residents turn out for their *paseo,* or stroll.

For a different slant on La Rioja's past, the **Museum of La Rioja ★**, Plaza de San Agustín, 2 (*✆* **94-129-12-59**), charts the history from Paleolithic times to the modern day. Though icons, altarpieces, and monastery contents are still present here, you'll also see artifacts from the Romanization of the region, which brought the cultivation of grapes and olives which still define La Rioja today. Admission is free. The museum opens on Tuesday to Saturday, 10am to 2pm and 4 to 9pm. On Sundays, it opens from 10am to 2pm.

Wine shops are ubiquitous in Logroño's old quarter, especially along Calle Portales and the nearby side streets. La Rioja has over 100 wineries, but which to choose? A short drive from Logroño, a less than traditional winery tour awaits you at **Bodegas Tritium ★★★**, Avenida de la Libertad, 9, Cenicero. (https://tritium.es; *✆* **62-915-28-22**). With a heap less formality than elsewhere, your tour here might last 3 hours and feel more like a catch-up with old friends. But you will certainly learn something at this family-run bodega, tucked away in a narrow backstreet. The building is over 500 years old, and a visit to the subterranean caves—where the wines are aged—is loaded with atmosphere. The emphasis is firmly on fun, and Itziar is a lively, lovely guide who is clearly enamored with wine. The two owners experiment, producing a new wine every year, using acacia barrels as well as traditional oak, and spending a decent portion of their waking hours with their noses firmly poked into a glass—in the interests of research, naturally. The cost is either 15€ with a two-wine tasting, or 20€ with four. Although they are flexible, reservations are essential. They're open year-round, with tours at 11am, 1pm, and 5:30pm.

Where to Stay in Logroño

Eurostars Fuerte Rua Vieja ★ Wrapped up in solid stone, this beautiful small hotel occupies a corner of one of Logroño's atmospheric, cobbled streets. The walls ooze old world charm, but the hotel itself only opened its doors in 2017. Renovated with care and consideration, it makes bold, modern statements with an ultra-contemporary styling that is pleasing on the eye. Rooms are spacious enough and the downstairs lounge is an eclectic mix of chic décor and comfortable sofas. In the basement, the small spa is a welcome surprise.

Calle Ruavieja, 22–28. www.eurostarshotels.com. *✆* **90-293-24-24**. 30 rooms. 75€–120€ double; 130€–240€ suite. Parking 20€. **Amenities:** Restaurant; bar, exercise room, Turkish bath, sauna, Jacuzzi; free Wi-Fi.

Hostal La Numantina ★   Santiago-bound pilgrims favor this bargain-priced, simple hotel. The weary walkers must negotiate the stairs to reach reception upstairs. The rooms are small, the furnishings are basic and a bit outdated, and it all feels a little like the guest bedroom in your great-aunt's house. On the plus side, you do get a TV and heating in the room, a comfortable bed with better-than-average linens, and a compact but scrupulously clean private bathroom. Complimentary coffee.

Calle Sagasta, 4. www.hostalnumantina.com. © **94-125-14-11.** 22 rooms. 60€ double. Closed Dec 24–Jan 6. **Amenities:** Free Wi-Fi.

Hotel Calle Mayor ★★   Small and perfectly crafted, the Calle Mayor is based around a 16th-century *palacio,* the one-time house of a wealthy resident. Beautifully restored, the original small hotel was expanded in 2016. Fortunately, the character remains undiluted, a comfortable blend of old stone and wood with ultra-chic furnishings. Look closely for the remnants of the original building: the Roman arch through which you enter, a stone pillar here, a sturdy staircase there. Adding further character are some large wall photos of old Logroño. Rooms are all spacious and bright, with soft relaxing colors. Unless you're in the market for a suite, choose a standard room over a superior one, but specify a *large* standard when booking—these are the same size as the superior units, but cheaper. A small patio provides outside space.

Marqués de San Nicolás, 71. www.hotelcallemayor.com. © **94-123-23-68.** 30 units. 75€–95€ double; 180€–210€ suite. Parking nearby 18€. **Amenities:** Library, exercise room, free Wi-Fi.

Where to Eat in Logroño

When it's time for dinner or just a few pre-dinner tapas, anyone who's anyone is to be found somewhere near the L-shaped junction of **Calle de Laurel** and **Travesia de Laurel,** two fun-packed streets fully loaded with bars and restaurants. Every self-respecting Spanish town has an area like this, but in Logroño each bar is a specialist. Look at the enticing posters outside, make your selection, and then plunge in. We recommend the garlic mushrooms at **Soriano,** Travesia de Laurel, 2; the octopus-centric delights at **La Universidad Pulpería,** Travesia de Laurel, 9; and the "lollipop of black pork sirloin with mushroom sauce" at **Letras de Laurel,** Calle Laurel, 22.

Pasión por Ti ★ RIOJANA/PINTXOS   Amidst the mayhem of Calle del Laurel (see above), this place is a shining star. In the front bar, sharpen your elbows and fight to the counter to order their star *pintxo,* crafted from foie gras, low-temperature egg, and truffled cream potatoes, with its accompanying "syringe" of olive oil (you may need instructions on how to eat it). In the restaurant, there are plenty of choices on their well-priced menus, everything from pork cheeks in a red wine reduction to grilled turbot or octopus. Owner Victor is a genial host and his wines are inexpensive.

Calle Laurel, 5. www.grupopasion.com. ✆ **94-122-00-39.** Entrees 18€; fixed-price menus 12€–25€. Daily 11am–5pm and 6:30–midnight. (Full meals from 1pm and 8:30pm, respectively.)

Restaurante Ikaro ★ RIOJANA/LATIN AMERICAN   Everything about this place shouts "cared for," from the designer furniture to the carefully thought-through lighting. But most of the love is rightly reserved for the food, with a short but elaborate menu that draws inspiration both from the region and from afar. The young owners Iñaki and Carolina, a Spanish/Ecuadorean couple, were awarded with a Michelin star in 2018, and their tasting menu is excellent value. If you go à la carte you can order half-portions—a true (and welcome) novelty.

Avenida de Portugal, 3 Bajo. www.restauranteikaro.com. ✆ **94-157-16-14.** Entrees 21€–25 €; set menus 25€–56€. Wed–Sun 1:45–3:30pm; Thurs–Sat 9–10:30pm.

Side Trip to San Millán de la Cogolla

Around 42km (26 miles) southwest of Logroño, **San Millán de la Cogolla** is often considered the cradle of both the Castilian and Basque languages. The small village was the home of 13th-century poet and author Gonzalo de Berceo, the first major literary figure to write in the Castilian dialect. He was educated here by the monks of **Monasterio de Yuso ★** (www.monasteriodeyuso.org; ✆ **94-137-30-49**), a magnificent compound whose current structure was built between the 16th and 18th centuries on the site of an earlier, 11th-century one. Nine Augustinian monks still reside here, and the sacristy holds secular and religious treasures, including the first written examples of both the Basque and Castilian languages, which were removed for safekeeping from the vacant Suso monastery nearby (see below). Visits are by obligatory guided tours between Semana Santa (Holy Week) and September, Tuesday to Sunday 10am to 1:30pm and 4 to 6:30pm (also open Mon in Aug); from October to Palm Sunday, hours are Tuesday to Saturday 10am to 1pm and 3:30 to 5:30pm, Sunday 10am to

---

WINE HARVEST festival IN LOGROÑO

During the week around the feast day of San Matéo, Logroño celebrates both the patron saint and the wine harvest with **Las Fiestas de San Matéo y de la Vendimia.** Activities include a carnival procession, gastronomic tastings organized by the social clubs, a round of *corridas*, a jai alai tournament, concerts, theater, live music in the streets, and fireworks over the Río Ebro. On September 21, two men in historic costumes tread barefoot to crush grapes from the first harvest, with the must then offered to Our Lady of Valvanera, the patron saint of La Rioja. For festival details and timetables, contact the tourist office (see p. 569)

1pm. The tour costs 7€ adults, 5€ seniors, 3€ ages 7 to 15. A minibus also departs from Yuso to the more ancient **Monasterio de Suso** ★ on the hill above town. Founded in A.D. 550, Suso consists of a Visigothic core with Mozarabic enlargements from the 11th century and a Romanesque section from the 13th. Tickets cost 4 €. Reservations are required to visit Suso; call ✆ **94-137-30-82.**

If you like tranquility, you can choose to stay in a wing of the Yuso monastery, converted into the **Hostería de San Millán** ★ (www.hosteriasanmillan.com; ✆ **94-137-32-77**). It offers 25 large and airy rooms, and huge suites with doubles between 77€ to 95€, suites from 135 € to 200 €. Choose between the mountain or courtyard view; we recommend the former. There's a restaurant on site, and breakfast is included.

HARO ★

Logroño may be La Rioja's regional capital, but Haro offers it stiff competition as the center of the region's world-renowned wine industry. Sometimes compared to Tuscany, Haro and its surroundings are home to many first-class bodegas, where tastings are available for connoisseurs and beginners alike.

Essentials

ARRIVING Four **trains** (www.renfe.com; ✆ **90-232-03-20**) run daily from Logroño (trip time: 45 min.). There are also three or four connections per day with Zaragoza (trip time: 2½ hr.). Six to seven **buses** per day run between Haro and Logroño (trip time: 45 min.–1 hr). For information, call ✆ **94-123-59-83.** If you're driving, follow the AP-68 expressway (south of Logroño) northwest to the turnoff for Haro.

VISITOR INFORMATION The **tourist office,** at Palacio Bendaña, Plaza de la Paz, 1 (www.haroturismo.org; ✆ **94-130-35-80**), is open mid-June to September Tuesday to Sunday 10am to 2pm and 4 to 7pm. The rest of the year (except Easter week, which keeps summer hours), it's open Tuesday to Friday 10am to 2pm, Saturday 10am to 2pm and 4 to 7pm.

SPECIAL EVENTS Every June 29, during the San Pedro festival, the **Battle of Wine** erupts. It's an amusing, mock-medieval brawl in which opposing teams splatter each other using wineskins filled with the output from local vineyards.

Exploring Haro & Visiting the Bodegas

Deserving a look before you head for the bodegas, Haro's Old Quarter is filled with mansions, some from the 16th century; the most interesting ones lie along **Calleja del Castillo.** The focal point architecturally is the **Iglesia de Santo Tomás,** Plaza de la Iglesia. Distinguished by its wedding-cake tower and Plateresque south portal, this 16th-century church has a Gothic interior. The tower's cupola is echoed in the bandstand on the nearby Plaza de la Paz.

You could spend days touring the wineries in and around town, but a few visits will satisfy your curiosity. **Bodegas Muga** ★, Av. Vizcaya 2 (www.bodegasmuga.com; ℂ **94-130-60-60**), near the rail station, is one of the best wineries for visitors. Tours (15€) are offered in Spanish and English Monday to Saturday by advance reservation. You can also simply pop into the *vinoteca* for a drink. The wine shop is open Monday to Friday 8:30am to 5:30pm and weekends 10am to 3pm. Nearby you can also visit the atmospheric underground cellars of **Bodegas La Rioja Alta** ★, Av. de Vizcaya, 8 (www.riojaalta.com; ℂ **94-131-03-46**). English-language tours, which cost 15€ and must be arranged in advance, are Monday to Friday at 10am.

If you arrive in Haro in August or the first 2 weeks in September, when many of the bodegas are closed, settle instead for drinking wine in the *tabernas* that line the streets between Calle Parroquia and Plaza de la Paz. A night spent there will make you forget all about bodega tours. Some of the finest red wines in Spain are sold at these bars, along with tapas—all at bargain prices.

If your interest in wine extends beyond drinking it, take the 6-mile trip to nearby Briones and the **Vivanco** ★ winery and museum (located off the N232; www.vivanco wineculture.com; ℂ **94-132-23-23**). This huge, modern complex displays wine-making equipment, shows short films, offers tastings, and has a bar and restaurant. One room is dedicated to wine-related art, expressed through sculpture, paintings, and even short film clips. (If that doesn't impress, perhaps the international collection of 3,000 corkscrews will.) Outside are 200 grape varieties growing in the aptly named Garden of Bacchus, and there's even a play area for kids. A variety of experiences are offered, from a simple museum visit to wine courses. The Vivanco Experience, which includes a museum visit, a tapa, a winery visit, and a 4-wine tasting, costs 43€. A museum visit

The entrance to Iglesia de Santo Tomás.

Bodegas Muga.

alone is 15€. Opening times vary throughout the year, so check the website

Where to Stay in Haro

Hotel Ciudad De Haro ★   Located outside of town on the highway, this bright, modern hotel is modeled on a Riojan country estate house, right down to the arched entrance from the road to the broad green lawns. Rooms are small but comfortable, and there's plenty of free parking. It's hard to walk into town from here, even though it's less than a mile. If it's summer, you will need to book well in advance. You might choose to stay here just for the swimming pool.

Carretera N-124, Km 41. www.ciudadeharo.com. © **94-131-12-13.** 57 rooms. 55€–95€ double. Free parking. **Amenities:** Restaurant; bar; outdoor pool; free Wi-Fi.

Hotel Los Agustinos ★★   Haro doesn't get any more historic than this building, an Augustinian monastery founded in 1373. During the 19th and early 20th centuries it served as a military garrison, a school, a hospital, and finally "did time" as a prison. Renovated by a Basque hotel group, it is now the most elegant and most desirable lodging in Haro. The neighborhood is a pedestrian zone, which keeps the noise level down at night.

The rooms are rather traditionally appointed, distributed on two floors. Ask for a large standard when booking, as rooms vary but prices do not. Most have some exposed stone or overhead beams in addition to white plaster. A huge glass-roofed central atrium provides a pleasant communal space for relaxation.

Calle San Agustín, 2. http://hotellosagustinos.com. ℂ **94-131-13-08.** 62 rooms. 72€–110€ double. Reserved parking 8€. **Amenities:** Restaurant; bar; free Wi-Fi.

Where to Eat in Haro

Beethoven I and II ★ RIOJAN Chef María Angeles Frenso forages her own wild mushrooms for this popular duo of restaurants which directly face each other in the middle of town. Beethoven I is the choice for a weekday daily menu; Beethoven II promises a modern touch to its Riojan cuisine and offers a slightly wider menu. If that's not enough, I also has a bar with tapas.

Calle Santo Tomás, 3–5. www.beethovenharo.com. ℂ **941-31-00-18.** Entrees 16€–24€. Reservations required in summer. Mon–Fri 1:30–4pm and 8:30–11.pm; Sat–Sun 1:30–4pm and 9–11:30pm. Beethoven I closed Wed evening and Thurs; Beethoven II closed Mon evening and Tues. Both closed Jan.

Terete ★★ RIOJAN Expertise has passed through six generations of the Gutiérrez family since Alberto Andrés Alonso opened Terete in 1867 to share "the fate God had chosen for him to perfect the art of roasting lamb and serving it with a glass of wine." In other words, eating here is divinely ordained. Menus change subtly during the year, boletus mushrooms giving way to asparagus or artichokes, but the staples they accompany stay the same. Meat is king here (though hake or cod may be on the menu) and nearly everyone takes the sublime oven-cooked lamb. Beneath your feet and out of sight, the house wine is ageing away in caves that date back 400 years. The smooth reds made in-house cannot be found elsewhere, so take advantage. In the kitchen, one family member creates the desserts, another tends the oven. Cuisine is rustic and hearty rather than overly fancy and elaborate, but very satisfying.

Calle Lucrecia Arana, 17. www.terete.es. ℂ **94-131-00-23.** Entrees 8€–28€. Set menu 38€. Reservations recommended. Tues–Sat 1:15–4pm and 8:30–11pm, Sun 1:15–4pm. Closed July 1–15 and Nov 15–30.

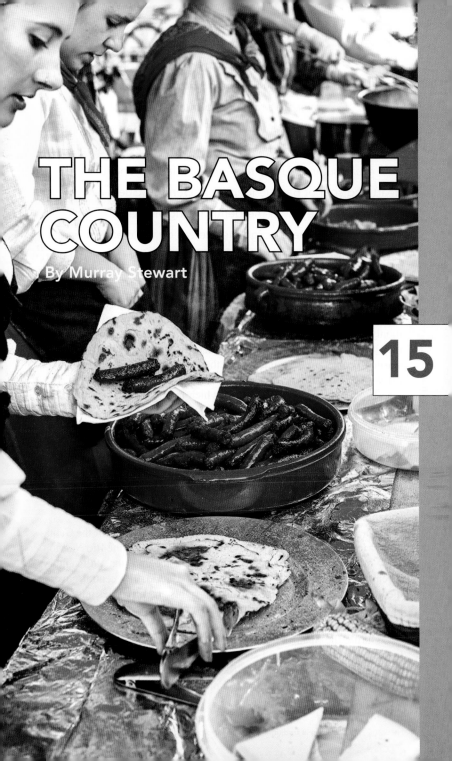

THE BASQUE COUNTRY

By Murray Stewart

T he Basque Country (El Pais Vasco in Castilian) is nothing if not seductive. Visitors come in droves to see the Guggenheim Bilbao Museum, only to discover that there is so much more: bold Bilbao city itself, beautiful *Belle Epoque* San Sebastián, the two joined by a coastline of long sandy strands, rocky promontories, and great surfing. Then, they venture farther and uncover the heart and soul of Basque identity at Gernika (Guernica in Castilian), feast their eyes on the gently rolling vineyards of Rioja Alavesa, and everywhere gorge themselves on the creatively crafted Basque cuisine, considered by many to be the finest in all of Spain.

The Basques are possibly the oldest traceable ethnic group in Europe. Their language, Euskera (also spelled Euskara), predates any of the commonly spoken Romance languages; its origins, like those of the Basque race itself, are enigmatically lost in obscurity. One theory holds that these spirited people are descended from the original Iberians, who inhabited Spain before the arrival of the Celts some 3,500 years ago.

The region calls itself Euskadi, which in the strictest sense refers to the Basque Autonomous Community, consisting of three provinces: Guipúzcoa (whose beautiful beachfront capital is **San Sebastián**), Bizkaia (with its capital the exciting, rejuvenated industrial city of **Bilbao**), and inland Álava, which contains the Basque administrative capital Vitoria-Gasteiz and the wine-growing region of **Rioja Alavesa.** Basque nationalists dream of uniting all the Basque lands in one independent nation; in their minds, Euskadi also includes the northern part of Navarre and three former provinces in France.

The Spanish Basque provinces occupy the eastern part of the Cantabrian Mountains between the Pyrenees and the valley of the Río Nervión. They maintained a large degree of independence until the 19th century, when they were finally brought to heel by Madrid. The central government continued to recognize the ancient rights and privileges until 1876, but the region lost its special status when it rebelled over succession to the Spanish throne.

During the Spanish Civil War (1936–39), the Basques were on the losing Republican side, and subsequent oppression under Franco led to deep-seated resentment against Madrid. The Basque separatist movement, ETA (*Euskadi ta Askatasuna,* or Basque Nation and Liberty), and

The Basque Country

the French organization Enbata (Ocean Wind) engaged unsuccessfully in guerrilla activity, mainly killings and kidnappings, between 1968 and 2011 to secure a united Basque state. ETA eventually declared a permanent unilateral ceasefire in 2011, and in 2017 they began to decommission their weapons. A year later they announced their intention to disband. Basque nationalists now express their fiercely protected sense of identity through the ballot box, and although you will still see nationalist graffiti and banners, the relative economic strength of this region has eroded the appeal of nationalism. The Basques are pragmatists, and compared to the rest of Spain, life is pretty good in Euskadi. Now keen to further bolster their economy through tourism, the people are friendly and welcoming to visitors keen to discover their unique, profound culture.

SAN SEBASTIÁN-DONOSTIA ★★★

Locals will tell you, "Before God was God and rocks were rocks, the Basques were Basques." San Sebastián (Donostia in Basque) is still a bastion of Basque culture and identity—as well as a resort on par with Nice and Monte Carlo, thanks to flowering gardens, year-round festivals, seafront promenades, sandy beaches, a scenic boat-filled bay, lively nightlife, and the best restaurants in Spain. Delightfully walkable, it's a city to be explored on foot.

Essentials

ARRIVING **Iberia** (www.iberia.com; ℃ **90-111-15-00**) offers three to six daily flights to San Sebastián from Madrid, plus two daily flights from Barcelona through its regional subsidiaries. The domestic airport is at nearby Fuenterrabía (Hondarribia). Airport buses (Line E20) run to the Plaza Gipuzkoa stop in central San Sebastián every 20 minutes Monday to Saturday from 6:30am to 9pm, and Sunday every 30 minutes from 7:40am to 9pm. Tickets are 2.55€. Contact **Ekialdebus** (https://ekialdebus.eus; ℃ **90-030-03-40**) for more information. If you're arriving in the region from elsewhere in Europe, note that the international airport in Biarritz, France (www.biarritz.aeroport.fr), is regularly connected to San Sebastián by direct bus (trip time: 40 min.).

From Madrid, RENFE **trains** run direct to San Sebastián (trip time: 5½–7 hr.). RENFE also provides three direct trains daily from Barcelona to San Sebastián (trip time: 5½ hr.). For RENFE information, visit www.renfe.com or call ℃ **91-232-03-20**.

San Sebastián is linked by a **bus** network to many of Spain's major cities, although Madrid is better reached by train. **Alsa** (www.alsa.es; ℃ **90-242-22-42**) runs a dozen daily buses from Madrid, taking around 6 hours and costing 37€. **Vibasa-Monbus** (www.monbus.es; ℃ **98-229-29-00**) operates three buses from Barcelona, a 7-hour trip costing 33€ one-way. Finally, **Transportes PESA/Lurraldebus** (www.pesa.net/www.lurraldebus.eus; ℃ **90-012-14-00**) runs buses from Bilbao every 30 minutes during the day, taking 1¼ hours and costing 12€ one-way. All these operators have offices at the bus station.

Driving from Madrid, take the A-1/E-5 toll road north to Burgos, and then follow the A-1 to Miranda de Ebro. From here, continue on the AP-1/E-80 68 north to Elgoibar and then the AP-8 east to San Sebastián. From Pamplona, take the AP-15 toll road north then the A-15, which leads right into San Sebastián.

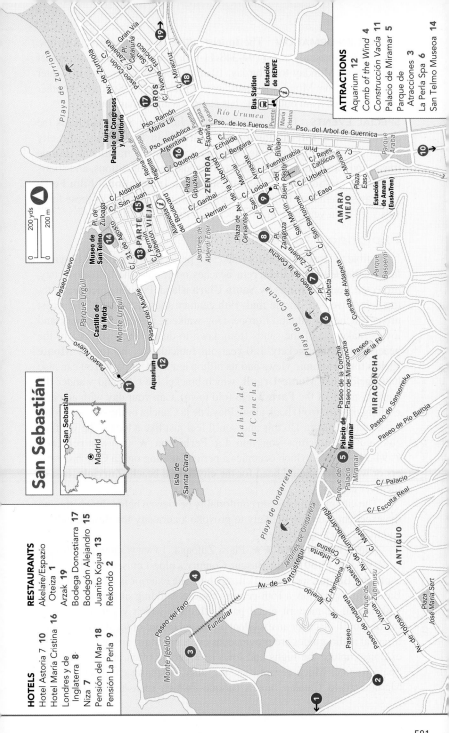

San Sebastián

HOTELS
Hotel Astoria 7 **10**
Hotel María Cristina **16**
Londres y de
   Inglaterra **8**
Niza **7**
Pensión del Mar **18**
Pensión La Perla **9**

RESTAURANTS
Akelaře/Espazio
   Oteiza **1**
Arzak **19**
Bodega Donostiarra **17**
Bodegón Alejandro **15**
Juanito Kojua **13**
Rekondo **2**

ATTRACTIONS
Aquarium **12**
Comb of the Wind **4**
Construcción Vacía **11**
Palacio de Miramar **5**
Parque de
   Atracciones **3**
La Perla Spa **6**
San Telmo Museoa **14**

The **tourist office** is at Boulevard, 8 (www. sansebastianturismo.com; 𝄞 **94-348-11-66**). The office opens in summer 9am to 8pm Monday to Saturday, 10am to 7pm Sundays, and in winter from 9am to 7pm Monday to Saturday and 10am to 2pm Sundays. Another office operates from outside the bus station, with similar hours.

SPECIAL EVENTS In the second half of July, San Sebastián hosts the **San Sebastián International Jazz Festival.** In mid-August, the city stages its annual party, **Aste Nagusia,** celebrating traditional Basque music and dance, along with fireworks, cooking competitions, and sports events. In mid-September, the **San Sebastián International Film Festival** draws luminaries from America and Europe. The dates of these festivals vary from year to year, so check with the tourist office.

Exploring San Sebastián

Irresistible to locals and visitors alike, the perfectly shell-shaped **Playa de la Concha ★★** and **Ondarreta** beaches open onto the half-moon bay, protected from the waves by **Santa Clara** island. Popular since sea-bathing was "invented" in the mid–19th century, these are two of the finest urban beaches in Atlantic Europe. Dog-walkers, joggers, swimmers, and lovers make use of the sands from dawn to dusk. When you tire of the beaches, take the rickety 100-year-old funicular to the top of **Monte Igeldo** for panoramic views and its hilltop amusement park. You can also hike Igeldo and **Monte Urgull,** which bracket the city, and wander the narrow streets of the **Parte Vieja** (old town). Cap your day with an early evening *paseo* (stroll) back along Playa de la Concha or the elegant promenade that flanks it. Do this and you'll feel just like a local. The whiff of chlorine might tempt you into **La Perla spa ★** (www.la-perla.net; 𝄞 **94-345-88-56**), which occupies a period building on La Concha. Surfers or wannabes should head for the city's third beach, **Zurriola,** east of the river estuary.

The city monuments can comfortably be viewed before lunch, though the excellent museum is likely to provoke a curiosity for Basque culture and make you linger longer.

San Telmo Museoa ★★, Plaza Zuloaga, 1 (www.santelmomuseoa. es; 𝄞 **94-348-15-80**), is the Basque Country's oldest museum dedicated to capturing Basque society and citizenship. The exterior is a typically bold Basque juxtaposition, a 16th-century convent building sitting side-by-side with a wall of modern metal panels through which vegetation grows. Inside, you'll discover an excellent presented record of local history. Multilingual audio-guides are provided, as excellent films, artifacts, and other exhibits capture the highs and lows of a people often at odds with the Spanish state. Much revered are the huge, stunning canvases by José Maria Sert—a Catalan, not a Basque—which recreate key events in

Basque history and are best appreciated from the upstairs gallery. Two hours here will be well spent. Located in the Old Town at the base of Monte Urgull, the museum is open Tuesday to Sunday 10am to 8pm. Admission is 6€ adults, 3€ students and seniors, free for under 18s.

The wide hilltop promenade **Paseo Nuevo** almost encircles Monte Urgull, one of the two mountains which bookend the city. (Monte Igeldo is the other one.) At one end of the *paseo* lies the city's **Aquarium ★**, Plaza Carlos, Blasco de Imaz, s/n (www.aquariumss.com; ℇ **94-344-00-99**), an oceanographic museum/aquarium with a mesmerizing collection of myriad marine species. A transparent underwater walkway allows a 360-degree view of sharks, rays, and other fish. A maritime museum upstairs presents a fascinating synopsis of humankind's precarious relationship with the sea through the ages. Here you can also see the skeleton of the next-to-last whale caught in the Bay of Biscay, in 1878. The aquarium is open Semana Santa (Holy Week) and July through August daily 10am to 9pm; from Easter to June and in September, it's open Monday to Friday 10am to 8pm, Saturday and Sunday 10am to 9pm; from October to Easter Monday it's open Friday 10am to 7pm, Saturday and Sunday 10am

The underwater walkway at San Sebastián's Aquarium.

SPEAKING basque IN STEEL & STONE

Eduardo Chillida (1924–2002) was the greatest Basque sculptor of the 20th century, known mainly for his monumental abstract works in steel and stone. Born in San Sebastián, he returned to the city in 1959 and worked at his beautifully sited studio in the hills outside town. Visitors don't have to go far to see one of Chillida's signature works, the "Comb of the Wind." It rises from the rocks at the base of Monte Igeldo, where it meets the sea at the west end of Playa de la Concha, ushering in the ocean breezes. Like his best works, it combines an abstract beauty of form with an analytical precision that makes the viewer contemplate both the object and the space it inhabits. Viewed from one direction, the "Comb of the Wind" resembles giant calipers, a tool associated with Basque mariners and their legendary charts. Across the bay behind the Aquarium (p. 583) is the "Construcción Vacía" ("Empty Construction"), the work of **Jorge Oteiza** (1908–2003), another revered Basque sculptor.

to 8pm. Admission is 13€ adults, 9€ students and seniors, 6.50€ ages 4 to 12.

The **Palacio de Miramar** stands on its own hill on the point dividing the two beaches, La Concha and Ondarreta. Once a summer palace, it was favored by Queen María Cristina (namesake of the grandest hotel in town), who was taken down to bathe in a carriage pulled by oxen. It was opened in 1893, but once the monarchy fled Spain, the building fell into disrepair before being restored in the 20th century. You can visit the gardens daily from 8am to 9pm, but the palace itself is closed to visitors.

For the best panoramic view of the city, bay, and coastline, ride the funicular to the top of **Monte Igeldo** ★ (www.monteigueldo.es; © **94-321-35-25**). From July to October, the funicular runs Monday to Friday 10am to 9pm, Saturday and Sunday 10am to 10pm. From April to June, it runs Monday to Friday 10am to 8pm, Saturday and Sunday 10am to 9pm. Round-trip fare is 3.15€ adults, 2.35€ children 7 and under. You can also drive or even walk, if you don't mind a fairly steep climb without sidewalks. A small amusement park with a variety of rides, **Parque de**

Atraciones, is located on top of Monte Igeldo. Open roughly the same hours as the funicular, it charges 1€ for most games, 2€ to 2.50€ for rides.

Where to Stay in San Sebastián

San Sebastián is in demand, so book well in advance for the best deals; during high season (May–Sept), many hoteliers will insist that you stay more than 1 night.

EXPENSIVE

Hotel María Cristina ★★★   This renovated landmark Belle Epoque hotel was built and named for royalty. It remains the most glamorous address in town, with rooms and suites decorated in subtle tones that recall the paint colors of Rolls-Royce automobiles. The María Cristina provides beautiful public rooms, with opulent onyx, marble, and faux painting, where celebrities can be photographed during the film and jazz festivals. The same glam public areas make the hotel a first choice for many society weddings. Even the least expensive guest rooms are spacious. Bathrooms feature very contemporary fixtures and beds are deeply luxurious.

Paseo República Argentina, 4. www.hotel-marriott.com. ✆ **94-343-76-00.** 136 units. 210€–445€ double; 400€–900€ suite. Parking 40€. Bus: 5 or 6. **Amenities:** Restaurant; bar; exercise room, free Wi-Fi.

Londres y de Inglaterra ★★   When the movie stars and Hollywood directors are in the María Cristina, the supporting actors and the film auteurs from struggling countries scramble to book into this dowager property on the northern edge of Playa de la Concha. It's grand in a Belle Epoque style but has loosened up its corset stays over the years. Its real advantage over the Maria Cristina is the sea view. The semiformal public rooms have large windows that overlook the beach and flood the spaces with light, and comfortable armchairs to sink into to enjoy the comings and goings of the guests. Guest rooms are commodious, with marble bathrooms. Specify a beach-view room when you book.

Calle Zubieta, 2. www.hlondres.com. ✆ **94-344-07-70.** 148 units. 80€–300€ double; 215€–650€ suites. Parking 23€. Bus: 5, 16, 18 or 25. **Amenities:** Restaurant; bar; free Wi-Fi.

MODERATE

Hotel Astoria 7 ★★   Which movie star will you spend the night with? That's the come-on at the Astoria 7, a snazzy contemporary hotel in the building that once held San Sebastián's first multiplex cinema. Developers decided to play to that strength, so the entire hotel is themed to classic films. Each room is named for an actor, actress, or director, and a small cinema in the basement screens films every night. The beautiful lobby library is replete with coffee-table cinema books, film critiques, and an extensive collection of DVDs you can check out and watch in your room. The neighborhood seems rather removed from the beach scene, but it's a quick bus ride to the center. Rooms are modern and spacious, and even kind of glamorous.

Calle Sagrada Familia, 1. www.astoria7hotel.com. ☎ **94-344-50-00.** 102 units. 60€–160€ double; 90€–230€ suite. Parking garage 19€. Bus: 21, 23, or 28. **Amenities:** Restaurant; bar; free Wi-Fi.

Niza ★★   We have a soft spot for this family-run hotel right on Playa de la Concha because the staff is so genuinely friendly and the hotel—owned by the Chillida family of sculpting fame (p. 584) oozes character. The rooms are bright and well ventilated, so you may not need the air-conditioning, provided only in the street-side rooms. Decor is minimal, occasionally old-fashioned. The 18 sea-view rooms are recommended, being slightly larger than those on the other side, which overlook a land-scaped square. Niza is easily the best-priced sea-view hotel in town.

Calle Zubieta, 56. www.hotelniza.com. ☎ **94-342-66-63.** 40 units. 80€–250€ double. Parking 16.50 €. Bus: 5, 16 25 or 28. **Amenities:** Restaurant; bar; free Wi-Fi.

INEXPENSIVE

Pension del Mar ★   East of the river, but still centrally located in the Gros district, this light and bright second-floor guesthouse is managed slickly by the delightful Antonio. Distinct Nordic styling gives added verve to the clean lines of the spacious rooms, 4 of which have private bathrooms. No breakfast is served, but guests have complimentary coffee 24/7 and there's a communal kitchen if the local cuisine has inspired you to cook. Adults only.

Tomas Gros 3. www.lapensiondelmar.es. ☎ **94-335-99-70.** 6 units. 36€–85€ double. Discounted parking 16€ per day, available nearby. Close to bus and train stations. **Amenities:** Free Wi-Fi.

Pensión La Perla ★   A simple, central option with a welcoming and relaxed atmosphere, La Perla has been thoroughly modernized with shiny wooden floors, but with interesting old photos of the city doing what it does best—celebrating its festivals. The wide entrance door is another vestige of yesterday, when it was known as the Hotel Sevilla: It was designed to let in horses. Rooms offer a microwave and fridge, and there's complimentary coffee at reception. Room number 7 has an enclosed balcony overlooking the street. Owner Juan Mari carries on the family business and constantly updates the décor.

Loiola, 10. www.pensionlaperla.com ☎ **94-390-04-75.** 10 units. 40€–110€ double. Bus: 26, 28. **Amenities:** Computer terminal, free Wi-Fi.

Where to Eat in San Sebastián

We once asked famed Spanish chefs Ferran Adrià and José Andrés where they would go for a gastronomic holiday in Spain. Both answered "¡San

Sebastián!" The city's chefs are the most acclaimed in the country. Gourmets devour local specialties such as cod al pil-pil in garlic or hake cheeks in green sauce. *Pintxos* (Basque tapas) are described as "grand dishes in miniature": Nobody does them better than this city.

EXPENSIVE

Akelaré/Espazio Oteiza ★★★ CONTEMPORARY BASQUE   A

genial legend of the new wave of Basque cuisine, Pedro Subijana works magic into his dishes in these two restaurants under one roof. **"Akelaré"** means "Witches' Sabbath" in Basque, and this is the gastronomic option for those who can afford it. There is no *à la carte,* just three variations of the tasting menu: The whole table must take the same one. One version is based on Akelaré classics, such as foamed foie gras or rice with periwinkles and snails. Under the same expert Subijana supervision is the less formal **Oteiza,** named in honor of the late sculptor (p. 584). Oteiza's prices are much more accessible, dishes are chosen *à la carte,* and you can dine outside with views over the Cantabrian Sea.

Paseo del Padre Orcolaga, 56. www.akelarre.net. ⓒ **94-331-12-09.** Akelaré: tasting menu 230€. Espazio Oteiza: entrees 20€–32€. Reservations required. Akelaré Wed–Sat 1–2:30pm and 8:30–10pm, Sun 1–2:30pm; July–Sept also open Tues. Oteiza daily 12:30–3pm and 7:30–10:30pm. Both closed Dec 23–Mar 1.

15

Pinchos *(pinxtos)* are traditional appetizers in Basque country.

Arzak ★★★ CONTEMPORARY BASQUE   The other progenitor of *la nueva cocina vasca,* Juan Mari Arzak, and daughter Elena partner up to run this flawless restaurant now in its fourth generation. Behind the scenes, a well-oiled kitchen operation, a sumptuous wine cellar, and an astonishingly well-equipped culinary laboratory combine to support the Arzak miracle. Their genius pairs spider-crab with a delicate ginger biscuit, or sources Mediterranean scarlet prawns to compliment crunchy krill. Is this art as food, or food as art? You will be torn between wanting to savor the subtle flavors in front of you and longing to try the next enticing dish. Whose curiosity would not be stirred by a meat dish titled "Clockwork venison and roe deer"? Efficient service peaks with the waiters' welcome interventions, and the charming Elena Arzak herself works the room, warmly engaging with her guests. An experience to treasure.

Av. Alcade Elósegui, 273. www.arzak.es. ℂ **94-327-84-65.** Entrees 48€–72€; tasting menu 237€, excluding drinks. Reservations required. Tues–Sat 1:15–3:15pm and 8:45–10:30pm. Closed June 13–30 and most of Nov.

MODERATE

Bodegón Alejandro ★★ BASQUE   Descend the stairs to find the 20 or so tables that constitute this casual family restaurant, where chef Inaxio Valverde cooks up excellent Basque delights in classic style. Dimly lit, the two rooms feature large illuminated murals of the city in times long past. Valverde always offers a version of cod *pil pil,* but this might be cleverly crafted into a spider-crab stew. The changing seasons could bring tuna to your table and if you can't decide, you can always default to the tasting menu—with paired wines as an extra treat. Valerde does a brilliant riff on apple pie, making it with tart green apples sided by cheese ice cream.

Calle Fermín Calbetón, 4. www.bodegonalejandro.com. ℂ **94-342-71-58.** Entrees 21€–25€; tasting menu 52€. Reservations recommended Fri–Sat. Sun and Tues 1–3:30pm, Wed–Sat 1–3:30pm and 8:30–10:30pm. Closed Dec 23–Jan 15.

Juanito Kojua ★ BASQUE/SEAFOOD   A destination for traditional Basque seafood dishes since 1947, this modest spot began as a meeting place for fishermen's eating clubs and has persisted over the years because its chefs always seem to manage to get the top of the catch. Fish and shellfish, prepared simply, are the headline acts: grilled, baked, sometimes steamed. The classic hake cheeks in *pil pil* is the dish the locals order here, but you could try char-grilled line-caught red sea bream (a member of the bass family), tangy with salt. Meat dishes are limited, but the chef is rightly proud of his filet mignon served with a torchon of foie gras, grilled red piquillo peppers, and sautéed mushrooms.

Calle Puerto, 14. www.juanitokojua.com. ℂ **94-342-01-80.** Entrees 16€–25€. Reservations recommended. Sun 1–3:30pm; Mon–Sat 1–3:30pm and 8–11pm. Closed last 2 weeks Dec.

Rekondo ★ BASQUE   You will likely smell the wood smoke from Rekondo even before reaching the old stone house containing this terrific Basque *asador*. A Basque trademark is roasting meat over open flame, adeptly grilling chops and steaks or spit-roasting haunches of beef or whole kid or lamb. Rekondo branches out to all manner of seafood, grilling garlic-marinated squid and roasting whole spider crab directly over the coals before breaking it down to finish in a casserole tucked into a corner of the grill. The sommelier favors red wines as bold as the food— old-style Riojas and premier cru Bordeaux. In 2014, *Wine Spectator* cited Rekondo for one of the five best restaurant wine cellars in the world.

Paseo Igeldo, 57. www.rekondo.com. ℂ **94-321-29-07.** Entrees 24€–40€. Reservations recommended. Thurs–Mon 1–3:30pm and 8:30–11pm. Closed 2 weeks in June and 3 weeks in Nov.

INEXPENSIVE

Bodega Donostiarra ★★   Approaching its centenary, this remains a hugely popular, informal place with crowds spilling out to the outside tables, even in cool weather. Try to reserve, though most tables are on a first-come, first-served basis. Of course, you don't need a table as the pintxos are inventive, elaborate, and varied; just stand, and they'll deliver. Main courses focus on deliciously tempting Basque favorites with the chance to feast on a *chuleton* (beef chop) or grilled hake; the lunchtime dish of the day, with wine, bread, and dessert included, is a bargain. Gluten-free bread and beer available.

Peña y Goñi, 13. www.bodegadonostiarra.com. ℂ **94-321-15-59.** *Pintxos* 1.60€–4.50€. Entrees 9€–20€. Dish of the day 10€. Mon–Sat 9:30am–11pm (until midnight Fri–Sat).

San Sebastián Shopping

South of the Old Town, the Zentroa district is home to many mainstream outlets. For something different, a good option is **Alboka,** Plaza de la Constitución, 8 ℂ **94-342-63-00,** where most handicrafts on sale are of Basque manufacture. A Basque beret can be sourced at **Casa Ponsol Sombrería,** Calle Narrica, 4 (www.casaponsol.com; ℂ **94-342-08-76**), San Sebastián's oldest hat manufacturer. For fine food, two markets take pride of place, **La Bretxa** and **San Martín.** The former is more traditional, the latter an innovative upstart with live music and fancy *pintxos* on Thursday evenings.

San Sebastián Nightlife

A good evening for the locals involves a civilized bar-crawl, hunting out the finest *pintxos* in the Old Quarter, or across the river in Gros or Egia districts. Groups of friends, known as *cuadrillas,* stumble from bar to bar with the emphasis more on food than alcohol.

A BEGINNER'S GUIDE TO *pintxos*

Listing every great *pintxo* bar in San Sebastián would fill a phone book. Groups of *pintxos* enthusiasts often spend their evenings on some 20 streets in the old town. **Calle Fermín Calbetón** is one of the most popular, but **Calle 31 de Agosto** and the adjacent side streets are equally lively. Locals rarely spend the evening in the same bar: They find a likely looking venue, grab a drink and a *pintxo*, then simply move on to the next bar and repeat the process. Locals will eventually retire…for dinner, but if you are enjoying the *pintxo* style of eating, just keep going with this "culinary speed-dating."

Here are a few good places to get you started: You'll stumble across many more. Opening times vacillate with the seasons, but pintxos are best had from around noon to mid-afternoon, and again from early evening until 8pm. After that, they lose a bit of freshness. Most *pintxos* run 2€ to 6€, depending on the base ingredients and level of craftmanship involved. Wine, cider, or beer is typically another 2€ to 3€ per glass. On Thursday evenings, away from the Old Town, many bars offer a *pintxo* and drink for a cut-price: It's known as *pintxo pote*. Try the Egia and Gros districts to join in the fun.

Bar Sport ★ BASQUE PINTXOS
Amid the mock-chaos and tongue-in-cheek humor of this small, central bar, you'll find tasty bites to die for. The frenzied crowds ebb and flow like the tides as you fight for attention. Place your order, give your name…and eventually something will happen. Something good, such as squid stuffed with crab, perhaps. Fermin Calbeton, 10. ✆ **94-342-68-88.** Open daily.

Bar La Cepa ★ BASQUE PINTXOS
Mushrooms, mushrooms, mushrooms! There's heaps of them on the back counter and hams hanging overhead. If that's not clue enough…guess what the bar's name means? You can gorge on the *pintxos* or trade up to *raciones* or full meals. 31 de Agosto 7–9. www.bar lacepa.com. ✆ **94-342-63-94.** Closed Tues.

Bar-Restaurante La Viña ★ BASQUE PINTXOS   Once one of the most traditional bars, La Viña got an injection of creativity when chef Santiago

The big cultural center is **Centro Kursaal,** Av. de Zurriola, 1 (www. kursaal.eus; ✆ **94-300-30-00**), an avant-garde building designed by Rafael Moneo and positioned on the waterfront by Zurriola beach. A cultural, sporting, and leisure center, it is the venue for almost any major event. Along with the Guggenheim museum in Bilbao, it has helped put the Basque Country on the architectural map. Its modern design is at odds with the city's essential Belle Epoque look, but it is really only the late 20th-century architectural equivalent. Most of San Sebastián's major festivals are staged here and there is an 1,800-seat theater for plays, music and *zarzuela* performances.

THE BASQUE COAST ★★

Between San Sebastián and Bilbao, the Basque coastline is characterized by the mountains of the Cordillera Cantábrico tumbling down to the sea,

Rivera took over from his parents in 2013. You can still get great standards such as ham and mushroom croquettes, but don't overlook the more inventive *pintxos*. Try the prize-winning "ice cream cone" filled with fresh cheese whipped up with white anchovy. Mushrooms and shrimps are also put to good use by the kitchen wizards. Calle 31 de Agosto, 3. www.lavinarestaurante.com. *©* **94-342-74-95.** Closed Mon.

Bergara Bar ★★★ PINTXOS CREATIVOS   In its third generation of family ownership, little remains of the scruffy old bar that once occupied this street corner in the Gros district. But the reputation has been built over the years and the quality persists. A fabulous spread awaits its visitors and the overly strong lighting only serves to illuminate the aesthetic beauty of the dishes on the counter and the awards and press eulogies that are unashamedly fixed to the walls. Yes, you will pay more here, but you won't regret it. The *cocktail de marisco* (seafood), served in a glass, is a true *txapeldun* (prizewinner). Calle del General Artetze, 8. www.pinchosbergara.es *©* **94-327-50-26.** Open daily.

Casa Alcalde ★ BASQUE PINTXOS Head to the *pintxos* bar at this restaurant for the best variety of ham, cheese, and ham-and-cheese *pintxos* in San Sebastián. The walls are bedecked with bullfighting posters, but once you've gorged yourselves on the delicacies on show, you'll have no energy to fight a *toro*. Calle Mayor, 19. www.casaalcalde.com. *©* **94-342-62-16.** Open daily.

La Cuchara de San Telmo ★★ PINTXOS CREATIVOS   The counter here is bare, but do not walk out. The culinary delights of this evergreen favorite are detailed on the blackboards or the menu, as everything is *al momento*, or cooked to order, guaranteeing its freshness. Black pudding is an excellent choice, but the squid ink "risotto" made with orzo, foie gras with applesauce, and roasted pig's ears are the signature dishes. Tender beef cheeks and suckling pig are favorites for those wanting a full meal. Popular and crowded—come early, pay more than elsewhere, go home happy. Calle 31 de Agosto, 28. www.lacucharadesantelmo.com. *©* **94-441-76-55.** Closed all day Mon and Tue lunch.

where their fractured faces form rocky cliffs and headlands that surround astonishing sandy beaches. Huge swells make for some of Europe's most spectacular waves. The coastal villages are beach resorts, fishing villages, or a combination of the two. Fishing plays a lesser part in the local economy than previously, when intrepid Basque whalers and cod fishermen plied the coast of North America a century or more before Columbus set sail. They knew the way to the New World, but exhibiting the Basque head for business, they didn't see the point in sharing their lucrative secret.

The coast is best explored by automobile, allowing you to stop when and where you please. Begin by driving west from San Sebastian on the AP-1/AP-8 for 20km (13 miles) to **Zarautz ★**. Originally a whale-hunting village, its claim to fame now is that it boasts the coast's longest beach. Waves crash along the 3km (1¾-mile) of sands, creating surf that rivals Mundaka (p. 593). The seaside promenade is lined with

The sandy beach at Zarautz is the longest on the Basque Coast.

contemporary avant-garde sculpture, giving Zarautz a hip, edgy look—matched by the ambience when the surfers are in town. Continue west for 7km (4 miles) on the scenic coastal road, N-634, to **Getaria ★★**, the best place to linger along this coast This village has spawned two heroes from different eras. Juan Sebastián Elkano was the first navigator to circumnavigate the globe (his better-remembered captain, Magellan, actually perished en route), a feat that merits no fewer than three Elkano statues in Getaria and an exhibition about him inside the tourist office. Contributing to the village's renown is fashion genius **Cristóbal Balenciaga,** whose museum (www.cristobalbalenciagamuseoa.com; ✆ **94-300-88-40**) is a must for clothes-conscious visitors. It opens daily in July and August, from 10am until 8pm; spring and fall it is open 10am to 7pm, winter (Nov–Jan) Tuesday to Sunday 10am to 3pm, closed in February. Tickets are 10€ for adults, 7€ for students and seniors. Still primarily a fishing port renowned for its anchovies, Getaria also has two beaches and a church with an unusual sloping floor. The hillsides above the coastal plain are known for their excellent grapes, which produce light, white *txakolí* wines. Taste them in the bustling bars of the main street, Kale Nagusia.

Just another 7km (4 miles) west on N-634, **Zumaia ★** has two great beaches flanking cliffs studded with fossils. The coastline's spectacular stratified rock formations are known as the *flysch,* some of them created over 100 million years ago.

Continue west on the N-634 and then take the GI-638 (8km/5 miles) to reach **Ondarroa.** Before you enter town, you'll see signs for **Playa Saturrarán ★**, a white-sand beach between two rocky headlands that is the Basque Country's best-known nudist beach. Ondarroa is firmly founded on its fishing industry but has two principal landmarks in town: the 15th-century **Torre Likon** watchtower and the fortress-like Gothic church of **Santa María,** which seems to have grown out of the rock on which it stands.

Twisted roads now follow seaside cliffs west to **Lekeitio ★**, 26km (16 miles) from Ondarroa. Two shallow swimming beaches flank the mouth of the town's River Lea, while the industry divides between fishing (tuna, mainly) and tourism. Overlooking the harbor, the 15th-century **Basilica de Santa María de la Asunción,** Calle Abaroa, s/n (www.basilicadelekeitio.com; *©* **94-684-09-54**), has dramatic flying buttresses. Its gold-plated Flemish altarpiece depicts scenes from the life of the Virgin and the Passion of Christ. It's open for (free) visits Monday to Friday 8am to noon and 5 to 7:30pm, with guided visits available on prior request.

Getting to the next coastal village calls for a long detour upriver. Go 22km (14 miles) west on BI-2238 to Gernika (p. 595), then 11km (6¾ miles) north on BI-2235 to **Mundaka ★**, a favorite for surfers who adore its renowned left-curling pipelines which race up the narrowing river mouth, creating some of Spain's top surfing conditions. Otherwise, it's a gentle little fishing town with great swimming beaches. The **Mundaka Surf Shop,** Paseo Txorrokopunta, 8 (www.mundakasurfshop.com; *©* **94-617-72-29**), rents gear and offers lessons, and sells a variety of cool Mundaka tees and sweatshirts.

This coastal tour westwards continues with the medieval fishing village of **Bermeo ★**, just 5km (3 miles) north on BI-2235. Pleasure boats have largely replaced fishing vessels in the pocket harbor, but big diesel-powered trawlers lie at anchor in deeper water just offshore. Renovated after suffering storm damage, the replica whaling schooner *Aita Guria Baleontzia ★*, Calle Lamera, s/n (www.aitaguria.bermeo.org; *©* **94-617-91-21**), can be visited in summer months. The ship is a reminder that Bermeo's whalers hunted along the Cantabrian coast until the late 15th century, but soon began to venture to Greenland, Canada, and Maine. Normally, it is open from Easter week through October, but exact times depend on tides and weather, so do call ahead. Cost is 5€ adults, 3€ ages 4 to 14. The last fortified tower of the town, the 15th century Torre Ercilla, is home of the **Museo del Pescador ★**, Torrontoroko Enparantza, s/n (*©* **94-688-11-71**). Exhibits focus mainly on the town's modern in-shore fishery, especially for anchovies. Stirring displays explain how the fishermen created their brotherhood in the 19th century to manage the fishery, extract a fair price, and help families of men lost at sea. It opens Tuesday to Saturday, from 10am to 2pm, then from 4 to 7pm, and on Sundays 10am until 2pm. Entrance is free on Saturdays, otherwise tickets cost 3.50€ adults, 1.75€ seniors and students, free for ages 11 and under.

Eleven kilometers (7 miles) further west along the BI-631, you will reach the impressive promontory of **San Juan del Gaztelugatxe ★★**, standing proud against the ocean waves with a small church on top. Already a major visitor attraction, its fame accelerated rapidly when it starred as the mystical island of Dragonstone in an episode of *Game of Thrones*. Beware that it is a long descent and then ascent to visit the church, where you can ring an external bell three times and make a wish. You can access the point at all times, free of charge, though it has become so popular that booking is required between June and September and on public holidays (www.tiketa.eus; ✆ **68-873-81-47**). The church itself is rarely open.

Where to Stay on the Basque Coast

Atalaya Hotel ★   Built in 1911 to emulate a British seaside lodging, the Atalaya is skillfully maintained, old-fashioned in a pleasant manner, and utterly charming. It sits next to a shady waterfront park in Mundaka. Walk past the trees and down a set of stairs, and you're on the point where you can catch a pipeline and ride it all the way upriver to the sandy beach. It is convenient for surfers, and charges low-season rates during the winter when the big waves roll in. Some sea-view rooms have galleried balconies, keeping out winter storms; others open terraces. The summer café opens to the public, sometimes with live music.

Calle Itxaropen, 1, Mundaka. www.atalayahotel.es. ✆ **94-617-70-00.** 13 units. 79€–120€ doubles. Free parking. **Amenities:** Café (in summer); sauna (in winter); free Wi-Fi. Closed mid-Dec–mid-Jan.

Katrapona ★★   Overlooking the fishing harbor in compact Getaria, this handsome guesthouse is home to bright, spacious rooms, some with balconies. In its 100-year history, the building served as a fish-processing center and a gastronomic society before becoming a hotel. Solid stone walls and wooden ceiling beams are brightened with colorful décor, and the establishment provides a warm, friendly welcome. Step out the door and all the town's main restaurants and bars are a short stone's throw away. Breakfast includes a generous spread of mouthwatering, home-made goodies, which vary daily.

Plaza Katrapona 4, Getaria. www.katrapona.com. ✆ **94-314-04-09.** 8 units. 65€–95€ doubles. **Amenities:** Free Wi-Fi.

Where to Eat on the Basque Coast

Gure Txokoa ★★ BASQUE   Joxe Mari Mitxelena and Elena Aizpurua took over this Basque classic restaurant in 2003 and built it into a sought-after dining destination in Zarautz. The menu on any given day depends on what's in the market, and the couple emphasizes seasonal dishes that employ garden vegetables. Even dishes such as oven-roasted crab, for example, are served with a salad of frisée wrapped in paper-thin slices of zucchini and carrot. The fish are purchased daily at the docks of several villages along the coast, and the couple buys their nicely marbled beef by entire sides. Like so many coastal cooks, Mitxelena works with charcoal and open wood fires to cook most meat and fish. The wine cellar has an excellent selection of the bright, slightly tart local Txakoli wines made in the nearby hills.

Calle de Gipuzkoa, 22, Zarautz. www.restauranteguretxokoa.es. ⓒ **94-383-59-59.** Entrees 20€–25€. Tues–Sat 1–3:30pm and 8–11pm, Sun 1–3:30pm.

Restaurante Elkano ★★★ BASQUE SEAFOOD   This legendary Getaria seafood grill, created by Pedro Arregui, was a pioneer in cooking all manner of fish outdoors over a wood fire. His son Aitor joined his father in 2002 and shared the cooking duties until the latter passed away in 2014. The succession is in good hands, though Aitor ponders whether the baton of Basque cuisine will endure through the next few generations. Elkano has a menu, of course, but do not arrive with a dogmatic urge to eat—for example—his signature dish, turbot. If the best quality turbot is not available that day, then Aitor will not compromise: It's simply taken off the menu. "The most important part of my day is spent with the fishermen," he asserts. Almost everything here is grilled, the choice changing with the seasons: mackerel in February, Getaria's famed anchovies in April. Steaks and chops are also available, but the fish are Elkano's signature plates.

Calle Herrerieta, 2, Getaria. www.restauranteelkano.com. ⓒ **94-314-00-24.** Entrees 18€–40€. Mon 8.30–10:30pm; Wed–Sat 1–3:30pm and 8.30–10:30pm; Sun 1–3:30pm. Closed last week Dec, and 1 week before or after Easter.

GERNIKA-LUMO

The subject of Picasso's most famous painting (the original is now displayed at the Reina Sofía Museum in Madrid; see p. 87), Gernika-Lumo was the spiritual home of the Basques and a seat of Basque nationalist sentiment. Destroyed by a Nazi air raid on April 26, 1937, during the Spanish Civil War, the town was targeted on its market day, ensuring maximum carnage. Estimates of casualties range from 200 to 2,000. The bombers reduced the town to rubble, but a powerful symbol of independence was born. Although activists around the world attempted to rally support for the embattled Spanish Republicans, governments everywhere, including that of the United States, left the Republicans to fend for themselves, refusing to supply them with arms.

Picasso gave his painting the town's Castilian name, but "Gernika-Lumo" is preferred here to the painter's "Guernica." The town has been rebuilt, but its significance is in its symbolism, not in any aesthetic beauty. A church bell chimes softly, and laughing children play in the street. In the midst of this peace, however, you suddenly come upon a sign: souvenirs . . . remember. A ceramic replica of Picasso's work can be seen at the north end of Calle Allende Salazar.

Essentials

ARRIVING Frequent **Bizkaibus** buses (www.bizkaia.es; © **90-222-22-65**) operate daily between Gernika and Bilbao, costing only 2.55€. If you're driving from Bilbao, head east along the A-8 superhighway; cut north on the BI-635 and follow the signs for Gernika. From San Sebastián, drive west along A-8, and take the BI-635 north. A more scenic but slightly longer route involves driving west from San Sebastián on A-8, branching off on the coastal road to Ondarroa and continuing on as the road turns south, following the signs to Gernika.

VISITOR INFORMATION The **tourist office** is at Calle Artekalea, 8 (www.gernika-lumo.net; © **94-625-58-92**). In summer, it's open Monday to Saturday 10am to 7pm, Sunday 10am to 2pm; off season, it is open weekdays 10am to 6pm, weekends 10am to 2pm.

Exploring Gernika-Lumo

The Assembly House and former Basque parliament, known as the **Casa de Juntas** ★, Juntetxea (© **94-625-11-38**), is a significant visitor attraction in town. Under a marvelous stained-glass ceiling, you can discover much about the Basque *fueros,* their laws and customs. You can also soak up the gravitas of the parliamentary hall, which is still used occasionally. It is open June to September daily 10am to 2pm and 4 to 7pm, October to May daily 10am to 2pm and 4 to 6pm. Admission is free. Outside is the Tree of Gernika, a powerful symbol of Basque identity under whose branches the Kings of Castile used to swear allegiance to the *fueros.*

Museo de la Paz de Gernika ★★, Foru Plaza, 1 (www.museodelapaz.org; © **94-627-02-13**), Gernika's Peace Museum, documents the 1937 bombing through photographs, video, and artifacts, including sobering bomb fragments bearing Luftwaffe markings. The attack lasted for up to 3 hours, as Nazi and Italian planes unloaded thousand-pound bombs on the helpless townsfolk. Exhibits include a framed letter from President Roman Herzog of Germany, dated March 27, 1997, acknowledging German responsibility for the indefensible act and calling for reconciliation and peace. Copies of Picasso's working drawings for *Guernica* are also displayed. While the atrocity is one focus of the museum, the exhibits also address wider, more global issues of war and peace, adding to the interest for the visitor. March to September, it's open Tuesday to Saturday 10am to 7pm, Sunday 10am to 2pm; between October and February (closed

Jan), hours are Tuesday to Saturday 10am to 2pm and 4 to 6pm, Sunday 10am to 2pm. Admission is 5€ adults, 3€ students and seniors, and free for kids under 12.

Where to Stay & Eat in Gernika

Bolina El Viejo ★ BASQUE TRADITIONAL   Sure, there are fancier places to eat in this region, but in an authentic Basque town like Gernika, you should be eating authentically. Amongst a crowd of workmen, beret-clad pensioners, and curious visitors, just tuck in to the daily menu, 3 courses for next-to-nothing with wine and bread included. Some of the efficient, matronly waitresses have done 40 years of service here, as the business has been passed down the generations. Out front is the town's main bar: Just push through the glass dividing door to reveal the modest dining room beyond.

Calle Adolfo Urioste 1. www.restaurantebolinaelviejo.com. ℂ **94-625-10-15.** Entrees 15€–22€; set menus 11€. Reservations not taken, so arrive early. Sun–Thurs 1–5pm, Fri–Sat 1–11pm.

Hotel Urune ★★   Gernika has slim pickings for accommodation, but this renovated Basque *baserri* (farmhouse) just south of town is well worth the short detour, set in rural hilltop bliss and painted in a brash indigo color. Alberto is an engaging host, his love for his hotel evidenced by the years of painstaking refurbishment invested in its creation. Inside, the classy rooms are each named after a Basque mythological creature. Beautifully furnished, the superior ones enjoy the benefits of a terrace. Outside, sun-loungers are available, with direct views to the rugged Bizkaian mountains opposite. Communal spaces occupy the former animal pens downstairs: Thankfully, the animals have long gone, their space now well-used with super-comfortable sofas and welcoming fireplaces.

Barrio de Txakale 8 (off the BI-635), Muxika, www.urunehotela.com. ℂ **94-465-16-63.** 12 units. 78€–160€ double. Free parking. **Amenities:** Airport transfers available, free Wi-Fi. Closed Feb, and Jan if no bookings.

BILBAO ★★★

The 21st-century edition of Bilbao (Bilbo in Basque) is a case study in the transformative power of art, or at least of architecture. As recently as the 1980s, Bilbao was a smoky steel-making and ship-building city on the banks of a severely polluted river. Today it is a graceful small metropolis with a global appeal. Instead of seeing smoke and grime, visitors behold broad avenues, lovely river vistas, a cornucopia of cutting-edge architecture, top-drawer cuisine, and an edgy, lively vibe.

The city government's audacity in courting the Guggenheim Museum in New York and engaging controversial architect Frank O. Gehry to design the Guggenheim Bilbao has paid off richly. The opening of the

Guggenheim in 1997 began the transformation of the riverfront and turned a provincial city of 355,000 into what Gehry has called a laboratory for contemporary architecture. Among architects, you're nobody these days until you have a building in Bilbao—and plenty of world-class names have followed in Gehry's footsteps.

Bilbao continues to flourish as a banking and services center, most of its manufacturing having fled. Although the city is best discovered by walking, the city government has significantly upgraded the transportation infrastructure, installing a new airport (designed by Santiago Calatrava), and an efficient and attractive metro system with futuristic entrances, glass hoods which locals call *fosteritos* in reference to their British designer, Sir Norman Foster.

Essentials

ARRIVING   **Bilbao Airport** (www.aena.es; © **91-321-10-00**) is 8km (5 miles) north of the city, near the town of Loiu. Flights arrive from not only from Spanish cities (Madrid, Barcelona, Alicante, Arrecife, Fuenteventura, Las Palmas, Málaga, Menorca, Palma, Santiago de Compostela, Sevilla, Tenerife, Valencia, Vigo) but also European cities including Brussels, Frankfurt, Lisbon, London, Manchester, Milan, Paris, and Rome. **Iberia**'s booking office in Bilbao is contactable via www.iberia.com or at © **90-111-15-00.** From the airport into town or to the main bus station, take bus number A-3247 for 3€.

The main **train** station, Estación de Abando (www.renfe.com; © **91-232-03-20**), is at Plaza Circular 2. From here, you can catch long-distance trains to Madrid, Barcelona, and elsewhere. Four trains per day run to and from Madrid on weekdays and Sundays, two on Saturdays (trip time: 5–6¼ hr.). Trains run twice daily to and from Barcelona (trip time: 6¼ hr.), with one on Saturdays. Next door, the ornate Concordia station is the jumping-off point for services to Santander and Léon. Shorter-distance trains to Bermeo, Mundaka and Gernika leave from Atxuri station, while those heading for San Sebastián leave from Casco Viejo (Matiko); both these last two stations are on the Euskotren (www.euskotren.eus) network.

PESA (www.pesa.net; © **90-012-14-00**), at the Termibus bus station in Plaza de Garellano (www.termibus.es; © **94-439-50-77**), operates more than twenty **buses** per day to and from San Sebastián (trip time: 1¼ hr.). **Alsa** (www.alsa.es; © **90-242-22-42**) also operates from the Termibus station, with 15 buses daily to and from Madrid (trip time: 5 hr.). The Termibus website carries details of all bus services from Bilbao. Use the services of **Bizkaibus** (www.bizkaia.eus; © **94-612-55-55**) to get to Gernika, with buses running at least every half-hour each weekday (trip time: 45 min.), hourly on Sundays.

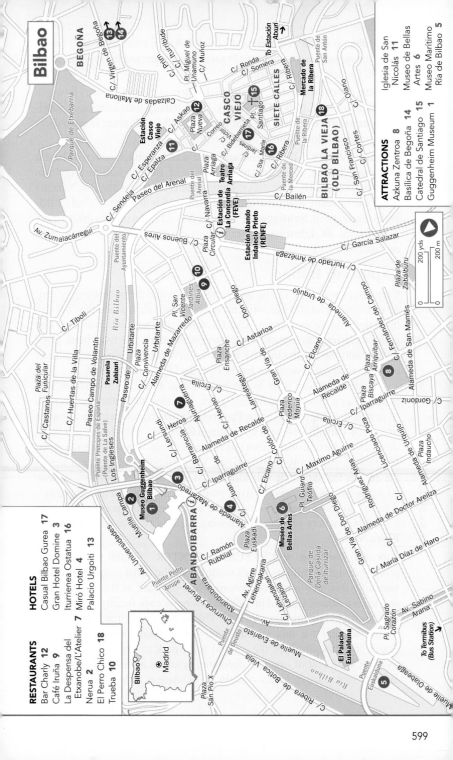

Bilbao

BEGOÑA

CASCO VIEJO

SIETE CALLES

BILBAO LA VIEJA (OLD BILBAO)

ABANDOIBARRA

ATTRACTIONS

Azkuna Zentroa **8**
Basílica de Begoña **14**
Catedral de Santiago **15**
Guggenheim Museum **1**
Iglesia de San Nicolás **11**
Museo de Bellas Artes **6**
Museo Marítimo Ría de Bilbao **5**

RESTAURANTS

Bar Charly **12**
Café Iruña **9**
La Despensa del Etxanobe/L'Atelier **7**
Nerua **2**
El Perro Chico **18**
Trueba **10**

HOTELS

Casual Bilbao Gurea **17**
Gran Hotel Domine **3**
Iturrienea Ostatua **16**
Miró Hotel **4**
Palacio Urgoiti **13**

Bilbao is on the A-8 toll road, which links the cities of Spain's northern Atlantic seacoast to western France. It is connected by superhighway to both Barcelona and Madrid.

VISITOR INFORMATION　　The **tourist office,** at Plaza Circular, 1 (www.bilbaoturismo.net; © **94-479-57-60**), is open daily 9am to 8pm. A **satellite tourist office** outside the Guggenheim Bilbao Museum is open daily 10am to 7pm (closes Sun at 3pm except July–Aug).

SPECIAL EVENTS　　The biggest and most widely publicized festival is **La Semana Grande,** dedicated to the Virgin of Begoña and lasting from mid-August to early September. During the celebration, the Río Nervión is the site of many flotillas and regattas. July 25 brings the festival of Bilbao's patron saint, **Santiago** (St. James); July 31 is devoted to the region's patron saint, **St. Ignatius,** and numerous events are held between these two dates.

Exploring Bilbao

Cargo ships no longer sail up the Nervión river into the once-smoggy center of Bilbao, a former industrial urban giant once nicknamed the "botxo," or "hole." Foundries, shipyards, and factories are long gone, with only one crane remaining as a reminder. Now a walk along the river bank gives insight into the renaissance of Bilbao: a new football stadium, cutting-edge skyscrapers, a designer footbridge, the Guggenheim itself.

Under a master plan by architect Cesar Pelli, the waterfront was reshaped as a green, human-scale place. The elegant footbridge over the river near the Guggenheim, the **Pasarela Zubizuri,** summarizes the spirit of the new Bilbao. Designed by Santiago Calatrava, it is sinuous and monumental, and exclusively reserved for pedestrians. Away from the river, the magnificent arrow-straight **Gran Via** boulevard cuts a swath across the city, its Parisian-style splendor dotted with designer shopping outlets. At its eastern end, across the river, you'll find the **Casco Viejo,** the atmospheric old town centered around the seven original streets of the city; now, this is where to enjoy an evening drink or two, particularly in the **Plaza Nueva.**

Azkuna Zentroa ★ CULTURAL CENTER　　French furniture and product designer Philippe Starck made his public debut as an architect by remaking this one-time Modernisme white elephant as Bilbao's cultural and leisure center. Opened in 1909 as a wine storage facility, the building was devastated by fire 10 years later. The shell of brick, iron, and concrete waited decades for this reincarnation before finally opening in 2010. Starck intentionally kept the ground level dark to encourage romantic trysts; it's a forest of ornately decorated columns in different whimsical motifs. Subterranean levels contain an exhibition gallery and a concert hall; the upper levels' brick and glass cubes contain a multimedia library, state-of-the-art gym, rooftop swimming pool, cafes, and restaurants. Plaza Arriquibar 4. www.azkunazentroa.eus. ℗ **94-401-40-14.** Admission free; 7€ per day to use gym or pool. Mon–Thurs 7am–11pm, Fri 7am–midnight, Sat 8:30am–midnight, Sun 8:30am–11pm. Metro: Indautxu or Moyua.

Guggenheim Museum ★★★ ART MUSEUM   Skeptics said Bilbao would get a temporary bump in tourism as curious people came to see what Frank O. Gehry had wrought on the once-industrial waterfront. Over 2 decades later, more than 1 million people each year visit the museum, and the flow shows no sign of abating. Truly, this is the engine that drove Bilbao onto the tourist map and kept it there. The strange building seemingly assembled of gargantuan parts from a titanium-clad fish no longer seems so alien. In fact, it has become as iconic as Eiffel's tower in Paris. Admittedly, there's something appealingly primitive about the squat beast, best viewed from across the river so you can take it all in.

The interior is radical. With a disorienting lack of right angles, the building is essentially a soaring 50m-high (164-ft.) atrium with exhibition floors cantilevered off a central support. Unless you've visited often, take the free audioguide when you enter, as it helps navigation.

Frank O. Gehry's Guggenheim Museum has transformed Bilbao into a tourist magnet.

THEY CALL IT puppy LOVE

Critics love to debate the merits of Frank O. Gehry's Guggenheim Bilbao Museum, but considering the museum in isolation misses the point. Bilbainos have embraced the surrounding plazas and made the pavements their own. Skateboard kids love the ramps and smooth-rolling runs, while soccer tykes kick balls against the walls. The greatest irony might be that Jeff Koons' goofy 43-foot-tall flower-sprouting puppy sculpture has almost upstaged the main limestone-and-titanium building. Installed as a temporary exhibit for the 1997 opening, the puppy was saved from demolition through a letter-writing campaign by local schoolchildren, and this magnificent send-up of kitsch is now more or less permanent. As locals joke, the museum is just the kennel for the puppy.

The permanent collection focuses on major post-1950 artists, including Picasso, Robert Motherwell, Robert Rauschenberg, and Antoni Tàpies. The Bilbao branch also shows contemporary Basque art, favoring sculptors, painters, and video artists who are still living and working. In addition, there's a vigorous temporary exhibition schedule, often featuring avant-garde work from China, Korea, and Japan. Signage is trilingual—in Basque, Castilian, and English.

Calle Abandoibarra, 2. www.guggenheim-bilbao.eus. © **94-435-90-80.** Admission generally 16€ adults, 9€ seniors and students, free for ages 12 and under. A 16€ Bono Artean ticket offers joint admission to Museo de Bellas Artes and Guggenheim Bilbao. July–mid-Sept daily 10am–8pm; mid-Sept–June Tues–Sun 10am–8pm. Closed Dec 25 and Jan 1. Bus: 1, 10, 13, or 18. Metro: Moyúa. Tranvia: Guggenheim. Underground parking garage accessed from Av. Abandoibarra.

Museo de Bellas Artes ★★ ART MUSEUM Don't feel sorry for this elegant fine arts museum, just because the Guggenheim gets all the attention. With around half of its 14,000-piece collection on display at any one time, it exhibits outstanding pieces of art you'd be sorry to miss. Big names of Spanish painting—Velázquez, Zurbarán, El Greco, Goya—are represented by mostly minor works, while Basque sculptors such as Chillida and Oteiza are well represented. Regional paintings from the early 20th century show both folkloric subjects and a striking sense of moral outrage, particularly about the mistreatment of miners and factory workers. With wide, welcoming staircases and spacious rooms, this is a super place for reflection and appreciation.

Plaza del Museo, 2. www.museobilbao.com. © **94-439-60-60.** Admission 10€ adults, 8€ seniors, free for under age 25. Free to everyone 6–8pm daily. A 16€ Bono Artean ticket offers joint admission to Museo de Bellas Artes and Guggenheim Bilbao. Wed–Mon 10am–8pm. Metro: Moyúa.

Museo Marítimo Ría de Bilbao ★ MUSEUM You know that an industry is really finished when the city builds a museum about it. Bilbao

The Museo de Bellas Artes.

was a great shipbuilding center on Spain's north coast from the beginning of the Industrial Revolution. Now it's a city about information and information technology, so this excellent maritime museum, built on the site of the last active shipyard, is a requiem for Bilbao's seagoing era. Start with the short semi-animated video, which graphically outlines the city's incredible post-industrial renaissance. Outdoor exhibits display several restored historic vessels, while a new workshop focuses on Basque wooden boat-building.

Muelle Ramón de la Sota, 1. www.museomaritimobilbao.eus. $\textcircled{C}$ **94-608-55-00.** Admission 6€ adults, 3.50€ students and seniors, free under age 6. Tues free to everyone except July–Aug. July–Sept daily 10am–8pm; Oct–June Tues–Fri 10am–6pm, Sat–Sun 10am–8pm. Metro: San Mamés. Tranvía: Euskalduna.

EXPLORING BILBAO'S CASCO VIEJO (OLD QUARTER) ★

Even though Bilbao was established around 1300, it has few medieval monuments. However, the Old Quarter of Bilbao—connected by four bridges to the much larger modern section on the opposite bank of the Nervión—has been declared a national landmark. To reach the pedestrianized Old Quarter on foot (the only way to explore it), take the Puente del Arenal from the Gran Vía, Bilbao's main boulevard. From the

Bilbao's Casco Viejo (Old Quarter).

Guggenheim Bilbao, hop on the Tranvía to Pio Baroja or the Metro to Casco Viejo—or enjoy the walk down the riverfront promenade.

A few paces north of the Old Quarter's center, 64 graceful arches enclose **Plaza Nueva,** also called the Plaza de los Mártires, completed in 1826. Its most important church, **Iglesia de San Nicolás** (Plaza de San Nicolás; ⓒ **94-415-36-27**), built in 1756, has a notable Baroque facade. It opens Monday to Friday from 10:30am to 1pm, then 5:30 to 7:30pm, and on Saturdays 10:30am to 1pm, Sundays 11am to 2pm. On most Sundays, a compact **flea market** starts at 8am in the Plaza Nueva.

If you climb 300 steps from Plaza Unamuno and do a 10-minute walk, you'll reach the **Basilica de Begoña,** Calle Virgen de Begoña, 8 (ⓒ **94-412-70-91**), built largely in the early 1500s. Inside, the dimly lit church features a brightly illuminated depiction of the Virgen de Begoña, patron saint of Bizkaia, dressed in long, flowing robes. Many boats are named for the Virgin, and a long-standing custom calls for sailors to sing the "Salve Regina" when they spot the church tower as they return to port. Hours are Monday to Saturday 8:30am to 1:30pm and 5 to 8pm, Sunday 9am to 2pm and 5 to 9pm. Buses 3, 30 or 38 will take you there, if the walk is too much.

The Old Quarter also houses the **Catedral de Santiago,** Plaza Santiago, built in the 15th century and dedicated to Bilbao's patron saint St. James. The church is an important pilgrimage site, and its neo-Gothic tower is said to demonstrate the "good taste of the cultured population of Bilbao." In July and August it opens daily 10am to 9pm, the rest of the year 10am to 7pm. Tickets cost 5 € adults, 4 € seniors, 3.50 € students.

Where to Stay in Bilbao

MODERATE

Gran Hotel Domine ★★　If you're going to Bilbao mainly to visit the Guggenheim, it's almost impossible to beat this whimsical, charming hotel located across the street. Iñaki Aurreroextea undertook a nearly impossible job: Create a hotel that looks good next to Gehry's museum without copying the form or style. He devised a skin of polished stone and cantilevered black glass windows. Their odd angles echo the Guggenheim in a fractured plane of small reflections. Inside, the interior was designed by Valencian artist Javier Mariscal; although fully refreshed in 2018, his zany artwork remains. Less expensive rooms overlook the central atrium or the back street. The price is right, and you can view the Guggenheim from the rooftop terrace every summer morning at breakfast.

Alameda de Mazarredo, 61. www.granhoteldominebilbao.com. *ⓒ* **94-425-33-00.** 135 units. 120€–310€ double; 220€–640€ suite. Valet parking 25€. Metro: Moyúa. Bus: 13, 27, 38, or 48. **Amenities:** Restaurant; bar; sauna, Turkish bath, exercise room; free Wi-Fi.

Miró Hotel ★　Almost as close to the Guggenheim as the Hotel Domine (see above), the Miró is the signature hotel of Spanish fashion designer Antonio Miró, who is to Spanish menswear what Calvin Klein is to American. The hotel exterior is a neo-Bauhaus checkerboard of gray steel and tinted glass. Inside, it's 21st-century minimalism all the way, with black carpets on the floors and so much black marble in the bathroom that you'll want to turn on all the lights to see. Some interior rooms are tight on size, but suites have plenty of room to stretch out. Exterior rooms with a view of the Guggenheim fetch a premium price. Discreet, professional service, soft leather sofas, and an honesty bar accentuate the relaxed ambience. A la carte breakfasts use quality local products.

Alameda Mazarredo, 77. www.mirohotelbilbao.com. *ⓒ* **94-661-18-80.** 50 units. 85€–230€ double; 210€–460€ suite. Parking 18€. Metro: Moyúa. Bus: 13, 27, 38, or 48. **Amenities:** Bar; exercise room; room service; steam bath, hydromassage bath; bikes for rent; free Wi-Fi.

Palacio Urgoiti ★★　Out of the city, but handy for the airport, this magnificently reconstructed delight welcomes those who prefer tranquility to the busy Bilbao center. A 17th-century creation, owned by the same family ever since, this "palace" was originally 10 miles away, but under threat from highway construction, was rebuilt in its current location. The result justifies the effort: a delightful hotel reminiscent of a stately manor house. It's wonderfully elegant, with super-spacious rooms, fine cuisine, and refined staff. Golfers will find a 9-hole, par-3 course waiting on the doorstep—equipment is provided.

Calle Arituagne, Bilbao-Mungia. www.palaciourgoiti.com. ✆ **94-674-68-68.** 43 units. 82€–180€ double; 140–220€ suite. Free parking. **Amenities:** Restaurant, bar; golf course, indoor pool, exercise room; free Wi-Fi.

INEXPENSIVE

Casual Bilbao Gurea ★   A bright super-central choice, this upstairs establishment, housed in a 250-year old building, is decorated in bright and bold colors. Given the full makeover, it is hard to imagine what it might have looked like when Joseph Bonaparte's Minister of Maritime affairs was born here in the mid-18th century. Double-glazed windows exclude street noise, and one unit is adapted for guests with wheelchairs.

Calle Bidebarrieta, 14. www.casualhoteles.com. ✆ **94-416-32-99.** 26 units. 55€–105€ double. Parking nearby 15 € Metro: Casco Viejo. **Amenities:** Free Wi-Fi.

Iturrienea Ostatua ★★   A modernized townhouse hotel in the old quarter is concealed behind a quaint, characterful entrance and a spiraling staircase. Once inside, reassuringly solid walls and exposed oak beams sit comfortably with clean lines and bright décor. Recently introduced air-conditioning keeps the summer heat at bay. Delightful Basque owners and staff give a cared-for feel to this tasteful gem, freshening up the décor year-by year: A new wall mosaic particularly catches the eye. Breakfast is below average for price, well above for quality.

Calle Santa María, 14. www.iturrieneaostatua.com. ✆ **94-416-15-00.** 9 units. 60€–85€ double. Parking 18 €. Metro: Casco Viejo. **Amenities:** Free Wi-Fi.

Where to Eat in Bilbao

EXPENSIVE

La Despensa del Etxanobe/L'Atelier ★★★ CONTEMPORARY BASQUE   A pillar of the Basque culinary infrastructure, Fernando Canales is a rock star among Bilbao chefs. Turn on any local food show and he's likely to pop up, showing viewers precisely how to make some avant-garde creation with three ingredients and a little magic. Canales has moved from the rather remote Palacio Euskalduna to this more central location, dividing his enormous talent between these two adjacent restaurants. For many, **La Dispensa**'s informal ambience, underscored with gentle music and clever use of lights and mirrors, will win the day. The **L'Atelier** styles itself as "gastronomic" and carries the Michelin star comfortably, but more formally. We are happier with the relaxed, less expensive Dispensa, but whichever option you select, the food from the extensive menus remains a true star. Roasted octopus with a potato and paprika foam competes for your attention with crayfish carpaccio, and that's just for starters. Canales goes the extra mile to get the very best product, simply because his super-knowledgeable clientele demands it. Everything here oozes class, so relax, enjoy—you won't be disappointed.

Calle Juan Ajuriaguerra, 8. www.ladespensadeletxanobe.com, https://atelier etxanobe.com. ☎ **94-442-10-71.** Entrees 22€–34€; tasting menus 60€–110€. Reservations required. Atelier: Mon and Wed–Sat 1–3pm and 8–10pm (Fri–Sat until 11pm). La Dispensa also open Tues. Closed Dec 30–Jan 15, late Jul–mid-Aug.

Nerua ★★ CONTEMPORARY BASQUE   Prodigy chef Josean Alija took just months to win his first Michelin star at this elegant fine-dining venue, its entrance behind the Guggenheim Bilbao. Alija collected accolades early in his career for prize-winning dishes like whipped milk-protein ice cream with candied violets, or roasted foie gras with candied carrots. His menu changes three times each year, after a lengthy planning process. Like many of the artists shown at the Guggenheim, Alija loves to confound expectation. "Without innovation, tradition dies," he asserts, but while he draws on Basque culinary know-how, he travels abroad, finding additional inspiration. Instead of serving roast pork with a leek sauce, he serves roast leek with an Iberian pork sauce and rice germ. To play off his famed foie gras, he makes a vegetarian version. To eat here is to enjoy dining as performance art.

Avda. Abandoibarra, 2. www.neruaguggenheimbilbao.com. ☎ **94-400-04-30.** Tasting menus 80€–170€. Reservations required. Tues 1–3pm; Wed–Sat 1–3pm and 8.30–10pm; Sun 1–3pm (Nov–Apr closed Wed evening). Metro: Moyúa. Bus: 1, 10, 13, or 18. Closed 1st 2 weeks Jan.

MODERATE

Café Iruña ★★ BASQUE   A true reference point for Bilbaínos, this elegantly furnished establishment offers its visitors two classic Basque options. You can stand at the bar, dazzled by its delightfully tiled walls, and sip your wine while grazing on reasonably priced *pintxos,* or take a table amid lively chatter in the dining room next door for a sit-down meal. Either way, you are following in the footsteps of thousands who have graced this institution since it opened in 1903. Iruña (the name is Basque for Pamplona) makes the most of its cachet, hosting concerts and events, but doesn't seek to overcharge on account of its beauty or fame.

Jardines de Albia www.cafeirunabilbao.net. ☎ **94-423-70-21.** Entrees 12€–21€; set menus 15€–29 €. Reservations recommended Fri–Sat. Mon–Fri 7am–1am, Sat 7am–2am, Sun noon–1am. Metro: Moyúa.

El Perro Chico ★ BASQUE   The "Little Dog" perches above the River Nervión, at the end of the bridge that connects the ragged La Vieja district with the Old Town. Inside, original tiled floors and walls lend character to this casual place. But the food is taken seriously, solid Basque ingredients such as hake given a subtle twist of modernity. Anchovies are brought to the table pegged to a miniature clothesline—there's a hint of fun going on. Asian influences can be evidenced, too: orange curry or oxtail stew with sake show a willingness to experiment. Outside, the gatherings of young Bohemians in this hipster quarter demand you take a window table to max your people-watching.

Calle Aretxaga, 2. www.elperrochico.com. © **94-640-26-65.** Pintxos 4€–6€; entrees 12€–17€. Reservations required for restaurant. Wed–Sun noon–midnight (Fri–Sat until 1am).

Trueba ★ BASQUE TRADITIONAL Aitor and Marián are friends, not husband and wife, but their partnership is a marriage made in heaven nevertheless. "Basque Traditional" means that the raw material will be the best, so the tomato served with fresh tuna shards will melt in your mouth—sensational. Aitor uses his tiny kitchen to best effect, his poché egg crafted with truffled potato and red peppers to start your meal with a fanfare. The ambience is refined, yet homey, and the clientele keep coming back.

Colon de Lareategui, 11. www.restaurantetrueba.com. © **94-423-83-09.** Pintxos 4€–6€; entrees 12€–17€. Reservations required for restaurant. Mon–Wed 1:30–4pm, Thurs–Sat 2–4pm and 9–11:30pm.

INEXPENSIVE

Bar Charly ★ BASQUE PINTXOS Don't be deterred by the slightly gaudy sign or the slightly goofy name, as this is as good a place as any to start your slow circular gastronomic crawl round the Plaza Nueva. The counter groans under the weight of tiny delicacies, but if you suffer decision paralysis, order a selection with a drink for a decent price. Great atmosphere matches the food, with outside tables if the weather is kind.

Plaza Nueva 7. www.barcharly.com. © **94-415-01-27.** Pintxos 2€–4€. Daily 10am–10pm (Fri–Sat until 11:30pm). Metro: Casco Viejo.

Bilbao Shopping

Many visitors can't resist buying a beret in Basque Country. The best selection is found at **Sombrería Gorostiaga,** Calle Victor, 9 (© **94-416-12-76**), a family-owned business since 1854. It opens Monday to Friday 10am to 1:30pm and 4 to 8pm, Saturdays 10am to 4:30pm. Elosegui is the authentic brand to buy. If you'd like to purchase high-end Basque art or artifacts, try **Galeria Llamas,** Calle Iparraguirre, 4 (© **94-423-97-35**), near the Guggenheim museum. It's open Monday to Friday 10am to 2pm and 5 to 9pm, Saturday 11am to 2pm and 6 to 9pm. They ship worldwide.

Even if you are not a foodie, check out the ship-shaped **Mercado de la Ribera,** Calle Ribera, 22 (© **94-602-37-91**). The 1929 Art Deco–style building sits on the site of markets dating back to the 14th century, and is a marvel of decorative tile, brick, and glass. It claims to be the largest covered market in Europe and opens Monday to Friday 8am to 2:30pm and 5 to 8pm, Saturdays 8:30am to 3pm (mid-June to mid-Sept, the afternoon openings are Fri only).

Bilbao Nightlife

For locals, going out for drinks and *pintxos* is the principal mode of evening entertainment. There is a good concentration of bars on **Calle Licenciado Poza,** between Alameda del Doctor Areilza and Calle Iparraguirre, in the Ensanche neighborhood, but the super-lively **Plaza Nueva** in the Old Quarter is the best compact choice for people-watching and bar-hopping. Amongst the plaza's options, **Café Bar Bilbao,** Plaza Nueva, 6 (www.bilbao-cafebar.com; ℂ **94-415-16-71**), has a classic look. Its house specials include fresh anchovies wrapped around green olives. When you need a change of scenery in this square, the next bar is mere yards away.

If you'd rather dance and mingle than eat, one of the most popular spots is **Cotton Club,** Calle Gregorio de la Revilla, 25 (www.cottonclub bilbao.es; ℂ **94-410-49-51**). A DJ spins the latest tunes for a crowd in their 20s and 30s. The club is most frenzied on Friday and Saturday when it opens from 8:30pm to 6:30am. There is no cover; beer begins at 5€. The **Teatro Arriaga Antzokia,** Plaza Arriaga, 1 (www.teatroarriaga.eus; ℂ **94-479-20-36**), on the banks of the Río Nervión, is the setting for world-class opera, classical music concerts, ballet, and even *zarzuelas* (comic operas). Advance schedule is on the website. Other festivals and cultural events are available via the tourist office website.

RIOJA ALAVESA ★★

San Sebastián and Bilbao may dominate the consciousness of visitors from abroad, but the southern Basque Country is gaining momentum as a visitor draw. Part of Alava province, the Rioja Alavesa region borders on La Rioja and produces world-class wines from bodegas that range from dusty caves to designer wineries sparkling in the sunshine. Less Basque in identity than the two coastal provinces, nevertheless this captivating region is firmly part of the Basque Country.

With its classic almond-shaped town layout, elevated position, imposing entrance gates, narrow streets full of wine caves, and characterful restaurants and cozy hotels, **Laguardia ★★★** is top choice for exploring this region. It stands guard over the surrounding vineyards and assuredly wears its official accolade as "One of Spain's Most Beautiful Towns." Wine is all around, with opportunities to taste and buy the precious products of the surrounding vineyards. Backed by the heights of the craggy Cordillera Cantábrica mountains, the scenery here is easy on the eye, a visual feast for the eyes as you sip on a full-bodied glass of red.

Exploring Laguardia

Wander compact **Laguardia**'s largely vehicle-free alleys and admire its town walls, with a winery tour or two thrown in. Be sure to catch the **Reloj Carillón,** the town clock which celebrates the hours of noon, 1pm, 2pm, and 8pm by emitting tiny Basque figurines who perform a delightful traditional dance, often to applause.

A guided tour of the **Iglesia Santa Maria de los Reyes** church is also worthwhile. This and a climb up the town's tower, the 13th-century **Torre Abbacial,** are best organized through the **tourist office,** Calle Mayor, 52 (www.laguardia-alava.com; ℰ **94-560-08-45**), which opens Monday to Saturday 10am to 2pm and 4 to 7pm, Sundays 10:45am to 2pm. Views from the tower are stunning.

For a winery visit that keeps you inside the town walls, try the magnificently named **Bodegas Carlos Pedro Pérez de Viñaspre,** located at Calle Páganos, 44, where daily tours with tastings let you access some of the hundreds of caves that lurk beneath the town. Call ℰ **94-560-01-46** to book a visit in English, which costs 5€.

Within easy walking distance of the town, pamper yourself with a spa visit to the **Wine Oil Spa Villa de Laguardia** at Paseo San Raimundo, 15 (www.hotelvilladelaguardia.com; ℰ **94-560-05-60**). For 20 € you can enjoy the pool and wine oil circuit, with a range of treatments and massages available at extra cost. Advance booking is required. Next door, the **Villa Lucia Wine Thematic Center** (https://villa-lucia.com; ℰ **94-560-00-32**) is a good choice for all, but especially for parents with children who might get bored by a winery tour. Here, a semi-animated film, humorous at times, will take you on an excellent 4-D tour of Rioja Alavesa. Don't panic when smoke appears to rise from the seat in front, it is all part of the fun. The 7€ admission includes a tour of the adjacent museum and

starchitect **MAKES WINE HOTEL**

Being designer of the Guggenheim Museum Bilbao (p. 601) is not Frank Gehry's only Spanish claim to fame. Another of his Basque Country creations is the luxurious **Hotel Marqués de Riscal ★★★**, Calle Torrea, 1, Elciego (www.hotel-marquesderiscal.com; ℰ **94-518-08-80**), deep in the center of the wine-producing region. The 43-room hotel shares many of the famous museum's architectural quirks. The roof, for example, is constructed from curved plates of titanium suspended at different angles and tinted silver, gold, and rose, while the exterior of the hotel is meant to evoke a "grapevine just before the fruit is harvested." Its elegant rooms are all about windows; there are even window seats that follow the zigzagging contours of the exterior glass. The architect said he wanted "to make the view part of the room." A stay in this work of art is expensive: 300€ to 550€ for a double, suites 550€ to 780€. A Michelin-starred restaurant is on site, as is an indoor heated swimming pool, a fitness center, and even a spa offering "wine treatment therapies."

The hotel is part of an entire complex that Gehry designed for the Marques de Riscal winery. The company modestly calls it **La Ciudad del Vino,** or "City of Wine" (www.marquesderiscal.com; ℰ **94-560-60-00**). Gehry incorporated many of the structures of the 19th-century winery into his grand gestures of fanciful style. The store and wine bar accept casual visits—you can easily taste and buy. If there's room, you might be able to join a tour, although reservations are advised. Tour and tasting costs 16€; call to arrange a time. The store and wine bar are open daily 10am to 7pm.

a glass of wine. A good wine shop and on-site restaurant includes a games room for the youngsters. The Center opens 10am to 8pm, though busy lunchtimes are not advised for the film/museum visit. It's closed for 2 weeks in January.

Where to Stay & Eat in Rioja Alavesa

Hotel Castillo el Collado ★★   Standing imperiously at the end of a pretty garden, this established hotel oozes history from every solid stone. It reflects class from its tiled floors and breathes charm from its wood-work. Each spacious room is different, with intriguing names such as La Fabula or Amor y Locura. (You'll be happy in any of them, but those two enjoy fantastic views to both north and east.) If you want a truly giant private Jacuzzi, ask for the room called Doña Blanca. All guests can climb the wooden stairs to the tower, for stunning vistas over vineyards, mountains, and the nearby wetlands

Paseo el Collado 1, Laguardia. www.hotelcollado.com. © **94-562-12-00.** 10 units. 99€–138€ doubles. **Amenities:** Restaurant, bar, free Wi-Fi.

Restaurante Ariño Jatetxea ★ BASQUE TRADITIONAL   Checkered tablecloths, open-stone walls, and wooden beams adorned with pictures hanging at a squint angle will make you feel instantly at home here, but it's the no-nonsense, traditional food and decent prices that'll tempt you back a second time. Boss Gaizka makes no apologies for the lack of pretension in his old-style cuisine. Why should he? Labastida is a town whose population swells in summer, as second-home owners stage an invasion and provide his main clientele. Nor does he change his menu, as for over 30 years everyone has gone home happy on meaty staples such as beef chop or entrecôte, or hake from a limited fish menu.

Calle Frontín, 28, Labastida. © **94-533-10-24.** Entrees 9€–15€. Weekday set menu 12€. Tues–Thurs and Sun 1–4pm, Fri–Sat 1–4pm and 9–11pm. Closed Sept.

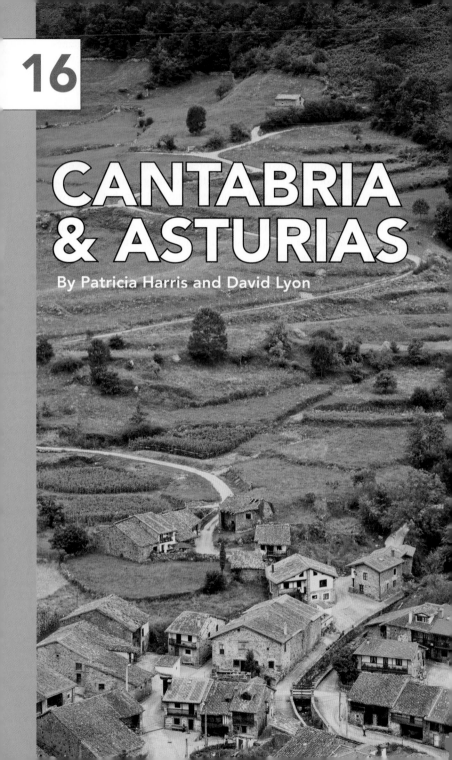

16

CANTABRIA & ASTURIAS

By Patricia Harris and David Lyon

W hen you arrive in the northern Spanish regions of Cantabria and Asturias, you'll be forgiven for thinking you somehow made a wrong turn and ended up in Ireland. Not only are the people more Celtic than Roman, the green lowlands and recurrent mist give even the landscape a Hibernian feel. But make no mistake: This is Spain, and some historically minded Spaniards would even argue that it's the very cradle of modern Spain, as this is where the Reconquest of Iberia began. The two regions are the core of "green Spain," flanked on the west by Galicia and the east by Basque Country. The high mountains of the Cordillero Cantábrico capture the moisture rolling off the Bay of Biscay and the Atlantic Ocean, dumping it on the green fields and mountain forests of both regions.

Some of the earliest evidence of human habitation in Europe (as long ago as 140,000 years) has been found in the limestone caves of this region. When the Romans arrived, they found thriving Celtic communities on the coast, and when the Moors came riding in, they were fiercely resisted by local Visigothic warlords.

Protected by mountains, many Christians took refuge on this northern strip during centuries of Moorish domination of lands farther south. By tradition, the Christian Reconquista began here with the A.D. 722 Battle of Covadonga, led by the warrior Pelayo, later crowned king of Asturias. A great deal of religious architecture remains in the region, including a handful of country churches in an intriguingly transitional style between Gothic and Romanesque.

This chapter begins in Cantabria and works westward toward Asturias. It is best seen by car, as connections between the coastal communities are not always convenient, and public transport in the interior is inadequate or nonexistent. **Santander,** a rail terminus and the regional capital, makes the best center for touring Cantabria; it also has the most tourist facilities. From Santander, you can get nearly anywhere in Cantabria within a 3-hour drive. To explore Asturias, the best base is its capital, **Oviedo.**

FACING PAGE: **A village in Cantabria's rugged green interior.**

The most attractive portion of the Cordillera is the scenic and topographic summit known as the **Picos de Europa,** located mostly in Asturias but creeping over the border into Cantabria. In 1918 the region was made Spain's first national natural park.

SANTANDER ★

Santander, capital city of Cantabria, has always been a rival of San Sebastián (p. 580), though it has never attained the status of that Basque resort to the east. Santander became a royal residence from 1913 to 1930, after city officials presented the English-style Magdalena Palace to Alfonso XIII. Don't expect much medieval ambience here, but there's plenty of more modern charm. After Santander's old quarter was ravaged by a 1941 fire, it was rebuilt in a grand resort style with wide boulevards, a waterfront promenade, sidewalk cafes, restaurants, and hotels.

Ferry service between the city and the United Kingdom and Ireland (see below) has made Santander especially popular with Brits and Irish, for whom the city is the first sandy toehold in Iberia.

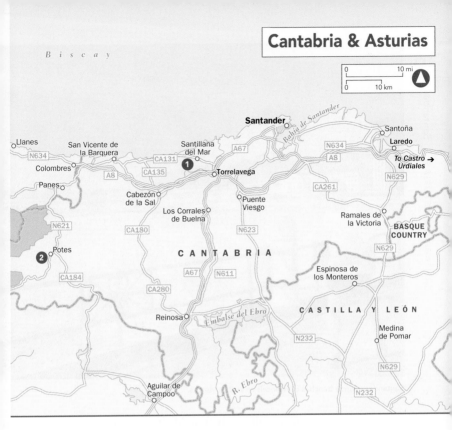

Many visitors to Santander head for **El Sardinero** ★★, a resort less than 2.5km (1½ miles) from the city center. Buses and trolleys make the short run both day and night. Besides hotels and restaurants, the area has three main **beaches:** Playa de Castaneda, Playa del Sardinero, and Playa de la Concha. If they become too crowded, take a 15-minute boat ride to **El Puntal,** a little-frequented but beautiful beach. If you don't like crowds or beaches, go up to the lighthouse, some 2km (1¼ miles) from El Sardinero, where the views are wide-ranging. A restaurant serves snacks both indoors and outdoors. Here, you can hike along the green cliffs or loll in the grass.

Essentials

ARRIVING   Five to 10 daily flights from Madrid and Barcelona land at **Ballesteros-Santander Airport** (www.aena-aeropuertos.es; ✆ **94-220-21-00**), a little more than 6.5km (4 miles) from the town center. Taxis to the town center cost 20€, but regular bus service between the airport and the train station costs only 3.50€ one-way. The local office of **Iberia** is at the airport (www.iberia.com; ✆ **90-240-05-00**).

Santander's sandy beaches draw locals as well as visitors.

There are six to nine **trains** daily from Madrid (trip time: 4–6½ hr.); a one-way fare costs 32€ to 53€. For national rail information, visit www.renfe.com or call ☎ **90-232-03-20.**

Buses are the best way to get to Santander from Bilbao or Oviedo. Buses arrive at Calle Navas de Tolosa (www.alsa.es; ☎ **90-242-22-42**). There are 31 connections a day to and from Bilbao (trip time: 1½ hr.); a one-way ticket costs 7€ to 16€.

Brittany Ferries (www.brittanyferries.ie) operates passenger and car ferry service to and from Plymouth and Portsmouth in the U.K. and to and from Cork in Ireland. One-way service starts at 139€. Ferries come into the city center at Calle Muelles de Maliaño, 21, 27 (☎ **94-236-06-11**).

VISITOR INFORMATION The **tourist information office** at Paseo Pereda (www.ayto-santander.es; ☎ **94-220-30-00**) is open July to August daily 9am to 9pm; the rest of the year it's open Monday to Friday 9am to 7pm, Saturday 10am to 7pm, and Sunday 10am to 2pm.

SPECIAL EVENTS The **Festival Internacional de Santander** in August is among the top music and dance events in Spain. This festival sometimes coincides with religious celebrations honoring St. James, Spain's patron. For information, visit www.festivalsantander.com.

Exploring Santander

The **Museo de Arte Moderno y Contemporáneo de Santander y Cantabria** ★, Calle Rubio, 6 (www.museosantandermas.es; © 94-220-31-20), will be closed for renovation until 2021. The museum has taken on a new mission to stage exhibitions of contemporary art, often featuring Cantabrian artists. When reopened, the museum will still display works from its permanent collection, including art by Goya and Zurburán, as well as some interesting northern Spanish landscape paintings from the 19th and 20th centuries, which give a real feel for the Cantabrian coast and countryside. In the same building, the **Biblioteca de Menéndez Pelayo,** Calle Rubio, 6 (www.bibliotecademenendezpelayo.org; © 94-223-45-34), represents the personal 50,000-volume collection amassed by historian/writer Marcelino Menéndez y Pelayo (1856–1912), Santander's most illustrious man of letters. It expects to offer guided tours on reopening.

Catedral de Santa María de la Asunción ★ CATHEDRAL   Greatly damaged in the 1941 fire, this restored, fortress-like 13th-century cathedral holds the tomb of historian/writer Menéndez y Pelayo (see above). The 12th-century **Capilla del Cristo,** sitting beneath the main church, consists of a trio of low-slung aisles that can be entered through the south portico. The Gothic cloister was restored after the fire. Roman ruins, discovered beneath the north aisle in 1983, are visible through a glass floor.

Plaza José Equino Trecu, Somorrostro, s/n. www.diocesisdesantander.com/catedral-2/. © **94-222-60-24.** Admission 1€ adults, 0.50€ children. Mon–Fri 10am–1pm and 4–7:30pm, Sat 10am–1pm and 4:30–8pm, Sun 10am–2pm and 5–8pm. Closed during Mass.

Museo Maritimo del Cantábrico ★★ MUSEUM   When you're ready for a break from the beach, this engaging modern museum does a good job of tracing the importance of the sea to the history and economy of the region. Children will probably be most interested in the aquariums and interactive exhibits. That will give parents time to study the photographs, artifacts, and displays that trace Cantabria's 3,000 years as a shipping port.

Calle Muelle de San Martín, s/n. www.museosdecantabria.es. © **94-227-49-62.** Admission 8€ adults, 5€ ages 5–12 and seniors. May–Sept Tues–Sun 10am–7:30pm; Oct–Apr Tues–Sun 10am–6pm. Bus 1–4, 7, 13.

Where to Stay in Santander

IN TOWN

Abba Santander Hotel ★   All the rooms in this long-standing hotel have outside windows with good insulation so that guests can enjoy maximum light with minimum disturbance from street noise. The location near the bus and rail stations is rather congested but is a bonus for those without a car. Furnishings in the mid-size rooms are rather spare, but marble bathrooms add a touch of style. More importantly, the rooms are fresh and

GAUDI'S summer palace & MORE

Lying 49km (30 miles) west of Santander and only a short drive west of Santillana del Mar, Comillas's major attraction is **El Capricho de Gaudí,** Barrio de Sobrellano (www.elcaprichodegaudi.com; ☎ **94-272-03-65**). Fabled Catalan architect Antoni Gaudí designed this summer palace in the Mudéjar Revival style. The tile-covered 1883 villa is open March through October 10:30am to 8pm daily (the rest of the year it's open 10:30am–5:30pm). Admission is 5€ adults, 2.50€ ages 7–14. The town also has the Modernisme **Palacio de Sobrellano** (☎ **94-272-03-39**) and **La Capilla Panteón,** designed in the late 1870s by Catalan architects Joan Martorell and Josep Llimona y Agapit Vallmitjana, respectively. The exteriors are updated Gothic buildings—the magical modern details are all inside. Admission to the palace and chapel is 3€ each. Visit the Centros Cultures de Cantabria website for hours and tickets (https://centros.culturadecantabria.com). Comillas' tourist office is at Calle Joaquín del Piélago, 1 (www.comillas.es; ☎ **94-277-25-91**). The

town cemetery gates (above the main beach) are a Modernisme masterpiece created in 1893 by Lluis Doménech i Montaner.

clean. Friendly staff is a big plus. They even arrange "room service" from a couple of local fast-food restaurants for those who need a quiet evening in.

Calle Calderón de la Barca, 3. www.abbasantanderhotel.com. ☎ **94-221-24-50.** 37 units. 56€–137€ double. Parking 9€. **Amenities:** Free Wi-Fi.

Hotel Bahía ★★ This long-time city social center received a makeover and reopened in 1999 to offer guests a more contemporary and relaxed sense of style. Liberal use of marble in the lobby sets the tone for the modern color schemes and traditional furnishings in the guest rooms, many of which have views of the ocean or of the cathedral. It's not right on the beach, but Bahia is convenient for exploring the waterfront and the old town and sits at the head of the Jardines de Pereda, a charming city park.

Av. Alfonso XIII, 6. www.hotelbahiasantander.com. ☎ **90-257-06-27.** 188 units. 91€–169€ double. Parking 16€. **Amenities:** Restaurant; bar; exercise room; spa; free Wi-Fi.

Jardín Secreto ★★   Hidden away amid the central city streets, this guesthouse offers six double rooms, each with private bath, and the eponymous green garden at the back of the property. It's run by a brother and sister and was decorated by their mother, whose taste runs to modern minimalism but in cheerfully bright colors. The rooms are on two floors—opt for those at the top to get maximum light. Breakfast is pastry and coffee, but it's enough to jump-start the day.

Calle Cisneros, 37. https://jardinsecretosantander.com. ✆ **94-207-07-14.** 6 units. 60€–90€ double. **Amenities:** Free Wi-Fi.

AT EL SARDINERO

Eurostars Hotel Real ★★★   Being part of a royal entourage can have its advantages. This gracious white hotel, located on beautifully landscaped grounds above Playa de los Peligros, opened in 1917 to accommodate the guests of King Alfonso XIII and his family on their annual summer vacations in Santander. Today's vacationers may not have the ear of the king, but they enjoy equally glamorous surroundings and impeccable service. All the spacious rooms have exterior views and sumptuous traditional furnishings that harmonize with modern technology and contemporary art. For even more relaxation, the old garages on the property have been renovated and converted into a thalassotherapy spa center. This is *the* address in Santander and one of the top properties in northern Spain.

Paseo Pérez Galdós, 28. www.hotelreal.es. ✆ **94-227-25-50.** 123 units. 102€–356€ double; from 469€ suite. Free parking. Bus: 1, 2, or 7. **Amenities:** Restaurant; bar; exercise room; spa; free Wi-Fi.

Las Brisas ★   This 19th-century palace turned boutique hotel is a good option for travelers seeking an intimate property with lots of character. The white building with red tile roof makes a great first impression, and once inside you won't be disappointed. Public areas and guest rooms feature a mix of antiques and traditional furnishings liberally enhanced with rich fabrics, artworks, plants, and flowers. Each small room is different, but all have sleekly modernized bathrooms.

Calle la Braña, 14. www.hotellasbrisas.net. ✆ **94-227-01-11.** 13 units. 54€–140€ double; 90€–170€ triple. **Amenities:** Free Wi-Fi.

Sercotel Palacio del Mar ★   About two-thirds of the rooms in this modern mid-1990s hotel are junior suites that feature a separate sitting area and can accommodate up to five people. All rooms are fairly large and have clean-lined modern furnishings and a terrace or balcony. Guests have access to a nearby health club with pool, though the hotel does have its own lovely terrace for catching the sun.

Av. de Cantabria, 5. www.hotel-palaciodelmar.com. ✆ **94-239-24-00.** 67 units. 60€–198€ double; 77€–231€ jr. suite. Free parking. **Amenities:** Restaurant; bar; access to nearby health club with pool; free Wi-Fi.

Where to Eat in Santander

Bodega del Riojano ★★ SPANISH   The decor of this restaurant in an ancient wine cellar could not be more fitting: The walls are covered with the ends of wine barrels that have been signed and decorated by contemporary Spanish artists. In 2009, new ownership injected fresh energy into this well-established and respected restaurant. The wines may be, as the name suggests, mostly from La Rioja, but the cuisine is Cantabrian through and through. You can count on some highly regional dishes, like mackerel dumplings and plates of meatballs surrounded by steamed clams and prawns. The kitchen goes the extra mile to make dishes special, even marinating fresh strawberries in Armagnac to serve with puff pastry for a simple seasonal dessert.

Calle Río de la Pila, 5. www.bodegadelriojano.com. ✆ **94-221-67-50.** Entrees 16€–28€. Mon–Sat 1:30–4pm and 7:30pm–midnight, Sun 1:30–4pm. Closed Mon Sept–June.

El Serbal ★★★ CANTABRIAN   This elegant, contemporary restaurant is a top spot to enjoy fine food paired with fine wines. The wine cellar features about 500 bottles from 15 different countries and the menu is short and sweet. Cod *a pil pil* is found all along the coast, but El Serbal is the only place we know where artichokes, clams, and octopus find their way into the dish. The contrast of colors and textures makes it look almost too pretty to eat. The classic roast suckling pig is sometimes roasted with oranges. In 2018, El Serbal earned its first Michelin star.

Calle Andrés del Río, 7. www.elserbal.com. ✆ **94-222-25-15.** Entrees 24€–26€; 4-course menu 44€; 7-course menu 70€. Reservations required. Tues–Sat 1:30–4pm and 8:30–11:30pm, Sun 1:30–4pm. Closed Feb 1–2. Bus: 7.

Zacarías ★★ CANTABRIAN   Chef Zacarías Puente and Inés Villanueva founded this locavore restaurant in 1989 to indulge their passion for the fish, cheese, and produce of the Cantabrian coast and countryside. They even called the cuisine "from the sea to the peaks." In 2015, they turned the restaurant over to their kids, who divided it into two very different dining menus. The "Always Zacarias" menu offers some of the specialty dishes that made the restaurant's reputation over the years, including local beef priced by the kilo. The "Zacarías Evolución" plates stand with the best of Spanish avant-garde cooking today. Sample dishes might include bonito with lemon mustard, or hake and prawn ceviche.

Calle Hernán Cortés, 38. www.restaurantezacarias.com. ✆ **94-221-23-33.** Entrees 12€–24€, set menu 35€. Daily 1–4pm and 8pm–12:30am.

Santander Nightlife

The most exciting thing to do in the evening is to head for the gaming tables of the **Gran Casino Sardinero,** Plaza de Italia (www.grancasino sardinero.es; ✆ **94-227-60-54**), which has a cover charge of 3€. The gaming room is open daily 8pm to 4am; the slot machine parlor is open daily 2pm to 4am. Be sure to bring your passport for entry. You must be 18 or older.

SANTILLANA DEL MAR & ALTAMIRA CAVES ★★
The Village of Santillana

Jean-Paul Sartre called the Cantabrian town of **Santillana del Mar** "the prettiest village in Spain," and we wouldn't dispute his esteemed judgment. Among the most perfectly preserved medieval villages in Europe, Santillana is now a Spanish national landmark. A monastery houses the relics of Santa Juliana, an Asia Minor martyr who refused to surrender her virginity to her husband. The name Santillana is a contraction of "Santa Juliana"; the "del Mar" is misleading, however, as Santillana is not on the water but inland. Despite all the tour buses, Santillana retains its medieval atmosphere and is very much a village of dairy farmers to this day.

Santillana del Mar is the traditional base for visiting the **caves of Altamira** (p. 622), which contain some of the most famous Stone Age

The medieval town of Santillana del Mar.

paintings in the world. The caves have been largely closed to protect them, but you can visit an amazingly faithful facsimile.

ESSENTIALS

ARRIVING Autobuses La Cantábrica (© 94-272-08-22) operates four to seven **buses** a day from Santander in summer but cuts back to four between September and June. Trip time is 45 minutes, and a one-way fare costs 11€. To drive, take the N-611 from Santander to the C-6316 cutoff to Santillana.

VISITOR INFORMATION The **tourist information office** is at Av. Escultor Jesús Otero, 20 (www.santillana-del-mar.com; © 94-281-88-12). It's open daily 9:30am to 1:30pm and 4 to 7pm.

EXPLORING SANTILLANA

Wander on foot throughout the village, taking in its principal sites, including **Plaza de Ramón Pelayo** (sometimes called Plaza Mayor), which is dominated by twin *paradors.*

A 15th-century tower, facing Calle de Juan Infante, is known for its pointed arched doorway. A walk along **Calle de las Lindas** (Street of Beautiful Women) will take you past many of the oldest buildings in Santillana. Two towers date from the 14th and 15th centuries. **Calle del Río** is named for a stream running through town to a central fountain.

Visit the 800-year-old church, **Colegiata de Santa Juliana ★**, Calle Santo Domingo (© 94-281-88-12), which shelters the tomb of the village's patron saint, Juliana. It has a lovely ivy-covered cloister and displays such treasures as 1,000-year-old documents and a 17th-century Mexican silver altarpiece. It's open Tuesday to Sunday (daily July–Aug) 10am to 1:30pm and 4 to 7:30pm. In winter, it closes at 6:15pm. The 3€ admission also includes the 400-year-old Convento de Regina Coelí, also called the **Convento de las Clarisas (Convent of the Poor Clares;** Museo Diocesano; © 94-281-88-12), which lies at the other end of the main street. The convent houses a rich art collection, inspired by a Madrid art professor who encouraged the nuns to collect and restore religious paintings and statues damaged or abandoned during the Spanish Civil War. The collection is constantly expanding. The convent is open Tuesday to Sunday 10am to 1:30pm and 4 to 8pm (until 6:30pm in winter).

The Altamira Caves

About 2.5km (1½ miles) from Santillana del Mar are the **Cuevas de Altamira,** famous for prehistoric paintings dating from the end of the Ice Age. The cave paintings at Altamira are ranked among the finest prehistoric paintings ever discovered, and, as a result, they are often called the "Sistine Chapel of prehistoric art." These ancient depictions of bison and horses, painted vividly in reds and blacks on the caves' ceilings, were not

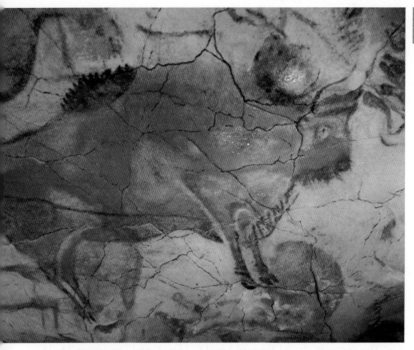

A prehistoric painting at the famed Cuevas de Altamira.

discovered until the late 19th century. Once their authenticity was established, scholars and laypersons alike flocked to see these works of art, which provide a fragile link to our remote ancestors. Bacteria from visitors caused severe damage, so the caves were completely closed for years. Now five visitors per week, selected at random from those visiting the museum 9:30 to 10:30am every Friday, are permitted to take a strictly controlled 37-minute tour of the caves.

Everyone else must settle for the **Museo de Altamira** ★★ (museo dealtamira.mcu.es; ⓒ **94-281-80-05**), not far from the original caves, where Altamira's main cave chambers have been painstakingly recreated with computerized digital-transfer technology. The faux cave has every crack, bump, and hollow of the original. The paintings of 21 bison in iron oxide pigment are perhaps the highlight. Modern museum exhibits go into considerable detail about the lives of the people who made this art. The museum is superb, but it does fall short of the magic of seeing one of these ancient caves. (See p. 624 for another cave option in the region.)

If you don't have a car, you have to walk from Santillana del Mar, as there is no bus service. From spring to fall, however, it's a pretty stroll past long green pastures filled with grazing milk cows. The museum is open

16   cave paintings **FROM 15,000 YEARS AGO**

Altamira isn't the only ancient cave in the region. Seven other caves are open, including **El Castillo ★★★**, found at Carretera N623 Km 28, 27km (17 miles) from Santander (*© **94-259-84-25***). Lying in the medieval hamlet of Puente Viesgo in the Pas Valley, this cave was excavated under the 350m (1,150-ft.) peak of the mountain, Monte del Castillo. Decorated by artists 15,000 years ago, the cave has several different sections. Admittedly, the art is not as advanced or concentrated as the works found at Altamira, but seeing the handprints, the clan marks, and the graceful images of deer, bison, and horses that must have seemed to dance in the flicker of firelight could make the hair stand up on the back of your neck. Small groups enter with a guide and must stay close, even in some of the palace-sized chambers. The caves are open mid-June to mid-September Tuesday to Sunday 10:30am to 2:30pm and 3:30 to 7:30pm; March to mid-June and mid-September to October Wednesday to Sunday 9:30am to 2:30pm and 3:30 to 6:30pm; November to February Wednesday to Friday 9:30am to 3:30pm. Admission is 3€ adults, 1.50€ for ages 4 to 12. Since numbers of visitors are strictly limited, you can save yourself some heartache by reserving admission at a particular date and time at http://cuevas.culturadecantabria.com.

Tuesday to Saturday 9:30am to 8pm (6pm Nov–Apr), and Sunday 9:30am to 3pm. Admission is 3€ for adults, free for students, seniors, and ages 18 and under. Admission is free to all on Saturday after 2pm and all day Sunday. The center is closed January 1 and 6, May 1, and December 24, 25, and 31.

Where to Stay in Santillana

MODERATE

Casa del Marqués ★★   For such a tiny place, Santillana del Mar has a lot of classy lodging, and this old manor house converted to a hotel is a terrific alternative to the two *paradors*. The foundations of the manor date from the 11th century, when this was a convent town, but the decor goes for generic antique. Exposed stone walls emphasize the antiquity of the structure; ceiling beams and broad wooden floors add to the effect. The staircase was carved in one piece from a 700-year-old oak tree when this version of the house was built in the 1440s. Guest rooms are comfortably furnished with rustic-looking furniture. The house is surrounded by lush gardens.

Calle Cantón, 26. www.hotelcasadelmarques.com. *© **94-281-88-88.*** 15 units. 91 €–167€ double; 175€–195€ triple. Parking 16€. Closed Jan–Mar. **Amenities:** Bar; free Wi-Fi.

Parador de Santillana Gil Blas/Parador de Santillana del Mar ★★★   If you want to stay in a 400-year-old noble house with all the attendant noble decor (including suits of armor), then book the Gil

Blas. If you just want to stay in Santillana in comfort, choose the Parador Santillana del Mar, which was created for overflow from the historic building but looks like it has been on the same square for centuries. The price is a little lower in the newly built hotel, and we especially like the rooms with big windows opening onto the square. Rooms in the Parador Gil Blas are exceptionally large, but all the plumbing, heating, and wiring systems are quite old.

Plaza de Ramón Pelayo, 11. www.parador.es. © **94-202-80-28** for Parador de Santillana Gil Blas; © **94-281-80-00** for Parador de Santillana del Mar. 56 units. Santillana del Mar: 90€–150€ double. Santillana Gil Blas: 100€–175€ double. Free parking. **Amenities:** Restaurant; bar; sauna; free Wi-Fi.

INEXPENSIVE

Casa del Organista ★   Make your own romantic music at this 18th-century stone manse originally built for the organist at the Colegiata de Santillana. Lovingly restored by artisan stonemasons and carpenters who specialize in heritage buildings, the three-story structure still has wooden balconies hanging off the exterior and exposed wooden ceiling beams inside. The guest rooms are surprisingly ample for a building its age and are furnished in a simple but warm style.

Calle Los Hornos, 4. www.casadelorganista.com. © **94-284-03-52.** 14 units. 60€–93€ double. Free parking. **Amenities:** Bar; free Wi-Fi.

Hotel Altamira ★   With its exposed stone walls, broad wooden floors, and wooden ceiling beams, the Altamira can hold its own for historic ambience with any old hotel in town, *paradors* included. This was not a noble residence, but judging by the spacious stairways and large rooms, it was constructed for someone of considerable means. It also boasts a pretty good restaurant specializing in local dishes (see below).

Calle Cantón, 1. www.hotelaltamira.com. © **94-281-80-25.** 32 units. 55€–100€ double. **Amenities:** Restaurant; bar; free Wi-Fi.

Where to Eat in Santillana

Restaurante Altamira ★ CANTABRIAN   Noted for its Cantabrian specialties, this hotel-restaurant is the best place in town to eat a full meal. The menu emphasizes the inland dishes of the region, notably "meat of the pasture"—as in lamb, mutton, veal, and beef. The grasses are thick and nutritious around Santillana, and the local meat is outstanding. The different stews, known as *cocido,* are always a good bet. Unlike the Madrid version, they emphasize either a lot of fresh vegetables or a lot of legumes. The *cocido montañes* is a little richer and meatier, containing bacon, sausage, pork ribs, lots of shredded white cabbage, and the local white beans.

In the Hotel Altamira, Calle Cantón, 1. www.hotelaltamira.com. © **94-281-80-25.** Entrees 14€–24€, set menus 16€–18€. Daily 1:15–4pm and 8–11pm.

LOS PICOS DE EUROPA ★★★

If you drive from León, your first sight of these magical mountains may well be a rainbow arching over the ridges. As part of the Cordillera Cantábrica on the northern Spanish coast, they block the moisture rolling in off the Bay of Biscay. The moisture falls as rain on the green countryside, and between the mists, the greenery, and the rainbows, one might almost expect to see unicorns.

The wildlife isn't quite *that* rare, but these mountains are the last stronghold for some unusual creatures. On the beech-covered slopes of these mountains and in gorges laden with jasmine, you might spot the increasingly rare Asturcón, a shaggy, rather chubby wild horse so small it first looks like a toy pony. Another endangered species is the Iberian brown bear. The park is also home to the sure-footed chamois goat, rare butterflies, peregrine falcons, buzzards, and golden eagles. All wildlife is strictly protected by the government.

Los Picos de Europa are the most famous and most legend-riddled mountains in Spain. Rising more than 2,590m (8,500 ft.), they are not high by alpine standards, but their proximity to the sea and sheer vertical drop makes their height all the more impressive. Romans constructed a north-south road whose stones are still visible in some places, but during the Middle Ages, the mountains were passable only with great difficulty. The abundance of wildlife, dramatic rocky heights, and the medieval battles that took place in the hills all contribute to the legends and myths of the principality of Asturias.

If you **hike** in this region, be prepared. Many slopes are covered with loosely compacted shale, so good hiking boots are essential. Inexperienced hikers should stick to well-established paths. In summer, the weather can get hot and humid, and sudden downpours sweeping in from the coastline are common in any season. Hiking is not recommended between October and May.

The best way to see this region is **by car.** Most drivers arrive in the region on the N-621 highway, heading southwest from Santander, or on the same highway northeast from the cities of north-central Spain (especially León and Valladolid). This highway connects many of the region's best vistas in a straight line. It also defines the region's eastern boundary. If you're driving east from Oviedo, you'll take the N-632, coming first to Cangas de Onís.

Bus travel is much less convenient but possible if you have lots of time. The region's tourist hubs are the towns of **Panes** and **Potes;** both have bus service from Santander (two buses per day in summer, one per day in winter) and León (one bus per day in summer). The same buses come to Panes and Potes from the coastal town of Unquera. From Oviedo, there are two buses daily to the district's easternmost town of Cangas de

Onís; they continue a short distance farther southeast to Covadonga. Within the region, a small local bus runs once a day, according to an erratic schedule, along the northern rim of the Picos, connecting Cangas de Onís with Las Arenas.

Exploring the Region

If you have a car, the number and variety of tours in this region are almost endless, but for this guide, we have devised three driving tours that form a loop. Any of them, with their side excursions, can fill an entire day; if your time is limited, you can omit some of the side excursions and make it a half-day drive.

DRIVING TOUR 1: **PANES TO POTES** ★★

DISTANCE: **29km (18 miles); 45 minutes**

Except for one optional detour, this drive extends entirely along one of the region's best roads, N-621, which links León and Valladolid to Santander. The drive is most noteworthy for its views of the ravine containing the Deva River, a ravine so steep that direct sunlight rarely penetrates it.

About two-thirds of the way to Potes, signs point you on a detour to the village of:

1 Liébana

In this village, .8km (½ mile) off the main road, you'll find the church of **Nuestra Señora de Liébana,** built in the 10th century in the Mozarabic style. Some people consider it the best example of Arabicized Christian architecture in Europe, with Islamic-inspired geometric motifs. If it isn't open, knock at the door of the first house you see as you enter the village; it's the home of the guardian, who will unlock the church if she's around. For this, she will expect a tip. If she's not around, content yourself with admiring the church from the outside.

Return to N-621 and continue another 5.6km (3½ miles) to Tama. Watch for turnoff to Centro de Visitantes de Sotama.

2 Centro de Visitantes de Sotama

This state-of-the-art **visitors center** for the Picos de Europa national park (http://parquenacionalpicoseuropa.es/english; ⓒ **94-273-81-09**) is filled with life-size photos and striking sound effects that bring the mountains alive. You will feel like you are hiking the trails and encountering the wildlife. An excellent section on cave life makes the Ice Age seem like yesterday. The center is open daily 9am to 6pm (July–Aug until 8pm). Admission is free.

Hiking the Picos de Europa near Fuente Dé.

Continue another 3.4km (2 miles) to reach the village of:

3 Potes

This charming place offers a view of well-kept alpine houses against a backdrop of jagged mountains.

Three kilometers (1¾ miles) southwest of Potes, near Turiano, stands the:

4 Monasterio de Santo Toribio de Liébana

Restored to the transitional Romanesque style of its powerful heyday, this 17th-century Franciscan monastery contains what is reputed to be a splinter from the True Cross, brought from Jerusalem in the 8th century by the bishop of Astorga. The monastery is also famous as the former home of Beatus de Liébana, the 8th-century author of *Commentary on the Apocalypse,* one of Spain's most notable ecclesiastical documents. Visiting hours are 10am to 1pm and 4 to 6pm daily. Ring the bell and one of the brothers will let you enter if you are dressed respectfully. For more details and Mass times, call ✆ **94-273-05-50** or visit www.santotoribiodeliebana.es.

Drive the 19km (12-mile) winding and beautiful road west from Potes, following the path of the Río Deva to the:

5 Parador de Fuente Dé

You can spend the night here (p. 635) or just stop for lunch.

6 Fuente Dé

Only a few hundred meters beyond the parador, a *teleférico,* the third-largest cable-car system in the world (www.cantur.com; *©* **94-273-66-10**), carries you 800m (2,625 ft.) up to an observation platform above a wind-scoured rock face. The cable car operates July to August daily 9am to 8pm, September to June daily 10am to 6pm. A one-way fare costs 11€; round-trip is 17€. At the top you can walk 5km (3 miles) along a footpath to the rustic **Refugio de Aliva** (*©* **94-273-09-99**), open between June and September 15. Double rooms cost 80€. If you opt for just a meal or a snack at the hostel's simple restaurant, remember to allow enough time to return to the *teleférico* before its last trip down.

DRIVING TOUR 2: **POTES TO CANGAS DE ONÍS** ★

DISTANCE: **85km (53 miles); 2 hours**

This tour includes not only the Quiviesa Valley and some of the region's steepest mountain passes, but also some of its most verdant fields and most elevated pastures. You might stop at an occasional village, but most of the time you will be going through deserted countryside. Your route will take you through several tunnels and high above mountain streams set deep into gorges. Occasional belvederes along the way always deliver on their promise of panoramic views.

The village of Potes (see "Driving Tour 1," above) is your starting point. Take N-621 southwest to Riaño. At Riaño, turn north for a brief ride on N-625. Then take a winding route through the heart of the region by driving northwest on N-637. Although it's beautiful all along the way, the first really important place you'll reach is:

1 Cangas de Onís

This is the westernmost town in the region, where you can get a hotel room and a solid meal after a trek through the mountains. It serves as base camp for many hiking and climbing expeditions into the mountains; you'll find a wealth of guides and outfitters along its main street. The biggest attraction in Cangas de Onís proper is an ivy-covered **Roman bridge,** lying west of the center, spanning the Sella River. Also of interest is the **Capilla de Santa Cruz,** immediately west of the center. One of the earliest remaining Christian sites in

The Roman Bridge in Cangas de Onis.

Spain, it was originally constructed in the 8th century over a Celtic dolmen and rebuilt in the 15th century.

About 1.5km (1 mile) northwest of Cangas de Onís, beside the road leading to Arriondas, stands the:

2 Monasterio de San Pedro

This Benedictine monastery, in the village of **Villanueva,** has a church built in the 17th century, enclosing the ruins of a much older Romanesque church. Inside you'll see some unusual carved capitals showing the unhappy end of the medieval King Favila, who was supposedly devoured by a Cantabrian bear.

DRIVING TOUR 3: **CANGAS DE ONÍS TO PANES** ★★

DISTANCE: **56km (35 miles); 1 hour**

This tour travels along the relatively straight C-6312 from the western to the eastern entrance to the Picos de Europa region. A number of unusual excursions can easily stretch this into an all-day outing.

From Cangas de Onís (see "Driving Tour 2," above), head west about 1.6km (1 mile). You'll reach the turnoff to:

1 Cueva del Buxu

Inside this cave you'll see a limited number of prehistoric rock engravings and charcoal drawings, somewhat disappointingly small. Only 25 people per day are allowed inside (respiration erodes the drawings). It's open Wednesday to Sunday at 10:30am, 11:30am, 12:30pm, 3:15pm, and 4:15pm. Advance reservation is essential and must be made by telephone (℃ **60-817-54-67**) Wednesday to Sunday between 3 and 5pm. Admission is 4€ adults, 2€ ages 7 to 12 and over 65.

Some 6.5km (4 miles) east, signs point south in the direction of:

2 Covadonga

Revered as the birthplace of Christian Spain, Covadonga is about 9.5km (6 miles) off the main highway. A battle here in A.D. 722 pitted a ragged band of Christian Visigoths against a small band of Muslim soldiers. The resulting victory established the first niche of Christian Europe in Moorish Iberia, and the leader of the Goths, Pelayo, was crowned king. The town's most important monuments are **La Santa**

The basilica in Covadonga.

Cueva ★★, a cave containing the sarcophagus of Pelayo (d. 737), king of the Visigothic Christians, in a slot tomb; and an enormous neo-Romanesque **basilica,** built between 1886 and 1901, commemorating the Christianization of Spain. At the end of the long boulevard that funnels into the base of the church stands a statue of Pelayo.

Return to the highway and continue east. You'll come to the village of Las Estazadas; then after another 11km (6¾ miles) you'll reach:

3   Las Arenas de Cabrales

Note that some maps refer to this town simply as Arenas. This is the headquarters of a cheese-producing region best known for Cabrales, a blue-veined cheese that's avidly consumed throughout Spain. Stop at any of the bars here to sample some Cabrales with the local hard cider. You can also see how it is made in the exhibition center at the **Cueva del Queso** ★, Barrio Pares, s/n (www.fundacioncabrales.com; ✆ **98-584-51-23**). The Cueva is open May through August 10am to 2pm and 4 to 8pm, September to April on weekends only. Tours begin quarter after the hour and cost 4.50€ adults, 3€ children.

Drive 5km (3 miles) south from Arenas, following signs to the village of:

4   Puente de Poncebos

Shown on some maps simply as Poncebos, this village is several miles downstream from the source of Spain's most famous salmon-fishing river, the Río Cares, which flows through deep ravines from its source near the more southerly village of Cain. Beginning at Poncebos, a footpath has been cut into the ravine on either side of the Río Cares. It's considered one of the engineering marvels of Spain, known for centuries as the **Divine Gorge.** The path crosses the ravine many times over footbridges, and sometimes through tunnels chiseled into the rock face beside the water, making a hike along the banks of this river a memorable outing. You can climb up the riverbed from Poncebos overland to the village of Cain, a total distance of 11km (6¾ miles). Allow between 3 and 4 hours. At Cain, you can

A DIFFERENT KIND OF brew

Asturias has only recently begun to make wine on a commercial scale—in part because it has such wonderful apple orchards and excels at making hard cider, or **sidra.** The drink is the perfect accompaniment to most Asturian cuisine, especially the tangy blue Cabrales cheese. The local cider, which is fermented exceptionally dry from rather tart apples, should ideally be poured with the bottle raised a meter (3 ft.) above the glass to oxygenate the brew. When you order *sidra*, you get a theatrical show with the drink.

take a taxi back to where you left your car in Poncebos if you don't want to retrace your steps.

After your trek up the riverbed, continue your drive to the village of:

5 Panes

This village lies at a distance of 23km (14 miles) to the eastern extremity of the Picos de Europa.

Where to Stay & Eat in the Los Picos de Europa Region

Once you leave Cangas de Onís, lodging options are very limited in these mountain towns. If you're planning an overnight stop, make sure you have a reservation. Directly north of Cangas de Onís, the unprepossessing little village of Arriondas has not one but two Michelin-starred restaurants. Nowhere in the Picos de Europa area can you dine so well as you can here.

IN ARRIONDAS

Casa Marcial ★★★ CREATIVE ASTURIAN   Londoners might know chef Nacho Manzano for his U.K. restaurant Ibérico, but to find such

The blue-veined cheese of Cabrales.

a culinary genius in this remote mountain town is a delightful surprise. The restaurant occupies the old farmhouse in the hilly country north of town where Manzano was born and grew up. His parents used to operate a small traditional Asturian restaurant here; since their son took over, it's become a mountain pilgrimage site for Spanish gourmands. Yes, he still serves a remarkably traditional *fabada*—Asturian pork and beans—but in a small portion with the beans still toothy and topped with a drizzle of very green olive oil. Lighter fare is where he shines, whether it's the cold cucumber soup poured over green pepper sorbet, local salmon sauced with melon gazpacho, or roast woodcock with oysters and mountain eels. Most diners opt for one of the three menus: a 7-course menu of traditional Asturian dishes, a 7-course classic *dégustación* menu, or the

10-course gastronomic menu where Manzano pulls out all the stops and serves his latest inventions. Reserve a week to a month ahead.

Carretera AS-342, La Salgar, 10, 4.5km (2¾ miles) north of Arriondas. www.casa marcial.com. ☏ **98-584-09-91**. Entrees 32€–39€. Set menus 90€–158€. Tues–Sat 1–4pm and 9–11:30pm; Sun 1–4pm. Closed 5 weeks Jan–Feb (dates vary).

El Corral del Indianu ★★★ CREATIVE ASTURIAN   Gastronomic pilgrims also beat a path to the door of Chef José Antonio Campo Viejo, who is something of a self-styled madman with wild hair and a penchant for reimagining traditional Asturian flavors in new ways. He glazes local organically raised veal with whiskey, herbs, and mushrooms, and he turns paella rice into Asian-style sticky rice with sautéed vegetables, meats, and local kelp. Asturian cuisine emphasizes fatty meats, strongly flavored fish, and lots and lots of beans. But in Campoviejo's hands, it becomes light and even delicate, with dishes like a *salmorejo* of wild strawberries and local heavy cream, or a shotglass–sized serving of *fabada* with perfect white beans enrobed with liquefied bacon and puréed cabbage and topped with a thin slice of raw onion and tiny cubes of blood sausage. The restaurant has a rustic yet modern dining room, as well as a glass-enclosed room that enjoys views of the patio gardens. The a la carte menu is brief, but most diners come for the 10-course tasting menu, which changes with Campoviejo's whims. Reserve at least a week ahead.

Av. de Europa, 14. www.elcorraldelindianu.com. ☏ **98-584-10-72.** Entrees 24€–36€, tasting menu 92€. Fri–Sat and Mon–Tues 1:30–4pm and 9–11pm; Sun and Wed 1:30–4pm.

IN CANGAS DE ONIS

La Palmera ★ ASTURIAN   Located by the river on the road heading east from Cangas de Onís to Covadonga, La Palmera serves rib-sticking Asturian cuisine at prices far lower than the mountain lakes area just a few miles up the road. The cooking is all about the bounty of the Asturian mountains, so look for excellent grilled beef steak, slow-roasted leg of lamb, and several versions of the local Atlantic salmon and trout. The owners support local farmers by carrying their farmstead cheeses—far less pungent than Cabrales, but delicious nonetheless.

Soto de Cangas s/n, La Rotunda. ☏ **98-594-00-96**. Entrees 12€–22€. Wed–Mon 10am–11pm. Closed Aug.

Parador de Cangas de Onís ★★   Occupying the beautiful former Monasterio de San Pedro de Villanueva, this hotel sits 2km (1½ miles) from the village center on the banks of the Río Sella. Public areas feature exposed beams and open stone work, while guestrooms are far more modernized—sedate and comfortable. Ask for one with a balcony to enjoy the surrounding landscape. Because Cangas de Onís is strategically located at the foothills of the Sierra Escapa, this hotel is favored by outdoors enthusiasts who flock to the area for fly-fishing, canoeing, and hiking in the mountains.

Villanueva de Cangas, s/n. www.parador.es. ℂ **98-584-94-02.** 64 units. 75€–169€. Free parking. **Amenities:** Restaurant; bar; free Wi-Fi.

IN COSGAYA

Hotel del Oso ★   You're really in the countryside by the time you reach Cosgaya, so it's a treat to encounter the Hotel of the Bear next to the Río Deva in the Liébana valley. The rooms are small and feature just a bed or two and a chair and table, but they all have modern private baths. Two-thirds of the rooms are in the main building, the remainder in a small annex. The main building also has the restaurant, Mesón del Oso, which serves big portions of local cooking. It's open daily for lunch and dinner, entrees are 12€–26€. In season, the best dishes on the menu feature trout from the river outside the door. Grilled steak with Cabrales cheese sauce is also a specialty. Desserts are all homemade; you can't go wrong with any of the tarts made with local fruits. From Potes, take the road signposted to Espinama 15km (9⅓ miles) south.

Carretera Potes–Fuente Dé, Km 14. www.hoteldeloso.com. ℂ **94-273-30-18.** 50 units. 72€–92€ double. Free parking. **Amenities:** Restaurant; bar; outdoor pool; outdoor tennis court; free Wi-Fi. Closed Jan 7–Feb 15.

IN FUENTE DÉ

Parador de Fuente Dé ★★   This modern mountain lodge attracts a clientele more interested in the mountains than in being pampered at a *parador.* It sits literally at the end of the road to Fuente Dé; to continue on into the mountains, you have to take the cable car (p. 629) to the ridgeline. There are two wings, with somewhat smaller rooms in the older wing, but even those are spacious enough to spread out a bit. In the summer, rooms are often filled with people who have come to hike in the mountains, or those who have come to climb and bring all their technical gear. In the fall, the *parador* is very popular with hunters, as the hills are full of wild game. The restaurant is open daily for lunch and dinner, with a set menu from 30€. To get here, drive 26km (16 miles) west of Potes.

At Km 3.5 de Espinama. www.parador.es. ℂ **94-273-66-51.** 77 rooms. 75€–100€ double. Free parking. Closed mid-Dec to early Feb. **Amenities:** Restaurant; bar; free Wi-Fi.

GIJÓN

The largest city in Asturias and the major port for shipping coal from the region's famous mines, Gijón (pronounced Hee-*hohn*) has remade itself as a summer resort destination with its pedestrianized streets, lively café and dining scene, and access to excellent beaches and nearby hiking trails.

Essentials

ARRIVING   Gijón itself doesn't have an airport, but **Aeropuerto Asturias** (www.aena.es; ☎ **91-321-10-00**) in Santiago del Monte, Ranón, 42km (26 miles) away, is shared with Oviedo. Service via a half-dozen airlines connects to most of Spain.

Gijón has good rail links, making it a good gateway into Asturias. High-speed **RENFE Alvia trains** (www.renfe.es; ☎ **90-232-03-20**) arrive from Madrid in 5½ to 6 hours; the one-way trip costs 34€ to 45€. There's also frequent **bus service** (☎ **90-242-22-42** for information), with two dozen buses per day arriving from Madrid (trip time: 5½ hr.), costing 24€ to 53€ one-way. There is also service from Bilbao with 18 buses per day (trip time: 4–5 hr.) costing 24€ to 51€. Service is three times a day from Oviedo; the 20-minute one-way trip costs 3€.

Driving from Santander in the east, head west along the N-634. At Ribadesella, you can take the turnoff to the N-632, the scenic coastal road to Gijón. To save time, continue on N-634 until you reach the outskirts of Oviedo, and then cut north on A-66, the express highway to Gijón.

VISITOR INFORMATION   The **tourist information office** is at Calle Rodríguez San Pedro (www.gijon.info; ☎ **98-534-17-71**). It's open in summer daily 10am to 10pm, off-season daily 10am to 2:30pm and 4:30 to 7:30pm.

Exploring Gijón

The most interesting quarter of Gijón is the barrio of **Cimadevilla,** with its maze of alleys and leaning houses. This fishing village, on a peninsula jutting into the ocean to the north of the new town, spills over an elevated piece of land known as Santa Catalina. It forms a headland at the west end of the **Playa San Lorenzo,** the city's best beach. The strand extends about 2.5km (1½ miles) and has good facilities.

After time at the beach, you can stroll through **Parque Isabel la Católica,** at its eastern end. You can also visit the **Termas Romanas,** or Roman Baths, at Campos Valdés (museos.gijon.es; ☎ **98-518-51-51**), which are underground at the end of the old town, opening onto Playa de San Lorenzo. Discovered in 1903, these baths are now fully excavated, and the town has opened a museum here. Near the baths are reconstructed parts of the old Roman wall. The baths are open Tuesday to Friday 9:30am to 2pm and 5 to 7:30pm; on Saturday and Sunday 10am to 2pm and 5 to 8pm. Admission is 2.50€, 1.40€ seniors and students, and free to all on Sundays. Audioguides are 1.50€ extra.

Gijón is short on major monuments. The city was the birthplace of Gaspar Melchor de Jovellanos (1744–1811), one of Spain's most prominent men of letters, as well as an agrarian reformer and liberal economist. (The notorious minister Manuel de Godoy had Jovellanos imprisoned for 7 years in Bellver Castle on Mallorca.) In Gijón, his restored birthplace is

jurassic park **IN ASTURIAS**

Dinosaur buffs from around the world flock to one of the most extensive dinosaur museums in the world, **Museo del Jurásico de Asturias ★★**, San Juan de Duz at Colunga (www.museojurasicoasturias.com; © **90-230-66-00**), 32km (20 miles) east of Gijón and 40km (25 miles) northeast of Oviedo. The 209km (130-mile) stretch of sandy beaches and towering cliffs along this coast have produced so many dinosaur bones that the area is dubbed "the Dinosaur Coast." In all, 800 fossils, representing dinosaurs that inhabited the earth 65 million to 280 million years ago, are displayed in a trio of large exhibition spaces. The bones are presented in life-size versions, and the museum itself is built in the shape of a big hoof print. Admission is 7.21€ adults, 4.75€ seniors and children 4 to 11; it's free on Wednesdays. From July to August, hours are daily 10:30am to 8pm; the rest of the year it's open Wednesday to Friday 10am to 2:30pm and 3:30 to 6pm, Saturday and Sunday 10am to 2:30 pm and 4 to 7pm. It's closed in January.

now the **Museo-Casa Natal de Jovellanos,** Plaza de Jovellanos (museos. gijon.es; © **98-518-10-40**), open Tuesday to Saturday 9:30am to 2pm and 5 to 7:30pm, Sunday 10am to 2pm and 5 to 7:30pm. Admission is free.

Where to Stay in Gijón

MODERATE

Hotel Hernán Cortés ★　Gijón's leading downtown hotel is just about midway between the harbor and Playa San Lorenzo, making it fairly convenient. The whole operation has been modernized, giving the hotel the largest rooms on average in the city. They are also a bargain for families, as they tend to have space for extra beds if you're traveling with children. Moreover, some of the suites have large lounges with an extra sofa bed. The hotel does not have its own restaurant, but there is a breakfast room and extra-early free coffee service. Moreover, the Casino de Asturias and its Restaurante-Cafetería As de Picas share the imposing neoclassical building, so you can get a bite to eat any time before midnight.

Calle Fernández Vallín, 5. www.hotelhernancortes.es. © **98-534-60-00**. 60 units. 51€–189€ double; 95€–229€ suite. Bus: 4 or 11. **Amenities:** Bar; free Wi-Fi.

Parador de Gijón (Parador Molino Viejo) ★★　Local color abounds at this charmingly old-fashioned hotel with an 18th-century cider mill at its core. It sits right in the middle of the Parque Isabel la Católica, a 10-minute stroll from the town center. Gardens wrap around the hotel, and a colony of swans makes its home in the stream running through the landscape. The rooms are quite modest but atmospheric with heavy wooden furniture, shutters on the deep windows, and broad wooden floors.

Parque Isabel la Católica, s/n. www.parador.es. © **98-537-05-11**. 40 units. 80€–185€ double. Free parking. Bus: 4 or 11. **Amenities:** Restaurant; bar; free Wi-Fi.

INEXPENSIVE

La Casona de Jovellanos ★ This 18th-century building once housed the Asturian Royal Institute of Marine Life and Mineralogy, established here in 1794 by the author Jovellanos. It is a boxy structure, often renovated over the centuries, but hardly grand. When it was built, it stood on the site where Gijón still had fortifications against pirates. Rooms are small but attractive, and the hotel is within easy walking distance of the yacht harbor and the beach.

Plaza de Jovellanos, 1. www.lacasonadejovellanos.com. ✆ **98-534-12-64.** 13 units. 60€–100€ double. Bus: 4 or 11. **Amenities:** Restaurant; bar; free Wi-Fi.

Where to Eat in Gijón

Auga ★★ ASTURIAN This spectacular contemporary restaurant is perfectly situated to get the top of the catch: It literally sits at the end of a pier in the middle of the harbor. The indoor dining room has wood floors and ceilings, but whenever the weather permits, most diners prefer to sit out on the terrace to eat and watch the boats. Chef Gonzalo Pañeda began his career as a pastry chef (his desserts are still fabulous). He was converted to the savory side of the kitchen after eating at Akelaré (p. 587) in San Sebastián and left a resort job to found his own place. He has since won a Michelin star of his own for his imaginative market dishes. He has an uncanny ability to combine flavors not usually associated with each other—for example, seared scallops with shavings of black truffle, green apple, and cauliflower, or roasted sea bass with lime zest on a bed of mushrooms and onions. All the plates are beautifully presented.

Calle Claudio Alvargonzález, s/n. www.restauranteauga.com. ✆ **98-516-81-86.** Entrees 22€–32€; tasting menu 80€. Tues–Sat 1–4pm and 9–11:30pm; Sun 1–4pm. Closed Mon and mid-Dec to mid-Jan. Bus: 10.

Casa Tino ★ ASTURIAN The Tino for whom the restaurant is named started in the trade as a waiter in 1940 and founded this restaurant in 1965 on a nearby street. (It moved here in 1969.) Pictures of Tino and his co-workers and friends are all over the walls, signaling before you even look at the menu that this is a friendly, family operation where they prize their customers. The menu is filled with Asturian and general Spanish home-cooking dishes like braised pig's feet with roasted potatoes, big meatballs simmered in gravy, and fish chowders filled with large pieces of hake, turbot, or cod. A cameo appearance on an episode of *Anthony Bourdain: Parts Unknown* has made Casa Tino a Mecca for fans of Bourdain and José Andres.

Calle Alfredo Truan, 9. www.restaurantecasatino.com. ✆ **98-513-84-97.** Entrees 8€–20€, set menu 17€. Mon–Sat 1:15–3:30pm and 8:45–11:30pm. Bus: 4 or 11.

OVIEDO ★★

Suddenly famous as the birthplace of Queen Letizia, wife of Felipe VI, Oviedo happily basks in the spotlight. The capital of Asturias and only

26km (16 miles) from the coast, the city can be temperately pleasant in summer, when much of Spain is unbearably hot. Despite its high concentration of industry and mining, the area has unspoiled scenery. Razed in the 8th century during the Reconquest, Oviedo was rebuilt in an architectural style known as Asturian pre-Romanesque, which predated many of the greatest achievements under the Moors. Remarkably, this architectural movement was in flower when the rest of Europe lay under the black cloud of the Dark Ages. And speaking of Dark Ages—Oviedo suffered the special enmity of dictator Francisco Franco, who made his reputation by crushing a miners' uprising in 1934. Yet for all of its dark past, Oviedo today is a lyrical and upbeat little city, where Celtic musicians and folk dancers take to the streets in the summer. Film director Woody Allen once gushed about the city, "It is as if it did not belong to this world, as if it did not exist. … Oviedo is like a fairy tale."

Essentials

ARRIVING Oviedo doesn't have an airport, but travelers can fly into Santiago del Monte, Ranón, 52km (32 miles) away, which also serves Gijón. Call ✆ **98-512-75-00** for information.

RENFE (www.renfe.com; ✆ **90-232-03-20**) offers three **trains** per day from Madrid; the one-way trip takes 4½ hours and costs 50€. **ALSA** (www.alsa.es; ✆ **90-242-22-42**) operates **buses** from Madrid; the trip one-way takes 5½ to 6 hours and costs 32€ to 43€.

Driving from the east or west, take N-634 across the coast of northern Spain. From the south, take N-630 or A-66 from León.

VISITOR INFORMATION The **tourist information office** is at Plaza de La Constitución, 4 (www.oviedo.es; ✆ **90-230-02-02**). Regular hours are daily from 10am to 2pm and 4:30 to 7pm, but from July to September it's open 9:30am to 7:30pm. For more detailed information, go to www.turismoasturias.es.

Exploring Oviedo

Oviedo has been rebuilt into a modern city around Campo de San Francisco, a large green park, but its historical and artistic monuments still cluster along the stone streets and plazas of the Old Quarter. The **Catedral de San Salvador ★**, on the Plaza de Alfonso II el Casto (catedraldeoviedo.com; ✆ **98-521-96-42**), is the most important landmark. The original church—now little more than the foundation—dates to the 8th century, but the Gothic cathedral was begun at the end of the 13th century and completed in the late 16th century. Inside is an altarpiece in the florid Gothic style, dating from the 14th and 15th centuries. The cathedral's 9th-century **Cámara Santa (Holy Chamber)** is famous for the Cross of Don Pelayo, the Cross of the Victory, and the Cross of the Angels, the finest specimens of Asturian art in the world. The pieces show the continuing evolution of the already highly sophisticated goldsmithing of the Visigoths.

Admission to the cathedral is 7€ adults, 6€ seniors, 5€ students and ages 12 to 18, 4€ pilgrims. The cathedral is open for tours Monday through Saturday 10am to 2pm and 4 to 6pm, until 8pm with no interruption July–August. Take bus no. 1.

Right near the cathedral, the **Museo de Bellas Artes de Asturias ★★**, Calle Santa Ana, 1 (www.museobbaa.com; ℗ 98-521-30-61), exemplifies a civic tendency in parts of Spain to dump all the art that used to be in churches and private collections into one big museum. This museum, where the majority of the work represents Spanish painting and sculpture from the 14th through the 19th centuries, does an admirable job. The representations of other European schools are only of passing interest, but there are some extraordinary works here, including one of only three sets of portraits of the apostles painted by El Greco and a marvelous multi-panel representation of the martyrdom and life of Santa Marina. (In one panel, she is miraculously resurrected from the split belly of a dragon.) Admission is free. The museum is open September to June Tuesday through Friday 10:30am to 2pm and 4:30 to 8:30pm, Saturday 11:30am to 2pm and 5:30 to 8pm, Sunday 11:30am to 2:30pm. In July and August, it is open Tuesday through Saturday 10:30am to 2pm and 4 to 8pm, Sunday 10:30am to 2pm.

From the cathedral plaza, walk down Calle Rúa, which becomes Calle Cimadevilla. It leads into the boxed-in square called **Plaza Constitución,** where the Ayuntamiento (town hall) makes the square the secular counterpart to the cathedral plaza. Calle de Fierro leads past the food market hall (p. 642) to **Plaza del Fontán** and adjacent **Plaza Daoíz y Vélarde.** Bagpipe and folk troupes often perform here during tourist season (May–Sept), and on Thursdays a vigorous street market takes over the squares. A flea market of antiques and collectibles sets up shop on Sundays.

Standing above Oviedo, on Monte Naranco, are two of the most famous examples of Asturian pre-Romanesque architecture. **Santa María del Naranco ★★** (turismoasturias.es; ℗ 638-260-163), originally a 9th-century palace and hunting lodge of Ramiro I, offers views of Oviedo and

VICKY cristina OVIEDO

Writer-director Woody Allen and Oviedo (the romantic getaway city in his 2008 film *Vicky Cristina Barcelona*) seem to have a mutual admiration society. In 2002, the Principality of Asturias, where Oviedo is the capital, awarded Woody the Premio Principe de Asturias de Las Artes (the Prince's Prize for the Arts). In accepting the award, Woody called Oviedo "delicious, exotic, pretty, clean, and agreeable." The Asturians liked that so much that they ordered a life-size bronze statue of the actor/director/author/comedian striding down Calle Uria in his characteristic slump. It's one of more than 100 sculptures that enliven the streets and plazas of the city.

Santa Maria del Naranco in Oviedo.

the distant snowcapped Picos de Europa. It was converted into a church in the 12th century. Its intricate stonework depicts hunting scenes, and barrel vaulting rests on a network of blind arches. The open porticoes at both ends were architecturally 200 years ahead of their time. From April to September, the church is open Sunday and Monday 9:30am to 1pm, and Tuesday to Saturday 9:30am to 1pm and 3:30 to 7pm. Off-season hours are Sunday and Monday 10am to 12:30pm, Tuesday to Saturday 10am to 2:30pm. Admission is 3€ and includes admission to San Miguel de Lillo. Entrance is free on Monday.

About 90m (295 ft.) away, **San Miguel de Lillo** ★ (turismoasturias. es; ✆ **638-260-163**) was also built by Ramiro I, originally as a royal chapel. It was no doubt a magnificent specimen of Asturian pre-Romanesque architecture until 15th-century architects marred its grace. The stone carvings that remain, however, are exemplary (most of the sculptures have been transferred to the archaeological museum in town). The church is open the same hours as Santa María del Naranco (see above). Ask the tourist office for its walking tour map from Oviedo center to the churches or take bus 10 from Calle Uría.

Shopping

Serious shoppers know that Oviedo offers some of Spain's best outlets for handbags and shoes. For a number of the finest boutiques, head for the intersection of **Uria** and **Gil de Jaz.** In this district, and on adjoining side streets, you'll find some of the country's best-known designer boutiques selling the same merchandise that often fetches higher prices in Madrid and Barcelona. You'll also come across good sales on Asturian ceramic ware. The Sunday flea market on **Plaza Daoíz y Vélarde** tends to focus on small items—everything from vintage jewelry to mid-20th-century cameras. The market operates 10am to 2:30pm. The **Mercado Fontán** (mercadofontan.es; ✆ **98-520-43-94**), the city's main fresh food market, is a delightful array of the fish of the coast alongside meat and produce from the green hillsides. It's open Monday to Saturday from 8am until 3:30pm.

Where to Stay in Oviedo

Eurostars Hotel de la Reconquista ★★★   It's hard to imagine that this elegant 18th-century building started life as an orphanage and children's hospital. Renovated and opened as a hotel in 1974, it quickly became a social center for the city. You might recognize the beautiful arcaded lobby from Woody Allen's film *Vicky Cristina Barcelona.* Spacious guest rooms all face outward and feature traditional furnishings in soothing neutral tones. In nice weather, guests enjoy two outdoor patios; in cooler weather, they relax in the huge lobby, with comfortable tables and chairs resting on a beautifully woven 250-sq-m (2,690-sq.-ft.) carpet. You get a lot of history and style for the relatively reasonable price.

Calle Gil de Jaz, 16. www.melia.com. ✆ **98-524-11-00.** 142 units. 90€–264€ double; 260€–630€ suite. Parking 23€. Bus: 1, 2, or 3. **Amenities:** 2 restaurants; bar; sauna; free Wi-Fi.

Exe Hotel El Magistral ★   This 1997 hotel is within easy walking distance of Oviedo's old town but provides an interesting counterpoint with its sleek chrome staircase in the lobby and cafeteria/bar constructed with glass bricks. The guest rooms cut back on the high style for an emphasis on comfort with parquet floors, simple bed coverings, and good lighting.

Calle Jovellanos, 3. www.elmagistral.com. ✆ **98-521-51-16.** 52 rooms. 43€–128€ double. Parking 10€. Bus: 1 or 2. **Amenities:** Cafeteria; free Wi-Fi.

Hotel Clarin ★★   Formerly a Room Mate hotel, the Clarin has opted to retain the Art Deco black-and-white décor while freshening all the draperies, rugs, and linens. The executive double rooms offer a substantial increase in size and many have an additional sofa bed and sitting area. Many top-floor rooms also feature skylights.

Calle Caveda, 23. www.hotelclarin.es. ✆ **98-520-95-97.** 47 units. 45€–90€ double. Parking: 10€. Bus: 1, 2, or 3. **Amenities:** Bar; free Wi-Fi.

Where to Eat in Oviedo

Casa Conrado & Suárez ★ ASTURIAN   Long the standard of old-fashioned fine dining in Oviedo, Casa Conrado changed hands in 2018. The new iteration still offers classic dishes such as beans with partridge, creamed prawns on croutons, or baked rice with clams, hake, and artichokes. But the menu now also focuses on beef roasts and steaks from a high-end cattle ranch that specializes in the heritage Asturian "casina" cattle. If you're not in the mood for a full meal, stop in the lovely bar, with its polished wood and stained glass, for tapas such as octopus with apple aioli and onion, or a small toast with ham and fresh duck liver. Reserve a few days ahead in the summer or during festivals.

Calle Argüelles, 1. https://casa-conrado-suarez.negocio.site. 🕾 **98-570-97-80.** Entrees 15€–40€. Mon–Sat 11am–5pm and 7:30pm–midnight, Sun 11am–5pm. Closed Aug. Bus: 1.

Casa Fermín ★★ ASTURIAN   The plates are so lovely that you'll want your camera at the ready when the waiter delivers your food to the table. And the food is as good—if not even better—than it looks. Using the best culinary techniques and local products, the chefs have transformed simple Asturian home cooking into elegant cuisine. Many of the novel dishes—roast loin of venison with fruit chutney, for example, or steak tartare with mustard ice cream and jalapeño peppers—go together so well that it's amazing no one has offered them before. Reserve ahead for weekend dining.

Calle San Francisco, 8. www.casafermin.com. 🕾 **98-521-64-52.** Entrees 26€–33€; tasting menu 70€. Mon–Sat 1:30–4pm and 9pm–midnight. Bus: 1 or 2.

El Fontán ★★ ASTURIAN   If you work up an appetite looking at the fresh meats, fish, produce, cheeses, and more in the Mercado Fontán (p. 642), there's a simple solution: Climb the stairs to the market restaurant, El Fontán, for hearty home cooking in a lively room overlooking the main floor of the 1885 market hall. The daily menu is a super-bargain, as it includes a half-bottle of wine. Market workers swear by the restaurant's *pote Asturiana,* a stew of white beans (of course), potatoes, assorted sausage, and shredded kale with a hambone tossed in for seasoning. The bean stew, *fabada Asturiana,* is always in the top running in annual contests for the best version in Spain.

Calle Fierro, 2. www.restauranteelfontan.com. 🕾 **98-439-62-47.** Entrees 11€–23€; set menu 16€. Mon–Wed 8am–5pm, Fri–Sat 8am–5pm and 8pm–midnight, Sun 9am–5pm.

GALICIA

By Patricia Harris and David Lyon

Galicia is a rain-swept land of grass and granite, much of its coastline gouged by fjordlike inlets called *rías*. The countryside is steeped in Celtic tradition. In many areas its citizens, called Galegos, speak their own language, closely akin to Portuguese. That's not surprising since the region extends above Portugal in Spain's northwest corner. Although much of the interior is mountainous, Galicia is famous across Europe for its fisheries, including swordfish and expensive goose barnacles, or *percebes*.

Nothing did more to put Galicia on the tourist map than the **Camino de Santiago,** the route of religious pilgrims. It is the oldest, most traveled, and most famous route in continental Europe, making Santiago de Compostela the first tourist city on the continent. To guarantee a place in heaven, pilgrims journeyed to the purported tomb of Santiago (St. James the Apostle), patron saint of Spain. From the ninth century on, they trekked across the Pyrenees by the thousands, risking their lives in transit. The Camino de Santiago contributed to the development and spread of Romanesque art and architecture across Spain and provided a rallying point for Christian armies to expel the Moorish conquerors. More than 230,000 people still make the trek each year—some out of religious conviction, some for the athletic challenge, and some to participate in the route's deep history.

The fisheries are Galicia's other pride—something you'll realize immediately upon perusing any menu. Boats trawling out of A Coruña land much of the hake *(merluza)* and several species of tuna so prized throughout the country. Much of Spain's swordfish catch hails from A Guarda. The marshy shores near Pontevedra and O Grove yield many of the various species of clams that are pickled and sold as tapas. Galicia's processors also produce the bulk of the country's tinned anchovies and other seafood delicacies so important to Spanish barroom dining. The region is especially celebrated for braised octopus. Surprisingly, inland Galicia produces some of Spain's finest beef.

A CORUÑA ★

Whichever direction you face in this financial and industrial capital of Galicia, the smell of the sea is always with you. The city perches on a fist

FACING PAGE: **Dancers in traditional costume celebrate the end of a pilgrimage in Santiago de Compostela.**

of land jutting into the Atlantic and pointing toward Ireland. Another Spanish city legendarily founded by Hercules, A Coruña was overrun in succession by Phoenicians, Celts, and Romans. Its defining historical moment, however, came in 1588, when it launched Felipe II's "Invincible Armada" on its ill-fated attack on England. Only half the ships made it back to Spain. The following year, Sir Francis Drake paid a visit, burning and looting A Coruña in reprisal.

Today it is a big-shouldered, rugged city that draws its living from the sea, as so many Galicians have since time immemorial. One side of its isthmus is lined with impeccable sandy beaches washed by gentle waves along most of their length. The area where Orzan and tiny Matadero beaches lie on either side of a rocky point gets sufficient waves to attract surfers. Because the peninsula is so narrow, it's easy to stay anywhere in the city and walk across to the beaches.

On the other side of the A Coruña peninsula, rocky headlands protect a deep-water port. It is split between container ships and the *lonja,* the fish market that feeds all of Spain and much of the rest of Europe. Glassed-in balconies along the high buildings at the edge of the port gave A Coruña its 19th-century nickname, "City of Crystal."

Essentials

ARRIVING   Up to 10 flights a day wing their way from Madrid to A Coruña. **Aeropuerto de Alvedro** (www.aena-aeropuertos.es; 𝄐 **90-240-47-04**) lies 10km (6¼ miles) from the heart of the city and is served by **Iberia** (www.iberia.com; 𝄐 **800-772-4642**), **Air Europa** (www.aireuropa. com; 𝄐 **911-401-501**), **Air Nostrum** (www.airnostrum.es; 𝄐 **96-196-03-19**), and **Vueling Airlines** (www.vueling.com; 𝄐 **807-20-01-00**).

Trains arrive at Estación San Cristóbal, Praza San Cristóbal (www. renfe.com; 𝄐 **90-232-03-20**). Depending on the train, the one-way ride from Madrid lasts 6 to 9 hours and costs 35€ to 54€. **Monbus** (www. monbus.es; 𝄐 **90-229-29-00**) runs **buses** between A Coruña and Santiago de Compostela every hour. The trip takes 30 to 90 minutes and costs 5€.

By **car,** A Coruña is reached from Madrid by the N-VI. You can also follow the coastal highway, N-634, which runs all the way across the northern rim of Spain from San Sebastián to the east.

GETTING AROUND   A Coruña is remarkably compact, since the ancient port city sits on a thumblike peninsula. It is easy to walk from one point of interest to another. Bus 3 makes a circuit of the peninsula; the fare is 2€ adults, 1€ seniors and students.

VISITOR INFORMATION   The **tourist office** at Praza María Pita, 6 (www. turismocoruna.com; 𝄐 **98-192-30-93**), is open February to October Monday to Friday 9am to 8:30pm, Saturday 10am to 2pm and 4 to 8pm, and Sunday 10am to 3pm; in off-season, it closes 1 hour earlier in the evening.

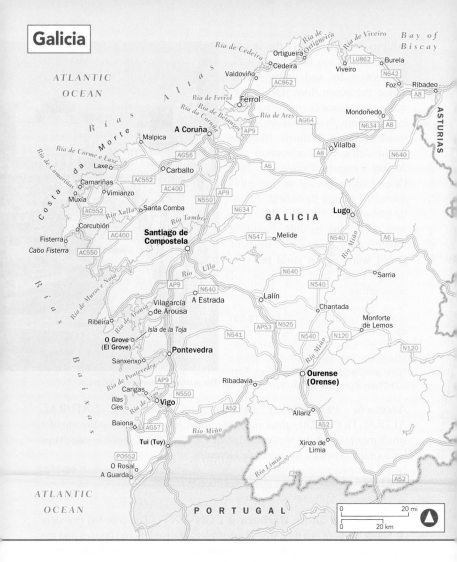

Galicia

ATLANTIC
OCEAN

Bay of
Biscay

Ría de Cedeira

Ría de Ortigueira

Ría de Viveiro

Ortigueira

Cedeira

Valdoviño

Viveiro

LU862

Burela

Foz

Ribadeo

N642

AC862

A8

Ría de Ferrol

Ferrol

Ría de Ares

Mondoñedo

ASTURIAS

Ría da Coruña

A Coruña

Vilalba

N634

A8

Malpica

AP9

AG64

R í a s

M o r t e

Ría de Corme e Laxe

Laxe

Carballo

A8

N640

Camariñas

Vimianzo

AC552

Santa Comba

AC400

N550

AP9

N634

GALICIA

Lugo

Muxía

Río Xalla

A6

Corcubión

Fisterra

AC400

Santiago de
Compostela

N547

Melide

N540

A6

Cabo Fisterra

AC550

Río Tambre

Sarria

Río Ulla

N640

N540

R í a s

AP9

N640

Lalín

Chantada

Vilagarcía
de Arousa

A Estrada

Monforte
de Lemos

Ribeira

Ría de Arousa

N541

AP53

N525

N540

N120

N120

Isla de la Toja

O Grove
(El Grove)

Pontevedra

Ourense
(Orense)

Sanxenxo

Ría de Pontevedra

Ribadavia

Cangas

AP9

N550

Illas
Cíes

Vigo

A52

Allariz

A52

Baiona

AG57

Río Miño

Tui (Tuy)

Xinzo de
Limia

PO552

O Rosal

A Guarda

Río Limia

A52

ATLANTIC
OCEAN

PORTUGAL

0   20 mi

0   20 km

Costa da Morte

Ría de Camariñas

Ría de Muros e Noia

B a i x a s

Exploring A Coruña

The port side of town (the east) has the working port, the seaside gardens,
and the old fort. The port area opens into **Praza (Plaza) de María Pita,**
which divides the Old Town from the newer city. It is an easy 10-minute
walk across the peninsula to Riazor and Orzan beaches on the west side of
the peninsula. The **Beach Promenade,** a paved walkway along the waterfront, covers 13km (8 miles) of the periphery of A Coruña's peninsula.

Acuarium Finisterrae ★★ AQUARIUM   Few subjects are so dear to
the hearts of Galegos as the ocean and its creatures, and one of the

exhibits here is literally the ocean, on the other side of a glass wall. Fish swim by and crabs scuttle across the ocean floor. The under-water experience is amplified in an exhibit room that simulates being inside Captain Nemo's *Nautilus* in the Jules Verne adventure tale *20,000 Leagues Under the Sea.* Other tanks replicate marine envi-ronments around the world. Atlan-tic harbor seals cavort in their own pool. Changing exhibits highlight subjects as diverse as the effects of global warming on coral reefs or the promises and problems of aquaculture.

Paseo Alcalde Francisco Vázquez, 34. www.turismocoruna.com. ✆ **98-118-98-42.** Admission 10€ adults, 4€ seniors and students. July–Aug daily 10am–8pm; Mar–June and Sept–Dec daily 10am–7pm; Jan–Feb Mon–Fri 10am–6pm, Sat–Sun 11am–7pm. Bus: 3, 3A, 11.

The seaside promenade in A Coruña.

Ascensor Panorámico Monte San Pedro ★ NATURAL ATTRACTION This glass elevator climbs 100m (328 ft.) to the top of a small mountain at the western edge of town—a great spot for sunsets or for looking down on the Torre de Hércules.

Parque San Pedro at the Millennium Obelisk. www.turismocoruna.com. ✆ **98-110-08-23.** 3€ each way. Operates June–Sept Tues–Sun 11:30am–9pm; Oct–May Tues–Sun 11:30am–7:30pm and Sat 11:30am–9pm.

Convento da Santa Bárbara ★ CONVENT The cobbled Prazuela de Santa Bárbara is a tiny, tree-shaded plaza flanked by old houses and the high walls of the Santa Bárbara convent. The Clarisas nuns (Poor Clares) are cloistered, but you might hear them singing their prayers at midday services, and you can purchase pastries from their *torno,* a small revolving window built into the convent's vestibule.

Prazuela de Santa Bárbara. *Torno* operates Mon–Fri 10:30am–12:30pm and 4:30–5:45pm, Sat 10:30am–noon.

Domus ★ MUSEUM If you're feeling philosophical on your beach vacation, the so-called "House of Man" is intended to provoke curiosity—starting with its unusual curved building designed by Japanese architect Arata Isozaki. The museum bills itself as the "first interactive museum in the world devoted to the human being." It explores such concrete subjects as the brain, the heart, and the senses and probes more intriguing and philosophical ideas such as identity.

Calle Ángel Rebollo, 91 www.turismocoruna.com. ✆ **98-118-98-40.** Admission 2€ adults, 1€ seniors and students. July–Aug daily 10am–8pm; Mar–June and Sept–Dec daily 10am–7pm; Jan–Feb Mon–Fri 10am–6pm, Sat–Sun 11am–7pm.

Jardín de San Carlos ★ PARK/GARDEN   These gardens near the Casa de la Cultura date from 1843 and cover the site of an old fortress that once guarded the harbor. Their views make the gardens a terrific picnic spot. Within the gardens is the tomb of Gen. John Moore, a British commander who fought unsuccessfully against Napoleon's troops. He retreated with his British forces to A Coruña, where he was shot in a final battle.

Paseo del Parrote.

Jardines de Méndez Núñez ★ PARK/GARDEN   These gardens in the center of town make a restful interlude while sightseeing. The scent of roses is almost overpowering during May and June.

Between the harbor and Los Cantones (Cantón Grande and Cantón Pequeño).

Museo Arqueológico e Histórico Castillo de Santo Antón ★ MUSEUM   The sturdy stone *castillo* was built in the 16th century to fortify the harbor after Drake's raid and later served to hold prisoners and sailors who arrived in port with infectious diseases. It became a museum in 1968. Some artifacts date back to the mysterious megalithic culture of the late Paleolithic era, while others were discovered in medieval burial sites. There's also Roman metalwork and pottery, but visitors are most amazed at the level of artistry in the Celtic gold jewelry created 2500 to 500 B.C.

Paseo Marítimo Alcalde Francisco Vázquez, 2. turismocoruna.com. ✆ **98-118-98-50.** Admission 2€ adults, 1€ seniors and children. July–Aug Tues–Sat 10am–9pm, Sun 10am–3pm; Sept–June Tues–Sat 10am–7:30pm, Sun 10am–2:30pm. Bus: 3 or 3A.

Praza (Plaza) de María Pita ★ SQUARE   Dividing the Old Town from the newer city, this plaza honors the memory of the woman who helped save many of A Coruña's citizens from slaughter by the English. According to legend, she spotted the approach of Drake's troops, and, risking her own life, fired a cannon to alert the citizens to an imminent invasion. Today the Praza is the social and political center of the city. It is hard to say where more business gets done: in City Hall or in the cafes and bars on this square.

Bus: 1, 1A, 2, 2A, 3A, 17, 23A.

Santa María del Campo ★ CHURCH   This 13th-century church can only be viewed from the exterior, but it offers extraordinarily beautiful architectural details. The west door is elaborately carved in the traditional Romanesque-Gothic style. Beneath its rose window you'll see a Gothic portal from the 13th or 14th century. The tympanum is carved with a scene depicting the Adoration of the Magi.

Calle de Santa María.

Torre de Hércules ★ LANDMARK   Europe's oldest working lighthouse, this structure was first erected by the Romans in the 2nd century, although continued modernization has obscured its origins. A climb to the top provides great views of A Coruña's bay and port.

Av. de Navarra, s/n. www.torredeherculesacoruna.com. ☎ **98-122-37-30.** Admission 3€ adults, 1.50€ seniors and students. June–Sept daily 10am–9pm, Oct–May 10am–6pm.

Where to Stay in A Coruña
MODERATE

Hesperia Finisterre ★   This high-rise hotel at water's edge is often booked by business travelers, but it must be hard to concentrate on work when the nearest beach is less than a half-mile away (it's also an easy walk into the old town). Recently refurbished guest rooms are of average size, with tasteful contemporary furnishings and bathrooms with hydromassage tubs. All rooms have sea views. Advance booking often garners discounts.

Paseo del Parrote, 2–4. www.hesperia.com. ☎ **98-120-54-00.** 92 units. 75€–158€ double; 135€–261€ suite. Parking 15€. Bus: 1, 2, 3, or 5. **Amenities:** Restaurant; bar; bikes; concierge; health club; Jacuzzi; outdoor pool; sauna; 2 outdoor tennis courts; free Wi-Fi.

Meliã Maria Pita ★★   The walls of this high-rise modern hotel appear to be made of glass–all the better for guests to enjoy the views from prime location on the point of the waterfront, across from both Orzán and Riazor beaches. Rooms are fairly large, and the decorators weren't afraid to add strong colors and patterned fabrics into the mix of tasteful traditional furnishings and wood floors.

Av. Pedro Barrié de la Maza, 1. www.melia.com. ☎ **98-120-50-00.** 183 units. 73€–197€ double; 149€–340€ suite. Parking 17€. Bus: 2 or 3. **Amenities:** Restaurant; bar; free Wi-Fi.

INEXPENSIVE

Eurostars Atlántico ★   This boxy modern hotel won't win any awards for architecture, but it sits in a prime location equally convenient to explore city sights or head to the beach. You might also run into a few high rollers here, since it also houses the Casino Atlántico. Guest rooms are of ample size and feature well-chosen contemporary furnishings. All rooms have exterior views, which can range from the beach or gardens to city buildings. Booking directly gets you free breakfast.

Avda do Porto da Coruña, 4A. www.eurostarshotel.com. ☎ **91-122-65-00.** 199 units. 59€–130€ double. Bus: 1, 2, or 3. **Amenities:** Restaurant; bar; sauna; free Wi-Fi.

Hotel Riazor ★   This hotel near the convention center overlooks the beach and boasts incredible views of the bay. It's only about a 20-minute walk into the center of town. The low-key modern decor takes its cues from the colors of sand and water. Some bathrooms have showers only, so if you prefer a tub, be sure to ask. Well-laid out room configurations include triples and quadruples, well-suited for families.

Av. Pedro Barrié de la Maza, 29. www.riazorhotel.com. ✆ **98-125-34-00.** 174 units. 68€–109€ double, 95€–130€ triple, 115€–159€ quadruple. Parking 15€. Bus: 2 or 3. **Amenities:** Restaurant; bar; free Wi-Fi.

Where to Eat in A Coruña

It's customary to go window-shopping here for dinner. The restaurants along two of the principal streets—Calle de la Estrella and Calle de los Olmos—all have display counters up front.

Adega O Bebedeiro ★ GALICIAN   Stone and wood—that's the theme of Bebedeiro, where stone walls, a stone fireplace, hardwood floors, and rustic pine tables and stools set the tone. Now in the second generation of the same family, the restaurant specializes in local fish and shellfish, mostly cooked in a wood-burning oven. Some unusual plates include turnip greens with fried cracklings served with a San Simon cheese puff pastry, and a beautiful plate of asparagus spears draped with *langostinos* and served with a pair of garlic mousselines. Puff pastry is popular in this kitchen (the heat of the fire makes it very dramatic); a great seasonal fish dish pairs roasted sea bass with puff pastry filled with scallops. Reserve ahead for weekends.

Calle Ángel Rebollo 34. www.adegaobebedeiro.com. ✆ **98-121-06-09.** Entrees 13€–25€; tasting menu 36€. Tues–Sat 1–4pm and 8pm–midnight, Sun 1–4pm. Closed 2 weeks in June and Dec. Bus: 2 or 3.

Casa Pardo ★★ GALICIAN   Easily the city's most elegant dining room, Pardo arrays black tables clad in white linen beneath very contemporary sculptural chandeliers. In the three decades since Ana Gago and Eduardo Pardo founded the restaurant, it's become known across northern Spain for elegant presentations of innovative seafood dishes. These might include such delights as sea bass braised in crab cream, pan-fried monkfish medallions, or the famous house *caldeirada* (seafood stew) based on monkfish and earthy Galician potatoes. Galician beef is famous throughout the country, and Pardo does a primo sirloin steak with foie gras.

Calle Novoa Santos, 15. www.casapardo-domus.com. ✆ **98-128-00-21.** Entrees 12€–30€; set menus 43€–60€. Mon 1:30–4pm, Tues–Sat 1:30–4pm and 9pm–midnight. Bus: Any city bus.

El Coral ★ GALICIAN/SEAFOOD   The front window of this family-run eatery may have a better and more varied array of sea life than any aquarium. The sole here is the real Dover sole, most of which is caught just outside the port. Icy waters guarantee that the local oysters from the Rias Altas and lobster and crab from all along the coast are sweet and briny. The selection of Galician wines is excellent.

Av. de la Marina Callejón de la Estacada, 9. www.restaurantemarisqueriacoral.com. © **98-120-05-69.** Entrees 16€–28€. Mon–Sat 1–4pm and 9pm–midnight. Bus: 1, 2, 5, or 17.

Pablo Gallego Restaurante ★★ SEAFOOD We ate here on the advice of a fishmonger the first time we visited A Coruña and will probably never eat *pulpo Galego*—octopus stewed with potatoes and paprika—anywhere else again. In fact, this charmingly casual spot just off Praza María Pita is where fishmongers and fishermen alike go to eat. The menu runs the gamut from simple anchovies to monkfish medallions and giant prawns roasted on skewers. The restaurant has a clay tandoor oven, which it uses to good effect with chicken dishes and fatty fish—like red tuna belly.

Calle Capitan Troncoso, 4 bajo. www.pablogallego.com. © **98-120-88-88.** Entrees 12€–28€. Mon–Sat 1:30–4pm and 8pm–midnight. Closed 2nd half Jan. Bus: Any city bus.

A Coruña After Dark

Some of the most appealing bars in A Coruña are atmospheric holes in the wall with a local clientele and decor that has remained virtually unchanged since the mid–20th century. Start your evening at **Mesón A Roda,** Capitán Troncoso, 8 (www.mesonaroda.com; © **98-122-86-71;** daily 1–4pm and 8pm–midnight), which is known for its tapas. For a late night, the town's most appealing and popular disco is **Playa Club,** Andén de Riazor (www.playaclub.club; © **98-127-75-14**). Set on an oceanfront terrace, a few feet from the waves of Playa Riazor, it typically does not open until 10pm.

Day Trips from A Coruña

THE COAST OF DEATH & THE END OF THE WORLD ★★

For the ancients, **Cabo Fisterra** ★ was the end of the world as they knew it. The 145km (90-mile) route takes you along some of the most majestic and rugged coastline in Spain. It carries the ominous nickname of **A Costa da Morte** (the **Coast of Death;** in Castilian, La Costa de la Muerte) because so many ships have wrecked on its shores.

Leaving A Coruña, take the coastal road west (Hwy. 552), heading first to the road junction of **Carballo,** a distance of 36km (22 miles). From this little town, many of the small coastal harbors are within an easy drive. **Malpica** ★, to the northwest, is the most interesting, with its own beach and offshore seabird sanctuary. From Malpica, continue to the sheltered fishing village of **Corme** ★ at Punta Roncudo. It has lovely beaches backed by sand dunes.

The lighthouse at Cabo Fisterra, one of the westernmost points in Europe.

From Corme, continue along the winding roads to the whitewashed village of **Camariñas ★★**, which stands on the *ría* of the same name. Camariñas is known as a village of expert lace makers; you'll see their work for sale in many shops. You can also see historic lacework at the **Museo do Encaixe ★**, Praza Insuela, s/n (www.camarinas.net; ✆ **98-173-63-40; 2€**). From Camariñas, a road leads all the way to the lighthouse at Cabo Vilán.

The road leads first to **Muxia ★** (shown on some maps as Mugia), below which stands the lighthouse at Cabo Touriñan. Continue driving south along clearly marked coastal roads that are sometimes perched precariously on cliff tops overlooking the sea. They will lead you to **Corcubión,** a village with a Romanesque church. From here, follow signs that lead you along a lonely southbound secondary road to the end of the line, **Cabo Fisterra ★★★**, for a panoramic view. This rocky promontory topped by a lighthouse is one of the westernmost points in continental Europe. The sunsets from here are among the most spectacular in the world. The bronze hiking boot mounted near the lighthouse commemorates the fact that diehard Santiago pilgrims continue walking from the cathedral to this distant westward point.

SCENIC RÍAS ALTAS ★

If you have the nerve to drive sinuous roads with steep drop-offs to the sea below, the Galician *rías* should be right up your alley. Comparable to Norwegian fjords, these tidal inlets have been cut into the rocky Galician coastline by the turbulent Atlantic Ocean pounding against its shores. Rías Altas is a modern name applied to all the estuaries on the northern Galician coast. The clifftop roads hug the coastline but give panoramic views. If your nerve fails, default to the adjacent coastal highway.

From A Coruña, head east on the AP-6 to pick up N-651 to **Puentedeume** (also spelled Pontedeume), on the Rías Ares. Historically, it was the center of the counts of Andrade. The remains of their 14th-century palace can be seen, along with the ruins of a 13th-century castle, rising to the east.

Continue north on C-642 to **O Ferrol** (**El Ferrol** in Castilian), which used to be called El Caudillo in honor of the late dictator Francisco Franco, who was born here. O Ferrol is one of the major shipbuilding centers of Spain, and since the 18th century has been a center of the Spanish navy. It's a gritty town, but it lies on one of the region's most beautiful *rías*. Few tourists linger at O Ferrol.

Rock formations on the Galician Coast outside of Vicedo.

Stay on C-642 to **Ortigueira,** a major fishing village at the head of the *ría* (estuary) from which it takes its name. Driving on, you'll notice the coastline becoming more saw-toothed as you approach **Vicedo.**

Next, you will enter the historic village of **Viveiro.** Part of its medieval walls and an old gate, Puerta de Carlos V, have been preserved. The town has many old churches of interest, including the Gothic-style Iglesia San Francisco. Viveiro is a summer resort, attracting vacationers to its beach, Playa Covas. A great place to stop for seafood here is **Restaurante Nito,** in the Hotel Ego, Playa de Area, 1 (www.hotelego.es; ☏ **98-256-09-87**).

The coastal highway (C-642) will take you through **Burela,** another fishing village. From here you can take the high cornice road east (N-634), where you will see the **Iglesia de San Martín de Mondoñeda,** part of a monastery that dates from 1112. It stands in splendid isolation atop a hill. The road continues down into the little town of **Foz,** a fishing village and summer resort with beaches separated by a cliff. Pick up E-70 west here for the 1½-hour inland drive back to A Coruña.

SANTIAGO DE COMPOSTELA ★★★

All roads in Spain once led to the northwestern pilgrimage city of Santiago de Compostela. A journey to the tomb of the beheaded apostle, St. James, was a high point for the medieval faithful—peasant and prince alike—who converged here from across Europe. They still do, at the rate of more than 230,000 per year.

Santiago de Compostela's link with legend began in A.D. 813, when an urn was discovered containing what were believed to be the remains of St. James, an apostle of Jesus who was beheaded in Jerusalem. A temple was erected over the spot, but in the 16th century, church fathers hid the remains of the saint, fearing they might be destroyed in raids along the coast by Sir Francis Drake. Somewhat amazingly, the alleged remains—subject of millions of pilgrimages from across Europe—lay relatively forgotten.

For decades no one was certain where they were. Then, in 1879, a workman making repairs on the church discovered what were supposed to be the remains, hidden

The Catedral de Santiago de Compostela, a beacon to pilgrims for centuries.

since the 1500s. To prove it was the actual corpse of St. James, church officials brought back a sliver of the skull of St. James from Italy. They claimed that it fit perfectly, like a puzzle piece, into the recently discovered skeleton.

In addition to being the third-most-holy city of the Christian world (after Rome and Jerusalem), Santiago de Compostela is a university town and a marketplace for Galician farmers. With its flagstone streets, churches, and shrines, it is one of the most romantic and historic of Spain's great cities. Santiago also has the dubious distinction of being the rainiest city in Spain, but the showers tend to come and go quickly.

Essentials

ARRIVING The only international airport in Galicia is **Aeropuerto de Santiago,** east of the city in Lavacolla (www.aena.es; ☎ **90-240-47-04**), 11km (6¾ miles) on the road to Lugo. There are at least seven daily flights from Madrid and three from Barcelona. During the summer, there is also nonstop service from London, Dublin, Milan, Basel, and Frankfurt.

From A Coruña, 21 **trains** make the 1-hour trip daily at a cost of 6€ to 16€. Six high-speed and one slower train arrive daily from Madrid; the 5- to 11-hour trip costs 23€ to 46€. For information, visit www.renfe.com or call ☎ **90-232-03-20.**

Buses, leaving on the hour, connect A Coruña with Santiago (trip time: 1 hr.) and cost 5€ one-way. For information, contact **Monbus** (www.monbus.es; ☎ **98-229-29-00**). Eight buses daily arrive in Santiago from Madrid, taking 7 to 9 hours and costing 13€ to 60€ one-way. For information, visit **Alsa** at www.alsa.es or call ☎ **90-242-22-42.**

If you're driving, take the express highway (A-9/E-50) south from A Coruña to reach Santiago. From Madrid, N-VI runs to Galicia. From Lugo, head south along N-640.

VISITOR INFORMATION The **tourist office,** at Rúa del Vilar, 63 (www.santiagoturismo.com or www.turgalicia.es; ☎ **98-155-51-29**), is open May through October 9am to 9pm daily, November through April Monday to Friday 9am to 7pm, Saturday and Sunday 9am to 2pm and 4 to 7pm. On Easter it is open 9am to 7pm.

Exploring Santiago

Santiago de Compostela's highlight is undoubtedly its storied cathedral, and you should take at least 2 hours to see it. Most of the other impressive buildings are on Praza do Obradoiro, also called Praza de España. After visiting them, take a stroll through this enchanting town, which has a number of other worthwhile monuments as well as many stately mansions along Rúa del Vilar and Rúa Nueva. One of the most important squares in the Old Town is **Praza de la Quintana,** to the left of the cathedral's Puerta de Orfebrería (Goldsmith's Doorway). It's dominated by **Casa de la**

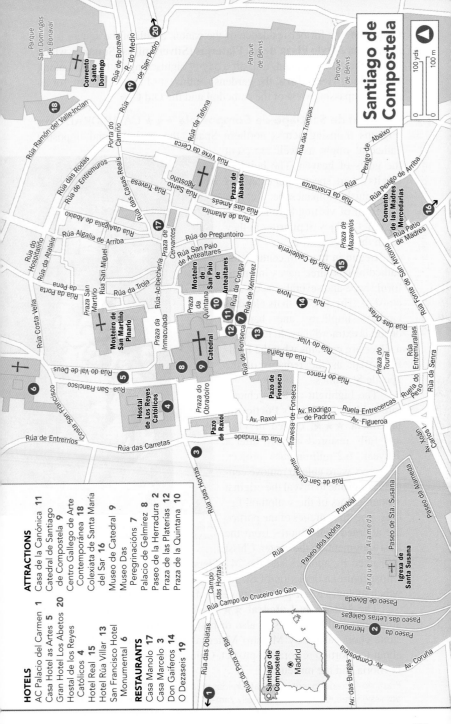

Santiago de Compostela

0 100 yds
0 100 m

HOTELS
AC Palacio del Carmen 1
Casa Hotel as Artes 5
Gran Hotel Los Abetos 20
Hostal de los Reyes
Católicos 4
Hotel Real 15
Hotel Rúa Villar 13
San Francisco Hotel
Monumental 6

RESTAURANTS
Casa Manolo 17
Casa Marcelo 3
Don Gaiferos 14
O Dezaseis 19

ATTRACTIONS
Casa de la Canónica 11
Catedral de Santiago
de Compostela 9
Centro Gallego de Arte
Contemporánea 18
Colexiata de Santa María
del Sar 16
Museo de Catedral 9
Museo Das
Peregrinacións 7
Palacio de Gelmírez 8
Paseo de la Herradura 2
Praza de las Platerías 12
Praza de la Quintana 10

657

Canónica, the former residence of the canon. South of the square is the Renaissance-style **Plaza de las Platerías (Silversmiths' Square),** which has an elaborate fountain. Cap off a day of sightseeing with a walk along **Paseo de la Herradura,** the gardens southwest of the Old Town, for an all-encompassing view of the cathedral and the Old City.

Catedral de Santiago de Compostela ★★★ CATHEDRAL

For pilgrims traipsing across northern Spain, this majestic and imposing cathedral might as well represent the gates of heaven. The building and its art are spectacular examples of Spanish Romanesque, but the real thrill of visiting here is seeing the relief and joy of pilgrims as they reach their destination.

Begun in the 11th century, the cathedral has three naves in cruciform shape and several chapels and cloisters. The altar, with its blend of Gothic simplicity and baroque decor, is extraordinary. In the crypt, a silver urn contains what the faithful accept as the remains of the apostle St. James.

The highlight of the architecture is Maestro Mateo's **Pórtico de la Gloria ★★★**, carved in 1188 and fully restored in 2018 after a 10-year, 6.2-million-euro project. Restorers were able to remove centuries of grime to reveal the original vibrant colors of the sculptural figures. The three arches of the portico are adorned with figures from the Last Judgment. In the center, Christ

A detail from the cathedral's elaborately carved Pórtico de la Gloria.

is flanked by apostles and the 24 Elders of the Apocalypse. Below the Christ figure, a depiction of St. James himself crowns a carved column, which includes a self-portrait statue of Mateo at the bottom.

The **Museo de Catedral ★★** displays tapestries, gold work, and archaeological fragments. It also displays the ruins of a circa-A.D.-1200 stone choir carved by Maestro Mateo along with a detailed exhibition about the portico restoration project. Guided tours include the Pórtico de la Gloria and the museum.

Praza do Obradoiro, s/n. www.catedraldesantiago.es. ℂ **98-156-05-27.** Cathedral admission free. Cathedral open daily 7am–8:30pm. Museum admission 6€, guided tours 10€–12€; reserve time slot in advance on website. Museum Apr–Oct daily 9am–8pm, Nov–Mar 10am–8pm.

Centro Galego de Arte Contemporánea ★ ART MUSEUM Portuguese architect Álvaro Siza Vieira took the traditional building material of granite and used it to create a sleek modern building that somehow manages not to look out of place in the historic center. Opened in the early 1990s, the center hosts changing exhibitions of contemporary art and is slowly building a permanent collection of work from Spanish, Portuguese, and Latin American artists. The terrace offers stunning views.

Rúa Valle-Inclán, s/n. www.cgac.org. ℘ **98-154-66-19.** Admission free. Tues–Sun 11am–8pm.

Colexiata de Santa María do Sar ★ CHURCH Although a little removed from the center of town, this church is one of the architectural gems of the Romanesque style in Galicia. Its walls and columns are on a 15-degree slant thought to be attributable to either a fragile foundation or an architect's fancy. Visit the charming cloister with its slender columns.

Castrón d'Ouro, .8km (½ mile) down Calle de Sar, which begins at the Rúa do Patio de Madres. www.colegiatadesar.com. ℘ **98-156-28-91.** Admission 2€, free with ticket from Museo de Catedral. Daily 11am–2pm and 4:30–7:30pm.

Museo das Peregrinacións ★ MUSEUM If you'd like to know more about the life of St. James and the growth of Santiago de Compostela as a pilgrimage site, it's worth spending some time here. Maps and

The Renaissance-style Plaza de las Platerías.

displays outline the major pilgrimage routes; exhibits discuss what motivates people to embark on this challenging journey.

Praza das Praterías, 2. http://museoperegrinacions.xunta.gal. ℂ **98-156-61-10.** Admission 2.40€ adults, 1.20€ students and pilgrims, free for seniors and under age 18. Tues–Fri 9:30am–8:30pm, Sat 11am–7:30pm, Sun 10:15am–2:45pm.

Where to Stay in Santiago
EXPENSIVE

Hostal de los Reyes Católicos ★★★   When this magnificent property opened in 1499, the first visitors slept on straw mattresses that were changed every 6 months. The traditional heavy wooden furniture, soft mattresses, and luxurious bedding in the guest rooms today are certainly much more comfortable. It's well worth a splurge to stay here so that you can soak up centuries of history as you explore the hallways, visit the cloisters, and simply sink into a chair in the stunning lobby. If you can't swing a stay, inquire about a guided tour, or enjoy a drink at the bar.

Praza do Obradoiro, 1. www.parador.es. ℂ **98-158-22-00.** 128 units. 167€–247€ double; 237€–370€ jr. suite. Parking 20€. **Amenities:** 2 restaurants; bar; free Wi-Fi.

MODERATE

AC Palacio del Carmen ★   If you'd prefer to get away from the crowds in Praza do Obradoiro, this property in a former convent is a good bet. It's very close to the plaza, but just far enough away so that you can enjoy the peaceful environment, lovely patio, and parklike grounds. Rooms are small to mid-size with traditional furnishings, wood-beamed ceilings, and tiled bathrooms.

Calle Oblatas, s/n. www.ac-hotels.com. ℂ **98-155-24-44.** 74 units. 88€–117€ double. Parking 15€. **Amenities:** Restaurant; bar; concierge; free Wi-Fi in public areas.

Hotel Rúa Villar ★   This 18th-century manor house with a graceful arched arcade sits practically next to the cathedral in the historic center of Santiago. The owners also collect art, and their sure sense of taste is evident in the harmonious mix of modern furnishings with the stone and wood of the old building. If you visit during winter, request a room with a gas fireplace. Two rooms have lovely, if small, glassed-in sitting areas with views.

Rúa do Vilar, 8–10. www.hotelruavillar.com. ℂ **98-151-98-58.** 14 units. 70€–90€ double. No parking. **Amenities:** Restaurant; bar; free Wi-Fi.

San Francisco Hotel Monumento ★★   From the hotel's indoor pool, big windows in the rough stone walls look out on gardens and a distant mountain. Yet this hotel in an 18th-century former convent building sits near the cathedral in the heart of the narrow streets of the Old Quarter. The public areas are rich in architectural details, while the rooms feature hardwood floors, wood-beamed ceilings, and traditional furnishings.

Campillo San Francisco, 3. www.sanfranciscohm.com. ℂ **98-158-16-34.** 82 units. 115€–185€ double. Free parking. **Amenities:** Restaurant; bar; indoor pool; free Wi-Fi.

INEXPENSIVE

Casa Hotel as Artes ★   This small hotel represents a real change of pace for history-soaked Santiago. Many of the rooms do feature lovely old exposed stone walls, but rather than play off the architecture, the innkeepers have named each room for an artist and have used that artist as inspiration for colorful and somewhat whimsical decor. The small size of the property makes it a nice choice for a romantic getaway.

Travesía de Dos Puertas, 2 (off Rúa San Francisco). www.asartes.com. ℂ **98-155-52-54.** 7 units. 50€–100€ double. Free parking. **Amenities:** Free Wi-Fi.

Gran Hotel Los Abetos ★★   About a 5-minute drive from the center of Santiago, this modern property calls itself a hotel but has many of the amenities of a resort, including an outdoor pool, tennis courts, and beautiful grounds with stone walkways. High-quality furnishings are in tasteful, classic style. Family rooms with two queen beds can sleep four guests.

Calle San Lázaro, s/n. https://granhotellosabetos.com. ℂ **98-155-70-26.** 148 units. 64€–110€ double; 74€–120€ family room. Free parking. **Amenities:** Restaurant; bar; exercise room; outdoor pool; sauna; outdoor tennis court; free Wi-Fi.

Hotel Real ★   Rooms here are on the small side, but each has a balcony which somehow makes the rooms seem more expansive. Simple furnishings in neutral colors are restful and let the views take center stage. Bathrooms are equally small but well maintained.

Calle Calderería, 49. www.hotelreal.com. ℂ **98-156-92-90.** 13 units. 60€–70€ double. **Amenities:** Free Wi-Fi.

Where to Eat in Santiago

MODERATE

Casa Marcelo ★★ CREATIVE GALICIAN   Created as a cutting-edge restaurant, Marcelo has evolved into a gastropub with an exposed kitchen that features exciting dishes. There's a distinct Japanese influence, especially in the beautiful presentation and use of bright colors to make the plates pop. Peru sneaks into some of the dishes as well, often by way

---

SLEEPING IN historic places

A network of historic inns and manor houses offers a marvelous new way to stay in Galicia. All the properties have been restored with an eye to comfort and quality. Now welcoming visitors, they are organized through **Pazos de Galicia** (www.pazosdegalicia.com). A map on the website shows historic homes around the cities of Galicia, with A Coruña, Santiago de Compostela, and Pontevedra being the most preferred choices. Of course, you'll need a car to reach these places, which lie outside cities or towns of historic interest. They include **Pazo La Buzaca,** Lugar de San Lorenzo, 36, Morana (www.pazolabuzaca.com; ℂ **98-655-36-84**), a 13-room 17th-century structure (part of the complex was a former hunting lodge), and **Pazo do Souto,** Calle Torre, 1, Carballo (www.pazodosouto.com; ℂ **98-175-60-65**), a restored rustic manor house with a pool.

of ceviche. If you're not ready for a full meal, sample the cuisine on the cheap by eating tapas at the bar. Since the restaurant won a Michelin star in 2019, dinner reservations via the website are essential.

Rúa Hortas, 1. www.casamarcelo.net. © **98-155-85-80.** Tapas 5€; *raciones* 12€; set menus 60€–75€. Reservations essential. Tues–Sat 1:30–3:30pm and 9–11:30pm, Sun 1:30–3:30pm. Closed Feb.

Don Gaiferos ★ GALICIAN   Old-fashioned and proud of it, this traditional restaurant next to the Church of Santa María Salomé emphasizes seafood, which arrives by truck from the *lonja* at A Coruña. Good starters include a plate of raw cockles or anchovies with giant capers. The fare is straightforward and simple—roasted hake with potatoes, peas, and, this being Santiago, a few scallops (symbol of Santiago). The beef and veal dishes are also quite good. Among the desserts, the almond tart is the best.

Rúa Nova, 23. www.dongaiferos.com. © **98-158-38-94.** Entrees 16€–24€; set menu 25€. Reservations required. Tues–Sat 1:15–3:45pm and 8:15–11:30pm, Sun 1:15–3:45pm.

O Dezaseis ★ TAPAS/GALICIAN   This subterranean haunt specializes in tapas and empanadas with the aim of communicating to non-Spaniards that it really is okay to make a meal of small plates. The dishes are not the creative concoctions you'd find at Casa Marcelo (above), but rather the small plates that sustain Spaniards all over the country. So expect *tortilla Española* (potato omelet), little casseroles of meatballs, sliced ham and cheese, sizzling plates of grilled chorizo or blood sausage, and the ubiquitous pieces of roast chicken. Or try slices of Galician empanada, which is akin to a pot pie with less runny filling. The traditional one is filled with chunks of fresh tuna, potato, onion, and carrot in a light béchamel sauce. "Sixteen" (as the restaurant's name translates) also grills whole fish.

Rúa San Pedro, 16. © **98-156-48-80.** Tapas 4€–14€; *raciones* 6€–14€; set menus 13€–22€. Mon–Sat 2–4pm and 8:30pm–midnight.

INEXPENSIVE

Casa Manolo ★ GALICIAN   As you might expect of a dining room only 100 paces from the cathedral, Casa Manolo feeds a lot of hungry pilgrims. In fact, there's just one choice of meal each day, called the Pilgrim's Menu, and it reflects the kind of pasta- and rice-heavy fare that sustains walkers on the road. So don't be surprised if the meal of the day is breaded veal cutlet on spaghetti with red sauce, or an approximation of paella. It's not fancy, but the price is right and the company terrific.

Praza Cervantes, s/n. www.casamanolo.es. © **98-158-29-50.** Set menu 12€. Mon–Sat 1–4pm and 8:30–11:30pm; Sun 1–4pm. Closed Jan.

Shopping

A favorite of most tourists is *tarta Santiago,* a tart sold at virtually every pastry shop in the city. Also very popular is *queso de tetilla,* a mild local cheese shaped like a woman's breast. The artful blue-and-white porcelain that is the town's trademark is available for sale at **Sargadelos,** Rúa Nueva, 16 (www.sargadelos.com; ✆ 98-158-19-05). **Amboa Maeloc,** Rúa Nueva, 44 (www.amboamaeloc.com; ✆ 98-158-33-59), stocks similar ceramics, plus a wide range of other regional handicrafts.

Many local wines, including assorted bottles of Ribeiro, Condado, and, most famous of all, Albariño, are sold without fanfare in grocery stores throughout Galicia. But for a specialist in the subtleties of these tipples, head for **Charcuterías Seco,** San Pedro Mezonzo, 3 (www.charcuteriaseco.com; ✆ 98-159-12-67).

Santiago After Dark

In the religious center of Galicia, there's a lot more to do after dark than pray. An estimated 200 bars and *cafeterías* are found on the Rúa do Franco and its neighbor, Rúa da Raiña. The pavement along those streets on weekend evenings at around 11pm is mobbed. One of the town's hot spots is **Pub Modus Vivendi,** Praza Feixó, 1 (✆ 607-804-140), where rock music blasts the night away in a cozy but too crowded interior. Its psychedelic decor attracts local students and young visiting foreigners Sunday to Thursday 6pm to 3:30am, Friday and Saturday 6pm to 4:30am. For a quieter experience, partake of a *queimada* (a punch made with local spirit) at **Retablo Café-Concerto,** Rúa Nova, 13 (www.retablocafeconcerto.com; ✆ 629-883-245), which is open daily 6pm to 5:30am.

PONTEVEDRA ★

The city of Pontevedra is an open-air museum to the evanescence of glory. The aristocratic old town on the Lérez River still has vestiges of an ancient wall that once encircled the town. In medieval days, it was called Pontis Veteris (Old Bridge), its sheltered harbor at the end of the Ría Pontevedra was a bustling port, and foreign merchants mingled with local traders, seamen, and fishermen. But the Lérez delta silted up in the 1700s and Pontevedra went into decline. The old town, a maze of colonnaded squares and cobbled alleyways, lies between Calle Michelena and Calle del Arzobispo Malvar, stretching to Calle Cobián and the river. The old mansions, called *pazos,* echo the city's bygone maritime glory, for the money to build them came from the sea.

Essentials

ARRIVING   From Santiago de Compostela, 17 **trains** per day make the 30- to 60-minute one-way trip to Pontevedra at a cost of 6.30€ to 7.60€. **RENFE** has an office on Praza Calvo Sotelo, s/n (www.renfe.com; ✆ 90-232-03-20), where you can get information. The rail and bus stations are 0.8km (½ mile) from the town center on Calle Alféreces Provisionales. From Santiago de Compostela, a **bus** leaves every hour during

Pontevedra's Old Quarter.

the day for Pontevedra (trip time: 1 hr.); the one-way trip costs 2€ to 5€. For information, visit www.monbus.es or call ✆ **98-229-29-00.** If you're **driving** from Santiago de Compostela, head south along N-550 to reach Pontevedra.

VISITOR INFORMATION   The **tourist office,** at Casa da Luz, Praza da Verdura (www.visit-pontevedra.com/ing; ✆ **98-609-08-90**), is open Monday to Saturday 10am to 2pm and 4:30 to 7:30pm, and Sunday 10am to 2pm.

Exploring Pontevedra

Pontevedra's **Old Quarter ★** is almost entirely pedestrianized these days, making it a pleasant place to stroll. The major attraction in the old part of the city is the **Basílica de Santa María la Mayor ★**, Avda de Santa María, 24 (www.santamarialamayor.org; ✆ **98-686-61-85**), dating from the 16th century. All the metal decoration on the church has taken on an avocado-green patina. Its most remarkable feature is its western facade, carved to resemble an altarpiece, with a depiction of the Crucifixion at the top. The church is open daily 10:30am to 2pm and 6 to 9pm.

The **Museo de Pontevedra,** Calle Pasantería, 10 (www.museo.depo. gal; ✆ **98-685-14-55**), contains a hodgepodge of everything from the

Pontevedra civic attic. Displays range from prehistoric artifacts to a still life by Zurbarán. Many of the exhibits are maritime-oriented, and there is a valuable collection of jewelry. The museum is open Tuesday to Saturday 10am to 9pm, Sunday 11am to 2pm. Admission is free. The museum opens onto a major square in the old town, Praza de Leña (Square of Wood).

Iglesia de San Francisco at Plaza de Ourense, 5, is another church of note, with a fine Gothic facade opening onto gardens. Founded in the 14th century, it contains the sepulcher of Don Payo Gómez Charino, noted for his part in the 1248 Reconquest of Seville, when the city was wrested from Moorish domination.

Where to Stay in Pontevedra

Hotel Rías Bajas ★   Built in the late 1960s when Pontevedra was a busy business center, the Rías Bajas has switched gears to cater to leisure travelers who have come to see the quaint stone buildings and narrow, pre-modern streets of the Old Quarter. Although the hotel is on a bustling street corner, it is less than a 5-minute walk from the Old Quarter. The decor of the public areas features lots of stone and paneled wood, and it is frequently used as a backdrop for political press conferences. The guest rooms are simpler and more traditional. They tend to be small (although some triples are available), but all feature a usable work desk.

Calle Daniel de la Sota, 7. www.hotelriasbajas.com. 1 ℂ **98-685-51-00.** 100 units. 54€–77€ double; 75€–95€ triple. Parking 12€. **Amenities:** Restaurant; bar; free Wi-Fi.

Parador de Pontevedra ★★   Once home to the counts of Maceda, this handsome Renaissance town house has been beautifully restored, with a carved stone staircase leading from the courtyard to the guest rooms. Quiet and regal, the *parador* makes a perfect base for exploring Pontevedra (the basilica is nearby) and for making day trips to O Grove to the west or to the wine country on the southwest coast.

Calle Barón, 19. www.parador.es. ℂ **98-685-58-00.** 47 units. 85€–130€ double; 128€–195€ suite. Limited free parking. **Amenities:** Restaurant; bar; free Wi-Fi.

Where to Eat in Pontevedra

Alameda 10 ★ GALICIAN   A little bit modern, a little bit traditional, Alameda 10 focuses mostly on making good, simple food without a lot of fuss. It has an extensive tapas menu that includes some unusual dishes like a small green salad with duck "ham," a Portuguese-style cornbread, chicken croquettes, and freshly fried potato chips with Cabrales cream.

Calle Alameda, 10. www.restaurantealameda10.com. ℂ **98-685-74-12.** Entrees 15€–30€, set menu 30€. Mon and Wed–Sat 1–4pm and 9–11:30pm, Tues 1–4pm.

Casa Román ★ GALICIAN   Calling itself a "restaurant *marisquería*," this branch of Casa Román is really all about the shellfish. Oven-roasted scallops are particularly popular, but the kitchen focuses on crustaceans.

Several dishes use the European lobster (somewhat smaller than its American cousin). Depending on what's on display on ice, you can also enjoy the big meaty crabs found all over the rocks along the *rías* (excellent roasted in the oven), steamed Norway lobster (what the Italians call *langostinos*), and several species of shrimp and prawns. The restaurant is in the new section of town, Praza de Galicia.

Calle Augusto García Sánchez, 12. www.casaroman.com. ⓒ **98-622-01-88.** Entrees 14€–25€. Tues–Sat 1:30–3:45pm and 9–11:45pm, Sun 1:30–3:45pm.

Solla ★★★ GALICIAN   Self-taught chef Pepe Solla is an original, and his embrace of the classic flavors of Galician cuisine is matched only by his determination to make it all new. The old country house where Solla has just nine tables has been a restaurant for many years, but the chef gave it a complete makeover in contemporary Spanish style. Having won one Michelin star already, Solla is a likely contender for another with dishes like a cream of oysters, hake roe, sturgeon caviar, and bluebell flowers. He matches the meatiness of sea bass with braised turnip greens, Galician cabbage (similar to kale), and an orange-lemon sauce. Solla is a prime regional exemplar of the *cocina de autur.* He has caught the "locavore" fever, so almost everything on his menus comes from within a 1-hour radius, and all the fish is caught inshore in sustainable fisheries. Reserve at least 2 weeks ahead.

Av. Sineiro 7, Km 2, San Salvador de Poio, 2km (1¼ miles) from center of town, toward O Grove. www.nove.biz/pepe-solla. ⓒ **98-687-28-84.** Set menus 59€–102€. Tues–Wed and Fri–Sat 1:30–4pm and 9–11:30pm; Thurs and Sun 1:30–4pm. Closed Dec 20–Jan 4.

Day Trips from Pontevedra

O GROVE & A TOXA ★

Only 34km (21 miles) west of Pontevedra on the PO-308, **O Grove** (El Grove in Castilian) is a summer resort and fishing village, surrounded by 8km (5 miles) of beaches and some of the most extensive shellfish flats on the Galician coast. The nominally 45-minute drive from Pontevedra is a pleasure. We say "nominally," because you'll be hard-pressed to drive through without stopping frequently for photographs. The road follows the north coast of the Ría de Pontevedra, part of the famous Rias Baixas wine district. Small vineyards hanging with Albariño wine grapes are on one side of the road, and the rugged coast with scenic vistas on the other.

When you do reach O Grove, you can get local information at the **tourist information office,** Praza Do Corgo, s/n (www.turismogrove. com; ⓒ **98-673-14-15**), which is usually open weekdays 11am to 2pm and 4 to 6pm, with shorter hours on weekends. Besides feasting on shellfish at **La Posada del Mar ★★**, Calle Castelao, 202 (ⓒ **98-673-01-06;** entrees 10€–24€, set menus 26€–35€; closed Mon), there are really only two other things to do. The first is to cross the bridge next to La Posada del

Mar to visit **A Toxa** ★ (La Toja in Castilian), an island holding Galicia's most famous spa and most fashionable resort. The casino and the golf course are both very popular. The island is covered with pine trees and surrounded by some of the finest scenery in Spain. A Toxa first became known for its health-giving properties when, according to legend, the owner of a sick donkey left it on the island to die. The donkey recovered, and its cure was attributed to the waters of an island spring.

The other principal attraction is the **Acuario de O Grove** ★, Punta Moreiras (www.acuariodeo grove.es; ℂ **98-673-23-27**). Renovations in 2013 to 2014 altered this aquarium's exhibits to focus mainly on the immediate coastal zone and converted the facility to being powered entirely by wind and solar cells. In addition to seeing a lot of the tastiest sea life in its natural

A working boat in the fishing village of O Grove.

environment, the aquarium has a few sea otters and other marine mammals. Admission is 10€ adults, 8€ seniors and ages 4 to 14. From mid-June to mid-October it is open daily 10:30am to 8:30pm; from mid-October to mid-June it is open Wednesday to Friday 10am to 6pm and Saturday and Sunday 10am to 7:30pm.

WINE & HISTORY ON GALICIA'S SOUTHWEST COAST ★★

The coastline from the Ría de Vigo to the Río Miño, which forms the border between Spain and Portugal, is steeped in history and blessed with a climate that favors the cultivation of Albariño grapes. It is also an area with some of the greatest fishing ports in the world, and consequently some of the best casual fish restaurants in Spain.

Begin at the village of **Baiona** ★, 57km (36 miles) south of Pontevedra; its moment of enduring fame came on March 1, 1493, when Columbus's vessel, *La Pinta,* made landfall here. The ship's navigator was from Baiona, which became the first place in Europe to learn of the Columbus's discoveries across the Atlantic Ocean. A replica **Carabela *Pinta*** (www. baiona.org; ℂ **98-638-59-21**) constructed for the quincentennial, bobs in the harbor among recreational sailboats. The ship is open daily 11am to 2pm and 4:30 to 7:30pm. Admission is 2€. Just above the harbor stand the picket-fence stone walls of Baiona's **Fortaleza de Monterreal** (www. baiona.org; © 98-668-70-67). The fort was constructed fitfully from the 12th century onward but was completed in the early 1600s. Its 3km (2 miles) of walls wrap around the headland above the harbor. It is open daily 10am to 9pm. Admission is 2€.

As you drive south on the PO-552 from Baiona, several pull-outs along the road allow you to enjoy the dramatic views. In 30km (19 miles), the fishing port of **A Guarda ★★** (La Garda in Castilian) nestles in a deep cove at the mouth of the Río Miño. This ancient Celtic port predates the Roman presence and is now home to Europe's most important sword-fish fleet. Pastel houses, restaurants, and bars form a Cubist wall around the harbor. The Paseo Marítimo leads to a breakwater with a walkway along the top, and to tiny **Museo do Mar ★** (http://museodomar.xunta. gal; © 98-661-00-00), set in a replica of the cannon emplacement that once guarded A Guarda. Exhibits include aquarium tanks and good expli-cation of traditional local fishing equipment and vessels. The museum is open early June to mid-September daily 11am to 2pm and 6 to 9pm, the rest of the year Saturday and Sunday 11am to 2pm and 4 to 7pm. Admis-sion is 1€, 0.50€ under age 14. If you're hungry, head to the road above the harbor for grilled swordfish or rice and shellfish casseroles at **Xeito Restaurante Mariquería ★★**, Av. Fernández Albor, 19 (www.restaurant exeito.es; © 98-661-04-74). The restaurant on the rocky headland has out-door tables for taking in the view. It's open daily for lunch and dinner. Main dishes cost 15€ to 30€.

The highway turns north at A Guarda to follow the Río Miño toward Túi. In about 11km (7 miles), you reach the important D.O. wine district known as **O Rosal ★** (a subdivision of Rías Baixas). The highway sud-denly sprouts side roads leading to vineyards. Grapes line the roadside in tracts as small as backyard gardens and as big as fields reaching over the hillside. The dominant grape is Albariño, which makes a fruit-forward, slightly acidic wine with a long finish for which the Rías Baixas region is justifiably famous. Several winemakers in O Rosal offer tastings, includ-ing **Bodegas Terras Gauda ★★**, PO-552 km 55 (www.terrasgauda.com; © 98-662-10-01). The tasting room is open Monday to Saturday 11am to 2pm and 4 to 8pm, Sunday 11am to 2pm. Free winery tours are offered Monday to Saturday at 5:30pm, Sunday at 12:30pm.

About 16km (10 miles) north, the cathedral city of **Túi** sits right on the border with Portugal near the two-tiered road-and-rail bridge over the Río Miño that links the two countries. The bridge was designed by Alex-andre-Gustave Eiffel. (He designed a tower in Paris you may have heard of.) A footpath along the river here represents the southern Iberian branch of the **Camino de Santiago.** Locals maintain it as a greenway, and fisher-men often come to the path to cast a line into the Río Miño. The winding

The Eiffel-built bridge outside Túi.

streets of Tuí's Old Quarter lead to the **Catedral** ★ (www.catedraldetui. com; © **98-669-05-11**), a national art treasure that dominates the *zona monumental*. The acropolis-like cathedral/fortress, built in 1170, wasn't used for religious purposes until the early 13th century. Later architects respected the original Romanesque and Gothic styles and made few changes in its design. It is usually open daily 9am to 2pm and 4 to 9pm. Admission to the church is free, but 2€ will also get you into the museum, cloister, tower, and gardens.

From Túi, it is a 40-minute drive north on PO-340/AP-55 to return to Pontevedra.

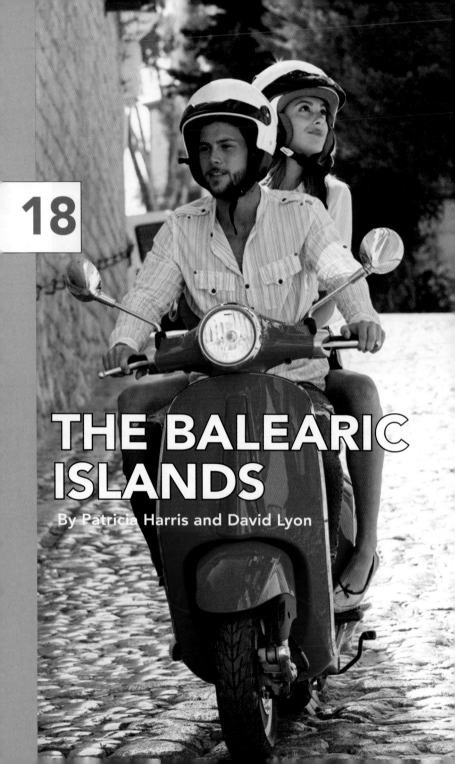

18

THE BALEARIC ISLANDS

By Patricia Harris and David Lyon

T he Balearic Islands (Los Baleares)—Mallorca, Menorca, and Ibiza, plus Formentera and other diminutive islands—stand at the crossroads of the western Mediterranean. They are due south of Barcelona, due north of Algiers, and due east of Valencia. Carthaginians, Greeks, Romans, Vandals, and Moors occupied and ruled them before Spain came along. Yet despite a trove of Bronze Age megaliths and some fine Punic artifacts, the invaders who have left the largest imprint are the sun-seeking vacationers who swoop in every summer.

After Jaume I expelled the Moors in 1229, the islands flourished as the kingdom of Mallorca, but declined after being integrated into the kingdom of Castilla in the mid–14th century. The 19th century provided a renaissance, as artists such as George Sand, Chopin, and, later, poets Robert Graves and Laura Riding established the islands as a haven for musicians, writers, and artists. The artists gradually paved the way for tourists of all stripes.

Very few visitors have time to explore all three major islands, so you'll have to decide early which one is for you. **Mallorca,** the largest, is the most commercial and touristy, with sprawling hotels and fast-food joints in all but the most scenic parts. Freewheeling **Ibiza** attracts the international party crowd, as well as seekers of white-sand beaches and sky-blue waters. The smallest of the major islands, **Menorca,** is the most serene. It is less touristy than Mallorca and Ibiza, and for that reason it is now experiencing an "anti-tourist" tourist boom. The government of the islands has recently safeguarded 35% of the entire island group from further development. Be aware that continuing strong demand and a short summer season means unusually high prices for Balearic Island hotels.

MALLORCA ★★★

The most popular of Spain's Mediterranean islands, Mallorca draws millions of visitors each year. About 209km (130 miles) from Barcelona and 145km (90 miles) from Valencia, Mallorca has a coastline 500km (311 miles) long. An explorer's paradise in its interior, it's overbuilt along certain coastal regions. The north is mountainous; the fertile southern flatlands offer olive and almond groves interrupted by windmills. The main city, Palma, is the financial and political capital of the Balearic Islands.

> ## Not an Island for All Seasons
>
> July and August are high season for Mallorca; don't even think of coming then without a reservation. It's possible to swim comfortably from June to October; after that, the water is prohibitively cold and many hotels and restaurants close until May.

The golden sands of Mallorca are famous, with lovely beaches such as **Ca'n Pastilla** and **El Arenal,** but tend to fill with package tourists. Both Cala Mayor and Sant Agustí have good beaches, including **Playa Magaluf,** the longest beach on the Calvía coast. **Cala de San Vicente,** 6.5km (4 miles) north of Pollença, is a beautiful beach bordered by a pine grove and towering cliffs. Stretches of golden beach lie between Cala Pi and Cala Murta on the Formentor peninsula.

Mallorca Essentials

ARRIVING   If you're coming in August, make sure you have a reserved return ticket. There are no empty airplane or ferry seats this time of year.

   Iberia (www.iberia.com; ℂ **90-240-05-00**) flies to Palma's **Aeroport Son San Joan** (www.aena.es; ℂ **90-240-47-04**) from Barcelona, Valencia, and Madrid. There are daily planes from Madrid and Valencia, and several daily flights from Barcelona in summer; more than 60 airlines serve Palma from all over Spain, Europe, North Africa, and the Near East during the summer season. An airport bus takes you to Plaça Espanya in the center of Palma for 3€, while a metered cab costs about 30€ for the 25-minute drive into town.

   Trasmediterránea, Estació Marítim in Palma (www.trasmediterranea. es; ℂ **90-245-46-45**), operates a daily **ferry** from Barcelona (trip time: 3½ hr.) from 37€ one-way. There are six ferries per week from Valencia (none on Sun), taking 7 hours and costing 54€ one-way. (A faster boat takes 4–6 hr. and costs 130€.) In Barcelona, book tickets at the Trasmediterránea office at Estació Marítim (ℂ **90-245-46-45**), and in Valencia at the office at Terminal Trasmediterráneo Muelle Deponiente, Estacio Marítima (ℂ **90-245-46-45**).

GETTING AROUND   At the tourist office in Palma, you can pick up a bus schedule that explains island routes. **Empresa Municipal de Transportes** (www.emtpalma.es; ℂ **97-121-44-44**) runs city buses from its main terminal, Estació Central D'Autobus, Plaça Espanya. The standard one-way fare is 1.50€ within Palma; at the station you can buy a 10-ride card that costs 10€. One of the most frequented bus routes, bus 412, goes from Palma to the Cuevas del Drach, a 1½-hour trip that costs 9€–14€ one-way. Other popular routes go to Deia (bus 210, 45 min.; 6€) and Valldemossa (bus 210, 30 min.; 4€). **Ferrocarril de Sóller,** Carrer Eusebio Estada, 1 (www.trendesoller.com ℂ **97-175-20-51**), off Plaça Espanya,

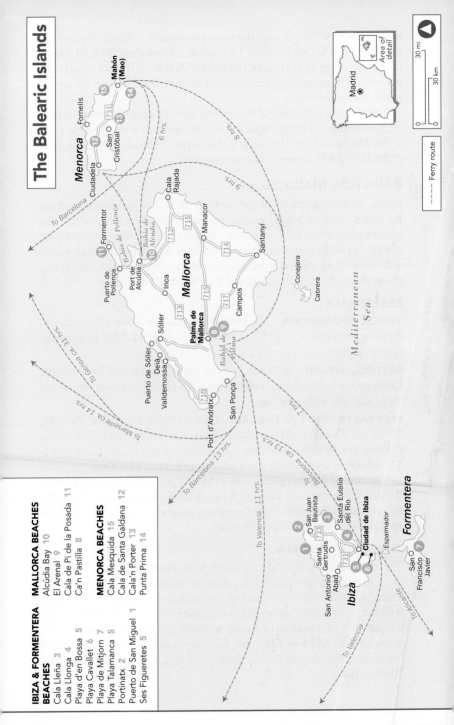

The Balearic Islands

IBIZA & FORMENTERA BEACHES

Cala Lleña 3
Cala Llonga 4
Playa d'en Bossa 5
Playa Cavallet 6
Playa de Mitjorn 7
Playa Talamanca 5
Portinatx 2
Puerto de San Miguel 1
Ses Figueretes 5

MALLORCA BEACHES

Alcudia Bay 10
El Arenal 9
Cala de Pi de la Posada 11
Ca'n Pastilla 8

MENORCA BEACHES

Cala Mesquida 15
Cala de Santa Galdana 12
Cala'n Porter 13
Punta Prima 14

Menorca

Fornells
Ciudadela
Puerto de Pollença
Formentor
Port de Pollença
Puerto de Sóller
Sóller
Deià
Valldemossa
Port d'Andratx
San Ponça
Palma de Mallorca
Inca
Manacor
Cala Rajada
Santanyí
Campos

Mahón (Mao)
San Cristóbal

Mallorca

Bahía de Pollença
Bahía de Alcúdia
Bahía de Palma

Conejera
Cabrera

Ibiza

Santa Gertrudis
San Antonio Abad
San Juan Bautista
Santa Eulalia del Río
Ciudad de Ibiza
Espalmador

Formentera

San Francisco Javier

Mediterranean Sea

To Barcelona
To Genoa ca. 31 hrs.
To Marseille ca 14 hrs.
To Barcelona 13 hrs.
To Valencia 11 hrs.
To Alicante
To Valencia

Madrid
Area of detail

----- Ferry route

30 mi
30 km

has train service through majestic mountain scenery to Sóller. These trains run daily April to October from 10:10am to 7:40pm (Nov–Mar 10:30am–6pm), also stopping at Mirador Del Pujol d'en Banya. The ticket costs 18€ one-way, 25€ round-trip. Tickets must be purchased in cash on day of travel (no credit cards).

If you plan to stay in Palma, you don't need a car. Otherwise consider such companies as Europcar, at the airport terminal (www.europcar.com; ✆ **90-210-50-55**), or Avis, also at the airport terminal (www.avis.com; ✆ **90-211-02-61**). Reservations are essential.

Palma de Mallorca ★★

Palma, on the southern tip of the island, is the seat of government and has the lion's share of hotels, restaurants, and nightclubs. Nearly half the island's population lives in Palma (islanders call Palma simply Ciutat [City]). It's the largest of the Balearic ports, its bay often filled with yachts and ocean liners. Arrival by sea is the most impressive, with the skyline characterized by Bellver Castle and the cathedral's bulk.

ESSENTIALS

VISITOR INFORMATION The **tourist information office** at Plaça Reina, 2 (www.visitpalma.cat; ✆ **97-117-39-90**), is open Monday to Saturday 8:30am to 8pm.

GETTING AROUND In Palma, you can get around the Old Town and the Paseo on foot. Otherwise, make limited use of taxis, or take one of the buses that cuts across the city.

FAST FACTS The **U.S. Consulate,** Edificio Reina Constanza, Porto Pi, B, 9D (✆ **97-140-37-07**), is open Monday to Friday from 10:30am to 1:30pm. The **British Consulate,** Carrer Convent dels Caputxins, 4 (✆ **97-171-24-45**), is open Monday to Friday from 8:30am to 1:30pm.

In case of an **emergency,** dial ✆ **112.** If you fall ill, head to **Clínica Rotger,** Calle Santiago Rusiñol, 9 (www.clinicarotger.es; ✆ **97-144-85-00**), or **Clínica Juaneda,** Calle Company, 30 (www.juaneda.es; ✆ **97-173-16-47**). Both clinics are open 24 hours.

EXPLORING PALMA

The Moors constructed Palma in the style of a casbah, or walled city, and those foundations are still visible, although obscured by high-rise hotels. The area immediately surrounding the cathedral epitomizes old Palma, with mazes of narrow alleys and cobblestone streets. In the Gothic quarter, the 10th-century **Banys Àrabs** ★ baths, Carrer Serra, 7 (www.visit palma.cat; ✆ **637-046-534**), are the only intact Moorish-constructed buildings remaining in Palma. Admission is 2.50€; they're open daily 10am to 7pm.

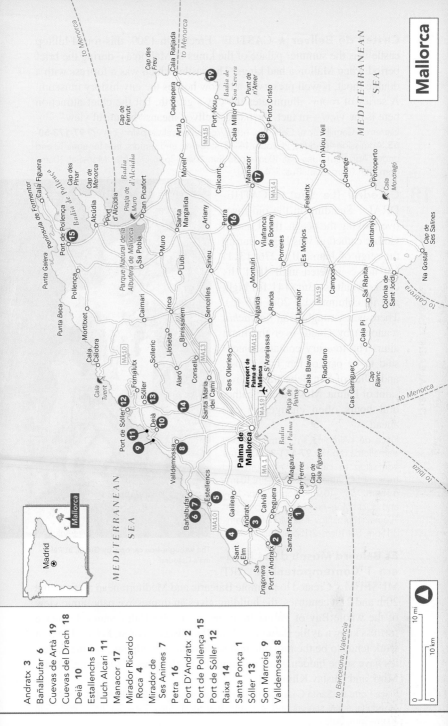

Mallorca

Castell de Bellver ★ CASTLE   Erected in 1309, this round hilltop castle was the summer palace of the kings of Mallorca—during the brief period when Mallorca had kings. The castle, which was a fortress with a double moat, is well preserved and now houses the city history museum. A series of rooms illuminates the city's growth, but the chief attraction here is the view—in fact, the name, Bellver, means "beautiful view."

Carrer de Camillo Josè Cela, s/n. https://castelldebellver.palma.cat. ⓒ **97-173-50-65.** Admission 4€ adults; 2€ youth 14–18, students, and seniors; free for ages 13 and under. Apr–Sept Tues–Sat 10am–7pm, Sun 10am–3pm; Oct–Mar Mon–Sat 10am–6pm, Sun 10am–3pm. Bus: 3, 4, or 20.

Catedral (La Seu) ★ CATHE-DRAL   Standing in the old town overlooking the ocean, this Catalan Gothic cathedral was begun during the reign of Jaume II (1276–1311) but not completed until 1601. Its central vault is 43m (141 ft.) high, and its columns rise 20m (66 ft.). There is a wrought-iron *baldachin* (canopy) by Gaudí over the main altar. The treasury contains pieces said to be part of the True Cross, and relics of San Sebastián, patron saint of Palma. Museum and cathedral hours often change, so call ahead.

Plaça de l'Almoina s/n. http://catedral demallorca.org. ⓒ **97-171-31-33.** Free admission to cathedral; museum and treasury 5€. June–Sept Mon–Fri 10am–6:15pm, Sat 10am–2:15pm; Apr–May and Oct Mon–Fri 10am–5:15pm, Sat 10am–2:15pm; Nov–Mar Mon–Fri 10am–3:15pm, Sat 10am–2:15pm. Bus: 15 or 25.

The wrought-iron canopy, by Gaudí, at Palma's Catedral.

Es Baluard Museu d'Art Modern i Contemporani ★ ART MUSEUM   Created to promote Balearic and Mediterranean art from the 20th and 21st centuries, the building gives an impressive panoramic view of the whole Bay of Palma from the site of the 16th-century defensive fortress known as the Baluard de Sant Pere (Bastion of St. Peter). The best work tends to be the monumental-scale outdoor sculpture, but the galleries have some hidden gems of paintings by the likes of Picasso, Chagall, Miró, and Gustav Klimt.

Plaça Porta de Santa Catalina 10. www.esbaluard.org. ⓒ **97-190-82-00.** Admission 6€ adults, 4.50€ seniors and students, free to all Tues. Tues–Sat 10am–8pm; Sun 10am–3pm. Bus: 1.

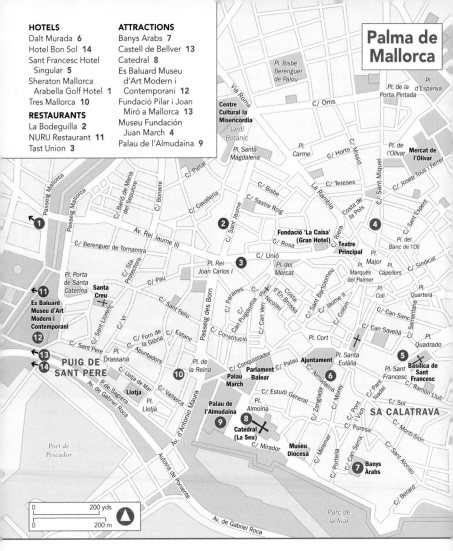

HOTELS
Dalt Murada **6**
Hotel Bon Sol **14**
Sant Francesc Hotel
  Singular **5**
Sheraton Mallorca
  Arabella Golf Hotel **1**
Tres Mallorca **10**

RESTAURANTS
La Bodeguilla **2**
NURU Restaurant **11**
Tast Union **3**

ATTRACTIONS
Banys Arabs **7**
Castell de Bellver **13**
Catedral **8**
Es Baluard Museu
  d'Art Modern i
  Contemporani **12**
Fundació Pilar i Joan
  Miró a Mallorca **13**
Museu Fundación
  Juan March **4**
Palau de l'Almudaina **9**

Palma de Mallorca

Fundació Pilar i Joan Miró a Mallorca ★★★ ART MUSEUM   This magical studio-museum captures the vivid vision of one of Spain's greatest abstract artists: Joan Miró, who lived and worked here from 1956 until his death in 1983. His widow Pilar Juncosa donated a treasure trove of his paintings, drawings, and graphic works along with personal documents. Rotating exhibitions deal with his life and work in the beautiful building designed by Rafael Moneo. The walk to the former chapel turned sculpture studio is a study in harmony with nature.

Carrer Joan de Saridakis, 29. https://miromallorca.com. ✆ **97-170-14-20.** Admission 7.50€ adults, 4€ children and seniors; free to all Sat 3–6pm. Mid-May to mid-Sept Tues–Sat 10am–7pm, Sun 10am–3pm; rest of year Tues–Sat 10am–6pm, Sun 10am–3pm. Bus: 3, 46, 20.

677

Museu Fundación Juan March

Palma ★ ART MUSEUM   Small but select, this museum has 70 works of 20th-century Spanish art representing the first generation of the Spanish avant-garde—Picasso, Miró, Dalí, and Juan Gris—as well as mid-century Spanish painters such as Carlos Saura and Antoní Tápies. Temporary exhibitions show contemporary work by Spanish painters as well as representative work from the international avant-garde.

Carrer Sant Miquel, 11. www.march.es. ℰ **97-171-35-15.** Free admission. Mon–Fri 10am–6:30pm; Sat 10:30am–2pm.

Palau de l'Almudaina ★ PALACE   The former Alcázar Real was built first by Moorish rulers in 1281, then significantly modified by the kings of Arágon who held sway here over the next few centuries; they made this their royal residence when they came to Mallorca. Opposite the cathedral, it is surrounded by Moorish-style gardens and fountains. The palace museum displays antiques, artwork, suits of armor, and Gobelin tapestries. The grounds have panoramic views of the harbor.

The sculpture garden at Fundació Pilar i Joan Miró a Mallorca.

Carrer Palau Reial, s/n. www.patrimonionacional.es. ℰ **97-121-41-34.** Admission 7€ adults, 4€ seniors and ages 5–16. Apr–Sept Tues–Sun 10am–8pm; Oct–Mar Tues–Sun 10am–6pm. Bus: 15.

AN unspoiled MEDITERRANEAN ISLE

Declared a National Reserve in 1991, **Illa de Cabrera** ★★, lying off the south coast of Mallorca, is the largest of the 19 islands that form the Archipelago of Cabrera. With its lush vegetation, dramatic coastline, and abundant animal life, it makes for an intriguing day trip. Large colonies of birds and marine animals await visitors. In the 13th and 14th centuries, pirates used Cabrera as a base to attack Mallorca. Ruins of a castle built in the 14th century can be seen at the entrance to the port. **Excursions à Cabrera** (www.excursionsacabrera.es; ℰ **97-164-90-34**) operates several tours from Colonia de Sant Jordi, 47km (29 miles) southeast of Palma, from May through September. Tours last 3 to 6 hours and cost 35€–58€.

PALMA OUTDOORS

BEACHES   You can swim from late June to October; don't believe the promoters who try to sell you on mild Mallorcan winters in January and February—it gets downright cold. There is a beach near the Palma cathedral, but beaches outside the city center are more appealing. Some hotels have private beaches, but the closest public beach to downtown is **Playa Nova,** a 35-minute bus ride. If you head east, you reach the excellent beaches of **Ca'n Pastilla.** The golden-sand beaches at **El Arenal** are well equipped with tourist facilities. Going to the southwest, you find good but often crowded beaches at **Cala Mayor** and **Sant Agustí.**

GOLF   Mallorca is a golfer's dream. The best destination is **Arabella Golf Mallorca,** Urbanización Son Vida, about 13km (8 miles) east of Palma along the Andrade Highway (www.arabellagolfmallorca.com; ✆ 97-178-30-00). It offers four golf courses, including a 3-par pitch-and-putt for beginners (12€–24€). Greens fees are 27€ to 93€ for 9 holes, 45€ to 155€ for 18 holes. Cart rentals are available for 20€ to 45€. For more on Mallorca golf, contact **Federación Balear de Golf** (www.fbgolf.com; ✆ 97-172-27-53).

Sunbathing at Playa Nova.

WHERE TO STAY IN PALMA

Almost all lodging on Mallorca requires guests to take breakfast. Most strongly encourage half- or full board, which you can decline (it's rarely economical). Prices here reflect room with breakfast. Please note that Palma outlawed Airbnb effective July 2019.

Expensive

Sant Francesc Hotel Singular ★★★   Imagine yourself as lord of the manor at this 19th-century city palace transformed into a low-key luxury hotel. It's set in the heart of the old quarter within walking distance of all of central Palma's attractions. The rooftop terrace has spectacular views as well as a very nice swimming pool and service bar. The "well-being treatment rooms" offer a wide variety of massages and other treatments—minus the hydrotherapy usually associated with Spanish spas. Décor in the rooms is subdued—all white, tans, and warm browns—but appeals as much to the sense of touch as sight. Most "privilege" rooms and suites also feature a balcony or terrace.

Plaza Sant Francesc, 5. www.hotelsantfrancesc.com. ✆ **97-149-50-00.** 42 units. 195€–485€ double; 295€–639€ jr. suite; 475€–1024€ suite. **Amenities:** Bar, 2 restaurants, spa; free Wi-Fi.

Sheraton Mallorca Arabella Golf Hotel ★★   You don't come to this Sheraton to lounge about on the beach—the hotel doesn't even have a shuttle to the strand. You come to play the nearby golf courses at Arabella Golf Mallorca (p. 679), including Son Muntanera on the property. There's also a 9-hole pitch-and-putt. The hotel offers a shuttle to the others, all less than a mile away. Spacious rooms have good views of the beautifully landscaped grounds.

Carrer de la Vinagrella, s/n. www.sheratonmallorcagolfhotel.com. ✆ **800-325-3535** in the U.S., or **97-178-71-00.** 93 units. 169€–369€ double; 76€–465€ jr. suite. Free parking. Bus: 7. **Amenities:** 2 restaurants; bar; bikes; children's center; 3 18-hole golf courses, 1 9-hole course; 3 pools (1 indoor); spa; fitness center; sauna; 3 outdoor tennis courts (lit); Wi-Fi (free in lobby, 21€ in rooms, but negotiable).

Tres Mallorca ★★   Located in the midst of Palma's historic center, this superb boutique hotel is entered through the 16th-century mansion that forms its core. Some architectural touches from the original structure are retained, such as colonnaded balconies and a tile floor on the ground level. But guest rooms are modern and spacious, with a breezy contemporary design that features either hardwood or marble floors and airy furnishings that give every room a spa ambience. Two roof terraces, linked by a bridge, have excellent views of the city rooftops and the port.

Calle Apuntadores, 3. www.hoteltres.com. ✆ **97-171-73-33.** 41 rooms. 150€–263€ double; 175€–313€ jr. suite. **Amenities:** Restaurant; bar; outdoor pool; sauna; free Wi-Fi.

Moderate

Dalt Murada ★ Built into a 16th-century manor in Palma's old Gothic quarter, this hotel has splendid views of the cathedral from the roof terrace. The rooms feature a mix of parquet wood and tile floors, exposed wooden beams on the ceilings, and dark wood window frames. Rooms vary a lot in size, with some being quite small, so ask to see the room before moving in. The location is perfect for sightseeing, less ideal for lying on the beach. Breakfast is served beneath lemon trees on the central patio.

Calle Almudaina, 6A. www.daltmurada.com. ✆ **97-142-53-00.** 16 units. 70€–140€ double; 110€–207€ suite. Bus: 3 or 7. **Amenities:** Restaurant; bar; free Wi-Fi in business center.

Hotel Bon Sol ★ Family-owned and -operated, this charming four-story hotel with a vaguely Moorish tower sits up on a cliff above the sea in Illetas. A walkway of about 200 steps winds through mature landscaped gardens down to the small beach below. About two-thirds of the rooms are in the original hotel complex, built in a few stages in the 1950s; some larger rooms and suites are distributed among outlying villas. The family has gone to great lengths to evoke a medieval Moorish fantasy with antique furniture and decorative elements.

Paseo de Illetas, 30. www.hotelbonsol.es. ✆ **97-140-21-11.** 147 units. 198€–298€ double; 260€–395€ suite. Free parking. Bus: Take bus marked illetas. Closed Nov 6–Dec 20. **Amenities:** 2 restaurants; bar; children's center; exercise room; 2 pools; spa; 2 outdoor tennis courts (lit); free Wi-Fi.

WHERE TO EAT IN PALMA

Surprisingly for an island, Mallorca's most typical main dish is *lomo,* or pork loin. If you order *lomo con col,* the meat comes enveloped in cabbage leaves and topped with a sauce of tomatoes, grapes, pine nuts, and bay leaf. The local version of *sabrosada* sausage is made with pure pork and red peppers. *Sopas mallorquinas* typically consist of mixed greens in soup flavored with olive oil and thickened with bread. The best-known vegetable dish is *el tumbet,* or lasagna of potato and eggplant with tomato sauce.

Moderate

La Bodeguilla ★★ MALLORCAN/SPANISH Run by two brothers who really know their wines, this place is equal parts wine shop, tapas bar, and restaurant. Wine-barrel tables with glass tops are arrayed on two stories. Downstairs, where all the hams are hanging, is ostensibly the tapas bar, but you can also get tapas upstairs, and you can ask for the restaurant menu in the bar. Dishes are quite sophisticated for the casual nature of the place—a starter of egg poached in a foie gras *veloute,* for example. The selection of Catalan wines is particularly strong.

Carrer San Jaume, 3. www.la-bodeguilla.com. ✆ **97-171-82-74.** Tapas 5€–8€, entrees 14€–42€. Daily noon–midnight. Bus: 2, 3, 7, 15, 20, 25, 46.

NURU Restaurant ★★ MEDITERRANEAN/FUSION Jesús Pérez de la Fuente—aka "Chus"—was born in the Santa Catalina neighborhood and felt he owed it to his barrio to lighten things up with a smart restaurant and bar. He hit the mark—NURU has become a convivial spot to see and be seen, with just 60 seats distributed between two levels and an outside terrace, and Santa Catalina has since taken off as Palma's hottest neighborhood. Chus's dishes balance fresh Mediterranean ingredients with Asian accents. Expect miso honey-roasted eggplant, for example, or dumplings filled with Peking duck and foie gras. He also serves dishes he attributes to his mother, such as Irish beef tenderloin with asparagus.

Carrer d'Anníbal, 11. www.nuru.restaurant. © **871-964-931.** Entrees 18€–29€; set lunch menu 13€–16€. Mon 7–11pm, Tues–Sat 1–3:30pm and 7–11pm. Bus: 3, 5, 44, 46.

Inexpensive

Tast Unión ★★ MALLORCAN You'll have to use your elbows to get in at meal time, but Tast Unión welcomes drinkers and diners at all hours. Like its sister tapas bar **Tast Avenidas** (Av. Comte de Sallent, 11; © **97-110-15-40**), it specializes in creative tapas, crafted by executive chef Patxi Castellano, that use seasonal produce and the catch of the day. His version of squid stuffed with *gulas* (imitation baby eels) and *sabrosada* was a big winner at the national Spanish tapas competition. The meltingly soft pan-fried duck liver is also popular. Don't worry if you can't get to the bar; tapas are also passed on trays, with plates color-coded to indicate the price.

Carrer Unión, 2. www.tast.com. © **97-172-98-78.** Tapas 3€–7€; entrees 12€–25€. Mon–Sat 12:30pm–midnight. Bus: 3, 7, 20, 46.

PALMA AFTER DARK

The island's northern tier has some clubs, but for a laser- and strobe-lit club, boogie in Palma, which is packed with bars and dance clubs. Right on the beach near lots of hotels, **Tito's,** Passeig Marítim (www.titosmallorca.com; © **97-173-00-17**), is the island's most popular disco, frequented by an international crowd. Tito's charges a cover of 18€ to 20€, including the first drink. Between June and September, it's open nightly 11pm to 6am; the rest of the year Thursday to Sunday 11pm to 6am. Palma's best beer hall is **Lórien,** Carrer de les Caputxines, 5 (© **97-172-32-02**), with 100 selections from two dozen countries.

Luckia Casino Mallorca lies on the harborfront promenade at Av. Gabriel Roca, 4 (www.casinodemallorca.com; © **97-113-00-00**). You'll need a passport (plus a shirt and tie for men) to enter and play table games or slots. The slot parlor is open daily 10am to 4am, the gaming tables 5pm to 4am. Entry is 8€.

Mallorca's West Coast

Mountainous Mallorca's dramatic scenery is best appreciated by driving. This daylong circuit of 142km (88 miles) begins and ends in Palma.

Deià, one of several charming towns on Mallorca's west coast.

As you leave Palma heading west on C-719, the Sierra de Tramuntana rises just a short distance from the sea. The road passes Palma Nova before coming to **Santa Ponça,** a town with a fishing harbor divided by a promontory. A fortified Gothic tower and a watchtower are evidence of the days when this small harbor suffered repeated raids and attacks. Jaume I's troops landed in a cove here on September 12, 1229, to begin the reconquest of the island from the Moors.

From Santa Ponça, continue along the highway, passing Paguera, Cala Fornells, and Camp de Mar, all beautiful spots with sandy coves. From Camp de Mar twisting, cliff-top roads lead to **Port D'Andratx.** Summer vacationers mingle with fishermen in this natural port set against a backdrop of pines. The place was once a haven for smugglers.

Continue northeast another 5km (3 miles) along C-719 to reach one of the loveliest towns on the island, **Andratx,** 31km (19 miles) west of Palma. Frequent raids by Turkish pirates forced this town to move inland. It's surrounded by fortifications and boasts a Gothic parish church.

From Andratx, take C-710 north, a winding road parallel to the island's jagged northwestern coast. Most of the road is perched along the cliff edge and shaded by pine trees. It's hard to drive and pay attention to the scenery, so stop at the **Mirador Ricardo Roca** for a panoramic view of a series of coves that can be reached only from the sea. The road continues to **Estallenchs,** a town of steep slopes surrounded by pine groves, olive and almond trees, and fruit orchards (especially apricot). Estallenchs sits at the foot of the Galatzo mountain peak. Stop to explore some of its steep, winding streets on foot. From the town, you can walk to Cala de Estallenchs cove, where a spring cascades down the high cliffs.

The road winds on northeast 8km (5 miles) to **Bañalbufar** (if you drive directly northwest from Palma it's about 26km/16 miles). Set 100m (328 ft.) above sea level, it seems to perch directly over the sea. **Mirador de Ses Animes ★,** a belvedere constructed in the 17th century, offers a panoramic coastal view. Many small excursions are possible from here. You might want to venture north to **Port d'es Canonge,** reached by a road branching out from the C-710 northeast from Bañalbufar. It has a beach, a simple restaurant, and some old fishermen's houses. The same road takes you inland to **La Granja** (www.lagranja.net/en/), a mansion originally constructed by the Cistercians as a monastery in the 13th century.

Back on C-710, continue to **Valldemossa,** the town where composer Frédéric Chopin and French novelist George Sand spent a now-famous winter (see also p. 685). Beyond Valldemossa, the road runs along cliffs some 395m (1,300 ft.) high until it reaches **Son Marroig,** the former residence of Archduke Lluis Salvador, who erected a small neoclassical temple on a slope overlooking the sea to give visitors a panoramic vista. From a balcony, you can enjoy a view of the famous pierced rock, the Foradada, rising out of the water. Inland a short distance lies **Deià,** the home of English writer Robert Graves for many years (see p. 686).

As you continue north along the highway, you come first to **Lluch Alcari,** a settlement that was once the victim of pirate raids. You can see the ruins of several defense towers. C-710 continues to **Sóller,** 10km (6¼ miles) past Deià, lying in a broad basin with abundant citrus and olive trees. Many painters, including Rusiñol, settled here and found inspiration. The historic center has no fewer than five 16th-century facades, an 18th-century convent, and a parish church of the 16th and 17th centuries. Travel 5km (3 miles) north on C-711 to reach the coast and **Port de Sóller,** perched on a sheltered round bay. A submarine base is here today, but it is also a harbor for pleasure craft and has a lovely beach. The **Sanctuary of Santa Catalina** has one of the best views of the inlet.

After leaving the Sóller area, you face a choice: If you've run out of time, you can head back along C-711 to Palma with two stops along the way (see below). Your other option is to continue north, following the C-710 and local roads, to **Cap de Formentor,** where even more spectacular scenery awaits you. Among the highlights of this coastal detour: **Fornalutx,** a lofty mountain village with steep cobbled streets, Moorish-tiled roofs, and groves of almond trees; the splendid, hair-raising road to the harbor village of **Sa Calobra,** plunging to the sea in one area and then climbing arduously past olive groves, oaks, and jagged boulders in another area; and the 13th-century **Monasterio de Lluch,** some 45km (28 miles)

Take the Train

Take the train from Palma to Sóller and everyone in your party can watch the scenery instead of watching the road. It's fun to ride Tren de Sóller's turn-of-the-20th-century narrow-gauge railroad. You can catch the train at the Palma Terminal on Calle Eusebio Estada, near Plaça d'Espanya. It runs daily April to October from 10:10am to 7:40pm (Nov–Mar 10:30am–6pm), also stopping at Mirador Del Pujol d'en Banya. The ticket costs 18€ one-way, 25€ round-trip. Tickets must be purchased in cash on day of travel (no credit cards). Visit www.trendesoller.com or call ℭ **97-175-20-51** for information.

north of Palma, which is home to the Black Virgin of Lluch, the island's patron saint. The well-known "boys' choir of white voices" sings there daily at noon and again at twilight.

Those not taking the coastal detour can head south along C-711 with a stop at **Jardines de Alfàbia,** Carretera Palma–Sóller Km 17 (www. jardinesdealfabia.com; ☏ **97-161-31-23**). This foothills estate, a former Muslim residence, includes a palace and romantic gardens where you can wander among pergolas, a pavilion, and ponds. In the palace you'll find a collection of Mallorcan furniture and an Arabic coffered ceiling. The gardens are open April to October daily 9:30am to 6:30pm, March Monday to Friday 9:30am to 5:30pm and Saturday 9:30am to 1pm; closed November through February. Admission is 7.50€.

From Alfàbia, the highway heads straight toward Palma, just 18km (11 miles) away. But before reaching the capital, consider a final stop at **Raixa,** a manorial estate and gardens owned by the island government and open to the public by guided tour (reserve at least 1 week in advance at https://raixa.conselldemallorca.cat; ☏ **97-123-76-36**). Built on the site of an old Muslim hamlet, it stands 1.5km (1 mile) outside the village of Buñola ("Small Vineyard"). The present building was once the estate of Cardinal Despuif and his family, who constructed it in the Italian style near the end of the 1700s; the artist Rusiñol came here, painting the place several times. Ruins from Roman excavations are found on the grounds. After Raixa, the route leads directly to the northern outskirts of Palma.

WHERE TO STAY & EAT IN PORT DE SÓLLER

Jumerirah Port Sóller ★★★ The clifftop location above the Port and the Cap Gros lighthouse gives the Jumeirah a bird's-eye perspective on one of the most dramatic spots on an already dramatic coast. Light floods into the hotel, though truthfully, you'll want to spend as many hours as possible on the outdoor terraces. Spacious rooms are decorated with clean lines, wooden accent pieces, and sumptuous monochromatic upholstery. All rooms have balconies with striking views, of either mountains or the sea. All rates include breakfast.

Calle Belgica, s/n, Port de Sóller. www.jumeirah.com. ☏ **97-163-78-88.** 121 units. 323€–821€ double; 464€–625€ jr. suite; 1,020€–2,754€ suite. Free parking. Closed Nov–Mar. **Amenities:** 3 restaurants; 2 bars; spa; 3 outdoor pools; free shuttle to port; free Wi-Fi.

Valldemossa & Deià ★★

Even if you choose not to do the entire coastal drive outlined above, you may want to make an excursion from Palma to these two historic towns. The graceful market town of Valldemossa is the site of the **Cartoixa Reial,** a royal residence turned Carthusian monastery. French writer George Sand and the tubercular composer Frédéric Chopin notoriously spent the winter of 1838-1839 here in **Cell 4 ★★**, Plaça de las Cartujas, s/n (www.celdadechopin.es; ☏ **696-405-992**). Shocked locals, fearing

A courtyard of the Cartoixa Reial in Valldemossa.

they would catch Chopin's tuberculosis, burned all but a small painting and a French piano after the couple left. But the cell preserves a sense of their presence with a few personal belongings and a great sense of how they heated their quarters with braziers and where they placed temporary walls for privacy from her children. The view across the gardens is remarkably romantic. Visits are available April through October Monday to Saturday 10am to 6pm, Sunday 10am to 2pm; February, March, and November Monday to Saturday 10am to 4:30pm; December through January Monday to Saturday 10am to 3:30pm. Admission is 4€ adults, 2€ under age 10. *Tip:* Buy tickets carefully, as there is a separate tour of the monastery does not include Cell 4.

After a visit to the Cartoixa Reial, wander the steep streets of Valldemossa's Old Town. The cloister of **Ses Murteres** has a romantic garden, and there's a late-18th-century **Carthusian church** where Goya's father-in-law, Bayeu, painted the dome's frescoes.

From Valldemossa, continue through the mountains, following signposts for 11km (6¾ miles) to **Deià.** Set against a backdrop of olive-green mountains, Deià is peaceful and serene, with stone houses and creeping bougainvillea. Small tile altars in the streets reproduce the traditional Christian Stations of the Cross. This town has long had a special meaning for artists. Robert Graves, the English poet and novelist *(I, Claudius),* lived in Deià and died here in 1985. He is buried in the local cemetery, **Campo Santo.**

You can visit Graves's home, **Ca N'Alluny** ★★, Carretera de Soller Km 1 (www.lacasaderobertgraves.com; ✆ **97-163-61-85**), a 5-minute walk from the center of town. Graves and his lover, poet Laura Riding, built the house in 1932. She directed much of the striking design, which remains as she envisioned it. Graves wrote: "I wanted to go where town was still town; and country, country." The couple fled in 1936, when Nationalist forces took over the Balearics at the beginning of the Spanish Civil War. The house has been restored to circa 1946, when Graves returned to the island. Visitors can see Graves' and Riding's studies, as well as the kitchen and dining room. It's open April to October, Monday to Friday 10am to 5pm and Saturday 10am to 3pm; November to April hours are Monday to Friday 9am to 4pm and Saturday 9am to 2pm (mid-Dec to mid-Jan 10:30am–1:30pm). Admission is 7€ adults, 5€ students and seniors, 3.50€ under age 12.

Bus Nort Balear (✆ **97-149-06-80**) goes to Valldemossa from Palma 13 times daily for a one-way fare of 4€, then continues on to Deià (6€). Buses leave Palma at Plaza España (Calle Eusebio Estrada). If you're driving from Palma, take the Carretera Valldemossa–Deià to Valldemossa and continue to Deià.

WHERE TO STAY & EAT IN DEIA

Hoposa Costa d'Or ★   Designed to blend into the landscape, this adults-only (14+) luxury hotel sits in a pine grove on a hill above the rugged coast on the road to Sóller, about 1.5km (1 mile) north of Deià. The gardens are filled with citrus trees, date palms, and gnarled old fig trees. A pathway leads through the forest down to a private and secluded cove beach. Rooms are simply furnished with comfortable beds, luxe linens, and marble bathrooms.

Carrer Lluch Alcari, s/n. www.hoposa.es. ✆ **97-163-90-25.** 41 rooms. 170€–232€ double; 282€–354€ suite. Free parking. Closed late Oct–Mar. **Amenities:** Restaurant; bar; bikes; exercise room; 2 pools (1 indoor); 2 outdoor tennis courts (lit); free Wi-Fi.

El Olivo ★★ CONTEMPORARY SPANISH   The rather rustic nature of the building—a former olive oil mill with stone walls and wicker furniture—belies the sophistication of the contemporary Spanish cuisine here. Chef Guillermo Méndez tends to gild the lily, serving such dishes as sweet Sóller prawns sautéed with pancetta and topped with a purée of Jabugo ham and celery. Even vegetarians can get the full treatment with a house classic of "carpaccio" of zucchini with goat cheese and basil vinaigrette.

Belmond La Residencia Hotel, Son Canals. s/n, Deià. www.hotel-laresidencia.com. ✆ **97-163-93-92.** Entrees 34€–46€; tasting menus 128€–150€. Summer daily 7:30–11pm, winter Wed–Sun 7:30–10:30pm. Closed Dec–Feb.

Es Racò d'es Teix ★★ MEDITERRANEAN   You're likely to get your best meal on the island at this delightful Michelin-starred and family-run restaurant in an old stone house with spectacular views of the mountains. The rather rustic dining room has tables on two levels. Chef Josef Sauerschell is an inventive sort who makes the most of local products, offering dishes like lobster ravioli with white peaches or slow-cooked suckling pig stuffed with spicy *sabrosada* sausage and glazed with honey. Make reservations as far in advance as possible.

Carrer de sa Vinya Veia, 6, Deià. www.esracodesteix.es. ⓒ **97-163-95-01.** Entrees 35€–40€, tasting menus 78€–164€. Reservations essential. Wed–Sun 1–3pm and 8–11pm. Closed mid-Nov to mid-Feb.

Port de Pollença & the Northwest Coast ★

Beside a sheltered bay between Cap de Formentor to the north and Cap del Pinar to the south lies **Port de Pollença,** 65km (40 miles) north of Palma. The town is flanked by two hills: **Calvary** to the west and **Puig** to the east. Calvary Chapel offers the best views of the resort and the bay. Low-rise hotels, private homes, restaurants, and snack bars line the very attractive beach, which, though narrow at its northwestern end, has some of the island's whitest sand and clearest water. Windsurfing, water-skiing,

Cap de Formentor.

and scuba diving are among the watersports offered in the area. Wednesday is **market day** in Port de Pollença—head for the town square between 8am and 1pm to browse through fresh produce, leather goods, embroidered tablecloths, ceramics, and more. Bargaining is part of the fun.

Sunday is market day in the town of **Pollença,** which is about 6km (3¾ miles) inland from Port de Pollença. Here, an 18th-century stairway, known as the **Monte Calvario (Calvary),** leads 365 steps up to a hermitage. (You can also reach the top by car via Carrer de las Cruces, which is lined with 3m-high/9¾-ft. concrete crosses.) Between Pollença and Port de Pollença, you can branch off on route 2203 to **Cala San Vicente,** a pleasant, sandy cove with notable surf and several small hotels and restaurants.

Heading northwest along the coast from Port de Pollença, the **Mirador de Colomer** provides an expansive view of the California-like coast from Punta de la Nau to Punta de la Troneta and includes El Colomer (Pigeon's Rock). But the island's most intoxicating views are on the 20km (12-mile) stretch of winding, at times vertiginous, road from Port de Pollença to the tip of **Cap de Formentor ★**, "the devil's tail." Cliffs rise more than 200m (656 ft.) high and rock-rimmed coves embrace turquoise waters. About halfway along this road, **Cala de Pi de la Posada** has a lovely bathing beach. Continuing on to the end, you'll come to the lighthouse at **Cap de Formentor.**

South of Port de Pollença about 11km (7 miles), you'll reach a long stretch of narrow, sandy beach along **Alcúdia Bay,** which is backed by countless hotels, whose crowds can overwhelm the area in peak season. The nightlife here is more abundant than in Port de Pollença. Between Port de Alcúdia and Ca'n Picafort, nature enthusiasts will enjoy the 800-hectare (1,977-acre) **Parc Natural de S'Albufereta,** Carretera Alcúdia–Artá Km 27 (en.balearsnatura.com; ✆ **97-189-22-50**), a wetlands area of lagoons, dunes, and canals where more than 200 species of birds have been sighted, with the largest numbers during spring and fall migrations. The park is open daily October to March from 9am to 5pm and April to September from 9am to 6pm. Entry is free, but you must get a permit at the reception center. No motor vehicles are allowed within the reserve.

Five **buses** a day from Palma's Plaça Espanya go to Port de Pollença; a one-way fare costs 9€–11€. If you're driving from Deià (p. 685), follow C-710 all the way to Pollença. Port de Pollenca's **tourist information office,** on Carrer Joan XXIII, 19 (www.ajpollenca.net; ✆ **97-186-54-67**), is open summer Monday to Friday 9am to 8pm, Saturday 9am to 4pm; winter Monday to Friday 8am to 11am and 11:30am to 3pm.

WHERE TO EAT & STAY IN PORT DE POLLENÇA

Stay Restaurant ★ MALLORCAN   A mainstay on the waterfront since the 1970s, Stay was rebuilt from scratch in 2006 to provide a great

Parque Natural de S'Albufera lies south of Port de Pollença on Mallorca's northwest coast.

harbor experience. Sure, the dining room has panoramic views, but the huge terrace all but puts you in the yachts anchored in the marina. Seafood dishes are plentiful and uniformly excellent, ranging from fillet of John Dory with caramelized onions to a mixed grill of whatever the fishermen bring in. The best meat dish is roasted leg of Mallorcan lamb.

Muelle Nuevo, Estació Marítim, s/n. www.stayrestaurant.com. ⓒ **97-186-40-13.** Entrees 19€–41€, set menu 38€. Daily noon–4pm and 7:30–10:30pm.

Son Brull ★★★ Probably the best residence in the area for gastronomes, this former 17th-century monastery was transformed into an ultrachic contemporary hotel without losing sight of its rustic roots. Although it's at least a 10-minute drive to the beach, the hillside country setting has its own appeal. The hotel offers cooking classes and dish tastings with chef Rafel Perello at the gastronomic restaurant 3/65, which has prix-fixe menus at 55€ and 77€ and a tasting menu at 108€.

Carretera Palma-Pollença s/n. www.sonbrull.com. ⓒ **97-153-53-53.** 23 units. 321€–593€ double; 422€–1,210€ jr. suite. Free parking. Closed Dec–Mar. **Amenities:** Restaurant; bar; bikes; 2 pools (1 indoor); spa; outdoor tennis court; free Wi-Fi.

Mallorca's East Coast: The Cueva Route ★

Less dramatic than the west coast, Mallorca's east coast is studded with caves and is often called the *cueva* (cave) route. Leave Palma on the freeway but turn onto Carretera C-715 in the direction of Manacor. About 56km (35 miles) east of Palma, you come to your first stop, Petra.

PETRA

At Petra, which was founded by Jaume II on the ruins of a Roman settlement, a statue commemorates native son Junípero Serra (1713–84), the Franciscan who founded California's San Diego, Monterey, and San Francisco missions. A walking tour of local history and Serra sites is on the town tourism website, www.visitpetramallorca.com/en.

CUEVAS DEL DRACH ★★★

After Petra, follow C-715 southeast 11km (7 miles) into Manacor, then take the road east 12km (7½ miles) toward the town of **Porto Cristo.** Go 0.8km (½ mile) south of town to **Cuevas del Drach (Caves of the Dragon;** www.cuevasdeldrach.com; ✆ **97-182-07-53**). The caves contain a forest of stalactites and stalagmites, as well as five lakes, where you can listen to a concert and later go boating. Martel Lake, 176m (577 ft.) long, is the world's largest underground lake. From mid-March through October, tours depart daily every hour (except 1pm) from 10am to 5pm; from November to mid-March, they depart daily at 10:45am, noon, 2, and 3:30pm. Admission is 15.50€ adults, 8.50€ ages 3 to 12. If you don't have a car, daily buses from Palma to Porto Cristo take roughly 2 hours.

Cuevas del Drach.

CUEVAS DE ARTÀ ★★★

Near Platja de Canyamel (Playa de Cañamel, on some maps), **Cuevas de Artà** (https://cuevasdearta.com; ✆ **97-184-12-93**) are said to have inspired Jules Verne's 1864 novel *Journey to the Center of the Earth.* Formed by seawater erosion, the caves are about 32m (105 ft.) above sea level, and some chambers rise about 46m (151 ft.). You enter a vestibule where torch smoke has blackened the walls. The Reina de las Columnas (Queen of the Columns) rises about 22m (72 ft.) and is followed by a lower room called the "Inferno" for its Dante-esque appearance. It is followed by a field of stalagmites and stalactites (the "Purgatory Rooms"), which eventually lead to the "Theater" and "Paradise." The caves were once used by pirates and provided a haven for Moors fleeing the persecution of Jaume I. The stairs in the cave were built for Isabel II for her 1860 visit. Tours depart daily July through September 10am to 7pm; April to June and October every hour from 10am to 6pm; November through March 10am to 5pm. Admission is 15€ adults, 7€ ages 7 to 12.

IBIZA ★★

Ibiza began to thrive as an art colony in the 1950s and became popular with hippies in the 1960s. Today, it attracts northern European package tourists, ravers, and many gay travelers. At 585 sq. km (226 sq. miles), Ibiza is the third largest of the Balearic Islands, with a jagged coastline, some fine beaches, whitewashed houses, secluded bays, cliffs, and hilly terrain dotted with fig and olive trees. Warmer than Mallorca, it's a better choice for winter, but swelters in July and August.

Ciudad de Ibiza boasts **Playa Talamanca** in the north and the white sandy beaches of **Ses Figueretes** and **Playa d'en Bossa** in the south. **Las Salinas,** in the south, near the old salt flats, offers excellent sands. **Playa Cavallet** and **Aigües Blanques** attract nude sunbathers. The long sandy cove of **Cala Llonga,** south of Santa Eulalia del Río, and the white sandy beach of **El Cana** to the north are sacred to Ibiza's sun worshipers. Set against a backdrop of pines and dunes, the pure white sand of **Es Pujols** makes it Ibiza's most popular beach.

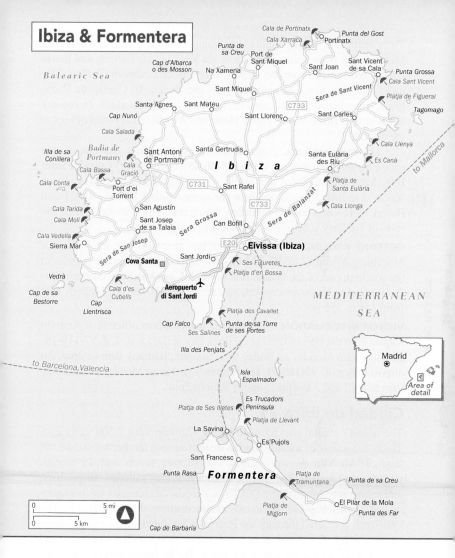

Ibiza & Formentera

Balearic Sea

Cala de Portinatx
Cala Xarraca
Punta del Gost
Portinatx
Punta de sa Creu
Port de Sant Miquel
Cap d'Albarca o des Mosson
Na Xamena
Sant Joan
Sant Vicent de sa Cala
Punta Grossa
Cala Sant Vicent
Sant Miquel
Sera de Sant Vicent
Platja de Figueral
Santa Agnès
Sant Mateu
C733
Sant Carles
Tagomago
Cap Nunó
Sant Llorenç
Cala Salada
Illa de sa Conillera
Badia de Portmany
Sant Antoni de Portmany
Santa Gertrudis
Cala Llenya
Santa Eulària des Riu
Es Canà
Cala Gració
Ibiza
Cala Bassa
Cala Conta
Port d'ei Torrent
C731
Sant Rafel
Platja de Santa Eulària
San Agustín
C733
Cala Tarida
Sant Josep de sa Talaia
Can Bofill
Sera de Balanzat
Cala Llonga
Sera Grossa
Cala Molí
Cala Vedella
Sierra Mar
E20
Eivissa (Ibiza)
Sera de San Josep
Sant Jordi
Vedrà
Cova Santa
Ses Figueretes
Platja d'en Bossa
Cap de sa Bestorre
Cala d'es Cubells
Aeropuerto di Sant Jordi
MEDITERRANEAN
Cap Llentrisca
Platja des Cavallet
SEA
Cap Falco
Punta de sa Torre de ses Portes
Ses Salines
Illa des Penjats
to Barcelona, Valencia
Isla Espalmador
Madrid
Area of detail
Es Trucadors Peninsula
Platja de Ses Illetes
Platja de Llevant
La Savina
Es Pujols
Sant Francesc
Punta Rasa
Formentera
Platja de Tramuntana
Punta de sa Creu
Platja de Migjorn
El Pilar de la Mola
Punta des Far
Cap de Barbaria

0 ___ 5 mi
0 ___ 5 km

Both soft drugs and hard sex are available, but there are dangers. Visitors can be deported for engaging in drunk and disorderly conduct; as a result, some young travelers have forsaken Ibiza for the more relaxed atmosphere of tiny Formentera (p. 701).

Ibiza Essentials

ARRIVING   As with Palma, if you come in July and August, be sure you have a return ticket and a reservation. Nine different airlines serve **Ibiza International Airport** (www.aena.es; ✆ **90-240-47-04**), 5.5km (3½ miles) from Ciudad de Ibiza. Several daily flights connect Ibiza with Palma.

There are at least 4 daily flights from Valencia and at least 5 from Madrid. Main service from points in Spain is via Vueling, Air Europa, and Iberia (as Air Nostrum). From the airport, **bus** service covers the 5.5km (3½-mile) ride into town. Sometimes taxis are shared. In Ciudad de Ibiza, buses leave hourly for the airport from Av. Isidor Macabich 24 (by the ticket kiosk), from 7am to 11pm. Hertz and Avis have car rental offices at the airport.

Trasmediterránea, Estación Marítima, Andenes del Puerto, s/n (www.trasmediterranea.es; © **90-245-46-45**), operates **ferry service** from Barcelona several times per week; a one-way ticket costs 41€. From Valencia to Ibiza, there's one boat per week, costing 14€ one-way. From Palma, there's one boat on Saturday, which costs 28€ one-way. Check the website for ferry schedules. It's easiest to book online.

GETTING AROUND The two main bus terminals are at Av. Isidor Macabich, 20 and 42 (© **97-134-05-10**). Mopeds and bikes are popular in the southern part of the island; rent through **Casa Valentín,** corner of Av. B. V. Ramón, 19 (www.casavalentin.es; © **97-131-08-22**). Mopeds cost from 25€ to 35€ per day.

VISITOR INFORMATION The **tourist information office** is at Antonio Riquer 2, in the port of Ciudad de Ibiza (www.ibiza.travel; © **97-119-19-51**). It's open Monday to Friday 9am to 6pm, Saturday 9am to 2pm. An airport office (© **97-180-91-18**) is open year-round Monday to Saturday 9am to 2pm and 3 to 8pm, Sunday 9am to 2pm.

Ciudad de Ibiza ★★

The island's capital was founded by the Carthaginians 2,500 years ago. Today it consists of a lively marina district around the harbor and an old town, **D'Alt Vila ★**, with narrow cobblestone streets and flat-roofed, whitewashed houses. The marina district is full of galleries, shops, bars, and restaurants. Much of the Old Town's medieval character has been preserved, with many Gothic-styled houses opening onto courtyards. The Old Town is entered through the Puerta de las Tablas, flanked by Roman statues. Plaça Desamparadors, crowded with open-air restaurants and market stalls, lies at the top of the town. Traffic leaves town through the Portal Nou. While Ibiza is primarily a beach destination, one attraction is worth visiting.

Museo Monográfico y Necrópolis Púnica de Puig des Molins ★
MUSEUM The old archaeology museum in the center of town has closed, but this new facility at an excavation site just outside the city walls houses all its artifacts. Most objects on display came from burials on Ibiza and Formentara and date back to prehistoric Iberian settlements. You'll see substantial collections of terra-cotta figurines from Punic (i.e., Carthaginian) burials, Roman artifacts, Muslim graves, and finally 14th- to 16th-century ceramics associated with Christian burials. Outside the

Ibiza's D'Alt Vila.

museum building, visitors can wander in the Punic necropolis, even entering one tomb with re-created but realistic human remains.

Carrer Via Romana, 31. ℂ **97-130-17-71.** Admission 2.40€ adults, 1.20€ students. Apr–Sept Tues–Sat 10am–2pm and 6:30–9pm, Sun 10am–2pm; Oct–Mar Tues–Sat 9:30am–3pm, Sun 10am–2pm.

BEACHES IN CIUDAD DE IBIZA

The most popular and crowded beaches near Ciudad de Ibiza are **Playa Talamanca** in the north and **Ses Figueretes** (also called Playa Figueretes) in the south. Don't be surprised to find a lot of nudity. The best beaches are connected to the city center by boats and buses; more remote ones are accessed by car or private boat. Another popular beach, **Playa d'en Bossa,** lies to the south.

To avoid crowds near Ciudad de Ibiza, continue past Playa d'en Bossa to **Las Salinas,** near the old salt flats farther south. Here, beaches include **Playa Cavallet,** one of the officially designated nudist strands.

WHERE TO STAY IN CIUDAD DE IBIZA

Cénit ★   These gay-friendly budget rooms and apartments perch on a hillside about a 10-minute walk to the beach (and a 20-min. walk *from* the beach). Floors are staggered so each room has a terrace, most on top of

Ses Figueretes beach, just south of Ibiza town.

another room. Studio and 2-bedroom apartments book up fast, but single rooms are also available. All accommodations are small, but the beds are comfortable, and you didn't come to Ibiza to stay in your room.

Carrer Archiduque Lluis Salvador, s/n. www.ibiza-spotlight.com/cenit. ✆ **97-130-14-04.** 63 units plus 55 apartments. 90€–196€ double, 118€–195€ apt. No parking. Closed mid-Oct to Apr. **Amenities:** Outdoor pool; Wi-Fi 15€.

Hotel La Ventana ★   If you want to be in the heart of the D'Alt Vila to soak up medieval history on the days you nurse your sunburn, it's hard to beat this quirky, colorful hotel in a four-level townhouse with great sunrise views. Curio cabinets full of knick-knacks, pastel walls, and winding staircases give the whole place a lot of distinctive charm. Breakfast is offered, and many cafes and bars line the surrounding streets heading toward the harbor. Most rooms have king-size four-poster beds and rather basic tile bathrooms or showers. Ask for a balcony room to get the best city views.

Sa Carrossa, 13. www.laventanaibiza.com. ✆ **97-139-08-57.** 13 units. 80€–170€. No parking. **Amenities:** Bar; terrace; free Wi-Fi.

El Pachá ★★   An Ibiza clubbers' legend, El Pachá sits close to the marina, and it channels an international party style. Rooms are spacious, and suites are huge. El Pachá affects a mostly white decor and Philippe Starck style, where the only noticeable color is the tan (or burn) on the guests. Glitterati without a friend's villa stay here when they visit Ibiza. One perk is guaranteed access to the Pachá Ibiza Club.

Paseo Marítimo, s/n. www.elhotelpacha.com. ⓒ **97-131-59-63.** 55 units. 120€–325€ double; 450€–950€ suite. **Amenities:** Restaurant; bar; bikes; outdoor pool; free Wi-Fi.

WHERE TO EAT IN CIUDAD DE IBIZA

Fresh fish has always been the mainstay of the local diet, though pork is equally important. Some islanders feed figs to the pigs to sweeten the meat. The most famous dessert is *flaó,* akin to American cheesecake but flavored with mint and anise. *Greixonera* is a spiced pudding, and *maccarrones de San Juan* is cinnamon- and lemon-flavored milk baked with cheese. Restaurant prices drop but quality rises the farther you get from the harbor.

El Zaguan ★ MALLORCAN   Friendly and relaxed, this tapas joint has a repertoire of more than 400 small plates. Of course, they change daily, depending on what's in season and what was landed at the fish dock. It's a good place for parties where one eater might be more adventurous than another, as the variety ranges from simple grilled fish to elaborate stews with exotic ingredients. You can always count on grilled dorada (sea bream) or the pork tenderloin with dates and bacon.

Av Bartolomé Roselló, 15. http://www.elzaguan.es. ⓒ **97-119-28-82.** Tapas and raciones 6€–18€. Daily 12:30pm–12:30am summer, 12:30–11:30pm winter.

Sa Brisa Gastro Bar ★★ INTERNATIONAL   With two outdoor terraces and a big open kitchen, this eclectic restaurant serves a wide range of international street food, from Japanese hamachi sushi to Mexican street cart tacos to Lebanese falafel. Plates are meant to be shared over drinks tapas-style. One favorite dish is a duo of sliders—one from Wagyu beef, the other from Iberian pork cheeks.

Passeig Vara de Rey, 15. www.sabrisagastrobar.com. ⓒ **97-109-06-49.** Tapas and raciones 8€–22€, tasting menu 45€. Daily 1pm–midnight.

SHOPPING

Ibiza developed its nonconformist style in the 1960s by combining elements of traditional local attire with more relaxed hippie garb. In recent years, Ibizan designs have become much more sophisticated and complex, but the individualistic spirit has not wavered. **Lovy Ibiza,** Plaça de la Vila, 2 (ⓒ **97-131-76-02**), sells high-quality leather goods made by local artisans. One-of-a-kind accessories, including bejeweled belts and leather bags, are designed for individual clients. **Campos de Ibiza,** Vincente Cuervo, 13 (ⓒ **97-193-42-89**), sells island-inspired candles, fragrances, and lotions along with beach accessories.

CIUDAD DE IBIZA AFTER DARK

El Divino, Puerto Ibiza Nueva (www.eldivino-ibiza.com; ℂ **97-131-83-38**), is the most beautiful disco on Ibiza. Open daily in summer only, it prides itself on attracting supermodels and other celebs. The club is open midnight to 6am. Cover ranges from 25€ to 50€. **Pachá,** Av. 8 de Agosto, s/n (https://pacha.com; ℂ **97-193-21-30**), one of Ibiza's oldest discos, still has its groove on. Three bar areas and dance floors, open only in the summer, attract the young and not-so-young, the bored, and the jaded. Overheated dancers cool off in a pool. Cover is 40€ to 60€. Opposite Pachá, everyone from supermodels to soccer stars floods into the **Bombay Lounge,** Av. 8 Agosto, 23 (www.bombay-lounge.com; ℂ **97-193-12-37**), the top cocktail lounge in the city. Drink *caipirinhas* to a soundtrack of jazz, soul, and house. Light bites as well as burgers and fries are served until 2:30am. The club opens at 10pm, but the A-list comes after midnight. No cover.

The modern **Casino de Ibiza,** Paseo Juan Carlos I (www.casinoibiza.com; ℂ **97-131-33-12**), has gaming tables and slot machines; it's open nightly 6pm to 6am. Within the casino, the **Heart** bar and restaurant is a unique collaboration with cuisine by Albert and Ferran Adrià and entertainment by Cirque du Soleil. Casino entrance is 6€. A passport is required for admission and you must be 18 or older.

The Northern Coast ★

Except for a few coves with good swimming—**Portinatx,** at the very northern tip, and **Port de Sant Miquel,** north of the small town of Sant Miquel—the north of Ibiza is less traveled by tourists. You'll find some of the island's prettiest countryside, with fields of olive, almond, and carob trees and the occasional *finca* raising melons or grapes.

EXPLORING IBIZA'S NORTHERN COAST

Off the road leading into Port de Sant Miquel (Puerto de San Miguel) is **Cova de Can Marçà** (www.covadecanmarsa.com; ℂ **97-133-47-76**). After a stunning descent down stairs clinging to the cliff's face, you enter a cave that's more than 100,000 years old and forms its stalactites and stalagmites at the rate of about 0.6cm (¼ in.) per 100 years. Once a favored hiding place for smugglers and their goods, it's now a smartly orchestrated surrealistic experience—including a sound-and-light display. The 40-minute tour, offered 10:30am to 7:30pm, is conducted in several languages for groups of up to 70. The cave is open from May to October; admission is 12€ for adults and 8€ for children.

At the island's northern tip, **Portinatx** has a series of beaches and bays marred by a string of shops and haphazardly built hotels. For a taste of its rugged beauty, go past the construction to the jagged coast along the open sea.

beach time **MINUS THE CROWDS**

If you want to escape to a lovely beach without hotel construction, head for **Playa Benirras,** just north of Port de Sant Miquel. An unpaved but passable road leads out to this small, pretty cove, where lounge chairs are available and pedal boats are for rent. You'll find snack bars and restaurants on the beach. On summer Sundays, a drum circle greets the sunset—a local party everyone is invited to join.

Rounding the island's northern tip to **Cala Sant Vicent** (San Vicente), a beautiful drive leads along the coast to **Sant Carles** (San Carlos). On Saturdays you might find a **flea market** just beyond Sant Carles on the road to Santa Eulalia on the east coast. Open from about 10am until 8 or 9pm, it offers vintage and new clothing, crafts, and the usual odds and ends.

WHERE TO STAY ON THE NORTHERN IBIZA COAST

Hotel Hacienda Na Xamena ★★★   Located on a promontory over-looking Na Xamena Bay 23km (14 miles) northwest of Ciudad de Ibiza, this utterly beautiful hotel is precisely what every magazine art director dreams that Ibiza should be like. Rooms are spacious and flooded with light, and the sea seems to be all around. Many rooms feature large oval freestanding tubs for soaking, and many have a private hot tub or a pool looking out at the ocean. This is CEO and celebrity heaven, where no matter how public your face back home, you can relax in anonymity here with attentive (but not obsequious) personal service.

Na Xamena, s/n, San Miquel. www.hotelhacienda-ibiza.com. ✆ **97-133-45-00.** 77 units. 347€–560€ double; 525€–2,450€ suite. Free parking. Closed Nov–Apr. **Amenities:** 4 restaurants; bar; bikes; exercise room; 3 pools (1 indoor); spa; outdoor tennis court (lit); free Wi-Fi.

Santa Eulalia del Río ★

Santa Eulalia lies at the foot of the Puig de Missa, on the estuary of the only river in the Balearics. The principal monument in town is a fortress church standing on a hilltop, or *puig*. Dating from the 16th century, it has an ornate Gothic altar screen.

You can reach the area's prime beaches by bus or boat, departing from the harbor near the boat basin. There are four buses a day to **Aigües Blanques,** one of the best beaches, 10km (6¼ miles) north. (It's legal to go nude here.) The long, sandy cove of **Cala Llonga,** 5km (3 miles) south, is served by 12 buses a day. Cala Llonga fronts a bevy of package-tour hotels, so it's often crowded. Boats depart Santa Eulalia for Cala Llonga every 30 minutes, from 9am to 6pm. **Es Caná,** a white-sand beach 5km (3 miles) north of town, is accessed by boats and buses that leave every 30 minutes, 8am to 9pm. Four buses a day depart for **Cala Lleñya** and **Cala Nova.**

Santa Eulalia's **tourist information office** at Marià Riquer Wallis, 4 (www.santaeulalia.net; ✆ **97-133-07-28**), opens in summer Sunday to Friday 9:30am to 1:30pm and 5 to 7:30pm, Saturday 10am to 1pm; the rest of the year it's open Monday to Friday 9am to 2pm. From Ciudad de Ibiza (departing from Avenida D'Isidor Macabich), **buses** run to Santa Eulalia del Río every hour; a one-way fare costs 3€. Seven **boats** a day run on the hour between Ciudad de Ibiza and Santa Eulalia del Río, with the first leaving Ciudad de Ibiza at 10:30am and Santa Eulalia del Río at 9:30am. The boat ride takes 45 minutes. For information, call ✆ **616-496-606.**

WHERE TO STAY & EAT IN SANTA EULALIA DEL RIO

Can Curreu Hotel Rural & Spa ★★★ MALLORCAN   Within the village of Sant Carles on PM-810, this spectacular hotel and spa features one of the best dining rooms on Ibiza. The pastel-decor rooms with soft lighting are romantic and spacious, and each has a balcony with a beautiful vista. Suites also have kitchenettes. The spa and wellness center offer Turkish baths as well as the usual spa and massage treatments. In addition to the dining room, the restaurant serves lunch and dinner on an outdoor terrace next to a 1,000-year-old olive tree. The menu (entrees 20€–40€; tasting menu 52€) incorporates just enough international dishes (duck breast in red wine, sea bass in a salt crust) to provide a change from such local fare as grilled red shrimp with gray sea salt, or skewers of grilled vegetables with romesco.

Ctra San Carlos, km. 12. www.cancurreu.com. *C* **97-133-52-80.** 7 units. 195€–295€ double, 250€–495€ suite. **Amenities:** Restaurant; bar; spa; horseback riding, free Wi-Fi.

FORMENTERA ★

For years, the island of Formentera was known as the "forgotten Bale-aric." The smallest island of the archipelago, it's a 78-sq.-km (30-sq.-mile) flat limestone plain marked on the east by La Mola, a peak rising 187m (614 ft.), and on the west by Berberia, at 96m (315 ft.). The Romans called it Frumentaria (meaning "wheat granary") when they oversaw it as a booming little agricultural center. But a shortage of water, coupled with strong winds, allows only meager vegetation to grow, notably fig trees and fields of wild rosemary. Its year-round population of 5,000 swells in summer, with most visitors coming over for the day from Ibiza to enjoy the beaches.

Formentera Essentials

ARRIVING Formentera is served by up to 36 **boat** passages a day in summer and about 8 per day in winter. Boats depart from Ciudad de Ibiza for La Savina, 3km (1¾ miles) north of Sant Francesc, the island's capital and largest settlement. The trip takes between 35 minutes and 1 hour. A round-trip fare costs from 40€. For information, contact **Trasmapi** (www.trasmapi.com; *C* **90-231-44-33**), or check at your hotel.

GETTING AROUND As ferryboats arrive at the quays of La Savina, taxis line up at the pier. One-way passage to such points as Es Pujols and Playa de Mitjorn costs 10€ to 15€; negotiate the fare in advance. To call a taxi in Sant Francesc, dial *C* **97-132-20-16;** in La Savina, *C* **97-132-20-02.** You can rent bicycles and motor scooters from **MotoRent Migjorn** in La Savina (www.motorentmigjorn.com; *C* **97-132-11-11**), or from **MotoRent Pujols** in Pujols (www.motorentpujols.com; *C* **97-132-21-38**). Motor scooters cost 25€ to 65€ per day, bicycles 8€ to 12€ per day.

VISITOR INFORMATION The **tourist office** at Calle de Calpe s/n, in Port de La Savina (www.formentera.es; *C* **97-132-20-57**), is open Monday to Friday 10am to 2pm and 5 to 7pm, Saturday 10am to 2pm.

Exploring Formentara

Beaches, beaches, and more beaches—that's why visitors come to Formentara. You can see the ocean from any point on the island.

Playa de Mitjorn, on the southern coast, is 5km (3 miles) long and is the principal area for nude sunbathing. A few bars and hotels occupy the

Es Calo beach.

relatively undeveloped stretch of sand. You can make **Es Copinyars,** the name of one of the beachfronts, your stop for lunch.

At **Es Calo,** along the northern coast, west of El Pilar, there are some small boardinghouses. From here you can see the lighthouse of La Mola, which was featured in Jules Verne's *Journey Round the Solar System.*

The town of Sant Ferran serves the beach of **Es Pujols,** darling of the package-tour operators. This is the most crowded beach on Formentera, with pure white sand, good windsurfing, and a backdrop of dunes and pine trees.

Westward, **Cala Sahona** is another popular tourist spot, lying near the lighthouse on Cabo Berberia. Pleasure vessels often anchor here on what is the most beautiful cove in Formentera.

MENORCA ★★

Barely 15km (9⅓ miles) wide and less than 52km (32 miles) long, Menorca, the second largest of the Spanish Balearic Islands, is one of the most beautiful islands in the Mediterranean. Its principal city is **Mahón** (also called Maó; pop. 25,000), set on a rocky bluff overlooking the great port, which was fought over for centuries by the British, French, and Spanish.

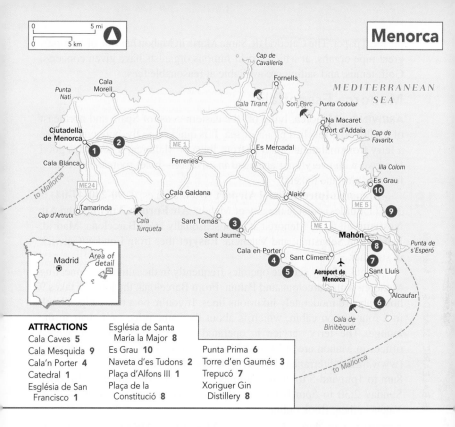

ATTRACTIONS

Cala Caves **5**	Església de Santa María la Major **8**	
Cala Mesquida **9**	Es Grau **10**	Punta Prima **6**
Cala'n Porter **4**	Naveta d'es Tudons **2**	Torre d'en Gaumés **3**
Catedral **1**	Plaça d'Alfons III **1**	Trepucó **7**
Església de San Francisco **1**	Plaça de la Constitució **8**	Xoriguer Gin Distillery **8**

Menorca has about 60,000 permanent inhabitants, and while it hosts half a million visitors a year, it is not overrun by tourism. The island has some industry, including leatherwork, costume-jewelry production, dairy farming, and even gin manufacturing. Life here is quiet and relaxed. Some clubs in Ibiza don't even open until 4am, but on Menorca nearly everybody is in bed well before then.

Beaches are the island's greatest attraction—Menorca has more beaches than Mallorca, Ibiza, and Formentera combined, stretching along 217km (135 miles) of pine-fringed coastline. Many are not connected by roads, and nude bathing is commonplace, though officially illegal. Our favorite beach is **Cala'n Porter,** 11km (6¾ miles) west of Mahón. Towering promontories guard the slender estuary where this spectacular beach is found. Another of Menorca's treasures, **Cala de Santa Galdana,** is 23km (14 miles) south of Ciudadela; its gentle bay and excellent sandy beach afford the most scenic spot on the island.

In addition to trips to the beach, there are some fascinating things to do for those interested in history, archaeology, music, and art. Many artists live in Menorca, and exhibitions of their work are listed regularly in the local paper. The Catedral de Santa María in Mahón has one of Europe's great pipe organs, at which world-famous organists have given concerts. Golf, tennis, and sailing are available at reasonable fees.

Menorca Essentials

ARRIVING   Menorca, lying off the eastern coast of Spain and northeast of Mallorca, is reached by air or sea. It is quickest to fly, but you can take a ferry from mainland Spain or from Ibiza or Mallorca. It is always good to arrive with everything arranged in advance—hotel rooms, car rentals, ferry, or airplane tickets.

Menorca International Airport (www.aena.es; *©* **90-240-47-04**) is 3km (1¾ miles) outside the city of Mahón. **Air Europa, Vueling,** and **Air Nostrum** all fly to Menorca at least seasonally from Barcelona, Madrid, Palma, San Sebastián, and Valencia. **Easyjet** flies from London/Gatwick in summer.

Regular **ferry service** operates frequently in the summer, connecting Menorca with Barcelona and Palma. From Barcelona, the journey takes 9 hours aboard moderately luxurious lines. If you're on a real budget, bunk in a four-person cabin, which is about the same price as a chair in the lounge. The ferry service is operated by **Trasmediterránea,** whose offices in Mahón are at Estació Marítim, along Moll (Andén) de Ponent (www.trasmediterranea.es; *©* **97-136-29-50**); it's open Monday to Friday 8am to 1pm and 5 to 7pm, Saturday 7 to 10pm. The office is also open Sunday 2:30 to 5pm but is mostly busy managing ferry arrivals from Valencia then. Book online.

GETTING AROUND   **Transportes Menorca (TMSA),** Cí Rodees, 5, Mahón (www.tmsa.es; *©* **97-136-04-75**), operates bus service around the island. Mahón's tourist office (see below) has complete bus schedules for the island. The Spanish-owned **Atesa** (www.atesa.es; *©* **97-136-62-13**) operates a rental-car desk at the airport, charging from 50€ to 117€ for its cheaper models. **Avis** (www.avis.com; *©* **97-136-15-76**) also operates out of the airport, asking from 58€. Car-rental firms will deliver a vehicle to the airport or to your hotel, but you must specify in advance. To summon a local taxi, call *©* **97-136-71-11.** The taxi stop is at Plaça s'Esplanada in Mahón. One-way cab fare from Mahón to the beaches is 18€.

Mahón ★★

Since 1722, Mahón (Maó) has been the capital of Menorca. With gorgeous Georgian architecture, Mahón still shows traces of British occupation. It was built where an old castle on a cliff overlooked one of Europe's finest natural harbors, some 5.5km (3½ miles) long. The castle and the town wall erected to dissuade pirates are long gone, however, except for the archway of San Roque. In 1287 Alfonso III of Aragón established a

Boats docked in Mahón.

base in the harbor, which became known as **Isla del Rey (Island of the King).**

Mahón is not a beach town, but it has some hotels and is the shopping and nightlife center. The closest beaches for swimming are at **Es Grau** and **Cala Mesquida** (see p. 706).

ESSENTIALS

ARRIVING & GETTING AROUND
From the airport, a bus goes to central Mahón every half-hour. It costs 2.65€. A taxi is about 10€. Mahón is the **bus** transport depot for the island, with departures from Calle José Anselmo Clave in the heart of town. Ferries from Barcelona (one-way fare around 125€) arrive at the Port of Mahon each morning—walk or take a taxi to your hotel. The most popular run is to Ciudadela (seven buses daily in summer, four daily in winter), but there are also connections to other parts of the island. The tourist office distributes a list of schedules, which is also published in the local newspaper, *Menorca Diario Insular.* Ticket prices vary but fares can be paid on board. Be sure to carry change.

VISITOR INFORMATION The **tourist office,** at Plaça Constitutió, 22 (www.menorca.es; © **97-136-37-90**), is open Monday to Friday 9am to 1pm and 5 to 7pm, Saturday 9am to 1pm.

EXPLORING MAHÓN
The main square of Mahón is **Plaça s'Esplanada.** Locals gather here on Sunday to enjoy ice cream, which some claim is the best in the Balearics. In summer, an artisans' market is held here on Tuesday and Saturday 9am to 2pm.

Mahón' 18th-century Town Hall, constructed in an English Palladian style, sits on **Plaça de la Constitució,** where you'll also find **Església de Santa María la Major** (© **97-136-39-49**). Founded in 1287 by Christian conqueror Alfonso III, this church has been rebuilt by every ruler since. (The major changes came in 1772.) Its celebrated organ, which has four keyboards and more than 3,000 pipes, was constructed by Swiss artisan

Johan Kyburz in 1810. From May to October there are organ concerts Monday through Saturday at 11am; tickets cost 5€. The church is open daily 7:30am to 12:30pm and 5:30 to 8pm; entry is free, but donations are welcomed.

The northern boundary of the city is formed by **Puerto de Mahón,** which has many restaurants and shops along Moll de Ponent. Mahón's port sits in the largest natural harbor in the Mediterranean. The best way to explore it is on an hour-long **catamaran tour** offered by **Yellow Catamarans,** Moll de Llevant, 12 (www.yellowcatamarans.com; ✆ **639-676-351**), which costs 12.50€ for adults, 6€ for ages 3–12. In addition to a couple of decks, the lower part of the hull is glass so you can observe underwater sea life. Tours run April 10:30am and noon, May to October between 10:30am and 2:30pm. On the harbor you can also visit the **Xoriguer Gin Distillery,** Moll de Ponent, 91 (www.xoriguer.es; ✆ **97-136-21-97**), to see how the famed Menorcan gin is made in giant copper vats over wood fires. The distillery is open May to October Monday to Friday 9:30am to 7pm, and Saturday 10am to 2:30pm; November to April it's open Monday to Friday 9:30am to 1pm and 3 to 6pm.

MAHÓN OUTDOORS

BEACHES **Cala'n Porter,** 11km (6¾ miles) west of Mahón, is one of the most spectacular beaches on the island. It's a sandy beach at a narrow estuary inlet protected by high promontories. **La Cova d'en Xoroi,** ancient troglodyte habitations overlooking the sea from the upper part of the cliffs, can also be visited. Going around the cliff face, you'll discover more caves at **Cala Caves.** People still live in some of these caves, and there are boat trips to see them from Cala'n Porter.

North of Mahón on the road to Fornells you'll encounter many beachside settlements. Close to Mahón, and already being exploited, is **Cala Mesquida,** one of the best beaches. To reach it, turn off the road to Cala Llonga and follow the signs to playa.

The next fork in the road takes you to **Es Grau,** another fine beach. Along the way you see the salt marshes of S'Albufera, abundant in migrant birds. Reached by bus from Mahón, Es Grau, 8km (5 miles) north of Mahón, opens onto a sandy bay and is crowded in July and August. From Es Grau you can take a boat to **Illa d'en Colom,** an island in the bay with some good beaches.

South of Mahón is the little town of Sant Lluís and the large sandy beach to the east, **Punta Prima.** Favored by local people, this beach is served by buses from Mahón, with six departures daily. The same buses will take you to an attractive necklace of beaches, the **Platges de Son Bou,** on the southern shore. Many tourist facilities are found here.

GOLF Menorca's only course is **Golf Son Parc** (www.golfsonparc.com; ✆ **97-118-88-75**), an 18-hole course.

WINDSURFING & SAILING The best spots are at Fornells Bay, which is 1.6km (1 mile) wide and several miles long. **WindFornells,** Carretera es Mercadel-Fornells, s/n (www.windfornells.com; ℂ **664-335-801**), supplies gear. Open April through October.

WHERE TO STAY IN MAHÓN

Hotel Capri Le Petit Spa ★
Simple and modern, every room in this pleasant hotel near the city center has hardwood floors and pale wooden furniture (meant perhaps to evoke a Scandinavian sauna). But each room also has a private balcony, and views of the city are excellent. The spa on the top floor includes a sauna and hot tub. The Artiem group has several hotels on Menorca, but only the Capri is family-friendly.

Carrer Sant Esteve, 8. www.artiemhotels.com. ℂ **97-136-14-00.** 75 units. 85€–160€ double. **Amenities:** Restaurant; bar; exercise room; outdoor pool; spa; free Wi-Fi.

Hotel Port Mahón ★★
A grande dame among Menorca hotels, the Port Mahón has been receiving guests since the 1950s—and some of the first are still returning. Taking advantage of Menorca's mild climate, it's open all year. Rooms can be on the small side, and the furnishings are less grand in the guest rooms than in the lobby. The gardens are quite beautiful, and the hillside location gives sweeping views of the town and harbor. Every room or suite has at least a small private balcony with potted geraniums.

Av. Fort de L'Eau, s/n. www.sethotels.com. ℂ **97-136-26-00.** 82 units. 98€–187€ double; 160€–240€ suite. **Amenities:** Restaurant; 2 bars; outdoor pool; free Wi-Fi.

WHERE TO EAT IN MAHÓN

Fish and seafood are the basis of the Menorcan diet. The most elegant dish, *caldereta de langosta,* consists of pieces of lobster blended with onion, tomato, pepper, and garlic, and flavored with an anise liqueur. Shellfish paella is also popular, as are the "warty Venus" shellfish, *escupinas.* Wine comes from the mainland, but gin is made on the island, a legacy of the British occupation. It's often drunk with lemon and ice (a *palloza*).

Jàgaro ★ SEAFOOD
With a large outdoor terrace and two indoor dining rooms, this bustling restaurant is one of the largest on Mahón's waterfront. Seafood is the emphasis, and the menu includes such regional dishes as fried lobster with poached egg and a *caldereta de langostina*—a soup studded with large prawns. One of the dining rooms is set up like a wine cellar as a nod to the excellent selection of largely Catalan wines.

Moll de Llevant, 334. www.jagaro.es. ℂ **97-136-23-90.** Entrees 15€–50€. Apr–Sept daily noon–4pm and 8pm–midnight; Oct–Nov and Mar Tues–Sat noon–4pm and 8pm–midnight, Sun noon–4pm. Closed Dec–Feb.

Ses Forquilles ★★★ MENORCAN
After all the designer dining rooms and frou-frou dinner plates, you owe it to yourself to visit this

top-rate but down-to-earth tapas bar with a huge counter, several tables where you can stand to eat, and an upstairs dining room. You can get olives or a plate of *patatas bravas,* but you can also get more creative fare such as fried artichoke chips, mini-cutlets of rabbit loin, and the house-cured tuna. Great ingredients, imaginative preparation, and reasonable prices.

Rovellada de Dalt, 20. https://sesforquilles.com. © **97-135-27-11.** Tapas 2.80€–6€; entrees 9.50€–22.50€. Daily 1:30pm–midnight.

Ciudadela ★

At the western end of the island, the town of Ciudadela (Ciutadella de Menorca) was the island's capital until 1722, when the British switched to Mahón to make use of its deeper harbor. The British then built the main island road to link the two cities. Today Ciudadela has a classic Mediterranean ambience, with the narrow streets of its historic center lined with 17th- and 18th-century mansions and numerous churches. Development stopped in Ciudadela when the capital was transferred, and many buildings still stand that might otherwise have been torn down in the name of progress.

Like Mahón, Ciudadela perches high above its harbor. Known as Medina Minurka under the Muslims, Ciudadela retains Moorish traces despite the 1558 Turkish invasion and destruction of the city. An obelisk in memory of the city's futile defense against that invasion stands in **Plaça d'es Born (Plaza del Born),** the main square overlooking the port.

ESSENTIALS

ARRIVING From the airport, you must take a taxi to Ciudadela, as there is no bus link. The cost is approximately 53€ each way. From Mahón (Plaça s'Esplanada), six **buses** go back and forth every day; a one-way fare costs 6€.

VISITOR INFORMATION The **tourist office,** Plaça d'es Born, 15 (© **97-148-41-55**), is open May to October Monday to Saturday 9am to 8:30pm; November to April, hours are Monday to Friday 9:30am to 2pm.

EXPLORING CIUDADELA

Since the days of Jaume I, the center of Ciudadela has been **Plaça d'es Born,** which overlooks the port to the north. The square was built around an obelisk commemorating the town's struggle against the Turks, who sacked the city in 1558. The **Ayuntamiento** (Town Hall) anchors the west side of the square. On the southwest corner of the square, the 14th-century Gothic **Església de San Francisco** has some excellent carved-wood altars. A once-splendid palace, Palacio de Torre-Saura, stands on the square's northwest corner. Still owner-occupied, it was constructed in the 1800s.

In the Middle Ages Ciudadela was completely walled to protect against pirate incursions, which were a serious threat from the 13th

megalithic **MENORCA**

One of Menorca's surprising assets is a number of easily accessed prehistoric relics. A quick excursion from Mahón, marked off the Mahón-Villacarlos highway, is **Trepucó,** where you'll find both a 4m (13-ft.) *taula* (huge T-shaped stone structure) and a *talayot* (circular stone tower). The megalithic monuments stand on the road to Sant Lluís, only about 1.6km (1 mile) south of Mahón. Of all the prehistoric remains on the island, this site is the easiest to visit.

Yet another impressive prehistoric monument, **Torre d'en Gaumés** lies 15km (9⅓ miles) west of Mahón off the route to Son Bou. (The path is signposted.) You can take a bus from Mahón to Son Bou if you don't have a car. This megalithic settlement spreads over many acres, including both *taulas* and *talayots*, along with ancient caves in which people once lived. The exact location is 3km (1¾ miles) south of Alayor off the road to Son Bou.

The island's best-preserved and most significant collection of prehistoric mega-lithic monuments, however, is the restored **Naveta d'es Tudons,** accessible 5km (3 miles) east of Ciudadela, just to the south of the road to Mahón. Its *naveta* (a boat-shaped monument thought to be a dwelling or a burial chamber) is said to be among the oldest monuments constructed by humans in Europe. Archaeologists have found the remains of many bodies at this site, along with a collection of prehistoric artifacts, including pottery and decorative jewelry (now in museums).

Plaça d'es Born.

century on. The fortresslike **cathedral,** Plaça Pío XII, was ordered built by the conquering Alfonso III on the site of the town's former mosque. The church's neoclassical facade was added in 1813. The church suffered damage during the Spanish Civil War but has been restored.

Ciudadela is at its liveliest at the **port,** with an array of shops, bars, and restaurants. Sailboats and yachts dock here in summer. **Carrer Quadrado,** lined with shops and arcades, is another street worth walking.

The Moorish influence lingers in a block of whitewashed houses in the **Voltes,** off the Plaça s'Esplanada. In Ciudadela, local people still meet at **Plaça d'Alfons III,** the square honoring their long-ago liberator.

CIUDADELA OUTDOORS: THE BEACHES

Buses depart from Ciuddela's Plaça d'Artrutx for most coastal destinations, including the best beaches. Known for its white sands, **Cala Santandria,** 3km (1¾ miles) to the south, is a sheltered beach near a creek, with nearby rock caves that were inhabited in prehistoric times. The coves of **En Forcat, Blanes,** and **Brut** are also near Ciudadela.

The bay of Santa Galdana.

Cala de Santa Galdana, not reached by public transport, is the most stunning bay in the area, lying 23km (14 miles) south of Ciudadela. The tranquil bay is ringed with a beach of fine golden sand. Tall, bare cliffs rise in the background. The road to this beach, unlike so many others on Menorca, is a good one.

WHERE TO STAY IN CIUDADELA

Hotel Menorca Patricia ★   Centrally located near the main square, Plaça d'es Born, the Patricia is a modern hotel built in the late 1980s to cater to leisure and business travelers alike. (It has good meeting rooms, so Spanish businesses often choose it for small "reward" junket meetings.) The decor is low-key and pleasant, and the rooms are spacious. During a 2014 renovation, the hotel installed all new hardwood floors, upgraded the modern furniture, and brought in new soft bedding and drapes in pale beige and taupe tones. It's about a half-mile to the nearest beach.

Passeig Sant Nicolau, 90–92. www.hotelmenorcapatricia.com. ℰ **97-138-55-11.** 44 units. 70€–139€ double; 88€–174€ jr. suite. Closed Nov–Mar. **Amenities:** Bar; outdoor pool; free Wi-Fi.

Hotel Rural Sant Ignasi ★★   This hacienda-style hotel sits outside of town in a 1777 mansion on beautifully landscaped grounds. Converted to a hotel in 1997, the hotel feels like a very rich friend's home. Instead of a lobby, there's a living room—although few guests stay indoors. Each ground-level room has a garden, each second-floor room a balcony terrace. Bedrooms are amply sized, and the decor is warm and low-key.

Carretera Cala Morell s/n. www.santignasi.com. ℰ **97-138-55-75.** 25 units. 110€–208€ double; 164€–295€ jr. suite; 250€–410€ suite. Free parking. Closed Oct–Mar. **Amenities:** Restaurant; bar; 2 outdoor pools; free Wi-Fi.

WHERE TO EAT IN CIUDADELA

Café Balear ★ MENORCAN   This is the kind of place every former commercial fisherman looks for in a port: a fish restaurant on the docks with its own boat anchored out front. The menu is flexible—it all depends on what the fishermen catch (it usually includes monkfish, sea bream, rock fish, and John Dory). Other fishermen supply lobster, prawns, and assorted clams. As an indulgence, take the mixed seafood plate with a little of everything.

Pla de Sant Joan, 15. www.cafe-balear.com. ✆ **97-138-00-05.** Entrees 12€–25€. Mon–Sat 1–4pm and 7pm–midnight. Nov–Mar closed Sun–Mon.

Smoix ★★ MENORCAN   Run by a friendly couple, this spot has a romantic garden setting and serves good local food based on seasonal produce and the catch of the day. Unlike many Ciudadela restaurants, Smoix offers many house specials of braised meat—lamb trotters, slow-cooked suckling pig. The house "hamburger" is made with freshly ground veal, presented in a nest of filo with a fried egg on top. When big sardines are in, order one grilled; the waiter will de-bone it before it comes to the table.

Carrer Sant Isidre, 33. www.smoix.com. ✆ **97-148-05-16.** Entrees 14€–29€. Mon–Sat 1–4pm and 7–11pm.

Fornells & the Northern Coast ★

On Menorca's northern coast, the tiny town of Fornells snuggles around a bay filled with boats and windsurfers. Built around four fortifications, including the Tower of Fornells at the harbor mouth and the now-ruined Castle of San Jorge, Fornells today is a flourishing fishing village noted for upscale restaurants featuring savory lobster *calderetas.*

West of Fornells is **Platja Binimella,** a beautiful beach (unofficially nudist) easily accessible by car. A snack bar is the sole concession to civilization.

It takes some effort to reach the promontory at **Cap de Cavalleria,** the northernmost tip of the island, marked by a lighthouse. At a bend in the road leading to Platja Binimella, a signpost indicates the turnoff to Cap de Cavalleria through a closed gate heading to a dirt road. The gate is shut to keep in livestock; you should close it after you pass through. As you follow the long dirt road, you will encounter several more gates and travel through cultivated fields and scattered grand *fincas.* Park shortly before the lighthouse, then pick your way across the scrub and rocks for the views. The best one is from a circular tower in ruins to the right of the lighthouse. The vista encompasses the whole of Menorca—a symphony of dramatic cliffs and jewel-blue water.

EXTREMADURA

By Peter Barron

19

S tretching from the Gredos mountains south to Andalucía, from Castile west to the Portuguese frontier,
Extremadura probably means "the land beyond the
river Douro." Many here will tell you it's not a coinci-
dence that in Spanish it also means "extreme" and
"hard". *Extremeños* are proud of their tough way of life, forged in
the harshly beautiful landscape and sometimes inhospitable climate. It has shaped their history.

The world knows Extremadura as the land of the conquistadors. Famous
sons include Hernán Cortés and Francisco Pizarro, who conquered the
Aztecs and the Incas in the 16th century. Driven by economic necessity to
seek a living far from their parched homeland, they imposed their iron
will on peoples half a world away. The riches they sent home financed
palaces and public structures that stand today as monuments to Spain's
imperial age. The marvelously preserved cities of Cáceres and Trujillo
evoke that history, while Mérida has some of the world's finest Roman
ruins. The civilizations who have ruled Spain since—Visigoth, Arab and
Christian—have all left their mark. Extremadura also has an abundance of
unspoiled nature: mountains, river gorges, and the rolling, oak-forested
dehesa where the famous *pata negra* pigs roam. Its wildlife—particularly
an exquisite bird population including eagles, vultures and storks—
attracts international acclaim. Yet wider tourism remains remarkably
undeveloped. Little English is spoken, though you'll be warmly welcomed, and visitors have an opportunity to immerse themselves in Spanish culture and traditions little changed in hundreds of years. Because
summer can get intensely hot, spring and fall are the best times to visit.

MÉRIDA ★★★

A UNESCO World Heritage site since 1993, Extremadura's regional capital provides an extraordinarily vivid picture of the pleasures and cruelties
of everyday life at the height of the Roman Empire. Founded by Emperor
Augustus in 25 B.C. as a colony for retired legionaries from his Spanish
campaigns, Emerita Augusta was the capital of the province of Lusitania
and one of the most important cities of the Roman Empire. Today, Mérida
is home to the most completely preserved Roman ruins outside Italy,
including an evocative theater complex, the longest Roman bridge still
standing, and a world-class museum of Roman artifacts. The ruins, many

of them excavated only in the last hundred years, sit cheek-by-jowl with shops and houses in the unremarkable modern city; the people of Mérida seem to take the ancient treasures in their stride. It's a great place to start a tour of historic Extremadura.

Essentials

GETTING THERE   **Trains** arrive at the station on Calle Cardero (www. renfe.com; ℓ **91-232-03-20**), a 10-minute walk north of Plaza de España. Each day there are four direct trains from Madrid (trip time: 5–6 hr., cost: 30€–45€) and two from Sevilla (trip time: 3½ hr.). The **bus** station on Avenida de la Libertad (ℓ **92-437-14-04**) receives eight buses a day from Madrid (trip time: 4–5 hr.; cost: 27€–40€), 10 from Sevilla (trip time: 3 hr.; cost: 10€–16€), and three from Cáceres (trip time: 1 hr.; cost: 7€). By **car,** take the A-5 superhighway from Madrid or Lisbon (A-6 in Portugal). The drive from Madrid by **car** is approximately 4 hours; from Lisbon, about 3 hours. From Sevilla, drive due north on the Autovía Ruta de la Plata A-66, about 2 hours. Half a dozen car parks are dotted around the old town, but ask your hotel for directions—most have parking arrangements.

VISITOR INFORMATION   The main **tourist office,** on Paseo de José Sáenz de Buruaga (turismomerida. org; ℓ **92-433-07-22**), next to the entrance to the Roman theaters, is open daily 9am to 6:30pm, until 9pm in summer.

Actors perform Euripedes's tragedy *Hipolito* at the Merida Classical Theater Festival.

EVENTS   In July and August, the **Mérida Classical Theater Festival** (www.festivaldemerida.es; ℓ **92-400-94-80**) presents Greek and Roman classical plays performed nightly in Spanish at the Roman theater. Even if you don't understand the language, the spectacular setting and lighting make these performances an unforgettable experience. Tickets from around 15€ to 50€ can be booked on the website; for the stony cheaper seats consider taking a cushion.

Exploring Mérida

The compact old city is easily explored on foot. The best way to explore the city's many archaeological gems is to buy a combined **Conjunto**

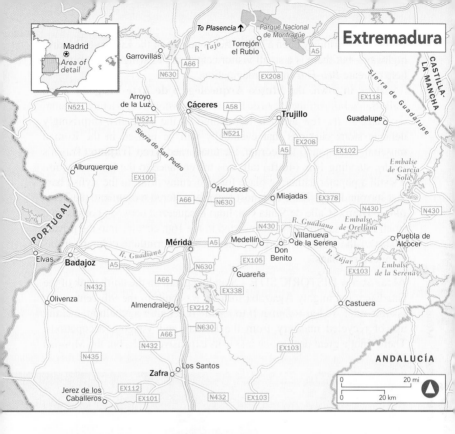

Monumental ticket for 15€ at the tourist office, which gives access to seven key sites, including the **Roman theater** and **amphitheater,** the **Circus Maximus,** and the **Alcazaba.** (Admission to these monuments individually costs 6€.) Other monuments, such as the **Roman bridge,** the **Temple of Diana,** and the city's two remaining aqueducts, can be visited for free. Most are perpetually uncrowded.

Besides the sites listed below, you can wander past the **Acueducto de los Milagros,** the more complete of the town's two remaining Roman aqueducts, which brought water from lake Proserpina (5km) 3 miles away. A dozen or so complete arches are still standing, 25m (82 ft.) tall, every one of them covered with nesting storks for much of the year. Further along the trickling river Albarregas, you reach the three remaining columns of the **Acueducto de San Lázaro,** which sits beside a modern house, one of its arches serving as a carport. (The lengthy aqueduct you see here is a 16th-c. rebuild along the original route.) Nearby the huge **Circus Maximus,** more than 400m (1,300 ft.) long, was probably built before the theater and amphitheater; it could hold up to 30,000 spectators for chariot races. There's not much left of the original structure—over the years it has variously been a barley field and part of the Lisbon-to-Madrid highway—but there is a small visitor center and viewing platform which help recreate *Ben-Hur* in the imagination.

Back in town, the **Museo Arqueológico de Arte Visigodo** ★ on Calle Santa Julia off the Plaza de España (admission free) is a tiny museum dedicated to the few artifacts left behind by the Visigoths, surprisingly delicate stone carvings that eventually will be housed in the Roman museum. Just around the corner, the unadorned **Arco Trajano** (Trajan's Arch), standing 14m (46 ft.) tall, was the entrance to the Roman forum; it's still a popular gathering place for an evening drink in the stylish bars that surround it (p. 722). The most recently restored monument, the **Templo de Diana** (Calle de Santa Catalina) is squeezed between houses on a small central square; it was converted in the 16th century into the private palace of the Count of Corbos, who used its Corinthian columns in his architectural plans.

Alcazaba ★ HISTORIC SITE   Standing guard on the north bank of the Guadiana, the mighty Alcazaba fortress was built in the 9th century by Islamic ruler Abd-ar Rahman II to restore order after a rebellion, making use of recycled masonry from the Roman and Visigoth occupations. There's not a great deal to see inside its expansive walls, but the Moorish

The Temple of Diana is the most recently restored of Mérida's Roman ruins.

cistern *(aljibe)*, incorporating floral Visigoth pillars and live goldfish in the still water, makes a beautiful oasis. Chillingly, during the Spanish Civil War both sides used the Alcazaba as a stronghold at different times. Today, the ramparts spark children's imaginations, and provide a perfect vantage point for photographs of the Roman bridge.

Paseo Roma s/n. turismomerida.org. ℂ **92-412-72-62.** Admission 15€ combined ticket, 7.50€ students and seniors, free for kids 11 and under. Apr–Sept daily 9am–9pm; Oct–Mar daily 9am–6:30pm. Closed Dec 24, 25, and 31 and Jan 1.

Anfiteatro Romano ★★ ANCIENT SITE   At the height of its glory in the A.D. 1st century, this amphitheater could seat up to 15,000 spectators, drawn here to watch wildly popular, and murderous, entertainment: gladiatorial battles and fights between humans and wild animals, a precursor to today's bullfight. The central pit is the *fossa bestiaria* where animals were kept before going to their deaths. It was probably also used to re-enact famous naval battles *(naumachia)* by flooding the arena with water from the city's aqueduct. As you enter, past descriptions of the various classes of gladiator with their plumed helmets, daggers, and nets, it's easy to imagine the roar of the mob.

Plaza Margarita Xirgú, s/n. turismomerida.org. ℂ **92-433-07-22.** Admission 15€ combined ticket, 7.50€ students and seniors, free for kids 11 and under. Apr–Sept daily 9am–9pm; Oct–Mar daily 9am–6:30pm. Closed Dec 24, 25, and 31 and Jan 1.

Casa del Mitreo ★ ANCIENT SITE   Next to the red-painted bullring, this Roman manor house offers a vivid snapshot of the life of a wealthy family in 2nd-century Emerita Augusta. An elevated walkway lets you survey excavated mosaics, murals, and columns. In some parts archaeological digs are ongoing. The **Cosmological Mosaic,** a tiled reception room floor depicting heaven, earth, and the sea, shows the level of opulence at play. Nearby, the **Los Columbarios** funeral site deals with the Roman way of death (they clearly believed you *could* take it with you). Information panels are in Spanish only, but include drawings of how the buildings originally looked.

Calle Oviedo, s/n. turismomerida.org. ℂ **92-433-07-22.** Admission 15€ combined ticket, 7.50€ students and seniors, free for kids 11 and under. Apr–Sept daily 9am–9pm; Oct–Mar daily 9am–6:30pm. Closed Dec 24, 25, and 31 and Jan 1.

Museo Nacional de Arte Romano ★★★ MUSEUM   The star attraction in town, this towering museum is Spain's most important repository of Roman artifacts. Designed in the 1980s by celebrated Spanish architect Rafael Moneo, the flat-brick edifice houses a beautifully curated collection of pieces recovered in and around Emerita Augusta (a veiled bust of Augustus himself is a highlight). Over three levels surrounding a huge, airy atrium, you're transported in time through sculptures, pottery, glassware, and coins, with clear information in Spanish and English. Walls are covered with almost-complete mosaics and murals, discovered in Roman houses in downtown Mérida. Part of the thrill is how the museum connects with the actual Roman ruins, incorporating a swatch of Roman road on the way to a crypt where you can explore the patios of Roman houses being excavated on-site.

Calle José Ramón Melida, s/n. www.museoarteromano.es. 📞 **92-431-16-90.** Admission 3€ adults, 1.50€ seniors, students, and kids 17 and under. Free after 2pm Sat and all day Sun. Tues–Sat 9:30am–6:30pm (in summer until 8pm), Sun 10am–3pm. Closed Mon and holidays.

Puente Romano ★★ ANCIENT SITE   Leading from the gates of the Alcazaba far across the Guadiana river, the Roman bridge is the world's longest surviving from antiquity, with 60 arches stretching nearly half a mile (792m). Constructed from granite blocks and concrete at the city's founding in 25 B.C., it has been renovated many times since. It's still in use today but was pedestrianized in the 1990s, when Santiago Calatrava's bowlike **Lusitania bridge** was built to take motor traffic. The two bridges complement each other beautifully. It's said that the rutted tracks still visible on the cobbled surface of the Roman bridge date from the age when wooden-wheeled carts delivered goods to the gates of the Alcazaba.

Admission free.

Teatro Romano ★★★ ANCIENT SITE   The jewel among Mérida's Roman ruins, this amphitheater is one of the world's most important

Mérida's Roman bridge is nearly half a mile long.

archaeological sites. Built at the order of the consul Agrippa in 15 B.C., it could seat 6,000 theater-goers. The spectacular stage wall *(scaenae frons)* with Corinthian columns and statues of deities was added in the A.D. early 2nd century under Emperor Trajan. The theater lay buried for more than a thousand years, leaving only the highest rows visible (the so-called *Siete Sillas,* the seven seats) until excavations began in the early 20th century under the direction of archaeologist José Ramón Melida. The columns were not fully restored until the 1970s. Today, the theater is the only one of Mérida's ruins still used for its original purpose, hosting a dazzling classical theater festival in July and August.

Calle José Ramón Melida, s/n. turismomerida.org. ℭ **92-433-07-22.** Admission 15€ combined ticket, 7.50€ students and seniors, free for kids 11 and under. Apr–Sept daily 9am–9pm; Oct–Mar daily 9am–6:30pm. Closed Dec 24, 25, and 31 and Jan 1.

Where to Stay in Mérida

MODERATE

Ilunion Mérida Palace ★★★ A restored 16th-century palace, the Ilunion has an unbeatable location close to the historic sites on the Plaza de España, where smartly-dressed locals gather for a late-night cocktail. From the iced water in the Moorish atrium to the spacious, mosaic-tiled rooms, everything is geared towards comfort and luxury. There's a gym, sauna, and tiny rooftop swimming pool (summer only) with fluffy towels and sunset views. The buffet breakfast and terrace restaurant serve good quality regional cuisine, although you can find other eating places in town with more character. Given the location and attention to detail, prices are remarkably reasonable.

Plaza de España, 19. www.ilunionmeridapalace.com. ℭ **92-438-38-00.** 76 units. 65€–200€ double. Valet parking 40€. **Amenities:** Restaurant; bar; room service; exercise room; rooftop pool; free Wi-Fi.

Parador de Mérida ★★ When you walk on the foot-worn tiles— terracotta dotted with blue octogram stars—you can sense the layers of history in this 18th-century convent. This spot was once a temple to the goddess Concordia and later a church, hospital, and prison; it combines Roman, Visigoth, and Mudéjar styles. In 1960 the *parador* played host to a meeting of two dictators, Spain's Franco and Portugal's Salazar. Rooms come in different shapes and sizes, some with four-poster beds, all splendidly outfitted with wood furnishings, coffered ceilings, and fine linen. At the salon installed in the cloister you can order a cooling drink and decipher the 19th-century graffiti carved into the columns. The lush garden has a small swimming pool, and the restaurant is top-notch, specializing in regional roasts of Ibérico pork and Retinto beef. Rates spike during the theater festival, but they are quite reasonable in the low season.

Calle Almendralejo, 56. www.parador.es. ℭ **92-431-38-00.** 82 units. 80€–200€ double. Parking 20€. **Amenities:** Restaurant; bar; room service; exercise room; outdoor pool; sauna; free Wi-Fi.

INEXPENSIVE

Apartamentos Capitolina ★★   The owners of Rex Numitor (p. 721) operate these stylish and spacious apartments next to the restaurant, just around the corner from Plaza Mayor. Clean and quiet, each has a separate living area with a small kitchen. The contemporary decor is peach and lime, the beds are good quality, and the terrace offers lovely views over the Alcazaba and Roman bridge. Breakfast is included in the nightly cost, as is daily maid service.

Calle de Castelar, 1. www.apartamentoscapitolina.com. © **92-431-86-54.** 4 units. 60€–160€ double. **Amenities:** Restaurant; kitchen; free Wi-Fi.

Nova Roma ★   Our value pick, this is a modern hotel aimed at the business traveler. It's not very exciting, but it is well managed, with a sparkling marble lobby and Roman-themed décor. The guest rooms are clean, well equipped, and have firm beds. There's plentiful hot water in the baths, just what you need after a long day at the ruins. The location, on a quiet side street, is just a short walk to the historic sites and the bullring. Good value parking is nearby.

Calle Suárez Somonte, 42. www.novaroma.com. © **92-431-12-61.** 55 units. 50€– 100€ double. Parking 11.50€. **Amenities:** Restaurant; bar; room service; free Wi-Fi.

Where to Eat in Mérida

Casa Nano ★★ EXTREMADURAN   On a quiet street just off Plaza de España, Casa Nano offers basic but delicious Extremaduran fare. You'll be ushered past the kitchen into the air-conditioned backroom, which feels like entering the *patrón*'s parlor. The *menú extremeño* is hearty and memorable—try *sopa de ajo,* involving a lot of garlic, soaked bread, and a poached egg. The lamb, slow cooked with plums *(cordero a la ciruela),* is sublime with the chilled red wine included on the set menu. Round things off with chocolate-coated figs or acorn tart and a complimentary liqueur. The friendly staff are attentive and appreciative. Cash only.

Calle Castelar, 3. © **92-431-8257.** Set menus 12€–23€. Mon–Sat 1:30–5pm and 8:30–11:30pm.

Fusiona Gastrobar ★★ FUSION   Many restaurants on the strip leading to the Roman Museum are sullen and over-priced, but this brightly-lit gastrobar bucks the trend, offering some of the most interesting cooking in town at bargain prices. In a casual atmosphere, sophisticated tapas combine the flavors of Extremadura with world cuisine—*croquetes* with truffles, *solomillo* with mascarpone and papaya, tuna tataki and quince. There are plenty of vegan-friendly options and an interesting selection of wine, artisanal vermouth, and beers. The hip-yet-friendly staff are clearly passionate about their culinary mission.

Calle José Ramón Mélida, 15. fusiona-gastrobar.negocio.site. © **92-410-29-36.** Tapas 4.80€, entrees 7.50€–12€. Mon–Tues 8:15pm–midnight, Wed–Sun 1:30–5pm and 8:15pm–midnight.

Plaza España, Mérida.

EXTREMADURA | Mérida

Mercado Gastronómico San Albín ★★ SPANISH   From the outside, Mérida's red-painted bullring looks a little run-down, but inside the porticos have been transformed into a lively gastronomic market. Grab a stool at one of the barrel-top tables surrounded by fading bullfight memorabilia and choose dishes from any of seven kiosks along the hallway, mixing it up as you go. We had simple tapas of *jamon, croquets,* and goats' cheese with caramelized onions, accompanied by a glass of cold *manzanilla,* but the Spanish extended family next to us ordered the huge set lunch based around roast suckling pig and lamb, and it looked like terrific value. It's an excellent pit-stop if you're doing a walking tour of the Roman ruins, as it's just across the road from the Casa del Mitreo.
Calle Vía Ensanche, 1. ✆ **64-759-12-61.** Tapas 2€–8€; entrees 10€–15€; set menu 15€. Daily noon–midnight.

Rex Numitor ★★ EXTREMADURAN   Right next door to Casa Nano (p. 720), Rex Numitor has a serenely spacious dining room, and in summer you can eat outside on the cobbles. The dishes, modern takes on Extremaduran classics, are as sophisticated as the decor, with swoops of sauce here and an architectural stack of proteins and vegetables there. The menu changes frequently, but recent standouts include a cherry gazpacho with olive oil ice cream; miso confit salt cod with pickled tomatoes and

721

mushrooms; and lamb sweetbreads with foie and truffles. Excellent cooking, friendly service, and modest prices.

Calle de Castelar, 1. rex-numitor.eltenedor.rest. © **60-958-64-41.** Entrees 12€–23€; set menus 16€–25€. Daily 1:30–5pm and 8:30pm–midnight.

Mérida Entertainment & Nightlife

The clutch of bars and restaurants around Arco Trajano are Mérida's modern-day forum. **A de Arco,** Calle Trajano, 8 (adearco.com; © **92-430-13-15**), leans more toward food, while its neighbor **Barocco,** Plaza de la Constitución (barocco-pub.negocio.site; © **69-143-34-50**), focuses heavily on cocktails. By midnight the clientele of both have merged into one big crowd spilling out over the square. Around the corner, **Jazz Bar,** Calle Alvarado, 10 (www.facebook.com/JazzBarMerida; © **92-431-99-00**), has high quality music and cocktails until around 3:30am. (Barocco keeps going until 4am.) In summer, the cocktail kiosks on Plaza de España also carry on late into the night, with young children playing in the square.

CÁCERES ★★★

The largest municipality in Extremadura, with a population of 95,000, Cáceres is a lively university town. It's also an UNESCO World Heritage Site, with honey-walled palaces, churches, and towers, largely financed by gold sent from the Americas by 16th-century conquistadors. These provide an enchanting backdrop for some high-end tourism and a burgeoning foodie scene

Cáceres was founded in the 1st century B.C. by the Romans as Norba Caesarina. After the Romans, it was settled by all the cultures that have made the south of Spain the cultural melting pot of influences it is today. Its name is derived from *alcázares,* an Arabic word meaning fortified citadel. Most visitors will head straight for the **Ciudad Monumental,** the medieval walled city, one of the most immaculately preserved in Spain.

Essentials

GETTING THERE The state of Extremadura's rail network has been a source of public anger for years, and getting to Cáceres by rail is slow going. There are five trains daily from Mérida (trip time: 1 hr.), costing 6€ to 8€, and four trains daily from Madrid, taking 3 to 4 hours, costing 24€ to 34€. There is only one direct train daily from Sevilla, taking 5 hours, costing 27.50€. The railway station is on Avenida Alemania (© **90-232-03-20**), near the main highway heading south.

Bus connections arrive at the bus station on Calle Túnez (© **92-723-25-50**) from Madrid (trip time: 5 hr.) and Sevilla (trip time: 4½ hr.) every 2 to 3 hours. There are also a handful of buses a day from Mérida and Trujillo. It's a 30-minute walk from the bus station to the city center, or wait for a green-and-white shuttle bus, which will drop you at the busy

LAND OF THE conquistadors

It's estimated that some 15,000 *extremeños* went to seek their fortune in the New World. The most fabled of these adventurers were Hernán Cortés (from Medellín), who went to Mexico, and Francisco Pizarro (from Trujillo), who went to Peru. Vasco Núñez de Balboa, who sighted the Pacific Ocean; Hernando de Soto, who discovered the Mississippi; and Francisco de Orellana, who explored the Amazon, all came from the region. Thanks to these tough and often ruthless men, the names of Extremaduran villages are sprinkled across the Americas—Albuquerque (New Mexico), Mérida (Mexico), Medellín (Colombia), and Trujillo (Peru), to name just a few. The conquistadors left Extremadura because they faced such difficulty making a living in the harsh land of their birth. One reason was that huge tracts of land, used for ranching, were owned by feudal absentee landlords. The estates, or *latifundios*, were home to tenant farmers and their families who paid the owners for the privilege of grazing a few goats or growing scant crops in the dry climate. Worse, a system of *mayorazgo* meant that all family property must be passed on to the eldest son, leaving younger sons penniless. It's not surprising that many set sail in search of a better life. Many conquistadors died or stayed in the New World, but others returned home with great riches to build magnificent palaces and monuments, many of which still stand. Bernal Díaz, who claimed to have fought 119 battles with Cortés in Mexico, was candid: "We came here to serve God and the king," he wrote, "and to get rich."

junction of Plaza de América. From there it's a 10-minute walk to Plaza Mayor and the old town.

By **car,** driving time from Madrid is about 3½ hours. Take the A-5 and exit onto the A-58 at Trujillo, driving another 45km (28 miles) west to Cáceres. From Mérida, it's a short drive north on the Autovía Ruta de la Plata. It's best not to try driving into the old town. **Parking Obispo Galarza** is close to Plaza Mayor. If your hotel is in the old town, ask them before you arrive about parking arrangements.

VISITOR INFORMATION The **tourist office** on Plaza Mayor (www. turismoextremadura.com; ✆ **92-711-12-22**) is open in summer daily 10am to 2pm and 5:30 to 8:30pm; in winter hours are Tuesday to Sunday 10am to 2pm and 4:30 to 7:30pm. The staff are extremely keen to help.

Exploring the Old Town of Cáceres

The first place you're likely to reach in old Cáceres is **Plaza Mayor,** which sits at the gateway to the walled city. It's a huge, coffin-shaped square, developed in the Middle Ages for fairs and gatherings, and it fulfils much the same function today, accommodating the annual WOMAD world music festival among many other events. It's a great place to relax in one of the cafés and contemplate the uncluttered façades, granite arcades and sturdy towers. Yet it's only the *hors d'oeuvre* to the old town proper, revealed through the oddly-angled **Arco de la Estrella.** Built by Manuel

Churriguera in 1726, the arch was commissioned by the nobleman Bernardino de Carvajal Moctezuma, who wanted the oblique shape to allow carriages easier access to his palace, next to the **Torre de Bujaco.**

If you have time, it's worth exploring the old town twice. By day, climb the winding, cobbled streets and stumble across the many magnificent palaces and churches, neatly signed with information panels (in Spanish only). By night, when the buildings and squares are beautifully lit and the air is cool, try one of the expert and entertaining guided tours; some are available in English. **Guias-Historiadores** (www. guiashistoriadorex.com; ✆ **68-429-36-43**) or **Cáceres al Fresquito** (✆ **66-683-63-32**) cost 8€ to 10€ per person. If mobility is an issue, try **Tuk and Go,** Calle Gran Via (tukandgo.com; ✆ **67-522-19-22**), which offers auto-rickshaw tours for 6.50€ to 12€.

The medieval quarter of Old Town Cáceres.

The extraordinarily well-preserved walls which enclose the old town of Cáceres were originally built by the Romans and fortified in turn by the Visigoths, Moors, and Christians. About 30 towers remain from the city's medieval walls. Originally much taller, they reflected the pride and independence of their builders; when Queen Isabel took control in the late 15th century, she ordered them cut down to size. Only the **Casa de las Cigüeñas** (House of the Storks) in **Plaza de San Mateo** was allowed to rise higher, demonstrating the value of loyalty to the queen. These unchanging streets and squares have provided a ready-made historical setting for many films and TV shows down the years, and in 2017 were the backdrop for season 7 of the hugely popular TV drama, *Game of Thrones,* alongside locations at the nearby natural monument of **Barruecos** and **Trujillo castle** (p. 733).

Plaza de Santa María ★ PLAZA   As you climb the **Calle Arco de la Estrella,** the first square you'll meet, and one of the most picturesque, is Plaza de Santa María. On all sides stand the honeyed façades of buildings once inhabited by the local nobles. Straight ahead is Cáceres' cathedral,

Concatedral de Santa María, a 15th-century Gothic structure to which many Renaissance embellishments were added when Cáceres became rich. It contains the tombs of several conquistadors and a beautiful cedar altarpiece from the 16th century (insert coins to light it up). Opposite the cathedral stands the bishop's palace **(Palacio Episcopal);** above its Renaissance doorway you'll see carved medallions with the heads of an Aztec and a Filipino, representing Spain's global empire. Felipe II, after whom the Philippines are named, stayed here in 1583 on his way back from being crowned king of Portugal.

Casa de los Toledo-Moctezuma ★ HISTORIC HOME   Just north of Plaza de Santa María is the domed palace bearing the name of **Isabel de Moctezuma,** daughter of the Aztec emperor, Moctezuma II. It was built by the conquistador **Juan Cano de Saavedra** with riches from his wife's dowry following their wedding in 1532. Isabel had quite a life. Married three times by the age of twelve, she converted to Christianity, married three conquistadors, had an illegitimate child with Hernán Cortés, and was widowed five times. Saavedra survived her and returned rich to Cáceres to complete his family pile. In 1559 his son Juan Cano de Moctezuma married Elvira de Toledo y Ovando, establishing one of Spain's grandest dynasties. The palace, which bears the crests of various noble families, is now a public-records office, hence the mirrored windows.
Plaza Conde de Canilleros, 1.

Palacio de los Golfines de Abajo ★★ HISTORIC HOME   Perhaps the most magnificent of all the palaces in Cáceres, the beautifully restored home of the Golfin family is brimming with artistic and historic treasures spanning 600 years. And, unlike many of the palaces in the old town, it is well set up for guided visits—it even has a shop. It was built in the 15th century in Gothic style, with over-the-top Plateresque embellishment

---

Eyes on Storks

Whenever you look up in Cáceres—as in many towns in Extremadura—the chances are you'll see **storks (cigüeñas)** alighting on their huge, untidy nests, built on rooftops, bell-towers, and pylons. The city is one of the most important stork-breeding sites in Europe, hosting scores of pairs. In nearby **Malpartida de Cáceres** they celebrate these mythical birds every May in a festival called the Week of the Stork (malpartidadecaceres.es), with photography competitions, nest-building workshops and ornithological trails. These days you can see them throughout the year, as fewer are making the trip across the Straits of Gibraltar to winter in Africa, preferring the rich pickings here. In some parts of the region, notably the **Monfragüe national park** (p. 738), you can observe the much rarer black stork.

added in the 17th century. The **Reyes Católicos** (Catholic Kings) used to stay here—you can see a signed letter from them asking the Golfins for military support in 1485—and in gratitude for numerous services they allowed their shield to be included on the façade. It sits, crowned by a cross, on top of the highest double windows. As if one sumptuous palace weren't enough, the Golfins had another at the top of the old town: **Palacio de los Golfines de Arriba** (Calle de los Condes). General Franco was declared head of state there in 1936; today, it houses a pleasant courtyard restaurant.

Plaza de Los Golfines, 1. www.palaciogolfinesdeabajo.com. © **92-721-80-51.** Admission adults 2.50€, seniors 1.50€. Tues–Sat 10am–6:30pm (7pm in summer), Sun 10am–1pm. Guided tours on the hour.

Museo de Cáceres ★★ MUSEUM The municipal museum, at the top of the old town, is a low-key gem. It occupies two historic houses, **Casa de las Veletas** and **Casa de los Caballos,** built on the remains of the Moorish fortress, or Alcazaba. The first holds archaeological and ethnographic collections illustrating life in Extremadura from the Paleolithic through the Middle Ages. A Bronze Age ceremonial stone boar, probably intended to protect the herd, shows how the region's preoccupations have

A 12th-century cistern is the last remnant of Cáceres' Moorish fortress.

endured. In the second is a collection of fine art and sculpture, including works by Picasso, Miró, and a luminous *Jesus Salvador* by El Greco. There's also a delightful large canvas from 1914 of women at a village fiesta, carrying a chicken and a head-held watermelon, by the Extremaduran impressionist Eugenio Hermoso. The greatest revelation, however, is the Moorish cistern *(aljibe)* which lies beneath the Casa de las Veletas. Dating from the 12th century, it is all that survives of the original fortress, and still collects rainwater which falls on the Renaissance cloister above. The golden reflection of its horseshoe arches in the water is a wonderful sight.

Plaza de las Veletas, 1. museodecaceres.juntaex.es. ⓒ **92-701-08-77.** Free admission for EU citizens, others 1.20 €, free Sun. Tues–Sat 9am–3pm and 4–7:30pm (8:30pm in summer), Sun 10am–3pm, closed Mon.

Centro de Artes Visuales, Fundación Helga de Alvear ★ ART MUSEUM

Just outside the old town, a modernist stone palace from 1910, beautifully remodeled by the architects Tuñón and Mansilla, houses the collection of the German/Spanish collector Helga de Alvear. She established a nonprofit foundation here in 2006, in partnership with the council of Extremadura, to share and promote the contemporary visual arts. Its white-box, concrete-floored rooms host long-term exhibitions drawn from one of the world's most important modern collections. On the wall beside each piece is a quotation from the artist who created it. The Cuban abstractionist Carmen Herrera sums up the mood: "The straight line is, for me, the beginning and the end."

Calle Pizarro, 8. fundacionhelgadealvear.es. ⓒ **92-762-64-14.** Free admission. Mon–Sat 10am–2pm and 5–8pm (6–9pm in summer), Sun 10am–2:30pm.

Where to Stay in Cáceres

Atrio Restaurant Hotel ★★★ To walk across a deserted Plaza de San Mateo, past the ivy-covered Torre de Sande towards the Atrio hotel, is to step into the glossy-magazine world of luxury travel. The building's design is dramatically bold. At the apex of this World Heritage site, next to a 15th-century church, architects Tuñón and Mansilla have created an ultra-modern hotel with all the artistry of the restaurant it houses. Once inside you're drawn into a world of white vertical slats and changing light straight out of an architectural journal. Hans Wegner chairs and Andy Warhol originals complement the spaces. The practicalities are all in place, too: impeccable service, beautifully appointed rooms, and, of course, *that* restaurant and wine cellar (p. 729). If all that isn't enough, the hotel offers exquisite additional food and wine experiences, with matching prices.

Plaza de San Mateo, 1. restauranteatrio.com/en. ⓒ **92-724-29-28.** 13 units. 290€– 320€ double. **Amenities:** Restaurant; bar; concierge; solarium; terrace; free Wi-Fi.

Parador de Cáceres ★★★ One of the oldest *paradors* in the system, this state-run beauty is set inside the 14th-century **Palacio de Torreorgaz** in the old town. Recent top-to-bottom renovation gives it a tastefully austere feel: clean white walls, granite doorways, and brick vaulting; LED lighting and 21st-century air-conditioning. The spacious guest rooms are coolly furnished in wood and natural fabrics with well-fitted-out modern bathrooms. They are great value in low season. Its restaurant, **Torreorgaz,** is a little expensive (set menu 35€) but has a lovely coffered ceiling and in summer a few tables in a leafy patio (ask to reserve). It specializes in regional dishes such as Ibérico pork with *Torta del Casar* cheese.

Calle Ancha, 6. www.parador.es. ✆ **90-254-79-79.** 33 units. 105€–225€ double. **Amenities:** Restaurant, bar; concierge; room service; terrace; free Wi-Fi.

Soho Boutique Casa Don Fernando ★★ If the uptown, upmarket hotels are beyond your means, this is a great value base from which to explore the city. A former grand townhouse, bang in the middle of the Plaza Mayor, it is neatly designed, clean, and well-run by the friendly staff, who are happy to help with advice about visiting the town. Some rooms are a little tight, but they are straightforwardly comfortable and—thanks to an enforced no-smoking policy—fresh-smelling. Given the location and quality of service, the rates in low season are scarcely believable. Discount parking is available at the Obispo Galarza car park nearby.

Plaza Mayor, 30. www.sohohoteles.com. ✆ **92-762-71-76.** 36 units. 40€–100€ double. Parking 10€. **Amenities:** Cafeteria; bar; babysitting; room service; free Wi-Fi.

NH Palacio de Oquendo ★★ Yet another converted stone palace, this primarily business and conference hotel is so spick-and-span it looks as if it had been built last week. Ideally located on Plaza de Juan, it's just a short stroll from the old city and the Plaza Mayor, and well placed for the restaurant nightlife which fills the pavements below. What the large rooms lack in character they make up for in cleanliness, high-quality fittings, and huge beds. You get a lot of comfort for your money.

Plaza de San Juan, 11. www.nhcollection.com. ✆ **92-721-58-00.** 86 units. 70€–185€ double. Parking 10€. **Amenities:** Restaurant; bar; terrace; concierge; room service; babysitting; free Wi-Fi.

Casa-Palacio Gran Lujo Cáceres ★★ There are plenty of good value rooms and flats to be had in Cáceres on Airbnb, but this one deserves a special mention. It's a luxurious apartment in a beautifully renovated 18th-century palace in the old town next to the Plaza Mayor, with vaulted ceilings, private patio, and fountains. You can rent a room or the whole open-plan space for up to 7 people (infants go free) for a fraction of what the luxury hotels will set you back. The location, cleanliness, and super host have earned rave reviews online.

Calle Moreras, 2. Search title on Airbnb.com or Booking.com. **Amenities:** Kitchen; free Wi-Fi.

A Foodie Paradise

Extremadura has always taken its food seriously, as the Bronze Age boar in the Museo de Cáceres (p. 726) attests. The delicatessens behind Plaza Mayor are packed with regional specialties: *jamón de bellota* from the acorn-grazing black pig; *patatera*, a humble, soft sausage made with potato and flavored with *pimentón de la Vera*, smoked paprika made from chilies first imported by the conquistadors; *Torta del Casar*, a gooey sheep's milk cheese best spooned out with a biscuit. But what has really turned Cáceres into a serious foodie destination has been the life's work of one man: Cáceres-born Toño Pérez, head chef at the fabled **Atrio** restaurant (see below), which opened here in 1986. Things really took off when it moved up to the old town in 2010, into a stunning renovation by star architects Tuñón and Mansilla, to serve the region's finest alta cocina. The effect has been to raise culinary standards and expectations across the city. A new wave of excellent taperías and gastrobars has sprung up, taking Extremadura's fine ingredients and traditions—and no doubt Toño Pérez—as inspiration.

Where to Eat in Cáceres

Atrio ★★★ EXTREMADURAN   Simply the best restaurant in Extremadura and one of the best in Europe, Atrio is something to be experienced—if you can afford it. Chef Toño Pérez marries the techniques of cutting-edge cuisine with hyper-local ingredients and traditional flavors; he has a particular penchant for local wild vegetables. Two fixed menus are available: nine courses of Atrio classics or twelve of adventurous new creations. Here's a taste: prawn carpaccio with mustard sprouts and sour cream; crunchy Ibérico pork with crayfish and game foam; and for dessert, Perez's take on *Torta del Casar* with quince and olive oil, and a double-take "cherry which is not a cherry." Courses are paired with wine from the 40,000-bottle cellar—sommelier José Polo is Pérez's partner—regularly named by *Wine Spectator* magazine as one of the world's finest. Visiting it is a highlight, but be careful—many are eye-wateringly expensive. The setting and service are as elegant as the fare, in a sleek, wood-slatted room hung with originals by Warhol and Tàpies. It is sometimes possible in low season to walk in and get a table at lunchtime, but reservations are strongly recommended.

At Atrio hotel, Plaza de San Mateo, 1. www.restauranteatrio.com. ✆ **92-724-29-28.** Fixed-price menus 149€. Mon–Sat 1:30–4pm and 9pm–midnight; Sun 1:30–4pm. Closed last 2 weeks July.

El Figón de Eustaquío ★★ EXTREMADURAN   If an old-fashioned Extremaduran feast is what you crave, head for this classic Cáceres establishment, founded in 1947 and apparently unchanged since. Set in the perfect society spot on Plaza San Juan, where tables spread across the pavement on summer evenings, the rustic interior is lined with old photographs of the family who still run it, while white-coated waiters move about expertly. The food is certainly traditional and hearty—roast suckling pig, *calderata de cordero* (lamb stew), *migas extremeño* (traditional fried breadcrumbs)—but the creativity and presentation nod to more recent culinary trends. There are excellent desserts, too—try the trademark fig ice-cream.

Plaza San Juan, 14. www.elfigondeeustaquio.com. ✆ **92-724-43-62.** Entrees 12€–30€; set menu 26€. Daily 1:30–4pm and 8–11:30pm. Closed July 1–15.

La Cacharrería ★ EXTREMADURAN   A good alternative to a heavy-set menu, this *tapería* serves adventurous small plates in a fashionably renovated stone building in the heart of the old town. You can share a handful of artfully presented tapas at 4.50€ apiece, served at high wooden tables. Mixing the modern and the traditional, the ravioli of *morcilla de Guadalupe* (blood sausage) and solomillo in *torta del Casar* sauce (served in a martini glass) are superb, though the gristly pig's ear with spicy *migas* may be a little too adventurous for some. There is also a good selection of vegetarian options, regional wines, and attractive *tapas dulces* (desserts).

Calle Orellana 1, ✆ **615-21-27-50.** Entrees 10€–18€. Thurs–Mon 1–4pm and 8:30pm–midnight. Closed Tues–Wed.

Mastropiero Gastrobar y Jardín ★★ FUSION   One of the new wave of eateries, Mastropiero serves superb fusion tapas in a lovely garden on the edge of the old town. The menus come in record sleeves, the bread in a paper bag, and the cooking is both witty and delicious. The *bombas crujientes* with kimchi and Ibérico pork, and the *cordero gyoza* (lamb dumplings with green curry) burst with flavor. Upbeat servers and a soundtrack of 1960s soul add to the family-friendly atmosphere. As the evening wears on, people turn to gin: Mastropiero's Gin Club has an astonishing selection, including more brands of tonic than your average bar has gins.

Calle Fuente Nueva 4. www.mastropierogastrobar.es. ✆ **92-721-48-37.** Tapas 6€–8€, entrees 10€–12€. Daily 7pm—late.

TRUJILLO ★★

The view as you approach the walled town of Trujillo, perched on a granite hill above the deserted plain, is much the same today as at any time over the past 500 years (electricity pylons aside). Its Moorish castle and city walls date from the 9th to the 12th centuries, the tower of the church Santa María la Mayor celebrates its Christian reconquest in the 13th. What really put the name of this modest settlement on the map, however, is that it produced many of the pugnacious *extremeños* who colonized the New World. Francisco Pizarro, who conquered the Incan empire with an army of just 180 men, was born here in the 1470s; his horseback statue and his family's lavish palace dominate the Plaza Mayor. Francisco Orellana, the first European to navigate the length of the Amazon river, was

The walled town of Trujillo became wealthy with conquistador gold.

another local boy made good; his birthplace is now a high-end hotel (Calle Paloma, 5–7; www.casadeorellana.com). Today, the name Trujillo can be found on towns and cities, rivers, even beer bottles across Latin America; it is said that 20 countries were born here. The stupendous wealth which the conquistadors brought back was used to build the 16th- and 17th-century manor houses, churches, and towers which make this small town such an architectural delight. Plaza Mayor on a warm night, with its flood-lit monuments, arcaded outdoor restaurants, and strolling families, is one of Spain's most pleasurable sights.

Essentials

GETTING THERE   There are **buses** every hour or so from Madrid to Tru-jillo, taking 3½–4½ hours, and half a dozen daily from Badajoz and Các-res. A one-way ticket from Madrid costs 22€–33€; from Badajoz 14€–23€; and from Cáceres 5.50€. Trujillo's modern, but rather bleak, bus station is on Avenida Extremadura on the south side of town (www.avanzabus.com; ✆ **92-732-12-02**). By **car,** Trujillo lies on the network of roads connecting Lisbon and Madrid via the A-5. Driving time from Madrid is around 3 hours; from Badajoz around 1½ hours; and from Caceres 40 minutes.

Exploring Trujillo

An economical way to get around the main points of interest is to buy the all-in **Zona Monumental** ticket for a guided tour offered by the tourist office at 11am and 5:30pm daily. It costs 7.50€ and gives you access to six sites, including the castle, churches, and the **Casa-Museo de Pizarro.** The tour is in Spanish but even if you don't understand the language it's worthwhile to tag along—you can always peel off and use your ticket later. Tours and audio-guides in English are available from Turismo Trujillo, Calle Tiendas, 3 (www.turismotrujillo.es; ✆ **92-732-05-10**). But first, and last, you should spend plenty of time in the lovely **Plaza Mayor.**

Plaza Mayor ★★★ PLAZA Trujillo's main square, sitting above the rather downcast modern town, is an irregular collection of historic buildings and monuments which, seen together, come close to perfection. Overlooking it all is a huge bronze **equestrian statue** of Francisco Pizarro by the American sculptor Charles Rumsey, given to Trujillo by Rumsey's widow in 1926. Although portrayed as tall and magnificent in his plumed helmet, Pizarro was in truth a thuggish illiterate whom many today would deem a war criminal. (An identical casting in Lima—the Peruvian capital Pizarro founded—has proven so controversial, it has had to be moved twice.) Behind the statue stands the solid **Iglesia de San Martín,** an enormous 14th-century granite church that was reconstructed in Renaissance style in the 16th century. In 1526 Emperor Carlos V stopped here to pray on his way to Sevilla to marry Isabel of Portugal. Inside it has an impressive vaulted nave and an 18th-century baroque organ, still in working order. In the diagonally opposite corner of the square is the **Palacio de la Conquista,** started in 1562 by Pizarro's brother Hernando for his wife (and niece) Francisca Pizarro

A statue of Francisco Pizarro presides over Trujillo's Plaza Mayor.

Yupanqui. She was the daughter of Francisco Pizarro and his mistress Inés Huaylas Yupanqui, the Incan emperor Atahualpa's sister. It's known locally as the **Palacio del Escudo,** or Palace of the Shield, after the enormous coat of arms and balcony which festoon its corner—a striking example of 17th-century Plateresque bling, featuring carved busts of this complex foursome. There are plenty more sights of interest in the square: the **Ayuntamiento Viejo** (Old Town Hall) with three tiers of arches, each squatter than the one below; the unusual facade of **Casa de las Cadenas,** a 12th-century house draped with a heavy chain to show that Felipe II, who stayed here, had granted the Orellana family immunity from taxes; and in a corner, the **Palacio de los Duques de San Carlos,** a 16th-century palace now used as a convent. After all that you'll have earned a cold drink at one of the square's open-air cafes, whose awnings spray cooling mist on hot afternoons.

Iglesia de Santa María la Mayor ★★ CHURCH   Climbing the hill above Plaza Mayor, you'll reach this Romano-Gothic church, the largest in Trujillo, built on the ruins of a Moorish mosque. Its proudest treasure is the *retablo* (altarpiece) with two dozen panels painted by Fernando Gallego in the late 15th century. You can see the tomb of another local celebrity, Diego García de Paredes, the so-called "Samson of Extremadura," who is said to have single-handedly defended a bridge against 200 attacking Frenchmen. He died in 1534 and gets a mention in Cervantes' *Don Quixote* as an example of a real-life hero, rather than the fictional ones in books of chivalry. The heroic climb up the bell tower is repaid with terrific views across the rooftops and Plaza Mayor.

Calle Santa Maria, 17. Admission 1.50€. Apr–Sept daily 10am–2pm and 5–9pm; Oct–Mar daily 10am–2pm and 4–7pm.

Casa-Museo de Pizarro ★ HISTORIC HOME   This small museum, in a house at the top of the old town where the young Francisco Pizarro is said to have lived, doesn't tell you a great deal about the life of Trujillo's most famous son, but the ground floor is a nicely-done recreation of a modest Extremaduran home of the 15th century. The bedroom, fireplace, and agricultural implements have the air of a folk museum. Upstairs is dedicated to Pizarro's adventures in Peru, with relief maps, timelines, and scraps of the Incan culture he did much to destroy. Although the information is mostly in Spanish, it offers an easily digestible glimpse of history which children, who go free, should enjoy.

Calleja del Castillo, 1. www.turismoextremadura.com. ✆ **92-732-26-77.** Admission 1.50€ adults, children free. Daily 10am–2pm and 4:30–7:30pm.

Castillo ★★ HISTORIC SITE   Built by the Moors on the site of a Roman fortress, this perfect example of a medieval castle stands at the summit of the granite hill known as **Cabeza del Zorro** (Fox's Head) on which Trujillo was founded. With its long crenelated ramparts, horseshoe arches, and dungeons, it's little wonder it was chosen as a location for

HBO's epic TV drama *Game of Thrones,* which should boost Trujillo's modest international appeal. Legend has it that the Virgin Mary appeared here in 1232, giving the Christians renewed courage to free the city from domination by the Moors. Climb its battlements for panoramic views of Extremadura's austere landscape, just before sunset for maximum medieval effect.

Plaza de Castillo, 1. turismoextremadura.com. Admission 1.50€. Apr–Sept daily 10am–2pm and 5–8:30pm; Oct–Mar 10am–2pm and 4–8pm.

Where to Stay in Trujillo

Eurostars Palacio Santa Marta ★★   The location and surroundings of this hotel, in a recently refurbished 16th-century palace just behind Pizarro's statue, are scarcely believable at these prices. It's a chain, but everything here is beautifully done: spotless, wood-beamed rooms, many with views of Plaza Mayor; large pillowy beds; an outdoor swimming pool in summer; and well-trained staff. Enjoy a buffet breakfast under granite arches before heading off to explore the old town on your doorstep.

Calle Ballesteros, 6. www.eurostarshotels.com. ✆ **91-334-21-96.** 50 units. 55€–140€ double. Parking 10€. **Amenities:** Restaurant; bar; room service; pool and terrace; free Wi-Fi.

Storks nest on many of the Gothic stone towers of Trujillo.

Parador de Trujillo ★★★ Set in the former Franciscan convent of Santa Clara, founded in 1533, Trujillo's *parador* has a hint of saintly austerity. Transformed into a state-run hotel in 1984, its rooms are former nuns' cells, now with luxurious touches such as canopied beds and marble-clad bathrooms. There's a small pool, a serene Renaissance cloister with fruit trees and a well, and a good restaurant serving a 30€ set menu with such regional specialties as *zorongollo* (tuna and red pepper salad) and *técula mécula* (almond and egg tart). The quiet location is not far from Plaza Mayor, but finding it (and its carpark) among the narrow streets can be tricky.

Calle de Santa Beatriz de Silva, 1. www.parador.es. ✆ **92-732-13-50.** 50 units. 80€–175€ double. Free parking. **Amenities:** Restaurant; bar; babysitting; outdoor pool; room service; free Wi-Fi.

Hotel Victoria ★★ Sedate and beautifully maintained, the Victoria is a 19th-century mansion with all the decorative elements of that era: wrought-iron capitals and balustrades, marble floors, and ornate tiles. Rooms are oversized, high-ceilinged, and quiet—the hotel is a short walk away from the town's main action. There's a large garden terrace and interior patio, where buffet breakfast is served.

Plaza del Campillo, 22. www.hotelvictoriatrujillo.es ✆ **92-732-18-19.** 27 units. 80€–120€ double. Breakfast included in room rate. Parking 10€. **Amenities:** Restaurant; bar; terrace; free Wi-Fi

El Baciyelmo ★★★ In a lovingly restored townhouse not far from the Plaza Mayor, these studio apartments run by Dutch couple Karla and Herman are the town's hot ticket. The new-meets-old decor, leafy shared garden, and small outdoor pool—but especially the warm hospitality of the hosts—earn glowing reviews online. Available in a variety of sizes, each has a small living area and kitchenette, and can be booked for a minimum of 2 nights.

Calle Margarita Iturralde, 25. www.baciyelmo.com. ✆ **92-732-08-42.** 6 units. 58€–72€ double. **Amenities:** Packed lunches; bike hire; free Wi-Fi.

Where to Eat in Trujillo

If you've just arrived in Trujillo from the foodie paradise that is Cáceres (p. 729), be prepared for things to be a little different around here. The cooking is generally hearty rather than sophisticated, and around the Plaza Mayor, quality and service can be hit-or-miss. That said, if you keep it simple and go for the good-value set menus, you can dine well, especially if meat is your cup of tea.

La Alberca Asador ★ EXTREMADURAN Well-located at the top of the old town with a lovely terrace, La Alberca specializes in local meat cooked simply and elegantly on the charcoal grill. Solomillo Ibérico pork and Ternera Retinto beef lead the way, while non-meat-eaters rave about the charcoal-roasted vegetables. The 15€ *menu del día* includes interesting options such as *revuelto de morcilla* (scrambled egg with blood sausage), which tastes better than it sounds in English. The welcoming and attentive service has earned lots of good reviews.

Calle de la Victoria, 8. www.facebook.com/albercatrujillo. ✆ **92-732-22-09.** Entrees 13.50€–27.50€, set menus 15€–25€. Thurs–Mon 1–4pm and 8:30–11:30pm. Closed Tues–Wed.

Corral del Rey ★★ EXTREMADURAN   By general consensus the pick of Trujillo's restaurants, Corral del Rey is the upmarket choice, with a group of brick-vaulted dining rooms and a better class of terrace, just off Plaza Mayor. Meats grilled on local *carbón de encina* (holm oak charcoal) are the specialty, coupled with some interesting flourishes: *bacalao* Corral del Rey (grilled salt-cod with zucchini and garlic), marinated tuna and red pepper salad, cold melon soup. There's an extensive regional wine list and good-looking desserts such as brandy-soaked figs dipped in chocolate. The set menus at 25€ and 40€ are at the higher end of the scale and if you go à la carte, it can all get rather expensive.

Plazuela Corral del Rey, 2. www.corraldelreytrujillo.com. ✆ **92-732-30-71.** Entrees 13€–30€. Mon–Tues and Thurs–Sat 1:30–4pm and 8:30–11pm, Sun 1:30–4pm.

Mesón la Troya ★ EXTREMADURAN   A Trujillo classic and one of the best-value restaurants in the region, Mesón la Troya serves massive portions at reasonable prices. Set in prime location right on the Plaza Mayor, it is equally interesting to sit outside or in, where old photographs and plates grace the white walls. The fixed-price menu gets you four courses, including bulky tortilla and paella openers, ideal for the ravenous backpacker. The tastiest main courses are traditional hotpots such as *prueba de cerdo* (garlicky pork casserole) and *calderata de cordero* (lamb stew). You may not need breakfast the next morning.

Plaza Mayor, 10. www.mesonlatroya.es. ✆ **92-732-13-64.** Entrees 7.50€–15€, set menus 15€–26.50€. Daily 12:15–11:30pm.

El 7 de Sillerias ★ EXTREMADURAN   Don't be put off by the underwhelming exterior; when the weather permits, this courtyard restaurant is buzzing with regulars going out for a big, sharing treat. After a

---

SHH . . . SPAIN'S BEST wine?

If you ask for a glass of red wine in any of Trujillo's better restaurants, the chances are you'll be offered the local superstar, Habla del Silencio. It's made in harsh, slatey vineyards a 10-minute drive south of town at an extraordinary avant-garde winery that looks more Bond villain's lair than bodega. Starting in 2000, Habla's philosophy has been to throw off the baggage of traditional wine-making and focus on quality. That approach has paid off, as this intensely purple, organic blend of varietals has been voted the best Spanish red wine several years in a row. You can visit the Habla bodega for a tour and tasting by appointment only via the website. You'll see the minimalist black bottle for sale, for a very reasonable 10€ or so, at most delicatessens in town.

Bodegas Habla, Autovia A-5, exit km 259; bodegashabla.com; ✆ **92-765-91-80.**

Trujillo, home to the Feria Nacional de Queso (National Cheese Festival), is a great place to try the local sheeps'-milk cheeses.

hunk of bread with delicious local olive oil, recommended dishes include an idiosyncratic house salad (involving smoked salmon, goat cheese, walnuts, and crunchy dried onions), smoked sardines on toast, and rock salt-sprinkled *entrecot de Retinto* steak, paired with a good regional red. If there's room after that, try the creamy *arroz con leche* (rice pudding) or cheesecake with fig marmalade.

Calle Sillerías, 7. www.el7desillerias.com. © **92-732-18-56.** Entrees 10€–20€. Daily 1pm–1am (Sun until midnight).

Trujillo Shopping

The best shopping in town revolves around edible Extremaduran specialties, and there are some appealing delicatessens on **Calle Tiendas.** Ibérico ham and sausage, goat and sheep cheeses, honey, olive oil, and wine can all be packaged up to take home. If you're visiting in May, look for the national cheese festival (www.feriadelquesotrujillo.es) that overruns Plaza Mayor, featuring some of the world's finest. There's also a burgeoning craft ale industry. And make sure you don't miss **Pastelería Basilio** at nearby Calle Herreros, 1 (www.facebook.com/pasteleriabasilio; © **92-732 01 63**), with its photogenic windowful of sticky regional cakes. For more durable souvenirs, try **Convento de la Merced,** Calle Merced, 2 (extremaadur artesana.blogspot.com; © **92-777-45-11**), which sells artisanal ceramics, wicker, and metal work. A lovely old ceramic billboard advertising **Nitrato de Chile** (saltpeter used as fertilizer) marks the spot.

MONFRAGÜE ★★

Arching like a broad, green brushstroke on the map north of Cáceres and Trujillo, the **Parque Nacional de Monfragüe** (pronounced *mon-frag-way,* or "broken mountain") became a national park in 1979 following a campaign by local conservationists. A UNESCO Biosphere Reserve since 2003, it covers 69 square miles (18,000 hectares) of untouched Mediterranean woodland, rocky gorges, and majestic water where the Tagus and Tiétar rivers converge. It's a must-visit destination for serious birdwatchers, home to most of Spain's protected bird species, including the Spanish imperial eagle, black stork, azure-winged magpie, and Europe's biggest population of black vultures (you'll see scores of them without even trying). Red deer, wildcats, genets, and otters roam the forests and riverbanks; some 200 different species live here. Unfortunately, facilities for wider tourism are still relatively undeveloped. It gets punishingly hot here in summer—the best times to visit are spring and autumn.

Essentials

It's not really practical to explore Monfragüe without access to a car or motorcycle. The one-street hamlet of **Villarreal de San Carlos** is the only place to stay within the park; it has a rugged backpacker feel. The larger village of **Torrejón el Rubio,** just south of the park, would be a more comfortable base for most visitors. Torrejón is a short drive from Trujillo (30 min. via EX-208) or Cáceres (45 min. via EX-390), making it a feasible day trip from either town; it's 2½ hours from Madrid via the A-5. Bus service from Cáceres and Trujillo runs just twice a week to Torrejón.

Exploring Monfragüe

Although the park covers a vast expanse, navigating it is straightforward. At the small tourist office in Torrejón el Rubio, Paseo de Pizarro, 1 (www.torrejonelrubio.com; © **92-745-52-92;** 10am–2pm and 4–8pm), you can pick up well-produced maps with color-coded suggested routes by car and foot. The red route (Ruta Roja) is the best-known, and a good place to start. Before you set off, visit the inexplicably un-signposted **Birdcenter,** Travesía la Jara (www.centrosurmonfrague.com; © **92-745-52-92;** 10am–2pm and 4–8pm), where the English-speaking staff can advise on everything from guided outings to local cave paintings; make sure to download their excellent app (search for **Birding in Extremadura**). The building itself is worth a look: a steel-and-stone representation of a pair of spreading wings. Then take the road north towards Villarreal de San Carlos.

Castillo de Monfragüe ★★ HISTORIC SITE   A natural first stop on entering the park, Monfragüe's castle—a heavily restored 9th-century Moorish ruin—is not much to look at. The thrill comes from the panoramic views it offers across the Tagus and its winding tributaries, banked by unspoiled woodland, with scarcely a building in sight for miles. Raptors hang in the air above and below you. To reach the castle, leave your vehicle in the carpark at the bottom of the hill and take the free shuttle which runs every 30 minutes Tuesday to Saturday.

Salto de Gitano ★★★ VIEWPOINT   The best-known image of Monfragüe and the highlight for many, the *mirador* at Salto de Gitano (Gypsy's Leap) looks across the craggy gorge to the **Peña Falcón** on the other side of the river, a dramatic outcrop colonized by scores of griffon vultures, who circle around so low and slow that they appear enormous. You might also see a rare black stork gliding along the water. Parking here is easy, and the authorities have provided wooden shelters with log backrests so you can gaze up for hours through a long lens to capture the perfect image. As the road winds towards Villa Real de San Carlos there are many other well-managed *miradors*. **Fuente del Francés** is a good place to spot red deer; **Puente de Cardenal** is a stone bridge ordered by the Bishop of Plasencia in 1450 to connect that city with Trujillo. It's said to have cost the same number of gold pieces as the stones it contains: 30,000. You may find, however, that it's invisible under the rising water.

Villarreal de San Carlos ★ TOWN   Despite its regal name, Villarreal is a tiny, slate-built hamlet, the only settlement for miles around. It was established at the end of the 18th century by Carlos III as a garrison to protect the area against the ravages of banditry, all too common at the

MONFRAGÜE'S cave paintings

Besides its abundance of nature, Monfragüe is blessed with many fine examples of prehistoric rock art *(arte repustre).* There are more than 100 sites within the park where cave paintings can be seen, ranging from the Mesolithic period (8,000 years ago) to the Iron Age (2,800 years ago). To view them, visit the Centro de Arte Rupestre de Monfragüe in Torrejón el Rubio (attached to the BirdCenter), where you can arrange a guided tour—with some English—for small groups. What's exciting is how unpackaged this experience is. The simple paintings, such as those close to the Castillo de Monfragüe, are as open to the elements as they've always been. Armed with just a torch and a laminated photocopy to help identify the ancient stick figures of people and animals, your legs dangle from a metal platform at the mouth of the cave as you explore. Tickets cost 4€. Travesía la Jara. www.centrosurmonfrague.com. ✆ **92-745-52-92.** 10am–2pm and 4–8pm.

time. Today, it provides a base for birdwatchers and backpackers with a couple of bars, a handful of basic places to stay, and an informative visitor center. Each February it hosts the International Ornithology Fair, whose photography competition produces mind-blowing results (go to fioextremadura.es).

Centro de Información del Parque Natural de Monfragüe, Villarreal de San Carlos. www.birdinginextremadura. ℭ **92-719-91-34.**

Where to Stay & Eat in Monfragüe

There's not much going on in **Torrejón el Rubio,** but a number of newly built self-catering apartments have popped up offering great value. Take care when booking as several have very similar names. Our picks are the spotless, comfortably air-conditioned **Apartamentos Rurales Natura,** Travesia del Pizarro (www.ruralnatura.es; ℭ **92-731-16-77**), which throw in cakes for breakfast; and **Apartamentos Rurales Monfragüe,** Calle Corchito, 27 (apartamentosmonfrague.es; ℭ **92-745-50-79**). Food in the village is fairly basic; there are a couple of just-okay hotel restaurants, plus friendly **Centro Social** in the Plaza España, which does a surprisingly good hamburger.

Villarreal de San Carlos also has a handful of rural apartments, of which **Casa Rural Al-Mofrag** (casaruralalmofrag.com; ℭ **68-645-43-93**) and **Apartmentos Rurales El Mirador de Monfragüe** (www.el miradordemonfrague.com; ℭ **68-645-43-93**) are our picks. If you plan to eat in Villarreal it more or less has to be **Casa Paqui** (ℭ **92-719-90-02**), where you can get *estofado de jabali/venado* (roast boar or venison) at 15€, accompanied by ice cold beer in frozen glasses.

Off the beaten track on the park's north side towards Plasencia, the extraordinary, ranch-like **Casa Rural La Sierra de Monfragüe,** Carretera EX-208, km13 (www.lasierrademonfrague.es; ℭ **63-891-54-65**), is well worth checking out.

Hospedería Parque de Monfragüe ★★ Located just north of sleepy Torrejón el Rubio on the way into the park, this huge, modernist construction is an unexpected sight. Completed in 2015 using traditional materials—slate, wood, concrete, red weathered steel—it is certainly impressive if not exactly beautiful. Inside it has all the amenities of a luxury hotel: floor-to-ceiling windows with marvelous views, spacious slate-and-wood bedrooms with huge TVs (who comes here to watch TV?), a gym, and spa. Outside there's a huge swimming pool and garden. The restaurant, **El Paraíso de los Sentidos** (Paradise of the Senses), over-promises, stuck in limbo somewhere between hearty and fancy cuisine. Despite its huge dimensions, the Hospedería is often fully booked, even off-season—such is the pull of the park for birdwatchers and walkers.

Carretera Plasencia-Trujillo, km. 37. www.hospederiasdeextremadura.es. ℭ **92-487-05-97.** 60 units. 75€–120€ double. Free parking. **Amenities:** Restaurant; bar; swimming pool; fitness center; free Wi-Fi.

THE dehesa: A WAY OF LIFE

As you travel in southwestern Spain, you'll see all around you the classic landscape of rolling pasture dotted with holm and cork oak trees: the **dehesa.** Extremadura has about a million hectares of it. It's not the natural landscape, but traditionally managed parkland—trees have often been planted in orderly rows—that for hundreds of years has been the basis for the region's agricultural economy. The *dehesa* provides an environment which farmers of pinky-black **pata negra** pigs depend upon to produce the prized *jamón ibérico de bellota*—ham from pure-bred pigs which have roamed freely in the woodland, munching protein-rich acorns. A leg of the best-quality ham will sell for hundreds of euros.

Farmers' income is supplemented by cork oaks, which are stripped of their bark once every 9 years—you'll see rust-colored trunks where they've recently been harvested. Oak branches are also pruned for firewood for cooking and heating.

As well as providing for human needs, the *dehesa* is a fertile habitat for Extremadura's diverse wildlife, from the Spanish imperial eagle to honey bees and even the Iberian lynx. It's a sustainable—if tough—way of life, and although the *dehesa* is currently protected and cherished, it's under threat as a younger generation moves away from the land to seek easier ways to make a living.

Palacio Viejo de Las Corchuelas ★★★   This family-run bed and breakfast, in a big, whitewashed farmhouse right on the edge of the park, is a proper paradise. Owner Carmen is passionate about the region where she grew up and wants to share it with visitors. She prepares traditional dishes, such as homemade hams and sausages, using ingredients grown on her own *finca*. The rooms have been renovated to a high standard with stone and tile floors, wood beams, and spacious bathrooms. Set in the foothills of the Sierra de las Corchuelas mountains, with a pretty garden and shared swimming pool, it's a 3-mile drive north of Torrejón el Rubio. Carretera EX-208, km 31. www.lascorchuelas.com. ⓒ **60-882-19-61.** 6 units. 110€ double (fixed price). **Amenities:** Dining room; swimming pool and lake; birdwatching; free Wi-Fi.

GUADALUPE ★★

Guadalupe is a medieval religious theme-park, and a magnificent one at that. Everything in this remote mountain village is geared around the pilgrims who flock to visit the black Madonna (**Our Lady of Guadalupe**) reputedly carved by St Luke and discovered here in the 13th century. The commanding centerpiece is the **Real Monasterio de Santa María de Guadalupe** (p. 742), a Hieronymite monastery built in the 14th century as a shrine to the Virgin.

The hilly whitewashed village which gathers around the monastery grew up to accommodate the pilgrims' needs, with porticoed shops and

The Real Monasterio de Santa Maria de Guadelupe houses the famous Madonna carving that has drawn pilgrims to Guadalupe for centuries.

hostelries. It's much the same today, though many of the shops have been overrun by the gaudy religious souvenir industry. Nevertheless, Guadalupe's medieval appeal remains largely intact. An atmospheric highlight is to stay at the **Real Hospedería del Monasterio,** the 16th-century lodgings that adjoin the monastery, for the complete pilgrim experience.

Essentials

It's not easy getting to Guadalupe. There are two **buses** a day from Madrid (check schedule at www.samar.es) taking around 3½ hours, but poor connections from other parts of Extremadura. By **car** from Madrid, follow the A-5 west to exit 171 at Navalmoral de la Mata and then south on the EX-118 to Guadalupe (trip time: 3 hr.). Once in Guadalupe, buses park just uphill from the town hall *(ayuntamiento).*

You can pick up a self-guided tour sheet from the tourist office on the square (guadalupeturismoblog.wordpress.com; ☎ **92-715-41-28**) for a detailed tour of 22 points of interest in the village. (Do use the map, the arrow directions on the streets themselves are deeply confusing.)

Exploring Guadalupe

The **Plaza Mayor** (also called **Plaza de Santa María**), at the base of the steps to the monastery's **Basílica,** is the hub of the village. You'll probably gravitate here so often that the friendly waiters who patrol the area will start to recognize you.

Real Monasterio de Santa María de Guadalupe ★★★ CHURCH

In the late 13th century, a farmer named Gil Cordero was searching for a stray cow when a vision led him to a statue of the Virgin buried in the soil.

A chapel was built on the site of his discovery, and in time, as the Virgin's reputation for miracles spread, it became the number-one pilgrimage destination in Spain. As royals and explorers spread its fame to the New World, Our Lady became the patron saint of all the territories conquered by Spain, generating great wealth. Columbus came here to give thanks for his safe return on discovering America, and even today many of the visitors you'll see are from Latin America and the Philippines.

Over the centuries the monastery has undergone numerous extensions and refurbishments in a variety of styles—Gothic, Mudéjar, Renaissance, Baroque—and it was even abandoned in 1835, with much of the church's property confiscated by the government. At the beginning of the 20th century, the site was restored by the Franciscan monks who maintain it today. It's stuffed with treasures and lavish decoration amassed through the Virgin's far-reaching fame.

To explore the monastery and see the Virgin up close you have to buy a ticket for one of the guided tours leaving the entrance hall every half hour. The tour, in Spanish only, is a fairly cursory race through various museums and chapels ahead of the main event. But the treasures are astounding. The **Museo de las Bordados,** in the old refectory, hosts a collection of richly embroidered vestments from as early as 1415, including a chasuble made from a cloak belonging to the Catholic Kings Isabel and Fernando. The **Museo de Miniados** contains mammoth leather-bound choir books with beautifully illuminated manuscripts; the paintings are miniatures, not the books. Much of the craftsmanship in these galleries was produced right here in the monastery's workshops. The **Museo de Esculturas y Pinturas** is a small collection containing works by El Greco, Goya, Zurbarán, and a porcelain crucifix attributed to Michelangelo. The artistic highlight of the tour is the intensely decorated **Sacristía,** known as the Spanish Sistine Chapel, which contains a series of eight superb paintings by the Extremaduran master Francisco de Zurbarán, in the setting for which they were commissioned in the 1630s. They depict scenes from the lives of the Hieronymite monks who lived and worked here; in the chapel hangs the *Apotheosis of St Jerome.*

After a quick look at the **Relicario,** crammed with bits of holy memorabilia, items from the Virgin's opulent dress collection and a table belonging to Philip II, you're handed over to habit-wearing monks for the last act. The statue of Our Lady of Guadalupe is found in the 18th-century **Camarín** chapel, where your monastic guide does the final build-up, describing a set of paintings by Luca Giordano of scenes from the life of Mary, plus polychromes of female biblical figures. By this point female pilgrims are fanning themselves as if to say "get on with it." At last, the monk swivels a gilded panel, rather in the manner of a game show, to reveal the black Madonna. Pilgrims queue to kiss a silver image of the Virgin (wiped down each time by the monk), and many leave the chapel deeply moved. After all that, you can unwind at leisure in the tranquil

15th-century **Mudéjar cloister** with its horseshoe arches, fruit trees, and fountain pavilion.

The Gothic **Basílica,** which can be visited separately (admission free), is understated by comparison with what has gone before. Highlights are the intricately carved wooden choir and a Renaissance wrought-iron grille, said to have been forged from the chains of freed slaves. As you contemplate the *retablo* (altarpiece), every few minutes the Virgin's statue appears again, swiveled back by the monk on the other side as another pilgrim group shuffles away.

Plaza de Santa María. www.monasterioguadalupe.com. © **92-736-70-00.** Admission to museums and sacristy 5€ adults, 1.50€ ages 7–14, free for kids 6 and under. Daily 9:30am–1pm and 3:30–6:30pm.

Where to Stay in Guadalupe

With so many pilgrims on the go, the village has lots of lower-key lodging options, although many are rather dingy and cheerless. Honorable exceptions are **Hostal Alba Taruta,** Calle Chorro Gordo, 2 (www.hostal albataruta.es; © **92-736-71-51**), just down the hill from Plaza Mayor, which is clean and comfortable with a lovely terrace; **Hotel Rural Posada de Rincón,** Plaza Sta. María de Guadalupe, 11 (posadadelrincon.com; © **92-736-71-14**), a recently renovated little hotel in the corner of Plaza Mayor; and the highly rated self-catering apartments at **Casa Rural llana 12,** Calle Llana, 12 (casaruralllana.com; © **60-956-78-95**), with spotless rural-chic rooms and spectacular mountain views.

Hospedería del Real Monasterio ★★★   As far as 75km (46 miles) away on the road to Guadalupe there are advertisements for the *Hospedería* and the *Parador* vying for the custom of approaching pilgrims. This time we recommend the *Hospedería* for the rare opportunity to lodge inside one of Spain's most beautiful monasteries. The feel is institutional and eccentric (your room number may not correspond to the number of the floor you're on). As your key clanks in the lock it really does echo down the red-tiled corridor. Foot-weary priests snooze in the worn

---

MATERIAL girl

Beneath her splendid robes, the statue of Our Lady of Guadalupe stands just 2 ft. (59cm) tall. She's made of carved cedar and her complexion was probably darkened by centuries of smoke from votive candles. According to legend, the statue was hidden by fleeing monks as the Moors invaded in 712, to be rediscovered 600 years later. Since the 14th century the figures of Mary and Christ have remained dressed in their extravagantly embroidered robes with just hands and faces showing; the original poly-chromed sculpture is rarely seen. Once a year, between the 6th and 8th of September, the statue is removed from the Camarín chapel, dressed up in a change of golden finery, and paraded through the thronged streets for the Fiesta de Santa María.

A bronze plaque commemorates Columbus's visit to Guadalupe, bringing captured Native Americans to be baptized.

armchairs of the *Sala de Estar* (sitting room). It's wonderful, and the prices are extremely pilgrim-friendly too, as little as 50€ for its ascetic rooms. Reserve well in advance, as pilgrim groups can book up the entire hotel, especially around religious festivals. And then talk to the friendly staff at the porters' lodge about your plans for dinner (see below).

Plaza Juan Carlos 1. www.hotelhospederiamonasterioguadalupe.com. © **92-736-70-00.** 47 units. Rooms 50€–150€ double. Free parking. Closed Jan. **Amenities:** Restaurant; bar; free Wi-Fi.

Parador de Guadalupe ★★★ The parador is a more upmarket affair, and while it's pricier than the *Hospedería* it can be remarkably good value outside peak times (it gets very expensive in Holy Week). This 15th-century former hospital, just around the corner from the monastery, once hosted Queen Isabella; explorers would meet royal representatives here to sign contracts before setting out for the New World. The courtyard, dotted with orange and lemon trees, is a lovely place to while away an afternoon; tables have little electronic bells with which to summon your bill, or maybe an ice cream. The rooms are large and characterful, some with four-poster beds, others with balconies, and all have unique pieces of furniture and art on the walls.

Calle Marqués de la Romana, 12. www.parador.es. © **92-736-70-75.** 80 units. 85€–250€ double. Parking 14€. **Amenities:** Restaurant; bar; concierge; room service; outdoor pool and terrace; free Wi-Fi.

Where to Eat in Guadalupe

Hospedería del Real Monasterio ★★ EXTREMADURAN   When you come down for dinner in the spectacular cloistered courtyard, you'll find a printed place card with your name on it at your table, preceded by a formal D. or Dña. They do things properly at the *Hospedería*. The food and service feel a little institutional, but it's hearty and excellent value, just what a hungry pilgrim needs. It's best to keep things simple and stick to the set menu at 15€—seasonal gazpacho with "a bit of everything," a huge *calderata de cordero* (slow-cooked lamb stew) accompanied by chilled red *vino de casa,* and fruit for dessert. Then maybe a snooze in the *Sala de Estar.*

Plaza Juan Carlos 1. www.hotelhospederiamonasterioguadalupe.com. (𝐶 **92-736-70-00.** Main dishes 10€–28€. Daily 1:30–3:30pm and 9–10:30pm.

Parador de Guadalupe ★★ EXTREMADURAN   The most sophisticated restaurant in Guadalupe, the *parador* serves regional cuisine with a creative twist. The set menu is relatively expensive at 32€, but the service, historic surroundings (whether you're dining in the courtyard or in the restaurant), and the quality of the local produce make this a memorable experience. In addition to excellent pork and lamb, signature dishes include a *zorongollo* salad of red peppers and pickled rabbit, and tomato soup with grapes and artisanal bread, followed by interesting regional puddings and cheeses.

Calle Marqués de la Romana, 12. www.parador.es. (𝐶 **92-736-70-75.** Entrees 18€–28€. Daily 1:30–4pm and 8:30–11pm.

Meson Cerezo II ★ EXTREMADURAN   Catering and accommodation in and around Plaza Mayor are dominated by the name Cerezo, but in fact the several establishments you'll see are run by two competing branches of same family. In this case competition clearly benefits the consumer. The basic set lunch, including a complimentary hunk of *morcilla de Guadalupe* (blood sausage) to start, plus bread, wine or beer, and dessert, comes in at an astonishing 8.90€. Cold *ajo blanco* soup and pork loin on a wood-fire grill are simple and excellent, the service chatty and swift. And the view from your table is a close-up of the Real Monasterio. The other Cerezo bar/restaurant in the square isn't bad either, but the hotels are best avoided.

Plaza Sta. María de Guadalupe, 33. www.hostalcerezo2meson.com. (𝐶 **92-715-41-77.** Main dishes 8€–15€. Daily 1:30–3:30pm and 8–10:30pm.

PLANNING YOUR TRIP TO SPAIN

By Patricia Harris and David Lyon

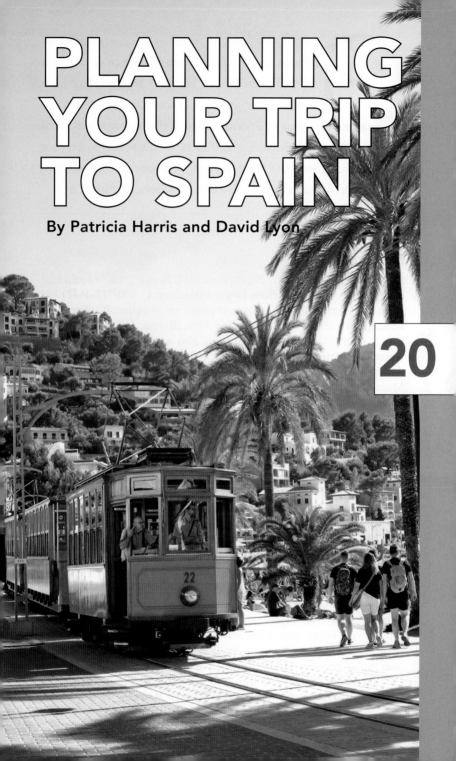

G etting to Spain is relatively easy, especially for those who live in Western Europe or on the East Coast of the United States. If all your documents are in order, you should clear customs and immigration smoothly. The staffs of entry ports into Spain usually speak English, and they tend to speed you on your way. In this chapter, you'll find everything you need to plan your trip, from tips on hotels to health care and emergency information.

ARRIVING

By Plane

FROM NORTH AMERICA   Flights from the U.S. east coast to Spain take 6 to 7 hours. **Iberia Airlines** (www.iberia.com; ✆ 800/772-4642) has more routes into and within Spain than any other airline. It offers daily nonstop service to Madrid from New York all year, and from Chicago, Boston, and Miami seasonally. Iberia flights are often codeshares with **American Airlines** (www.aa.com; ✆ 800/433-7300), which runs daily nonstop service to Madrid from New York (JFK), Philadelphia, and Miami. Iberia's main Spain-based competitor, **Air Europa** (www.aireuropa.com; ✆ 011-34-90-240-15-01), offers nonstop flights from New York (JFK) to Madrid and seasonal nonstop flights from Miami to Madrid. Air Europa makes connections from other U.S. cities through its codeshare partner **Delta** (www.delta.com; ✆ 800/221-1212), which also runs daily nonstop service from Atlanta and New York to both Madrid and Barcelona. European discount carrier **Norwegian** (www.norwegian.com/us; ✆ 800/357-4159) offers nonstop service to Spain from Los Angeles, Newark NJ, Fort Lauderdale, and Oakland CA.

FROM THE U.K. & IRELAND   The airfare market from the U.K. and Ireland is highly volatile. **British Airways** (www.britishairways.com; ✆ 0844-493-0787, or 800/247-9297 in the U.S.) and **Iberia** (www.iberia.com; ✆ 0870-609-0500 in London) are the two major carriers flying between England and Spain. More than a dozen daily flights, on either British Airways or Iberia, depart from London's Heathrow and Gatwick airports, about seven flights a day to Madrid and back, and at least six to Barcelona. Flights from Manchester and Birmingham serve travelers from the Midlands or Scotland. **Vueling** (www.vueling.com) offers bargain flights between London Gatwick and several points in Spain, and **EasyJet** (www.easyjet.com) flies from several U.K. airports to Madrid, Barcelona, Málaga, and the Balearic Islands. **RyanAir** (www.ryanair.

com) flies to Madrid, Barcelona, Girona, Valencia, Sevilla, and Málaga from London Stansted, Dublin, and Shannon.

By Train

If you're already in Europe, you might want to go to Spain by train, especially if you're traveling on a **Eurailpass** (p. 750). Even without a pass, you'll find that the cost of a train ticket is relatively moderate. Rail passengers from Britain or France should reserve couchettes and sleepers far in advance. To go from London to Spain by rail, you'll need to transfer stations in Paris to board an express train to Spain.

By Car

Highway approaches to Spain are across France on expressways. The most popular border crossing is near Biarritz, but there are 17 other border stations between Spain and France. If you plan to visit the north or west of Spain (Galicia), the Hendaye-Irún border is the most convenient frontier crossing. If you're going to Barcelona or Catalunya and along the Levante coast (Valencia), take the expressway in France to Toulouse, then the A-61 to Narbonne, and then the A-9 toward the border crossing at La Junquera. You can also take the RN-20, with a border station at Puigcerdà.

By Bus

Bus travel to Spain is possible but not popular—it's quite slow. (Service from London will take 24 hr. or more.) But coach services do operate regularly from major capitals of Western Europe and, once they're in Spain, usually head for Madrid or Barcelona. The major bus line from London to Spain is **FlixBus** (www.flixbus.com; ✆ **0855-626-8585**).

GETTING AROUND

By Plane

By European standards, domestic flights within Spain are relatively inexpensive, and considering the distances within the country, flying between distant points sometimes makes sense. For reservations on **Iberia,** visit www.iberia.com, or call ✆ **800/772-4642. Air Europa** (www.aireuropa. com; ✆ **90-240-15-01**), **Vueling** (www.vueling.com), and **Ryan Air** (www.ryanair.com) fly even more connections in Spain than Iberia.

By Train

Spain is crisscrossed with a comprehensive network of rail lines on RENFE, the national rail line. High-speed AVE, AVANT, ALVIA, and ALTRIA trains have reduced travel time between Madrid and Sevilla, Madrid and Valencia, and Madrid and Barcelona to 2½ hours or less. Trains are now so fast that few hotel trains (sleeper trains) are offered, apart from those going to Portugal or France. The RENFE website has possibly the world's easiest-to-use online schedule. Pay close attention to

Jetting Around Europe

If you plan to travel to a number of cities and regions, the **OneWorld Visit Europe Pass** (www.oneworld.com) can be a good deal. Sold only in conjunction with a transatlantic ticket from American, Iberia, or British Air airlines, it's valid for most airports in Europe, but you are required to choose up to four different cities in advance in the order you'll visit them. Restrictions forbid flying immediately back to the city of departure, and you're only allowed one change within the preset itinerary once the ticket is issued. The dates and departure times of the actual flights, however, can be changed without penalty once you arrive in Europe. Costs depend on what kind of ticket you are issued—consult the folks at your OneWorld transatlantic carrier if you're interested in a multi-stopover ticket and see what the best deal is at the time of your visit. The ticket is valid for up to 60 days after your initial transatlantic arrival in Europe.

prices on the schedule; AVE trains often cost twice as much as other high-speed trains but are not much faster. Reservations are required on all high-speed trains, even with a discount card or pass, and reservation fees vary depending on the class of train.

JUNIOR & SENIOR DISCOUNT CARDS If you are between 14 and 25, you can purchase the **Tarjeta Joven Renfe,** which gives you a year of purchasing tickets within Spain for a 30% discount regardless of class, type of train, or day of the week. The pass costs 22€ and must be purchased at a RENFE customer service window. Travelers age 60 and older may purchase a **Tarjeta Dorada** for 6€ at any RENFE customer service window. Also good for a year, it provides 40% discounts on AVE and AVANT tickets Monday to Thursday, 25% Friday to Sunday, and 40% every day on MD *(media distancia)* and *cercanías* (commuter rail) trains.

SPANISH RAIL PASSES RENFE also offers discounted rail passes that must be purchased before arriving in Spain. The **Eurail Spain Pass,** which entitles you to unlimited rail travel in Spain, is available for 3 to 8 days of travel (within a month's span) in either first or second class. The pass works most economically for long-distance travel—the kind of routes you might otherwise fly if trains weren't more convenient and faster (Madrid to Barcelona, for example, or Barcelona to Málaga). For 3 days, the cost for an adult is $267 first class or $201 second class; for 8 days, the charge is $439 first class, $331 in second class. Children 4 to 11 pay half-fare on any of these discount passes. *Note:* This pass must be purchased before arriving in Spain. In the U.S. and Canada, contact **Rail Europe** (www.raileurope.com; ✆ **877/272-RAIL** [272-7245]).

EURAILPASS The **Eurailpass Global** (purchase online at www.eurail.com) permits unlimited first-class rail travel in any country in western Europe except the British Isles (it is valid in Ireland). Purchase passes before you leave home—not all passes are available in Europe, and passes purchased in Europe will cost more. This pass permits unlimited travel in

21 Eurail-affiliated countries. You can travel on any of the days within the validity period. The time period and season determine the price. Generally speaking, the Global Pass offers more convenience than savings. See the Rail Europe website and run the numbers.

OTHER RAIL PASSES Many different rail passes are available in the United Kingdom for travel in Britain and continental Europe. Stop in at the **International Rail Centre,** Victoria Station, London (© **0870-5848-848** in the U.K.). Some of the most popular passes, including **Inter-Rail** and **Euro Youth,** are offered only to travelers ages 25 and under; these allow unlimited second-class travel through most European countries. The main North American supplier, **Rail Europe** (www.raileurope.com; © **877/272-RAIL** [272-7245]), can also give you informational brochures and counsel you on which passes work best for your circumstances.

By Bus

Bus service in Spain is low-priced and comfortable enough for short journeys. The efficiency of train travel has cut drastically into available bus routes. Almost every bus schedule in Spain is available on the **Movelia** website (www.movelia.es), which also allows you to buy tickets on-line, provided you have access to a printer.

By Car

A car offers the greatest flexibility while you're touring, even if you're just doing day trips from Madrid. But don't plan to drive in the congested cities. Rush hour is every hour.

RENTALS All the major international rental car firms maintain offices throughout Spain. These include **Avis** (www.avis.com; © **800/331-1084**), **Hertz** (www.hertz.com; © **800/654-3001**), **Budget** (www.budget.com; © **800/472-3325**), **Enterprise** (www.enterprise.es; © **90-210-0101** in Spain, 855/266-9289 in the U.S.), and **Europcar** (© **91-110-0000;** www.europcar.com). Prices vary little among the companies, but you can find the best deals at **www.holidayautos.com**. Tax on car rentals is 15%, so factor it into your travel budget. Prepaid rates don't include taxes, which will be collected at the rental kiosk.

Most rental companies require that drivers be at least 25 years of age and, in some cases, not older than 72. To be able to rent a car, you must have a passport and a valid driver's license; you must also have a valid credit card or a prepaid voucher. Citizens of non-E.U. countries should obtain an **International Drivers Permit** before arriving in Spain. Without one, some agencies may refuse to rent you a car.

DRIVING RULES Spaniards drive on the right-hand side of the road. Spain has two kinds of express highways: *autopistas,* which charge a toll, and *autovías,* which don't. To exit a highway, follow the *salida* (exit) sign (except in Catalunya, where exit signs read *sortida*). On most express highways, the speed limit is 120kmph (75 mph). On other roads, speed

20

PLANNING YOUR TRIP TO SPAIN

Getting Around

limits range from 90kmph to 100kmph (56–62 mph). You will see many drivers far exceeding these limits.

If you are fined by the highway patrol *(Guardia Civil de Tráfico),* you must pay on the spot, either to the officer or online using a cellphone and credit card. There are stiff penalties for driving while intoxicated.

BREAKDOWNS   On a major motorway you'll find strategically placed emergency phone boxes. On secondary roads, call for help by asking the operator for the nearest Guardia Civil. The Spanish affiliate of AAA, **Real Automóvil Club de España (RACE;** www.race.es; © **90-240-45-45**), provides limited assistance in the event of a breakdown.

GASOLINE (PETROL)   Service stations abound on the major arteries of Spain and in such big cities as Madrid and Barcelona. They are open 24 hours a day. On secondary roads, most stations open at 7am daily, closing at 11pm or midnight. All gas is unleaded—*gasolina sin plomo.* Many vehicles run on clean diesel fuel called *Gasoleo A* or on more expensive Biodiesel. Fuel prices change often—to check prices and available stations, visit http://geoportalgasolineras.es/. *Tip:* We generally rent diesel vehicles for much better gas mileage for a given vehicle size.

MAPS   For drivers who don't like or trust GPS, there are still old-fashioned paper maps available. Michelin map 990 (folded version) or map 460 (spiral-bound atlas) cover Spain and Portugal. **Google Maps** (http://maps.google.com) are pinpoint accurate in cities, but the database can be sketchier on rural roads.

TIPS ON ACCOMMODATIONS

From castles converted into hotels to modern high-rise resorts overlooking the Mediterranean, Spain has some of the most varied hotel accommodations in the world—with equally varied price ranges. Accommodations are broadly classified as follows:

ONE- TO FIVE-STAR HOTELS   The Spanish government rates hotels by stars, plus the designation "GL" (Grand Luxe) for the most luxurious properties. Note that many criteria in the star system are based on suitability for business meetings, but since each property is reviewed on the same criteria, the stars can be useful for comparing lodgings in the same area.

HOSTALES   Not to be confused with a youth hostel, a *hostal* is a modest hotel without services. They're often a good buy. You'll know it's a *hostal* if a small s follows the capital letter h on the blue plaque by the door.

YOUTH HOSTELS   Spain has about 140 hostels *(albergues de juventud)* and they are not limited to young people. Some are equipped for persons with disabilities. Many hostels impose an 11pm curfew. For information, contact **Red Española de Alberques Juveniles** (www.reaj.com; © **91-522-70-07**).

PARADORES   The Spanish government runs a series of unique state-owned inns called *paradores* that blanket the country. Castles, monasteries, palaces, and other grand buildings have been taken over and converted into hotels. Several newer properties were simply built from scratch to look monumental. To book or learn more, contact **Paradores de España** (www.parador.es; ✆ **90-254-79-79**). Make reservations directly with the network's website, as third-party bookers tend to slap on additional charges. *Paradores* offer good discounts when one of the travelers is under 30 or over 65, or if you purchase 5 nights (which can all be in different *paradores*).

SHORT-TERM RENTALS If you'll be based in one place long enough to justify paying a cleaning fee, most major cities have agencies that specialize in short-term apartment and even house rentals. They are particularly nice if you want your own kitchen and even laundry facilities. Internet-based "sharing rentals" like **Homeaway** (www.homeaway.com) and **Airbnb** (www.airbnb.com) have encountered stiff municipal opposition, especially in Barcelona, Madrid, Bilbao, and San Sebastián. Palma de Mallorca has banned **Airbnb** outright, and several cities have cited the company for violating health and safety codes. As of early 2019, several Spanish cities—including Barcelona, Madrid, and Valencia—were considering following Palma's lead.

TOURS

It would be impossible for us to list all the tours that are offered for visitors to Spain. We list here some of the most well-respected and long-established tours, but do your own research as well; even the most long-running company can experience financial difficulties and go out of business. When purchasing a tour, it's often a good idea to buy travel insurance from a third party, as tours can be expensive.

Active Travel

Backroads (www.backroads.com; ✆ **800/462-2848** or 510/527-1555) offers bicycling and hiking/walking trips in Basque country, on the Balearic Islands, and from the Costa Brava to the Spanish Pyrenees. One walking tour of Mallorca also includes yoga. You'll pedal between 48km and 81km per day (30–50 miles) on bike tours led by **Easy Rider Tours** (www.easyridertours.com; ✆ **800/388-8332** or 978/463-6955). Routes are often along back roads; the most appealing tour follows routes trod by medieval pilgrims on their way to Santiago.

Madrid-based **Bravo Bike** (https://bravobike.com; ✆ **91-758-29 45**) offers several city cycling tours as well as day trips to nearby cities such as Toledo, Segovia, and Ávila (with van transportation to the destination). The company also offers multiday Spain options such as trips along the Costa Blanca or through La Rioja wine country.

Cultural Tours

Featuring groups ranging in size from 15 to 25 participants, **ACE Cultural Tours** (www.aceculturaltours.co.uk; ✆ **44 01223 841055**) engages

If you are interested in walking the Camino de Santiago across the north of Spain, **Spanish Steps** (www.spanishsteps.com; ℂ **877/787-9255**) offers a comprehensive program of walks of differing numbers of days and difficulty levels. Options include the Camino Finisterre from Santiago to the so-called "end of the earth." **Classical Pursuits** (www.classicalpursuits.com;

ℂ **844/378-2869**) usually includes a Camino route in its culturally oriented excursions. **The Natural Adventure Company** (www.thenaturaladventure. com; ℂ **020-3151-4250** in the U.K., 011-44-20-3151-4250 international) offers a wide range of self-guided Camino walks, including several along the Camino Portugués from Portugal.

art historians to lead tours such as a Madrid/Toledo focus on Spain's master painters. ACE also has options for travelers with an interest in wildlife. **Context Travel** (www.contexttravel.com; ℂ **800/691-6036**) offers excellent scholar-led tours of Barcelona and Madrid. To facilitate conversation, maximum group size is six and custom tours are also available.

Custom Tours

If you prefer to travel at your own pace and on your own schedule, Heritage Tours (www.heritagetours.com; ℂ **800/378-4555** or 212/206-8400) creates customized itineraries that might focus on Spanish Jewish history or on architecture and gastronomy in Barcelona. Saranjan Tours (www.saranjan. com; ℂ **800/858-9594**) specializes in custom tours on the Iberian peninsula. Options include walking and bicycling journeys on the Camino de Santiago, a gourmet tour of Extremadura and Sevilla, or a painting sojourn in La Rioja.

Escorted General-Interest Tours

Escorted tours are structured group tours, with a group leader. The price usually includes hotels, meals, tours, admission costs, and local transportation. Inquire about airfare. Escorted tours—whether by bus, motorcoach, train, or boat—take you to the maximum number of sights in the minimum amount of time with the least amount of hassle. The downside of escorted tours is that you'll have little opportunity for serendipitous interactions with local people; tours often focus on heavily visited sites and cannot deviate from the schedule and itinerary. They can be convenient for people with limited mobility, but be sure to discuss your needs before booking. **Trafalgar Tours** (www.trafalgar.com; ℂ **866/513-1995**) offers a number of tours of Spain, including a popular 15-day trip called "The Best of Spain." Other companies offering Spain itineraries include **Go Ahead Tours** (p. 755), **Globus** (www.globusjourneys.com; ℂ **866/755-8581**), and **Insight Vacations** (www.insightvacations.com; ℂ **888/680-1241**).

Food & Wine Trips

Spain Taste's food and wine tours in Catalunya, designed for serious gastronomes, may include dinners at Michelin-starred restaurants, wine tastings, and cooking lessons. For more information, contact www.spaintaste.com (© **619-52-72-77**). Similarly named **A Taste of Spain** (www.atasteof spain.com; © **85-607-96-26**) offers an 8-day "ultimate foodie tour" for groups, visiting Madrid, La Rioja, Basque Country, and Barcelona. Many more options are available for individual travelers, including a 5-day tour of Santiago de Compostela and the Rías Baixas and a 2-day tour in La Mancha. The company has a number of intriguing 1-day activities such as a visit to cava country from Barcelona or an excursion to Jerez de la Frontera from Sevilla or Cádiz. **Go Ahead Tours** (www.goaheadtours.com; © **800-590-11-61**) offers a comprehensive 12-day food and wine tour of Spain that covers Barcelona, San Sebastián, Bilbao, La Rioja, the Ribera del Duero, and Madrid, with an option to add 3 days in Andalucía.

Touring by Train

For a taste of old-fashioned glamour, **Palace Tours** (palacetours.com; © **800/724-5120** or 786/408-0610) books trips on three luxury trains, El Transcantabrico Clasico (which began service in 1983 as Spain's first luxury train), El Transcantabrico Gran Lujo, and Al Andalus. Excursions range from a 6-night journey through Andalucía to a 7-night trip across northern Spain from Santiago de Compostela to León.

[FastFACTS] SPAIN

Business Hours Banks are open Monday–Friday 9:30am–2pm and Saturday 9:30am–1pm. Most other offices are open Monday–Friday 9am to 5 or 5:30pm; the longtime practice of early closings in summer is dying out. In restaurants, lunch is usually 1–4pm and dinner 9–11:30pm or midnight. Major stores are open Monday–Saturday 9:30am–8pm; smaller establishments often take a siesta, doing business 9:30am–1:30pm and 4:30–8pm.

Disabled Travelers Because of Spain's many hills and endless flights of stairs, visitors with mobility issues may have difficulty getting around the country,

but conditions are slowly improving. Newer hotels are more sensitive to the needs of those with disabilities, and the more expensive restaurants, in general, are wheelchair accessible.

Organizations that offer a vast range of resources and assistance to travelers with disabilities include the **American Foundation for the Blind** (AFB; www.afb.org; © **800/232-5463**) and **SATH** (Society for Accessible Travel & Hospitality; www.sath.org; © **212/447-7284**). For information on travel agencies that offer customized tours and itineraries for travelers with disabilities, visit **Disabled Travelers.com,** which also has a wealth of information

on accessible house swaps and other independent travel. Minneapolis-based **Dignity Travel** (www.dignity travel.biz; © **612/381-1622** or 877/337-4272) specializes in group travel for people who have trouble walking or use a wheelchair. British travelers should contact **Tourism for All** (www. tourismforall.org.uk; © **0845-124-9971** in the U.K. only) to access a wide range of travel information for seniors and those with disabilities.

Drinking Laws The legal drinking age is 18. Bars, taverns, and cafeterias usually open at 8am, and many serve alcohol to 1:30am or later.

Drugstores To find an open pharmacy (farmacia) outside normal business hours, check the list of stores posted on the door of any drugstore. The law requires drugstores to operate on a rotating system of hours so that there's always a drugstore open somewhere.

Electricity The U.S. uses 110-volt electricity, Spain 220-volt. Most low-voltage electronics with transformers, such as laptops, tablets, and cellphone chargers, do fine with 220-volt. Spain uses the European standard rounded two-prong plug; North Americans and residents of the British Isles will need adapters.

Embassies & Consulates If you lose your passport, fall seriously ill, get into legal trouble, or have some other serious problem, your embassy or consulate can help. These are the Madrid addresses and contact information: **Australia:** Torre Espacio, Paseo de la Castellana 259D; www.spain.embassy.gov.au; ☎ **91-353-66-00; Canada:** Torre Espacio, Paseo de la Castellana 259D; www.canadainternational.gc.ca; ☎ **91-382-84-00; Ireland:** Paseo de la Castellana 46-4, Ireland House; www.irlanda.es; ☎ **91-436-40-93; New Zealand:** Calle Pinar 7, 3rd Floor; www.nzembassy.com/spain; ☎ **91-523-02-26; United Kingdom:** Torre Espacio, Paseo de la Castellana 259D; www.gov.uk/government/world/organisations/british-embassy-madrid; ☎ **91-714-63-00; United States:** Calle Serrano 75; es.usembassy.gov; ☎ **91-587-22-00.**

Emergencies Call ☎ **112** for fire, police, and ambulance services.

Health Spain should not pose any major health hazards. Tap water is safe to drink. During the summer, limit your exposure to the sun. Use a sunscreen with a high sun protection factor (SPF) and apply it liberally.

Internet & Wi-Fi Wi-Fi—pronounced "wee-fee" in Spanish—is becoming ubiquitous in Spain. Most lodgings offer free Wi-Fi, at least in public areas. For Wi-Fi on a phone or tablet, download the GOWEX free Wi-Fi app from Google Play or the Apple Store. Internet cafes are vanishing, but if you find one, expect to pay 2€ to 4€ per hour.

Language The official language in Spain is Castilian **Spanish** (or *Castellano*). Although Spanish is spoken in every province of Spain, local tongues reasserted themselves with the restoration of democracy in 1975. **Catalan** has returned to Barcelona and Catalunya, even appearing on street signs; this language and its derivatives are also spoken in the Valencia area and in the Balearic Islands, including Mallorca (though natives there will insist they speak Mallorquín). **Basque** is widely spoken in the Basque region (the northeast, near France). Likewise, **Galego,** which sounds and looks very much like Portuguese, has enjoyed a renaissance in Galicia (the northwest). English is spoken in most hotels, restaurants, and shops.

LGBT Travelers Spain is one of the most culturally liberal and LGBT-friendly countries in the world. Discrimination based on sexual orientation has been illegal for more than a generation. Madrid and Barcelona are major centers of gay life in Spain. Popular resorts for gay travelers are Sitges (south of Barcelona), Torremolinos, and Ibiza.

Lost & Found To report a lost credit card, contact the following numbers: American Express at ☎ **90-237-56-37;** Diners Club at ☎ **91-547-40-00;** MasterCard at ☎ **90-097-12-31;** or Visa at ☎ **90-097-44-55.**

Mail Sending a postcard or letter to the U.S. starts at 1€. To calculate the price, visit http://correos.es. You can also buy stamps at any tobacconist shop.

Mobile Phones If you have a GSM phone with a SIM card, you can pick up a local prepaid SIM once you land in Spain to have local service with a local number. **T-Mobile** and **Google Fi** customers can use their phones in Spain with only a small charge for calls and data. **AT&T** customers should inquire in advance about roaming charges, which can be substantial. Phones that work on **Verizon** and **Sprint** systems don't work in Spain. Most mobile phones from the U.K. are compatible.

Many travelers opt to buy a pre-paid mobile

phone on location. **Voda-fone** (www.vodafone.com); **Movistar** (aka Telefónica; www.movistar.com); **Orange** (www.orange.es); and **Yoigo** (www.yoigo.com) are the four largest and most reliable mobile phone service providers in Spain.

Money & Costs Before you leave home, exchange enough petty cash to cover airport incidentals, tipping, and transportation to your hotel. After that, best exchange rates are usually from ATMs. Avoid exchanging money at commercial exchange bureaus and hotels, which generally have the highest transaction fees.

Safety Spain's crime rate more closely resembles Canada's than the U.S. That said, muggings and robberies do occur, so be careful. Stay out of dark alleys and don't go off with strangers. Exercise caution by carrying limited cash and credit cards; leave extra cash, credit cards, passports, and personal documents in a safe location, and don't leave anything visible in a parked car. Loss or theft abroad of a passport should be reported immediately to the local police and your nearest embassy or consulate.

Safety can be a concern for **women** exploring on their own. Avoid deserted streets and do not hitchhike. Dress conservatively, especially in remote towns. If you're a victim of catcalls and vulgar suggestions, look straight ahead and just keep walking. If followed, seek out the nearest police officer.

Separatist protests in Catalunya or the Basque country rarely pose more than an inconvenience for visitors.

Senior Travel Major discounts are available to seniors in Spain, including reduced rates on most admissions and reduced fares on public conveyances. Special room rates are also available at the national *parador* network.

Smoking Like most of Europe, Spain bans smoking in the workplace, restaurants, bars, and nightclubs, as well as on public transportation and in cultural venues. When in doubt, light up outside and away from children.

Taxes The internal sales tax (known in Spain as IVA) ranges from 8% to 33%, depending on the commodity being sold. Food, wine, and basic necessities are taxed at 8%; most goods and services

(including car rentals), at 18%; luxury items (jewelry, all tobacco, imported liquors), at 33%; and hotels, at 8%.

Telephones **To call Spain:** Dial the international access code (**011** from the U.S.; 00 from the U.K., Ireland, or New Zealand; or 0011 from Australia), dial the country code **34,** dial the city code, and then the number.

To make international calls from Spain, first dial 00 and then the country code (U.S. or Canada 1, U.K. 44, Ireland 353, Australia 61, New Zealand 64). Next dial the area code and number. For example, if you wanted to call the British Embassy in Washington, D.C., you would dial 00-1-202-588-7800.

For **directory assistance:** Dial ✆ **1003** in Spain. For **operator assistance** in making an international call, dial ✆ **025.** Numbers beginning with **900** in Spain are **toll-free.**

Time Spain is 6 hours ahead of Eastern Time in the United States. Daylight saving time is in effect from the last Sunday in March to the last Sunday in October.

Tipping Don't overtip. The government requires

CHANGES IN credit cards

The **SmartChips** embedded in most European credit cards and those in cards issued in North America differ, as Spain uses a "chip and PIN system" still not adopted by North American card issuers. North American patrons must still swipe the magnetic strip on their cards and usually sign a receipt. American Express cards will work where an Amex logo is displayed, but they are not as widely accepted as Visa and MasterCard.

that restaurant and hotel bills include their service charges—usually 15% of the bill. However, that doesn't mean you should skip out of a place without dispensing an extra euro or two. Some guidelines:

Your **hotel porter** should get 1€ per bag. **Chambermaids** should be given 1€ per day, more if you're generous. Tip **doormen** 1€ for assisting with baggage and 1€ for calling a cab. For **cabdrivers,** add about 10% to the fare as shown on the meter. At airports, and major train terminals, the **porter** who handles your luggage will present you with a fixed-charge bill. Service is included in restaurant bills, but it is the custom to tip extra—in fact, the **waiter** will expect a tip.

Tour guides expect 2€, although a tip is not mandatory. Theater and bullfight **ushers** get from 1€.

Toilets In Spain they're called *aseos, servicios,* or *lavabos* and are labeled *caballeros* for men and *damas* or *señoras* for women. If you can't find any, go into a bar, but you should order something before using their facilities.

Visas For visits of less than 3 months, visas are not needed for citizens of the U.S., Canada, Ireland, Australia, New Zealand, and the U.K.

Visitor Information The Tourist Office of Spain's official website can be found at **www.spain.info**.

USEFUL TERMS & PHRASES

Most Spaniards are very patient with foreigners who try to speak their language. That said, you might encounter several difficult regional languages and dialects in Spain: In Catalonia, they speak *Catalan* (the most widely spoken non-national language in Europe); in the Basque Country, they speak *Euskera;* in Galicia, you'll hear *Gallego.* However, Castilian Spanish (*Castellano,* or simply *Español*) is understood everywhere; for that reason, we've included a list of simple words and phrases in Spanish to help you get by.

Basic Words & Phrases

English	Spanish	Pronunciation
Good day	Buenos días	**bweh**-nohs **dee**-ahs
How are you?	¿Cómo está?	**koh**-moh es-**tah**
Very well	Muy bien	**mwee** byehn
Thank you	Gracias	**grah**-syahs
You're welcome	De nada	deh **nah**-dah
Goodbye	Adiós	ah-**dyohs**
Please	Por favor	pohr fah-**vohr**
Yes	Sí	**see**
No	No	**noh**
Excuse me	Perdóneme	pehr-**doh**-neh-meh
Give me	Déme	**deh**-meh
Where is . . . ?	¿Dónde está . . . ?	**dohn**-deh es-**tah**
the station	la estación	lah es-tah-**syohn**
a hotel	un hotel	oon oh-**tel**

English	Spanish	Pronunciation
a gas station	una gasolinera	**oo-nah gah-so-lee-*neh*-rah**
a restaurant	un restaurante	**oon res-tow-*rahn*-teh**
the toilet	el baño	**el *bah*-nyoh**
To the right	A la derecha	**ah lah deh-*reh*-chah**
To the left	A la izquierda	**ah lah ees-*kyehr*-dah**
Straight ahead	Derecho	**deh-*reh*-choh**
I want . . .	Quiero . . .	***kyeh*-roh**
to eat	comer	**ko-*mehr***
a room	una habitación	**oo-nah ah-bee-tah-*syohn***
How much is it?	¿Cuánto cuesta?	***kwahn*-toh *kwehs*-tah**
When?	¿Cuándo?	***kwahn*-doh**
What?	¿Qué?	**keh**
Is there . . . ?	(¿)Hay (. . . ?)	**aye**
Yesterday	Ayer	**ah-*yehr***
Today	Hoy	**oy**
Tomorrow	Mañana	**mah-*nyah*-nah**
Good	Bueno	***bweh*-noh**
Bad	Malo	***mah*-loh**
Better (Best)	(Lo) Mejor	**(loh) meh-*hor***
More	Más	**mahs**
Less	Menos	***meh*-nohs**
No smoking	Se prohibe fumar	**seh proh-*ee*-beh foo-*mahr***
Do you speak English?	¿Habla usted inglés?	**ah-blah oo-*sted* een-*glehs***
Is there anyone here who speaks English?	¿Hay alguien aquí que hable inglés?	**aye *ahl*-gyehn ah-*kee* keh *ah*-bleh een-*glehs***
I don't understand Spanish very well.	No (lo) entiendo muy bien el español.	**noh (loh) ehn-*tyehn*-doh mwee byehn el es-pah-*nyol***
The meal is good.	Me gusta la comida.	**meh *goo*-stah lah koh-*mee*-dah**
What time is it?	¿Qué hora es?	**keh *oh*-rah es**
May I see your menu?	¿Puedo ver el menú (la carta)?	***pweh*-do vehr el meh-*noo* (lah *car*-tah)**
The check, please.	La cuenta por favor.	**lah *kwehn*-tah pohr fah-*vohr***
What do I owe you?	¿Cuánto le debo?	***kwahn*-toh leh *deh*-boh**

NUMBERS

English	Spanish	Pronunciation
1	uno	***oo*-noh**
2	dos	**dohs**
3	tres	**trehs**
4	cuatro	***kwah*-troh**

English	Spanish	Pronunciation
5	cinco	**seen**-koh
6	seis	**says**
7	siete	**syeh**-teh
8	ocho	**oh**-choh
9	nueve	**nweh**-beh
10	diez	**dyehs**
11	once	**ohn**-seh
12	doce	**doh**-seh
13	trece	**treh**-seh
14	catorce	kah-**tohr**-seh
15	quince	**keen**-seh
16	dieciséis	dyeh-see-**says**
17	diecisiete	dyeh-see-**syeh**-teh
18	dieciocho	dyeh-see-**oh**-choh
19	diecinueve	dyeh-see-**nweh**-beh
20	veinte	**bayn**-teh
30	treinta	**trayn**-tah
40	cuarenta	kwah-**rehn**-tah
50	cincuenta	seen-**kwehn**-tah
60	sesenta	seh-**sehn**-tah
70	setenta	seh-**tehn**-tah
80	ochenta	oh-**chehn**-tah
90	noventa	noh-**behn**-tah
100	cien	**syehn**
1,000	mil	**meel**

Travel Terms

Aduana Customs

Aeropuerto Airport

Avión Airplane

Aviso Warning

Correo(s) Mail, or post office

Dinero Money

Embajada Embassy

Entrada Entrance

Este East

Frontera Border

Hospedaje Inn

Norte North

Oeste West

Pasaje Ticket

Puerta de salida Boarding gate

Salida Exit

Tarjeta de embarque Boarding card

Vuelo Flight

Index

Restaurants

PHOTO CREDITS